and Up to Date Style Turban 99 Cents.

No. 39T3922 A very neat and dressy Turban, made of good quality black felt, very tastily trimmed in the front with a bird and imported fancy spangled feather. The brim on the left is overlaid with a nicely designed wool felt, same extending well to the right of the crown and falling to the left over the brim and onto the bandeau, which is embellished with twists of black silk finished velvetta. A handsome buckle in the front completes the trimming of this exceedingly becoming hat. Shape can be ordered in black only, while other trimmings any color desired. Price, each.....99c

Real Paris Style Hand Made Swell Turban $2.19.

$2.19

No. 39T3925 This is a hand made tan colored draped felt Turban on a buckram frame. The trimming consists of two large wings which are held to the felt with a handsome buckle. A drape of pink silk taffeta drawn through buckle, falling over the wings and extending over the brim in two places, same material covering the black velvette bandeau with handsome made loops and bows completes the trimming of this beautiful hat. Can also be ordered in black, gray or brown with contrasting trimmings to match. Price, each.........$2.19

Richness and Simplicity This Newest Black and White Turban $2.48.

39T3923 This is an extraordinary becoming Turban of the latest black and white combination. The entire facing, as well as the top of the brim is made of very fine wool hairy felt. In the draping and the brim around the crown consists of silk finished velvetta. A handsome bow in the front from which falls a twist of fine velvetta over the hair in effect. The trimming rich but plain, consists of a bow of wide velvet over which is drawn a black breast. The velvetta bandeau is faced with pink silk and roses. We recommend you order the hat as described, but can also be had in other combinations desired, excepting the breast which comes in black and white only. Price, each.........$2.48

No Small City Milliner can Produce as Stylish a Hat as This at $2.48.

No. 39T3926 This is the new Marlborough shape, raised high on both sides and falling back closely to the hair. The buckram frame is covered with black silk finished velvetta. Same is overlaid with a handsome design of black chantilly lace all around the brim. A large fold of blue taffeta silk, underlined with black silk finished velvetta, caught by cabochon, extends all around the crown and gives it the new desired effect. A cabochon on the left, from which is drawn a black imported breast, and bandeau of black velvetta covered with blue silk and velvet roses completes the trimming of this very handsome hat. Price, each.....$2.48

Board, one year $180.00

Gasoline, one year $35.00

Oldsmobile

"The Best Thing on Wheels"

This graceful and practical Automobile will ... of six horses at an average cost of $15.00 a ... miles). Board alone for one horse costs $180.00 ... the economy is very evident.

The Oldsmobilist has the satisfaction of knowing ... chine is always ready. Its practicability was demo...

Price $650.00 Visit our ... fifty-eight selling agents or write for ...

THE OLDS MOTOR WORKS, DETROIT, MICH.

Going Like the Wind

BILLIARDS and POOL at HOME

BURROWES Portable Table. $15. to $27.

Sizes 2½ x 5 and 3 x 6 ft. Weight 28 and 39 lbs. From $15 to $27

As practical and interesting for experts as for beginners in BILLIARDS AND POOL. Book explains many other fascinating games for all players, young or old.—Place on any table in any room, or on our folding stand—quickly leveled—set away upright. Made for use, cannot warp, recent improvements, frame of rich mahogany, best green broadcloth cover, 16 balls and 4 cues of finest quality, 40 implements with table. A source of daily enjoyment at all seasons. Sent on Trial. Write for local agents' addresses. Description and colored plates FREE.

THE E. T. BURROWES CO.
108 Free Street Portland, Maine
NEW YORK, 277 Broadway.
SAN FRANCISCO, 402 Battery St.
Also Largest Manufacturers in World Fine Wire Insect Screens—Made to Order—Won't Rust. Send for Screen Catalog F.

Costs But 2 Cents a Week To Have Your Washing Done by Electricity

Washes in Two to Six Minutes!

Does Both the Washing and Wringing A Fine Wringer Furnished Free

The 1900 Motor Washer Run by Electricity

The 1900 Motor Washer (Either Electric Motor or Water Power Motor) Sent Anywhere On 30 DAYS' FREE TRIAL

1900 Motor Washer Run by Water Power

This Washing Machine can also be run with Gasoline Engine Power

Which Book shall we Send,—"Electric" or "Water Power"

The 1900 Washer Co., 3332 Henry St., Binghamton, N. Y. or Canadian 1900 Washer Co., 355 Yonge St., Toronto, Canada

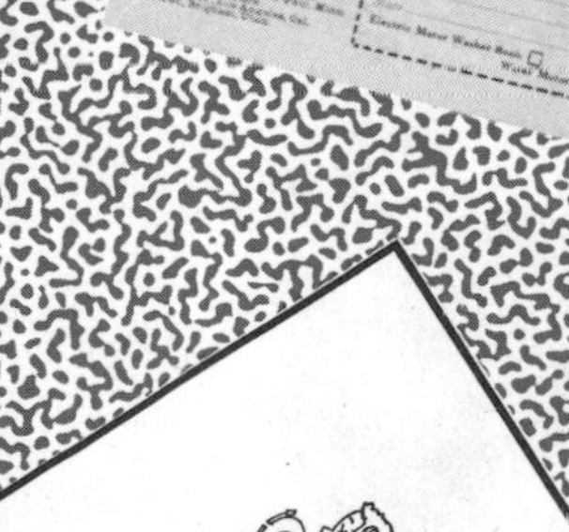

WEBER PIANOS

Are Used and Enthusiastically Endorsed by the World's Greatest Singers

Because of that Pure, Rich and Sympathetic Tone in the Possession of Which They Stand Alone.

WAREROOMS:
108 Fifth Avenue, New York
266 Wabash Avenue, Chicago
181 Tremont Street, Boston

WANTED

INFORMATION AS TO THE WHEREABOUTS OF

CHAS. A. LINDBERGH, JR.

OF HOPEWELL, N. J.

SON OF COL. CHAS. A. LINDBERGH

World-Fam...

This chil...

THEY WERE WONDERFUL YEARS

CONFIDENT YEARS —

SPIRITED YEARS —

ABOVE ALL, THEY ARE THE

NOSTALGIC YEARS —

They bring back the fabulous fascinating golden eras that introduced our American heritage and world events to history.

Relive our past with these priceless pictures and descriptions — once you start, it is difficult to stop reading until the end.

YES, THEY WERE

TRULY WONDERFUL YEARS

NOSTALGIA

OUR HERITAGE IN PICTURES AND WORDS

CRUSADE BIBLE PUBLISHERS

NASHVILLE, TENNESSEE

NOSTALGIA represents a bringing together editorially of four
NEWS FRONT/YEAR pictorial history volumes:
GREAT PIONEERS OF AMERICAN INDUSTRY, TURBULENT 20TH CENTURY (1900-1950),
HISTORIC DECADE (1950-1960), CRISIS OF CHANGE: THE INCREDIBLE DECADE (1960-1970).

Printed and bound in the United States of America

Library of Congress Card No. 74-20376

International Standard Book No. ISBN 0-91348247-1

Foreword

The years depicted in *nostalgia* are the most eventful in recorded history. Never before in so short a space of time have conditions of life, as affecting the individual, the nation, and the international community changed so rapidly.

In a cultural sense the period has been dominated by vast discoveries in the various fields of fundamental science and their application to all aspects of human life; to the substitution of machines for human labor; to the development of transportation facilities which have annihilated distance; to the alleviation of human suffering and the conquest of disease; to the luxurious amenities of every-day living; to the destructive instruments of war.

It is a tribute to the quality of the normal human being that during this period of steady growth and constant disturbance he has been able to find opportunity for the development of his individual interests, literary and artistic, and satisfaction of the need of relaxation that is found in sport. Above all, it is highly significant that, in this country at least, the vigor of our individual opinions, and of all the American people continues unabated. That is the essence of a free democracy and it gives us faith in our future.

—Baldwin H. Ward, Editor

CONTENTS

Great Pioneers of American Industry

Turbulent 20th Century

IN CONGRESS, JULY 4, 1776.

The unanimous Declaration of the thirteen united States of America,

When in the Course of human events it becomes necessary for one people to dissolve the political bands which have connected them with another, and to assume among the powers of the earth, the separate and equal station to which the Laws of Nature and of Nature's God entitle them, a decent respect to the opinions of mankind requires that they should declare the causes which impel them to the separation. — We hold these truths to be self-evident, that all men are created equal, that they are endowed by their Creator with certain unalienable Rights, that among these are Life, Liberty and the pursuit of Happiness. — That to secure these rights, Governments are instituted among Men, deriving their just powers from the consent of the governed, — That whenever any Form of Government becomes destructive of these ends, it is the Right of the People to alter or to abolish it, and to institute new Government, laying its foundation on such principles and organizing its powers in such form, as to them shall seem most likely to effect their Safety and Happiness. Prudence, indeed, will dictate that Governments long established should not be changed for light and transient causes; and accordingly all experience hath shewn, that mankind are more disposed to suffer, while

of our people. — He is at this time transporting large Armies of foreign Mercenaries to compleat the works of death, desolation and tyranny, already begun with circumstances of Cruelty & perfidy scarcely paralleled in the most barbarous ages, and totally unworthy the Head of a civilized nation. — He has constrained our fellow Citizens taken Captive on the high Seas to bear Arms against their Country, to become the executioners of their friends and Brethren, or to fall themselves by their Hands. — He has excited domestic insurrections amongst us, and has endeavoured to bring on the inhabitants of our frontiers, the merciless Indian Savages, whose known rule of warfare, is an undistinguished destruction of all ages, sexes and conditions. In every stage of these Oppressions We have Petitioned for Redress in the most humble terms: Our repeated Petitions have been answered only by repeated injury. A Prince, whose character is thus marked by every act which may define a Tyrant, is unfit to be the ruler of a free people. Nor have We been wanting in attentions to our British brethren. We have warned them from time to time of attempts by their legislature to extend an unwarrantable jurisdiction over us. We have reminded them of the circumstances of our emigration and settlement here. We have appealed to their native justice and magnanimity, and we have conjured them by the ties of our common kindred to disavow these usurpations, which would inevitably interrupt our connections and correspondence. They too have been deaf to the voice of justice and of consanguinity. We must, therefore, acquiesce in the necessity, which denounces our Separation, and hold them, as we hold the rest of mankind, Enemies in War, in Peace Friends. —

We, therefore, the Representatives of the united States of America, in General Congress, Assembled, appealing to the Supreme Judge of the world for the rectitude of our intentions, do, in the Name, and by Authority of the good People of these Colonies, solemnly publish and declare, That these United Colonies are, and of Right ought to be Free and Independent States; that they are Absolved from all Allegiance to the British Crown, and that all political connection between them and the State of Great Britain, is and ought to be totally dissolved; and that as Free and Independent States, they have full Power to levy War, conclude Peace, contract Alliances, establish Commerce, and to do all other Acts and Things which Independent States may of right do. — And for the support of this Declaration, with a firm reliance on the protection of divine Providence, we mutually pledge to each other our Lives, our Fortunes and our sacred Honor.

John Hancock

UNANIMOUS DECLARATION OF THE THIRTEEN UNITED STATES OF AMERICA WAS APPROVED BY DELEGATES FROM 12 COLONIES, JULY 4, NEW YORK ORIGINALLY ABSTAINING.

Declaration of Independence Signed

As early as the spring of 1776 sentiment for a complete rupture with England became manifest in the Colonies. The North Carolina Convention instructed its delegates to vote for a declaration of independence. Richard Henry Lee of Virginia put forth a resolution (June 7) that the United Colonies "are, and of right ought to be free and independent States." It was decided to postpone a decision on the resolution until a committee composed of Jefferson, Franklin, John Adams, Robert Livingston and Roger Sherman drew up a formal declaration. A draft of this was presented to Congress on June 28 and on July 2 the declaration was passed. Minor amendments were made, the changed document being approved without dissent and the first signatures were affixed July 4.

"We hold these truths to be self-evident, that all men are created equal . . ." wrote Thomas Jefferson

Declaration of Independence, Constitution and Bill of Rights

America's enduring framework for democracy.

"AN ASSEMBLY OF DEMI-GODS," wrote Jefferson from Paris when he read the list of delegates to the Constitutional Convention at Philadelphia in 1787. George Washington is shown addressing the members who elected him their presiding officer, average age 42. Small farmers and working men were not represented. Most delegates were educated, professional men who had wide experience in public affairs. All had business or financial interests to guard, yet the document they wrote protected civil and political liberties as well as property rights. The meetings were secret, but James Madison (standing, center) kept detailed notes, published years later.

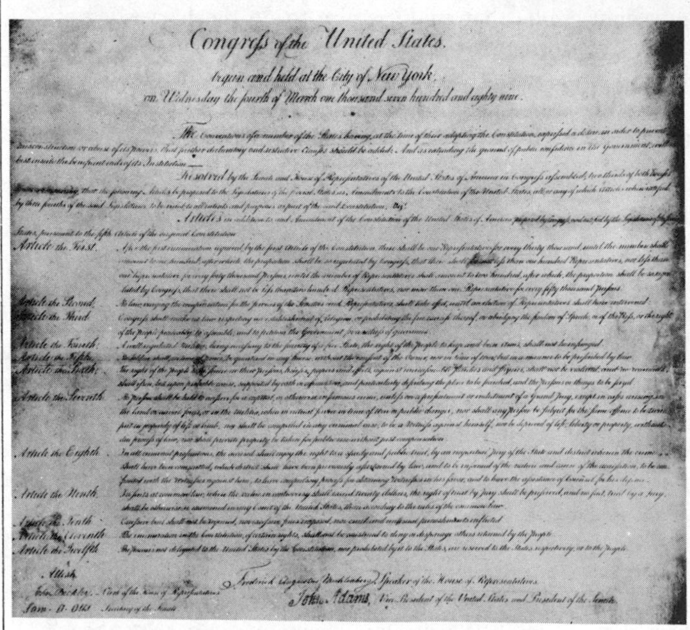

Congress of the United States,
begun and held at the City of New-York, on Wednesday the fourth of March one thousand seven hundred and eighty nine.

BILL OF RIGHTS Many Americans objected to the Constitution because they felt their individual rights were not guaranteed sufficiently. James Madison submitted 12 amendments to Congress Sept. 9, 1789, and 10 of these were ratified by Dec. 15, 1791, to make up the Bill of Rights. Its provisions: (1) freedom of religion, speech, press and assembly; (2) establishment of a militia; (3) no forceful quartering of soldiers in private homes; (4) freedom from unreasonable searches and seizure; (5) due process of law; (6) trial by jury; (7) right of common law; (8) prevention of excessive fines, bail, punishment; (9) listing of certain rights in Constitution would not deny other rights retained by the people; (10) powers not delegated to the United States by the Constitution be reserved to states or to the people.

HARVESTER OF THE

McCormick's reaper opened up wheat wealth of the West, began transformation, mechanization of agriculture throughout world.

On a hot Virginia afternoon in 1831, a 22-year-old farmer gave the first public demonstration of a mechanical reaper that could harvest grain four times as fast as a man with a cradle and scythe.

The young farmer was Cyrus McCormick; his invention was to revolutionize agriculture and lay the foundations for today's multi-billion-dollar agricultural equipment industry and one of its major corporations, International Harvester Co.

In 1831, farmers in the U.S.—and all over the world—were still harvesting grain with hand tools that had hardly changed since the days of the ancient Egyptians.

A strong man could cut only two acres of grain in a day of backbreaking labor.

Most farms in the North, worked by their owners with a hired hand or two, were necessarily small; in the South, operation of huge plantations was made possible only by slave labor. The great plains of the West were still waiting to be settled and sown with grain, and it is difficult to imagine how they could have been conquered if mechanized harvesting had not become a reality when it did.

Dozens of inventors before Cyrus McCormick had tried to produce a mechanical reaper and failed.

One of these inventors, in fact, was Cyrus' own father, Robert McCormick, a well-educated, well-to-do farmer of Scotch-Irish descent who also operated grist mills, sawmills, a smelter and a smithy in Rockbridge County, Va.

Robert McCormick began working on his reaper in 1816, when his eldest son was seven years old, and he did not give up until May of 1831.

By then, Cyrus had already shown considerable mechanical ability. When he was 15, he had built himself a lightweight cradle that enabled him to do the harvesting work of a grown man; a few years later, he invented a hillside plow. He had spent hours on end in the family blacksmith shop, watching his father tinker with reaper models—and when Robert McCormick decided to give the reaper up as a bad job, Cyrus took it over.

By mid-July, he had a reaper that worked.

He had abandoned the principles of his father's machine, which was pushed into the grain by two horses while the wheat was pressed against stationary convex sickles by rapidly revolving beaters, and developed a set of principles of his own—principles which lie behind every piece of grain cutting machinery at work today.

Basically, the first horsedrawn McCormick reaper had seven essential elements: a straight knife with a serrated edge and reciprocal or vibrating motion; a platform behind the knife to receive the cut grain; fingers or guards extending from the platform to keep the grain from slipping sideways; a revolving reel to hold the grain against the knife and lay the cut stalks on the platform; forward draft from the right or stubble side by means of shafts attached in front to the master wheel; a divider on the

Modern McCormick reapers are power-driven, vastly faster and more efficient than 1831 model; but, like all other grain cutting machinery in use today, they incorporate the seven basic elements first combined by Cyrus McCormick.

PRAIRIES

CYRUS McCORMICK

left side to separate the grain to be cut from that to be left standing; and a master wheel to carry most of the weight of the machine and furnish power.

McCormick had originated all seven of these elements independently; as far as he knew, no one but his father and himself had ever even thought of a mechanical reaper.

Actually, six of the seven had already been developed by other inventors; only the master wheel was his alone. But he first combined them into a working machine.

He first discovered that other inventors were interested in the reaper, too, in 1834, when he read in *Mechanics' Magazine* a description of a reaper just invented by a Cincinnati candlestick maker named Obed Hussey, based on principles similar to his. (Hussey was later to be one of his many competitors.)

He immediately sent a description of his own machine to the magazine's editor, explaining that it was three years old, and filed a patent claim in Washington.

However, he went on improving the reaper for six years more, selling only an occasional machine to a friend or neighbor. In 1840, he finally decided that it was good enough to be marketed on a broader scale.

He could hardly have picked a worse time to go into business. The McCormick enterprises had been hit hard by the panic of 1837; in 1841, he and his father had to sell their iron furnace and plunge deep into debt to keep the little plant in the black smith shop in operation.

Blacksmith shop on Walnut Grove Farm where McCormick invented the reaper also served as his first manufacturing plant

FIRST POWER-DRIVEN FARM MACHINERY

Moreover, he found out almost immediately that the reaper was not as thoroughly perfected as he had believed; the first two sold to customers outside Rockbridge County broke down in heavy grain in the 1841 harvest.

Another winter of work eliminated the flaw that had produced the clogging, and, in 1842, for the first time, the reaper was offered with a money-back guarantee.

The small business began to grow. Seven reapers were sold in 1842, 23 in 1843, 50 in 1844, at $100 each.

During the next year or two, he began licensing Western manufacturers to produce McCormick reapers.

But, both because he was dissatisfied with the quality of the work turned out by his franchise holders and because he was so sure that the real future of the agricultural equipment industry lay in the West, he became more and more anxious to move his plant westward.

In 1847, he went to Chicago, built a factory there, and manufactured and sold 500 reapers.

During the 1850s, sales soared into the thousands.

However, competition in the infant industry was getting tough. Both McCormick and Hussey had applied for extensions of their 1834 patents in 1848; both had been refused, and the field was thrown open to dozens of rivals.

If McCormick's talents for sales, advertising and marketing had not been as great as his inventive genius, his company could never have held its own.

He began to establish a chain of sales agencies throughout the grain-growing areas of the nation almost as soon as he moved to Chicago.

In the early '50s, he became the first major manufacturer to introduce consumer credit. A farmer could buy a McCormick reaper—then priced at $125—for $35 down at harvest time and the balance on December 1.

McCormick had begun advertising in the 1840s, and his ad budget grew as fast as his competition. (Early ads for the "Patent Virginia Reaper" usually showed a reaper being pulled at a trot by a pair of high-stepping horses, with a man dressed in his Sunday best raking the platform.)

He was one of the first advertisers to make use of testimonials—usually from socially or politically prominent men who had never seen a reaper, much less operated one, but who could be persuaded that the machine was a boon to the hard-working farmer—and one of the first to use direct mail campaigns.

The Civil War brought the agricultural equipment industry into its own once and for all.

"The reaper is to the North what slavery is to the

First McCormick reaper (l.) made a hit with local farmers at Steele's Tavern, Va., in July of 1831. Competitive field trials with other manufacturer's machines were later a favorite McCormick publicity stunt.

McCormick's first Chicago factory (r.) was destroyed by fire in 1851, rebuilt on same site. After great Chicago Fire of 1871, a giant new plant was built on a new site, today the location of International Harvester's McCormick Works.

APPEARED ABOUT 1900

South," declared Secretary of War Edwin M. Stanton, "and without McCormick's invention, I feel the North could not have won and the Union would have been dismembered."

McCormick himself, as a Southerner by birth and a Midwesterner by adoption, had hated to see war come. In 1860, he founded the *Expositor,* a religious periodical, bought the Chicago *Times,* and published both until April, 1861, using them to urge preservation of the Union.

A big man with seemingly inexhaustible energy, he was constantly on the move; he often held conferences in his hotel bedrooms while he shaved.

He was considered cold and aloof by most of those who knew him. In September of 1857, however, he met a pretty girl from upstate New York, Nancy Fowler, and four months later he married her.

By 1874, he was the father of five children; in 1879, the McCormick family moved into a lavish Chicago mansion, and there, five years later, Cyrus McCormick died.

His eldest son, Cyrus H. McCormick, succeeded him as president of McCormick Reaper Works.

By then, the company was producing a harvester, mowers, reaper-mowers and binders as well as reapers; sales passed the 50,000-unit mark the year of Cyrus' death.

McCormick reapers had won top honors at a dozen international expositions, and were selling briskly in Europe as well as in the U.S.; in 1879, Cyrus had been elected to the French Academy of Sciences as "having done more for agriculture than any other living man."

International Harvester Co., today the giant of the industry (its 1959 sales were $1.36 billion), was formed in 1902—at just about the time when the first power-driven reapers were going on the market—by a merger of McCormick Reaper Works with six competitors. Cyrus H. McCormick became the new company's first president, and his grandson, Brooks McCormick, is now its executive vice president.

The giant strides that mechanized agriculture has made since the invention of the original McCormick reaper can perhaps be best summed up by a single set of statistics: harvesting one acre of wheat, a job that took 46 hours in 1829, takes less than half an hour today.

McCormick's sales strategy matched his inventive genius

Before Cyrus McCormick's reaper appeared in 1831, farmers used the cradle to harvest grain. This tool enabled men to cut two acres a day.

By 1858, harvesting machinery used canvas aprons to raise the grain to a table where two men riding on the reaper bound it as fast as collected and tossed the bundles overboard.

BALTIMORE celebrated laying of B&O cornerstone on July 4, 1828. First spade of earth was dug by 92-year-old Charles Carroll of Carrollton, Md., last surviving signer of the Declaration of Independence, who said that he considered his honorary task to be "among the most important acts of my life," second only to his signing of the Declaration, if even to that.

ALL ABOARD!

Philip Thomas founded Baltimore and Ohio, first U.S. railroad, opened the way to the Middle West

THE 220,000-MILE network of railroads that crisscrosses the U.S. today began to grow in 1827, when a group of Baltimore businessmen decided to do something to boost their town's sagging share of commerce with the fast-growing pioneer West.

What they did was to charter the nation's first railroad, the Baltimore & Ohio—now 6000 miles long and sixth among U.S. railroads in revenue, with income of $389.4 million at the start of the Sixties.

The leader of the group, and the man who guided the B&O through its first nine years, was a Quaker banker, Philip E. Thomas.

The U.S. in 1827 had a population of just over 12 million, and Baltimore, with 80,000 inhabitants, was its third largest city.

The great surge of growth that was to carry the nation to the Pacific by mid-century had already begun.

The toll roads and turnpikes that were the only links between the coastal cities and the pioneer country West of the Alleghenies were overcrowded and inadequate.

A new form of transportation was clearly needed, and most Eastern businessmen were betting on canals.

New York's Erie Canal had opened in 1823; construction of the land-and-water Pennsylvania System of Public Works had begun in 1824.

Canal transportation was proving itself to be fast and cheap, and as "canal fever" mounted, Baltimore's trade—still dependent on the old National Road to Wheeling on the Ohio River—declined.

Work on the Chesapeake and Ohio Canal was under way at Georgetown, but, by 1826, Baltimore businessmen had decided that this new southern waterway, which would bypass their city, would do them no good at all. (Philip Thomas, then a Chesapeake and Ohio project commissioner, resigned his post in indignation.)

Baltimore's future looked so dark that several leading families had already moved away.

Then, in the fall of 1826, Philip Thomas began to listen to his brother, Evan, talk about railroads.

Evan had just returned from a visit to England, and had been dazzled by the newly completed Darlington & Stockton line.

Philip Thomas was 50 years old in 1826. He had begun his career in the hardware business, had risen to the presidency of the National Mechanics Bank and was one of Baltimore's most respected citizens.

According to John H. B. Latrobe, another of the B&O's founders, "his

Thomas' persistence overcame difficulties early

persuasiveness was remarkable. Never thrown off his balance, quiet in his speech, laborious in his search for the facts, and, above all, eminently successful in his own business, people listened to him with conviction."

Philip Thomas spent the last months of 1826 searching for the facts about railroads.

He was joined in his research by George Brown, a director of the National Mechanics Bank, who had also been receiving glowing accounts from a brother in England.

By February, 1827, the two men were convinced that a railroad was just what Baltimore needed, and on Feb. 12 they invited 27 Baltimore business leaders to a meeting at Brown's home to discuss the project.

A few days later, the group met again to listen to a highly favorable report by a subcommittee it had appointed to investigate details.

The report concluded, "it is the opinion of many judicious and practical men that these roads will, for heavy transportation, supersede canals as effectually as canals have superseded the turnpike roads."

For 1827, such a statement was little short of revolutionary.

The world's first known "rail road" had been built in England in 1602, for horsedrawn carts traveling from a mine to a nearby canal.

It had consisted of parallel strips of wood, laid on wooden crossties, which reduced friction so effectively that horses and mules could pull two-and-one-half times as much weight as before.

The wooden tracks were soon overlaid with iron, and by the early 19th century the basic principles of railroad construction, still in use today, had all been developed.

However, the only "rail roads" in the U.S. were short, privately owned colliery lines. Even in Great Britain, where 2000 miles of track had been laid, railroads were just beginning to be thought of as a general, public means of transportation for people and freight.

The cars were still all horsedrawn, although scientists and inventors had been experimenting with steam power for almost 200 years.

Once the Baltimore businessmen had decided on their daring project, they moved fast.

The Baltimore and Ohio Railroad's charter, which was to serve as a model for dozens of railroad charters in the years to come, passed the Maryland state legislature on Feb. 28. (One of its notable provisions was exemption of the railroad from state taxes.)

With Thomas as president and Brown as treasurer, the new company began to sell stock.

The idea of a railroad had aroused so much popular enthusiasm that the initial offering of $3 million was soon oversubscribed.

Practically every citizen of Baltimore with any cash to spare owned a piece of the B&O, and the laying of the railroad's cornerstone, on July 4, 1828, was the occasion for a giant civic celebration.

Army engineers had surveyed the route from Baltimore to the Ohio River, and work on the first 13-mile line of track began in October.

The B&O began carrying passengers on a 13-mile run early in 1830.

Later the same year, the U.S.'s first steam engine — Peter Cooper's tiny *Tom Thumb* — puffed triumphantly down the B&O's track, and the B&O began switching to steam power as fast as it could commission the design and manufacture of engines. Within four years, seven locomotives were hauling the railroad's 44 passenger and 1078 freight cars.

By 1834, rails were running to Harper's Ferry, and in 1835 passenger service between Baltimore and Washington began.

In 1836, Philip Thomas retired. Every mile of B&O track had meant exhausting challenges—technical and administrative, financial and political—for the company's first president.

The $3 million stock issue of 1827 had been woefully inadequate as construction costs—over $4000 per mile of track—had mounted, and, in the depression years of the 1830s, capital was hard to come by.

The B&O's political troubles stemmed from its rivalry with the Chesapeake and Ohio Canal Co., whose president also happened to be chairman of the Roads and Canals Committee of the U.S. House of Representatives.

It was not until 1852 that the line finally reached its original goal—the Ohio River at Wheeling.

But it pushed on to reach St. Louis in 1857, Chicago in 1874.

Almost half a century after the pioneer railroad's birth, the great days of railroading in the United States were just beginning.

HISTORIC *Tom Thumb*, first U.S. locomotive, made trial run out of B&O's Baltimore station on Aug. 25, 1830, reached hitherto undreamed of speed of 18 miles per hour.

HORSEDRAWN RAILROAD CARS PROVIDED SERVICE DURING FIRST MONTHS OF B&O OPERATION, WERE SOON REPLACED BY STEAM.

PHILIP E. THOMAS, first president of B&O, was born in 1776, son of a prosperous Maryland planter, lived to see B&O carry Lincoln to first inaugural *(r.)*. Thomas died in 1861, as Civil War, in which B&O played a vital role as supply lifeline of North, was beginning.

SURVEYING, construction of pioneer railroad's route across Alleghenies, was for 1830s, a stupendous engineering feat.

HIGHLIGHTS OF U.S. RAILROADING

1825—First steam locomotive operated experimentally.
1828—Construction of Baltimore & Ohio begun.
1830—Scheduled steam service begun on South Carolina Rail Road (now part of Southern Railway).
1831—First U.S. mails carried.
1837—World's first sleeping car service.
1840—Total track miles 2808.
1853—Chicago linked by rail with East.
1854—Rails from East reach the Mississippi.
1856—California's first railroad opened.
1859—Rails from East reach the Missouri.
1860—Track miles pass 30,000.
1862—President Lincoln signs bill authorizing transcontinental lines.
1869—First transcontinental rail link completed.
1883—Standard time adopted.
1886—Standard gauge adopted throughout U.S.
1893—Locomotive reaches 100 miles per hour.
1900—Total railroad investment passes $10 billion.
1917—Federal Government takes over rails during World War I.
1920—Trackage reaches all-time high—230,000 miles.
1934—First Diesel streamliner in service.
1952—More Diesel-electric than steam locomotives.
1965—Total rail investment reaches $35.5 billion

HE KEPT THE WORLD "IN STITCHES"

Singer's global empire spans 67 nations, has sold over 100 million sewing machines

In 1850, a highly talented machinist and not-so-talented Shakespearean actor named Isaac Merritt Singer built a sewing machine that worked.

That original Singer machine was the first of 100 million that have stitched their way into every habitable corner of the globe over the past 110 years.

Today, Singer Manufacturing Co. has 5000 sales centers in 67 countries, hands out instruction booklets in 54 languages. Its sales volume exceeds a half billion dollars.

The firm has not had a major U.S. competitor since Civil War days, and a dozen years ago, two-thirds of all the sewing machines sold in the U.S. were Singers. (Singer's current share of the U.S. market has declined to a still respectable one-third. The Japanese have grabbed 56%, and European manufacturers account for the remaining 11%.)

When Isaac Singer perfected the sewing machine, he did what at least half a dozen other inventors had failed to do over the 60 years since the first crude stitching device was patented by Thomas Saint.

All the pre-Singer machines had serious mechanical defects, and none had achieved commercial success.

The first U.S. sewing machine patent went to Elias Howe, Jr., in 1846.

But Howe failed to launch his product successfully on the U.S. market. He departed for England to try there, failed again, and returned penniless in 1849 to discover that two new machines—each with some original features, but basically infringing his patent—had been patented in his absence and were being marketed.

He began legal proceedings against their inventors, and launched the "sewing machine war" that was to continue until 1854.

By 1850, the year Singer himself saw his first sewing machine, other manufacturers had entered the fray.

But to the public, the sewing machine was still an unreliable gadget.

No machine on the market could sew more than a few stitches before the operator had to remove the cloth and make a fresh start. None could keep the thread from breaking and tangling. None could sew on a curve.

Sales, accordingly, were very small —in spite of a huge potential market both in the garment and leather working industries and among housewives who did all their family sewing by hand and professional seamstresses who could barely eke out a living with 18-hour days of slow, laborious hand stitching.

Isaac Singer was, in a way, the last man on earth who should have been responsible for anything as innately respectable and domestic as the sewing machine.

He was a colorful, lusty adventurer whose ideas of domesticity were, to say the least, unconventional.

He produced 24 children by two wives and three mistresses.

And, after his sewing machines began to make money, he set the prim New York of the 1860s on its ear by his lavishly exuberant ways.

Singer was born in Pittston, N. Y., in 1811, the son of poor German immigrants. His formal education ended at the age of 12, when he ran away from home and became an apprentice machinist in Rochester, N. Y.

The partnership of rambunctious Isaac Singer (above) and staid Edward Clark (below) was as uncongenial—and as profitable—as any in business history.

He was soon a qualified journeyman, but he decided that the stage was more to his liking than the work bench.

Those were the days when the arrival of a barnstorming road company was a major event in small towns where any entertainment more daring than a church social was rare.

Practically any company, good, bad or indifferent, could play everything from Shakespeare to *The Stumbling Block, or Why the Deacon Gave Up His Wine,* to packed houses nightly.

In 20 years, he held only three jobs outside the theater.

Early in the 1840s, stranded in Fredericksburg, Ohio, he went to work in a local woodworking plant.

He invented a carving maohine, patented it, and scraped up the money to go east and into business.

In New York, he teamed up with a printer named George Zieber, and the two of them moved on to Boston.

There they rented space to display the carving machine in the workroom of Orson C. Phelps, a struggling sewing machine manufacturer.

Nobody came to buy carving machines, so Singer had plenty of time to study Phelps' sewing machine, a model patented by John A. Lerow and S. C. Blodgett, and decide that he could make it work.

In 11 days, living on a $40 loan from Zieber, he did just that.

He replaced the circular shuttle that twisted the thread with a horizontal one, and designed a table to support the cloth and a presser foot to hold it down against the upward stroke of the needle, so that the machine would sew continuously on any kind of seam. He also replaced the cumbersome hand crank of all the sewing machines then in existence with a foot pedal.

Singer, Zieber and Phelps immediately went into partnership to manufacture the new machine.

Their first big order, for 30 machines at $100 each, came from a New Haven, Conn., shirt manufacturer before the end of 1850.

By summer of 1851, the small company was doing a brisk business —but, like every other firm in the sewing machine field, it was being sued by Elias Howe, Jr.

A well-to-do attorney named Edward Clark agreed to come into the business, advancing cash and guaranteeing legal counsel for 20 years, in exchange for the one-third interest of Phelps, who had dropped out.

In the fall, Zieber fell ill and sold his interest to Singer and Clark.

The resulting partnership was one of the oddest—and most successful—in the annals of business.

Flamboyant Singer found staid Clark ideal partner, business balance wheel

During the Civil War, proudest Singer boast was that "We clothe the Union Armies."

Singer Manufacturing began advertising early (first New York ad, 1853) and was first U.S. corporation to spend $1 million a year on promotion.

Clark was an ultra-conservative manufacturer's son, and a college graduate. He was distressed by his partner's cultural deficiencies (to the end of his days, Singer could barely spell) and shocked by his personal life.

But, fortunately for Singer Manufacturing Co., he was fascinated by sewing machines, and he had tremendous talents as executive, salesman and promoter.

Clark's first major contribution to the company—and to the industry—was the settlement, in 1854, of the legal battle with Elias Howe.

He set up a "patent pool," to be shared by Howe, Singer, and two other inventors whose machines had some claim to true originality.

All the remaining manufacturers agreed to pay a $15 fee, to be divided by the pool members, on each machine they produced until the patents expired.

Then Clark settled down to selling sewing machines.

In the first years, Singer sales were largely to industry—in part, because the price of the original Singer sewing machine, $125, was a major investment for a private owner at a time when average U.S. family income was $500 a year.

To boost sales of sewing machines for home use, Clark introduced trade-in allowances (on competitors' machines as well as Singer models) and installment buying. Singer Manufacturing was the first major U.S. corporation to adopt either of these practices.

He also developed the company's sales agency system, and—most important of all, perhaps—launched its foreign operations.

Isaac Singer, in the meantime, went on improving the machines themselves, swapping jokes with the boys in the machine shop, and making good copy for New York newspapers.

The most spectacular of his extravagances was a two-ton, 31-passenger traveling carriage, equipped with all comforts of home but a kitchen.

After 1860, he spent most of his time in Europe.

His last love and second wife was a young French girl, with whom he seems to have settled down at last.

He died, in 1875, in the $500,000 Greco-Roman-Renaissance palace he had built on the English coast and called The Wigwam.

Edward Clark was to remain at the helm of Singer Manufacturing, which had been incorporated in 1863, until his death in 1882.

By then, the company had assumed the dominant position in the U.S. sewing machine industry which it has never lost, and the machine Mahatma Gandhi was to call "one of the few useful things ever invented" was well launched on its world travels.

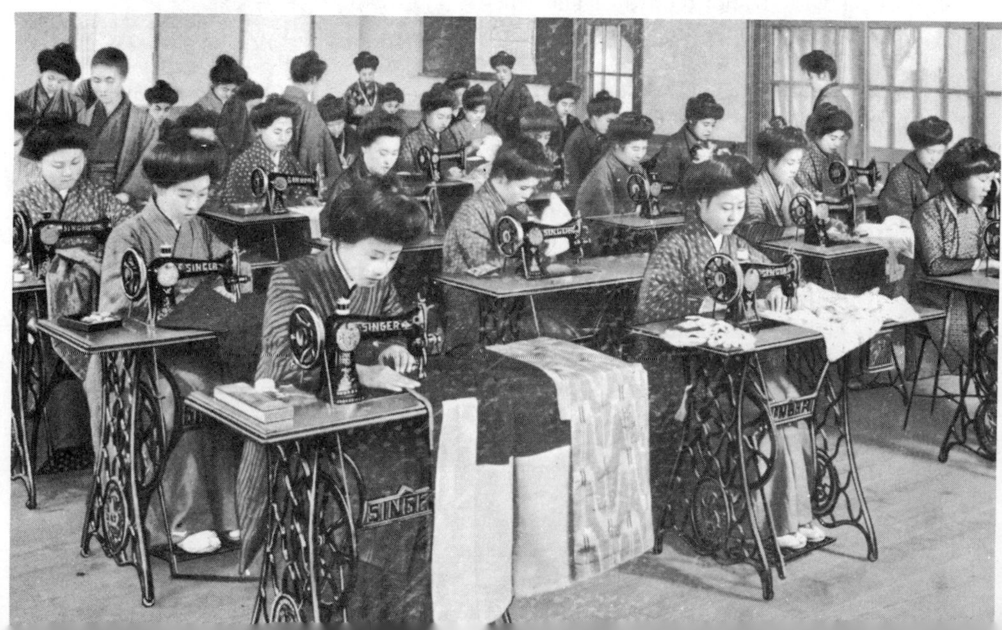

Florida's Seminole Indians dressed drably till Singer salesmen arrived late in 19th Century. Now the machines stitch elaborate, multi-colored costumes.

Singer lost $100 million in Russian Revolution (r., St. Petersburg headquarters of Czarist days). Soviet government returned $3 million in 1959.

Before World War II, Singer machines sold briskly in Japan (l.). Today, Japan's own sewing machine industry is Singer's main U.S. competitor.

BILLION DOLLAR BY-PRODUCT

Impurities, adulteration of mid-19th-Century drugs outraged young Navy Surgeon Squibb; unintended result of lifelong campaign was modern pharmaceutical industry, vast enterprise still bearing his name

TODAY'S pharmaceutical industry in general, and E. R. Squibb & Sons in particular, was pioneered by a maverick. Dr. Edward Robinson Squibb was a crusading scientist rather than a business man, and vehemently distrusted such business staples as patents, salesmen, advertising, and even corporations themselves.

Squibb spent his life battling for the standardization and purity of drugs, laying the basis of modern pharmacy and launching the movement that produced the first Pure Food and Drug Act.

Squibb was just as stern a moralist away from his laboratory. He considered certain passages of the opera Lohengrin "offensive," and was horrified to learn once that his wife had had European earrings smuggled past customs for her. He brought the earrings back to customs, had them assessed and paid the duty.

His campaign against commercial drug adulteration started during his years as a young assistant surgeon in the Navy in the 1840s and 50s. A self-administered dose of rhubarb made him violently ill; analysis revealed that it was worm-eaten and full of sand. Later examinations in the ship's dispensary disclosed many other medical supplies unfit for use. He promptly dumped half the supplies overboard.

Repeated discoveries of such flagrant impurities as 21 pounds of sand in the gum arabic, and rhubarb in the opium, added fuel to his obsession.

Determined to replace the adulterated drugs issued to the Navy, he wangled an assignment to the New York Shipyard (popularly known as the Brooklyn Navy Yard). There he obtained permission to set up a laboratory to make his own pure drugs.

When Squibb found that the existing supply of commercially made ether varied so much in strength that its clinical effect was unpredictable, he manufactured his own.

He then went on to make chloroform, which had recently come into use as an anesthetic. In 1855 he successfully administered his first dose to a brother-in-law before extracting a decayed tooth with a pair of pliers.

Dedicated as he was, however, Squibb needed to earn more money than the $1800 a year which the Navy paid him. He had married soon after arriving at the Brooklyn Yard, and already had two sons, Charles and Edward, to support.

His young wife was rather extravagant and frivolous, insisting on expensive bedroom furniture, imported clothes and a summer house during the hardest times. And to add to his burdens, she was subject to epilepsy.

Squibb resigned from the Navy in 1857, worked for a year in a new commercial laboratory in Louisville, Kentucky, and then, on the strength

FIRST BROOKLYN laboratory *(above)* of E. R. Squibb & Son produced ether and other drugs of dependable purity, standard strength, established today's "ethical" industry.

MASKED TECHNICIANS *(below)* in modern New Brunswick, N.J., plant manufacture antibiotics, undreamed of in Dr. Squibb's day, under strictly controlled sterile conditions.

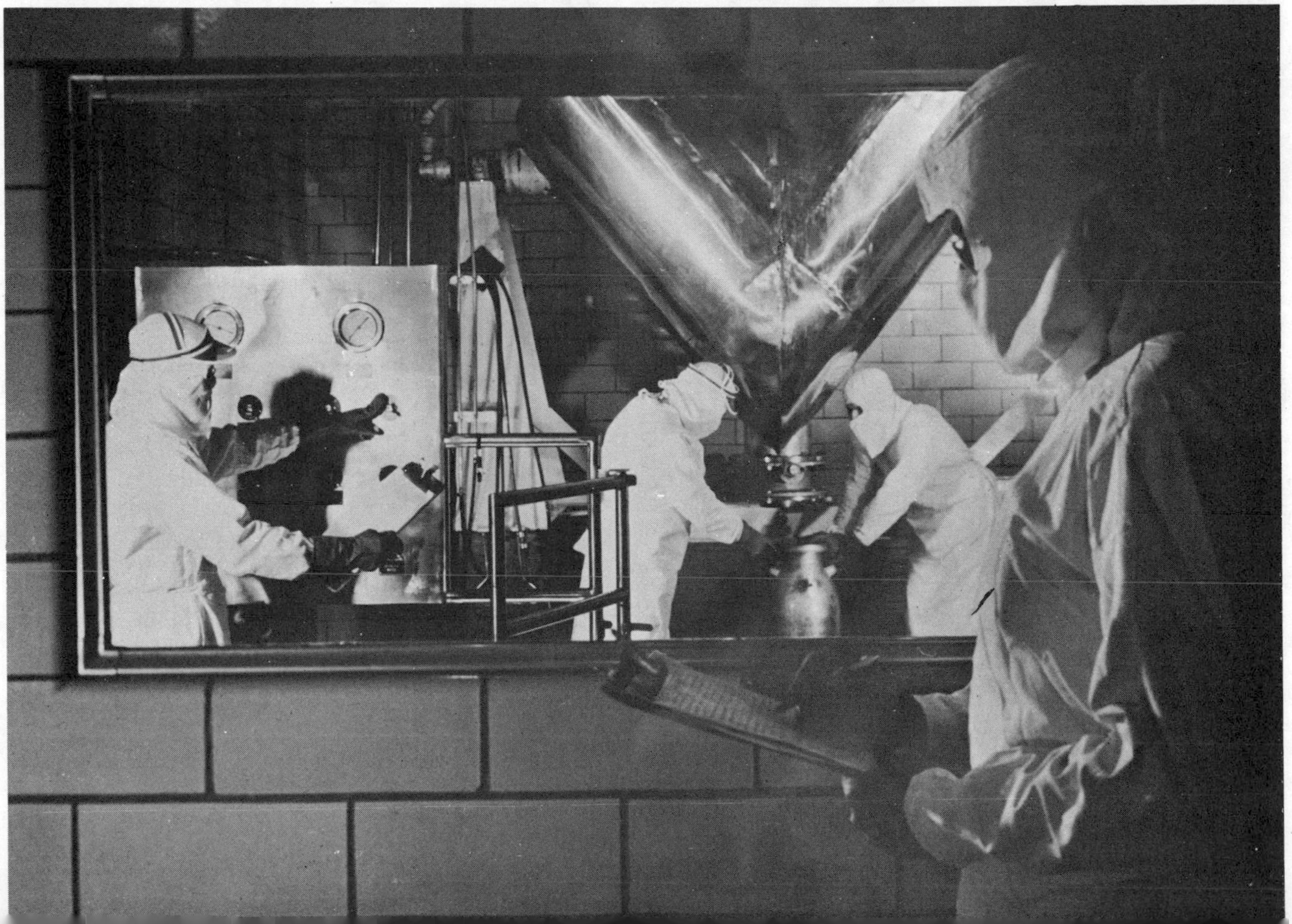

Fires, frustrations could not halt Squibb campaign, company progress

of a promised army contract, borrowed $1300 and set up his own laboratory in Brooklyn Heights.

His only concession to advertising was the 320 circulars stating his qualifications which he sent to physicians and pharmacists.

In 1858 the firm of Edward R. Squibb, M.D., shipped its first order —18 pounds of chloroform. In less than six weeks more capital was needed for expansion.

OLD BUILDING near entrance to Brooklyn Bridge housed first Squibb laboratory, started in 1858. A century later, Squibb's Brooklyn plant, whose gleaming lights welcome bridge traffic from Manhattan, fills 13 large buildings on the same spot.

Soon after, a young assistant, faint from ether fumes, dropped a bottle of it, thus starting the first of many fires which were to demolish Squibb's laboratories.

Squibb himself was severely burned but not beaten. He rebuilt the laboratory with $2100 raised by friends. Business recovered so quickly that the loan was repaid in three years.

Receipts from May to December, 1859, totalled over $5000. The Civil War broke out and the long-promised Army orders materialized. The firm was soon straining to keep up with production.

Concern for his private and business affairs never lessened his concern about drug adulteration. In 1860 he received an appointment to the Committee of Revision of the U.S. Pharmacopeia (the basic code of U.S. Pharmacy), where he began to take his first whacks at the quacks.

After melting down a cask of commercial aloes, from which he separated the debris, he mailed both to the Committee. The debris weighed half as much as the aloes.

During the War years Squibb petitioned Congress to enforce the Act of 1848, (which prohibited the import of adulterated drugs) by replacing politically appointed inspectors with those of scientific background. Congress took no action.

Some years before, he had petitioned Congress on quite a different matter. After flogging had been abolished in the Navy, he wrote a 2500-word demand for its restoration, which also went unheeded.

Just before the war ended Squibb

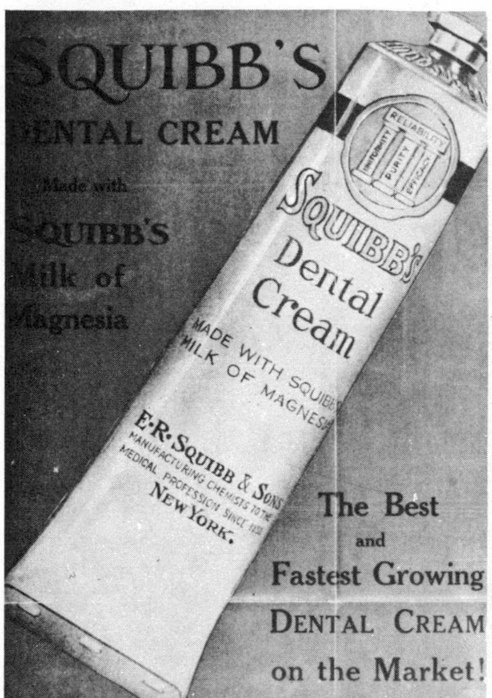

MASS ADVERTISING, started after death of Squibb, made firm's products household staples throughout entire nation.

MAJOR INTEREST of the young Dr. Squibb, shown here as assistant surgeon in the Navy, was production of pure, standard drugs, end to adulteration and quackery. Existing enormous industry was by-product of his lifelong, bitterly waged crusade.

expanded his laboratory to handle increased Army orders.

The timing was bad. Peacetime slowdown of orders, cost of expansion, and a general post-war depression left the company in a slump. Squibb was in debt for $6000—barely able even to renew a $25,000 mortgage on the laboratory.

The new structure remained almost idle for over five years while taxes and debts mounted. In 1867 alone, the loss was $8,000. The discouraged doctor began buying cemetery plots.

In 1871, despite another fire, the family finances took an upward swing. Squibb invested in and helped organize the National Chemical Wood Treatment Company to distil acetic acid from wood.

He took over personal management of the plant, and after five years the company was selling $33,000 worth of acid annually. The net earnings of the corporation in 1879 were over $10,000.

Meanwhile, business at Squibb's own laboratory had been improving. In 1873 sales were up 45%.

The problem of meeting debts and taxes reduced, Squibb once again turned his attention to the fight for pure drugs.

In 1876, convinced that the Pharmacopeia could never establish genuine standards until it was taken out of the hands of patent medicine profiteers, he asked the American Medical Association to take over control. The A.M.A. tabled the proposal.

Disgusted but not discouraged, he wrote a rough draft of a Pure Food and Drug Act, versions of which were enacted in 1880 by both the New York and New Jersey Legislatures. Powerful patent medicine lobbies stalled Federal passage, however, until six years after his death.

The A.M.A. had also rejected his plan to publish a periodical to keep the medical profession abreast of scientific development, so he founded his own publication, "An Ephemeris." It not only evaluated new medicines and techniques but also took a resounding whack at quacks and charlatans, as well as attacking Medical Journals for accepting advertising.

By this time he was in his 80s and not well. The business had prospered as his reputation for pure, ethical products grew—annual sales before his death came to $414,410. In 1882 he retired and his sons took over, but he refused to incorporate, feeling divided responsibility destroyed initiative.

Until his death in 1900 from a heart attack, he disapproved from the sidelines while his son Charles introduced modern business techniques such as the opening of a Manhattan showroom, enlarging the sales force from a counter attendant and stock man to 13 men.

In 1901, a year after the elder Squibb's death, the company was finally incorporated, and four years later control was sold to Lowell Palmer and Theodore Weicker. The business began to expand beyond the doctor's dreams.

In 1952 Mathieson Chemical Corp. purchased the company and two years later merged with Olin Industries to form Olin Mathieson Chemical Corp. Squibb sales today are in excess of $100 million. This corporate immensity would have surprised Dr. Squibb, who as a go-it-aloner, often said while fighting the whole world, "God and One is a Majority."

LET THERE BE LIGHT

Edison's incandescent lamp lit up world

OF ALL THE GIANTS of late 19th century technology, Thomas Alva Edison was probably the greatest.

He was certainly the most prolific.

As every schoolchild knows, Edison invented the incandescent electric light; he also planned and put into operation the first complete electric lighting and power system.

But even before his spectacular triumph with the incandescent bulb, he had made contributions to the development of telegraphy and the telephone that established him as one of the greatest inventors of his day.

During the course of his long career, he also invented the phonograph, the motion picture camera, and the first practical electric storage battery.

Merely as a byproduct of his work on the electric light, he discovered an electrical phenomenon, the "Edison Effect," that helped lay the foundations for 20th century electronics.

And, last but by no means least, while other 19th century inventors were tinkering in their basement or backyard workshops, Edison pioneered the development of the modern industrial research laboratory.

He was born on Feb. 11, 1847, in Milan, Ohio, the son of a lumber and feed dealer, and grew up in Port Huron, Mich.

Went to Work at 12

Until he was 12, he was educated at home by his mother, a former school teacher; then he went to work as a railroad newsboy and "candy butcher."

When he was 15, a friendly local stationmaster taught him telegraphy, and a year later, he began roaming the Middle West as a tramp telegraph operator.

In his spare time, he read all the scientific literature he could lay his hands on—as he had been doing ever since his newsboy days. And he experimented with the equipment in every Western Union office he worked in, often to his employers' dismay.

In Louisville, he recalled years later, "I went one night into the battery room to obtain some sulphuric acid. The carboy tipped over, the acid ran out, went through the ceiling to the manager's room below, and ate up his desk and all the carpet. The next morning I was summoned before him and told that the company wanted operators, not experimenters."

By the time he was 18, he was seriously at work on his first great invention—the system of multiplex transmission that revolutionized telegraphy by making possible the sending of two or more messages along a single wire.

In 1867, he moved to Boston, then the center of electrical technology in the U.S.

At 21, "Full Time" Inventor

Just two years later, a notice appeared in a telegraphy trade journal, announcing that Thomas A. Edison, formerly a Western Union employee, would "hereafter devote his full time to bringing out his inventions."

At 21, Edison was in business as a freelance inventor.

His first patent was granted for a notably unsuccessful invention—electromagnetic "vote recorder" to speed the taking of roll call votes in Congress and the state legislatures. Each legislator would merely push a button on his desk to record his "aye" or "nay."

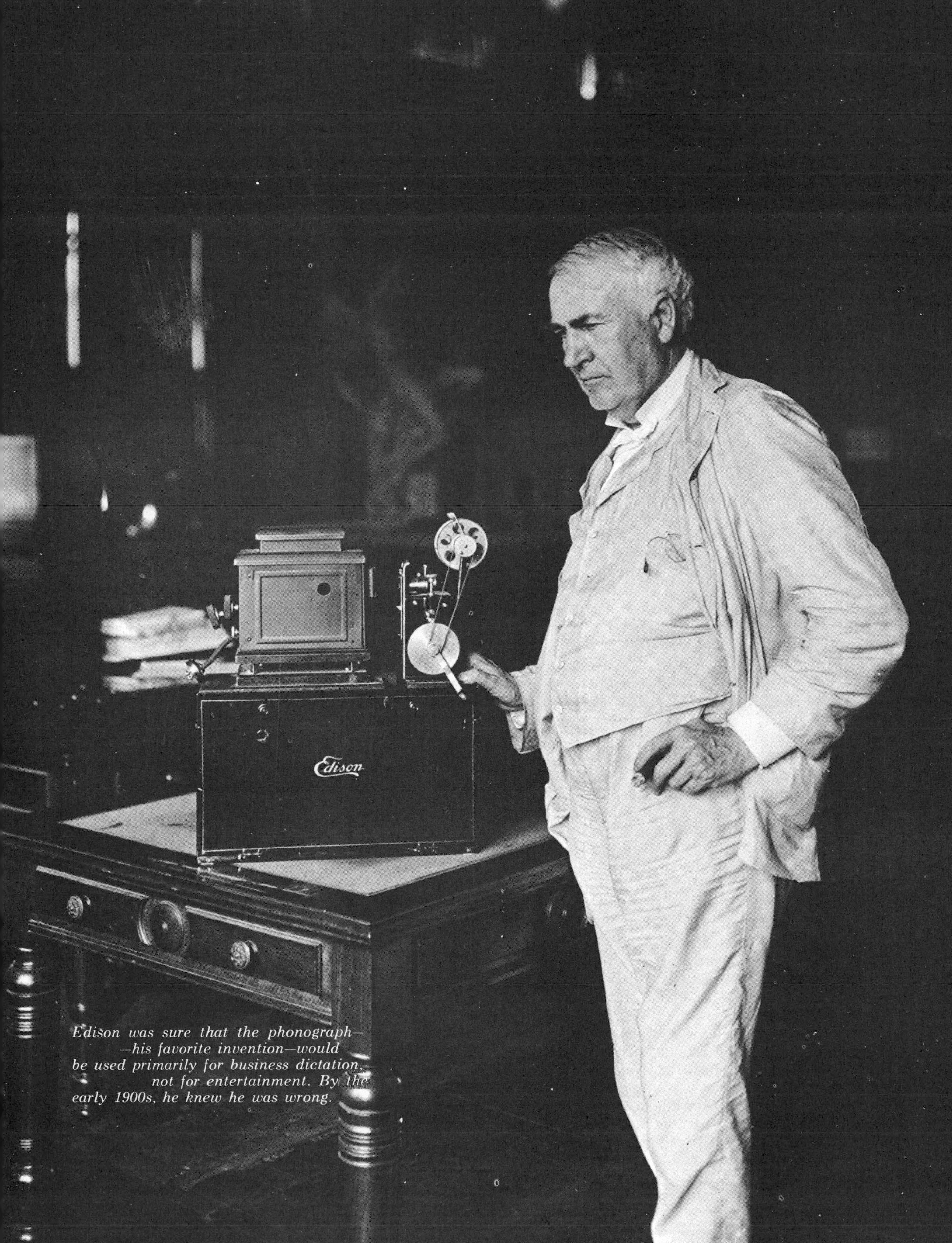

Edison was sure that the phonograph—his favorite invention—would be used primarily for business dictation, not for entertainment. By the early 1900s, he knew he was wrong.

EDISON PUT RESEARCH ON BIG BUSINESS BASIS

Not surprisingly, he was told in no uncertain terms—first by the Massachusetts legislature and then by Congress—that automated voting was the last thing any politician wanted; it would eliminate too many opportunities for speech-making.

Edison had his first stroke of luck in the middle of 1869, when he moved from Boston to New York and met Franklin Pope, an electrical engineer who worked for Gold Indicator, a wire service that supplied gold and stock quotations to half Wall St.

Coffee and Dumplings

Edison's funds had run out, and he was subsisting on a steady diet of coffee and apple dumplings; Pope was letting him sleep on a cot in the Gold Indicator Co. battery room.

Then, one day while Pope was showing him the mechanisms of the indicator, the whole transmitting apparatus came to a halt.

So did business in the Wall St. firms that were serviced by Gold Indicator; a few hours' delay in repairing the breakdown would have created enough ill will to send the company's customers running to a rival wire service.

Edison, who was working on a stock ticker of his own, quickly spotted the trouble and made the repair.

The next day, he was retained by Gold Indicator to work on improving the machine, and he was never out of work again.

$40,000 Fee

Over the next year, he patented his own stock ticker and took out seven other patents, covering a series of minor improvements in telegraphy, that earned him a $40,000 fee from his old employer, Western Union.

In 1871, he opened a small factory in Newark, N. J., and began turning out stock tickers and other electrical equipment for Western Union.

Over the next three years, while running his business and patenting scores of minor inventions, he returned to concentrated work on his multiplex telegraph.

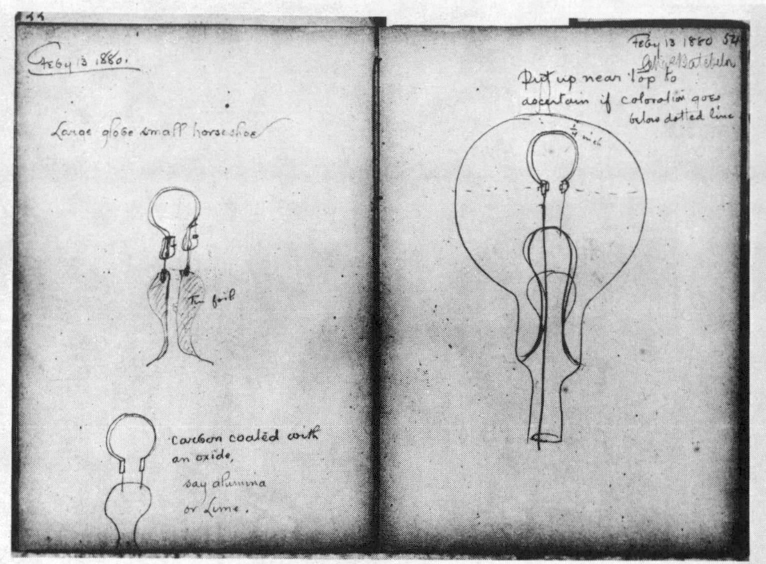

Edison's laboratory notebook for February, 1880, records his discovery of the "Edison Effect," related to the generation and movement of free electrons in space, vital to the development of modern electronics.

In 1874, the "quadruplex," which could send four messages on one wire (two in each direction) at a rate of 142 telegrams an hour, was finally perfected, and Edison's reputation as a major inventor was made.

Patent War

The quadruplex also triggered the first of many "patent wars" over Edison inventions—between Western Union, which had contracted for the system and then delayed in paying for it, and Jay Gould's Atlantic & Pacific Telegraph Co., which had taken the young inventor off the financial hook.

Shortly after the quadruplex was completed, Edison moved to Menlo Park, N. J.

The laboratory he built there was the first of its kind—virtually a pilot plant for the great industrial research laboratories of the 20th century.

Industrial R & D

It was an "invention factory," magnificiently equipped, staffed by the most talented mechanics and technicians from the Newark factory and also by several university-trained scientists—a radical departure in a day when practical technology and "pure" science were considered to be light years apart.

The first major invention to come out of Menlo Park was the carbon telephone transmitter, patented in 1878.

Alexander Graham Bell had patented his telephone three years earlier but its transmitter was so weak that its users had to shout over the wire.

It was the combination of Bell's receiver and Edison's transmitter that made the telephone a success.

While he was working on the telephone, Edison noticed that the diaphragm of the receiver vibrated when the instrument was in use—and decided that these vibrations could be used to reproduce the human voice.

Edison regarded the research scientists on the staff of his Menlo Park, N. J., laboratory (below) with a

"Just tried experiment with a diaphragm having an embossing point and held against paraffin paper moving rapidly," he wrote in his laboratory notebook in July, 1877. "The speaking vibrations are indented nicely."

Four months later, the first phonograph played "Mary had a little lamb" to an astonished employee group. Early in 1878, it was patented.

The 1877 phonograph was extremely crude, however, and, although Edison always declared it was his favorite invention, he did not find time to perfect it until 1888.

The electric light came first.

Tired inventor posed with his improved phonograph in June, 1888, after 72 straight hours of work.

mixture of respect and friendly contempt. Edison said, "I can hire mathematicians, but they can't hire me."

Scientists had been learning how to turn electric power into light all through the 19th century.

In 1878, a few arc lights were already in use, but they were too large and glaring, and consumed too much current, for general use.

Half a dozen well-known inventors were already trying to develop a smaller light, and find a means of subdividing the current in an electric circuit so that a number of lights could be powered and turned on and off individually.

Enters Light Race

Edison entered the race in the fall of 1878, backed by a group of financiers headed by J. P. Morgan.

He announced to the press that he would have his light ready within six weeks—an estimate that was far too optimistic.

As he said in 1905, the electric light "caused me the greatest amount of study and required the most elaborate experiments" of any of his inventions. He was not ready to take it to the patent office until November, 1879.

The principle he worked on was that of the incandescent bulb, which earlier inventors had tried unsuccessfully to develop: a slender rod in a vacuum or near vacuum of glass, heated to incandescence by electric current and kept from burning out or melting by the absence of oxygen.

"Just consider this," he wrote while the work was in progress. "We have an almost infinitesimal filament heated to a degree which it is difficult to comprehend, and it is in a vacuum under conditions of which we are wholly ignorant. You cannot use your eyes to help you, and really know nothing of what is going on inside that tiny bulb."

Over the months, Edison made it his business to find out what was going on. He devoured all the available literature on high vacuums, an area in which research had only recently begun.

The bulb he finally produced was a vacuum of one-millionth part of an atmosphere, by far the highest ever produced in the U.S.

He tested hundreds of materials to find the right filament for the light, finally settling on a carbonized cellulose fiber.

On Oct. 20th, 1878, a lamp was turned on in the Menlo Park laboratory that burned for 13½ hours, according to laboratory records, 40 hours, according to tradition.

It would take only minor improvements, Edison knew, to make lights that would burn for hundreds of hours.

At 31, he had reached the pinnacle of his career.

During the year he spent on the light, he had also been studying the already successful gas distribution industry, and planning an electricity distribution system that, he believed, would put the gas companies out of business.

And he spent most of the next 10 years out of the laboratory, trying to put the system into operation.

His success was only moderate—partly because of financial conservatism of his backers, partly because of his own failing as a big businessman, and partly because he failed, astonishingly, to recognize the superiority of alternating current over direct current for large power installations. (The champion of A-C was George Westinghouse.)

By 1892, the Morgan group had formed the General Electric Co. (to engage in both power distribution and electrical manufacturing) and frozen Edison out of its active management.

After a brief and unsuccessful fling at mining, he returned to the laboratory.

He had patented his first motion picture camera in 1891, and its development occupied him during most of the decade.

In 1904 came his last major contribution to modern technology, the dry storage battery.

Although he had retired from the power industry, his days in the business world were by no means over. By the 1920s, his various manufacturing enterprises, combined into a single corporation as Thomas A. Edison, Inc., were grossing over $20 million a year.

Edison died in 1931, one of the most honored men of his generation.

The value of his gifts to the 20th century can hardly be calculated—even in billions of dollars or trillions of kilowatt hours.

John Dryden (at desk) launched Prudential Insurance from unpretentious basement office in 1874.

INSURANCE FOR EVERYBODY

John F. Dryden tapped the mass market for life insurance with low-cost, pay-by-the-week "industrial" policies

BEFORE THE 1870s, life insurance was a luxury item.

It was John F. Dryden, co-founder of the Prudential Insurance Co. of America, who broadened the base of the life insurance industry in 1874 by making small "industrial" policies available to factory workers for only pennies a week.

Today, life insurance is part of the financial planning of seven out of every 10 American adults, including two thirds of those with family incomes between $3000 and $5000 a year and half of those whose family incomes are under $3000.

(Some 78% of all U.S. families now own insurance, compared to 74% who own automobiles, 60% homes (non-farm families), 38% liquid assets of savings bonds, savings and other bank accounts, etc., and 14% corporate stocks).

These 132 million Americans were buying nearly $78 billion of new insurance by 1960, to bring total policies to almost $685 billion, and collected $8 billion in benefits.

As for John F. Dryden's Prudential Co., it is one of the giants of the industry, second only to Metropolitan Life in size. (It has 36 million policy holders with $90.4 billion worth of life insurance in force, and it is paying $1.7 billion, including $509 million in dividends, to policyholders and beneficiaries).

The story of insurance goes back almost to the dawn of civilization. The early maritime peoples of the Mediterranean had primitive forms of marine and other property insurance. The military and religious fraternal organizations of classical Rome paid death benefits to their members, and so did the guilds of medieval Europe and cooperatives in 16th century England.

The development of true life insurance began in the 17th century, when the foundations of actuarial science were laid by mathematicians. (It was Dr. Edmund Halley, discoverer of the comet that bears his name, who constructed the first scientific mortality table.)

From the late 17th century on, the life insurance business grew rapidly in England and more slowly on the European continent. (For a time, British gamblers considered it a sporting wager to take out a policy on the life of anyone from the King on down. Parliament stopped this practice in 1744 with the Gambling Act, which prohibited buying life insurance except where "the person insuring shall have an interest in the life or death of the person insured.")

Churchmen pioneered

The first American life insurance company was established in 1759 by the Presbyterian Synods of New York and Philadelphia. Its sonorous title was "Corporation for the Relief of Poor and Distressed Presbyterian Ministers and for the Poor and Distressed Widows and Orphans of Presbyterian Ministers," later shortened by just "Presbyterian Ministers' Fund."

The Episcopalians followed suit with a non-profit insurance company of their own in 1769. But after that, the business grew only slowly until the mid-19th century.

Twenty-four marine and property insurance companies were chartered in the 1790s, but only one of them, the Insurance Co. of North America, appears to have sold any life insurance. This kind of protection was little needed in a predominantly rural society where the sons of the family simply took over the farm when the breadwinner died.

The first profit-making life insurance company, the Pennsylvania Co. for Insurance on Lives and Granting Annuities, appeared in 1809.

A number of others followed, but they were all low-pressure concerns that did little advertising, hired few, if any, agents, and were content with a small volume of business.

These early 19th century insurance firms were ordinary stock companies, owned and controlled by their stockholders like any other corporation, although a few of them did pay special dividends to policyholders who did not own stock.

The first mutual companies, owned and controlled by policyholders who automatically earn dividends from their "participating" policies, appeared in 1843.

And for the next 25 years, the industry enjoyed rapid growth. By the end of the 1860s, $2 billion worth of life insurance was in force in the U.S., and the agency system was well established.

However, only the well-to-do could afford the high annual premiums of ordinary life insurance.

The factory workers whose numbers swelled as the Industrial Revolution gained momentum had virtually no way to protect their families.

All that was available to them were the death benefits provided for members by some lodges and fraternal organizations and the embryonic labor unions; and the "assessment insurance" offered by businesses known, as the 16th century English cooperatives had been, as "Friendly Societies."

A Friendly Society simply assessed its members for small fixed sums, either at regular intervals or only when somebody died, for a fund from which to pay benefits to deceased members' families.

At worst, the Friendly Societies were completely fraudulent; at best, they were inefficient and liable to collapse under the weight of claims, since they ignored actuarial tables and accumulated no substantial cash reserves.

The upshot of all this was, of course, that the families that needed life insurance most—accumulating a personal nest egg of any size on a 19th century factory worker's wage was very difficult indeed—were least likely to have any.

A huge mass market for life insurance was ready and waiting to be

In 1892, the flourishing Prudential Co. moved to new building, a turreted, gray stone structure inspired by French chateau.

Established insurance firms weren't interested in idea of pennies-a-week industrial policies

tapped when John F. Dryden went into the insurance business shortly after the Civil War.

Dryden understood this mass market for the very good reason that he came from a factory family.

He was born in 1839, the son of a mechanic who, after a brief fling at farming in Maine, returned to work in the mills of Worcester, Mass., and settled his family there.

John Dryden, Sr., died when young John was 10. He had been a skilled worker, undoubtedly earning good wages for the 1830s, and he left his family better off than most.

They owned their own home, and Mrs. Dryden took in roomers to help make ends meet. Nevertheless, young John Dryden's adolescence was hard. He worked as a bakery delivery boy in the early mornings and as a machinist's apprentice after school, putting a strain on his health from which he never entirely recovered.

After graduating from high school, he worked in a machine shop for several years. By 1861, he had saved enough to go on to Yale – a very unusual accomplishment for a 19th century workingman's son.

He spent four years in New Haven, married his landlady's daughter, and was prevented from earning a degree only by a complete physical breakdown his senior year.

He and his young wife moved to Ohio, where his married sister had settled – and where the climate was proverbially heathful. And it was there that his insurance career began.

Dryden had become interested in the insurance business—and particularly in the idea of low-cost policies for workingmen – while he was still in college. He had studied the growth of the Prudential Assurance Co. of London, which had been selling industrial insurance in England since 1854, and he was positive that the same type of business could succeed in the U.S.

To all the established U.S. insurance companies, however—including Dryden's first employer, Aetna Life Insurance Co. – the thought of selling small policies to factory workers for a few cents a week, collected weekly by agents from the policyholders' homes seemed completely unsound.

Dryden spent his first two years in the business selling ordinary insurance for Aetna.

His Columbus, Ohio, agency failed, and in 1866 he brought his family back East (Forrest Dryden, a future president of Prudential, had been born at the end of 1864) and settled in Brooklyn, where he began selling insurance again.

The late 1860s were a boom time for the insurance business, but even so, it was not until the end of the decade that Dryden was able to interest anyone in expanding into the untried field of industrial insurance.

Then, when he did find a partner – a wealthy insurance man named H. H. Goodman – New York State refused to grant his projected industrial insurance company a charter, and the partnership collapsed.

So in 1873, Dryden moved on to Newark, N.J., and rented desk space in the office of a real estate man named Allen Bassett.

Family protection

In the meantime, the worst economic depression of the century had struck the nation. Insurance companies, like business of all kinds, were folding by the dozen, and conditions for launching a radically new venture could hardly have been less favorable.

On the other hand, however, the Panic of 1873 underscored the desperate need of industrial workers for some kind of family protection. With thousands thrown out of work, there

Prudential offered good jobs to "typewriter girls" of 1900; today, company has 55,000 employees

"Prudential girls" enlivened company ads at turn of the century.

were more burials in pauper's graves —and more destitute families—than ever before.

And Dryden, who was more determined than ever to found his industrial insurance company, could hardly have chosen a better location than Newark.

Newark in 1873 was the third largest industrial city in the U.S. Its population was 115,000, swelled by 70,000 new arrivals in 15 years—most of them industrial workers, many Irish and German immigrants. The average Newark worker earned just $513 a year.

Dryden quickly made a convert of his well-to-do office mate, Bassett.

Next he approached Dr. Leslie Ward, a young Newark physician from a wealthy and prominent family. Dr. Ward's active social conscience had led him to hang out his shingle in a working class neighborhood, and he liked the idea of an insurance company that would help his patients and people like them.

Dryden still had to sell a number of hard-headed businessmen — enough to raise $30,000 of capital — on the idea that industrial insurance could be not just another kind of charity, as many of them were inclined to believe, but a sound business proposition.

And even with two prominent citizens like Bassett and Ward as partners, the task of persuasion took many months.

But in February, 1875, the Prudential Friendly Society — named after its successful British counterpart — was finally chartered.

All through the spring and summer of 1875, Dryden labored over actuarial tables, figuring rates, costs and commissions.

The new company actually went into business in September, with only $5900 in the bank and the rest of its $30,000 capitalization pledged but still unreceived.

Shortly thereafter, a New Jersey state actuary was told by his supervisors to visit a "peculiar little company which is doing a novel kind of insurance business in Newark."

And, to any established insurance firm, the description would have seemed quite accurate.

On a shoestring

Prudential was operating on the thinnest of shoestrings. Bassett, as president, was paid $150 a month, Dryden, as secretary, $100. The only other employees were a $40-a-month bookkeeper and a $3-a-week office boy.

The company still used Bassett's basement real estate office, refurbished with $52.40 worth of second-hand furniture, and defrayed its $116.67 monthly rent by subletting a back room to a Penn Mutual Life Insurance agent and renting desk space to a representative of J. M. Bradstreet & Sons.

However, this "peculiar little company" did have the backing of leading businessmen. "No institution in Newark," wrote the conservative *Newark Register*, "has a board of directors that can more strongly claim the confidence of our people."

Dryden began advertising for agents in December, but he himself was the company's star salesman during its first months.

He visited factory after factory during lunch hours, and shocked the business community by staying open in the evening so that workers could

Life Insurance — 1895 to 1964
Figures from Institute of Life Insurance (millions)

	Ordinary Life		Industrial		Group Life	
	No. of Policies	Amount	No. of Policies	Amount	No. of Policies	Amount
1895	2	$ 4170	7	$ 818	....	$........
1900	3	6124	11	1449	....	....
1905	5	9585	17	2278	....	....
1910	6	11783	23	3125	....	....
1915	9	16650	32	4279	.120	100
1920	16	32018	48	6948	2	1570
1925	23	52892	71	12318	3	4247
1930	32	78576	86	17963	6	9801
1935	33	70684	81	17471	6	10208
1940	37	79346	85	20866	9	14938
1945	48	101550	101	24874	11	22172
1950	64	149071	108	33415	19	47793
1955	80	216600	112	39682	32	101300
1960	95	340268	100	39563	44	175434
1964	104	458029	92	39833	54	252182

*Refers to number of individual policies, not "master certificates" held by organizations

New Prudential Co. was in the black by 1877

come in and talk insurance.

The first Prudential policies offered sickness benefits of $3 to $25 a week; $100 a year after age 65; $50 to $500 in death benefits for adults, and $10 to $50 for children.

This was minimal coverage, but it paid for funeral expenses, a crushing financial blow to an uninsured working class family, and could provide a small nest egg, too. (Five hundred dollars, after all, was almost a year's wages for an average worker.)

And all claims were paid within 24 hours.

By the end of 1875, Prudential had 279 policies in force. By November, 1876, the number had risen to 7000 – and claims came in so fast that the company was dangerously in the red. "I am afraid that we are likely to be swamped by this expensive kind of success," wrote one member of the board of directors.

Turn of the tide

At one point during the summer of 1876, it was only Dr. Ward's medical skill that kept Prudential in business. He saved the life of a dangerously ill patient who also happened to be the holder of a $500 policy; and just then, a $500 claim would have driven the company into bankruptcy.

By the end of the year, Prudential's directors were begining to think that their investment in the company had been nothing but a charitable contribution, after all.

They agreed, however, to send Dryden to England, on a $250 expense account, for consultation with Prudential Assurance of London.

Rather to the disenchanted directors' surprise, the trip was a triumph. Dryden interviewed Henry Harben, head of the giant British enterprise, which by then was selling 1.5 million policies a year and collecting an annual $5 million in premiums, and won his enthusiastic support.

He got advice on every aspect of operation, from agent organization to bookkeeping, and a full set of the work-saving forms that Prudential of London had developed.

After two weeks in London, Dryden returned with a complete plan for reorganization of the U.S. Prudential—and for its eventual expansion from coast to coast.

Economy measures adopted immediately included—in addition to the streamlined bookkeeping with the new forms—the abandonment of sickness benefits and a slight rate increase; the actuarial tables that had been used for the company's original rates were based on the experience of ordinary insurance companies, whose customers were better heeled and healthier.

1877, the worst year of the depression, was the year the tide turned for Prudential.

With company finances on a sound footing, profits began to appear. The first branch office was opened in Paterson, N. J., in April.

J. Walter Thompson came up with Prudential "Rock" idea in 1895.

Two years later, the company—whose name had been changed to The Prudential Insurance Co. of America—began to expand on a larger scale, with offices in New York and Philadelphia.

There was still some criticism of industrial insurance from conservative quarters; it was even said that the small policies on children's lives encouraged poor mothers to murder their babies. Less dramatic but no less ludicrous was the charge that Prudential agents deliberately let policies lapse to reap bigger profits for their employers. Actually, the company did far better on policies that stayed in force.

When the first Prudential office opened in New York, the *Sunday Mercury* said, "It may be known to some of our readers that a small, one-horse insurance company with its headquarters in Newark, N. J., is actually endeavoring to scoop in a harvest of victims in this city and state . . . On the 31st day of July, its agents crossed the Hudson River and invaded this city like microscopic pestilence or an army of worms or hornets."

But none of this kept the people who needed them from buying Prudential policies. By the end of 1879, 43,715 were in force, amounting to $3,866,913.

And in the same year, two of the biggest ordinary insurance companies, Metropolitan and John Hancock, accorded Prudential the sincerest form of flattery by moving into the industrial insurance business.

Six years later, with one million industrial policies in force, Prudential returned the compliment by entering the rapidly growing ordinary insurance field.

John Dryden took over the presidency of his big company in 1881, and held the office until his death in 1911, when he was succeeded by his son Forrest.

During all those years, Prudential's spectacular growth continued —from the million policies of 1885 to 2.5 million in1896, 10 million in1911.

In this century, Prudential, like all major insurance companies, has derived more and more of its income from ordinary insurance, less and less from industrial.

With the steady rise in their living standards and aspirations, U.S. workers have tended to "move up" to ordinary insurance for more coverage and the convenience and lower cost of annual payments by mail.

And group insurance (introduced in 1911 by Equitable Life) has also risen in importance.

But industrial insurance, which contributed so much to the growth of the insurance business, is still very much alive. It is the sole source of protection for millions of low-income families. And although their dollar volume is far lower than that earned by either ordinary or group insurance, there are actually more industrial policies in force today than any other type.

CHARLES A. GOODYEAR

RUBBER FOR INDUSTRY

Charles Goodyear turned the impractical novelty called "India rubber" into a vital raw material with hundreds of industrial applications

GOODYEAR was born in 1800 in New Haven, Conn., the son of a small manufacturer and inventor.

He would have liked to study for the Congregational ministry, but family finances kept him from going beyond high school – and anyway, his father, Amasa, who had decided to go into hardware sales, had the mistaken notion that young Charles would make a good merchant.

The hardware business, at that time, consisted entirely of manufacturer-wholesalers who sold to traveling peddlers. A. Goodyear & Sons, which Charles joined after an apprenticeship with a Philadelphia firm, also had a retail store—probably the first in the U.S.

It did fairly well for a few years, but went under, like hundreds of other small businesses, in the depression that hit the nation at the end of the 1820s.

And Charles, who had assumed the responsibility for his elderly father's debts, began making the trips to debtors' prison that punctuated most of the rest of his life.

Seldom in all business history has one man's devotion to a product borne such amazing fruits as the devotion of Charles Goodyear to the sticky, temperamental material that his generation called India rubber.

Early in the 1830s, when Goodyear first noticed a line of rubber goods in a Manhattan store window, rubber was hardly more than a curiosity. When he died in 1860, it was the basis of a flourishing industry an industry that owed its very existence to Goodyear's process of vulcanization, and its rapid growth, in large part, to his enthusiasm.

Charles Goodyear was a spectacularly unsuccessful businessman. But he deserves to be remembered as the pioneer of the rubber business not only because he turned rubber into a versatile, reliable, all-weather material with hundreds of industrial applications, but also because he saw its potentialities and devoted all his time and energy – and a small fortune—to developing and promoting them during the last 15 years of his life.

The Goodyears were stubbornly determined not to declare themselves bankrupt; Charles was in New York trying to raise yet another loan on the day in the early '30s when he saw a rubber life preserver in the Roxbury India Rubber Company's show window.

The near-bankrupt young hardware merchant walked into the company's showroom—and into history.

Rubber had been discovered by the Western world when Columbus came back from Santo Domingo with some of the odd little bouncing balls that the natives there played games with.

But it was given no practical application whatsoever until late in the 18th century, when somebody noticed that the stuff could rub out pencil marks.

This fact gave it its name, and a small market as an artists' supply;

but it was still so little in demand that ships were carrying it as ballast early in the 19th century.

Scientists and manufacturers alike were beginning to get curious about it, though.

In 1823, a Scotsman named Charles Mackintosh developed a solution of rubber and benzene that could be spread between two layers of cloth. He began manufacturing waterproof coats that gave commercially processed rubber its first toehold in the consumer market – and added a new word to the language.

The only trouble with Mackintosh's macintoshes was that they turned sticky and odoriferous when the wearer stood near a hot stove, and got as hard as boards in extreme cold.

But even this partial success stimulated enough excitement about rubber's potentialities to start dozens of experimenters on the search for the perfect rubber compound – a search that was to end almost two decades later with Goodyear's discovery of vulcanization.

French manufacturers began using rubber in garters and suspenders.

And the material made its first major appearance on the U.S. market when an enterprising importer began selling rubber shoes handmade by South American Indians. The shoes were a luxury item at $5 a pair, and an impractical one at that, since they too turned sticky in heat and rigid in cold; but they caught the popular fancy.

Then, late in the '20s, a Boston factory foreman named E. M. Chaffee came up with a rubber-turpentine compound that looked better than any of its predecessors. He also invented a spreading machine, and, with the backing of a group of local financiers, founded Roxbury India Rubber in 1828.

Rubber coats, hats, and shoes were soon flooding the market; in fact, just about anything that could be rubberized was. Other small companies followed Roxbury into the field, and for about five years, the industry enjoyed a small boom.

The boom was still on when Charles Goodyear saw the life preserver in the Roxbury display window. Intrigued by the device itself as well as by the new material, he went in to see how it worked, and decided when it was demonstrated to him that the valve was extremely inefficient.

He bought the life preserver, took it home and, in the little spare time that staving off his creditors allowed him, began developing a better valve.

A few months later, when he took the perfected valve back to the Roxbury Co., the rubber bubble had burst.

Toward the end of his life, in his two-volume treatise on rubber production, *Gum Elastic,* Goodyear listed the defects of rubber in its natural state:

"1. It becomes rigid and inflexible in cold weather.

"2. It is softened and decomposed in the sun and hot temperatures.

"3. It is very soluble and quickly dissolved when brought into contact with grease, essential or common oils, and though more slowly, yet as surely dissolved by perspiration.

"4. It is in its nature so very adhesive that when any two surfaces are brought into contact, they become by slight pressure one mass that cannot be separated.

"5. It loses its elasticity by continued tension or constant use.

"6. It has a very unpleasant odor."

And none of this formidable array of flaws had been more than partially or temporarily corrected by Chaffee's compound. It was hardly surprising that once the novelty appeal of the rubber goods made from it had worn off, their sales collapsed like a rubber coat in a heatwave.

But Goodyear, completely lacking as he was in both financial resources and scientific training, decided that a better compound could be found and that he was the man to find it.

Roxbury India Rubber, impressed by his new valve, encouraged him to try, but was in no financial position to offer him a retainer.

At least, he discovered when he began his work in 1834, rubber was an inexpensive subject for experimentation; its market price had plummeted to about five cents a pound.

Working in the kitchen of his New Haven home, with only small loans from friends to buy his rubber—and pay the family grocery bills—Goodyear began developing new compounds.

In 1835, he went alone to New York and persuaded friends there to set him up in a tiny laboratory and supply him with chemicals. Within a few months, he had developed a rubber - magnesia - lime compound that looked good enough to win medals at two trade fairs that fall.

He brought his family down from New Haven, launched a small manufacturing firm, and enjoyed a short period of relative prosperity.

The birth of the automobile industry in the 1890s (below, Frank and Charles Duryea in their first auto) created vast market for rubber products

Rubber plus sulphur plus heat

But he soon found out that the magnesia-lime coating was neutralized by the slightest touch of acid, leaving the rubber as sticky, adhesive, and temperature-sensitive as ever.

Out of business and back in debt, he began experimenting again.

The second apparently successful compound was the result of an accident. Trying to remove the color from a piece of rubber fabric that he had embossed, he used nitric acid—and saw that where the acid fell, the material turned black, lost its stickiness, and acquired a perfect finish.

If Goodyear had had enough chemistry to know that nitric acid is largely composed of sulphuric acid, he might have hit upon the secret of vulcanization then and there.

As it was, he decided that the nitric acid coating was the answer to the problem.

He began manufacturing again. In 1837, he was granted a patent for the process, and soon found a wealthy backer to help him expand the manufacturing operation.

When the panic of 1837 hit the nation a few months later, the new business was wiped out. But Goodyear was able to move on, with his patent, to his old friends from Roxbury India Rubber.

In 1838, the revitalized Roxbury Co. received a sizeable government contract for mail bags—and disaster struck again.

After a month in storage, the mail bags were found to have disintegrated into the old, familiar, sticky mess.

The trouble was — as Goodyear realized too late—that the nitric acid process worked successfully only on very thin rubber sheet.

The unfavorable publicity resulting from the mailbag fiasco, only three years after the failure of the magnesia-lime compound, was a near death blow to the infant rubber industry – and Goodyear's reputation.

He was already considered something of a crank; it was a standing joke among businessmen that "if you meet a man who has on an India rubber cap, stock, coat, vest and shoes, with an India rubber money purse without a cent in it, that is Charles Goodyear."

And now his hopes for the financial backing he would need to try again appeared so slim that he was almost ready to go back to the hardware business.

But this time, the real breakthrough was only months away.

It came when he found his assistant in the Roxbury plant experimenting with a sulphur coating that seemed to give excellent results when dried in the sun.

Sulphur might be the magic ingredient—but how to make it permeate not just sheets, but solid masses of rubber?

The final discovery, when it came, was another happy accident; Goodyear dropped a lump of sulphur-treated rubber on a hot stove and saw that although it charred on the surface, it did not melt.

He left the accidentally heat-treated lump outdoors overnight and found that it also resisted cold. The search was over.

However, although he now believed that rubber plus sulphur plus heat produced the perfect compound, he still had to develop an exact formula; and for that, he needed better equipment than a kitchen stove.

Close to 40 years old, in failing health, and still thoroughly discredited in the business community, he somehow scraped up the money to build a small test plant at Woburn, Mass., and there, with the help of his father and brothers, he experimented for four more years.

He finally applied for a patent on the vulcanization process in 1843, and received it in 1844.

He likened vulcanization to the tanning of hide or the conversion of iron to steel, and said of his invention: "While the inventor admits that these discoveries were not the result of *scientific* chemical observation, he is not willing to admit that they were the result of what is commonly termed accident; he claims them to be the result of the closest application and observation."

Goodyear never went back to manufacturing; he devoted the rest of his life to experimenting with, writing about, and promoting rubber.

Licensing rights and royalties earned him close to $200,000, a sizeable fortune for the mid-19th century; but he poured most of it right back into the industry.

He spent $30,000 on "Goodyear's Vulcanite Palace" at the Great Exposition of 1851 in London, and $50,000 on an even more ambitious display at the Paris Exposition Universelle in 1855.

In *Gum Elastic,* he detailed close to 1000 applications for his favorite substance, virtually all of which have proved to be practical.

The rubber industry's great spurt of growth did not come until the end of the century, when the developing automotive and electrical industries created vast new demands for the material that not even Goodyear could have foreseen.

But it was solidly established, with capital investment of $7 million and annual sales of $4-5 million, well before Goodyear's death in 1860.

"If the search had failed," one of Goodyear's biographers has written of his discovery of vulcanization, "he would have been remembered, if at all, as a ruthless, crazy eccentric who sacrificed all the ordinary comforts of life in pursuing a shadow. The search succeeded, and laid the foundations for a great industry. The eccentric became the genius."

Small rubber companies of 1850s turned out products from combs and corset stays to furniture like that displayed by Goodyear at London Exposition.

Woolworth opened his first five and ten in Lancaster, heart of Pennsylvania Dutch country, on June 21, 1879.

KING OF THE FIVE-AND-DIME

Nickels and dimes added up to a multi-million-dollar merchandising empire for Frank W. Woolworth

FRANK WINFIELD WOOLWORTH was a man obsessed with an idea. In the best Horatio Alger tradition, he clung tenaciously to his vision of becoming *somebody* throughout early years of poverty, depression and failure.

He pioneered the "five-and-ten" merchandising concept which was to become an integral part of American life just as the Sunday funnies or Little League baseball.

By creating a gold mine out of nickels and dimes, Woolworth helped to develop mass production at low unit prices, and he brought thousands of items within reach of the lowest economic group. Ten-cent dentifrices and cosmetics put toothbrushes in every bathroom and cold cream on every woman's vanity.

When Woolworth started out in the decades after the Civil War, his idea of a small change store was looked down upon by established merchants. But the once-startling five-and-ten has blossomed into a billion dollar annual business.

Frank Woolworth was born in Jefferson County, upper New York State, in 1852. For generations the Woolworths had been tied to the soil, sometimes as tenant farmers, sometimes as landowners. Men of the family were trained for no other work. Woolworth's father owned 108 acres and eight cows. Principal crops were potatoes and dairy products.

At 16, when Woolworth finished his education, he went to work full time on the family farm. But he hated the long winters and rough. monotonous work. He dreamed of escaping to a clerking job behind a store counter, but no one would hire the inexperienced youth. Business was slow and prices had skyrocketed after the Civil War.

At the age of 21 he landed a job of sorts with Augsbury & Moore, a leading drygoods store in Watertown, New York. He received no salary for the first three months. His tasks were sweeping the floor, delivering packages and dressing windows.

During the next six years Woolworth rose to the position of clerk at a weekly salary of $10, married a young Canadian girl named Jennie Creighton, bought a four-acre farm, and saw the birth of his first child. But the dream of making his mark in the world was nowhere in sight.

"No one thought Woolworth would rise higher than a clerkship," a friend recalled years later. But his mother had more confidence. "Someday, my son, you'll be a rich man."

A new merchandising craze – the five-cent counter – flared up briefly during these hard years. Merchants with superfluous stock dumped it on a "five cent counter" to get rid of it. Unwanted items quickly disappeared and customers usually bought some of the store's regular merchandise as well.

However, the boom in five-cent selling soon faded because goods were shoddy and merchandise lacked variety. Profits were small and experienced retailers dubbed the idea a passing fad.

But to Woolworth, another man's failure was his opportunity. His lifelong ambition to be somebody finally found a concrete objective – to open a store of his own stocked only with five-cent items.

In 1879, he borrowed $300 from his employer and set out to find a town where he could locate. He discovered that Utica, New York (35,000 population) had been untouched by the new merchandising strategy.

He rented a small store and distributed flyers announcing the grand opening of his "Great Five Cent Store". He stocked such items as candlesticks, biscuit cutters, pie plates, tin spoons, thread and handkerchiefs. (Woolworth's affinity for the color red showed itself in brilliant displays of red jewelry and turkey red napkins and later in the

60-story Woolworth Building, once world's tallest building, celebrated 50th anniversary in 1963. Company still maintains its headquarters here.

Woolworth's low prices brought many items within reach of the poor

now-familiar red store fronts.)

Trade was heavy during the first two weeks but customers soon lost interest and returned to higher-priced stores.

But Woolworth was convinced that failure was not due to his idea but to Utica. The biggest handicap was lack of sufficient five-cent merchandise so he decided to raise the figure to ten cents and look for another town.

One month later he opened the first five-and-ten in Lancaster, Pennsylvania. Years later one of the three women clerks in the store remarked that "Mr. Woolworth sat on a platform on a winding stairway at the back of the store, guarding the sales box and watching the clerks at work."

The store proved highly popular with the thrifty Pennsylvania Dutch housewives and soon Woolworth began to broaden his horizons. His next ventures were in Harrisburg and York, but they proved repetitions of the Utica experience and he was forced to close the stores.

Scranton was the next Keystone State city to feel the Woolworth touch. This time a brother, Charles, was brought into partnership and for the remainder of Woolworth's career, relatives and trusted friends were to fill key positions within the company. And nearly 100 employees – buyers, managers – were to become millionaires.

Early records show that Woolworth sales reached $18.000 in 1881 and climbed to $24.125 by 1882. Although three of his five early attempts ended in failure, Woolworth was now the proud proprietor of one flourishing and one fairly successful store.

Old dreams of expansion soon returned to haunt him. It was obvious that the five-and-dime business needed more outlets. A chain of stores would enable him to buy goods in quantity, to attract new kinds of merchandise, and to sell more cheaply.

To expand, he needed more capital. He searched for partners with cash who would share half the risk in opening each new store in return for half its profits. By 1886, Woolworth had seven stores in Pennsylvania, New York and New Jersey. Annual sales climbed over the $100,000 mark.

Woolworth personally bought every item that appeared for sale on his counters. Profits depended upon intelligent buying and, since most jobbers were located in New York, he moved there in 1886.

Taking a $25-a-month room in Chambers Street and moving his family into a house in Brooklyn, he began a quest for low-priced articles. He soon learned that prices were kept high by jobbers who had the inside track with manfaucturers and they didn't want to be bothered by selling to him directly.

A Mother Hen

As he was walking along lower Broadway one day, he happened on a small candy shop whose proprietor was willing to supply him with candy at the low price of 20 cents a pound. Woolworth jubilantly ordered 100 pounds for his stores and thus began one of the most profitable dime store lines. Today Woolworth sells 250 million pounds of candy a year.

He tried the same tack with a small Christmas tree ornament factory and eventually built up a stable of suppliers.

In 1890, he made the first of many pilgrimages to Europe to buy toys and knickknacks directly from German and Austrian factories.

The dime store king watched over his business like a mother hen. He would send out memorandums to the effect: "Be sure and not have more clerks than you can use and don't turn all the gas burners on every night."

He also kept his employees alert with anonymous visits. His favorite trick was to stroll through a store and fill his pockets with postcards, rubber balls, etc. Then he would dump the lot on the manager's desk and remark acidly, "I could have filled a delivery truck."

Discovery of a wasted penny never failed to annoy Woolworth, even when he became fabulously rich. He was notorious for the low wages he paid his female clerks. He felt "when a clerk gets so good, she can get higher wages elsewhere . . ."

When labor troubles plagued him and clerks went on strike for higher wages, he instructed his managers to

SUPERMARKET OF MERCHANDISE

Sales of dime stores – or variety stores as they prefer to be called – totals about $1.1 billion, but only a small portion comes from five and ten cent items. (As far back as 1932, the limit jumped to 20 cents and a no-limit policy was established in 1935).

Even the name five-and-ten is no longer completely valid. Today, the dime or variety store rivals the big department store in merchandise and prices. One may buy a diamond ring for $99.95, caviar at $1.29 an ounce or a mynah bird for $44.95.

The modern Woolworth store resembles a supermarket. A 42nd Street outlet in New York City recently sprouted a fresh fruit and vegetable stand. Biggest similarity, however, stems from introduction of a self-service system. Over 75% of the 3607 Woolworth stores in the U.S. and overseas now have check-out counters.

Woolworth sells more dolls than any other retailer in the world. It is one of the leading sellers of brassieres – now about seven million – and also does brisk business in rose bushes and turtles.

Its restaurants are without peer in quantity of food served.

Nearly one million meals are prepared daily.

Recently Woolworth entered the discount race and opened the first of 18 self-service department stores under the name of Woolco in Columbus, Ohio. Woolco stores sell everything from clothing to furniture to major appliances. In addition, the discount shops offer specialized departments for auto service, drug prescriptions, beauty salons and portrait studios. Parking lots can accommodate 5000 cars.

In the present age of spiraling living costs and dim memories of nickel cups of coffee and five-cent subway rides, Woolworth remains a refreshing oasis for budget-minded Americans. It offers something no one can resist – a bargain.

Woolworth maintained his policy of "Nothing in this store over 10 cents" until 1930s. Today stores derive major business from $1-and-over items.

Woolworth entered mass merchandising field in 1962. Shoppers flocked to opening of the first Woolco discount department store in Columbus, Ohio.

"remember all such girls and when the dull season comes give them the bounce."

The great tide of immigration was beginning to hit the U.S. and to Woolworth those millions of poor were ripe for his dime stores. In 1891 he astonished his managers with the grand pronouncement: "I have been looking over a census of the United States and I am convinced there are 100 cities and towns where we can locate five-and-ten cent stores and we can sell a million dollars of goods a year!"

If anything, his prediction was short-sighted. Sales for 59 stores in 1900 surpassed $5 million, and the modest Brooklyn brownstone was replaced by a 30-room mansion on fashionable Fifth Avenue.

Woolworth clearly saw that his business could not remain a one-man show. He was a victim of nervous attacks and constantly worried over the fate of his empire should he die.

Accordingly, in 1905, a $10 million stock corporation came into existence under the name F. W. Woolworth & Co. All stock was held within the company so the five-and-ten still remained a family affair.

By 1909, the dime store was firmly implanted on the American scene. Woolworth, now a portly 57, decided to invade England by opening a "three and sixpence" store in Liverpool. English newspapers quipped that he chose Liverpool to be near the boat when failure came.

Woolworth sank $64,000 into the venture and by 1962 there were 1078 "Wooly's" in Great Britain with net income of $46 million.

Soon Woolworth began to feel the pinch of competition. Names like Kresge, Kress and McCrory began to crop up. Individually, they did not worry him but, collectively, he began to feel their mounting threat.

He also experienced friendly rivalry — his brother, Charles, a cousin and other early partners who had branched out on their own along the Pacific Coast and in Canada where Woolworth had no stores. They often purchased large quantities of items together and, as a group, controlled 276 stores in addition to Woolworth's 318.

In 1911, holdings were consolidated into one company to increase profits and ward off competition. A $65 million corporation was formed with F. W. Woolworth retaining 50% interest.

Although his commercial success was assured, Woolworth's last years were filled with poor health and tragedy. Nervous attacks of weeping and insomnia sent him in search of expensive cures at European spas. His closest aides, who had been with him since the beginning, began to die. His beloved daughter, Edna, passed away suddenly from an ear ailment and his wife, Jennie, whose mind had failed completely, retreated into the past.

As business flourished, Woolworth grew fatter and became more lackadaisical. He gorged on soft, rich foods, over-ripe bananas being a favorite, and he refused to exercise or even take short walks.

He died in April 1919 at the age of 66 from a combination of gallstones and uremic and septic poisoning. An editorial in the *New York Sun* summed up his life and labors: "He won a fortune, not in showing how little could be sold for much, but how much could be sold for little."

HE BROUGHT ORDER TO TROUBLED OIL

Rockefeller ended industry chaos

IN 1863, a 24-year-old Cleveland commission agent named John D. Rockefeller went into the oil business.

Edwin L. Drake had struck oil at Titusville, Pa., just four years earlier; the infant industry was chaotically competitive, with dozens of small producers and refiners jockeying for position.

Over the next 20 years, Rockefeller put an end to the chaos — and to most of the competition. By the 1880s, his Standard Oil Trust controlled 85% of all U.S. oil production and distribution.

He launched an industry whose total 1960 sales approximated $30 billion; even more importantly, he pioneered the development of modern, large-scale industrial organization.

The future Oil King was born in Richford, N. Y., in 1839.

His father, William Avery Rockefeller, was an intelligent, irrepressible and irresponsible salesman of patent medicines who was described by a reminiscing friend, after the family became famous, as having had "all

Structure of Rockefeller empire was completed before advent of automobile, which increased demand for petroleum tremendously.

the vices but one." (He was a teetotaller.)

His mother, on the other hand, was frugal, strict and devoutly religious; and it was she who set the tone of family life, since William spent most of his time on the road.

The family drifted West, and settled in Cleveland when John was 15. A year later, he graduated from high school and began looking for work.

It took John D. Rockefeller six weeks to find his first job.

Business was bad in Cleveland, and the quiet, serious young man did not impress prospective employers as a "hustler."

As the weeks dragged on, his father began trying to persuade him to give up and come home to the rural community near Cleveland where the family was living.

"It makes a cold chill run down my spine when I think of it," he declared as an old man. "What would have become of me if I had gone to the country?" But he added hopefully, "Maybe I would have gotten a start in business later."

Before his father became adamant, however, he managed to find a bookkeeper's position, at $25 a month, with a firm of commission merchants called Hewitt & Tuttle.

All through his life, one of Rockefeller's most striking characteristics was the sheer fun he got from his work. He was drivingly ambitious, and the charges of money and power-madness that his enemies heaped upon him were, from one point of view, justified; but it is equally true that he loved business for its own sake.

He used to recall that from his first day, Hewitt & Tuttle was "delightful to me—all the method and system of the office."

Within a year or two, he had taken over most of Mr. Tuttle's work; his salary rose to $700 a year.

But the firm was doing poorly, and, early in 1859, he decided to begin working for himself. He and a young Englishman, Maurice B. Clark, went into business together as commission merchants in farm produce.

It was in that same year that the first U.S. oil well was drilled.

"Seneca Oil," as petroleum was called, had long been highly esteemed as a medicine; it was believed that, if it could be extracted in commercially profitable quantities, it would rival whale and other oils as an illuminating fluid.

Rockefeller, in heyday of power, dressed, looked like "richest man in world."

The land of Western Pennsylvania was known to be oil-rich, and a development company, the Pennsylvania Rock Oil Co., had been at work there for two years.

Its agent, a former railroad man named Edwin L. Drake, had decided to try to get at the oil by drilling, using techniques similar to those of salt mining.

Battling rain, mud, and the jeers of his neighbors (the idea of pumping oil from the ground seemed so far fetched that he was hard put to find men willing to work for him), Drake brought in his first well at Titusville in August, 1859.

Within 24 hours, oil fever set in. Land values skyrocketed as prospectors poured into the area.

In January, 1860, Luther Atwood obtained the first patent for "cracking" crude oil, thus making possible mass production of light illuminating oils; in November of the same year, the first refinery went into production.

News of each of these exciting events soon reached Cleveland, where Rockefeller and Clark were busily and successfully marketing produce.

The new industry seems to have attracted the two young men from the beginning; here was where fortunes could be made in the years ahead.

In the early 1860s, it was as easy to open a refinery as it is to start a gas station today; in 1863, Rockefeller and Clark opened theirs.

In 1865, Rockefeller bought out Clark and Clark's brother for $74,500, and entered a new partnership with his own brother, William, and Samuel Andrews, the technical expert of the firm. A fourth partner, Henry M. Flagler, soon joined them.

Later the same year, the new firm of Rockefeller, Andrews & Flagler opened its second refinery. In 1866, William, who had inherited his father's gregarious nature and talent for salesmanship, went to New York to open an office there and begin an export business.

By 1868, the Rockefeller firm was the nation's largest oil "manufacturer" and in 1870 it was reorganized as the Standard Oil Co. of Ohio.

It had already begun making the railroad rebate deals that were to help it grow to monolithic size and power—and contribute to its unsavory public reputation.

Hard bargaining between railroads and shippers was the rule in the 19th century, and rebates were often granted to favored customers in exchange for guarantees of business. Standard Oil simply bargained harder — and more successfully — than any of its competitors, and therefore came in for perhaps more than its share of public enmity when the rebate system began to be attacked and investigated later in the century.

Rockefeller had decided that, if the industry was to move ahead, its production and distribution facilities would have to be concentrated in one gigantic organization; and he wanted that organization to be his.

To some extent, at least, the state of the industry in the early 1870s bore him out.

Too many adventurers had rushed into the new field too fast; prices were dropping and small firms were going bankrupt.

If a business genius like Rockefeller had not come along, the industry probably would have consolidated itself into three or four large organizations instead of only one; but a high degree of consolidation was almost inevitable.

As the 1870s moved along, one Cleveland company after another was absorbed by Standard Oil. In all, over 20 were drawn in, some willingly, others unwillingly.

Absorption of oil interests in other states followed; and in 1882, the Standard Oil Trust was capitalized at $70 million.

By 1885, the structure of Standard Oil was complete, although its greatest years of growth lay ahead in the era of the automobile.

The company had acquired wells and potential oil producing land; it had taken over pipelines and built added ones to create a network worth $31.5 million; its 20 component companies operated at least 50 refineries.

Standard plants were producing a wide variety of products and by-products, and the trust's marketing department was wiping out independent distributors as efficiently as Standard of Ohio had absorbed independent refiners a decade earlier.

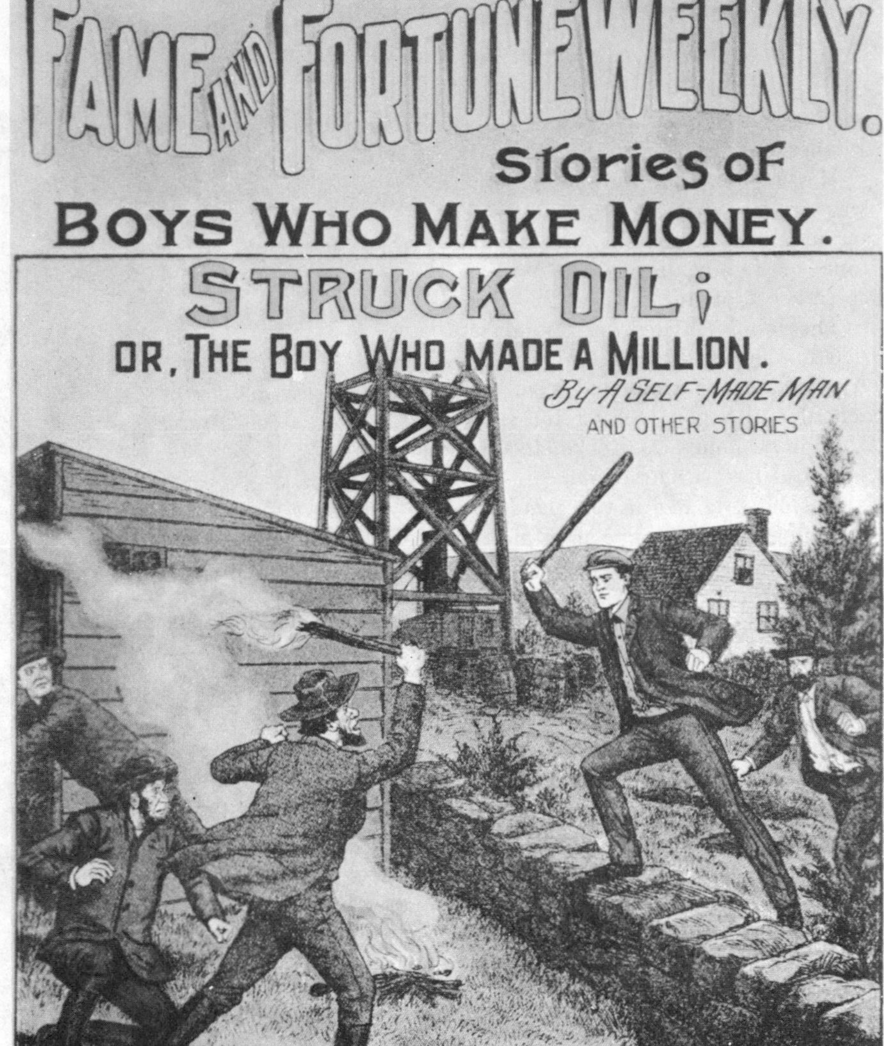

Poor boy who rose to millionaire through own efforts and luck was widespread American dream of the period. Rockefeller's oil career was outstanding inspiration.

Rockefeller's vast industrial empire could not have been built without the use of ruthless competitive tactics; but these tactics could not have succeeded if the company's internal organization had not been superb in every administrative and technical department, and the complex structure would have fallen apart if its efficiency had not increased in proportion to its size.

It was not to fall apart, of course, until 1911, when the trust was "busted" by the U.S. Supreme Court.

Rockefeller himself retired from the active management of his companies in 1896, the richest man in the U.S.—and one of the most unpopular.

His real contribution to U.S. business received little objective evaluation before the Standard Oil monopoly was destroyed.

Harvard president Charles W. Eliot wrote in 1915 that the "organization of the great business of taking petroleum out of the earth, piping the oil over great distances, distilling and refining it, and distributing it all over the earth, was an American invention."

It could almost be said to have been the invention of one American, John D. Rockefeller.

Horse-drawn Standard Oil tank wagon symbolizes past, future of transportation.

GEORGE EASTMAN

HE CLICKED THE SHUTTER FOR BILLIONS OF SNAPSHOTS

George Eastman invented film, low-priced camera, created $2-billion-a-year industry, turned whole U.S. into nation of camera fans

THE MAN who turned the U.S. into a nation of shutter-bugs — and photography into a multi-million-dollar industry — was George Eastman, founder of Eastman Kodak Co.

Back in 1877, when Eastman, then a 23-year-old Rochester, N. Y., bank clerk, took up photography as a hobby, taking a picture called for a back-breaking 70 pounds of equipment, considerable knowledge of photographic chemistry and infinite patience and skill.

Not surprisingly, amateur photographers were a very small, dedicated band—and even professionals were considered slightly crazy by the general public.

Today, photography is probably the No. 1 U.S. hobby. One American in three is a camera fan. Over 2 billion snapshots are shot each year, and total retail sales of cameras, film, and other photographic supplies and equipment are over $2.5 billion.

Eastman Kodak alone had 1960 sales of $945 million — about three quarters from photographic products, the rest from synthetic fibers, plastics and chemicals.

And, while Eastman is the giant of the field simply because it produces every type of photographic goods, it has plenty of competition, both domestic (from such firms as Ansco, Bell & Howell, Polaroid, Du Pont) and foreign, in all its product lines.

George Eastman's contributions to photography were dazzling in their simplicity—he invented film, and he invented a box camera that anyone could use.

Before Eastman came along, the only suitable negative material was glass. Every picture required a separate glass plate, and, since photographic emulsion would not keep, it had to be made on the spot and then applied to the plate, exposed and developed while still wet.

This meant that a photographer setting out for an afternoon's shooting had to take along a camera as big as a soap box, a heavy tripod, a "dark tent" for preparation and developing of his glass plates, a supply of plates in a heavy folder, chemicals, developing tanks and water.

George Eastman, unlike the other photographers of his day, decided that there must be a way to make all this

KODAK SLOGAN made advertising history in late 19th Century, got sales of first box camera off to a fast start.

The Kodak Camera

"You press the button, - - - - we do the rest."

The only camera that anybody can use without instructions. Send for the Primer free.

The Kodak is for sale by all Photo stock dealers.

A Transparent Film For Roll Holders.

The announcement is hereby made that the undersigned have perfected a process for making transparent flexible films for use in roll holders and Kodak Cameras.

The new film is as thin, light and flexible as paper and as transparent as glass. It requires *no stripping*, and it is wound on spools for roll holders.

It will be known as *Eastman's Transparent Film*. Circulars and samples will be sent to any address on receipt of 4 cents in stamps.

Price $25.00—Loaded for 100 Pictures.

The Eastman Dry Plate and Film Co.

ROCHESTER, N. Y.

PICTURE-SNAPPING became a popular hobby in the 1890s, when Eastman's small cameras, flexible film eliminated wet-plate photography's 70-pound equipment.

misery unnecessary—and set about finding one.

Eastman had left school at 14 and gone to work as a $3-a-week office boy to help support his widowed mother and two sisters. He had studied accounting at home in the evenings, joined the Rochester Savings Bank as a junior clerk at 20, and moved up to a bookkeeper's job and a salary of $800 a year—a fairly substantial one for 1870s.

He was a thrifty, hard-working, intelligent young man who might very well have become a successful banker if he had not almost succumbed to a streak of wanderlust when he was 23. He began planning a vacation trip to—of all places—Santo Domingo, and a friend at the bank urged him to take up photography so that he could bring home pictures of the Central American jungles.

He gave up Santo Domingo for a less adventurous trip to the Great Lakes, but he did become a thoroughly competent wet plate photographer.

By 1878, he was more interested in photography than in banking, and was avidly reading about the attempts of British photographers to make gelatin emulsions that would remain sensitive when dry so that their plates would not have to be exposed and developed immediately.

Although he had never spent a day in a chemistry class, he began experimenting with a gelatin emulsion of his own in his mother's kitchen.

His hobby became a passion. He worked at the bank all day, mixed emulsions all night, and, as his mother told the story years later, slept through from Saturday night to Monday morning every week.

By 1879, he had invented not only a practical dry-plate emulsion, but also an emulsion coating machine for mass production of the plates.

In 1880, he began running a dry-plate business at night in the loft of a factory building.

And a year later, he went into partnership with Henry A. Strong, a Rochester buggy whip manufacturer who boarded with the Eastman family, and left the bank to devote full time to photography.

Strong, as the older of the two and the more experienced businessman, became president of the new company; Eastman was treasurer and general manager.

By 1883, the Eastman Dry Plate Co. was flourishing, and moved into a four-story building at what is now 343 State St., and still the headquarters of Eastman Kodak.

Eastman then began turning his attention to the development of a light, flexible negative material to replace glass plates, which, even when they could be used dry, were still too bulky, inconvenient and expensive.

By 1885—also the year in which the firm opened its first foreign office, in London—he was advertising that "shortly will be introduced a new sensitive film, which, it is believed, will prove an economical and convenient substitute for glass dry plates, for indoor or outdoor work."

This first film was made of paper, and carried in the camera on a roll holder which substituted for the plate holder.

It was not entirely satisfactory, because the grain of the paper was likely to appear in the print.

CAMERA that revolutionized photography was the 1888 model No. 1 Kodak, basically similar to today's simple models.

FIRST FACTORY of Eastman Dry Plate Co. occupied site where Eastman Kodak's administrative offices stand today.

Eastman pioneered in employe benefits, climaxed career by huge gifts

So Eastman coated the paper with a layer of plain, soluble gelatin, and then a second layer of insoluble, light-sensitive gelatin. After exposure, the gelatin was stripped from the paper, transferred to a sheet of clear gelatin, and varnished with collodion.

This type of film produced satisfactory prints, but Eastman kept on trying to get rid of the paper base. In 1886, he hired a full-time research chemist.

In the meantime, he and Strong were discovering that the professional photography market was far too small for their production potential.

The way to make real money, they decided, was to reach the general public, and the way to do this was to invent a small, light, easy-to-use camera.

In 1888, the first Kodak appeared on the market.

The trade name was invented by Eastman himself; he wanted a short, catchy word that would be easy to spell and pronounce in any language, and he liked the letter "K".

Eastman also coined the famous Kodak advertising slogan, **"You press the button—we do the rest."**

This was literally true. The No. 1 Kodak Camera sold for $25, loaded with enough film for 100 exposures. When all the pictures had been taken, the owner simply mailed the camera to Rochester with $10 for developing and printing of the old film and reloading with a new roll.

In 1889, the first non-paper-based film—a transparent roll on a base of cellulose nitrate—was marketed, and one of its first buyers was Thomas Edison, who used it to produce the first 35-millimeter motion pictures.

The first folding Kodak camera was introduced in 1890, the first daylight-loading camera and film in 1891.

Use of Kodak dry plates for X-ray began in 1895.

And in 1900, the first Brownie camera—priced at $1 with film that sold for 15¢ a roll—made photography a hobby that practically anyone could afford.

Eastman did not become president of his own company until 1919, when Strong retired. He became chairman of the board in 1925, and served until his death in 1932.

He accumulated a personal fortune of over $100 million, and gave most of it away during his lifetime—$51 million to the University of Rochester, $20 million to Massachusetts Institute of Technology, and millions more to schools, hospitals, dental clinics and civic associations in Rochester and throughout the world.

His favorite project was probably the launching of the Rochester School of Music and Symphony Orchestra.

He loved music, although his talents as a performer were non-existent; as a young man, he had bought a flute and spent two years trying unsuccessfully to learn to play "Annie Laurie."

He visited Europe every year, and went on a number of African safaris.

Quiet, shy, and straight-laced, George Eastman was nevertheless a popular employer. (Eastman Kodak was among the first major companies to introduce payment for employe suggestions, profit-sharing, a company stock plan and similar fringe benefits.) He was also, for years before his death, the best-known and best-loved citizen of Rochester, N. Y.

And his life's work, the development of photography, still deserves to be called—as it was by the *New York Times* in an obituary editorial—"a stupendous factor in the education of the modern world."

PHOTOGRAPHIC PAPER, film and other photo supplies pour in endless stream from Eastman's giant, highly automated modern Rochester plant, still centered on the original site.

PHILANTHROPIST EASTMAN was camera-shy but posed in 1931 with Rush Rhees, president of Univ. of Rochester, which received $51 million of Eastman fortune.

Thomas Edison, right, was guest of honor at announcement ceremonies of Kodacolor film in 1928 at Eastman House. Although Eastman, left, and Edison had worked together through their companies on the development of the motion picture, this occasion marked their first personal meeting.

Lighting contract for Chicago's 1893 World's Fair went to George Westinghouse and his new AC system.

HE ELECTRIFIED INDUSTRY

Westinghouse's AC transformer made economic distribution of electric power possible

In December, 1880, George Westinghouse of Pittsburgh paid a visit to Menlo Park, N. J.

The purpose of his trip was to see the first public demonstration of Thomas Alva Edison's newly perfected electric light—a dramatic night-time illumination of the entire park.

Like the hundreds of other spectators, Westinghouse went home that night dazzled by the potentialities of electric power. But he had also spotted the weak point in the Edison system—the short range of the direct current produced by its generators—and decided that he could improve upon it.

At 34, Westinghouse was already a noted engineer, inventor, and industrialist.

But in the years ahead, his contributions to the development of electric power—not only as a light source, but also as the workhorse of industry and transportation—were to win him a place among the greatest technological pioneers of his amazing era.

Westinghouse was born in 1846, the son of a well-to-do machine shop owner in upstate New York.

He began working part-time in the shop while he was still in his early teens, rigging up ingenious devices to speed his chores and spending most of his time building model engines.

Then, after two years of active service in the Civil War and a semester at Union College—all that was needed to persuade his culturally ambitious father that he had no bent for the liberal arts—he went into the family business full time.

Before he was 21, however, he had patented his first major invention and launched his own manufacturing firm.

The invention was a railroad "car replacer"—a mechanism that hoisted derailed cars (frequently seen in those pioneer days of railroading) back onto the track in a fraction of the time it had taken train crews to do the job manually.

The fast-growing business of railroading was as challenging as a young engineer of the 1860's and 70's could find. It gave Westinghouse his start, and he never lost his enthusiasm for it. (By a pleasant coincidence, he even met his wife—with whom he was to spend over 40 unusually happy years—on a train trip.)

Shortly after he perfected his car replacer, he began working on the device that the railroads needed most urgently — an efficient, quick-acting brake.

The trains of the 60s were brought to a halt by a cumbersome arrangement of handwheels on each platform, linked to chains that ran

George Westinghouse spotted weak point in Edison's system, put together transformer used in today's AC.

Early (1886-89) Westinghouse power plants grew rapidly. Many small belt-driven alternators were used.

beneath the cars and tightened brakes as the wheels were turned.

A crew of skilled brakemen needed half a mile's leeway to bring a train to a smooth stop, and disastrous collisions were common.

Lack of the right brake was holding back the railroad's expansion more than any other single factor —bigger, faster trains could have been built and put into operation, but they almost literally could not have been stopped.

For more than a year, Westinghouse experimented with various steam-powered braking devices, but they were all too cumbersome.

Then he came across a magazine article that described the revolutionary compressed-air drilling equipment being used in the construction of the Mont Cenis tunnel through the Alps.

There, he saw, was the answer— compressed air could be used equally well to power a compact braking system.

Within a few months, he had applied for patents on his air brake and was trying to peddle it to the railroads. But railroad men from Commodore Vanderbilt on down simply laughed at the idea that air could be used to stop a train.

In the meantime, Westinghouse's car replacer business was running into trouble. Sales were falling off, and the young inventor's partners (both older men and business veterans) were trying to edge him out of the company and keep the patents for the device.

Westinghouse managed to win the patent fight, however, and left the family home in Schenectady to head for Pittsburgh, the fast-growing center of the iron and steel industry. There, he hoped, he would find a larger company interested in taking over the car replacer.

He not only succeeded in this venture, making a profitable arrangement with the firm of Anderson & Cook, but also, within a few months, found a local railroad that was willing to give the air brake a try.

In April, 1869, the air brake got its first run—from Pittsburgh to Steubenville and back on the Steubenville Division of the Panhandle Railroad.

And a few minutes out of Pittsburgh, it showed what it could do.

The train was chugging along at 30 miles an hour when its horrified engineer saw a horsedrawn wagon no more than two blocks ahead of him on the tracks. No team of brakemen could have stopped the train in time to avert disaster.

But the air brake did—just four feet from the horses, which had gone out of control in their fright and were plunging sideways toward the locomotive.

The rest of the run, during which all scheduled stops were made smoothly, was anticlimactic — the brake had already sold itself to Panhandle, and to every other railroad in the business.

Three months later, the Westinghouse Air Brake Co. was chartered, with a capitalization of $500,000. Westinghouse, at 23, was on his way.

For most of the next two decades, he devoted himself primarily to the railroad equipment business, developing scores of automatic safety and control devices that made vital contributions to the program of rail transportation.

His second company, Union Switch & Signal, was founded in the year of 1881.

In the mid-80s, almost as a sideline, he turned his attention to natural gas.

His interest was aroused when he discovered a natural gas well on his own property. Within a matter of months, he had developed and patented a "system for conveying and utilizing gas under pressure" that overcame hitherto insurmountable obstacles to the efficient use of the hard-to-handle fuel. Then he organized a public utility company to serve all of Pittsburgh, and went back to business.

As the 80s moved on, Westinghouse was increasingly involved with electrical as well as mechanical engineering. He experimented with — and finally rejected — electricity as a supplementary power source for a bigger and better airbrake for long freight trains that he perfected in 1886.

And, from the day of his visit to Menlo Park in 1880, he was con-

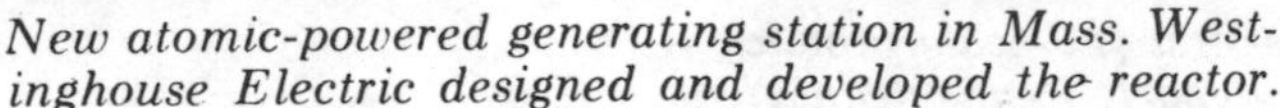

New atomic-powered generating station in Mass. Westinghouse Electric designed and developed the reactor.

Westinghouse tapped gas on grounds of own home, later developed effective methods of drilling, conveying.

cerned with the problem of electrical distribution.

Like Edison himself, and unlike most of the other inventors of the day, Westinghouse had seen the value of staff work in science and engineering, and had hired a brilliant team of research workers. It included men like Nicola Tesla, Guido Pantaleoni, and Oliver Shallenberger, whose formal education and scientific understanding were greater than his own.

And this team joined him in the task of finding a substitute for the Edison direct current system.

The trouble with DC was that it could only be generated at low voltages, and that distribution of electricity was thus limited to a very short range—only a mile at the time of the demonstration.

Westinghouse wanted to develop a system that would permit generation at very high voltages, and delivery of power to points near and far at whatever voltage was needed—in other words, to "alternate" current from high to low pressure.

The difficulty—so great that it seemed insurmountable to Edison and to most of the other electrical engineers of the day—was control of those very high voltages.

The first breakthrough came when Westinghouse heard about the development in England of a device called a "transformer" to reduce voltages in electrical circuits.

He promptly dispatched Pantaleoni to England to obtain the U.S. patent rights for the transformer and bring it home.

When it arrived, he pronounced it theoretically sound but faulty in mechanical design—and began literally taking it to pieces and putting it together again.

Soon he had a working model of the transformer used in all alternating current systems today.

He patented it in 1886—six years after Menlo Park—and, in the same year, established the Westinghouse Electric Company.

Westinghouse Electric's revenues were to soar to $4 million by 1890, making Westinghouse, at the peak of his career, the head of a giant corporation as well as of half a dozen smaller ones. (By 1960 Westinghouse Electric Corp. sales totaled $1.2 billion and Westinghouse Air Brake's $170 million.)

The transformer was the last of the many developments that made possible the distribution of electricity by alternating current.

By the fall of 1886, the first AC system—supplying power to Lawrence, Mass., from a Westinghouse experimental laboratory at Great Barrington, Mass., four miles away—was ready to go into operation.

It was a complete success, and demonstrated not only that AC could carry power farther than DC, but also that it was much cheaper.

However, Edison and his coworkers refused to admit that AC was safe, and a substantial proportion of the public agreed with them.

The battle between Westinghouse and Edison interests was to rage for 10 years—until Westinghouse Electric and Edison General Electric pooled their patents in 1896.

Each side bombarded the public with newspaper and billboard advertising; Edison himself wrote an article for the influential *North American Review* on the dangers of AC, and Westinghouse offered a rebuttal in the next issue.

Newspaper editorials took sides in the controversy.

Charges of bribery, fraud, and criminal libel flew back and forth.

Of course, there were occasional fatal accidents when AC wires were strung too low; and these were greeted with newspaper headlines like: "THE WIRE'S FATAL GRASP:" "ONE MARTYR MORE;" "AGAIN A CORPSE IN THE WIRES."

AC got perhaps it worst advertisement when New York State announced that in the future, criminals would be electrocuted (by alternating current) rather than hung.

Nevertheless, AC gained ground.

The turning point came in 1892, when the city of Niagara Falls called for bids on a complete power system—and Westinghouse won out over Edison G.E.

The following year, Westinghouse brought off one of the most spectacular coups of his career—one that proved that he (again, like Edison) had a sense of public rela-

Downtown Pittsburgh reflects peaceful benefits of world's first full-scale atomic-electric generating station for civilian needs only (Shippingport, Pennsylvania).

tions that was far ahead of his time.

The sponsors of the Chicago World's Fair had announced that the Fair would be illuminated by no less than 250,000 electric lights.

Westinghouse Electric and Edison General Electric were the only two firms in the country able to bid for the gigantic contract — and Westinghouse underbid its rival by more than $1 million.

The Fair, Westinghouse believed, would provide such a magnificent showcase for the powers of electricity—and the products of the firm that won the contract—that he was willing to lose hundreds of thousands of dollars to get the job.

But Edison refused to admit defeat, and promptly went to court to challenge Westinghouse's right to use the Sawyer-Mann electric light bulb, on the ground that this bulb—the patent for which Westinghouse had recently acquired—was so similar to the Edison bulb as to be a patent infringement.

The court decided in favor of Edison.

Westinghouse met the challenge by the simple expedient of designing a new bulb that worked on a different principle. It was by no means as good as the Edison bulb, but perfectly adequate for a few months' service at the Fair.

Then came the crash production program. New machinery was built and installed in a new factory, and in a bare five months, the 250,000 light bulbs were produced.

The bright lights of the Fair's "Magic City" drew "ooh's" and "ah's" from thousands of visitors, and rave notices in the nation's press. And the giant Westinghouse installation that supplied the power, open to the public, proved to be one of the most popular attractions.

Moreover, Westinghouse did better than break even on the deal, and prompt cash payment from the grateful Fair management helped tide the company over the Panic of 1893.

By the turn of the century, with the Westinghouse-Edison patent war a thing of the past, alternating current was accepted as—in the words of the great British scientist, Lord Kelvin—"the only practical and economical solution for the problem of electrical distribution."

George Westinghouse, in the meantime, had turned his attention to the problems of electric power for industry.

A British engineer, Charles Parsons, had invented a turbine engine in 1884. And Westinghouse, once again recognizing a good thing when he saw it, bought the U.S. patent rights for the equipment and began the job of perfecting it.

The result was the Westinghouse-Parsons turbine generator, the most powerful engine ever built. (He provided his own showcase for the new advance by immediately scrapping all the power-producing devices in his factories and replacing them with Westinghouse-Parsons generators).

Also in the 90s, he went to work on the world's first electrically powered urban transit system; the motor that made possible large-scale development of electric trolley lines was perfected in 1902.

Then, in the early 1900s, he rounded out his career by developing the first electric locomotive for the railroads.

Two years before his death in 1914, he won a particularly satisfying honor. To his already impressive collection of awards, decorations, and honorary degrees, he added the Edison Medal—an annual award granted by the American Institute of Electrical Engineers in commemoration of the career of the great inventor of the incandescent bulb.

"It is perphaps somewhat ironic," the award read, "that he whom we are to honor tonight has disagreed violently over a long period of years with the man in whose honor this medal was founded. But those of us who know Thomas Edison as a generous and just man know that he regards his defeat in one battle as a great victory in the march toward progress."

Today's engineers would put it another way — George Westinghouse did as much as any man of his generation to advance the "state of the art" in electricity.

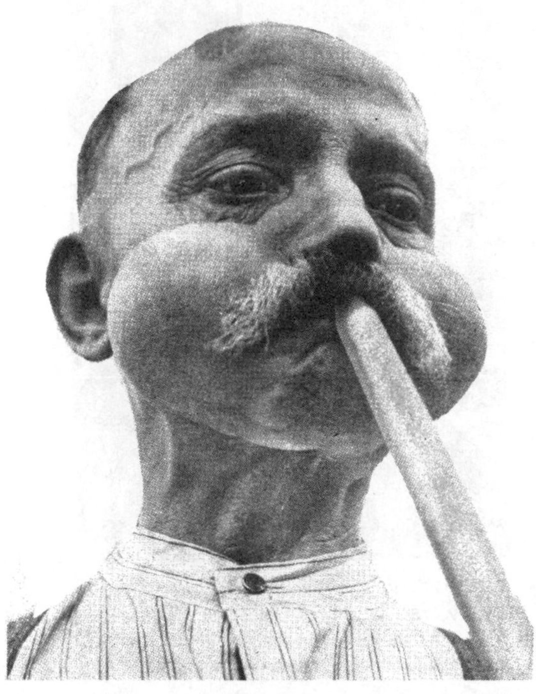

GLASS GIANT

Untutored Mike Owens replaced blowpipe with machine, founded $2-billion-a-year glass industry

Painting, made in 1910 to symbolize revolution in glass production, shows Owens standing in front of early model automatic bottle machine, inspecting a clear glass bottle which the machine has just produced.

AT THE TURN of the century, glass was made much as it had been for over 2000 years.

The last major advance in glass production had been the invention of the blowpipe around 300 B.C.

Then, in 1903, a West Virginian glass blower named Michael J. Owens perfected a machine that produced glass containers mechanically.

A few years later, a second Owens machine made possible automatic production of plate glass.

These two inventions catapulted the ancient craft of glassmaking into the ranks of modern industry.

Horatio Alger Career

And they launched Mike Owens on one of the least publicized but most spectacular Horatio Alger careers in the annals of U.S. business.

Today, the annual sales volume of over 200 U.S. glassmaking firms is more than $2 billion, and "Owens" is probably the most famous name in glass.

The direct descendants of Mike Owens' companies, Owens-Illinois Glass Co. and Libbey-Owens-Ford Glass Co., are second and third in the industry (Pittsburgh Plate Glass is first). And the leading producer of glass fiber for insulating materials and fabric is Owens-Corning-Fiberglas Corp., largely owned by Owens-

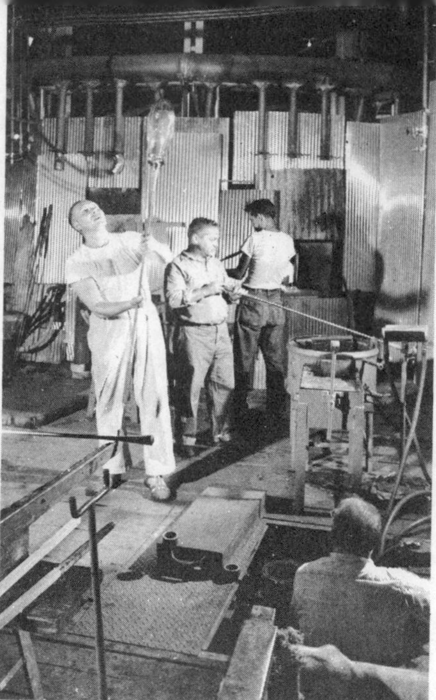

Some 750 highly skilled craftsmen still employ age-old "hand blowing" for special products. Photos show (l. to r.) worker blowing air pocket in molten glass, "spinning" container into shape, then lowering it into mold. Bulk of such work today is to meet specifications for specialized laboratory equipment.

Illinois and the industry's fourth largest firm, Corning Glass Works.

Mike Owens was born in Mason County, W. Va., in 1859, and went to work as a furnace stoker in a Wheeling, W. Va., glass plant when he was only 10.

The master blowers in the Wheeling plant dipped "gathers" of molten glass from the furnace by hand, formed it by blowing it through pipes, and gave the finished glass containers their final shape with hand tools.

Hand glassblowing was—as it still is today, although it plays a much smaller role in the industry—a highly skilled and highly paid craft.

But the unskilled work of the glass plants was done by children like Mike Owens, who earned 30¢ for a 12 to 14 hour day.

Owens' mechanization of the industry, 30 years later, was to help put an end to its use of child labor.

His first invention, hit upon when he was still in his early teens, eliminated the job of the "mold boy," who squatted on the floor beside the master blower, opening and closing his mold. Young Owens sank the mold into the floor, and provided a foot treadle so that the blower could open and close it himself.

Owens was a master blower at the age of 15.

And by the time he was 20, he had become a leader in the American Flint Glass Workers' Union.

He first came into contact with his future employer, sponsor and partner, Edward Drummond Libbey, when he was sent to Cambridge, Mass., to organize a strike at Libbey's New England Glass Co.

He was so successful that the New England Glass Co., a family business founded in 1818, turned "runaway shop" and moved to Toledo, Ohio, where it was renamed Libbey Glass.

Union Leader

However, the budding young labor organizer seems to have made a quick decision that he was really more interested in the production end of the glass business.

Six months later, he turned up in Toledo, asked Libbey for a job, and —surprisingly enough—got one.

He rose quickly to become Libbey's plant manager, and soon began thinking about a machine to replace the glass blower in bottle production.

Mike Owens was perhaps unique among inventors in that he could not really invent.

Totally lacking in technical training, he could not even read a blueprint. And he would probably have had a hard time operating one of his own machines.

But he knew glass, and had an almost instinctive understanding of the principles upon which a glass blowing machine would operate.

When he had decided how his machine would work, he told his parish priest about it. His description was so clear that the priest warned him against telling anyone else — "from what you've told me, I could go out and have this thing built."

However, Mike Owens had gone as far as he could go—somebody else would have to build the machine.

With Libbey's backing, he took his idea to a talented engineer and designer named Emil Bock.

"Put It in Iron"

"Put it in iron," he said when Bock handed him his first baffling set of blueprints.

And "put it in iron" Bock did.

The first crude machine, christened the "bicycle pump," sucked up molten glass, placed the gob inside a steel mold, and puffed a mechanical breath of air into the mold to produce a glass bottle.

The first few bottles were so misshapen that they could never have gone on the market, but they proved that the machine worked.

Slowly over the next few years, it was perfected, enlarged, and put into motion.

Six, then eight, and finally 15 "bicycle pumps" were mounted on a rotating steel framework that circled like a merry-go-round in front of a pot of molten glass. As each unit passed over the pot, it dipped, scooped up a measured quantity of glass, and went on. When it returned, seconds later, it had blown and discharged a standard-sized bottle.

The machine that went into production in 1903 weighed 100,000 lbs., contained 10,000 parts, and could turn out 400,000 bottles every 24 hours. (Top production for a master hand blower with four assistants was 216 bottles in a 14-hour day.)

Libbey and Owens then went into partnership to form the Owens Bottle Machine Co.

At 44, the erstwhile labor organizer was a management man, and—as companies throughout the industry began leasing the revolutionary new machines—an extremely wealthy one.

Plate Glass Machine

Owens next turned his attention to mechanization of flat or plate glass production, still an expensive, small-scale operation in which workmen blew huge glass bubbles and flattened them by hand.

He developed a machine that drew glass automatically from the furnace in sheet form, and established a second company, still in partnership with Libbey – the Libbey-Owens Sheet Glass Co.

In 1917, the first Libbey-Owens plant opened in Charleston, W. Va. —a plant in which no human labor was needed from the time the raw materials entered it until the continuous sheet of glass came from the oven ready for cutting.

Mike Owens died in 1923, and Edward Libbey two years later.

In 1930, Libbey-Owens Sheet Glass Co. merged with Edward Ford Plate Glass Co. to become today's Libbey-Owens-Ford.

In 1929, Owens Bottle Co. acquired the Illinois Glass Co. and became Owens-Illinois. And six years later, Owens-Illinois absorbed the original Libbey Glass Co., where plant manager Mike Owens had gotten his start and the glassmaking revolution had begun.

Owens never retired, died in harness at directors' meeting in 1923.

Latest model of automatic glass container machine is expected to increase production rate to 1200 per minute.

Ottmar Mergenthaler

HE UNPLUGGED PRINTING'S BOTTLENECK

Mergenthaler's Linotype transformed typesetting

In 1884, a young German-American inventor named Ottmar Mergenthaler unveiled a machine that Thomas A. Edison — himself perhaps the super-inventor of all time—was to call the "Eighth Wonder of the World."

The machine was the Linotype—the world's first fast, dependable, economical instrument for composition of printer's type.

With its introduction, the printing industry—born 400 years earlier when Johann Gutenberg invented movable type—can be said to have come of age.

Today's printing and publishing industry is a multi-billion-dollar giant, with its volume by 1960 of over $14 billion in the U.S. alone. And Mergenthaler Linotype Co. is one of its major suppliers. The company's 1960 sales were $47.2 million; it produces 65-70% of the hot-metal type-composing machinery in use in the U.S., and its share of the overseas market is slightly higher.

Ottmar Mergenthaler was born in 1854, and grew up in the small German town of Ensingen.

When he was 14, he was apprenticed to a nearby watchmaker. His father was a schoolmaster, and would have liked to send him to high school, but two older brothers were there already, and family funds were running low.

The watchmaker was undoubtedly delighted to get him. A few years earlier, he had created a minor sensation in Ensingen by sneaking into the church tower and repairing the town clock, which had seemed to be hopelessly broken down.

And young Ottmar, who had already decided that he wanted to be an engineer, was perfectly happy with the arrangement.

He spent four years working for the watchmaker by day and attending technical school in the evening.

"Above all, watchmaking taught me precision," he wrote years later, after he had invented one of the world's most complex pieces of machinery. "I learned to temper a spring to the finest degree, to combine the constituents of metal alloys in exact proportions. I learned how to cut out the finest teeth, to make pins. I realized that, if a movement was to work, it must be considered as a whole, that each part had to be perfect in itself and also harmonize with every other."

At the end of his apprenticeship, Mergenthaler emigrated to the

Linotype was christened by *New York Tribune* publisher, Whitelaw Reid. "It's a line of type," he exclaimed when Mergenthaler, demonstrating the complexities of the new typesetting machine, handed him a metal slug.

U.S., and went to work for the son of his former master, who owned an engineering workshop in Washington D. C.

The workshop's main business was the building of patent models for inventors – and, when Mergenthaler was 22, an inventor named Charles T. Moore walked in to ask for a model of a machine he had just developed.

ASSIGNMENT CHANGED LIFE

Mergenthaler got the assignment, and it changed the course of his life.

Moore's invention was a kind of typewriter that produced a transfer of a page for printing by lithography.

It gave Mergenthaler his first glimpse of the printing industry, and he was immediately fascinated by printing's great, unsolved problem–the mechanical composition of type.

He spent seven more years in the Washington workshop, the last five as a partner, devoting all the time he could to experiments with composing machines.

In 1883, when he went into business for himself, his first working model was just a year away.

INDUSTRY NEED DESPERATE

Printers and publishers – especially newspaper publishers, who were just beginning to build up mass circulations – had for several decades been literally desperate for the kind of machine Mergenthaler was trying to invent.

Over the four centuries since Gutenberg's invention of movable type, dramatic progress had been made in printing and most of its related crafts. Printing press design and operation and papermaking had been improved; electrotyping, lithography, photoengraving and photogravure had been developed.

But type was still composed by hand, as slowly and laboriously as it had been in Gutenberg's day.

And the typesetting bottleneck was blocking the entire industry's progress toward high speed, low cost mass production.

By 1892, when Mergenthaler introduced "star-base" model (above), over 1000 linotypes were in use.

Over 200 19th century inventors had tackled the problem; a number of inventions had been hailed with enthusiasm, won medals and prizes at trade fairs–and promptly broken down in the print shop.

One group of experimenters tried to eliminate type altogether by directly producing an inked transfer for lithographic printing. A second group tried to make use of the principles of stereotyping, with machines that stamped letters one after another onto papier-maché molds for casting in metal. A third simply tried to make machines that could set lead type automatically instead of by hand.

The typesetting machines came closest to success, but they were all too cumbersome, required so many operators that they offered no real economy (the first to be actually installed in a print shop, in 1840, had to be tended by no less than seven men), and, above all, were unable to keep the small pieces of lead type from breaking or sticking.

Ottmar Mergenthaler, during his years of experimentation, tried variations of all three types.

From the papier-maché molds of the stereotype devices, he progressed to metal molds, or matrices, one for each character.

The machine he finally perfected composed these matrices in lines, "justified" their spacing, cast lines of type in molten metal, and redistributed the matrices to repeat the operation. It required only one operator, and set up to 7 lines of type a minute, or more than three times the speed of hand composition. And the sturdy matrices, with sunken impressions of letters, to replace delicate, raised founder's type and to produce solid plates for printing, eliminated breakage.

PROTOTYPE IMPERFECT

Mergenthaler's prototype machine, demonstrated in 1884, did not provide for automatic justification, and its matrices moved on bars rather than independently.

It took him two more years of hard work to correct these deficiencies; but on July 3, 1886, the first Blower Linotype began setting type for the *New York Tribune*.

There was still a danger that the new machine would prove to be uneconomical because of the high cost of the matrices.

When Mergenthaler approached a Baltimore type founder to order 1200 matrices at 6 cents apiece, he was told that the job could not be done for ten times the price.

MADE OWN MATRICES

He solved this problem by designing machinery for high quality, low cost production, and going into the matrix business himself.

He also kept on improving the Linotype.

Before the inventor's death in 1899, three Mergenthaler Linotype plants in Brooklyn, Germany, and England were in full swing, and over 3000 machines were in use.

Today, close to 100,000 Linotypes are setting type–at up to 12 lines a minute–all over the world.

An unsuccessful compositor invented in 1887 by James Paige was called "Mark Twain Machine" because the writer lost fortune promoting it.

The New York Tribune *used first Merganthaler Linotype in 1886. Actual machine with its original operator John T. Miller re-united in 1936.*

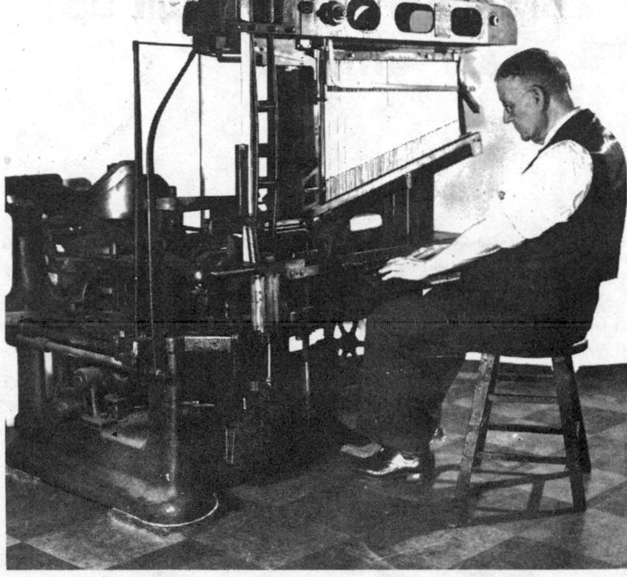

By 1902, sixteen years after New York Tribune *began using machine in U.S., Linotypes had replaced the old hand-typesetting methods at London's Daily Telegraph.*

Mergenthaler Co. exhibits model at an international trade fair in Ceylon where mechanization is catching up.

Today Linotypes are setting type in all corners of the world. Group of Eskimos get demonstration from a compositor working on the Fairbanks, Alaska, News-Miner.

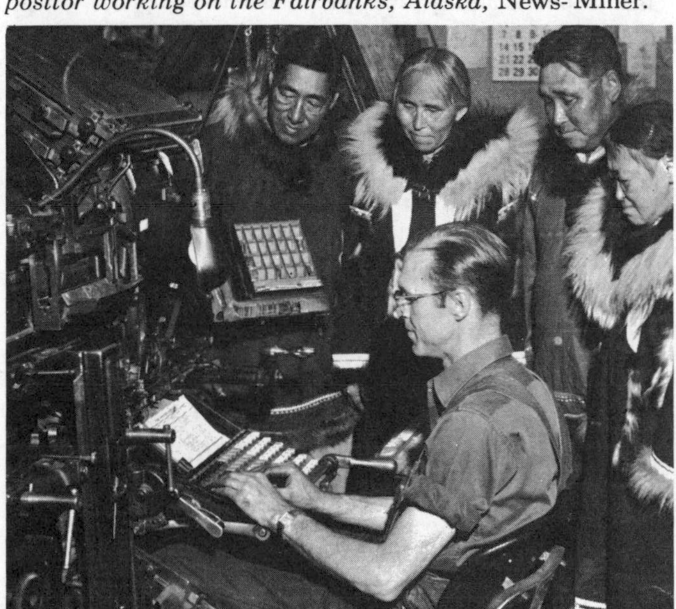

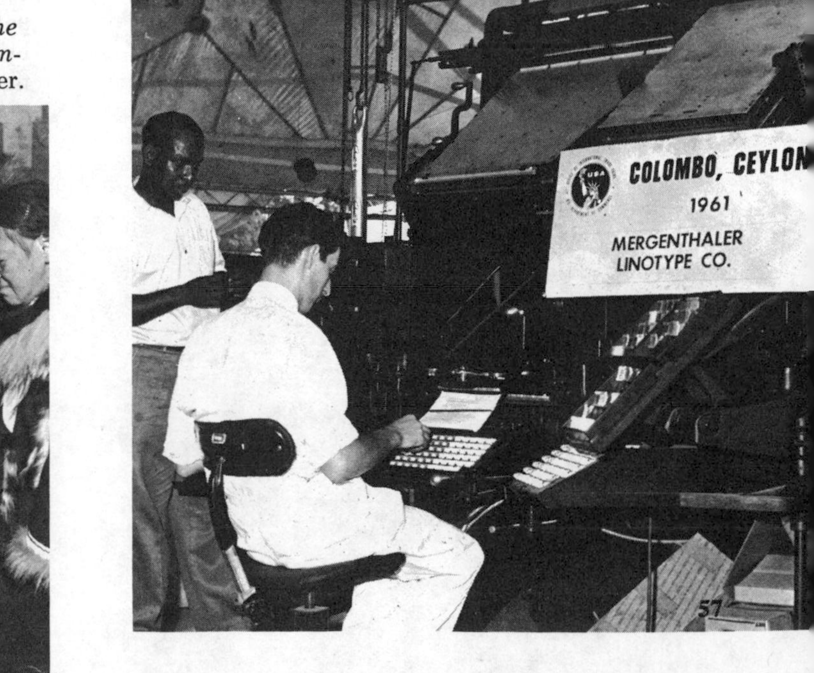

LONG LINES LIFETIME

Theodore N. Vail's faith and flair made long distance telephone practical reality, built up AT&T "empire"

THEODORE N. VAIL

COAST-TO-COAST telephone service became a reality in 1914. (*Below,* wires are strung across Nevada-Utah state line.) Vail had begun securing interstate rights 35 years earlier, when idea of a New York-Chicago call had seemed fantastic.

THE MAN who did more for the telephone than anyone else but Alexander Graham Bell, who invented it, was Theodore Newton Vail.

Vail was the first general manager (1878-1885) of the original Bell Telephone Co., and twice president of American Telephone & Telegraph Co., which was formed in 1885 as Bell's long distance division and later took the position of parent company which it holds today.

His faith in the future of the telephone was so limitless that he would probably hardly bat an eyelash at the modern AT&T, which has 59.6 million telephones in service. By the early Sixties it was grossing $8.4 billion and leading U.S. industry in assets ($24.6 billion), profits ($1.33 billion) and number of employees (567,000).

He began dreaming of coast-to-coast telephone service in the 1870s, when the telephone appeared to be no more than an ingenious gadget for local communication. He saw that only a national network of affiliated companies under a single top management could provide this kind of service. And he saw—in an age when the typical corporate public relations philosophy was still best expressed by Commodore Vanderbilt's "the public be damned"—that a public utility like the telephone company, near-monopoly though it might be, was peculiarly dependent upon public good will.

Theodore Vail was born in 1845, and grew up in rural New Jersey, the son of an iron manufacturer.

His first few years out of high school were spent as a telegraph operator, first in New York City and then, after the Vail family moved west, in Pinebluff, Wyoming.

In 1869, he joined the U.S. Railway Mail Service as a route agent on an 1100-mile Union Pacific run through the wilderness from Omaha, and began a rise that can only be described as meteoric; seven years later, he was in Washington as General Superintendent of the department.

By 1878, he was getting tired of government service and looking for a job in private business.

The telephone was then barely two years old; Alexander Graham Bell had sent his historic message, "Mr. Wat-

ALEXANDER GRAHAM BELL

son, please come here," to his assistant in the next room of his boarding house on March 10, 1876; he and a few associates had formed the Bell Telephone Co., and were trying to exploit the new gadget's commercial potentialities.

The president of Bell Telephone, Gardiner Hubbard, knew Theodore Vail, and persuaded him to come into the company as general manager.

Vail's Washington friends were staggered.

The First Assistant Postmaster General wrote him, in part:

"I can scarcely believe that a man who holds an honorable and responsible position should throw it up for a damned old Yankee notion (a piece of wire with two Texan steer horns attached to the ends, with an arrangement to make the concern bleat like a calf), called a telephone!"

But Vail was fascinated by the "Yankee notion," and by the administrative challenge of the new business.

Launching a telephone company was very different from manufacturing and marketing an ordinary new consumer product or piece of machinery.

The Bell group had already decided that phones should be rented, rather than sold, to customers, and that service should be provided by central exchanges.

Demand for telephones was mushrooming, but rental fees were not bringing in enough to meet manufacturing costs, and the infant company was facing a law suit against the giant Western Union, which had gone into the telephone business on its own and was violating Bell's patents.

In the summer of 1878, the Western Union telephone was, in fact, far superior to the Bell unit.

Thomas Alva Edison had designed its transmitter, and conversation over a Western Union phone was practically static-free; use of a Bell phone was still, as the inventor's aide, Thomas Watson, had said, "more calculated to develop the American voice and lungs" than to encourage conversation.

Vail spent his first months with the company raising money, struggling to keep up the morale of discouraged Bell franchise holders who wanted to sell out, and negotiating with Western Union.

By fall, the crisis was past. The company had been reorganized with a capital of $450,000 — a $400,000 increase — and a Boston inventor, Francis Blake, Jr., had come up with an excellent transmitter for the Bell phone.

A year later, Western Union was advised by its attorneys to get out of the telephone business, and the suit was settled out of court.

Vail had not quite put the company on its feet single-handed; the devotion and personal sacrifice of the other Bell executives had counted for a great deal, and Blake's transmitter was a magnificent piece of luck.

But the new General Manager's energy and optimism, the administrative genius that had carried him to the top of the Railway Mail Service in only seven years, and his vast talents for dealing with people and for fund-raising

INSTITUTIONAL AD CAMPAIGN launched by Vail in 1907 was aimed at removing public distrust of Bell "monopoly." One of the arguments it advanced was that only a national company could afford to maintain service in unprofitable areas.

Can you imagine a city, as cities once existed, made up of several "quarters," to each of which was confined a population which spoke a separate language?

You, as the average citizen, would be forced to learn several languages, or to go about the city with an interpreter - a process that would seriously interfere with your business.

If, instead of using different languages, the people of a city used *different telephone systems*, the result would be exactly the same. You would have to keep *each particular brand* of telephone.

It is nobody's *fault* that this is so. The Bell companies are not responsible for the fact that a nation's convenience demands the use of one telephone system, any more than they are that *one language* for a nation is better than a collection of provincial dialects.

The associated Bell companies, with their singleness of purpose and unity of service, *are* responsible, however, for doing their utmost to *provide the system that wholly fits this recognized condition*—that prevents the endless and expensive confusion of many systems.

The Telephone's Burden is to embrace in *one* comprehensive system all that a city, or the whole country, needs in the way of telephone service.

This has made the telephone universal.

To-day's work of carrying sixteen million messages—some of business, some of joy and some of sorrow—is not all of the *day's burden*, either.

Preparing for to-morrow's quota of message-passengers on this great national highway of speech is a labor quite as heavy as to-day's actual work.

For in the Bell service to-morrow never comes.

The associated Bell companies' eighty thousand workers are *always* preparing for it—always working to keep pace with the new requirements, forecast by to-day's routine.

People have rapidly developed this *new sense*—the sense of projecting speech. As the sense develops they are learning more about the telephone's possibilities. Twenty million minds are constantly finding new uses for it.

We must immediately adapt the entire Bell system to these new uses.

A realization of this widespread work should clear your mind of doubt, if any exists, that the associated Bell companies are working *with* and *for* the public, striving by the most progressive methods to provide a telephone service that will take your voice anywhere that your thought goes, or your friend goes, or your letter will travel—sometimes even farther than your imagination will carry you—, whether it is half way across the town or half way across the country.

The Bell service is diligently keeping pace with the country's progress, in full knowledge of existing conditions and the necessities of the future.

It goes to the public with such statements as this, in order that all telephone subscribers may understand the position it occupies as a utility, may make their demands on the service intelligently; may readily see that rates must perforce be regulated and continue on an equitable business basis in order to provide the maximum number of subscribers—to make the system universal, that they may fully understand that co-operation of subscriber and telephone company is the *surest guarantee* of good service.

American Telephone & Telegraph Company

And Its Associated Bell Companies

LOCAL AND LONG DISTANCE TELEPHONE

One Policy—One System Universal Service

UNITING OVER 4,000,000 TELEPHONES

Set corporate public relations pattern

had done a great deal to turn the tide. And from then on, these same qualities, coupled with almost prophetic vision and with a rare gift for taking the right step at the right time, were to make him largely responsible for his new company's spectacular success.

Expansion speeded up; it was easy, in a town of any size, to find a young man who wanted to organize and sell stock in a local Bell telephone company.

Vail insisted on the building of exchanges that linked two or more towns, although there was still little demand for such service and most local companies were reluctant to spend the money.

He even began securing inter-state rights.

He was already envisioning a national telephone network in which Bell would be a permanent partner.

Bell stock was soaring; it rose from $50 a share in 1878 to $1000 a share after the Western Union settlement. Vail, who had substantial holdings in the parent company and in the flourishing New York City subsidiary as well, was a millionaire at 35.

When Vail joined the company, in 1878, there were fewer than 10,000 Bell telephones in the U.S. By 1881, there were over 130,000, serviced by 408 exchanges.

In 1884, the first New York-Boston circuit was completed; Vail's dream of a transcontinental network was a few miles closer to reality, and in 1885, the American Telephone & Telegraph Co. was formed for further development of the Bell System's long lines, with Theodore N. Vail as president.

In 1887, with over 50,000 miles of long lines in operation, Vail left the telephone company.

He was in poor health; he wanted more time for his investments; and, very probably, his passion for growth was bringing him into conflict with the increasingly conservative management of the company.

He had moved during the '80s, with his wife and son, to a magnificent home in Boston, bought a farm in Vermont for summer use, and begun entertaining lavishly and almost continuously at both establishments. His hobbies, with which he expected to keep busy during his retirement, were carriage horses, sailing and stocks.

Ever since he had begun to earn money (or been able to borrow it—thrift was about the only business virtue which Theodore Vail did not possess), he had speculated, always enthusiastically, often brilliantly, sometimes disastrously in ventures ranging from the manufacture of electric storage batteries to a California ostrich farm.

Over the 20 years between 1887 and 1907, his most notable speculative accomplishments were losing practically his whole fortune on a scheme for heating cities by piping hot water underground, and then recouping it in an Argentine electric power development project.

In 1907, AT&T—now the parent company of the Bell System—invited him to come back as president, and he accepted.

During his 20 years of absence, the system had grown prodigiously—and had run into serious trouble.

Insufficient provision had been made for maintenance of existing telephone installations and for purchase of new equipment; many Bell exchanges throughout the country had become badly run down.

And competition had reared its head again—this time, in the form of small, independent, local companies, which, with brand new equipment, shoddy though it often was, were able to offer better service.

The local companies had a psychological advantage,

FIRST BELL EXCHANGES, following example of telegraph offices, hired teen-age boys as operators *(far l.)*. By 1885, women operators, who proved to be more courteous and conscientious, had virtually taken over *(c.)*; telephone companies were among first to offer opportunities to working women. Today, while the traditional "voice with a smile" is still an essential part of telephone service, automation is playing an ever-increasing role. Dial telephones for local calls began coming into use in the 1920s; the Direct Distance Dialing system which makes a long-distance call as simple as a local one began to grow in 1951, and by 1965, linked 95% of all U.S. telephones. AT&T workers call the room housing its elaborate Distance Dialing equipment *(l.)* "Crossbar Canyon."

too; anti-big business feeling was running high in the early years of the new century, and the Bell System was a perfect target for attacks as a "monopoly."

However, the public soon found out that competition in the telephone business meant that the average homeowner or storekeeper had to install two or more telephones and keep track of which service his friends or customers patronized.

And, as the new companies began making the same mistake Bell had made and allowing their equipment to run down (many of them had been able to offer low rates by making no provision for maintenance whatsoever), Bell, which had been repairing and refurbishing, began getting business back.

This did not, however, make the giant any more popular.

Back in the presidency, Vail met the challenge of the independents by offering them consolidation practically on their own terms—and many of them were happy to accept.

Then he turned his attention to the public relations problem. He launched an "institutional" advertising campaign—one of the first—with a six-figure budget. He began issuing annual reports of the type common today but practically unheard of then, in which the company's problems and policies were fully and frankly discussed. He encouraged newspaper publicity, and himself wrote a stream of magazine articles on public utilities, in which he did not even hesitate to use the dread word, "monopoly."

He seems to have sincerely believed that the truth—attractively presented whenever possible, of course—could not possibly hurt the Bell System.

In 1908, when Bell's advertising agency, N. W. Ayer, presented an ad with the headline, "One Policy, One System, Universal Service," the company's own advertising director suggested that it might attract the unfavorable attention of trust-busting politicians.

"Is it true?" Vail asked.

The advertising director admitted that it was.

"Very well, then," Vail replied, "let's print it and beat them to it."

Vail's design for public relations, which he was to continue developing until his retirement from the presidency in 1919, has served as a model for the best corporate public relations programs of the present day.

THEODORE VAIL IN HIS 70'S

MAIL ORDER

Richard Warren Sears, founder of the $4 billion Sears,

SEARS *(above)*, clean shaven in his 20s, later cultivated handlebar mustache to match partner Roebuck's *(below)*. Rosenwald's *(r.)* was more sedate.

THE U.S. mass consumer market of the late 19th Century was less opulent than today's—but it was hungry and fast-growing, and offered dazzling opportunities to imaginative merchandisers.

One of these merchandising pioneers was Richard Warren Sears, founder of Sears, Roebuck & Co., which started this decade with sales of over $4 billion.

Young Sears went into the mail order business in 1886, when large-scale mail order merchandising was a relatively new idea. (His firm's only major competitor, Montgomery Ward, had begun operations in 1873.)

FIRST SEARS STORE was North Redwood, Minn., railroad station where young Sears sold watches. Most small town station agents of 1880s had businesses on the side.

MAGICIAN

Roebuck mail order empire, wrote catalogs that talked hard-headed buyers' language

Mail order catalogs were aimed primarily at the nation's largest consumer group, farmers and small town residents, who in 1880 made up 71.8% of the U.S. population.

As Richard Sears, who had grown up in Minnesota farming towns, knew, farmers had little money to spare, and did not want frills.

They did want agricultural equipment, home furnishings and supplies and sturdy work clothes at rock-bottom prices. When they splurged a few dollars on a Sunday suit or a watch, they were interested in price first, quality second.

Sears knew, too, that in an age of stock jokes about country bumpkins and city slickers, the average farmer was afraid of being cheated, or made to look foolish, or both, if he did business with city folks.

It was his knowledge of these facts of rural life, together with a natural talent for and unbounded love of selling, that gave Richard Sears his phenomenal success.

He offered his customers the goods they needed at unbeatable prices, and wrote his catalog copy in such reassuringly folksy terms that fears of city slickers in Chicago vanished when the farmer opened the big book.

Sears, who had left high school and gone to work as a telegraph operator at 16, was 23 years old and working as a station agent in North Redwood, Minn., in 1886, when one day a shipment of watches arrived from a Chicago jewelery company, addressed to a local jeweler.

The jeweler had not ordered the watches and refused to accept them, so Sears promptly wrote to Chicago and offered to sell them himself.

Then he began telegraphing his fellow station agents up and down the line, letting them know he was in the watch business.

The watches vanished, and Sears ordered more.

He made a $500 profit in six months, moved to Minneapolis, and set up the R. W. Sears Watch Co., in a $10-a-month office furnished with a kitchen table and a few 50¢ chairs.

Business (still conducted largely through station agents) boomed, and in 1887, Sears moved to Chicago, the rail hub of the Middle West.

About then, however, the watches began to come back for repairs, and Sears advertised for a watchmaker.

His ad was answered by a young man his own age, Alvah C. Roebuck, who was hired to repair the watches, and became a partner in Sears' fast-growing enterprise within a few months.

Roebuck does not seem to have been exceptionally talented, but he had what Sears wanted — boundless admiration for the talents of Richard Warren Sears, and plenty of capacity for hard work. (Sears himself was already working from seven in the morning to 10 or 11 at night.)

The company issued its first catalog in 1887, and began selling to the general public in 1888.

1960 MODEL STORE is part of Tampa, Fla., shopping center. Sears entered the retail field when the automobile made its customers less dependent on mail order catalogs.

Sears decided that a successful mail order merchant had to offer his customers three things: absolute assurance of honesty, a chance to see the goods before being committed to buy, and prices low enough to make up for the fact that mail ordering was still unconventional.

The first catalog, like all its successors, offered a flat money-back-if-not-satisfied guarantee.

The ethical standards of merchandising in the 1880s were not high, and Sears was by no means above bamboozling customers with extravagant adjectives and sky-high claims when he thought he could get away with it.

However, he and other mail order pioneers did a great deal to raise the standards of merchandising.

A catalog had to offer a fixed price and stick to it, unlike a retailer, who could—and often did—charge whatever he thought the customer would pay.

And it had to offer the money-back guarantee to win the business of the suspicious farmers.

So, within a few years, retailers began to realize that they had to adopt the same "customer is always right" policies or lose all their business to the mail order houses.

And manufacturers had to meet the new demand of mail order houses and retailers alike for goods of reliable quality that would not bring a flood of returns.

By 1893, the year in which the Sears, Roebuck & Co. name was adopted, Sears' catalog was offering furniture, dishes, clothing, harnesses and saddles, guns, wagons and buggies, bicycles, shoes, baby carriages, musical instruments and sewing machines as well as watches and jewelry.

Sears wrote every line of catalog copy himself, and supervised its makeup, violating every rule in the advertising man's book.

"White space" was kept to an irreducible minimum, pages were crowded with tiny type and blurred woodcuts.

But Sears, Roebuck customers obviously liked it. The company's 1892 sales volume was $296,368.

The catalog was supplemented by heavy advertising in the so-called "mail order magazines," small monthlies popular with rural readers.

For Richard Sears, there was simply no such thing as too many orders. In fact, he liked to get orders first, then worry about filling them.

His 1895 promotion of men's suits was typical.

He advertised 2000 suits at $4.98 C.O.D., and another 1000 at $8.95, describing them in glowing terms and asserting that "we are the largest handlers of clothing in America."

Orders came flooding in. The clerks in Sears, Roebuck's Chicago offices were swamped; buyers began scouring the market to find the suits, which had existed only in Sears' imagination when the ads were placed, and the shipping department hopelessly jumbled colors, sizes and fabrics.

Such spectacular promotions increased sales volume to $750,000 in 1895.

They also brought the company to a state of complete administrative chaos, and Alvah Roebuck to physical collapse and early retirement.

The firm's liabilities had risen to more than three times the amount permitted under its charter of incorporation, and Sears began looking for new investors.

He found them in Aaron Nusbaum, who had made a fortune with a soda pop and ice cream concession at the 1893 Chicago Columbian Exposition, and Nusbaum's brother-in-law, Julius Rosenwald, a clothing manufacturer.

Sears retained the presidency of the company, recapitalized at $150,000. Rosenwald became vice president and Nusbaum treasurer.

Julius Rosenwald's talent for administration and finance was as great as Sears' for advertising and sales; from 1895 on, he ran the business while Sears concentrated on the promotion that kept it growing.

Among his promotional schemes were free gift offers, a Customers' Profit Sharing Premium Plan which was, in effect, the forerunner of today's trading stamp plans, and a catalog distribution system under which regular customers got catalogs to pass along to their friends, and received merchandise bonuses for their friends' orders.

Sales passed the $10 million mark in 1900. Sears, Roebuck had gained, and was never to lose, undisputed first place in the mail order field.

Its chief opposition came from country general stores and small town retailers, who were so afraid of mail order competition that they organized public catalog-burnings.

Both Rosenwald and Nusbaum had a preference, incomprehensible to Sears, for knowing how they were going to fill an order before advertising for customers.

Nusbaum was the more conservative of the two, and he and Sears found it impossible to work together. He sold out in 1903.

The clash of personalities between Sears and Rosenwald was less acute; the two men seem to have had the greatest respect for each other.

When Sears retired in 1908, leaving Rosenwald in the presidency, ill health was his most important reason; he died in 1914. His departure ended the most colorful era of Sears, Roebuck history.

Today, over half of Sears' $4 billion sales volume comes from its chain of retail stores, begun in 1925, and more ordering is done by telephone than by mail. But the catalog that Richard Sears made a part of everyday U.S. life is still the cornerstone of all mail order merchandising.

LEADING MAIL ORDER HOUSES

Company	1900 Sales ($ million)	1900 Profits ($ million)	1920 Sales ($ million)	1920 Profits ($ million)	1940 Sales ($ million)	1940 Profits ($ million)	1960 Sales ($ million)	1960 Profits ($ million)
Sears, Roebuck	10.6	0.9	245.4	11.8	704.3	36.1	**4036.2**	**198.7**
Montgomery Ward	8.8	0.5	101.7	7.9	474.8	27.0	**1222.6**	**30.7**
Spiegel	.....	.....	n.a.	n.a.	53.5	1.8	**268.8**	**11.8**
Aldens*	.....	.....	7.0	−.3	26.7	.3	**114.7**	**3.4**
National Bellas Hess**	n.a.	n.a.	47.7	−1.3	3.4	−.2	**48.9**	**1.3**
New Process	.....	.....	n.a.	n.a.	5.1	.3	**22.1**	**.7**

* Known as Chicago Mail Order Co. until 1946.
** Present firm purchased receivership of earlier company of same name in 1932. Original National Bellas Hess was known as National Cloak and Suit Co. until 1927.

TYPICAL PAGES OF EARLY CATALOGS FEATURED ELECTRIC BELT (SUPPOSED MALE DISEASE CURE-ALL), HAND-CRANKED WASHING MACHINE

CATALOG STYLE grew more conservative after Sears retired. 1913 page shows use of fewer adjectives, more "white space."

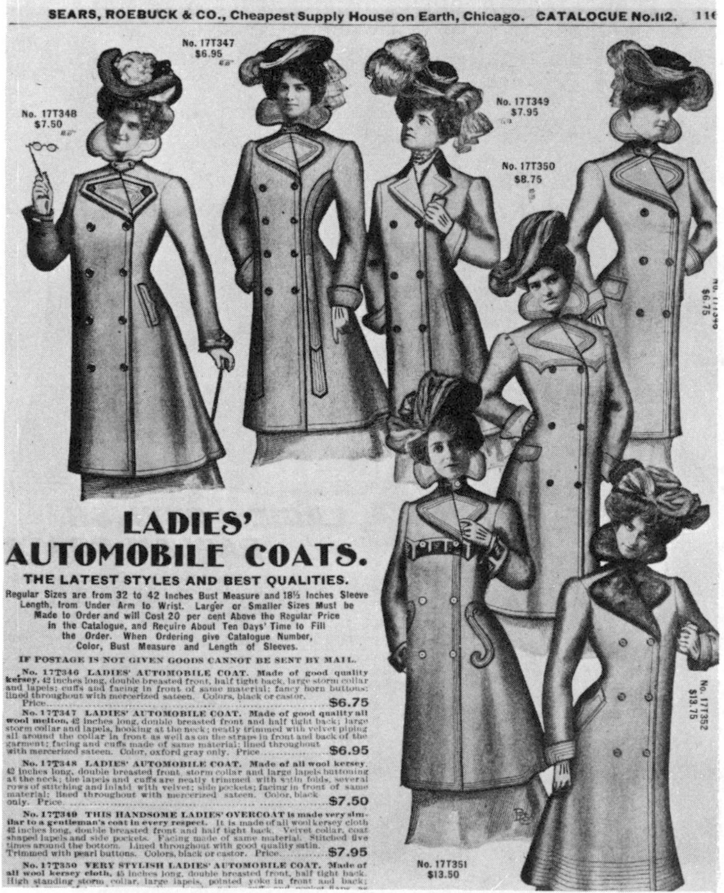

1897 CATALOG COVER emphasized company's financial stability, listing bank references and new $150,000 capitalization.

CHAMPION OF U.S. LABOR

Gompers dedicated his life to elevation of the masses, improvement of factory conditions. He made the voice of U.S. labor heard around the world

IN THE 1850s a commonplace sound echoed through the narrow streets of London's East Side slums:

"God, I've no work to do. Lord, strike me dead – my wife, my children want bread . . ."

The pitiful wailing of the unemployed had a profound effect on young Samuel Gompers.

"That cry, ringing through the streets day after day, never failed to draw me to the window . . . to watch these men struggling against despair," he wrote 60 years later in his autobiography.

It became the most important influence to shape his life.

More than any one of the powerful merchant princes in U.S. business history, Samuel Gompers was responsible for the emergence of modern industrial America. By his insistence on "more, more" for labor, he forced mechanization and spurred our industrial revolution.

During his lifetime Gompers towered over all other labor leaders; his legacy remains the bedrock on which present-day unionism rests. For more than 40 years he served as president of the American Federation of Labor, from its feeble birth in 1886 until his death in 1924.

As time went on he was regarded by most of the nation as labor's elder statesman and, although the AFL only included one-tenth of the total employed, he took it upon himself to speak for all labor. Few questioned his right to do so.

Despised both by reactionary industrial czars and radical left-wing elements (for entirely different reasons), he was revered by millions who looked to him as their champion.

Born in 1850 into a poor family of Dutch Jews who had migrated to London, Gompers had a brief four-year education and, at 10, was apprenticed to a shoemaker. However, he complained the noise of the shoemaking establishment hurt his ears and he switched over to cigar-making, his father's trade.

Persistent poverty soon prompted the Gompers family to make a second move, this time to the United States. The Cigarmakers Society of England had established an emigration fund. Instead of paying unemployment benefits, it helped pay members' passage to America.

The Gompers family arrived in New York in 1863 after seven weeks at sea. Their new four-room home on Houston Street looked more spacious than the one-room flat in London, but the neighborhood was similar. Gompers recalled that opposite their house was a slaughterhouse, behind it a brewery.

For the first year and a half he and his father made cigars at home. But always of a gregarious nature, he soon found many friends, attended night school at Cooper Union, and joined local social clubs. Eventually he almost forgot he was not a native-born American. (He fathered the AFL's anti-immigration policy.)

At 14 Gompers joined the Cigar-

AFL President Samuel Gompers (sixth from right) often met with prominent leaders of the business community, steel scion Charles M. Schwab (fifth from right) and Presidential aspirant Herbert Hoover (2nd from left).

National guardsmen were called in to quell rioting of striking American Railway Union members during the famous 1894 Pullman Strike in Chicago.

Steelworkers battled federal troops during bloody 1892 Homestead riots.

makers' Local No. 15. He went to work in a factory and immediately began to participate in union activities. So evident were his qualities of leadership that when fellow employees, some of them 40 years his senior, wanted to present grievances to the boss, he was selected as their spokesman. His level-headed arguments often won the desired terms.

On his seventeenth birthday he married a girl who worked in the same shop and 20 months later their first child was born. Five more followed and, because his income for many years was small and irregular, the family often suffered privations.

Gompers became more and more involved with union activities, especially when the depression of the 1870's caused severe unemployment among the cigarmakers.

Gompers and Adolph Strasser, another active labor man, obtained control of the weak Cigarmakers International Union and tried to strengthen it. Their reforms, startling for those times, included uniform initiation fees and dues, centralized control over strikes, and the levy of $2 per member for a strike fund.

Finally in 1878, when the cigarmakers' distress had grown extreme, the union risked its first walkout. "It was a wonderful fight," said Gompers, despite the fact the union was forced to capitulate after five months.

"Although we did not win, we learned the fundamentals . . . which would assure success later."

The strikers went back to work, but Gompers was blacklisted for many months.

Gompers' spirit of combat was to be of great use, for the country was entering a dynamic and turbulent era when modern industrial America began to emerge from its infancy.

From colonial days until the Civil War, few workers had any consciousness of class. Those few unions which did organize found themselves stymied by the old common law of conspiracy.

But the ending of slavery assured industrial capitalism a dominant role in the U.S. economic system. Overnight the economy mushroomed. By 1894, the U.S. had jumped to first place in world production of industrial goods.

Rapid growth was accompanied by heavy concentration of capital and the birth of giant corporations. Monopolies sprang up in many branches of industry. Survival often depended on cutthroat competition.

With the introduction of machinery, most workers were no longer individual, dignified craftsmen, but generally adjuncts to the machine.

"There are too many millionaires and too many paupers," editorialized the *Hartford Courant*. America was indeed a land of contrasts.

Furious speculation and overbuilding came to a brief halt with the depression of 1873. It lasted seven years. Wages were slashed and labor unions crushed. The new industrialists used the same ruthless tactics on workers as they did on competitors.

"I can hire one-half of the working class to kill the other half," boasted railroad magnate Jay Gould.

Warfare was declared and from the 1870s on, guns, spies, and troops played a prominent role in U.S. labor relations. Many industrial battles were settled in this way.

During these chaotic times the first important national labor organization began to make itself known. Activities of the Noble Order of the Knights of Labor were cloaked in darkest secrecy with rituals similar to the Masons and Odd Fellows. But in 1878 when the depression had produced a new consciousness in American workers, it came out into the open, rallying all labor to its slogan: "An injury to one is the concern of all."

Labor solidarity was its main objective and no group of workers was excluded – skilled and unskilled, white and Negro, male and female. The Knights even admitted employers.

Its goals were lofty; elevation of humanity, education, political action. Workers were urged to found producers' co-operatives or work in harmony with employers.

"I shudder at the thought of a

American unionism owes its life to crusading efforts of Gompers

strike," said one of its leaders. It was this non-militant attitude, so out of keeping with the rebellious times, which brought its demise.

In the meantime a rival, the American Federation of Labor, had risen, with Samuel Gompers as its president and co-founder. Its aims and methods were a far cry from the Knights.

"A struggle is going on . . . between the oppressors and the oppressed of all countries," the preamble to its constitution declared, "A struggle between capital and labor . . ."

While the AFL recognized the struggle, it did not intend to change the system. It merely wanted a bigger share of the pie.

"Pure and simple unionism" was their philosophy. Concentrate on immediate objectives; never mind about grandiose ultimate goals.

In structure the AFL was founded on voluntarism or "a rope of sand," as Lenin called it. Each local had complete independence.

A serious flaw in their organization was a snobbish emphasis on skilled workers, labor's aristocracy. It had little interest in the non-skilled, even though mass production would eventually put the majority of labor into that category.

When Gompers took on the job of its presidency (no one else wanted it), the youthful organization became his personal baby. At an annual salary of $1,000, he settled in an 8 x 10 office with tomato crates for files and enthusiastically set out to build the Federation. He worked tirelessly, doing every conceivable job including that of errand boy.

He wrote in March 1887: "My official duties are taking up my entire time and energy . . . I have not had the pleasure of partaking of afternoon or evening meals (Sunday included) with my family for months."

Evidently there were other reasons for his absence from home. A member of the AFL Executive Council wrote to a friend in 1892: "I am rather inclined to think Sam is a model husband as the haunts that used to know him now mourn his absence; his favorite pool room has closed up its doors."

Physically a startling person, he had a huge torso, short legs, and a pipe-organ voice. He used all his incongruous parts to gain and hold attention; his contemporaries described him as "a born actor."

He combined this personal dynamism with shrewdness. His old battles in the cigarmarkers union had taught him the value of a strong treasury. Accordingly, the AFL charged high dues and initiation fees. Strike funds, unemployment insurance, sickness, old age and disability benefits – all were available to members. (Gompers later opposed Federal unemployment insurance, workmen's compensation and social security on the grounds that unions should provide for their own.)

In politics he advocated nonpartisanship, refusing to identify the AFL with either major party. "Reward our friends and punish our enemies" was his policy.

In fighting for better conditions he tried to make the AFL respectable in the eyes of the general public. Even though he once studied German to read Karl Marx in the original, he hated being labeled a radical.

His later violent animosity toward socialism and communism was partly because these ideologies bore a foreign connotation. He insisted the U.S. labor movement should be purely American and work out its own philosophy and techniques.

His idea of unionism reflected typical American practicality. He set up an efficient, business-like union, not unlike the workings of business itself.

The Federation grew slowly during its early years, from less than 150,000 members in 1886 to 278,000 in 1898. But powerful industrialists administered many devastating defeats to it.

Immigrants formed backbone of early U.S. labor movement. N. Y. strikers demand 8-hour working day, rally to slogan "In Unity is our Strength."

Corporate Staying Power

Two bitter strikes proved to Gompers that his strongest unions could not yet withstand the attack of a giant corporation.

For nearly five months in 1892 the Carnegie Steel Co. and the Amalgamated Assn. of Iron and Steel Workers, one of the most powerful unions in the country, waged war at Homestead, Penna. The steel company imported 300 armed Pinkerton detectives and 8,000 National Guardsmen to crush the union. A triumphant Carnegie re-established the 12-hour day and cut wages to subsistence level. Forty years elapsed before the industry effectively organized again.

In 1894, the American Railway Union, led by Eugene Debs, struck the Pullman Palace Car Co. in Illinois. Despite a call for Federal troops, trains stood still all over the country. Finally the strike was broken by a court order against the union for interfering with the operation of mail trains.

(Although the injunction was not a new legal instrument, this was its first important use against labor. Afterward, it became a popular weapon.)

The ARU sent an urgent telegram to Gompers, asking him to come to Chicago to support a city-wide strike. Gompers came but refused to give his blessing. He said the railway strike was already lost and further agitation might endanger the long-run interests of labor.

For this stand he was severely criticized by both radicals and some sections of labor.

Management and labor rub elbows during Union Square labor rally in N. Y. Outdoor meeting (above) afforded workers opportunity to air grievances. Even the ladies had their say in early labor disputes. Below, group of striking telephone operators line up for picket duty in Boston, 1916.

Labor's Magna Carta

Despite his individualism, his disdain of money (he died a poor man) and his selfless devotion to labor, Gompers was pompous and self-righteous.

Consistently throughout his long tenure as AFL leader, he defied the membership when it favored radical programs. For all of his progressive speeches, he became exceedingly conservative as the years passed.

He often was not able to rise above flattery and adulation. In 1914 his lobbying finally resulted in a bill which would exempt unions from being sued for restraint of trade. To him, the Clayton Act was labor's Magna Carta.

But so pleased was he with the friendly spirit of Congress and so emotionally insistent on the exact wording of his favorite theory — "... the labor of a human being is not a commodity or an article of commerce" — that he compromised on a crucial clause.

It originally stated "nothing contained in the anti-trust laws . . . shall apply to labor . . .", but the final wording was considerably weaker. His oversight enabled the courts to interpret the Act very liberally. Not until 1935 did the Wagner Labor Relations Act change the situation.

The period of World War I was one of great activity and gratification for Gompers. Rising above labor partisanship, he renounced his previous pacifism and became a national leader and patriot.

The favorable Wilson administration helped labor get a fairer hearing in industrial disputes and AFL membership doubled. After the war Gompers was disappointed not to be included in the peace delegation, but he was sent to Europe as head of a labor goodwill mission.

There he felt doubly betrayed when the post-war era brought a retrogression in industry-labor relations. With war-time restrictions lifted, prices soared. Labor, asking for higher wages to meet increased living costs, found itself threatened with the open shop and lockouts.

Its power and prestige went into a temporary decline as Gompers reached the end of his life. As a result of a half century of intense exertion and free living, his health began to deteriorate. He contracted Bright's disease and became almost blind.

In December, 1924, he traveled to Mexico City for a meeting of the Pan-American Federation of Labor but became ill. He wished to die on American soil and was moved across the border to San Antonio.

For more than 50 years he had struggled to further organized labor.

"The trade union is the great fact of my life," he said. His monument is today's approximately 18 million union members.

HE BEAT THE HEAT

Willis Carrier, inventor of mechanical air conditioning, designed world's first temperature-humidity control system for a Brooklyn printing plant in 1902, founded Carrier Corp. in 1914. Today, air conditioning is a $4-billion-dollar industry and has brought cool comfort to millions of homes

NEW YORK was even hotter and damper than usual in the summers of 1900 and 1901, and as the summer of 1902 drew near, a Brooklyn printing firm decided that it had to stop just talking about the weather.

The paper the plant used was one size on dry days, another on humid ones. Colors overlapped, color runs rarely matched from day to day, and flow and drying rate of ink were irregular.

So the company, Sackett-Wilhelms, called in the Buffalo Forge Co., manufacturers of blowers, heaters and exhausts, to design a temperature-humidity control system.

Buffalo Forge turned the problem over to its most promising young employe, engineer Willis Carrier.

In August, 1902, the world's first industrial air conditioning went into operation at Sackett-Wilhelms—and today's $4 billion air conditioning industry was born.

Willis Carrier came from an upstate New York farm family. He was 25 in 1902, and a year out of Cornell, where he had taken a degree in electrical engineering.

He took the Buffalo Forge job after graduation with some misgivings, since the company had nothing to do with electricity. But a campus recruiter (they were around, even then) had made him a good offer, and he liked the idea of living with relatives in Buffalo.

Carrier spent his first months at Buffalo Forge designing drying systems for coffee and lumber and a forced draft system for boilers.

He soon decided that the branch of engineering he had stumbled into was woefully lacking in basic data. So he started working overtime on development of formulas and compilation of tables — and, within six months, had prepared a formula for selecting draft fans for maximum boiler efficiency, minimum fan horsepower.

The Buffalo Forge management was sufficiently impressed to establish a research department and put Carrier in charge of it.

He next came up with data on heater coils which—once he had persuaded the older engineers to use his tables—saved the company $40,000 in the next heating season.

So it was hardly surprising that when the temperature-humidity control order arrived from Sackett-Wilhelms, Willis Carrier got the job.

Mechanical temperature control was already a reality in 1902—although decidedly a luxury item.

The first commercial ice-making machine had been invented by a Florida doctor, John Gorrie, in 1851, and in the 1880s, mechanical refrigeration began to spread throughout the U.S. Madison Square Theatre and Carnegie Hall were ice-cooled; so was the New York Stock Exchange, after its members asked, "if they can cool dead hogs in Chicago, why not live bulls and bears in New York?"

But, although air could be cooled, circulated and moistened fairly successfully, its humidity could not be reduced — and, especially for industrial use, humidity control was just as important as cooling.

Years later, Carrier described his first humidity-control experiment:

"We rigged up a roller towel arrangement with loosely woven burlap which we kept flooded with a saturated solution of calcium chloride brine. We drew air through the burlap with a fan. Readings of dry-bulb and wet-bulb temperatures told us the amount of moisture removed from the air by the brine.

"Everything about the test was operated manually except the fan—a man dipped brine from a barrel and poured it over the cloth, and a man turned the rollers."

This test was abandoned in a week. The calcium chloride did reduce moisture, but it left the air so salty that it would have rusted machinery.

The next experiment involved circulation of cold air through heater coils, balancing the temperature of the coil surface and the rate of air flow to produce the dew point temperature at which the air had the right humidity for printing.

This method worked. On July 12, 1902, Carrier turned in finished drawings to Sackett-Wilhelms.

But it was not until several months later, in the fall of 1902, that Carrier hit upon the principle of "dew point control," the basis of modern air conditioning engineering.

He was waiting for a train on a foggy night in Pittsburgh, and suddenly realized that he was pacing back and forth in the ideal medium for moisture control.

If he could create "fog" by saturating air with water, and then control its temperature at saturation, he could produce exactly the desired amount of moisture in air.

Since he was still supposed to be working on heaters, blowers and exhausts for Buffalo Forge, it was spring of the next year before he was able to start working on his new idea.

His "Apparatus for Treating Air" was finished in 1904 and patented on January 2, 1906.

As orders started coming in, Carrier—now head of the company's Engineering Department at 29—began to take an interest in the marketing of his moisture-providing brainchild.

He compiled a sales catalog, including technical data which, when published in 1911 as "Rational Psychrometric Formulae," would establish air conditioning as a full-fledged branch of engineering.

The catalog also listed potential markets for cooling apparatus—theatres, churches, restaurants, ships, soap, leather, glue and textile factories, tobacco warehouses.

Home air conditioning was still only a day dream, and for the next 20 years, cooling installations were to be sold primarily for improvement of products and processes — the textile industry was the first large-scale customer—rather than people comfort.

In 1908, the air conditioning in Buffalo Forge's business was grow-

OPENING of New York's first air conditioned movie theatre, the Rivoli, on Memorial Day, 1925, was a highly publicized event. It was also a nerve-wracking one for Carrier, who had spent all night in the theatre setting up the new equipment.

ing so fast that the company decided to form a subsidiary, Carrier Air Conditioning Co. of America.

Carrier was the new company's vice-president, and Irvine Lyle its sales manager.

Lyle was another of Buffalo Forge's most promising young men. As New York district sales manager, he had brought in the Sackett-Wilhelms order six years before, and he and Willis Carrier were close friends.

Carrier Air Conditioning flourished for six years, winning new customers in industry after industry.

In 1914, however, with the threat of war making business conditions uncertain, Buffalo Forge decided to cut back — and the new subsidiary was the first to go.

Carrier and Lyle were promised that their jobs with the parent company were safe, but they were still heartsick over the decision.

Together with five of the subsidiary's other key men, they decided to go into business on their own.

The seven pooled their savings—and their borrowing power—to form Carrier Engineering Corp. with a total capital of $32,600.

Salaries in the new company were at what one of the founders later described as "subsistence level," and its two-room headquarters in Buffalo was sparsely furnished with secondhand furniture.

But 40 contracts came in during the first year, and Carrier Engineering was soon in the black.

Renamed Carrier Corp. after a 1930 merger with Brunswick Kroeschell and York Heating & Ventilating, it still holds an important place in the industry Carrier pioneered.

The industry as a whole has now

MONSTER refrigeration machines used in early air conditioning systems were complex and cumbersome. Carrier's development, in early 1920s, of simpler refrigeration equipment for manufacture by Carrier Corp. was vital growth.

RAILROAD AIR CONDITIONING was introduced by Baltimore & Ohio on its crack New York-Washington trains in 1930. Cool comfort of pullman cars and diners aroused businessmen's interest in air conditioning for their plants, offices, homes.

placed air conditioning units in 5.5 million U.S. homes. Factory air conditioning is commonplace, and summer comfort is offered by 90% of the nation's theatres, 50% of hospitals, 27% of Class A office buildings, 35% of motels, 20% of stores, and 3% of churches.

Willis Carrier's dream of the air-conditioning of whole cities from a single central plant may be just around the corner.

SACKETT-WILHELMS air conditioning equipment, Carrier's first installation (in artist's conception, *above,* with young Carrier at center) was designed to provide temperature of 70 degrees in winter, 80 in summer, constant humidity of 55%. To maintain these conditions, it had to remove 400 pounds of water an hour from the air.

FIRST AIR COOLED HOME was Minneapolis mansion of Charles G. Gates. Equipment, specially designed by Carrier, was 20 feet long, six feet wide, seven feet high. Small home units, introduced in the late 1920s, were not common till 1940s.

THEY TAUGHT THE WORLD TO FLY

Wright brothers made first powered flights, founded today's huge industry

Orville (l.) and Wilbur (r.) in 1909 at Ft. Myer, Va., where first military plane was tested for Signal Corps.

BACK IN DECEMBER, 1903, taxpayers who felt like complaining about governmental extravagance could point to the $100,000 Federal grant made to the Smithsonian Institution for—of all things—development of a heavier-than-air powered flying machine.

The machine, built by one of the nation's leading scientists, Dr. Samuel Pierpont Langley, had been tested twice. And, as most sensible citizens had felt sure it would, it had plunged ingloriously into the Potomac on both occasions.

Few people even noticed the short, garbled accounts that appeared in a handful of newspapers a week later, describing a successful flight made at Kitty Hawk, N. C., by two scientific unknowns named Orville and Wilbur Wright.

Today, of course, the Wright brothers are ranked with Edison and Bell among the handful of inventors who made the most dramatic and decisive contributions to 20th Century technology.

It is less well remembered that they were also pioneer aircraft *manufacturers,* founders of today's $6.5 billion U.S. aircraft industry.

Wilbur and Orville Wright (born in 1867 and 1871 respectively) were two of the five children of Milton Wright, a bishop of the United Brethren church.

They were the only members of their family who did not go to college.

Instead, they went into business together in Dayton, Ohio as soon as they left high school, and, by the mid-1890s, were moderately successful bicycle manufacturers.

Then, toward the turn of the century, a casual interest in aeronautics that they had shared ever since their teens began turning into a full-fledged hobby.

It was hardly surprising, in a world that had seen the making of so many technological miracles over a few decades, that there were scientists, inventors, and amateurs like the Wright brothers who believed that

New era of history confronts panoplied old during Wilbur Wright's triumphal 1908 tour.

man would one day fly.

In fact, a great deal of progress in aerodynamic theory had already been made.

Men had been taking to the air for short flights in lighter-than-air balloons for over a century, and in heavier-than-air, unpowered gliders for several decades.

Toy models of powered heavier-than-air craft had been flown.

But all attempts to get a man-carrying "flying machine" off the ground had failed.

Part of the trouble was that nobody knew enough about flying to build a craft that would fly, and to handle it in the air.

The glider enthusiasts were just beginning to put the theories of flight to practical test for seconds at a time; most of the would-be aircraft builders who preceded the Wrights had never been off the ground.

The inventor of the airplane would have to be his own test pilot. He would need not only the scientific understanding and mechanical talent required for any great invention, but also a high degree of physical courage and skill.

And he would have to be lucky. Even unpowered gliding, the indispensable preliminary to powered flight, was an extremely dangerous sport.

In 1899, Wilbur wrote to the Smithsonian Institution, explaining that he wanted to begin experiments in flight "to which I expect to devote what time I can spare from my regular business," and asked for a reading list.

After a year of intensive study, the brothers began building their first glider, and by the spring of 1900 were corresponding with the U.S. Weather Bureau about the best location for flying it.

They also wrote to Octave Chanute, a retired civil engineer who was one of the nation's leading students of aeronautics.

Both Chanute and the Weather Bureau recommend-

AT FIRST, FEAT WAS IGNORED

ed the Carolina coast as having the desired winds.

So, in September, 1900, the brothers set off for their first "vacation" in Kitty Hawk.

They returned in 1901, and again in 1902.

By the end of their third season, with the advice and encouragement of Chanute, they had consolidated, revised and in certain respects completely revolutionized the existing body of aerodynamic theory.

Their 1902 glider was larger and more airworthy than any ever built. It contained all the control elements necessary for stable flight. It was, in fact, an airplane without motors or propeller.

These the brothers built over the winter, and in the fall of 1903 they went back to Kitty Hawk for the fourth time.

"I see that Langley has had his fling and failed," Wilbur wrote to Chanute in October, after the Smithsonian Institution flying machine had lurched into the Potomac for the first time. "It seems to be our turn to throw now, and I wonder what our luck will be?"

On December 15th, after two more months of gliding practice, they flew the powered plane.

The longest of the four flights they made that morning (before the wind overturned the little plane on the ground and damaged it beyond repair) lasted only 57 seconds.

But, in Orville's words, it was the "first in history in which a machine carrying a man raised itself by its own power into the air in full flight, sailed forward without reduction of speed, and landed at a point as high as that from which it started."

Triumphantly, Wilbur and Orville telegraphed their brother Lorin, back in Dayton, to give the news to the Associated Press.

However, public cynicism about flying machines was at its height after the recent fiasco on the Potomac, and the Dayton AP man turned down the scoop of a lifetime with the comment that if the flight had lasted 57 *minutes,* Lorin might have a story.

Spain's King Alfonso sits in plane, chats animatedly with Wilbur, after demonstration during 1908 tour.

Brothers flank President Taft after he presented them Aero Club of America Medal at White House, 1909.

Inaccurate Accounts

A few accounts of the flight, most of them wildly inaccurate, did leak into the press over the next few weeks. But the first full report (written by Chanute for *Popular Science Monthly)* did not appear until March, 1904.

By then, Wilbur and Orville had decided to stop pretending to be bicycle manufacturers who flew for a hobby, and became aircraft manufacturers.

They finished their second plane, larger and heavier than the first, in May, and began flying in a 68-acre cow pasture.

In September, they reported joyfully to Chanute that they were able to "circumnavigate the field." Before the year's end, they were making five-mile flights.

Then, in November, they began trying to negotiate the aircraft industry's first government contract.

It took them three years.

Their first letter to the War Department got a form reply, obviously designed for "flying machine" cranks, completely ignoring the fact that the Wrights had asked for no development funds, but had actually offered to build a practical aircraft for military reconnaissance and communications. It added up to "no."

Extremely disappointed and desperate for customers (their savings from the bicycle business were fast running out), the Wrights began negotiating with the French and British governments.

But a year later, when they were making 25-mile flights and drawing hordes of curiosity-seekers and reporters to the cow pasture, they were still waiting for business.

It was not until early 1907 that President Theodore Roosevelt (who had helped launch the Langley project when he was Assistant Secretary of the Navy in 1896) read about the Wright plane and passed the word along to the War Department to do something about it.

The red tape began to unwind.

In the summer of 1907, an Aeronautical Division of the Signal Corps was formed, and shortly thereafter advertised for bids on a two-passenger aircraft with a useful load of 350 pounds, a 125-mile range and a 40-mph cruising speed.

The public, the press and even most of the nation's aeronautical experts — everybody, in fact, but the Wright brothers — decided that the government had finally taken leave of its senses.

The Wrights, however, had practically written the Signal Corps' specifications (bids were merely a legal formality) and knew that they could build the plane.

The brothers' year of triumph was 1908.

Wilbur, flying in France (where negotiations with the French and British were coming to a successful conclusion) became a popular hero almost overnight. So did Orville, flying under War Department auspices in the U.S.

Birth of Industry

In 1909, the Wright Company became big business.

The brothers, who had earlier refused several offers of substantial financial backing, accepted an offer from an impressive group of multimillionaires (including Cornelius Vanderbilt and Howard Gould).

In exchange for all rights to their U.S. patents, they received $100,000 in cash, 40% of the stock of the new corporation, and a 10% royalty on every plane it sold. Wilbur became company president.

Two years later, Wilbur died, and Orville retired shortly thereafter.

Even before Wilbur's death, the aircraft industry had started to grow, and a bitter patent war between the Wright Co. and its first major competitor, Glenn Curtiss, had begun.

The court battles dragged on until 1917, when they were ended by the formation of an aircraft industry patent pool for wartime production.

In 1914, Curtiss, who was fighting for his business life, took to the air in the 1903 Langley flying machine (so drastically remodeled that Langley would never have recognized it) in an attempt to prove that the Wrights had not invented the first airplane at all.

Orville Wright was so angered by the Smithsonian Institution's support of Curtiss' claims for the Langley machine that he sent his and Wilbur's original Kitty Hawk plane to a British museum.

The Smithsonian did not publish an official retraction until 1934, and the Kitty Hawk plane did not come home until 1948, the year of Orville's death.

By then, the aircraft industry had long since come of age, under the leadership of men like Glenn L. Martin, Donald Douglas and William E. Boeing.

But it was the Wrights who, as a plaque in the Smithsonian Institution states today, "as inventors, builders and flyers . . . developed the airplane, taught man to fly and opened the era of aviation."

First Wright plane made four free, controlled, powered flights, first in history, at Kitty Hawk Dec. 15, 1903.

Wilbur (r.) piloted first Army test plane at speed of 42.5 mph July 30, 1909.

HOW MAGAZINES WENT NATIONAL

Cyrus H.K. Curtis led the turn-of-the-century publishing revolution that created the mass circulation magazine; S.S. McClure dramatized its power as a national opinion-maker

IN 1883, A 33-YEAR-OLD publisher named Cyrus H. K. Curtis launched an unpretentious little women's magazine called *The Ladies' Journal*, edited by his wife.

Ten years later, 36-year-old Samuel Sidney McClure, owner of a small newspaper feature syndicate, brought out the first issue of a general-interest monthly called *McClure's Magazine*.

By the turn of the century, *The Ladies' Home Journal* (the extra word crept into the magazine's title early in its life) had almost a million readers; *McClure's* had 360,000.

And a dozen other magazines—*Munsey's*, *Delineator*, *Cosmopolitan*, *Pearson's*, to name a few—had reached circulation heights (300,000 to 700,000) that would have dizzied any publisher back in the 1870s and 80s, when probably only *Harper's* boasted more than 100,000 readers.

Magazine publishing was coming into its own—as a big business and a major social and economic force.

Cyrus Curtis was the leader of this publishing revolution.

His *Journal* was the first magazine to win and hold the loyalty of a truly national audience.

He pioneered modern techniques of magazine circulation-building, promotion, distribution, and market research.

He was the first magazine publisher to grasp the potentialities of advertising as a money-maker.

He laid down the principles upon which the relationship between advertiser, advertising agency, and magazine are still based.

And, because he wanted his readers to trust the advertising pages in Curtis publications as they did the editorial pages — he fought for high standards of advertising ethics.

S. S. McClure's career as a publisher was short, and his influence on the industry far less pervasive than Curtis'.

But, between 1902 and 1906, he made magazine reading more exciting for more people than it had ever been before—and demonstrated the power of the national magazine as a molder of public opinion.

The influence of *McClure's* during the years when it was running exposes of business and politics was so great that William Allen White (writing in Curtis' *Saturday Evening Post*) called McClure one of the 10 most important men in the

Curtis, a now successful publisher of a successful women's magazine, takes over the Saturday Evening Post in 1899.

Ladies' Home Journal began as Mrs. Curtis' women's page in small weekly. Shown is art room of early Curtis offices.

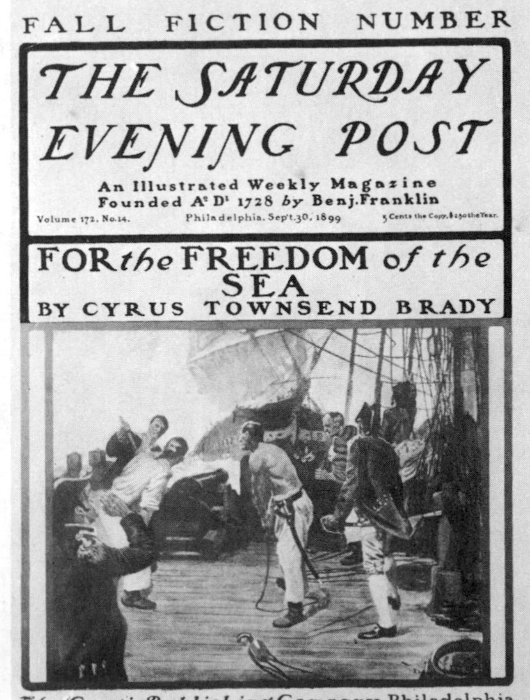

United States.

Although magazine publishing did not become a major industry in the U.S. until the days of Curtis and McClure, it has a long, honorable history that begins in 1740 with the publication of Benjamin Franklin's *General Magazine and Historical Chronicle for all the British Plantations in America.*

(Even earlier, in 1729, Franklin had founded the *Pennsylvania Gazette*, which was to be renamed *The Saturday Evening Post* 100 years later and which became a Curtis publication in 1899. But during its first century of life, the *Gazette* was more newspaper than magazine.)

By the end of the 18th century, 98 small magazines—most of them written by and for the intellectual elite of the 13 colonies—had appeared, and many of them had already disappeared.

All through the 19th century, magazines multiplied (there were 700 by 1865), their audience broadened and their influence grew.

Only Local Circulation

Outside the big cities, books were scarce and expensive, libraries few and far between, public education rudimentary and public entertainments practically non-existent; magazines were a major source of fun for thousands of Americans.

They attracted the finest talents of their day—Thoreau, Poe, Emerson, Hawthorne, Richard Harding Davis, James Russell Lowell were all "magazinists."

High Level Reading

Many of them *(Harper's, Atlantic, North American Review)* were solidly highbrow, and even those that catered more to popular taste (like the rechristened *Saturday Evening Post*) offered pretty substantial fare along with serialized fiction and light features.

Special-interest publications began to spring up. The first women's magazine, *Godey's Ladies' Book*, was founded in 1830, the first farm magazine, *Country Gentleman* (later to become the third Curtis publication), in 1853.

A sampling of new magazine titles from the late 1860s includes: *Carriage Monthly; National Baptist; Christian Witness: Good Health; Temperance Advocate; Art Journal; Ball Players' Chronicle; Sporting Times; Velocipedist, Communist.*

All the magazines of the first three quarters of the century, however, had small circulations.

And while a few of the more distinguished were known throughout the country, circulation was generally local or regional.

Advertising was a minor source of revenue. Before the 1860s, in fact, many reputable publications simply refused to accept it—and with some reason, since most of the advertising that did find its way into magazine pages was for dubious patent medicines.

After the Civil War, however, things began changing fast.

The new railroads that spanned the continent made national distribution feasible for the first time; the Postal Act of March, 1879, gave second class mailing privileges to magazine publishers—an important economic incentive for circulation-building.

The nation's economy was growing by leaps and bounds — total value of U.S. manufactures rose from $2 billion in 1860 to $5 billion in 1880 and $9 billion in 1890.

New Advertising Media

And manufacturers who aspired to reach a national market began planning advertising campaigns and looking for advertising media.

Americans were as hungry for reading matter as ever—and more of them belonged to the educated middle class with money to spend. New magazines began springing up faster than ever; there were 1200 in

LEFT *Women employees' rest, off-duty room had well stocked library.*

Cyrus Curtis spent a great deal of energy promoting his magazines as a medium for mass advertising, and one year spent $310,000 in his own national advertising campaign.

1870. 3300 in 1885. Many of today's leaders *(McCall's, Good Housekeeping, Popular Science, Cosmopolitan, National Geographic,* and *Vogue)* were founded between 1870 and 1885.

Mass Magazine

The stage was set for the entry of the national magazine — and then came Cyrus Curtis.

Curtis was born in Portland, Me., in 1850; his father was in the home furnishings business.

He began his career in the magazine business at the age of 13, when he bought an ancient handpress for $2.50 and started turning out a two-cent weekly called *Young America* that sold briskly to Portland's teenagers.

In 1879, after a few years as a drygoods salesman in Portland and an advertising solicitor in Boston, he settled in Philadelphia and founded a small weekly called *The Tribune and Farmer.*

The Tribune and Farmer soon acquired a women's page, edited by Louisa Knapp Curtis, who was to keep her job in her husband's organization until 1889.

The page was so successful that Curtis decided to make it a separate magazine, issued monthly as a supplement to *The Tribune and Farmer.* The first issue of the Ladies' Journal appeared in 1883, containing articles on gardening, fashion, child care, cooking, and needlework, plus an illustrated serial.

Journal's circulation hit 25,000 at the end of its first year, 100,000 in 1885 and 700,000 in 1889.

In that year, it came of age.

Curtis arranged a $200,000 line of credit with N. W. Ayer & Son (one of the leaders in the new business of advertising) and launched a massive ad campaign for his magazine; before the year was over, he was to spend a total of $310,000. He doubled the *Journal's* subscription price—from 50c to $1 a year—and hired a professional editor, a brilliant 25-year-old named Edward Bok.

The price rise cost the magazine about 250,000 low-income readers; Curtis immediately set about rebuilding his circulation by announcing a subscription contest with $500 as first prize to the reader who brought in the most new subscribers.

Wide Editorial Interest

Bok began broadening the magazine's editorial content with culture ("Forgotten Graves of Famous Men," "Gladstone's Love of Reading and Bismarck's Literary Taste"); exotic people and places ("How Zulu Women Sew"); and human interest ("Unknown Wives of Well-Known Men").

He introduced a column for girls, in which "Ruth Ashmore" (he wrote it himself until he found a suitable woman contributor) told her young readers to "learn to say no" and advised them on dress, manners, and romantic problems.

But the *Journal* remained primarily a service magazine for housewives, and the quality of its service was high. By the mid-90s, Curtis and Bok had hired a doctor to run the magazine's health column, and experts in their fields to head its other service departments — child care, household management, cooking, beauty.

Model Home Plans

In 1895, the *Journal* began running plans for simple, practical, well-designed model homes that led one eminent American architect, Stanford White, to say a few years later, "I firmly believe that Edward Bok has more completely influenced American architecture for the better than any man of his generation."

"Get the right editor and you'll have the right magazine," Curtis once said. "Then it's only a selling proposition."

All through the '90s he worked at "selling" the *Journal* to readers and national advertisers.

By the end of the decade, the *Journal's* circulation was breaking even its own records, Curtis Publishing Co. was solidly in the black, and its owner was ready to perform his second publishing miracle—the transformation of the *Saturday Evening Post.*

Cyrus H. K. Curtis

Edward Bok

Samuel Sidney McClure

THE MAGAZINE WITH A MILLION

The Ladies' Home Journal

Christmas 1903

DECEMBER TEN CENTS

THE CURTIS PUBLISHING COMPANY, PHILADELPHIA

By 1903 The Ladies' Home Journal *had a million readers, the first magazine to win a national following.*

The Ladies' Home Journal for January 1903 — Page 33

Mrs. Sangster's Girls' Problems

The Journal *set a format for women's magazines to come, with columns on beauty, department, health problems.*

By the turn of the century, the Journal *had become the fashion style-setter for women all over the country.*

32 THE LADIES' HOME JOURNAL October, 1899

THE NEW FALL HATS AND THE LITTLE THINGS

By Emily Wight

DESIGNS BY THE AUTHOR

TWO lace handkerchiefs may be used in making a fichu: one for the two points on the shoulders; the other to be drawn through the knot of net in front. Lace edging may be used. Another very pretty fichu is made of embroidered chiffon.

To Match the Costume

WHEN the season arrives for the doffing of straw and donning of winter materials, the home milliner begins to look about for ideas.

The small hat of felt in the popular shape, turned up on the sides and down in front, shown in the illustration, is trimmed with taffeta silk matching the dress in color.

Hat with an Upturned Brim

THE black felt hat illustrated has two bands of black velvet under the brim and a rosette of narrow ribbon where it is turned up in front. A half-wreath of roses extends across the front; the stems are apparently held close to the low crown by flat bows of black satin. There are upstanding velvet loops of the satin at the left side of the hat.

A Group of Neck Arrangements

Black silk passementerie revers are joined to a black velvet stock, and finished with cross-pieces and bows of ribbon.

The jabot and collar shown in the illustration are of white chiffon. The vest front is made in one box-plait of tucked white satin with turquoise buttons.

The other two yokes are of lace, combined with tucked and shirred chiffon, and velvet.

A Dainty Affair in Mousseline de Soie

This fall, high collars attached to yokes of many shapes are shown in great variety. The very dainty one of white *mousseline de soie*, shown in the illustration, is made with tuck-

The Stylish Picture Hat

The picture hat of this season has a brim wide in front and narrow at the back, where it is curved gracefully to suit any style of hair-dressing. The one shown in the illustration is trimmed with black velvet ribbon and ostrich plumes. Strings may be worn with it if one fancies them, starting from beneath the bow at the back and tying under the chin.

Round Hat for Shopping

THE round hat with a slightly rolling brim, shown in the illustration, is bound with velvet, trimmed with a torsade of silk and one of velvet in shades to harmonize, each ending in a full rosette, between which are thrust two long quills of the shade of the velvet. It is adapted to walking or shopping.

The Fashionable Velvet Toque

The green velvet toque in the illustration is made with a wire frame, and is trimmed on the side with an arrangement made by twisting the velvet around a wire circle and fastening it with a gilded ornament set with stones. Above and below are two large rosettes made of crinkled silk in a lighter

A Pansy Evening Hat

THIS little evening hat is nearly covered with bunches of blue-purple pansies. A bow of velvet matching the pansies in color is placed in front and caught with a gold ornament. Loops of the velvet show between the pansies on the back and sides.

To Wear with a Cloth Suit

THE brown hat of felt braid, shown in the illustration, has heavy cream-colored lace draped about the crown, and large loops of stitched silk on the left side. Bunches of violets lie under the slightly raised brim.

Variations of the Fichu

THE fichu will be much in evidence this season. A black one will be a useful adjunct to one's wardrobe. *Mousseline de soie* is the material, and narrow white lace edges the ruffles of the one shown.

Velvet Appliqué A Cloth Bolero

THE novel trimming to the little cloth bolero, as shown in the illustration, is narrow flowered ribbon, with tiny twisted rosettes at regular intervals. The bolero of velvet appliqué shown has straps composed

THE LADIES' HOME JOURNAL

FROM MR. GIBSON'S NEW BOOK "THE SOCIAL LADDER" PUBLISHED BY R.H. RUSSELL. COPYRIGHTED 1902, BY ROBERT HOWARD RUSSELL

MR. GIBSON'S AMERICAN GIRL

FEBRUARY 1903 TEN CENT

THE CURTIS PUBLISHING COMPANY, PHILADELPHIA

CONQUEST OF THE BEARD

King Gillette's invention of the safety razor changed the face of the times by ending male bondage to whiskers

ONE EARLY MORNING in 1895, a 40 year-old traveling salesman with a well-lathered face glared into his shaving mirror and muttered words that men have said for centuries when confronted with a dull razor.

The frustrated shaver was King Camp Gillette, successful peddler of bottle caps and a man who had dreams of inventing something—he didn't know what.

As he stood staring at his straight razor, the picture of what is known today as the safety razor came to him, crystal clear in every detail.

His vision was destined literally to change the face of men in the 20th century and to create a new U.S. industry which now has annual sales close to $500 million (including accessories).

The safety razor gave men an easy, quick, economical shave for the first time in history. It vastly altered the fashions of the times by fostering the rapid demise of the beard.

King Gillette was a self-made man. Born in Fond du Lac, Wisconsin, in 1855 and educated in Chicago, he was forced to shift for himself after the Chicago Fire of 1871 wiped out his father's business.

From the age of 21 on, he prospered as a traveling salesman in the U.S. and England.

Although untrained mechanically and possessing no particular technical ability, Gillette, the salesman, yearned to invent something. Once he systematically went through the alphabet, listing every conceivable item which man might need.

In 1891, Gillette took a new job with the Baltimore Seal Company, a manufacturer of bottle stoppers. He became good friends with William Painter, inventor of the stopper and originator of the cork-lined tin cap known as the Crown Cork. (Baltimore Seal later became Crown Cork & Seal Company.)

King Camp Gillette's mustachioed face has appeared on 100 billion blade packages over last 60 years.

On a visit to Painter's home in Baltimore, the talk drifted to inventions, a fascinating topic to both men. One of Painter's remarks had a profound effect on Gillette.

"King," he said, "you are always thinking of inventing something. Why don't you try to think of something like the Crown Cork? When once used, it is thrown away and the customer keeps coming back for more."

After this advice, Gillette became obsessed with inventing a device which could be used and thrown away.

It occupied his thoughts for four years until the summer of 1895.

"I was living in Brookline (Mass.) at the time," Gillette reminisced in a 1918 article. "On one particular morning I started to shave and found my razor dull. It was not only dull but it was beyond the point of successful stropping and it needed honing, for which it must be taken to a barber or cutler.

"As I stood there with the razor in my hand, my eyes resting on it as lightly as a bird settling on its nest—the Gillette razor was born.

"I saw it all in a moment, and in that same moment many unvoiced questions were asked and answered more with the rapidity of a dream than by slow process of reasoning."

The cumbersome straight razors of the 1890s consisted of a sharp edge backed by a bulky support. Gillette saw that the backing was a waste when the same result could be had by putting a fine edge on a small piece of steel.

Why not sharpen two opposite edges of a thin, uniform steel strip, and hold the blade in place with a clamp and a handle?

"I stood there in a trance of joy," Gillette later recalled. "Fool that I was, I knew little about razors and practically nothing about steel."

Before invention of the safety razor, daily shaves were a luxury only the wealthy could afford. An 1861 engraving shows Virginia gentleman relaxing with his newspaper while waiting patiently for his turn in the chair.

So great was his delight that he immediately wrote to his wife who **was** visiting in Ohio:

"I have got it. Our fortune is made!"

His enthusiasm was somewhat premature. Eleven years of work and experimentation were to pass before he would collect a single dollar in dividends on the invention.

At a Boston hardware store he purchased pieces of brass, steel ribbon used for clock springs, a small hand-vise, and files. With these raw materials and no mechanical training Gillette produced the first model of the safety razor with disposable blades.

He made endless sketches (some used later in patent suits) and then came, in Gillette's own words, "the hour of trial." Eight years of trial, in fact, before the safety razor was introduced on the market in October, 1903.

Gillette believed that razor blades could be made cheaply since steel ribbon sold for 16 cents a pound. He calculated a pound would yield 500 blades.

"I did not know then that the steel to be used must be a particular quality and it would cost many times what I supposed per pound."

He was to spend over $250,000 in laboratory tests before this question of steel was solved.

To his surprise, he found that no one was interested in his razor. Investors were cold and technicians didn't think the idea worth bothering with.

Even his friends regarded the razor as a joke and often greeted him with: "Well, Gillette, how's the razor?"

Charles Evans Hughes, U.S. Supreme Court Justice, sported popular 1900 beard-mustache combo.

For nearly six years he experimented with blades, searching out machine shops in Boston, New York and Newark for advice on how to harden and temper thin steel. Everywhere he was told to stop wasting his money and drop the radical idea.

"But I didn't know enough to quit," he said later. "If I had been technically trained, I would have quit."

During this period of discouragement all he had to show was the crude model he had fashioned himself in 1895.

The first significant development came in 1900 when William E. Nickerson, a graduate of the Massachusetts Institute of Technology, entered the picture. While the idea of the safety razor belongs solely to Gillette, its development into a practical instrument was the work of Nickerson.

In a loft over a fish store located next to a wharf where Boston's garbage was dumped, Nickerson refined the original razor and developed a process for hardening and sharpening sheet steel.

In 1901, Gillette finally persuaded some friends to raise $5000 to help him form a company and start manufacturing the razor.

The first razors appeared on the market in 1903. Sales for that year came to 51 razors and 168 blades.

But the following year razor sales leaped to 91,000 and blades to 123,000. By 1908, annual blade sales had passed the 13 million mark and, by 1917, one million razors and 120 million blades were being sold yearly.

The conquest of the beard seemed well underway.

But thousands of years before Gillette provided an easy method to "Look Sharp," the removal of hair from men's faces had been a concern of kings, generals and poets.

Early Egyptian razors were made of flint and copper and sharpened with sandstone. The invention of bronze made possible a sharper razor which retained its cutting power longer. About 2500 B.C., iron and steel furnished even more efficient materials for razors.

Romans wore long beards until 200 B.C. when Scipio Africanus, conqueror of Hannibal, became the first daily shaver. The unshaven face soon became the mark of peasants and slaves.

Luxuriant whiskers have swelled masculine egos since dawn of time

The first time a young Roman noble shaved was the occasion for a feast day. His shorn beard was dedicated to the gods. Nero preserved his beard in a gold box set with pearls.

About this time the first barber shops came into existence.

Beards became popular again in Rome around 120 A.D. when the Emperor Hadrian grew one to hide ugly scars on his face. For the next 200 years beards were in style until the time of Constantine the Great in 300 A.D. His shaving made a smooth face fashionable once more.

Barbers flourished in the Middle Ages. They not only shaved customers and cut hair, but also practiced the painful art of bloodletting which was a popular remedy for all ailments.

Shakespeare made numerous references to shaving in his plays. In "Love's Labor Lost" there are mentions of "the razor's edge invisible" and "I could not endure a husband with a beard on his face."

Shaving in the U.S. has had a long and varied history. American Indians pulled out their beards, using clam shells as tweezers. George Washington owned a fine set of straight razors and was kept clean shaven by a servant.

In Civil War days whiskers were back in style, a fashion which continued through the 1890s. By that time the Egyptian bronze razor had changed only slightly to the straight edged concave razor. Only the rich could afford a daily shave by a barber or valet. Others possessed one or two hook-type straight razors and shaved once or twice a week.

During World War I, razors began to sell in quantities never dreamed of by its inventor.

When the U.S. entered the war, Gillette's output went almost exclusively to the Armed Forces. Men who had never heard of the safety razor were issued a Gillette. As a result, self-shaving became widespread and servicemen carried the habit over into peacetime.

In 1921, Gillette weathered his first storm of competition. The company's basic patents were due to expire, leaving the field open for anyone to make the razor and blade. Other manufacturers prepared to flood the market with imitations.

Six months before the expiration date, Gillette brought out a new model to sell for $1. (Until that time razors had sold for $5 or higher.) The company made record profits that year.

Biggest Little Thing

In 1930, Gillette merged with a competitor, the Auto-Strop Company, and continued to expand through the years prior to World War II. During this time the one-piece razor was developed. A new manufacturing process produced the Gillette Blue Blade. A thin blade followed and shaving creams were later added to the product line.

There are few U.S. companies whose advertising is better known to the public than Gillette's. In 1939, the company decided to take a gamble and invest a substantial share of its annual advertising budget in radio sponsorship of the World Series.

The Yankees took the Series in only four games and Gillette sold 2.5 million razors. Since then, sports events have formed the backdrop for the company's advertising.

Gillette Safety Razor Company is also among the oldest television advertisers. It sponsored boxing events on TV back in 1944.

Major product improvements mark the company's recent history. In 1947, the company brought out a blade dispenser which did away with paper-wrapped blades and permitted insertion of the blade directly into the razor.

The first adjustable razor was introduced in 1957 and was followed by the Super Blue Blade in 1960.

In the 60 years since King Gillette sold his first razors, the company has turned out over a billion razors and 40 billion blades. It now has factories in Argentina, Australia, Brazil, Canada, England, France, Germany, Switzerland and Mexico.

In 1948, the company embarked upon a diversification program. It acquired The Toni Company, manufacturers of home permanent wave kits. In 1955, it bought up the Paper-Mate Company, producer of ball point pens. The company entered the hospital supply field in 1962 with the purchase of Sterilon Corporation.

Recently Gillette Safety Razor set a new sales record of $276 million. About 72% came from the Safety Razor Division.

The company's trademark, the face of King Gillette with wavy black hair and a full mustache, has been reproduced on blade packages over 100 billion times.

Just before Gillette died in 1932 at the age of 77, he was heard to remark:

"Of all the little things that have been invented, the razor is one of the biggest little things ever issued from the U.S. Patent Office."

Royalty promoted bearded elegance in late 1800s. King Leopold of Belgium (left) and Austria's Emperor Franz Joseph (center) were models of European fashion. U.S. journalist Jos. Pulitzer (right) wore shaggy Vandyke.

Young, successful Henry Ford poses proudly in office, had already bought out early partners.

HE MADE THE FORDS ROLL BY

Ford made first car in 1896, in 1908 concentrated on low-cost Model T, sold 15 million by 1927

HENRY FORD's Model T, first marketed in 1908, was the original "compact" car.

The development of the "T", which almost overnight turned the automobile from a toy for the rich into an adjunct of everyday U.S. life, makes Ford the key figure of an industry whose early days are crowded with illustrious names.

Henry Ford was born on a Michigan farm in 1863.

The only side of farm life that attracted him was the opportunity it afforded for tinkering with machinery, and when he was 16 he left home to become an apprentice machinist in Detroit.

For the next few years, as apprentice and journeyman, he worked on steam and gasoline engines; in 1888, he joined Edison Illuminating Co. as a mechanical engineer.

Four years later, in 1892, Charles Duryea invented the first U.S. automobile. And Henry Ford, like every other young mechanic in Detroit, was electrified by the event.

The first gasoline-powered motor car had been demonstrated in Paris by Gottlieb Daimler, inventor of the high speed internal combustion engine, only six years earlier, and the first practical automobiles were already being manufactured by the French firm of Panhard & Levassor, whose engineers had added to Daimler's vehicle such basic features of automobile design as clutch, gear-box, and transmission.

The U.S. industry, which was to surpass the French in production in 1903 —coincidentally, the year in which Ford Motor Co. was founded—got off to a slow start in the '90s.

The horse and buggy hung on because, as Charles Duryea ruefully remarked, "oats were too cheap."

The first U.S. automobiles, made almost entirely by hand, were not only too expensive for most potential customers, but also so undependable that "automobileers" were the laughing stock of their horsedrawn friends and neighbors.

And the noisy, dirty "horseless carriages", which ran—when they did run—at such breathtaking speeds, were considered by many citizens to be a menace to life and limb.

When Thomas Edison declared in 1895 that the "horse is doomed," few Americans agreed with him.

Among those who did, however, was a fast-growing group of manufacturers in Detroit, which was the natural capital of the new industry because it was

Bearded naturalist John Burroughs, inventor Thomas Alva Edison, share ride in sturdy Model T piloted by Henry Ford himself.

MODEL T CONCEPT REBORN IN MODERN COMPACT

already the center of the carriage, bicycle, and marine engine industries, and had plenty of machine shops, metal working establishments, and skilled labor.

Ransom Olds turned his Olds Motor Works to automobile production in 1899; Henry M. Leland, a manufacturer of bicycle parts and marine engines, formed the Cadillac Motor Co. in 1900.

But the first Detroit-made automobile had made its jerking, sputtering maiden run in 1896, and its builder had been Henry Ford.

Ford began working on a car of his own as soon as he read the reports of Duryea's triumph.

Still working full time for Detroit Edison, he turned out three experimental models between 1896 and 1899.

Then, in partnership with Tom Cooper, a retired bicycle racing champion, and C. H. Wills, an engineer, and with the backing of a group of Detroit financiers, he founded the Detroit Automobile Co.

This first business venture was a financial fiasco; so was the Ford Automobile Co., formed with the same partners under the auspices of another group of financiers in 1901.

The trouble was that Ford and his associates were trying to sell a high-priced racing car, even further out of the average buyer's reach than the Oldsmobile and Cadillac, which were by then enjoying considerable success in a limited market.

However, Ford was making a reputation for himself, both as a brilliant engineer and as a daring racing driver. (He raced his own cars in competition until 1904.)

In the summer of 1902, he produced his last and most famous racer, the "999," which was so fast that neither Ford, Cooper nor Wills wanted to risk bringing their business careers to an untimely end by taking it into competition.

Driven by Barney Oldfield, one of the first great professional auto racers, the "999" won a spectacular triumph in a major meet, and attracted the attention of a prosperous coal dealer, Alex Y. Malcomson.

Ford and Malcomson became cofounders of the Ford Motor Co. in the fall of 1902, and their first car, practical and relatively inexpensive, priced at $850, went on the market in 1903.

"The most reliable machine in the world," its advertisement in *Motor World* Magazine ran. "A two-cylinder car of ample power for the steepest hills and muddiest roads. The same genius which conceived the world's record maker — the "999" — has made possible the production of a thoroughly practical car at a moderate price."

Ford Motor Co. sold 1700 of these cars in 15 months, and earned small fortunes for its backers.

Malcomson, intoxicated by this quick success, promptly invested in another automobile company, failed, and in 1906 had to sell out his Ford holdings to avoid bankruptcy.

Ford and the company's business manager, James Couzens, who was to be number two man in the organization until 1915, bought him out for $175,000.

Public suspicion of "horseless carriages" was melting away in the early years of the new century, and Ford Motor Co., like its competitors, continued to prosper.

All the cars on the U.S. market, however, were still luxury items.

Ford Motor Co. introduced five models between 1903 and 1908; the cheapest—the original $850 model—was competitive with the least expensive of the "merry Oldsmobiles," and the others ran as high as $2000.

But Henry Ford had begun to dream of a really cheap "farmer's car."

And quite suddenly, early in 1908, he decided that henceforth his company was going to produce one single low-priced model, and that all Ford cars would be as standardized as "pins or matches."

The result, of course, was the Model T, a light, tough, accessoryless black box on wheels.

The "T" bore some resemblance to earlier Fords, and to Oldsmobile, Cadillac, and French Renault models.

But the design features that, together with its overall simplicity and economy, made it unique, were the work of Ford and the men around him.

These included an ignition system with a built-in magneto; a system of "splash" lubrication; a new and superior type of rear axle; three-point suspension and "planetary" transmission.

Even in its first year, when it was priced at a moderate but not rock-bottom $850 (in the years ahead, its price was to drop to $575), the car was a spectacular success.

For one thing, it was far easier to drive than other cars on the market—an important feature in a day when most prospective buyers still had to learn to drive.

And it could travel the roughest country roads, climb stony hills and slog through mud—even more important when the vast majority of roads throughout the U.S. were still relics of the horse-and-buggy era.

Famous "999" was so fast Ford, himself a racing driver, relinquished controls to champion Barney Oldfield (at wheel).

Assembly line, which eventually turned out car a minute, brought Ford international fame as genius of mass production.

The Ford assembly line was born of necessity as Model T sales soared.

It was obviously impossible to turn out thousands of cars a year in a factory where mechanics wasted time moving from job to job or waiting for stockboys to bring them parts.

First came the grouping of machines, with parts and tool bins, in the order in which they would actually be used, rather than in separate departments for each type.

Then came the installation of inclined slide, leading from one bench to the next, to eliminate the need for carrying or passing of parts from man to man.

Equally important was the increasing specialization of each worker's task; a skilled mechanic who formerly would have put an entire part together now merely performed a single operation on the part-in-the-making and passed it along.

By 1913, "line production" was in use on all the feeder lines that led to the final assembly floor.

There, men still moved from chassis to chassis, and, with parts arriving from the feeder lines faster and faster, chaos reigned.

In 1914 came the final step—a moving belt powerful enough to carry cars along the final assembly line was developed.

In the summer of 1913, it still took 12 hours and 28 minutes to put a Model T together; eight months later, the time had been cut to 98 minutes.

And on February 7, 1920, Ford attained his "life's desire"—a car-a-minute production rate.

The Model T was discontinued in 1927. It died because the car buyers of the prosperous '20s were beginning to demand elegant styling and solid comfort, and, as yearly model changes became fashionable, a new institution—the used car lot—sprang up to meet the needs of low-income customers.

A trend in automobile manufacture and marketing that did not begin to reverse itself until the late 1950s had begun.

However, the "T" had made automotive history. It had sold 15 million units for a $7 billion gross, and could take most of the credit for launching the U.S. public's love affair with the internal combustion engine.

FLYING THE MAILS

Early air mail routes blazed trail for today's commercial airlines; first private air mail contractor was William Boeing, aircraft manufacturer and airline magnate-to-be

Late in 1919, the U.S. Post Office Department awarded its first air mail route to private contractors.

The route was a hazardous run over 48 miles of water from Seattle, Wash., to Victoria, British Columbia; the contractors were pilot Edward Hubbard and aircraft manufacturer William Boeing.

Ten years later, Boeing's United Air Transport and other fledgling airlines were flying the mails – and a few thousand adventurous passengers – from coast to coast.

The era of commercial aviation had begun, and the story of its beginnings is a remarkable one in which private enterprise, government initiative, and personal heroism all play their parts.

Bill Boeing deserves to be singled out as a pioneer of air transport because of his leadership in the development of the airlines and aircraft manufacture.

But few industries have so many pioneers.

There were manufacturers like Glen Curtiss and Glenn L. Martin, both of whom were in business before World War I, and Donald Douglas, who built the great DC-3, probably the plane in which most

First contract air mail route was flown by Eddie Hubbard (l.) *and Bill Boeing in converted Navy plane*

of today's jet passengers first rode.

There were the Post Office Department officials who staked their careers on the success of a new way of carrying the mails. And there were the pioneer pilots who risked — and very often lost — their lives flying primitive aircraft over uncharted routes.

It is safe to say that the airlines probably would never have gotten off the ground without the financial support of the Post Office; large scale commercial air transport was simply too costly a venture for private business to undertake unaided.

And the Post Office's interest in air mail goes all the way back to the years before World War I, when planes were awkward, unreliable, and slow (60 mph was a spectacular speed), and the very idea of flying still fantastic to most people.

Air mail appropriations were introduced in Congress from 1910 on, usually to the sound of laughter from the House floor as one representative or another suggested that the Post Office Department should "get down to earth."

A few trial mail runs — by both balloon and heavier-than-air craft —were actually made in the pre-war years. (The first regular passenger run was also a pre-war venture — for a single Florida tourist season in 1914, the Tampa Air Boat Line shuttled back and forth between Tampa and St. Petersburg.)

But the first air mail appropriation did not come through until 1916, and then, when the Post Office asked for bids on a route in Alaska and one between New Bedford and Nantucket, it had no takers. The infant aircraft industry was too busy with war production.

Amateur Pilot

It was in the same year the 35-year-old William E. Boeing entered the industry.

Born in Detroit in 1881, he had studied engineering at Yale and Washington State College, and then settled in Seattle to go into the family lumber business.

In 1915, he learned to fly from Glenn Martin in Los Angeles, and bought a Martin plane for pleasure.

Like most of the amateur pilots of his day, he didn't have long to wait for his first accident. It was only a hard landing on Puget Sound, but the new plane was greatly damaged.

Plans for air mail service in the U.S. are described by Major R. H. Van Fleet to Pres. Wilson at first Washington-New York run.

Pioneer passenger service, Tampa Air Boat line, drew crowd for its first flight in 1914 (below), *but was a commercial failure.*

Aviation's early days take high toll in human lives

In the course of a do-it-yourself repair job, Boeing decided that he could build a plane just as good as the one he had cracked up—and that building planes was what he was going to do.

He drew plans, set up shop in his hangar, and turned out two aircraft, which sold with such encouraging speed that he promptly incorporated his company and moved to a larger site -- a shipyard south of Seattle. A few months later, in the fall of 1916, the Boeing Airplane Company was in full swing – just in time for the World War I boom.

Fighter and reconnaissance planes had begun proving their worth in the earliest days of the war in Europe, and U.S. aircraft manufacturers, whose business had been growing steadily but very slowly before 1914, were suddenly swamped with orders.

Then, when the U.S. itself entered the conflict, they were completely overwhelmed. An industry that had built only about 200 aircraft in its entire history was asked to turn out no less than 29,000 practically overnight.

Only a few thousand of the planes had been built before the war ended. But wartime research and development had produced aircraft – notably, the Curtis "Jenny" – far faster and better than those of the prewar years; thousands of young men had learned to fly; the public, dazzled by the valor of the airmen in the skies over France, was beginning to take aviation seriously; and last but not least, mail was traveling by air.

The first regular airmail service was inaugurated in 1918, by the Post Office and the Army in cooperation, to give Army air trainees some flying practice.

Its routes linked Boston, New York, Philadelphia, and Washington.

Then, shortly before the end of the war, in August, 1918, the Post Office took over the mail routes from the Army. It was to keep them – with the single exception of the

For Air Express attempt to fly nonstop to Chicago, Handley Page WW I bomber is loaded at Mitchell Field, N. Y., Nov. 1919. Engine trouble forced completion of delivery by train. Regular AE started in 1927.

experimental Seattle-Victoria franchise awarded to Hubbard and Boeing in 1919 — until the mid-1920s.

The wartime trial run was not a financial success; patriotic business men who had applauded the venture found the rates too high (24 cents for half an ounce) and the service not as good as advertised. (Overoptimistically, the Post Office and the Army had promised same-day delivery between New York and Washington — a feat that has yet to be accomplished.)

Perilous Venture

It did prove — at least, to the satisfaction of air-minded Postmaster General Albert Sidney Burlson and Assistant Postmaster Otto C. Praeger — that air mail could be a practical proposition.

But the real value of air mail obviously would lie in long runs, not short ones.

And long runs, with the aircraft and equipment of 1918, were easier to talk about than to fly. Of the first 40 pilots hired by the Post Office, 31 were to die in service.

The first air mail from New York reached Chicago in 1919, Omaha and then San Francisco in 1920.

At first, transcontinental air mail was flown only by day and transferred to trains at night, taking almost as long for the trip as did the mail on the fast, through trains.

Night flying — with no navigation aids, poor maps, no ground lighting to mark the airways, and few and inadequate airfields — was almost incredibly dangerous.

But Burlson and Praeger believed that it had to be tried — and so did their war veteran pilots.

Coast-to-Coast Service

The first coast-to-coast day-and-night flight was attempted in February, 1921. Of the four planes that took off, two from New York and two from San Francisco, two were grounded by weather, and one crashed.

That the fourth got through was largely due to the nerve and stamina of one pilot, Jack Knight, who later flew with United Airlines until 1941.

Knight had the third leg of the flight, from North Platte, Nebraska, to Omaha; but when he reached Omaha, he found that the westbound plane which was to have met him there, turned around and taken the mail back east, was grounded in Chicago. He flew on to Chicago himself, with only a Rand McNally road map to guide him. And in two more relays, the plane reached New York. It had taken a total of five pilots 33 hours and 20 minutes to make the trip.

This kind of thing couldn't be done every day; it was not until 1925 that regular cross-country night flights began.

By then, the Post Office in cooperation with General Electric and American Gas Accumulator Co., had designed, developed, and installed a system of lighted airways, with emergency landing fields every 25 miles along the transcontinental route and powerful, revolving electric or acetylene beacons every ten miles — a giant step forward in aviation safety.

It was also in 1925 that the Post Office, now headed by Postmaster General Harry S. New, began turning the mail routes over to private contractors — a move that marked the end of seven lean postwar years for the aviation industry, and the beginning of the growth of the airlines.

Among the pioneer pilots of air mail's first years were Army Lt. Torrey H. Webb (below, r., *with wife, before takeoff with first official load of air mail ever flown*) *and Jack Knight* (below, l.) *hero of Post Office Department's first transcontinental mail run. Start of regular New York-Chicago night flights* (above) *came in 1925.*

Cmdr. Richard E. Byrd, who led the first flight to the North Pole in 1926, made important contributions to air safety by navigational aids.

Early manufacturer Claude L. Ryan (r.) supplied mail planes to Pacific Air Transport whose owner Vern Gorst is shown with Ryan after record flight from Frisco to Seattle.

Boston-New York mail route of the Colonial Air Transport opened in 1926. Gen. mgr. Juan Trippe (r.) later founded Pan American Airways.

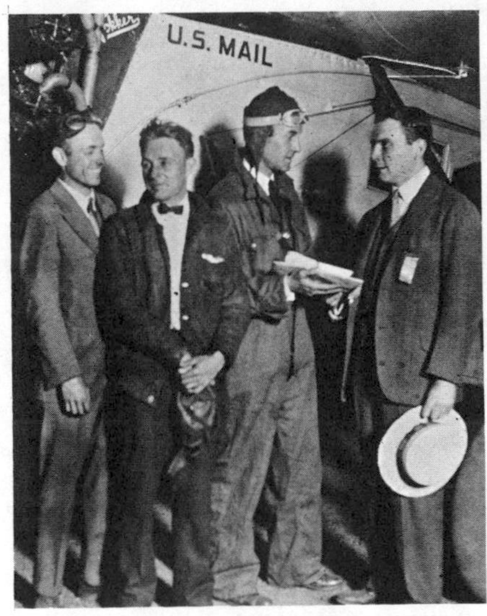

Gen. Billy Mitchell (r.), here with humorist Will Rogers, was court-martialed for his outspoken criticism of armed forces for their failure to recognize military value of plane.

Christening of a Ford Trimotor by Amelia Earhart and Grover Whalen on July 7, 1929 launched the first coast-to-coast air line in the U.S.

Charles Lindbergh got New York's traditional hero's welcome on return from epoch-making transatlantic flight in 1927. His feat made millions of Americans air-minded, gave overnight boost to infant U.S. industry.

FLYING THE MAILS Part 2

Commercial air transport began to grow when Post Office gave mail routes to private contractors; Boeing's United was first major line

On February 2, 1925, Congress passed the Kelly Bill—"An act to encourage commercial aviation and to authorize the Postmaster General to contract for the air service."

Commercial aviation in the mid-1920s needed all the encouragement it could get. And the Post Office, which had at its disposal the chain of potentially lucrative air mail routes that it had been developing—and flying with its own planes and pilots—ever since 1918, was in the best position to provide the needed shot in the arm.

"Lindy" with ace pilots Al Williams, Jimmy Doolittle; with wife; with official of Guggenheim Fund (l. to r.)

Air mail contracts ended aviation's postwar slump

Air travel in the '20s was dangerous and uncomfortable, but hardy passengers like these (ready for takeoff in Pacific Air Transport Boeing 40B-4, above, and Colonial Airlines Fokker, below) kept coming back.

The aircraft industry had plunged into the doldrums at the end of World War I.

Out in Seattle, William Boeing had been reduced to turning out furniture to stay in business when the wartime contracts stopped coming in – and other manufacturers had been no less hard-pressed.

Most of their business, in the early '20s, still came from the armed forces, whose peacetime needs were small.

The Post Office Department's air mail appropriations were not large enough to allow for purchases of many new aircraft – most of the early mail routes were flown in converted World War I reconnaissance planes.

And the commercial market was practically nonexistant. Opportunities in the air for private enterprise were very limited before 1925.

Hundreds of tiny airfields had sprung up across the country; there were plenty of war surplus planes around, and plenty of ex-military pilots who wanted to go on flying. But the best that most of these young men could hope for was to earn a precarious living from teaching, exhibition stunt flying, or taking up joyriders on Sunday afternoons, or from such aerial odd jobs as crop dusting and photography.

Many small-scale passenger operations were launched, but at best, they were no bigger than today's air taxi services, and most of them were short-lived.

The business community was keeping an eye on the skies, but the cost of large-scale development of air transportation was too huge and the risks too great -- until the Kelly Bill came along.

Industry interested

Within two months of the act's passage, the Post Office was flooded with inquiries from prospective bidders for airmail routes – over 5000 of them.

And among the bidders were some of the best-known names in U. S. industry.

The directors of one newly formed company, National Air Transport

(NAT), included Philip Wrigley, Lester Armour, William A. Rockefeller and C. F. Kettering; another bid came in from Henry Ford, who had been interested in aviation ever since 1923 and had backed designer W. B. Stout in the development of a transport plane called the Ford Tri-Motor. (Ford's career in air transport was to be short; he found the field too unprofitable and sold out to Boeing's United Airlines in 1929. It was important, though — the fact that the manufacturer of the beloved Model T was willing to take to the air did a great deal to increase public acceptance of aviation.)

Coming of age

By the end of 1926, airmail routes had been assigned to 12 companies, NAT and Ford Air Transport among them, all with solid financial backing. The routes were short, and only one of the 12 lines (Western Air Express) showed a profit in its first year — but it was clear that air transportation was coming of age.

Another boost from Washington came during 1926, with the passage of the Air Commerce Act. This piece of legislation made the government responsible for licensing of interstate operators, investigation of accidents, extension and maintenance of the lighted airways that the Post Office had begun developing in 1924. It also gave the new Aeronautical Division of the Department of Commerce the job of making aerial maps and running a weather service to provide meteorological reports.

All these provisions made air transport — though still a hazardous business — a sounder investment for industry and a safer bet for the public.

Most people still considered flying the least likely way to get from one place to another; but more and more passengers were beginning to climb aboard the now privately-run mail planes.

Boeing bid

Then, in 1927, the Post Office took the next step — calling for bids on two longer routes, from the West Coast to Chicago and Chicago to New York.

When the bids were opened, the Post Office — and the industry — received a staggering surprise.

William Boeing of Seattle was offering to fly the mail east to Chicago for just $2.85 a pound — twice as low as any competing bid.

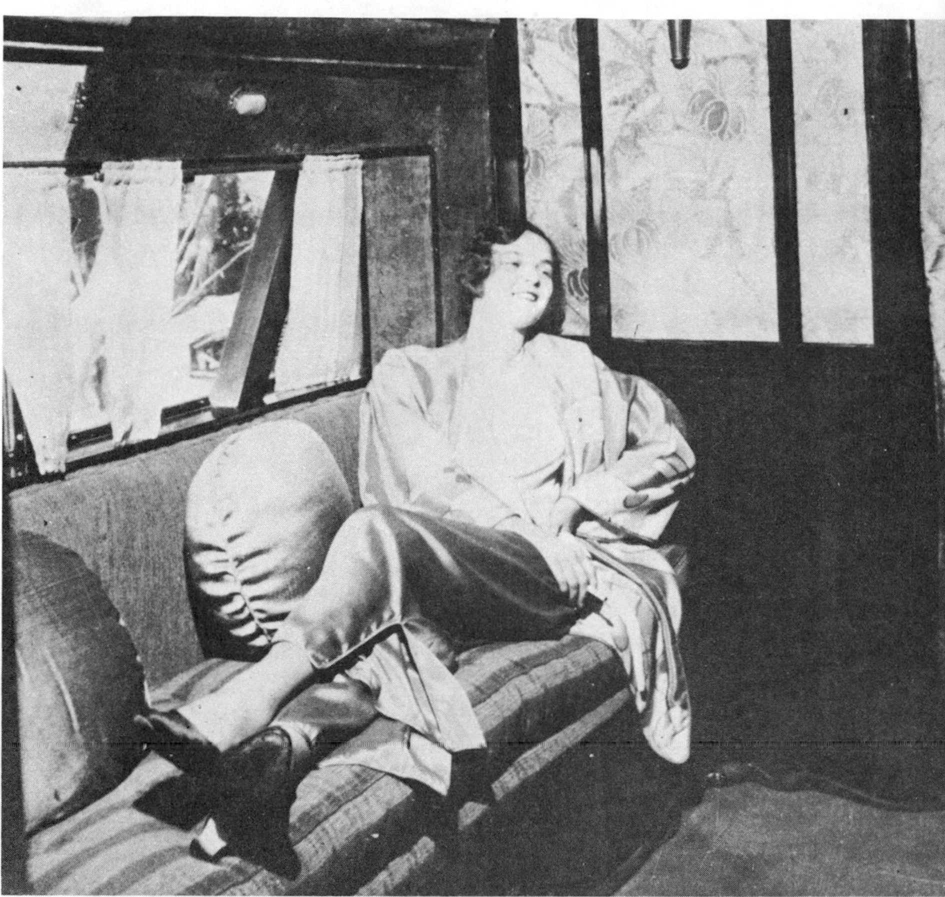

By the end of the '20s, fast-growing airlines were luring passengers with deluxe accommodations (lavishly appointed Western Airlines cabin, above) and personal service (below, stewardess serves coffee in flight).

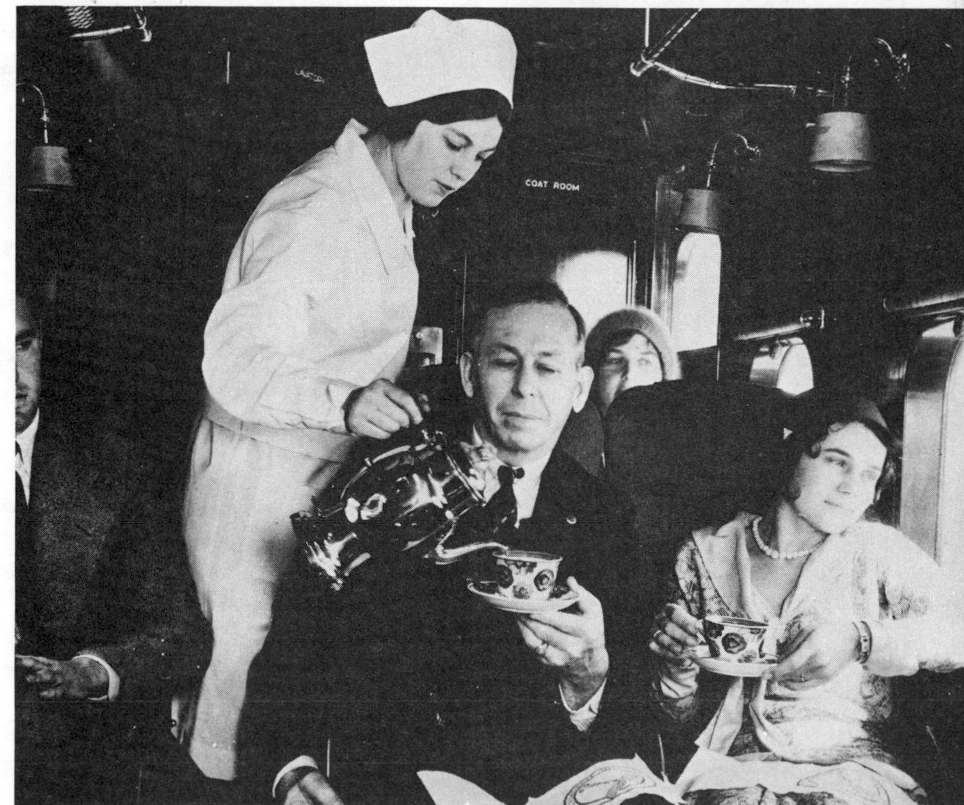

Franklin Delano Roosevelt brought the airlines to the brink of disaster in 1934; but F. D. R. was the first President to make campaign flights.

These eight stewardesses – all of them registered nurses – were hired by Boeing Air Transport in 1930 for the San Francisco-Chicago flights.

Airlines indispensable by mid-1930s

Boeing had not been among the original bidders in 1925; but he had bought out one of them, Pacific Air Transport, less than a month after the routes were assigned. Although not a profit-maker, Pacific had had a fairly successful first year, carrying 1000 passengers along with the mail bags.

His low bid for the Chicago route was a gamble; but it must have seemed to him that a bet on the development of commercial air transport was the shrewdest one an aircraft manufacturer could place.

And the next few years, in which Boeing Air Transport, as his new company was named, grew into the first of the great airlines, United, were to prove him right.

Naturally, Boeing's bid was accepted. He had the experience and the equipment that the Post Office wanted, and Boeing Airplane was as stable a firm as any in the industry. If the $2.85 rate seemed ridiculous, that was his worry – and that of his disgruntled competitors.

Boeing always maintained that he designed and built the Boeing 40 mail plane between February, 1927, when the airmail contract came through, and July, when service started. It's hard to believe that the planes were not even on the drawing board before February – but in any event, they were flying only five months after the contract award.

The Boeing 40s were single-engine craft, with an enclosed cabin for two passengers and an open cockpit for the pilot. They were the first planes to be equipped with two-way, shortwave aircraft radio, perfected and installed in the Boeing plant and a major contribution to air safety.

In its first year, Boeing Air Transport carried 230,000 pounds of mail and 525 passengers. (The first was a Chicago newspaper woman named Jane Eads, who was taken along for a publicity ride and was ecstatic over her flight to the coast.)

The Model 40 had flown 2 million miles in two years before it was retired by the Boeing 80, which, for 1929, was a positively luxurious passenger plane.

The tri-motor 80 had a cabin for

12, with upholstered seats, reading lights, and cabin instruments to show the travelers their altitude and airspeed. It even had a lavatory (until then, planes had grounded for "comfort stops"), with hot and cold running water. And—another "first" — box lunches were served by a male steward. (In 1930, the first girl hostesses appeared on the San Francisco-Chicago run).

At the end of 1928, Boeing Airplane merged with Frederick B. Rentschler's Pratt & Whitney Aircraft to form the nucleus of United Aircraft & Transport Corp., the most powerful corporation the industry had yet seen. Chance Vought, a builder of military planes, and two propeller manufacturers, Hamilton and Standard Steel, soon joined up with Boeing and P&WA.

United Airlines, the transport arm of UA&T, was born in mid-1929, when Boeing won a bitter struggle with NAT (which had been flying the mail from Chicago to New York since 1927) for control of the coast-to-coast air route.

Boeing and Rentschler set the pattern for the rapidly developing industry.

Curtiss Airplane and Wright Aeronautical also merged in 1929, and began buying up smaller manufacturing firms to form North American Aviation. NAA too had its airline — Transcontinental Air Transport. (TAT surmounted the hazards and discomfort of night flying, which were still considerable, by transferring its passengers to trains at night. It got them from coast to coast in 48 hours, with red carpet service all the way).

The third of the corporate giants — and probably the most complex in structure, with dozens of manufacturing and transportation affiliates—was Aviation Corp., or AVCO.

Nowhere but up

As the 20s drew to a close, it appeared that the aviation industry had nowhere to go but up. Public enthusiasm for flying had soared after Charles A. Lindbergh's history-making Atlantic flight; so had aircraft and air transport stocks. In 1929, the U.S. airlines outstripped those of Europe for the first time, flying more air miles than the French, English, German and Italian lines combined.

But serious trouble lay ahead. Like so many other industries, aviation was dealt a stunning blow by the depression. It was given a new lease on life in April, 1930, by the McNary-Watres Bill, which gave airmail carriers a flat per-mile subsidy, regardless of the amount of mail they carried. At the same time, the bill gave the Postmaster General the authority to consolidate lines and assign routes in the public interest.

Postmaster General Walter Folger Brown lost no time in making his new authority felt. Under his direction, the mergers proceeded at a faster clip than ever, and more and more of the smaller lines were pushed to the wall.

A number of AVCO's airline subsidiaries were forged into a new transcontinental line, American Airways (later American Airlines). And a merger negotiated by Brown between TAT and Western Express created another of today's great lines, TWA.

By the end of 1931, the Brown reorganization was complete. Three major lines, United, American, and TWA, were flying coast to coast; their parent companies, UA&T, AVCO, and NAA, dominated the industry.

Then, in 1933, Congressional investigation of the "spoils conferences" between Postmaster Brown and industry leaders began; charges of graft, collusion, and excessive profit-taking by the manufacturing branches of the three great corporations were hurled. And on Feb. 9, 1934, President Franklin D. Roosevelt cancelled all commercial airmail contracts and turned the mail routes over to the Army.

The McNary-Watres Bill had, in effect, pushed the airlines out of the frying pan into the fire.

But the Roosevelt experiment didn't work. The Army pilots were totally inexperienced in night and distance flying, and 12 of them were killed in crashes before the month was up.

The airlines got the mail contracts back in May. However, the industry was completely reorganized, with the strict separation of manufacturing and transportation interests that still prevails today.

As for William Boeing, he retired from the presidency of UA&T in 1933, with a Guggenheim medal for "successful pioneering in aircraft manufacture and air transportation." He returned to Boeing Airplane Co. during World War II, and lived until 1956—long enough to see the dawn of the jet age.

The modern era of air transport dawned when Douglas DC-3 hit airport runways in the mid '30s. One of the all-time great aircraft, the Douglas DC-3 made flying a habit for a new generation of travelers.

BARON OF BROADCASTING

Lee De Forest's invention of the audion brought millions within reach of the very best in entertainment, education

ON ELECTION NIGHT, 1920, thousands of Americans throughout the nation gathered in front of local newspaper offices to read the returns of the Harding-Cox election.

Meanwhile, in East Pittsburgh, Pennsylvania, history of another kind was in the making. As officials of the Westinghouse Works sat in a small shack atop a factory building, they read the latest election bulletins into a primitive microphone. Their voices, transmitted to an antenna on the roof, wafted out on the night air.

No more than 500 amateur "ham" operators heard this initial broadcast over station KDKA. Yet the next morning news of the sensational feat was splashed across front pages from coast to coast. For weeks afterward, people marveled at the new miracle which could bring up-to-the-minute news into their living rooms.

Behind the birth of broadcasting lay 20 years of frustration for Lee De Forest, the father of radio. Without his invention of the audion tube, neither radio nor television would have been possible. For that matter, we would not have radar, loudspeaker systems, sound movies or photographic transmission.

One of the most important uses of De Forest's vacuum tube was to amplify the feeble current produced by radio waves.

No ivory tower engineer, De Forest not only perfected the technical means to make broadcasting possible, but he also gave his invention a social conscience. In 1910, he envisioned radio as "a medium for bringing into each home the very best in entertainment, education, and information."

He accurately gauged the cultural impact of radio a decade before it came into being. He saw it as a means of widening the intellectual horizons of people who had no direct access to music, culture and news. He believed it would create new ties of understanding between people all over the U.S. and even throughout the world. "A new world cement," he termed radio.

All these goals—and more—broadcasting achieved during De Forest's lifetime.

As far back as 1865 an English physicist, James C. Maxwell, predicted the existence of electromagnetic waves, but it was not until 1884 that Heinrich Hertz of Germany actually proved such waves existed.

Then Guglielmo Marconi, the Italian inventor, produced a wireless

Westinghouse Station WBZ in Springfield, Mass., occupied cramped quarters during early broadcast days.

telegraph in 1896. The device was first used on ships, but its messages were confined to dots and dashes. The idea of transmitting speech evidently did not occur to Marconi.

The next step toward radio was made by an enterprising American engineer, Reginald Fessenden, who came up with the improbable idea of replacing the clatter of telegraph keys with music and speech.

Fessenden is credited with making the first radio broadcast in history from Brant Rock, Mass. On Christmas Eve, 1906, Morse code operators on ships along the Atlantic coast were mystified to hear singing and violin music instead of the familiar dots and dashes.

Constantly plagued by financial troubles, Fessenden became convinced that wireless telephony would not be possible or profitable for many years and, instead, he turned his attention to telegraphy.

It was left to Lee De Forest to develop the audion, a tiny glass and wire gridiron which could both detect and generate radio waves. The audion was perfected in 1906 but De Forest did not apply for a patent until 1907 because he could not afford the $15 fee required by the Patent Office.

Born in Council Bluffs, Iowa, in 1873, Lee De Forest was the son of a Congregational minister who soon moved to Talladega, Alabama, to head a school for Negroes.

The boy's childhood was a lonely one. Northerners were not particularly welcome in the small Southern community after the Civil War. Also, his father's position did not add to the boy's popularity.

Reared in genteel poverty, he dreamed of great riches and fame. He grew up in an era of spectacular new inventions: the gas engine, telephone, electric light. Science fascinated him and De Forest was determined to become an inventor.

He entered Yale University where he was encouraged by his professors to study electrical engineering and to do post-graduate research in the field of wireless communication. In 1898, he received a doctorate but the best job he could get was in the Chicago plant of Western Electric Company at the munificent salary of $8 a week.

One advantage of his routine, tedious job was that it left his mind free to work on wireless experiments at night.

Eight years and a score of preliminary inventions later, his diligence paid off with the audion.

During the summer of 1907, he made a test broadcast in New York City with a Swedish concert singer, Madame Eugenia Farrar. She had scarcely launched into a rendition of "I Love You Truly" when a wireless operator at the Brooklyn Navy Yard sprang from his chair and relayed the phenomenon to the officer in charge.

The earphones were passed from one astonished officer to another. Finally, someone reported the incident to the *New York Herald*. It duly appeared the next morning on page 5; a short paragraph accorded no more importance than a street fight.

De Forest's flair for publicity and his ambition to create a market for the audion led to further feats. In 1908, he broadcast from the Eiffel Tower in Paris. The program of phonograph music, heard as far away as Marseilles, caused a brief sensation.

Two years later, he broadcast a performance of "Cavalleria Rusticana" from the stage of the Metropolitan Opera House in New York. This was the first "live" broadcast of an opera. Unfortunately, the audience was limited to 50 listeners in the New York metropolitan area and one music-loving wireless operator on the *S.S. Avon* at sea.

But success of the audion also brought many troubles for De Forest. He had become an easy target for promoters. Frenzied stock selling had already landed him, and the companies to which he loaned his name, in considerable hot water. He had been involved in a patent infringement suit with Fessenden; had heard his audion derided in a courtroom as a hoax; been told by an eminent judge to "get a common, garden variety of job and stick to it," and had narrowly escaped criminal conviction for stock fraud.

During his lifetime, in which he was continuously entangled in patent litigation, he made and lost four fortunes.

Further misfortune came in 1911. The American Marconi Co. instituted a suit against him for infringement, while dissatisfied stockholders in his radio company complained they had been swindled. The bad publicity of the trial, in which De Forest was exonerated but his associates convicted, ruined his company beyond repair.

Meanwhile, he had succeeded in increasing the capacity of the audion to amplify signals up to 27 times. In 1913, he was able to sell the wire-telephone right of the audion to the American Telephone and Telegraph Co. for $50,000, retaining the right to manufacture audion tubes for sale to hams.

LEE DE FOREST

Early programming was chaotic, sporadic, unimaginative

When the U.S. entered World War I, the government ordered all amateur wireless equipment dismantled and De Forest began making equipment for military use. In 1917, he sold his remaining rights in the audion to AT&T.

After the war, leadership soon passed from his hands. He retired from radio and concentrated on other areas of electronics.

If De Forest is the father of radio, David Sarnoff was surely his prophet. Born in Russia in 1891, Sarnoff came to the U.S. at the age of 9, taught himself the Morse Code, and became an operator with the Marconi Co. By 1916, when he was 25, he had become assistant traffic manager at Marconi. In that year he submitted to his boss a memo which became the Magna Carta of radio:

"I have in mind a plan of development which would make radio a household utility in the same sense as the piano or phonograph. The idea is to bring music into the home by wireless."

He went on to predict almost every phase of radio programming: music, entertainment, sports, news and special events.

Sarnoff suggested the radio music box could be sold to the public for about $75 and he thought one million sets might be sold within three years. In this respect his vision was short-sighted. The Radio Corporation of America, set up in 1919 with Sarnoff as commercial manager, reported sales of $84 million during the two year period from 1922 to 1924.

After World War I, there were about 10,000 hams in the U.S. Their interest became a major factor in the development of radio because they made up the first audience.

Dr. Frank Conrad, an engineer at Westinghouse, began to broadcast from his garage in Pittsburgh in 1919. Ham audiences soon complained about his dull monologues and asked him to play phonograph records. As time went on, his fans became critical and he began to receive mail saying, "Play something lively" or "How about playing 'My Old Kentucky Home'?"

Thus began the career of Station KDKA, the first commercial station in the U.S. Others followed shortly: WBL (Detroit); WJZ and WOR (Newark); KYW (Chicago) and WEAF (New York). Within a few years the number of stations approached 1000.

By 1929, the price of a set remained as high as $135, but there were over 12 million owners.

In those early days one epoch-making broadcast followed another. Listeners heard the Dempsey-Carpentier fight, the first World Series broadcast in 1921, messages from Presidents Harding and Wilson, and the Republican and Democratic national conventions in 1924.

In between the special treats were long hours of dull talks — "The Art of Billiards," "How to Raise Bees" — screechy songs and ear-splitting instrumental numbers.

Musical performers, most of whom were unpaid, left a great deal to be desired. Most frequent was the studio pianist who filled in dead air time and appeared under different names a half dozen times a day.

Almost every singer was flamboyantly billed — "Princess Waukomis, contralto, full-blooded Indian princess" or "Solos by B. Paladino, mandolin player, recently arrived from Russia."

There was no such thing as regular programming. Stations went silent during lunch and dinner hours, so that its staff might eat. No broadcasting was done on Sundays or holidays.

Early reception was chaotic, requiring dedication on the part of the listener. A multitude of stations, particularly in metropolitan areas, operated on the same wave band, jumbling and blanketing each other's signals. It was common to hear two or three programs at once.

Secretary of Commerce Herbert Hoover urged all stations to abide by a gentlemen's agreement but his words went unheeded and even brought a telegram from the broadcasting evangelist, Aimee Semple McPherson. It called on him to tell his "minions of Satan to leave my stations alone."

Order arrived in 1926 when Congress created the Federal Radio Commission. It was superseded by the Federal Communications Commission in 1934.

Commercials have been a part of broadcasting almost from the beginning. The question of how to pay for the new medium brought a variety of suggestions. Initially, David Sarnoff thought costs should be met by a levy on set manufacturers and, later on, he hoped to find a billionaire philanthropist to subsidize the

In early 1930s Milton Cross hosted Metropolitan Opera broadcasts from anteroom of grandtier box at Met.

Sports events always attracted wide radio audiences. Babe Ruth, Graham McNamee in '27 over NBC Radio.

operation. Secretary Hoover didn't have anything as specific in mind but he was sure the American public would never permit the medium "to be drowned in advertising chatter."

Nevertheless, on August 28, 1922, AT&T's Station WEAF broadcast the first commercial. It was a stodgy, 10-minute talk extolling Hawthorne Hall, a new cooperative apartment house in Jackson Heights, N.Y. The talk brought complaints from listeners and the press, but AT&T continued to build its roster of sponsors. Four months later it had 16, including a department store, an advertising agency and the YMCA.

At first each station broadcast only its own programs, but soon they began to link together for specials. AT&T was in the most favorable position for network programming because it had the advantage of its telephone lines. By 1925 it owned 26 stations, as far west as Kansas City, which were regularly hooked up. AT&T refused others use of the company's lines.

As a result, RCA's stations were forced to use telegraph lines which were not constructed to carry voice. Quality was poor and RCA fared badly.

In 1926, AT&T withdrew from radio, selling its stations to RCA which immediately set up the National Broadcasting Company. Since it then owned two stations in many cities, RCA opened a second chain which it called the Blue Network. The original chain was dubbed Red Network.

In April, 1939, NBC televised the formal dedication of RCA pavilion by David Sarnoff at World's Fair.

In January, 1927, a rival, United Independent Broadcasters, Inc., appeared. When the Columbia Phonograph Company assumed control, it became known as the Columbia Broadcasting System.

Mutual Broadcasting Company came on the scene in 1931 and, in 1943 when the government ruled that a company could not operate more than one network, NBC's Blue Network was sold and re-named the American Broadcasting Company.

The Amalgamated Broadcasting System, organized by comedian Ed Wynn in 1933, has long been forgotten. Wynn went to Hollywood, leaving the details to others. The opening night appeared to have been arranged by the Marx Brothers.

Five thousand New Yorkers, selected at random from the phone book, tried to squeeze into a studio seating 200. Pastrami sandwiches and beer were *sold* to the guests. The master of ceremonies challenged an irate newspaper reporter to a duel, and a Federal radio commissioner got stuck between floors in an elevator. ABS forgot to pay its employees and the operation expired a month later.

If radio didn't upgrade the cultural and intellectual life of its listeners, it wasn't for lack of trying. Arturo Toscanini presided over the NBC Orchestra and the Metropolitan Opera was available every Saturday. Such news commentators as Lowell Thomas, Elmer Davis and William Shirer analyzed current events.

NBC and CBS conducted schools of the air. Discussion programs like Town Meeting of the Air and documentaries such as March of Time were plentiful.

On the other side of the coin, of course, were Gang Busters and its ilk, as well as that vast afternoon wasteland of soap operas.

Aside from elections, prize fights and President Roosevelt's Fireside Chats, the most popular programs were variety shows.

In 1929, Rudy Vallee pioneered the first variety program, a tabloid edition of vaudeville with music, comedy and light drama. His Fleischmann's Yeast Hour and his theme song, "A Vagabond Lover," ushered in the Great Depression.

In the world of variety shows there were no soup lines, no goose-stepping dictators, no budget deficits. Only Jack Benny, Kate Smith, Burns and Allen, Fred Allen, Edgar Bergen and Charlie McCarthy, and Fibber McGee and Molly.

A startling event in 1938 called widespread attention to a fact that many in the industry were already aware of: radio was a dangerous and powerful weapon.

On a quiet Sunday evening, several million citizens heard a series of news bulletins and listened to eye witness accounts describing an invasion by Martians armed with death rays. Orson Welles and his Mercury Theater had prefaced the program by announcing it was a dramatic performance of H. G. Wells' "War of the Worlds."

New Jersey highways were flooded with people fleeing the nonexistent invaders and hospitals treated patients for shock.

A week after NBC made its debut in 1926, David Sarnoff announced that "television is just around the corner." In 1930, RCA began experimental television in New York and, a year later, CBS inaugurated the first regular TV programs.

At the beginning of World War II, there were 7500 TV sets in New York City. In 1965 there were 64 million sets and 678 TV stations in the U.S.

The change in American life was obvious: increased consumption of cigarettes and liquor, re-arrangement of living room furniture, and tray dinners. The home enjoyed a revival as the center of family life but nobody talked much.

Radio listening declined abruptly. The industry feared it had nourished a parricide and predicted that radio was doomed.

On the 40th anniversary of his invention of the audion, Lee De Forest bitterly assailed the broadcasters. "What have you done with my child?" he asked. He had conceived of it as an instrument to upgrade the mass intelligence but he said it had become "a stench in the nostrils of the gods of the ionosphere."

Despite De Forest's indictment, much of his vision had come true. Radio brought within the reach of everyone an immense range of experience. It was available every day, whether one lived in Manhattan or on a snow-bound farm. Most important, by shattering regional and cultural barriers, it transformed the U.S. into a cohesive community for the first time.

The 20th Century

Nationalism, science, mass production . . . these were the forces of conflict which created the turbulent years of the 20th century

No other period in history has seen so much drama and change, such heights of human achievement and depths of infamy as the 20th century. Of the dominant forces of this age, nationalism, harnessed to militarism, took a toll of some 22 million in two world wars. The empires of Germany, Austria, Italy, Japan, Turkey and Czarist Russia were overthrown. Victory came at Pyrrhic cost for Britain and France. The United States surged to supremacy among free nations. War built a Communist empire which runs from the Baltic to the China Sea, dominating one third of the world's 2,725 million inhabitants.

Science, a second world-shaping force of the century, opened new vistas in every major field of human endeavor. Medicine, with new surgical techniques, psychoanalysis, antibiotics, sulfa and other drugs achieved a number of victories over man's last natural enemy, disease, and added 17 years to his life expectancy. Transport and communications were revolutionized by the radio, radar, airplane and television—by electric, diesel, jet and rocket propulsion. And most important, atomic energy, an inexhaustible new source of power illumined the future.

America in high gear

To apply science required adequate means of production and these means were available. Standardization of parts, specialization of workers, assembly lines were all established industrial methods by the turn of the century. It remained for Henry Ford and others to combine them into the technique of mass production which resulted in a second industrial revolution.

Materially, it has been an American century. The United States population, 75 million in 1900, has more than doubled. With about six percent of the world's population, she produces about one third of the world's goods. The work week has decreased by one third, but the real wages of workers buy far more commodities. Steel output, backbone of industry, multiplied by nine by 1950, electrical output by 300. The automobile industry is the largest of all, producing more than twice as many motor vehicles as all other nations combined.

Organized labor, growing too, has more than 20 times as many members as in 1900. U.S. government more than keeps pace. Its cost to the citizen is 70 times higher, but it provides vital new services in public health, power, finance, social security, conservation and agriculture. The major item, defense took 68% of the budget in 1953, a high. Since then, the average defense budget uses somewhat more than 50% of the total national expenditure.

"THE HUMAN RACE"

The years of decision

Opening in the serene majesty of the Victorian *Pax Britannica,* the 20th century has seen the British Empire give many of her colonies the right of self-government. The world has been split into two camps, both armed with atomic weapons. There are two years which were decisive in this century of crises. The first was 1917, year of the Russian Revolution and U.S. entry into World War I. It was the beginning of U.S. isolation, though remnants yet survive.

The second critical year was 1945 when the forces of science, mass production and nationalism joined in climax: Hiroshima and the atom bomb. In that year of the war's end, Hitler, Mussolini and Roosevelt died. Shortly after, the United Nations was born, marking the beginning of U.S. leadership in world affairs. But also in 1945 at the Yalta and Potsdam conferences Russia forged her claim to an empire. Soon Eastern Europe and China fell to Stalinist forces and militant communism dictated the lives of approximately 933 millions.

With the promise of a free world through the United Nations and with a limitless source of power within its grasp—atomic energy—modern civilization might have anticipated a great renaissance. Instead the world is split in two, the Communist and the free. The United Nations has not been able to prevent the perpetual flare-ups of fighting which threaten to turn the Cold War into World War III. Nuclear energy, which has tremendous potential for both war and peace, occupies much scientific research for more effective arms.

MAN OF THE HALF CENTURY, EDISON AFFECTED EVERYDAY LIFE THROUGH HIS DYNAMIC APPLICATION OF SCIENCE

In an age of applied science, Thomas Alva Edison (1847-1931) more than any other man shaped the daily living of the first half of the 20th century. The era's greatest discovery, atomic energy, made theoretical scientist Albert Einstein the man of the future. But many of Edison's 800 patents, among them the electric light, movies and the phonograph, were common items by mid-century. Edison's credo is clear in his definition of genius: 1% inspiration and 99% perspiration.

WORLD REVOLUTIONISTS V. I. Lenin and J. V. Stalin made the greatest changes in 20th century international history. Lenin, mastermind of world Communism *(l.)*, led Bolsheviks to victory in Russian Revolution. Stalin, his successor *(r.)*, raised USSR to world's second most powerful nation.

WORLD DEMOCRAT Woodrow Wilson's League of Nations was designed to ensure a permanent world peace. Although the League failed, Wilson's ideal of international democracy is the great motivating force of the present United Nations and it is the common cause of free men all over the world.

HISTORIANS AND EDITORS SELECT THE GREAT MEN OF THE 20th CENTURY

SCIENTIST Alexander Fleming's discovery of penicillin placed him foremost in half century of medical advances, which included Freud's development of psychoanalysis, Pavlov's reflex work.

PRAGMATIST John Dewey led in the two fields of Education and Philosophy. His theories caused great changes in U.S. teaching although they were criticized by humanist Robert Hutchins.

ORGANIZER Samuel Gompers headed the U.S. labor movement during its early years. He was a founder of the American Federation of Labor and served as its president until his death.

COMPOSER Richard Strauss began his musical career at the age of four and left a massive volume of work when he died in 1949. Arturo Toscanini ranked first among the world's conductors.

MAN OF GOD Albert Schweitzer renounced fame and fortune as a musician, a philosopher, an author and a physician and became a medical missionary, serving among native Africans.

MAHATMA, Hindu word for "great soul," was title of gentle Mohandas K. Gandhi. India's liberator and crusader for human rights was named first in Advancing the Dignity of Man.

DEFENDERS OF THE FREE WORLD Winston Churchill *(l.)* and Franklin Delano Roosevelt *(r.)* are shown in Quebec during World War II. History-maker Sir Winston, balloters agreed, was the world's leading statesman of the half century. Roosevelt was selected as having greatest effect on U.S. history of any man, also led in the U.S. Statesman, Great President, and Outstanding Man categories.

Great men had an effect on the 20th century of which history alone must be the final assessor. Conscious of this and of the fallibility of human judgment, YEAR asked a group of historians, each eminent in his field, to select the outstanding men in the main branches of human endeavor.

In some fields no decisive choice was possible. Adolph Ochs (first in Journalism) and Babe Ruth and Jim Thorpe (who shared the lead in Sports) appear elsewhere (see Index.)

Surprisingly few women were mentioned in the polling; most prominent was Mrs. Eleanor Roosevelt. Of the final choices pictured, products of many social climates, not all had a benevolent effect on their time, but all had a truly great one.

DRAMATIST Eugene O'Neill, first great U.S. playwright, opened new dimensions in his field. Winner of four Pulitzer Prizes, he died in 1953.

UNIVERSAL scientist Albert Einstein was the most prominent figure in the forty years between publication of the Quantum Theory in 1901 and development of the Atom Bomb during WW II.

PAINTER, ceramist and all-around artist of the half century, Pablo Picasso was unsurpassed in originality. Oddly enough, he supported communism even after it had condemned his art.

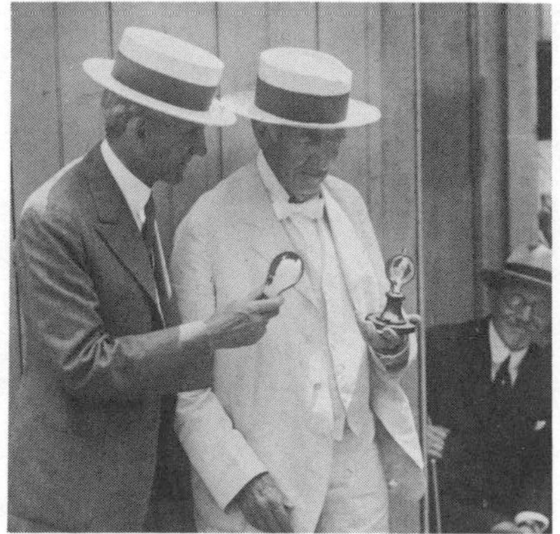

INDUSTRIAL mind of Henry Ford *(l.)* led to a revolution in production methods. Thomas Edison *(r.)* changed daily living since 1900 with such inventions as phonograph, electric light, movies.

SOLDIER of the half century, General Dwight D. Eisenhower commanded the greatest striking force in history in invasion of Normandy, June 6. 1944, and led Allied armies to victory over Nazism.

Turn of the Century

"Good Old Days" witness rise of the U. S. to a World Power with Science and Industry combining to shape the future

With the British Royal Navy supreme on the seas and European states precariously balanced in power, the early years of the century were years of relative security and peace. As Winston Churchill recalled, "The old world in its sunset was fair to see." Americans too looked back on the pre-war era as the Good Old Days.

The half century's most popular form of music—jazz—and a big share of its popular songs originated before 1914. Concert and theatre-goers welcomed works of Debussy, Richard Strauss, Stravinsky and Puccini, the singing of Caruso and Chaliapin, the acting of Bernhardt and Duse, and the dancing of Pavlova and Nijinsky, under the auspices of impressario Serge Diaghilev. In 1913 the N.Y. Armory Exhibition introduced modern art to the U.S. But generally Americans preferred to watch the greatest of double-play combinations, Tinkers to Evers to Chance on the baseball diamond, or Jim Thorpe, whose feats in the 1912 Olympics and elsewhere made him the athlete of the half century.

The brewer's big horses hadn't yet yielded the right-of-way to the tin lizzie. After a 9 or 10-hour day a man could stop in the corner saloon for a 5¢ beer and free lunch. He probably sported a mustache and celluloid collar and rode a bicycle. Of a winter evening he might read a lurid newspaper account of the Thaw-White murder case, or a sentimental novel by Gene Stratton Porter, or the latest exposé of the "Muckrakers," whose outspoken journalism helped correct many industrial and political abuses. If he "took sick" he was apt to be treated with tonic or castor oil. The great medical discoveries were still to come. But science, in the realm of physics, made enormous progress—with very few to mark it.

QUEEN VICTORIA died in 1901, after a 63-year reign during which the British Empire reached its acme of prosperity and power. Her legacy of peaceful progress lasted over a decade, until the outbreak of World War I.

Max Planck propounded the Quantum Theory. Einstein equated matter to energy in the famous equation E equals mc^2 (E represents energy, m is mass, c the speed of light) which eventually led to the atomic bomb. The inventors were about to transform daily living. The Wright Brothers flew successfully, Edison presented the first movies, Marconi and De Forest developed radio in the half century's great surge of creativeness.

The revolution in production, like the inventions which it mass-produced, was a new arrangement of old ideas. Interchangeable, standardized parts had been known to American manufacturers since Eli Whitney began making guns in 1798. Assembly lines, integration of parts, job-specialization were also known principles. Henry Ford had the genius required to organize the process. Mass production and science, vital forces of the half century, stood ready. A third force, imperial nationalism, had been years in rehearsal.

On the international scene the most significant event was the emergence of the U.S. as a first-class power. U.S. industrial production more than doubled during the era, and by 1914 surpassed that of its chief rivals.

Production took manpower; the U.S. admitted nearly a million immigrants a year. It was an era of trusts and financial giants such as J. P. Morgan. Keeping pace with business growth were organized labor and government. For a vigorous era, Teddy Roosevelt was ideal spokesman. His theatrical gestures gave notice that the U.S. meant to take its place on the world stage.

Meanwhile Imperial Russia faced revolt and defeat in war with Japan. The 1905 revolution, pushed underground, smouldered to explode in 1917. There were other revolutions—in China, Mexico, Portugal; and other wars—the Boer War, Boxer Rebellion, the Balkan Wars; signposts enroute to World War I. Europe was divided: Britain, France and Russia in the Triple Entente confronting the Triple Alliance of Germany, Italy and Austria-Hungary. The pre-war drama with its Victorian pomp and prudery was ending; the setting for the new era was almost complete.

◂ **ROUGH RIDER,** Trust Buster, Bull Moose, popular Theodore Roosevelt personified the "Good Old Days." As President (1901-1908), Roosevelt gloried in the limelight and loved to wield the "Big Stick" of power. In typical form he bulled through the Panama Canal, won the Nobel Peace Prize for his part in ending the Russo-Japanese War, and using the Navy as an instrument of foreign policy, sent the White Fleet around the world to dramatize the new status of the United States as a leading world power. Tough TR was idolized along with Mary Pickford and the Gibson Girl.

THE REPUBLICAN IDEALS of Vice-President Theodore Roosevelt *(r.)* differed from those of President William McKinley, who, like his conservative predecessors for three decades, believed government should not interefere with the economic life of the nation. The growing demands that government safeguard the public welfare from excesses of vested political or economic interests were reflected in the actions of outspoken Roosevelt. Party bosses had pushed Roosevelt, then New York governor, into the vice-presidency against his wishes, in the hope of ending his crusading political career.

PROGRESSIVE ERA BEGINS

Roosevelt enacts new policies in domestic and foreign affairs

The nation was shocked on Sept. 6, 1901 when President McKinley was shot. At his death young Vice-President Theodore Roosevelt confidently assumed office. Conservative opposition to Roosevelt arose, led by Republican Party boss Mark Hanna, who feared "radicalism" now that Teddy, "that damn cowboy," was President.

Hanna's fears of an attack on big business were partly justified when in 1902 TR aligned himself with the miners against the operators in the Great Coal Strike. He applied pressure in financial circles and threatened to seize the mines, forcing the operators to agree to submit the dispute to a board of arbitration. This board marked the first successful intervention of government in a capital-labor conflict.

Roosevelt launched his assault on business combinations by calling the Northern Securities Co., which had consolidated the railroad properties of Hill and Harriman, "a hideous monster." Prosecuted for violating free competition in 1902, it was ordered dissolved by the Supreme Court in 1904. Thus Roosevelt gained a reputation as a "trust buster," winning against Standard Oil Co. of N.J., the beef, sugar and other commodity trusts. Congress passed the Expediting Act, giving precedence in federal courts to cases arising from the Sherman and Interstate Commerce Acts. In 1903 Congress helped further by passing the Elkins Act which gave the Interstate Commerce Commission power to curb the evils of the railroad rebate system. The ICC was empowered by the Hepburn Act (1906) to require uniform bookkeeping for railroads, to extend jurisdiction over other carriers.

Muckraking journalists and TR forced food processors and drug producers to improve scandalous conditions; the Meat Inspection and Pure Food and Drug Acts came in 1906. Another success of the Roosevelt Administration was conservation of natural resources. Assisted by Gifford Pinchot, TR arrested wasteful exploitation of lumber, coal, petroleum and minerals, created forest reserves and boosted development of water power projects through the National Conservation Commission (1908).

Roosevelt's aggressive interest in world affairs was largely responsible for America's rise as a world power. His "big stick" policy virtually made the Caribbean "an American lake." The success of his policies and his great popularity gave the Republicans four victories during his tenure: 1902-04-06-08. His Democratic opponent in 1904, Judge Alton B. Parker, repudiated policies of his party's previous candidate, Bryan, but was swept under by TR's large vote.

ASSASSIN Leon Czolgosz, an anarchist, approached Pres. McKinley after a speech in Buffalo Sept. 6, 1901 and, with a gun hidden in a handkerchief, shot him twice. McKinley died on the 14th. Next day Roosevelt was sworn in.

THIS POWERFUL QUARTET represents the formidable forces with which Roosevelt had to contend. Andrew Carnegie, on extreme left, dominated the steel industry before retiring to philanthropic works. Beside him is William Jennings Bryan, popular Democratic leader, who backed agrarian interests. Next to him sits railroad magnate J. J. Hill, who battled for control of transportation in the Northwest. John Mitchell, on the far right, was the energetic leader of the United Mine Workers.

OLD GUARD LEADER Senator Marcus A. Hanna (Ohio) opposed many of Roosevelt's departures from conservative Republican policy, but was devoted to the cause of aiding relations between capital and labor. TR, barely contained by constitutional limits of his executive powers, boasted that he "caused to be done many things not previously done by the President," shocked Old Guard.

◀ **THE "OPEN DOOR"** policy in China was sponsored in 1899 by John Hay, Secretary of State under McKinley. Once private secretary to Lincoln, Hay also served TR as Secretary of State. In 1903 he framed treaty with Panama which made possible Panama Canal.

ELIHU ROOT, a distinguished statesman, was Teddy Roosevelt's second Secretary of State (1905-1909). He was influential in maintaining peace during Franco-German conflict over Morocco in 1905, won Nobel Peace Prize in 1912.

DYNAMIC TR, given to theatricalism, operates a steam shovel on Panama Canal construction site. Roosevelt's political career began in N.Y. State Assembly. He resigned as McKinley's Asst. Sec. of the Navy to join Rough Riders in Spanish-American War. A hero at San Juan Hill in '98, he returned to win the governorship of N.Y.

ROOSEVELT, TAFT IN POLICY SPLIT

Progressives of Republican Party break away, form Bull Moose Party

President William Howard Taft, who had served under Roosevelt and been his close friend, proved to be independent of TR's influence. He faced progressive opposition, led by Sen. LaFollette (Wisc.), as insurgent Republicans united with Democrats against Taft on tariff and other issues. The Republican Party rift deepened. Held responsible for the split, Taft was severely criticized despite his progressive measures. He had (1) brought twice as many anti-trust suits as had TR; (2) furthered conservation by buying timber tracts and withdrawing oil and coal lands from public leasing; (3) vastly broadened powers of ICC to regulate business by sponsoring Mann-Elkins Act (1910).

LaFollette and TR entered the race for presidential nomination in 1912, but the conservative machine effected Taft's re-nomination and the Bull Moose Party formed with TR as its candidate. His opposition divided, Democratic candidate Woodrow Wilson won the election.

CAUGHT IN CROSSFIRE between progressives and conservatives within Republican party, President Taft failed to unite warring factions. He lacked political dexterity of his predecessor, Roosevelt, who had helped him win office and whose policies he had been expected to follow. Taft was blamed for ruinous party split which threw 1912 election to Democrats. Shown with him are his sons Robert *(l.)* and Charles.

UNCLE JOE CANNON, *(l.)* ultra-conservative Speaker of the House from Illinois, appointed Rules Committee members, influenced legislation, blocked progressive action. Insurgent Republicans and Democrats joined to end his autocratic rule. This bi-partisan group drove wedge into Republican ranks.

REFORMER Robert M. LaFollette *(l.)* beat Wisconsin Republican bosses to become progressive governor (1900-1906), helped found Progressive Party in 1911. AF of L leader Samuel Gompers fought use of federal court injunctions to break strikes, opposed Taft.

CONSERVATIONIST Gifford Pinchot, aide to TR and Chief Forester under Taft, became a martyr to the cause of conservation after losing his job for attacking policies of Sec. of Interior R. A. Ballinger. The Ballinger Controversy over private leasing of public lands welded the progressives against Taft and widened breach within the party.

PROGRESSIVE Hiram Johnson, elected governor of California in 1910, had fought organized graft in state politics. A new progressive party—the Bull Moose—was formed in 1911 and Johnson was Roosevelt's running mate on the party's ticket the following year.

WILSON--A SCHOLAR IN POLITICS

Brings "The New Freedom" and strong leadership to American government

NEW DEMOCRATIC ADMINISTRATION is ushered into office. Retiring President William Howard Taft escorts President-elect Woodrow Wilson to waiting carriage outside White House for trip up Pennsylvania Avenue to Capitol for Wilson's inauguration as 28th President of the United States. March 4, 1913 marked beginning of "The New Freedom"—a concept of strong presidential government originated and followed by Wilson—in which business and the country at large felt the close touch of governmental regulation in banking, commerce, anti-trust laws and personal income taxes.

Wilson took office in 1913 at the peak of a reform wave with Democrats in control of both House and Senate. His New Freedom platform meant freedom from coddling Big Business. In this vein he pushed through five key bills: (1) Underwood Act removed or reduced tariff on many articles; (2) Federal Reserve Act, 1913, fathered by Sen. Carter Glass, Va., instituted currency controls; (3) Federal Trade Commission which regulated methods of competition by those engaged in interstate commerce; (4) Clayton Anti-Trust Act which controlled monopolistic practices in industry; (5) the first graduated income taxes. Other new measures included the Seaman's Act to improve living and working conditions of America's seamen; Workingmen's Compensation Act, giving disability allowances to civil servants; and rural credit laws.

When four railway brotherhoods threatened to strike in 1916, Wilson went before Congress and won, by law, the 8-hour day for railroad workers. In this record of reform Woodrow Wilson's re-election battle was won with 9,129,600 votes to Charles Evans Hughes' 8,538,200.

CHARLES EVANS HUGHES, Supreme Court Justice, resigned to be Republican presidential candidate in 1916. He retired election night assured of victory, but morning revealed California's vote had gone Democratic and Wilson had been re-elected by narrow margin.

PACIFIST Jeannette Rankin, first woman representative in Congress (Mont.), voted against participation in World War I and again refused to approve entry into war in 1941. She was only dissenter.

RIGHT-HAND MAN to Wilson was Joseph P. Tumulty *(l.)*, a graduate of early Jersey City politics. Day by day for ten years, as Governor of New Jersey and later as president, Wilson depended on his loyal private secretary. The two worked effectively as a team. Tumulty, with House and Kerney of N.J., chose Wilson's cabinet.

U. S. BUSINESS EXPANDS

America produces more than Germany, England and France combined

American business all but grew up in the years 1900-1913. A decade of business consolidation culminated in 1901 with formation of the United States Steel Corporation. Capitalized at $1,400,000,000, it combined the activities of twelve of the largest companies in the U.S.

Production methods were also being rapidly perfected. More than 1,000,000 bicycles were turned out in 1900, an achievement dwarfed when Henry Ford began in 1908 to mass-produce Model-T automobiles. By 1913 Ford had means to produce 1,000 cars a day, his annual output exceeding 250,000. The nation's railroad network reached its peak of some 250,000 miles of track by 1914. Both big and little business began to advertise on a larger scale to sell in an increasingly competitive economy.

But with adulthood came restriction as well as power. In 1904 the courts invoked the Sherman Anti-Trust Act against mergers and holding companies. The way was open for the Roosevelt administration's program of trust-busting, during which 37 cases—among them the famous indictment of Standard Oil Co. —were brought against big firms.

Although the depression of 1907-1908 was brief, it provoked a hue-and-cry about manipulation by the so-called "Money Trust." Widespread public demand enabled President Wilson in 1913 to get through Congress the Federal Reserve Act, a law which put bank reserves and the control of credit under jurisdiction of Federal Reserve Banks.

Poor working conditions and employer abuses created serious labor discontent. For this reason and because of a great influx of immigrants with new ideas about labor organization, the power of organized labor grew immensely. The American Federation of Labor under Samuel Gompers had in its ranks over 2,000,000 by 1904. The extremist Industrial Workers of the World, agitating for social as well as labor ideas, also flourished but eventually disbanded.

The entire tax structure of the U.S. was revamped in 1909 when Congress first levied a tax on corporations for the privilege of doing business, and at the same time an amendment to the Constitution was adopted to pave the way for the personal income tax of 1913.

Agriculture thrived as markets expanded because of growing urban industrial population. Such developments as the gasoline tractor were making farming more profitable.

As a whole the American economy was healthy and growing despite labor strife, regulation and bank panics. By the start of World War I U.S. business had acquired something of its mid-century character.

J. PIERPONT MORGAN, SR. with his daughter, Mrs. Louise Morgan Saterlee and his son, J. P. Morgan, enter the Capitol to testify before a Senate Committee prior to adoption of the disputed 1913 personal income tax law.

JOHN D. ROCKEFELLER, SR. built Standard Oil Company which became anti-trust target in 1892. Re-organized as Standard Oil Co. of N.J., it was ordered dissolved in 1911, and stock in 37 companies distributed to stockholders.

ANDREW CARNEGIE *(c.)*, one of America's leading philanthropists, and Charles M. Schwab figured in the formation of U.S. Steel Corporation, the first billion dollar corporation, in 1901. Carnegie sold to the Morgan combine.

EARLY AUTOMOBILE FACTORY produced vehicles by old-fashioned, time-consuming methods. Then came Henry Ford's Motor Company (1908) with a new theory of manufacture—the assembly line system. Car production climbed from 1700 in 1903 to 250,000 in 1913. First Standard Oil Service station appeared in Ohio in 1912. It had two pumps, cost $250.

AMERICAN INDUSTRY was showing considerable advances in size and diversity while the promise of gold in Alaska and silver in Nevada continued to lure men and money into the development of another area of the nation's resources. Gold production in the famous Klondike region began with the gold rush of 1896, reached its peak in 1900.

FACTORY FIRE TOLL: 145
Expose of working conditions in New York City's garment industry followed tragic Triangle Shirtwaist Factory fire in 1911. Women trapped at their machines perished in the flames while some workers jumped to their deaths.

CHILD LABOR RESTRICTED
After 1910 social pressure led to laws curbing use of child labor. "Sweat shop" working conditions, one of labor's major grievances, contributed to union growth.

STATE MILITIAMEN attempt to keep strikers away from textile mills at Lawrence, Mass. This strike was one of many outbreaks in the growing discord between organized labor and management. Forced by the growing power of organized labor to recognize labor's problems, employers began to develop new techniques of personnel and labor relations.

BANK PANIC resulted in a run on the Knickerbocker Trust Company, New York City in 1907, caused an investigation of the alleged "Money Trust." Effective public pressure for regulation of banking and credit led to congressional enactment of the Federal Reserve Act of 1913 which remains a permanent monument to that panic and a valuable safeguard.

A Vigorous Age in American Journalism

Growth of mass-circulation dailies and yellow press

WORLD'S JOSEPH PULITZER

JAMES GORDON BENNETT, JR.

GIANT OF JOURNALISM—W. R. HEARST

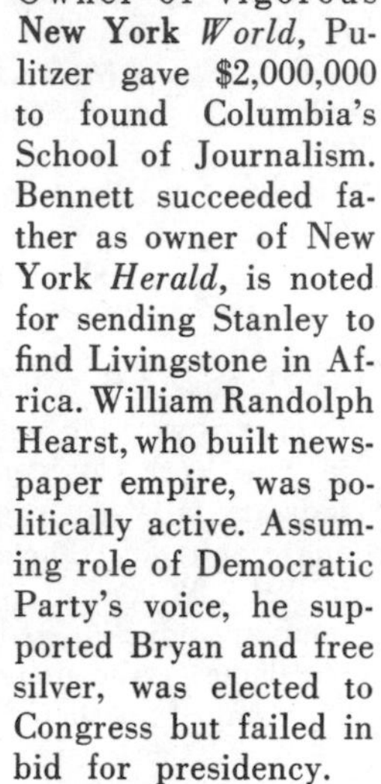

POWERS OF PRESS

Owner of vigorous New York *World*, Pulitzer gave $2,000,000 to found Columbia's School of Journalism. Bennett succeeded father as owner of New York *Herald*, is noted for sending Stanley to find Livingstone in Africa. William Randolph Hearst, who built newspaper empire, was politically active. Assuming role of Democratic Party's voice, he supported Bryan and free silver, was elected to Congress but failed in bid for presidency.

At the turn of the century the press reflected America's vast expansion and its attendant evils. It was a time of titans in journalism, when embattled newspapermen became advocates of economic and political reforms.

In New York Hearst bought the *Journal* in 1895 and declared war on Pulitzer's mighty *World*. He paid fabulous salaries to such famed writers as Mark Twain, Richard Harding Davis, Edgar Saltus and Stephen Crane. Both papers played up accidents, disasters, crime and corruption, a type of reporting labeled "yellow journalism." Bennett, who inherited the successful *Herald*, entered the fight. Adolph S. Ochs took control of the *Times* in 1896 to mold its greatness.

While Hearst and Scripps were building newspaper empires in the U.S., Lord Northcliffe's *Daily Mail* in Great Britain was printing 1,000,000 copies by 1900. But the foreign press was largely controlled by the political power in office.

THE MUCKRAKERS

King of the "Muckrakers" was Lincoln Steffens who did most of his early writing for *McClure's Magazine*. One of his most vivid articles "Ohio: a Tale of Two Cities" exposed political corruption in Cincinnati and Cleveland. Another trenchant writer, Ida M. Tarbell published a two-volume *History of the Standard Oil Company* attacking it as a giant trust. A third crusading author was Upton Sinclair who combined a political career as a Socialist with the writing of exposé-type books. His bitter indictment of the packing industry, *The Jungle*, eventually resulted in reforms. His other works include *King Coal* and *The Brass Check*.

PRESS SERVICES GROW

The Associated Press was formed in 1900 under leadership of Melville E. Stone. In 1908 E. W. Scripps formed United Press and Hearst International News Service. Reuters was operating in Great Britain and Europe. In this period press photography came into its own. Remarkable "shot" at left by *World* press cameraman shows shooting of New York's Mayor Gaynor.

EDITOR-BIOGRAPHER IDA TARBELL

JOURNALIST L. STEFFENS

AUTHOR, SOCIALIST SINCLAIR

IMPERIALISM IN LATIN AMERICA

Expanding U.S. control in Caribbean; dollar diplomacy and Canal defense

Economic and defense interests were responsible for extension of U.S. influence in Latin America. A canal through the isthmus between Mexico and South America would strengthen naval defense of both U.S. coasts, but the needed consent of Colombia, owner of the chosen route, was refused in 1903. Roosevelt then recognized a revolutionary government in Panama, signed a canal treaty and warned Colombia to keep out.

To defend the canal's approaches it was important to prevent rival naval powers from gaining a foothold in nearby Latin nations. Such a danger had loomed in 1902 when Germany, Britain and Italy had blockaded Venezuela to force payment of debts. The blockade was withdrawn, but it was feared that debt collection might be used by European powers as pretext for obtaining bases. Thus Roosevelt developed a "corollary" to the Monroe Doctrine.

In 1904 the Dominican Republic, threatened by European creditors, became a semi-protectorate of the U.S. In 1909 Taft sent Marines to protect Americans during Nicaragua revolt. They aided overthrow of Dictator Zelaya and remained to reorganize government. Latin Americans grew wary, resenting "Yankee menace."

THE "BIG DITCH" was begun in 1908. Construction *(l.)* of the Panama Canal was a great achievement of engineering and medical science. As important as actual work of digging and building three huge locks at each end were measures to control yellow fever, malaria.

STRONG MAN Porfirio Diaz brought rapid economic development to Mexico by encouraging and protecting foreign investments during his long dictatorship. But Mexico's masses, failing to benefit, helped overthrow him in 1911.

CARTOONIST draws his conception of Theodore Roosevelt's policy toward threat of intervention in Dominican Republic by European creditors. To uphold Monroe Doctrine, Roosevelt claimed, America must intervene.

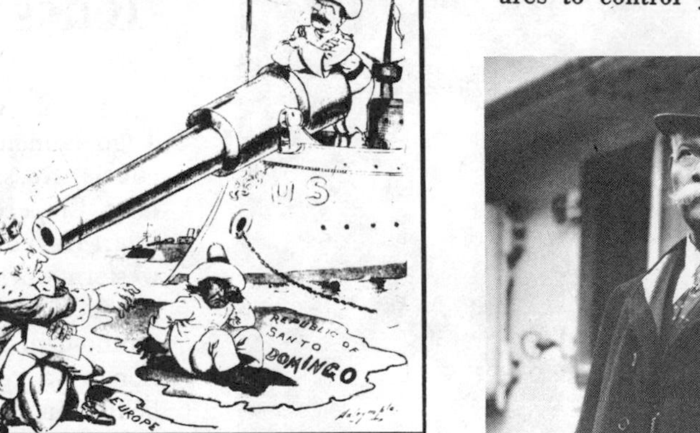

"A BLOT upon the history of Nicaragua" according to Secy. Knox, was Dictator Jose Santos Zelaya. He was overthrown in 1909 revolution after U.S. had intervened with President Taft ordering Marines to Nicaragua.

"PANCHO VILLA" *(l.)* had his hopes for the Mexican presidency dashed by President Woodrow Wilson's recognition of a rival, Carranza. The bandit-general's men raided Columbus, New Mexico in 1916, killing 17 U.S. citizens. Wilson sent troops under General Pershing *(r.)* to capture Villa. Critical European situation halted the hunt.

First Russian Revolution

At the turn of the century Russia was a backward country trying to industrialize. Its social structure was antiquated, its agriculture primitive and its standard of living extremely low. The discontented peasants looked to the Czar, "The Little Father," for deliverance. But weak-willed Nicholas II, tool of reactionary advisers among the nobility and the hierarchy of the Orthodox Church, was apt symbol of the regime's advanced decay.

After Russia's defeat by the Japanese a mass of unarmed workers, led by Father Gapon, marched peacefully on January 22, 1905 to the Winter Palace to petition the Czar. Troops fired on them. This "Bloody Sunday" united the opposition. Peasant uprisings and political strikes broke out throughout the country. In September a congress of the *zemstva,* or popular consultative assemblies, demanded establishment of representative government. In October a transport strike paralyzed the nation, followed by a general strike at St. Petersburg. The army and navy then mutinied.

On October 17th the Czar agreed to give the people freedom of speech, assembly and conscience and proclaimed that a popularly elected Duma (legislature) would have the power of consent to all laws. Soon reverting to absolutism, however, he reduced Duma to a debating society. But the big revolution was brewing.

POPULAR REBELLION MET BY MASSACRE AND DECEIT
Hunger and poverty ignited the First Russian Revolution. A wave of protest demonstrations swept the country. Unable to suppress the legitimate desires of his people for representation, the Czar gave some concessions. The first two Dumas (legislatures) were composed of liberal elements but the Czar dissolved them. The third, reactionary and powerless, remained until 1917 while underground revolt smouldered.

Russo-Japanese War

On February 8, 1904, a Japanese fleet led by Admiral Togo launched a surprise attack on Port Arthur, Manchuria, Russia's main Far Eastern naval base. Two days later Emperor Meiji declared war. Like the attack on Pearl Harbor 37 years later, it was a surprise assault. The western world praised Japan's aggression. Japan wanted primacy in Korea, as did Russia, and Japan sought a foothold in Manchuria where Russia had a favored position as a result of the settlement after the Boxer Rebellion in China in 1900.

Admiral Togo took immediate control of the Yellow Sea and the Sea of Japan, and when Russia's Baltic Sea Fleet reached the Straits of Tsushima he virtually annihilated it. On land Japan decimated enemy armies.

Peace came with the Treaty of Portsmouth in 1905, concluded on the initiative of President Theodore Roosevelt, and Japan became the leading Far Eastern power. Only the revolutionists' lack of organization kept the Imperial Russian Government from sudden collapse.

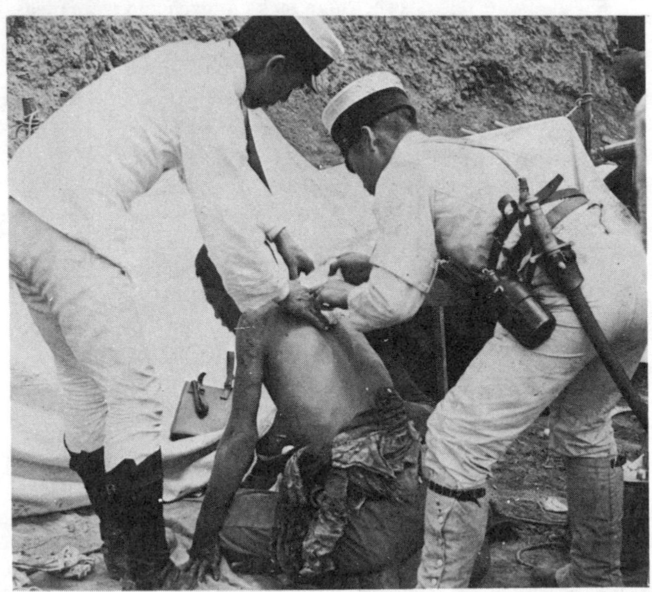

WORLD STUNNED BY JAPAN'S VICTORY OVER RUSSIA
Bravery displayed by Japanese soldiers and their crushing defeat of Russia astonished the world. The *London Times* reported admiringly, "The Japanese Navy, thanks to the masculine decision of the Mikado Meiji and his advisers, has taken the initiative of opening the war by an act of daring."

JAPANESE NAVAL COMMANDER WINS WORLD ACCLAIM
Admiral Heihachiro Togo (1847-1934), one of the heroes of the war, toured the world afterward, receiving ovations everywhere. He lived to be a demi-god to the Japanese people.

EDWARD VII *(l.)* was the successor to his mother, Victoria, in 1901, and like her gave his name to an age. During his brief reign (he was nearly 60 when he assumed the throne), he won the people's affectionate respect, contributed to international understanding, and was admired as a patron of the arts and a sportsman. In 1910 he was succeeded to the throne by his second son, George V, who reigned from 1910 to 1936. A conscientious, tireless worker, he personified British dignity in his handsome but colorless person. Royal family *(above)*, left to right are: the Prince of Wales (later Edward VIII and then Duke of Windsor), Princess Mary, the Duke of Gloucester, George V, Duke of York, Queen Mary, the Duke of Kent.

THE EDWARDIAN ERA

End of the Victorian Age sees mounting rivalry for colonial expansion

The 20th century found Europe divided into two triumvirates: The Triple Entente of England, France and Russia versus the Triple Alliance of Germany, Austria-Hungary and Italy.

The South African Republic rebelled against Great Britain and the bloody Boer War ensued, ending with the Treaty of Vereeniging (May 31, 1902), a pact benevolent to the Boers. The colony turned from revolt to staunch support of the Empire. Africa was again a trouble spot when France tried to subjugate Morocco and Germany's Wilhelm II sped to Tangier. Growing tension brought England into the situation.

England needed to re-establish a favorable balance of power in Europe, threatened by Germany's rising industrial and military power. When Queen Victoria died in 1901 her son Edward VII prepared the way for the Entente-Cordial of 1904 by his visit to Paris in 1903. England also signed an alliance with Japan (1902) to preserve the status quo in the Far East.

Through the offices of Theodore Roosevelt an international conference was held at Algeciras, Spain in January 1906. There France won a free hand in Morocco.

FRANZ JOSEPH, Emperor of Austria-Hungary, reigned for 68 years, from 1848 to 1916. Conservative and autocratic, he exercised great personal power, succeeded in holding together loosely-bound nations of the Empire.

DREYFUS AFFAIR was one of the major scandals of the Golden Days. Anti-Semites on French general staff helped frame Dreyfus for treason. Condemned to Devil's Island, he was rescued with help of novelist Emile Zola *(J'accuse)*.

GERMAN NAVY second to none was goal of Adm. Alfred von Tirpitz (1849-1930). As Minister of Marine he encouraged development of submarines, resigned in 1916 as protest against Kaiser's reluctance to use navy fully.

THREAT OF WAR AVERTED

Kaiser's visit to Tangier in 1905 almost precipitated World War I. Frightened, Great Powers, with TR's aid internationalized the city.

CONFLICT RAGES BETWEEN BRITAIN AND BOER S. AFRICAN REPUBLIC 1899-1902

Boer War was led by Stephanus Kruger *(r.)*, President of the South African Republic. Conservative and tenacious, he and his aides fought for four years against British forces of almost half a million, including Lord Roberts, Lord Kitchener, Winston Churchill (then a journalist), Cecil Rhodes, and Baden Powell (founder of Boy Scouts). After the war Boer properties were restored and a grant of £3,000,000 was made to rebuild the farms.

BELGIUM GAINS IN CONGO

Leopold II of Belgium spearheaded development of the Congo but his exploitation of its people and resources led to scandal and then reform.

Africa--Battleground for Imperialism

Nationalist, economic drives spur exploitation

To the Western world, stirred by reports of Africa's wealth, the "Dark Continent" lay like a ripe plum. Europeans established trading companies, exploratory expeditions, sought gold and other minerals and dealt in slaves. Africa was divided among England, France, Portugal, Germany and Spain during the period 1884-1890.

The French conquered North Africa and using its colonies as bases developed a huge empire in Central Africa. The British subdued the Boers, uniting South Africa to the Empire. Cecil Rhodes, who built an empire by developing the Kimberly diamond mines, pushed South Africa's frontiers into Rhodesia. In 1908 the Congo became a Belgian colony, ending Leopold's abusive personal rule. Germany, who in 1890 owned one million square miles in Africa, won 100,000 square miles of Equatorial Africa by concession from France in 1911 in return for recognition of French rights in Morocco. Italy was defeated in its bid for Ethiopia but controlled Eritrea and Somaliland.

TURKISH REVOLT WINS FREEDOM

Turkish army officers Niyazi Bey and Mahmud Shevket Pasha instigated the Young Turk revolution in Macedonia, ending "Red Sultan" Abdul Hamid II's 33 years of rule, April 26, 1909.

OTTOMAN EMPIRE

Dismemberment of the Ottoman Empire created world problems. Russia, seeking a Mediterranean outlet, encouraged nations of the Empire to revolt. Bulgaria gained independence; Austria annexed Bosnia and Herzegovina. Italy attacked Tripoli in 1911 and Turkey had to cede the city.

Turkish defeat by joint Balkan powers was followed by victory in the second Balkan War, but her military decline invited rearmament and reorganization of the Empire under Prussian generals such as Liman Von Sanders Pasha and led to secret alliance between Turkish leaders and Wilhelm II. Thus in uneasy peace the seeds of war germinated.

PRO-GERMAN COUP IN TURKEY

Defeated by Balkan nations, Turkey lost most of her European lands (Treaty of London, 1913). A *coup d'etat* led by Minister of War Enver Bey put pro-German nationalists into power.

20th CENTURY STIRS FAR EAST

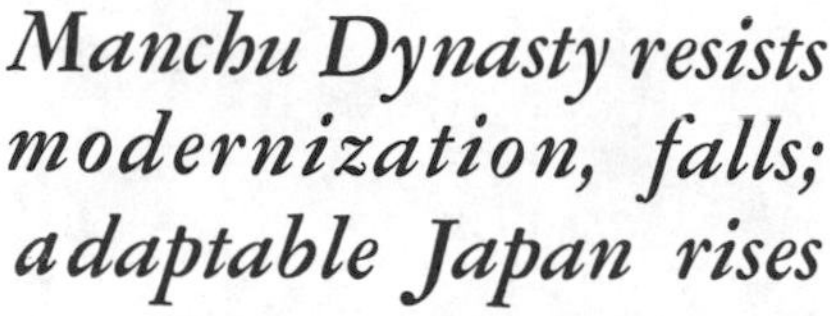

Manchu Dynasty resists modernization, falls; adaptable Japan rises

Revolt erupted in 1911 at Wuchang and spread rapidly through China. The revolutionists established a provisional government at Nanking, elected Dr. Sun Yat-sen president, and the Republic of China was born. The emperor's abdication proclamation authorized Yuan Shih K'ai to head a provisional republican government. Sun resigned and Yuan soon defied the Kuomintang and disbanded Parliament. In 1913 Sun and his followers in Canton tried unsuccessfully to unseat him.

Meanwhile Japan had been swiftly Westernized, won a stunning victory over the Russians and grown rapidly as a world power. In 1914 Japan declared war on Germany and captured its possessions in Shantung. Fearing war with Japan, Yuan signed treaties granting Japanese demands designed to guarantee her position in China. At Yuan's death in 1916, Li Yuan-hung became president. Parliament was reassembled only to be dismissed when Tuan Chi-jui seized power. Denouncing the Peking government as illegal, Sun formed a new provisional government at Canton in 1917. But a unified China was still distant.

MANCHU RULER, the Dowager Empress Tzu-Hsi ruled China during most of the period from 1862, when she became co-regent for her son, until her death in 1908. Manchu court encouraged Boxers, hoped to eject alien powers.

FIRST PRESIDENT of the Chinese Republic, Dr. Sun Yat-sen aided movement to eject Manchus from China, later formed the *Kuo Min Tang*, or Nationalist Party, championed a system of parliamentary government.

AMERICAN SOLDIER relieves the thirst of a wounded Japanese *(l.)* as U.S. and Japan join to suppress Boxer Rebellion in China. Other western powers also sent troops in May 1900 when Chinese militia forces, supported by a Manchu court clique, rebelled against expanding imperialism by attacking foreigners. The uprising was crushed and U.S. Secretary of State John Hay formulated an "Open Door" policy of equal opportunity to all nations, saving China from dismemberment.

PRINCE HIROBIMI ITO, who studied European systems of government, influenced Japanese reform. Prime Minister during much of Meiji period, he drafted a constitution which carefully guarded the rights of the emperor, established a bi-cameral *Diet* (legislature), reorganized Cabinet on German lines.

EMPEROR MITSUHITO, known as the Meiji Emperor, was put on the throne at the age of 14 by the *daimyos* (great lords) when they overthrew the last Shogun and ended almost 700 years of feudal military government. During his reign (1867-1912) Japan was modernized and emerged as a world power.

BASEBALL RECORDS held by the great Tyrus Raymond (Ty) Cobb include highest batting average (lifetime .367), most stolen bases, most total bases and others. Cobb led the American League in batting for 12 seasons, nine consecutive, top average—.420.

OUTSTANDING as a second baseman in the early era was peppery Eddie Collins, also noted as a hitter, base runner and field captain. Collins was a member of the Philadelphia Athletics' famous "$100,000 infield." In 1939 he was elected to baseball's Hall of Fame.

NATIONAL LEAGUE'S Honus (Hans) Wagner is considered all-time top shortstop by many baseball experts. "The Flying Dutchman" retired in 1917 but remained in the record book with most hits, runs and stolen bases for N. L. He is also in the Hall of Fame (1936).

AMERICAN ATHLETES ON THE RISE

Baseball becomes the national sport, boxing grows as sport scene widens

The National League fought to maintain its status as baseball's only major league, but American League magnates raided its stars and by 1903 the NL asked for a truce. In the first World Series in 1905 between the New York Nationals and the Philadelphia Americans, famous names on the rosters included Christy Mathewson, Rube Waddell, Tris Speaker and Walter Johnson.

Boxing gained in 1892 with adoption of Marquis of Queensbury rules, requiring gloves and three minute rounds. In track and field the U.S. early won world supremacy. In 1904 Olympics, U.S. team won 21 events.

FRANK CHANCE was first baseman in the famous "Tinker to Evers to Chance" double-play combination of the Chicago Cubs. Chance served as Cubs' player-manager. In his first full season as manager (1906) Cubs took the pennant with 116 victories, major league record. The noted baseball star joined the roster of the Hall of Fame in 1946.

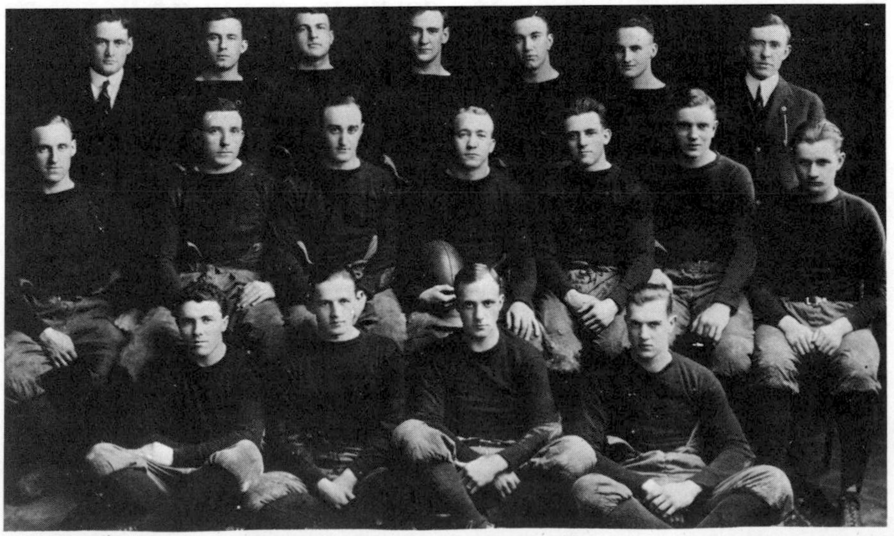

NOTRE DAME in 1913 made famous the forward pass, which had been introduced in 1906. A great Army team, playing the "easy" South Benders, was leading 13-0 when Gus Dorais, Notre Dame quarterback, started passing to ends Knute Rockne (holding ball) and Pliska, winning 35-13. This combination made American gridiron history.

JIM CORBETT IN FINAL DEFEAT

Winning the heavyweight crown from John L. Sullivan, James J. Corbett was champion from 1892 to 1897. He was knocked out by Bob Fitzsimmons who then lost the title to Jim Jeffries. Boxing Jeffries in 1903, Corbett *(l.)* lost.

BURNS CLAIMS CHAMPIONSHIP

Shown here in typical boxing stance of the time is Tommy Burns who claimed the title in 1905 when Jim Jeffries retired undefeated. But heavyweight contender Jack Johnson challenged Burns in Australia in 1908 and beat him.

JOHNSON THE VICTOR AT RENO

Undefeated champion Jim Jeffries came out of retirement to fight Jack Johnson in 1910. Johnson defeated him by a knockout in fifteen rounds at Reno and in so doing the powerful fighter won the heavyweight championship.

THORPE—GREAT ALL-AROUND ATHLETE OF ALL TIME

A sportsman who excelled in many areas of the athletic arena, Jim Thorpe won fame for the quality and variety of his skills. He was an All-American football player at Carlisle University, and outstanding enough at baseball to play with a major league team (New York Giants). He reached his peak in 1912 at the Olympic Games when he won both decathlon and pentathlon events. Later his trophies were taken away on charges of professionalism.

BASKETBALL IS BORN, GROWS INTO MAJOR SPORT

James A. Naismith (above, not in uniform), invented basketball at the YMCA College, Springfield, Mass. in 1891. He is shown with the first team to play the game. Its popularity mushroomed and by 1950 basketball was a major U.S. sport.

PIONEERING IN GOLF

Walter J. Travis was the American Amateur Champion 1900-1903. Francis Ouimet beat Ray, Vardon in 1913.

THE SPORT OF KINGS FEATURES FAMOUS NAMES IN THE GRANDSTAND AND ON THE TRACK

Horse racing attracted many celebrities, such as Lillian Russell, noted entertainer. Top horses of the era were Sysonby, who lost only one race, the unbeaten Colin, and the fine Roseben. Greatest of the harness racers was Dan Patch *(right)*, a pacer. His mile record of 1.55¼, set in 1905, was not beaten until Billy Direct's 1.55 record was set in 1938.

GERMAN ENGINEER and pioneer auto maker, Nikolaus August Otto built the first successful internal combustion engine operating on four-cycle principle for which he secured an American patent in 1877. His co-worker, Gottlieb Daimler *(above)*, went on to develop the engine, making the automobile practicable, and was the first to use a carburetor.

HENRY FORD built his first car in 1896 and in 1903 formed the Ford Company. He produced racing cars, trained famous driver Barney Oldfield. By 1908 he had turned out his famous Model T. That same year Henry Leland, who began making Cadillacs in 1902, produced precision-made auto parts which were interchangeable, advancing mass production potential.

VANDERBILT CUP RACE *(above)* was a grueling annual endurance test for drivers, cars and audience. Spectators had to leave New York at midnight to reach the hundred mile Long Island track in time for the starting gun which cracked at dawn. The first Indianapolis race was held in 1911.

"GET A HORSE!"

Derision, mud-holes and flats fail to stop the new vehicle

In 1900 Americans traveled by train or boat, horse and buggy or stage coach. A few eccentric individuals owned that new contraption, the horseless carriage, which clattered down New York and Detroit streets in a confusion of backfires and shying horses. Rugged enthusiasts went for drives in the country or raced at 8 mph between towns around Flint, Michigan, where Ransom Olds had his Motor Works, and Chicopee, Massachusetts, where Charles Duryea made his car.

James W. Packard put a steering wheel on his 1901 model. Henry Ford, Ransom Olds and Alexander Winton produced cars steered with a tiller and the motor under the seat. By 1905 there were more than 10,000 owners of automobiles—the French name which came into use. William C. Durant of Buick organized General Motors. In 1911 the first Indianapolis Speed Race was run. But the Automobile Age in America did not arrive until 1912 when Leland put Charles F. Kettering's self-starter on his Cadillacs and replaced the burdensome hand-crank.

MASS PRODUCTION on Ford's assembly line at Highland Park linked cars together so that they seemed to march like elephants in a circus parade. Bodies skidded down a ramp onto the chassis as they moved along below. Ford borrowed the assembly line idea from the slaughterhouse in the stockyards and began the technique of mass auto production.

ELECTRIC CAR Milady goes modern in an electric car, advertised as "safe, noiseless, immaculately clean and docile vehicle." Driving in this early era of the auto usually meant donning goggles, dusters, veils and gauntlets.

FIRST SUCCESSFUL FLIGHT of a powered heavier-than-air machine was made at Kitty Hawk, N. C., on Dec. 17, 1903 by Orville Wright (lying in plane). Duration of the flight was 12 seconds. Later the same day brother Wilbur (standing) made a flight of 852 feet in 59 seconds. Wrights financed their aviation experiments with proceeds from their bicycle shop.

SCIENTIFIC AMERICAN award winner was designer-pilot Glenn Curtiss, shown seated in his biplane the *June Bug* at Hammondsport, New York, in 1908. On July 4, 1908 he made a flight of 5,090 feet, exceeding the distance of one kilometer, thereby becoming the winner of the first aeronautical trophy ever offered in competition in the United States.

FIRST FLIGHT

Wright Brothers, Curtiss and Zeppelin vie for early honors

In a race against time, Orville Wright, on December 17, 1903 officially became the first human being to pilot a heavier-than-air machine. Actually, three days before, Wilbur flew the same plane for more than 100 feet, but records give the December 17th date as the first flight, probably because of the public exhibition at that time. Man's first flight was financed by proceeds from the Wright bicycle shop.

Earlier attempts to conquer the air date back to 1783 when the balloon was developed. 1900 saw men in various parts of the world working on the prototype of modern aircraft. Clement Ader of France experimented with steam-powered planes as early as 1886. Some French historians maintain Ader should have the honor accorded the Wright brothers. In the U.S. Samuel Langley developed his *Aerodrome* in 1903. Powered by a five cylinder gas engine, the plane failed because of a faulty launching rack. The Wright brothers' greatest rival, from another U.S. bicycle shop, Glenn Curtiss first flew his craft in '08.

DAREDEVIL AERONAUT
Public interest in flying was sharpened by aeronautical exploits. Crowds lined the streets to watch daredevil English pilot Claude Grahame-White take off from West Executive Avenue, Washington, D. C. on Oct. 14, 1910. In the background are the Navy Dept. buildings and the White House offices.

DIRIGIBLES DEVELOPED
The world was astounded in 1907 when Ferdinand von Zeppelin flew 11 passengers 218 miles in eight hours in the LZ-3 *(r.)*. A German count, Zeppelin retired from a military career to devote himself to experimental work on dirigible balloons. He became the world's leading authority on dirigible aircraft.

STEAM POWER

Before the advent of diesel and electric motors, coal-burning engines pulled cars on the El trains above N.Y. streets *(l.)* and hauled trains in and out of Pennsylvania Station. Horse-drawn fire wagons answered alarms, careening down city streets, the pumper billowing smoke from its steam boiler. In 1893 the famous old No. 999, N.Y. Central's *Empire State Express*, set a locomotive speed record of 112.5 miles an hour.

EXPANSION OF ADVERTISING

Start and development of new commercial phenomenon on American scene

The turn of the century saw, for the first time, large-scale advertising used to sell goods and services on a nationwide basis.

Advertising was in its infancy, but the public was already being acquainted with Eastman Kodaks, Campbell's Soup, Hoover Suction Sweepers, Cream of Wheat, Remington Typewriters, Studebaker Automobiles and many other products through the use of advertising.

Early advertisers, meanwhile, were reaping the impressive results of increased sales from this great new force. This period also marked the real beginning of advertising agencies in the role of special service organizations: writing copy, selecting media and conducting market analyses.

Advertising was off to a good start. It was not until the end of World War I, however, that one of its most powerful allies—"cheesecake," the pretty girl appeal—would be used as a powerful selling force.

HORSELESS CARRIAGE advertising heralded the end of the horse and buggy era by featuring such famous slogans as Packard's "Ask the man who owns one" and Ford's "Boss of the Road." However, it took Oldsmobile in 1903 to strike a final blow at the defenseless horse in this vivid example of automobile advertising.

TALKING MACHINES at $15-$50 had "His Master's Voice" trademark and advertising's most cautious testimonial by John Philip Sousa, "It is all right."

FORM REDUCING techniques to produce a fashionable feminine figure were announced by corset manufacturers such as this one promising "Happy Symmetry" to those of too ample form. "All Hand Finished, at $1.00 to $5.00."

SEARS, ROEBUCK & CO. built acceptance for catalogues, featured descriptive copy, testimonials. This one in 1902 had 1,200 pages, offered such values as sewing machines selling for $10.45.

LABOR AND TIME-SAVING devices such as this automatic washer were starting to appear on the market. They were to be only the beginning of a flood of automatic home appliances designed to aid the nation's harried housewives.

FIELD TRIPS for college students were gaining popularity in 1911. College girls *(above)*, wearing popular skirt and blouse costume, are shown attending an art appreciation class at the Municipal Art Gallery in New York City.

NOTED EDUCATOR, philosopher and father of progressive education in the U.S. was John Dewey, who opened his first "child-centered" school at Univ. of Chicago in 1900. Dewey believed education of child must be functional.

BIGGEST CHAUTAUQUA attraction was silver-tongued orator William Jennings Bryan, who always filled the house. Chautauqua circuit plan, which developed in 1904, brought music, lectures and entertainment to the country.

EDUCATION

Little red schoolhouse outgrows its goal and curriculum as educational aims mature

Mastery of the three R's was the goal of education at the turn of the century. Teachers, usually women, received average annual wage of $325. In rural areas high schools were almost unknown and usually education ended with completion of grammar school. In 1900, 75% of high school graduates went on to college to become teachers, lawyers, doctors, ministers or engineers. Harvard gave impetus to study of business administration by establishing its graduate school of business in 1910.

Rumblings of the revolt in elementary and secondary education, still unresolved 50 years later, had begun, with Dewey leading "progressive" movement. Eventually public schools began to adopt his progressive education techniques and doctrines. Education was chief beneficiary of many philanthropists like Rockefeller and Carnegie, whose funds made possible wide educational research.

POPE PIUS X, (1903-1914), who succeeded the aristocratic Leo XIII, was a Venetian of humble birth. He condemned religious modernism in 1907. As Pontiff, he reorganized the entire church. In 1951 Pius X was beatified by the church.

A HALF CENTURY of crusade ended when Mary Baker Eddy, founder of the Christian Science movement, died in 1910. Her doctrine, that healing may come through faith and understanding the teachings of Christ, spread widely.

FUNDAMENTALIST, evangelist and best-selling author, "Pastor" Charles Russell *(above)* preached against Charles Darwin's theory of evolution and the atheism of lawyer-lecturer Robert Ingersoll in bitter three-way feud.

RELIGION TESTED BY MODERNISM

A theological conflict swept Christian countries at the century's start, stirred by science and studies of liberal scholars. Modernists questioned the literal interpretation of the Scriptures, held that modern scientific knowledge disproved them. Papal decrees charging heresy hushed the storm within the Catholic Church. Fundamentalists took shelter in new churches: The Pillar of Fire, Nazarene, Seventh-day Adventist, etc. Liberals turned Unitarian and Humanist, radicals became agnostics. Controversy inspired evangelists, whose zeal swelled U.S. church membership from 36 million in 1900 to 52 million in 1914. Immigration increased Catholic ranks 62% but Protestants still outnumbered them 3 to 1. In 1908, 33 churches formed Federal Council of Churches of Christ.

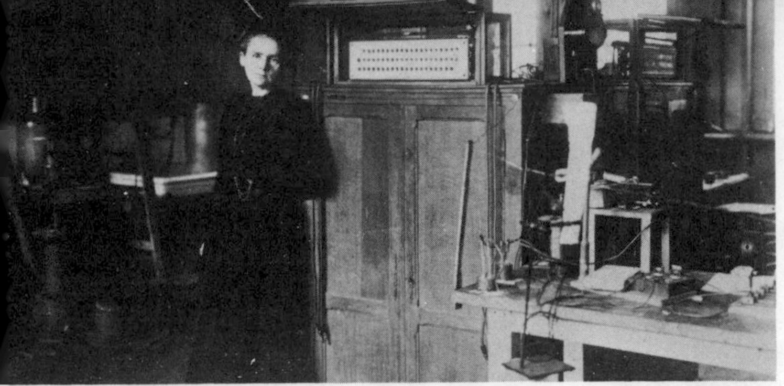

STUDY OF RADIO-ACTIVITY in uranium led Madame Curie and her husband to the discovery of radium. As early as 1903 Curie and Laborde found that one gram of radium yielded over 100 calories of heat per hour, suggesting tremendous possibilities of this new energy source. Rutherford and Soddy were other early workers in studies of radio-activity.

SCIENTISTS

New theories reveal new horizons

Public appreciation of the work of the pure scientist was lacking in the early years of the century, although the foundations for the Atomic Age were being laid. Rutherford, Bohr, Lenard, Thomson and others studied atomic structure and the nature of radio-activity. By 1903 it was known that radio-active elements held great power.

Greatest achievement in scientific thought was probably the overthrow of the Newtonian explanation of the universe by the new theory of relativity introduced by Einstein in 1905. He and Debye used Planck's quantum theory of light to explain the phenomena of specific heat.

GIANTS OF SCIENCE, Albert Einstein *(l.)* and Charles Steinmetz were both German-born and both sought the American atmosphere in which to continue their careers. Brilliant theorist and mathematician, Einstein created formula for mass-energy relationship (Relativity) which proved basis for atomic bomb. Steinmetz was electrical genius.

PHYSICIST Werner Heisenberg proposed formal statement of the laws of probability in a Principle of Uncertainty, held that no phenomenon can be uniquely defined by physical formulae, margin of uncertainty always exists.

MAX PLANCK *l.*, together with Einstein, provided the basis for modern physics with his Quantum Theory (1901). His assumption was that radiant energy was discontinuous and it appeared in specific bundles or quanta.

FRIEND OF EDISON, Luther Burbank *(l.)* devoted his life to creating new or improved varieties of plants by the crossing of species (hybridization) and selection. The hardy Burbank potato ended food shortages in many areas.

POLAR EXPLORATION

Conquest of both poles was accomplished within a period of two years. Admiral Robert Edwin Peary, American arctic explorer, made three attempts to find the North Pole before he finally attained the ice-cap on April 6, 1909. Frederick A. Cook claimed to have preceded Peary, but after investigation the government gave Peary the credit. Raold Amundsen of Norway started his expedition to the South Pole in 1910, taking along Eskimo dogs, sledges and enough supplies to last nine men two years. He reached the South Pole on December 16, 1911, and set up a flag found by explorer Robert F. Scott a month later.

NORTH POLE CONQUEROR PEARY

RAISING FLAG ON SOUTH POLE

AMUNDSEN, SOUTH POLE VICTOR

SCIENCE IN ACTION

Discoveries applied successfully

Practical scientists, led by Edison, Marconi, Burbank and Sperry, utilized findings of pure scientists to improve living conditions. In 1904 a bulb detecting radio waves, forerunner of the vacuum tube, was invented. Electric lighting spread and movie theatres appeared as Edison and others worked on cameras and projectors. Ships were safer, equipped with Sperry's gyroscope compass and stabilizer. Wilbur and Orville Wright proved man could fly in 1903 at Kitty Hawk, North Carolina.

At mid-century man was trying to harness cosmic rays, discovered in 1903. The isotope theory which led to discovery of plutonium from which first atomic bomb was made, dates back to 1913.

RADIO

Guglielmo Marconi invented the wireless receiving apparatus which first spanned the Atlantic. On the Newfoundland coast on Dec. 13, 1901 he picked up the Morse telegraphic "S" coded as three dots, sent from Poldhu, England. Lee De Forest *(r.)*, father of radio broadcasting, invented the audion tube, making possible radio with a loudspeaker.

MEDICINE ADVANCES

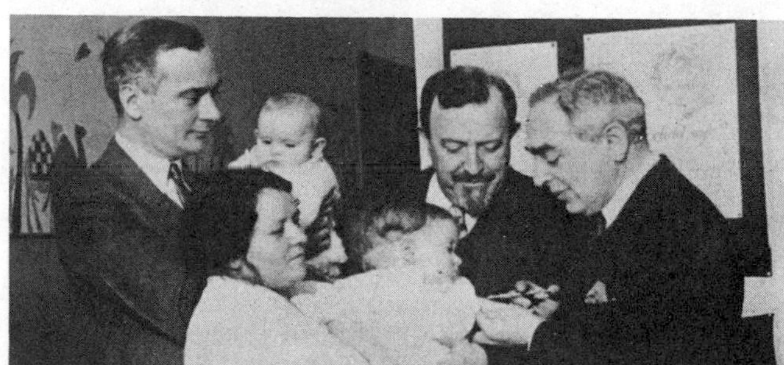

CONQUEST of dread diphtheria by development of immunization saved lives of thousands of children. Dr. Bela Schick, who developed test for determining susceptibility to the disease and introduced the term allergy, gives injection.

HOSPITAL DEMONSTRATION of operating technique in 1901 is seen in Roosevelt Hospital, N. Y. as Dr. McBurney shows new method for appendectomy. Women nurses became accepted due to Florence Nightingale's pioneering work.

PAUL EHRLICH'S discovery of salvarsan which curbed syphilis was a step forward in "incurable" ills. Ehrlich received a Nobel award in 1908, Progress also came in mental treatment, led by Freud, Jung and Adler.

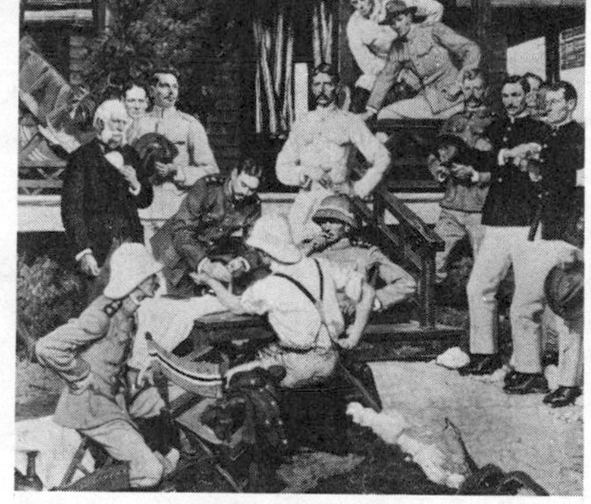

DR. WALTER REED proved in 1901 through experiments on volunteer soldiers that yellow fever was caused by a filterable virus which was transmitted to man by the mosquito *Aedes aegypti*. Reed was U. S. Army doctor.

ROBERT KOCH, shown in laboratory, is considered one of the founders of modern bacteriology. He discovered the germ of tuberculosis. In 1901 Dr. Karl Landsteiner revealed principle of blood groups and transfusion became safe.

EVA TANGUAY, music hall favorite early in the century, was noted for singing *I Don't Care.* Another music hall singer, Gaby Deslys, was brought to U.S. by the Shuberts for sensational tour.

NOTED BEAUTY and singer, Lillian Russell, toast of the land at the turn of the century, made plump figures fashionable and was publicized for the number of her husbands. With start of the annual Ziegfeld Follies in 1907, the Ziegfeld Girl became an American institution.

ANNA HELD, French import, was the wife of Florenz Ziegfeld. She was famous for her hourglass figure, milk baths and her rendition of the song, *I Just Can't Make My Eyes Behave.*

BABES IN TOYLAND *(above)*, produced in 1903, was one in a long list of hit operettas that flowed from the prolific pen of Victor Herbert to charm the public. The Irish-born composer's melodic works continued to win wide popular acclaim during this period, included *Mlle. Modiste* in 1905; *The Red Mill* in 1906; and *Naughty Marietta* in 1910.

THE STAGE

Personalities, not plays, dominant

In the first era of the century the American theatre was hitched to the star system. Managers like Charles and David Frohman, Belasco and Klaw & Erlanger sought plays primarily as showcases for their stars.

David Warfield played *The Music Master* more than 1,000 times; E. H. Sothern and Julia Marlowe presented Shakespeare; Maxine Elliott managed her own theatre; Frances Starr acted for Belasco; George Arliss performed *Disraeli* in New York and on the road for almost five years. Otis Skinner, Blanche Bates, Mrs. Leslie Carter, Cissie Loftus and Jane Cowl were achieving success.

ELLEN TERRY made her first appearance as Mamilius in *A Winter's Tale* at the age of nine. Later Henry Irving engaged her as his leading lady for the Lyceum, where she played such roles as Lady Macbeth *(above)*. Her great charm made her the foremost Shakespearean actress of the stage.

POPULAR leading man, Joseph Jefferson, is shown as Bob Acres in *The Rivals.* Another favorite, William Gillette, portrayed Sherlock Holmes in dramatizations of Conan Doyle's stories.

MAUDE ADAMS played *The Little Minister* in 1904 opposite Robert Edeson. The play, written by James M. Barrie was produced by Charles Frohman. Two other Barrie plays made memorable by the celebrated Maude Adams were *What Every Woman Knows* and the perennially delightful fantasy, *Peter Pan.*

PERFORMING FAMILY, The Four Cohans, Jerry J., Helen F., Josephine and George M., were famous vaudeville headliners at the beginning of the century. During this period vaudeville and music halls flourished. The popular Cohans turned to the Broadway stage in 1901 when they appeared together in George's musical, *The Governor's Son.*

"FLORADORA," a 1900 musical, won real success through publicity when wealthy men began falling for girls of the famous Sextette *(above)*. Original members were Marjorie Relyea, Vaughan Texsmith, Agnes Wayburn, Daisy Greene, Margaret Walker and Marie Wilson. The song, *Tell Me, Pretty Maiden*, became a popular hit.

THEATRE GROWS

Maturing influences and monopoly

In a day of posturing melodrama and romance, the first moves toward realism were being made. Belasco insisted on real props; the "organic," realistic acting style of the Moscow Art Theatre and Stanislavsky was affecting American directors. In 1905 Shaw's *Mrs. Warren's Profession* battled past censors and police. Sociological dramas of Shaw and Ibsen became influential.

The Theatre Trust, a monopoly of bookers and managers, controlled some 700 theatres across the nation. Asbestos fire curtains were being installed as a result of 1903 Iroquois Theatre fire in Chicago in which 602 died.

A FAVORITE COMIC TEAM
Weber and Fields, comedy stars for years, put on revues like *Whoop-de-doo* at their New York Music Hall.

FAMED FRENCH ACTRESS
"The Divine Sarah" toured U.S. many times. In plays such as *L'Aiglon*, the great Bernhardt scored triumphs.

THEATRE PIONEER
David Belasco, a name synonymous with theatre, insisted on stage realism in such hits as *Du Barry*, 1902; *The Girl of the Golden West*, 1905; *The Easiest Way.*

ANNA PAVLOVA, Prima Ballerina of international fame, made the first of her tours of America in 1911, under the aegis of the impressario Diaghilev, after she had achieved a fantastic reputation in the Imperial Russian Ballet. Her performance as the "Swan" in the classic ballet *Swan Lake* was hailed as the "greatest ever seen" and still ranks high.

A SLICE OF LIFE in 1912 saw brother and sister John and Ethel Barrymore *(l.)* in their first leading roles together. Ethel had been a stage favorite since her performance as Mme. Trentoni in *Captain Jinks of the Horse Marines* in 1901. John's important roles lay in the future. Third member of the famous theatrical family was brother Lionel.

MARY PICKFORD, 1912
Known only as "the girl with the golden curls," Biograph Studio was forced to reveal her identity and start star system after *The New York Hat.*

GEORGE BARNES, 1903
Spectators screamed when George Barnes fired pistol at camera in *The Great Train Robbery*, the first movie which utilized a connected story.

FIRST MOVIES APPEAR

Early years of the century see birth and rapid growth of film industry

The movies were already taking shape as an embryonic industry in 1900. Edison's Kinetoscope, the peep show through which one person could view a strip of film, had been supplanted in 1896 by Armat's Vitascope which projected the film on a screen. Little equipment was needed to make the early films. Scenes were taken from life, and were filmed on the street, with bystanders taking part.

The movie industry began to grow rapidly between 1903 and 1908. The business of filming a picture became more complex. In the industry, there evolved many specialized jobs. The public's appetite for the new medium drew hundreds of enterprising men into the field and saw companies like Biograph, Kalem and Essanay manufacture pictures as fast as they could.

Others like Carl Laemmle, William Fox and the Warner Brothers bought projectors and showed the films in tents and improvised theatres. Public demand for novelty was met by constant advances by the filmmakers. Simple actions of human beings gave way to stories with plot. Close-ups and movement by the camera were introduced. By 1914, movies were becoming big business.

EARLY THEATERS
Early years of the movies were not without trial. Exhibitors had to improvise theaters *(above, right)* while the producers were caught in a morass of litigation over patents and fled to California.

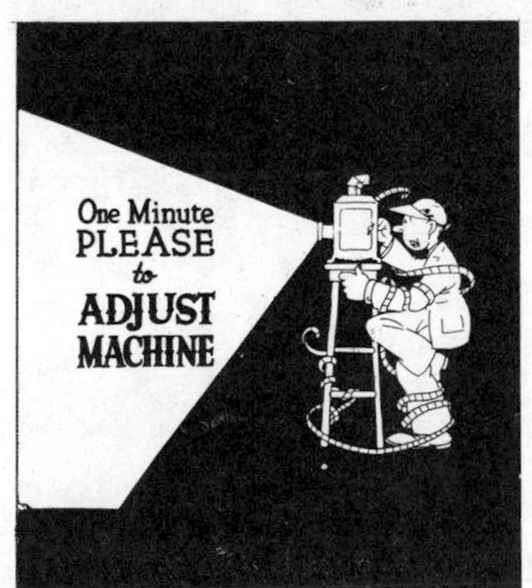

THE AUDIENCE HAD TO READ
Among the limitations of the early movies was the necessity of carrying on a stream of card explanations to the audience. On Oct. 6, 1927 Warner Brothers presented *The Jazz Singer* starring Al Jolson, the first feature length film with speech and music to be produced by any company.

DIRECTOR DE MILLE
Showman Cecil B. De Mille (seated on running board) fled to California seeking a good climate. He was the first to produce feature length movies. His *Squaw Man* (1913) established Hollywood as new industry center.

AMERICANS AND MUSIC

Golden Age in opera, sentimental ballads and pianolas in the home

Group singing of popular ballads was a widespread form of entertainment at the turn of the century. Young and old joined in singing such sentimental songs as *A Bird in a Gilded Cage*, *Tell Me, Pretty Maiden*, and *In the Good Old Summertime*, while barbershop quartets spent many hours perfecting their renditions of *Sweet Adeline*.

The taste of the average American for classical music was largely undeveloped at the turn of the century. The music of the masters was seldom heard outside of a few large cities, and the possession of a box at the 18-year-old Metropolitan Opera House was chiefly important as a measure of social position.

In 1901 there were only thirteen major orchestras in the country. Boston and Philadelphia were soon to challenge New York's standing as the nation's music center. The phase of music which flourished most vigorously was the opera, which was enjoying its "Golden Age" of great singers and conductors.

Those who supported the nation's musical life were little interested in the work of the American musician. Fame and fortune belonged to European artists who were imported to satisfy musical desires in the United States. Some Americans Europeanized their names.

In 1900 Ignace Jan Paderewski attempted to aid the unrecognized American composer by setting up a fund of $10,000 from which a prize of $1,000 was given every three years to a worthy native composer. *The Star Song* by Horatio Parker won him the first award in 1901.

The turn of the century saw the piano make enormous gains in popularity, with the battered upright becoming almost a household staple. Newest craze was the player-piano or "pianola," which swept the country between 1900 and 1920 before the hey-day of the phonograph.

RAGTIME became the national craze when Irving Berlin *(above)* introduced his hit song *Alexander's Ragtime Band* in 1912 and set all-time records.

CONDUCTOR of eight memorable seasons at the Met, Arturo Toscanini *(l.)*, is shown with General Manager Gatti Casazza, who brought him from Italy in 1928, and soprano Geraldine Farrar.

OPERETTAS of Victor Herbert dominated the Broadway stage from 1900 to 1910, included such favorites as *The Red Mill*, *Babes in Toyland* and *Naughty Marietta*, his greatest hit.

FIGHTING serious competition from Oscar Hammerstein *(above)* Met bought his Manhattan Opera House, and by contract, prohibited him from producing opera in New York City.

FARRAR AND CARUSO

Two stars of the Golden Age at the Met were the lovely Geraldine Farrar, idol of American womanhood after her debut as Juliette in 1906, and Enrico Caruso. He made his debut Nov. 23, 1903 and was an instant success. The golden-voiced Italian tenor symbolized the magic of operatic music.

MODERNIST HENRI MATISSE UPSETS THE U.S. MORALISTS
"The Beasts" was the term angrily applied to the "moderns" who exhibited side by side with established artists at the New York Armory Show (1913). Paintings such as Henri Matisse's *Odalisque (above)* attempted to create design rather than photographic likeness, shocked critics and moralists. "The Armory show is *pathological!* It is hideous!" said the *New York Times.*

ARTIST OF THE MODERN SCHOOL
Prim Victorianism vied with shocking radicalism. John Sloan, who had served his apprenticeship as a magazine illustrator, distressed many of the critics.

Turmoil in Art World of U.S.A.

Public undecided in battle of modernists

The opportunity for art appreciation in America was largely restricted to the wealthy who acquired art collections in their own homes in the 1900 era. There were galleries only in large cities and these were so hampered by lack of funds that they failed to give the public adequate sampling of the art of the day. Most Americans had little opportunity to see great masterpieces and failed to form opinions in the clash between conservative and modern schools.

Enthusiasm expressed itself in unprecedented attendance at art exhibits of the great expositions of the period, suggesting the average American's hunger for art experience.

Most accepted American artists worked abroad, fostering the preachings of the academy that to be good, art must be European. Those who remained at home became the vanguard of a true American art.

AMERICAN IMPRESSIONIST
Mother and Child by Mary Cassatt (1845-1926) depicts a theme frequently utilized by this artist, an admirer of Degas and Manet.

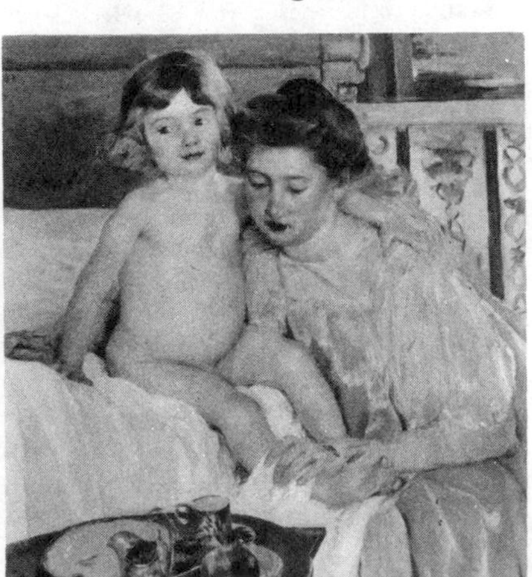

NOTED AMERICAN ARTIST SPURNS FOREIGN INFLUENCE
Rebelling against accepted standards for art and artists, Winslow Homer refused to study or work abroad. In rigid seclusion he painted such canvases as *Gulf Stream*, above. This painting sold to the Metropolitan Museum of Art for $5,000 in 1910. Within 20 years, similar canvases sold for over ten times this amount.

America Reads Romance, Religion

Era of prolific activity

Romance, morality, sentiment and religion were the literary subjects which sold in turn-of-the-century America. The simple homilies of Harold Bell Wright and Gene Stratton Porter stayed in demand while Charles Shelton's *In His Steps* (1897) became the bestseller of the half century with more than 8 million copies.

Deeper channels of American writing were well represented by Mark Twain and Henry James. Upton Sinclair's bitter indictment of the packing industry, *The Jungle*, caused reforms to be instituted. Death ended the short career of Frank Norris in 1902. Theodore Dreiser had trouble publishing his *Sister Carrie*.

Overseas Rudyard Kipling continued to glorify the empire, and H. G. Wells pioneered in science-fiction. In France, the great realist, Emile Zola died in 1902. Classical ironist Anatole France composed some of his finest work, while Marcel Proust crystalized pre-war society in *Remembrance of Things Past*.

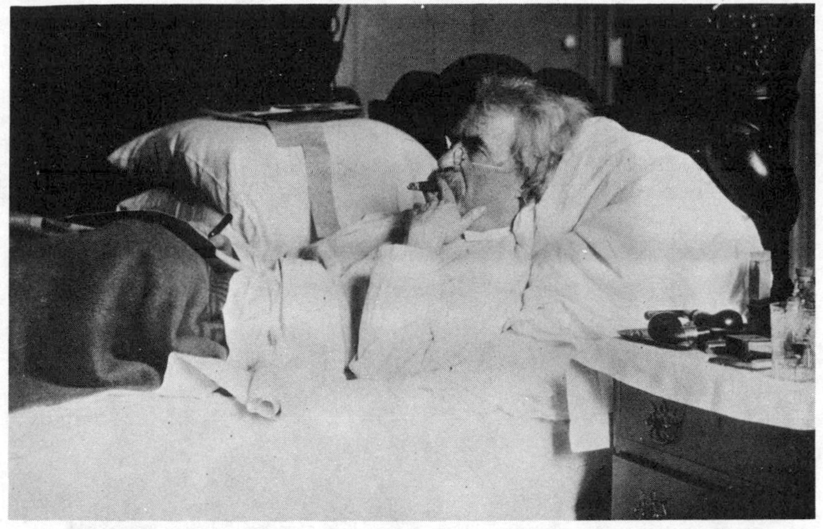

MARK TWAIN'S FAVORITE SPOT FOR WRITING WAS HIS BED

The irascible humorist, whose real name was Samuel L. Clemens, died in 1910. His classic *Huckleberry Finn* swelled the branch of American literature which was characterized by U.S. idiom and subject matter.

THE CHAMPION OF EMPIRE

British author Rudyard Kipling (1865-1936) produced numerous, immensely popular poems, novels and short stories dealing chiefly with life in India, where he was born, glorifying imperialism.

ELEGANT OSCAR WILDE

Century's end found him professing, like Baudelaire, Mallarme and others of the *fin de siècle* cult, a belief in art for the sake of art.

RUSSIAN NOVELISTS MEET

Maxim Gorki *(r.)* on a visit to Leo Tolstoy *(l.)* found the great novelist living the life of an agrarian mystic. The author of *War and Peace* and *Anna Karenina* died in 1910; Gorki lived on to become the first Soviet author, writing of revolt against society.

SUCCESSFUL AMERICAN NOVELIST

Jack London, the era's highest paid writer, foreshadowed the hard boiled school, is perhaps best known for his novels *The Sea Wolf* and *The Call of the Wild*, published in 1905.

AUTHOR OF POPULAR NOVELS

Teacher, newspaper woman, and Pulitzer prize winner in 1922, Willa Cather used material from her early days among immigrants who were pioneers in Nebraska, as in *My Antonia*.

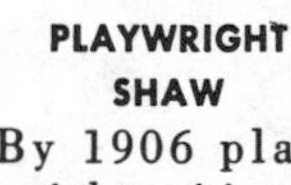

PLAYWRIGHT SHAW

By 1906 playwright, critic and Fabian Socialist George Bernard Shaw was already a recognized master of English prose. Well known for his many plays he wrote his best after 1912, among them *Pygmalion*.

EARTHQUAKE, FOLLOWED BY THREE DAYS OF FIRE, BRINGS DEATH AND DESTRUCTION TO SAN FRANCISCO IN 1906

Early in the morning of April 18, 1906 San Franciscans were awakened by the jolt of a severe earthquake, which started one of the most devastating fires in history. In three days an area of four square miles in the heart of the city was reduced to ashes and tangled debris. Looking down California Street from fashionable Nob Hill the gutted homes and buildings stand as mute testimony to the extent of the damage done by the quake and fire. The picture above was taken from the Fairmont Hotel, whose walls were left standing although the interior was completely burned out. Note Ferry Building, extreme upper left,, which withstood effect of the disaster. More than 450 people lost their lives in the destructive quake and fire.

DISASTERS

MESSINA, Sicily was a thriving and beautiful city until one of the most disastrous earthquakes ever recorded destroyed it totally in 1908. Fire and tidal waves followed the tremor that shook Sicily and Calabria, added to the tragedy which claimed the lives of 84,000 terrified people.

BLOWING STEADILY for 18 hours and reaching a velocity of 135 miles an hour, a violent West Indian hurricane piled up enormous waves engulfing the coastal city of Galveston, Texas in 1900, killing 5,000 and destroying property valued at $17,000,000. Higher sea wall saved the city in hurricane of 1915.

ERUPTION of Mount Pelee in 1902 completely destroyed St. Pierre, the leading city on the island of Martinique in the West Indies. Ashes fell from April 25 to May 8, when a disastrous fire swept the city, killing 40,000 people. Lone survivor of the disaster was an imprisoned convict.

MAIDEN VOYAGE of the White Star luxury liner, *Titanic*, ended disastrously on night of April 14, 1912, when the British liner struck an iceberg off Newfoundland. Carrying 1,513 persons to their death, many of them Americans, the *Titanic* had supposedly been non-sinkable. Half-filled lifeboats rescued only 711 survivors, picked up by the *Carpathia*. The terrible scene depicted above was painted by a German artist from vivid descriptions given by survivors.

STEAMSHIP FIRE
Steamship General Slocum became a raging inferno, killing 1,021 when it burst into flames going through Hell Gate, East River on June 15, 1904. The passengers were mainly women and children out on a Sunday school picnic.

VICTIMS TRAMPLED
Fire killed 602 patrons in Chicago's Iroquois Theatre on December 30, 1903. Most of the victims were trampled to death in the mass hysteria which accompanied the blaze. Burned out theater seats testify to the extreme heat.

BALTIMORE FIRE
In Baltimore's great fire of February 7, 1904 which started at the waterfront, 2,500 buildings were destroyed and damage was estimated at $150,000,000, largely due to the inadequacy of fire fighting equipment as shown.

CRIME
New weapons develop

THAW-WHITE CASE, 1906-1909, wrung dry by a growing sensational press, provided excitement for Americans. Millionaire Harry K. Thaw shot noted architect Stanford White atop Madison Square Garden, designed by White. Motive: intimacies with Thaw's girlish wife, Evelyn Nesbit *(above)*. Thaw's lawyer coined the term "brainstorm" during trial.

The science of criminology grew with the development of fingerprinting by Sir F. Galton and the work of Cesare Lombroso and Dr. Bertillon (see below). At the same time criminals were acquiring better weapons: automobiles, slicker mouthpieces, and better organization. The U.S. crime rate was already the highest in the world, and with organization, it was bound to rise.

DR. CRIPPEN *(r. arrow)*, first murderer trapped by wireless, and companion Ethel Le Neve *(l.)* leave the steamer *Montrose*, whose captain had radioed Quebec (1910). Dr. M. Bertillon (pictured with sample specifications) invented the system of recording a suspect's physical description.

NEW YORK'S UNDERWORLD of the turn of the century preferred the fabulous law firm of Howe and Hummel *(below)*, pioneers of organized crime. The shysterly firm managed to keep a gamut of criminals at work until 1907.

CARRIE NATION'S campaign against the evils of drink centered in Kansas where she was repeatedly jailed for hatchet forays on local saloons. Her target here is another evil, smoking.

DARING DANCERS of the Gay '90's were the Can-Can girls, tossing their skirts high in an "abandoned manner." Genteel ladies, who had "limbs" rather than legs, avoided knowledge of such "license."

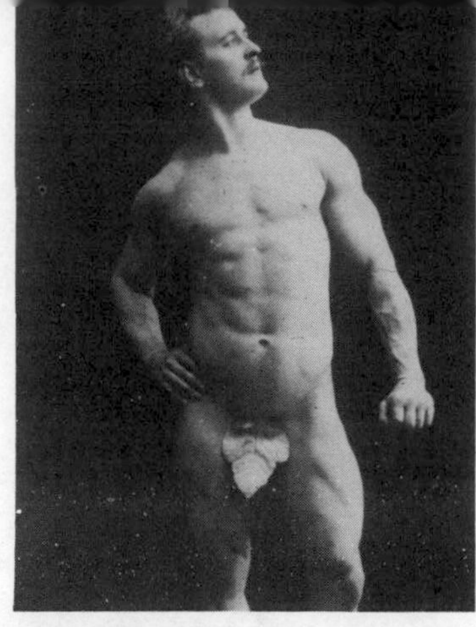

SANDOW, the strong man, became the secret passion of thousands of swooning women. A find of the Great Ziegfeld, he posed attired modestly in a fig leaf.

SUFFRAGETTES were seldom taken seriously in the early 1900's, despite their yearly increasing agitation for the right to vote.

IMMIGRANTS, carrying in their arms or on their backs all their worldly possessions arrived at Ellis Island by the thousands each year. Few spoke English but all believed in the miracle that was America.

YOUTH IN BLOOM was personified by the Gibson Girl, created by Charles Dana Gibson, famous artist and cartoonist. Each young girl tried to look as much like his drawings as nature would permit. Gibson used the foibles of high society, current fads and suffragettes as subject matter.

EXPONENT of free love was the dancer Isadora Duncan *(r., above)*, whose two illigimate children and free thinking scandalized the nation. Miser Hetty Green *(l., above)* became the nation's first great woman financial wizard. Despite her shabby appearance, she was worth millions of dollars.

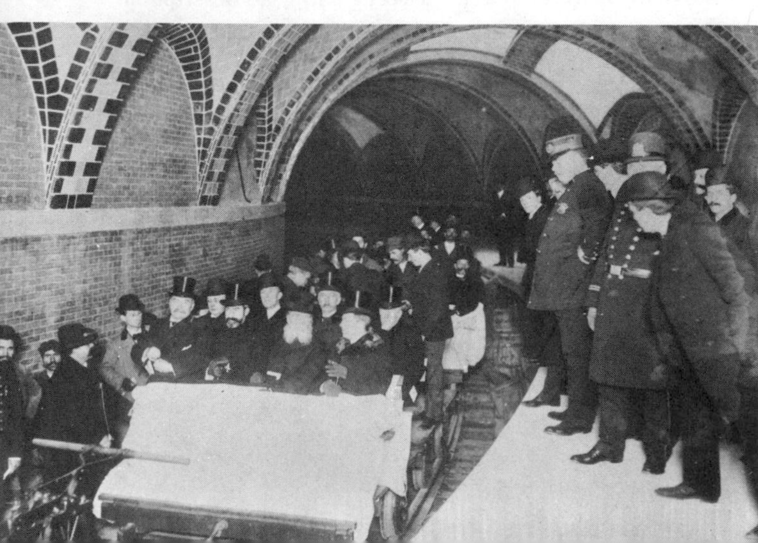

BUSINESS AND CIVIC leaders vied for a chance to ride on New York City's first subway, which opened in 1904. Construction began four years earlier. Cost of the subway was entirely defrayed by sale of bonds issued by the City of New York. Work on additional tubes started two years later.

LEADERS OF AMERICA'S ARISTOCRACY IN THE GILDED AGE

Society's "Four Hundred" first assembled in Mrs. William Astor's art gallery-ballroom in 1892. As 400 was the greatest number the room could accommodate, only that many were invited and the term was born. Mrs. Cornelius Vanderbilt II, another leader of society, was "At Home" in the stone mansion at right. Its wrought iron gate was opened for state occasions.

FAVORITE American outdoor sport for high society was the carriage drive. In Central Park, Mrs. O. P. M. Belmont reflects how the fashionably dressed matron should look while "taking the air." Mrs. Belmont later abandoned society to promote the cause of suffrage.

MARRIAGE of Consuela Vanderbilt *(l.)*, at 18 to the Duke of Marlborough produced angry editorials which thundered their protest against these "international mesalliances," and branded them as human sacrifices for a title. The marriage ended in divorce in 1921.

ACROSS TOWN from New York's marble mansions the city's slums were growing, fed by a continuing stream of immigrants and by the growing migration from the farm to the city. Large families lived in one room with no toilet or bathing facilities, often without a window.

MOST AMERICANS did not move in the luxurious atmosphere of the Astor and Vanderbilt set but were able to find enjoyment in their more simple pleasures. Family singing around the piano in the evenings brought happy moments to many, as it did to this group pictured at right.

FASHIONS were changing at the turn of the century, and by 1913 style had dictated a new freedom in women's clothing. Skirts were ankle length and loose back-interest was important. The popularity of the dusty automobile ride influenced the design of the duster and the sailor hat tied on with a scarf. The hobble skirt *(left)* was the rage of 1910, while the embroidered skirt topped with straight jacket was a hit in 1907. Swimming suits that could actually be worn in the water, although still too modestly confining for active swimming, became popular about 1910. A day at the beach became a holiday for the entire family about the same time, and weight guessing was a popular sport. Note how the woman at the left has gone to great trouble to protect herself from the sun, in an era still favoring pale complexions.

FIRST WORLD WAR

Imperialism and industrial expansion plunge Europe, then world into bloody conflict

Europe's uneasy peace was shattered by a shot at Sarajevo on June 28, 1914, when a Serbian-trained terrorist killed the heir to the Austrian throne. Assured of German support, Austria made unacceptable demands of Serbia. Russia, protecting the Serbs, ordered partial mobilization against Austria. That brought Germany in. In the first three days of August, Kaiser Wilhelm declared war on Russia, on its ally, France, and marched on neutral Belgium. London's lights blinked out. Europe was at war.

The Western Front, after the Germans were stopped at the Marne, settled down to a muddy stalemate. Both sides expended millions of men on a few miles of No Man's Land. But on the fluid Eastern Front Hindenburg's armies won the war's bloodiest fighting against Russian troops, some of whom went into battle unarmed until they could take weapons from the German dead.

RUSSIAN REVOLT

Early in 1917 the regime of Czar Nicholas, shaken by revolution and defeat, suddenly collapsed. The succeeding democratic Provisional Government, at first dominated by moderates, was taken over by the better disciplined Bolsheviks. Their exiled leader, Lenin, with German aid, came from Switzerland to lead what he hoped would be the Communist world revolution. To him the war was secondary. He negotiated a separate peace with Germany, releasing huge German armies for the Western Front.

In the U.S., President Wilson, reelected in 1916 on the slogan, "He Kept Us Out of War," had tried to steer a neutral course. With Britain controlling communication channels, the Allied case was far better publicized. Inept German diplomacy and violation of Belgium made a strong public impression. Overshadowing all other pro-Allied factors was German submarine warfare. Beginning with the sinking of the *Lusitania*, Americans had been recurrently shocked by U-boat attacks. Early in 1917 when Germany renewed its campaign of unrestricted submarine warfare, Wilson decided to abandon neutrality. On April 6, 1917, the President asked Congress for a declaration of war.

POSTERS extoled Military Service. Later Navy could boast, not one life lost at sea in transport maneuvers.

The Allies, fortified in 1918 by "Black Jack" Pershing's A.E.F., seized the offensive on all fronts. Austria, Turkey and Bulgaria capitulated. As the German home front rocked with mutiny, the Kaiser finally stepped down. A new German government was formed and in November requested an armistice. Thus after four years of battles involving 65 million men, of whom 57% were casualties, costing $350 billion and untold human misery, the war ended. The U.S., whose entry had broken the stalemate and was in that sense decisive, got off comparatively cheaply, losing 125,000 men. By contrast, Russia lost 1,700,000.

HOLLOW VICTORY

At the Versailles Peace Conference Wilson met a web of secret agreements and hard-headed politicians. His idealism made scant impression but he did succeed in writing into the treaty his cherished dream of a League of Nations. At home, meanwhile, Congressional leadership had fallen to isolationists. Wilson returned to carry the League issue to the people. Failing in that hope and in health, he lived only a few more years.

Among other casualties were four empires: Germany, Russia, Austria, Turkey; and a fifth, Britain, had been grievously bled. The U.S., however, had climbed to industrial supremacy, and many Americans, led by Wilson, felt that isolation was now impossible. Many, but not enough. For in repudiating its international responsibilities and rejecting the League of Nations the United States left the world's future in the hands of stricken, embittered and impoverished Europe.

★ ★ ★

HOPE OF THE WORLD for a just peace rested in the 28th President of the United States, Thomas Woodrow Wilson (1913-1920). During war, his plea for "peace without victory," based on his Fourteen Points, acting continually as a corroding factor, weakened the enemy's determination to fight. When in the Autumn of 1918 the Germans faced military defeat, they turned to Wilson, offering to accept his Fourteen Points as the basis of peace. Despite his world-wide popularity, Wilson's internationalism lost him support in an isolation-minded Congress, rejecting his League of Nations.

BACKGROUND OF WORLD WAR I

Assassination in Sarajevo ignites a powder train that explodes into war

Gavrilo Princip, Serbian terrorist, shot and killed Archduke Ferdinand of Austria and his wife in a street in Sarajevo on June 28, 1914. He was acting on behalf of a movement aimed at uniting the Southern Slavs under the banner of Serbia. Russia favored this movement but the Austria-Hungary leaders opposed it completely.

Austrian leaders, wanting to crush troublesome Serbia, presented an ultimatum with unacceptable terms. After the Serbian rejection, Austria on July 28 declared what she intended to be a local war, but Russia was bound by military alliances to Serbia and the Czar, against his own judgment, ordered a partial mobilization. When Germany, allied to Austria, began to mobilize, so did France, since she was committed by treaty to Russia.

On August 1 Germany declared war on Russia, and two days later on France. When German armies marched into Belgium, England, as a member of the Triple Entente, countered by declaring war on Germany on August 4.

In 1914 there were so many potential causes for war among the European nations that only a slight incident was needed as a spark to produce the explosion.

With military and industrial expansion of the Central Powers (Germany, Austria-Hungary and Italy), the balance of power in Europe had been broken. Germany's new navy made her a rival of England's hitherto undisputed leadership in world trade. The defeat of France by Prussia in 1870 had forced France to ally herself with Russia, while Russia's Pan-Slav policy clashed with Archduke Ferdinand's desire to annex the Southern Slavs and make Austria-Hungary a triple monarchy.

Now, with the assassination of a relatively unimportant Austrian nobleman, the world suddenly found itself committed to a war which European statesmen and soldiers had long been expecting and preparing for. Perhaps wise rulers could have avoided war, but European leadership was at an extremely low ebb.

Once begun, World War I lasted four years, involved almost every nation on the globe, and cost an estimated total of 11,093,500 deaths—a tragic loss to the world.

KAISER WILHELM II of Germany *(r., pointing)* was an enthusiastic militarist and made no effort to avoid the war. A grandchild of Queen Victoria, he had once boasted, "We can hold the sky on the top of German bayonets," but with the collapse of the German government and revolt of the navy in 1918, the Kaiser was forced to abdicate and flee to Holland.

FAMILY TIES linked England's King, Germany's Kaiser, Russia's Czar. George V of England (standing beside Edward VII and Duke of Windsor) and Kaiser Wilhelm were grandsons of Queen Victoria. During the war, King George made personal appearances and visits to the front lines in France to encourage the British. He was a cousin of Czar Nicholas II of Russia (shown with his son) who, although he knew that his country was unprepared for war, yielded to the pressure of his officials and ordered mobilization only a month after the assassination of Archduke Franz Ferdinand at Sarajevo. The Czar and his family were executed by Revolutionists in 1918. George V ruled until his death in 1936.

ASSASSINATION of Austrian Archduke Franz Ferdinand *(above, pointing)* took place on June 28, 1914 at Sarajevo. The assassin was Gavrilo Princip (shown under arrest) who was acting on behalf of the Serbian society "Union or Death," a terrorist organization. Viennese officials professed to be convinced of the complicity of the Serbian government. Although they failed to find conclusive evidence, the Austrian crown council favored war against Serbia, delivered an ultimatum to Belgrade on July 23 while assuring Russia that no Serbian territory would be annexed. The Russian council decided on military action if Serbia were attacked, and with Austria's declaration of war (July 28) World War I began.

SIR EDWARD GREY, hoping to avoid a war, proposed mediation on the Austro-Serbian issue. The Kaiser called Grey's offer "British insolence," and Austria also refused. Said Grey sadly, "The lamps are going out all over Europe."

GERMAN CHANCELLOR Theobald von Bethmann-Hollweg lost support of both political and military men, earned the first vote of censure ever passed on a chancellor by the Reichstag because of his inadequacy during World War I.

RAYMOND POINCARE served as President of France from 1913 to 1920 (shown *r.* with King Victor Emmanuel III of Italy). Aware of the threat of war, he tried to re-establish the balance of power in 1913 by system of alliances.

ABDUL HAMID II was ruler of the Ottoman Empire from 1876 to 1909. He opposed attempts at reform, prorogued first Turkish parliament in an effort to retain absolute power. He was deposed by "Young Turks" (1909), died in exile.

RUSSIAN PEOPLE fought bravely under leadership of Czar and his officers, despite political unrest. Russia's Czars, instead of granting civil liberties and government reforms, concentrated on eliminating liberal leaders. Russia had already undergone general strikes and localized revolts aimed at winning concessions from the government. Disastrous war losses of men and territory, including Poland, Finland, Bessarabia, other Baltic states, and grave economic problems sped Revolution.

"THE BIG THREE" CONDUCTED OVER-ALL SUPERVISION OF GERMAN FORCES
Hindenburg and Ludendorff (*l.* and *r.* of Kaiser) functioned admirably as a team. Hindenburg's quiet strength enabled him to restrain impetuous, brilliant Ludendorff. As the war advanced they became national heroes and actual rulers of Germany.

WESTERN FRONT

The fight on the Western Front began when German armies invaded neutral Belgium on Aug. 4, 1914 as a northeast route into France. Heroic Belgian resistance gave French time to draw up battleline at the Marne, where the first battle was fought.

1915: Germans attacked French who had been reinforced by British, Dominion and Colonial troops. Battles of Ypres, Artois and Champagne cost many lives, caused little change in battle fronts.

1916: Bloody battle of Verdun, despite more than million lives lost, made little change in lines.

1917: Britain lifted burden from French by sending large numbers of troops to fronts. After setbacks, Al-

FRENCH HEROES PETAIN AND JOFFRE COMMANDED OUTNUMBERED FRENCH ARMY
Petain (*l.*) and Joffre (*r.*) were national heroes after Allied success at battles of the Marne and Verdun. On the strength of his reputation, Petain dominated the French War Council between World Wars I and II, resisted every attempt at modernization, was responsible for French lack of preparation against Germans in 1939.

THE LAST "GENTLEMAN'S WAR"
British "Tommies" give water (*below*) to a German "Jerry." Similar acts were common at the various fronts in W.W. I.

HAIG ORIGINATED "POPPY DAY"
Haig succeeded Field Marshal French as commander of British troops. For his part in breaking Hindenburg Line, Sir Douglas was given the title of Earl.

ALLIED HELP ALMOST TOO LATE
General Cadorna built Italian army into fighters, failed to realize an army can suffer from battle fatigue. Italians were desperate for the promised Allied aid.

GERMAN ARMY ADVANCES TO A POSITION ONLY 18 MILES FROM PARIS ➧
Taxis sent by General Gallieni, military Governor of Paris, helped in moving French troops to the front during the desperate early days of the German invasion. It was actually General Gallieni who was the real savior of Paris, since it was he who mapped out the strategy used by General Joffre to win the Battle of the Marne.

GERMANY'S NEW HORROR WEAPON ➧
Poison gas was used for the first time by Germans at Ypres. Failure to take advantage of the resulting confusion was one of the major mistakes of the German high command. Clouds of the gas often blew back into German lines.

lies decided to wait for American troops before renewing attacks on Germans, who had been heavily reinforced by release of Eastern troops after the Russian Revolution and the Russo-German armistice.

During these three years, Germany had lost her colonial empire to the Allied forces. Her submarine warfare had failed to blockade England, and in 1914 a fleet under Count von Spee, was defeated by the British in the Battle of the Falkland Islands.

The only major sea battle between German and British navies occurred off Jutland on May 30, 1916. The German navy, except submarines, then retired until the Armistice.

ITALY-AUSTRIA FRONT ➧
Italy, after being persuaded by generous Allied promises, attacked Austria in May, 1915. In two years of fighting against Austrian mountain troops *(r.)* Italians gained only ten miles, suffered great losses.

IRISH REBELS GIVE ALLIES A STAB IN BACK
The Irish Revolution broke out in April, 1916, when the Sinn Fein (Irish underground), with the help of Germany, revolted. Sir Roger Casement, caught in the act of leaving a German U-boat, was executed along with many others. Suppression of revolt was severe.

ABORTIVE SOMME OFFENSIVE INTRODUCES NEW WEAPONS
Tanks and flame throwers were used for the first time by the British during the battle of the Somme. Total losses at Somme were 400,000 British and Dominion troops, 200,000 French, over 400,000 Germans.

1917 OFFENSIVES
Arras *(l.)* Aisne and Champagne were bloody, futile battlefields. Germany repulsed all attacks, Allies awaited arrival of the U.S. forces.

PRISONERS
Shown *(r.)* are French prisoners in Germany. The greatest number of prisoners were Russian, Austrian and Italian.

BATTLE OF TANNENBERG began when the Russians under Samsonov invaded East Prussia and were met by Germans led by Generals von Ludendorff and von Hindenburg. Fighting took place Aug. 26-30, 1914; resulted in annihilation of two Russian corps, reduction of three others to half strength, the capture of 100,000 Russians, and suicide of Gen. Samsonov.

HEROIC SERBIANS succeeded, with help of Montenegro, in repelling invasions. The Austro-German campaign in Serbia was strengthened when the Central Powers secured the aid of Bulgarians, who crossed Serbian frontier on Oct. 11, 1915. Allies had failed to supply Serbs with modern equipment, and by November they were forced to retreat into Albania.

EASTERN FRONT

In 1914 Russians and Serbs withstood Austrian offensives, but Germans struck them mortal blows at Tannenberg and Masurian Lakes.

1915: Despite initial successes against Austrians, Russians were finally thrown back with German help and Warsaw was occupied. By Sept., Russia had lost almost a million men, all Poles and Lithuanians.

1916: Russian offensives and Austro-German counter-offensives cost a million men without military gains. Russia was demoralized by losses. On Aug. 27 Rumania declared war on Austria and was occupied in January of 1917 by German forces.

1917: Russian forces completely demoralized by internal revolution. Greece entered war against Germany.

GERMAN MARSHAL von Mackensen *(l.)* was master of the offensive, enjoyed great successes on the Eastern Front, at Galicia, Brest-Litovsk and Pinsk. He overran Serbia, invaded Rumania. Russian Grand Duke Nicholas Nicolaievich *(r.)* as Supreme Russian Commander was forced to carry out strategy devised by others. In 1915 he was relieved, sent as viceroy to the Caucasus. Czar assumed command.

ALLIES WITHDRAW, TURKS WIN

Dardanelles and Gallipoli, Turkey, were attacked by Allies in attempt to open route to Russia. Campaign combined naval bombardments with troop landing attacks on Turkish forts *(l.)*. Allies lost 6 battleships and casualties were 250,000 on each side. After 10 months, Allies withdrew and abandoned attack, leaving Russia cut off from Allied shipping of needed supplies. Failure of this plan caused resignation of First Lord of the Admiralty Churchill.

BRILLIANT BRITISH STRATEGIST GENERAL ALLENBY ENTERS JERUSALEM

Unarmed and on foot in accordance with Biblical prophecy, conqueror Allenby entered Jerusalem Dec. 8, 1917, almost 1000 years after the Crusaders. His leadership of Anglo-Egyptian army foiled Turkish attempts to take the Suez Canal, lifeline of the British Empire. Allenby's Egyptian campaigns are classic examples of the use of mounted troops and of the value of mobility as a strategic weapon. In both his great battles against the Turks he completely deceived enemy as to his plans, thus had decisive advantage.

THE WAR IN ASIA AND AFRICA

The Ottoman Empire entered the war on the side of the Central Powers on Nov. 2, 1914, when her fleet bombarded Russian ports on the Black Sea. Britain retaliated by annexing Egypt and Cyprus. At the same time, Russia launched an unsuccessful attack on Turkey.

1915: The Turks, fighting on several fronts, failed in their attempt to wrest the Suez Canal from British. Actions by both sides in Mesopotamia and Persia were indecisive. In the Caucasus the Turkish offensive resulted in heavy casualties.

1916: Allied defeat at the Dardanelles prevented aid from reaching Czarist troops, thus helping to precipitate the Russian Revolution. Parts of Palestine and Mesopotamia, including Baghdad, were occupied by the Allies. The ill-equipped Ottoman troops began to buckle.

TURKS GERMAN ALLIES

Anti-German sentiment developed when Turkish troops *(l.)* joined Germans in joint operation. Germans took dominating attitude, treated Turkey as their colony.

However, Germans gave Turks valuable leadership and military aid on the fronts.

BEST JUNGLE FIGHTER

Gen. von Lettow-Vorbeck (on horse) earned Allied admiration by defending German East Africa for four years with native troops. Battle terrain was mostly jungle.

On his surrender, 13 days after Armistice, Allies permitted him to retain his sword.

JAPANESE CAPTURE GERMAN COLONY

Japan attacked Germany's major Chinese colony, Kiaochow, in 1914. German governor, Meyer-Walldeck, put up heroic resistance with his 6000 men, making his stand in Tsingtao, which was finally occupied by the Japanese *(r.)*. Germany lost her Pacific islands to Australia, New Zealand, Great Britain and Japan.

ADEQUATE DEFENSES to forestall any attack on the U.S. were the aim of President Wilson. In December 1915 he asked Congress to increase nation's armed strength, continued to hope war might be avoided. To arouse the public to possible danger, the President and Gen. Leonard Wood, a great advocate of preparedness, led a demonstration in N. Y.

GERMANY ANNOUNCED in February 1915 that she would destroy all merchant ships caught in English waters. On May 7 off the Irish coast, the *Lusitania* was sunk with the loss of 1,198 lives. including many Americans. She was carrying a part-cargo of small arms and munitions. Stiff U.S. notes of protest to Berlin were sent by new Sec'y. of State Lansing.

U. S. GOES TO WAR

Production shifts into high gear, women enlist, millions sail for France

With great parades and grand slogans America entered World War I. Idealistic President Wilson, the advocate of "Peace without Victory" and a return to the status quo changed his attitude to favor just compensation for the oppressed nations. He effectively publicized the Allies' fight for democracy and became the idol of Europe.

When the U.S. declared war her armed forces totaled only 378,000, and until the establishment of convoys, the movement of troops to Europe was slow. Meanwhile, conscription brought millions of Americans into the war.

Germany, after making powerful gains against the Italians, transferred more than a million additional troops to the Western Front in an attempt to break the deadlock there. She also intensified her submarine warfare, and the number of Allied ships sunk jumped threefold to total over 850,000 tons a month. However, the Allies' development of the convoy system of shipping and their great increase in shipbuilding capacity finally cancelled Germany's advantage on the Atlantic.

The Allies' loss of Russia and their setbacks on the Italian front were more than offset by the tremendous industrial capacity of the U.S. and the one million American troops in Europe by July of 1918.

By the end of 1917 the most pressing Allied problem was the unification of command; since the beginning their forces had been hamstrung by lack of coordinated planning.

ANTI-WAR GROUPS were a natural development in U.S., where one-fifth of the population was of Germanic descent. German propagandists worked to keep America neutral while German agents tried to persuade Congress to embargo munitions shipments to Allies. Failing this, mysterious fires and explosions occured, including "Black Tom" disaster in N.J.

DECLARATION OF WAR with Germany was made by the U.S. on April 6, 1917 following President Wilson's plea "to make the world safe for democracy." U.S. had severed diplomatic relations with Germany on February 3 following German notification of unrestricted submarine warfare. During February and March several American ships were sunk.

SEC. OF WAR BAKER DRAWS FIRST DRAFT NUMBER
Drafting of U.S. troops began July, 1917 with 3,706,544 in Class I—subject to immediate call. Tennessee earned name of "Volunteer State" by filling military quotas entirely from volunteers. By September of 1918, 24,000,000 men were registered and at the Armistice armed forces totaled 4,791,172.

WAR MEANT MUD FOR THE U.S. ARMY DOUGHBOYS
Volunteers and draftees were trained at sixteen camps with capacities of 48,000 each. These had been constructed in a period of only four months in various parts of U.S. Because of the acute shortage of U.S. officers, Allied officers helped to train the men both in the home camps and in Europe.

PATRIOTIC APPEALS
Posters helped in enlistments, in saving food, warning against saboteurs, and in selling Liberty Bonds.

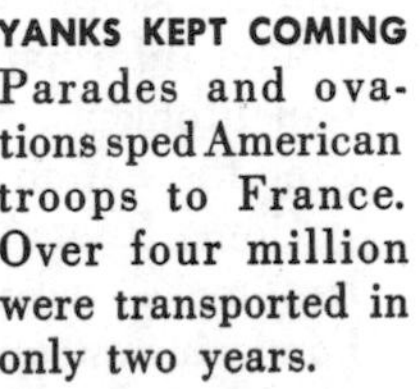

YANKS KEPT COMING
Parades and ovations sped American troops to France. Over four million were transported in only two years.

HEAVILY CONVOYED TROOPSHIPS TRANSPORTED ARMY
Sailings of troops to France aboard former enemy ships such as the German liner *Leviathan* were widely publicized at the beginning of the war. Although the first contingents to reach France with Gen. Pershing were very small, they helped boost French morale, badly shaken by tremendous losses.

BAPTISM BY FIRE BY U.S. SOLDIERS IN FRANCE
Heavy casualties suffered by first U.S. troops under fire in 1917 were due mainly to inexperience. After this the troops were trained behind the front lines by seasoned officers. Arrival of 175,000 U.S. troops in Europe by end of 1917 helped to tip the balance of war in favor of the Allies.

FIFTH AVENUE during the War was a pageant of uniforms, banners and flags as in the Liberty Loan parade shown here. Avenue was a show place in which to keep before the public the many branches of endeavor necessary to the success of the war effort. Secretary of the Treasury McAdoo appealed directly to the people in his sale of war bonds, rather than follow usual procedure of issuing bonds to bankers who would then offer them to the public.

HOME FRONT SHARES BURDEN OF WAR

Americans unite behind Wilson to make world safe for democracy

Wilson's battle cry, "The world must be made safe for democracy," and the U.S. declaration of war dissolved internal dissension and America entered the war in the spirit of a crusade. Facing the task of building and training a citizen army, Selective Service began conscripting men from 21 through 30, eventually registering those from 18 to 45, while the Council of National Defense mobilized material resources and productive power.

Bernard Baruch's War Industries Board controlled all manufacturing; Herbert Hoover's Food Administration stressed conservation, changed eating habits; Harry A. Garfield's Fuel Administration directed the use of coal and oil supplies; George Creel headed a Committee on Public Information. In the face of mounting transportation problems, Secretary of the Treasury McAdoo took over the nation's railroads.

Home front Americans were "hooverizing" with meatless meals, wheatless days, and buying Liberty Loan bonds in amounts that totaled only $3 billion less than the total cost of the war ($21.8 billion). Aided by Felix Frankfurter's War Labor Policies Board, labor achieved the eight-hour day and equal pay for women workers.

MADAME ERNESTINE SCHUMANN-HEINK, great Wagnerian opera singer, worked tirelessly for the Allied cause. Her sons, in a dramatic illustration of war's cruelty, fought in both German and Allied armies. During the war, Americans felt that almost anything German was subversive.

SUPPORTING LIBERTY LOAN, Senators Thomas Walsh, Warren Harding (who was to be the next president) and Frank Kellogg (later the author of famous peace pact) are first, third and fourth in a bond-buying queue at the Capitol. Vice-President Thomas R. Marshall mans the sales booth.

MOVIE STARS Charlie Chaplin and Douglas Fairbanks, Sr. were among the most successful "bond salesmen." Others; W. S. Hart, Mary Pickford, Marie Dressler.

"THE CASTLES" were a famous husband-wife dance team. Vernon Castle, RFC., was killed early in the war. His lovely widow, Irene, was active home-front worker.

PROPAGANDA MACHINERY created by George Creel was one of the major successes of the mobilization. As head of the Committee on Public Information, Creel *(l.)* had the job of stirring up national enthusiasm for the all-out effort and mobilizing and unifying the public mind. America's response was tremendous, reflected in huge sale of Liberty Loan bonds.

FOOD ADMINISTRATOR Herbert Hoover *(r.)* taught the nation to "hooverize" their meals with meatless dishes and wheatless days, thus releasing food for shipment overseas to the European front. The American housewives cooperated with his efforts to reduce food consumption at home, saved 500,000 tons of sugar, conserved fats and oils necessary to manufacture munitions.

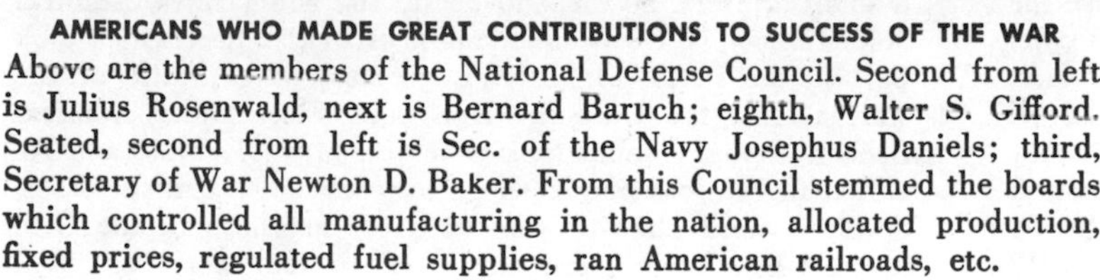

AMERICANS WHO MADE GREAT CONTRIBUTIONS TO SUCCESS OF THE WAR
Above are the members of the National Defense Council. Second from left is Julius Rosenwald, next is Bernard Baruch; eighth, Walter S. Gifford. Seated, second from left is Sec. of the Navy Josephus Daniels; third, Secretary of War Newton D. Baker. From this Council stemmed the boards which controlled all manufacturing in the nation, allocated production, fixed prices, regulated fuel supplies, ran American railroads, etc.

WOMEN WORKED in war plants, proved to be equal to men in manual dexterity and patience as well as patriotism. Their numerous activities during the war as members of the armed forces and as industrial or office workers helped to hasten the passage of the 19th Amendment which granted woman suffrage.

AMERICAN TROOPS *(above,* in the Argonne) finally began to arrive in Europe in large numbers in 1918, and shifted balance of war to favor the Allies. French and British forces were still fighting on separate fronts independently of each other. On March 21-April 5 the Germans under von Ludendorff launched their great offensive against British, but French reinforcements stopped his advances.

SUCCESS followed appointment of Marshal Foch (April, 1918) as Supreme Allied Commander. Although he had no real power to coordinate the armies, he proved to be an excellent mediator. Allied cooperation soon forced German retreat, and doughboys began liberating occupied French territory.

QUEEN OF SPIES, Dutch Mata Hari, posing as an Oriental dancer, spied for German intelligence service. She was caught and executed by the French after a scandalous trial which involved many prominent people.

BRITISH archaeologist T. E. Lawrence (1888-1935) was able to unite the Arabs against the Turks by promising them independence. After the war, Allied refusal to honor his promises and fulfill agreement broke his heart and health.

MYSTERY MAN of Europe, Sir Basil Zaharoff, sold munitions to the highest bidder and supplied either Germans or Allies impartially. A Greek by origin, Zaharoff acted as the representative of Vickers, Schneider, and Krupp.

WAR AT SEA

GERMAN SHIPS disguised as merchant vessels preyed on Allied and neutral shipping. Most famous of these were the *Meowe*, *Wolff*, and the *Seeadler*, which was under the command of Count von Luckner *(above, l.)*. A legendary figure, he never sank a ship without due warning, and carried all prisoners to neutral ports. At Scapa Flow in the Orkney Islands where the German fleet was interned after surrendering to the British at Rosyth, the fleet was scuttled by its crews by order of German Admiral Reuter on June 21, 1919 *(center)*. Fleet consisted of 10 battleships, 9 armed cruisers, 8 small cruisers, 50 torpedo boats, 102 submarines. Admiral John Jellicoe *(r.)* was commander of British fleet which took part in the Battle of Jutland, greatest naval battle of the war, against the German High Seas Fleet under Admiral Scheer. Actual combat took place on May 31, 1916, and resulted in the loss of six ships by each side. British losses, however, were almost twice as great as those of the Germans, when losses were computed in tonnage.

WAR IN THE AIR

CAPTAIN Eddie Rickenbacker *(c.,* with other aviators of the 94th U.S. Pursuit Squadron) was America's leading ace. Others were Floyd Bennett, Billy Mitchell, Doug Campbell. Rickenbacker shot down a total of 25 enemy planes.

TANKS AND WARPLANES were new products of World War I. When British engineer Ernest Swington's tank projects were rejected by Asquith and Lord Kitchener, he went to Winston Churchill. First tanks held four guns, eight men.

ACE HERMANN GOERING COMMANDED GERMAN FLYERS
"Red Knight of Germany" was name given to Baron Alfred von Richtofen *(upper l.)* who painted plane red, shot down 80 Allied planes. French pilot Rene Fonek *(c.)* was credited with 75 planes, Canadian William Bishop *(r.)* with 72. Hermann Goering *(l.)* led Flying Circus Squadron after Richtofen's death. Refusing to surrender after the armistice, Goering fled to Sweden where he worked as a mechanic.

HAND GRENADES and throw-mines are being loaded on a German Fokker. Anthony Fokker, designer of these planes, was a Dutchman, tried to sell his war plane to Holland but failed. Then he built them for the Kaiser.

ALLIED BALLOON is hit by a German Fokker. These balloons were filled with highly inflammable hydrogen. They were used by both sides for observation purposes on the Western Front.

PLANES IN WORLD WAR I

GERMAN FOKKER TRI-PLANE

U.S.A. PLANE, THE SPAD

FRENCH BOMBER

BRITISH BRISTOL FIGHTER

AIR RAID alarm sounds in London. Allied air raids concentrated on Rhine industrial centers, but London was the main target for the Germans. Total casualties: 1,316 killed, 3,000 injured.

COMMANDER of U.S. expeditionary forces, General Pershing *(l.)* lacked warmth but had extraordinary administrative ability and talent for getting things done. It was he who kept American Army separate, resisted French plan to absorb it into their forces.

MARSHAL Ferdinand Foch signed the Armistice for Allies at Compiegne. Hostilities ceased November 11 at 11 a.m. Of his job as Allied coordinator Foch, hailed as a victorious leader, said later, "I was no more than conductor of an orchestra . . . say that I beat time well."

ORIGINAL "Big Berthas" were 42 cm. howitzers made in Austria-Hungary and used by Germany to batter the forts at Liège and Namur in 1914. The name was later applied to the German 21 cm. guns used to shell Paris in 1918. These guns had a range of 75 miles, the greatest that had ever been attained. World War I brought about many changes in the forms of artillery and in its uses. The mortar, which had been considered obsolete, made its reappearance with the new, close-range fighting for position; gas and smoke shells were introduced, and the ranges of all weapons increased.

VON LUDENDORFF struck for the second time at Ypres on April 9, 1918 as part of a great German offensive. He broke through British lines after heavy bombardment. Ypres was left in ruins *(above)*. Due to lack of reinforcements he was unable to follow up advantage. His attack at Aisne was stopped 37 mi. from Paris. After this, German losses were greater than the intake of recruits, and military strength slowly waned.

WILSON'S 14 POINTS

1. Open covenants with all nations.
2. Freedom of navigation.
3. Removal of economic barriers.
4. Reduction of armaments.
5. Adjustment of colonial claims.
6. Evacuation of Russia, free determination of own political policy.
7. Evacuation of Belgium.
8. Evacuation of French territory.
9. Redrawing of Italy's frontiers.
10. Freedom for Austro-Hungarian minorities.
11. Evacuation of Rumania, Montenegro, access to sea for Serbia.
12. Turkish, other nationalities of Ottoman Empire given sovereignity. Dardanelles opened to all nations.
13. Independence for Poland.
14. A league of nations to be formed.

PRESIDENT WILSON in an address to Congress on Jan. 8, 1918, had set forth Fourteen Points he felt essential to a just and lasting peace. In the autumn of 1918, when Germany and Austria-Hungary realized they were defeated, they agreed (October 4, 1918) to accept the Fourteen Points as a basis for peace negotiations. Wilson's idealism and insistence upon justice as the necessary basis for a peace settlement won him great prestige among the peoples of both the Allied and the enemy nations, but the leaders of the Allied nations were reluctant to accept his liberality as a model because they feared that it might lead to the loss of the advantages of their costly victory. Conflicting views and interests at the Peace Conference soon forced the Fourteen Points into the background of the negotiations.

NIKOLAI LENIN was the master-mind of the Bolsheviks, and it was he who recognized the opportunity and took advantage of the split in the Kerensky government with the Bolshevik *coup d'etat* which resulted in formation of The Union of Soviet Socialist Republics. Several members of Lenin's family had been executed because of their anti-Czarist activities. Among these was Lenin's daughter, who had joined a revolutionary students' society. Lenin's real name was Vladimir Ulianov. He had spent many years in exile, directing the activities of his party from outside Russia.

RUSSIAN REVOLUTION

Lenin overthrows Kerensky as Bolsheviks found first communist state

Widespread hunger, corruption and inefficiency in government increased discontent in Russia during the war. In March 1917 strikes and hunger riots broke out in Petrograd. Czar Nicholas II ordered the garrison to fire on rioters and dissolved the Duma, but the troops revolted and the Duma ignored him. The Czar found himself abandoned. On March 15 he abdicated, and the Romanov dynasty was over.

A provisional government was formed by liberal Prince Lvov. Royalist regiments in the army sided with the Duma and Lvov's government while peasants, troops and workers supported the Petrograd Soviet, the strongest of the rebel factions.

Prince Lvov was replaced by Kerensky, who tried a new drive against Central Powers, which failed. Meanwhile, taking advantage of the new freedom of speech, press, assembly and organization won by the Revolution in March, the Bolsheviks agitated furiously with promises of *peace* for soldiers, *bread* for workers, and *land* for peasants.

On November 6, 1917, with the revolutionary slogan "All power to the Soviets," Lenin, with perfect timing, marshalled his meager forces (180,000) and took possession of government buildings, communication centers, railway stations, and other strategic points in Petrograd.

LEON TROTSKY BUILT RED ARMY
Trotsky, as commander of the new Red Army, played part almost as important as Lenin's in the Russian Revolution.

Lenin, with other Bolshevik leaders, had been transported from Switzerland to Russia with the aid of Germans, who hoped these extremists would undermine the pro-Allied provisional government. Soon after seizing power, Bolsheviks made their peace with Germany.

The new regime organized a *Cheka* (secret police) to stop all counter-revolutionary activity. The peasants were told that all land was theirs, workers took control of factories, the property of the Russian Orthodox Church was confiscated, foreign debts were repudiated.

After a lengthy civil war, the Anti-Bolshevik forces, led by former Czarist generals and supported by the Allies, were defeated by the newly organized Red Army under Trotsky.

Perhaps the most significant social phenomenon of the half-century, the Russian Revolution had begun the creation of a new way of life.

RASPUTIN, THE MAD MONK Rasputin (with beard) was for a while the most powerful man in Russia. By treating Crown Prince, he gained great power over Czarina. His scandalous behavior led to his assassination.

MURDERED BY BOLSHEVIKS Czar Nicholas II, his wife and children were finally executed July 16, 1918, after a long imprisonment in Ekaterinberg, Siberia. Autocratic Nicholas had done nothing to help the Russian masses.

ALEXANDER KERENSKY'S moderate and short-lived provisional government achieved declaration of Russia as a republic, release of political prisoners from Siberia. Kerensky fled abroad.

STREET FIGHTING during Bolshevik Revolution in Petrograd, November, 1917, marked beginning of Russian Civil War. By end of the month Bolsheviks held power throughout the country.

SMALL FORCE of revolutionary marines and workers *(l.)* succeeded in capturing key points in St. Petersburg on Nov. 6, 1917. Success of this Bolshevik *coup d'etat* meant downfall of the moderate Kerensky government, followed by civil war. Red Army was soon organized under Trotsky, consisted mostly of workers and deserters from Czar's army.

GENERAL WRANGEL *(above)* and Generals Kolchak, Denikin and Yudenitch commanded the various "White Russian" troops in unsuccessful fight against Bolsheviks. Heroes of the Red Army were (below, *l. to r.)* Budenny, Timoshenko, Voroshilov, who conquered the Allied-supported White Army.

ALLIES AID ANTI-BOLSHEVIKS, KEEP GERMAN SUBS FROM RUSSIAN PORTS In the spring and summer of 1918, when Russian ports, Archangel and Murmansk were ice-free, 15,000 British and American troops were sent there. They overthrew the local Soviets and set up the Provisional Government of the North. When Kolchak's government failed, political influences forced the Allies to withdraw.

ARMISTICE

Conflict ends in Allied victory

After defeating Russia (Treaty of Brest-Litovsk, March 3, 1918), Germany was free to turn her full power upon the Western Front. She had occupied Serbia, Montenegro and Rumania, and was striking mortal blows at Italy. By transferring her Eastern Front troops to France, she intended to put an end to the war with a decisive *coup de grace.*

Meanwhile Allied armies kept advancing in Mesopotamia and Palestine, and the Turks were obliged to follow Bulgaria's lead of Sept. 30 and sign an armistice (Oct. 30).

Declarations of independence by Czechoslovakia and Yugoslavia split Austria-Hungary, and the armistice on this front was concluded Nov. 3. After the abdication of Emperor Charles, Austria and Hungary became two independent republics.

With the Central Powers surrendering in quick succession, the Allies pressed their offensive. American troops, now more experienced, advanced strongly. The Germans, their morale broken by the loss of their allies, began a general retreat. Kaiser Wilhelm's authority was weakening and Prince Max of Baden, a Liberal, became Chancellor.

On Oct. 4, at the insistence of von Ludendorff, the German government appealed to Wilson, proposing to use his 14 Points as a basis for peace. With all German forces in general retreat, von Ludendorff was replaced by Gen. von Gröner. By Nov. 10, Americans had followed Germans to Sedan, near the Belgian border.

With chaos at home, a German delegation headed by Mathias Erzberger met Marshal Foch near Compiègne to sign the Armistice Nov. 11, 1918.

As a result of the war, several new nations were formed including the Baltic States, Yugoslavia, Czechoslovakia, Austria, Hungary, Finland, Poland.

DOUGHBOYS CELEBRATE the ending of "the muddiest war in history." Until the Armistice was signed, not a foot of German territory had been occupied by Allies. Hitler later was able to claim that Germany had been defeated from within, not by Allied forces. German navy had mutinied, popular revolts broken out.

In Memoriam

U. S. War Department Estimates (all figures in thousands)

	Total Mobilized Forces	Killed and Died	Wound Casualties	Prisoners and Missing	Total Casualties in Per Cent of Total Mobilized
ALLIES					
Russia	12,000	1,700	4,950	2,500	76.3
France	8,410	1,357	4,266	537	73.3
Brit. Emp.	8,904	908	2,090	191	35.8
Italy	5,615	650	947	600	39.1
U.S.	4,355	126	234	4.5	8.0
Japan	800	0.3	0.9	0	0.2
Rumania	750	335	120	80	71.4
Serbia	707	45	133	152	46.8
Belgium	267	13	44	34	34.9
Greece	230	5	21	1	11.7
Portugal	100	7	13	12	33.3
Montenegro	50	3	10	7	40.0
Total	42,188	5,152	12,831	4,121	52.3
CENTRAL POWERS					
Germany	11,000	1,773	4,216	1,152	64.9
Austro-Hungary	7,800	1,200	3,620	2,200	90.0
Turkey	2,850	325	400	250	34.2
Bulgaria	1,200	87	152	27	22.2
Total	22,850	3,386	8,388	3,629	67.4
G. Total	65,038	8,538	21,219	7,750	57.6

CIVIL WAR brought street fights to Berlin in the winter of 1918-19, when German Communists tried to overthrow the government by force. Their effort was defeated, but militaristic and nationalistic elements began to defy the new-born Weimar Republic.

VICTORY PARADES were numerous and colorful in New York in 1919 as thousands of troops came home. Greatest spectacle of all was watched by an estimated two million New Yorkers who lined Fifth Avenue to cheer General John J. Pershing as he led his returning soldiers in their triumphant march up the thoroughfare.

WILSON WAS FORCED TO CONCEDE ALMOST ALL OF HIS 14 POINTS IN ORDER TO SECURE THE LEAGUE OF NATIONS

"The Big Four" were *(left to right)* Orlando of Italy, Lloyd George of Britain, Georges Clemenceau of France, and U.S. President Woodrow Wilson. Orlando, frustrated in his attempt to enlarge Italy's frontiers according to his wish, walked out. France wanted to crush Germany. England was more lenient, while the U.S. took an extremely liberal stand. France, England, and the U.S. combined kept Wilson from realizing his vision of a just and permanent world peace.

BATTLE OF VERSAILLES

Wilson fails to get U. S. participation in the League of Nations

After the Armistice the whole world looked to Woodrow Wilson as the man who would save the world from future catastrophies through his League of Nations. The President's prestige in Europe was tremendous. He was received with great enthusiasm in England, Paris and Rome before he went to Paris for the Peace Conference, but, although the Republicans captured both houses in the 1918 congressional elections, he failed to include Republican leaders among the men who accompanied him to the Conference. Through his error, Wilson lost the backing of the U.S. Congress.

When the delegates from 27 nations met at Versailles their varied and opposed objectives quickly became apparent, and Wilson's position lost strength as he continued to insist on maintaining an impartial attitude.

When the Treaty was finally drawn up it had very little resemblance to Wilson's 14 Points. Germany protested that the terms were not in keeping with the agreement they had accepted in laying down their arms, and that many of the conditions would be impossible to fulfill. However, the German delegation under Brockdorff-Rantzau finally signed at Versailles, June 28, 1919.

Germany ceded Alsace-Lorraine to France; Eupen-et-Malmedy to Belgium; Upper Silesia, Posen and the Corridor to Poland; and her colonies to various Allies. Danzig was made a Free State, the Saar was internationalized, and the Rhineland occupied. The German army was reduced to 100,000 and her merchant marine and fishing fleet to almost nothing. She agreed to pay indemnities and the cost of the armies of occupation. The Treaty also included provision for the establishment of the League of Nations, and Wilson believed the League provided the mechanism for correcting errors in the Treaty.

Wilson returned home to face a hostile Congress. Republican opposition blocked ratification of the Treaty as it stood. The Senate proposed amendments, but Wilson would not allow Democrats to vote for the changed form. The Treaty of Versailles was therefore never ratified by the U.S. government, which also refused to ratify the treaty of alliance signed with France and England. U.S. abstention and rivalries among Western powers were among the chief causes of the League's failure to be effective.

LEAGUE OF NATIONS PALACE, GENEVA, SWITZERLAND

The League of Nations had only an advisory capacity with no power to enforce its recommendations. It was composed of the Council (executive branch) with 9 members (5 were permanent), and the Assembly, made up of all the member nations.

WOODROW WILSON, trying to save his League of Nations in spite of Republican opposition, took the issues directly to the public. Over-exertion caused a breakdown from which he never recovered. In spite of his broken health, he continued to fight, died bitterly disappointed in 1924.

CHIEFLY RESPONSIBLE for congressional defeat of the Versailles Treaty and Wilson's downfall was Senator Henry Cabot Lodge of Massachusetts. The group of isolationist senators who helped kill the League included *(l. to r.)* Lodge, Borah, Brandegee and Hiram Johnson.

IGNACE PADEREWSKI, one of the greatest pianists of his time, was Poland's champion in the fight for independence at Versailles. Poland gained her freedom from Russia and Paderewski became his country's first premier in January, 1919.

PHILOSOPHER PRESIDENT Thomas Garrigue Masaryk (1850-1937) fought for the independence of Czechoslovakia, and when the dreams of the Czech nationalists were realized at Versailles, Masaryk was elected first Czech President.

BRITISH ROYALTY welcomes U.S. President Wilson and his wife. Wilson was greeted by a hero's welcome on his arrival in Europe. In every city of every nation he visited, the people turned out to see and to cheer the "Modern Messiah." In the picture above are *(left to right)* Mrs. Wilson, Queen Mary, President Wilson, King George V and Princess Mary of England.

DISTURBED by the cynical attitude the European diplomats had displayed at Peace Conference, weary Pres. Wilson arrives home *(above)* to face unexpected hostility from U.S. opponents of League and Treaty.

U. S. TURNS TO PEACE

Strikes and unrest follow demobilization in America's period of postwar transition

AEF COMMANDER General John J. Pershing came up Hudson River in this tug in 1918 with General Peyton March *(l.)* and Sec'y. of War Baker *(r.)* on his return from Europe. Americans knew that the war was really over when doughboys and generals alike began returning to their homes.

FEAR of Red plots caused public alarm over all radicalism. Congress refused to seat Socialist Victor Berger of Wisconsin in the House of Representatives until staunch supporters elected him three consecutive times. Berger, a critic of the war, served a long prison sentence. The New York State Legislature expelled five of its members because they were Socialists. All unorthodox beliefs were suspect.

After the false report of an Armistice on November 7, 1918 had set off premature celebrations, Americans were happy but more subdued when the actual signing took place on November 11.

Returning servicemen from overseas found homefront conditions changed. A war-mobilized economy had expanded industry and business. Labor had higher wages and shorter hours. The number of millionaires increased from 16,000 to 20,000.

The years of 1919-1920 were an era of change. The speakeasy, rum-running, bootleg problem had its start with the ratification of the 18th Amendment. Americans found new dangers in radicalism and communism. Attorney General A. Mitchell Palmer tried to suppress all unorthodox political and social ideas. The Ku Klux Klan grew to 4,000,000 members in the '20s.

Strikes in 1919 increased 350 percent over 1918, and strikers were counted in the hundred thousands. In November 1919, John L. Lewis called a strike of miners for more pay and better working conditions. Attorney General Palmer ended the strike with injunctions. Public opinion forced shortening of the 12 hour working day in the steel industry.

A changing pattern appeared in business. Geared to wartime consumption, business found itself over-expanded. Products glutted the home market and prices fell. A two year depression, with 4,750,000 unemployed, settled over the nation. Railroads were returned to private control under the watchful eye of the Interstate Commerce Commission.

The 19th Amendment gave women the right to vote.

PACIFIST Eugene Debs was a perennial Socialist presidential candidate after 1900. Sentenced to 10 years in prison for anti-draft speeches, he polled 919,000 votes while still in the penitentiary during the 1920 election. Earlier Debs had been jailed for his part in the 1894 Pullman strike.

CALVIN COOLIDGE, Massachusetts' governor, won acclaim when he broke Boston police strike (1919) with National Guard troops, rebuked Gompers' offer to intercede. "There is no right to strike against the public safety by anybody, anywhere, any time." Loyal policeman directs guardsman.

CROOKED WORLD SERIES in 1919 shook public confidence in organized baseball. It was established that eight Chicago players from the White Sox team *(r.)* which won the American League Pennant conspired to throw victory in the fall classic to the Cincinnati Reds. To re-establish public trust after the "Black Sox" scandal, baseball officials in 1921 elected respected Judge Kenesaw Mountain Landis *(l.)* as baseball commissioner (a post he held until his death in 1944) with absolute power to weed out corrupt practices.

FAMED HITTER Babe Ruth had great pitching record from 1914-1919, winning 66 and losing 35 games. He set World Series record of 29 consecutive scoreless innings.

DYNAMIC PUNCHING featured battles of old-time heavyweight champions. Jess Willard (on canvas *above)* winner of the championship in 1915 against Jack Johnson, was knocked out in the fourth round at Toledo in 1919 by Jack Dempsey. Willard was knocked down seven times in the first round.

SPORTS

Preoccupation with the war in Europe and preparation for America's later entry channeled the energies of U.S. youth into military rather than athletic channels during World War I.

Baseball increased its hold as America's national sport, but came dangerously close to being discredited by the "Black Sox" scandal of 1919 in which some of the greatest stars were convicted of having sold out to gamblers. Also in 1914, an organization known as the Federal League demanded recognition as a major league and raided organized baseball for stars. The move proved a failure and the League disbanded in 1915.

Famous performers in other sports included R. Norris Williams and W. Johnston in tennis, Mel Sheppard in track, Fanny Durack in swimming, and the great Walter Hagen in golf.

The lull soon gave way to the great sporting era which marked the Twenties.

FIRST GREAT STAR of early automobile racing was famous Barney Oldfield who set record of 131 mph. in 1910. Here a later star, Ralph de Palma, takes the lead from Oldfield in 1914 race. Oldfield's friend, Henry Ford, taught him to drive the famous "999."

MAN O' WAR shattered horse racing records. The greatest horse of the era, Man o' War started his sensational career in 1919 as a two year old. In that year and the next he won 20 of his 21 races, set five records and earned $239,465. He lost only to the prophetically named Upset at Saratoga.

CHAPLIN AND EDNA PURVIANCE
Chaplin worried whether the public would accept *Shoulder Arms* (1918), a picture which defended "the little man," but it turned out to be his biggest hit.

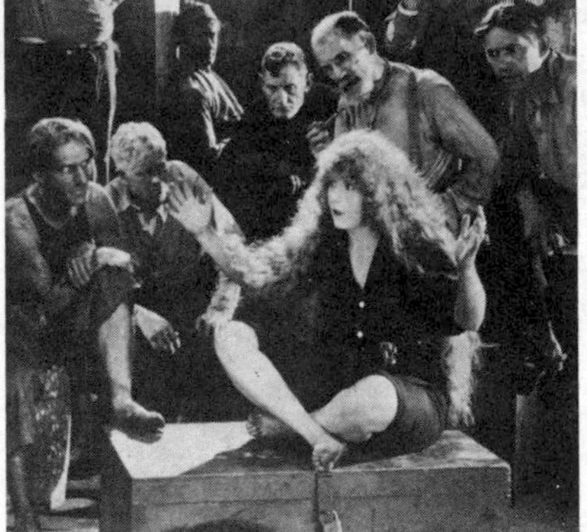

MOVIE QUEENS OF THE 1900s
The Perils of Pauline put serial queen Pearl White in jeopardy every episode, every week *(above)*. By 1919 Gloria Swanson *(below)* had graduated from Sennett comedies to full-length *Male and Female*, directed by C. B. DeMille.

THEDA BARA OOZED SEX APPEAL
Shown above is a scene from William Fox's production of *A Fool There Was*, which epitomized Miss Bara's vamping. Her real name was Theodosia Goodman.

ONE-REEL COMEDY SERIES
Mack Sennett's serial, *Keystone Cops (left)*, carried on its preposterous roster such zanies as Ben Turpin, Chester Conklin, Hank Mann and Ford Sterling.

FOUR FORM UNITED ARTISTS
"The lunatics have taken over the asylum," scoffed producers when Douglas Fairbanks, Mary Pickford, Chaplin and Griffith *(r.)* made their own films.

THE MOVIES

They develop artistically and mature into a strong industry

In 1914 *Traffic in Souls* grossed $450,000 and Mary Pickford signed a contract with Adolph Zukor at $2,000 a week. In 1915 *The Birth of a Nation* was shown at $2 admission; "The greatest motion picture of all time" was the work of D. W. Griffith, who with his camera-man, Billy Bitzer, introduced the close-up, the flashback, the fade. It established Griffith as a master of cinema technique and it made outstanding stars of its players: Lillian Gish, Henry B. Walthall, Mae Marsh and Wallace Reid.

Mack Sennett was responsible for the first full-length comedy, *Tillie's Nightmare*, starring English Music Hall comedian Charlie Chaplin with Marie Dressler and Mabel Normand.

WILLIAM HART AND BESSIE LOVE
Hart played the strong, silent two-gun man of the West better than anyone else of his time. Scene above is from Thomas Ince's production of *The Aryan*.

RIDE OF THE KU KLUX KLAN
The Birth of a Nation was D. W. Griffith's masterpiece *(above)*. Roscoe "Fatty" Arbuckle began as a Keystone Cop, but soon starred in his own films for Paramount. Scene of triumph below is from *His Wedding Night* (about 1917).

THEATER

Important year of 1914 sees techniques improve

In August Elmer Rice's first play *On Trial* was a hit. It borrowed in technique from the cinema, utilizing for the first time on stage the device of the flashback.

The same year the Washington Square Players formed and produced plays. Five years later the group had developed into the Theater Guild and produced its first hit.

Dramatic hits included George M. Cohan's version of *Seven Keys to Baldpate*, Jane Cowl in Bayard Veiller's *Within the Law* and Doris Keane in Edward Sheldon's *Romance*.

JOHN AND LIONEL BARRYMORE
The brothers appeared together for first time in Du Maurier's *Peter Ibbetson*, with Laura Hope Crews and Constance Collier. Play ran successfully in 1917.

GIRLS NOT ONLY ATTRACTION
W. C. Fields, Will Rogers, Lillian Lorraine and Eddie Cantor *(below)* were in 1917 *Ziegfeld Follies*. In the same cast were Bert Williams, Fannie Brice.

BALLET DANCER
Vaslav Nijinsky, "world's greatest male dancer," was brought to U.S. in 1916 by Diaghilev. He is shown in *Specter of the Rose.*

CO-AUTHOR AND STAR FRANK BACON
Lightnin''s record run of 1,291 performances made Bacon's reputation and fortune. Also in the homespun drama were Beatrice Nichols, Jessie Pringle.

THE DANCING DOLLY SISTERS
Rose and Jennie Dolly were hit of *Ziegfeld Follies* before they starred with Chevalier at the Casino de Paris and reputedly broke bank at Monte Carlo.

MUSICIANS

Great stars, like Madame Schumann-Heink and Enrico Caruso, devoted most of their time to entertaining troops, promoting the sale of Liberty Bonds and stimulating patriotic fervor on the home front. Every doughboy knew George M. Cohan's "Over There" and Irving Berlin's "Oh, How I Hate to Get Up in the Morning."

While America was concentrating her musical talents on the war, France suffered a great musical loss. Claude Debussy, one of the great composers of the century, died in 1918. A painter of mood pictures, Debussy had an elusive charm which musicians of many lands tried to emulate.

GALLI-CURCI RECEIVES THANKS ➧
Opera star Madame Galli-Curci gave many concerts for servicemen during the first World War. Franklin D. Roosevelt, then Assistant Secretary of Navy, thanks her *(r.)* for her patriotic service.

ENTERTAINER
Sweetheart of the AEF, Elsie Janis *(l.)* dared enemy attacks in her zeal to entertain troops. Doughboys crowded to hear her.

BLUES COMPOSER AND PLAYER
Trumpet player William C. Handy was the greatest exponent of the Blues. Vocally and instrumentally, his "St. Louis Blues" became the most recorded and arranged composition in jazz field.

MOTORING was a precarious experience in pre-war days. Breakdowns were frequent, eliciting shouts of derision from self-satisfied buggy-drivers. Women learned to drive, but blowouts made it unwise to motor without menfolk along.

Automobiles

New industry expands

During the First World War American automobiles changed little in outward appearance, but came out with many mechanical improvements.

Charles F. Kettering developed the self-starter and electrical system in 1912 which eliminated the risk of a broken arm from a balky crank, resulting in more people driving.

The automobile was a boon to the country doctor, the trucking industry and the government, which used 30,000 trucks during the war. Henry Ford's assembly line production resulted in one out of every 13 Americans owning an automobile by 1920.

PLANES SPAN ATLANTIC

By the end of World War I, the airplane was beginning to fulfill its promise of becoming a useful instrument, one in which man could speed across oceans and span continents. As early as 1909, Louis Bleriot had flown a monoplane across the English Channel from Calais to Dover in 37 minutes. Spurred by the use of planes during the war, aircraft design and construction improved rapidly, and in 1919 had progressed sufficiently to make possible the first successful flights across the Atlantic Ocean.

FIRST successful non-stop flight across the Atlantic was made by two British flyers. Leaving St. Johns, Newfoundland on June 15, 1919, in a Vickers-Vimy biplane, Capt. John Alcock and Lieut. Arthur W. Brown flew the 1,936 miles to Ireland in 15 hours and 57 minutes. The flight ended with a crash-landing into an Irish bog *(l.)*

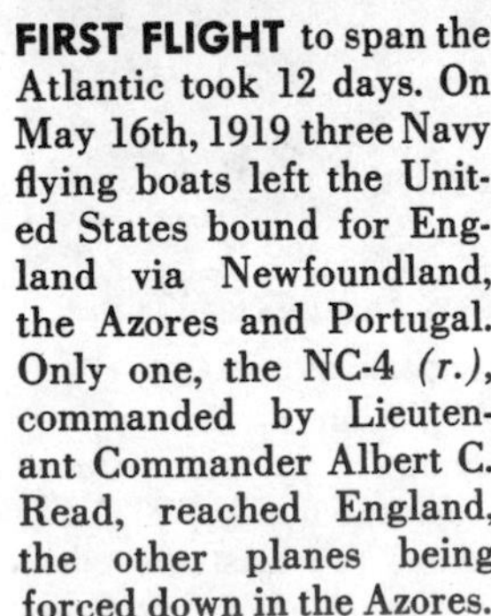

FIRST FLIGHT to span the Atlantic took 12 days. On May 16th, 1919 three Navy flying boats left the United States bound for England via Newfoundland, the Azores and Portugal. Only one, the NC-4 *(r.)*, commanded by Lieutenant Commander Albert C. Read, reached England, the other planes being forced down in the Azores.

DISASTERS Fire destroyed a large part of Salem, Mass. on June 25, 1914, as shown in the picture at the top. More than 15,000 were left homeless after the blaze, and the total damage exceeded $12,000,000. German saboteurs were held responsible for the mysterious Black Tom explosion that rocked the area of Perth Amboy, N. J. on July 30, 1916. The blast destroyed munition docks and spread the wreckage for blocks as shown above. Two lives were lost and the damage totaled $22,000,000.

BASIS for cathode ray tube, the heart of present-day television sets, was laid by researchers such as Dr. Irving Langmuir *(above)* and Harold Arnold, whose work was based on Lee De Forest's discoveries early in the century.

INVENTOR of the telephone in 1876 when he was at the age of 29, Alexander Graham Bell is shown at official opening of first transcontinental line in 1915. Bell was then 68 years old. Transatlantic telephone service began in 1927.

HIRAM MAXIM, shown above, was the inventor of the automatically operating machine gun, the most deadly weapon of the First World War. He also developed a gun silencer, experimented extensively with airplane design.

WAR STIMULATES INVENTIONS

During World War I, both sides contributed to great advances in aviation. Germany developed the first synthetic rubber and built the greatest chemical industry in the world. Dr. Leo Baekeland made discoveries in field of plastics.

UNIVERSITY of Minnesota was among the few colleges and universities converted for use during World War I as special military training centers. GI's received instruction in an airplane propeller workshop from civilian teachers.

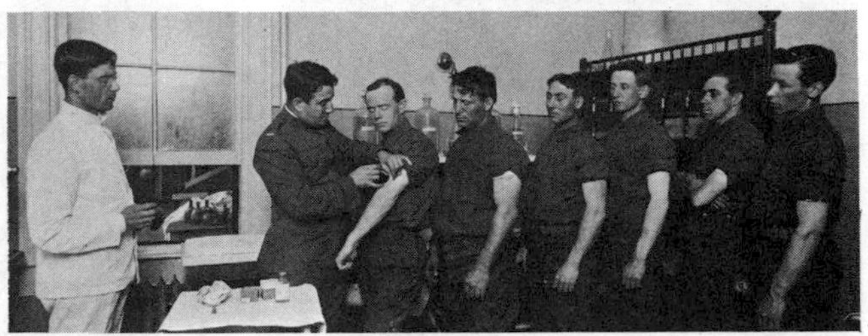

INOCULATIONS to combat disease were used to good effect on soldiers forced to live in trenches under insanitary conditions. Earlier research on the nature of immunity helped develop serums that stimulated creation of antibodies.

EDUCATION

Testing for intelligence quotients had begun in the United States in 1907, when Alfred Binet, noted French psychologist, introduced the Binet scale. In the intervening years up to World War I, educators had sought means to test mental ability scientifically. The information obtained from the Army Alpha and Beta tests, given to all inductees during the war, became the foundation of present-day testing to determine ability, learning and aptitudes.

GREAT NEGRO educator and president of Tuskegee Institute in Alabama, Booker T. Washington *(right)* was deeply mourned when he died in 1915.

MEDICINE

The shortage of doctors to treat casualties during the war necessitated amazing feats performed by corpsmen in the field. Treatment of "shell-shocked" soldiers led to a greater understanding of the relation of mind and body.

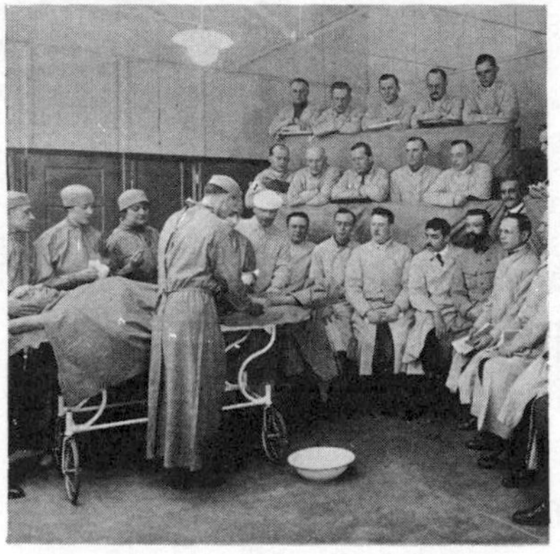

NEW surgical technique developed by Dr. Alexis Carrel *(l., in white cap)* saved the lives of many soldiers. His methods of draining wounds cut down the healing time from the previous average of approximately thirty days to one week, won official praise.

PASSING SCENE

BARBARA LAMARR was typical of beauties in the entertainment world early in the century. She made one contribution without effort when her last name was appropriated for use in American movies by Viennese Hedy Kiesler.

AVOWED ANARCHISTS, Emma Goldman and Alexander Berkman made no effort to conceal their attempts to interfere with this country's war preparations. Both were convicted, imprisoned and deported from the U.S. in 1919.

BILLY SUNDAY, the spectacular evangelist, led thousands down his "Sawdust Trail." His tent show revival meetings were crowded from coast to coast and huge crowds enjoyed a return to the "fundamentals" of the old-time religion.

EXTOLLING the therapeutic values of wine in parades such as this failed to halt the victory of prohibition forces during the period 1915-1920. The 18th Amendment went into effect in January, 1920 and the U.S. was officially "dry."

Illustrated Daily News

GERMANS BLOCK SIGNING OF TREATY

Newport to Entertain Prince of Wales in August

FIRST "TABLOID" picture newspaper in the U.S. appeared in 1919. By mid-century, as the New York *Daily News,* its circulation had become the largest in America with sales amounting to more than 2,000,000 copies daily.

VICTORY for women came in 1920 when the 19th Amendment went into effect, and assured them of equal voting rights with men. Pioneer suffragettes like those parading above had waged a long hard battle before winning.

WARTIME FASHIONS Pure silk undergarments similar to bloomers shown at left began to enter milady's wardrobe just prior to World War I, although many women considered such brief attire quite daring. Mannequins wearing designer's creations were seen at many society affairs such as the Astor Cup Races in a forerunner of the present-day fashion show. The models mixed with the crowds to demonstrate what the well-dressed woman should wear. Strolling beauties pictured *(above)* reflect the variety of styles that characterized the period of 1918-19. Spats worn over low street shoes *(r.)* continued to hide dainty ankles from male eyes.

WORST EPIDEMIC of modern times spread around the globe in 1918-19. The outbreak of influenza, attributed by France to Spain, by Spain to France and by America to eastern Europe, appeared almost simultaneously among the nations of the Western Front, and then spread to the Central Powers and their neighbors during 1918 and 1919. As the death toll rose in the United States, home-made "preventives" like the gauze masks worn by San Franciscans *(above)* became common.

THE CASTLES, Vernon and Irene, raised the standard of ballroom dancing to new heights in the U.S. Her short haircut at first scandalized nation but soon became the fashion. Their career ended in 1917 when he died in a plane crash.

LITERATURE IN WARTIME

Fiction during World War I foreshadowed the realism of the '20s. Bored and frustrated by war, American readers wanted fiction that depicted their own problems; they demanded realistic themes instead of tales of sentiment, morality and religion. The patriotic fervor of the times, often almost fanatical, was reflected in popular literature. However, more important and more lasting were the novelists who treated different phases of the war in a realistic and critical manner, writers like John Dos Passos, E. E. Cummings, Thomas Boyd and Laurence Stallings.

John Dos Passos' *Three Soldiers* dealt directly and naturalistically with the war, showing the effect of regimentation on men of different types of character. In *The Enormous Room* (1922), E. E. Cummings attacked the common conception of a heroic and chivalrous France, telling of tortures endured by an artist in a French military prison. The reactions of the normal American soldier were realistically treated in Thomas Boyd's *Through the Wheat* (1923). Laurence Stallings in 1924 authored a novel entitled *Plumes* which reflected the post-war disillusionment.

POLISH-BORN Joseph Conrad grew up speaking French and Polish. Only at 21, did he begin to acquire English, the language of his metaphysical fiction. Among his novels are *Lord Jim* (1900), *Nostromo* (1904) and *Victory* (1915).

BALLAD SINGER and collector, Carl Sandburg wrote of America with dedication, creating equally well the mood of city and prairie. Among his books of poems are *Smoke and Steel* (1920) and *Slabs of the Sunburnt West* (1922).

IRISH POET, playwright, and a lover of folk-lore, William Butler Yeats was the leading figure in the Irish Renaissance which called forth the fine talents of Synge, "AE," James Stephens and other distinguished writers in Ireland.

NOVELIST and historian, H. G. Wells' interests lay in politics and in civilization as a whole, with an eye to a better future. In 1916 he wrote *Mr. Britling Sees It Through*, describing Britain's home front during the war years.

Gay Twenties...1920-1929

Flivvers, flagpole sitters, dance marathons, jazz . . . sheiks and flappers, prohibition and prosperity—hail and farewell!

Like all wars, the First World War left moral as well as physical scars. By making life seem cheap and transient, war encouraged the eat-drink-and-be-merry school of thought. It raised again the paradox which plagued all religions, the co-existence of evil and a just God.

Bootlegging became one of America's leading industries, paving the way for organized crime. The prosperous automobile industry was a partner in crime in aiding escape from authority, police and parental. The sheiks and flappers of what Gertrude Stein called the "lost generation" had their fling.

It was the generation of Texas Guinan's "Hello Sucker," Lindbergh's triumphant flight, of companionate marriage, Freudian preoccupation with sex, dance marathons, the Charleston, ukuleles, and flagpole sitters. Sports entered its Golden Age. Women demanded equal rights. Jazz emerged from New Orleans as the musical theme of the times.

Despite it all, college attendance doubled. Science and the ouija board both flourished. Americans read cheap magazines as well as the novelists and poets of their day. It was a wayward, but productive era.

Affairs abroad

Towards events abroad, the attitude of most Americans agreed with President Harding's ". . . prosper America first." The League of Nations looked to Americans too much like an entangling alliance. Their attitude was not altogether unreasonable. Europe, its trade throttled by high tariffs, was unable to pay its war debts. Finding in the Versailles peace no security but an armistice, the Old World had returned to pacts reminiscent of the prewar vintage. International conferences set ratios of naval strength and even "outlawed" war, in theory. In practice they were backed by nothing stronger than good intentions, while the sum spent on armaments in 1928 would have run the League for 500 years at the rate then current.

When Communist uprisings overseas coincided with a postwar wave of strikes in the U.S. a bitter reaction against "un-Americanism" developed. It flared up in 1920 with the Wall St. bombing and reached a climax five

POLICE CONFISCATE STILL

years later with the Sacco-Vanzetti case. Reaction took various forms. The Ku Klux Klan grew into an invisible empire of four million members, by 1925 actually outnumbering organized labor at the time. Religious fundamentalism opposed by Clarence Darrow and upheld by William Jennings Bryan, triumphed at the Scopes trial. The old-time religion, along with isolation and a conservative economy, was good enough for many Americans who felt that any tampering with cherished institutions might jeopardize the national prosperity, for the Republicans' campaign promise of a "return to normalcy" had been more than fulfilled and Calvin Coolidge, taking office in 1923, believed with his predecessor in prospering America first.

Boom and bust

Laissez-faire and economy were Coolidge's watchwords. "The business of America is business," said Cautious Cal coolly. With that, industry forged ahead. Mass production, the industrial revolution of the half century, really came into its own. Everywhere new buildings of all kinds went up, especially in Florida and California.

Manpower was replaced by electrified machines and electrical output doubled. The threat of technological unemployment was a hint of the crash to come but, like the agricultural recession, it was generally disregarded. Sixty percent of American families were living on twenty-four percent of the national income.

Corporations grew to giant size, controlled by management in the name of the stockholders scattered throughout the country. Twenty-five million Americans, viewing the market with rose-tinted visions of an unending plateau of prosperity, invested in the Great Bull Market of 1929. Stock became increasingly speculative. The market rested more on optimism than on proven values.

In September the structure began to totter. On October 29, 1929, 16 million shares were traded on the N.Y. Stock Exchange. Averages fell 40 points. In 71 days, General Electric fell 228 points and the era of the hip flasks, big butter-and-egg men, and stockbrokers in their tower suites came to an end. The Great Bull Market was gone.

Such were the Twenties. Boom they lived and Crash they died.

◀ **HENRY FORD,** more than any individual, was responsible for putting America on wheels. Chief originator of the mass production revolution, Ford dominated the early automobile industry with the company he founded in 1903. By 1914 he was prosperous enough to announce a $5-a-day minimum wage. In 1924, Fords could be bought for $290 F.O.B. Detroit. No thing of beauty, the Model T had to be cranked by hand, and "Tin Lizzie" jokes were standard vaudeville fare, but Americans bought them by the millions. In 1928, competition from General Motors led to the introduction of the Model A.

FAMOUS FORD Model T gets ready for the road in 1924 with some finishing touches on the assembly line. Automobiles were mass produced by Ford during the first decade of the century, but the industry made its biggest economic contribution after World War I. More than 15,000,000 Model T automobiles were built by Ford in less than twenty years.

ENDLESS STREAM of Chevrolets comes down the assembly line at Flint, Michigan in 1920. Early model trucks are on the line at right and passenger cars on the left. This General Motors plant closed after World War II.

MORE OF EVERYTHING

Mass production and distribution bring golden era to U. S.

The Twenties were climactic years for American business. The fruits of mass production were reaped. Old products and new were coming off the assembly line and distributed at home and abroad.

The development of the automobile industry was spectacular. America recognized the need for streamlined distribution methods to keep pace with production. Chain and department stores and mail order houses multiplied. Montgomery Ward, Sears and Roebuck and A&P became household words. Great sums of money were spent on advertising, giving a boost to popular weekly magazines, the new medium, radio, as well as enriching the advertising field. There was greater efficiency in distribution channels. General Foods, Standard Brands and Borden's became to distribution what U.S. Steel had been to production.

While new techniques for mass production provided the answer to most of America's business problems during the Twenties, they were not enough in some sectors of the economy. Serious difficulties arose in agriculture, coal and textiles, which had over-expanded during World War I.

Labor relations in the Twenties seemed easy, and trade union membership, which stood at nearly 5,000,000 in 1920, dropped to about 3,400,000 in 1929. The workingman apparently was satisfied to allow management more of a free rein than during the period immediately preceding and after the First War.

The government, too, was good to business, and devoted itself to reducing the national debt by $9,000,000,000 in 11 years. The Federal Trade Commission had been set up more as a means of arbitrating between businesses than as a curbing power to private enterprise. According to statisticians—and the meaning was everywhere apparent—value of goods and services available to the average consumer increased from $592 in 1919 to $625 in 1929.

There was a tremendous growth in corporate business, with room for both the big and small investor. By 1929 corporations were responsible for 62 percent of the national income produced by business. The number of shares on the New York Stock Exchange grew from 493,449,000 to over 1,000,000,000 between 1925 and 1929. Real estate was a favorite form of speculation. Foreign securities looked good, $15,000,000,000 in American money was invested in them in the decade. In 1929, prior to the crash, trading on the New York Stock Exchange exceeded 4,000,000 shares per day on 122 days and 5,000,000 shares on 37 days.

The stock market crash of October 29, 1929 suddenly ended all of this. In the course of a few weeks, thirty billion dollars in paper values vanished into thin air. American business found that consumers would no longer buy all the goods they could produce. The Great Depression was on its way, and by 1932 industry was operating at less than half its maximum 1929 volume. Not until long after did it become clear that this decade of 1920-29 was a crucial one in the development of America's mighty industrial machine and the achievement of an increasingly higher standard of living.

FIRESTONE RUBBER TYCOON
Harvey S. Firestone founded one of world's largest rubber concerns, developed farm machinery tires, organized "ship by truck movement" in WWI.

PIONEER AIR PULLMAN, the tri-motor Boeing 80A replaced single engine Boeing 40 on coast to coast route of United Air Lines in 1928. Trip took 27¾ hours. Scheduled airlines, aided by technical and safety advances, grew rapidly after starting operations in 1926.

TRUCKING TIME on coast to coast run was shaved when this 3 ton Packard rolled into N.Y. 13 days after leaving Los Angeles. The trucking industry came into its own during the '20s with the rise of automotive production. Conflict with railroads soon developed.

AGGRESSIVE salesmanship, including door-to-door contact, and advertising, were the two most important ingredients in America's mass distribution system.

OIL AT SIGNAL HILL ➧
Oil gushes in the big Signal Hill oil field at Long Beach, California in 1923. Oil industry grew enormously during 1920's as automobile ownership multiplied.

MIAMI BUILDING BOOM
Real estate in Florida and elsewhere, like "cat and dog" stocks, was popular with big and small investors. Real estate speculation continued until the crash.

FARM SURPLUSES, for the first time in history, became a major problem. Adjusted to high level production demanded by World War I, American farmers suddenly found they were producing more than they could sell. Congressional action on bills to solve the problem was not taken until the more severe years of the depression.

PRESIDENTIAL CABINET members, some of whom were to be involved in the scandals of the Harding administration, are pictured. Seated *(l. to r.)* are Secretaries of War, John W. Weeks; Treasury, Andrew W. Mellon; State, Charles Evans Hughes; Harding; Vice-Pres. Coolidge; Navy, Edwin Denby. Standing are Secretaries of the Interior, Albert B. Fall; Atty. General Daugherty; Agriculture, Henry C. Wallace; Commerce, Herbert Hoover; Labor, James J. Davis.

BACK TO NORMALCY

Harding era is climaxed by the revelation of scandals in government

Warren Gamaliel Harding, of Marion, Ohio, with his running-mate, Calvin Coolidge, defeated the Democratic ticket of Cox and Roosevelt to become President in the 1920 elections.

War with Germany was brought to an official end with the Knox Resolution, passed by a special session of Congress in 1921. In the same year, foreign immigration was limited for the first time in history. In 1922, the Fordney-McCumber Tariff raised import duties, and U.S. industry began heading for the prosperity that marked the mid-Twenties.

A good-natured, trusting man, lacking administrative experience, Harding appointed to important positions men who became involved in scandals of waste, bribery and collusion. After Harding's death the most infamous of these scandals was uncovered when it was discovered that Interior Secretary Fall had secretly leased the oil lands of Teapot Dome (Wyoming) and Elks Hill (California) to oil tycoons Harry F. Sinclair and Edward L. Doheny, and received "loans" totaling $325,000 from them. Also in-involved in the scandal was Attorney General Daugherty.

◀ **THE HARDINGS WITH VISITOR**

DEMOCRATIC CANDIDATES, James M. Cox of Ohio and Franklin D. Roosevelt of New York were the unsuccessful opponents of the Harding-Coolidge ticket in the 1920 presidential election.

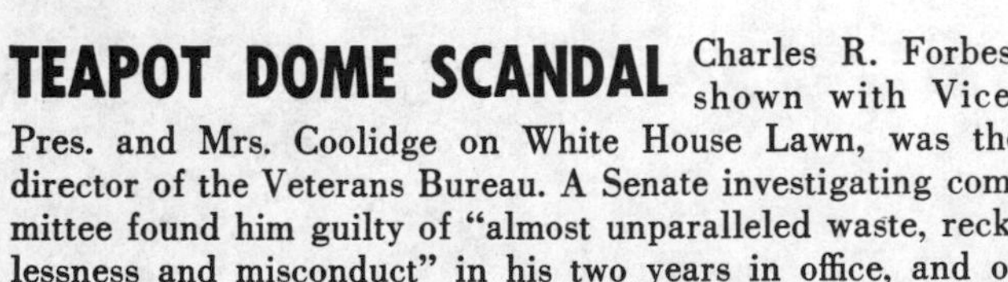

TEAPOT DOME SCANDAL Charles R. Forbes, shown with Vice-Pres. and Mrs. Coolidge on White House Lawn, was the director of the Veterans Bureau. A Senate investigating committee found him guilty of "almost unparalleled waste, recklessness and misconduct" in his two years in office, and of misappropriating $200 million. He was sent to Leavenworth, Kansas, penitentiary in 1924. Edward Doheny, Calif. oil baron (and lawyer Frank Hogan), was tried for bribery and acquitted as an aftermath of Teapot Dome Scandal involving oil leases. Harry Sinclair is seen with Interior Secretary Fall (bow tie) who was convicted of taking bribes.

Keeping Cool with Cal

Republicans retain power while business prospers

THE GREAT WHITE FATHER from Vermont, who practiced the art of "saying much in little and often in silence," succeeded Harding to the presidency. President Coolidge wears the war bonnet while attending Indian ceremonies at Deadwood, South Dakota. He could have had the Republican nomination again in 1928, but true to his nature he said briefly, "I do not choose to run," and ended speculation.

Harding died suddenly on August 2, 1923, and Calvin Coolidge became the nation's chief executive. Running in the 1924 elections with Charles G. Dawes, he managed to defeat both the Democratic ticket of John W. Davis and Charles W. Bryan and the Progressive Party candidates, LaFollette and Wheeler. Despite the scandals of the Harding administration, "Silent Cal" appealed successfully to the voters by emphasizing tax reductions, national debt retrenchment and his slogan, "Keep Cool With Coolidge."

"The business of America is business," said Coolidge, and business prospered under a lenient Federal Trade Commission and an Attorney General who was not inclined to press for indictments under the Clayton Anti-Trust Act. Although Congress had passed a veterans' bonus bill over Coolidge's veto, an attempt to solve the farm problem failed when he vetoed the McNary-Haugen bill, and the Norris proposal of a government-operated hydro-electric power development at Muscle Shoals in the Tennessee Valley was also vetoed. In 1928, however, he signed into law the Boulder Canyon Project to build a dam (Hoover Dam) on the Colorado River for irrigation and power purposes.

CALVIN COOLIDGE poses with his family *(l. to r.)* son John, Mrs. Coolidge, Coolidge, son Calvin and father John Coolidge. When news of Harding's death in August of 1923 reached the Coolidge family in Vermont, Justice of the Peace John Coolidge swore in his son as President of the United States in the dead of night before eight witnesses.

PROGRESSIVE "Fighting Bob" LaFollette of Wisconsin, shown with son Robert, ran on the Progressive Party ticket in 1924 backed by American Liberals.

TWO ITALIAN IMMIGRANTS, Nicola Sacco and Bartolomeo Vanzetti, were arrested in Boston and charged with murder of a paymaster and a guard. Though evidence was flimsy and contradictory, trial brought out that both were atheists and philosophical anarchists. Convicted in hysterical atmosphere of 1921, they were denied a retrial though new evidence was uncovered. Their execution in 1927 set off world-wide protests.

KU KLUX KLAN grew to 4,000,000 members during the Twenties. Fed by American disillusionment at the aftermath of World War I, by reaction against the League of Nations and foreign entanglements of any sort, and by widespread fear of radical or "Bolshevik" ideas, the KKK preached suppression of all "dangerous" minority groups, including foreigners, Catholics, Jews, Negroes. Here the Imperial Wizard of the Ku Klux Klan kisses the flag and stands before a fiery cross, both used as symbols by the Klan organization.

GERMANY UNDER WEIMAR REPUBLIC

After the war Germany, under the Social Democratic Party, suffered Communist *(Spartacist)* revolts. Following the crushing of the uprising, two top Communist leaders, Karl Liebknecht and Rosa Luxembourg, were murdered while under arrest by members of the "Free Corps," volunteer ex-soldiers of tough character and doubtful loyalty formed to crush the uprisings (1919).

The moderate parties established a democratic republic known as the Weimar regime. However, Germany's economic situation was deteriorating rapidly and by the elections of 1930 the Nazis had obtained enormous support and the moderate parties lost heavily. The Nazis and Communists combined forces against the government and Chancellor Bruening thought it necessary to resort to government by emergency decree. With democracy thus paralyzed, the scene was set for the rise of Adolf Hitler.

GUSTAV STRESEMANN *(l.)* became foreign minister under the Weimar Republic, served in every cabinet from 1923 until his death (1929), and tried to lead Germany on the road towards cooperation with other nations.

DISASTROUS inflation crushed the middle class. After the currency stabilization of 1924 there was brief prosperity but soon depression saw breadlines *(r.)* form in every city; suffering drew many Germans to the Nazis.

ADOLF HITLER and Rudolph Hess *(l.)* are shown comfortably lodged in their fortress jail where Hitler dictated *Mein Kampf* which later became the bible for the Nazi party.

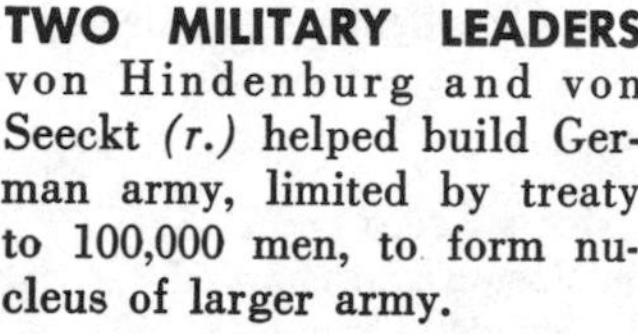

TWO MILITARY LEADERS von Hindenburg and von Seeckt *(r.)* helped build German army, limited by treaty to 100,000 men, to form nucleus of larger army.

FASCIST ITALY

Events of 1914 to 1919 set the stage for a collapse of the old regime in Italy. Under the leadership of Mussolini the Fascist Party gained power. He had organized cells in all parts of Italy that were prepared to take up arms for the Fascist cause. In 1922, after seizing control of the city governments of Bologna and Milan, the Fascists marched on Rome. The King invited Mussolini to form a government, and granted him dictatorial powers. In 1929 the Vatican became an independent state.

Having made his Fascist state work in Italy, Mussolini looked abroad for further conquests.

"ON TO ROME" was the cry of thousands of Fascists on the march assembled from all parts of Italy. The famous march climaxed Fascist plans for the control of Italy. Mussolini, former Socialist, was to be Dictator of Fascist Italy for 21 years. De Veechi, Marshall Italo Balbo and *Il Duce* lead the Fascisti *(above)*.

LEON TROTSKY stood next to Lenin in the leadership of Russian Revolution. As People's Commissar for War, he built the Red Army which won the civil war but lost in Poland. Stalin later exiled him and he was murdered in Mexico (1940).

JOSEPH STALIN *(l.)* built his office of secretary-general of the Russian Communist Party into the key position, and after Lenin's death in 1924 he grabbed absolute domination, eliminated all other contenders and instituted the first Five-Year Plan.

VLADIMIR LENIN was the dominant spirit of the Bolshevik Revolution and sponsor of the "New Economic Policy." He had been the target of an assassination attempt in 1918, and in 1922 a stroke left him partially paralyzed until his death in 1924.

COMMUNIST RUSSIA

Russia industrializes by Communist methods to strengthen position

The Polish-Russian armistice placed the "Whites" (anti-Bolshevik troops) in an untenable position and by November, 1920, the Bolsheviks had won complete control. Russia was left prostrate, with famine and unrest rampant. Lenin called a retreat to a more moderate system, the "New Economic Policy" (NEP). After Lenin's death in 1924 Stalin, Zinoviev and Kamenev took control. The comparitive mildness of the NEP was replaced by the rigor of the first Five Year Plan. Russia, hitherto an agricultural country, was to be industrialized. Communist civil servants, engineers and scientists were being trained. The collectivization of the peasants began in earnest. Spearheaded by the terrorist methods of the OGPU (security police), 55% of them were driven into state farms.

By 1933, the end of the first Five Year Plan, Russia had achieved considerable stability and power, both internally and internationally. The wave of purges lay ahead.

DEATH OR IMPRISONMENT WAS THE FATE OF THREE-QUARTERS OF THE RUSSIAN LEADERS IN THE GREAT PURGES

With Kirov's assassination in 1934, Stalin realized his hold was not as firm as he thought. The purges included all those suspected of plotting with the exiled Trotsky or Nazi Germany against Stalin. Leo Kamenev *(l.)* had helped Stalin defeat Trotsky but that did not protect him—he was executed. Karl Radek *(c.)*, the most brilliant journalist of the Revolution, was imprisoned. Nikolai Bukharin *(r.)*, the leading theoretician of the Communist Party, co-founder of the Communist International and a highly educated man of international fame, was executed in the great purge of 1937.

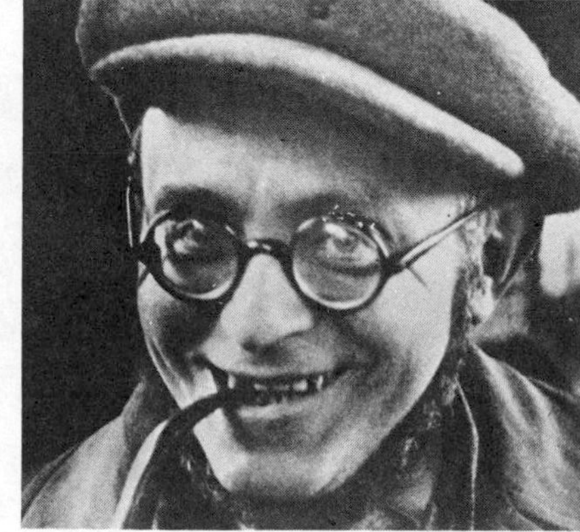

FIRST Labor Cabinet in Britain was formed in 1924 by Ramsay MacDonald *(l.)*. He helped build the Labor Party and the League of Nations and was re-elected Prime Minister in 1929.

BRIAND *(c.)*, Baldwin *(r.)* and Churchill *(top r.)* are shown on their return from Lausanne where they had decided upon future status of Alsace-Lorraine, Germany and areas of Turkey.

WORLD FINDS BRIEF PEACE

Series of conferences fail with tension and civil wars all over world

The threat of an armament race in 1921 caused Harding to summon the Washington Disarmament Conference. In Europe a Permanent Court of International Justice developed. The British Imperial Conference made the Dominions virtually autonomous in 1926.

While civil wars raged in China, Communism began to infiltrate the country, guided by such Russians as Michael Borodin. Despite Chiang Kai-shek's efforts towards modern reorganization in 1925, the country remained in chaos.

The Ottoman Empire finished the war the most crippled of the vanquished states. While Sultan Mohammed VI accepted the humiliating conditions of foreign occupation, the Turkish revolution began under Mustafa Kemal Pasha. In 1923 Turkey regained independence from the Allies. Arab nations were also seeking independence.

MARSHALL Pilsudski (in uniform) defeated the Russians and was president of Poland until 1923. He ruled later as dictator (1926-33).

"NO, NEVER" was Ulster's answer to Eire. The revolutionaries in Eire were demanding withdrawal of all British rule. Sinn Fein was the party of rebels that in 1919 had proclaimed Ireland an independent republic with Eamon de Valera as president.

DICTATOR OF SPAIN Gen. Primo de Rivera (1923-1930), after bringing the fighting in Spanish Morocco to an end, talks with the son of Raisuli, the Moroccan chieftain.

FAMOUS Greek leader, Eleutherios Venizelos, premier and revolutionist, was responsible for attack on Turkey which ended in Greece's defeat.

ARMED mostly with weapons taken from their enemies, Turkish troops under capable leaders heroically resisted the invading Greeks.

JAZZ. BORN RAG-TIME IN NEW ORLEANS, BECOMES A MUSICAL SCORE FOR THE TIMES, A NATIVE AMERICAN MUSIC

"Is everybody happy?" became for Ted Lewis *(l.)* in his battered hat—and for the Jazz Age—a trademark. Equally famous was Rudy Vallee's creamy tenor *(c.)*. No less successful, Paul Whiteman hired front line talent including Bing Crosby (in the middle of the Rhythm Boys) to help him "civilize" jazz. Meanwhile jazz, born in New Orleans' Storyville, beat its way upriver in the Twenties in the persons of Jelly Roll Morton, King Oliver, Louis Armstrong, Bessie Smith and others, to Chicago, where Bix Beiderbecke heard it. From there it echoed and set feet tapping everywhere.

PROHIBITION BUREAU AGENTS

HOME BREW AFTER AGENTS' RAID

SMASHING RUM RUNNERS' GOODS

JAZZ AGE JEWELRY: A FLASK

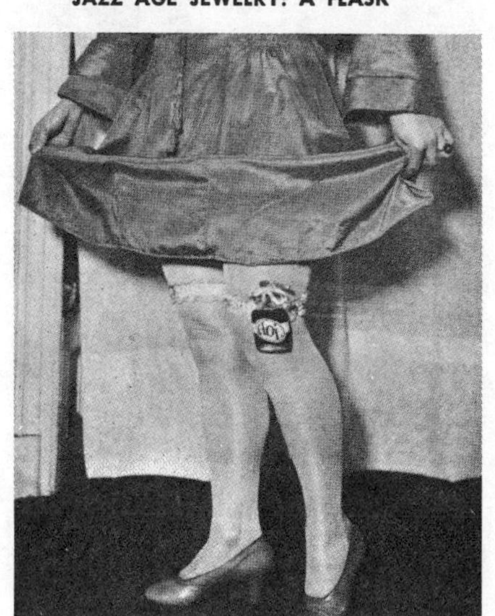

PROHIBITION

The legal sale of intoxicating liquor in the U.S. ended June 30, 1919 and resumed 14 years later. During the interim, respect for the law suffered a serious decline. Bootlegging became a major American industry with ample sources: rum runners, "near-beer" brewers and stills. There were home brews of every variety.

The Prohibition Bureau employed 3,000 agents: the two most famous, Moe Smith and Izzy Einstein *(above, l.)* made 4000-odd arrests. Not more than 5% of the rum-running and 10% of the stills were being stopped. Prohibition went against the grain of the pleasure-seeking Jazz Age.

SPEAKEASY WITH ITS PEEPHOLE

THE GYRATIONS OF BLACK BOTTOM AND CHARLESTON DANCES WERE TYPICAL EXHIBITIONS IN JAZZ AGE

The shimmy *(l.)* originated with Gilda Gray and was immortalized in the jazz classic, "I Wish I Could Shimmy Like My Sister Kate." Its name came from her phrase, "shaking my chemise." The dance-happy '20s, like other eras, had steps that later looked funny—witness Arthur Murray in 1923, already noted for his ballroom style. The Charleston craze swept the country with an epidemic of knock-knees and angled elbows. Dance contests blossomed from coast to coast. Even elderly men and women tried the new steps. A staggering variety of dances enjoyed a brief popularity.

MAH-JONG A POPULAR PASTIME OF THE 20s

Some pastimes of the '20s survived, as did the popularity of many writers of the era and the great crop of jazz musicians whose music has never died.

JOHN HELD, JR. CARTOON DEPICTS JAZZ AGE CHARACTER

Drawing with consummate skill, John Held both created and preserved the era of the '20s for memory and history with his racoon-coated Joe-collegiates, his knee-skirted flappers and his sobbing saxophonists.

AUTHOR ANITA LOOS

Her handbook for golddiggers, *Gentlemen Prefer Blondes,* was a chronicle of Jazz Age. Later it became a Broadway musical.

FITZGERALD AND FAMILY

F. Scott Fitzgerald left a testament of the era in *This Side of Paradise* (1921), *The Beautiful and the Damned* (1922) and *The Great Gatsby* (1926). His writings might have served as text for Held's drawings.

LIFE OF PARTY TEXAS GUINAN

She greeted sugar daddies who visited her famous New York speakeasy with "Hello, Sucker!" and made them like it, ensuring herself a profitable career.

TABLOID CELEBRITIES
The romance of Peaches and Daddy Browning *(l.)* was aired in court and the newspapers. Others in the news were Queen Marie of Rumania, murderers Leopold and Loeb and playgirl Starr Faithfull.

DANCE MARATHONS ▶
The Jazz Age, in its craving for sensation, fostered a Golden Age of sport but also went to unhealthy extremes. These young amateurs were in their 3,327th hour of the grueling spectacle when photographed.

FLAGPOLE SITTING CRAZE
Spectacles of every variety appealed in the '20s. Alvin "Shipwreck" Kelly *(above)* was the most celebrated flagpole sitter.

DR. COUE POINTS HIS FINGER AT ONE OF THE VICTIMS OF HIS PSYCHOLOGY
The formula of Dr. Coué, "Day by day in every way I'm getting better and better," was used to treat all kinds of ailments in the '20s. Meanwhile, Freudian psychology became popular and brought a whole new vocabulary—"libido," "inferiority complex," "inhibition," "super-ego," "frustration"—into fashion. Psychoanalysis was highly in vogue.

HIS HONOR THE MAYOR JIMMY WALKER OF NEW YORK
Walker, like Big Bill Thompson of Chicago, fronted for a slightly soiled political machine and each typified his time and city. However, the mayors were opposite in their approach to royalty: Big Bill threatened to punch the King of England if he showed up in Chicago; in New York Jimmy welcomed celebrities, including the Prince of Wales.

MAE WEST, VOLUPTUOUS QUEEN OF THE MOVIES
As Diamond Lil, Mae West had her greatest popularity. It was a role she played, with variations, through the '20s and later decades. Audiences never tired of it. When Mae said her famous and oft-quoted line, "Come up and see me sometime," in a husky voice, audiences were always delighted.

CLARA BOW had "It," an elusive quality which nobody quite succeeded in defining. Fortunately, definitions proved unnecessary, since "It" was evident in all of her pictures. She made some 30 movies during the decade.

CELEBRITIES of the '20s, Mark Hellinger and Gladys Glad accept congratulations on their marriage from producer Florenz Ziegfeld. Miss Glad was one of the girls "glorified" by Ziegfeld in the popular *Follies* of the era.

INTERNATIONAL TRIO of star entertainers met on shipboard. Shown from left to right are America's adventurous Douglas Fairbanks, the grand old Scotsman Harry Lauder, and the cosmopolitan Frenchman Maurice Chevalier.

GEORGE GERSHWIN'S compositions made him a Jazz Age legend. Along with hit tunes, he wrote *Rhapsody in Blue, Concerto in F* and the opera *Porgy and Bess* which helped make jazz acceptable to American concert-goers.

FUNERAL of Rudolph Valentino, famous in the '20s for his portrayal of the Sheik, drew 40,000 women to Broadway in 1926 and caused almost as much emotional upset as the 1929 crash. Brief career included six star roles.

XANTIPPE, as interpreted in 1928 by Sophie Tucker at a charity affair in London. The indestructible Sophie, who was to become famous as the "last of the Red Hot Mammas," made up in volume what she may have lacked in voice.

FASHIONS

Women cast away their corsets in the '20s. Fashions became at once boyish and defiant. With bobbed hair, cloche hats, flat chests and hips they reflected the spirit of Dorothy Parker's lines: "And if I do not suit you so, to hell, my love with you." Marion Nixon, Kay Francis and Evelyn Brent show styles.

THE BIG SHOT of Chicago crime in the '20s was Al Capone *(l.)*. He was finally convicted on a charge of income tax evasion. Capone died in the last stages of syphilis, but his elaborate criminal organization (see text) survived him.

HENRY LANDRU, called "Bluebeard" by the French, murdered ten of the women he had married. He was condemned to the guillotine after a sensational trial in 1921, and died at Versailles in 1923.

CRIME

Organized underworld becomes a big business

In the '20s criminal organization in the U.S. grew rich, powerful and complex. Prohibition opened a new source of criminal income rivaling that of the steel industry.

In Chicago, the center of a spectacular crime wave, the organization was led by Al Capone. After some bloody gang wars, he came into undisputed control of liquor sales to 10,000 speakeasies. He and other criminals profited from prostitution, narcotics and "protection" rackets. Capone's annual "take" from gambling was an estimated $25,000,000.

Organized crime encouraged police corruption, vice and public cynicism. Its cost in cash, while high, was less than its moral cost which left respect for the law seriously weakened.

MASTER CROOK Gerald Chapman shown in custody *(above)*, pulled a $1,500,000 mail truck robbery in 1921. After his capture he escaped from the Atlanta Penitentiary and killed a policeman. He was soon recaptured and ultimately executed for murder.

LEOPOLD AND LOEB, the two bored neurotic youths who, without any motive, killed little Bobby Franks in 1924, got life imprisonment after a brilliant plea by the famous criminal lawyer Clarence Darrow. Loeb was stabbed to death in 1936 by a fellow inmate.

HANGING Charley Birger didn't stop the Birger-Shelton gang wars which raged in southern Illinois. The two gangs used armored cars and a plane, feuded throughout the decade. Three of the five Shelton boys were dead by 1950.

GANG WARFARE in Chicago culminated in the St. Valentine's Day Massacre of 1929 when seven of Al Capone's competitors were machine-gunned in a bloody bid for power. There were 500 Chicago gang murders in the '20s.

LINDBERGH

FIRST SOLO Atlantic flight was made when Lindbergh flew a Wright-powered Ryan monoplane, *Spirit of St. Louis,* from Roosevelt Field in New York to Le Bourget Airport in Paris, France, a distance of 3610 miles in 33½ air hours on May 20-21, 1927.

A lone aviator in a silver monoplane rose into a drizzling overcast and disappeared over the Atlantic. This was Lindbergh's first step in winning the $25,000 Raymond Orteig Prize.

Charles A. Lindbergh had arrived in New York City on May 11, 1927 to find the other contestants awaiting more favorable weather. With his relatively flimsy equipment the lone flyer soon caused a press sensation in New York. His more cautious competitors, among them Byrd and Chamberlin, were well known pilots while young Lindbergh had never been heard of in the East. Further, his avowed intentions of flying without co-pilot or navigator made a dramatic situation. The trip won him world-wide fame as well as the prize.

STEEL AND CONCRETE canyons of lower Manhattan filled with a hail of cheers and confetti, and the heart of the nation filled with affection for the 25-year old flier who had flown the Atlantic alone. Lindbergh was decorated by France, England and the U. S.

GRAF ZEPPELIN, a German airship, made headlines in August of 1929 by being the first commercial aircraft to fly around the world. The 21-day flight from Lakehurst, New Jersey and back was important in aviation for a second reason: it was also the first successful direct crossing of the Pacific Ocean by any aircraft. The dirigible was soon put into regular passenger service.

COMMANDER Richard E. Byrd and Floyd Bennett *(above* with decorations, DFC) were the first men to fly over the North Pole. They took off from Kings Bay, Spitsbergen, in the Fokker monoplane *Josephine Ford,* on May 8, 1926, and returned there 15½ hours later, after having flown non-stop for 1545 miles.

AROUND THE WORLD flight was attempted from Seattle, Washington on April 6, 1924 by four of these Douglas Army planes. Two of the biplanes were successful in completing the 26,345 mile journey. The total elapsed time was 175 days. Actual flying time, however, was 363 hours. The biplanes used pontoons or wheels, detachable to minimize weight.

AIRMAIL FLIGHTS on a regularly scheduled basis were inaugurated between Los Angeles and New York on July 1, 1924. During the following year, Congress passed the Kelly Airmail Bill, which authorized the U.S. Post Office Department to contract with private airlines to carry the mail on a subsidized basis.

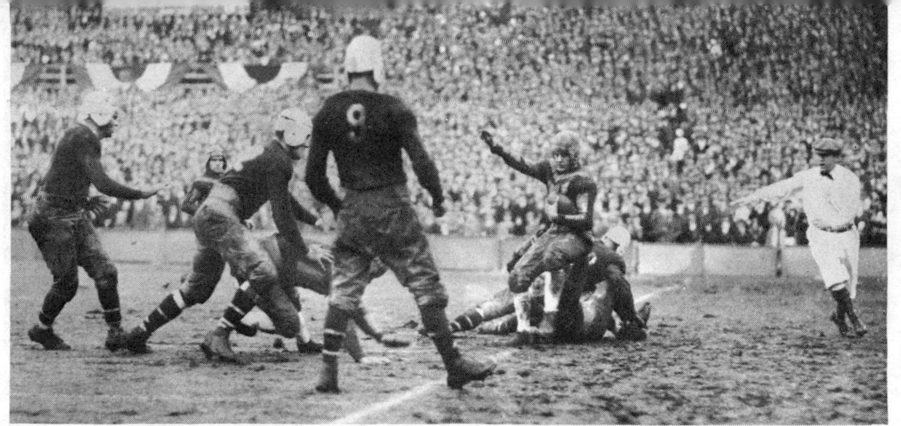

"RED" GRANGE. THREE-YEAR ALL-AMERICAN, LATER TURNED PROFESSIONAL
Known as the "Galloping Ghost" of Illinois, the great Harold "Red" Grange was probably finest running back football has known. Chosen All-American every year of his varsity career, "Red" gained a phenomenal 3,637 yards rushing in 1923-4-5. Induced to turn pro by C. C. Pyle, he gave impetus to the pro game. Grange was the mainstay of the Chicago Bears. He is shown above in a Chicago-N.Y. game.

FOOTBALL SENSATIONS OF 1929
Mighty mite of Eli, sensational Albie Booth, jackrabbited through opposing lines in 1929, the same year that Carideo piloted a great Notre Dame team and Nagurski was tackle at Minnesota.

SPORTS

The fabulous Twenties produce a Golden Age

The Twenties in the sporting world produced top players who were so colorful that they caused a tremendous expansion of interest in their particular sport.

Baseball zoomed to an unprecedented popularity and prosperity largely because of the imagination-catching power of the great Babe Ruth, whose home runs made turnstiles click, boosted his own salary up to a dazzling $80,000 per year and gave magnates the financial power to build big stadiums.

No one, not even the great Joe Louis, could equal the drawing power of Jack Dempsey, whose explosive fists drew the fans to the ring. He drew his biggest crowd, over 120,000 people, when he lost his title to Gene Tunney in 1926. Tunney, defending the title a year later against Tom Heeney, drew a pallid 45,000.

Big Bill Tilden skyrocketed tennis receipts as enthusiasts crowded in to see him blast opponents off the court. Tommy Hitchcock made the American public polo conscious. The elusive "Red" Grange, striking for touchdowns from anywhere on the field, glamorized football and gave the needed impetus to the newly formed professional leagues. *Man O' War* shattered horse-racing standards. The near-invincibles, Charlie Paddock and Paavo Nurmi, made track and field a major spectator sport. Indeed, sports were America's chief relaxation.

SOUTHERN CALIFORNIA TEAMS
"Thundering Herd" was the name given to the mighty Southern California teams of the Twenties which included such great players as Drury and Pinckert. The team was coached by Howard Jones *(above)* and featured off-tackle smash.

NOTRE DAME WINS WITH ROCKNE
Knute Rockne gained fame in the sports world when he coached the Notre Dame football team from 1918 to 1930. He chalked up an outstanding record of victories for his Fighting Irish team with a total of 105 wins and only 12 defeats.

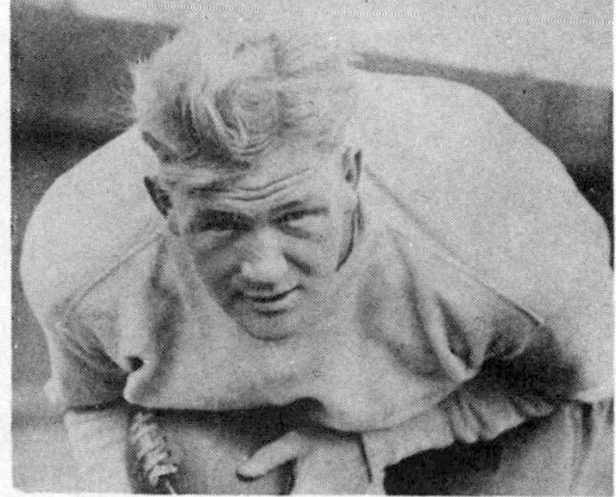

NOTRE DAME TEAM RUNS RIOT ON GRIDIRONS FROM COAST TO COAST
The Four Horsemen of Notre Dame *(l. to r.)*, Harry Stuhldreher, Don Miller, Jim Crowley and Elmer Layden, rambled through opposing teams from 1922 to 1925. All but Don Miller later became successful football coaches. Grantland Rice gave them their nickname. The stalwart of the Stanford team of 1925, Ernie Nevers *(r.)* was considered by many the all-time football great. The Notre Dame team, which defeated Stanford in Rose Bowl 27 to 10, named him their greatest opposing player.

MIGHTY BAT of Babe Ruth was box office magic for baseball, put the National Pastime in the big business class by drawing huge crowds through the turnstiles. The Babe is shown *(c.)* posing with some of his teammates of the early Twenties, the first "Murderers Row" of the Yankees. They are *(l. to r.)* Wally Pipp, Ruth, Peckinpaugh, Bob Meusel and "Home Run" Baker. Picture at left shows Ruth with his home run twin, Lou Gehrig, of the 1927 Yankee team, hailed as one of the finest ever assembled. Using his familiar slugging stance *(r.)*, the Babe set record of 60 home runs in 1927.

SMART CATCHER, Mickey Cochrane, set new style with his great speed. He played a total of 1,482 games and had a lifetime batting average of 320, was elected to the baseball Hall of Fame.

GREAT MANAGERS of the Twenties, John J. McGraw of the New York Giants *(l.)* and Connie Mack greet each other at the 1913 World Series. Mack's Philadelphia Athletics went on to win the series, 4 games to 1. Both piloted their teams through many pennant-winning seasons.

STALWART SLUGGER of the National League was Rogers Hornsby, who held National League batting crown for seven seasons between 1920 and 1928. In 1924 he set the modern era batting record of .424.

HARDY PERENNIAL of big league pitchers was Grover C. Alexander of the Philadelphia Phillies. In his 20-year career he won 373, lost 208, holds record for most shut out games in a single season (16 in 1916).

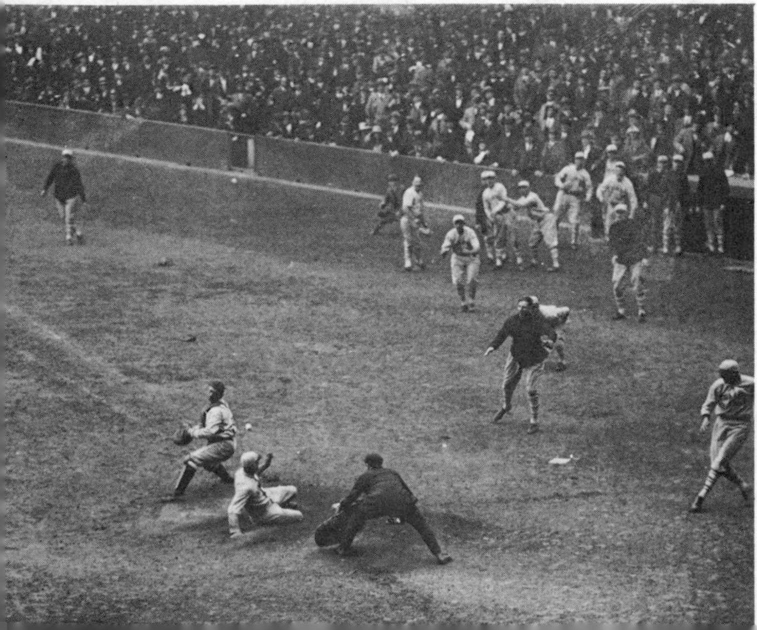

DEVIL MAY CARE base running was revived by the Fordham Flash, Frank Frisch, who often headed into the bag on his stomach. Frisch later became manager of the St. Louis club and won a World Series victory.

TREMENDOUS EXCITEMENT shown by players *(l.)* was generated by inside-the-park home run hit by Casey Stengel in the first game of the 1923 World Series between Giants and Yankees. Series was taken by Yankees, four out of six.

MAN O' WAR WINS HIS LAST RACE IN 1921 AGAINST SIR BARTON AND ZEV TRIUMPHS IN THE KENTUCKY DERBY

Man O' War's last race was a match race against Sir Barton in 1921, held at Kenilworth Park, Canada for $80,000. Man O' War, a three-year-old, defeated his four-year-old rival *(l.)* and then retired. His owner Samuel D. Riddle, refused a $1,000,000 offer for him; and he made a fine stud record, siring such greats as War Admiral, Crusader and American Flag. Kentucky Derby winner, Zev *(r.)* beat English Derby winner, Papyrus, by five lengths in International Classic at Belmont Park in 1923. Papyrus, a truly great horse, was hampered by unfamiliar conditions of the track.

OLYMPIC STAR

Blazing finish marked the running of Charlie Paddock *(l.)*, shown here winning the Olympic 100-meter dash.

BREAKS RECORD

Great distance runner from Finland, Paavo Nurmi, broke world's record for the mile in 1923-24.

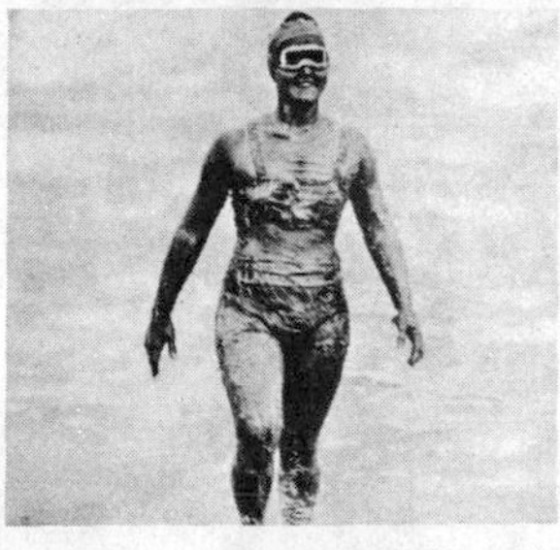

FIRST woman to conquer the English Channel was Gertrude Ederle, who made the long swim successfully in 1926 and set woman's record of 14 hours 31 mins.

SWIMMING CHAMPION of the era was famous power-stroking Johnny Weismuller, who succeeded in lowering the world's record for the 100 yard free style by two seconds in five years.

GRAND SLAM WINNER of the U.S. and the British Open and Amateur golf titles in 1930, and greatest golfer of the Twenties was Robert Tyre "Bobby" Jones *(l.)* who made life miserable for the greatest of the era's pros, Walter Hagen *(r.)*. Rising popularity of the game set off a miniature golf craze.

HEAVYWEIGHT WRESTLING CHAMP

The paralyzing grip demonstrated here *(l.)* by Ed "Strangler" Lewis, former heavyweight wrestling champion, became famous throughout the world as his "trade mark."

BASKETBALL'S CELTICS

Original Celtics of 1922-23 are still considered by many experts the greatest basketball team of all time. Shown here *(l. to r.)* are John Beckman, John Whitney, Nat Holman, Jack Barry and Chris Leonard. Game was becoming a major sport.

DEMPSEY DISPOSES OF SURPRISING CHALLENGER FROM SOUTH OF THE BORDER IN BRIEF BUT EXCITING BATTLE

The greatest fight of Dempsey's career may well have been his match with the Argentine, Luis Angel Firpo, in New York in 1923. Firpo, a huge man, unleashed a terrific right in the first round which drove Dempsey through the ropes and into the laps of the sports writers. They helped him back into the ring, and many claimed that the referee should have awarded the fight and championship to Firpo. Dempsey climbed back in fighting mad and belabored Firpo into unconsciousness in the second round. The knockout was one of the most devastating exhibitions of sheer punching power ever seen.

DISPUTED LONG COUNT

Dempsey *(l.)* went to wrong corner following knock-down of Tunney in their second fight (1927). Tunney rallied to retain championship, later retired undefeated.

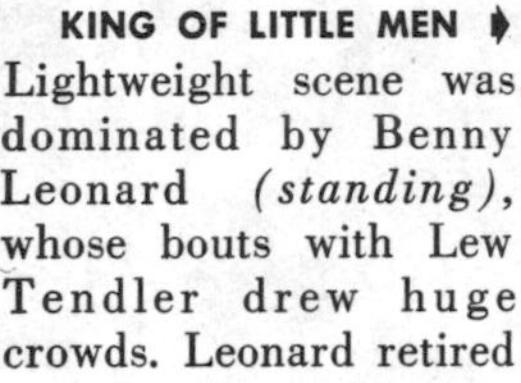

KING OF LITTLE MEN ▶

Lightweight scene was dominated by Benny Leonard *(standing)*, whose bouts with Lew Tendler drew huge crowds. Leonard retired undefeated in 1924.

DOMINANT IN WOMEN'S TENNIS

France's Mlle. Suzanne Lenglen regularly beat America's best woman, Molla Bjurstedt Mallory, at Wimbledon before turning professional in 1926. Here Queen Mary greets her at Wimbledon.

FINESSE AND POWER ON DISPLAY

Greatest tennis player was William T. Tilden, virtually unbeatable in 1920-1926. He guided the U.S. to seven Davis Cup triumphs until France won with Barotra the Bounding Basque in 1927.

GIRLS' CHAMPION IN 1923

Helen Wills developed a poker face, ice in her veins, and magnificent strokes. She completely dominated the women's tennis scene both here and abroad in the late Twenties and early Thirties.

HEMINGWAY AN AMATEUR BOXER

Ernest Hemingway, with a simple, direct style, was successful and popular at an early age. Among his famous novels are *In Our Time* (1924), *The Sun Also Rises* (1926), *Farewell to Arms* (1929).

THE NOVELS OF SINCLAIR LEWIS REFLECT AN ERA OF DISILLUSIONMENT

In Lewis' novel *Main Street,* he satirizes dreariness of small towns. In *Babbitt* (1922) he exposes small business mores; in *Arrowsmith* (1925) he treats the medical profession rather gently, but in *Elmer Gantry* (1927) he bears down hard on religious hypocrisy. Lewis' novels are prime examples of the reaction from idealism. He is shown here with his wife in a small town typical of the one in *Main Street.*

BOOKS

After the war, as the great Victorians died one by one, the literary pioneers of the "lost generation" emerged. Their attitude was wary and a little cynical, perhaps as a result of the war. But they were vigorous and not afraid to break with tradition.

They preferred realism to sentiment, although sentiment still sold well. Bruce Barton's biography portraying Christ as a businessman was as much a part of the times as Sinclair Lewis.

Science, particularly the new psychology of Freud and the behaviorists, opened up new channels of characterization. James Joyce, Virginia Wolfe, Aldous Huxley, D. H. Lawrence and other British writers pioneered in the technique of chronicling the mind's adventures.

Sherwood Anderson helped to free the short story from several hidebound conventions. Subsequently the form was raised to a new peak of excellence by such writers as Ernest Hemingway and Erskine Caldwell.

Poetry in America was highlighted by such great names as Robert Frost, Edna St. Vincent Millay and George Santayana. The spirited Twenties kindled many talents.

GERTRUDE STEIN AND HER FRIEND ALICE B. TOKLAS

Gertrude Stein is known as a leader of extremism in modern literature. She was never a popular success in America. Her writing was controversial but as a brilliant conversationalist she influenced Thornton Wilder, Hemingway and others.

JOYCE AND GRANDSON

James Joyce's novel *Ulysses* (1920), was revolutionary in its technique. It was barred from the U.S. by censorship until 1933.

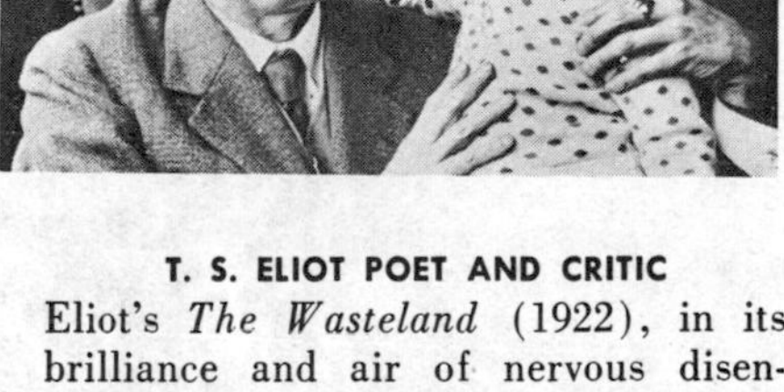

POPULAR SHORT STORY WRITER

Ring Lardner (shown with Mrs. Lardner) used the short-story form and fashioned some of the most biting satires in the language. *Haircut,* for example, is found in many anthologies.

TWO REALISTIC NOVELISTS

John Dos Passos, author of *Manhattan Transfer* (1925), later in decade worked on his massive trilogy *U.S.A.* Theodore Dreiser, dean of the genre, is best known for his *An American Tragedy.*

T. S. ELIOT POET AND CRITIC

Eliot's *The Wasteland* (1922), in its brilliance and air of nervous disenchantment, contributed a touchstone for the decade. "The Love Song of J. Alfred Prufrock" is Eliot at his finest.

ARTIST'S MECCA AND RETREAT moved from Paris, France to Greenwich Village, New York City. Aspiring artists displayed their paintings on back alley walls. Occasionally, amidst the clutter of mediocre art, could be found the work of a new genius not yet moved to Fifth Avenue.

REVOLUTIONARY WOOLWORTH BUILDING in New York City finally gained official recognition for its architect Cass Gilbert in 1929. The building had been completed in 1913. Although recognition came late, people could not help but feel the influence of the skyscraper's long, clean lines on New York's rapidly emerging sky-line of goliaths.

MILLIONAIRE PHILANTHROPISTS opened their extensive collections to the public for viewing or gave them to the American people. Pictured above is the Freer Gallery in Washington, D. C. It was the gift of millionaire Charles L. Freer. The Gallery exhibited rare and precious collections of antique Asiatic and recent American art.

HARVEST TIME FOR U. S. ART

Seeds of art interest sown by the great expositions of the first decade were reaped in the 20's. American artists were home to stay. Art schools, museums, and galleries blossomed. Magazines grew, and newspapers began staffing art editors. Villages all over the land formed art associations and held exhibits.

Although the country was more enthusiastic about art than in previous years, it was not yet ready to accept "modern" art. When the Paris Exposition in 1927 stipulated that exhibits must be "modernistic," the cautious Coolidge administration refused to participate. In 1927 Customs officials refused to classify as art work the abstractionist sculpture of Brancusi.

The American government became an art patron by erecting battle monuments in Europe. These monuments were, of course, in the classic design.

The American people began to acquire a new taste in art. They liked the smoothness and simplicity, later to be called "functionalism" and "streamlining," which appeared in commercial buildings and vehicles.

Progressive museums and galleries worked with industry to foster the fledgling profession of industrial design. Their aim was to couple genius for mass production with artistic skill in order to bring harmonious design into everyday living.

The idea that American art should be native, free of its cultural subjection to Europe, was taking hold in the country. The way was opening for fresh and independent work to gain recognition and acceptance. Artists discovered the artistic and pictorial possibilities of the skyscraper and the machine. They turned for inspiration to their own country, its land and its people.

This era of art belonged basically to the industrialist and the philanthropist whose importance was shown by gifts amounting to millions and by Henry E. Huntington's purchase of Gainsborough's *Blue Boy* for $640,000.

ARTISTS, professional and amateur both, were drawn to scenes like this one *(r.)* at Provincetown, Mass. Art was now as much for the average American as for the artist. Art colonies from coast to coast became favorite vacation spots. Dabblers found themselves rubbing elbows with established artists at Laguna Beach, Taos, Brown County, Asheville and Provincetown.

BAPTISM IN KANSAS by John Steuart Curry *(l.)*, hangs at the Whitney Museum of American Art. This oil painting established Curry as one of the foremost artists in the U.S. and a leading member of regionalist school.

LECTURERS WERE A NEW TYPE of museum personnel. They were needed when museums began presenting well planned educational programs. Pictured above is John D. Rockefeller, Jr.'s museum "The Cloisters" in Fort Tryon Park, N. Y.

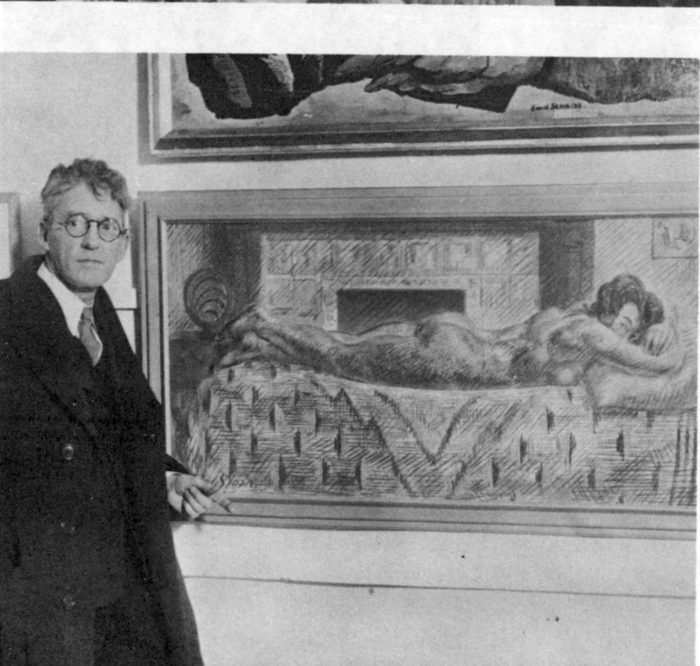

LEADER OF THE INDEPENDENTS, John Sloan, exhibits his work *Nude, Four Senses*. The Society of Independent Artists was very unregimented and its exhibit rule of "no jury, no prizes" helped to increase its membership.

MOVIES in the TWENTIES

The great movie idols of the 1920's were unsurpassed in any other decade. The all-time greats were Barrymore, Bow, Chaney, Chaplin, Colman, Fairbanks, Garbo, Gilbert, Keaton, Lloyd, Pickford, Swanson and Valentino. The movies' emphasis on the theme of sex evoked so much criticism from church officials that the producers were forced to create a censorship office and Will Hays, Harding's Postmaster-General, was appointed its head.

BEAUTIFUL GRETA GARBO and John Gilbert set hearts to pounding with intense scenes like this one *(above)*. A *Variety* poll found Garbo greatest woman film star of all time. John Barrymore made love to Dolores Costello in *The Sea Beast (below)*. He was one of first to act in a film using sound accompaniment provided by "Vitaphone" process.

TOM MIX AND TONY galloped across the screen shooting and capturing stagecoach robbers and Indians. Exponents of the motion picture at its best, they moved and performed against very photogenic backgrounds. Fox Films paid Tom Mix $20,000 a week for performing in these cowboy epics. His films were good family fare. Justice triumphed.

"THE COVERED WAGON" was one of the first large-scale productions to utilize the winning of the American West as its theme. This extravaganza moved westerns into a higher class of film fare. James Cruze, the director, shot the exteriors in Nevada. The attack on the wagon train is shown above. Cruze and his stars, J. W. Kerrigan, Lois Wilson, Ernest Torrence, returned with one of the big hits of 1923. This film convinced the movie industry that big grosses were readily obtainable for spectacular films.

GISH SISTERS, Lillian and Dorothy, made *Orphans of the Storm (above)* for Griffith in 1922. Lillian had won a personal triumph in *Broken Blossoms*, 1919, in which she played opposite Richard Barthelmess. Both sisters had previously appeared on the stage. Dorothy: a comedienne; Lillian played ingenues.

GREAT actor and pantomimist was Charlie Chaplin. With Jackie Coogan *(r.)*, he made *The Kid* in 1920. As a tramp, Chaplin combined laughter with pathos. Chaplin portrayed same tramp in *The Gold Rush* and *The Circus.* Coogan played the waif so poignantly that he became a great star overnight.

YOKEL parts made a star of Harold Lloyd. He was foolish but likeable. Audiences roared while he tried to extricate himself from fantastic predicaments. Shown *(l.)* is a scene from *Safety Last*, made in 1923. Other popular Lloyd movies were *The Freshman* and *Grandma's Boy*, both hilarious hits.

CHARIOT RACE in *Ben Hur* was one of the biggest movie thrills in 1926. Niblo directed Francis X. Bushman *(l.)*, Ramon Navarro *(r.)*, Betty Bronson, Carmel Meyers and Fay McAvoy in early hit.

GREAT LOVER Rudolph Valentino *(far left)* had more fans than any actor known. Douglas Fairbanks *(l.)* fought duels and rescued damsels in distress with an athletic grace which captivated fans. Ghoulish Lon Chaney *(below, center)* was master of macabre, frightening characterizations.

"THE TALKIES"

Although Edison's kinetoscope synchronized sound with pictures, his invention was never fully developed. In 1922 the inventor of radio's audion tube, Lee De Forest, said he could perfect "talking movies". However, sound was not used until 1926 when Warner Brothers, in financial difficulties, seized upon Western Electric's Vitaphone to attract audiences to theatre. *Don Juan* used a musical accompaniment, played from discs. "Musical shorts" were made by Warners and Fox.

The Warners again took the lead in sound pioneering by using music with dialogue in *The Jazz Singer* (1927), with Al Jolson. There was no planned dialogue, but Jolson adlibbed and "Talkies" were born.

IN BLACK FACE, singer Al Jolson got down on his knees and helped make "talkies" a success with *The Singing Fool* (1928) and *The Jazz Singer (above)* in which he sang his famous song, *Sonny Boy,* to young Davey Lee.

MACK SENNETT continued to produce comedy hits in the 1920's. His slapstick gags convulsed audiences. Ben Turpin *(center)* was his biggest name at this time. Comics Snub Pollard and Marie Provost flank funny-man Turpin.

LAURETTE TAYLOR created the title role in *Peg O' My Heart* on Broadway in 1912 for 603 performances, enacted it again in films, married play's author.

"IT GIRL", Clara Bow, epitomized the flapper of the Twenties. She got her title from Elinor Glyn who wrote the widely-read book *It.* In *True to the Navy* she charmed Frederic March.

"SEVENTH HEAVEN" (1927) won Academy Awards for Janet Gaynor and director Frank Borzage. She and her co-star Charles Farrell played lovers.

"THE BIG PARADE" (1925) was first American film to show the war realistically. The stars were Renée Adorée, John Gilbert. King Vidor directed.

WALT DISNEY drew his first animated cartoon in 1920 featuring Oswald the Rabbit. In 1928, when he developed a friendly mouse named Mickey, his true genius became apparent. *Steamboat Willy,* Mickey's second short, used sound and became immediate success.

LAVISH MUSICALS flourished and became extremely popular with the inception of sound. One of the first "backstage" stories was *The Broadway Melody* (1929), starring Charles King.

BOBBY CLARK *(r.)* and Paul McCullough went to Broadway from Burlesque to star in *The Ramblers* in 1926. Phil Silvers, Bert Lahr and Ben Blue were other baggy-pants comedians who left burlesque for the legitimate theatre.

GREAT COMICS, The Marx Bros. — Groucho, Zeppo, Harpo and Chico —went from vaudeville to musical comedy and then to the movies. Their 1928 hit was a madhouse named *Animal Crackers,* written by Kaufman and Ryskind.

THEATER

BOMBASTIC W. C. FIELDS careened through several Ziegfield *Follies* and starred in *Poppy (above).* A big red nose was his famous trade-mark.

PART INDIAN, Will Rogers was a gum-chewing rope-twirler from Oklahoma. He developed into a laconic comedian and starred in the *Follies,* became "best loved actor in America."

EUGENE O'NEILL'S *Emperor Jones* was 1921 sensation with Charles Gilpin starring. The same year, O'Neill's play *Anna Christie* opened; *Desire Under the Elms* 1924; *Strange Interlude* 1928.

ELEANORA DUSE, Italian actress, was compared with Bernhardt as "world's greatest actress". She died on her farewell American tour in 1924.

BEAUTIFUL GIRLS and lavish scenery made Florenz Ziegfield, Jr. synonymous with American musical revues. His famous *Follies* (1910-27) had top casts.

MOST SUCCESSFUL couple acting in the modern theatre, Alfred Lunt & Lynn Fontanne, gave Theatre Guild its 1924 hit with Ferenc Molnar's *The Guardsman.* His *Liliom* was 1921 Guild hit.

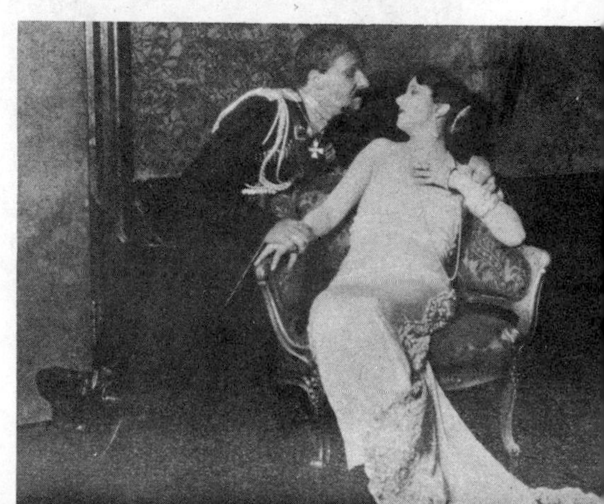

SCIENCE

In the 1920's, the machine dominated hand labor. Automobiles, busses and trucks practically replaced the horse for transportation and hauling purposes. The smallest villages installed electricity, and the new ease of telephone communication changed social and business habits. A new apparatus *(above, l.)* transmitted photos by radio to New York from London. Press associations hailed the likenesses *(r.)* as good enough to publish.

SPEED OF LIGHT, long thought to be 186,000 miles per second, was found to be 227 miles faster by Prof. Albert A. Michelson of University of Chicago, after many years of extensive research.

X-RAY RESEARCHER was Prof. Arthur H. Compton who shared the 1927 Nobel prize for physics with Professor Rees Wilson of England. Professor Compton is shown above with his invention, the revolutionary X-ray spectrometer.

BOON TO HOLLYWOOD was the Pallo-Photo-Phone, invented by Charles A. Hoxie in 1922. This device recorded both picture and voice, synchronized them perfectly on the same film. Hoxie and Pallo-Photo-Phone shown above.

THEORY OF RELATIVITY was demonstrated by Prof. Lundendorf, director of the Potsdam Observatory in Germany. The astronomer is shown here with Albert Einstein (in white suit), the man who originated the theory.

FORERUNNER OF TUBES now used in television sets was the huge cathode ray tube developed in 1928. Tube produced as many electrons per second as one ton of radium. The new device was developed by scientist Coolidge.

MEDICINE

The Twenties were the era in medicine during which the public became vitamin conscious. A major achievement was the discovery that liver extract could be utilized in the treatment of anemia (1926). A serum developed in 1922 helped check the dread Rocky Mountain spotted fever.

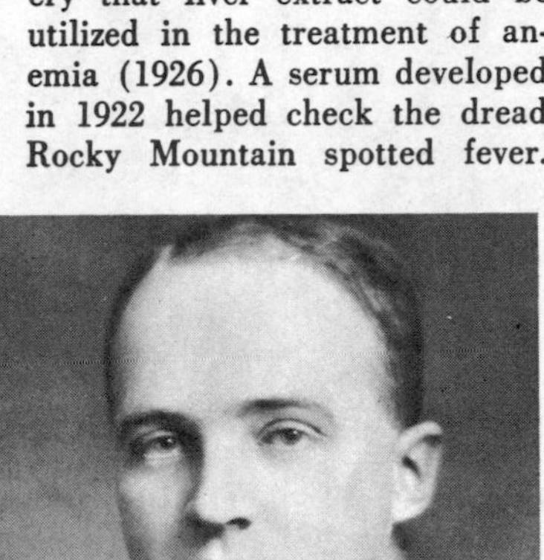

HELP FOR DIABETICS came when Drs. Charles H. Best *(above)* and F. G. Banting *(below)* discovered insulin. Their work in 1921 helped diabetics live normal lives by using insulin.

"CRIMSON NEWS" was featured by the tabloids of the 20's. New York *Graphic* printed "composite" photos of "Daddy" Browning, a married real-estate man who gave young girls luxurious gifts and took them to expensive places. He was shown with his "dolls," Mary, Peaches (his wife) and Sunshine.

PAPERS MERGE

Tabloids gain big circulation; Press caters to the advertiser

After World War I most of the world's press was linked closer than ever to the government and largely regulated by political censorship. This was especially true in Communist Russia.

Even in America there was an air of self-imposed censorship as control of more and more newspapers shifted from "fighting editors" to cautious, dollar-conscious businessmen.

As newspapers became mainly business ventures, their function as molders of public opinion became largely subordinated to the wishes of the advertisers. As production costs increased, publishers were more dependent upon advertisers to stay in business. Hence, the Twenties was an era of mergers. Newspapers were killed or bought out in order to build up circulations large enough to attract advertisers. By 1924, 30 chains controlled 150 dailies. Frank A. Munsey bought the New York *Herald* and merged it with the *Sun*. He also bought the *Telegram* which he later sold to Scripps-Howard who merged it with the *World*. Hearst expanded his chain by buying the Los Angeles *Herald*, San Francisco *Call-Post*, Baltimore *News*, and other papers. Frank A. Gannett started his chain by gaining control of three up-state New York papers in 1923. In 1929 he purchased the 87-year-old *Brooklyn Eagle*.

In America the Twenties saw the rise of the tabloid, based on the highly successful London *Mirror*. The first American tabloid was the *Daily News*, founded by J. M. Patterson. Others were Hearst's *Mirror* and MacFadden's *Evening Graphic*. Primarily "picture" newspapers, tabloids were soon locked in a battle for circulation supremacy, sought to attract readers by printing sensational and intimate pictures and stories about murder and sex.

FAMOUS EVOLUTION TRIAL made big news in 1925. John T. Scopes, a high school science teacher in Dayton, Tenn., was publicly tried for teaching Darwinism. He was defended by the greatest free-thinking lawyer of the time, Clarence Darrow. Scopes and Darrow were defeated by Fundamentalist William Jennings Bryan. Mississippi (1926), Arkansas (1928) and Texas (1929) followed Tennessee by passing laws forbidding the teaching of evolution in state-supported schools. Country was not ready to accept man's descent from animal.

PUBLISHER HENRY R. LUCE established a new style and trend in news journalism with his *Time* magazine in 1923. *Time's* lively summarization of the news gained it a large circulation. The first issue is shown at the right. Other popular magazines of the 20's were the *Saturday Evening Post*, *Liberty*, Western and "confession" magazines.

FOUNDER of New York *Daily News* was Joseph M. Patterson. Established in 1919 as a sensational tabloid, *News* became the largest circulation daily in the United States.

ADOLPH OCHS built New York *Times* from 10,000 circulation in 1900 to one of the world's greatest and most respected papers. Its famous slogan was "All the news that's fit to print."

CHURCH was victor in Lateran Treaty of 1829. Mussolini gave Vatican rights of a sovereign state. The Pope became temporal ruler of the Vatican. Pius XI ended voluntary confinement *(l.)*.

SOUL-SAVER Aimee Semple McPherson *(r.)* employed old time religion and Hollywood theatrics to thrill members of International Church of the Four Square Gospel in Los Angeles. Advertising helped win her converts.

RELIGION THRIVES IN TWENTIES

On the whole, the Twenties represented boom years for churches in America. Their edifices alone soared to a $3 billion evaluation and they spent $5 million a year.

Although the Sunday automobile ride and the new diversions outside home and church reduced Protestant ranks by three per cent, membership still topped 35 million.

The outstanding Protestant phenomenon of the decade was Fundamentalism, which expressed the opposition of religiously conservative rural groups to urban notions of evolution and to the changing moral standards.

Catholics had solved their differences with Italy and Mexico. The Church won its battle against the free-thinkers within and there were few issues during the decade. The Pope spoke against the godlessness of Communists and the greed of capitalists, but Catholics were secure enough not to feel deeply involved. Immigration had swelled U. S. Catholics to 19 million and world membership was over 322 million.

The record was marred only in the Balkans and Russia. Jewish refugees from pogroms in Bessarabia and the Pale of Settlement fled to America. In America, they had escaped their endless persecution, yet many were still nervous about the future and embraced Zionism.

In Russia Marxian Communism was trying to remove religion from the masses, and 100 million Orthodox Russians were deprived of their religious freedom. Communists called religion "the opiate of the people" and condemned the pious.

SOCIAL CONSCIENCE grew in U.S. when Jane Addams, shown at Chicago's Hull House, called attention to deplorable slum conditions. She won a Nobel prize and served as chairman of Women's League for Peace and Freedom.

BERTRAND RUSSELL believed that science must be free from teleology. The philosopher quarreled with Pietists who believed God was the essential end for science. Russell favored working on questions man can solve.

DAREDEVIL CODY often defied death. Woman daredevil Mabel Cody made news by performing the death defying feat pictured above. She was one of the first stunt performers to thrill onlookers by changing from a speeding auto to an airplane. The daring act was done by means of a rope hanging from airplane. Cody successfully performed this maneuvre at Daytona Beach, Florida.

PASSING SCENE

"BIG RED SCARE" swept U.S. in the early 1920's. The Revolution in Russia created an hysterical atmosphere. Labor struck often. Employers felt improving labor conditions was "bolshevistic". Attorney General Palmer made mass arrests, was instrumental in passing a peace-time sedition act, deported the above group of aliens. Five N. Y. Socialist assemblymen were denied seats.

LOUD SPEAKERS were first used by Calvin Coolidge when he campaigned for re-election in 1924. Radios were still luxuries, but enough advancement had been made to put loud speakers in cars which cruised the streets. More radios by 1928 made it worthwhile for Herbert Hoover to campaign over air.

PLAYWRIGHT George Bernard Shaw won the Nobel Prize for Literature in 1925. He established Anglo-Swedish Alliance with his prize money. Purpose of the Alliance was to familiarize Britons with Swedish literature.

DOG STAR adored by U. S. children was Rin-Tin-Tin, famous dog motion picture star. The idol of every American boy and girl, he earned millions for Warner Brothers. He is pictured above with Mrs. Rin-Tin-Tin and their pups.

PRINCE OF WALES made front-page. Edward, Prince of Wales, was the favorite subject of society columnists in the 1920's. The Prince made headlines when he was thrown *(l.)* during a horse race in England in 1928.

AMERICAN OPERA *The King's Henchman* written by Deems Taylor *(r., center)* was premiered at the Metropolitan Opera House in New York in 1927. Edna St. Vincent Millay wrote libretto; tenor Edward Johnson starred.

WALL STREET EXPLOSION KILLS 30, INJURES 200

On September 16, 1920, a mysterious explosion rocked Wall Street. The police traced the blast to a small junk wagon which had been abandoned by four men in front of the Sub-Treasury building. Although many people were held for questioning, the police were baffled. Crime remains unsolved.

FLOYD COLLINS DIES PINNED DOWN IN SAND CAVE

In 1925, rescuers failed to save Floyd Collins' life when he was pinned by the foot while exploring a Kentucky sand cave. While his rescuers worked to reach him from a shaft through the limestone rock, Collins lived in the above position for 19 days. He died the day before they reached him.

DISASTERS

FOURTEEN CREW MEMBERS KILLED

The dirigible *U.S. Shenandoah* finally landed near Sharon, Ohio after it was torn apart in a thunder storm in 1925. Fourteen of the crew lost their lives.

TORNADOES BATTERED MIDWEST

High winds tore off the side of this home in Lorain, Ohio in 1924 while the state had its worst tornado. Midwest areas were damaged in 1924 and 1925.

MISSISSIPPI TAKES HIGH TOLL

The 1927 Mississippi River flood left thousands homeless. Blasting of Poydras, La. dikes relieved pressure on New Orleans dikes and city was saved.

SICILIAN VOLCANO ERUPTS

Mount Etna erupted in 1928 sending lava streams 100 feet wide cascading down the mountain. The town of Mascati, Sicily was completely wiped out and the total damage from the eruption was estimated at $10,000,000.

HURRICANE BEATS GULF STATES

Hurricane in 1926 killed 372 people and destroyed 5,000 homes. This Miami hotel was blown off its foundation. A second twister struck Cuba, killed 600.

ADVERTISING

With improved publications and the new medium of radio, advertising emerged in the 1920's as a new selling force. It deeply affected American habits, tastes, and aspirations.

Advertising created the mass demand needed for mass production. People were told that, now, they too could and should have the new autos, refrigerators and radios. These no longer were luxuries but items necessary for pleasant daily living.

Within advertising, also, strides were made. Cheesecake appeared when Holeproof Hosiery raised skirts and showed legs. Women appeared in cigarette ads. Men blessed advertising for promoting collars that were softer and non-detachable.

Within a single decade, millions were sold new heights of enjoyment.

THE FIRST WOMAN IN CIGARETTE ADVERTISING MADE SHOCKING HISTORY

The Chesterfield advertisement *(above)* appeared in 1926. It established a new precedent in cigarette advertising by subtly enticing women to smoke. This ad paved the way for a Lucky Strike ad in 1929 which urged its readers, "Reach for a Lucky Instead of a Sweet." This slogan infuriated the National Confectioners Assn. but doubled the sales of George Washington Hill's American Tobacco Company.

SLOGANS BECAME AN IMPORTANT PART OF SELLING

Slogans began to be used more and more as a popular selling device. They were excellent devices for succinctly conveying one outstanding idea to the public. "I'd Walk a Mile for a Camel" was created in 1921 and appeared in all Camel advertising. It played a big role in increasing Camel sales.

THIS DRAMATIC AD BOOSTED JORDAN MOTOR CAR SALES

This famous Edward S. Jordan ad was much read, discussed and remembered. It caught the dashing spirit of the time and set afire dreams of owning a car. It appealed to the reader's desire to please "the woman in his life" and to the longing for a charming companion to spend carefree hours with.

CHRYSLER Corporation was formed in 1925 by Walter P. Chrysler *(l.)*. Company manufactured the Plymouth, DeSoto, Dodge, Chrysler cars.

HENRY FORD and son Edsel stand beside the "Model A" Ford in 1928 Automobile Show. Their "Model T" was long the nation's favorite car.

TRAVEL

Americans on wheels

FIRST RADIO for use in automobiles required an aerial a great deal taller than the Dodge which carried it, could hardly have been a handy gadget.

U. S. railroads reached their peak about 1920. In that year they operated 263,821 miles of track and recorded 47,369,906,000 passengers. Their assets were estimated by the Interstate Commerce Commission at $18.9 billions—amounting to about one-tenth of the nation's wealth.

Americans were now beginning to consider their motor cars a necessity rather than a hobby. In 1927 the Holland Tunnel under the Hudson river was opened and hard-surfaced highways encouraged the use of automobiles for travel. By 1929, 26,501,000 vehicles were registered, including 34,000 busses and 3,408,000 trucks. The automobile industry had produced an enormous volume in its 30 years and vigorous rivalry developed among its three giants—the General Motors, Chrysler, and Ford corporations.

WHITE-BUILT BUS was used by Prumer Coach Line on its first scheduled run to Miami in 1924. Greyhound Line later absorbed Prumer into its own system.

WILLIAM C. DURANT, President of Durant Motors, got $348 for his 1922 *Star*. Ex-head of General Motors, he tried to undersell Ford and Chevrolet.

MAXWELL CAR here has Mary Pickford, "America's Sweetheart," at the wheel. Until about 1910, almost all cars were open-bodied touring or roadsters.

"BREMEN," the North German Lloyd liner won her right to the title Queen of the Seas in 1929. Her time for crossing the Atlantic from Cherbourg to Ambrose Channel was 4 days, 17 hours and 42 minutes. Competition in luxury and speed characterized the '20s in all modes of transportation.

RAILROADS responded to the lively competition for customers and business by improving designs and schedules. In 1925 the New York Central's famous luxury train *20th Century Limited* began its mile-a-minute schedule, making New York to Chicago run in 960 minutes—fabulous speed in '20s.

RADIO BROADCASTING began with this mass of wires and coils in Dr. Frank Conrad's garage in Pittsburgh. Listeners heard the Westinghouse engineer's voice and recorded music from this experimental station. On November 2, 1920, Conrad's station became Station KDKA in Pittsburgh. In 1926 the Radio Corporation of America formed the National Broadcasting Co. as a subsidiary. The Columbia Broadcasting System was organized a year later by William S. Paley.

RADIO

America on the air

Radio's tremendous popular appeal and its immediate acceptance by the public helped it grow from the experimental crystal set to a great new industry by 1929.

Assembling the various parts of an early radio was quite a chore—first came the "box" itself, then aerials, grounding apparatus, headphones, loudspeakers, and even battery mats to "protect the rugs" were available in confusing variety.

By 1927 the airwaves were so crowded with broadcasting stations that the Federal Radio Commission was formed with power to license stations and to assign wave lengths.

PERSONALITIES in early broadcasting were soon local and national favorites. Here Station WEAF's sports announcer Graham McNamee covers the first game of the 1926 baseball season. Sports, jazz bands and comedians were popular.

VOICES, especially coloratura soprano voices, proved difficult to broadcast. Singers of popular music, grand opera stars (Lucrezia Bori, *above*), orchestras and comedians were tested to determine what the audiences wanted.

RADIO LISTENING became a part of almost everyone's life with the rapid improvement in loudspeakers and sets. The Patter Teams, Billy Jones, Ernie Hare, The Happiness Boys, and Roxie's Gang were among the early performers.

SOUND EFFECTS were crude *(l.)* and difficult to achieve because transmission by radio distorted many sounds beyond recognition. To make a Victor recording in early 1920s, musicians crowded around the recording horn *(r.)* with amplifying devices attached to the violins for maximum volume. By 1925 Victor had developed an electrical recording method which produced a richer, truer tone and permitted the musicians to perform from their normal positions without the use of amplifiers.

THE CRASH!

Financial disaster ends Golden Era

On Black Tuesday, October 29, 1929, the value of many popular stocks was cut in half on the floor of the New York Stock Exchange *(r.)*. In panic selling, over 16 million shares changed hands in the single day's trading.

Hoping for a reversal of the downward spiral, anxious crowds waited outside the Exchange for news *(lower r.)*. With "hot tips" and "inside information," many speculated, buying 90% of stock on credit. Inside broker's offices clients watched the ticker tape *(l.)* as dreams of retirement and affluence were wiped out. With heavy trading, quotations on the tape fell so far behind as to be useless, and negotiations were completed without any idea of the prices offered or received.

The sudden and ruinous decline ended the seven year idyll of a continuous market advance. In a little over two months' time the Dow Jones Industrial Average fell from its all-time high of 381.17 on September 3, 1939 to 198.69 on November 13, 1929. In three days, October 26 to 29, the Average had dropped 68 points.

Within three weeks, losses were near 30 billion in securities on the Exchange alone. Total paper declines for listed and unlisted securities throughout the nation were probably well over $100 billion.

POWERFUL investment banker Samuel Insull controlled a $4 billion public utility empire with an investment of less than 10%. The artificially inflated structure he had built collapsed disastrously after stock market crash of 1929.

CHARLES M. SCHWAB, early associate of steel titan Andrew Carnegie, was still active as the head of Bethlehem Steel in the Twenties. Schwab was one of original founders of the U.S. Steel Corp.

LEADERS IN AUTO industry were Edsel Ford, Walter P. Chrysler and Charles W. Nash. Chrysler Corp. was organized in early '20s. In 1927-28, when Ford was changing over to Model A, General Motors was largest producer with sales totalling 40% of market.

ELEVEN MEMBERS of Cabinet that worked with Hoover are shown with the President in a traditional White House lawn picture. Left to right, seated: Secretary of Treasury Mills, Vice President Curtis, President Hoover, Secretaries Stimson of State and Hurley of War; standing, Secretaries Chapin of Commerce, Wilbur of Interior, Attorney General Mitchell, Postmaster-General Brown, Secretaries Adams of Navy, Hyde of Agriculture and Doak of Labor.

AL SMITH, four times governor of N.Y. and 1928 Democratic presidential nominee, was a colorful campaigner. His Tammany Hall political background, his opposition to temperance movement and his religion worked against him.

BOOM TURNS INTO BUST

Hoover's efforts to maintain prosperity fail to retard growing depression

Despite good business prospects and continuing prosperity, the 1928 presidential elections were exceedingly bitter. Republicans nominated Herbert Hoover of California, while the Democrats chose Alfred E. Smith. A vicious whispering campaign and Hoover's attack on Smith's ideas of farm relief and hydroelectric power as "state socialism" helped defeat the "Happy Warrior."

On March 4, 1929, Hoover was inaugurated. Forewarnings of depression had appeared. There were 2,000,000 unemployed; the building boom was over by 1928; America's two economic indicators, steel and automobiles, were slowing up due to over-production; world trade was greatly hampered by high tariffs. Despite the Farm Bloc's efforts to lower tariffs, Congress raised rates even higher with the Hawley-Smoot Tariff.

The Crash came October 29, 1929; industry declined and unemployment grew. Hoover sought to aid the stricken nation by creating the Reconstruction Finance Corporation to lend money to banks and businesses.

Amid rising economic crises, the 1932 presidential campaign was fought with Roosevelt and Garner against Hoover and Curtis. The Democrats called for Federal aid to farmers and unemployed, reciprocal trade treaties, regulation of the Stock Exchange "and continued responsibility of government for human welfare."

On March 4, 1933, at the depth of the depression, Franklin Roosevelt was inaugurated.

DEMOCRATIC candidates, Governor Franklin Roosevelt of New York and John N. Garner of Texas, are shown on train platform during '32 campaign.

REPUBLICAN candidate for 1932 reelection, President Hoover speaks at Madison Square Garden in New York. Vice-Pres. Curtis was also renominated.

BONUS ARMY marched on Washington to lobby for veterans' bonus payments, camped on the outskirts, was dispersed with tear gas and tanks.

DEPRESSION DECADE

Troubled years of the thirties give birth to FDR's New Deal as world diplomacy tries appeasement in the face of totalitarian aggression

"Prosperity," said President Herbert Hoover, "is just around the corner." To men in breadlines, hobos riding the rods, Okies in Hoovervilles, the Bonus Marchers herded out of Washington and the nation's 12½ million unemployed, the remark was a bitter irony and Hoover, in spite of his good intentions, became a symbol of the country's misfortunes.

The whole world was sinking into bankruptcy and depression. World trade had declined by 70%. Nations were forced by inflation to abandon the gold standard, and the German Republic fell apart. Governments failed, monarchies were abolished, and there were revolutions in ten Latin American countries. French ministries changed almost monthly, Labor was swept from power in England, and everywhere demagogues offered panaceas to the discontented.

The New Deal

In the U.S. there was a drastic change in thinking. It started with the crash of '29, was strengthened by the exposure of dishonest business practices among powerful industrial barons such as Samuel Insull, and reached a climax when banks failed, mortgages were foreclosed, and business proved incapable of providing jobs. National morale was dangerously low.

Franklin Delano Roosevelt, elected President in 1932, told the nation that "the only thing we have to fear is fear itself," and set out to prove it. His New Deal reform departments—the Tennessee Valley Authority, Civilian Conservation Corps, Works Project Administration and others—increased the national debt from $20 billion to $34 billion by 1936. However, the national income rose from $40 billion to $60 billion during that period, and the worst was over.

Meanwhile, the 14 years of Prohibition had ended with Repeal in 1933, Theodore Roosevelt's "Big Stick" had been discarded for the "Good Neighbor" foreign policy, and John L. Lewis had organized the CIO and its 1936-37 sit-down strikes.

FDR frankly termed his program experimental—designed to meet an emergency. Some of it, such as the National Recovery Act and the Agricultural Adjustment Act, was ruled unconstitutional by the U.S. Supreme Court, and Roosevelt's subsequent attempt to pack the Court failed, as did his abortive "purge" of Congress.

The New Deal had become so large and so controversial that it was accused of political favoritism, blamed for the economic recession of 1937 and even—by its most rabid critics—for the Dust Bowl drought.

Most Americans, however, supported FDR. In the 1936 elections the Republicans suffered their worst defeat by carrying only two states.

The recovery under the New Deal, although costly, kept the U.S. free of the panic and desperation that were breeding dictatorships in many of the European countries.

HUNGER IN A LAND OF PLENTY

People could not believe the reports the American press printed on Adolph Hitler, who seized the German chancellorship in 1933. The world-wide depression was spiritual as well as economic, and made possible the anti-semitism, bookburnings and Nazi Germany's other incredible crimes against humanity and civilization.

Roads to War

Japan took advantage of China's civil wars and invaded Manchuria in 1931. Neither the League of Nations nor any government registered an effective protest, and aggression flourished. In 1935 Mussolini sent his new Italian army to occupy tiny, backward Ethiopia. The Spanish Revolution began in 1936 when Insurgents under General Franco revolted against the government. Nazi Germany and Fascist Italy, arrogant now, promptly sent arms to Franco; Russia aided the Loyalists, but the democracies remained neutral. 1937 brought the sinking of the *USS Panay* by Japan. By 1938 the Rome-Berlin-Tokyo Axis was formed and existing security pacts were worthless.

In 1933 Hitler withdrew Germany from the League of Nations; in 1936 he reoccupied the Rhineland; in 1938 he annexed Austria. When Prime Minister Chamberlain and French Premier Deladier decided on "appeasement" at the Munich Conference, Hitler proved insatiable, and by March 1939 he was in Prague. The Nazi aim was to unite all German people into one "Totalitarian State."

After the occupation of Czechoslovakia, Hitler began his demands on Poland regarding Danzig and Pomorze (the "Polish Corridor" to Warsaw). Poland, supported by Britain and France, refused to make concessions. Europe now knew that the Nazis intended to fulfill the boast they sang, "Today Germany is ours; tomorrow the whole world."

RENDEZVOUS WITH DESTINY, a phrase he used to describe this period, applied even more aptly to FDR himself. Franklin Delano Roosevelt, elected President for the first of four terms in 1932, had been the Governor of New York, vice-presidential candidate, and Assistant Secretary of the Navy. An eloquent speaker with a compelling voice, he was able to communicate his personal courage and faith to the nation by use of radio addresses he called "Fireside Chats."

ROOSEVELT CLAN gatherings made lively affairs of White House holidays during the 1930s. Shown here with the President are his wife, his mother, three of his five children, and four grandchildren. The activities of young Roosevelts provided abundant newspaper copy. As First Lady, Mrs. Roosevelt had a greater influence than any other President's wife in history. Despite criticism of her frequent jaunts, she earned recognition as a humanitarian.

NEW DEAL TACKLES DEPRESSION

Restoring individual security and national stability creates big government

Increasing unemployment and poverty sent national morale to its lowest point during the four months between Franklin Delano Roosevelt's election and his inauguration (Mar. 4, 1933). Meeting head-on the problems of the dislocated economy, the President called Congress into an emergency session to enact his promised New Deal program. The next "One Hundred Days" were without precedent—never in history had a presidential program been enacted into law so quickly. Bills were presented to Congress with a terse recommendation that they be passed—and passed they were.

With enactment of the emergency measures the federal government now assumed responsibility for the welfare of the individual and asserted itself in a number of areas never before considered within the sphere of the United States government.

Quick funds were made available by means of the Federal Emergency Relief Administration. Four million people were given jobs in the Civil Works Administration, and half a million men and boys were absorbed into the Civilian Conservation Corps.

New Deal help for the farmer came primarily through the Agricultural Adjustment Act, which fixed prices and limited the acreage under cultivation. The National Industrial Recovery Act was designed to protect workers and help business recover.

The "Gold Standard" was abandoned in 1933, and the gold content of the dollar was cut from 100% to 59.06%. Despite fierce opposition to this devaluation, Roosevelt's New Deal Democrats polled a tremendous majority in the 1934 elections, and economic recovery was soon evident.

The U.S. foreign policy during the '30s concentrated on maintaining neutrality. The 1935 Senate voted down U.S. participation in the World Court and Congress passed the Neutrality Act, forbidding Americans to furnish money or munitions to foreign belligerents. American determination to avoid war was shown by acceptance of Japan's reparations after her aircraft sank *USS Panay*.

SHANTY TOWNS sheltered thousands when the depression of the early '30s gripped the nation. Liberty Bonds had been sold and homes mortgaged for cash to play the "Hoover bull market". By midsummer of 1929 about 300 million shares of stock were being carried on margin and "paper millionaires" were plentiful. When the market crashed the nation's buying power was paralyzed. Banks failed, mortgages were foreclosed, foreign trade dropped, and there were 20,000 business failures in 1930 and 29,000 more in 1931. When the number of unemployed rose to 12 million, many people were forced to live in "Hoovervilles" *(r.)*, earned a few pennies a day for sorting bottles and cans.

HARRY HOPKINS *(l.)* had been a director of the New York Tuberculosis and Health Association and he became a friend of President Roosevelt at that time. In 1933 FDR appointed him Administrator of the New Deal relief and unemployment bureaus; later he became Secy. of Commerce.

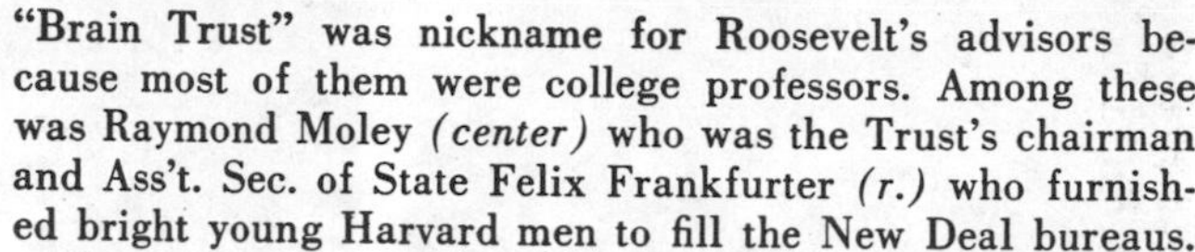

"Brain Trust" was nickname for Roosevelt's advisors because most of them were college professors. Among these was Raymond Moley *(center)* who was the Trust's chairman and Ass't. Sec. of State Felix Frankfurter *(r.)* who furnished bright young Harvard men to fill the New Deal bureaus.

HENRY A. WALLACE was New Deal Secy. of Agriculture, responsible for administering Agricultural Adjustment Act. AAA was designed to raise farm produce prices, eliminate the serious overproduction and relieve nation's farmers, who had a mortgaged indebtedness of $8.5 billion. Farmers' income rose from $5.3 billion in '32 to $8 billion by '35.

NEW DEAL CABINET was composed of *(seated, l. to r.)* George Dern (War), Cordell Hull (State), Pres. Roosevelt, Wm. Woodin (Treas.) and Homer Cummings (Attorney Gen.). Standing *(l. to r.)* are Henry Wallace (Agric.), Harold Ickes (Int.), Claude Swanson (Navy), James Farley (Post. Gen.), Daniel Roper (Comm.) Mme. Perkins (Labor).

REPUBLICAN nominee Alf Landon of Kansas *(l.)* had the support of Democrats Al Smith *(r.)* and ex-Secretary of State Bainbridge Colby, former Roosevelt sponsors. In his campaign bid for the Presidency, Landon condemned the New Deal, yet at the same time promised to continue with its recovery program. This unconvincing platform helped FDR and Democrats to win their landslide victory of 1936.

DEMOCRAT WINNERS in 1936 were President Roosevelt, campaign manager James A. Farley and Vice-President John Garner. Dissension in the Democratic party, opposition by big business and utility companies, and the formation of a new political party (Union Party) were factors in the pre-election predictions of a possible Democratic defeat, but Democrats carried all states except Maine and Vermont.

FIRST DEFEAT for the New Deal was the Supreme Court's decision that the National Industrial Recovery Act and the Agricultural Adjustment Act were unconstitutional. Six of the Supreme Court justices were over 70, and Roosevelt sent a bill to Congress proposing the addition of 6 new justices to the Court. His bill created a national uproar and met with solid opposition led by Democratic Senator Burton K. Wheeler *(above, left)*. The President then attempted to "purge" Congress of those Democrats who opposed his program, but the voters returned many of his opponents to office in 1938 mid-term elections. The Supreme Court justices who passed NRA, AAA rulings were *(standing l. to r.)* Roberts, Butler, Stone, Cardozo and *(seated)* Brandeis, Van Devanter, Hughes, McReynolds, Sutherland.

DICTATOR in his home state of Louisiana, Senator Huey Long won many followers with his Share the Wealth scheme which promised an annual income of $5000 to every American. Long was most dangerous of the depression demagogues, but his assassination dissolved his expanding political empire. Father Charles Coughlin *(upper r., center)* was a rabble-rousing radio priest of the 1930s who attempted to oust Roosevelt in the 1936 elections by forming a new party. He joined forces with Gerald K. Smith *(on his right)* and Dr. Francis Townsend *(on his left)* to form the Union for Social Justice party. Party also included the political heirs of Huey Long, nominated Rep. Wm. Lemke for President. The bitterly fought 1934 gubernatorial campaign in California ended in defeat for socialistic Democratic candidate Upton Sinclair *(above)*. Influx of migrants from the Dust Bowl had made California a breeding ground for radicals.

ORGANIZED LABOR made its greatest advances during the New Deal. The National Industrial Recovery Act recognized labor's right to bargain collectively. Strikes causing violence and bloodshed were wide-spread (a Bethlehem Steel striker above), but the CIO imported a new weapon from France called the "sit-down strike." Workers intrenched themselves in the factory and refused to work or allow others to enter and work. Union leaders Frankenstein, Martin and Reuther *(second, fourth and fifth from left)* led a United Automobile Workers strike against Gen. Motors.

LABOR UNIONS in 1935 were of two types: the old AF of L "craft union" and the new CIO "vertical union," which included all workers in a given industry. CIO leaders shown conferring in 1937 were *(left to right above)* Sidney Hillman, John L. Lewis, Philip Murray and John Brophy. AF of L president William Green is shown *(right)* with New Deal Secy. of Labor Frances Perkins, first woman in a Cabinet post.

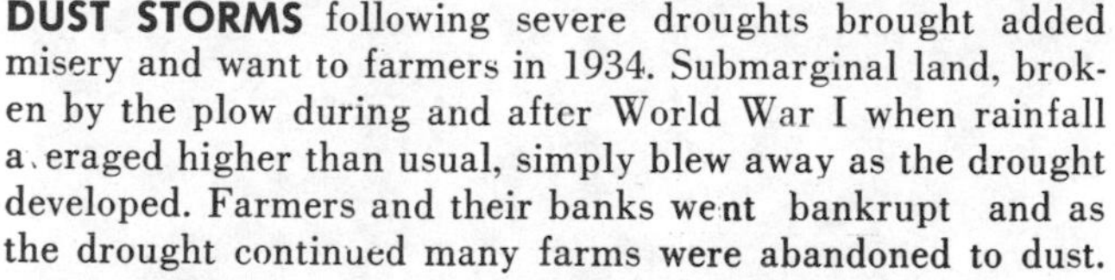

DUST STORMS following severe droughts brought added misery and want to farmers in 1934. Submarginal land, broken by the plow during and after World War I when rainfall averaged higher than usual, simply blew away as the drought developed. Farmers and their banks went bankrupt and as the drought continued many farms were abandoned to dust.

A MILLION AMERICANS took to the roads. Refugees from the Dust Bowl, uprooted tenant farmers and unemployed laborers—all called "Okies"—piled their few possessions into wagons, dilapidated cars or on their own backs and headed west, hoping to find employment as migratory workers among California's fertile truck farms and lush orchards.

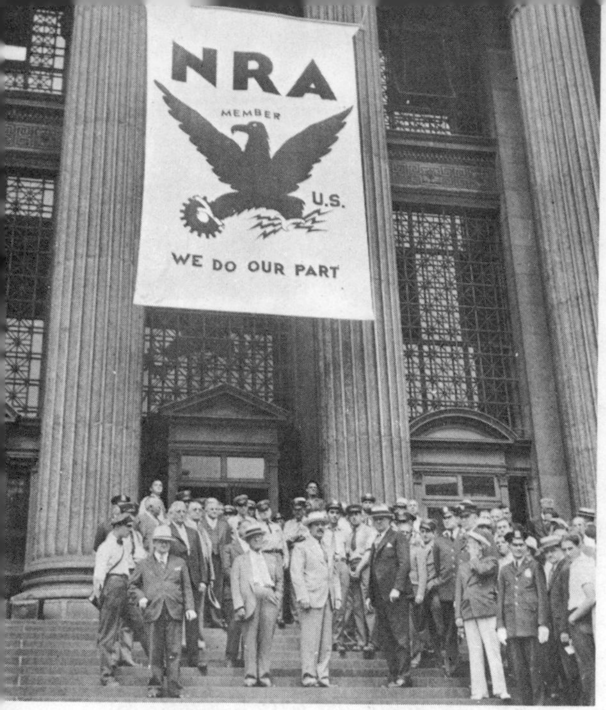

EMBLEM OF RECOVERY for business was the Blue Eagle, denoting participation in the National Recovery Administration. Under NRA 700 industries imposed codes of fair competition upon themselves and recognized labor's right to collective bargaining. Works Progress Administration *(above)* undertook public projects, especially those of building and repair.

MOST POPULAR of the New Deal emergency measures was the Civilian Conservation Corps, which put 500,000 youths to work in national forests and parks. Program included soil conservation, reforestation, and the draining of wastelands.

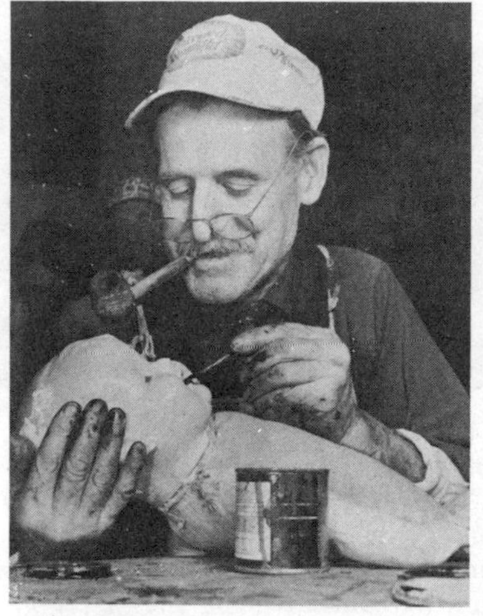

WPA jobs included a great many unexpected tasks, even repairing dolls for Christmas gifts for the children of the poor *(l.)* With the creation of this relief program in 1935, the federal government assumed the responsibility for finding work for the 3.5 million "employables" throughout the nation. Charges of "boondoggling" (made work) plagued the program's administrator, Harry Hopkins.

JUNIOR WPA was the National Youth Administration, which trained students for specialized jobs and provided funds to help the needy pupils by providing part-time work. During depression this program aided over 650,000 students.

WPA PROJECT was musical show *Pins and Needles* with a cast made up of unemployed members of the International Ladies Garment Workers Union. Music for dance shown at right was called *Sing Us a Song of Social Significance.*

DESPITE BITTER OPPOSITION from public utility companies, Congress created the Tennessee Valley Authority in 1933, ending the fight Sen. George W. Norris had waged since 1920 to harness the great Tennessee river and prevent the yearly floods that devastated the region. Serving seven states, TVA built 16 dams on the river and its tributaries, provided tremendous power to operate great war plants at Oak Ridge and Muscle Shoals. Norris Dam *(above)*, named for the Senator, is located on the Clinch river in eastern Tennessee. TVA electrified half a million homes in the area.

FUNDS FOR DAMS came from Public Works Administration appropriations. Bonneville Dam *(above)* was first of a series of multiple-purpose dams designed to utilize the power of Oregon's Columbia river. Spillway is 1,090 feet long; lock permits ocean vessels to ascend river 192 miles.

IRRIGATION WATER from the Grand Coulee Dam on the Columbia river in Washington opened up 1.2 million acres of former desert land for farming and industry in the Columbia basin. Picture above shows the dam when it was 50 percent completed. Dam is the world's largest masonry structure.

MIDTOWN HUDSON TUNNEL between New York City and New Jersey was a Public Works Administration project. The PWA, headed by Harold Ickes, built municipal airports, city sewage systems and water supplies, highways, bridges and public buildings in every state in the nation during '30's.

SLUM CLEARANCE programs inaugurated under the Public Works Administration made Uncle Sam landlord to thousands. The first of these projects to be completed was the Techwood development in Atlanta, Ga., a portion of which is shown below. Monthly rents here ranged from $16.50 up.

WORLD'S LARGEST coffee producer, Brazil, faced economic problems in the Thirties when coffee prices dropped due to overproduction. Surpluses were dumped into the sea to bolster prices.

BLINDFOLDED Bolivian prisoners taken during the Caco War. Disputed ownership of forest region set off conflict in 1932. Truce was concluded (1935) at the instance of U.S., five other states.

MOST RADICAL stage of Mexico's social revolution was reached under the leadership of President Lazaro Cardenas *(l.)* between 1934 and 1940. The high point of the Cardenas administration was marked by the expropriation of the property holdings of foreign oil companies when they refused to increase the wages of workers by one-third. The value of the expropriated lands was placed at $450 million.

GOOD NEIGHBOR POLICY

U. S. paves way for cooperation by accepting non-intervention

Antagonists in the Twenties, Latin America and the United States learned to be good neighbors in the Thirties. By 1936 the marines had been withdrawn from Haiti and Nicaragua and the distasteful Platt amendment abrogated. Recognizing the obstacles to cooperation raised by an interventionist policy, the United States at the Buenos Aires Conference in 1936 agreed to a treaty stating that "intervention . . . in the internal or external affairs" of any nations is "inadmissible."

Difficulties arose when the nationalist Latin American governments adopted economic programs which provided for high tariffs and exchange controls, intended to combat depression but also acting as barriers to inter-American trade.

As the threat of war grew in the late Thirties, however, the American nations buried their economic differences in order to strengthen the political bonds that joined them. At the Buenos Aires and Lima Conferences in 1936 and 1938 they agreed: (1) that they believed in the principles of nonintervention, the peaceful settlement of disputes and the equality of nations, (2) that they would defend these principles against foreign aggression, and (3) that any threat to the peace of the American nations would be cause for a meeting of their foreign ministers to consult on what common action should be taken.

With the beginning of World War II in 1939, these agreements faced their first real test, and the Panama Conference in October produced plans for mutual defense.

"THE WIZARD" is what Venezuelans called Juan Vicente Gomez, their iron-handed dictator from 1909-1935 while he served either as president or chief of the army. His rule was marked by material progress, including the opening of rich oil fields in 1918, administrative reforms and financial stabilization.

CHIEF ARCHITECTS of Good Neighbor policy in the U.S. Department of State were Cordell Hull, Roosevelt's Secretary of State, and Under-Secretary Sumner Welles (shown together *r.)*. Hull served in the cabinet until 1944 when he resigned because of poor health, was succeeded by Stettinius.

JAPAN ATTACKED China in June, 1937 and by the end of July had captured Peking and Tientsin. Landing party *(above)* guards bridge to Shanghai.

SHANGHAI CAMPAIGN took place Aug. 8-Nov. 8, 1937. Merciless day and night bombing raids *(above,* victims being removed) shocked world opinion. With Shanghai's fall, Japanese quickly took Soochow and began drive up the Yangtze. By 1939 they had captured almost all key cities, including Nanking, Canton, Hankow.

PRESIDENT Chiang Kai-shek moved the Chinese capital from Nanking to Chungking where he directed the ill-equipped but determined Chinese troops resisting the Japanese. He is shown with the three famous Soong sisters, *(l. to r.)* Mme. Chaing Kai-shek, Mme. Sun Yat-sen and Mme H. H. Kung.

CHINESE COMMUNISTS dropped political disagreements to unite with the Nationalists in fighting the Japanese invaders. Pictured at the Communists' Yenan headquarters in the Thirties are *(l. to r.)* Mao Tse-tung; Earl Leaf, a United Press corresondent; Chu Teh; and Madame Mao Tse-tung.

BANZAI!

Japan attacks China

In 1931-1932 the Japanese succeeded in occupying Manchuria and creating there the "independent" puppet state of Manchukuo, over which she promptly established a close protectorate. Refusal of the League of Nations to recognize Manchukuo was without effect.

Continuing to nibble at China's sovereignty, Japan applied pressure to compel removal of anti-Japanese officials, increased her garrisons in the northern provinces, made increasingly impossible demands.

Chiang's Nationalist government continued its campaign against the Communists. In December, 1936, General Chang Hsueh-liang kidnapped Chiang, sought to force an end to anti-Communist activities and a declaration of war against Japan. Demonstrations of loyalty to Chiang, even by the Reds, helped effect his release and testified to the moral unity of China.

In January, 1937, negotiations terminated the anti-Communist campaign, and six months later an incident at Lukouchiao, near Peking, marked the beginning of the Japanese attack on China.

The fighting spread rapidly throughout China, and within two years the poorly-equipped Chinese had been driven from control of most of the ports, the majority of the key cities and the larger part of the railroads. Nevertheless, there was no sign of any weakening of the Chinese determination to resist, and after 1939 the war continued with sporadic, inconclusive fighting over a large area. Japan was unable to force a decision, although her troops occupied a large part of China, and the long-continued stalemate did not end until Chinese and Allied troops joined to drive out the last of the Japanese invaders in World War II (1945).

"I HAVE FOUND it impossible to . . . discharge my duties as King . . . without the help and support of the woman I love." Thus King Edward VIII abdicated throne of England to marry American divorcee, Wallis Warfield Simpson in 1936 (wedding picture *l.*). Romance thrilled public, and world-wide audience heard abdication message on radio.

PRIME MINISTER Stanley Baldwin *(r.)* led Dominion ministers in refusal to consent to a morganatic marriage, felt it would lessen crown's prestige. The ex-King became the Duke of Windsor.

BRITISH COMMONWEALTH

The 1931 Statute of Westminster illustrated the adaptability of the British Commonwealth of Nations to changing conditions. It provided that the London Parliament should no longer make laws applicable to the Dominions unless requested to, while it retained the Crown as a symbol of the common allegiance of all the member nations. The Dominions had become independent, sovereign nations, bound together in fraternal association under the King.

In 1937 the Irish Free State became the sovereign nation of Eire, while the northern counties (Ulster) remained part of the United Kingdom. Chief center of interest in the Commonwealth, however, was India where growing unrest and desire for self-government appeared. The National Congress Party of Mahatma Gandhi and the Moslem League under Mohammed Ali Jinnah emerged as leading political parties. Their agitation led to the Government of India Act in 1935 which established virtual self-government in the provinces of British India and looked to the federation of the many princely Indian states with the provinces.

Although numerous crown colonies, protectorates and mandated territories were still governed directly from England, some observers felt the Empire was falling apart, and doubts were raised concerning the strength and solidity of the Commonwealth. With the outbreak of World War II, however, the Dominions promptly rallied to the side of Great Britain and fought vigorously for her cause.

GEORGE VI succeeded Edward on the throne, reigned until his death in 1952. Always careful to avoid interference with the British Parliamentary government, he proved a hard-working, dutiful monarch, raised royalty's prestige.

BRITISH delegation to the Ottawa Imperial Economic Conference of July 21-August 20, 1932, is shown at the right. The conference produced agreements for imperial preference system to improve economic conditions in the Empire. Free-trade liberal members of the British cabinet resigned in protest.

ROUND-TABLE Conferences were held in London to seek solutions to unrest in India. Gandhi was released from prison to attend the first of these meetings which produced the Delhi Pact ending second passive resistance campaign. Results of the discussion were eventually embodied in the 1935 Government of India Act which transformed India's government.

INDIAN LEADERS included poetess Sardjini Naidu and Mohandas K. Gandhi, famed for his practice of passive resistance, his championing of In--dia's untouchables and his fasts while imprisoned. Revered Mahatma Ghandi was assassinated, 1948.

CANADA

New surge of growth

Canada entered the twentieth century with a population of 5,371,315 and a larger land area than any other British Dominion. Her agricultural growth continued steadily, and her mining and manufacturing industries received a stimulus from World War I that led to continued expansion.

Canadian troops had distinguished themselves in World War I in such battles as Ypres, the Somme, Vimy Ridge and Amiens. Canada supplied the Allies with 640,886 men and spent $1.5 billion on her war effort.

Canada's chief trade relations after World War I were with the United States, and American high-tariff legislation increased her economic difficulties during the depression until the conclusion of a reciprocal trade agreement in 1935 with the United States eased the situation.

The Thirties gave birth to two new political parties, the Cooperative Commonwealth Federation (CCF), a socialist movement, and the radical Social Credit Party. High point of the decade came in 1939 with the visit of King George VI and Queen Elizabeth, the first reigning sovereigns ever to visit Canada.

LORD TWEEDSMUIR, *(r., above)* served as Governor General of Canada from 1935 to 1940, was also famous (under name of John Buchan) as author of the spy-chiller, *The Thirty-Nine Steps.*

FAMOUS CANADIAN prime ministers were Sir Alfred Laurier *(l.)*, French Canadian leader of the Liberal Party, and Sir Robert Borden, Conservative Party leader during and after W.W.I.

PRIME MINISTER of Canada, W. L. Mackenzie King (shown with Franklin Roosevelt) first took office in 1921 and retained his position with only brief interruptions until 1948.

BOTH FRENCH and English are used as official languages in Canada's House of Commons. Welding together French and English elements in Canada has presented officials with many problems.

EVERY YEAR THE NAZI PARTY HELD A PUBLIC DISPLAY OF MIGHT IN THE ANCIENT CITY OF NUREMBERG

NAZI DICTATORSHIP

Hitler remilitarizes Germany, strengthens his dictatorship and prepares for war

When Heinrich Bruening became German Chancellor in 1930, he faced the bitter opposition of both Communists and Nazis who made orderly parliamentary government impossible. He therefore decided to rule by decree and through presidential emergency powers. The moderate parties lost heavily in the next elections, with the Communists gaining by 40% and the Nazis emerging as the second strongest party.

President Hindenburg, elected in 1925, was re-elected in a run-off election in 1932. The Nazis had pressed hard for Hitler's candidacy but Hindenburg won over 19 million votes. Hitler, however, polled over 13 million, gaining one third of the seats, while the Communist Thaelmann lagged behind with 5 million votes.

Bruening, the architect of Hindenburg's victory, rapidly lost his power and was replaced by von Papen. Later, von Papen in turn was replaced by von Schleicher. On Jan. 30, 1933 Hitler was appointed to the chancellorship through the efforts of von Papen, and the Third Reich began.

Hitler at first formed a coalition regime in which only three Nazis were present. But the atmosphere of terror following the burning of the Reichstag virtually eliminated opposition. One by one all non-Nazis were dropped from the Cabinet or joined the Nazi party. A bloody purge, in which about one thousand people were killed, eliminated all possible competitors to Hitler's power within the Nazi party; a few "private accounts" were also settled.

Now began the task of putting Germany "back on the map." Conscription was revived, the armament industry began to hum and the general staff was restored.

After the remilitarization of the Rhineland in 1936, Austria was terrorized into surrender in 1938. Then Hitler turned to the Sudeten region of Czechoslovakia and, at the famous Munich meeting, acquired it from Chamberlain and Daladier. Though Hitler declared himself satisfied, it was only a few months later that he occupied the rest of Czechoslovakia and turned it into a so-called protectorate. Next was to come the conquest of Poland and war.

THE REICHSTAG FIRE which broke out in February of 1933 marked the beginning of the drastic measures that were utilized against all real or potential anti-Nazis. The Communists were accused of being guilty of the crime, and some of their leaders were actually tried. Later it was established that Goering and his fellow Nazis had started the fire.

HINDENBURG, commander-in-chief of the German armies in World War I and twice president of Germany, appointed Hitler in 1933. Although politically inept, he had prestige. Here he visits Tannenberg Victory Monument.

A MIGHTY MAN is Ernst Roehm, chief of Brownshirts, as he talks to Elite Guard Chief Himmler *(wearing glasses)*. A few months later, Himmler was responsible for having Roehm killed in the purge of 1934.

◀ **IL DUCE MUSSOLINI** became Hitler's ally during the Ethiopian war. He and Hitler formed the Axis which was later joined by Japan. Mussolini visited Berlin in 1937 and reviewed German Labor Corps.

THE HAND of friendship ▶ was clasped by two dictators, Hitler and Franco, when they met at frontier between France and Spain in 1940. When Hitler's end seemed imminent, Franco's friendliness cooled.

AUSTRIA, land of Hitler's birth, was his first conquest. Its government, headed by Kurt von Schuschnigg, was terrorized into submission by threat of force. Austrian Nazis aided the German cause. On March 11, 1938, German troops crossed the Austrian frontier without firing a shot. In 1939 Hitler's soldiers marched into Czechoslovakia. German anti-aircraft contingent is shown *(r. above)* entering Prague.

BOTH SMILED but for different reasons. British Prime Minister Chamberlain, shaking hands with Hitler at Bad Godesberg, believed that he had saved the peace in 1938. Hitler knew better. The Munich Conference was a pivotal point, for with the abandonment of Czechoslovakia came the inevitability of war or Nazi dominance of Europe, rather than, "Peace in our time", as Chamberlain had believed.

SOVIET UNION concentrated a major portion of its national effort on military matters. The Nazis, the U.S. and Great Britain copied Red Army technique of mass parachute jumping.

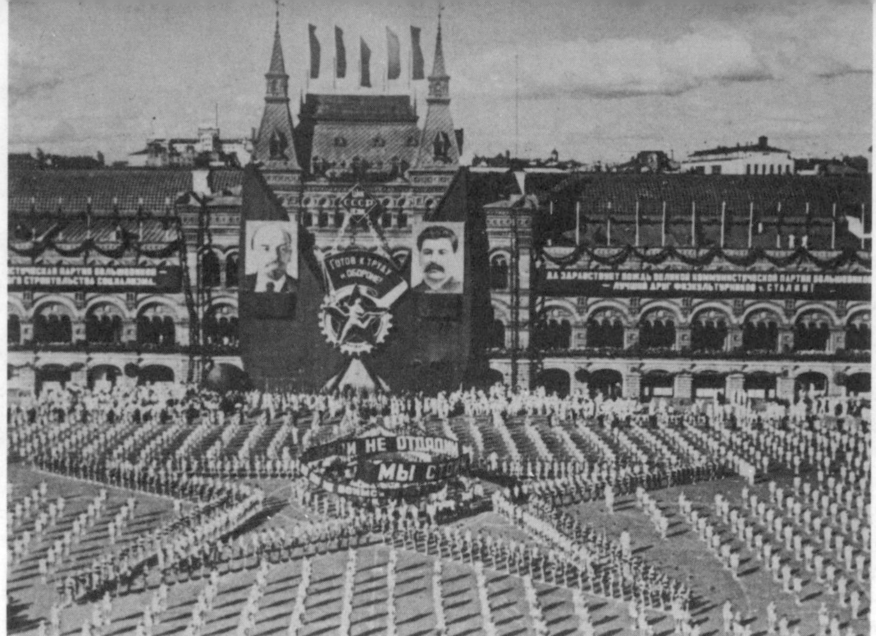

RED SQUARE IN MOSCOW is the scene of many great spectacles. A sports parade is shown above. Participants come from various republics of the Soviet Union. Until 1931, sports had been confined to the army and the big cities. At that time, as a part of Stalin's program for better living, better health and higher education, sports were introduced to the peasants under the collective farm system

L. P. BERIA replaced Yezhov, who had succeeded Yagoda as Chief of the OGPU (later the NKVD. He executed those practicing gross abuse and helped to restore some order.

SOVIET POWER

Stalin's purges eliminate all competitors for leadership

The rise of the Soviet Union to the rank of a first class world power was made clear by the Franco-Soviet alliance of 1935.

The Political Bureau (Politburo) of the Communist Party, headed by Joseph Stalin, ruled Russia without restraint; Communist parties all over the world obeyed the same command through the Communist International (Comintern). However the murder of Stalin's friend Kirov gave evidence to Stalin of the instability of his regime and a wave of purges began. At the same time there was a general tightening of controls.

Foreign relations of the USSR did not remain unaffected by the internal tumult. Foreign Commissar Maxim Litvinov made great diplomatic strides in dealing with the West, conferring with Daladier and Chamberlain in the attempt to strengthen Russia's prestige in the eyes of the world. After Munich Litvinov resigned and was replaced by Vyacheslav Molotov who knew little about the West. Soon secret talks began between representatives of Hitler and Stalin. When Hitler turned his attention to Poland, British and French military missions were dispatched to Moscow to no avail. On August 23, 1939 the world received the shocking news of the German-Soviet non-aggression pact which enabled Hitler to start World War II.

Russia remained neutral but supported the Germans with certain raw materials. The provinces of Lithuania, Latvia and Estonia were annexed to Russia as a reward for this subtle alliance. Finland, on the other hand, had to be subdued in a costly war. In spite of the alliance German armies invaded Russia on a 2,000-mile front on June 22, 1941 and the USSR attained new world importance.

BUKHARIN

SERGEI KIROV

TUKHACHEVSKY

GENRIKH YAGODA

MURDER OF KIROV brought on the great wave of purges which shocked the world. Nearly the entire leadership of Communism in Russia as well as the army high command was sent before execution squads or to prisons—all suspected of plotting with the exiled Trotsky or Nazi Germany against Stalin. Panic ruled the entire country. Tukhachevsky, Assistant People's Commissar for Defense, was among the generals executed in the trial of 1937. Yagoda, president of OGPU, and Bukharin were tried for treason in 1938 in the last of four sensational trials.

KING OF KINGS, Conquering Lion of Judah and Elect of God, Haile Selassie (with his family) was helpless when Fascist hordes of Mussolini launched a barbarous attack on his undeveloped Ethiopia to expand Italian colonial empire.

ADDIS ABABA was looted by the frenzied Ethiopians when their emperor fled to Palestine. Haile Selassie went on to Geneva where he appealed to the League of Nations unsuccessfully. After entering the city, Italians restored order.

ITALIAN TROOPS occupied Makale without resistance and are shown rejoicing over it. However, guerrilla activities and night attacks in mountainous country unfit for tanks harassed the Italians who were already weary from hot climate.

ITALIAN BOOT ON THE MARCH

The foreign policy of Benito Mussolini and his Blackshirts was aggression. By 1930 Mussolini had his Fascist machine functioning smoothly; his uncontrollable desire for conquest turned Italy's eyes to Ethiopia.

In November, 1934 an Italian consulate was attacked by Ethiopian warriors. A note of deep regret was sent by Haile Selassie and accepted by the Italian government—Mussolini was not ready for his Ethiopian adventure. After another skirmish in December, Ethiopia appealed to the League. In February, 1935 Italy began to mobilize. During the spring and summer the League vainly looked for a peaceful solution to the crisis, as Italy demanded and received apologies and indemnities.

On October 3 Fascist legions entered Ethiopia, invading from Somaliland and Eritrea. On October 19 the League's proposal of an embargo to restrict Italy's oil imports failed. Great Britain's efforts to close the Suez Canal also failed. The war progressed indecisively until late January, when Italian superiority began to tell. By the end of February 1936, the heroic Ethiopians were suffering defeat after defeat.

After Addis Ababa fell and the Emperor fled, Ethiopia was annexed by Italy. Preparing for further conquests, Mussolini withdrew from the League in 1937.

ITALIAN TROOPSHIP bound for Ethiopia is shown in the Suez Canal. The League's attempted boycott of Italy and England's protests against the use of the Canal failed because of British-French disunity. Lack of success in Ethiopia dealt a mortal blow to the League.

ETHIOPIANS went into battle armed only with weapons used in tribal warfare. Christian and Moslem, brave but undisciplined troops came from all parts of Ethiopia to fight the aggressor. Against Mussolini's modern tanks and airplanes, they did not stand a chance.

HOMELESS REFUGEES are always hit harder by civil than by international war. This tragic fact was demonstrated during the Spanish Civil War, when homeless civilians were driven from city to city before the advancing soldiers. Some of them were fortunate enough to escape to France on ships provided by the British; others *(shown above)* made their way slowly on foot to the French frontier where they were interned. The war's end did not stop this migration.

SPANISH CIVIL WAR

Insurgent forces under Franco conquer Loyalist Spain

The Spanish Civil War (1936-1939) was a prelude to World War II, but its roots lay buried in the history of Spain itself: the feudal Spanish agricultural system; financial barons restricting industrial growth; lack of a middle class; a powerful Catholic church owning land and industry, and controlling education. All of these forces were pro-monarchy until a republic was formed in 1931, when they turned to fascism.

Strikes and riots raged from 1931 until Franco's mutiny of July 1936 in Spanish Morocco. The Rebels had the army, its equipment, and aid from Germany and Italy. Spring of 1937 saw Loyalist holdings split by a Rebel drive east to the Mediterranean. Early in 1938, northern Loyalists stood firm near Barcelona, but dwindling supplies forced retreat. Franco took the city with ease, marched into helpless Madrid March 28.

GENERAL FRANCISCO FRANCO was little known until his mutiny in Spanish Morocco in July of 1936. He took command of the Rebels Oct. 1, 1936 and became dictator of Spain Aug. 4, 1939.

VICTORY PARADE, in the Fascist style, was held in Madrid, May 19, 1939 after Spain had been ravaged by three years of bitter fighting between the Rebels, supported by Germany and Italy, and the Loyalists, supported by the International Brigade. Spanish marines passing in review *(below)* were but a small part of the 150,000 German, Italian and Spanish troops taking part in the celebration.

AMELIA EARHART PUTNAM with her navigator, Fred Noonan, in a Lockheed twin-engine plane, attempted a flight around the Equator to gather scientific data. After leaving New Guinea, they disappeared over the Pacific, and no trace of them has ever been found.

DISASTER STRUCK HINDENBURG on May 6, 1937, as it was preparing to moor at Lakehurst, New Jersey. In one of the worst tragedies in the history of aviation, this German dirigible exploded into flames, killing 36 of the 97 aboard and injuring many others.

AVIATION

Aviation records were made and broken in the Thirties. In 1931 Wiley Post and Harold Gatty set a round-the-world flight record. Amelia Earhart was the first woman to solo across Atlantic in 1932. In 1933 Post soloed around the world via stratosphere, wearing an oxygen suit. Millionaire sportsman-pilot Howard Hughes broke records circling the globe in 1938.

However, U.S. Navy experimental lighter-than-airships were marked by disaster. The sister ships, Akron and Macon, crashed: the Akron in the Atlantic in 1933, the Macon in the Pacific in 1935.

A regularly scheduled air route over the Pacific began in 1935 with China Clippers. Aviation in the Thirties was no longer just a brave experiment, but had true commercial value.

"WRONG WAY" Corrigan took off ostensibly for Los Angeles, California from Brooklyn, N.Y. July 17, 1938, in his nine-year old $900 plane. When he landed in Dublin the next day, he told authorities he somehow got "mixed up."

WILL ROGERS and Wiley Post attempted to fly to Alaska, but their plane crashed August 15, 1935 near Pt. Barrow and both men were killed. The noted American actor and humorist *(l.)* is pictured with Post before the crash.

FIRST PACIFIC NON-STOP FLIGHT was made October 4, 1931 by Clyde Pangborn and Hugh Herndon, Jr. They flew the 4860 miles in 41 hours 30 minutes from Japan to Wenatchee, Wash. The landing gear on their single-engine plane was dropped after take-off, necessitating a belly landing.

CHINA CLIPPER flights from the United States to Manila were inaugurated on November 22, 1935. The flight of this 4-engine plane, shown flying over the partially constructed Golden Gate Bridge, marked the start of regularly scheduled commercial air traffic over the Pacific to the Philippines.

SPORTS IN THE 'THIRTIES

MAX SCHMELING and Jack Sharkey vied for heavyweight title after Gene Tunney retired in 1928. In their fight of November, 1930 Schmeling won on a foul in the fourth round. This was first time the title had been won this way.

SHARKEY won the title by decision in a 1932 return match with Schmeling. In 1933 huge Primo Carnera, an immensely powerful Italian cleverly promoted as a new superman, knocked Sharkey out in sixth round with a right uppercut.

MAX BAER, noted for his tenth round knockout of Schmeling, exploded Carnera myth by knocking out the "Ambling Alp" in 11th round of 1938 fight.

BROWN BOMBER, Joe Louis, skyrocketed to fame with a string of sensational knockouts climaxed when he downed Carnera with a 6th round KO.

JIMMY BRADDOCK, once considered "washed up" by the experts, came back amazingly in 1935, winning the title from Max Baer in a fifteen round bout.

CAREER OF JOE LOUIS

Joe Louis' rise to fame was amazing. Max Baer was knocked out in the fourth round of their fight in Sept. '35. Opponents were often so scared before the match that occasionally one would go down just from the breeze generated by Joe's deadly punches. He was thought unbeatable until he met Max Schmeling in '36, and went down in the twelfth. The defeat didn't stop Joe, but seemed to improve him. Matched with the champion, James Braddock, in 1937, he went down dramatically in the first round, but knocked the game Irishman out in the eighth to win the title. He eagerly welcomed a return match with his only conqueror, Max Schmeling, and knocked him out in 1938.

JOE LOUIS VS. MAX SCHMELING ➧

FIREBALL EXPERT Bob Feller set a new single game strikeout record of 18 on Oct. 2, 1938, beating Dizzy Dean's National League record of 17 set in 1933. Feller was baseball's boy wonder.

JEROME "DIZZY" DEAN was clown prince of baseball in the Thirties. He made an outstanding record during 1934 season, winning 30 games. He later became successful sports commentator.

HANK GREENBERG, Detroit slugger, hit 58 home runs in '38, threatening the Babe's record of 60. He gained in self-confidence to become great player, later a Cleveland Indians' executive.

CARL HUBBELL, pitching mainstay of Giants, led league in '36 and '37. He set record of 24 straight victories, winning last 16 of 1936, first 8 of 1937.

JOE DIMAGGIO *(l.)*, joined N.Y. as Ruth and Gehrig faded. A great center fielder, Yankee Clipper led American League in '39 with .381 batting average.

LOU GEHRIG *(r.)* nearly always came through in a pinch for Yanks. He led league in batting and home runs in '34, and was perennial runs-batted-in champ.

SLUGGING ATHLETES of Connie Mack gained reputation of "wonder team" in the early '30's, aided by such powerful sluggers as Jimmy Foxx *(below)*, who led the league in '33, Al Simmons, batting champ in '30 and '31, and Cochrane.

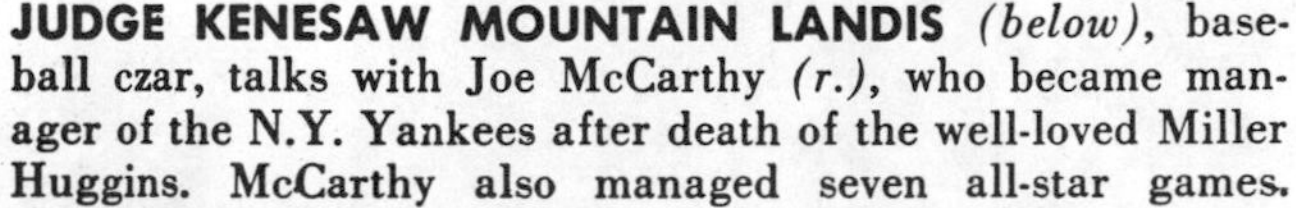

JUDGE KENESAW MOUNTAIN LANDIS *(below)*, baseball czar, talks with Joe McCarthy *(r.)*, who became manager of the N.Y. Yankees after death of the well-loved Miller Huggins. McCarthy also managed seven all-star games.

POETRY IN MOTION was sportswriters' description of the running style of Jesse Owens, shown tying the world's 100 yard mark of 9.4. Owens broke three world's records and tied one on May 25, 1935, when he set the men's world record for the broad jump, leaping 26 feet, 8¼ inches. He later enhanced this triumphal track and field record by winning three championships in Olympic Games of 1936.

STORMY petrel of one Olympic team, Eleanor Holm created furor by drinking champagne en-route to a meet. She won 100 meter backstroke title in 1936 Olympics.

GREATEST woman athlete was title given Mildred "Babe" Didrickson, shown *(second from right)* setting new world and Olympic record for 80 meter hurdles of 11.7 in the 1932 Olympic Games.

EAST BEAT WEST in thrilling Rose Bowl game on New Year's Day, 1934. Photo shows Columbia's quarterback, Cliff Montgomery, getting away for a gain as Columbia defeated favored Stanford team 7 to 0.

EXPLOSIVE FULLBACK Bronko Nagurski *(l.)*, an All-American tackle, wrecked opposing lines for many years as mainstay of professional Chicago Bears in the '30s. Slingin' Sammy Baugh, Texas Christian's All-American of 1936, carries the ball *(r.)* in 1937 All-Star game against Green Bay. Baugh became one of football's greatest professional stars.

DARK LIGHTNING of the turf was the gallant *Equipoise,* whose great speed set the mile record of 1:34 2/5 in 1932 at Arlington Park track, carrying 128 pounds. Among other great horses of the era were *Gallant Fox, Jack High, Blue Larkspur* and *Twenty Grand.*

TENNIS crown held by Tilden went to H. Ellsworth Vines *(below)*, U. S. champ in 1931-32. He later became golf pro.

THE ICEMAN, Jockey George Woolf, shown on *Seabiscuit,* won record purse of $108,400 on *Azucar* in 1935 Santa Anita Handicap. Besides *Seabiscuit,* noted horses were *War Admiral, Bold Venture, Challedon.* Woolf was killed in accident, is honored by statue.

◀ **UNION PACIFIC** was one of the pioneers of railroad industry in working out the diesel streamliner. Satisfied with a three car pilot model which did over 100 mph, U.P. put this sleek seven car train on regular runs in 1945.

FIRST TEST RUN of the Burlington ▶ *Zephyr* was in 1934. High speed efficiency and performance of this three car diesel train cut to 13 hours the Chicago-Denver run, and set the pattern for today's fast streamlined trains.

"NORMANDIE," pride of the French Line, made her maiden voyage and triumphal entry into New York harbor in 1935, one year before her famous rival, the *Queen Mary*. Both luxury vessels received N. Y.'s traditional welcome.

TRANSPORTATION

ON MAIDEN VOYAGE the Cunard White Star superliner *Queen Mary* reached New York June 1, 1935. Sailing up the Hudson past lower Manhattan, the 81,235-ton, 975-foot ship was greeted by boat whistles, flags and crowd.

◀ **SIX MILES** a minute and London fur dealer John Cobb breaks world's land speed record. In special 24-cylinder Railton racer, Cobb set mark of 368.85 mph, August 23, 1936 on Utah track, famous Bonneville Salt Flats.

RADICAL streamlining for motor ▶ cars was tried first by Chrysler with the Airflow in 1934. While it proved an efficient and comfortable model, it was too advanced for its time. Later, streamlining became standard.

FROM QUAGMIRE TO CONCRETE is the story of twenty years of improvement on the same stretch of road between Washington, D.C., and Richmond, Virginia. In 1919 motoring on a dirt road was rough in rainy weather. The following year gravel assured a smoother ride, no bogging down. In 1927 the road had a concrete surface and was designated U. S. Route 1. The last picture, in 1939, shows the stretch had become a three-lane, one-way highway. By 1944 there were approximately 3,000,000 miles of public rural road in the U.S. The steadily increasing number of motor vehicles in use on American roads has necessitated continuous highway expansion and improvement projects throughout the nation.

REMARKABLE DEVICE is mechanical heart designed by famous surgeon Dr. Alexis Carrel and Col. Charles A. Lindbergh. Showing heart functions, it was exhibited at New York World's Fair.

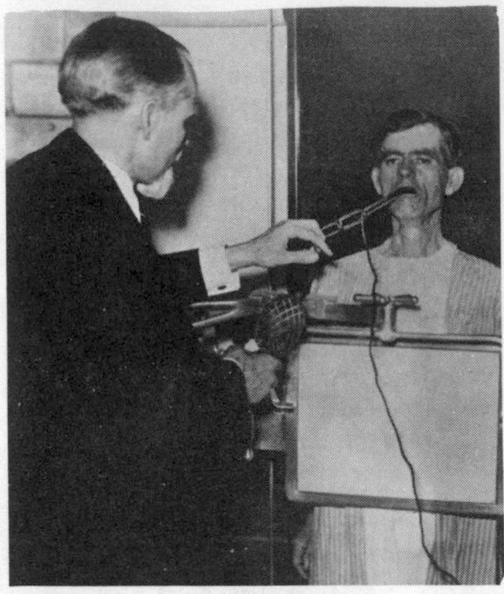

MEDICAL CAMERA so small it could be easily swallowed was invented in 1934, enabled physicians to study stomach disorders through photos. It took sixteen pictures of stomach interior.

MEDICINE

Medicine in the Thirties continued to make important progress in its struggle against disease. Discovery and synthesis of vitamins made news. Discovery of blood groups helped make transfusions safe, earned 1930 Nobel Prize for Dr. Karl Landsteiner. Knowledge of glandular functions grew; evidence in 1933 showed that the pituitary gland produced hormones affecting growth, sexual activity, and sugar and milk production. Surgery was used to lower high blood pressure in 1935. In 1939 metrazol shock therapy was found effective in treating dementia praecox.

SULFANILAMIDE was produced in large quantities to meet the growing demand for the drug after discovery of its effectiveness against streptococcic infections and some forms of influenza.

NOBEL PRIZE IN MEDICINE in 1934 was awarded jointly to Doctors George Minot and William Murphy *(below, l.)* for their discovery that liver in the diet in sufficient quantities is a specific in the treatment of pernicious anemia. Beside them is Dr. Thomas Hunt Morgan, biology professor at California Institute of Technology, who won 1933 Nobel Prize for work on the genetic functions of chromosomes. Another medical researcher was Dr. E. V. McCollum, leader in the work on vitamins.

EDUCATION

ROBERT M. HUTCHINS, appointed head of U. of Chicago in 1929, was nation's youngest college president at 30. Founder of Chicago Plan, he stressed great books, "humanizing" curriculum.

MANY SCHOOLS were closed during the depression due to lack of funds. Others like this Kentucky school hired older students to teach their younger brothers and sisters. Note homemade desks, seats, all community could afford.

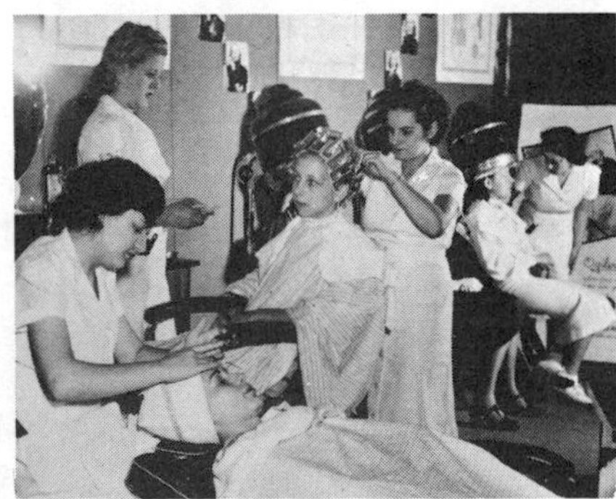

VOCATIONAL TRAINING had been introduced into most city high schools by mid '30s. Students who wish to become beauticians are shown attending a beauty culture class in Jane Addams vocational high school in New York.

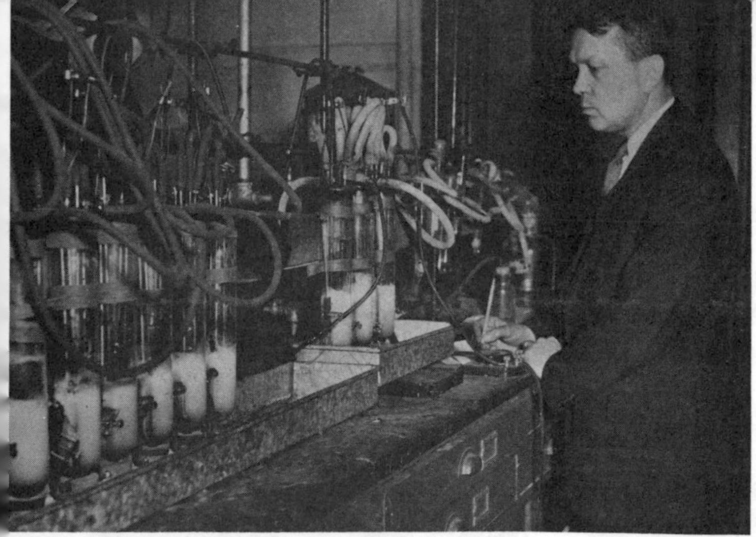

UNLOCKING MOLECULES is job for which this apparatus was invented. It is used in making "heavy water" which differs from water in that it contains twice the amount of hydrogen by weight. Its co-discoverer, Prof. Harold C. Urey, later was on wartime atom bomb team.

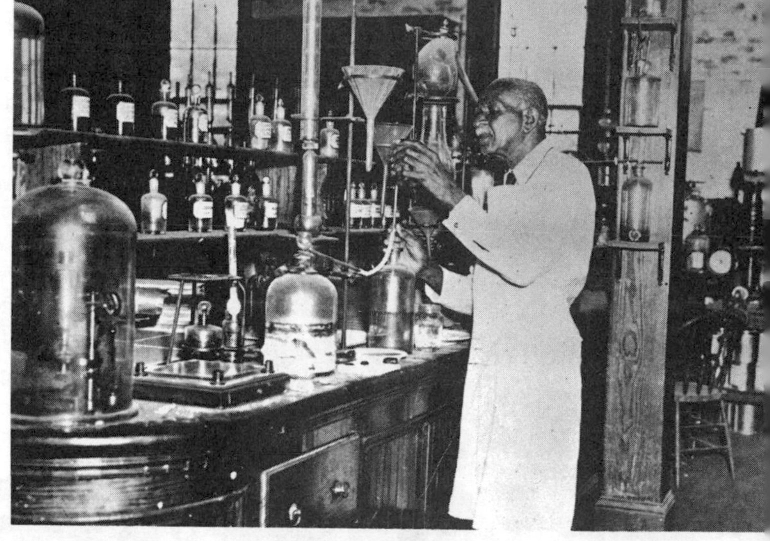

BOON TO SOUTH was work of famed Negro scientist, Dr. George Washington Carver, Director of Agriculture at Alabama's Tuskegee Institute. He developed 285 products from peanut, 185 from sweet potato, used native clay to make paints, helped raise living standard.

SCIENCE

Splitting the atom creates great new source of energy

Many discoveries of scientists of the '30s were later used in military devices of World War II. One of the most effective was radar; experimentation in this area was a factor in developing television. In 1939 high-frequency radar was developed; it recorded solid objects which were reflected on "scanning" screens, helped track ships or planes.

More important was work done in unleashing atomic energy. In 1932 Compton, Urey, Thibaud and Joliot were working at the problem of splitting the atom and transforming part of its mass into energy. The cyclotron developed by U. of California's Lawrence succeeded in obtaining intense streams of protons and deuterons with energies as high as 16,000,000 volts. Later experiments developed isotopes U-235 and U-238, useful in making the atomic bomb. But not until development of the atomic pile with "moderators" to control nuclear reaction was atomic fission controlled.

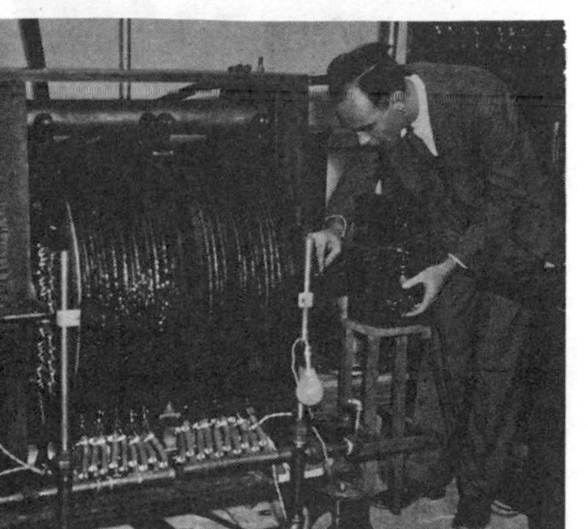

MECHANICAL BRAIN, device to save engineers repetitive calculations, was designed by Dr. Vannevar Bush *(r.)* at Mass. Institute of Technology in 1932. In another area, the Geiger Counter was developed for detecting radioactivity.

EARLY ATOM SPLITTER was built by Dr. Karl D. Anderson *(above)* and Nobel Prize winner Dr. Robert A. Millikan in 1931. Supplying important information about atomic energy, such apparatus assisted scientists in nuclear study.

SCIENTISTS of many nations worked on atomic problems. The British team *(l.)* who worked under the direction of the famed scientist Lord Rutherford *(center)* to split the atom were youthful Dr. E. T. S. Walton *(l.)* and J. D. Cockroft *(r.)*. The photograph on the right shows a new planet *(see arrows)*, discovered at the Lowell Observatory, Flagstaff, Arizona in 1930. Situated beyond the planet Neptune, it is the ninth planet in our solar system.

SHIRLEY TEMPLE, curly-haired blonde charmer, was the greatest child star. From 1934-39 her Fox films grossed $35 million; "Shirley" dolls and clothes were popular. In *The Little Colonel* in 1935 she danced with Bill Robinson.

ONE VOICE allegedly saved Universal Studios from bankruptcy in 1937. It belonged to Deanna Durbin, who in *Three Smart Girls* and *100 Men and a Girl (r.* with Stokowski), sang her way to fame. Pasternak was the producer.

LAUREL AND HARDY, popular partners in bumbling humor, became worldwide comic favorites under tutelage of Hal Roach, who made *Our Gang* films.

DICKENS' DAVID COPPERFIELD was brought to cinema life by Freddie Bartholomew who was teamed with W. C. Fields. The child star also appeared with Spencer Tracy in *Captains Courageous,* which won for Tracy an Oscar.

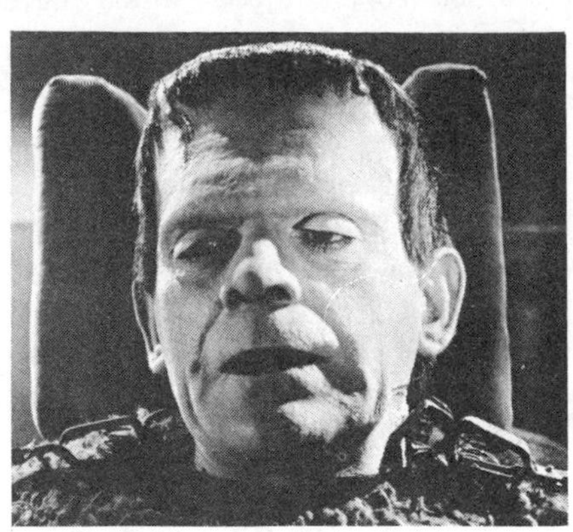

MONSTERS stalked the screen in 1931-32. Boris Karloff played Frankenstein's creation. Another terror, *Dr. Jekyll and Mr. Hyde,* won Fredric March award.

INNUENDO, charm, exuberance were trademarks of French star Maurice Chevalier, and marked such musicals as *Love Parade* and *The Smiling Lieutenant.* In him director Ernst Lubitsch's famed "sly touch" found expression.

HISTORICAL portraits were forte of George Arliss, who acted on stage and screen with equal skill. He brought *Disraeli* to the screen, with Joan Bennett, after having played it on stage for five years in N. Y. and on the road.

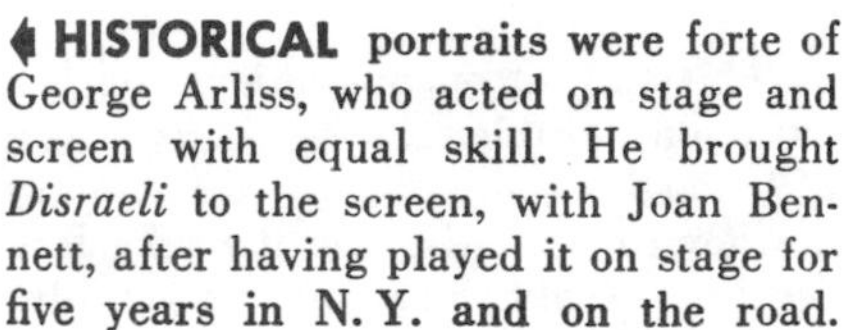

GERMAN side of the war was shown in *All Quiet on the Western Front,* adapted from Remarque's novel and judged best picture of 1930. Lewis Milestone directed and Louis Wolheim *(l.)* and Lew Ayres were principal actors.

MOVIES

The all-star cast and self-censorship

In a decade that opened with depression, movies needed special drawing powers. Merely announcing "Garbo Talks!" sold *Anna Christie*, but soon new devices were required. One tried successfully was the all-star cast; *Grand Hotel* in 1932 had Garbo, John and Lionel Barrymore, Joan Crawford, Wallace Beery. Responsible for such casting was MGM producer Irving Thalberg. Testament to his greatness was Thalberg Memorial Award.

Evidence of film industry maturing came in 1934 with formation of Production Code Administration (self-censorship) under Joseph Breen. In 1935 Zanuck and Schenck merged their 20th Century studio with Fox.

JEAN HARLOW, "platinum blonde," blazed to fame in *Hell's Angels (upper photo*, with Ben Lyon), the sensational Howard Hughes production. Later, under Thalberg's guidance at MGM, she enlivened *Red Dust*, with Clark Gable.

UNIQUE short subjects, displaying the satiric wit of Robert Benchley, were written and acted by the one-time critic. The problem above: *How To Sleep*, one of Benchley's humorous lectures.

◀ FIVE AWARDS went to *It Happened One Night*. This 1934 romantic comedy, starring Clark Gable and Claudette Colbert, was directed by Frank Capra. A highly successful Columbia picture, it served to revitalize Clark Gable's career, previously type-cast.

MAE WEST continued on screen the same type of bawdy entertainment she had offered on stage. The provocative blond performer appeared in *I'm No Angel* with the coming star, Cary Grant.

PRIZE tear-jerker of 1931 was *The Champ*, with Wallace Beery as a fighter and Jackie Cooper playing his son. Beery won Academy Award for his acting, as did writer Frances Marion.

WALTER HUSTON portrayed *Dodsworth* opposite Ruth Chatterton in 1936, in the film version of Sinclair Lewis' novel. William Wyler was director of this impressive Goldwyn production.

◀ **MOST POPULAR** dancers in pictures, the famous team of Ginger Rogers and Fred Astaire raised film musicals to new heights. Their polished style and grace were evident in such movie musical comedies as *Gay Divorcee*, *Top Hat*, and *Swing Time*, and *Follow the Fleet*. First-rank composers such as Jerome Kern, Cole Porter, Irving Berlin and George Gershwin wrote the musical scores for their RKO motion picture hits.

FOREIGN FILMS grew more popular in America. Charles Boyer, Dannielle Darrieux *(above, in Mayerling)* became U.S. stars, as did Jean Gabin *(below, arm in sling, in Grande Illusion)*. German *M* of Lang, Hitchcock's British film work also drew audiences.

"KING KONG" was only two feet high, but with RKO trick photography he frightened millions of movie patrons. This Hollywood "monster epic," replete with thrills, chills and panic, still ranked high among terror films.

CHARLES LAUGHTON starred in *Mutiny on the Bounty (below, center*, with Clark Gable), directed by Frank Lloyd and judged best picture of 1935. His memorable *Henry VIII* won an Award.

PAUL MUNI brilliantly interpreted *Zola*. For another biographical role, *Pasteur*, he won an Award in 1936. Muni worked at Warners under Wallis.

A GOLD MINE for MGM was Andy Hardy series, thanks to Mickey Rooney who enacted young Andy's adventures. Object of passion was Lana Turner.

MARLENE DIETRICH had made reputation in German *Blue Angel* with Jannings. American films like Von Sternberg's *Shanghai Express*, 1932, emphasized her exotic quality. The name Dietrich became synonymous with glamor. ▶

DISNEY'S GENIUS flowered in full-length *Snow White and the Seven Dwarfs* in 1938. Dubbed into 15 languages, it was largest modern money-maker. Color helped Disney's work.

ROBERT DONAT, in title role of *Goodbye, Mr. Chips,* 1939 adaptation of Hilton's story of English school master, won an Award. Film introduced Greer Garson.

NEWCOMER Katharine Hepburn appeared with John Barrymore in *Bill of Divorcement* in 1932. A year later she won Award for *Morning Glory.* Barrymores, Ethel, John, Lionel, were in *Rasputin.*

LEO McCAREY made two of the decade's best motion pictures with actress Irene Dunne: *The Awful Truth* with Cary Grant and Ralph Bellamy *(above),* and *Love Affair,* which co-starred Charles Boyer.

CAMILLE was Garbo's triumph, but with George Cukor directing, the Swedish star also helped establish a young leading man just rising—Robert Taylor.

DOCUMENTARY realism distinguished *Grapes of Wrath,* saga of the "Okies" by John Steinbeck. Henry Fonda played the son of Jane Darwell under John Ford's direction, the latter two winning "Oscars." Nunnally Johnson wrote the fine screenplay.

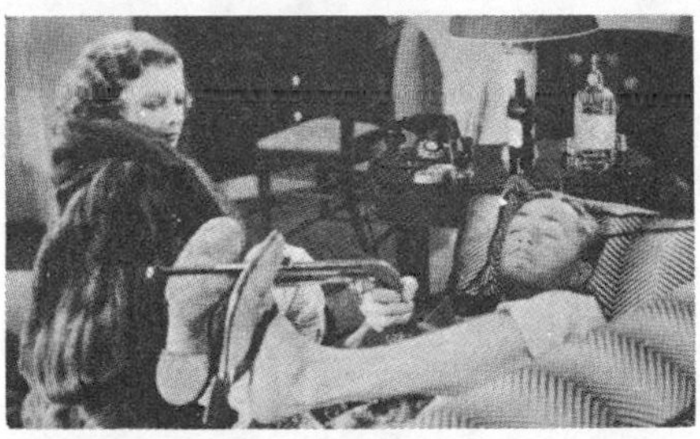

M-G-M HITS included *The Thin Man,* Dashiell Hammett's tale of an urbane detective, with William Powell, Myrna Loy. Another success was *Arrowsmith.*

FANTASY *Wizard of Oz* featured Judy Garland singing *Over the Rainbow* to *Tin Man* Jack Haley, *Straw Man* Ray Bolger and *Cowardly Lion* Bert Lahr. Another winning performance was given by Bette Davis in *Dark Victory* in '39.

DRAMATIC *Wuthering Heights* starred Laurence Olivier and Merle Oberon, under the direction of William Wyler. Script from the Bronte novel was by Ben Hecht and Charles MacArthur, who had collaborated on *Front Page.*

SWING SESSION for charity, a contest for "amateurs," enlisted this stellar sextet: *(left to right)* Jack Benny, violin; Dick Powell, cornet; Ken Murray, flute; Bing Crosby, drums; Shirley Ross, piano; Tommy Dorsey, trombone.

ORSON WELLES demonstrated the power of radio in October, 1938, when in the course of a dramatic presentation, he described the imaginary landing of a "machine from Mars" and caused some listeners to panic.

RADIO'S CREATION was Charlie McCarthy. a ventriloquist's wooden dummy, endowed with humanity and charm by his creator, Edgar Bergen. The brash antics of Charlie and the doltish Mortimer Snerd highlighted Sunday radio.

RADIO'S BIG ERA

Despite the Depression, radio sales climbed until 8,000,000 were sold yearly by 1937. Besides daytime soap operas, radio offered a diversified diet: comedy with Eddie Cantor, Jack Benny, Fred Allen, Fibber McGee and Molly, as well as Information Please, New York Philharmonic and Chicago Round Table discussions.

Mutual Broadcasting System added a third coast-to-coast network; 80,000,000 Americans felt close to world events as they heard FDR's fireside chats, the abdication of Edward VIII and the Munich crisis reported.

AMOS AND ANDY spanned two decades of broadcasting. Freeman F. Gosden (Amos) and Charles J. Correll (Andy), operators of the Fresh Air Taxi Cab Co., first played all roles.

AMATEUR HOUR hit radio in the '30s. Major Bowes took over the "Roxy Gang" from the Capitol Theatre in New York, later developed touring troupes of amateurs like Veronica Mimosa.

SPECIALISTS developed in the field of radio reporting. Ted Husing *(below, l.)*, with his rapid, vividly detailed style, became one of the best known sports announcers. In the area of news, H. V. Kaltenborn *(center)*, with his clarifying explanations of the Munich crisis in 1938 on CBS, showed how far news reporting had progressed from first election-returns broadcast of Harding election in 1920. "Commentator" became a new job for political writers and world-travelers such as Lowell Thomas *(r.)*. Another popular personality was Mary Margaret McBride with her program for women.

FASHIONS

BRENDA FRAZIER was most famous debutante of the era and set fashion vogue. Copies of her many strapless ball gowns in all colors and fabrics swirled on dance floors across the nation. Here she poses in white velvet.

SLACKS made style news when Marlene Dietrich hid her celebrated legs in them and thereby launched a popular new fashion that has come to mean millions to the sportswear industry.

STARLET Rita Hayworth, in great demand as bathing suit model in the '30s, helped sell Cole of California's first Matletex swim suit, which used diagonal shirring to insure form-fit.

PRESS

MOST FAMOUS woman columnist of this era was Dorothy Thompson, later the wife of writer Sinclair Lewis. Noted for her criticism of anti-American groups, she is shown here at a 1939 German-American Bund rally.

FOUNDER of Guild of New York Newspaper Men and Women in 1933 was columnist Heywood Broun, whose feuds with Pegler, etc. were famed.

PRESS AGENT Steve Hannagan (with actress Ann Sheridan) publicized Miami Beach with photos of bathing beauties. Another leading agent was Ivy Lee, public relations man for Standard Oil Co., Rockefellers.

RISE OF COLUMNISTS marked the '30s. Damon Runyon wrote brilliantly of sports, Broadway. Many of his tales of Broadway became literary classics.

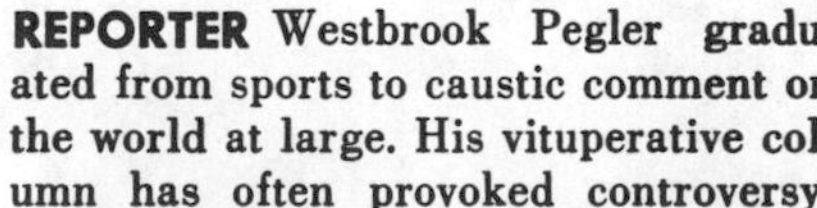

REPORTER Westbrook Pegler graduated from sports to caustic comment on the world at large. His vituperative column has often provoked controversy.

SPORTS WRITER Grantland Rice, an outstanding critic and reporter of athletic events, gained fame by his selection of football's All-American teams.

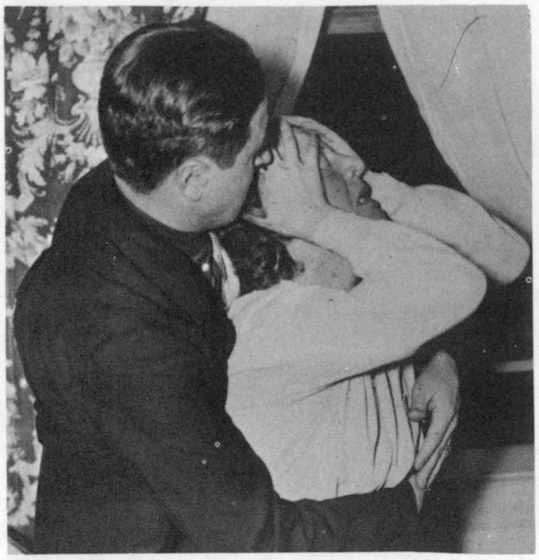

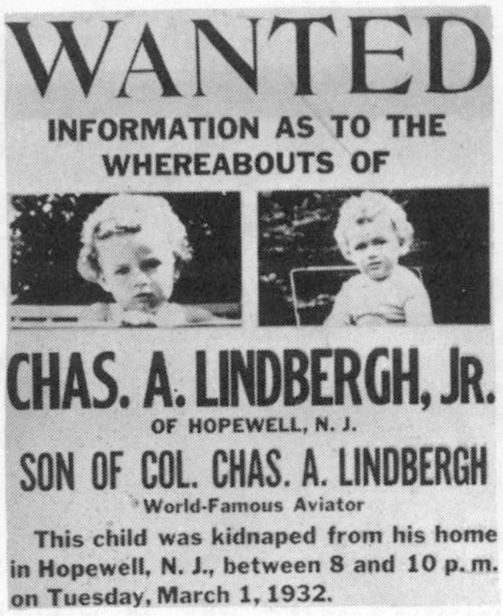

WANTED
INFORMATION AS TO THE
WHEREABOUTS OF
CHAS. A. LINDBERGH, JR.
OF HOPEWELL, N. J.
SON OF COL. CHAS. A. LINDBERGH
World-Famous Aviator
This child was kidnaped from his home
in Hopewell, N. J., between 8 and 10 p.m.
on Tuesday, March 1, 1932.

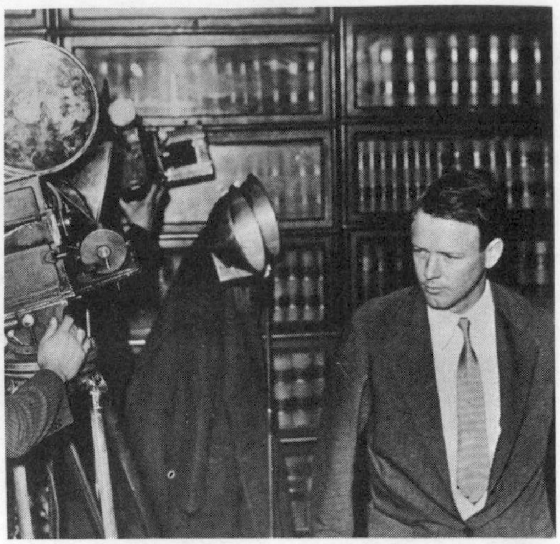

LINDBERGH KIDNAPPING shocked the nation and led to legislation to curb kidnapping. The son of Anne Morrow Lindbergh and Col. Charles A. Lindbergh *(above c.)*, disappeared March 1, 1932 and 72 days later his body was found a few miles from Lindbergh home at Hopewell, N. J. Bruno Richard Hauptmann *(below, with guard).* was executed for the murder April 3, 1936; his wife *(above r.)* collapsed at news. Dr. John F. Condon *(below c.)* contacted Hauptmann, who maintained his innocence to the last. But part of the $50,000 ransom was found in his garage; this and other evidence convinced jury and public of his guilt. The case resulted in a law that made kidnapping a federal offense, and was enacted under Atty. Gen. Homer S. Cummings and J. Edgar Hoover, Director of the FBI *(below right)*. This action checked wave of kidnapping to which criminals had turned after Repeal had ended bootlegging.

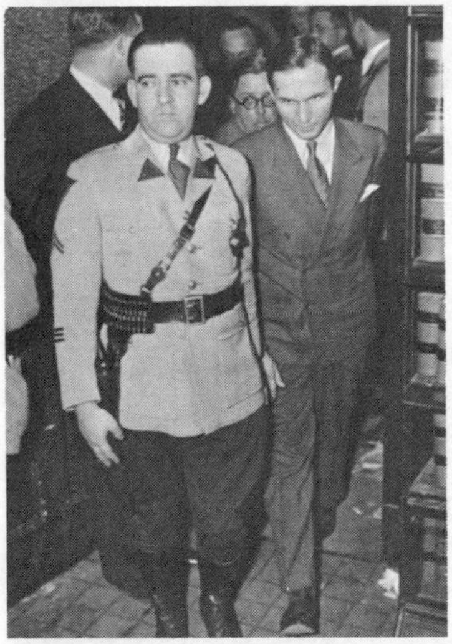

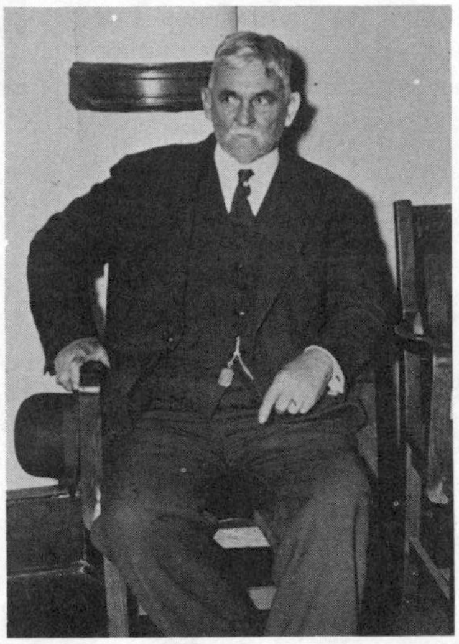

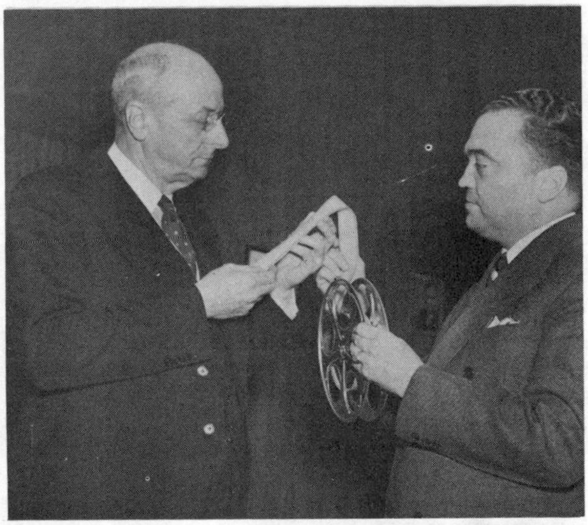

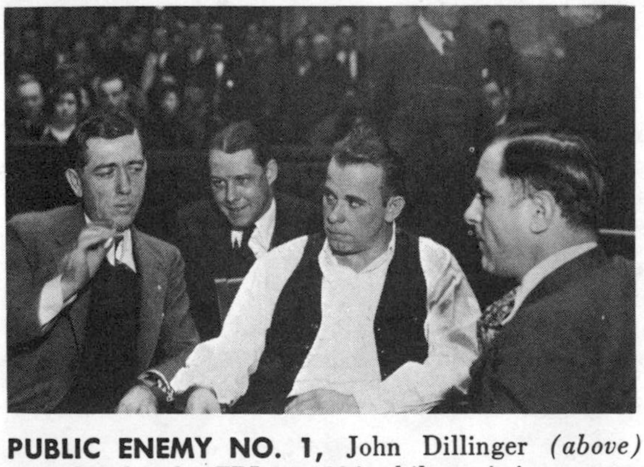

PUBLIC ENEMY NO. 1, John Dillinger *(above)* was shot by the FBI in 1934 while resisting arrest. Among others who met same fate were "Pretty Boy" Floyd, "Baby Face" Nelson, Ma and Fred Barker. Alvin "Old Creepy" Karpis was caught in 1936 by G-men led by J. Edgar Hoover. Appointed in 1924, he made FBI one of world's top police agencies.

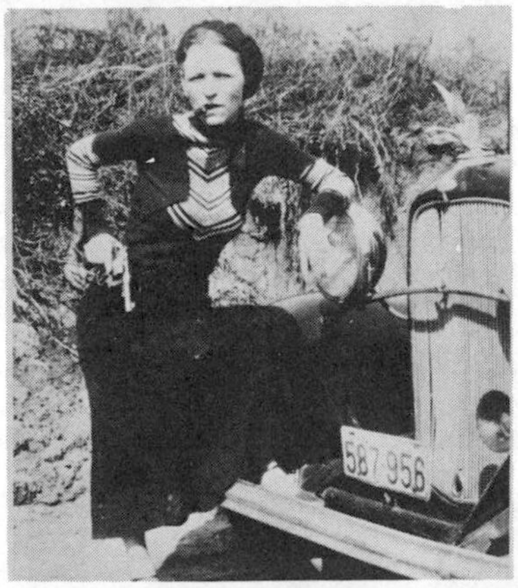

"GUN MOLL" Bonnie Parker and Clyde Barrow, wanted for murder, were ambushed by G-men in Louisiana in 1934. Lonely-hearts killer H. F. Powers admitted 5 murders.

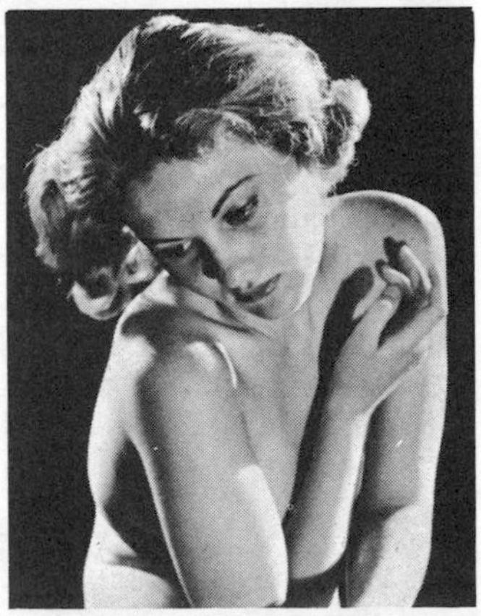

MODEL Veronica Gedeon and two others were slain in 1937 by psychotic youth prematurely released. Case emphasized inadequate psychiatric care.

BOOKS

Historical novels lead best-sellers

Readers of the Troubled Thirties, seeking escape from Depression doldroms, looked for bulky books—preferably racy and hypnotic novels. Hervey Allen's *Anthony Adverse*, prototype of the genre, dominated best-seller lists in 1933-34. Topping this came Margaret Mitchell's *Gone With the Wind* in 1936. It was one of three most popular novels of the half century; the other two: *In His Steps* by C. M. Sheldon, 8 million copies; Hubbard's *Message to Garcia,* 4 million.

While quantity prevailed,the quality of writing fell short of the high standard of the previous decade. Ernest Hemingway's *To Have and Have Not* did not match *The Sun Also Rises* and *A Farewell to Arms* of the '20s. Sinclair Lewis' *Ann Vickers* and *Work of Art* did not measure up to *Dodsworth* (1929), nor did Erich Maria Remarque's *The Road Back* (1931) rank with *All Quiet on the Western Front.*

But the '30s produced several vital literary talents—John Steinbeck, Thomas Wolfe, William Saroyan. There were also non-fiction classics, such as Lawrence's *Seven Pillars of Wisdom,* Douglas Southall Freeman's *R. E. Lee,* Clarence Day's *Life With Father.* Lloyd C. Douglas began mining the religious vein with *Magnificent Obsession* (1932) and with *Green Light* (1935) and *White Banners* (1936) became very popular.

"COME AND GET IT," call to meals in logging camps, was title of Edna Ferber's 1936 novel of lumber industry. Twice she had been top seller: *So Big* (1924), *Cimarron* (1930). Another popular author was Ellen Glasgow.

SCHOLAR-NOVELIST Aldous Huxley of the noted British family, wrote *Point Counter Point* (1928), the trenchant satire *Brave New World* (1932) and *Eyeless in Gaza* (1936). His works include philosophy, essays and criticism.

THOMAS WOLFE sent *Of Time and the River* manuscript to Scribner's by trunk to be edited by Maxwell Perkins, mentor of Hemingway and Fitzgerald. Wolfe's first novel was *Look Homeward, Angel,* last, *You Can't Go Home Again.*

NOBEL PRIZE was presented to Pearl Buck by King Gustav of Sweden in 1938. Her fine novels of China won wide acclaim: *The Good Earth* led best-sellers of '31-'32. All of the five most popular novels of '31 were written by women.

SOUTHERN THEMES and psychological depth of William Faulkner (between members of his Miss. household) were seen in *The Sound and the Fury* (1929) and *Sanctuary* (1932).

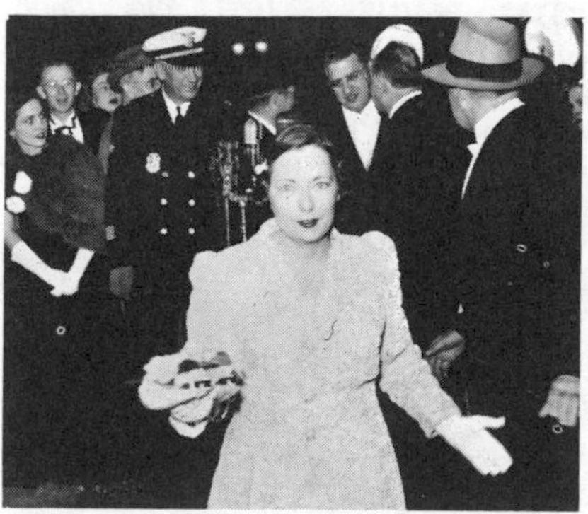

LEGEND of the South and of publishing trade, *Gone With the Wind* (1936) won Pulitzer Prize and had sold more than 3.5 million copies by '49. Author M. Mitchell *(above)* died in accident.

WRITER in several media on varied themes, Thornton Wilder pioneered as a playwright with *Our Town* and *Skin of Our Teeth;* his novels: *Woman of Andros* and *Heaven's My Destination*

HELEN HAYES performed a *tour de force* as *Victoria Regina*, aging 60 years in the Laurence Housman play. Vincent Price played Prince Albert in this Gilbert Miller production of 1935.

"TOBACCO ROAD" opened Dec. 4, 1933 for a record run until May 31. 1941. Adapted by Jack Kirkland from Caldwell's book, it starred Henry Hull.

NOEL COWARD *(l.)* wrote *Design for Living* for Lynn Fontanne, Alfred Lunt and himself to perform. It was hit of 1933 as was his *Private Lives* in 1931.

THEATER

In an era of richly diversified fare, Broadway offered comedy—Kaufman and Hart's *You Can't Take It With You*, 1937; musicals by the Gershwins, Cole Porter, Rogers and Hart.

New writers of social comment emerged: Lillian Hellman with *The Children's Hour*, 1934; Clifford Odets' *Waiting for Lefty*, 1935; Sidney Kingsley's *Dead End*, 1935; Irwin Shaw's *Bury the Dead*, 1936.

"GREEN PASTURES," 1930, adapted from Roark Bradford's tales, was Old Testament story of Negro Sunday school teacher. Harrison *(l.)* was "De Lawd."

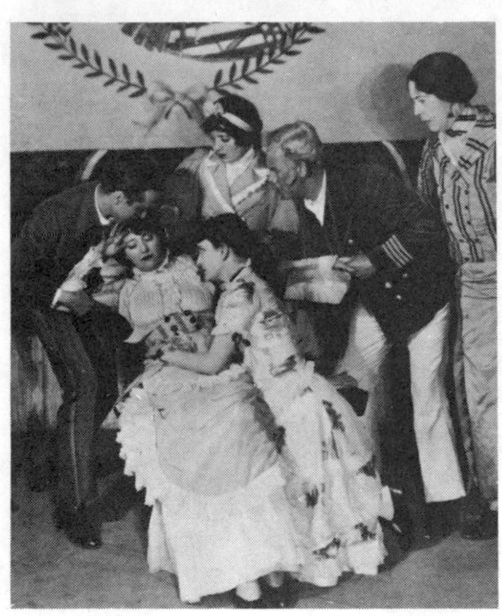

◀ **"SHOW BOAT"** opened in 1927, played through '30s in road companies and revivals. Helen Morgan *(fainting)* and Charles Winninger were in original cast of Kern-Hammerstein show.

IN CAST of *Roberta*, 1933, were, ▶ George Murphy, Ray Middleton, Tamara and Bob Hope. Sydney Greenstreet was comedian in Kern show.

FIRST MUSICAL to win Pulitzer Prize. *Of Thee I Sing* (1931) had a score by the Gershwins, book by Kaufman and Ryskind. Leads were William Gaxton. George Murphy and Victor Moore.

NOTED REVUE of 1931, *The Band Wagon* starred Fred Astaire and sister Adele *(below)*, Frank Morgan and Helen Broderick. Produced by Max Gordon, it had Schwartz-Dietz score.

FIRST HIT of the Group Theatre in 1933 was Sidney Kingsley's *Men In White*, realistically staged by Lee Strasberg. Alexander Kirkland starred; in bit parts: Clifford Odets and E. Kazan.

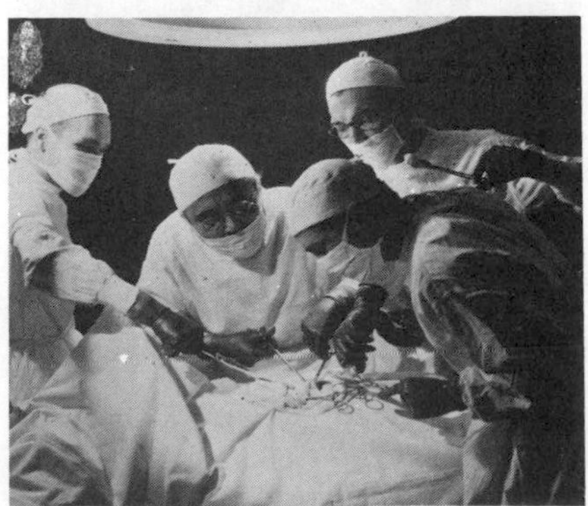

ETHEL WATERS sang *Heat Wave* in *As Thousands Cheer* and stopped the show, one of 1933's best. Written by Irving Berlin and Moss Hart, produced by Sam Harris, it also starred Marilyn Miller and Clifton Webb, whose big number was *Easter Parade.* In 1930 Webb had played in *Three's a Crowd;* left, with Libby Holman and Fred Allen.

KATHARINE CORNELL became producer as well as star in 1931, with Rudolf Besier's romantic *Barretts of Wimpole Street,* staged by her husband, Guthrie McClintic, with settings by Jo Mielziner. Her earlier plays had included *Bill of Divorcement,* 1921; *Candida,* 1924; *The Letter,* 1927. As actress-manager she presented successful *Romeo and Juliet* in 1934, and *St. Joan* in 1936, in New York and on tour.

THREE SEASONS, 1934-36, saw three hits: *The Petrified Forest* by Robert Sherwood, Noel Coward's *Tonight at 8:30, Winterset* by Maxwell Anderson. Leslie Howard was in *Forest* with Humphrey Bogart. Coward and Gertrude Lawrence *(r.)* played his work.

THORNTON WILDER'S *Our Town* told of "life, love and death" in a small town. On a bare stage with few props, the action was interpolated by "stage manager" Frank Craven. His son John and Martha Scott *(above)* played lovers.

CHORUS GIRL was the role played by Polly Walters in *She Loves Me Not* in 1933. In a scene from the production *(above),* the costumed chorine startles John Beal in his Princeton room where she has been hiding.

MARGARET SULLAVAN portrayed a hopeful young actress in *Stage Door,* 1936 drama by George Kaufman and Edna Ferber. Miss Sullavan moved between Hollywood-NY.

EUGENE O'NEILL in 1931 became America's greatest playwright with *Mourning Becomes Electra,* trilogy based on Greek tragedy; Nazimova and Alice Brady in six-hour Theatre Guild opus.

STORM CENTER of U.S. art, Thomas Hart Benton, whose *Susanna and the Elders* shocked some, fought Indiana on fee for Century of Progress murals.

INDIVIDUALISM marked the new American artists. Kansas-born John Steuart Curry drew on Middlewestern themes, as seen here in *Wisconsin Landscape.* He is grouped with Benton and Iowan Grant Wood as an exponent of "American Scene" painting. For Rockwell Kent, vivid symbolism expressed highly personal art.

Art Matures

New ideas, techniques as appreciation grows

Historians may call the '30s the Golden Decade of American Art. People had time to look and learn and the artist had a new patron—the U.S. Government. It was a Depression Renaissance in art: the mural in the post office, the WPA show in the public library. Chicago's Century of Progress, featuring modern design drew millions.

Unable to afford entertainment, people flocked to museums and galleries. Pocket art histories appeared and artistic merit penetrated comics via *Prince Val* and *Flash Gordon.* Some art patrons continued to give or lend collections while others were forced to sell, in both cases to the public benefit. Through great fairs on both coasts in 1939, Americans anticipated "A World of Tomorrow."

FAR AHEAD of his times, architect Frank Lloyd Wright was ignored, then ridiculed; by the '30s only a few could afford his daring designs. "Fallingwater" at Bear Run, Pa. was built of cantilevered concrete over a waterfall.

EXPERIMENTALIST Pablo Picasso influenced modern art in Europe and America. Often studiedly crude, he sought feelings and ideas in place of photographic images, and expressed them on canvas, in sculpture and in ceramics.

◆ **MEXICAN ARTIST** Diego Rivera, a communist, commissioned as Rockefeller Center muralist, painted Lenin with Washington, Lincoln—mural destroyed.

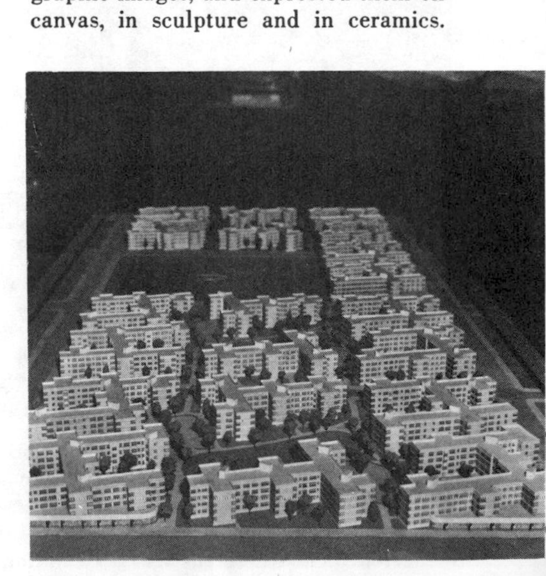

PLANNED improvement of U. S. ◆ cities through recovery spending seen in Williamsburg Housing Project, uniform without monotony, huge but uncrowded.

DUKE Ellington's *Solitude* won $2500 ASCAP award, 1934. Eddie De Lange and Irving Mills were lyricists. Ellington hits include *Mood Indigo, Sophisticated Lady;* also elaborate studies.

JITTERBUGS refused to remain seated when Benny Goodman played at New York Paramount in 1938. Fine clarinetist and jazz innovator, Goodman, holding microphone, looks askance at couple dancing on stage. Music by "The King of Swing" inspired such demonstrations.

MUSIC—LOUD AND SWEET

Jazz gave way to swing in the '30s and as dance orchestras increased in size so did their volume. Popular music began to depend more on the arranger and less on originality. *Time On My Hands* and *Bye, Bye Blues* were hits and the depression was reflected in such songs as *I Found A Million Dollar Baby* and *Brother Can You Spare a Dime.* Freak hit of the decade was *The Music Goes Round and Round.* But American music gained stature with the work of George Gershwin whose folk opera *Porgy and Bess* opened in 1935.

In the realm of classical music a major force was Arturo Toscanini who resigned as director of the N.Y. Philharmonic Symphony Orchestra in 1936 and went home to Europe to retire. But he returned to the U.S. the next year at the urging of David Sarnoff and Samuel Chotzinoff who offered to create for the maestro the NBC Symphony Orchestra. He was given *carte blanche* with the new orchestra and its first concert on Christmas night, 1937, was the birth of a series of broadcasts that were among the era's most exciting musical events.

CONTRALTO Marian Anderson was championed by Mrs. Eleanor Roosevelt who sponsored the great Negro artist in capital concert. Beautiful Rosa Ponselle *(below)*, introduced to Met by Manager Gatti-Casazza, became an opera favorite.

JAZZ MASTER Louis Armstrong and torrid trumpet made thousands of devotees. With singer Maxine Sullivan, he does number from *Swinging the Dream.*

KATE SMITH first sang *God Bless America* on Armistice Day, 1938. Its lyric simplicity soon made Irving Berlin song an unofficial national anthem.

◀ **VIBRANT** Ethel Merman introduced her famous *I Got Rhythm* in hit show *Girl Crazy* in 1930. Meanwhile sultry Helen Morgan perched on a piano in supper clubs and theatres across nation and sang blues rendition of *My Man.*

LEOPOLD STOKOWSKI became ▶ conductor of the Philadelphia Symphony Orchestra in 1912 and thereafter it became one of the country's best. The distinguished maestro also helped develop other leading U. S. orchestras.

THE MORRO CASTLE caught fire off Asbury Park, New Jersey on Sept. 8, 1934, taking a toll of 135 lives. Carrying 318 passengers and a crew of 231 from Havana to New York, the American ship was saved from greater destruction by quick response to her call.

DISASTERS

DISASTROUS EARTHQUAKE struck northwestern Formosa in 1935, killed over 5,000. Refugees are given water by Japanese rescue crew *(above)*. Twelve years earlier Japan had suffered one of the worst earthquakes in modern times in which 143,000 persons were killed.

TERRIFIC BLAST destroyed the Consolidated Public School in New London, Texas on March 18, 1937, caused the deaths of 294 students. Natural gas that had been piped in for heating purposes had exploded. School was completely modern, one of the largest in U.S. Only one corner of main building was left standing *(r., center)*. Frantic parents and rescue workers search the ruins.

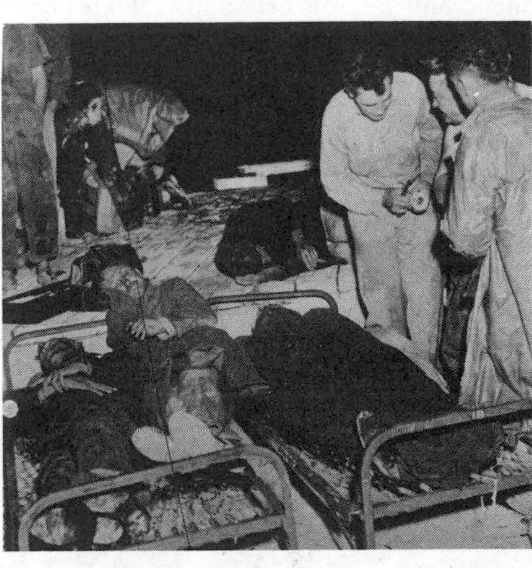

HURRICANE swept the Florida Keys in September, 1935 and three hundred World War I veterans encamped there were killed. Relief workers, rushed to stricken area, are shown *(above)* aiding scores of wounded.

WORST FLOOD in Kentucky history struck in January, 1937, when the Ohio River overflowed its banks. The business and residential districts of Louisville were inundated to the second story *(below, l.)*. Railroad round houses were more than half submerged *(r.)* when the Ohio swept over its banks at Portsmouth, Ohio, in the same winter floods. Refugees were evacuated from the city by train. Mississippi and Allegheny rivers also flooded in 1937, causing extensive damage.

RADICAL were Franklin D. Roosevelt's press conferences, the first time a president met reporters informally, answered direct questions. Also new were radio "fireside chats" which brought vital issues to the people.

ASSASSINATION of King Alexander in Marseilles, Oct. 9, 1934, almost led to war between Yugoslavia and Hungary, since it was a Croat revolutionary from Hungary who committed the crime. The assassin was killed immediately by guard *(on horse, l.)*, but Alexander lay dying, as did M. Barthou, French foreign minister riding with him. Inset shows *(l. to r.)* Alexander and Barthou.

PASSING SCENE

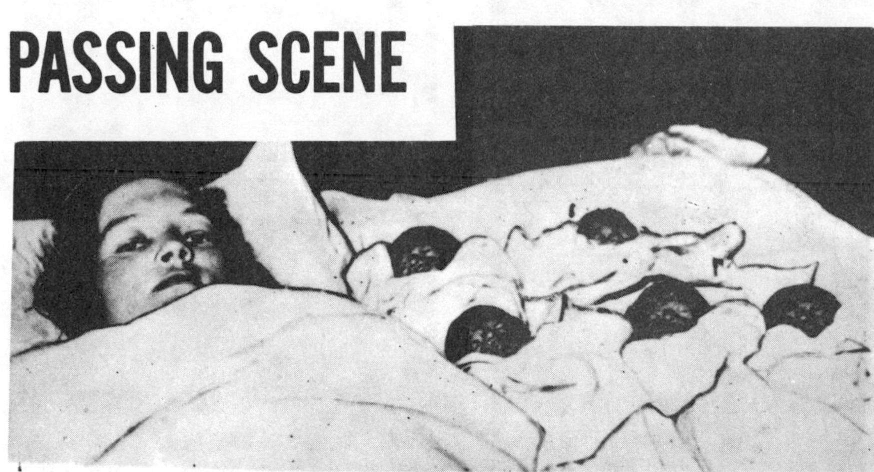

THE DIONNE QUINTUPLETS were born to Oliva and Elzire Dionne, May 28, 1934, on a farm near Callander, Ont., Canada. Dr. Allan R. Dafoe *(l.)*, the attending physician, worked with little equipment, saved the infants' lives to register a success then unknown in medical history. A week after birth, Marie, Annette, Cecile, Emilie and Yyonne, all together weighing 12 pounds, and living in an incubator supplied by Chicago paper, were world's most famous babies.

SKYSCRAPERS were an architectural development purely American. Skyline views taken 25 years apart show lower Manhattan. Tower in top view is Singer Building, 47 stories. Tallest tower in lower view is Bank of Manhattan, 71 stories. Second highest structure in world, 77 stories, is the Chrysler Building *(c.)*, erected in 1929. Tallest in world, Empire State Building *(r.)*, 102 stories, was begun Oct. 1, 1929, four weeks before the stock market crash, and completed in 1931.

◀ **SWALLOWING GOLDFISH,** a fad of college students in the '30s, was as inexplicable as earlier campus fads. Allegedly begun at Princeton, the craze spread *(l.* is a Missouri co-ed) and as sudden as its rise was its demise.

SCOTTSBORO CASE, in Alabama, ▶ 1931, involved nine Negroes accused of assaulting two white girls, one of whom later declared the case a frame-up. Masterful defense by Samuel Liebowitz reached Supreme Court, saved youths.

PASSING SCENE

REPEAL legalized liquor sale after almost 14 years of Prohibition. The 72nd Congress in Feb. 1933 passed a joint resolution for the 21st Amendment, repealing the 18th; within ten months states ratified. Pres. Roosevelt made Prohibition's end official Dec. 5, 1933.

JOHN D. ROCKEFELLER, SR. died in 1937, aged 97, having become one of the richest men in history through control of Standard Oil. Worth almost one billion dollars, he donated 500 million dollars to various philanthropies, was founder of the University of Chicago.

RUTH BRYAN OWEN, daughter of William Jennings Bryan, was the first woman to become U.S. Minister. Assigned to Denmark in 1933, this pioneer woman diplomat served there until '36, when she was married to Boerge Rohde, a Danish subject, and resigned her post.

◀ **FOOD PRICES** at typical A&P store in 1938 included hamburger steak at 19¢ a pound, porterhouse steak, 45¢, pork chops, 25¢. Retail food prices were 20% above those of 1933, when food cost less than at any time since 1915. By 1948 prices had doubled over 1938.

SOPRANO GRACE MOORE successfully brought opera to the screen and amazed producers. Her movie hit, *One Night of Love,* a 1934 Columbia picture, featured Tullio Carminati. Another opera star, Lawrence Tibbett of the Metropolitan, was making hit films. ▶

NANCY ASTOR, born in Virginia, wed Lord Waldorf Astor in 1906 (*l.*, when he became Lord Mayor of Plymouth). She entered House of Commons in 1919, first woman to do so.

HOLLYWOOD quartet in 1933 shows Franchot Tone and Joan Crawford (married 1935-39), Elizabeth Allen and Gilbert Adrian. Designer Adrian added "Letty Lynton" dress to fashions.

FATHER DIVINE, evangelist leader of N. Y.'s Harlem, bought estate in 1938 as "Heaven" for followers. Neighbors protested; his reply: "Peace, it's wonderful!"

SALLY RAND was a favorite at the Century of Progress Exhibition in Chicago during summers of 1933-34. Visited by 38 million people, the Fair made $63 million. American industry exhibited products, as did many foreign countries.

"MARCH KING" John Philip Sousa died in 1932, after a long career as brass band conductor; ex-Marine Corps bandmaster, he wrote *Stars and Stripes Forever.*

LARGEST THEATRE in the world, Radio City Music Hall in New York's Rockefeller Center opened in 1932. It seats 6,200; proscenium arch is high as five-story building; weekly receipts often total $150,000. Theatre presents movies and stage shows featuring precision dancers, the Rockettes.

MINIATURE GOLF became a sudden nation-wide fad in 1930. Inexpensive to operate, courses sprouted like weeds. On vacant lots little courses were laid out, featuring hazards like tunnels, drawbridges and 45-degree slopes. Garnet Carter of Tennessee claimed invention of the popular game.

-©Karsh Ottawa-

World War II . . . 1939-1945

Twenty-five-year armistice ends with Axis conquest of Europe and Asia, but the Allies, armed with the A-Bomb, win the final battle

Adolf Hitler in 1939 engineered the opportune and cynical Nazi-Soviet nonaggression pact which shocked the world. On September 1, Hitler, his Russian front secure, struck at Poland. Britain and France declared war, but proved unready. After a ruthless month-long blitzkrieg, the Nazis were able to partition Poland with their Soviet cohorts, who then invaded Finland. The Western Front settled down to a winter's "sitzkreig" behind the Maginot and Siegfried lines.

Next spring, Hitler struck at Denmark and Norway and by May stood poised for the great drive west. Stabbing as usual without warning, his mechanized Panzers and dive-bombing Stukas crushed the Netherlands, Belgium, Luxembourg and, after 45 days of fighting, France. From the incredible debacle, Britain, led now by the indomitable Winston Churchill, salvaged 337,131 troops from Dunkirk, and with inspiring bravery held firm through the air blitz which followed. Officially neutral, the U.S. managed to offer aid through Lend-Lease to Britain and to Russia, attacked by Hitler in 1941.

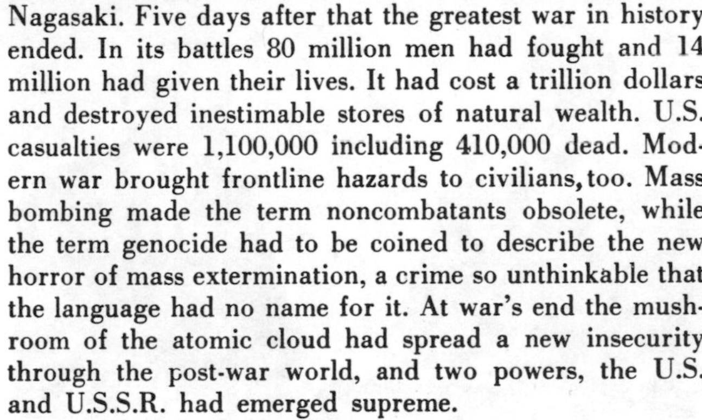

Stunned by the disaster at Pearl Harbor, outraged Americans built an army of 8,300,000 men; a two-ocean navy; war industries which produced a 10,000 ton ship in 78 days, 9,000 planes a month; and the atomic bomb. It could not be done in time, however, to prevent the conquest of the Philippines, Burma, Singapore and the Indies. In 1942 the Navy turned back the Japanese in the Coral Sea and Midway battles and China held out under Chiang Kai-shek. In 1943 the U.S. was ready for the weary three-year island hopping campaign from Guadalcanal to Tarawa . . . Kwajalein . . . Saipan . . . Leyte . . . Iwo Jima . . . Okinawa . . . and a climax over Hiroshima.

The Allies, meanwhile, had won El Alamein, invaded Africa (fall of 1942), then Sicily and Italy, which soon capitulated, leaving the Germans to fight at Salerno, Monte Cassino and Anzio. The Russians, marshalling as in Napoleon's day their ancient defenses of distance and winter, fell back on the Leningrad-Moscow-Stalingrad line and there fought epic battles. At Stalingrad, after three months of fighting involving a million men, Hitler's fortunes and the war reached a crisis. By January, 1943, he was in retreat. During the previous month the Allied Big Three had met to plan the second front and, in preparation, the U.S. 8th Air Force had dropped the first of 1,500,000 tons of bombs on Hitler's *Festung Europa.*

D-Day for the vast Allied landing in Normandy came on June 6, 1944. Its success ensured Hitler's doom. After a breakthrough into the interior the Allies surged powerfully across France, though gains were not made without heavy casualties. That winter the Germans struck back in the Battle of the Bulge, but it was a last attempt of the weakened Wehrmacht to regain the offensive.

The year of 1945 was one of more than military decision. In April Italian partisans caught and killed their onetime Duce, Mussolini. Franklin D. Roosevelt, then serving his fourth term, died on the eve of victory, and the presidency passed to Harry S. Truman. During the same month, U.S. and Russian soldiers made a juncture in Germany and the Allies met in San Francisco to establish the United Nations. In May Admiral Doenitz announced Hitler's suicide and Germany surrendered unconditionally. Only Japan was left, and the stage was set for the last act, not only of war but of an epoch.

On August 6, 1945, a B-29 dropped the first atomic bomb on Hiroshima and left the city devastated. Three days later a second bomb leveled Nagasaki. Five days after that the greatest war in history ended. In its battles 80 million men had fought and 14 million had given their lives. It had cost a trillion dollars and destroyed inestimable stores of natural wealth. U.S. casualties were 1,100,000 including 410,000 dead. Modern war brought frontline hazards to civilians, too. Mass bombing made the term noncombatants obsolete, while the term genocide had to be coined to describe the new horror of mass extermination, a crime so unthinkable that the language had no name for it. At war's end the mushroom of the atomic cloud had spread a new insecurity through the post-war world, and two powers, the U.S. and U.S.S.R. had emerged supreme.

◀ **BRITISH BULLDOG SPIRIT** manifest in ages past in the battles of Agincourt, Trafalgar, Waterloo, came into the custody of Winston Churchill during World War II. Taking over the government as Hitler marched on France, Churchill rallied his people for their great national effort at Dunkirk and the aerial Battle of Britain. As the war drew to a victorious close, his Conservatives were defeated at the polls, but Churchill never surrendered. World statesman of his time, he championed his ideals of freedom, democracy and justice wherever he found them in jeopardy.

RUSSO-GERMAN ALLIANCE gave the green light for World War II. Negotiations were concluded in the Kremlin on August 23, 1939, with the signing of the German-Russian pact by Stalin and Ribbentrop *(l.)*. Preceded by a trade agreement which supplied Germany with vital raw materials, the pact provided for abstention from attack on each other, partition of Poland and Russian occupation of Baltic states. English and French missions negotiating in Moscow were caught unprepared, and the news of this Nazi-Communist alliance shocked the world. Soon after, with Danzig as his excuse, Hitler marched into Poland *(above)* from the west, and on September 17, Russia attacked from the east. Despite the nonaggression pact Russo-German relations remained delicate.

HITLER STARTS WORLD WAR

Seeds of World War II were planted by the Allies when they failed to stop German rearmament. Hitler, believing in the Nazi principle of *Herrenvolk*, had as his first objective the inclusion in the Reich of all German-speaking minorities outside of Germany.

First on his list was the Saar, which voted overwhelmingly for reunion with Germany (1935). The Rhineland was occupied in 1936, Austria annexed in 1938 followed by the 3,000,000 Sudenten Germans living in Czechoslovakia (1938). Hitler took Memel from Lithuania and, turning to Danzig, decided not only to risk war with Poland but also to make a deal with the Russians for dividing the whole country. Finally, without formal declaration of war, Germany attacked Poland September 1, 1939. England and France declared war on Germany two days later.

Other contributing factors to World War II were the arbitrary national boundaries drawn after the first World War, and the indecision and lack of unity among the Allies. England was headed by Chamberlain who had apparently never read *Mein Kampf*. France was in constant political turmoil. Germany's smaller neighbors were helpless. In addition, Germany's industrial expansion needed new markets and raw materials. Nazi regime had been built on a foundation of persecution and conquest. To stay in power, Hitler needed more triumphs and new scapegoats. The unpreparedness of the democracies made it easier.

JOSEPH BECK, Polish Foreign Minister (1932), concluded a 10-year nonaggression pact with Germany in 1934. Pact was re-affirmed by Hitler in January, 1939, only to be abrogated a few months later. Beck had the unenviable task of trying to save his country at once from Hitler and from Stalin.

THE STEEL PACT of May 22, 1939, between Italy and Germany was a manifestation of the solidity of alliance between the two nations. Hitler *(c.)* sits between foreign ministers Ciano of Italy *(l.)* and Ribbentrop of Germany *(r.)* as they sign pact. Behind Hitler stands Marshal Goering.

POLAND On Sept. 1, 1939, lightning struck in Eastern Europe. In a conflict lasting less than a month, Poland, three times the size of England with over 30 million people, fell like a house of cards before the invaders.

Using 45 German divisions, the Reich completely paralyzed the Polish war brain within 48 hours of the war opening. While the Poles were thinking in the leisurely terms of the contact patrols of 1914, the Germans were waging an all-out aerial campaign. This resulted in the total destruction of the Polish Air Force and absolute German air supremacy within two days after the first German troops had crossed the Polish border. On the ground, trained armored units of tanks combined with infantry *(above)* and based more on speed than on fire power, penetrated deep into the Polish lines. Sept. 17th Russia, without a declaration of war, invaded the Polish eastern frontier. The third week of the war saw the first large scale bombing on a civilian population. On Sept. 27th, an armistice was declared after more than a week of continuous air and artillery bombardment, and two days later the 120,000 man garrison surrendered.

FINLAND The Finnish government rejected Russian demands similar to those accepted by other Baltic states, and on Nov. 30, 1939, the Red Army began an invasion of Finland on three fronts. Hero of Finnish resistance was Baron Karl Mannerheim *(above, r.)* who, in 1918, had defeated a Communist uprising in Finland.

Despite great numerical superiority (100 divisions against three), the Russian attack bogged down in the face of determined resistance and Arctic cold. Finally, on Feb. 2, 1940, Marshal Timoshenko led a 27-division assault on the Mannerheim line. Through ten days of bitter fighting, the Finns held their ground, but were finally forced to withdraw on February 15. Successful breaching of the Mannerheim Line proved the beginning of the end. Unable to resist the Russian hordes in the open, Finland surrendered on March 12, 1940. Peace treaty, negotiated at Moscow, ceded to Russia islands and territories totaling 16,173 square miles, including the Karelian Isthmus and a naval base at Hangoe.

GRAF SPEE IS SCUTTLED at the mouth of the river Plata, just outside the entrance of the neutral port of Montevideo, Uruguay. The German pocket battleship was scuttled and sunk by her own crew on Dec. 17, 1939. Fast, heavily armored, carrying six 11-inch guns, the 10,000 ton pride of Germany had sought refuge in the neutral port Dec. 13 after an 11-hour battle with the British light cruisers *Ajax* and *Achilles* and the heavy cruiser *Exeter*. When his time for repairs ran out, the Captain of the *Graf Spee* decided to scuttle her rather than face the waiting British ships.

INVASION OF NORWAY

The conquest of Norway would insure the Germans of safe transportation of Swedish iron ore down the Norwegian coast. German ships advanced towards Norway April 7th. Norwegian forces were mobilized and Englis' troops came to their defense. The Germans took Oslo and destroyed the Norwegian Navy. Norway resisted for two months, finally surrendered on June 9, 1940. Major Vidkun Quisling, who collaborated with the Germans, was made Minister President.

ERICH RAEDER was made Commander in Chief of the German Navy in 1935, a post he held until 1943. In Oct. 1946 he was sentenced to life imprisonment at Nurnberg, as a war criminal.

CONTROL of Scandinavia was complete after the successful attack on helpless Denmark, April 9, 1940. The Danes, fiercely resentful of their conquerors, are shown *(above)* during the occupation as they honor their King on the 30th anniversary of his government, a celebration which violates Nazi orders.

VIDKUN QUISLING'S name was to become a dictionary word meaning "one who traitorously assists an enemy power to invade his country." Quisling *(l.)* is shown with Nazi Heinrich Himmler.

MESSERSCHMITT 109 SWEPT THE SKIES OF INFERIOR AIRCRAFT

HEINKEL 111, GERMAN MEDIUM BOMBER, AIDS LAND ADVANCES

FRANCE CRUMBLED before the onslaught of the ruthlessly efficient Germans. General von Brauchitsch launched a new attack on June 5. Within a week virtually all opposition faded. On June 22 Premier Reynaud capitulated, as the victorious Germans entered the capital *(l.)*. French army had never recovered from the Panzer attack at Sedan.

BETWEEN May 29 - June 4, 337,131 French and English troops were evacuated from Dunkirk in 887 ships. Most of these were small craft, hastily assembled for the emergency and included fishing trawlers and lifeboats which braved Channel waters to aid in the rescue. All equipment on the Continent and about 30,000 troops were lost.

HOLLAND, BELGIUM, FRANCE FALL

With the occupation of Scandinavia completed, the German war machine next turned its attention to the West. On May 9, 1940 German paratroops entered Holland. After the disastrous bombing of Rotterdam, the Dutch surrendered on May 15th.

An attack on Belgium had come simultaneously. The German advance forced Belgian troops to withdraw to the Antwerp-Namur line where they merged with French and British forces.

But the big German push began May 10 through Ardennes into France. The Germans overcame second-rate troops to take the east bank of the Meuse. From there on the German attack was meteoric.

On May 28, the last Belgian troops capitulated and left the British to extricate themselves from Dunkirk.

By the 17th of June the Swiss frontier was contacted, and the entire Maginot line boxed. Paris had been reached and France fell June 22nd.

CAPTURED towns were systematically looted by German soldiers for their government, as shown here in Belgium. Many of Europe's art treasures fell into the hands of the high German officials.

HITLER AT NAPOLEON'S TOMB, which was designed to necessitate this act of homage, is forced to bow his head to view the last resting place of the great man of France.

FRANCE WAS OCCUPIED when her armies were defeated and her government surrendered. In the same railway coach where Marshal Foch granted Germany an armistice in 1918, Hitler had his revenge on June 21, 1940. Here a Frenchman cries as he watches Germans march into Paris.

BATTLE OF BRITAIN

After the disaster of Dunkirk, the fight began to safeguard England herself against invasion. In a move to keep ships from falling into the hands of the enemy, the British sank or destroyed the major units of the French fleet anchored at Oran, Algeria. All-out bombing attacks began on England August 8, 1940. On August 15 Britain withstood a 1000-plane attack. By September 10 the casualty rate in London alone had risen to between 300-600 killed a day and 1000-3000 wounded. The raid on Coventry climaxed the Nazi bombings. Winston Churchill is shown inspecting cathedral ruins there.

NORTH AFRICA

With the French army at the mercy of the Germans, and the French government on the verge of collapse, Italy entered the war on the side of Germany, June 10, 1940. The first real offensive of the Italians came in North Africa. On Sept. 13, 1940, a large force under Marshal Graziani struck at Egypt. The Italians advanced to Sidi Barrani where British troops under Gen. Wavel completely routed the Italians. Within the next few months Italy was driven out of Ethiopia *(l.)*. Germany organized her Afrika Korps under the brilliant Gen. Erwin Rommel *(above)* who soon took the offensive. Had the German invasion of Russia not deprived Rommel of supplies, Egypt might have fallen in the summer of 1941.

BISMARCK SUNK

The most powerful battleship afloat, the German *Bismarck (l.)* caused great alarm when she set out into the Atlantic in 1941. Intercepted by the British off the coast of Greenland, May 24, this 35,000-ton ship sank the 42,000-ton British battlecruiser *Hood (r.)* and damaged the battleship *Prince of Wales*. But the *Bismarck's* speed was reduced by a hit of at least one aerial torpedo and a shell in her bow. After a three day running battle, the ship was sunk on May 26 with all except 100 of her 2400 officers and men aboard.

WAR IN BALKANS

In a swift campaign of three weeks beginning April 6, 1941 the Germans overran the only Balkan countries yet unconquered, Yugoslavia and Greece. To crush them the Germans used 30 divisions of modern mechanized forces. The Italians had been held off by an almost weaponless Greek army, yet the Germans, in spite of 74,000 British troops aiding the Greeks, broke the Metaxas Line in two days and forced the British to evacuate, leaving some 30,000 Imperial troops behind to be captured. Tens of thousands of Greek civilians were left homeless after the battle (as Greek boy *l.)*. The airborne invasion of Crete was one of the most amazing of the war. Using 3,500 paratroops to seize the airfields, the Nazis soon landed about 35,000 airborne troops on the island *(above,* unloading from German plane). Crete was captured ten days after the start of the invasion, May 20, 1941. About 13,000 British troops were either killed or taken prisoner. Survivors were sent to Cyprus and Egypt.

BENITO MUSSOLINI and other Fascist leaders are shown inspecting troops. The Italians generally proved very poor fighters in the war and they were often a liability to the Germans rather than an asset. In North Africa the Italian troops were physically weak and always homesick. They showed little desire to fight and usually surrendered at the first sign of real danger. It was from Albania, which the Italians had captured in a matter of days in the spring of 1939, that Mussolini invaded Greece on October 28, 1940. In the group left is Victor Emmanuel III, the nominal King of Italy, who in 1922 had requested Mussolini to form a government for Italy and had granted him dictatorial powers, which were never relinquished.

HITLER INVADES RUSSIA

Hitler attacked Russia with 127 divisions, 3000 aircraft, on June 22, 1941. On a front of nearly 2000 miles the Nazi forces were organized into three groups. Von Lieb advanced through the Baltics, Von Bock directly toward Moscow and Von Rundstedt swept through the Ukraine toward Kiev *(below, r.)*. The chief strength of the Russians lay in their inexhaustible reserves *(below, l.)*. The Germans failed to achieve a decisive victory. The seige of Moscow was halted by winter and the German troops went into defensive position. A safe Moscow doomed the hopes of destroying Russia and proved that the Red Army could withstand the invaders. Subsequent to the attack on Hitler's life, engineered by German officials, Der Fuehrer took over control. It was the beginning of the end for German hopes in Russia and the entire war.

U. S. MAINTAINS NEUTRALITY

War in Europe forces nation into all-out aid to belligerent Allies

Hitler's designs for conquest were obvious by late 1939, but Americans were slow to recognize the danger. Until early 1941, U.S. foreign policy was to strengthen the European democracies, while maintaining neutrality.

As early as April, 1939, Roosevelt asked Congress to revise the Neutrality Act to provide Great Britain and France with more aid in case of war. The arms embargo remained law, preventing the sale of arms to the Allies, but allowing our ships free travel in combat zones if they did not carry war materials. The President's second request to lift the embargo came in Sept., 1939, and was heeded reluctantly after 6 weeks of heated debate. The Allies could then buy arms on a cash-and-carry basis. At the same time, Congress designated parts of Europe as "danger zones" from which U.S. ships and citizens were barred.

THE ATLANTIC CHARTER was the result of this memorable 1941 meeting between F.D.R. and Churchill on *HMS Prince of Wales.* It outlined the principles on which a democratic peace would be based.

Americans felt the Maginot Line and the British blockade would contain Hitler, but when Denmark, Belgium, Holland, Luxembourg and France all fell in the spring of 1940, the U.S. began to realize its desperate situation.

In Sept. 1940 Congress passed the first peacetime conscription act, 14 months before war was declared. By Oct. 1941, over $17 billion had been appropriated for defense, and American industry had slowly converted and expanded to begin full wartime production.

Meanwhile, common defense plans among Western Hemisphere nations resulted in the formation of a Joint Board of Defense with Canada, and an agreement with Latin American countries to pre-occupy and jointly administer any Dutch, Danish or French colonies in danger from the Nazis.

Anti-Japanese sentiment was revealed by two large loans to China and an embargo on the export of scrap metal and aviation gas to Japan.

Allies received favoritism: British warships were repaired in U.S. shipyards, British pilots were trained in Florida and 105 obsolete tanks went to Canada for training purposes.

In March 1941 Lend-Lease became law, permitting the U.S. to lend "defense articles" to Great Britain and other nations whose defense was considered vital to the U.S. Two months later, on May 27, almost a year after the British evacuation from Dunkirk and the fall of France, President Roosevelt declared a limited national emergency; by Nov., 1941 the U.S. was neutral in name only. Within days, Japan's attack on Pearl Harbor was to explode U.S. neutrality into full-fledged belligerency.

CONSCIENTIOUS objectors *(above)* protested conscription. Their viewpoint was little noted and the draft went ahead.

GERMAN SUBMARINES prowled Atlantic approaches to the British Isles, threatened British survival. Without imports, Britain's heroic people would have been incapable of carrying on. Warships from British and American navies convoyed merchant ships, kept ocean lanes open.

50 OVERAGE destroyers were given Britain during dark days of 1940. In exchange, U.S. was leased a number of vital air and naval bases in the Atlantic.

GERMAN-AMERICAN VOLKSBUND was chief Nazi organization active in U.S. Bund members are shown at a meeting in New York's Madison Square Garden, where they presented a strange sight, decked out in storm troopers' uniforms and Hitler Youth regalia, complete even to the swastikas.

MOUNTING FURY of Nazi blitz against England and heavy casualties caused many Britishers to evacuate their children to the U.S. Here British liner *Scythia* is docking in N.Y. with a group of 71 children, among the first to arrive.

AMERICA FIRST COMMITTEE voiced strong opposition to U.S. aid to the Allies before the attack on Pearl Harbor. Preparing to address an "America First" rally are Senator Burton K. Wheeler, Charles Lindbergh, Novelist Kathleen Norris and Norman Thomas *(l. to r. above)*.

PEACE TALKS began Nov. 17 among Secretary of State Hull, Japanese Ambassador Admiral Kichisaburo Nomura *(l.)*, and Kurusu. Disturbed by U.S. alarm at their advances in Thailand and Indo-China, Japan rushed this "peace envoy" in an attempt to ease relations. Conferences were still going on as Japanese task force steamed to Pearl Harbor.

CHINESE AMERICANS protested the continued shipment of American scrap iron to Japan, since the Japanese were using it in manufacturing munitions for their fight against China. Picture at left shows a group picketing a scrap iron pile in Portland, Oregon. These Chinese Americans were successful in stopping departure of freighter bound for Japan.

WENDELL WILLKIE was a dark horse at the Republican National Convention, but he gained steadily in stature. While FDR was busy with the country's rearmament, Willkie was proving himself to be a capable and imaginative campaigner. With Mrs. Willkie at his side, he is shown here driving triumphantly to make acceptance speech at Elwood, Indiana.

HENRY WALLACE (shown with Roosevelt) was the Secretary of Agriculture during Roosevelt's second term. In 1940 he was nominated for the Democratic vice-president to replace Garner who opposed FDR's bid for a third term. Roosevelt insisted upon Wallace's nomination despite the bitter opposition from the political bosses at the convention.

NATION VOTES FDR 3rd TERM

The political world was in a turmoil in 1939 over the next year's elections. Various state legislatures recommended that Congress propose a constitutional amendment that would bar any president of the U.S. from a third term in office. Many voters who might have agreed with this in ordinary years were reluctant to "swap horses in mid-stream" during a war year.

Although strongly opposed by many prominent friends and party members President Franklin Roosevelt decided to run for a third term. He was nominated on the first ballot at the Democratic National Convention held in Chicago in July. Henry Wallace was selected for his running mate.

The Republican National Convention, meeting in June at Philadelphia, chose Wendell Willkie on the sixth ballot as their presidential nominee. Senator Charles L. McNary of Oregon was nominated for vice-president.

There was little difference between Roosevelt's and Willkie's foreign policies. Both pledged their aid to nations resisting aggression and declared their opposition to a "foreign war." Organized labor generally supported Roosevelt because of the great encouragement given labor during the New Deal recovery period. Willkie aimed much of his campaigning at the war workers, key voters in the election.

Roger Babson ran for president on the Prohibition Party ticket, Norman Thomas on the Socialist ticket, and Earl Browder on the Communist. However, the Hitler-Stalin agreement of 1939 damaged Browder's chances so effectively that he received only 46,251 votes, less than half of what Norman Thomas polled.

In the November, 1940 elections Willkie received 22,304,755 popular votes, more than had ever been cast for a Republican candidate. But Roosevelt, with 27,243,466 popular votes won by a landslide of 449 to 82 in the electoral college.

SECRETARY OF WAR Henry L. Stimson *(blindfolded)* drew the first draft numbers soon after France fell in June 1940. An army of 800,000 men was mobilized. Neutrality had been repudiated and United States moved toward an active role in the Second World War.

VICHY FRANCE Although France was completely defeated, Germany did not force her to accept an unconditional surrender. After the fall of France an authoritarian regime was established in the south under the surveillance of the invaders; its capital was at Vichy. Under the constitution of this puppet state, Marshal Pétain became chief of the French state and Pierre Laval became its Chief of Government (shown right flanking Admiral Darlan, the Commander of the French Navy). Trying to hold off the Nazis in his own way, Pétain collaborated to some extent with Hitler and with the Japanese in Indo-China. Both Pétain and Laval were tried and sentenced as traitors after the war was over. Anti-British Vichy forces fought against the Allies in Syria, Lebanon, North Africa, Madagascar and Dakar. A Free France movement, named the French National Committee, was recognized by England and functioned as a government-in-exile in London. It was headed by Charles de Gaulle and was formed to organize the restoration of France.

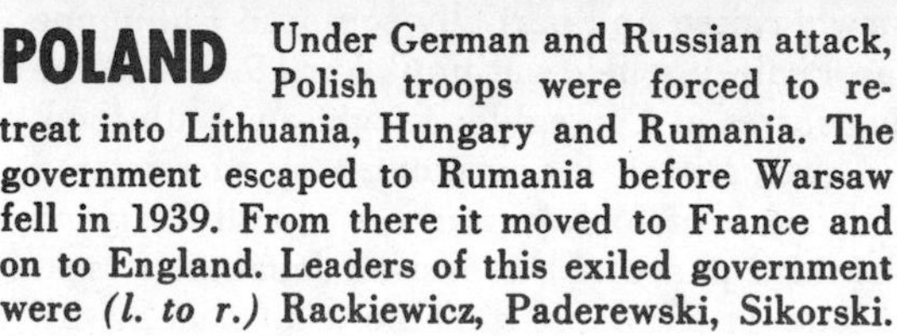

POLAND Under German and Russian attack, Polish troops were forced to retreat into Lithuania, Hungary and Rumania. The government escaped to Rumania before Warsaw fell in 1939. From there it moved to France and on to England. Leaders of this exiled government were *(l. to r.)* Rackiewicz, Paderewski, Sikorski.

NAZI-SOVIET RELATIONS The news of the non-aggression treaty between Germany and Russia, signed by Stalin and von Ribbentrop on Aug. 23, 1939, shocked the world. The pact provided for the partition of Poland and the Russian occupation of the Baltic states. Despite the treaty, Russo-German relations remained delicate. While Russia prepared, Molotov and other Soviet officials made visits to Berlin *(above)*, attempting to ferret out the German Chancellor's next move. After Germany invaded and gained control of the Balkans and other Russian satellites in 1941, Hitler made a friendship agreement with Turkey which guaranteed that nation's neutrality and prepared the way for Germany's attack on Russia.

U.S. NAVAL FORCES were devastated at Pearl Harbor. Of eight battleships on hand the *Arizona* was wrecked, the *Oklahoma* capsized and three others, including the *West Virginia* (shown burning *above*), were badly damaged. In all, 18 ships were hit, 177 aircraft destroyed, and the dead or missing listed at 3,219. Pres. Roosevelt characterized the attack as "a date that will live in infamy," and Americans had a new watchword: *Remember Pearl Harbor!* Had the Japanese known the extent of their victory, a fact concealed by the U.S., they might have invaded the Hawaiian Islands.

PEARL HARBOR ATTACKED

Fleet crippled as Japanese bombers catch U.S. military outpost off guard

At 7:50 a.m. (Hawaiian time) the morning of Dec. 7, 1941 Japanese planes attacked Pearl Harbor. Without a declaration of war, the attack on the Hawaiian naval base was made by 360 planes in three waves. The first bore down on ships, airfields and barracks and was met with little or no opposition. The second wave also met with only scattered fire, but the third was partially beaten off by heavy resistance from a combined ship and shore barrage. By 9:45 the Japanese planes were flying away from the damage they had wrought in one hour and forty-five minutes.

Less than 20 per cent of the attacking aircraft were shot down by the American forces and of this number most were accounted for on the last wave of the attacking force. The Japanese had accomplished their purpose. A large portion of the U.S. Fleet, excluding aircraft carriers of which none were in the harbor at the time, was destroyed or damaged so badly as to be inoperative for more than a year. Of the other operations launched simultaneously by the Japanese, the two most extensive were the invasion of the Philippines and the attacks on Malaya and Hong Kong.

General Masaharu Homma, who later gained the name of the "Butcher of Bataan" and instigated the infamous "death march," led the first raid on the Philippines. A systematic bombing of the airfields destroyed about 60 percent of the American aircraft. Garrisoned by 19,000 U.S. troops, 12,000 Philippine Scouts, and about 100,000 men of the newly raised and partially equipped Philippine Army, Bataan Peninsula held out until April 9, 1942. The last remaining forces at Corregidor fought on. With food, medicine and ammunition running out, they surrendered May 6. The invasion of Malaya and the assault on Hong Kong was the third phase of the over-all Japanese attack. Hong Kong, one of the most vital ports of the British Empire, was doomed from the start because of its totally inadequate forces, and surrendered on Christmas Day, December 25, 1941.

CARRIER WAR

After the disaster at Pearl Harbor, U.S. naval units began to strike back at the enemy. In February, 1942, carrier forces raided the Marshalls, Rabaul and Wake Island. In March Marcus Island was bombed, and April 18 Gen. Jimmy Doolittle's carrier planes raided Tokyo from the *USS Hornet.* The first naval engagement, however, was the Battle of the Coral Sea, May 7-8 in which two Japanese carriers were sunk and another damaged. American losses included the carrier *Lexington* and the destroyer *Sims.* But the decisive battle was to be at Midway June 4-7 when planes from the *Enterprise, Hornet* and *Yorktown,* aided by Marine air units, won a victory so complete that Japan's carrier strength never again equalled that of the U.S. in the Pacific. Picture shows the *Wasp* after submarine attack.

JAPANESE INVADED Malaya Dec. 7. 1941, same date as assault on Pearl Harbor. Sinking of the great British battle cruisers *Repulse* and *Prince of Wales* by air attack enabled Japanese to repeatedly flank defending Australian *(l.)* and other British Empire forces from sea. This, plus bungling British generalship, caused loss of all Malaya within two months, and opened up supposedly impregnable Singapore to land assault from north. Defense was badly organized and, when the city surrendered Feb. 15, 1942, 60,000 Imperial troops and their equipment became prisoners of the Japanese forces.

GUADALCANAL

On August 7, 1942, units of the 1st and 2nd U.S. Marine divisions landed on Guadalcanal, Florida and Tulagi Islands, and began a series of violent land and naval battles. In a surprise encounter on August 9 near Savo Island, Australian and U.S. ships suffered heavy loss and damage, but the Japanese unexpectedly withdrew, apparently unaware of their victory in the half-hour battle. On land heavy fighting continued, while the naval supply-line fight was climaxed by the Battles of Santa Cruz and Tassafaronga. Below, action at Guadalcanal.

NORTH AFRICA INVADED

Encircling Tobruk, Gen. Rommel's army was confronted by a British counterattack which relieved the city. He regrouped his forces and swept into Egypt in May, 1942. Tobruk fell on June 21, and the Germans rolled on until stopped only 70 miles from Alexandria at El Alamein. The battle of El Alamein with Gen. Bernard Montgomery leading the British 8th army, began Oct. 23, 1942, and the Germans were forced to retreat. Allied forces, led by Eisenhower, landed at Casablanca, Oran and Algiers, Nov. 8 *(l.)*. Axis troops were pursued to the Mareth line, a belt of former French fortifications built to protect the Tunisian frontier. Reinforced on Feb. 14, 1943 the Nazis fell upon the Americans and the battle of Kasserine Pass followed. On the 25th Rommel was driven back and Axis forces retreated until their surrender at Cape Bon, May 12, 1943.

ALLIED LEADERS *(l. to r.)* Sir Andrew Cunningham, Admiral Darlan and General Eisenhower. The French Navy opposed Allies at Casablanca till Darlan, who broke with Petain, ordered cooperation. Darlan was assassinated on Dec. 24, 1942.

SAN MARCO *(l.)*, Lord Mayor of Tripoli, is shown as he surrenders to the British 8th Army's General Montgomery. With the collapse of Axis resistance in Africa, the Italian dream of an African empire was dead. It had cost the Axis powers an estimated loss of 950,000 men killed or captured, 8,000 airplanes and 2,400,000 tons of shipping.

FEAST IN TUNISIA
General Mark Clark is seen feasting *(left)* as guest of Caid El Ayadi, chief of the powerful Rehamna tribe.

CASABLANCA MEETING
Roosevelt and Churchill met at Casablanca in Jan. 1943 and conferred with French leaders Giraud and de Gaulle, in regard to differences between French forces.

ALLIED TROOPS SWARM ONTO ANZIO BEACHHEAD

ALLIED TROOPS ROLL THROUGH STREETS OF SICILY

ITALIAN CAMPAIGN

After the successful invasion of Sicily July 10 to Aug. 16, 1943, Italy was invaded Sept. 3-9. On the first day of the invasion, war-weary Italy surrendered unconditionally. But the Germans had established themselves as far south as Naples. The main invasion assault was the landing at Salerno, Sept. 9 where U.S. troops gained a secure foothold and pushed to Naples Oct. 1. At Anzio Jan. 22 the Allies made a surprise attack on the Germans. By mid-February Nazi counter-attacks had hemmed in the beachhead. Cassino was demolished in the battle which began Feb. 1, 1944. On June 4 Rome fell and the Italian campaign became the "forgotten front" while Allied troops were fighting in France. The final Allied Italian offensive began April 9, 1945. With their homeland defenses falling, Germans surrendered in large numbers and hostilities officially ceased May 2, 1945.

CASSINO PULVERIZED BY AERIAL BOMBARDMENT

WILDLY CHEERING crowds of Rome's civilians made certain that the Yanks realized their gratitude for being liberated from the Nazis. The building in the background is the Victor Emmanuel monument. Anglo-American troops entered Rome on June 4, 1944.

WITH THE ALLIES threatening Italy itself, Mussolini's prestige declined. He was imprisoned and his place taken by Marshal Pietro Badoglio. Later rescued by German parachutists *(below)* he returned to organize a new government, but was eventually re-captured and executed without trial.

ALEUTIANS In the Pacific offensive of 1942, the Japanese forces occupied Attu, Kiska and Agattu in the Aleutians. Forces for an immediate counter attack were not available. When they were at hand an invasion was made on Attu, westernmost island, rendering Kiska untenable for the Japanese who left Aleutians Aug. 15.

BOUGAINVILLE

After the Papua Gona campaign in the fall of 1942 *(r.* Australian soldiers wounded there) the conquest of the Solomons centered on Bougainville. There, Allied forces landed at Empress Augusta Bay Nov. 1, 1943. By sea and air attack, the American command cut the supply line to Rabaul and bombed Japanese positions. On March 8, 1944 the remaining Japanese began a series of fierce attacks.

SUPREME Allied Pacific Commander, Liberator of the Philippines, General Douglas MacArthur promised, "I shall return."

NEW BRITAIN NEW GUINEA

A series of air bombardments in Nov. 1943 weakened the Japanese base of Rabaul in the Pacific. Cape Gloucester on the opposite end of New Britain from Rabaul was the scene of the beginning of the invasion for control of the island. The conquest of New Britain was completed by April, 1944. On July 30, 1943 the New Guinea campaign had concluded at Sanspor.

ADMIRALS Ernest J. King, Chief of Naval Operations *(c.)*, Chester W. Nimitz, Commander in Chief, Pacific Fleet, *(l.)* and William E. Halsey.

LT. GENERAL Joseph Stilwell *(l.)*, U. S. Commander of China-Burma-India theatre, with Maj. General Claire Chennault of Flying Tiger fame.

MARINE LEADERS shown here conferring were *(l. to r.)* Generals Henry L. Larsen, Roy S. Geiger, Holland S. Smith and A. A. Vandergrift.

TARAWA The first islands to be conquered in the Gilberts were Makin and Tarawa. On Nov. 20-24, 1943 the 27th Infantry army took Makin with no trouble. At Tarawa in a bloody battle, capture of the heavily fortified outpost cost the Marines 1,026 killed and 2,556 wounded.

KWAJALEIN After an air bombardment, the 4th Marine Division invaded Kwajalein Feb. 1, 1944. Essentially a mopping up job, the total American casualties were 1,516 and Japanese lost 8,122. Flame throwers were used successfully against pill-boxes and barricades.

TRUK This main Japanese base in the Pacific was bypassed by invasion troops, but fell victim to several carrier strikes during the war *(above)*. Carrier based aircraft attacked Truk Feb. 16, 1944, destroying 201 planes and 23 ships, though main Japanese fleet left island earlier.

SAIPAN U.S. attacks in the Marianas were directed against Saipan, Tinian and Guam. On June 16, 1944 the 2nd and 4th Marines landed on Saipan *(above)*. Organized resistance ceased on July 9. Guam was invaded on July 21, and Tinian three days later. Losses were heavy.

WIDOW of Army flyer Colin Kelly is shown with a portrait of her husband, the first U.S. war hero. He was killed in the Philippines early in the war.

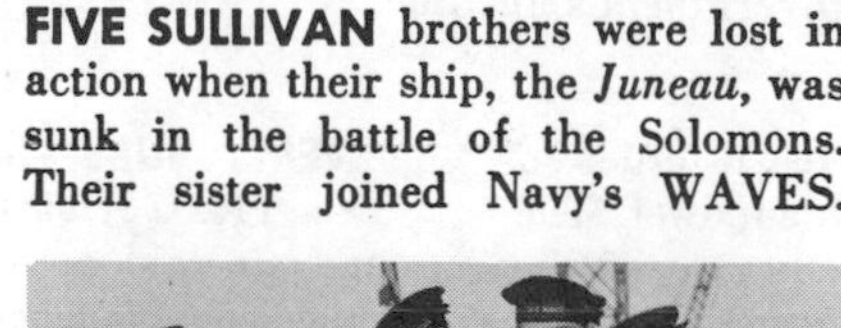

FIVE SULLIVAN brothers were lost in action when their ship, the *Juneau*, was sunk in the battle of the Solomons. Their sister joined Navy's WAVES.

OUTSTANDING ACE, Army Major Richard Bong was credited with destroying 39 Japanese planes and was awarded Congressional Medal of Honor.

CROWDED RAILROAD TERMINALS, CLOTHING DRIVES, G.I.-FILLED GIN MILLS WERE FAMILIAR HOME FRONT SIGHTS

With gasoline rationed and the demand for travel greatly increased., the nation's trains were swelled to overflowing. New York's Grand Central Station *(l.)* was packed with servicemen and civilians twenty-four hours a day. Gin mills *(r.)* mushroomed around military installations. Copacabana girls *(c.)* joined others in contributing clothing to the war effort.

WARTIME AMERICA

Mass draft, rationing, and all-out production change home front scene

Even before President Franklin D. Roosevelt announced on Dec. 15, 1940 that the U.S. must become the "Arsenal of Democracy," preparedness against attack was underway. Aliens were required to register, mass production of planes and ships had begun. Co-ordination of industrial activity was achieved by the Defense Production Board under "Big Bill" Knudsen. A Lend-Lease Agreement signed March 10, 1941 started munitions to European countries.

After Pearl Harbor, the draft was extended and the anti-inflation bill of Oct. 2, 1942 stabilized prices and wages. The Office of Price Administration (OPA) became the bureau of appeals for gasoline, tires and sugar. By 1943, 110,000 Japanese-Americans had been sent to re-location centers. Production of automobiles ceased Feb., 1942 and was not resumed until 1945. The "excess profits tax" on corporations added to the government's income.

The country was unified in the struggle. The AFof L and CIO pledged no strikes. Newspapers provided excellent battle coverage. Servicemen were given free entertainment tickets, while business advertising encouraged home front workers.

President Roosevelt died April 12, 1945, on the eve of victory. Postwar planning went on with the initial United Nations conference April 25. Nazi Germany collapsed May 7, and Japan surrendered on Aug. 14, 1945.

COLLEGE GIRL farmers took over farm chores in order to save the crops, where there was insufficient manpower. The coed farm battalions harvested crops and took care of the stock. Many city dwellers helped by raising Victory Gardens.

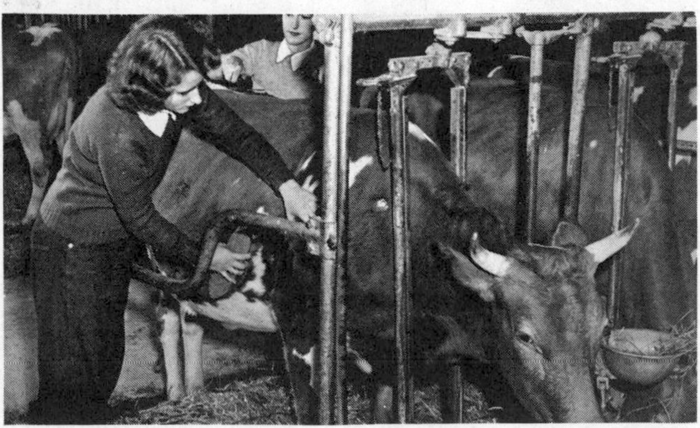

ENEMY SUBS shelled Santa Barbara, Calif. oil fields in Feb. 1942 *(below)*, did little damage, but coastal blackouts and air raid alerts increased. In Washington and Oregon, submarine-launched "fire balloons" caused forest fire damage.

MARINE WOMAN RESERVE

WOMEN'S ARMY AUX. CORPS

FLIGHT NURSE, U.S.N.R.

U.S. NAVY WAVE

WOMEN IN WAR Women's Army Auxiliary Corps was authorized by Act of Congress May 14, 1942, under the direction of Oveta Culp Hobby. Six weeks later the WAVES, Women's Auxiliary Volunteer Emergency Service, were organized by the U. S. Navy. The women reserves of the Coast Guard were known as SPARS and served as yeomen, storekeepers, radio operators and seamen. The WAFS, Women's Auxiliary Ferrying Squadron, performed the all-important job of ferrying military planes to the front before the Air Corps had enough trained pilots. The newest service was the Marine Women's Reserve. The women released trained men from noncombatant duties.

USO CLUBS were established all over the U.S. Club hostesses ranged from the girl next door to the movie queen. The Hollywood Canteen and the New York Stage Door Canteen were especially popular on the east and west coasts. The millionth service man to the Hollywood Canteen, Carl Bell *(above, r.)* is greeted by Carey Wilson, Lana Turner, Deanna Durbin and Marlene Dietrich. USO entertainment units went overseas to boost morale at the front. Most clubs had a "no dating" rule which was not often scrupulously observed. The USO was financed by private contributions.

ANOTHER ARMY revered by GIs for its work at home and overseas was the Salvation Army, whose tireless workers performed a multitude of services, selflessly and without publicity.

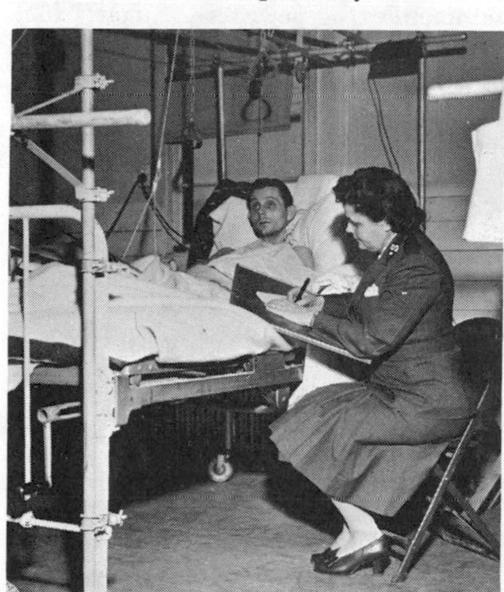

MRS. HISAKO TANOUYE, with six sons in service, is honored at Gold Star Mothers banquet in a Wyoming relocation camp, one of several to which Japanese civilians were sent during war.

WAR MARRIAGES were hastily arranged according to when furloughs were granted. Most brides followed their husbands from camp to camp. Proxy marriages took place by phone.

MEAT RATIONING began early in 1943 when each person was alloted 2½ pounds per week. Even though a variety of meat substitutes like fish and poultry were exempt from rationing, black markets were common among many meat suppliers. Under-the-counter dealings were an inevitable result of the pressure of high wartime income on short supplies.

BLACKOUTS dimmed bright lights of cities during war. Atlantic and Pacific coasts were especially alerted. Photos show New York before and during a blackout. Lights of Upper Manhattan and Queens frame blacked-out area.

RATION REGISTRATION was required in order to get stamps necessary to buy food that was scarce. 5,600 War Price & Ration Boards were set up in public schools, empty stores or any vacant space. Here citizens are applying for sugar stamps in N. Y. City in 1942.

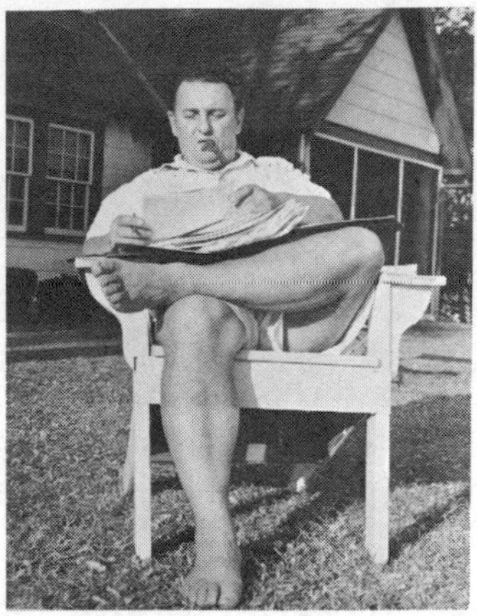

O.P.A. CHIEF was Leon Henderson. Office of Price Administration was established in 1941 to prevent hoarding and profiteering which could result from wartime shortages.

CIGARETTES were rationed and name brands disappeared from the open market. Some other items rationed on the consumer level were tires, gasoline, automobiles, typewriters, sugar, fuel oil, processed foods and meats.

VICTORY DRIVE posters like one at left promoted sale of war bonds and stamps. Workers signed up for automatic payroll deductions. Talent shows, school and business drives and dances were among the many methods used to swell the sale of war bonds.

AIR RAID WARDEN Wm. G. Hoppe commanded the first air raid warden corps in Milwaukee. The units were patterned after those in Great Britain. Volunteers were trained in fire prevention, handling incendiary bombs, first aid and the use of gas masks.

DETROIT RACE RIOT on June 21, 1943 was one of the country's worst clashes between whites and Negroes. More than 700 were injured, 34 were killed and 1300 arrested *(above, l.)*. Tension at home during wartime was eased by the vigorous antics of jitterbugs dressed in the latest vogue of sloppy zoot-suits *(above, r.)*, especially popular in California.

EIGHT NAZI AGENTS landed in Florida and New York from a U-boat in June, 1942. They buried explosives but were caught in 10 days by F.B.I. Six were found guilty and electrocuted. Above, ambulances remove bodies.

WOMEN WAR WORKERS in plants were affectionately named Rosie the Riveter. The percentage of women holding jobs increased from a prewar 25.8% to 33.9% by December of 1945.

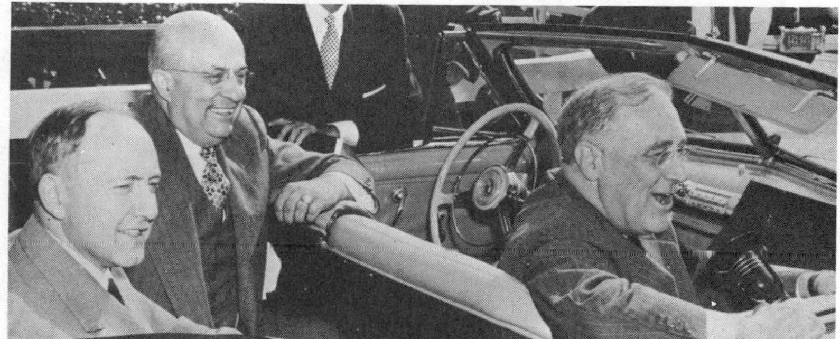

PRESIDENT FRANKLIN D. ROOSEVELT addresses Kaiser workers on his inspection tour of the Oregon Shipbuilding Corporation. Shipbuilder Henry J. Kaiser *(rear seat, center)* contributed much toward attaining "Victory Fleet" of 8,000,000 tons in 1942 and 16,000,000 tons in 1943.

AIRCRAFT ASSEMBLY LINE of P-38 *Lightnings* ran full blast at Lockheed plant. Airplane production under government contracts hit 96,318 by 1944 from 5,856 in 1939. Aircraft industry was concentrated on West Coast with bulk of plants in Los Angeles. Netting camouflaged them from aerial attack.

"USS WASHINGTON," christened at a U.S. Navy Yard in 1940, was 35,000-ton battleship which carried nine 16-inch guns. She was built at a cost of 65 million dollars.

REPUBLICAN PRESIDENTIAL CANDIDATE DEWEY

PRESIDENT ROOSEVELT DURING 1944 CAMPAIGN

1944 ELECTIONS

The question of whether FDR would run for a fourth term hinged less on the breaking of tradition then on the condition of his health. Accepting the nomination, Roosevelt arranged for the selection of Senator Harry S. Truman of Missouri as his running mate. Republican standard-bearer was Governor Thomas E. Dewey of New York. Roosevelt did little campaigning, but the powerful support of groups such as the CIO Political Action Committee under Sidney Hillman helped the Democratic ticket to victory. Twelve weeks after his inauguration, President Roosevelt died suddenly on April 12, 1945 and Harry Truman assumed the presidency. Truman had won prominence with his chairmanship of a Senate Committee investigating the costs of national defense. Now the problems of the atomic bomb and the U.N. were his.

VICE-PRESIDENTS BARKLEY, WALLACE, TRUMAN

LEND LEASE

Cabinet members *(l. to r.)* Morgenthau, Knox, Hull and Stimson framed policy with Senate Foreign Relations Subcommittee, sent $31 billion in aid to England, $11 billion to Russia; total lend-lease aid was over $50 billion. Wide variety of supplies contributed included P-39's *(lower l.)*, locomotives *(below)*.

INVASION OF NORMANDY on June 6, 1944 was the first step in the liberation of Europe. Greatest amphibious operation in history was commanded by Gen. Dwight D. Eisenhower. Following preliminary landing of airborne troops, over 4,000 ships disembarked ground forces. Over 11,000 Allied aircraft covering the invading armies flew more than 32,000 sorties, dropped over 27,000 tons of bombs. Within a week a 60-mile-long strip of beach was occupied and artificial harbors constructed. Ten days after an Allied landing in southern France (August 15), Paris was free.

ALLIES INVADE FRANCE

Hitler's "fortress of Europe" stormed in all-out offensive for final victory

After months of intensive preparation, during which the Allies had trained troops, collected supplies in Great Britain and methodically bombed German factories, power plants and transportation centers, the Allies were ready to invade France. D-Day was June 6, 1944. Covered by air and naval power, the invading forces secured a beachhead, and by June 27 the capture of Cherbourg had placed a major port in Allied hands. During the 100 days following the invasion 2,200,000 men, 450,000 vehicles and 4,000,000 tons of stores were landed. In July, Allied tanks broke through German defenses at St. Lo onto the Brittany plains. On September 15 at Dijon the Normandy invaders were joined by Allied forces who had invaded southern France. Following the Battle of the Bulge, Allied troops advanced into Germany. The Rhine was crossed March 8, 1945 at Remagen. By April 20, rapidly advancing Soviet forces were fighting in Berlin and six days later Russian and American troops met at Torgau. With the Third Reich collapsing, Germany signed the terms of surrender on May 7, 1945 at Reims.

"FULL VICTORY, NOTHING ELSE" were the famous orders given by General Dwight D. Eisenhower to these paratroopers while briefing them on tactics before their landing in Normandy. They were first troops to hit Normandy.

GERMAN V-1 ROCKET was a deadly robot bomb shot at England from bases in France. About 8000 were launched and 2300 hit London. By August 1944 English defense system destroyed nine out of ten bombs before they hit London.

DEATH STILL STALKED PARIS as small bands of Nazi snipers refused to surrender to the Allies. At the Place de la Concorde, Parisians *(l.)* frantically sought cover in the midst of their victory celebration Aug. 26, 1944. Disgraced Frenchwomen *(above)* who had collaborated with the Germans, were forced to march through the city half-naked, barefoot, with shaven heads and swastikas painted on their faces.

BATTLE OF THE BULGE

Using their last reserves, German forces under Von Rundstedt attacked the American First Army in the Ardennes on December 16, 1944. Allied forces were driven back to the Meuse. Outnumbered six to one, the Americans used cooks, clerks and others not usually considered combat infantry in the fight, as well as ski troops *(l.)*. Helped by poor weather, the Nazis advanced rapidly, cut off Bastogne and threatened Allied supply lines. On December 26 Patton's Third Army saved Bastogne and by the end of January, 1945 the Allies had flattened the "bulge" the Nazi attack had put in their lines. The Germans suffered 220,000 casualties and lost over 1,400 tanks and guns.

AMERICAN TROOPS were enthusiastically greeted upon their arrival in Belgium. On November 27, 1944 Antwerp was seized by the Allies and used as a center for Allied supply. In spite of the heavy attacks of German guided missiles, the center proved effective.

RUSSIA suffered heavy lasses in early years of war. Germany had occupied land which gave Russia 2% of its oil, 40% of its machinery and 50% of its wheat and livestock. In summer of 1942 Germany attacked Stalingrad. City held out until the winter when Russians defeated invaders. Battle was war's turning point. By early 1945, Eastern Europe was Russia's.

WAR CAME HOME to the German people *(above)* as Allied air offensive intensified and 31 Nazi cities suffered destruction of 500 acres or more, 305,000 Germans were killed and 780,000 wounded. At war's end, Germany had received 315 tons of explosive for every ton dropped on Britain.

GERMANY SUFFERED the heaviest continued series of air bombardments in history. From the advent of the war to May, 1945, British and American bombers flew over 4,000,000 sorties. American planes dropped 2,453,595 tons of bombs. Entire cities were wrecked *(above,* Berlin), industries ruined.

SIEGFRIED LINE *(above)* was Germany's last strong line of resistance against the invading Allied armies. The Germans thought Line was impregnable. However, Germany was so weakened by her defeat in the Battle of the Bulge that she was unable to stop Allied breakthrough into Cologne Plain.

CAPTURE OF COLOGNE, Mar. 6, 1945 set stage for Rhine crossing. March 25 the Saar was taken, April 23 Third Army reached Czechoslovakian frontier; May 1 the Seventh occupied Munich. The Russians took Berlin on May 2, and on May 7, with Hitler dead, Germany signed the final surrender.

UNSUCCESSFUL ASSASSINATION attempt was made on Hitler's life July 20, 1944 by members of his staff who foresaw Germany's defeat. Photo was taken two hours ofter bomb exploded. Shown are *(l. to r.)* Mussolini, Bormann, Doenitz, Hitler (note bandaged hand), Goering, Skorzeny, Loerzer.

AMERICAN SOLDIER stands guard over German soldiers who surrendered in the Ruhr pocket. They are imprisoned in an enclosure in Remagen, Germany. On April 1, 1945 the Allied armies captured the Ruhr basin and with it twenty-one Nazi divisions which included some 400,000 German troops.

MILITARY REPRESENTATIVES at the Berlin conference to grant the Allies full supremacy over Germany are *(l. to r.)* England: Field Marshal Montgomery, United States: General of the Army Eisenhower (Allied Commander-in-Chief), Russia: Marshal Zhukov, and France: General de Tassigny.

TAKING MUCH NEEDED relaxation after a conference in France, Generals *(l. to r.)* Courtney Hodges, Commander of First Army; Omar Bradley, Commander of Twelfth Army Group and George Patton, Commander of Third Army appear relaxed, cheerful and confident of an Allied victory.

"HERO of the Soviet Union" was Marshal Semen Timoshenko. He showed great valor and judgement and played an important role in defending Soviet Union against invading German armies.

NO MIRACLE, said Field Marshal von Runstedt, but a direct blunder of Hitler's let the British off so easily at Dunkirk. The Marshal was key German General in the Battle of the Bulge.

WORLD WAR II PLANES

B-17 FLYING FORTRESS

B-25 MITCHELL

P-51 MUSTANG

P-38 LIGHTNING

P-47 THUNDERBOLT

B-26 MARTIN MARAUDER

PHILIPPINES RETAKEN

On Sept. 15, 1944 marines and infantry hit Peleliu Island. Forces under MacArthur invaded Morotai Island. Meanwhile, on Sept. 11 carrier forces hit the central Philippines, destroying 501 Japanese planes and 173 ships. Raiding Manila Bay area, Task Force 58 damaged 103 ships, destroyed 405 planes. The U.S. 6th Army supported by the 3rd and 7th Fleets invaded Leyte in Oct. MacArthur waded ashore *(r.)* fulfilling his vow, "I shall return!" A major naval action followed and Feb. 4 Manila was reached. Mopping-up operations continued *(l.* Japanese prisoner) until July 5 when MacArthur declared the Philippine Islands liberated.

AFTER JAPAN OCCUPIED the China coast and established a naval blockade, the Burma Road was built in 1938. China's lifeline to the world *(above, c.)* was protected by the Flying Tigers, an American volunteer group headed by Gen. Claire Chennault. The conquest of Burma closed the road and left China stranded. The air force resorted to "flying the hump" over the Himalayas *(above, l.)*. By the end of 1943 a greater tonnage was coming into China than had ever gone over the Burma Road. Well-supplied *(above, r.* U.S. tank), China's armies took the offensive in spring, 1945.

USO CAMP SHOW units brought welcome entertainment to Allied troops throughout the world. Below, Bob Hope clowns with comic Jerry Colonna while Hope's troupe looks on amused.

FAMOUS Joe E. Brown grin was known by G.I.'s stationed all over the world. He brought much needed cheer to homesick, wounded men. Below, Brown with a friend while in China.

JACK BENNY, shown below with Papuan native boy, traveled miles to joke for soldiers. Entertainers wore army uniforms so that in case of enemy capture they would not be shot as spies.

While Manila was being stormed, a direct attack was being launched against the home islands of Japan. The occupation of the Marianas enabled land-based aircraft to bomb Tokyo, but because of the excessive distance (3,130 miles round-trip) a closer base was needed. It was decided to neutralize Formosa and Okinawa by bombing, and to invade Iwo Jima *(above)* with the 3rd, 4th and 5th Marine divisions. The invasion was the hardest and most costly assault in the history of the Marine Corps. Casualties numbered 19,938 with 4,360 killed or missing. The invasion against strongly fortified Japanese positions began on Feb. 19, 1945. Organized resistance apparently ended on Feb. 23 with the capture of the summit of Mt. Suribachi *(l.,* dramatic flag raising there). However, the island's rugged terrain offered perfect asylum to scattered Japanese troops who continued to resist from caves dug into the cliffs. The island was not finally secured until March 16. The entire Japanese garrison of 21,000 was killed except for 100 prisoners.

OKINAWA INVADED

Using over 1300 ships, Army and Marine forces invaded Okinawa on April 1, 1945. Island was needed as a springboard for invading Japan. On June 8, after Oraku Peninsula was taken, Gen. Bruckner asked Gen. Ushijma to give up. Although their position was hopeless, the enemy fought until June 21. Japanese losses were 110,549 killed and 8,696 taken prisoner. U.S. casualties were 11,250 killed, 33,769 wounded. Pictures *(l. and r.)* show American Army and Marines in action.

JAPANESE KAMIKAZE PILOTS made suicide attacks upon American ships. From October, 1944 to June, 1945, 2,500 missions were flown of which 475 were effective. Approximately 45 American ships were sunk and many more damaged. Left, a carrier hit in a Kamikaze attack. Above, a pilot wears ashes of friend killed in battle around his neck.

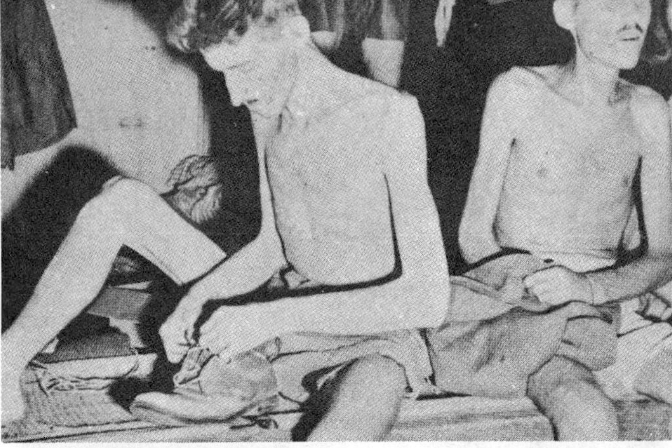

JAPANESE PRISON CAMPS were infamous for their brutality. Rescued from one of the prisons on August 29, 1945, by mercy squadrons from the U.S. Navy, two prisoners are emaciated, gaunt and barely alive. Stories told by those fortunate enough to survive months and years of torture and starvation were violent tales which shocked the free world.

HARA-KIRI, traditional Japanese suicide act, was committed in their dugout at Tarawa by these soldiers who preferred death to surrender. Lacking a customary ceremonial dagger, they used their guns. One man still has his toe on the trigger of his gun. The proper method of committing the act of hara-kiri is self-disembowelment using a special dagger.

AMERICAN AND RUSSIAN infantrymen meet at Torgau on the Elbe River in central Germany on April 25, 1945. Some of the forward units of the American First Army met Russians advancing from the east. Shortly after Russians captured Berlin, English took Bremen and Hamburg. On May 5, the German troops in the north also surrendered.

U. S. DROPS ATOM BOMBS

A series of concentrated air and naval attacks against Japan's home islands was begun in 1945. Long-range bombing began as early as June, 1944 and carrier war started February, 1945. With Japan still unwilling to surrender, on August 6 the first atom bomb ever used in warfare was dropped on Hiroshima. The huge explosion left 92,133 dead or missing and destroyed a big portion of the city *(below)*. Two days later, Russia declared war on Japan. On August 9 the second A-bomb was dropped on Nagasaki killing 73,000. The effects of the two bombs did as much in demoralizing Japan as they did in actual destruction. Japan unconditionally surrendered on August 14, and signed the formal articles of surrender aboard the *U.S.S. Missouri* in Tokyo Bay on September 2, 1945. So ended the most costly war in history.

WILD CELEBRATIONS GREETED THE NEWS OF PEACE AFTER THE BLOODIEST AND COSTLIEST WAR IN HISTORY

ALLIES WIN WAR

Bloodiest conflict comes to an end as Russian moves create new world problem

Allied invasion of France opened the final chapter of the war. With increasing fanaticism, Hitler invaded former allied countries to consolidate his defense positions. Hungary and Rumania were occupied. In Finland Germans and Finns fought each other as well as the Russians. Guerrilla activities increased everywhere. King Michael imprisoned General Antonescu and brought Rumania into the Allied camp by declaring war on Germany.

Totalitarian governments under Moscow-trained Communists were formed in eastern European countries in violation of former agreements between the Big Three. Stalin terminated the 20-year-old Turkish-Russian friendship treaty. All this indicated Russia's return to the expansionistic policies started originally by czars.

All in all, the common man rejoiced to hear of the surrender of Germany and Japan. The war had cost $1,154 billion. Total number of dead was in excess of 22 million, not including the toll of concentration camps. War's end, however, failed to bring hoped-for political stability and peace of mind. Neighbors of totalitarian Russia were already listening to the march of a new kind of goose step.

GERMAN DRAFT towards the end of war included young boys. Here 16-year-old is crying at defeat of his country.

EMPEROR HIROHITO helped MacArthur in the task of transforming militaristic Japan into workable democracy.

RUSSIAN SOLDIERS hoist the Soviet flag over the Reichstag building in Berlin after entering the German capital.

YALTA CONFERENCE of Churchill, FDR and Stalin was advantageous to Russia. Roosevelt trusted Stalin's word on the formation of democratic governments in Eastern Europe after its liberation and made many secret concessions such as giving Russia influence zones in Korea, Manchuria, Poland.

ROOSEVELT'S DEATH on April 12, 1945 brought sorrow to millions. His body was taken from the capital for burial at Hyde Park *(above)*. FDR was succeeded by vice-president Truman who faced a difficult task because he was not informed on top level policies, especially in foreign affairs.

GERMAN ARMISTICE was signed May 7, 1945 at Reims. After the death of Hitler, Admiral Doenitz became the Fuehrer. He finally accepted unconditional surrender. General Jodl signed for Germany and General Bedell Smith for Eisenhower. Representatives of Russia and France also attended.

POTSDAM CONFERENCE consisted of Attlee, Truman and Stalin. Churchill, who attended the opening sessions, was defeated in British elections and replaced by Attlee. At Potsdam it was decided to reduce German industry, establish reparation scales and discuss German and Polish boundaries.

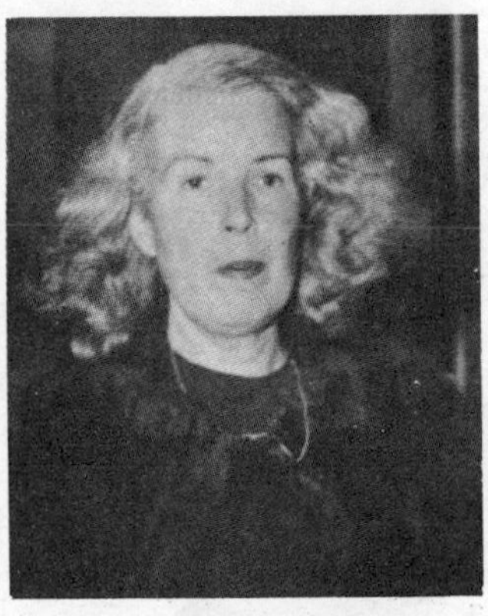

TOKYO ROSE AND AXIS SALLY were tried as traitors after the war was over. The purpose of their insidious broadcasts over enemy radio stations during war was to demoralize Allied forces fighting in Pacific area and in Europe. Sally, whose real name is Mildred Gillars, was sentenced to a prison term of 10-30 years. Tokyo Rose, actually Iva Toguri D'Aquino, received a sentence of 10 years and a $10,000 fine.

PIERRE LAVAL *(standing)*, Chief of Government in the Vichy Regime, was condemned to death as a traitor in 1945. Marshal Petain *(r.)* Chief of the French State, also received a death sentence. However, in view of his age and former service, his sentence was commuted to life imprisonment.

MUSSOLINI was hanged with other Fascists in Milan after being caught and executed by Italian partisans while trying to escape to Switzerland with his mistress, Clara Petacci *(center)*.

HITLER is pictured here with Eva Braun. Long Hitler's mistress, she was married to him just before the fall of Berlin. It is believed their bodies were burned after they committed suicide.

PREMIER HIDEKI TOJO, Japan's wartime leader, was tried by International Tribunal in 1947 and found guilty of war crimes. He was hanged with six other Japanese leaders Dec. 23, 1947.

NAZI ATROCITIES

War's end revealed one of the darkest pages in human history. Widespread evidence was found in German concentration camps of mass murder through gas chambers, cruel medical experiments by Nazi doctors and starvation of millions of men, women and children. At Dachau concentration camp *(l.)* most prisoners, who were Jews, Poles and anti-Nazis, were starved to death after being subjected to slave labor. Inmates of the camp at Buchenwald *(r.)* lived in inhumane dormitories with hardly space to turn. Though the exact total is unknown, the Nazis are believed to have murdered more than 5,000,000 people in Poland alone, of which 3,000,000 were Jews. The greatest sufferers were the Jews and the Slavs. Most Germans blamed Nazi party leaders for genocide.

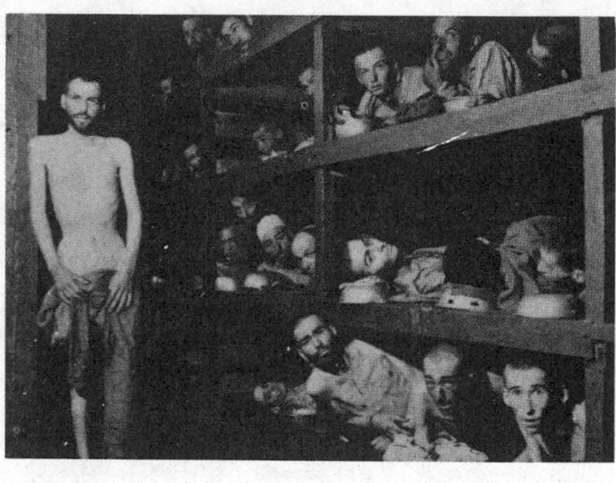

GERMAN WAR CRIMES TRIALS were conducted by the Allies in Munich after Germany surrendered unconditionally. Hitler, Goebbels and Himmler all committed suicide, thus escaping arrest by the Allies. However, the Allies did indict the remaining top war criminals *(l.)* for crimes against humanity and for plotting to wage aggressive warfare. Among those charged with these crimes were Goering, Hess, von Ribbentrop and Keitel, shown standing in forefront of the dock. Three of the defendants were freed, seven were sentenced to prison terms and twelve were executed. Goering escaped hanging by a last minute suicide in his prison cell.

FOUNDING OF THE U.N.

With war at an end the hopes of the world were reflected in a new international organization. The planning began in January of 1941 when the Allied countries that had declared war on the Axis powers designated themselves as the United Nations. By the end of the war 50 nations were a part of this group. On April 25, 1945 their representatives met in San Francisco to draft a charter of incorporation. On October 24 of the same year U. S. Secretary of State James Byrnes announced that the United Nations Organization was born. The major forum of the U.N. is the Assembly. Every member nation is authorized to send five representatives, but is allowed only one vote. Any matter which affects the peace of the world can be discussed. The Assembly can propose solutions to international problems directly to those states involved, or it can petition the Security Council to consider any warlike situation. The Council is composed of the "big five" plus six other member states. Since each of the major world powers has the veto, this body is often powerless. The U.N. had a more fortuitous beginning than the ill-fated League of Nations. Progress toward a just peace had been made before the U.N. was in operation. Germany was being demilitarized and her leaders were indicted for their crimes against humanity. The U.N. made efforts to prevent the recurrence of such crimes as the Nazi atrocities. On January 10 the first assembly of the U.N. met in London and elected as its secretary-general Trygve Lie of Norway.

RELIGION DURING THE WAR

Heroic chaplains of the *USS Dorchester* inspired America and the world by their great act of selflessness. Rabbi Alexander D. Goode, Father John P. Washington and two Protestants, George Fox and Clark Poling, gave up their lifejackets so that soldiers might be saved. They were last seen praying on deck as their ship sank. A new U.S. postage stamp was printed to commemorate their deed. Makeshift altars were found on many battlefields from Europe to the Pacific. American soldiers are shown praying during a comparatively quiet moment in the battle on island of Ie Shima.

"GONE WITH THE WIND" entranced movie audiences as it had readers of Margaret Mitchell's novel. After testing dozens of actresses, Producer Selznick cast English Vivien Leigh as Scarlett O'Hara. Clark Gable was the obvious choice to play Rhett Butler; he had to be borrowed from MGM. In exchange for him, MGM was given the rights to distribute the film. Cast included Olivia de Havilland, Leslie Howard, Thomas Mitchell and Hattie McDaniel; the latter won an Academy Award as did Vivien Leigh and director Victor Fleming. The Technicolor film cost $3,800,000 to produce, and ran 3 hours and 47 minutes.

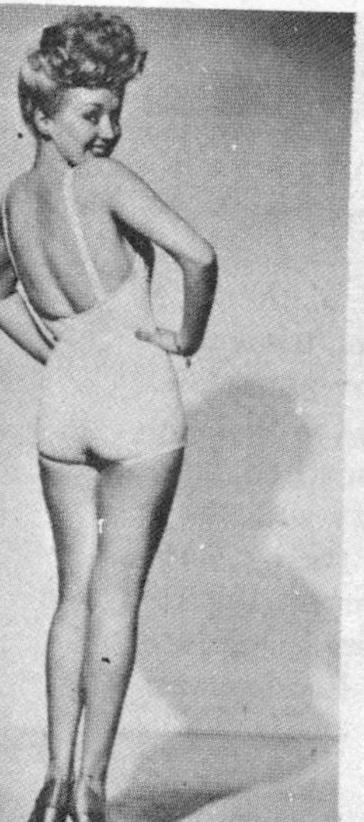

GLAMOR QUEENS, Betty Grable and Jane Russell, were big box office attractions. Betty was most requested G.I. pin-up *(l.)*. Jane, Howard Hughes' discovery, received much publicity; censors kept *The Outlaw* (1943) off many screens.

WARTIME MOVIES

Diversified entertainment

The years 1939-45 saw the beginning of Ingrid Bergman's U.S. career, which was to culminate in her being voted by her peers the best actress of sound pictures. Rita Hayworth, Lana Turner and Betty Grable proved their box-office appeal. For the first time, studio and theater annual income topped one billion dollars (1943). The industry's most important single event was David O. Selznick's 1939 production of *Gone With the Wind,* which had grossed an astonishing $33.5 million by 1956.

In 1940, Alfred Hitchcock directed *Foreign Correspondent,* a thriller in the tradition of his *39 Steps.* James Cagney left gangster roles in 1942 to play George M. Cohan in *Yankee Doodle Dandy.* In 1943 *Casablanca* and its director, Michael Curtiz, won "Oscars"; Ingrid Bergman and Humphrey Bogart starred. The same year Jennifer Jones was named best actress for her performance in *Song of Bernadette.* In *Cover Girl* (1944) and *Anchors Aweigh* (1945), Gene Kelly proved himself to be a talented dancer. *Laura,* with its haunting background music, starred Gene Tierney and Dana Andrews, and marked Clifton Webb's cinema debut. Also notable were: *Double Indemnity* (1944), based on James Cain's novel; *State Fair* (1945), with a musical score by Broadway's Rogers and Hammerstein; *Leave Her to Heaven,* one of 1945's top grossers, with Gene Tierney; *National Velvet* (1944), with the enchanting 12-year-old Elizabeth Taylor.

During the war, the armed forces used films in huge volume for indoctrination. Frank Capra's *Why We Fight;* John Huston's *San Pietro* and *Let There Be Light; Fighting Lady,* supervised by Edward Steichen and Louis de Rochemont, were documentaries at their best.

◀ **MRS. MINIVER,** touching story of family plight in wartime England, starred Greer Garson and Walter Pidgeon *(l.)*, won numerous Academy Awards as the best picture of 1942.

DANNY KAYE went to Hollywood in 1943 after becoming overnight comic sensation in N.Y. His first picture was *Up in Arms,* musical with Dinah Shore.

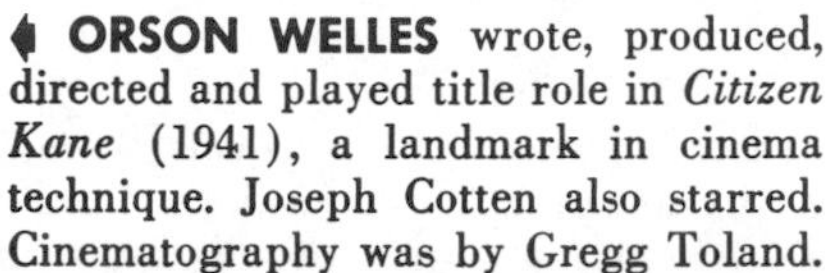

◀ **ORSON WELLES** wrote, produced, directed and played title role in *Citizen Kane* (1941), a landmark in cinema technique. Joseph Cotten also starred. Cinematography was by Gregg Toland.

SLAPSTICK comedy team, Abbott and Costello, were popular on radio as well as in the box office. *Buck Privates* (1941) was their first movie together.

EXPERT BLENDING of tears and belly-laughs made *Going My Way* the sensation of 1944. Bing Crosby and Barry Fitzgerald starred; Leo McCarey produced and directed for Paramount.

FROM THE OBSCURITY of several Dr. Kildare "B" pictures, Van Johnson shot to popularity. He gave a fine performance in *30 Seconds Over Tokyo* (1944).

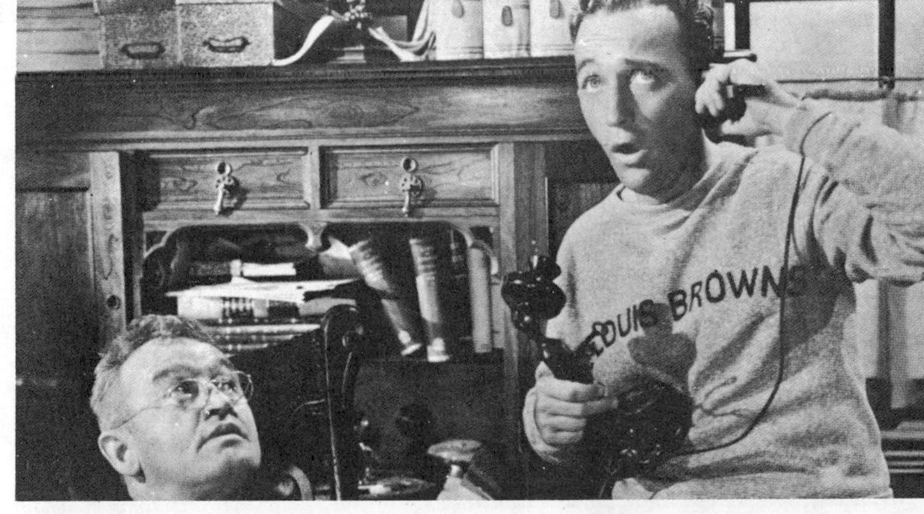

FRIGHTENINGLY frank story of an alcoholic was 1945's winner of several Awards. *Lost Weekend* starred Ray Milland and Jane Wyman.

◀ **INGRID BERGMAN** and Gary Cooper starred in *Saratoga Trunk,* a Warner Brothers film of 1945 based on the novel by Edna Ferber.

EXCITING PAIR in movie version of Hemingway's *To Have and Have Not,* were Lauren Bacall and Humphrey Bogart. They later married. ▶

SCIENCE AND MEDICINE IN WARTIME

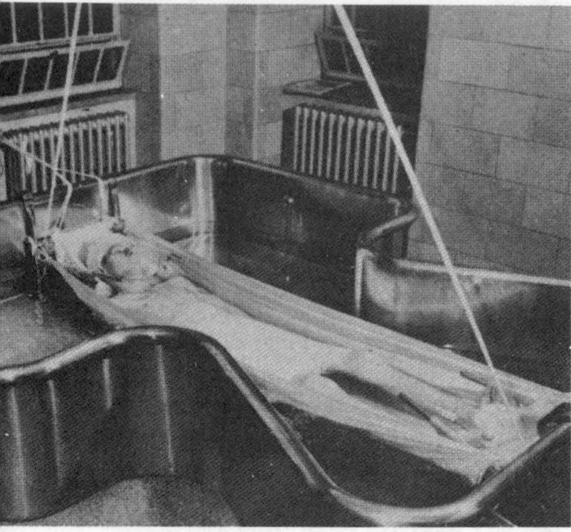

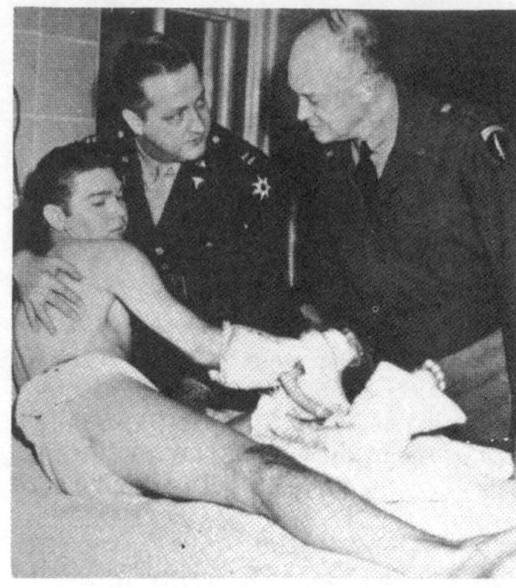

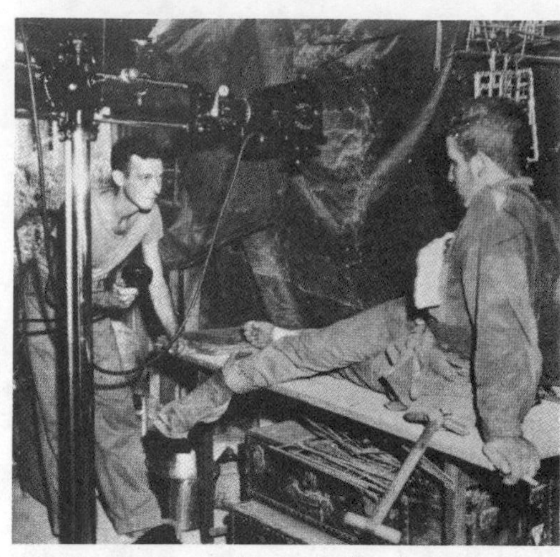

RECOVERIES set an unprecedented wartime record during World War II, due in part to Army technique of evacuating wounded under fire to advanced surgical centers. Picture at left shows a wounded soldier in a hydrotherapy bath, used to exercise arm and leg muscles. The center picture shows General Dwight D. Eisenhower *(r.)* while inspecting Fitzsimmons General Hospital in Denver. An example of new surgical techniques is the treatment of this patient's leg wound with a tube of flesh and blood that links his arm and leg. On the right, a marine, still in battle dress, is getting his wounded foot X-rayed at a field hospital only a short distance behind the front lines, during the battle for Saipan Island.

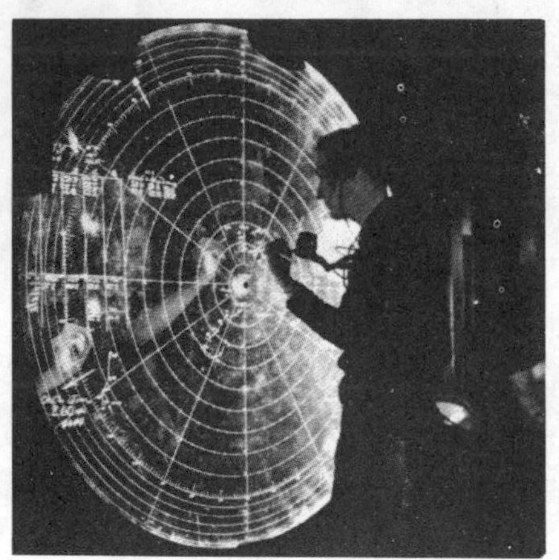

◀ **CHALLENGE** of attacks by enemy bombers was met by science with development of radar. The British, particularly vulnerable to bombs, led the field. Picture shows electronic eye used for the detection of approaching planes.

GOURMET'S NIGHTMARE is this ▶ rotary die machine that can turn out vitamin pills in great quantities. The vitamins are encased in gelatin capsules. Vitamin-conscious public in U.S. continued to boost sales.

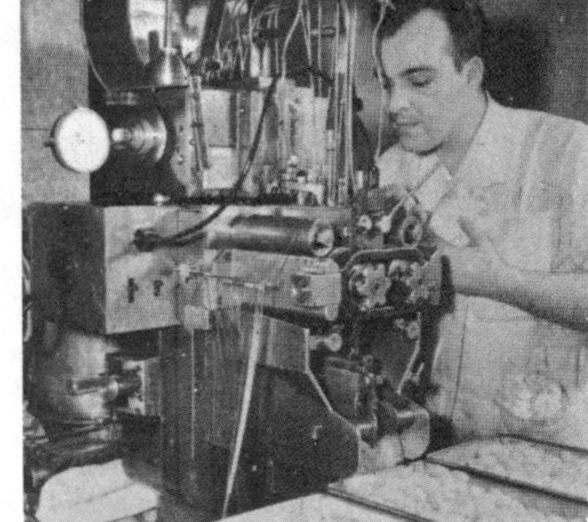

BOOKS Literature during World War II compared favorably in quality with output of First World War. Thomas Mann *(l.)*, shown with his daughter Erika, produced *The Beloved Returns*, a Goethean story on which he had worked intermittently for 28 years. John Steinbeck *(c.* with his wife and publisher) wrote *Grapes of Wrath* which led all sales in 1939, later published a best selling novel of the Norwegian resistance, *The Moon Is Down.* His earlier works, *Tortilla Flat* and *Of Mice and Men* were no less memorable. Somerset Maugham's *(r.)* masterwork *Of Human Bondage* was 29 years old when *The Razor's Edge* became a best seller in 1944. Koestler's *Darkness at Noon,* a powerful indictment of Moscow trials and Hemingway's *For Whom the Bell Tolls,* a tale of Spanish Loyalists, also won praise.

DISASTERS

EMPIRE STATE BUILDING was scene of air tragedy when B-25 bomber struck 78th floor, July 28, 1945. Three crew members and 10 people in building were killed, 25 injured. The plane, unable to land at LaGuardia, was Newark bound.

THE NORMANDIE, France's luxury liner, was built for $60,000,000. Interned after outbreak of war, she was bought by U.S. During her conversion into a troopship, a fire caused damage beyond salvage and she had to be sold for scrap.

BIG TOP FIRE at the Ringling Bros. Barnum and Bailey circus in Hartford, Conn., on July 6, 1944, turned post-holiday fun to grim tragedy. The sudden blaze during an afternoon performance caused a stampede in which 107 were killed and 412 injured. Most of the casualties were young children.

COCOANUT GROVE became the symbol of tragic fire when the Boston night club burned November 28, 1942. The only means of exit for a capacity crowd of 750 were two revolving doors. The fire and resulting hysteria caused 491 deaths and hundreds of injuries. Scene above shows removal of the dead.

MURDER INC.

Professional killers Goldstein and Strauss *(l.)* were successfully prosecuted by William O'Dwyer, later mayor of N. Y. They were part of national crime syndicate which got its name by killing at least 63 persons. Thomas E. Dewey *(r.)* convicted Lepke Buchalter and had international "bigshot" Lucky Luciano deported, but failed to break up syndicate completely.

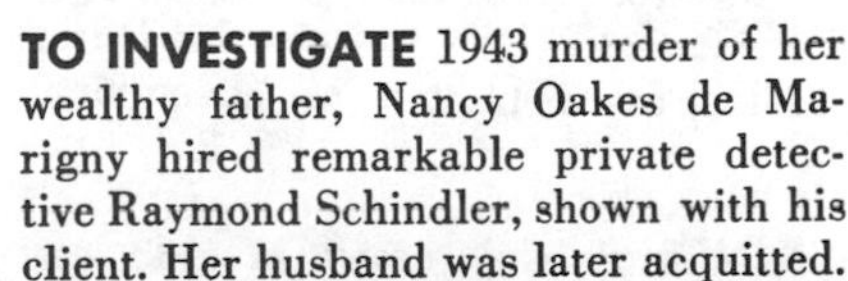

TO INVESTIGATE 1943 murder of her wealthy father, Nancy Oakes de Marigny hired remarkable private detective Raymond Schindler, shown with his client. Her husband was later acquitted.

SPORTS DIMOUT

The amazing enthusiasm of the American people for competitive sports of all sorts was never more strikingly demonstrated than during the dark years of World War II.

In baseball, the major leagues carried on with older players. The armed services made athletic programs an integral part of their training schedules. Fine football teams were composed of former college stars: the Great Lakes Naval Training Center produced one of the country's most powerful teams.

Many outstanding athletes entered the service and distinguished themselves by displaying the same "never-say-die" spirit they had contributed to their teams. American interest in sports never waned.

BEN HOGAN began surge to top in early '40s, was tabbed as future champ because of nerveless play. Other great golfers of war years were Byron Nelson, Sam Snead, Craig Wood, L. Little.

SUCCESSOR to Helene Madison as America's best girl swimmer was Ann Curtis who at one time held 18 records, won all free-style championships from 100 yds. to 1500 meters, 19 AAU titles.

TENNIS KING J. Donald Budge took amateur honors during war until he turned pro. After that, Bobby Riggs, Ted Schroeder, Don McNeill, Joe Hunt, Frank Parker rotated as champions.

LONG AND LANKY stars like George Mikan of DePaul University took over basketball scene. Mikan is shown in 1945 game in which DePaul took championship from Indiana State. Other stars of era were George Glamach, Stan Modzelewski, Geo. Senesky.

TOP TENNIS player Helen Wills Roark lost her position to Alice Marble *(above)*. Alice in turn gave way to Pauline Betz.

WINNER of triple crown in 1943 was *Count Fleet (below)*, Longden's choice as greatest horse he ever rode until *Noor* later came up to challenge for the title. His closest rival was *Blue Swords*.

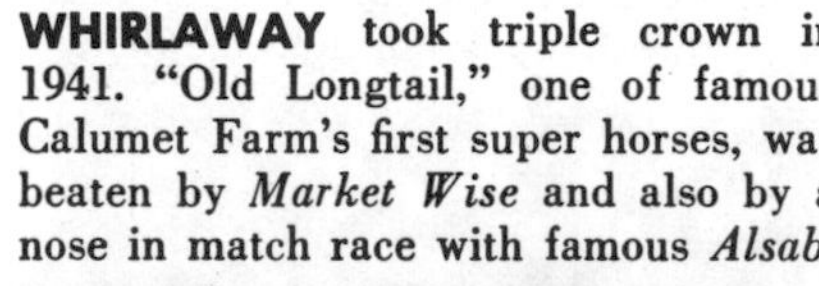

WHIRLAWAY took triple crown in 1941. "Old Longtail," one of famous Calumet Farm's first super horses, was beaten by *Market Wise* and also by a nose in match race with famous *Alsab*.

QUEEN OF TURF was title given to Louis B. Mayer's *Busher* after she beat colts in Arlington Handicap at Chicago in 1945. She was voted best horse of year as was *Twilight Tear* in 1944.

"MISTER OUTSIDE" of the great Army teams of 1944-45-46 and three times All-American, was Glenn Davis, one of the greatest all-around athletes to enter West Point. Sensational runner, Davis was named to all-time All-American team.

FRANK LEAHY became coach in 1941, re-established greatness of Notre Dame football, instilled the spirit of invincibility.

"MISTER INSIDE" of the Army juggernaut which also featured Davis in backfield was Felix A. ("Doc") Blanchard, also three times All-American and winner of Heismann and Maxwell trophies.

HIGHEST VAULT is achieved here by Cornelius Warmerdam as he set a world record of 15 ft. 8½ in. in 1943. The first man ever to vault over 15 feet, Warmerdam performed feat 43 times.

GUNDER HAEGG, shown here at Gilbert Dodd's heels, lowered mile record to 4:01.4 in 1945 and set new two-mile record of 8:42.8 in 1944 in Stockholm, Sweden. His rival was Arne Anderson.

HIGH-JUMPERS' target since sport began was the elusive seven feet. This dream jump was almost achieved by record-holder Les Steers, who kangarooed to an amazing 6 ft. 11 in. in 1941.

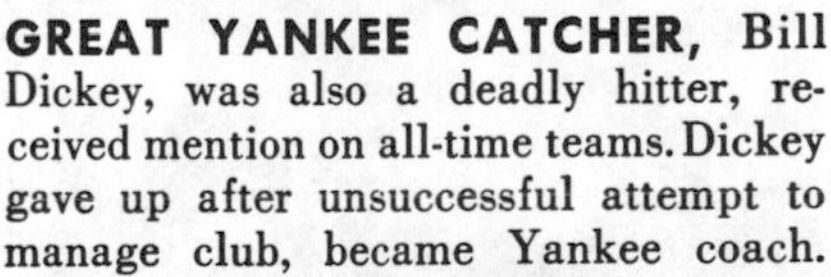

GREAT YANKEE CATCHER, Bill Dickey, was also a deadly hitter, received mention on all-time teams. Dickey gave up after unsuccessful attempt to manage club, became Yankee coach.

HARDY PERENNIAL, Lou Gehrig, was honored with ovation at Yankee Stadium in 1937 after playing days were ended by incurable illness. His consecutive game record, 2130, still stands.

NEW SWAT KING, Ted Williams of Boston Red Sox, won home run and batting championships of the American League in 1941-42, had explosive bat and temper, greatest swing since Ruth.

PASSING SCENE

"THE VOICE," Frank Sinatra, had the bobby-soxers swooning whenever he clasped a microphone to his breast and whispered the latest romantic ballad into it. Grandmothers, too, succumbed to his charm when the lean idol crooned melancholy love melodies.

BAND LEADER Glenn Miller is shown with Air Force Band during the war when the popular orchestra leader served as a captain in the Air Forces Training Command. The musician supplied striking new arrangements for marching songs, using standard tunes. Long favorite of dance fans, Miller was mourned by many at his death in air crash.

NEW YORK'S WORLD'S FAIR opened April 30, 1939, commemorating 150th anniversary of George Washington's inauguration, and attempting to envision the world of tomorrow. Costing $150,000,000, it covered 2 sq. miles of former city dump. Participants included 62 foreign nations, 33 states, territories; over 600 varied concerns.

SEWELL AVERY, head of Montgomery Ward Company, relaxed defiantly as he was carried from his office by U.S. soldiers. The incident occurred when the government took over the strike-bound plant as a wartime measure and Avery refused to leave premises.

SKATER-BUSINESS WOMAN Sonja Henie won world figure skating crown ten times and was Olympic champion three times in a row. In 1936 the Norwegian skater turned professional, began touring extensively with her own ice show and achieved success.

RITA HAYWORTH won international fame during the war through cheesecake photos, movies *(Blood and Sand,* 1941; *Cover Girl,* 1945), association with "names." She married and divorced Orson Welles.

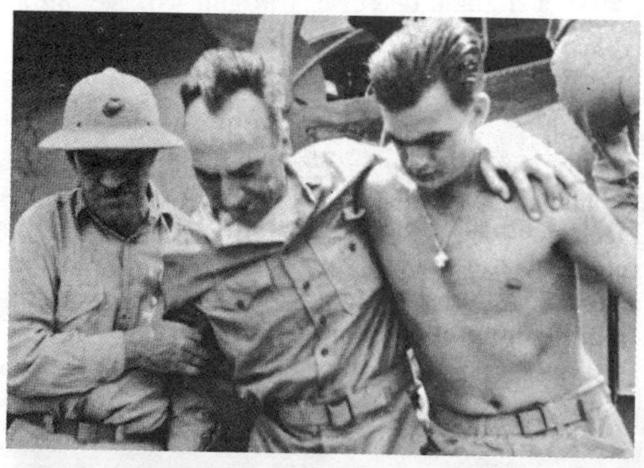

EDDIE RICKENBACKER was lost in South Pacific Oct. 21, 1942, when plane in which he was making official inspection tour was forced down due to lack of fuel. After 22 days on rafts, he and 6 crewmen were rescued.

APPROACHING WAR could not deter dedication of the National Gallery of Art, March 17, 1941. Andrew W. Mellon's gift of this $15,000,000 building to house 16,000 art treasures climaxed an era of public philanthropy, and provided a timely haven for the many art masterpieces of war-ravaged Europe.

SQUARE shoulders, trim waistline marked wartime fashion silhouette. Government regulation L-85 restricted the use of fabrics.

ON BOND selling tour in 1942, Carole Lombard died in plane crash near Las Vegas, Nev. Actress was the wife of Clark Gable.

THEATER

Fine plays succeed

The war years were boom years for the New York theatre. Of ten productions which in 1950 led the long-run list, six opened during 1939-45, including *Oklahoma*, longest-playing musical, 2,248 performances; *Harvey*, 1,775; *The Voice of the Turtle*, 1,557; and *Arsenic and Old Lace*, 1,444.

First dramatic hit of 1939 was *The Little Foxes*. Lillian Hellman's ruthless probing of a Southern family starred Tallulah Bankhead and competed for honors with Robert Sherwood's *Abe Lincoln in Illinois*. Then came the Lindsay-Crouse hit, *Life With Father*. These two produced *Arsenic and Old Lace* in 1941 and in 1945 wrote the successful *State of the Union*. Brilliant musical fantasy of 1941, *Lady in the Dark*, written and staged by Moss Hart, had Gertrude Lawrence surrounded by Danny Kaye, Victor Mature and Macdonald Carey.

Dorothy McGuire starred in Rose Franken's *Claudia* in 1941 while Vincent Price reveled in terror in Patrick Hamilton's *Angel Street*. In 1942 the Army Relief Fund gained millions through Irving Berlin's *This Is the Army;* the Fund also profited from Moss Hart's 1943 *Winged Victory*. The great hit *Oklahoma*, from a play by Lynn Riggs, supplied songs which have become popular classics since 1943. That year also saw John van Druten's *Voice of the Turtle*, a triangle tale of charm and wit. Sex on a more adolescent level appeared in F. Hugh Herbert's *Kiss and Tell*.

In 1944 Brock Pemberton presented *Harvey*, Mary Chase's comedy about an invisible rabbit, with Frank Fay and Josephine Hull. Rodgers and Hammerstein produced their first play, *I Remember Mama*, which Van Druten adapted from Kathryn Forbes' stories. In 1945 the famous team wrote the score for *Carousel*, which had been adapted from Ferenc Molnar's drama, *Liliom*. This hit show became a popular motion picture a decade later.

GREAT AMERICANA, *Oklahoma* opened in 1943, the first collaboration of Richard Rodgers and Oscar Hammerstein II. In the surrey with the fringe on top are Alfred Drake and Joan Roberts; at left stands Celeste Holm. One of the biggest hits in show business, it featured Agnes de Mille ballets, was directed by Rouben Mamoulian for Theatre Guild.

ALL-TIME RECORD was set by *Life With Father* which opened Nov. 8, 1939 and ran 3,224 performances. Co-author Howard Lindsay and Mrs. Lindsay (Dorothy Stickney) appeared as parents of Day family. Dramatized from reminiscences of Clarence Day, play was directed by Bret. Windust.

POETIC DRAMA *The Glass Menagerie* brought writer Tennessee Williams to Broadway in 1945. Julie Haydon played the sensitive daughter of Laurette Taylor *(seated)*, who gave a memorable performance as a mother who lives in the past.

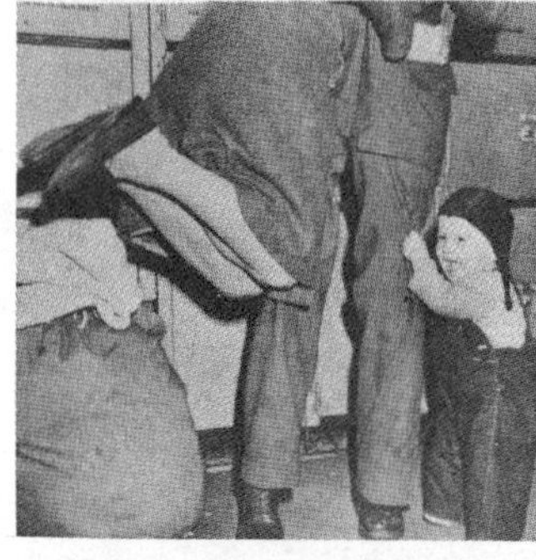

OUT AT LAST! Wherever discharged, servicemen enjoyed that giddy "school's out" feeling on leaving separation center. Wonderful too was family reunion. But there were homefront problems. When Congress weakened price controls in 1946, there were demonstrations against inflation.

BACK TO PEACE

Change from war strains U. S.

As in 1919, so in 1945, demobilization shook America with strikes and inflation. Three years and eight months of war had worn deeper grooves in American thinking than had the war 25 years before. Compulsory price and rent control and rationing had replaced voluntary methods of World War I. There were stamps for sugar, cooking fats, gasoline and recapped tires.

Demobilizing the "arsenal of democracy" which had produced such great quantities of war materiel as 86,338 tanks and 297,000 planes in five years, disturbed U.S. economy. The War Production Board lifted priority controls on hundreds of items. The Office of Price Administration took gasoline, fuel oil, many canned goods off the ration list. Fighting inflation, veteran and consumer groups rallied in support of price control.

OPA tried to hold price controls but opposition prevailed. By the summer of 1947 only rents were still controlled. With the control lid off, prices rose in a sharp inflation. Labor struck such big industries as steel, autos and coal for wage increases. After President Truman broke the 1946 railroad strike, Americans hopefully settled down to producing their way out of the inflation spiral.

HOUSING SHORTAGE hit the nation when 12 million servicemen came home. Wisconsin sheriff let family of eleven stay in county jail.

READJUSTMENT was problem of a whole nation as well as of returning veteran. Columbia student Maj. Jean L. Wood and wife work as baby sitters, tending six infants with microphones, loudspeakers.

BUTTER at 93 cents a pound brought this reaction from Sioux Falls, S. D. grocer. With steak at $1.10, housewives held off buying.

WAR BRIDES came by the shipload from England, France, Holland, Belgium, Italy, Austria, Luxembourg and Australia. GIs who had married overseas had to hustle to find jobs and provide homes for their wives. The housing shortage added to woes of many young couples. ➧

Postwar Years

Involved in crucial Cold War, America strengthens itself and Allies in desperate effort to halt spread of Soviet Communism

America emerged from World War II to find herself in a position of momentous responsibility. Although the Twentieth Century had proved an era of enormous material progress, it was also a confused age in which a troubled world was trying to adjust to doubts and disillusionment and new fears of nuclear destruction. For those who sought a magic cure-all for doubts and fears, for poverty and discontent, the lure of communism was powerful. As the most powerful of the democracies, the United States slowly and sometimes reluctantly, began to accept responsibility for leading the free nations of the world in the Cold War to preserve their political and economic freedoms.

With a somewhat naive optimism that everything would turn out all right in the end, Americans generally embraced the United Nations Organization with enthusiasm and assured themselves that United States participation would prevent a repetition of the tragic failure of the League of Nations. It soon became apparent, however, that the U.N. was no panacea. While Soviet diplomats cast crippling vetoes in the Security Council and proclaimed their propaganda from the U.N. rostrum, Soviet-sponsored coups were winning power in one democratic country after another.

America's belated answer came with new security arrangements and programs for economic assistance to war-weakened nations. With military aid to Greece and Turkey under the Truman Doctrine, with economic help to Western Europe through the Marshall Plan, with Point Four assistance to undeveloped countries, and with the dramatic Berlin Airlift to counter the Russian blockade, the advance of Communism began to stall. A defense organization was set up by the North Atlantic Treaty and strengthened in 1954 by rearming West Germany. It began to appear as though traditional United States isolationism was a thing of the past.

Meanwhile, the West's mistreatment and neglect of Asia was reaping its reward. Anti-colonialism swept through the Near East and the Far East in one of history's great upheavals, with Communism fanning the flames, fostering civil war in Indo-China and Malaya, driving Chiang Kai-shek out of China, leading the invasion of South Korea. In the Near East, Egyptian seizure of the Suez Canal followed by Israel's attack and the Anglo-French invasion of Egypt seemed to strengthen the Communist appeals to growing Arab nationalism, while in Jordan young King Hussein blamed Communist influences for the disorders there.

The world settled for a negotiated peace in Korea in 1953, and France surrendered half of Indo-China. The South East Asia Treaty Organization (SEATO) was formed as a counterpart of NATO. A U.N. force was organized to occupy the troubled Suez area while the diplomats continued to search for final solutions.

Gradually the United States came to understand that more than military treaties and H-bomb stockpiles were needed to meet the challenge of Communism. Vigorous economic health had to be maintained as a refutation of the Communist doctrine of capitalism's inevitable collapse. The nation continued to seek a satisfactory solution to the problems of sagging farm prices and continuing surpluses, and to establish the proper position of government in labor-management relations and public power, while it fought the twin evils of inflation and depression.

Even more important was the maintenance of a position of moral and cultural strength to offset the appeal of Communist doctrines. The Supreme Court struck a blow against Communist charges of racial discrimination when it ordered an end to school segregation. The excesses of some investigators in their hunt for domestic Communists aroused new vigilance over traditional civil liberties.

While the postwar years witnessed disconcerting rises in juvenile delinquency and divorce rates, there were hopeful signs of a growing maturity. Non-fiction books were outselling fiction; classical records were challenging the lead of jazz; local symphony orchestras, art classes, little theatre groups multiplied. In politics the practice of voting the straight ticket began to shown signs of declining in favor of more independent judgment at the ballot box.

With the announcement that artificial satellites would be launched by both the United States and the Soviet Union, the world found itself balancing between dreams of the conquest of space and fears of the horror of nuclear destruction. No nation could call itself safe from the fantastic weapons contrived by man's ingenuity in the Atomic Age, but the dream of peace, too, belonged to every man. While the forces of democracy and Communism struggled in uneasy "co-existence," hopes for a better world still flourished.

◀ **MOST POWERFUL** dictator in history was Joseph Vissarionovich Dzhugashvili. Born a shoemaker's son in 1879, he was expelled from a theological seminary in his youth and entered underground politics in Russia. There he adopted the name "Stalin," a Russian word meaning "steel." He conspired masterfully during the Revolution and afterward to become head of the Communist Party, and succeeded in capturing full power after the death of Lenin in 1924. He led the Soviet Union to its position as a great world power and maintained his iron control until his death in 1953.

THE COLD WAR

Less than one year after the end of hostilities, the West learned that to the Kremlin, peace meant an opportunity to spread Communist influence to all parts of the world. Casting aside the solemn promises made at Yalta and Potsdam, Soviet leaders fomented disorders in France, Italy, Greece and the Far East. Communist puppets came to power in Poland, Albania, Hungary, Rumania, Bulgaria and Czechoslovakia. Russia herself moved into Manchuria and Mongolia. On December 19, 1946, fighting broke out in Indo-China when the French refused to accede to Communist demands there.

The United States soon awakened to the dangers of revolution and war, and began to accept a position as leader of the free world in the "cold war" which had developed. Throughout Europe and Asia the democratic leaders faced battles with Russian-inspired domestic Communists. A major test came in 1948 when Italy was faced with a possible Communist victory in her national elections. A democratic coalition led by Alcide de Gasperi managed to emerge victorious, however.

In 1948 the Western democracies agreed to an international plan for control of Germany's steel-rich Ruhr. Seeking a counterbalance to Soviet power in central Europe, the Allies planned the creation of a friendly German state. In June 1948, England and France merged their occupation zones to form the nucleus of a new Germany. With the success of the Berlin Airlift, the new nation, under the leadership of Konrad Adenauer, was further strengthened. The North Atlantic Treaty Organization, born in 1948, presented the Soviets with a united front in the west, augmented when the United States, England and France guaranteed the integrity of the German Federal Government in 1950.

Meanwhile, the Chinese Communists under the leadership of Mao Tse-tung and aided by the Kremlin, had consolidated their control of China by September, 1949. In June of the next year, fighting again erupted in Asia when North Korean troops crossed the 38th parallel in a drive to win the entire Korean peninsula for communism. Despite early successes and the aid of Chinese "volunteers," the hastily-dispatched U.N. forces held back the invaders until a truce was negotiated in 1953.

AMERICAN SOLDIERS *(l.)* remained on duty in Germany with U.S. occupation forces while tension mounted over fast-growing Soviet influence in Europe.

RUSSIAN SOLDIERS represented terror of Soviet armed might to citizens of those occupied nations held in check by the Russian military forces there.

RAPID EXPANSION of Soviet power after World War II is indicated on this map. Poland, Rumania, Bulgaria, Hungary, Yugoslavia, Albania, Czechoslovakia and parts of Austria, Germany had succumbed to Communist domination by mid-1948.

FRAMERS of Soviet foreign policies *(l. to r.)*, Stalin, Molotov, Vishinsky and Gromyko soon demonstrated that Russia had no intention of accepting the *status quo* after World War II. Stalin violated the Yalta agreement by refusing to allow free elections in eastern Europe; Molotov tried to counter the benefits of the Marshall Plan with a "Molotov Plan" which tied the economies of the satellites even closer to Russia; Gromyko headed the Soviet's U.N. delegation.

CHINESE COMMUNISTS received supplies from Russia, Nationalists from the U.S., although neither nation threw its full weight into the struggle. Nationalist government was driven to Formosa in 1949. Captured Reds are shown here.

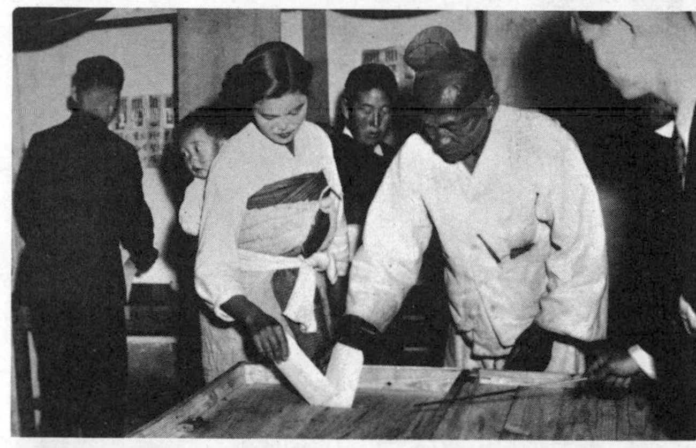

KOREA WAS SPLIT by Russian occupation north of 38th parallel, U.S. to the south. In May, 1948, South Koreans held their first free election *(above)* in 4000 years. At the same time the Russians proclaimed a "People's Republic."

GREEK FORCES fighting Communist rebels received U.S. arms, money, military direction while Reds were obtaining aid from Russia's Balkan satellites. Here a U.S. Army officer watches Greeks fire a 25-pounder at guerilla positions.

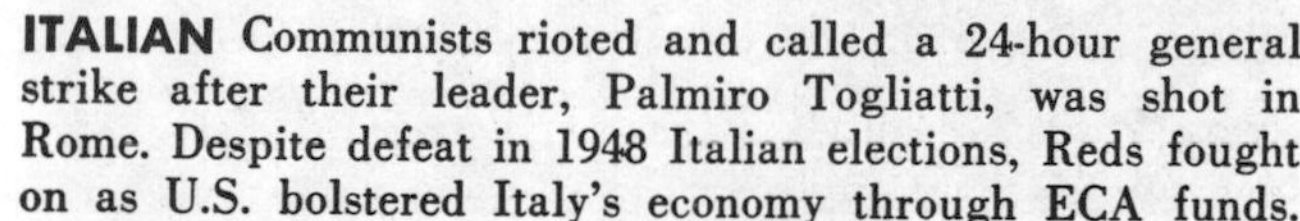

ITALIAN Communists rioted and called a 24-hour general strike after their leader, Palmiro Togliatti, was shot in Rome. Despite defeat in 1948 Italian elections, Reds fought on as U.S. bolstered Italy's economy through ECA funds.

U.S. prosecuted Communist Party leaders under Smith Act for conspiracy to overthrow government in record trial, Jan.-Oct. 1949; above *(l. to r.)* W. Z. Foster, Jacob Stachel, Henry Winston, Ben Davis, Eugene Dennis, John Williamson.

FRENCH Communist leader Jacques Duclos, strict adherent to Moscow line, replaced Maurice Thorez as Party head in 1950, after latter showed nationalistic leanings. A power in Communist world, he influenced U.S. Party to oust Browder.

POSTWAR Germany, under military government of occupying powers, was divided into French, British, U.S. and Russian zones. The mounting "Cold War" was evidenced in constant conflicts between Allies and Reds in this area, especially in the splintered administration of Berlin. U.S. soldiers in Germany *(above)* came face to face with Russian soldiers. Brandenburg Gate *(r.)*, main entrance to Soviet section, bears sign reading, "Who is splitting Germany, aids reaction!" a reference to efforts of Western powers to set up West German Government. As efforts to unify Germany failed repeatedly, American, British and French zones were merged in May 1949 and the German Federal Republic was established. Five months later the Soviet Union set up the German Democratic Republic in East Germany. Between 1949 and May 1955 the Western powers yielded their authority as occupying powers and the new West German Republic emerged a sovereign state under Chancellor Adenauer.

BARBED WIRE proved no barrier to these German women who illegally entered British zone from Soviet sector at Helmstedt, Germany, aided by German policeman. Border control was tightened by Russians as refugees fled East.

THE MARSHALL PLAN

America answers Europe's postwar plight and Communist threat

CONGRESSIONAL LEADERS WITNESS BIRTH OF THE MARSHALL PLAN AS PRESIDENT TRUMAN SIGNS AUTHORIZATION

To revive the devastated economy of Europe and counteract the march of communism, the United States evolved the Marshall Plan. This vast American aid program, unparalleled in history, was acclaimed "a masterstroke of modern diplomacy."

The idea of the plan, presented by Secretary of State George C. Marshall in a speech at Harvard University in June 1947, called for concerted European reconstruction with US assistance in the form of gifts and loans conditional upon the nations helping themselves. The Foreign Assistance Act was passed by Congress April 3, 1948 and the Economic Cooperation Administration was launched. Also called the European Recovery Program, the four-year plan provided that each participating nation be pledged to carry the major responsibility for its economic reconstruction.

The nations who joined were: Britain, France, Austria, Belgium, Denmark, Eire, Greece, Iceland, Italy, Luxembourg, Netherlands, Norway, Portugal, Sweden, Switzerland and Turkey. The countries of Eastern Europe were invited to participate but declined under Soviet pressure. In early 1949 the Russians switched from denunciation of the Marshall Plan to formation of a rival organization, the Council for Economic Mutual Assistance or "Molotov Plan," under which satellite states were bound closer to the USSR.

From 1948 through 1952 ERP expenditure totaled $12 billion. The influx of American machinery, livestock and raw materials was designed to raise national economies by 25%. Appraisal of the Program upon completion showed its goals had been successfully met. It took seven years after World War I for Europe to regain prewar production levels, while by 1951 industrial production was 41% above prewar levels, surpassing the target set. Europe also experienced a great revival in trade. During this period, too, vital economic-political steps were taken: a program for liberalization of trade, the European Payments Union, the Schuman Plan, the European Defense Community.

Successor to ECA was the Mutual Security Agency with a program combining economic and defense support. This included Point Four which provided American aid to underdeveloped countries. Thus the scope of aid was broadened in the cause of democratic progress and the growth of free nations.

BIPARTISAN SUPPORT of the Marshall Plan was reflected in this 1948 meeting where *(l. to r.)* Sen. Arthur Vandenburg (R.), John Foster Dulles (later Sec'y of State) and Sen. Tom Connally (D.) united in urging approval of ECA bill.

MARSHALL PLAN author, Sec'y. of State George C. Marshall, received honorary degree from Harvard together with Army Chief of Staff, Gen. Omar N. Bradley. Between them is Harvard University's President James Bryant Conant.

FIRST CARGO OF FOOD for Europe under the ERP arrived on the Victory Ship *John H. Quick,* which entered the French port of Bordeaux in May, 1948. U.S. ambassador to France, Jefferson Caffery (on flag-draped box) is shown addressing the French. Private groups such as CARE had sent food to Europe since war's end.

AMERICAN AID meant winter clothing for many in Western Europe like youngsters at Schoenberg, Germany.

TOP MAN in Economic Cooperation Administration was Paul Hoffman *(bottom r.)*. ECA sent largest portion of the ERP funds to the United Kingdom.

RUSSIA'S SATELLITES

Eastern European nations are firmly bound to the Soviet Union

Following World War II, Russian leaders seized the slightest of pretexts to continue the occupation of Eastern European nations and delay elections until Communist control was secure enough to establish "people's democracies." Despite their name, these satellites were ruled in dictatorial fashion by Communist leaders who took orders only from Moscow. Georgi Dimitrov was an absolute ruler in Bulgaria until his death in 1949. So were Ana Pauker in Rumania, Klement Gottwald in Czechoslovakia, Boleslaw Bierut in Poland, Rakosi in Hungary, Hoxha in Albania and Tito in Yugoslavia.

The nature of Russia's control was recognized early in 1946 by Winston Churchill, who warned that the Kremlin had raised an "iron curtain" around Eastern Europe. The Soviet Union controlled its satellite states by means of the Communist Information Bureau (Cominform). When Tito took an independent course, the Communist bloc was shaken by the possibility of "nationalistic" communist governments escaping the control of Moscow, and Titoism was promptly condemned as "deviationist."

CHIEF RUMANIAN Red was Ana Pauker, who had been instrumental in the dethroning of Rumania's King Michael, and held office of Foreign Minister. She is shown here with Erik Molnar, the Hungarian Minister of Foreign Affairs.

COMMUNIST LEADERS, Premier Georgi Dimitrov of Bulgaria and Marshal Tito of Yugoslavia, salute during Yugoslavian anthem. When Tito followed course independent of Moscow, Stalin "excommunicated" him from "Soviet church."

STRONG MAN of Hungary was vice-premier and Communist Party general secretary Rakosi *(r.* with AP correspondent Daniel DeLuce), who was put in power by Soviets during occupation. Hungary saw first great clash between Communism and Catholicism when Hungarian Cardinal Mindszenty *(l.)* was sentenced to life imprisonment for opposition to the government. The Pope condemned Hungarian government, excommunicated Communists, but Church found it could exercise little power in a police state. Mindszenty confessed at trial, but warned in advance any confession would be false.

POLAND'S vice-premier, Wladislaw Gomulka, was dismissed in 1949 and accused of deviationism. He had endorsed Tito, supported Polish nationalism. He regained power following the 1956 uprising.

"GERMAN LENIN," Communist Party Leader Ulbricht, listens to Otto Grotewohl, Premier of East Germany's "Democratic Republic." The ruling Socialist Unity Party was put into power by the Soviet Army and Soviet-trained Communists were given the top positions.

DEATH OF A DEMOCRACY

Following the 1946 elections, in which Communists got 38% of the popular vote, a coalition government was formed under Czechoslovakia's Pres. Benes. Communist leader Klement Gottwald became premier, and interior ministry, controlling police, also went to Reds. With 1948 elections approaching, the Reds announced discovery of a plot for armed revolt, took over industries and organizations, forced Benes to name a Communist cabinet *(below l.,* Gottwald watches Benes inspect list of proposed members). Although the elections offered only a single slate of candidates, Czechs cast 700,000 blank ballots. Benes resigned, to be succeeded by Gottwald. Ex-foreign minister Jan Masaryk *(below)* had committed suicide as democracy died in Czechoslovakia. At his funeral *(l.),* the Czechs wept for a great liberal and for their own liberty.

THE BERLIN AIRLIFT

Russian blockade is defeated by unprecedented air operation

BERLIN CHILDREN WATCH FROM A WAR-MADE RUBBLE HEAP AS C-54 PREPARES TO LAND AT TEMPELHOF AIRPORT

The terms of peace had left Berlin divided between Allied and Russian-controlled sectors. Since the city was surrounded by the Soviet Occupation Zone, the Western Powers could send supplies to their section of Berlin only over Red-controlled rails and roads.

In 1948 Russia halted all ground transportation in a blockade intended to force the West to give up Berlin and convince doubtful Germans that their future depended on Moscow. The West met the challenge. From June 19, 1948, to May 12, 1949, when Russia lifted the blockade, Berlin was supplied by a day-and-night armada of aircraft carrying food and fuel. By mid-August of 1948, the American and British planes were bringing in 4100 tons of food and coal within a single 24-hour period, and the constant drone of airplanes overhead had become an established part of life in Berlin.

The Berlin Airlift cost the United States $150,000,000 and Britain $50,000,000 to operate, but returned big dividends by impressing Russia with the West's determination and Germany with democracy's strength.

EAST BERLIN GOVERNOR SOKOLOVSKY

WEST GERMAN GOVERNOR CLAY

BAMBOO CURTAIN CLOSES

Communist China, only 11 years old in 1960, managed to set an unprecedented record of brutality and aggression in a remarkably short space of time. Napoleon's "sleeping bear" had finally awakened—only to find that nightmare could become reality.

Under the whiplash of pudgy Mao Tse-tung, the most populous nation in the world was led to expel the disorganized, demoralized Nationalists to Formosa. What followed was equally as frenetic and bloody.

Millions of landowners were killed, some 500 million peasants were first pushed through a land redistribution program, then a collective farm system and finally, in 1958, into the dehumanized revolutionary commune.

Designed to increase production, the commune program also was aimed at the destruction of the "economically wasteful" family unit. Parents were forced to turn their children over to State-operated nurseries and whole villages were integrated into single housing complexes.

So far, none of these experiments had proven to be particularly successful. Even Moscow had criticized the commune system, implying that it was impractical and too severe.

In the drive toward industrialization every available cent in the treasury was spent on capital goods. As a result, food supplies were continually short and rice was cut in mid-1960 to an allotment of five ounces a day, barely enough to sustain life.

To keep the population occupied elsewhere, Peking used the U.S. as the chief focus of hate, spewing venom at Washington at every chance.

While food production did not even keep pace with the birth rate, industrial output soared. By 1960, crude steel production had reached 13 million metric tons; coal output reached 347 million metric tons and oil production, non-existent before the Communists came to power, had reached 42 million barrels a year.

RED GUARD grimly reminds passersby that "Bamboo Curtain' is a reality.

China's neighbors fared a little better than its peasants. Tibet was overrun and the Dalai Lama forced to flee; UN forces in Korea, just when they seemed on the brink of winning the war, were pushed back by Chinese troops intervening on North Korea's behalf and had to settle for an uneasy truce at Panmunjom. Even India, one of Red China's defenders in the UN, had its troubles with its land-hungry neighbor. Discarding existing agreements, China built roads into India's northern frontier area, killed some border guards and camped detachments of troops on Indian soil.

On June 20, 1960, the International Commission of Jurists found Red China guilty of systematic extermination of the Buddhist religion in Tibet, a deed which horrified the Buddhist nations of Asia.

But even though the crimes of Red China had become well-known throughout the world, the UN General Assembly recorded an increasing number of supporters for that nation's membership. Whether Red China itself would ever be a sincere member was another question.

AMERICAN GENERAL, George C. Marshall, shown here with Chiang Kai-shek and Madame Chiang, was sent to China by President Truman to seek an equitable peace. He served as special envoy 1945 to 1947, finally announced failure.

CHINESE ARTILLERYMEN prepare, as the official Communist Chinese caption for this picture reads, for the "fight against the Chiang Kai-shek clique." Red program aimed for a universal army to include men, women and children.

MOCK TRIALS *(above)* sentenced millions of minor landlords to death, imprisoned others, in typical Red purge. Mao Tse-tung and N. Khrushchev *(below)* bolster USSR-Red Chinese solidarity in a series of "comradely" talks.

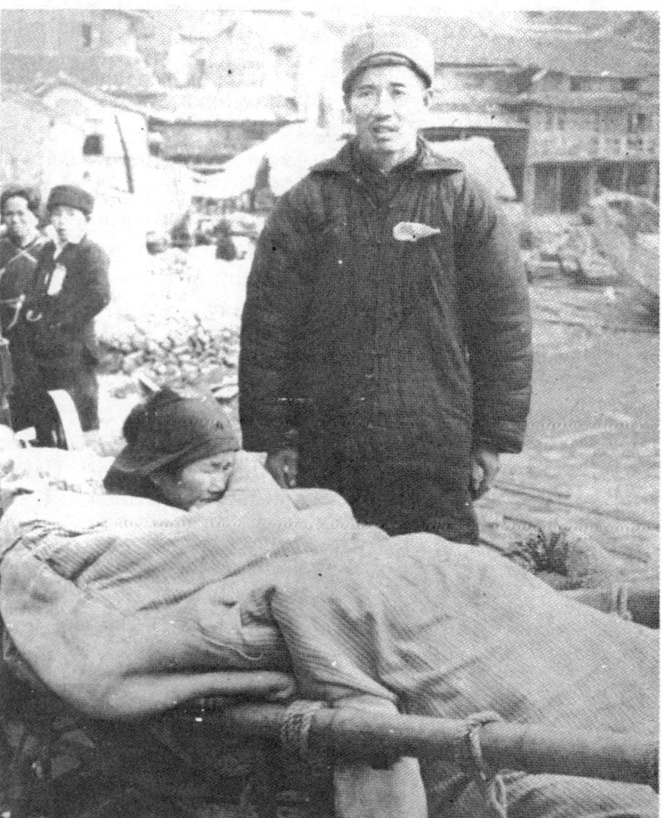

BEWILDERED CIVILIANS *(above)* found the evacuation of the Tachen Islands hard to understand. In five days U.S. and Chinese Nationalist ships removed 14,500 civilians and as many soldiers to permit the Reds to take over the islands without precipitating a major war. Tachens were too far north of Formosa for strategic value, while disputed islands of Quemoy and Matsu lay too close to the mainland for effective defense, were a moral and political issue.

FLAGS OF MEMBER STATES FLY IN FRONT OF UNITED NATIONS HEADQUARTERS AT LAKE SUCCESS, NEW YORK

UN FIGHTS TO KEEP PEACE

The United Nations passed its 15th anniversary in the same role it had begun: the primary force for peace.

Spearheaded by and comprised mainly of U.S. troops, a UN army entered the Korean conflict in 1950, thwarting a Communist attempt to overrun South Korea. After a truce was arranged at Panmunjon in 1954, the UN helped South Korea rebuild.

Two years later, in 1956, a more representative UN force entered the Suez crisis following the 1956 Israeli-Egyptian War and Anglo-French intervention. While remaining on guard there to prevent a renewal of hostilities, the UN Truce Commission continued its alert along Israel's northern and eastern borders.

And, since 1958, a UN Observation Group had been helping maintain peace in Lebanon following the withdrawal of U.S. forces.

But one of the most dramatic steps for peace and international stability taken by the UN began in mid-summer of 1960. A joint UN force, made up of contingents from the smaller (including African) members, and commanded by Swedish Gen. Carl von Horn, was flown into the heart of Africa to restore order to the just-born, previously Belgian Congo Republic (Leopoldville), which was disintegrating in a welter of tribal jealousies and "backstage" foreign intervention.

The impetus for all of this action, the original spark, came into being in 1945 when 29 nations ratified the charter in San Francisco. In 1950 the UN formally took

PALESTINE ISSUE provided an early test for U.N. effectiveness. The explosive question is being discussed here by Dr. Oswaldo Arnaha *(l.)* of Brazil and Soviet Union delegate Andrei Gromyko during debate on partition in 1949.

ELECTED FIRST Secretary General of the United Nations was Norway's Trygve Lie *(l.)*, shown with Francis Sayre and Warren Austin of U.S. Lie resigned in 1953 after seven years of service in "the most impossible job on earth."

KOREAN DEBATES in 1950 were charged with drama when U.S. delegate Warren Austin pulled a Russian-made North Korean sub-machine gun from his desk to support charges of Soviet aid to North Korea. Soviet delegate Malik *(above)* failed to respond, stalked abruptly from Council chamber.

SUEZ CRISIS prompted UN to send Emergency Force to Suez Canal, Sinai area. Canadian and Indonesian troops manned outposts, prevented outbreaks.

possession of its New York headquarters, a glass and steel landmark that soon became a symbol of peace and freedom the world over. Through the years emphasis was also shifted—the focal point of activity passed from the Security Council (composed of the Big Five and six member nations), which was too often paralyzed by the USSR's free-wheeling use of its veto power, to the General Assembly, which could act on majority decisions.

During the 15-year period, membership had increased to 99, mainly from the newly-independent Afro-Asian nations. In a sense these new members changed the character of the UN. No longer was it the exclusive stamping ground of the large powers.

All nations have but one vote in the General Assembly and most of the new nations saw their role as a buffer zone between East and West. Whatever their eventual effectiveness, the addition of these small nations made both the U.S. and USSR more conscious of the hopes and desires these shared in common—peace, dignity, growth.

By 1960, UN results had included the International Assistance program, set up in 1950; the first systematic exploration of potential Asian and Latin American resources; scientific training in agriculture for underdeveloped nations, and an aggressive world health program.

As it moved into the sixth decade of the 20th century with increased power and respect, the UN seemed to be opening at least a faint first trail toward British poet Lord Tennyson's dreamed-of "Parliament of Man."

U.N. MEDIATOR in Palestine was Sweden's Count Folke Bernadotte who was assassinated by extremists in 1948. Truce finally came through efforts of Bernadotte's successor, Ralph Bunche.

U.S. ADMIRAL Chester Nimitz, wartime commander in the Pacific, served Trygve Lie as administrator of the first United Nations plebiscite, held in Jammu and Kashmir in 1949.

DURING CIVIL STRIFE in Greece, United Nations' observers kept regular patrols, watched for incidents that might break the peace. Patrols were established in other trouble spots.

UN SECRETARY GENERAL Dag Hammarskjold *(l.)* carefully notes the accusations, threats and assertions of the "Czar" of all the Russias, Nikita Khrushchev. Thwarted in the Congo by Hammarskjold's swift action and policy of strict neutralism, the Red leader angrily denounced the UN Secretary General in an astonishing display of bombastic rhetoric. He proclaimed distrust of his Swedish adversary, demanded his resignation. Khrushchev lost; vote was 70-0.

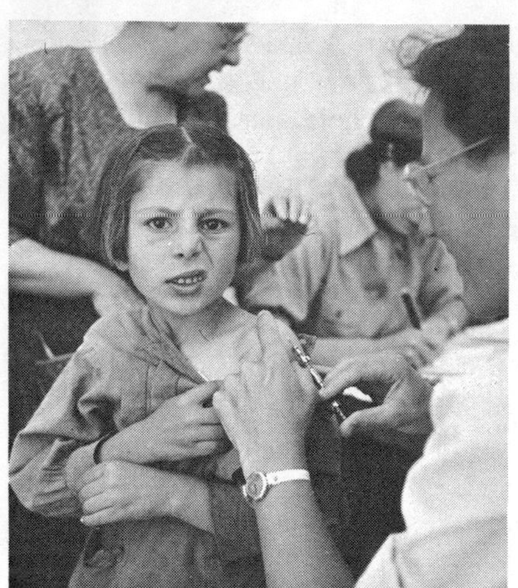

THE WORLD'S HEART

The nations of the world combined their efforts to fight disease, ignorance, malnutrition and human suffering through various U.N. welfare bodies including the World Health Organization, UNESCO, UNICEF and others. Campaigns against tuberculosis, malaria and other widespread killers reached millions of persons. UNICEF, special children's fund organization, distributed half a million milk rations daily *(r.)* to youngsters in Africa. Little Greek girl *(l.)* receives an anti-tuberculosis shot.

DEATH OF COLONIALISM is graphically illustrated by simple check of nameplates for new African nations by UN official. All of above countries were once ruled by European powers, only the Congo proved to be clearly unstable. Casting their first votes during stormy 1960 General Assembly meeting that drew leaders from nearly all Communist states, the new nations demonstrated their maturity through a policy of sincere neutralism matched in intensity only by their devotion to the UN as a badge of respectability and instrument for peace and progress.

THE SEVEN AND THE SIX

Map shows how Outer Seven, Great Britain, Norway, Sweden, Denmark, Austria, Switzerland and Portugal, lie around the fringes of the Common Market area composed of France, West Germany, the Netherlands, Belgium, Luxembourg and Italy.

Common Market forms a natural geographic unity; Seven do not.

EFTA Countries	EEC Countries
1. Austria	8. Belgium
2. Denmark	9. France
3. Norway	10. Germany
4. Portugal	11. Italy
5. Sweden	12. Luxembourg
6. Switzerland	13. Netherlands
7. United King.	

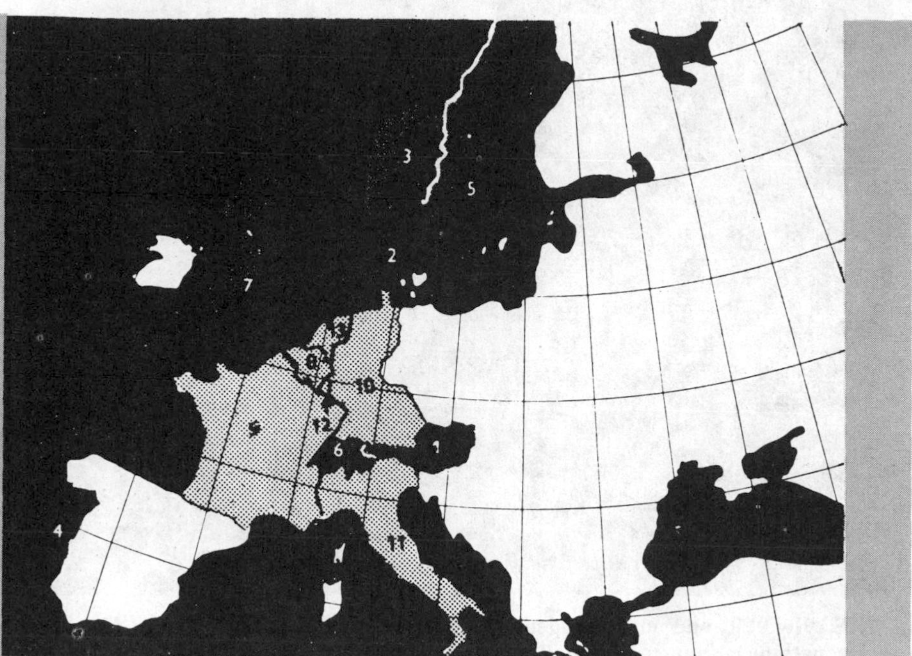

EUROPEAN AID AND DEFENSE

NORTH ATLANTIC TREATY was signed by President Truman in 1949 *(above r.)* and united nations of the North Atlantic community in a 20-year mutual defense pact, but provided for review of the agreement after ten years.

Western Europe, following World War II, took substantial strides towards its age-old goal of unity.

Massive U.S. aid laid the foundations for economic recovery and subsequent unprecedented prosperity.

The North American Treaty Organization joined Great Britain, France, West Germany, Italy and the smaller states in a firm military alliance to contain the Communist threat. (France, however, weakened NATO's strength by shifting most of her ground forces to meet the Algerian rebellion and ousting U.S. nuclear weapons from her territory—and then set up her own nuclear force.)

Belgium, the Netherlands and Luxembourg united in the Benelux union, and France, West Germany and Italy joined Benelux in establishing the Common Market, the Iron and Steel Community and the European Atomic Energy Commission. Great Britain, Norway, Sweden, Denmark, Switzerland, Austria and Portugal set up the counterpart "Outer Seven."

BIG FOUR MEETING in Paris in 1950 was one of many such conferences held in an attempt to keep the "cold war" from becoming hotter. Here Robert Schuman, then Foreign Minister of France, shakes hands with U.S. Secretary of State, Dean Acheson. Looking on are Britain's Ernest Bevin and Soviet Foreign Minister, Andrei Vishinsky.

THE WINNER! and new President of the USA was Harry S. (for nothing) Truman. He polled 49.5% of the votes after an active campaign covering 31,500 miles and 600,000 words and had his revenge on pro-Dewey press, pollsters and commentators by holding up this unfortunate early morning edition of Col. R. R. McCormick's anti-Truman Chicago *Tribune.*

TRUMAN AND FAIR DEAL

Bipartisanship ends isolation, "Cold War" turns hot, the Fair Deal fails

Harry S. Truman from Independence, Mo. was a man of independence in the White House. His administration aroused criticism from both sides. Taking the oath after Roosevelt's death, with the nation still at war, Truman was confronted with major problems of international importance: the U.N. formation at San Francisco, the Potsdam conference, the atomic bombing of Japan.

The period of post war readjustment was a difficult one. There was much unrest between labor and management. Popular pressure forced an end to price control. With the slogan "Had Enough?" the Republicans gained control of the 80th Congress.

Truman's Fair Deal program was blocked by southern Democrats and GOP conservatives. Little action was taken on his proposals.

To meet the Soviet-backed aggression, a bi-partisan foreign policy was developed. The Truman Doctrine gave aid to Greece and Turkey, while the Marshall Plan sent aid to western Europe. For the first time in history the U.S. was committed to a peacetime military alliance by the North Atlantic Treaty. The Point Four Plan was designed to assist backward nations economically. In 1950 Truman sent American troops to defend South Korea. The "Cold War" remained hot as he retired to private life.

AFTER the unexpected 1948 defeat of Thomas E. Dewey *(l.)*, Harold Stassen of Minnesota was considered a powerful contender for the Republican candidacy for the 1952 elections.

PROGRESSIVE PARTY leaders Henry Wallace *(l.)* and Glen Taylor polled even less than was expected. Votes given Wallace defeated Democrats in New York, Maryland, Michigan.

EARL WARREN shakes the hand of his victorious rival, Vice-President Alben Barkley. The loss of Calif. to Democrats by 17,865 votes was one of the major surprises of the election. Gov. Warren had the answer: "Truman got too many votes."

TRUMAN replaced Edward Stettinius, Roosevelt appointee to office of Secretary of State, first with James F. Byrnes, later with George C. Marshall (walking with Byrnes).

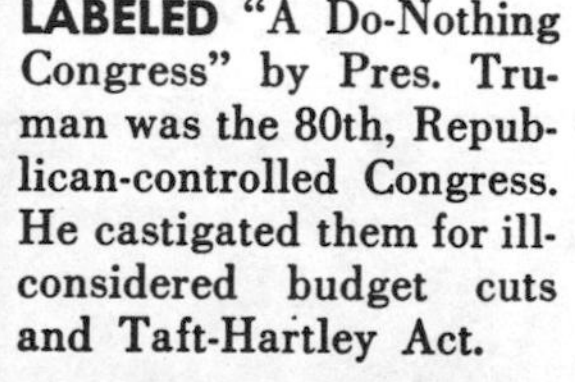

LABELED "A Do-Nothing Congress" by Pres. Truman was the 80th, Republican-controlled Congress. He castigated them for ill-considered budget cuts and Taft-Hartley Act.

IN 1949, Truman made third appointment to the office of Sec. of State, Dean Acheson (shown with Edward Stettinius), a choice which drew Republican fire. Acheson had considerable experience in diplomacy. Since 1941 he had been assistant to four Secretaries of State: Cordell Hull, Stettinius, James F. Byrnes and George Marshall. In 1947 he had made proposal which was to become Marshall Plan, aid to Europe.

TWO EXTREMES among Senate Republicans, liberal Wayne Morse of Oregon *(l.)* and Robert A. Taft of Ohio, won election in 1950. Widely known as "Mr. Republican", Taft survived bitter opposition of organized labor which blamed him for fathering restrictive Taft-Hartley Act. Morse advocated labor's stand, became an Independent, then a Democrat.

GEN. MacARTHUR'S DISMISSAL came with dramatic suddenness six months after Pres. Truman flew to Wake Island to confer with him on Korean War strategy *(above)*. U.S. Far East military commander, MacArthur was relieved, reportedly for insubordination. Back in U.S. for first time in fourteen years, he addressed Congress in 1951 in defense of policies.

KOREAN WAR

Uneasy truce writes an unemphatic end to the UN's first "police action"

On June 25, 1950 North Korean Communist forces, equipped with Soviet-made weapons and equipment, crossed the 38th parallel to invade South Korea. Two days later President Truman reversed American Far Eastern policy and ordered U.S. ships and warplanes to the battle zone. Gen. Douglas MacArthur was ordered to push back the Communists. But unprepared and outnumbered, American and South Korean troops were unable to repel the Communist hordes.

North Korean troops, well trained and equipped, met with little resistance in their initial drive south. The UN Security Council, meeting in special session, declared the North Korean attack an act of aggression and demanded that the invaders withdraw. The cold war, after more than four years, suddenly became the hottest kind of shooting war.

Momentum of the Communist invasion swept UN troops back into a tiny beachhead around the port of Pusan on the southern tip of Korea. The tiny pocket was held against overwhelming odds while a steady flow of men and material poured into the area in preparation for an Allied offensive. MacArthur's brilliantly staged amphibious landing behind enemy lines at Inchon on Sept. 15, 1950, coupled with the 8th Army's burst out of the beachhead, set the stage for linking the two forces as the UN armies drove north. Pynongyang, the North Korean capital, soon fell as U.S. troops landed on the east coast at Wonsan to complete the pincer movement.

American units were within sight of the Manuchurian border, victory seemed in sight, when disaster struck. Thousands of Chinese staged a counterattack which sent the Allies reeling south in retreat. Stranded in Northeastern Korea and cut off from escape routes by a human sea of fanatical Chinese, five divisions, 17,500 vehicles and 91,000 civilians were safely evacuated under a curtain of naval gunfire in a miraculous military operation. But again the UN forces counterattacked until, in summer 1952, the two armies seesawed in bloody combat for control of key points like "Heartbreak Ridge" and "Old Baldy."

Cease-fire negotiations, begun July 10, 1951, droned on. The front settled into deadly trench warfare, cost the Allies a weekly average of more than 200 killed and wounded as the Air Force stepped up the grim tempo of its raids on North Korean power plants and supply centers. Then both sides, unable or unwilling to push for a clear-cut victory on the battlefield, signed a precarious truce July 27, 1953. Cessation of hostilities came after 37 months and 2 days in one of the most cruel, atrocity-laden wars of modern times. Faced with a military stalemate, for the first time in their history, the American people saw a war end without victory.

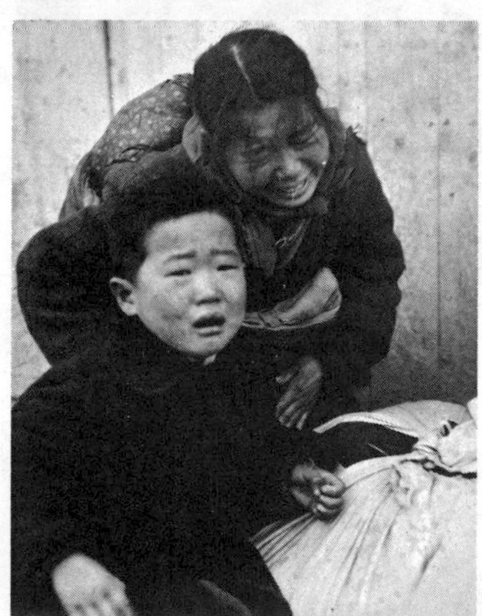

WAR WREAKED civilian disaster worse than Ukrainian famine of early '20s or aftermath of World War II. Sobbing mother halts with child in grim exodus.

VICTIMS amid war's rubble: a woman of Seoul seeks to comfort her wounded husband as an older member of the family squats beside them. When Seoul was recaptured March 14, the population of one million had shrunk to mere 120,000.

UN FORCES in Korea learned "superb professional competence." Morale and co-operation in 17-nation force were good. Here wounded Canadian is aided.

HARDEST HIT were Korean children; 100,000 orphans roamed the streets, scavenging or begging from soldiers. GI's, U.S. funds provided some relief.

AMERICAN weapons developed since World War II were used by U.S. Marines in Korea, in closer air-and-artillery support of Infantry, shown below.

DARING INCHON LANDING *(l.)* was staged by Gen. MacArthur miles behind Pusan front on Sept. 15, 1950. 1st Division Marines and Army's 7th Infantry division captured the harbor and drove toward Seoul as 8th Army advanced south to close trap on 25,000 Reds. Tide of war reversed when Chinese Reds entered conflict and trapped UN forces in similar situation. Marines and infantrymen fought their way to sea through icy corridor from Changjin Reservoir *(r.)*.

GEN. DOUGLAS MacARTHUR commanded UN forces in Korea until he was recalled abruptly by President Truman April 10, 1951. Above, MacArthur *(r.)* tours warfront with his successor, Lt. Gen. Matthew B. Ridgway, former 8th Army commander, and Maj. Gen. Thomas Hickey.

8TH ARMY COMMAND passed to Lt. Gen. James Van Fleet after Ridgway replaced MacArthur. Van Fleet (combat helmet), Ridgway and U.S. Secretary of Defense George Marshall tour front *(above)*.

CONCRETE PROOF of the Communists' refusal to recognize rules of war was evidenced in the way Chinese murdered hundreds of POW's who had been bound *(left)*.

DISTORTED MASK of hate marks the face of Red prisoner *(r.)*. Relatively few prisoners were taken by UN forces; Reds fought fanatically until dead or were severly wounded.

MIG-15, *(far r.)* most modern and advanced Soviet Jet, was the Russian equivalent of the U.S. F-86 *(r.)*. Although the F-86 claimed world's speed record (670.981 mph.) many air experts considered the MIG engine superior. MIG's entered war Nov. 8, 1950 as eight planes attacked four U.S. F-80's in first jet plane battle in history. Jets in Korean war provided an umbrella for the ground operations.

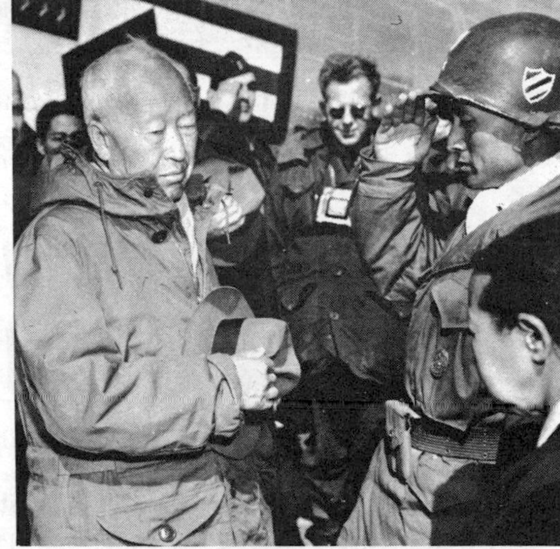

PATRIOT AND FIGHTER for his country's cause was Pres. Syngman Rhee *(above)* who served as inspiration to Koreans through bloody war years and undertook task of rebuilding.

SEVERE WINTERS were another enemy soldiers fought in Korea, as did nearly 12 million homeless Korean civilians. U.S. soldiers killed numbered 54,246 while 103,284 were wounded.

HEAVY ARTILLERY like the 155-millimeter "Long Tom" rifles *(below)*, rained destruction on enemy troops. Self-propelled, the "Long Tom" had an accurate range of approximately 15 miles, was first used in advance to Chorwon.

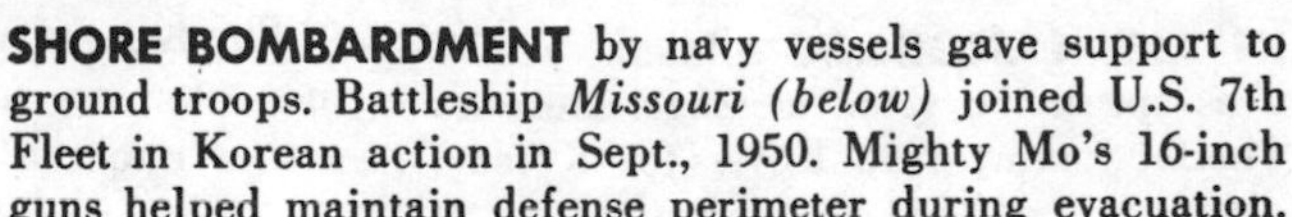

SHORE BOMBARDMENT by navy vessels gave support to ground troops. Battleship *Missouri (below)* joined U.S. 7th Fleet in Korean action in Sept., 1950. Mighty Mo's 16-inch guns helped maintain defense perimeter during evacuation.

GLOUCESTERSHIRE BATTALION survivor is presented citation by Lt. Gen. Van Fleet for battalion's heroic 80-hour stand against Reds at Imjin River, when outnumbered 16-1.

FIGHTING TURKS were labeled "bravest of the brave" for fierce hand-to-hand battle tactics. Above, Lt. Gen. Walker, 8th Army commander, decorates troops with Bronze Star.

17 U. N. NATIONS FIGHT IN KOREA

United Nations forces in Korea were the first example of the free world's united effort against Communism's imperialistic thrusts. Troops of 17 nations were fighting in Korea by mid-1951. Total allied strength was estimated at 600,000 men. From the U.S. had come most of the manpower which supported forces of the Korean republic. The UN forces were also largely dependent on America's arsenal for fighting equipment, although Britain provided many ships, tanks and planes.

The Korean war offered proof that men of many nations could work together under a unified command.

NON-COMBAT ASSISTANCE was sent by some UN members in lieu of troops; ambulance team from India.

FRENCH VOLUNTEERS led by Lt. Col. Monclar, fought savagely with bayonets. Above, the battle "cuisine" is sampled.

IN ANY LANGUAGE soldiers' goodbyes speak the same message. Here a Thailand army man leaves for Korea.

REORGANIZATION of Philippine troops in Nov., 1950 placed Lt. Col. Ojeda in charge. Below, armed patrol.

EXPRESSIONLESS FACES of repatriated American and Puerto Rican prisoners at Freedom Village were indicative of Chinese attempts to "brainwash" them with hours of lectures. Many were mental and physical wrecks from ordeal.

SOUTH KOREAN STUDENTS riot in Seoul streets, incensed at alleged ballot stuffing by Rhee confederates to elect Lee Ki Poong *(below,* with Syngman Rhee*)*. Rhee chose exile, Ki Poong died in family suicide, shot by his Korean army son.

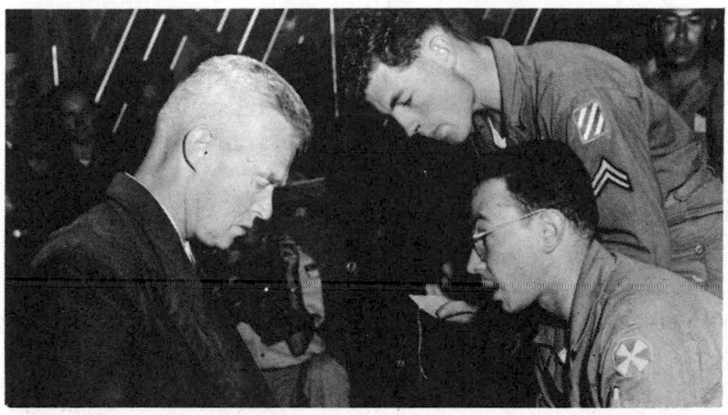

MISSING IN ACTION 17 months, Maj. Gen. William F. Dean *(above)* was believed dead until Dec., 1951 when his name appeared on Communist list of UN prisoners. He was repatriated under terms of exchange, operation "Big Switch."

REJECTING COMMUNISM, these Chinese prisoners of war also rejected repatriation to Red China. Displaying picture of Sun Yat Sen, they are leaving Panmunjom for processing at Inchon and the eventual trip to Formosa and freedom.

ATTEMPTS TO ARRANGE a truce in Korea were inaugurated in July, 1951. Meetings were held in Kaesong between representatives of the two opposing forces. The first problem was to locate a boundary between the armies. The Communists insisted that the 38th parallel be the truce line, while the UN demanded that the current battle lines, somewhat to the north, be the demarcation. Negotiations were marked with violent disagreements, charge and countercharge. After lengthy discussion of the prisoner of war issue and veiled threats of an invasion of China itself, the truce was signed.

TRUCE SPLITS COUNTRY

Geneva agreement divides Indo-China and Ngo Dinh Diem rises to power

Japanese wartime occupation kindled a nationalistic resistance in Northern Indo-China. Core of the resistance was the Vietminh, the "League for Independence of Vietnam," run by Ho Chih Minh, a Moscow-trained Communist. When French forces returned to Indo-China in early 1946 they found the Vietminh in control of North Vietnam. Negotiations with Ho broke down and the French drove him out of Hanoi in mid-1946. Thus began a military struggle which lasted eight years and cost the French $6 billion and 60,000 lives.

From the beginning the French found themselves surrounded in a hostile countryside. In 1953 the Vietminh drove across the Kingdom of Laos to the border of Siam. French General Henri Navarre sent his paratroops behind the Vietminh lines into the town of Dien Bien Phu, where the 14,000 French were enveloped in a Vietminh trap. The French called for direct American aid to supplement the billion dollars a year in arms and economic assistance which the U.S. was pouring into the conflict. President Eisenhower refused but sent additional aircraft.

Dien Bien Phu fell to the Communists in June of 1954. The defeat was a death blow to French morale and Premier Pierre Mendes-France signed a peace agreement at Geneva on July 20, 1954. The agreement partitioned Vietnam at the 17th parallel but left Laos and Cambodia free of Red domination. The Communists won 77,000 square miles of territory and 12 million people. General public reaction in France was one of relief from war and resulting high taxes.

When the western nations agreed to a humiliating armistice in Geneva to stop the southern march of the Communists in Indo-China, most observers agreed that only a miracle could save the south from eventually falling into the lap of the Communist north. That miracle seemed to have happened, thanks to the resolute efforts of one man—Ngo Dinh Diem. When the last French troops pulled out of Vietnam in 1956, they left behind them a united nation resolved to keep its independence.

●

On Oct. 23, 1955 a referendum between playboy Emperor Bao Dai and Diem had proved a crushing defeat to the Emperor and the French. With United States economic and military support, Diem proceeded to weld the nation together by destroying the Hoa Hoa sect, bringing the Cao Daists to bay, and exterminating the Binh Xuyen river pirates, who were running Saigon's police force for Bao Dai. Saigon's world-famous opium dens, gigantic brothels and gambling halls were closed. Refugees from the north were being resettled by the thousands.

On March 4, 1956, grateful Vietnamese by an overwhelming vote ousted Bao Dai, declared a republic, and Diem became its first president. Since Vietnam had not signed the Geneva Agreement, Diem repudiated it and refused to hold elections to unify north and south.

Neighboring Cambodia ended officially its 100 year association with France. Former King, Premier Prince Sihanouk asserted his independence with glowing praise of Red China and Russia while accepting aid from the United States, technical assistance and financial aid from China.

BATTLES fought in fields and rice paddies of French Indo-China ended in defeat for West, partition for Vietnam.

COMMUNIST LEADER in the war against French was Ho Chih Minh *(above)*, the Moscow trained head of Vietminh and president of N. Vietnam.

JUNGLE FIGHTERS of the Vietnam army included French officers and troops *(above)*. The French had trained few Vietnamese officers, and the lack of trained officers hampered the new Vietnamese army in independent operations.

MILITARY GENIUS of the Vietminh movement was Vo Nguyen Giap, commander of Communist forces built with Chinese advisers, Russian equipment.

FRENCH COMMANDER Col. Christian de Castries won worldwide acclaim for his gallant fight at Dien Bien Phu, and promotion to brigadier general. He was captured by Reds, later released.

HEROIC NURSE, Lt. Genevieve de Gelard-Terraube of French air force, only woman in Dien Bien Phu when it fell to Reds, refused evacuation until last of seriously wounded were removed.

◀ **CEASE-FIRE TALKS** between French and Vietnam and Vietminh delegations began at Grung-Gia, Vietnam and concluded in Geneva where Vietminh Gen. Quang Buu signed document ending Indo-China war *(l.)*.

PREMIER Ngo Dinh Diem gained ▶ popularity in South Vietnam as his government pushed a program of land reform and created an elected National Assembly. Diem won 1955 referendum vote over Emperor Bao Dai.

EISENHOWER ADMINISTRATION

GOP returns after twenty years, but Democrats win both houses

The eight years of Dwight D. Eisenhower's administration were marked by international, domestic and personal crises, but the President, with his middle-of-the-road and "above politics" policy was able to maintain his high prestige with the U.S. people.

The Administration that had inherited the Korean War was plagued by economic recession in 1953-1954 and again in 1958 and 1960. The President was struck down by a heart attack and ileitis in 1955 and had to deal with growing Democratic majorities in Congress. His personal staff was touched by scandal when Sherman Adams, key Eisenhower aide, resigned after being charged with intervening for a friend, Boston industrialist Bernard Goldfine, in federal agencies.

A series of international incidents struck the Administration and brought sharp Democratic charges that U.S. prestige in the Cold War had been seriously lessened as Communist influence continued its enormous growth in Latin America and Africa. Repeated "firsts" by the USSR in space developments, which began with the launching of the first man-made satellite, Sputnik I, Oct. 4, 1957, the shooting down of a U-2 "spy plane" flown by a U.S. aviator over the USSR, and the failure of the 1960 summit conference torpedoed by the unacceptable demands made on President Eisenhower by Soviet Premier Khrushchev as a result of the U-2 incident, all contributed to the alleged decline of U.S. world influence.

To enforce the Supreme Court desegregation decision the President used federal troops. Defiance of the Federal court order by Arkansas Gov. Orval Faubus forced the President to send paratroopers to Little Rock to enforce the order in previously all-white Central High School.

Secretary of State John Foster Dulles, the man President Eisenhower relied most upon to run the Cold War struggle, died from cancer May 24, 1959. Dulles guided foreign policy through the Korean truce negotiations, and the Suez crisis in the fall of 1956. He refused to back Great Britain and France when they, in conjunction with Israel, invaded Egypt after it had seized the Canal.

It was Eisenhower and Dulles who decided to prevent the overthrow of the pro-Western Lebanese government in 1958 through a "show of the flag" by dispatching U.S. ships, planes and troops. Christian Herter assumed Dulles' position after his death, to run headlong into a new Berlin crisis and the Summit failure.

On the domestic front, the eight Eisenhower years were marked by usually successful budget balancing and "compromise" government with Democratic cooperation. As they ended, budget balancing was under fire for "starving" Defense, and the mushrooming farm surplus problem was as far from solution as in 1953.

PRESIDENT John F. Kennedy, former Democratic Senator from Mass., and Vice Pres. Lyndon B. Johnson of Texas, former Senate leader, were elected in 1960, defeating Vice-Pres. Richard M. Nixon and Sen. Henry Cabot Lodge.

MOST CONTROVERSIAL bill to be signed *(above)* by Eisenhower was the Tidelands Bill, transferring title to oil lands from federal govt. to the states.

SPEAKER OF THE HOUSE for many sessions and member since 1924, Joseph W. Martin of Mass. shows redwood gavel he keeps on display in his office.

JIM HAGERTY, Pres. Eisenhower's Press Secretary, reads 1953 notice of U.S. troop withdrawal from So. Korea.

AILING JOHN FOSTER DULLES, Secy of State (1953-59) greets two old friends, Pres. Eisenhower and Sir Winston Churchill, in Walter Reed Hospital shortly before his death May 24, 1959. Staunch resister of Soviet pressure, he died of cancer.

SHERMAN ADAMS, *(r.)* Presidential Asst. to Eisenhower, leaves White House shortly before resigning due to alleged intervention with federal agencies for Bernard Goldfine.

PRESIDENTIAL PRESS CONFERENCE PLAYED POTENT ROLE

PHYSICAL FITNESS of the President was a major question after heart attack in September 1955. Daily reports from his physicians at the Fitzsimmons Army Hospital in Denver were given to the nation. Prayers were offered from all over the country and encouraging messages poured in from foreign countries, including Russia. By Feb. 29, Ike had announced he would run again, and despite a June abdominal operation, he stuck to his decision. Dr. Paul Dudley White, Boston heart specialist *(r. above)* told reporters after examining the President that the outlook for Ike's future health was favorable. White later went to Moscow to study Russian heart treatment techniques. Vice President Nixon *(l. above)* was ready to take over; interest grew in legislation to define responsibility in the event of presidential incapacity.

1956 ELECTIONS

Eisenhower and Nixon were endorsed unanimously at the 1956 Republican National Convention, receiving 1,323 votes, the total number cast. Harold E. Stassen had made an unsuccessful attempt to propose Gov. Christian Herter (Mass.) for vice-president. Herter refused the nomination and Stassen transferred his support to the incumbent Nixon. Adlai Stevenson worked hard to secure the Democratic nomination for president. After an upset primary defeat in Minnesota, he went on to outpoll his strongest rival, Sen. Estes Kefauver, in the Florida and California primaries. His refusal to pick a running mate left the choice open to the convention. After the first ballot vote, Kefauver, who had earlier urged his delegates to support Stevenson, led, followed by Sen. John Kennedy of Mass. The Republicans won the election decisively with 457 electoral votes in 41 states, but the Democrats held control of both houses of Congress.

THE BIG RED SCARE

Congressional committees hunt Communists in and out of government

SENTENCED TO DEATH, for giving atomic bomb scerets to Russia, were Ethel and Julius Rosenberg *(above)*. Ethel's brother, David Greenglass, turned state's evidence, received 15 years.

TREASURY DEPARTMENT Assistant Sec., Harry Dexter White, implicated by Whittaker Chambers, was also linked to underground by adverse FBI reports allegedly received by Pres. Truman.

OFF TO PRISON went Alger Hiss, March 22, 1951. Named as a Communist by ex-*Time* editor, Whittaker Chambers, former State Department official was convicted of perjury, given 5 years.

Sen. Joseph R. McCarthy's no-holds-barred method of investigating suspected Communists, "McCarthyism," evoked bitter criticism as "witch-hunting" and equally vigorous defense. In 1954 he was condemned by a Senate vote for misuse of his position. Communists were also attacked by the Senate Internal Security Sub-Committee under Chairman William Jenner (R-Ind.) who won headlines with charges against Harry Dexter White, Harold G. Glasser and Nathan G. Silvermaster.

Republican Harold H. Velde, chairman of the House Committee on Un-American Activities, subpoened former President Truman, Gov. James Byrnes (S. C.) and Tom C. Clark, Associate Justice of the Supreme Court in 1953, in connection with their knowledge of Harry Dexter White's activities. All three refused to answer the summons.

Investigation of Communist activities continued under the direction of Sen. James Eastland (D-Miss.). Study of Red infiltration of the entertainment and newspaper industries was highlighted by charges that Eastland was "after" the New York *Times* for personal reasons. Following Senate censure of McCarthy, public interest in Red-hunting began to diminish, and liberals hoped McCarthyism was dead.

JOSEPH R. McCARTHY and Roy M. Cohn *(seated)* were key figures in an investigation following an attack by McCarthy on the handling of the Peress case by the Army. When McCarthy pressured Gen. Zwicker and Army Sec. Stevens, the army counter-attacked with accusations against Cohn, claiming he had sought special favors for Private G. David Schine, former unpaid member of McCarthy's staff. McCarthy cried blackmail, and a televised investigation, lasting two months, turned up evidence of a "doctored" photograph, resulted in Cohn's resignation, subsequent resignation of Stevens in 1955 and Senate inquiry into McCarthy's conduct.

STALIN'S DEATH was announced on March 5, 1953. An autopsy was performed to protect his doctors from future charges of "murder." Principal funeral orations were delivered by Beria, Malenkov and Molotov. Beria predicted that nothing could break the unity of the rulers who would succeed Stalin. Shown here are the leaders of the Soviet Union following the coffin of Joseph Stalin as it is carried on a gun caisson through Red Square. From right to left: N. Khruschev, L. Beria, Chou En-lai, Premier of China, G. Malenkow, Marshal K. Voroshilov, L. Kaganovich, Marshal N. Bulganin and V. Molotov. As soon as the funeral ceremonies ended the new leaders began to revise many of Stalin's plans.

POSTWAR RUSSIA

Khrushchev brings new look, more power to USSR

When Stalin died in 1953, the leaders of the West carefully watched the long line of mourners. From that grim line of relatively unknown Communists would come the next ruler of the largest empire the world had ever seen.

Lavrenti Beria, head of the Secret Police, was liquidated; Premier Georgi Malenkov made a public confession of his failings and retired to a minor post in the hinterlands. The pudgy ex-Premier did not have to wait long for company. In a new style of "humane" purges, Bulganin, Zhukov and Molotov faded into the background.

Even Stalin was denounced, albeit posthumously, by the new boss of all the Russias—grinning, crafty Nikita Khrushchev, a man with the appearance of a lovable teddy bear and the bite of a full grown wolf. He had come up the hard way in the USSR; through purges, wars, doctrinal disputes. In such an atmosphere, the top position was won only by the one most clever and most strong.

Khrushchev brought changes to the USSR. The new line was co-existence, a policy he personally pushed in every part of the world. True or not, the Kremlin's new face gave it the offensive in the cold war struggle. And undeniably, the Russian people, who had never seen their wispy dream of utopia materialize, were better off. Police restrictions were lessened, consumer goods became more available and the Iron Curtain was transformed from an actual barrier to an ideological one. For the first time since the revolution the USSR was open to tourists.

The general effect of all this was actually to increase the Russian people's desire for peace and prosperity. A new bourgeoisie had formed in the Communist world. Marxism was still the accepted doctrine but a glimpse of the "good life" had considerably softened Communism's attitude toward the West. "We will bury you," said Khrushchev, but he said he meant it economically. Yet for all his talk the West still waited for sincere disarmament proposals and genuine co-existence.

THREE FACES OF NIKITA KHRUSHCHEV

BOMBASTIC. The Soviet Premier makes a hard point before members of the press during 1959 tour of the U.S.

CAUTIOUS. Mr. Khrushchev gingerly takes a bite of his first hot dog at Des Moines, Ia. He declined a second one.

CLOWNING. An old hand at different faces for different people, Khrushchev entertains crowd below USSR embassy.

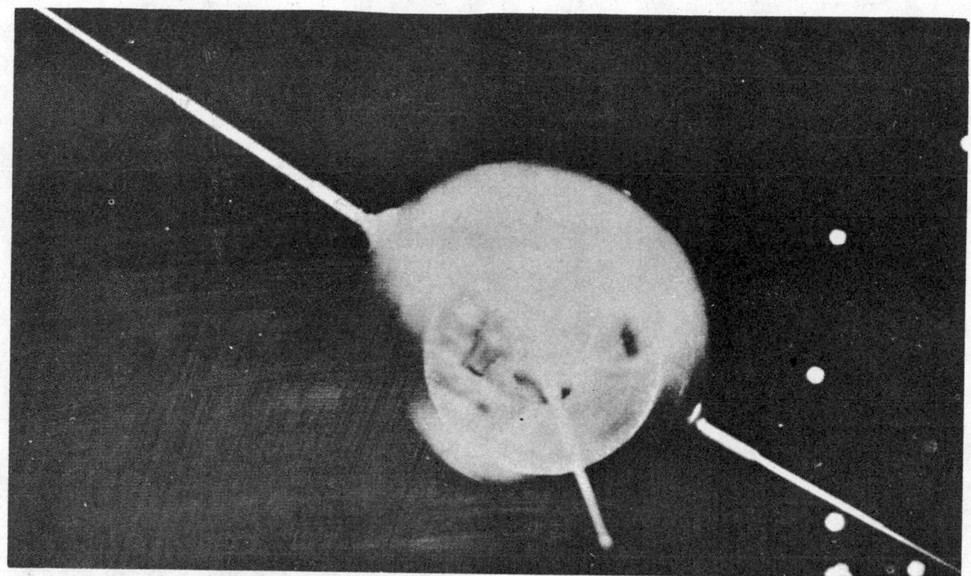

SPUTNIK, Russian word for satellite, became part of language Oct. 4, 1957 when USSR launched in space first man-made moon, like model shown above, catching U.S. flat-footed. Russians fired three before first U.S. one.

SOVIET LEADERS met with their seven European satellite allies at Warsaw to sign a mutual security agreement designed to counterbalance the West's NATO. High caliber of delegation, *(l. to r.)* Defense Minister Georgi Zhukov, Premier Nikolai Bulganin, Foreign Min. Molotov, Marshal Konev, showed importance of move.

U-2 SPY, Francis Gary Powers, was shot down over USSR May 1, 1960, given 10-year sentence by Russians. Incident caused breakdown of Summit.

GENEVA "SUMMIT" CONFERENCE of 1955 began July 18 and lasted 6 days, saw a concerted effort to ease tensions in the post-Stalin world. A hopeful tone looking toward a new era was set by President Eisenhower during the meetings. At that time he called for a program of "atoms for peace" and "open skies" for inspection of atomic plants. Topics discussed at the meetings dealt with European security, unification of East and West Germany, disarmament, and lifting of the iron curtain. Big Four pose on lawn of the Palais de Nations: *(l. to r.)* Premier Nikolai Bulganin of Russia; President Eisenhower; French Premier Edgar Faure; and Prime Minister Sir Anthony Eden of Great Britain.

REVOLT FLARED in East Berlin as Germans rioted against Russian rule on June 17, 1953. Gen. Dibrova, Soviet commanding officer, ordered tanks to clear streets of rioters in vicinity of East Berlin government headquarters, but East German demonstrators carrying banners marched triumphantly through Brandenburg Gate into the Western sector.

REVOLTS PLAGUE SOVIET EMPIRE

Subsequent to Stalin's death and the fall of Beria in 1953, symptoms of decay within Russia's satellite empire multiplied. From behind iron-curtained Eastern Europe with its 120 million people controlled by 43 Soviet divisions came signs of festering discontent and rumblings of revolt. Kremlin leaders alternated in reaction from a "softening up" policy to renewed Stalinist toughness.

After Communist Party boss Khrushchev denounced Stalin's tyranny at the 20th Party Congress in 1956, a general relaxation of pressures was seen. Then came the Poznan uprising in Poland, followed by official admissions of failure. In October, Gomulka who had been purged for nationalism in 1949, was restored to leadership. That same month the fuse was lit in Hungary and the gallant battle waged by Hungarian freedom fighters was cheered by the Western world. But here Soviet rulers reverted to the old pattern of brutality, unleashing the Red Army to crush the revolt. Reports of unrest from other quarters mounted: "incipient rebellion" in Rumania and Bulgaria with many arrests noted; rioting in East Berlin and widespread army desertions to the West.

While the satellites had gained some measure of independence, events made clear the pressure of anti-Communist sentiment and the tough "new Stalinism" was enforced. The cult of personality was in disfavor but the cult of the party and Red Army might remained.

POLISH UPRISING in Poznan on June 28, 1956 began as workers marched through the streets shouting for "Bread!" Tanks and troops entered the city; bloody anti-Communist demonstration reportedly cost hundreds of lives and thousands of arrests. Below, Polish workers carry a flag stained with the blood of a 16-year-old boy killed in the rioting.

THE HUNGARIAN REVOLT

The long-smouldering discontent of the Hungarian people, fired by successful anti-Communist action in Poland, erupted into brief but brutal warfare in the fall of 1956. On October 23 a student-worker demonstration toppled a huge statue of Stalin; security police opened fire. The next day Soviet tanks entered Budapest and general fighting broke out. Imre Nagy, removed in 1955, became Premier as the nation rallied to battle the Reds. Soviet troops withdrew November 1 but in three days returned to smash the revolt. Nagy appealed to the UN which in emergency session called on Russia to withdraw her forces from Hungary. But Nagy was ousted and replaced by puppet Janos Kadar and by Nov. 12th the revolt was all but crushed. Labor leaders ordered a general strike and the underground resistance regrouped its forces.

OBEDIENT SATELLITE, Czechoslovakia was one of the mainstays of Communist industrial might since its absorption into Russian empire following WW II. Czech arms and machinery turned up in Korea, other spots where Reds fought.

IRON CURTAIN consisted mostly of barbed wire, machine guns. In an attempt to check steady flow of refugees to West, Communists increased vigilance, as in Hungary *(above).*

SOVIET HEGEMONY over Eastern Europe was constantly emphasized, as in 1954 Warsaw Pact meeting in Moscow. Satellite leaders followed every Kremlin directive on West.

HUNGARIAN REBELS WAVE NATION'S FLAG OVER CAPTURED SOVIET TANK IN STREETS OF BUDAPEST DURING 1956 ABORTIVE REVOLT.

WANING OF COLONIALISM

Nationalism of peoples of Asia and Africa conquers colonial past

GIANTS OF INDIA, Mohandas Ghandi *(r.)* and Jawaharlal Nehru, popular pacifist leaders, fathered the Republic of India. When the British withdrew from their rich colony in 1947, free India emerged as a member of the British Commonwealth. At Ghandi's death (1948) Nehru continued rule.

FIRST PRESIDENT of Israel and a pioneer Zionist, Chaim Weizmann led Israel to freedom until his death Nov. 9, 1952. Itzhak Bon-Zvi became president Dec. 8, 1952. David Ben-Gurion, Premier, successfully met problems of unfavorable trade balance, large immigration numbers, need for capital.

Colonialism, which had been a major source of European wealth, became a "bad" word and a disappearing entity in the years following WW II.

Great Britain and France were the important colonial powers. Although weakened by the struggle against Japan and Germany, their military strength could probably have retained their colonies for them, but it could not have countered the changing tide of public opinion and economic common sense. Colonies just did not seem to be worth all the trouble any more.

Most graceful exit from the colonial scene was made by Great Britain. India, Pakistan, Ceylon, Cyprus, and all her vast African holdings, with the exceptions of Kenya, Tanganyika and the Rhodesia, were handed over to native governments. The British left behind a good civil service and a more than average amount of good will.

Until Gen. Charles de Gaulle came back to power in 1958, France had not made much progress with the colonial problem. Indo-China was lost in a futile and costly war; chaos was the order of the day in Algeria; below the Sahara civil unrest was ruining the drive toward industrial and economic growth.

DeGaulle strengthened ties with the old French colonies of Morocco and Tunisia. In a surprising move he gave the sub-Saharan colonies a choice of complete freedom or independence within the French Community. Only Guinea chose freedom.

Other nations that lost colonies were the U.S., Philippines; the Netherlands, most of Indonesia after a brief war, and Belgium, which abruptly left the huge Congo—the worst example of independence too soon. As soon as Belgian troops vacated the Central African state it disintegrated in a welter of tribal disputes and political jealousies, forcing the United Nations to intervene.

BURMA gained independence in 1948 after 122 years of British rule. Clement Atlee *(l., signing)* witnessed historic freedom document for Great Britain as Burma's Prime Minister Thakin Nu looked on. Burma led Southeast Asian countries in postwar movement toward greater social and economic reform.

INDONESIA became independent in 1949 after UN mediation ended 4-year Dutch-Indonesian battle. Reluctant to give up $1.5 billion holdings, the Dutch fought Indonesian nationalists. Rebels lost revolt but won freedom. Pres. Soekarno *(r.)* of U.S. of Indonesia spoke as nation became 60th UN member.

THE SUEZ CRISIS

Egypt's Premier Nasser triggered conflict in the seething Middle East when he seized the Suez Canal July 26, 1956. This action, following United States refusal to finance the Aswan Dam, billion-dollar pet project of the Egyptian dictator, critically threatened the West's oil supply. At a 22-nation London conference Aug. 16th, the "Dulles Plan" was evolved for operation of the canal by a non-profit international body, but Nasser rejected any foreign control and remained adamant in further discussion. On October 31st British and French forces attacked Egypt. Within one week Egypt's Soviet-equipped air force and small fleet were crippled, her land forces wrecked. Concurrently Israel defeated Egyptian forces in the Sinai Peninsula. United Nations reaction was swift; in emergency session November 1st an immediate cease-fire was demanded; on the 8th an emergency international police force was voted; then Britain and France later withdrew.

CAIRO CROWD wildly hailed Nasser as he drove through the streets of Egyptian capital during height of the British-French assault. The two Western powers initially refused a U.N. appeal for a cease-fire, but bowed to U.N.-U.S. pressure.

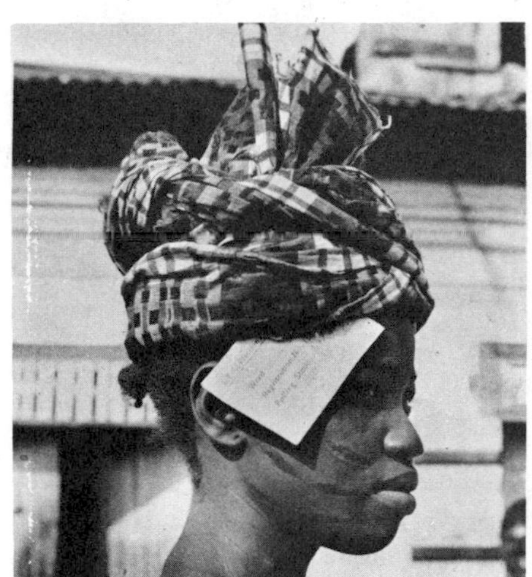

TATTOOED NIGERIAN woman keeps symbol of new freedom, a poll slip, carefully tucked inside her headgear.

RUGGED ETHIOPIAN TROOPS were flown to Leopoldville by U.S. planes to join other contingents of the UN Emergency Force. Other troops included Moroccans, Ghanaians, kilted Irish troops, Swedes and a detachment from Red-tinged Guinea.

NEWLY INDEPENDENT SOMALIS CELEBRATE FREEDOM IN 1960 WHILE DEMANDING SAME FOR THEIR EAST AFRICAN NEIGHBORS

GERMANY

Total defeat is followed by remarkable recovery

The Allied victory in Europe resulted in a partitioned Germany, divided into four occupation zones, Russian, British, French and U.S. East Germany, under Communist domination, made a slow recovery which was marked by bloody riots that culminated in near revolt in 1953.

Instead of further weakening Germany, the Allies bolstered their sections economically, paving the way for eventual German participation in Western defense. This liberal policy was largely responsible for West Germany's miraculous economic recovery, spurred on by over $4 billion in U.S. aid. West Germany soon became a major competitor on world markets, especially in automobiles, steel, electronics, coal and machine tools.

Chancellor Adenauer signed a virtual peace treaty with the Western Allies in 1953, restoring Germany's independence in exchange for supporting the West militarily. Full sovereignty came May 5, 1955, after 10 years of occupation, when Bonn formally joined the North Atlantic Treaty Organization. Adenauer, thrice victorious in elections during the 50s, established close accord with France but left the choice of his successor a troublesome question mark.

WILLY BRANDT, Socialist mayor of West Berlin, and German Chancellor Konrad Adenauer confer in Berlin in 1960. Both leaders rejected any change in city's status despite Soviet threats.

REFUGEE camps overflowed in Germany with displaced persons of Central Europe, residue of Nazi slave labor. Forced from East Berlin home during blockade, children wait at Russian zone border.

RAPID recovery of German economy began with currency reform in 1948. Initial Allied policy of denazification, demilitarization, decartelization was changed to counter the Russian threat.

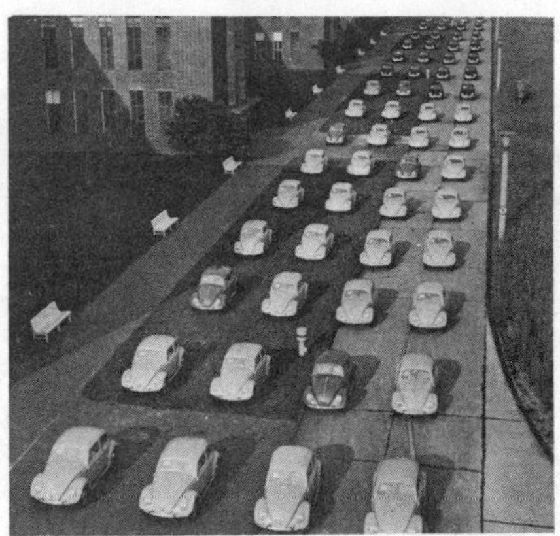

"PEOPLE'S CARS," which Hitler had vainly promised every German worker, were produced in mass quantities after recovery. German goods flooded world market as mark became sound currency.

HISTORIC handshake seals agreement between West German Chancellor Konrad Adenauer *(r.)* and Soviet Premier Bulganin as wartime enemies established diplomatic relations in Sept. 1955. At the five-day conference in Miscow arrangements were also agreed upon for return of prisoners of war.

SPRING 1956 saw the new West German Army, the Bundeswehr, on the march. Supplied with American uniforms and weapons, these soldiers approach shooting range near Coblenz for military drill. Rebuilding of German armed might was the Allied tactic to counter Russian military strength.

EMPEROR HIROHITO abolished old tradition and appeared for the first time in public, abandoning his divine role. After defeat, Japan was turned toward democracy, paving way to end military and caste systems. Although ruled by the U.S. army, the Japanese political, police officials functioned.

CONTROVERSIAL SECURITY TREATY, which led to Communist-dominated student riots and cancellation of Pres. Eisenhower's good-will trip to Japan, was signed by U.S. Ambassador Douglas MacArthur 2nd *(l.)* Japanese Foreign Minister Alichere Fujiyama. Riots failed to break pact.

JAPAN

Japan's surrender after the 1945 atomic destructions of Hiroshima and Nagasaki was followed by U.S. military occupation under Gen. Douglas MacArthur.

His rule brought sweeping changes, effecting a social revolution: the Emperor relinquished divinity; a democratic constitution was adopted; Japan emerged in September, 1951, as a free, democratic nation, but was beset with political troubles.

Following an inflationary period that accompanied the Korean War, Japan began to soar economically, increasing steel and electric output and capturing the shipbuilding lead from Great Britain.

Student riots cancelled a 1960 visit by Pres. Eisenhower, caused the resignation of Premier Kishi, and almost shattered the new Mutual Defense pact. Between East and West, Japan walked a shaky tightrope.

CROWN PRINCE Akihito (l.) and his "commoner" bride, Michiko Shoda, made a good-will trip to U.S. in 1960 to counter the unfavorable publicity resulting from violent anti-U.S. riots.

PEACE TREATY, signed by Premier Yoshida on Sept. 8, 1951, restored Japanese sovereignty. Russian disagreement caused delay in signing. But the U.S. signature ended the military occupation.

VIOLENCE erupted in Japanese Diet as liberal and socialist members clashed over Police Nationalization bill on June 3, 1954. Fifty people were hurt before the police quelled the rioting which resulted in further political turmoil.

CHAOTIC MOB is pushed back by cordon of helmeted Tokyo police trying to quell frenzied student rioters. The worst rioting in Japan's post-war history, it caused many futile deaths and downfall of pro-U.S. Kishi government.

GREAT BRITAIN

The Labor Party wielded the power in Great Britain from 1945-1951, inaugurating a program of economic reform which included nationalization of the Bank of England, major industries, transportation and communication. Wartime rationing and controls were largely retained but an economic upsurge halted austerity programs, socialization, and the rise of the Labor Party.

The Conservatives returned to power in 1951, with Winston Churchill, again in 1954 with ill-fated Anthony Eden and still again in '57 and '59 with Harold Macmillan. Great Britain's miraculous economic recovery weakened Labor's appeal to the voters and sparked doctrinal disputes that threatened to split and even eclipse the Labor Party as a major political force.

Abroad, Great Britain was a good loser. Its graceful departure from most of its old colonies was generally effected in a far superior manner than that of any of the other European powers. Most important, the British left behind good will and stable governments with trained personnel.

And even though the Union Jack no longer flew alone in every part of the globe, Great Britain maintained its position as a major power, a supporter of NATO and the Free World, and a close ally of the United States.

ELIZABETH II, crowned amid pomp and splendor on June 3, 1953, had been on tour of Commonwealth countries when King George died. Britons were proud of their young Queen, who earnestly applied herself to the role of monarch, aided by her husband, Prince Philip, the Duke of Edinburgh.

END OF RATIONING in Britain was delayed until July, 1954, when meat, the last item, was freed. The austerity era seemed over, but rationing returned with the crisis in Suez.

BRITISH COMMONWEALTH" CLUB," assembled for conference in London in 1957, called together all Prime Ministers. Major problem concerned S. Africa's policy of *apartheid* (segregation).

NO. 10 CHANGED hands in April, ➧ 1955 when Churchill retired in favor of Sir Anthony Eden. "Old age" and lull in political situation prompted decision. In succeeding election, May 26, Eden's Conservatives won a 59-seat majority.

OLD PATRIOT Eamon De Valera casts his ballot in Dublin during 1957 Irish parliamentary elections which returned his *Fianna Fail* party to power. In 1960 he retired to the presidency.

PRINCESS MARGARET and groom, Antony Armstrong-Jones, leave Westminster Abbey after their wedding, May 5, 1960. Jones, a commoner, had worked as society photographer before match.

DEFEATED in 1959 parliamentary elections, Oxford-educated Hugh Gaitskill found his Labor party leadership threatened by split among top union bosses.

HAROLD MACMILLAN succeeded Sir Anthony Eden as Prime Minister of Great Britain. Taking over during Suez crisis, he hoped to repair U.S.-British relations, strained over Suez invasion.

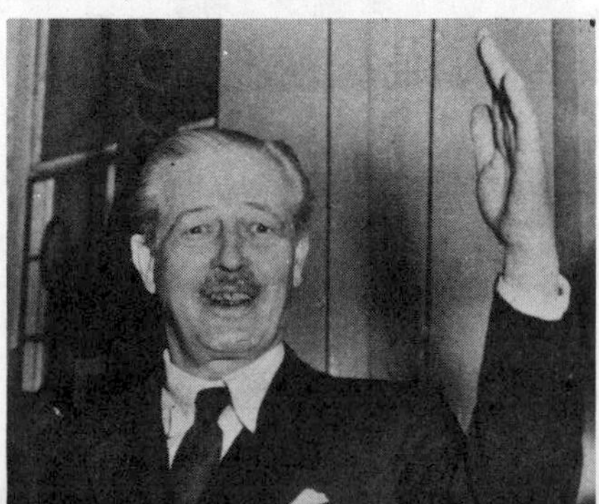

PERSONAL DIPLOMACY is exercised by tall, aristocratic Gen. Charles de Gaulle, President of France, during his 1958 tour of Algeria. Despite his efforts, no solution of the Algerian revolt developed. Rebels continued their raids.

PLAGUED BY DISSENT, former premiers Guy Mollet *(l.)* and Pierre Mendes-France tried to work out a political compromise. Before return of Gen. de Gaulle to power, it was virtually impossible to stabilize French government.

FRANCE

During its 13 post-war years of life, France's Fourth Republic saw the dissolution of enough parliaments to last 50 years. This haphazard "revolving door" system of government hampered the nation's recovery.

Indo-China was relinquished after a costly, bitter war. In Algeria France expended billions in wealth and the lives of seven soldiers every day. On May 13, 1958, French settlers and army leaders revolted against Premier Pierre Pflimlin, fearing he planned a "sell-out" to Algerian rebels.

Public clamor then returned wartime hero Gen. Charles de Gaulle to power. He became premier June 1 after demanding six months of full power to revise the constitution.

While the Algerian revolt still posed a serious problem, de Gaulle had strengthened—*pour la gloire*—the prestige, spirit, economy and military strength of his beloved France. He set up an independent nuclear striking force, virtually ignored the UN and threatened to disrupt the NATO alliance. But all of this was accomplished on the basis of de Gaulle's mighty personal prestige. At 70, he could not be expected to guide France for many more years and greatness cannot be handed down. Who could replace him?

HUMBLE APOLOGY is made by Thami El Glaoui, Berber chieftain, to reinstated Sultan of Morocco *(seated)*. El Glaoui once helped dethrone Sultan.

COMMUNIST CAMPAIGN against the Atlantic Pact was waged with protest demonstrations. This is a gathering of Parisian construction workers.

PIERRE POUJADE explains his anti-tax crusade at news conference. Rapidly gaining a large following, Poujade was worrying government officials, until movement showed signs of weakening.

OUSTED BY DE GAULLE, Jacques Soustelle, former Minister of the Sahara, Atomic Energy and overseas possessions continued his defense of Algerian colonists in French Assembly.

FORMER ENEMIES deGaulle and Adenauer attempted to bring France and Germany closer together in face of constant Red threats to both countries.

JOHN DIEFENBAKER, Saskatchewan lawyer, and head of the Progressive Conservatives, became Prime Minister in March, 1958, overthrowing the Liberals who were in power for 22 years.

MAURICE DUPLESSIS, iron-fisted "dictator" of Quebec, died Sept. 7, 1959. End of his 15-year rule of the province signalized weakening of French particularism, increased sense of nationhood.

DEATH of former Prime Minister Louis St. Laurent, following the defeat of the Liberals, made Nobel Prizer Lester B. Pearson *(above)* chief of the opposition.

NEW GOLIATH RISES

Canadian mining unlocks new industrial potential

Canada came to full maturity in the 20th century, adding a fresh, new voice to the councils of the Free World while retaining membership in the British Commonwealth.

Its economic advance was equally rapid. Population rose to 18 million; its Gross National Product soared to $18 billion in 1959; industrial production increased two-thirds, making it the world's sixth largest nation in industrial output, and immense new mineral wealth was opened up—oil and natural gas in the West, iron and copper in the bleak Northeast.

Internationally, Canadian troops played an important role in Korea and in the UN force sent to Suez following the 1956 cease-fire. This was largely arranged by Nobel Prize winner Lester Pearson, External Affairs Secretary during the long years of Liberal power.

The major political event of recent years was the overthrow of the Liberals, after 22 years of power, by the Progressive Conservatives headed by lawyer John Diefenbaker.

The death of Maurice *("le chef")* Duplessis, premier of Quebec for 15 years, paved the way for another surprising political upset. Jean Le Sage, a Liberal, became premier in 1960. Liberals hoped this would be the beginning of a national comeback.

Economically and militarily strong, Canada had come of age as a full and equal partner in Western defense.

NATIONHOOD did not weaken strong ties with Commonwealth, Great Britain or greatly loved Elizabeth, Queen of Canada. On royal visit she attended her first square dance with Prince Philip.

ST. LAWRENCE SEAWAY opened the heart of North American continent to foreign trade and provides anti-submarine continental waterway. Built by U.S. and Canada after Canadians threatened to build it alone, the Seaway opened in April, 1959.

CANADA'S FIRST native born Governors General were Maj. Gen. Georges Vanier *(above)* and Vincent Massey. 20th Century predecessors in Vice Regal post were Duke of Connaught, Lord Tweedsmuir, Lord Alexander of Tunis.

ARAMBURU TAKES OATH as president in Buenos Aires Nov. 1955. Pedro Aramburu pledged a firm provisional government by the military. He hoped to bring to his people a fully constitutional government which was partly realized May 1, when he restored original Liberal Constitution of 1853.

FIDEL CASTRO, guerrilla fighter who overthrew unpopular Cuban dictator Fulgencio Batista on Jan. 1, 1959, gained wide popular support on Batista collapse. In "utopian radical" program Castro promised land to peasants, moved to the Marxist camp and turned on one-time supporter, the U.S., with vitriolic attacks.

LATIN AMERICA

Instability, Red infiltration mark postwar period

Democracy and dictatorship, Communism and coffee, riot and revolt—all were problems that plagued Latin America after World War II, offering little comfort to the "gringo" neighbor to the north.

In Argentina, Peron was overthrown and forced to flee, as was Jimenez of Venezuela. Governments came and went against a background of gunfire in Guatemala, Bolivia, Colombia, Haiti and, most unfortunate of all for the U.S., in Cuba. Only 90 miles off the coast of Florida, Fidel Castro's Cuba was rapidly becoming a satellite of the Soviet bloc. Castro had confiscated all U.S. property, vilified Washington constantly, and cast threatening eyes on the U.S. Navy base situated on Guantanamo Bay.

But economically, much of Latin America prospered. Former Pres. Juscelino Kubitschek launched Brazil on an adventurous expansion program and built a strikingly beautiful capital, Brazilia, on land that was once deserted scrubland.

Throughout the rest of Latin America, foreign, particularly U.S. capital poured in, helping develop natural resources and industrialize countries which until the war were primarily agricultural.

The unhappy Cuban situation prodded the U.S. government into a belated expansion of its aid program in 1960 to stem the rising tide of anti-Americanism and Communism.

GENERALISSIMO Rafael Leonidas Trujillo Molina was 68 in 1960, ruled Dominican Republic for 29 years. He had relinquished presidency to brother Hector, but kept iron-fisted control.

ORGANIZATION OF AMERICAN STATES held its first meeting of heads of state, Panama, 1956, was kept busy since founding with problems ranging from economic problems to charges of U.S. "aggression" against Cuba by Castro. 18 western hemisphere presidents attended informal talks.

PET PROJECT OF JUSCELINO KUBITSCHEK, president of Brazil (1956-1960) was new capital, Brazilia. Typical of nation's determination to build for a new and modern future, the multi-million dollar project, under direction of architect Oscar Niemeyer, was aimed at opening Brazil's "backlands."

CAPITAL AND LABOR

Postwar prosperity based on industrial expansion, consumer spending

War acceleration of industry had produced by 1945 the prosperity lacking in the '30s. At war's end, many feared an economic collapse. Instead came unequalled prosperity, fostered initially by savings. Consumers' unspent overtime pay and industry's surplus profits motivated powerful forces of demand. Assured of markets, companies spent their surplus on plant modernization and expansion. Consumer demand steadily promoted this expansion. Trends toward consolidation were also evident, especially in the auto industry; one of the many big mergers resulted in formation of American Motors.

The post-war economy withstood three slight recessions in 1948 and 1949. By late 1954, economists felt that expansion was the new formula for prosperity. With national props of defense spending, home construction, and public works, it seemed likely that prosperity would continue.

Prosperity did not weaken labor. Union membership rose from 13 million to 17 million between 1946 and 1953. Most union contracts contained "fringe benefits" by 1955. Rising wages were usually offset by higher costs. A new trend came in 1954 when Studebaker union members voted a wage cut to keep the firm in business.

Strikes were frequent. When 650,000 steel workers struck for 53 days, President Truman seized the industry, blamed management, but the Supreme Court held the seizure unconstitutional. Passed over presidential veto in 1947, the Taft-Hartley Act restricted such practices as secondary boycotts, provided for strike-ending injunctions, and raised a continuing storm of controversy.

Red infiltration was a major postwar problem. Both the AFL and CIO opposed Congressional attempts to clean out Communists, held the job could best be done by labor itself.

FORD FAMILY gave up sole control of Ford Motor Company in 1956 with biggest common stock offering in history. Pres. Henry Ford II is shown *(standing)* with brothers William and Benson

CONRAD HILTON built greatest hotel chain in nation by acquiring old hotels and building new ones. In 1954, he bought the Statler chain. Hilton also operated hotels in foreign countries.

LABOR'S BIG FOUR *(above l. to r.,* Green, Murray, Meany and Reuther) met in 1951 to discuss government-imposed wage freeze directed under the mobilization program. After Green and Murray both died in Nov., 1952, Labor put Meany and Reuther in top AFL, CIO spots. By 1956, the two unions had merged, forming AFL-CIO. John L. Lewis *(l.)* led coal miners in major strike for more pension benefits in 1949. He was found guilty of contempt of a court injunction against strike; union was fined nearly \$1½ million.

HENRY J. KAISER *(l.)*, shown at 1955 opening of his Honolulu hotel, rose from paving contractor to versatile industrialist with billion dollar interests in cement, steel, aluminum, gypsum and engineering.

VIOLENCE BEGAN when Supreme Court decision banned segregation in public schools May 17, 1954, and ordered integration to proceed with "all deliberate speed." President Eisenhower sent federal troops to quell "mob violence" that barred Negroes from entering Little Rock Central High School, Ark. By 1960, though integration was resisted in many areas violence dropped off except for isolated spots.

ALBERT CAMUS *(l.)* French existentialist, gained wide U.S. audience with his symbolic masterpiece *The Fall* relating to man's heritage of guilt. Andre Gide, French Nobel Prize winner for Literature, died in '51. *The Counterfeiters* was his best known work in the United States.

BORIS PASTERNAK "refused" Nobel Prize for his *Doctor Zhivago*, story of reaction to Soviet Revolution. The Russian died of cancer in 1960. Ernest Hemingway *(r.)* won the 1953 Nobel Prize for his story *The Old Man and The Sea.*

VETERANS took advantage of the GI Bill and crowded U.S. colleges after the war. Older, often married with children, they were serious students and helped raise scholastic levels. The increased tuition fees pleased educators. By 1951, college enrollments dropped, rose again after Korean "police action".

EDUCATION

"Our great race with the Soviet Union is in education," said Vice Adm. Hyman Rickover as he sought to awaken the U.S. people to the problem of accelerating technical and scientific training in U.S. schools. This was not the only, or gravest, problem. U.S. education lacked the money, teachers, facilities and an adequate curriculum to meet the full needs of the mid-century.

Because of low salaries (teachers in 1960 were averaging less than production workers) only 35,000 of the 150,000 new teachers needed yearly were entering the profession. Although the U.S. in 1960 was spending $17 billion for education, authorities believed that to serve the growing numbers of new students (in elementary and secondary schools enrolment was 2.5 million above estimated capacity in 1960), this sum needed to be doubled.

Numbers of U.S. students reached high school and sometimes college without having mastered basic reading and mathematics skills, while the Soviet Union continued to turn out three times as many engineers and technicians than U.S. educational institutions.

Although many thought federal aid was the only solution, Congress in 1949 and 1954 voted down emergency aid measures. Additional problems of compulsory loyalty oaths for teachers, the value of progressive education and the lack of classrooms further complicated the crisis.

BOOKS

By the end of the 1950s, book publishing annual revenue topped the $1 billion mark. Although the U.S. reading public decreased from 21% to 17% of the population, as a result of the advent of television, book publishers announced that at the close of the '50s sales had increased 60% over the 1952 level. Annual volume of books sold rose well above the 550 million mark.

"Supermarket-style" paperback book stores cropped up throughout the country and burgeoned into a $60 million annual business, with some 300 million copies under 1912 titles in print. Among the paperbacks were to be found quality reprints and originals selling for 25¢ to $1.25.

From Here to Eternity, by James Jones, Herman Wouk's Pulitzer Prize winner *The Caine Mutiny* and Nicholas Monsarrat's *The Cruel Sea* were among the top sellers of the 1950s. J. D. Salinger's first novel, *The Catcher in the Rye*, scored a sweeping success. John O'Hara's *From the Terrace*, although considered by some critics to be his poorest work, sold briskly. *Exodus*, Leon Uris' glowing but not very literary work was popular.

A flood of memoirs like Sir Winston Churchill's *Triumph and Tragedy*, a personal history of World War II, poured from the presses. Such vivid, vibrant works as Ernest Hemingway's *The Old Man and The Sea*, 1953 Pulitzer Prize winner, showed trend toward realism.

GRANDMA MOSES, born in Eagle Bridge, N. Y., began painting after age 70. Her "primitive" oils of country scenes won recognition from art authorities, great popularity with the public.

SALVADOR DALI, best known surrealist, declared his work was produced in a state of psychological trance. He maintained that since problems of the subconscious are common to all, his paintings should be understandable. Whether laymen could accept this was problematical, but *The Face of War (above)* carried a direct message. Early surrealists included Chagall, Rousseau, Picasso, Klee and Ernst.

ART

New York's Museum of Modern Art celebrated its 25th anniversary in 1954. Art authorities agreed it could take much of the credit for more general acceptance accorded revolutionary new art forms which had come to birth in Europe in the early years of the century. The Metropolitan Museum of Art underwent a face-lifting with the addition of new galleries and a stunning new decor. From its 8th Street Abode, the Whitney Museum moved to larger quarters in the mid-town area.

The coveted Arensberg Collection of early modern paintings, include *Nude Descending A Staircase* by Marcel Duchamps, was offered first to the Los Angeles County Museum. They declined because of the provision that the collection be housed as a unit in a special gallery. It went finally to Philadelphia's Museum of Art.

More Americans were painting than ever before, professionally and as amateurs, producing everything from landscapes to surrealistic, symbolic art.

BERNARD BUFFET is shown working in his Paris studio. The 28-year-old Frenchman and his subjects personify post-war misery and despair, but the fabulous prices his paintings brought permitted the artist to live on a luxury level.

BERNARD BERENSON, one of world's most perceptive art critics, died in Italy in 1959, at 94. Born in Lithuania and educated in Boston, Berenson was foremost authority on Renaissance art. Many collections were built on his advice.

JACOB EPSTEIN, N.Y. born sculptor, is shown modeling bust of actress Anna Neagle. His revolt against conventional, ornate forms created controversy, but he won acclaim for his *Adam, Jacob and the Angel,* and for bronze portraiture.

UNDER THE BATON of Leonard Bernstein, the New York Philharmonic won unprecedented popularity. For the first time in many years, tickets were difficult to get. Bernstein and Philharmonic performed on TV with "specials" and concerts.

ARTURO TOSCANINI climaxed a great career with an all-Wagner program of the NBC Symphony on April 4, 1954, and retired at 87. World's foremost conductor, he died Jan., 1957.

MUSIC

Disc jockeys, rock and roll, record clubs, high sales of LPs and Hi-Fi, jazz and classical music festivals, the revival of the New York Philharmonic under the baton of Leonard Bernstein and the increased popularity of the opera were all part of a general surge of interest in music.

The U.S. was even spending more money for tickets to concerts than for baseball. Aside from news programs, radio time was almost entirely given over to music.

On Broadway the best-sellers were musicals, which consistently grossed higher than straight drama. Newcomers to the musical scene were Victoria de los Angeles, Eileen Farrel, Mario del Monaco, Maria Callas and, lest we forget, hip-swinging Elvis Presley.

ELVIS PRESLEY, TV and recording idol of the teenagers, swings into his much-publicized rock 'n roll antics during performance at Dallas, Texas. Many thousands came to bemoan or cheer.

OPERA STAR, Maria Meneghini Callas, revived traditions of the *prima donna* with headlined outbursts. U.S.-born soprano made Metropolitan debut in '56 after successful Chicago season.

POPULAR TROUBADOUR of the Caribbean, Harry Belafonte gained an army of fans with his renditions of folk songs, but outraged many purists. Belafonte also organized his own choral group. Here he serenades his young daughter.

VAN CLIBURN, a little known, 23-year-old concert pianist from Texas, won first prize in the International Tchaikovsky Piano Concert in Moscow, May 14, 1958. On return to U.S. he received a ticker tape parade, first for a musician.

◀ **READJUSTMENT PROBLEM** of veterans was the theme of *The Best Years of Our Lives* which evoked great audience sympathy. Harold Russell, Dana Andrews and Frederic March starred.

LAURENCE OLIVIER produced, directed and starred in a technicolor film of Shakespeare's *Henry V (r.)* in 1945. He made *Hamlet* in 1948, was praised for production and his performance. ▶

HOLLYWOOD HAS ITS PROBLEMS

Studios and theaters rode the inflationary boom, grossing an all-time high in 1947 of $1.5 billion.

However, new problems arose. The U.S. Government filed and won an anti-trust suit to divorce studios from their theaters. The profitable English market became shaky as the Labor government restricted U.S. products and limited the dollars returnable to Hollywood (in 1950, $19 million). A Congressional probe into Communist activity in Hollywood uncovered a conspiracy to influence movie-making, but implicated no one of major importance.

Meanwhile, Hollywood was losing its adult audience. The French sent *Devil in the Flesh,* uncensored, the Italians their refreshingly honest *Shoeshine* and *Bicycle Thief*, the British their *Red Shoes* and *Third Man.* Japan sent *Rashomon.*

Hollywood turned to new techniques and hitherto taboo subjects. *Boomerang* was a "documentary" crime story. *Lost Boundaries* dealt with the Negro-white social problem. *The Jolson Story* was a phenomenon —Al Jolson sang while Larry Parks, playing Jolson, gestured appropriately. The illusion was perfect, the profits staggering. Screen journalism was recognized by the Academy in 1949, when *The March of Time* received an award. Hollywood turned back to the time-tested Western for sure success.

Television proved to be Hollywood's most overpowering threat. By 1951 many theaters had closed after a strong drop in movie attendance. By 1952 the movie-TV battle flared in full force. A fantastic increase in the purchase of TV sets was countered by an increase in theaters, drive-ins and super-colossal color pictures but the theaters could hardly make ends meet. TV's adverse influence on movie attendance forced Hollywood to find a sensational solution.

In 1953, a previously-ignored process called 3-D was introduced. Audiences thronged the box offices to see the novelty. Soon wide screen, stereophonic sound were added as 20th Century-Fox introduced CinemaScope (screen ratio, 2.55:1) to give the industry standardization as each studio vied to develop its own techniques—Cinerama, Vista Vision, Todd-AO among others.

An ailing industry had at last received the shot in the arm it so urgently needed. Bigger and better, but fewer pictures were being made. Backlogs of feature films were profitably sold to TV. Audiences were getting their best entertainment in years. Prosperity returned to Hollywood.

CHAMPION starred Kirk Douglas. Successful $585,000 film pointed a way to produce in shrinking market.

BEST PICTURE of 1949, *All the King's Men* won Oscar for Broderick Crawford *(l.)* and Mercedes McCambridge, who were starred in this political drama.

CONFLICT FLARED in the *Seventh Veil*, a 1946 British film with psychological undertones. The tense drama starred James Mason and Ann Todd.

HIT OF 1950, *Sunset Boulevard* was an eerie drama about a silent movie star. It brought Gloria Swanson back to films and co-starred William Holden.

AFRICAN QUEEN involved alcoholic Humphrey Bogart and spinster Katharine Hepburn in a love affair and an attempt to sink gunboat in deep Africa.

GARY COOPER won great sympathy and an Academy Award in Stanley Kramer's *High Noon.* It featured song *Do Not Forsake Me, Oh My Darlin'.*

MOST DESIRABLE French export was Brigitte Bardot, shown in *And God Created Woman.* Combining sex with piquancy, BB threatened U.S. stars, others.

"THIS IS CINERAMA," produced in 1953 by Lowell Thomas, left viewers gasping. Though highly effective, Cinerama's defects included high installation cost, imperfect blending of three images shown on same screen. Some of the three-dimensional techniques first tried in 1952 required polarized glasses.

SEVEN ACADEMY AWARDS went to *Bridge on the River Kwai* in '58, including Best Actor to Alex Guiness *(above)*. It cost $3 million, grossed 30.

JAMES DEAN, in his last role before fatal accident, Elizabeth Taylor and Rock Hudson starred in movie version of Edna Ferber's epic novel *Giant.*

"AROUND THE WORLD IN 80 DAYS," had 50 stars in brief appearances. It won five "Oscars" in 1957, including Best Film award. David Niven and Cantiflas starred. Movie was produced by the late Michael Todd.

"TEN COMMANDMENTS," first of "blockbusters," was produced by late Cecil B. De Mille in 1957. Production cost $13 million, earlier De Mille version $1 million; by '60 it grossed $32 million. Film starred Charlton Heston.

SOUTH PACIFIC starred Mary Martin and opera basso Ezio Pinza and caused a minor revolution in casting, directing. Score featured several hit tunes.

HIT STAR was discovered in a hit musical of 1950. Bug-eyed Carol Carol Channing cavorted through *Gentlemen Prefer Blondes* in hilarious comedy antics. She is shown above with Yvonne Adair. Lyrics were by Leo Robin, the choreography by Agnes deMille.

THE KING AND I, an adaptation of best-seller *Anna and the King of Siam,* starred Gertrude Lawrence as the prim, unruffled British governess, until her untimely death in 1953. Yul Brynner proved a great Broadway find as sharp-tongued but likeable monarch.

THEATRE

The years following World War II were richly creative in the theatre. *Annie Get Your Gun, Born Yesterday,* and *Mister Roberts* delighted audiences. Sky-rocketed production costs increased Broadway's biggest problem — the financing of plays. "Angels" became increasingly wary of anything not certain of success.

The revival of classics and *avant garde* works were offered by small companies in converted movie houses, basements and lofts throughout NYC.

Such outstanding foreign companies as the Bolshoi Ballet from the USSR, the Old Vic from England, the Grand Kabuki from Japan and France's Comedie Français delighted enthusiastic audiences in the U.S.

Playwrights of the '50s who particularly captured the imagination of theatre-goers were Tennessee Williams, William Inge, John Osborne, Eugene Ionesco and Jean Anouilh.

BRIEF MOMENT of happiness in life of Jewish family soon to be torn apart by Nazis is enacted by Susan Strasberg as Anne and Joseph Schildkraut as her father in *The Diary of Anne Frank.*

INTENSE DRAMA characterized Tennessee Williams' *A Streetcar Named Desire.* Directed by Elia Kazan, it brought stardom to Marlon Brando and starred Jessi Tandy and Kim Hunter.

MY FAIR LADY, musical adaptation of Bernard Shaw's *Pygmalion,* was an immediate and lasting success. Julie Andrews learns to pronounce the letter "h" with help from Rex Harrison.

THREE PENNY OPERA, the Kurt Weill-Marc Blitzstein version of *The Beggar's Opera* made a triumphal return in 1956 for a long N.Y. run. Scott Merrill, Jo Sullivan played nuptial pair.

"GOOD NIGHT AND GOOD LUCK" was Edward R. Murrow's familiar sign-off. Considered by many as the dean of commentators, he became the prototype of the electronic journalist, dispensing weighty opinion, considered judgments.

JACKIE GLEASON enacted a variety of characters in short comedy skits and surrounded himself with beautiful girls on Saturday night hour. He is shown as Fenwick Babbitt, who takes jobs anyone in his right mind would refuse.

TV WESTERNS, such as *Gunsmoke (above)*, liked to call themselves adult. Mixing Freud with oats, stories had boys liking girls, paranoid killers, heroes with feet of clay. But they still continued to "head 'em off at the pass."

TELEVISION

By 1960 television broadcasting had burgeoned into an industry that billed $1.5 billion in advertising and reached 65 million people in a single show through a complex of almost 600 stations and three major networks. Nearly 90% of U.S. homes had sets (about 50 million) by 1960.

Live programs were almost entirely supplanted by film and tape shows. Westerns and detective series drew wide audiences and took prime viewing hours from quiz and variety programs. Although scandals resulting from Congressional probes into TV quiz cheating rocked the industry, the public's interest in "give-away" shows continued, if somewhat dampened.

TV became an educational factor. Programs like "Sunrise Semester" were aired in the early morning for students and teachers. New York State bought over $300,000 of network time for educational programs.

FEIGNED PENSIVENESS of Carl Van Doren figured in furor created over fixing in TV quiz shows. Van Doren and many of other contestants admitted they had been fed answers beforehand.

ARTHUR GODFREY "simulcast" daily morning show and two weekly night shows, *Talent Scouts* and *Arthur Godfrey and His Friends* on radio and TV. Informal manner won large following.

FIRST COAST-TO-COAST telecast and first presidential TV address to public was made by President Harry S. Truman in 1951. Occasion was the opening session of Japanese Peace treaty talks.

I LOVE LUCY zoomed to popularity and stayed there. Lucille Ball *(under table)* and husband Desi Arnaz *(r.)*, starred as Lucy and Ricky Ricardo, signed a 2½-year, $8 million contract.

MIRACLE MILE, a mile in four minutes, was first shattered by Roger Bannister, a medical student at Oxford, who ran it in 3:59.4 on May 6, 1954 at Oxford.

Nation	Gold	Silver	Bronze	Total
U.S.S.R	43	29	31	103
U.S.A.	34	21	16	71
GERMANY	12	19	11	42
ITALY	13	10	13	36
AUSTRALIA	8	8	6	22
HUNGARY	6	8	7	21
POLAND	4	6	11	21
GREAT BRITAIN	2	6	12	20
JAPAN	4	7	7	18
RUMANIA	3	1	6	10
TURKEY	7	2	0	9
CZECHOSLOVAKIA	3	2	3	8
BULGARIA	1	3	3	7
DENMARK	2	3	1	6
SWEDEN	1	2	3	6
SWITZERLAND	0	3	3	6
FINLAND	1	1	3	5
FRANCE	0	2	3	5
BELGIUM	0	2	2	4
IRAN	0	1	3	4
NETHERLANDS	0	1	2	3
NEW ZEALAND	2	0	1	3
SOUTH AFRICA	0	1	2	3
ARGENTINA	0	1	1	2
AUSTRIA	1	1	0	2
BRAZIL	0	0	2	2
BRITISH WEST INDIES	0	0	2	2
PAKISTAN	1	0	1	2
UNITED ARAB REP.	0	1	1	2
YUGOSLAVIA	1	1	0	2
CANADA	0	1	0	1
CHINA (NATIONALIST)	0	1	0	1
ETHIOPIA	1	0	0	1
GHANA	0	1	0	1
GREECE	1	0	0	1
INDIA	0	1	0	1
IRAQ	0	0	1	1
MEXICO	0	0	1	1
MOROCCO	0	1	0	1
NORWAY	1	0	0	1
PORTUGAL	0	1	0	1
SINGAPORE	0	1	0	1
SPAIN	0	0	1	1
VENEZUELA	0	0	1	1

1960 OLYMPIC SCOREBOARD

SPORTS

GOLD MEDAL goes to U.S. team in '60 Olympics as Tennessee State's Wilma Rudolph *(foreground)* hits tape first in women's 400-meter relay in Rome.

BEN HOGAN made a gallant comeback in the 1950 Open after an almost-fatal automobile accident the year before. He lost the match in playoff with Sam Snead, went on to win Masters, U.S. Open and British Open in 1953.

CONGRATULATORY KISS is given to Althea Gibson by her finals opponent, Darlene Hard, after Miss Gibson became first Negro to win a Wimbledon championship and coveted gold trophy.

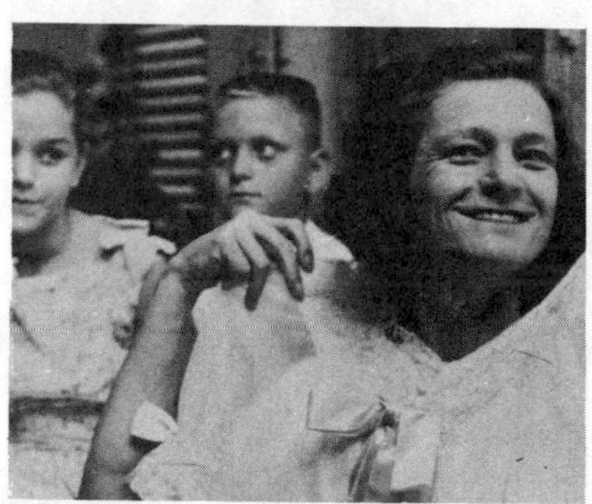

MILDRED ZAHARIAS, great woman athlete and golfer known as "Babe", made a courageous comeback but fought a losing battle against cancer.

CITATION (on rail), Calumet Farm's brilliant son of Bull Lea, became first horse in history to win more than million dollars on turf. "Big Cy" went to the post 45 times between 1947 and 1951, earned $1,085,760 and was retired in 1951.

CONNIE MACK, beloved "Mr. Baseball" and manager of Philadelphia Athletics for 50 years, died at 93 on Feb. 8, 1956. Above from left are: Bill Dickey, George Sisler, Frank Baker, Mr. Mack, Lefty Grove, Honus Wagner, W. Johnson.

THE GAME IS BUT A RUMOR if you happen to be sitting in the end zone, yet baseball-happy Los Angelenos do not seem to mind. A record crowd of 93,000 L. A fans watched Walter O'Malley's Dodgers win the 1959 World Series contest with Chicago White Sox in the mammoth Coliseum, a football stadium. In the equally exciting 1960 World Series, the New York Yankees and the once habitual occupants of the "cellar," the Pittsburgh Pirates, brought it right down to the line in a full seven-game series. Casey Stengel's Yankees batted in a record number of series runs, yet lost the final game to Pittsburgh in a thrilling series climax. Stengel was replaced by Ralph Houk, an ex-coach.

REGAINING BOXING TITLE for the third time, Sugar Ray Robinson, 20 years a great boxer, scores a smashing right to the head of Carl "Bobo" Olsen during middleweight bout in December, 1955 *(above)*. In the heavyweight division, Sweden's Ingemar Johansson scored a surprising upset over the U.S. champ, youthful Floyd Patterson in a 1959 bout ending in a kayo. Patterson caught the cocky Swede with a hard left hook *(r.)* in the 1960 return bout. Ingo was out for 10 minutes. Patterson, crushed by the first defeat, trained in complete seclusion for the return bout with Ingo.

PETER ARNO and the *New Yorker* laughed at man's troubles in a world of gadgets.

"Touche"

DELINEATOR of his anxious generation, writer and cartoonist James Thurber brooded over human bewilderment, the underground wars among men, women, dogs, children, machines, and nature in his work.

"WHY THE HELL COULDN'T YOU HAVE BEEN BORN A BEAUTIFUL WOMAN?"

WILLY AND JOE, Bill Mauldin's war-weary GI's of World War II, won both home-front and service audience with their wistful resignation and realism.

"IT'S BROCCOLI, DEAR."
"I SAY IT'S SPINACH, AND I SAY THE HELL WITH IT."

PROGRESSIVE mothers and their children were a Carl Rose specialty.

WIDE-LENSED and linear eye of Gluyas Williams was best at mirroring mores of the middlebrow community.

WIT AND HUMOR

American humor underwent marked changes during its Twentieth Century progress. During the pre-World War I years, the national wit tended to be hearty and concrete but gentle. The foremost American humorist, Mark Twain, died in 1910.

During the first World War, the influence of the British stiff upper lip touched American humor. Gradually the tough-minded school became prominent in songs and soldiers' jokes. The Twenties spawned a rich hodge-podge of crazy songs, slapstick, and flivver, flapper, divorce and Prohibition jokes.

Depression years brought a note of bitterness and satire at the expense of businessmen and politicians. Mid-century wit reflected mid-century anxieties with a tense, grisly cast that provoked the wry smile more often than the rousing belly-laugh.

MACABRE HUMOR of Charles Addams became world famous but proved hard to appreciate in many countries outside the U.S. with its unequivocal acceptance of the physically impossible, light-hearted approach to the sinister.

COMIC STRIPS were a well-developed form by the turn of the century. Among the most popular was Bud Fisher's *Mutt and Jeff*. By the Thirties comic books had become most popular juvenile reading material, worried educators.

CLUB LIFE IN AMERICA
Graduates Gather to Support the Team

ANDREA DORIA, Italian luxury liner, collided in heavy fog with the Swedish-American liner *Stockholm* on the night of July 25, 1956. The *Stockholm* stayed afloat despite a crushed bow and picked up 533 survivors from the *Doria*, which sank the following morning *(above)*. More than 12 ships responded to the SOS. Casualty count totaled four dead, 51 missing and presumed dead.

BASKETBALL became a game of giants like "Wilt the Stilt" Chamberlain, basketball's "Man Who Has Everything." He achieved national fame as a Kansas All-American *(right*, with ball), then went on to break all scoring records as a 1959-1960 rookie with the professional Philadelphia Warriors. 7′2″ star quit the game in 1960 over a dispute, then later re-signed contract.

DEFENSE

Jet bomb carriers link sea-air, land-sea commands

MASSIVE TRAP DOORS open to let huge courier of destruction, Titan ICBM, emerge into firing position. Protected by these 200-ton doors, missile is almost immune to an enemy air attack.

In the era of hydrogen bombs, intercontinental ballistic missiles and space-orbiting "spy satellites," the U.S. reshaped its defense posture. The concept of "massive retaliation" stressed the striking power of the Strategic Air Command, missile's offensive and defensive capabilities and less manpower.

The Defense Department cut its manpower total to 2.5 million in 1960. The Army streamlined itself into pentomic units that have increased mobility and are less vulnerable to atomic destruction than the outmoded regiment.

1951 saw the first peace-time Universal Military Training Law and the establishment of the Counter Intelligence Agency.

In 1959 the $136 million Air Force Academy, opened in 1955, had graduated its first officers. In that year also the first U.S. ICBMs were ready on their launch-pads both at home and abroad. Although missile attack seemed almost unstoppable, anti-missile defense featuring the Nike anti-missile missile was rushed ahead. Defense networks spread around the globe. Even in the silence of the cold arctic wastes the Distant Early Warning Line listened for the enemy that might bring war to the U.S.

"FATHER" OF ATOMIC SUB, Rear Adm. Hyman G. Rickover drew praise and criticism because of his views on U.S. defense and education. He was called a "military non-conformist."

USS FORRESTAL, 59,500 ton, $218 million aircraft carrier, could launch atom-bomb-carrying aircraft, as could the similar super- carrier, *USS Saratoga.* Carrying A3D Skywarrior atomic bombers, F3H Demon jet fighters, the *Forrestal* was hastily dispatched to patrol the eastern Mediterranean during 1957 Jordan crisis. She is shown above during her shakedown cruise in Guantanamo Bay, Cuba.

FIRST POLARIS MISSILE to be launched from a sub roars skyward, leaving an awesome stream of air and water in its wake. The missile was successfully launched from the nuclear sub, *USS George Washington,* 50 feet under ocean's surface while cruising 30 miles off the coast of Florida.

SLIDING DOWN the runway like a huge and angry goose, this USAF supersonic bomber, the B-58 "Hustler" gathers speed for its climb into the California sky. First produced in 1956, the delta-wing bomber is powered by four GE J-79 jet engines with afterburners. Plane carries a crew of three.

ATOMIC ENERGY

The smashing of the atom and the controlling of nuclear fission had given scientists the key to a basic secret of the universe and opened an era of great promise as well as inevitable fears.

Although atomic research for military purposes continued with undiminished vigor, the peaceable uses of the atom received greater and greater emphasis. In 1955 some 1200 scientists from 72 countries gathered at Geneva "to explore means of developing the peaceful uses of atomic energy through international cooperation." The future importance of nuclear fission (or atomic fusion, as in the H-bomb) as a source of power was especially stressed in the light of the world's dwindling coal and oil reserves.

The Soviet Union announced that a 5,000 kilowatt reactor near Moscow was in use, and in the United States work was pursued on nine atomic-power projects expected to develop 700,000 kilowatts. With the 1957 launching of the *Skate* the United States could point to three nuclear-powered submarines in service.

Radioisotopes, by-products of reactors, found increasing uses, ranging from industrial wear studies (tire wear, engine wear) to Carbon-14 dating methods in archaeology.

THERMONUCLEAR PROGRESS was marked by the explosion in 1952 of a "thermonuclear device" (generally regarded as a hydrogen or H-bomb). The blast completely destroyed the test island of Elugelab in the Marshall Islands where the bomb was detonated, left a crater in the Pacific Ocean floor 175 feet deep and a mile wide. In 1956 a hydrogen bomb was dropped successfully from an airplane. Russia also detonated an H-bomb, and both countries were stockpiling the bombs.

BEVATRON atom smasher, installed at University of California in 1954, had produced energies totaling five billion volts. Using Bevatron, physicists Segre, Wiegand and Chamberlain discovered the anti-proton. In Duquesne, Ohio, the first commercial-scale atomic-powered plant was scheduled for completion in 1957 and industrial utilization of radioisotopes had increased rapidly.

PROMINENT PHYSICIST, Dr. J. Robert Oppenheimer *(below r.)* directed development of first atomic bomb, became head of Princeton Institute of Advanced Studies. Shown with him is ex-AEC Chairman David Lillienthal.

RADIOACTIVE contamination created international complications in 1954 when Japanese fisherman, Aiki Kuboyama, died after accidental exposure to radioactive ash from Bikini H-bomb test. Others exposed recovered.

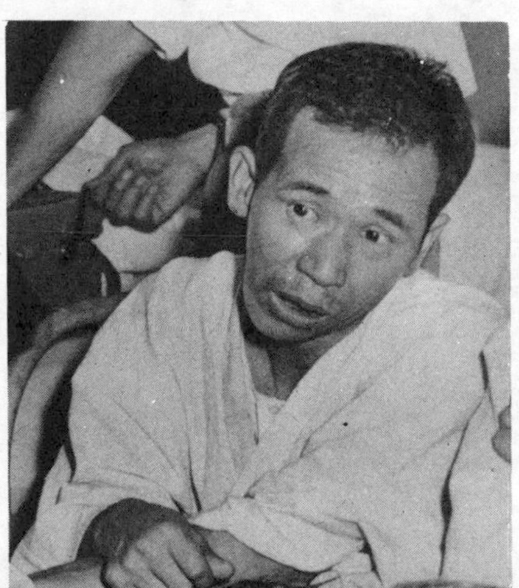

TREATMENT of cancer through radiation was bright side of atomic picture. Radioactive cesium, sodium, gold and other radioisotopes were utilized, as was University of Chicago's $250,000 microwave linear accelerator *(below)*.

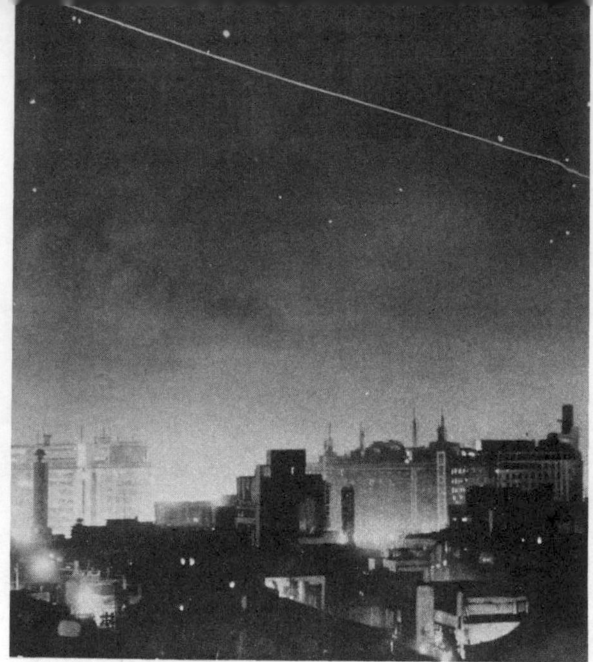

SOVIET SATELLITE *(l.)* streaking over Tokyo symbolized USSR's lead in race for space. The space traveler served as a reminder and warning of Russia's expert technology, prompted U.S. scientists *(r.,* from *left* to *right)* like Dr. William Pickering, Dr. James Van Allen and Dr. Wernher Von Braun to speed work on Explorer I, launched in 1958.

NEW HORIZONS IN SCIENCE

Storehouse of knowledge grows to meet challenge of the future

Science crept out of the laboratory and captured the imagination of the average man in the 1950's. Technological developments made possible through scientific discovery increased man's life span, raised living standards, tranquilized his mental troubles, relieved pain, immunized him from disease and opened unknown horizons to his ever-probing mind.

The National Aviation and Space Administration's X-15 rocket-plane carried a man 100 miles up to the edge of space in 1960. The Navy's Bathyscaph *Trieste* brought Lt. Don Walsh and Jacques Picard, in man's deepest dive, to the bottom of the Mariana Trench—36,000 feet below the Pacific.

The most exciting development was the possibility of space travel. Lunik I, four-ton Soviet prober, was launched on Jan. 2, 1959, becoming the earth's first artificial planet. Since 1957, 35 space satellites and probers had been launched by the U.S. and USSR. All of these collected valuable information on solar radiation, magnetic fields, interplanetary matter, to help fill the void in space knowledge.

The destructive nature of nuclear bombs was increased by the U.S. and USSR. Over 300 earth-shaking explosions spread potentially dangerous radioactive dust through the atmosphere. The U.S. engineered the largest nuclear blast, a 30 megaton (30 million tons of TNT) bomb. The original Hiroshima bomb was equivalent to only 20,000 tons of TNT.

The International Geophysical Year began 1958 with 64 nations participating in the 18-month study of the earth, its oceans, sun and space.

The giant question mark in the '60s was whether man would use his newly found powers constructively or destructively, to give life or to take it.

GIANT BRAINS, electronic computers such as the X-RAC *(below)* brought new speed to the solution of complex design, engineering, research problems, saved millions of man-hours. With development of transistors to replace vacuum tubes, considerable reduction in size of computers was made.

DR. JONAS E. SALK received a special citation from President Eisenhower in 1955, "for his extraordinary achievement . . . as a benefactor of mankind," in developing a vaccine for poliomyelitis (infantile paralysis). As vaccine supplies increased, a nation-wide inoculation program began.

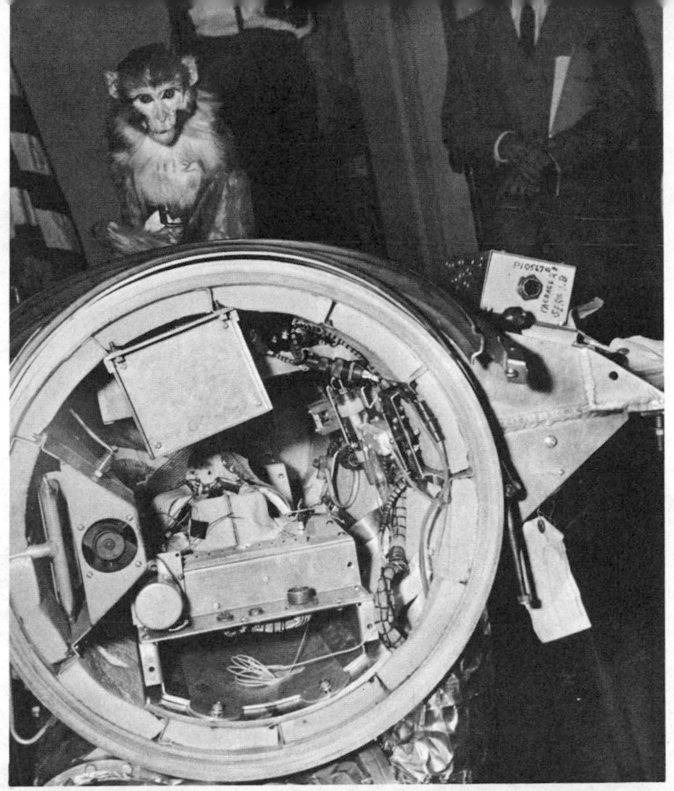

"SPACE MONKEYS" preceded human astronauts into space in U.S. program, as opposed to dogs used by USSR, to determine extent of hazards space would present to man. Sam *(l.)* pulled lever during capsule ride, Able *(r.)* rode in nose-cone.

SPATIAL LISTENING-POST was designed for construction in 1959. When operational the giant precision instrument would be able to pick "signals" from remote regions of space.

ELECTRONIC BRAIN of air defense is manned by skilled team of technicians. The first computer especially designed for air defense, the FSQ-7 was developed at the Lincoln Laboratory, Lexington, Mass. In the event of an enemy raid, the electronic brain would be fed information from radar posts hundreds of miles away, then give instructions for defense.

GIANT telescope is located at Mt. Palomar observatory in California. The 200-inch lens registered the image of nebulae one billion light years away—six billion trillion miles. World's largest telescope was completed in 1948 after 19 years of work and an expenditure of $6,500,000. At Harvard, a radio-telescope was being used by astronomers to study the structure of the galaxies in outer space.

TWO DISCOVERERS, Dr. Selman A. Waksman and Sir Alexander Fleming, examine cultures used by Dr. Waksman in his discovery of streptomycin. Fleming's discovery of penicillin was developed by Dr. Howard Florey and his group into a practical therapeutic agent in 1943.

HISTORIC DECADE 1950-1960

The story of the turbulent 10 years during which man pierced space, U. S. scaled new heights of prosperity but . . . Cold War deepened.

President Eisenhower's desire to melt Cold War ice is symbolized by State Dinner given for Khrushchev and his wife at the White House, during Khrushchev's 1959 visit to the U.S. A truculent Khrushchev refused to sit at the conference table with President Eisenhower unless the latter abjectly and publicly apologized for the U-2 flight over Soviet territory.

This was at Paris, only a few months later. Khrushchev thus wrecked the Summit conference before it could convene.

These were the two faces of Communism, its alternate images, which throughout the decade masked the same unflagging intent to weaken, then destroy, then replace the Free World with a universal Communist empire. How to counter this intent was the unsolved problem inherited by the '60's.

FOREWORDS

President John F. Kennedy

Our concern must be with the future. For the world is changing. The old era is ending. The old ways will not do.

Abroad, the balance of power is shifting. There are new and more terrible weapons—new and uncertain nations—new pressures of populations and deprivation. One-third of the world, it has been said, may be free—but one-third is the victim of cruel repression—and the other one-third is rocked by the pangs of poverty, hunger and envy. More energy is released by the awakening of these new nations than by the fission of the atom itself.

The world has been close to war before—but now man, who has survived all previous threats to his existence, has taken into his mortal hands the power to exterminate the entire species.

Here at home, the changing face of the future is equally revolutionary. We stand today on the edge of a New Frontier—the frontier of the 1960s—a frontier of unknown opportunities and perils—a frontier of unfulfilled hopes and threats.

The harsh facts of the matter are that we stand on this frontier at a turning-point in history. We must prove all over again whether this nation—or any nation so conceived—can long endure—whether our society—with its freedom of choice, its breadth of opportunity, its range of alternatives—can compete with the single-minded advance of the Communist system.

Can a nation organized and governed such as ours endure? That is the real question. Have we the nerve and the will? Can we carry through in an age where we will witness not only new breakthroughs in weapons of destruction—but also a race for mastery of the sky and the rain, the oceans and the tides, the far side of space and the inside of man's minds?

Are we up to the task—are we equal to the challenge? Are we willing to match the Russian sacrifice of the present for the future—or must we sacrifice our future to enjoy the present? The answer lies with the people of the U.S.

President John F. Kennedy and Mrs. Kennedy

SEAL OF THE PRESIDENT OF THE UNITED STATES

NATIONAL AFFAIRS 1950-1960

Foremost political fact of decade was President Eisenhower's vast popularity, an almost unique phenomenon in U.S. history

POLITICALLY, the decade was an era in which, until the very end, the U.S. people never seemed quite able to make up their minds. But they did "like Ike."

They voted General of the Army Dwight D. Eisenhower, running as a Republican, into the Presidency in 1952 with 33.7 million votes, the largest number ever cast for any candidate. They increased that total to 35.6 million when he was re-elected in 1956.

His rival in both elections, Adlai Stevenson of Illinois, received 27.3 million in 1952, only 25.7 million in 1956.

Meanwhile, however, after giving him a Republican congress by only one-vote margins in both houses in 1952, they swung completely over to the Democrats, who won majorities in both houses in 1954, and kept on increasing them. When the voters went to the polls in November, 1960, the Democrats had nearly two-to-one majorities in both houses, and, however the voting went, they were assured of retaining control of the Senate.

Yet, at the same time, many political experts were convinced that, should he have wanted—or had been constitutionally able—to run again, President Eisenhower would have been re-elected once more, although with perhaps a greatly reduced plurality.

What was the explanation?

The attempt to provide one provided the psychologists, professional as well as amateur, with a field day.

But the consensus was that President Eisenhower moved into the White House already entrenched in the minds of the masses as a transcendent world hero, the victor of World War II, the man who knew more than any one else about defense, the man better equipped than any one else to deal with the increasingly recalcitrant Soviet leaders.

Add to this, said the experts, that he was also the perfect type of "father figure," one whose calm, friendly yet dignified public personality aroused almost instinctive trust and respect. In Eisenhower's hands, it seemed certain, the country was "safe."

Whatever the truth of such attempts at analysis, President Eisenhower's popularity was a self-evident fact, and, while undergoing some erosion recently, it remained the foremost political fact through both his terms of office.

MISSILE AGE DEEPENED DEFENSE DEBATE

It survived, undiminished, two sieges of illness which, in almost any other president, might have aroused serious debate on his physical fitness to continue to function under the great strains inherent in his demanding office.

It also survived long absences from the White House which, in another president, might have aroused fiercely hostile criticism.

In this it was helped by an almost universally friendly (and Republican) press, but this alone would not have been enough to preserve it largely undiminished.

President Eisenhower's vast popularity was, under all the circumstances, an almost unique phenomenon in U.S. history, and it was the result, at bottom, not of any synthetic campaign, but of his own character and talents—as the mass of the people saw them.

The Eisenhower popularity meant, politically, both a lot and, strangely, a little.

It meant that, in his struggles with a Democratic Congress he generally was able, not only to put over most of his own program, but to block what he considered excessive spending proposals. In this he was helped by the Democratic moderation both symbolized and imposed by Senate Majority Leader Lyndon B. Johnson and his fellow Texan, House Speaker Sam Rayburn.

It meant also that, when the chips were down and he finally decided to act, he won an easy victory over Sen. Joe McCarthy, despite the latter's own large popular following.

But the Eisenhower magic could not be transferred to other GOP candidates, even when he personally campaigned for them, as the Congressional elections showed.

So, too, the much talked of "Eisenhower Republicanism," of the early '50s dissolved into nothingness as the President himself seemed to be turning more and more to orthodox, budget-balancing conservatism.

The mantle of Republican liberalism was assumed, instead, by Nelson Rockefeller, who won the New York Governorship in an upset 1958 victory, and by 47-year-old Richard M. Nixon, Vice President in both terms.

In 1960 the Eisenhower era was over, whether Nixon or his even younger Democratic rival, John F. Kennedy, won the 1960 elections and moved into the White House.

PRESIDENTIAL PRESS CONFERENCE PLAYED POTENT ROLE IN KEEPING EISENHOWER ON FRONT PAGES, SUSTAINING WORLD POPULARITY

IKE'S CABINET and other advisors through much of the Administration were: (Clockwise from lower left). Pres. Asst. Wilton Persons; Amb. to UN Henry Cabot Lodge; Interior Sec. Fred Seaton; Treasury Sec. George Humphrey (succeeded by Robert Anderson); Vice Pres. Nixon; Atty. Gen. Herbert Brownell (succeeded by William Rogers); Commerce Sec. Sinclair Weeks (succeeded by Frederick Mueller); Welfare Sec. Marion Folsom (succeeded by Arthur Flemming); Civil Defense Administrator Val Peterson; Budget Director Percival Brundage (succeeded by Maurice Stans); Defense Mobilizer Gordon Gray; Labor Sec. James Mitchell; Postmaster Gen. Arthur Summerfield; Sec. of State John F. Dulles (succeeded by Christian Herter); the President; Defense Sec. Charles Wilson (succeeded by Neil McElroy, T. Gates); Agric. Sec. Ezra Benson; Sec. to Cabinet Maxwell Rabb; Asst. to the President Sherman Adams.

IKE STAYS ON TOP

Keeps upper hand despite own illnesses, Dulles' death, Democratic Congresses

PRESIDENT DWIGHT DAVID EISENHOWER closed out his term in the White House and looked back on eight years of international, domestic and even personal crises.

It was an Administration that inherited a war in Korea, that ran head on into an economic recession, that saw the President himself struck down by a heart attack and ileitis, that found itself dealing with larger and larger Democratic majorities in Congress, and that was touched by scandal.

But when the Eisenhower years ended, Republicans had found much to cheer about. The Korean war had ended, The nation had pulled out of the recession. The President had recovered his health. The Democratic majorities had not been too difficult to get along with.

This was the picture the Republicans painted, but the Democrats saw it differently. To their minds, the Eisenhower Administration ended at a time when U.S. prestige, wounded by a series of international incidents which included the failure of the 1960 summit conference, the capture of a confessed U.S. spy on a mission over the Soviet Union and repeated "firsts" by the Soviets in space, had sunk to a new low in world affairs.

The decade began with a bang, both literally and figuratively, for the man then in the White House, Harry S. Truman. The Korean War, creating enough sparks to start four World Wars, began on June 25, 1950. The President acted without delay. Within a week U.S. troops were on their way to the Asian country that was to cost 34,000 American lives.

As if this had not been enough to concern the President, he also had his troubles with Congress, particularly when investigations turned up a rash of irregularities by Federal employes in the Reconstruction Finance Corporation, the Internal Revenue Service and other agencies. Moreover, on Nov. 1, 1950, Puerto Rican fanatics tried to assassinate him.

Other notable '50s events in the Truman Administration included the first hydrogen bomb explosion Nov. 1, 1952 (not officially confirmed for more than a year), the official end of Marshall Plan economic aid, as such,

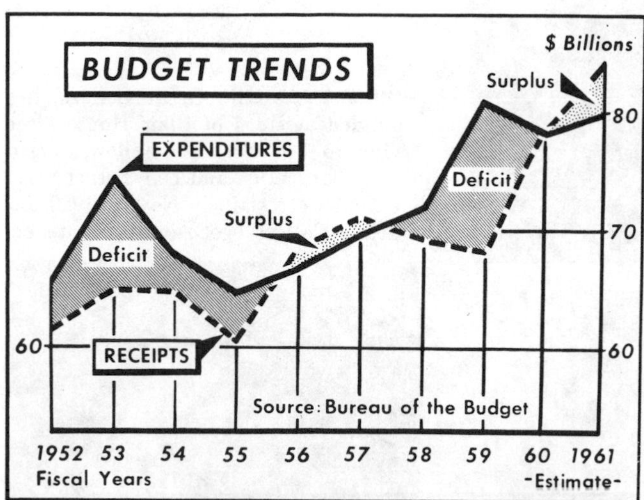

EARLY HOPES for a $60 billion budget faded when Eisenhower officials saw government expenses rise to record peacetime level of $80 billion. But the President managed a surplus; predicted one of $4.2 billion for the fiscal year of 1961.

with the Economic Cooperation Administration being replaced by the Mutual Security Agency, the firing of Gen. Douglas MacArthur as commander of U.S. and UN troops in Korea and his subsequent retirement and the seizure of the nation's steel mills, later held unconstitutional by the Supreme Court.

Although President Truman was himself exempted from the constitutional amendment that came into effect while he was in office limiting Presidents to two terms, he announced he would not run again.

When President Eisenhower took office in January, 1953, ending 20 Democratic years, he had his work cut out for him. While domestic affairs occupied much of his attention, he found the problems of the Cold War, of the Middle East, of Berlin, and of Latin America generally increasingly demanding.

Stalin died six weeks after President Eisenhower took office, and there was some hope that Soviet-U.S. relations would improve. For a while they did, but, by the time the President had completed his eight years at the nation's helm, relations had reached a low point, with Soviet Premier Khrushchev directing almost weekly attacks at the President.

The USSR scored a major victory in the world propaganda battle by launching the first man-made satellite, Sputnik I, Oct. 4, 1957. Democratic critics of the Administration's space and defense programs became increasingly vocal, and were not stilled when the Administration finally succeeded in matching the achievement by sending up the first U.S. satellite Jan. 31, 1958. The alleged "missile gap" became the battle cry of Administration critics.

The President also found it necessary to use Federal troops to enforce the Supreme Court anti-segregation decision. Faced by Arkansas Governor Orval Faubus' defiance of a Federal court, the President ordered paratroops to Little Rock to back the order to integrate the previously all-white Central High School.

The President was favored with only two years of Republican control of Congress, 1952 to 1954, and, as his term rolled on, the Democratic majorities in both the Senate and the House swelled. But, brandishing the power of veto and welcoming the spirit of compromise often exhibited by Democratic leaders, he managed to get most of what he wanted.

In 1959 the President lost the man he had relied upon most to run the Cold War struggle—Secretary of State John Foster Dulles. Together they had helped bring about a Korean truce in July, 1953; worked to end fighting in the fall of 1956 when Israel, France and Great Britain invaded Egypt after it had seized the Suez canal; decided to send troops to Lebanon in July, 1958, to avert overthrow of the pro-Western regime; and pressed forward to bring about a disarmament agreement with the USSR.

After Dulles' death, the President and his new Secretary of State, Christian A. Herter, found themselves preoccupied with the Soviet threat to turn over to Communist East Germany control over all communication lines to West Berlin. Also a grave problem was the capture by the Soviet Union of Frances G. Powers, whose U-2 reconnaissance plane was downed over the USSR.

TRUMAN'S ADVISORS included *(l. to r.)* W. Averell Harriman, who later became New York's Governor; George C. Marshall, then Defense Secretary; and Dean Acheson, Secretary of State. Truman had just returned from 1950 Wake Island conference with Gen. MacArthur.

WOULD-BE ASSASSIN, Oscar Collazo, lies wounded at steps of Blair House after trying to kill Truman. Fellow Puerto Rican Nationalist and U.S. Secret Service man were slain in Nov. 1, 1960, incident. Collazo got a life sentence.

GENERAL MACARTHUR, after being relieved of his command in the Far East on April 11, 1951, returned to Washington to address a joint session of Congress. The five-star general warned Congress against Communist appeasement, then said he would just "fade away." Senate inquiry found that MacArthur had failed to clear his policy statements through the Defense Dept.

HOOVER COMMISSION completed its series of proposals, after two years of study, on streamlining the government. The commission included (seated *l.* to *r.)*, James Farley, Joseph P. Kennedy, Herbert Hoover, Sen. McClellan, ex-Sen. Ferguson. 350 proposals were submitted by the group on methods of curbing expenditures. It estimated that waste cost U.S. $200 million yearly.

EISENHOWER'S GOLF brought the President many hours of relaxation but also much criticism from Democrats who complained that the Chief Executive spent too much time away from the White House. Eisenhower brushed off criticism. His favorite spots: Burning Tree Club in Washington, Augusta, Ga., and Newport, R.I. His score: about 90.

PRESS SECRETARY James A. Hagerty figured prominently in the operation of the government during presidential illnesses. He was, in effect, acting President for 48 hours when Eisenhower passed word after heart attack in 1955 in Denver for "Jim to take over."

MAJOR INQUIRIES by Congress during Eisenhower years included charges of favoritism in such regulatory agencies as the Federal Communications and Power Commissions. Drug investigation headed by Sen. Estes Kefauver (D.-Tenn.) turned up testimony that Dr. Harry Welch *(below)*, head of Food and Drug's Antibiotics Division, received $287,000 for outside activities on drug publications. He resigned after "conflict of interest" questions arose.

SHERMAN ADAMS, key Eisenhower aide in White House, resigned in 1958 following charges he intervened with federal agencies on behalf of a friend, Boston industrialist Bernard Goldfine. He had been regarded one of the most important of Administration officials.

VICE PRESIDENT NIXON met a hostile reception during his trip to Venezuela in May, 1958. Mobs attacked his car and smashed windows, showering Nixon with glass. Democrats saw in trip failure of Administration's policy toward Latin America. Republicans in turn blamed the Communists for the demonstrations. Nixon promised new look at our Latin American relations.

JOHN FOSTER DULLES served as President's chief advisor, representative to Congress, agent abroad in realm of foreign affairs. He served as Secretary of State for six years until his death from cancer on May 24, 1959. He travelled 560,000 miles as Secretary, including trips to see Tito *(l.)*, to meet South Korea's Pres. Rhee *(l., above)*, and to confer with Generalissimo Chiang Kai-shek on Formosa *(above)*. President Eisenhower mourned Dulles' death deeply. To fill the gap he began taking more good-will foreign trips himself.

VISITORS to Walter Reed Hospital where Secretary Dulles was confined during illness included President and Winston Churchill, nineteen days before Dulles' death. Despite controversy, Dulles was considered by all as strongest personality in Pres. Eisenhower's cabinet and the most vigorous.

CHRISTIAN A. HERTER succeeded Dulles as Secretary of State though handicapped by severe arthritis. Former Under-Secretary of State, Herter served out last two years of Eisenhower Administration at time when USSR stepped up anti-American attacks and serious problems arose with Cuba.

GOODWILL TRIPS by President highlighted last two years in office. In August, 1959, he went to Western Europe. In December, 20,000 mile trip took him to eleven nations in Europe, Middle East and Asia, including stopover at New Delhi, India *(l.)*. In February and March he traveled 16,000 miles touring Latin America. In June he traveled to Far East, including visit to Philippines where huge crowd greeted him at Manila airport *(above)*. President had scheduled trip to Moscow in June but Khrushchev withdrew invitation at summit meeting because of U-2 flight.

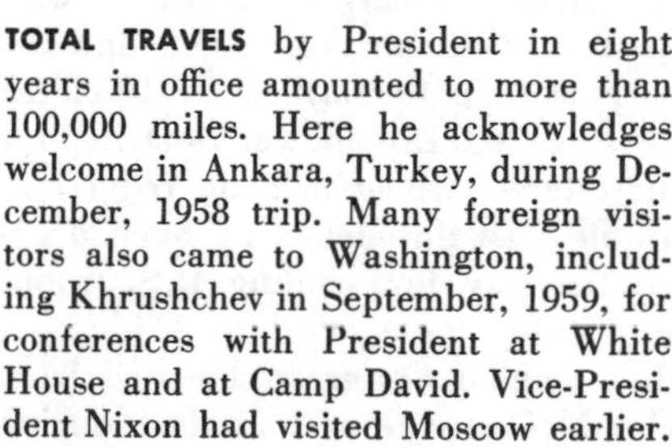

TOTAL TRAVELS by President in eight years in office amounted to more than 100,000 miles. Here he acknowledges welcome in Ankara, Turkey, during December, 1958 trip. Many foreign visitors also came to Washington, including Khrushchev in September, 1959, for conferences with President at White House and at Camp David. Vice-President Nixon had visited Moscow earlier.

COMPROMISE ON CAPITOL HILL

Congress, Administration, "muddle along" through most of the '50s

STATEHOOD finally came for Alaska in 1958 and Hawaii a year later. Alaska, where the good news was spread all over front pages in the new state *(above)*, proceeded to send all Democrats to Congress, E. L. Bartlett and Ernest Gruening to the Senate and Ralph Rivers to the House. Hawaii divided Senate representation, sending GOP's Hiram Fong and Democrats' Oren Long there and Dem. Daniel Inouye to the House. Kennedy and Nixon both stumped new states.

CONGRESS in mid-1960 found itself at a politically-charged, post-conventions session intent on doing something about raising the minimum wage, helping the aged pay the cost of high medical care, and aiding in school construction.

But both parties were even more intent on helping themselves in the national elections that followed.

Present were the two presidential nominees—Sen. John F. Kennedy for the Democrats and Vice President Richard M. Nixon for the Republicans, plus the Democratic Vice Presidential candidate, Sen. Lyndon B. Johnson. So were the national committee chairmen of both parties.

In domestic affairs, over the past 10 years, Congress found itself busy appropriating some $700 billion as the annual expenses of government rose from $40 billion in 1950 to $80 billion by 1960. It approved—among other things—the St. Lawrence Seaway project, authorized reorganization of the Defense Department, voted to give states title to submerged coastal lands, began a multi-billion dollar road building program, increased repeatedly the Federal limit on the national debt, voted a labor reform bill it hoped would keep racketeers out of the councils of union and management, passed the first comprehensive civil rights bill since the Reconstruction era, struggled with, but failed to solve the nation's farm problems, raised postal rates, and finally cleared the way for the addition of two new states—Alaska and Hawaii.

In the field of foreign affairs, Congress began the decade with the Korean war on its hands. But new concern came toward the end of the decade with the threat of possible Soviet superiority in missiles. The Soviet coup in sending the first satellite circling the earth stirred Congress into setting up a National Aeronautics and Space Administration, and into voting more money in many instances than the Administration had sought for the over-all defense budget.

The Senate approved security pacts with New Zealand, Australia, Japan and the Philippines. Greece and Turkey came into the North Atlantic Treaty Organization with Senate approval. The West German Agreement and the Japanese Peace Treaty were both ratified in 1952. In 1957 it approved the so-called Eisenhower Doctrine for the Middle East. This offered armed help on request to any nation in the Middle East threatened by outside aggression, and cleared the way for sending U.S. troops to Lebanon in 1958.

Much of the headlines about Congress stemmed from its investigations. The McCarthy era flourished during the two years of the decade the Republicans held majorities in Congress, from the elections in 1952 to those in 1954. The hearings on his dispute with the Army over whether he had applied pressures to get favors for his friend and assistant, draftee David Schine, took 36 days of testimony.

Other congressional investigations which made news were those in 1951 by Senator Estes Kefauver (D-Tenn.) into interstate crime; by the Senate Rackets Committee headed by Senator McClellan into labor racketeering; by the House Legislative Oversight Subcommittee into television quiz shows and the regulatory agencies, and by the Senate Anti-Trust Monopoly subcommittee into the high cost of drug prices.

Generally, until the end of the two Eisenhower terms, Administration relations were good. The Democratic majorities, firmly led by Johnson and by House Speaker Sam Rayburn, both Texans, largely "went along" with Administration proposals, permitting at least working compromises on many issues which were controversial.

SPEAKER SAM RAYBURN began his 47th year in the House March 4, 1959, for a new record surpassing that of Rep. Joseph Cannon, Ill. He also held the record for the most years as Speaker.

JOSEPH MARTIN JR. *(r.)* stepped down in Jan. 1959 after 20 years as House GOP leader. Victor in the unexpected revolt was Charles A. Halleck *(left)*.

SENATE LEADERS open 1956 session. Two left Senate before decade ended; Walter F. George (Dem., Ga.), former Foreign Relations chairman *(l.)*, died, and Wm. F. Knowland *(r.)*, (R-Calif.), Senate GOP leader, left to run for Calif. Governor. Between them are Harry Byrd (D-Va.), Senate Democrat leader Lyndon Johnson (D-Tex.), and Vice President Nixon.

McCARTHY HEARINGS in 1954 attracted a nationwide television audience when the Wisconsin senator sought to refute Army charges that he tried to win favored treatment for his aide, David Schine. A dramatic moment came when former Sen Flanders (R-Vt.) handed McCarthy *(above)* notice that he would make a speech against him in the Senate. Senator McCarthy *(below)* inadvertently catches his favorite target, Secretary Dean Acheson, on the Senate elevator.

McCARTHY OPPONENTS included Army Special Counsel Joseph Welch *(above)* master showman who livened proceedings with sardonic humor and later became a performer on television and screen. Sen. William Benton (D-Conn.) *(below)* submitted evidence to Rules Committee that McCarthy had been deliberately deceptive and introduced a resolution to expel him from the Senate. McCarthy was later condemned for his activities by the Senate. He died May 2, 1957, at Bethesda Naval Hospital.

CONSERVATIVE Southern Democrats who often teamed with Republicans to uphold Administration were *(l. to r.)* Senators Spessard Holland (Fla.) Walter George (Ga.), Harry Byrd (Va.), Allen Ellender (La.) and A. W. Robertson (Va.), shown after helping beat the 1955 Democratic tax cut bill.

IMMIGRATION was a specialty of the late Senator Pat McCarran (D-Nev.) when he was in the Senate. He co-sponsored a basic revision of the law with Rep. Francis E. Walter (D-Pa.). The law known as the McCarran-Walter Act, has often been called too restrictive.

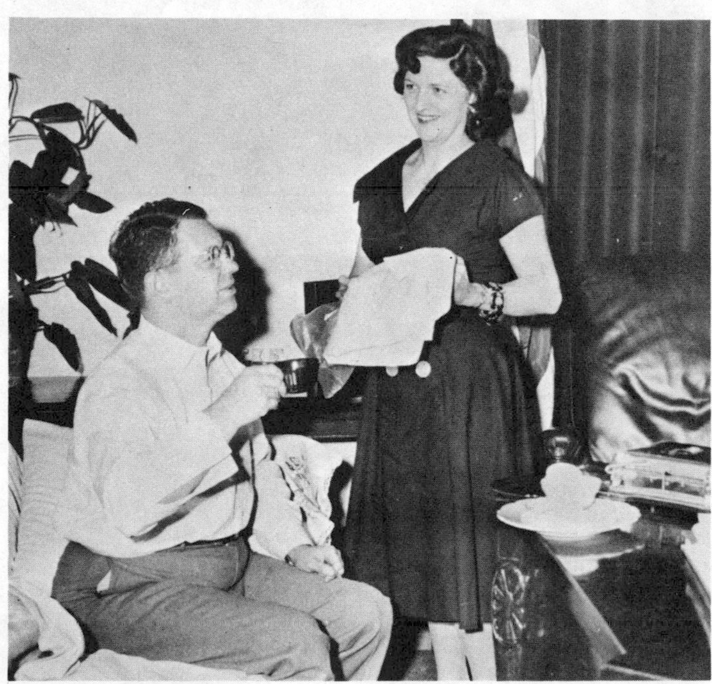

CIVIL RIGHTS legislation stirred controversy in virtually every legislative session of the decade. The first civil rights act of major importance since the Reconstruction era was passed in 1957, setting up a Federal Commission on Civil Rights. Hotly-disputed during the debate was a controversial jury-trial amendment. Among senators who voted for the successful amendment in photo to the left were *(l. to r.);* Senators Frank Church (D-Ida.), Joseph O'Mahoney (D-Wyo.), Lyndon Johnson (D-Tex.), Richard Russell (D-Ga.) and Estes Kefauver (D-Tenn.). Voting rights bill in 1960 brought round-the-clock session before passage. Sen. Vance Hartke (D-Ind.) spent night *(above)* on the couch during the filibuster.

GUNFIRE IN CONGRESS March 1, 1954, from three Puerto Rican nationalists wounded Representatives B. F. Jensen of Ia. (A); Kenneth Roberts, Ala. (B); George Fallon, Md. (C); Alvin Bentley, Mich. (D); Clifford Davis, Tenn.

HIGHWAY CONSTRUCTION program got under way after 1958 Congress authorized $1.8 billion highway bill. However, program ran into serious financing obstacles later and Congress considered ways to raise the necessary revenues.

PACKING PAYROLLS with relatives by Congressmen created a storm in 1959. Mrs. Randall Harmon ran her Congressman husband's office from her front porch and got $100 rent and $344 per mo. salary. Members defended such practices.

SEN. RICHARD NEUBERGER died in 1960 at the age of 47. The Oregon Democrat fought for civil rights, removal of highway billboards, funds for cancer research, and for bringing Congress under "conflict of interest" laws. He was a vigorous and forthright liberal.

ADVOCATE for the peaceful uses of atomic energy, Sen. Brien McMahon sponsored in 1946 the law establishing the Atomic Energy Commission. He also served as chairman of the Special Committee on Atomic Energy. The Connecticut Democrat died on July 8, 1952.

"MISTER REPUBLICAN" was title given to late Sen. Robert A. Taft (R-Ohio) whose bid for the Presidency failed when the GOP convention in 1952 selected Eisenhower. Later, he campaigned for Eisenhower and supported his programs.

SEN. JOHN W. BRICKER *(l.)* stirred a controversy in 1954 by sponsoring a constitutional amendment to limit the treaty-making powers of the President. Former Republican Governor of Ohio, he was defeated in a bid for re-election to the Senate in 1958 by Democrat Stephen M. Young in a surprise victory.

SEN. ARTHUR H. VANDENBERG (R-Mich.) played key role in the Senate as architect of so-called "bipartisan" foreign policy. A sponsor of the Marshall Plan, he served as chairman of the Foreign Relations Committee after Republican party gained Senate control in the '46 elections. He died on April 18, 1951.

CLOSEST ELECTION in U.S. history was the 1960 race of Sen. John F. Kennedy (l. with his wife) and Vice Pres. Richard M. Nixon (shown above during campaign). Out of a total of 68.8 million votes, Kennedy won by a margin of 119,450.

NATION SPLITS BALLOTS

Eisenhower twice wins Presidency; Democrats' Congress margin swells

IT WAS the Eisenhower era in politics.

Not since the late Franklin D. Roosevelt had any one man so dominated the scene yet, unlike Roosevelt, Dwight D. Eisenhower was unable to extend this popularity to other members of his party.

This emergence of Eisenhower as a political figure had its ironic touches. He rose to fame under two Democratic presidents, Roosevelt and Harry S. Truman, but ran as a Republican. More ironic was an abortive attempt by the Democrats to run Ike on their ticket in 1948 elections.

REPUBLICAN NOMINEES for the presidency and the vice-presidency in 1960 were Richard M. Nixon *(l.)* and Henry Cabot Lodge, shown responding to an ovation at the Republican convention in Chicago. Nixon intended to rely heavily on his 7½ years experience as vice-president to help swing election.

STANDARD BEARERS Sen. John F. Kennedy and Senate majority leader, Lyndon B. Johnson, were named the Democratic Party's candidates for the same office in a turbulent convention in Los Angeles which ended on a surprising harmony note after Johnson accepted second place on the ticket.

FRIEND OR FOE was what Nixon had to find out from N. Y. Gov. Nelson Rockefeller *(r.)*, when two breakfasted in Oct. '58 to end reports they were at odds. Again in 1960 Nixon had to make a secret flight to New York during GOP convention to iron out platform differences with the New York governor. Old Guard accused Nixon of "selling out" to liberals.

"DARK HORSE" left at post was Missouri's Sen. Stuart Symington, who hoped for Democratic nomination if delegates deadlocked between Kennedy, Johnson.

SMILING HUBERT HUMPHREY, apparently undismayed by crushing defeat in crucial West Virginia primary, makes friendly point to elated victor Kennedy at latter's campaign headquarters. Kennedy triumph over Minnesota senator in predominantly Protestant West Virginia, on heels of Wisconsin victory, helped clinch nomination.

TWICE PRESIDENTIAL NOMINEE Adlai E Stevenson *(l.)* arrives at the Los Angeles Democratic Convention in 1960 where his followers hoped to pull the same trick again. They failed, partly because Stevenson never openly announced he wanted nomination. Darling of the GOP conservatives was Arizona's Sen. Barry Goldwater *(r.)*, who became the spokesman for the party's Old Guard, inheriting emotional mantle that once had encircled late Sen. Robert A. Taft, long considered its leader.

CAMPAIGN REMINISCENCES were indulged in by President Eisenhower and Adlai Stevenson when they met at a White House lunch in 1953. Ike took all but 9 of the 48 states' electoral votes in breaking the 20-year hold of Democrats.

GLUM LOSER Sen. Taft (Ohio) waved morosely for cameramen after losing 1952 GOP Presidential nomination to Eisenhower. Taft actually lost nomination in Credentials Committee fight over the seating of contested Ike-Taft delegates.

Sen. Robert A. Taft of Ohio, known as "Mr. Republican," was Eisenhower's chief opponent for the 1952 nomination. But apparent control of the convention machinery was Taft's downfall when the Credentials Committee sought to prevent the seating of certain pro-Ike delegations, forcing a floor fight. In an emotion-packed session, the convention voted in favor of Eisenhower and, in effect, he won the nomination at this point.

Nominated as his running mate was a young freshman Senator from California, Richard M. Nixon.

A new national figure emerged from the Democratic convention, too—Adlai E. Stevenson, governor of Illinois, who won the nomination from leading contender Sen. Estes Kefauver.

The Democrats sought to smooth over a split with Southern delegates over civil and states rights by nominating for the Vice President Sen. John Sparkman (Ala.), but it was to no avail.

Ike swept the election, even making inroads in the "Solid South," and captured all but nine of the 48 states. He was aided by such Democrats as the governors of Texas and S. Carolina, who openly campaigned for him.

Additionally, he was backed by 80% of the press. Two great emotional issues were alleged Communism in the Government, which had been successfully exploited by Sen. Joseph McCarthy (Wis.), and the Korean War. Eisenhower promised to go to Korea, if elected, implying he would end the war there.

A different story was the Congressional contests, which left the GOP in control by a two-vote margin. Among the defeated was Henry Cabot Lodge, Ike's campaign manager. His successor was boyish-looking, 35-year-old John F. Kennedy of Massachusetts. The death of Sen. Taft in 1953 further upset Republican plans for effective Senate control.

The Democrats captured Congress, winning the House by 29 seats and the Senate by one, in the off-year elections of 1954. But what made the Republicans despair even more was Eisenhower's heart attack in September, 1955. This was followed by an operation for ileitis, an intestinal malady, in June of the following year.

RELUCTANT CANDIDATE Adlai Stevenson, then governor of Illinois, was named Democrats' 1952 Presidential candidate along with running mate Sen. John Sparkman (Ala.). Despite polls predicting close race, he lost by 6 million votes.

FIVE-WAY HANDSHAKE demonstrating party solidarity was given by Veep nominee Sen. Estes Kefauver, Gov. Averill Harriman, ex-President Truman, Sen. Johnson, Presidential nominee Stevenson at Democrats' 1956 Chicago convention.

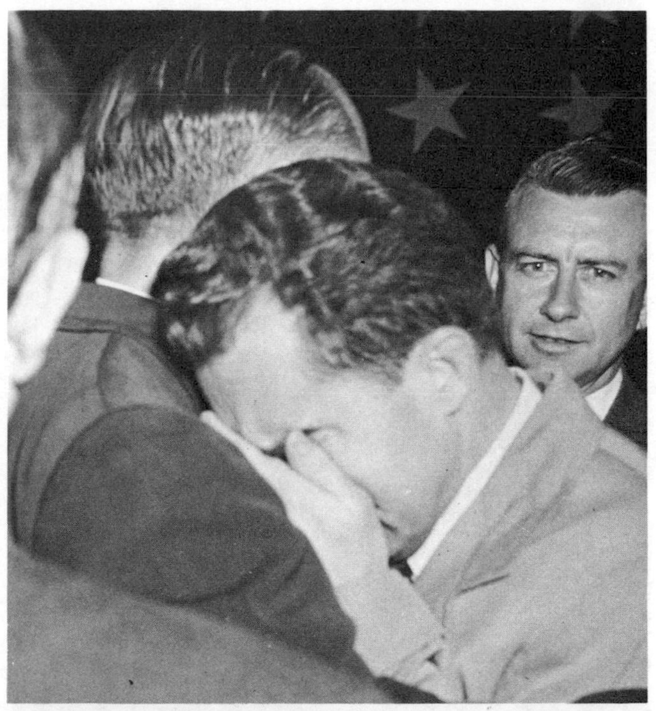

EMOTIONAL HIGHPOINT of 1952 campaign was Vice-Presidential candidate Nixon taking to national radio, TV networks to vindicate self against Democratic charges of fraud because of $18,000 fund raised by friends for personal use. Gift of dog "Checkers" figured prominently in his rebuttal.

Despite this he was renominated for the Presidency, along with Vice-President Nixon, while the Democrats again named the urbane and witty Stevenson and, as his running mate, Senator Kefauver.

Eisenhower was re-elected with the largest vote ever received by a Republican candidate and the highest in U.S. history, polling 57 per cent of the popular vote and again breaking the "Solid South," carrying every state but seven. His plurality, however, did not reach Roosevelt's record-breaking 11 million in 1936.

Again the Eisenhower charm failed to rub off on other GOP candidates and Ike found himself the first President-elect since 1848 to face opposition control of both Senate and House of Representatives. Some ascribed the defeat of Stevenson to the eruption of the Suez Canal crisis, which weakened his campaign appeal for ending conscription and hydrogen-bomb testing.

Following the death on May 24, 1959, of John Foster Dulles, Secretary of State since Eisenhower's administration began, and in the wake of the retirement of his own administrative aide, Sherman Adams, amid charges of scandal, Ike began to take personal control of affairs.

He invited Nikita Khrushchev to visit the U.S., which the Soviet premier did, made a 11-nation tour of three continents, and accepted an invitation to visit the USSR. This was withdrawn following the collapse of the Summit conference in Paris in May, 1960, when Eisenhower became the target of invective from Khrushchev, the like of which was unparalleled in modern diplomacy. Then a proposed trip to Japan had to be cancelled because of riots there over a new U.S.-Japan military treaty.

Domestically the decade was marked by the admission of Alaska and Hawaii as the 49th and 50th states and the seating of their first Senators and Representatives in '59.

Eager to take the spotlight were two young men—Sen. Kennedy and Vice-President Nixon—who were 43 and 47 years old respectively in 1960.

Each was his party's nominee for the Presidency and each was noted for his political acuity and cool and calculating manner. Both their running mates—Democratic Majority Leader Sen. Lyndon B. Johnson and U.S. Chief Delegate to the U.N., Henry Cabot Lodge—were older.

Indeed, it looked as if the next political era would be that of "the cool young men" who seemed to have more the look of management than they did of politics.

'I LIKE IKE' Eisenhower's supporters screamed at Chicago convention in 1952, echoing it in blinking, portable neon sign *(foreground)* and it soon became campaign slogan, with a strong emotional appeal transcending any and all issues.

BACK AGAIN for a second four years, "Ike and Mamie" acknowledged election-night cheers with "Dick and Pat" Nixon. Though victory over Stevenson was even more decisive, Republicans lost control of Congress to the Democrats.

TICKET SPLITTING helped former mayor of Philadelphia, Joseph Clark, to beat incumbent Sen. James Duff, an original Ike backer, in 1956 elections, though Pennsylvania was carried by Ike by big plurality. Democrat Clark went on to become an outstanding champion of civil rights legislation in Senate.

THREE RUSSIAN OBSERVERS, (top *l.*), study U.S. politics, got first-hand information at 1956 Eisenhower campaign headquarters in Washington, D. C. but no one expected L. N. Solevyev, M. I. Rubenstein and V. L. Kudryavtsev to work any changes in the election methods of the Soviet Union.

NEW STAR on political horizon was millionaire Nelson A. Rockefeller (l.) who wrested GOP New York gubernatorial nomination from Leonard Hall, former national chairman, and went on to win governorship in 1958. He antagonized party leaders by criticizing many of Eisenhower's policies.

WISCONSIN DEMOCRATS' first Senate victory in 25 years was won by William E. Proxmire (*above* with wife) when he overwhelmed ex-governor Walter J. Kohler in race to fill late Sen. Joe McCarthy's unexpired term. Proxmire was the absolute antithesis of his headline-hunting predecessor.

LABOR LEADERS George Meany (*l.*), AFL-CIO president, and Walter Reuther, head of United Auto Workers and AFL-CIO vice president, continued to be potent behind-the-scene factor in Democratic politics, but operated less openly than before to forestall "labor dominated" tag against their favorites.

NEW LOOK in California politics occurred when Edmund G. (Pat) Brown was elected governor in 1958 in clear-cut decision for Democrats after elimination of state's cross-filing law which had allowed candidates to file in both primaries. It was first time Democrats entered full slate.

AS MAINE GOES so would the rest of the nation—maybe—Democrats thought after normally rock-ribbed Republican state elected Edmund S. Muskie *(hands raised)* first Democratic governor in 20 years in 1954. It was part of off-year elections where Republicans lost the House and Senate.

DUAL VICTORY was scored in Oregon by Democrats when Richard Neuberger *(r.)*, a free lance writer and conservationist, became the first Democratic U.S. Senator in 40 years in 1954 and Republican Sen. Wayne Morse *(l.)* re-registered as a Democrat, later was re-elected under new party label.

PARTY SPLIT in New York lined Tammany Boss Carmine De Sapio *(above l.)* against Gov. Harriman in fight over 1958 U.S. Senatorial candidate. De Sapio won, but his nominee lost election, leaving Democrats badly divided in key state just before the crucial 1960 Presidential campaign.

THROUGHOUT FIFTIES, Democrats kept on increasing their margins in both houses of Congress, although the Republicans twice captured the Presidency by enormous majorities. Usual explanation was that nation's voters preferred Democrats as a party, but "liked Ike" as White House's occupant.

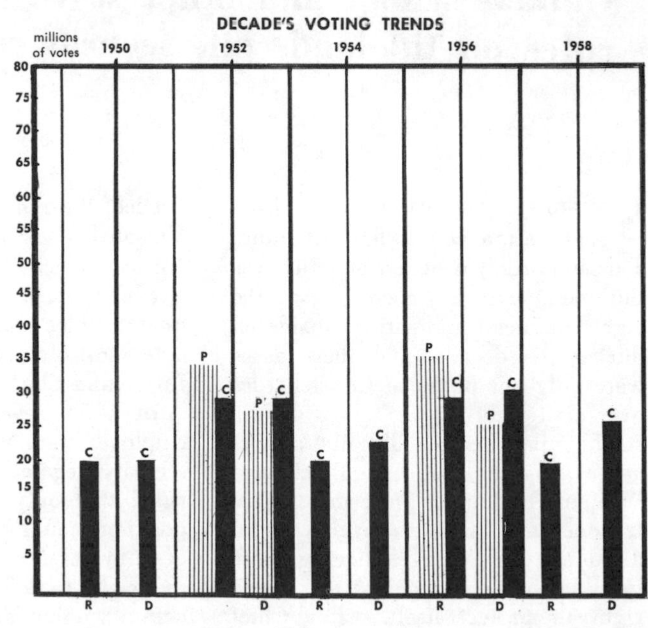

JUSTICES OF THE U.S. SUPREME COURT ARE (seated l. to r.) WILLIAM O. DOUGLAS, HUGO L. BLACK, CHIEF JUSTICE EARL WARREN, FELIX FRANKFURTER, TOM CLARK. (Standing) CHARLES WHITTAKER, JOHN M. HARLAN, WILLIAM J. BRENNAN, POTTER STEWART.

HIGH COURT MAKES HISTORY

Outlaws school and other segregation in far-reaching decisions; also rules on tidelands oil, security regulations, Congressional committees

SAY "SUPREME COURT" and school desegregation comes first to mind. This important decision actually was but one of many cases concerning the rights of racial minorities considered during the decade, and these cases were only one phase of Court battles over civil rights.

The nine Justices did not always agree. Justices Hugo L. Black and William O. Douglas were most deeply concerned about the rights of individuals, the others believing these must be balanced against the state's right to protect itself. After Chief Justice Warren succeeded Fred M. Vinson in 1953, he often voted with Justices Black and Douglas. Justice Brennan, appointed in 1956, also frequently sided with them. On the other side, most often, were Justices Frankfurter and Clark.

In 1956, several million Federal employes were removed from under security regulations when the court ruled that only those in "sensitive" positions could be dismissed because of subversive associations. In 1957, the right to advocate revolutionary action without any attempt to incite it was upheld, and the court ruled that a contempt citation was invalid when questions were asked outside the scope of the inquiry, as prescribed in the Congressional resolution creating the committee.

In 1958, laws requiring state and city officials and employes, and also officers of trade unions, to sign loyalty oaths were upheld, but a law requiring persons and organizations to sign such an oath to qualify for tax exemption was not. It was decided that citizens cannot be denied passport for foreign travel because of their beliefs and associations, but the court refused to upset the ruling of a California court dismissing the complaint of movie writers unable to get work because they declined to answer questions during a Congressional investigation, citing the 1st and 5th Constitutional Amendments.

The right of a discharged soldier to a jury trial instead of a court martial, when accused of a crime during service, was affirmed, as was the same right of civilian employes and the families of service men stationed abroad, except in cases where the accused came under the jurisdiction of foreign courts.

Close decisions—often five to four—were common in loyalty and contempt cases, but all nine Justices agreed in the public school desegregation decision, May 17, 1954, and in the 1955 definition of reasonable promptness in complying. Segregation in public recreation facilities such as swimming pools and golf courses also was prohibited.

In 1956, the Supreme Court upheld a Federal Court decision that segregation in any tax-supported colleges and universities also was illegal. (The '60 "sit-down protests" against lunch room and restaurant segregation were carried on chiefly by students.)

In spite of "double jeopardy" rulings, it was decided that a person can be tried in a Federal and a State court for the same crime; that "unreasonable searches" do not include routine health inspections made without a court warrant; and that a murder confession obtained by a psychiatrist through hypnotism was a violation of "due process" (1954).

The decision granting tideland rights extending 10 nautical miles offshore to Texas and Florida for historical reasons, while establishing a three mile limit for Louisiana and other Gulf states (1960), the ruling against secondary boycotts (1951) and a new definition of head of a household for taxation purposes, including unmarried men and women who were the chief support of family groups, were other major decisions.

A ruling that professional football was an interstate business and not a sport reversed an earlier decision and made the leagues subject to the Sherman Anti-Trust Act.

CHIEF JUSTICE Fred M. Vinson *(left)* former Kentucky Congressman, Federal Judge, Economic Stabilization Director, served from 1943 until his death in 1953. He was succeeded by Earl Warren *(right)*, former Alameda Cy. D. A., Attorney General and three-term Governor of California, 1948 Republican vice-presidential candidate.

EXULTING LAWYERS congratulating themselves after Supreme Court outlawed segregation in public schools are *(above, l. to r.)* George E. C. Hayes, Thurgood Marshall and James M. Nabrit. Legal champions of losing side were *(below, l. to r.)* J. Lindsay Almond, then Virginia Attorney General and later governor, John W. Davis, the 1924 Dem. Presidential candidate against Pres. Coolidge, and T. Justin Moore.

NEWEST HOPE of the Strategic Air Command was the B-58 Hustler. Capable of twice the speed of sound for short distances with nuclear bombs aboard, the first squadron of Hustlers began training in March, 1960. While the development of a nuclear-powered bomber and the tri-sonic B-70 remained in doubt, the B-58 might become the last and fastest.

DECADE OF DILEMMA

Progress in missiles strains defense budgets, outruns ability to defend nation against them, forces cutbacks in other arms

THE '50s were hardly six months old when the headlines screamed the news, from Korea, of the first air battles in history between jet planes.

At decade's end headlines spoke of long-range missiles —and of the junking of plans for new aircraft. Missiles had forced reorganization of military forces (as had, too, the Eisenhower Administration's insistence on a $40 billion annual defense budget ceiling).

The U.S. in 1951 saw its first peace-time Universal Military Training law and also the establishment of the Central Intelligence Agency—which was to play a bigger part in the nation during the next 10 years than UMT.

Aircraft production rose in 1952 as jets and helicopters, in Korea, helped alter basic tactics. The Navy, finally, was able to begin construction of its first $20 million super carrier.

In 1953, President Eisenhower named Charles E. Wilson, of General Motors, Defense Secretary. At the same time, Congress focused publicity on the fact that small business had been getting only 14% of defense contracts.

That same year, Congress approved reorganization of the Defense Department to accelerate service unification. Thule air base was completed on the northern tip of Greenland. The Army tested an atomic cannon, but missiles were making it an obsolete item even then.

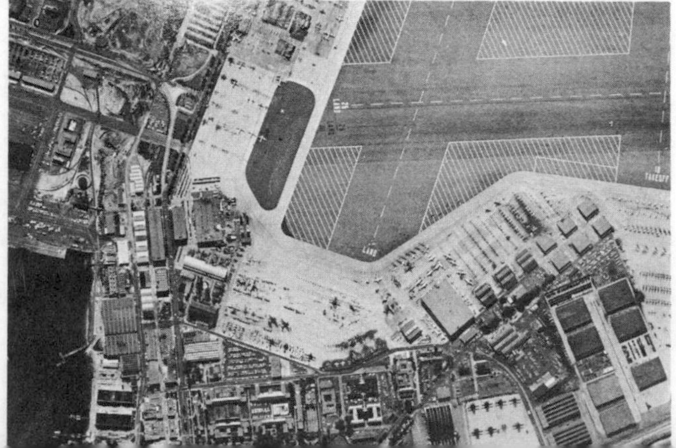

AERIAL RECONNAISSANCE from 70,000 feet is incredibly sharp, President Eisenhower demonstrated to a TV audience, using this shot of San Diego air base. The sharp camera eye was disclosed to be free world's newest defense weapon. The parallel lines clearly visible are 25″ wide; it was said the camera could discern 6″ lines. The U.S. U-2 "spy" plane shot down by Russia on May Day, 1960, was said to carry one.

By 1954, not only the U.S. but the USSR had exploded hydrogen bombs, and a new "defense posture" was called for. It placed new emphasis on air power—the Strategic Air Command became the tool of "massive retaliation"—and stressed new weapons, less manpower and over-all economies. In the same year, the Navy launched the first atom-powered submarine, the *Nautilus,* the Army announced its Corporal guided missile, and the Air Force admitted reporters to Cape Canaveral (for the first time) to disclose its Matador.

The $136 million Air Force Academy opened in 1955. The first "Texas Tower" off-shore radar warning station was constructed. The Seventh Fleet showed its strength in the Formosa Strait, and perhaps deterred the Red Chinese from war.

The Defense Department cut its manpower total, in 1956, to 2.8 million (by 1960 it was down to 2.5 million). Congress refused to appropriate $12 billion for bomb shelters. Unification of all services remained a distant goal.

Expensive radar networks, including the Distant Early Warning (DEW) system, were stretched across the North American Arctic against the threat of Soviet bombers. Meanwhile, engineers drove ahead to perfect an Intercontinental Ballistic Missile, only to learn, in 1957, the USSR already had one.

In 1958 the Army set up six newly streamlined divisions into a Strategic Army Command, ready to cope with small "brush fire" wars anywhere the Air Force could fly it. The Air Force set up its own Composite Air Strike Force, counterpart of STRAC. In July, both, with the Navy's Sixth Fleet, helped prevent an anti-West coup in Lebanon.

That same summer the *Nautilus* crossed the Arctic Ocean beneath the ice from Alaska to Greenland—a demonstration to the USSR that its Arctic coasts were vulnerable.

But it was not until late in 1959 that the first U.S. ICBMs, the intercontinental Atlases, were ready for their launching pads.

Anti-missile defenses, meanwhile, were being rushed. A ballistic missile early warning station was established at Thule, and two more were to follow elsewhere. The Midas detection satellite project was advancing, as was the improved, anti-missile Nike-Zeus missile. But these were no ground for optimism; missile attack seemed virtually unstoppable.

Successful firing of the intermediate range Polaris from a submerged atomic submarine gave the U.S. movable, almost undetectable and thus invulnerable bases which brought almost all the USSR in range. (It also led to Navy-Air Force controversy over control of such strategic weapons.)

Missile advance caused cancellation of F-108 fighter plane programs and cutback of schedules for the mighty B-70 bomber. In compensation, the Air Force was given a top role in missile planning.

The decade ended, in the opinion of many experts, with the nation's defense (like those of all the rest of the world) weaker than at its beginning, despite brilliant technical and research advances. Some blamed over emphasis on budgets. But the primary reason, there seemed little doubt, was scientific advance—man could make, and was making, weapons he could not guard himself against.

TITAN MISSILE was slimmer, more sophisticated intercontinental missile than the Atlas, equally capable of carrying a nuclear warhead many thousand miles. The 270 Titans and Atlases ordered by Congress by 1963 would retire as soon as Defense could put the Minuteman—second generation missile—in service. Minutemen would be solid-fueled, easier to handle, protected underground, elusive on railroad cars.

ELUSIVE RETALIATION is contained in new atomic-powered submarines capable of launching Polaris missiles while submerged. Two tests, three hours apart, in summer 1960, showed Polaris virtually ready to counter Soviet threats. Mobile targets, the subs are nearly invulnerable to attack.

NEW SUPER CARRIERS are one-fifth of a mile long, a block wide, cost $200 million or more. They can hold the enormous loads of jet fuel and weapons to support six squadrons—including bombers big enough to carry nuclear weapons. Carriers nearly went down for the count when Congress at first thought they made easy targets. During the Korean War, Congress saw future need for super carriers, approved six, the last to be the nuclear powered *Enterprise. USS Forrestal* was first in 1954; pictured at left is *Saratoga*, second.

NATO FORCES became strongest under Gen. Alfred Gruenther. Their ability to delay and counter-attack Soviet advances became less certain as missiles joined the arsenals and France pulled out forces to fight in Algeria, while insisting U.S. planes with A-bombs move off French soil. West Germans began reinforcing NATO with authorized divisions after 1957. U.S. A-bombs and planes moved into W. Germany.

SIXTH FLEET remained strong, while the Navy sent many ships into mothballs. In the Mediterranean, its ships showed up to influence the Suez settlement in 1956, to land troops on Lebanon in 1958 and, discreetly, to "show the flag" where European, African and Middle East nations would note. The Seventh Fleet carried out similar chores in East Asia, softening at least two Red Chinese threats on Nationalist Chinese islands. In 1960, both gained carriers.

NATO MISSILES included the U.S. Army's Honest John. In 1959 Italian trainees learned to operate them. Missiles aided NATO forces' modernization and ability to fight limited wars. Tactical missiles force enemy to disperse troops, help wipe out small concentrations.

MOBILE WARFARE included atomic cannon *(above)* which was the first weapon to give atomic punch to ground forces. Missiles later replaced them. Army divisions were reorganized in "pentomic" form which made everything mobile. Marines *(below)* likewise utilized helicopters in fast-moving amphibious warfare which works on the principle of vertical envelopment of the enemy and his territory. Helicopter companies were attached to Army pentomic divisions. Missile firing units were already in Europe and Asia, in position to support Free World forces or reinforce policy during crises.

NORTH POLE was visited for third time by a U.S. nuclear submarine on Feb. 9, 1960. Here, the *Sargo* surfaces through the ice. Gathering oceanographic data as they cross and re-cross the Arctic Ocean under ice, these submarines also demonstrated that any point in the USSR could be reached by missiles.

ARMY MISSILES were limited to 200-mile ranges at first, and later to 10,000 pound maximum weights. This 1955 exhibit of first Army missiles shows their versatility. Honest John, *(l.)*, is an artillery missile of medium to long range. Nike *(center)* is a high-speed destroyer of enemy bomber and fighter planes; Ajax version was succeeded by longer-range Hercules, and anti-missile Zeus was under development. Corporal *(r.)* is a long-range surface missile. All can carry nuclear or conventional warheads. Pershing would succeed the Honest John, and Sergeant would succeed Corporal.

CIVIL DEFENSE TEST cleared Times Square, one of New York City's busiest intersections, almost completely in July, 1956. Civilians cooperated in tests, but were apathetic about spending money for shelters against bombs or radioactive fallout. Congress refused Eisenhower request for $12 billion shelter funds in mid-'50s; NY in 1960 had to reduce state program.

TOUGH MARINE TRAINING came under fire in 1956 when six recruits lost their lives on training march under Sgt. Matthew McKeon. This was the scene at Parris Island camp investigated by tribunal. Training was softened, as a result, and hazing eliminated. But many Marines and ex-Marines questioned whether eased training would produce the kind of men demanded for missions.

DEFENSE BUDGET was a subject of constant controversy. Post-Korean War budgets rose from $31.8 billion to $40 billion where they were stabilized for at least two years. Congressmen Howard Smith (D-Va.) *(l.)*, and John Tabor (Rep.-NY) symbolized their intent with budget and scissors in 1957. Rockefeller Foundation report stated the nation could afford — and needed — expenditure of $5 billion more.

JOINT CHIEFS OF STAFF grew stronger with each reorganization, as the nation sought to get true unification and good defense posture. Leaders in 1959-60 were *(from left)*: Army Gen. Lyman Lemnitzer; Navy Adm. Arleigh Burke; Gen. Nathan Twining (Air Force), chairman; Air Force Gen. Thomas White; and Marine Gen. Randolph Pate, who later went into retirement.

ARMY DISSENT to reductions of forces and funds, as well as criticism of its potency, was voiced by Army Sec. Wilber Brucker and Gen. Maxwell Taylor, chief of staff in 1956. Taylor was one of several Army generals who retired promptly, or early, as a form of protest against limitations on manpower, modernization funds, and ranges of missiles.

NUCLEAR SUB ADVOCATE had been Hyman Rickover. When the public learned he had been passed over for promotion to rear admiral, they successfully championed him with their congressmen. As a vice admiral, Rickover continued his fight for more nuclear submarines, and outspokenly pleaded for scientific education, more home discipline for children.

1950s: BOOM WITHOUT BUST

As decade ended GNP passed $500 billion annual rate. Despite temporary setbacks, such as '58 slump, '59 steel strike, '50s saw almost constant rise in production, individual incomes, consumer spending, price of stocks.

ECONOMICALLY, in the 50s, the U.S. experienced the greatest quantitative growth on record, and it was accompanied by a mass prosperity unprecedented in all history.

Gross National Product (total of all goods and services) jumped from $329 billion in 1951 to an estimated $505 billion in 1960.

Significantly, while the GNP was increasing 53%, the consumer price index rose only 13%, demonstrating that this prosperity was not merely on paper and mostly the result of inflation, but had a solid, three-dimensional reality, as anyone who looked around himself in mid-1960 was bound to realize.

At decade's end, however, there were some scattered storm warnings.

Unemployment hung doggedly at close to 5 million, and scattered areas throughout the U.S. were being hit, proportionately, much harder. (This seemed, however, one of the growing pains accompanying the increasing—if still rather slow—shift to mechanization and automation. But this was callous comfort for the miner or textile worker without a job.)

The national growth rate, largely because of complacency-induced reluctance to rationalize production and operating methods, or to plow back a larger share of profits, was lagging behind that of Western Europe, Japan and the USSR. (But, in 1960, both major Presidential candidates were pledged to stimulate it.)

In addition, as the decade progressed, the U.S. seemed to be pricing itself out of world markets, principally because of high unit production costs. (High wages were usually blamed, but obsolescent methods and equipment also seemed guilty.) Many U.S. firms were moving production, especially for foreign markets, abroad. Total private U.S. investment in foreign countries jumped from less than $15 billion to well over $40 billion. (At least one-third was in Canada, the result of the inextricable economic interdependence of the two neighbors.) While most of this was a healthy expansion which served to bolster the Free World, at least a portion had alarming implications for U.S. producers.

And foreign-made goods, for example Japanese radios and European automobiles, were winning a larger and larger share of the U.S. domestic market.

The European small car challenge was one which Detroit, after much soul-searching (and further spurred by the meteoric rise of the Rambler, which made American Motors one of the decade's great corporate success stories), decided to meet head on. By the late '50s, General Motors, Ford and Chrysler all were successfully producing and marketing "compact cars."

The decade saw stocks on the major exchanges reach the highest price levels on record. (The Dow-Jones industrial average, in early 1960, passed 685.) It also saw the entire monetary and credit system function with unparalleled smoothness, thanks to the alternate checks and stimuli applied by the Federal Reserve and other independently functioning government financial agencies. Despite constant alarmist talk, there was no runaway inflation, no stock collapse, no genuinely serious depression (although there were substantial setbacks after Korea and in 1957-58).

The dollar, backed by almost $20 billion in gold, retained its world strength.

Chief "glamor" industry of the '50s was electronics which, stimulated by TV, defense and industrial demands, and "miracle" scientific advances, increased output from $3.5 billion in 1951 to $10.6 billion in 1960.

The '60s seem even more promising.

GNP was expected to jump, in terms of 1959 dollars, to $605 billion in 1965 and $710 billion in 1970, a 42% rise, while population increases from 180 million to 206 million, only 14%.

But, if the '60s merely equalled the "fabulous '50s," U.S. industry and business could be more than satisfied.

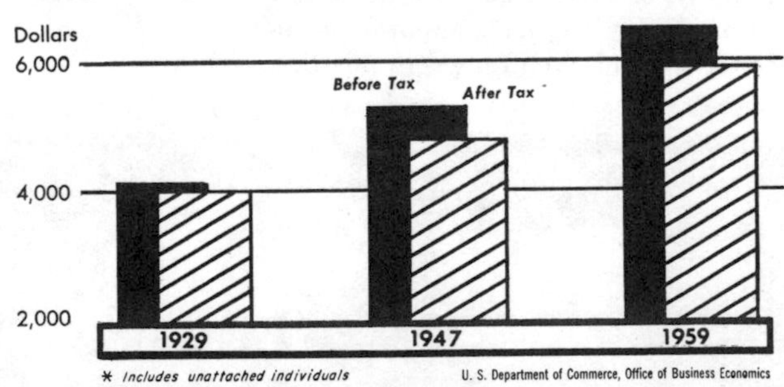

Industrial production and industrial inputs of man power and electric power, 1950-60, seasonally adjusted

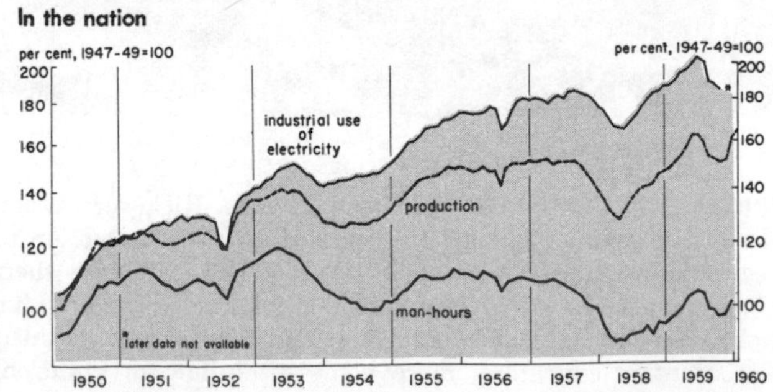

STOCK OWNERSHIP was shared by 12.5 million persons by 1960, almost doubling the shareholder population at the start of the decade. A.T.&T. had to hire world's biggest armory *(above)*, NYC, to seat 12,000 owners at annual meeting.

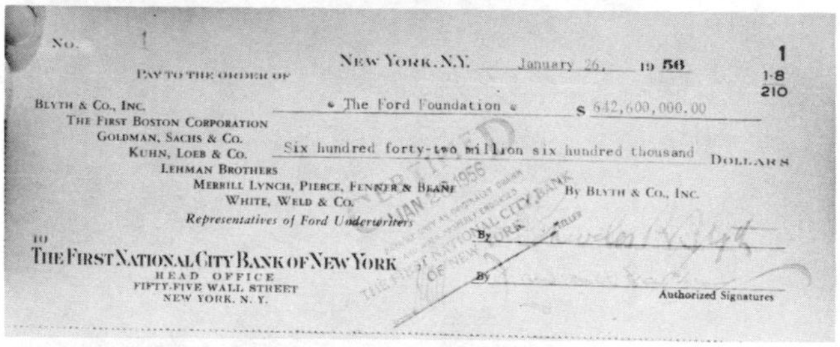

No. 1

NEW YORK, N.Y. January 26, 19 56

1
1-8
210

PAY TO THE ORDER OF The Ford Foundation $ 642,600,000.00

Six hundred forty-two million six hundred thousand DOLLARS

BLYTH & CO., INC.
THE FIRST BOSTON CORPORATION
GOLDMAN, SACHS & CO.
KUHN, LOEB & CO.
LEHMAN BROTHERS
MERRILL LYNCH, PIERCE, FENNER & BEANE
WHITE, WELD & CO.
Representatives of Ford Underwriters

BY BLYTH & CO., INC.

By
By
Authorized Signatures

TO
THE FIRST NATIONAL CITY BANK OF NEW YORK
HEAD OFFICE
FIFTY-FIVE WALL STREET
NEW YORK, N. Y.

$642.6 MILLION CHECK, result of first public sale of Ford Motor Co. stock, was turned over to Ford Foundation Jan. 26, 1956. Altogether, 10.2 million shares were marketed by syndicate of nation's top underwriting houses. Previously all stock, since organization of company in 1903, had been held by founder, Henry Ford, members of family. Present generation includes Henry II *(standing)*, Benson *(l.)*, William shown when they announced family would relinquish 60% of stock. Above them are portraits of their father Edsel *(l.)*, grandfather Henry. Ford 1959 sales totaled $4.36 billion.

SEWELL AVERY, Montgomery Ward chairman, gives victory sign after turning back Louis Wolfson's bid to control company in its publicized proxy fight.

AUTO SALES CYCLES alternately cheered, worried economists as sales volume dropped from record 7.2 million units in 1955 to a low of 4.65 million in 1958, then passed 6 million in 1960. Sales stunts had little effect on public's response.

STEEL'S BASIC importance in nation's economy was demonstrated by lengthy 1959 steel strike, which sharply cut production in auto, allied industries, produced drop in jobs. It caused only a temporary slowdown in over-all advance.

ANTI-TRUST impasse over duPont owning 63 million GM shares was ended when Federal Judge Walter J. La Buy ruled it could keep stock but without vote.

ELECTRONICALLY CONTROLLED MACHINE TOOL LINE EXEMPLIFIES TREND TO AUTOMATION WHICH ACCELERATED AS DECADE PROGRESSED

VAST PETROLEUM INDUSTRY, WHICH MADE POSSIBLE AUTOMOBILE, AVIATION, TRANSFORMED WORLD, CELEBRATED CENTENNIAL IN 1959

HUMBLE OIL REFINERY IN TEXAS TURNS OUT AVIATION GASOLINE. U.S. PRODUCES ABOUT TWO-FIFTHS OF WORLD'S PETROLEUM

LABOR'S MOMENTUM SLOWED

Prosperity turns workers conservative, eases strike pressures; racket disclosures lessen prestige of unions; CIO, AFL amalgamate, end rift

IN 1960, as in 1950, U.S Labor was optimistic, but its optimism was based more on hope than the solid expectations with which the decade began. Ten years of buffeting had dissipated its dreams of doubling union membership by organizing white collar workers, of relaxation of the sterner provisions of the Taft-Hartley Act, of increased fringe benefits.

The reality of the decade turned out differently. Although the American Federation of Labor and Congress of Industrial Organizations successfully merged, the 1950 goals largely remained "pie in the sky." White collar unionization expanded very little. Taft-Hartley remained on the books. The most important blow to union strength and prestige came with the disclosures of the Senate Rackets Committee. The public began to consider measures to curb unions like the Teamsters, whose power was greater in many areas than that of corporations and was led by dubious characters, ex-criminals and thugs.

Meeting these new challenges were new faces. Philip Murray, leader of the CIO and William Green, head of the AFL, died within 12 days of each other in 1952. They were succeeded by Walter Reuther and George Meany The former had risen to prominence as head of the United Automobile Workers. In 1955 Reuther gained a guaranteed annual wage for his membership, probably the decade's single most important development in union demands. Within a year of this victory, the CIO merged with the AFL, and Meany became the new organization's first president while Reuther became a vice-president and its most articulate spokesman. He was Labor's man of the decade.

As Reuther rose, so did Dave Beck, President of the powerful Teamsters. Considered a "labor statesman" in 1953, Beck was consulted by the government on many matters concerning labor. In 1956 and 1957, however, disclosures of his shady past took place. Beck was convicted, forced to resign his post and was sentenced to jail.

As a movement, Labor became more conservative during the decade. Gone were the crusading zeal and the dreams of worker's utopias of previous decades. As the workers of the U.S. became more affluent, they became more conservative. Now that they had more to lose, they were less ready to gamble. This was the most important long range change of the '50s.

STEEL STRIKES in 1952 and 1959 had widespread repercussions. The 1952 walkout resulted in higher wages, more fringe benefits, but also brought an increase in steel prices, inflationary pressure. Truman's seizure of the steel mills was declared unconstitutional in one of the most important decisions of the decade. The 1959 strike saw the workers return *(above)* under Taft-Hartley bill. Eventual settlement gave workers a pay raise, and, it was hoped, would prove not too inflationary.

GRAND OLD MAN of the United Mine Workers, John L. Lewis *(l.)* gained pay raises for his members, but was unable to do anything about the declining consumption of coal. Such other fuels as natural gas, oil and atomic power cut into consumption, and brought economic misery to the West Virginia fields and elsewhere. At the same time, technological improvements in extraction and processing cut rate of employment.

CHAIRMAN AND CHIEF COUNSEL of the Senate Rackets Committee, Sen. John McClellan (D-Ark) and Robert Kennedy probed wrongdoing in management and labor for more than three years. The committee demonstrated that there were strong ties between known criminals such as Johnny "Dio" Dioguardi and prominent labor leaders. The most important result of the hearings was the reorganization of the Teamsters, the jailing of Dave Beck and the meteoric rise of Hoffa.

JIMMY HOFFA'S first meeting with the probers took place in 1957, and soon thereafter the Teamster official became one of the best known figures in the nation. As Teamster president, he could paralyze the entire nation with a strike.

DAVE BECK was considered a clean, conservative unionist when he first appeared before the McClellan Committee. Kennedy and others soon showed that Beck had blackmailed employers and had conspired with trailer manufacturer Roy Fruehauf to win a company proxy fight. When questioned about the more than $320,000 he took from the Teamster treasury, Beck pleaded the Fifth Amendment. As a result, Beck was suspended, replaced by Hoffa and later convicted and sent to jail.

WETBACKS illustrate one aspect of the continuing problem of immigrant labor. Mexican seasonal workers get lower wages, live in near starvation misery in the American Southwest. On another level was the problem of southern migrants who moved to midwestern cities, where they tended to disrupt a once-stable market. Puerto Ricans in New York joined unions, but still received sub-standard wages. In New York, in 1959, P.R. workers in hospitals struck, won battle for higher wages.

SAMUEL GOMPERS founded the AFL, which followed his policy of craft unionism. CIO under John L. Lewis later broke away to organize the unskilled. In 1956 the federations merged. New complex boasted 15 million members.

A FAMOUS DUET of Harry Truman on piano and James Petrillo on horn bowed in during 1954, shortly before the American Federation of Musicians leader stepped down. George Meany, David McDonald and Walter Reuther *(below)* led the new AFL-CIO as president and vice-presidents. McDonald's steel workers staged decade's most costly strike in 1959-60. The walkout was ended only after use of the Taft-Hartley bill and intervention and mediation by Vice-President Nixon and others.

FARM SURPLUS KEEPS SWELLING

Federal stocks pass $8 billion; science, mechanization enable fewer farmers to produce more from less land; research may solve problem

THE FARM "PROBLEM," what to do with the ever swelling flood of agricultural commodities which nature, science and politics combined to pour forth in the U.S. in accelerating abundance (while much of the world was hungry), remained even further from solution at the decade's end than at its beginning.

Government guarantees assuring the farmer at least 82.5% of "parity" (averaged maximum) prices had piled up in Federal storage more than $8 billion of surplus commodities, including more than $3 billion in wheat, $2.2 billion in corn, $1.3 billion in cotton and the rest in everything from barley to tung oil.

Outstanding price support loans, by 1960, had reached some $2.5 billion, compared to $923 million at the beginning of 1951, and the loss sustained by the government had passed $9 billion.

Persistent efforts by President Eisenhower's Secretary of Agriculture, Ezra T. Benson, to scale down and, eventually, liquidate the program were repeatedly repudiated by a farm-vote-minded Congress.

There was no prospect whatever of a substantial change in the program at least until 1961, when the elections would usher in a new Administration and Congress.

One solution, backed strongly by Vice President Richard M. Nixon and approved by Congress, was free distribution of the surpluses among hungry foreign nations, but to this there were many practical difficulties and the opposition of such nations as Canada, which complained this would undercut it in its own traditional grain markets.

But, underlying the political aspects of the surplus problem was the inexorable fact that, while the farm population was shrinking from 25 million to 21 million, output per man rose two-thirds and output per acre as much as one-third. At the beginning of 1960, 90.7% of all marketed crops were being produced by only 44% of the nation's farmers, while the remaining 56%, mostly on small subsistence or "spare-time" farms (whose operators also held jobs in factories) were producing only a scant 9.3%.

This was the result of vastly increased mechanization, and of greatly improved cultivation methods, including new seed strains, chemical fertilizers and pesticides.

Outstanding examples were wheat, 1.1 billion bushels from 53 million acres in 1959, compared to 1 billion bushels from 62 million acres in 1950; corn, 4.4 billion bushels from 85 million acres in 1959, compared to 3.1 billion bushels from 82 million acres in 1950; and cotton, 14.7 million bales from 15.2 million acres in 1959, com-

CRANBERRIES are tested for traces of weed killer, use of which had been banned. Sale of 1959 crop was held up until samples from growers were checked, causing loss in Thanksgiving sales.

DROUGHT destroyed millions of acres of grazing land and grain feed crops in 1951-3. Ranchers had to open their winter feed stocks and send cattle to market prematurely. "Operation Haylift" saved many range cattle. Only by 1960 were herds rebuilt to their earlier size. To utilize the bumper corn crop grown in 1960, farmers fattened their livestock for a longer time on the farms throughout the country.

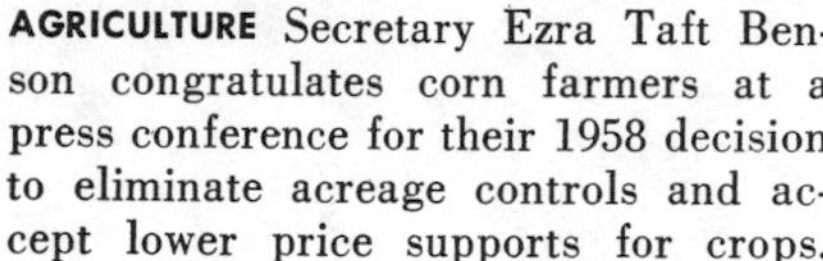

AGRICULTURE Secretary Ezra Taft Benson congratulates corn farmers at a press conference for their 1958 decision to eliminate acreage controls and accept lower price supports for crops.

1960 WHEAT CROP was estimated at 1.25 billion bushels. With the carryover, this meant at least 2.5 million bushels on hand—a four-year supply. Storage costs came to $1.5 million a day. Some of the surplus was used for school lunches and relief. Where there were crop failures and famines overseas, grain was sold at low prices to those hard pressed nations, and in some cases, given outright to them.

pared to 10 million bales from 17.8 million acres in 1950.

Livestock production similarly, despite shrinking range lands, reached an all-time high, with 1959 sales totaling $11 billion.

Gross farm income rose from $33 billion in 1950 to $37 billion in 1959 but, thanks to the multiplicity of small and inefficient subsistence farms, average income per farm remained at $2400 a year, and net profit actually fell to $11.2 billion from $13 billion.

Annual agricultural exports rose in value to $3.7 billion from 1950's $3 billion, but in share of total exports fell from one-third to less than one-fourth. Farm imports held constant in value at just under $4 billion, but, in proportion of total imports, fell from almost one-half to less than one-third.

Widespread drought and, in other sections, floods, plagued the nation's farmers during the decade, as did such pests as gypsy moths, locusts and Mediterranean fruit flies.

Increasing use of chemical insecticides raised the question of their possible harmful effects in foods and, as 1960 drew to an end, Congressional committees were considering bills to control them. Additives and chemical fertilizers also were under investigation.

A major new hope in disposal of surpluses was increased industrial use of farm products. Developments in this field included corn starch for sausage cases and frozen food wrappings, and important improvements in "miracle" cotton textiles.

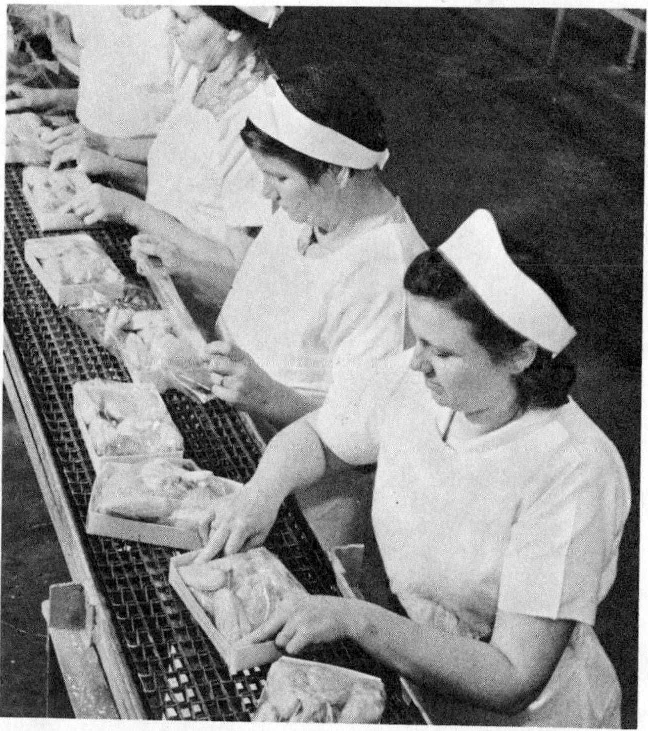

INSURING FRESH FOOD all year, food stores and homes installed cold storage compartments for meat, vegetables and fruits. New products and processing plants were added each season and sales rose during the decade from $1.2 billion to over $2.6 billion, with greatest growth in precooked "Jiffy meals."

UN
UN

WORLD AFFAIRS 1950–1960

World war averted, but crises, tensions mount from Korea to Congo

THE DECADE muddled through.

It managed to evade, and possibly avert, open outbreak of full-scale East-West war, the hydrogen holocaust that could consume mankind.

That, for the U.S. and the rest of the Free World, was about the best that could be said of it.

While the West was, in 1960, still far stronger in military potential and, very probably, in actual striking power, than its rivals, it still had lost considerable ground.

It had more to lose, so that the idea of total war was more repellent to it than, probably, to all the Communist bloc and, certainly, to Red China.

And the same tide of global economic upsurge which had swept the U.S., the British Commonwealth and West Europe to unprecedented heights of prosperity also had vastly increased the industrial capacity of the Soviet Union and its European satellites—with an accompanying amelioration of living conditions—and of the Communist Chinese—at the cost of millions of human lives and untold suffering.

The decade opened with Korea, where the Communist threat, thanks to prompt and resolute action by the U.S. and the United Nations, was contained after a bloody struggle—but not eliminated.

It saw Indo-China slip from French control but, if the South became free to attempt to rule itself, the North became the protege, if not puppet, of Peking.

CLOSE TOGETHER — AND WORLDS APART

It ended with Khrushchev contemptuous (if still nominally seeking "co-existence"), Castro in Cuba and the Congo in chaos.

During the decade, well over a score of new "nations" achieved juridical sovereignty (net UN membership increased 22), most of them, like the Congo, in Negro Africa. But all of them had very hard rows to hoe economically (everywhere, local politicians were trying to make personal hay out of rival Western and Communist offers of help) and few had any traditions of popular government. Too many, again like the Congo, were purely synthetic creations, the accidental offspring of 19th Century colonial rivalries.

While independence for each of the world's peoples remained an ideal goal (pending genuine world union), the permanent viability of a large number of these new states remained, to say the least, a matter of doubt.

Meanwhile, they furnished just that many more cockpits of East-West rivalry, where a single spark might set off, if not a world conflagration, at least another Korea.

In Latin America, the decade saw the end of all but three dictatorships, and their replacement, everywhere but in Cuba, by popular, democratic-minded regimes, intent on economic and social advance instead of personal aggrandizement. But, in Cuba, a traditional (and traditionally cruel) military dictator was replaced by increasingly Communist and hysterically anti-U.S. Fidel Castro. This seemed to give Communism, after two previous failures (in British Guiana and Guatemala), its long-sought foothold in the Western Hemisphere (and at the southern tip of the United States.)

It was a decade of conferences, over Korea, Indo-China, Berlin, disarmament, banning of nuclear weapons. They were held on the ambassadorial level, the foreign ministers' level, the chief of government level. Some met, on the Western side, with hope, and some, like the abortive Paris summit, thanks to Khrushchev's rudeness, never met at all.

But all were abortive. In all, the single Soviet purpose seemed to be to win concessions while offering none, to make propaganda, to split the Free World alliance.

To the same end, but unsuccessfully, Moscow attempted to exploit the UN, British labor and the return to power of De Gaulle in France.

Nevertheless, there were ominous Red successes. Vice President Nixon was endangered by South American mobs; Japanese mobs forced cancellation of President Eisenhower's long-planned trip.

But the Communist world, too, during the decade, showed internal stresses. Poland won limited freedom, East Germany sought it, Hungary's revolt was drowned in blood. And Communist China, truculently conscious of its immense manpower and growing industrial might, openly contested Kremlin primacy, assailed Khrushchev's "softness" and proclaimed itself the one font of Marxist orthodoxy.

Meanwhile men poised on the edge of space, preparing to enter the cosmos, but were themselves unable to establish ordered, united freedom on their own small planet.

WORLD'S WISH FOR PEACE TOOK CONCRETE FORM IN UN FORCES KEEPING VIGIL IN PALESTINE, SINAI, KOREA AND THE CONGO

NO AGREEMENT—BUT NO WAR

Khrushchev torpedoes '60 Summit to climax decade of fruitless talks

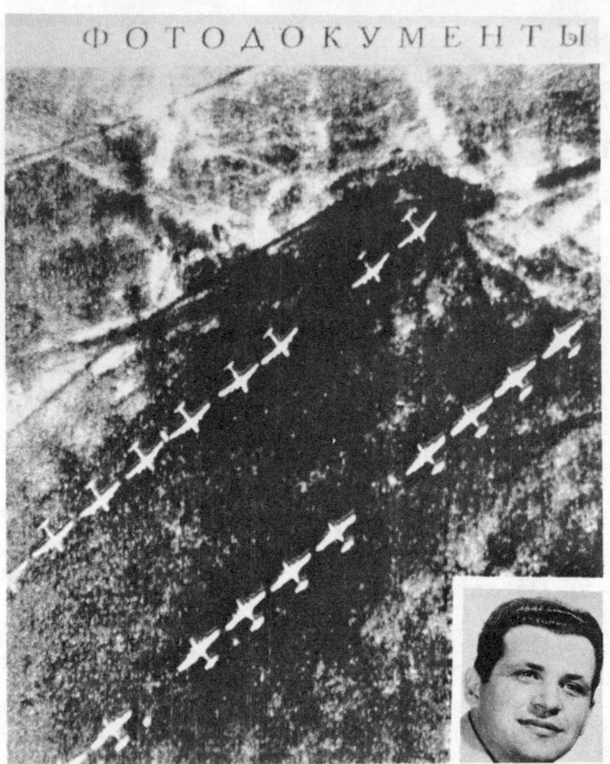

U.S. SPY PILOT, Francis Powers *(insert)*, snapped this photo of Soviet air base before being downed 1200 miles inside Russia. *Pravda* published photo May 1, 1960, helping torpedo Big Four talks. Soviet trial Aug. 19, gave Powers 10 years.

THE SENSATIONAL disclosure by Soviet Premier Nikita Khrushchev that a U.S. jet pilot on an espionage "overflight" had been shot down deep inside Russia wrecked a scheduled Big Four Summit conference May 16, 1960, in Paris.

The drama, which killed long-nurtured hopes of easing East-West tension, unfolded slowly. In Turkey on May 3, U.S. officials announced that a plane belonging to the National Aeronautics and Space Administration—an independent civilian agency in charge of all U.S. non-military space projects—had been missing since May 1 on a flight from an air base near Adana.

On May 5, Khrushchev, in an address to the Soviet parliament, solemnly declared:

"I am duty bound to report to you on the aggressive acts directed in the last few weeks by the United States of America against the Soviet Union."

He then told how on April 9, a U.S. plane had violated Soviet space and went "unpunished." He added that, when a second violation occurred on May 1, the U.S. jet plane—which bore "no identification signs"—was shot down.

In Washington, NASA said that the plane missing since May 1 had been a single-seater jet U-2 which was on a high altitude weather research flight. It said the pilot—later identified as Francis Gary Powers, 30—reported he was having trouble with his oxygen equipment and implied he had strayed off course near the Soviet frontier.

But on May 7, in a second parliamentary speech, Premier Khrushchev dropped his bombshell. He said the pilot was "alive and kicking" in Moscow, had confessed he was on a spy flight across the heart of Russia from Pakistan to Norway, and had been downed 1200 miles inside Russia.

Khrushchev held up photographs of Soviet airfields he said had been taken by the pilot. He branded the U.S. version of the flight a "complete lie," and said he had withheld details in his original announcement to see what kind of "fabrication" the State Department would issue. He again warned that "Turkey, Pakistan and Norway should become aware that they are participants in this hostile act." The premier had scored a damaging propaganda blow against the U.S.

The next week the U.S. officially acknowledged that the U-2 plane was on a surveillance mission. Even before this admission, critics of the government had argued that pains should have been taken to avoid any incidents in the Soviet area on the eve of the Summit talks.

President Eisenhower flew to Paris, but Khrushchev refused to hold the parley unless he apologized and promised to punish those responsible for the espionage. The president rejected the vehement demands of Khrushchev,

FURIOUS PREMIER Nikita Khrushchev raised a finger in anger during a news conference May 18, 1960, in Paris. He attacked the United States bitterly because of the admitted spy flight. He blamed the U.S. for failure of Summit talks.

and was backed up by British Prime Minister Harold Macmillan and French President Charles de Gaulle.

Eisenhower had been scheduled to go to Moscow in June, to return the Khrushchev visit to the U.S. the previous September. Khrushchev cancelled the invitation.

The Kremlin chief accused the U.S. of torpedoing the summit talks which he himself had sought for so long. U.S. officials countercharged that he deliberately inflated the spy case for propaganda reasons, and that he had had no intention of attending the summit conference because he realized he would not get any concessions on the Berlin and German unity issues.

Some observers said that Khrushchev had no choice except to spurn the Summit meeting. They speculated that he had to take a tough stand against the U.S. because his "peaceful coexistence" policy was under attack by other Soviet Communist Party officials. Knowing that his policy already was under attack by the Chinese Communists, they also speculated that Khrushchev's job might be imperiled.

But a month later, in a speech in Bucharest, Rumania, Khrushchev made it plain he was still the top boss in his Red household. The man whose "de-Stalinization" speech rocked the Communist world in February, 1956, used some sharp words in rebutting the Chinese critics. The Chinese Reds had maintained that a showdown war between Communism and capitalism was inevitable because of the inherently aggressive nature of capitalism.

"Only madmen," he said, "and lunatics, can now call for another world war. As for the men of sound mind—and they account for the majority even among the most deadly enemies of Communism — they cannot but be aware of the total consequences of another war."

Khrushchev ridiculed Lenin's old doctrine of inevitable "frightful collisions" between Communism and capitalism. He compared Communists who "mechanically now repeat" what Lenin said "many decades ago' to children first learning to read.

The Soviet premier restated Kremlin policy, which has not changed. That policy had three goals: to isolate the U.S.; woo the underdeveloped lands; and attain "peaceful coexistence." He said he had been ready to talk at the Summit conference in Paris in May, but the U.S.—through the "piratical" U-2 flight—had "crucified" the conference.

Another Soviet goal, one that has not changed since the Berlin blockade more than a decade ago, had occasioned the scheduled Summit parley—and thus the resulting intensified cold war. Khrushchev had been maneuvering to seize Berlin for the East German Communist government ever since he became the No. 1 Communist after Stalin's death in 1953.

The USSR's leader had promoted the Big Four parley of the President, his front-man, Premier Nikolai Bulganin, Prime Minister Sir Anthony Eden, of Britain, and Premier Edgar Faure of France, in Geneva in July, 1955. In the Western view the only constructive proposal that came out of that fruitless parley was President Eisen-

BIG THREE Western leaders pause on steps of Elysee Palace in Paris after discussing Soviet Premier Khrushchev's refusal to join in long-planned executive parley on world issues. Khrushchev demanded an apology from President Eisenhower because of the U.S. U-2 jet flight across the Soviet border. Mr. Eisenhower refused. The tall French president, de Gaulle, and British Prime Minister Macmillan sided with U.S. The Cold War thereafter grew more inflamed.

hower's "open skies" plan of mutual aerial surveillance to guard against surprise attack. The Reds rejected it.

Recalling it after the U-2 incident, Western Allied officials said Khrushchev could not have been too surprised that the U.S. used a surveillance plane in view of Khrushchev's own frequent boasts of Soviet missile capability. They speculated that his fury stemmed mainly from the fact that the U-2 flight revealed the weakness of Soviet defenses, and the fact that the USSR did not have a comparable high-flying plane.

Khrushchev began maneuvering for another Summit parley in November, 1958, when he threatened to sign a separate peace treaty with the East German Communist regime in six months unless there was a settlement of the "Berlin question." He demanded that Allied troops withdraw from West Berlin and that it be made a "free city," or, as U.S. Secretary of State Christian A. Herter described his aim, a "slave city". Khrushchev later withdrew the time limit on his threat after talking with President Eisenhower during Khrushchev's trip to the U.S. But he repeated the threat. The implication was that, if the East German Reds clamped a blockade on West Berlin and the Allies used force to break it, the USSR would go to the aid of the East German regime.

The U.S. and Great Britain, following the Soviet lead, suspended atomic tests in 1958 and met in Geneva in October to try to work out a Big Three ban on tests. Delegates reached a measure of agreement on methods of detection and control of high-powered atomic blasts. But they could not agree on the feasibility of detecting, hence

CHIEF AUTHOR of President Truman's foreign policies was Secretary of State Dean Acheson *(r.)*. He drew praise, but also fire, especially for his caution toward Red China during Korean war, and ouster of UN commander Gen. MacArthur.

TOP ADVISER to President Eisenhower was the late John Foster Dulles. The Secretary of State, in this 1953 photo, is seated between the then French Foreign Minister, Georges Bidault, *(l.)*, and British Foreign Secretary, Lord Salisbury.

ILL-FATED Big Four conference opened July 18, 1955, amid high hopes in Geneva, Switzerland. Soviet Premier Nikolai Bulganin ostensibly headed the Soviet delegation, but the real boss, even then, was believed to be Nikita Khrushchev. Bulganin later disappeared from the political scene. President Eisenhower first introduced his famous "open skies" mutual aerial inspection plan at the parley. Ever since, the USSR has rejected this proposal to reduce tension.

Seek to disarm, ban nuclear tests

controlling, small underground explosions. Another 10-nation parley on broader disarmament questions began in March, 1960. As usual, the West demanded a careful step-by-step control plan of disarmament, while the USSR spoke of controls—but did not spell out what form they could take. The Soviet delegation quit the disarmament parley June 27, 1960, while the nuclear parley continued. Three days later the USSR shot down another U.S. plane, an RB-47, claiming it was over Soviet territory. The United States charged the plane was shot down in international waters. Moscow refused an impartial check.

BIG FOUR OF 1955, were *(l. to r.)* Soviet Premier Nikolai Bulganin, President Eisenhower, French Premier Edgar Faure and British Prime Minister Sir Anthony Eden. Cordiality marked this July session in Geneva, but no results.

"LUNCHEON DIPLOMACY" session of Foreign Ministers in Geneva in July, 1959, failed to solve Berlin dispute. On lawn are *(l. to r.)* Selwyn Lloyd, Great Britain; Couve de Murville, France; Gromyko, Russia; Christian Herter of the U.S.

MARATHON East-West negotiations aimed to halt nuclear tests began in Geneva in October, 1958, when U.S. and USSR suspended further tests. Ten-nation East-West disarmament talks convened in March, 1960, but the USSR walked out.

WORLD TRAVELER Nikita Khrushchev, wearing topcoat against rain, talked for hours with French President de Gaulle, March 24, 1960, in advance of Summit parley he torpedoed in May. The guards salute top Russian with their swords.

DAG HAMMARSKJOLD *(l.)* in 1952 succeeded first Secretary General, Trygve Lie *(r.)*, was in second term as decade ended. In carrying out delicate, demanding job, Hammarskjold paid diplomatic visits to Communist China, Near East, Hungary and Africa.

UN WAGES PEACE FIGHT ON FAR-FLUNG FRONTS

Guards chief trouble spots from Korea to Congo; world-wide programs hasten development of new nations, needy areas

THE UNITED NATIONS ended the decade, as it had begun it, on the front lines of world peace.

In 1950 a UN army, spearheaded by and made up mostly of U.S. troops, turned back the Communist attempt to overrun South Korea. Following the truce, the UN helped Korea rebuild.

In mid-summer of 1960 a joint UN force, made up of contingents from the smaller (including African) members, and commanded by Swedish Gen. Carl von Horn, was flown in to restore order in the just-born Congo Republic, disintegrating in a welter of tribal jealousies.

Earlier, another composite UN force moved into the Suez area following the 1956 Israeli-Egyptian War and Anglo-French intervention. It remained on guard to prevent a resumption of hostilities. The UN Truce Commission continued its alert along Israel's northern and eastern borders.

And, since 1958, a UN Observation Group had been helping maintain peace in Lebanon, following the withdrawal of U.S. forces.

At its New York headquarters, the glass and steel landmark first occupied in 1950, the UN continued to function as a world forum. But emphasis was shifted from the Security Council, too often paralyzed by the Soviet veto, to the General Assembly, which could make majority decisions.

During the decade, the UN increased its net membership from 60-82. It added, from Europe, Albania, Bulgaria, Finland, Hungary, Ireland, Italy, Portugal, Rumania and Spain, and, from Asia and Africa, Cambodia, Ceylon, Ghana, Guinea, Indonesia, Japan, Jordan, Laos, Libya, Malaya, Morocco, Nepal, Sudan and Tunisia.

The International Technical Assistance Program, set up in 1950, aided 140 countries and territories.

By 1960, results included the first systematic exploration of potential Asian and Latin American resources; penicillin treatments for yaws, a scourge of all tropical areas, administered to 10 million persons, and, for farmers in many areas, the first modern tools and first training in scientific methods and use of fertilizer and pest controls. Expenditures had averaged $30 million a year, but were to be expanded.

The International Atomic Energy Agency, suggested by President Eisenhower, began functioning in 1957.

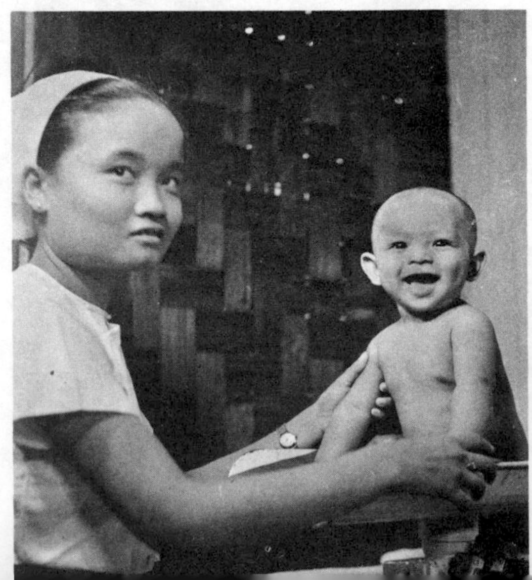

YUGOSLAV SAPPERS, part of UN composite force organized to meet 1957. Suez crisis, clear mines from railway tracks in Sinai Desert following withdrawal of Israelis. UN, in '60, was still on guard.

The Trusteeship Council, through Nobel Prize winner Ralph Bunche of the U.S., Under Secretary for Special Political Affairs, smoothed the path for the new African states.

The Food and Agricultural Organization, in 1960, launched a five-year program to feed the hungry half of the world's population.

The Office of the High Commissioner for Refugees coordinated aid for displaced Hungarians, Jews, Koreans, Algerians and Chinese.

Refugee activities included aid to almost 1 million Arab refugees from Palestine (the UN set up 380 schools for children in the camps and provided vocational training for adults) and aid in resettling 171,000 refugees following suppression of the 1956 Hungarian revolt. A major UN target was the emptying of each refugee camp in Europe by finding all inmates new homes and jobs.

Less publicized, but of equal importance, were "specialized" activities in telecommunications, uniform sea law, meteorology, scientific cooperation, labor and education.

As the decade ended, the UN seemed to be opening at least a faint first trail toward Tennyson's dreamed of "Parliament of Man."

SWORDS INTO PLOUGHSHARES symbolized UN post-Truce actvities in South Korea, where, as part of reconstruction program, 12 farm equipment plants were set up, run by trained Korean workers.

CHORTLING BURMESE BABY *(l.)* and wide-eyed Arab refugee children *(r.)* are both unknowing recipients of UN help. UN Children's Fund (UNICEF) operated 500 child and maternal care centers in Burma. Some 60,000 refugees forgotten in DP camps in Arab lands on Israel's border depended entirely on UN, through Relief For Palestinian Refugees Organization and UNICEF, to survive. By 1960, funds were scarce.

EUROPEAN BARRIERS LOWERED

But split into Outer Seven, Common Market slows progress after gains of '50s; French weaken NATO command unity

COUNCIL OF EUROPE, oldest European unity organ, formed in 1949, had primary job of reconciling Germany and France, which it did; also produced Saar settlement. The influence of this unofficial parliament, meeting in Strasbourg, faded when powerful economic organizations it had fostered went into operation.

West Europe's unity drive, which had progressed swiftly during most of the decade, was set back as it ended by a split into rival economic blocs. The U.S.-backed North Atlantic Treaty Organization also faced divisive military problems, mostly raised by France.

First steps toward European unity had come in 1949, the same year NATO was formed, when an unofficial parliament, the Council of Europe, met in Strasbourg, France. Council influence soon declined, but that body gave birth to the European Coal and Steel Community in 1953, the European Economic Community (Common Market), and the European Atomic Energy Community (Euratom). All these were pooling arrangements by six nations—France, Germany, Italy, Belgium, Luxembourg, the Netherlands—out of the 15-member Council of Europe. Great Britain backed away from these supranational bodies aimed toward a federated Europe, especially the Common Market. It hoped, in effect, to both have its cake and eat it too by arranging membership in all-European free trading area while retaining Imperial Preference, mutual tariff concessions among all Commonwealth nations. The European split was, instead, widened when Great Britain, Sweden, Norway, Denmark, Switzerland, Austria and Portugal formed the European Free Trade Association, known as the Outer Seven. Both groups began raising and lowering tariffs. Common Market members aimed to eliminate gradually all tariffs within their group, while raising a common customs wall to outsiders. The Outer Seven members planned to eliminate tariffs within their group, but individually decide on rates toward outsiders. Friction and bitterness among the rival blocs already had begun in 1960, although the two groups agreed to examine exports and imports on a product-by-product basis and try to find a compromise.

An example of the problem: Beginning Jan. 1, 1961, British tire-makers would pay 22% duty entering their products in the Netherlands. West German or French tires would pay only 17%. This gap would widen as the years went on, costing the British an important actual or potential market. This would be "discrimination," but it was inherent in the formation of such blocs.

Common Market members hoped within the next two decades to achieve complete economic integration in an area with a population of 165 million. Tariff reductions of the Outer Seven, at a rate of 10% a year, would produce a free internal market for 90 million in a decade.

For the U.S., whose recent decline in exports had caused concern, the potential difficulties of trading with either bloc involved high stakes. Even with the considerable decline of U.S. exports toward the end of the decade, the two European blocs together accounted for nearly 25% of the $15.8 billion total of commercial exports.

The Common Market group, in 1959, together took some $2.4 billion, in net value of actual goods shipped, of U.S. exports, or nearly 15%, with Germany as the biggest single buyer taking $735 million. The Outer Seven group accounted for nearly $1.4 billion, or about 10% of all U.S. commercial exports. Great Britain, the single largest buyer, took $840 million, more than half the total.

How the U.S. would maintain export markets in Western Europe had been a problem that had been building up for many years, and the end of the decade offered no solution in sight. Two possible solutions had been considered, however. Either the U.S. could lower its trade barriers further in exchange for European tariff concessions or through investments its industries could jump the European barriers with branch plants, as some U.S. firms had done. Most could not afford such costly leaps.

Settlement of Franco-German problem, a basic task of the original Council of Europe, had been attained. But on the central issue of the role of NATO, the attitudes of Chancellor Konrad Adenauer and President Charles de Gaulle differed at the end of 1960. The French leader proceeded with plans for creating an independent atomic striking force. He proclaimed his unwillingness to be bound by any agreement reached among Great Britain, the USSR and the U.S. in the Geneva negotiations for a ban on testing atomic weapons. De Gaulle also made clear his belief that the "system that has been called 'integration' has had its day. . . . She (France) has no need of a protector." Adenauer might face a choice: NATO or de Gaulle.

The strain on the NATO alliance brought about by the 1960 Congo crisis also was manifest. Belgium reacted bitterly to Allied support of UN moves to get Belgian troops out of the Congo. Premier Gaston Eyskens said Belgium might have to re-examine her NATO relationship, possibly withdrawing some troops from NATO.

THE SEVEN AND THE SIX
Map shows how Outer Seven, Great Britain, Norway, Sweden, Denmark, Austria, Switzerland and Portugal, lie around the fringes of the Common Market area composed of France, West Germany, the Netherlands, Belgium, Luxembourg and Italy.

Common Market forms a natural geographic unity; Seven do not.

EFTA Countries	EEC Countries
1. Austria	8. Belgium
2. Denmark	9. France
3. Norway	10. Germany
4. Portugal	11. Italy
5. Sweden	12. Luxembourg
6. Switzerland	13. Netherlands
7. United King.	

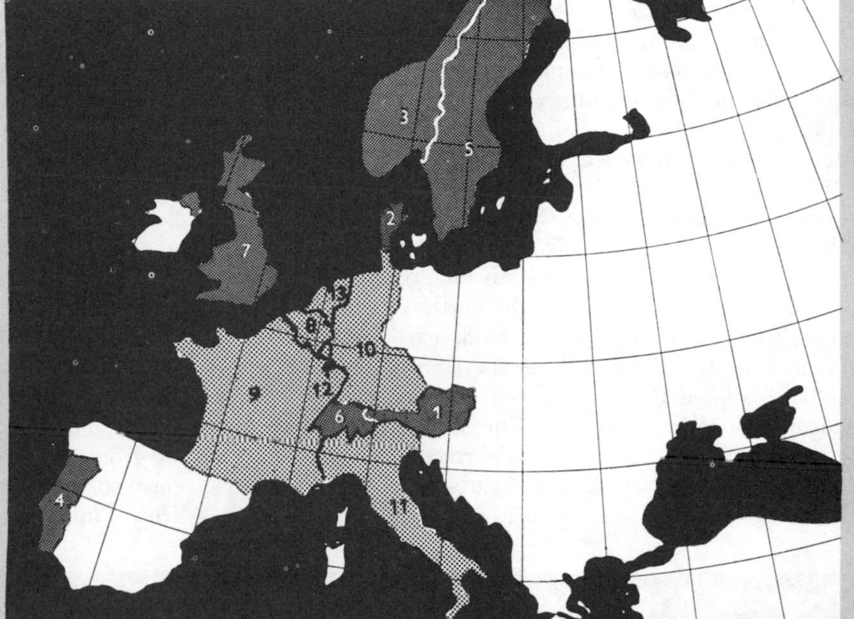

BELGIUM'S Paul-Henri Spaak *(top)*, first president of Council's Consultation Assembly, became NATO secretary-general. France's Robert Schumann *(below)* was "father" of Coal-Steel Community.

WEST GERMAN plants like Hunkingen Works produced 25 million tons steel in '59, form backbone of the Community.

KHRUSHCHEV SUCCEEDS STALIN

Party boss siezes Kremlin helm after stop-gap Malenkov rule; purges potential rivals

DRASTIC CHANGES occurred in the USSR in the years after the dictator, Joseph Vissarionovich Djugashvilli, known as Stalin, died March 5, 1953. But Moscow's cardinal foreign policy remained the world-wide triumph of Communism. The Kremlin's new strong man, Premier Nikita S. Khrushchev, proclaimed an era of "peaceful coexistence"—and threatened to rain hydrogen bombs on the West. He told the Soviet parliament in January, 1960, that Moscow had a "fantastic" new superweapon "in the hatching stage," adding: "We already possess nuclear weapons . . . and rockets to wipe any country or countries which attack us off the face of the earth."

Khrushchev, a short, stocky, bald, earthy extrovert, dominated most of the decade in the USSR. Georgi Malenkov and Nikolai Bulganin served for a time after Stalin's death, but Khrushchev, as Communist Party Secretary, had been the real power. Through the years he discarded such other well-known figures as V. M. Molotov, L. P. Beria (Stalin's secret police chief who was shot), and Lazar Kaganovich, Stalin's brother-in-law who also had done so much to aid Khrushchev, a former miner, in his climb to power. Although he denounced Stalin as a mass murderer of party members, he later told diplomats "when it comes to fighting imperialism, we are all Stalinists." His version of "peaceful coexistence" had the fixed goal: "Hands off" Eastern Europe for the West while Communist parties remained free to work actively against other governments.

Yet it also became a fact that under Khrushchev the USSR amassed great prestige among some underdeveloped nations. Moscow scored many firsts in space technology, developed an operational intercontinental ballistic missile, announced a one-third cut in ground forces, opened Soviet and satellite borders to western travelers as never before, and hiked living standards.

Emphasis remained on heavy industry but consumer goods rose in volume as Khrushchev declared the USSR would surpass the U.S. in per capita production in another decade. Some annual production statistics: "Virgin lands" program boosted grain production from 81 million metric tons in 1950 to 128 million in 1958; milk output up from 33 million metric tons to 58 million; gross industrial production up 90% since Stalin died (1953); iron output up 57%; oil 145%; electric power 97%.

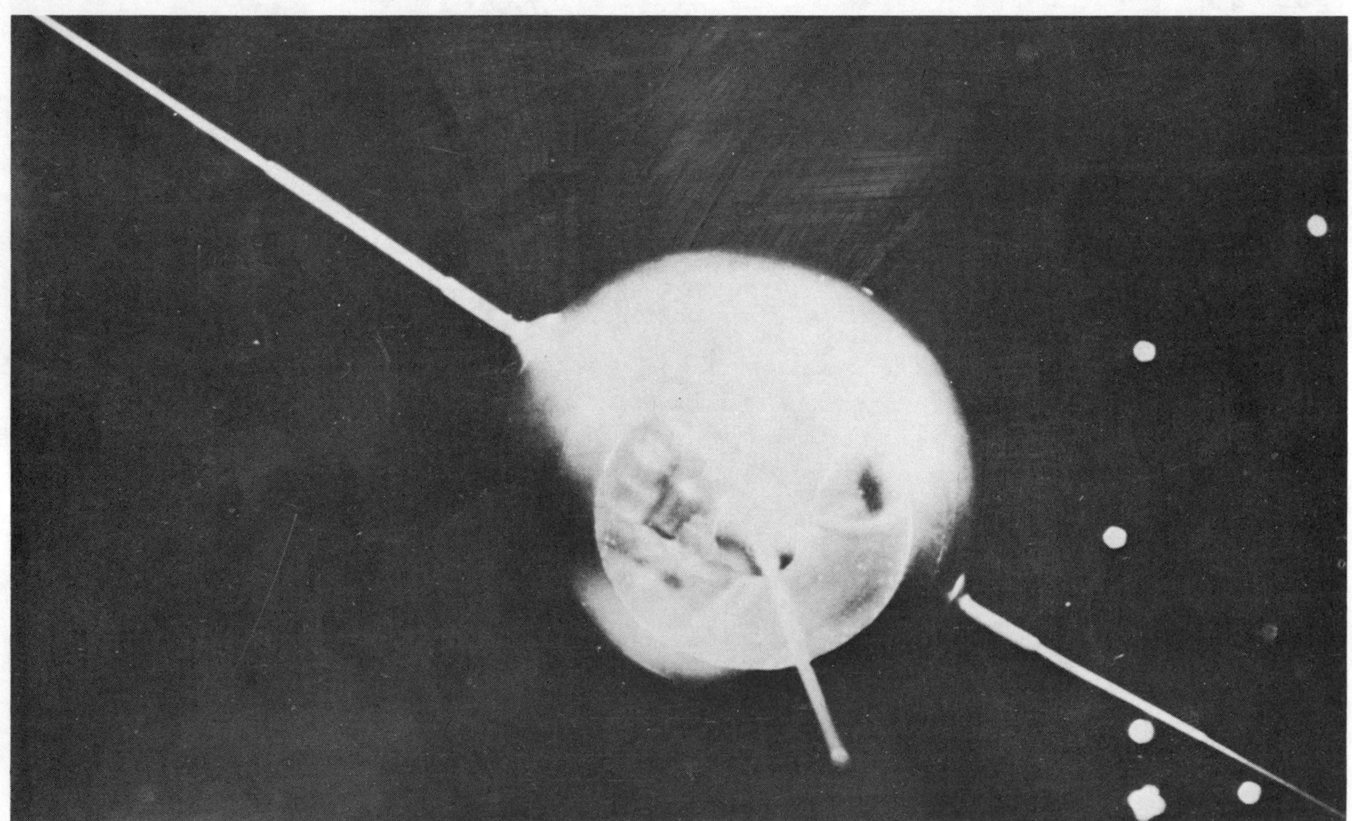

SPUTNIK, Russian word for satellite, became part of language October 4, 1957, when the USSR launched in space first man-made moon, catching U.S. flat-footed. The Russians fired three satellites, like model shown above, including one carrying dog Laika Nov. 3, 1957. Dog died later from effects of oxygen lack. USSR got to moon first, also into solar space.

MAN OF MANY MOODS, Soviet Premier Nikita Khrushchev, lived up to his advance billing as tough, aggressive, wily and astonishingly energetic when he visited the U.S. in Sept. 1959. This was to be prelude to May, 1960, Summit parley he called off because of U.S. spy plane incident. He displayed earthy humor, quick mind, at Washington's National Press Club appearance. But hard core also showed. Asked what he was doing during Stalin's tyranny, he dismissed question as "provocative." Reminded of Soviet suppression of Hungarian revolt, he snapped that the subject "stuck in some people's throats, like a dead rat." Chief USSR propagandist, he did not deviate from Red themes. Just before his arrival, Red scientists hit moon with rocket; May 15, 1960, they launched a 10,000-pound "space ship."

Soviet industry vastly expands as science triumphs in the race for space

DICTATOR'S END: Stalin's death March 5, 1953, brought some relief to the Soviet people and sharp conflicts in leadership before Khrushchev emerged on top of heap. Khrushchev, in a famous party speech, February, 1956, branded Stalin a mass murderer and a coward. At previous party congress, October, 1952, Khrushchev had proclaimed: "Millions turn in love and faith to Comrade Stalin . . . he defended the purity of Lenin's teachings." Stalinist police chief Beria, was executed Dec. 23, '53.

IN BIG PURGE Kaganovich (2), Malenkov (3), Molotov (4), Pervukhin (8) vanished in 1957 from the 11-man Presidium (formerly Politburo) of Soviet Communist Party. All had been accused of anti-Party activities. Mikoyan (6) and Suslov (7) remained. Marshal Zhukov was elevated to group, fired later. Khrushchev *(l.)* stayed through decade.

STRONG MAN Khrushchev is flanked by Marshal Georgi Zhukov, defense chief *(l.)* whom he fired Oct. 26, 1957, and Premier Nikolai Bulganin, who resigned March 27, 1958. Trio seemed happy at time of this photo, May Day, 1957. Marshal Rodion Y. Malinovsky succeed war hero Zhukov as defense chief.

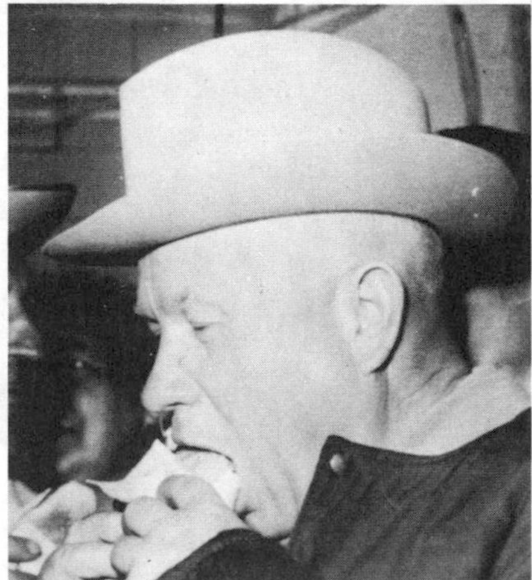

IN TALL CORN of Iowa on visit to farm Sept. 22, 1959, Nikita Khrushchev ate his first hot dog. He enjoyed the snack.

GLOBE-TROTTER in New Delhi with then Premier Bulganin, garlanded party boss waves goodbye to Indian hosts.

MECHANIZED MACHINERY used on Soviet collective farms came in for wrath of Communist Party Central Committee in 1960. It complained about faulty design of machinery and ordered tighter party control for collective farms, including organizational changes to spur agricultural production. Committee said production had been good in 1959, but not good enough because of mismanagement of farm land.

DRUM BEATER Khrushchev, with Burmese defense minister U Ba Shwe instructing, tries his hand at the Burmese drum during his 1955 India-Burma trip. The star salesman for Communism kept up drum fire of speeches criticizing U.S., England.

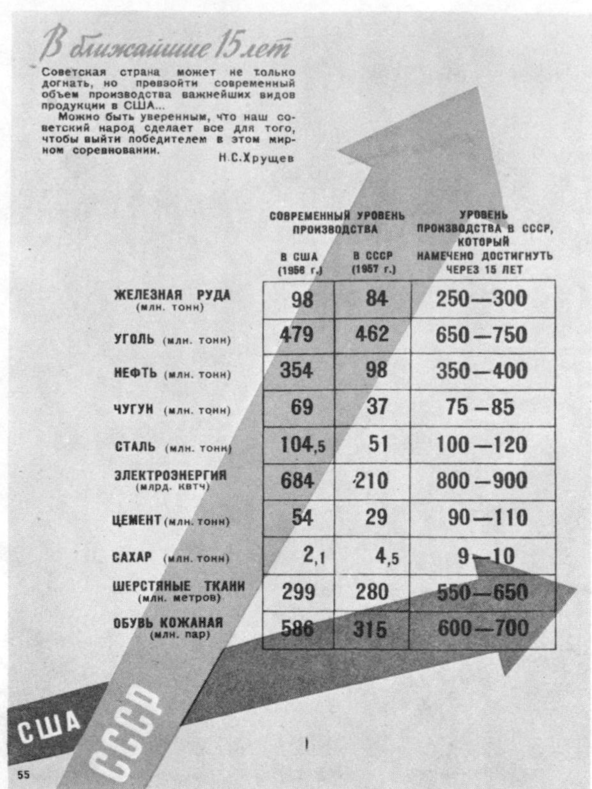

	Современный уровень производства		Уровень производства в СССР, который намечено достигнуть через 15 лет
	В США (1956 г.)	В СССР (1957 г.)	
ЖЕЛЕЗНАЯ РУДА (млн. тонн)	98	84	250—300
УГОЛЬ (млн. тонн)	479	462	650—750
НЕФТЬ (млн. тонн)	354	98	350—400
ЧУГУН (млн. тонн)	69	37	75—85
СТАЛЬ (млн. тонн)	104,5	51	100—120
ЭЛЕКТРОЭНЕРГИЯ (млрд. квтч)	684	210	800—900
ЦЕМЕНТ (млн. тонн)	54	29	90—110
САХАР (млн. тонн)	2,1	4,5	9—10
ШЕРСТЯНЫЕ ТКАНИ (млн. метров)	299	280	550—650
ОБУВЬ КОЖАНАЯ (млн. пар)	586	315	600—700

PRODUCTION poster in 1959 quoted Khrushchev as saying that "in the next 15 years the Soviet Land can not only catch up with but surpass the present volume of production of the most important type of goods of the U.S.A." It listed U.S. output in steel, oil, electric power and coal compared to anticipated Soviet output. Posters urged ever greater efforts.

STUDENTS filing into Moscow University lecture rooms include many young women. Yekaterina Furtseva, highest-ranking woman in the Soviet Communist Party, reported in 1960 that nation had 1,283,000 women teachers, including 1000 women professors in Moscow University. She said most Soviet specialists are women—engineers, physicians, scientists.

"LITTLE SUMMIT" debate between Premier Khrushchev and Vice President Nixon occurred in July, 1959, in kitchen area of U.S. Exhibition in Moscow's Sokolniki Park. Argument on merits of capitalism versus Communism grew quite heated. Nixon relayed invitation to Khrushchev to visit the U.S.

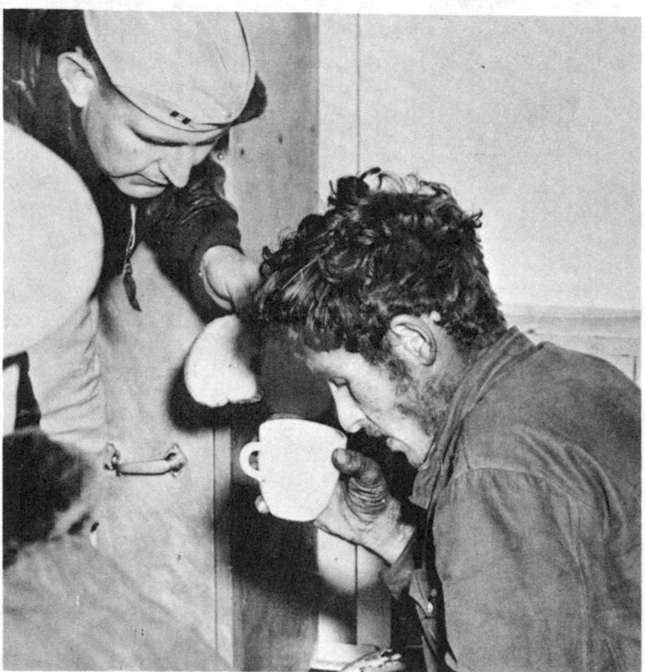

RESCUED AT SEA, Red Army Private Ivan Fredoto, 21, drains coffee after he and three other Soviet soldiers had been picked up from amphibious landing craft which drifted in Pacific 49 days. Bearded and grimy, Fredoto was cared for by U.S. Marines aboard the aircraft carrier *USS Kearsage.*

HUNGARIAN PATRIOTS FLY HUNGARIAN RED, WHITE AND GREEN FLAG ATOP CAPTURED SOVIET TANK IN BLOODY, ABORTIVE 1956 REVOLT

SATELLITES GROW RESTIVE

East German workers rise; Hungarian revolt is drowned in blood; Poland attains limited freedom; "slave" industry output up

THE KREMLIN, in a decade punctuated by revolts, wholesale purges and terror, slowly tightened its control over a belt of satellite states comprising nearly 400,000 square miles and nearly 100 million people.

Most heartbreaking development in the Khrushchev era of Soviet grip on the captive peoples behind the Iron Curtain began Oct. 23, 1956, when the Hungarian anti-Soviet revolt exploded. Even before Stalin died in 1953, Hungarians had watched Tito's Yugoslavs break with Moscow. Polish workers also had rioted to force better terms. In Budapest that day Red police fired on rioting students and the revolt erupted. Imre Nagy, a Communist, but not a Kremlin favorite, became premier by popular demand of the demonstrators. He replaced Andras Hegedus. By Oct. 28, Nagy announced Soviet troops had agreed to withdraw from Hungary. But this turned out to be a Red trick. The Soviet commander merely called up reinforcements, launched a massive surprise attack Nov. 1, and crushed the rising of the Hungarian people. Estimates of the dead ranged up to 35,000. Thousands vanished in deportation. A total of 200,000 more fled into Austria and Yugoslavia. Nagy was among those executed later. All UN efforts to send inquiry teams into Hungary failed, and the Soviet troops remained there. Moscow's new puppet in Hungary, Janos Kadar, obtained great doses of goods from Russia, but by 1960 had not healed the wounds.

Hungary, Poland, Czechoslovakia, East Germany, Rumania, Bulgaria and Albania had been bound militarily to Moscow by the 1955 Warsaw Pact aimed to counter NATO, and to Soviet economy through their COMECON, Red counterpart of the Common Market in West Europe. Fear of another revolt in Poland simultaneous with the Hungarian uprising led Khrushchev to make such concessions as withdrawing Soviet Marshal Konstantin Rokossovsky as head of Polish armed forces. But Poland under Communist Party chief Gomulka did not dare stray far from the Soviet pattern in its "liberalization."

Polish Reds battled against meat shortages and industrial discontent at the end of a decade of strain; other satellites had similar problems, including peasant resistance to the drive for total land collectivization. But a UN report told of an over-all better lot for the consumers in the Soviet bloc. Industrial production steadily picked up, although Soviet planning still gave the edge to production of capital goods over consumers' goods. Rumania reactivated an oil industry thought to be on its last legs; people had more food and clothes in East Germany; Czechoslovakia flourished; and Bulgaria renewed its diplomatic relations with the United States.

AFTER EIGHT YEARS' imprisonment, Josef Cardinal Mindszenty, spiritual leader of Hungary's 71% Catholic majority, was temporarily freed by 1956 revolt. When Russians ruthlessly crushed rebels he took refuge in U.S. legation.

THIS WOMAN REFUGEE sidesteps her way to freedom in Austria on improvised bridge of tree branch and guide rope flung across canal on border. Communists destroyed bridges to halt flight; 200,000 escaped within a few months.

GIRL PATRIOT leads band of workers who started June, 1956, bread riots in Poznan, Poland. Workers carry a flag stained with the blood of a 16-year-old boy killed in the uprising outside the huge International Trade Fair the day before. The workers marched through the streets chanting, "bread, bread, bread!" Red authorities officially admitted that at least 38 persons had been killed and 270 wounded in quelling revolt; also they admitted workers' grievances were just.

"BLOODY WEDNESDAY" workers' revolt in East Berlin broke out, June 17, 1953, as climax of general strike. East Germans marched through famed Brandenburg Gate into free West Berlin in brief, despairing insurrection. Russians declared martial law, crushed rebellion with vicious street slaughter.

LINES OF SOVIET T-34 TANKS clear rioters from streets in the vicinity of East Berlin government headquarters during fierce 1953 uprising. Soviet commander, General Dibrova, became furious when booed by angry German workers and at showers of Russian-language, anti-Communist leaflets.

CARDINAL WYSZYNSKI, Primate of deeply Catholic Poland, formed uneasy alliance with ideological enemy, Gomulka, to maintain limited liberty in native country of both. But, as decade ended, relations between Church, State were strained.

WLADYSLAW GOMULKA, Polish Communist Party secretary, announced to Warsaw crowd of 500,000 on Oct. 24, 1956, that Soviet troops would not enter country despite anti-Red riots; Poland compromised to avoid Hungary's fate.

CZECHOSLOVAKIAN INDUSTRY served as a front for Soviet political ambitions in the Middle East. Such factories as Skoda furnished Egypt with arms that it could not obtain elsewhere. Workers received higher wages to increase production. Docile satellite nation also became a big exporter to Latin America.

MILOVAN DJILAS, former Yugoslav vice president, got seven-year prison term because he denounced the Tito regime and Soviet suppressions in Hungary.

ALOYSIUS CARDINAL STEPINAC, spiritual leader of Yugoslavia's 7 million Roman Catholics, and outspoken foe of Marshal Tito, died February 10, 1960, aged 62. This picture shows him in his austere prison cell in 1951. He had been jailed four years before on charge of wartime Nazi collaboration.

PUPPET Hungarian Premier Ferenc Muennich warmly greeted Premier Khrushchev *(r.)* on latter's 1959 visit to Budapest. Soviet troops remained in force in Hungary after revolt.

YUGOSLAVIA'S DICTATOR, President Tito, gets light from smiling host, United Arab Republic chief Gamal Abdel Nasser, on 1959 visit to Cairo. Both proclaimed "neutralism", but Nasser gladly accepted Soviet aid, Tito got U.S. aid. Tito remained only big Communist leader to defy Kremlin.

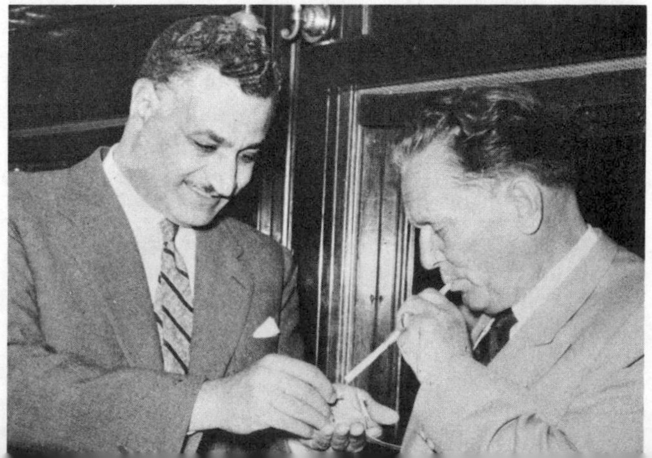

ATOMIC REACTOR, the first to be set up in Hungary, went into operation March 25, 1959. Soviet Union technicians, using Russian equipment, helped build the unit in the town of Csilleberg. It had a capacity of two megawatts, and would be used for research and the training of scientists. The Russians gave ample aid to puppet leaders after revolt.

CZECH PREMIER Antonin Novotny *(l.)*, Poland's Gomulka *(r.)* smile on beaming Khrushchev at 1960 Kremlin meeting of Warsaw Pact powers which called for separate peace treaty with East Germany. Pact is equivalent to West's NATO.

IRON CURTAIN, lifted momentarily by ill-fated Hungarian revolt, falls again between Hungary and Austria. Barbed wire, fierce dogs and mines, at end of decade, guarded all Red frontiers, made flight to freedom virtually impossible.

REJUVENATED WEST GERMANY BECOMES KEY NATO LINK

Nation, prostrate after World War II, takes economic lead in Europe, builds strong army; Adenauer triumphs in three successive elections

WEST GERMANY soared from the ashes of World War II defeat during the decade. Its amazing recovery bolstered West European unity and alarmed competitors. Its booming business, based on free enterprise, private capital and ownership, was heartening to the Western world.

Konrad Adenauer, 84-year-old elder statesman, aided by Ludwig Erhard, his Economic Minister, led the country to new political and industrial dominance. Adenauer firmly tied Germany's future to the Western Allies, his big hope in his long-range dream of a reunified Germany.

The "Miracle on the Rhine" began in 1951 when the Allies lifted limits on production. Unemployment then was 1.3 million but, at the end of the decade, manpower was actually short, despite the flow of millions of refugees from East Germany. Marshall Plan funds sped the remarkable recovery. U.S. aid, aside from vast military expenditures, totaled about $4 billion in a decade. But hard work and the skills of "Der Alte" Adenauer and his aides put Germany back among the top industrial nations, second only to the U.S. in the West.

Chancellor Adenauer signed a virtual peace treaty with the Big Three Western Allies in 1952, restoring Germany's independence in exchange for supporting the West militarily. Full sovereignty came May 5, 1955, after 10 years of occupation, when Bonn formally joined the North Atlantic Treaty Organization.

It was free to establish its own foreign policy, conduct its own peaceful atomic research and build a fast, highly-mobile army. Germany intended to have a force of 250,000 in the field by 1961, a revision of an original goal of 500,000 soldiers. Its first rocket battalion became operational in 1959.

West Germany paid more than $1.4 billion to Israel and individual Jewish victims of Nazism under a 1952 pact scheduled to expire in 1963. The I. G. Farben chemical trust and the Krupp steel empire agreed separately to pay a total of $8.8 million to former Jewish slave laborers.

Adenauer, thrice victorious in elections during the '50s, established a close accord with France and gained back the Saar territory in 1957. A big political question: who will be his successor? Politicians said it might be team mate Ludwig Erhard.

KONRAD ADENAUER, West Germany's Chancellor since 1949, tied his nation to NATO, spurred economic boom.

LUDWIG ERHARD, *(r.)* Economic Minister, effected truce with Adenauer in 1959. Coolness developed when Adenauer decided to retain job as Chancellor, not retire to Presidency. Erhard wanted the job. Heinrich Luebke became President.

POLITICAL MOAT in Europe is the divided German nation. West Germany is firmly fixed to the western allies; East Germany is anchored in the Soviet satellite camp. Both are strong industrially, West Germany being second only to U.S.

ALFRED VON KRUPP *(in doorway)* leaves the Landsberg Prison after 1951 pardon. Ruhr steel baron was war criminal.

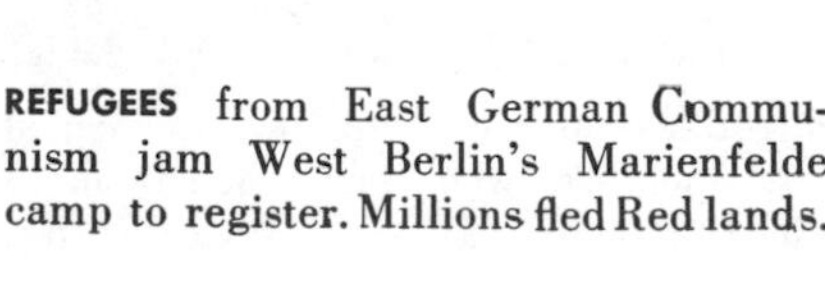

REFUGEES from East German Communism jam West Berlin's Marienfelde camp to register. Millions fled Red lands.

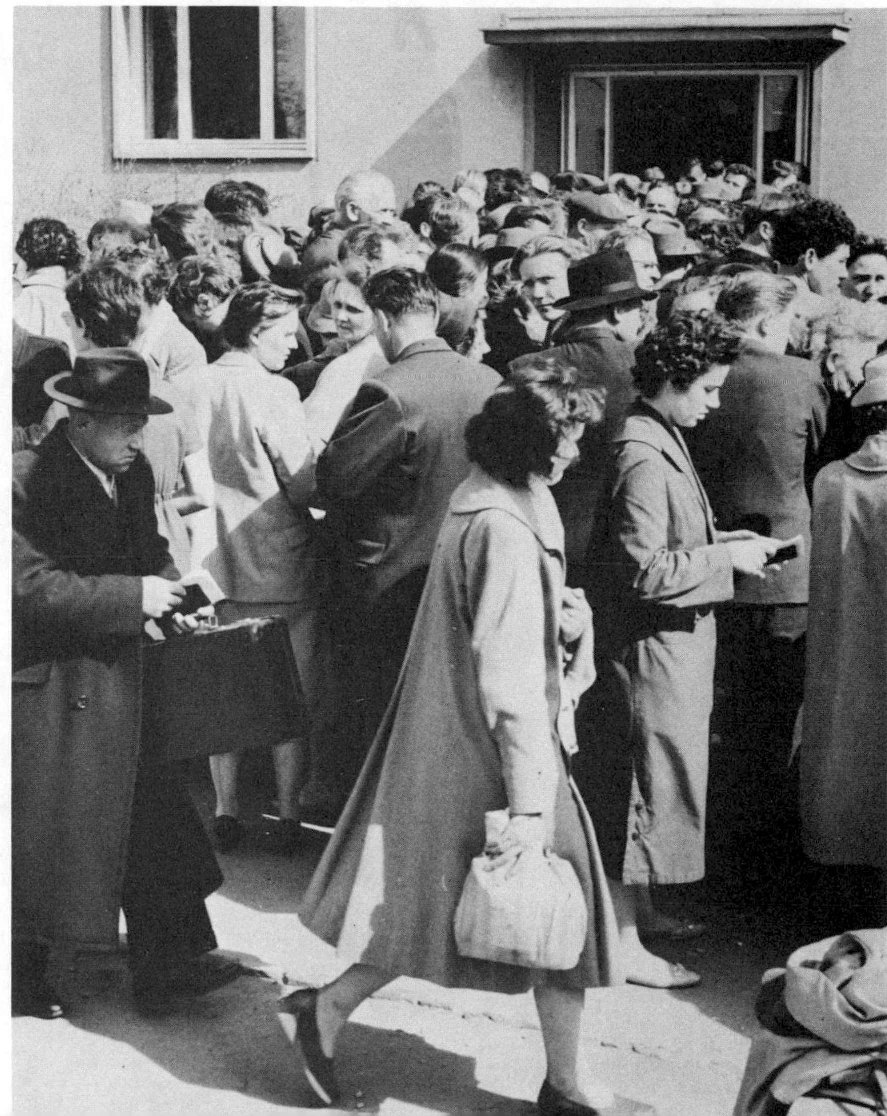

NEW ARMY of West Germans, equipped with U.S.-supplied arms and uniforms, gets first workout April 19, 1956, after the Bundeswehr was legalized despite much resistance. Original goal was 500,000 men. Plan now calls for 250,000 by 1961. All air force and navy force are recruited voluntarily.

SMEARERS of Jewish synagogue in Cologne, Paul Schoenen, 25, with raised hand, and Arnold Strunk, *(l.)* go on trial. Christmas Eve, 1959, desecration set off world wave of anti-Semitic acts.

A NEW SOURCE of energy for West German industry will come from such nuclear reactors as this one, the nation's largest, being constructed at Karlsruhe. Attempts of Chancellor Adenauer to introduce atomic weapons into Armed Forces were blocked by Socialists who feared such a move would put Germany in the middle in a third world war.

FIREWORKS explode over Homburg in Saar to celebrate Jan. 1, 1957, return to Germany from France of coal rich area, now 10th state of West Germany.

GIANT KRUPP FACTORY at Rheinhausen typifies vast Ruhr coal and steel complex. heart of West German heavy industry. Nation's steel production reached an all-time high in the 1950-1960 decade. Alfred von Krupp himself owns the vast, 150-plant Krupp group, largest single German combine in all West Germany.

VOLKSWAGEN assembly line pours out cars for foreign market. West German exports multiplied five times in decade.

WILLY BRANDT, popular West German mayor, talks with Chancellor Adenauer before addressing city parliament January 11, 1960. Chancellor Adenauer said that any change in West Berlin's status would surrender freedom to the Reds.

SERIOUS YOUNG Elizabeth II, queen of the world's largest community of nations, the British Commonwealth, wears crown, carries orb and sceptre in procession in Westminster Abbey following her coronation June 2, 1953. Foreign royalty and distinguished official guests stand in homage as she passes. She actually succeeded when father died in 1952.

GREAT BRITAIN STAYS IN SUN

Prosperity helps Conservatives triumph in three successive elections; Winston Churchill retires; Queen Elizabeth II succeeds father George V

THE BRITISH Conservative Party, led by Sir Winston Churchill, Sir Anthony Eden and Harold Macmillan, enjoyed a decade of smashing political and economic successes, marred only by the abortive invasion of Egypt which permanently dimmed Eden's political star.

The Labor Party reeled in defeat, split sharply into quarreling leftist and rightist factions. Macmillan's campaign of "you've never had it so good" prosperity paid off in the Oct. 8, 1959, elections which gave the Conservatives a 100-seat majority in the House of Commons, almost double that won in 1955.

In 1960, the facts justified British optimism for a bright future. Although the British had not regained the unique world dominance they enjoyed in the mid-19th century, they had established themselves as the major economic "third force" in the world between the U.S. and the Soviet bloc. Exports exceeded imports. Gold and dollar and other hard currency reserves had increased past the $3 billion mark. A $250 million loan from the U.S. obtained after the Suez muddle had been paid back over five years before it was due. British grants and loans to other nations from the end of World War II totalled more than $5.5 billion, with the outflow accelerating. The United Kingdom, despite war losses and transformation of the former empire into a "commonwealth," still remained a creditor nation, second only to the U.S. as a source of aid, loans and investment for the entire non-Communist world. Quotas on most imports from the dollar area had been abolished, opening wide a market of 52 million people with more money than ever before.

CLEMENT ATTLEE, former laborite prime minister, entered the House of Lords.

EX-MINER Aneurin "Nye" Bevan, most dynamic Laborite, died July 6, 1960.

HUGH GAITSKELL rose from obscurity to Labor Party helm in only a decade.

Churchill's Conservatives got back into office in 1951, defeating Prime Minister Clement Attlee's laborites, who had established a "welfare state" after ousting Churchill near the end of the war in 1945. Even then, the Laborites had been feuding among themselves, because of Attlee's decision to expand the arms program during the Korean war. Minister of Labor Aneurin Bevan led a group into resigning. Bevan, artisan of the free National Health Service, also became angered when the Attlee regime decided to make recipients pay at least half of the price of once free spectacles and false teeth. From then on, until his death in 1960, Bevan and left-wing followers fought against Attlee, and later party leader Hugh Gaitskell. After labor's crushing defeat in 1959, Bevan conceded in a House of Commons speech that "Our (Labor) name became identified with grayness, dullness, frugalities and shortages."

In 1953 Prime Minister Churchill imposed no new taxes (for the first time in 24 years) and even reduced some existing ones. Food controls eased. Britain's adverse trade balance improved. After Stalin's death, he proposed that the major powers informally meet to ease tensions and try for an East-West agreement. After years of refusing honors bearing titles, he finally, in 1954, accepted knighthood in the Garter, highest British order. He resigned in May, 1955, in favor of Sir Anthony Eden, 57, his "heir apparent," who had served long years as Foreign Secretary.

Sir Anthony ran into trouble almost immediately. Cypriotes fought and killed British soldiers in their drive for independence. His own party men charged him with "timidity" and "half measures." Then, in 1956, Nasser seized the internationally-owned Suez Canal. Sir Anthony protested to no avail. Finally, in cooperation with France and Israel, the British bombarded and invaded the Canal Zone. But the war halted quickly under U.S., Soviet and UN pressure. Sir Anthony resigned Jan. 9, 1957, and was succeeded by Macmillan. Faced with ill health, and politically disavowed, Prime Minister Eden ended his distinguished career.

OLD WARRIOR Sir Winston Churchill made way for Sir Anthony Eden in '55.

SIR ANTHONY EDEN quit prime ministership after the 1956 debacle at Suez.

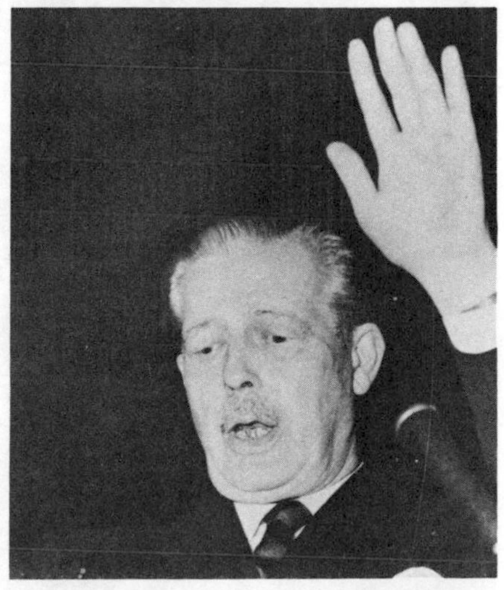

POST-SUEZ prime minister, Harold Macmillan, succeeded Sir Anthony Eden.

Macmillan did not disavow the Suez adventure, but he soft-pedalled it, and began retrenching to pay for the costly debacle. After a year of retrenchment, however, Great Britain emerged in an economic and political position of greater strength. By 1960, aside from winning an unprecedented victory at the polls on "prosperity and free enterprise" themes, Macmillan ordered a big defense boost to a record $4.5 billion. While dedicated to relaxing tensions and striving for a settlement with the Soviet Union, he constantly warned Great Britain must keep up its guard. Meanwhile, he had restored diplomatic relations with the United Arab Republic, broken after the Suez invasion.

Sadness and joy swept over the British Royal Family during the decade. The beloved King George VI died of a circulatory ailment Feb. 6, 1952. His elder daughter, Elizabeth, on an African vacation with her husband at the time, became Queen and was crowned June 2, 1953, in a procession watched by more than 2 million persons. Dowager Queen Mary, her grandmother, never lived to see the coronation. She died the previous March 24, aged 85. The cry of "It's a boy" went up Feb. 19, 1960, to signal the birth of a third child and second prince to Elizabeth II. Next in line to the throne after Prince Charles, the son became Prince Andrew.

On March 26, Princess Margaret, 29, only sister of Elizabeth, announced her engagement to a fashion photographer, Antony Armstrong-Jones, 30, ending a decade of speculation on her eventual choice. They married May 6, 1960. Four years before, she had ended her romance with Group Capt. Peter Townsend, one of the heroes of the Battle of Britain, because he had been divorced.

In neighboring Ireland, New York-born Eamon de Valera, at 77, resigned as premier, and became president.

HAPPY COUPLE, Princess Margaret Rose, 29, sister of Queen Elizabeth, and Antony Armstrong-Jones, 30, a photographer, waved from Buckingham Palace balcony May 6, 1960, after their marriage in Westminster Abbey. Capt. Peter Townsend, *(l.)*, was considered suitor, but Margaret yielded to Church of England, Royal Family, announcing Oct. 31, 1955, an end of her romance with Townsend, a divorced man.

RACE RIOTING caused a great deal of trouble in England in 1958. In this photo, taken the night of Aug. 31, police seize a white man and woman during a race riot in the Notting Hill district of South London. More than 400 persons were reported involved in Notting Hill clashes. The night before, violence erupted in the city of Nottingham, 123 miles northwest of London. Big influx of West Indians looking for work, needing housing, led to the violent outbreaks.

OPEN HEARTH furnace such as this one at Ebbw Vale, South Wales, aided British steel production and swelling export boom at end of decade. Auto and steel makers both did extremely well and planned further expansions which Britons hoped would extend eventually to the depressed shipbuilding industry.

MASS PROTEST, England's largest, and most significant, attracted nearly 75,000 persons to Trafalgar Square in London April 18, 1960. Crowd roared its approval of demands for unilateral nuclear disarmament by Great Britain, end of U.S. and British nuclear bases in United Kingdom, withdrawal from alliances like North Atlantic Pact.

EAMON DE VALERA, whose name is synonymous with Irish independence, at 77 years of age, finally gave up 40-year political grip. Veteran New York-born premier retired to the Presidency.

HER MAJESTY Queen Elizabeth poses with Commonwealth prime ministers who met in London in June, 1957. They are *(l. to r.)* John Diefenbaker, Canada; Harold Macmillan, Great Britain; R. G. Menzies, Australia; E. H. Louw, South Africa; H. S. Suhrawardv, Pakistan; J. Nehru, India; Sir Roy Welensky, Central African Fed.; Kwame Nkrumah, Ghana; Thos. McDonald, N. Z.; M. H. DeSilva, Ceylon.

DE GAULLE RETURNS, RULES 5th REPUBLIC

Resumes power to restore stability, end Algerian revolt; sweeps new elections

"MAN OF DESTINY" Gen. Charles de Gaulle enters Elysee Palace to talk with President Rene Coty after becoming premier June 1, 1958, during army revolt on Algerian policies. He later became president of "Fifth Republic," exercising strong executive powers. France underwent most dramatic changes since Napoleon.

FRANCE, in two and one-half years under Gen. Charles de Gaulle, saw the most drastic changes since the days of Napoleon. The nation averted civil war, got a new constitution, stabilized its economy, became the world's fourth nuclear power by exploding a test bomb, and exploited the petroleum riches of the vast Sahara. Despite the bloody drain of the Algerian rebellion, the nation under the tall, wartime hero spoke with a stronger voice on the world stage. De Gaulle's swift certainty ended a decade of ineffective rule.

The General had resigned as provisional president of the postwar government in 1946, and in 1953 had quit politics in disgust at what he called the "parliamentary game" of the Fourth Republic. Once, in 1951, his party, the Rally of the French People, was the strongest single group in parliament, but coalitions of others reduced its effectiveness.

During the 12 years de Gaulle was out of office, France had more than a score of premiers, but none was able to hold power long in the face of weaknesses in the constitution and costly conflicts abroad.

Premier Pierre Mendes-France wrote off the lost war in Indo-China with the 1954 truce in Geneva. In 1956, France granted independence to the protectorates of Tunisia and Morocco, but not to Algeria, which long had been regarded as part of metropolitan France. French had been settled in Algeria since 1830.

French settlers and army leaders revolted May 13, 1958, against Premier Pierre Pflimlin, fearing that he planned a "sell-out" to Algerian guerrilla leaders who had been waging war since 1954 in their drive for complete independence from the French. Mobs demanded the return of de Gaulle. Military-civilian juntas took control in Algeria, then seized Corsica. Pflimlin resigned, and de Gaulle became premier June 1 after demanding six months of full decree power. He also demanded, and got, after threatening to resign, power to revise the constitution.

Voters overwhelmingly approved a Fifth Republic constitution Sept. 28, 1958, giving a president strong executive powers, including dictatorial power in times of an emergency.

ANTOINE PINAY shakes hands with U.S. Gen. Matthew B. Ridgway, NATO chief, in 1952 when France enjoyed its most stable post-war government up to that time. The popular premier managed to slow price spirals and lessen the number of strikes. He took firm action against Communist rioters demonstrating against Ridgway's arrival in Paris. Police arrested key Reds, including veteran chief Jacques Duclos.

PIERRE MENDES-FRANCE (r.), a Radical Socialist (conservative) premier, obtained peace in Indo-China in 1954, but at a stiff price. He and Socialist party leader Guy Mollet *(l.)*, premier in 1956, were brief political allies. Mollet balked at Mendes' wish to rush the Algerian rebel talks.

STARTLING NEWCOMER in French politics, Pierre Poujade gained his followers 52 seats in 1956 National Assembly elections. He helped rupture Mollet-Mendes-France's Republican Front. He championed small businessmen's complaints on taxes. His group, however, later disintegrated in assembly.

Gaullists won a large majority in new assembly elections; Communist strength was cut from 143 deputies to 10; a new economic program produced a $1.15 billion favorable balance of payments in 1959 after three years of net losses; new "French Community" of nations replaced the former French African Empire and other overseas territories, only Guinea voting to cut all ties with France; a five-year $4 billion development program for Algeria began; de Gaulle, at 68, became president of the Fifth Republic Jan. 8, 1959, for seven years.

De Gaulle's offer of self-determination to Algeria brought another settler insurrection in Algiers a year later. He smashed it, shook up the army command, and also his cabinet of "technicians." He fired Jacques Soustelle, one of those who led the original revolt that returned de Gaulle to power. The assembly granted him decree-rule power, and Feb. 13, 1960, he gained prestige when an atomic bomb was tested successfully. This occurred just before his triumphant visit to the U.S.

FRANCO-GERMAN accord of President de Gaulle and Chancellor Adenauer *(r.)* gave basis to European economic and defense cooperation. In this December, 1959, meeting, De Gaulle reportedly calmed Adenauer's fears about French wish to revise NATO pact in such a way as to jeopardize the U.S. contribution to European defense. The French leader had objected to the integration of European air forces; De Gaulle also demanded seperate French atomic arm.

WARTIME COMMANDERS President de Gaulle, bareheaded, and President Eisenhower, examine a Civil War cannon while touring the famous Gettysburg battle field during de Gaulle's '60 visit.

PROTEST banners in French, Arabic, and English fly above crowd in Tunis, Jan. 25, 1960, demonstrating against France's planned Sahara atomic test. French exploded atomic bomb Feb. 13.

TRAGEDY, worst in history of auto racing, occurred at Le Mans, France, June 11, 1955, during famed 24-hour classic when driver Pierre Levegh hit another car at 140 miles per hour and hurtled into crowd. Toll: 82 dead; 73 injured.

BIGGEST SUSPENSION BRIDGE in Europe was built in 1959 at Tancarville, France, 20 miles upstream from Le Havre on the Seine River estuary. Workers at right, using a small gondola, rivet the king-size cables on 2000-ft.-long bridge.

ANGRY FARMERS gather at war memorial in Perigueux to demonstrate March 14, 1960, against French government agricultural policy which they claimed produced low incomes and high debts. De Gaulle refused special parliament session.

MILK DRINKING school children *(below, r.)* respond to Premier Pierre Mendes-France's program to boost consumption of dairy products and reduce French wine imbibing. His drive in 1954 to get adults on milk instead of winc collapsed.

FINE EXAMPLE of Italian craftsmanship is 32,000-ton ocean liner, Leonardo da Vinci, moored *(above)* in dry dock at Genoa, Italy, after successful May, 1960 trial run to test engines. It is the biggest liner built in Italy since World War II. Andrea Doria, sunk on July 25, 1956, off Nantucket, weighed 29,083 tons.

PROSPEROUS PENINSULA

Italian output soars; Christian Democrats continue shaky rule

ALCIDE DE GASPERI, long-time leader of the Italian Christian Democratic Party, was a firm friend of the West, and retained uneasy control of Italy while he was premier from 1947 to 1953. He held together a shaky combination of conflicting philosophies in his party as bulwark against the Communists. He died Aug. 19, '53.

SILVIO MILAZZO, rebuked by Church, Christian Democrats for accepting Communist support in local Sicilian parliament, bolted ruling party in 1959, formed own group. He won victory in elections, resumed office as regional president.

PALMIRO TOGLIATTI, leader of the Italian Communist Party of two million — largest outside the Iron Curtain — kept pressure on Italian governments ever since the war. In 1958 national elections the Reds and allies won 33% of votes.

ITALY, plagued by Communist-inspired strikes and turmoil, nevertheless ended the decade with an industrial production which broke all previous records. With 1953 as the base of 100, the production index rose to a high of 154 in 1960. A sensational further increase in gold and hard currency reserves brought, by 1960, a record total of $3.3 billion. Since 1953, Italy's Gross National Product had risen at a rate only slightly under West Germany's, the same as in France, and 2.5 times that of U.S. Italian recovery, like that of the rest of Western Europe, began with huge U.S. aid of $2.9 billion. Italy still had a tough job exporting enough to create a favorable balance of trade. But the adverse balance dropped to $170 million in 1960 from $718 million in 1957. Unemployment declined to 1.9 million from more than 2 million in 1951, although population rose from 46 million to 49 million.

Politically, the decade ended as it began, with the Christian Democratic Party—led brilliantly by Premier Alcide de Gasperi from 1947 until his death in 1953—clinging to power only with the consent of rivals and by entering coalitions to fend off the Communists, led by veteran Palmiro Togliatti. Christian Democrat Amintore Fanfani could form a cabinet in 1960 only after five months punctuated with riots, squabbles and uncertainy.

ITALIAN PRESIDENT Giovanni Gronchi *(r.)* visits Red host, Soviet Premier Khrushchev, at latter's country house near Moscow Feb. 7, 1960, while on state trip. Beside him is Mrs. Khrushchev, while Signora Gronchi talks to premier.

PIETRO NENNI heads Left Socialists, was firm Togliatti ally throughout most of decade. Attempts to reunite Togliatti 's group with right wing led by Pietro Nenni failed, and Nenni deputies usually supported Christian Democrat rule.

NEO-FASCISTS turned out in strength to raise arms in salute before bust of former Italian dictator, Benito Mussolini, at the tomb in his birthplace, Predappio, mountain town in North Italy. Estimated 5000 made Aug. 31, 1958, "pilgrimage" to Predappio. The trip was organized by Italian Social Movement, noisy neo-fascist group. Mussolini was executed near end of World War II by Italian partisans while trying to escape to Switzerland. Until 1957, when the Italian government turned over his corpse to the widow, Donna Rachele Mussolini, body had been secreted in a monastery.

TEMPEST IN TRIESTE occurred Nov. 6, 1953, after the Anglo-U.S. decision to turn Zone A of the disputed area over to Italian administration. Pro-Italian demonstrators, adding fuel to an already explosive situation, are watching flames consume office furniture belonging to the Independence Party, which had favored a "Free State" of Trieste. At least six persons were killed in Italian-Yugoslav rioting before U.S. and British troops were called in to restore order. After long negotiations, Italy and Yugoslavia signed an agreement Oct. 4, 1954, dividing the 320 square-mile area.

U.S. AMBASSADOR to Italy, Clare Booth Luce, arrives in April, 1959, with her husband, Time-Life-Fortune publisher Henry R. Luce. Although warmly received, she stirred a lively controversy when she strongly intimated U.S. aid would halt if Italy went to totalitarian extreme, Red or right.

L'AFFAIRE MONTESI: A Neo-Fascist editor, trying to upset Premier Mario Scelba's shaky government in 1954, told a wild story of a narcotics ring orgy resulting in the death of Rome playgirl Wilma Montesi. Prominent people with political ties were named in welter of inconclusive charges.

"FREE AND INDEPENDENT" reads the newspaper waved by joyous Austrian couple after May 15, 1955 signing of Four-Power treaty ending the post-war occupation.

AUSTRIA REGAINS SOVEREIGN STATUS

"Neutrality" pledge ends Soviet occupation

AUSTRIA EMERGED from the historic decade as the only winner of an international chess game in which the Allies (France, Great Britain, U.S.) and USSR were continually, often frenetically, checking each other, only to have checkmate go to their pawn.

Central European tensions being what they were, Austria was forced, in 1955, to accept neutrality in exchange for freedom and withdrawal of occupation troops. But just how far legal neutrality extended was evidenced by the chilly welcome afforded Khrushchev on his 1960 visit.

In a decade scarred by change and tensions, Switzerland managed to maintain tranquility and peace, attracting numerous foreign minister conferences, disarmament negotiations and international organizations.

Switzerland did as well economically as it did diplomatically. Over 300 hydroelectric plants tapped the small nation's abundant water supply. Heavy exports of watches, precision instruments and dairy products, coupled with its enviable import of tourist dollars, gave the Swiss one of the highest standards of living in Europe.

As a neutral state Switzerland entered into no military alliances, but served as common ground for all.

CHEERING AMERICAN students parade at Communist-sponsored Viennese Youth Festival. 11,000 young people from 100 countries gathered in summer of 1959.

JULIUS RAAB, blunt, right-wing Austrian Chancellor since 1953, led his Catholic People's Party government coalition with Socialists, maintained neutrality.

GENEVA'S STATELY, formal Palais des Nations was the scene of often turbulent international meetings of scientists, diplomats, and state leaders.

LOW COUNTRIES DRAW CLOSER

Benelux economic union nears completion, setting pattern for rest of West Europe; Belgian exports double during decade; Leopold, King of Belgians, abdicates in favor of eldest son, Baudouin

LEOPOLD OF THE BELGIANS signs away rights to throne July 16, 1951, making eldest son Baudouin *(r.)* a reluctant king who retained loyalty to his father.

THE "LOW COUNTRIES," the Netherlands, Belgium, and Luxembourg moved close during the 50s to a resumption of their historic unity, broken in the 16th Century by the Netherlands' revolt against Philip II of Spain.

The Benelux union, planned by the three governments while in exile during the Nazi occupation, came near completion with ratification of the treaty of 1958. (Luxembourg has been economically united with Belgium since World War I.)

Under the treaty, frontiers within the area virtually ceased to exist, and foreign trade and economic and social policies were almost completely coordinated. (The existence of three separate dynasties made formal political union seem more remote.)

The union of the three, all highly industrialized, was setting the pattern for West European economic union, which all three championed as charter members of the Common Market, the Iron and Steel Community, and the N. Atlantic Treaty Organization.

The prosperity of both the Netherlands and Belgium-Luxembourg depended largely on foreign trade (their great ports, Rotterdam in the Netherlands and Antwerp in Belgium, were respectively, third and fourth largest in Europe) and exports of both doubled during the decade.

In internal politics, developments were much alike. Both were ruled throughout the '50s by Socialist-Catholic coalitions (the Netherlands, once predominantly Protestant, found itself with a Roman Catholic majority), and cabinet posts were shuffled among the same groups of leaders in an endless game of musical chairs.

Both, too, ended the decade without the foreign possessions which had played important parts in their economies. The Netherlands lost Indonesia in 1949, just before the decade began, and, in 1960, Belgium granted independence to the Congo. (Belgian troops, however, remained to prevent total anarchy in the new nation, pending a full take-over by the UN.)

Personal drama was furnished mostly by royalty.

Leopold, King of the Belgians, in 1951, was forced to abdicate in favor of his son Baudouin. Leopold was unpopular because, it was perhaps unfairly claimed, he had been too quick to surrender to the Germans in 1940 and because, during the Occupation, he had remarried — to the lovely daughter of an industrialist. And until he moved from the royal palace, late in the '50s, tempests were stirred by his alleged "undue influence" over his royal son.

Loyal Netherlanders, in mid-decade, were upset by rumors of rifts between Queen Juliana and her husband Prince Bernhard. Again it was "undue influence," that of a faith-healer tending one of the royal children.

AN AGE-OLD STRUGGLE intensified when furious 1953 winter storms smashed dikes, swamped nearly a million acres, took 1800 lives. Nevertheless, Netherlands, in '50s, added thousands of acres by filling in most of Zuider Zee, former North Sea inlet.

TENSION EASED July 2, 1959, when Albert, bachelor Baudouin's younger brother and heir, wed lovely Donna Paola Ruffo di Calabria, of old Italian noble house. In 1960 she gave birth to son, thus providing ultimate successor to crown.

U.S. PAVILION proved center of attraction at 1958 Brussels World's Fair, which drew 15 million visitors. U.S. display, which provided "samples" of American life, and Soviet exhibit, which stressed industry, science, drew biggest crowds.

SWEDISH NAVY has an atom age "garage" *(above)*. "Operation Granite," launched after World War II, has scooped tunnel-like harbors into cliffs along coastline.

FINLAND won concession from USSR in 1956 when Porkkala Naval Base, leased by Soviet Union in 1944, was returned, Finnish flag was raised again *(above)*.

EUROPE'S FREE NORTH

Scandinavia shares in world prosperity, remains staunchly independent despite Red saber-rattling

NORWAY, Sweden and Denmark enjoyed a decade of peace and prosperity, marred only by occasional rocket-rattling from nearby USSR.

NATO members Norway and Denmark and neutral but staunchly democratic Sweden were subjected throughout the decade to a barrage of alternating Soviet insults, threats and cajolery, but refused to withdraw from their pro-Western position.

Finland, smaller, weaker, and menaced by the Soviet Union across 650 miles of common border, was forced to maintain strict neutrality in the East-West struggle as the price of freedom. Prime Minister Urho Kekkonen summed up his nation's perilous position when he said, in 1951, "We live on fine distinctions."

Finland could not, for instance, have run the risk of annoying its giant neighbor by joining the European Free Trade Association, or "Outer Seven," as Norway, Sweden and Denmark did in 1960.

The EFTA, whose geographically scattered membership included, in addition to the three Scandinavian countries, Great Britain, Austria, Switzerland and Portugal, was formed as a competitive counterpart to the Common Market (France, West Germany, Italy, and the Benelux group.)

But its leaders—especially in Scandinavia—hoped that it would prove to be a stepping stone to complete economic integration of Free Europe, and that it would eventually be amalgamated with the Common Market.

ICELAND lived from the sea. It squabbled during decade with Great Britain over coastal fishing, and with U.S. and NATO over presence of U.S. troops.

POPULAR constitutional monarchies were firmly established in Norway, Denmark, Sweden. Norway's King Haakon, who died in 1958, greets his great grandson.

SPAIN AND PORTUGAL, while anti-Communist bastions, also were enclaves of totalitarianism and poverty in the midst of booming, democratic Western Europe.

In Spain, Generalissimo Francisco Franco rode high through his second decade of one-man rule. There were undercurrents of opposition to the Franco regime, but the people of Spain remembered the horrors of the Civil War of the '30s too well to want to risk another.

Early in the decade, Spain got a badly needed economic boost when the U.S. decided that whether it (and its NATO allies) liked Franco or not, his country was too strategically located to be ignored, and would be given dollar aid in exchange for air and naval base sites.

Between 1953 and 1960, $400 million worth of military installations went up in Spain, while over $1 billion in cash, loans and commodities poured into the country.

The psychological importance of U.S. friendship to Spain was almost as great as its material value. It raised the prestige of the Franco government, which had been something of a diplomatic outcast among free nations ever since it came to power in 1939, at home and abroad.

By decade's end, the Spanish economy was undeniably expanding—and paying the price of expansion with inflation so severe that a drastic fiscal reform program had to be launched in the summer of 1959. Franco pinned his hopes for continued economic growth on development of an oil industry in the Spanish Sahara, increased private foreign investment in Spain itself and more U.S. aid.

WHO WILL FOLLOW FRANCO?

Young prince groomed to restore monarchy when dictator departs; U.S. bases aid Spanish economy; Salazar retains Portugal rule

PORTUGAL, as poor as its larger neighbor, was also ruled by a dictator—Dr. Antonio de Oliveira Salazar *(above)*, a 71-year-old former economics professor who celebrated the 32nd anniversary of his rise to power in 1960. He had little real opposition until 1958, when fiery Gen. Humberto Delgado astonished the nation by running—and running hard—for the figurehead presidency against the official candidate. He lost, was "retired" from the military, and departed for Brazil, vowing to continue his fight from exile. Unrest seemed to mount during 1959 and 1960, but the anti-Salazar forces still had a long way to go.

NEXT RULER of Spain would be a king, Franco had decided—either 21-year-old Prince Juan Carlos *(above)* or his 47-year-old father, Don Juan of Bourbon.

FRANCO, 67 in 1960, was the boss. His tight curbs on civil rights, notably religious freedom for non-Catholics, made his regime unpopular in Free World.

U.S. AIR BASES *(r.)* bolstered European defenses, Spanish economy alike. In 1960, West Germany began negotiating for Spanish bases of its own; move was strongly opposed by its NATO allies.

TURKEY OUSTS MENDERES; CYPRUS STRIFE SETTLED

Military coup ends 10 years of increasingly harsh rule, opposition sweeps new Turkish elections; Makarios heads Cyprus republic

THE MEDITERRANEAN island of Cyprus was a trouble spot throughout most of the decade.

Great Britain ruled it, NATO partner Greece wanted it, NATO partner Turkey wanted it split.

As for the Cypriotes themselves the majority (70%) were of Greek extraction, and desperately wanted *enosis*, or union with Greece.

However, it was felt — by Great Britain and by the NATO alliance as a whole—that the island was too strategic to be turned over to Greece, the weakest member of the partnership. Turkey was determined to safeguard the rights of the Turkish Cypriotes.

In 1954, Greek Cypriotes launched a campaign of violence against British authority. The next year, Archbishop Myriathefs Makarios III *(below)*, religious and political leader of the Greek population, was exiled by the British on the grounds that he was backing pro-*enosis* agitation.

And for the next four years, a sporadic but savage civil war raged on the island between Greeks, British and Turks (who organized own underground as attacks on the Turkish people by Greek partisans mounted).

In 1959, peace by compromise was finally achieved; it was decided that Cyprus would become an independent republic, barred by international agreement from union with either Greece or Turkey, with Great Britain keeping control of its defense bases.

An elaborate blueprint for the new nation's government was drawn up to insure equitable representation to Greek and Turkish Cypriotes.

In 1960, the soon-to-be republic elected Archbishop Makarios its first president (he had returned from exile a year earlier) and Turkish Cypriote leader Fazil Kucuk as vice president; it chose its first parliament, 70% Greek, 30% Turkish, and welcomed with only mild enthusiasm its Independence Day, August 16.

BARBED WIRE separated Greek, Turkish districts of Cyprus capital, Nicosia, when violence was at peak in 1956; but Greek and Turkish Cypriotes did business across it *(above, l.)* Though feeling ran high on both sides as island's fate hung in balance, many Cypriotes wanted no part of civil war.

TURKEY began the decade with the first free elections in its history, and ended it with a revolution that overthrew the regime that had been elected 10 years before.

In 1950, the Democratic (conservative) party of Adnan Menderes *(below)* won a landslide victory over the Republican People's party (somewhat leftist) of Ismet Inonu, which had ruled ever since the revolution of Kemal Ataturk, after World War I, and this victory started the nation on the road to Westernization.

In 1954, the Democrats, who had gone all out to increase Turkey's agricultural and industrial capacity and were enjoying considerable success, triumphed at the polls again.

In the second half of the decade, however, the government began running into economic troubles.

And, as spiraling inflation provoked popular criticism and parliamentary opposition, Menderes began moving sharply toward the totalitarian right.

His suppression of dissent brought still more opposition, which in turn was more and more ruthlessly suppressed, and by 1960, the nation was ripe for revolution.

Student riots began the revolt; a neat military coup, headed by Gen. Cemal Gursel, carried it through on May 27, 1960.

The Gursel regime took over efficiently, reaffirmed Turkey's alliance with Free Europe, and promised to hold elections in the near future. It appeared, at mid-year, that Turkey would have another chance to make a go of parliamentary democracy.

TURKISH STUDENTS sparked revolt against government of Adnan Menderes. Riots began on April 28; martial law was proclaimed, and a few days later, the universities were closed. Uprising was caused by Grand National Assembly's voting of almost dictatorial powers to commission set up to investigate opposition parties.

LEADER of Turkey's almost bloodless revolution was 65-year-old Gen. Cemal Gursel *(below)*. His overthrow of Menderes regime was greeted with almost universal popular rejoicing and relief.

GREECE kept a precarious hold on parliamentary democracy throughout the decade, in spite of unrest over Cyprus and worst poverty in Europe. '60 premier was Constantine Karamanlis *(below)*.

ANTI-WEST LEADER, former Premier Mohammed Mossadegh, known as "Old Mossy," became a virtual dictator Aug. 16, 1953, but was overthrown three days later by royalists. The aging premier, who became famous for his habit of weeping and fainting, continued his antics Nov. 19, 1953, when a Tehran military court tried him for treason. He got a three-year prison sentence.

OIL RICHES of Iran are concentrated near Abadan on Persian Gulf. Angry Premier Mossadegh nationalized the British-owned Anglo-Iranian oil company April 30, 1951, but settlement was achieved Aug. 5, 1954.

SHAH OF IRAN Mohammed Reza Pahlevi, holds land deed in his right hand as he lifts a peasant in the act of kissing the ruler's toe during Dec. 1, 1955, Tehran ceremony, when the shah distributed crown land to 287 landless peasants.

SHAH OUSTS MOSSADEGH

Pro-West ruler settles oil crisis; takes third bride

IRAN'S SHAH, Mohammed Reza Pahlevi, during the decade opened war on his nation's feudal system, which held more than 1 million farm families in virtual land serfdom. Through legislation and his own example, he planned to set up for Iran's 20 million people a model state.

The 41-year-old, thrice-wed ruler, who still yearned for a male heir to the throne, began his reform moves in the early '50s, selling, on small payments, chunks of crown land. But his example was not followed by the "thousand families," the all-powerful landlords.

Premier Ali Razmara tried to hike Iran's percentage of royalties from the British-owned Anglo-Iranian Oil Company as the decade began. A fanatic of Fadayan Islam, an extremist group which accused Razmara of being too soft with the British, assassinated him March 7, 1951. The new premier, Hussein Ala, also failed to come to terms with British interests and the move to nationalize oil spread. Serious trouble began when Dr. Mohammed Mossadegh became premier. This National Front leader despised all foreigners. The Communist-led Tudeh party, sensing a back door to power, enthusiastically supported Mossadegh, who nationalized the British oil interests on April 30, 1951. Attempts to settle the differences were abandoned Sept. 6, when Great Britain refused to talk to mob-backed Mossadegh. British oil men left Oct. 3.

BEAUTIFUL EMPRESS Soraya, then 19-years-old *(l.)*, married Shah of Iran Feb. 12, 1951, but was divorced, childless, March 4, 1958. Shah first wed Egyptian Princess Fawzia, who produced a daughter, Chahinaz, but no male heir. That marriage began March 15, 1939, ended November 19, 1948.

IN 20-YEAR QUEST for an heir to the monarchy, the Shah married 21-year-old commoner, Farah Diba, on Dec. 21, 1959, when he was 40 years old. The "King of Kings" was said to be eager to have a son to display on the festive 2,500th anniversary in 1961 of the founding of Persia.

In 1952 Iran presented the free world with its most serious crisis since Korea. Near bankruptcy, swept from border to border by bloody riots, oil-rich Iran was regarded as a tempting prize for the USSR. The Anglo-French depended on Iranian oil, but their needs could be filled by oil from the West. Iran could not produce or sell its oil when the British left, and began going into the red, in both senses, at an alarming rate.

Mossadegh was a crying, sobbing and fainting old man who received foreign ambassadors in his pajamas and who feared assassination. To consolidate his position, he began manipulations to seize control of the army from the Shah. On Aug. 15, 1953, when Mossadegh dissolved parliament, the Shah countered by naming Gen. Fazollah Zahedi, arch-foe of Mossadegh, the new premier. The Shah had this constitutional right, but when palace guards went to Mossadegh's home they were disarmed, and pro-Mossadegh and Communist mobs started to riot. Zahedi went into hiding and the Shah fled into exile. Mossadegh now was a dictator, but his rule was brief. Three days later, on Aug. 19, peasants and royalists rose up and Mossadegh was arrested. The Shah returned to Iran, and a military court sent Mossadegh to prison for three years, which he served in solitary confinement.

Relations with Great Britain were patched up and, by 1954, oil was flowing under an agreement between Iran and an international oil consortium, which included the U.S. Iran got 50% of all earnings. Iran's oil revenues in 1960 amounted to about $250 million yearly.

Despite Soviet threats of "dire consequences," Iran joined the Central Treaty Organization (former Baghdad Pact), and signed a defense treaty with the U.S.

WEEPING MOTHER holding her child, was among victims of Christmas quake in 1957 which killed 900 farmers and shepherds. Premier Manoucher Eghbal is handing money to the woman in crushed village of Farsinaj. Iran was hit by another earthquake April 24, '60. New disaster killed more than 200 persons, mostly women and children; injured 3,000 in southern town of Lar.

NEW-BORN LAND GROWS STRONG

Israel doubles population, shows military might, increases exports; but help from abroad still needed

DEATH CAME on Nov. 9, 1952, to Chaim Weizmann, Israel's first president and a pioneer Zionist. The 77-year-old leader had been confined to his bed for a year. An honor guard surrounds his catafalque as the new nation mourns its loss.

ISRAEL, the johnny-come-lately of the nations, completed its first decade and, like most people, was experiencing growing pains.

Founded in 1948 under incredible difficulties, the tiny republic, no bigger than the state of Massachusetts, found that its rapid growth, from approximately 1 million people in that year to 2,105,530 in 1960, was somewhat of a mixed blessing.

Statistically, its accomplishments were tremendous. It had brought 947,825 immigrants to its arid, sun-drenched land from 80 different countries.

In 1953 only 15% of the nation's imports were balanced by exports and, in that year, the country set up a 10-year plan designed to make it self supporting by 1963.

Although this goal was still distant, the gap between imports and exports had been decreased. In 1959 it exported $182.9 million worth of goods, imported $432 million.

The southern seaport city of Elath, on the Gulf of Aqaba, had boomed from 500 people in 1955 to 7000. It was partly turned into a thriving oil export center by waiving income taxes for residents. These normally ran as high as 60% on $5000.

Two basic problems were dependence on externally raised funds for income and a ring of hostile neighbors led by arch-enemy President Nasser of the United Arab Republic.

In 1959 alone, Israel received an estimated $180 million from reparations and restitution from the West German Government as well as from the proceeds of Israeli Government bonds floated in the United States.

In the mid-'60s, the reparations were to come to an end and the 12-year bonds fall due. To balance this, the government hoped to attract foreign-investments and reduce the trade gap.

Already a five-year-development plan had gone into effect with emphasis on developing mining and industry. Slowest expansion was expected in agriculture, because of limited water resources.

Dominant in Israel was the trade union federation Histadrut, whose membership included more than half of all Israel. It, with the government, owned and operated at least 60% of the nation's business, ranging from the historically-famous King Solomon's copper mines to a fancy resort hotel in Elath.

Without its army, which required two and one-half years service from all men and two from women, Israel long ago would have been gobbled up by its two pugnacious neighbors, Egypt and Syria, united in the UAR.

In 1956 Israel went to war with the latter in a struggle that caused the entry of Great Britain and France, which issued an ultimatum to both countries to halt hostilities, and then landed troops in the Canal area.

Eventually the United Nations—under strong urging from the U.S. and the USSR – occupied the disputed canal zone. It was an uneasy peace, broken by continuing extensive military preparations by the UAR, armed with Soviet weapons. In early 1960, sporadic fighting broke out along the Israeli-Syrian border. This warfare, it seemed likely, would continue intermittently as Israel's water needs increased and Egypt continued to deny the right of Israeli products to be shipped through the Suez.

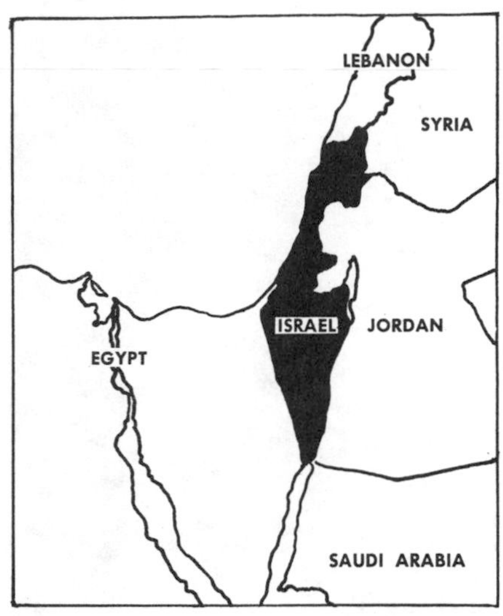

PALESTINE PARTITION adopted by UN Nov. 29, 1947, caused Palestine Arabs to revolt. After a bitter struggle, border was established along 1949 cease-fire line.

ARMED MEN guard two workmen *(foreground)* as they weld together two sections of pipe just a few hundred yards from the Jordan border during the construction of the Elath-Beersheba oil pipeline that snaked 135 miles, linked the port city with inland Beersheba. Elath also got a new railroad link across desert.

SEARCH FOR WATER is a day-to-day necessity in arid Israel, which hopes to reclaim a large portion of the Negev desert with a giant water pipeline.

NUMEROUS ARABS who fled Israel in 1948 stayed on in the war-torn Gaza strip to be cared for by the United Nations. Total of 750,000 displaced Arabs continued to be a major problem. Many of them were bitter toward border states which had encouraged them to fight against Jews and then forsook them when truce was signed.

ISRAEL FOREIGN minister Mrs. Golda Meir *(l.)* listens carefully with Chief United Nations delegate Abba Eban to discussion of the Suez Canal crisis.

OPEN WARFARE broke out again in October, 1956, when Israeli forces swept across Egypt's Sinai peninsula *(above)*. British and French forces both later invaded the Suez area to protect the canal and issued a cease-fire ultimatum to both sides. United Nations then sent a multi-nation expeditionary force, took over control.

PART OF AN INDEPENDENCE DAY PARADE, CRACK ISRAELI SOLDIERS SHOW THE VIGOR OF A CITIZEN ARMY WHICH WON TWO WARS

NEW IMMIGRANTS came pouring into Israel and were sent to towns being developed in Galilee, Lachish and the Negev. With a tremendous housing shortage throughout the new land, the first job of refugees was to build homes *(above)*.

DAVID BEN-GURION *(l.)*, talked things over with Israeli President Izhak Ben Zvi at the latter's home in Jerusalem in July, 1959, after he had submitted his letter of resignation as the Prime Minister. It was his fifth such resignation.

ISRAEL'S PREMIER David Ben-Gurion *(l.)*, chatted with West German Chancellor Adenauer in New York in March, 1960.

PORT OF HAIFA, Israel's largest, increased its capacity by widening the Kishon River, yearly handles four million tons.

"BLACK SATURDAY," Jan. 26, 1952, left Cairo a smouldering ruin after anti-British rioters ran amok. Mobs burned the Rivioli Theater *(l.)*, making bonfire of furnishings in street. Old Shepheard's Hotel, setting of many a Middle East thriller and memoir, also was burned. Day's riots left 60 dead, 80 wounded. Burned factories left 30,000 jobless.

NASSER RULES THE NILE

Takes over Egypt after Farouk ouster, adds Syria to "United Arab Republic"

ENERGETIC Gamal Abdel Nasser, president of the United Arab Republic of Egypt and Syria, set off a dynamite blast Jan. 9, 1960, to start construction of the long-planned Aswan High Dam on the Upper Nile. Denial of American-British funds for this dream project led the young revolutionary to seize the Suez Canal in defiance of the West and provoke the Anglo-French-Israeli invasion in 1956. The $15 million yearly profit from the canal, plus a $93 million Russian loan and a promise of more, made possible start of the ambitious program, costing at least $1 billion and taking decade to complete.

Within the decade Egypt had made some surprising economic gains. Nasser's maneuvers for dominance in Arabian affairs naturally figured strongly in his drive to industrialize Egypt. He wanted to be more than an economic match for his arch-foe, Israel. He wanted an industrial base of his own in case some shift in world politics should curb his Soviet arms supplies. And he wanted to tap the wealth of the oil states indirectly by making Egypt their source of supply for chemicals, textiles, paper, and many other things. But his drive also was an effort to cope with the same population explosion affecting the rest of the world. Egypt's population had doubled since 1900; now 25 million, it will be 30 million by 1970.

PLAY-BOY King Farouk married Narriman Sadek, 17, his second wife, in 1951; was forced to abdicate July 26, 1952. After a year in exile, she left him and their year-old son.

BRITISH TOMMIES leave the Suez Canal after a July 27, 1954, agreement giving Great Britain reoccupation rights under certain situations. Egypt seized the canal two years later.

The USSR had been, at decade's end, the big bankroller for Nasser's staggering 10-year plan, aimed to hike living standards. Moscow had put up $178 million plus a promise of $300 million more for the Aswan Dam despite Nasser's attacks on Communism in his feud with Iraq.

Nasser intended to expend $10.4 billion in ten years on industries, a staggering effort for a country whose national income was only $2.8 billion yearly, and whose per capita income was only $118 a year.

The foreign exchange source for Nasser's big schemes so far had been loans and credits from the USSR, West Germany, Japan, East Germany, the U.S., Yugoslavia, and Switzerland, in that size and order. Most of the swift industrialization had been government-directed.

The big Economic Development Organization, a semi-autonomous government agency, had an investment of $179 million in 75 companies. This made it the largest and most powerful voice in Egyptian economy —but second to the voice of Nasser.

The Egyptian strong man had come a long way since he began plotting against the monarchy a decade ago. He was embittered by corruption, so evident in faulty arms used by the army in the losing 1948-49 battle with Israel. He was among the army officers who seized power July 23, 1952. Maj. Gen. Mohammed Naguib was named commander-in-chief. But the real leader was Nasser. He forced the abdication of Farouk and Naguib became premier Sept. 7. On June 18, 1953, ancient Egypt, after 5000 years of rule by pharaohs, foreign viceroys and kings, was declared a republic, with Naguib president. Naguib, a kindly man, was very popular with the people. When he sought to establish civilian rule he clashed with Nasser, who wanted continued rule by the military as the best means of achieving reforms. Nasser removed Naguib and succeeded him as premier April 18, 1954. On June 23, the voters elected him president with a declared 99.9 per cent of the votes.

TEST OF STRENGTH between Egypt's two strong men, Gen. Mohammed Naguib, and Lt. Col. Gamal Abdel Nasser *(l.)* was won by Nasser. Strikes and rioting preceded the ousting of Naguib, who was enormously popular among the Egyptians and who wanted to return Egypt to civilian government rule. Junta made Naguib give up premiership April 18, 1954, then ousted him as president Nov. 14, 1954. At his right, in this 1953 picture, is army commander Marshal Abdul Hakim Amer.

FORLORN Egyptian youngster stands before British tank in ruined city of Port Said. Air and sea attack preceded Anglo-French invasion Nov. 5-6, 1956.

RUSSIAN T-34 tank, abandoned by Egyptian army while retreating across Sinai desert before swift advance of Israeli army, was evidence of quantities of Soviet arms sent to Egyptians and poor use Egyptians made of them.

WEST'S WITHDRAWAL OF BID to finance Aswan High Dam, part of which is shown above, led Nasser to seize Suez Canal July 26, 1956, to get its revenues for the project. Dam on Upper Nile, begun Jan. 9, 1960, will cost more than $1 billion, take at least 10 years to build and provide water for millions of acres. Dam also was expected to aid neighboring Sudanese farmers, one of whom *(below)* is seen controlling water flow to a Sudanese cotton farmland.

STRONG MAN in the Sudan, south of Egypt, was Gen. Ibrahim Abboud. His nation, formerly an Anglo-Egyptian condominium, became independent Jan. 1, 1956. Abdullah Khalil, head of the Umma party, became premier. But Abboud set up an army ruling body Nov. 18, 1958; finally seized full powers in March, 1959.

NATIONALIZATION aroused fears for future of Suez Canal, and a belief the Egyptians could not run it profitably. Volunteers joined the Egyptians for a trial, and many were retained. Here a Soviet pilot gets instructions about the canal. In 1960, the Suez waterway was exceeding its old traffic records.

UN-CHARTERED salvage crews began big job of clearing Suez Canal December 29, 1956, after a cease-fire was effected. Italian crewmen of the winch ship *Squalo*, anchored at left, swarm over hulk of Egyptian LST Akka at southern end of Lake Timsah below Ismailia. Egyptians filled Akka with cement and sank her in canal.

MERGER of Egypt and Syria in February, 1958, produced the Egyptian-led United Arab Republic. President Nasser and Syrian President Shukri al-Kuwatly invited other Arab nations to join. Yemen "adhered," but did not join.

Keeps seized Suez, Soviet Aswan Dam aid

The 36-year-old Nasser, after ousting Naguib and becoming premier and president himself, embarked on the goal of making himself leader of the Arab world.

His opening maneuver was a barter deal; Egyptian cotton for Czech arms. Soviet influence swelled.

Nasser quickly parlayed his increasing prestige in the Arab world by pressuring other Arab states into joint military pacts. Ostensibly directed against Israel, it was soon clear that these alliances were to thwart the Baghdad Pact.

In December, 1955, the U.S. and Great Britain made a firm offer to finance the Aswan Dam. The Egyptian dictator hesitated for seven months. Meanwhile, he engineered the ouster of British Gen. John Glubb as commander in Jordan, recognized Red China, and aided the rebellion in Algeria.

Western powers became aware that Nasser's "neutralism" included a willingness to accept both Western money and Soviet arms and advice. On July 19, 1956, when he decided to accept its help for the Aswan Dam, the West said "no." Angered, Nasser nationalized the internationally-owned Suez Canal Company.

Israel, Great Britain and France struck Egypt in late October in one of the strangest wars in history: the victors lost and Nasser, through U.S. and UN intervention, won. The invaders withdrew with Nasser still in full control of the canal, whose use he still denied to Israel.

With greatly increased prestige, Nasser formed the United Arab Republic in February, 1958. It was a union of Egypt and Syria. Nasser became president, with another Egyptian army chief, Field Marshal Abdel Hakim Amer, vice-president and Nasser's strong hand inside Syria. Most of the extremist Syrian political leaders were quietly curbed or replaced.

Almost all of the Egyptian press was in effect nationalized in 1960. Newspapers were "reorganized" under the National Union. The government sponsored a single party for the whole UAR.

Nasser was the "New Pharaoh."

FRENZIED Egyptians in Port Said dynamite huge statue of Suez Canal builder Ferdinand de Lesseps, shown here, after Anglo-French troops withdrew.

GRATEFUL HOST President Nasser gives a party May 14, 1958, for Soviet premier Nikita Khrushchev and other Russians in Moscow, and clinks glasses with the chunky Communist leader. The Russians not only sent big quantities of arms to the Egyptians, but also gave millions of dollars—on loan—for Aswan dam.

WOMEN'S HERO in Egypt is President Nasser, who not only successfully defied the British and French, but who adopted a constitution giving women the right to vote. Egyptian women voted for the first time in the post-revolution general election for a 350-member parliament July 3, 1957. Despite opposition, women were getting jobs formerly held only by men. Veiled women were becoming rare in Cairo; coffee shops were hiring waitresses and college girls sought such jobs.

TWO YEARS AFTER the July 14, 1958, revolt in which Gen. Abdul Karim Kassem vaulted to power in Iraq, the revolution began faltering. People seemed to be disenchanted. Some feared the nation was being swept toward another of those recurrent crises that had shaken Iraq ever since the monarchy toppled. Red threats remained.

A decade earlier, real reforms were taking place in Iraq, which most of the time disassociated itself from the rest of the Arab world. Land ownership and educational opportunities widened; dams were built to increase cultivation and to restore its original fertility to the country.

Twin coronations of the boy rulers and cousins, King Faisal II of Iraq and King Hussein of Jordan, produced a happy atmosphere May 2, 1953. Iraq was prosperous from its huge oil fields, and by 1955 had begun a vast internal improvement plan. The nation of 5 million also was able to repay $6.3 millions to the World Bank, the balance of a loan incurred in 1950 for flood control.

In 1955, Iraq and Great Britain joined the alliance between Turkey and Pakistan, the beginning of the controversial Baghdad Pact. Iraq also severed diplomatic relations with the Soviet Union. Egypt became angry, seeing the alliance as a defection from Arab League ideas.

IRAQ IS TROUBLED

BOY KINGS, Faisal II of Iraq *(l.)*, and Hussein of Jordan, ascended thrones May 2, 1953. The cousins were both 18 years old and British-educated. On July 14, 1958, army-led rebels revolted and killed young Faisal, proclaimed a republic, withdrew from the Arab Union of Jordan and Iraq, and entered a mutual defense alliance with Nasser's United Arab Republic. Hussein declared himself head of the Arab Union, but that union was dead, and his own rule was shaky.

ANTI-WESTERN HERO of the revolt which knocked Iraqis from the Baghdad Pact was machinegun-toting Brig. Abdul Karim Kassem, who became premier of the republic which replaced the monarchy. Kassem was wounded in an assassination attempt Oct. 7, 1959. He blamed so-called "imperialists" as plotters against him. Kassem put down a pro-Nasser revolt in March, 1959. He put severe checks on the Communists, fending off Soviet inroads, while also attacking the West.

A new wave of nationalism swept Arab states after Egypt's President Nasser seized the Suez Canal in 1956. Even Iraq, only Arab member of the Baghdad Pact, and Egypt's foremost Arab rival, enthusiastically supported the action. Nationalists plotted against Faisal's throne.

In February, 1958, Nasser's Pan-Arabic pressure on Iraq and Jordan grew with the union of Egypt and Syria as the United Arab Republic. Faisal and Hussein shortly countered by announcing merger of their two kingdoms as the federated Arab Union.

Less than six months later, the Arab Union was dead, as was Faisal. Kassem and his revolting "Free Officers" killed the young king, his uncle, Crown Prince Abdul Illah, and the veteran pro-Western premier, Nuri as-Said, under whom Iraq had made great strides with its public works program, the best in the Middle East.

Kassem took a middle-road nationalist course, fending off both the Nasserites and the Communists. In March, 1959, he put down a pro-Nasser revolt in Mosul, using Communist aid. He executed 13 army officers and four civilians Sept. 20, 1959—and survived an assassination attempt the next month. Though Kassem had a 50,000-man army, an estimated yearly oil revenue of $280 million, he lacked his own party. Popular support was ebbing.

Kassem survives plots as popularity ebbs

LOYALTY DEMONSTRATION for Premier-General Kassem in Baghdad is staged on Rashid Street in support of the leader who suppressed a military revolt in northern Iraq early in March, 1959. The hero of the 1958 revolution which put the nation on a fumbling road toward a republic was under pressure to join Iraq to Gamal Abdel Nasser's United Arab Republic when a group of officers set off the uprising in Mosul. It was all over within a few days, but an estimated 500 persons were killed. The premier (in front of the knot of officials to the extreme right on the roof of the Ministry of Defense building) obtained his victory only at the cost of accepting more Communist help than seemed healthy. On Sept. 20, 1959, the Kassem regime executed thirteen of the army officers involved in the revolt, and also four civilians of the monarchial regime of the late Nuri as-Said.

IN HAPPIER DAYS Nuri as-Said, Iraqi premier, posed for this Baghdad Pact Council picture June 1, 1957, in Karachi, Pakistan. The premier, left, was killed the next year when a military coup overthrew the monarchy. (In center is Premier H. S. Suhrawardy of Pakistan, and at right is Turkey's premier, Adnan Menderes, who was ousted May 27, 1960.) The Baghdad Pact was formed in 1955 as a bulwark against Communist expansion in the Middle East. Its members were Britain, Pakistan, Iran, Turkey, and Iraq. The United States, although not formally a member, cooperated closely. After Iraq, which had been its only Arab member and whose capital had given it its name, withdrew from the Pact, the ministerial council met in Washington in October, 1959, and changed its name to the Central Treaty Organization. Pact leaders still feared Soviet inroads through Iraq.

THORN IN THE SIDE of both Iraqi Premier Kassem and Egypt's Nasser was the 25-year-old King of Jordan, Hussein, a friend of the West, and enemy of Communism.

He warned the Arab world of the dangers of Red infiltration from Iraq, and he warned Nasser in a June 26, 1960, broadcast of the "dark fate" awaiting every dictator. He called the president of the United Arab Republic conceited, an opportunist and a tyrant of the worst type.

This bitter broadcast was prompted by a speech in which Nasser, without mentioning Hussein by name, said there were still a few traitors in the Arab world who had inherited kingdoms from their fathers and grandfathers. Hussein inherited his Hashemite kingdom from Abdullah, his grandfather who was assassinated in 1951, and from his ailing father, Talal, who ruled briefly.

Hussein, who actually took over from a regency council in 1953, yielded to anti-British demonstrations in 1956 when he dropped British Lt. Gen. John Bagot Glubb, known as "Glubb Pasha," commander of the Arab Legion, the Jordanian army which was the best-trained Arab force in the Middle East. But Hussein scored a triumph in 1957 when pro-Egyptian elements tried to overthrow him and force Jordan into a union with Egypt and Syria. Suleiman Nabulsi was premier that year. Under

Hussein holds throne despite Nasser pressure

ASSASSINATION of King Abdullah of Jordan, *(r.)* by an Arab extremist on July 20, 1951, created a crisis in that hotbed of troubles, the Middle East. His eldest son, Talal *(l.)*, was proclaimed king Sept. 5, 1951. But Parliament removed Talal as mentally unfit, installing his son, Hussein, May 2, 1952. Ever since, Hussein had been fighting Nasser and Communist intrigues. Jordanian troops *(below)* are checking a civilian's papers during a precautionary curfew.

JUBILANT CROWDS celebrated when King Hussein dismissed British Lieut. Gen. John Bagot Glubb *(r.)*, who was leader of the Arab Legion—the most efficient Arab military force in the Middle East. This act, March 2, 1956, came as a result of two months of riots and unrest in Jordan over the British pressure to join the Baghdad Pact. Egypt, Syria, and Saudi Arabia went directly to Jordan's people over their rulers, with agents, broadcasts and bribing to incite mass unrest.

his rule pro-Egyptian and pro-Communist elements in the army and government were being promoted. In March, the army displayed signs of revolt. Hussein made a dramatic bid to his wavering troops and won back their loyalty; Nabulsi and two successive chiefs of staff fled to Syria. Then Saudi Arabia and the U.S. rallied to Hussein with financial aid. The throne was saved.

When Kassem and his Iraqi rebels unexpectedly attacked in their coup in 1958 and killed Faisal, Hussein's cousin, and the monarchy, pro-Nasser forces again threatened Jordan. The king called in British troops, while U.S. marines landed in Lebanon. All troops withdrew later.

BRITISH PARATROOPS shown here landed in Cyprus, then flew into Jordan July 17, 1958, to protect that land after a military coup toppled the pro-Western Iraqi regime. U.S. Marines rushed into Lebanon July 15 at Lebanon's request.

LEBANON KEEPS INDEPENDENCE

Revolt to oust pro–West Chamoun, add nation to Nasser's United Arab Republic, fizzles out after U.S. sends Sixth Fleet, air–borne troops

U.S. MARINES maintain vigil on Beirut rooftop as traffic in Lebanese capital proceeds normally only block away. 1958 intervention was U.S. military's largest since Korea, met no opposition except scattered sniping. Marines were landed from Sixth Fleet, airborne troops from N. Carolina, W. Germany.

Lebanon, most westernized and most Christian of the "Arab" nations, survived the decade as an independent nation—but it was a close call, and only the dispatch of 13,000 U.S. troops made it possible.

After years of Pan-Arab agitation, whose aim was to absorb the tiny, mountainous Mediterranean land into Egyptian President Nasser's United Arab Republic, open revolt erupted May 11, 1958.

Proclaimed objective was to force the resignation of President Camille Chamoun, a Maronite Catholic (Lebanon's constitution provides that the President always be a Christian, the Premier a Moslem), chief stumbling block to union with the UAR.

After initial rebel seizure of about one-third of the country, there was little serious fighting. Most of the Lebanese ignored the crisis. Bikini-clad beauties continued sun-bathing on the beaches of Beirut, not only the capital but favorite playground of oil-rich Arab princes, despite distant, desultory machine-gun fire. Gen. Fuad Chehab, army commander, remained "unavailable" at his country estate, and his troops showed little aggression.

FORMER PREMIER Saeb Salem *(above)* led pro-Nasser revolt against President Camille Chamoun *(below)* which fizzled out after arrival of U.S. troops. Salem is Moslem, Chamoun Christian, but outbreak did not spark religious conflict which could have torn apart country, almost evenly divided between two faiths. Riots *(l.)* in Beirut were chief open violence. Leaders of both groups backed compromise under which Chamoun "voluntarily" resigned. Things otherwise remained very much as before and 1960 elections indicated the majority of the people were satisfied.

Nevertheless, as the weeks passed, rebel pressure mounted dangerously. After an appeal by Chamoun to the UN brought no action, President Eisenhower ordered the Sixth Fleet and U.S. airborne forces flown from the U.S. and West Germany to occupy strategic areas.

Radio Cairo raved, and Moscow muttered about dispatching "volunteers."

Actually, the U.S. force met no resistance. Chamoun, his face saved, resigned two months before his term constitutionally ended. The canny Chehab, a Christian with strong Moslem family connections who undoubtedly had "planned it that way," was elected Chamoun's successor by Parliament. Tension eased and, in October, the last U.S. troops were withdrawn.

Beirut settled back as convenient common ground where Arab Nationalism, the West and Communism could wage discreet propaganda war. (Most of its many newspapers are subsidized.) Camille Chamoun, in the 1960 elections, was re-elected to Parliament.

ARAMCO, and other Western companies, were not only pouring vast wealth into coffers of native rulers, but training a new generation of technicians, helping breed Arab middle class used to modern ways. Result may transform Arab society.

MAP SHOWS minor states, disputed areas of Arabian peninsula, as well as Riyadh, Saudi capital. Saudi Arabia also borders on Jordan, approaches within few miles of Israel. Rub al Khali Desert, famed "empty quarter," may have oil.

ARABIA AWAKES

Oil wealth, nationalism, East-West struggle, signal end to age-old patriarchal system

THE ARABIAN Peninsula, seedbed of Islam, continued in uneasy balance during the decade, but signs multiplied that oil wealth, Arab nationalism and Communist aggression might soon shatter it.

The petty sheikhdoms along the Persian Gulf remained allied to Great Britain — and British oil companies. The ruling house of huge, mostly empty Saudi Arabia, which occupied the bulk of the Peninsula, grew rich on oil royalties from the U.S.-owned Arabian American Oil Co.

Border disputes, principally over the Buraidi Oasis, reflected oil rivalries, as did an Oman revolt and unrest in Kuwait. In Saudi Arabia there was a covert power struggle between King Saud and his brother and heir Faisal, spokesman for the rest of the family, premier, foreign minister and Nasser protege.

Medieval Yemen, in the extreme south, became a Nasser ally and staged a comic opera "war" with Great Britain over the Aden frontier.

KING SAUD, son of great Ibn Saud, has lost ground to brother in struggle to control nation, oil wealth. Dhahran, in Saudi Arabia, is site of big U.S. base.

SHEIKH SULEIMAN al-Khalifa, ruler of Bahrein Island, typifies petty Arab dynasts on oil-rich Persian Gulf. He is staunch British ally, holds knighthood.

FERHAT ABBAS, *(l.)* pharmacist from Setif, was made premier of Algerian Provisional Government. Ben Bella, now in French jail, was rebel army leader. The rebel Algerian regime holds meetings in Tunis.

REBELS SPURN FRENCH TERMS

Algerian war continues after de Gaulle offers independence vote

ARMED "COLON" MOBS in Algiers challenged French President Charles de Gaulle's middle-road policy in an emotion-drenched uprising in 1960, but he weathered the storm and shook up the army command. Also, for the first time since the Algerian native rebellion began, peace representatives of both sides met face to face. But the rebels rejected French terms for negotiations to try to end the slaughter which began more than six years ago. The odds remained heavily against an early peace.

The Algerian war began Nov. 1, 1954, but its organizers started a decade earlier. Mohammed Ben Bella, whom the French decorated in World War II as a warrant officer in a hard-fighting Moroccan regiment, and his confederates, robbed an Oran post office in a daring raid that put more than 3,000,000 francs into the rebel organization. The French convicted him, but he escaped from prison and made his way to Cairo. He subsequently settled in Libya, directed arms traffic into Algeria, and then became commander of the rebel forces. Believed a militant leftist, he nevertheless rejected Communism. But this did not keep him from appealing to the Soviet bloc in 1956 for arms. He said his weapons-hungry forces would take aid from Communists or "even the devil himself."

Ben Bella and other rebels were captured by a ruse Oct. 22, 1956. The group flew from Morocco, where they had been guests of the king, en route to Tunisia. The French pilot landed the plane at Algiers instead.

The rebel National Liberation Front organized headquarters in Tunis after Tunisia obtained its independence from France. The rebels set up arsenals and training centers in both Tunisia and Morocco, and fed men and arms into Algeria. They fought mostly in hit-and-run attacks and ambushes. Estimates of their strength varied. The French said the rebels numbered only about 30,000 regulars. The rebels claimed they could put 120,000 men into the field. Whatever their strength, they kept nearly 500,000 French troops in the field, including 100,000 gendarmes. They put a drain of $1 billion yearly on the French treasury and killed an average of seven French soldiers daily. They disrupted European defenses.

FEARFUL ALGERIAN lies prisoner at the feet of French soldier during France's attempt to halt native rebellion. Revolt began Nov. 1, 1954, caused a heavy drain in men and money, and kept nearly 500,000 French troops pinned down. Native demands for independence came as a shock to French, who had regarded Algeria as a part of metropolitan France.

French forces, smarting from the debacle in Indo-China, poured into Algeria, which was legally part of metropolitan France. While a long succession of cabinets tried to settle the rebellion politically, the military used a revolutionary concept to try to defeat the guerrillas. The army "regrouped" about 2 million Moslems, or about one-fifth of the native population. Officers theorized that the rebels fighting for complete independence from France needed the support of the civilian population "as a fish needs water." Without it, the rebels would be without food, shelter, and other necessities. The French also electrified barbed wire fences along sections of the Tunisian and Moroccan borders. They enlisted nearly 130,000 Moslems as auxiliaries and armed them to guard their villages. Troops sought to "saturate" the native guerrillas by sheer weight of numbers. But Algeria is a vast land and the rebels kept popping up in unexpected places after dark. The French could not run trains, for fear of ambush, nor could they use the rural highways. They abandoned farms after dark. Rebels planted bombs in crowded stores and cafes. Nobody felt safe even in the middle of big cities like Algiers. Rebels executed pro-French Moslem leaders.

French settlers of European descent, outnumbered almost 10-1 by Moslems, distrusted the Paris government. They feared a "sell-out" to the Algerian rebel government in Tunis. French troops, particularly some of the "political" colonels, backed them. Thus a revolt within a revolt occurred May 13, 1958, when army officers joined the European settlers, or "colons," to create a "Committee of Public Safety" that defied the Paris regime. These committee movements spread to Corsica and France, and rightist mobs demonstrated in Paris as well as Algiers.

To avert the danger of civil war, President Rene Coty yielded to rightist demands and asked de Gaulle to form a government. He took office June 1 as premier, then as president the following January.

On Sept. 16, 1959, he offered his long-awaited peace plan. He promised to let the people of Algeria choose their own future—even independence—within four years after a cease-fire had restored peace. This stunned the Algerian "colon" conservatives who had demanded full integration of Algeria with France. The rebel government under Premier Ferhat Abbas rejected the plan because Paris refused to recognize him as spokesman for all Algerian Moslems. By January Brig. Gen Jacques Massu, military commander in Algiers, was fired by de Gaulle for his criticism of the president. At least 24 persons were killed and 141 wounded in resulting riots that began Jan. 24 in Algiers. Insurgents erected barricades in the streets, defying de Gaulle, but capitulated Feb. 1.

On June 14, 1960, de Gaulle again invited the rebels to Paris to talk peace terms. A delegation accepted but the talks failed when Paris refused diplomatic recognition.

FAMED CASBAH, native quarters of Algiers, holds 80,000 Moslems in an area meant for 14,000. Tens of thousands more live in bidonvilles (oil-can towns) despite housing projects. French officers, armed with rifles, patrolled the approaches to the native quarters in January, 1957, during a general strike designed to influence the UN debate in New York.

WAR LESSONS were taught to small groups in the 30,000-strong Algerian rebel Army of Liberation. These guerrillas are getting instructions in the field on how to strip a light machine gun captured from the French during an ambush. Picture was taken at a hideout for the hit-and-run army deep in the barren Sahara Atlas Mountains of northwest Algeria.

ALGERIAN REBEL LEADERS seized by the French Oct. 22, 1956, while on a flight from Morocco, where they had been guests of King Mohammed V, to Tunis. They are *(l. to r.)* Dr. Mustafa Lachera; Mohammed Boudiaf; Ait Ahmed Hocine; Mohammed Khider; Ben Bella, commander of "Algerian Liberation Army." Their arrest set off new anti-French rioting.

MOSLEMS AND EUROPEAN settlers marched together in a spirit of unity in May, 1958, in Algiers to demand the return to power of Gen. Charles de Gaulle. The French commander-in-chief, Gen. Raoul Salan, later addressed this crowd and spoke of the "90 million Frenchmen who are determined to remain French." Frustrated and disillusioned by the Paris government's handling of the nationalist Moslem revolt, a group of French army officers revolted and joined European civilians to create a "Committee of Public Safety" that defied the Paris regime. Newly-appointed Premier Pierre Pflimlin was unable to cope with the angered army.

GEN. CHARLES DE GAULLE became premier June 1, 1958, and later president in an office patterned after the United States executive branch. In the effort to settle the Algerian native revolt, and restore French "grandeur," he visited Algeria and mingled with the people. On this Dec. 4, 1958, visit he shakes hands with Moslem school children. But the rebel forces continued to defy him, and so also did some Frenchman.

JACQUES MASSU, a general and a tough paratrooper commander, led the soldiers who seized all of Algeria's key cities in the May, 1958, revolt against the Paris government. Massu, working under General Salan, paved the way for de Gaulle's return to power. Massu, however, was dismissed Jan. 22, 1960, from his post as military and civil commander of the Algiers area because of his criticism of President de Gaulle.

INSURGENTS among Europeans arose against de Gaulle in Algiers Jan. 24, 1960, after the French president dismissed Massu. Scores of persons were killed and wounded in fights between the demonstrators and the police. Insurgents erected street barricades.

JACQUES SOUSTELLE, a leading spokesman of the French colonialists in Algeria, was ousted Feb. 5, 1960, by de Gaulle from his post as minister of the Sahara, atomic energy and overseas possessions. Soustelle had been a strong supporter of de Gaulle at the time of the first revolt of the settlers in the spring of 1958. Many original Gaullists turned against the president when he favored a conciliatory policy toward the Algerian insurrectionists.

UPRISING of Europeans collapsed on ninth day, and the insurgents were put in trucks after leaving barriers. Some 420 of the insurgents were taken to a rest camp of legion paratroopers at Zeralda, 25 miles outside Algiers. A face-saving formula was provided by the French Army command, which agreed to let insurgents join an army unit: some just quit and went home.

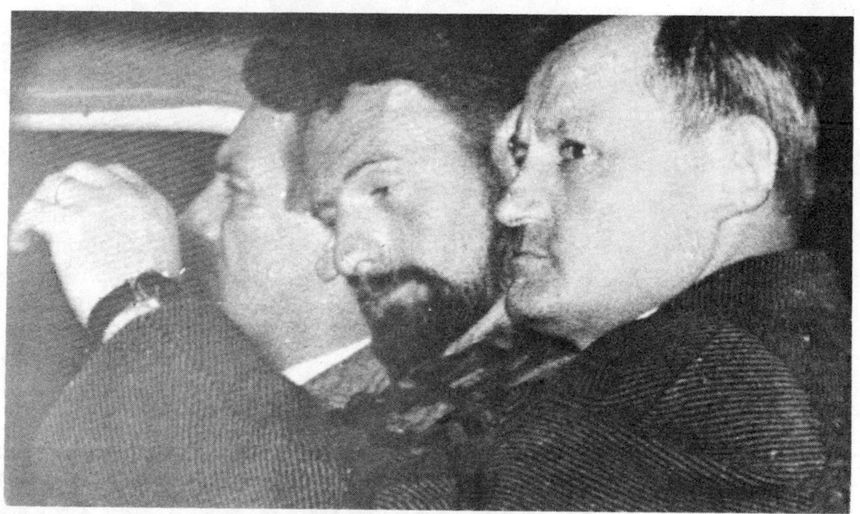

PIERRE LAGAILLARDE, defeated, bearded leader of the Algiers insurgents, appeared weary as he sat in car between two policemen upon his arrival at Santè prison in Paris Feb. 1, 1960. The 28-year-old extremist deputy of the French National Assembly was flown to Paris in a military plane only a few hours after he marched out of the Algiers barricades at the head of his dispirited followers. The Santè prison was the one where the French government first incarcerated Mohammed Ben Bella, Algerian rebel leader.

UNVEILED Algerian women are voting Nov. 30, 1958, for members of the National Assembly of the new French Fifth Republic established after Gen. de Gaulle returned to power on June 1 of that year. Final returns in the election showed that, in France, voters smashed the once-powerful Communist Party, cutting its parliamentary representation to a mere handful, and giving a third straight landslide victory to de Gaulle. The French leader's prestige was also very high among Moslem moderates when he took power. He increased that prestige when he promised on Sept. 16, 1959, to let the people decide own future within four years.

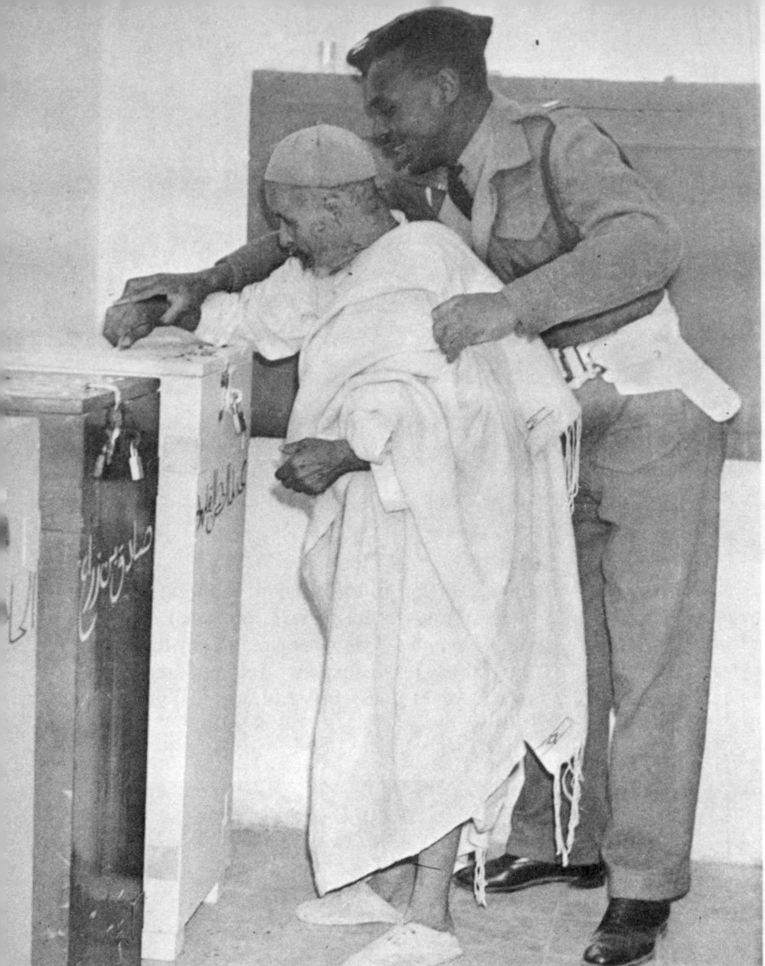

BLIND MAN is led to colored ballot boxes by Libyan policeman who guides his hand and card to the opening. For the first time in history people of the new kingdom went to polls Feb. 19. 1952. Libya was the first country to get independence fully under UN auspices. The King was Idris I.

MOROCCO AND TUNISIA WIN FULL FREEDOM

French protectorates end with both nations under nationalist pressure; U.S. giving up Moroccan air bases

THE DECADE brought full independence to two more North African nations, Morocco and Tunisia.

The "Sherifian Empire," one of the first states to recognize the infant U.S., won full freedom after 35 years in which France "protected" most of Morocco, Spain the northwest shoulder of Africa. The internationally famous port of Tangier, under anomalous "international" rule, had become a smugglers' and speculators' paradise.

Tunisia, the ancient Carthage, and for centuries part of the Ottoman Empire, had been a French protectorate since 1881.

Both received independence in March, 1956.

Chief architects of freedom for the two nations were Sultan Mohammed V, who exchanged his ancient title for that of King, and Habib Bourguiba, who turned from premier into President after the Constituent Assembly, in 1957, had ousted the aged hereditary Bey and declared Tunisia a republic.

While both leaders were pro-West (Bourguiba's wife was French), relations with France were severely strained at the end of the decade, largely because of great popular sympathy with the rebels in Algeria, which lay between them. Tunis was the site of the Algerian rebel "government" and its military base, and French pursuit of rebel forces and reprisal raids, such as the bombing of a village in 1958, led to bitter exchanges.

In Morocco, there was popular resistance throughout the decades of French rule, resistance which mounted in intensity after World War II, when Mohammed V, tired of his puppet role, became the nationalist leader. He was deposed and exiled in 1953, and replaced by his aged uncle, Mohammed Ben Moulay, after a contrived show of strength by the Berber feudal lords of the south, who were practically French clients, to intimidate the nationalists. But agitation continued, the new regime proved unworkable, and Mohammed V was brought back in triumph in November, 1955.

Independence, however, did not bring solutions to either political or economic problems. The nationalists, once united behind the Sultan as symbol, had less regard for him as King, and split into right and left factions. In 1958 a deliberative assembly and a cabinet responsible to it were set up. But in 1960 the King felt compelled to replace the leftist premier, Abdallah Ibrahim, with his son, Crown Prince Moulay Hassan, who was denounced

RUBBLED VILLAGE of Sakiet Sid Youssef leaped into world prominence Feb. 8, 1958, when French airmen raided obscure Tunisian hamlet near border of war-torn Algeria, killing 68 persons, wounding 100. Tunisia charged aggression; French defended action as raid on Algerian rebel base.

WHEELUS FIELD in Libya on the North African coast is the U.S. Air Force link to the Middle East. Present government is comparatively friendly toward the United States. More than one-quarter of the national income is derived in one form or another from the U.S.; Britain also has a base.

by the leftists as being a potential "fascist dictator."

But left-wing pressure had, in 1958, induced Morocco to accept a Soviet Embassy and Czech arms and to join the Arab League.

In 1960 the U.S. began evacuating its $400 million Air Force installations, set up in 1950 under an agreement with France. A sop to nationalist pride, it was a blow to the shaky economy, since they brought in $30 million a year.

Both Morocco and Tunisia were pressing for withdrawal of the remaining French garrisons, but both continued to depend on France for more than half of all foreign trade.

Libya, Tunisia's eastern neighbor, saw in an oil strike by a U.S. firm the possible end of its age-old poverty.

PENITENT PASHA of Marrakesh, famed El Glaoui, kneels before Sultan Mohammed V, after latter's triumphant return from exile. El Glaoui, chief pro-French Moroccan potentate, was later stripped of his own great possessions and power.

GENTLE OLD BEY of Tunis (receiving credentials of new French Ambassador Georges Gorse) was political figurehead under French. He was ignored by Premier Habib Bourguiba *(c.)* and was ousted July 25, 1957, as Tunisia became a republic. Bourguiba was North Africa's chief pro-West leader, anti-French, anti-Nasser, anti-Red but friendly toward the United States.

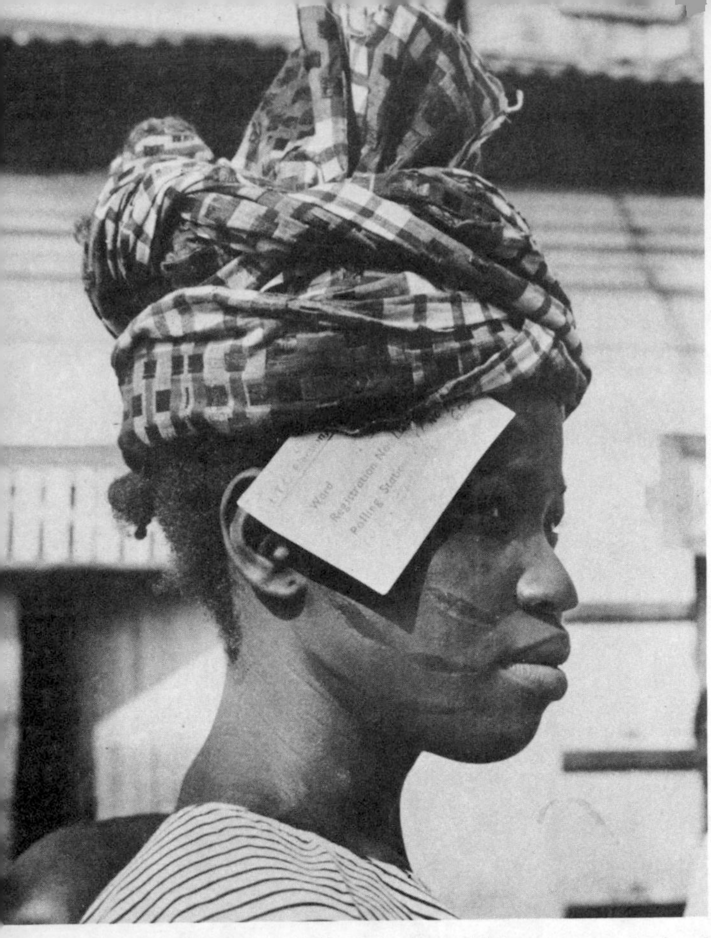

BALLOT SLIP, symbol of the new Africa, is worn in headdress of Nigerian voter. With freedom, franchise has been extended to more than 50 million people below the Sahara. Most are illiterate, need drawings to identify candidates and parties.

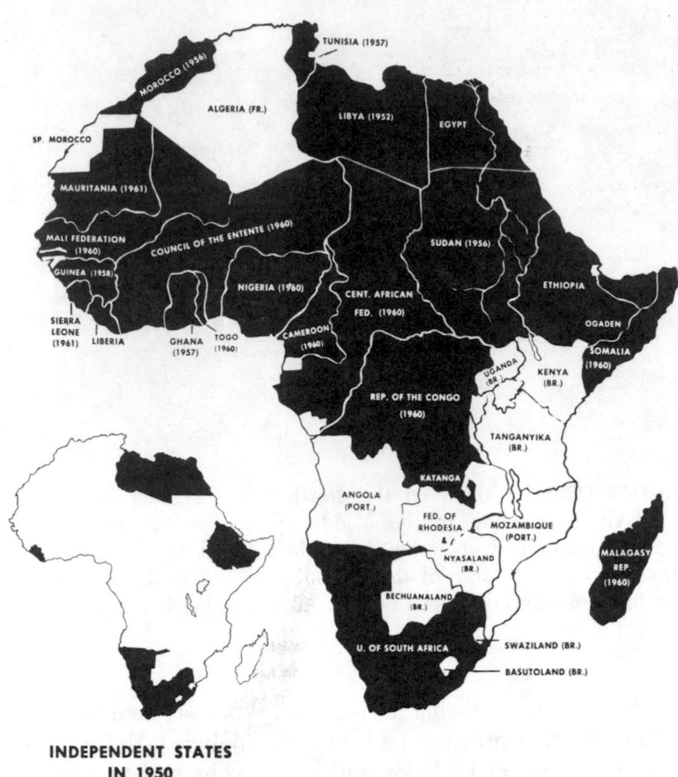

AFRICA covers 11.5 million square miles. In 1950, only one tenth of this area was free. By 1961, more than two-thirds of the entire continent will consist of independent nations, including 150 million of Africa's 200 million population.

AFRICA ERUPTS

Chaos sweeps Congo as Belgian, French, British west coast colonies gain independence; unrest spreads in eastern areas, Rhodesia, South Africa

TO THE OUTSIDE WORLD 10 years ago, Africa was the personal playground of Tarzan. By mid-1960, the "Dark Continent" appeared to have vanished overnight. In its place had risen a political, economic and social colossus representing the most massive and least violent transfer of power in the history of revolution. The change had taken place so rapidly it seemed almost furtive.

Actually, the rash of free nations that broke out over the face of Africa could be traced to the end of World War II, even though the transformation was scarcely noticeable for more than a decade. But the aspiration was there, not to mention a built-in axe to grind: colonialism. The European powers had made great strides in establishing western frameworks of government and justice, but these blessings were often less than apparent to the indigenous populations. Education was appallingly inadequate; a widespread color bar rubbed salt in the wound. By 1958, a flood of nationalism was sweeping the continent at a pace equaled by the almost frantic haste with which the colonial powers liquidated their stewardships.

The take-over was a mixed blessing. Independence was an undeniable affirmation of human rights. But there was also much concern that the mass-grants of self-rule had been a disastrously premature abdication of responsibility. Whatever the faults of the European powers, they had undertaken to prepare the African people for the time when they would run their own affairs efficiently. Few nationalist leaders could honestly claim that they were anywhere nearly prepared; their countries might well be on the road to banana-republic status. And the difficulties were compounded by the challenge from the East, although Communism might first appear as a boon. The result could be a new and worse type of colonialism.

However, on the credit side of the ledger were the strong ties between most new African nations and the countries that once ruled them. The U.S., too, was rapidly entering the picture, as investor, teacher and friend. If and when Africa's democracies reached true maturity, it would be due in large measure to the help and understanding of those they termed the "imperialists."

CZECH ARMS ARE UNLOADED AT CONAKRY, CAPITAL OF GUINEA. COUNTRY'S "NEUTRALISM" MAY BE NEUTRALIZED BY COMMUNIST AID.

DE GAULLE IS HERO IN MALI FEDERATION.

THE POSTWAR FRENCH dream for her African empire (roughly the size of the U.S.) was until recently a Greater France, with every overseas possession ultimately functioning as an equal part of the metropolitan country. At the end of the war, the status of colonial populations was changed from French subject to Citizen of France. In 1957, universal male suffrage was introduced. But these major advances failed to keep pace with nationalist goals. In September 1958, President De Gaulle offered the 13 French African dependencies a revised relationship permitting complete internal autonomy. Territories rejecting the offer would be given immediate independence. The proposal was enthusiastically endorsed in French Africa, particularly by the moderate and highly influential Felix Houphouet-Boigny, Ivory Coast president. The lone dissenter, Guinea—led by Houphouet-Boigny's arch-rival, left-wing nationalist Sekou Touré—wanted and got out, was angrily snubbed by France, has since become Africa's first potential Iron Curtain satellite. Prospects initially looked excellent for the new French Union, but soon leaders of large blocs were demanding total sovereignty. De Gaulle, sensing the inevitable, supported them. By 1961, 99 44/100 percent of French Africa will enjoy independence in a French Community bearing increased resemblance to the British Commonwealth. France's good grace in acceding to nationalism should help enormously in strengthening the ties of her former colonies to the West.

HARBOR OF ABIDJAN, IVORY COAST CAPITAL, IS SPANNED BY NEW FOUR-LANE BRIDGE

TOURE

DE GAULLE

HOUPHOUET-BOIGNY

FEATHERED NIGERIAN FINANCE MINISTER.

NEAR RIOT IN ACCRA WHEN GHANA'S NKRUMAH WAS RELEASED FROM PRISON.

THE IDEA of the British Commonwealth—a loosely knit union of free nations bound by ties of friendship and economic interdependence — was perhaps best seen in the newly sovereign states of Ghana and Nigeria. Their emergence to self-rule reflected the highest credit on Great Britain's policy toward its West African possessions, and on Prime Minister Harold Macmillan's progressive aims. The road to freedom in the two young countries had been marred by a minimum of disorder. Ghana—the former Gold Coast Colony — suffered only a temporary setback when its nationalist leader, Kwame Nkrumah, was briefly imprisoned in 1951. But by 1957 Ghana had become Britain's first sub-Sahara territory to achieve independence and remained in the Commonwealth as a republic. Nigeria's path was even smoother, although bitter political rivalries helped delay independence until 1960. The new nations were not without their special headaches. President Nkrumah had been sharply criticized for imposing strongman rule against deep-seated tribal opposition. Prime Minister Sir Abubakar Tafawa Balewa found Nigeria's progress retarded by 16th Century Moslem conservatism in his own Northern Province. But, thanks to civil service cadres trained in the highest British tradition, Ghana and Nigeria seemed far better prepared to govern themselves than any other new nation on the continent. Also due for independence in short order: former free-slave colony of Sierra Leone, more stable politically than most African states, and — thanks to its diamond industry—economically sound.

NKRUMAH

MACMILLAN

DIAMOND MINING, SIERRA LEONE'S MAJOR INDUSTRY, COVERS 500 SQUARE MILE AREA.

BALEWA

RHODESIA'S KARIBA DAM IS SECOND BIGGEST IN AFRICA.

MAU MAU TOOK 13,000 WHITE AND BLACK LIVES IN KENYA.

VERWOERD

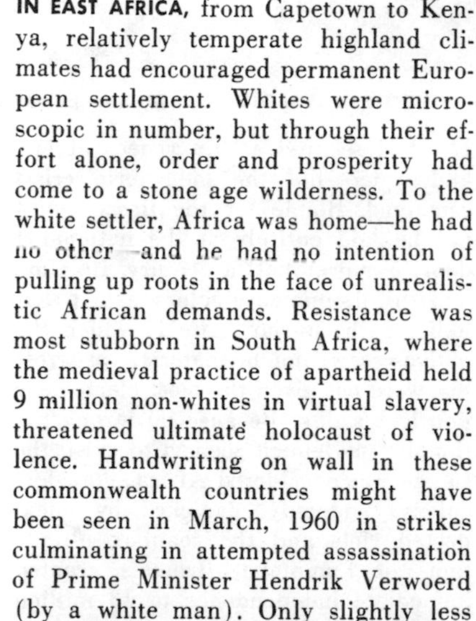

IN EAST AFRICA, from Capetown to Kenya, relatively temperate highland climates had encouraged permanent European settlement. Whites were microscopic in number, but through their effort alone, order and prosperity had come to a stone age wilderness. To the white settler, Africa was home—he had no other—and he had no intention of pulling up roots in the face of unrealistic African demands. Resistance was most stubborn in South Africa, where the medieval practice of apartheid held 9 million non-whites in virtual slavery, threatened ultimate holocaust of violence. Handwriting on wall in these commonwealth countries might have been seen in March, 1960 in strikes culminating in attempted assassination of Prime Minister Hendrik Verwoerd (by a white man). Only slightly less explosive was the Federation of Rhodesia and Nyasaland; here Prime Minister Sir Roy Welensky took firm stand for "partnership" control in "civilized" hands, whether white or black. But Africans, needled by firebrand nationalists like Dr. Hastings Banda, wanted to take over at once. Most temperate was Kenya, where whites, despite unspeakable Mau Mau horrors in early '50s, reluctantly prepared to accept African majority in government, as urged by Colonial Secretary Iain MacLeod. But demagogues such as Tom Mboya demanded immediate release of extremist Jomo Kenyatta, "freedom" 10 minutes later. Urgent need throughout "White Africa": moderation on both sides. But South African whites and Rhodesia-Kenya blacks seemed determined to thwart any effort toward moderation.

BANDA

ASSEMBLY LINE FUNERAL FOLLOWS MACHINE-GUNNING OF SOUTH AFRICAN NEGROES.

WELENSKY

KENYATTA

MACLEOD

MBOYA

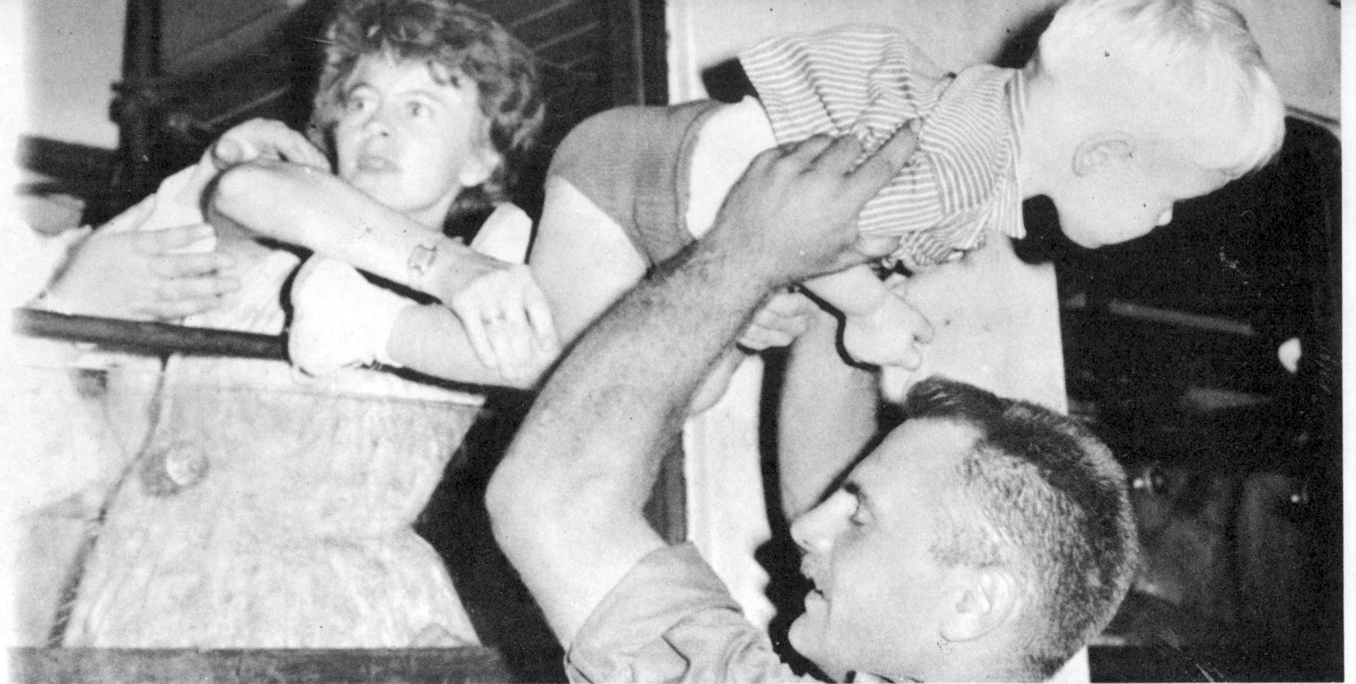

TERRIFIED MOTHER PASSES CHILD THROUGH TRAIN WINDOW IN LEOPOLDVILLE DURING EUROPEAN FLIGHT FROM STRIFE-TORN CONGO

INDEPENDENCE, which came to the Belgian Congo June 30, 1960, brought almost immediate chaos. The army mutinied against its Belgian officers (there were no commissioned natives), and went on a spree of rape and pillage. Hundreds died in inter-tribal conflict. Europeans fled in a massive air-ground exodus. Mineral rich Katanga Province, keystone of the economy, was led by pro-Belgian Moise Tshombe into secession. Belgian troops took over the chief cities. Goateed Premier Patrice Lumumba shrieked for the military aid Moscow hastened to offer. It seemed another Korea might develop. But a multi-nation emergency force, organized by night-and-day efforts of United Nations Secretary General Dag Hammarskjold, poured in. By early fall the UN had secured a thin veneer of law and order—but the long term crisis remained. Blame for the fiasco could not be laid entirely at the nationalist door. For over half a century, Belgium had run its immense colony as a paternalist authoritarian state in which the natives saw much material progress but were not given the most elementary political rights. Because no strong nationalist movement seemed to exist, the Congo was considered Africa's "model" colony. Suddenly, panicked by unexpected riots and the soapbox ultimatums of Lumumba, Brussels granted immediate independence to 13 million Africans who had never even seen a ballot box. The result: a full-fledged "republic" with nobody trained to run it. The Congo's near future: not good.

LUMUMBA

TSHOMBE

HAMMARSKJOLD

CONGO POLICE RESTRAIN FELLOW-AFRICANS IN RIOT

COPPER SMELTING PROCEEDS APACE IN ORE-RICH KATANGA

SOMALIS CELEBRATING NEWBORN INDEPENDENCE IN 1960 DEMAND THE SAME FOR THEIR NEIGHBORS

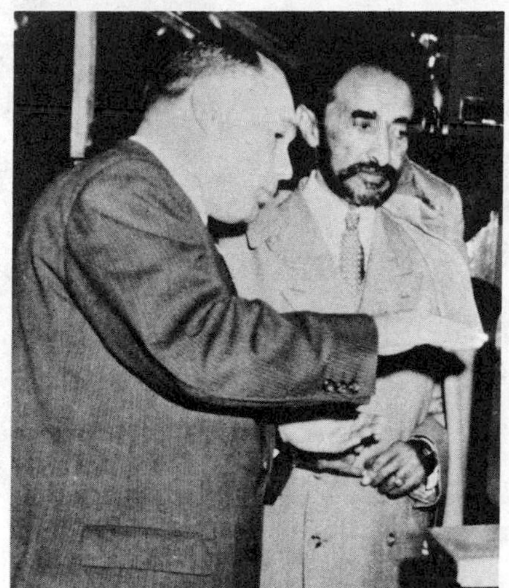

ETHIOPIA'S EMPEROR HAILE SELASSIE

AFRICA'S MORE PUBLICIZED newborn nations were not the only trouble spots on the continent. Least-known but most potentially potent powder-keg was Somalia — whose independence July 1, 1960, was overshadowed by the Congo farce. The proud, warlike Moslem Somalis had an international axe to grind: Ethiopia's vast Ogaden region which, they asserted, belonged to them. Ogaden had long been the arena of savage border skirmishes, previously kept under control by European administration. However, should the now-independent Somalis ever press their claims, the result might be war. Ethiopia, determined to hold the Ogaden, was ready. No stranger to major armed conflicts, it had a tough, well-trained army. Logistics could be handled expertly by the U.S.-operated Ethiopian Airlines, one of the world's most efficient. The UN, at decade's end, could do little more than keep its fingers crossed. But perhaps the king-size question mark of Africa was to be found in the Portuguese colonies of Angola and Mozambique, the only territories on the continent where politics were ruthlessly suppressed. Portugal's dictator, Dr. Antonio Salazar, considered the regions part of the metropolitan nation and no deviation—whether white or black—was tolerated. Yet the tidal wave of nationalism could not help but rub off on the Portuguese areas, although as the decade ended, there seemed small enough likelihood that it would put more than an insignificant dent in the iron-fist rule of Africa's last real colonies.

"OLD FORT" OF MOZAMBIQUE, BUILT IN LATE 16TH CENTURY TO GUARD ROUTE TO INDIES, TYPIFIES "DIEHARD" PORTUGUESE COLONIALISM

BRILLIANT GLARE OF ARTILLERY NIGHT-FIRING ILLUMINATES THE BLACKNESS OF KOREAN WAR FRONT DURING FINAL DAYS OF THE WAR.

KOREA SURVIVES RED ASSAULT

THE POPULAR UPHEAVAL that convulsed the Republic of Korea in April, 1960, forcing its 85-year-old founder and president, Syngman Rhee, from office, climaxed a decade of internal strife and full-scale Communist invasion.

For 12 years the Rhee government had served as a rallying point against aggression from Communist-ruled North Korea. But, as Rhee grew older, he ruled with a heavy hand, silenced democratic opposition and allowed his party to grow corrupt. Charges of rigged elections in March, 1960, proved the final blow to his career.

The Communist invasion began June 25, 1950, when 60,000 North Koreans armed with 100 Russian-built tanks smashed across the 38th Parallel. South Korean forces were weak, U.S. troops on hand only a token force and reinforcements available in Japan were scanty. Overwhelmed and fighting desperately, the defenders were reduced to a slim 4000 sq. mile foothold around Pusan.

Meanwhile, the United Nations, with U.S. initiative, reacted swiftly Within two days the UN (the Soviet delegate was boycotting the Security Council) met and quickly authorized military action.

During the following month, 17 UN states poured fighting forces (most were U.S.) into beleaguered South Korea and 22 others sent food, clothing, money and medical aid. Gathering strength, UN forces smashed out of the tight Pusan perimeter and began the roll-back. Simultaneously, on Sept. 15, Gen. Douglas MacArthur, UN commander, stormed ashore with U.S. troops deep behind the Communist lines at Inchon, trapping 35,000.

Suddenly, on Nov. 25, when the fast-moving UN forces had crossed the 38th Parallel and were nearing the Manchurian border, 200,000 Chinese "volunteers" swarmed across the Yalu River and drove the UN back again to the Parallel.

MacArthur, urging the military necessity of striking at bases within Chinese territory, chafed at restraints imposed by the political necessity of limiting the conflict to prevent World War III. On April 10, he was abruptly recalled to the United States by President Truman.

GEN. DOUGLAS MACARTHUR, RECALLED BY PRES. TRUMAN IN 1951, AND LT. GEN. MATTHEW RIDGEWAY TOUR PUSAN DOCKS.

U.S., UN, in bitter fighting, smash drive to overrun young republic

Two years of weary truce talks at Panmunjom—while the battle line see-sawed in bloody trench warfare along the 38th Parallel—yielded a cease-fire on July 27, 1953. Under neutral supervision, 75,799 prisoners returned to North Korea and China, 12,760 to UN contingents.

With 1 million known civilian casualties, 2 million displaced persons and 100,000 orphans, South Korea turned to the grim task of rebuilding its economy.

Aid and relief from the U.S. and UN, totaling $2 billion during the decade, gave backbone to the reconstruction program. By 1956, 5000 new homes had been built, and 110 new irrigation and flood control dams had doubled rice production. Industrially, while coal and paper output doubled by 1956, over-all production by 1959 had not advanced much beyond the 1949-50 level, nor had it kept pace with population growth. However, expansion in chemicals, textiles, rubber, glass and clay, food processing, machinery and metals gave new balance to Korea's traditional agriculture-mining economy. In '60, South Korea made a major bid for U.S. investments.

Strained relations with Japan over lingering World War II claims and rivalry for fishing grounds were further aggravated in 1959 when Japan permitted some of the 612,924 Koreans living in Japan to return to Communist North Korea. Then when in protest, South Korea cut trade ties with Japan, inflation sent Korean prices soaring. At the time of the ban 19.5% of South Korea's imports ($40.6 million) and 76.2% of its exports ($11.2 million), were with Japan.

Threatening again, North Korea violated the 1953 "status quo" truce agreement almost immediately, built up its military forces to include 30 major air bases equipped with Russian-built MIG-17 fighters and twin-jet bombers. In 1957, North Korea had an estimated 350,000 troops plus an equal number of Chinese forces, with 1 million more poised just across the Yalu River.

South Korea, with only 600,000 men and U.S. forces down to two divisions, feared a repetition of 1950. In 1957 the UN, to meet the new threat, sent in U.S. F-100 Supersabre jets and supplies to help redress the balance.

END-RUN at Inchon, 150 miles behind enemy lines, caught Reds completely off guard and turned tide of war. Daring amphibious attack was part of strategy unleashed by Gen. MacArthur that forced checkmated North Koreans to Manchurian border. LST's shown above were part of 261-vessel armada that landed troops, and then kept them supplied.

WEARY PUERTO RICAN soldiers carry machine-gun along desolate Korean road. Puerto Rican troops fought for first time as unit (Sixty-fifth Regiment) in Korea, made gallant stands at beleagured Hamhung and Hamnung. Fiercely proud of their U.S. citizenship, only commonwealth of U.S. contributed far more volunteers than 65th was able to absorb.

THEY CHOSE COMMUNISM: 21 Americans and one lone Briton who decided against UN repatriation are shown at Panmunjom, where they stayed during interrogation period. A five-nation neutral commission supervised the exchange. While some turncoats later returned to U.S., majority disappeared behind Bamboo Curtain. Their shocking betrayal resulted in military issuance of *Code of Conduct* to U.S. servicemen. In contrast, 14,000 Red POW's refused repatriation.

MURDERED AMERICANS lie in filth of Korean trench. Taken prisoners of war, atrocity victims were found in wake of Red retreats. North Koreans and Chinese refused to recognize humane rules of warfare whenever it was convenient. Thirty Americans *(above)* were tied and shot by North Koreans at Taejon, others slain by Chinese retreating from Hoengsong.

CANADIAN TROOPS joined other UN units early in 1951. First group to arrive was Princess Pat Battalion, which reinforced U.S. outfits during battle for Chipyong in February. A wounded Canadian officer *(above)* maintains vigil of enemy outposts. Other UN forces included detachments from Turkey, Philippines, Greece, Great Britain and 12 others.

UNEASY TRUCE was declared in Korea in 1953, ending 37 month war. Signing for UN is Supreme Allied Cmdr. Gen. Mark Clark. Truce ended two years of talks.

OUTNUMBERED BUT VICTORIOUS, U.S. troops take rest after successfully executing dawn assault on Chinese Communist positions on Western front. An estimated 300 Reds were killed by the raiding party, triumphing over mass-attack technique employed by the poorly-trained, ill-equipped, inferior Communist forces.

Rhee grows increasingly dictatorial, is ousted by popular upheaval

In spite of reconstruction problems and the Red threat, South Korea held elections. In 1956, although Syngman Rhee entered and won the elections for a third term by a plurality of 3 million votes, growing opposition registered 1.5 million posthumous ballots for his opponent, P. H. Shinicky, who died during the campaign.

However, in the March, 1960, elections widespread suspicion was aroused when Rhee's running mate, Lee Ki Poong—defeated decisively four years earlier by incumbent Vice President John M. Chang—rolled up 8.2 million votes to take *every* constituency and defeat Chang by a four-to-one margin. President Rhee, already 85 years of age, was charged with stuffing the ballot boxes to insure the selection of his own choice as successor.

These charges, and grievances accumulated during Rhee's 12 years of rule, sparked frenzied rioting which left an unofficial 250 dead and thousands injured. With riots at fever pitch, and stung by sharp official U.S. criticism, Rhee resigned April 27, 1960.

On June 15, a caretaker government passed a constitutional amendment reducing the power of the president and introducing a British-style cabinet system responsible to the National Assembly. Elections on July 30, 1960, gave the Democrats, the party of John M. Chang, more than two-thirds of the Assembly seats.

After a decade of war, uneasy truce, and political strife, Korea, the "Land of the Morning Calm," was still looking for a break in the storm.

NEW RULERS of Korea retain shaky hold. Acting president Huh Chang *(c)*, with aides Lee Ho *(l.)*, Kwon Soong-Yul.

SOUTH KOREAN STUDENTS rioted in Seoul streets, incensed at alleged ballot-stuffing by Rhee confederates to elect Lee Ki Poong. Bloody sidewalk frays resulted in capitulation of government, Rhee's self-imposed exile. New elections were held.

DEATH WAS PRICE of election rigging for Lee Ki-Poong *(r.)*, Vice-Pres. elect, shown with Rhee before family suicide.

GRIM FACE of Communist regime is reflected in Red guard at Hong Kong border. Although border is under heavy guard, uncounted thousands have fled into British colony. Red policy was to give exit visas only to disabled, aged.

RUSSIAN-TYPE trucks began rolling from Manchurian assembly line in 1958. But the amount was only a fraction of number needed. First trucks were of poor quality and needed many repairs.

DEATH IN DAYLIGHT came to millions during purges in early years of Communist regime. Usual practice was to try land owner before so-called Peoples Court, where neighbors or relatives would testify to accused's counter-revolutionary activities. Summarily convicted, accused would be shot as warning to others. Mass executions were designed to pave way for collectivization of land and eliminate even remote possibility of opposition from once landed class.

RUTHLESS DRAGON

Red China industrializes at own people's cost; might menaces West

COMMUNIST CHINA, one-year-old in 1950, grew mightily in the decade and by 1960 had emerged as a behemoth threatening the Western world.

Under the whiplash of chubby Mao Tse-tung, the vast Chinese mainland was cowed into submission and shoved along a Marxist path.

Uncounted millions were killed in blood purges of alleged counter-revolutionaries; some 450 million peasants were herded first into cooperatives and later, in a giant stroke of disregard for human values, placed in ant-like communes.

What happened in China in the past decade was one of the most significant events of the 20th Century, boding ill for the U.S. and its allies.

On October 1, 1950, the People's Republic of China celebrated its first anniversary. Chiang Kai-shek's Nationalists had been driven into exile on Formosa.

The question experts asked then was how long would the alien political phenomenon last in China. But as the years rolled by, the Reds consolidated their gains and by 1960 were hurtling headlong toward industrialization.

The cost was in blood and hunger. Mao Tse-tung, leader of the Chinese Communist Party since 1931, eliminated millions of landowners who were considered "unsafe." Peking admitted to 800,000 executions, but other estimates ran as high as 20 million.

In the drive toward industrialization, every available cent in the treasury was spent for capital goods. The result: Food supplies were continually short and the rice ration was cut in mid-1960 to an all-time low of some 5 ounces a day, barely enough to sustain life.

To keep the population occupied elsewhere, Peking used the U.S. as the chief focus of hate, spewing venom at Washington at every opportunity. The "Hate America" campaign never slowed during the decade. It reached a high point shortly before the Chinese Reds entered the Korean War in October, 1950.

While food production inched up barely in proportion to the birth rate, industrial output soared. By 1960, crude steel production had reached 13 million metric tons; coal output reached 347 million metric tons and oil production, non-existent before the Communists took power, had increased to 42 million barrels a year by 1960.

But possibly the most significant event in China during the decade was the start of the revolutionary commune system in 1958. Designed to increase production, it forced families into giving up their children to State-operated nurseries to free mothers for labor in the fields. It established under one roof feeding and living facilities.

One of the first reactions was the escape of thousands of peasants into Portuguese Macao and across the guarded border into Hong Kong. Even the Soviet Union took adverse notice of the harsh commune system, implying that Moscow considered it impractical and too severe.

Harsh as it sounded, there was no opposition from the Communist hierarchy to the pet scheme of Mao Tse-tung. Mao did lash out at what he called "rightists," but there were no purges of Red leaders such as occurred in 1955 when Kao Kang, Communist chieftain in Manchuria, was arrested as a counter-revolutionary for opposing the centralizing of power in Peking. He later took his own life.

Mao himself stepped down voluntarily as chairman of the government on April 27, 1959, and turned over the honorific post to Moscow-trained Liu Shao-chi. But he retained the reins of policy as chairman of the Chinese Communist Party, the world's largest, with a membership of almost 13 million.

While Mao enjoyed success in welding the most dynamic and powerful government in China's 3000-year history, he failed miserably to achieve the goal of winning recognition for the Communists as the legitimate government.

Few nations recognized Red China during the decade and there was little trade with nations outside the Communist orbit. Aside from an initial rush (Great Britain, the Scandinavian countries and the Red satellites) in 1950 to recognize Peking, Egypt (1956) was the only major power to exchange diplomats in the next nine years.

The Peking regime's aggressive actions in Asia alienated its Far Eastern neighbors.

On June 20, 1960, the International Commission of Jurists found Red China guilty of systematic extermination of the Buddhist religion in Tibet. The crime, in legal terminology, was genocide and it horrified the Buddhist nations of Asia.

Yet Peking pushed the extermination campaign in a brutal attempt to smash rebellion in its Tibetan "region," and thousands of refugees poured into Nepal and India with tales of massacre by Red Chinese troops.

Suddenly, in August, 1960, Peking appeared to shift. Prime Minister Chou En-lai, for the first time, seemed to support Moscow's proposals of peaceful coexistence with the West.

But whether it portended a genuine shift away from aggressive policies awaited solid gestures—something the Chinese Communists had not displayed for 10 years.

DESPITE RECORD CROPS, harsh austerity was imposed upon peasants in winter of 1959-60. Ration reductions were in line with policy of cutting food consumption in winter, when work is supposed to be less arduous than during crop-growing seasons. Rice soup and sweet potatoes was typical fare.

FLEEING WITH FEW belongings, refugees line up at Lowu border at Hong Kong in hope of escaping totalitarian regime in 1950. Population of British colony at edge of mainland more than doubled in short time, and in 1957 officials closed colony to free entry because of water and housing shortage.

VIOLENT ARTILLERY barrage from Communist guns *(r.)* greeted President Eisenhower's arrival on Formosa on goodwill trip in 1960. Barrage killed eight civilians on tiny Nationalist-held Quemoy island off mainland coast. Reds announced barrage was designed to show "contempt" for the U.S. President who ordered U.S. fleet to protect island.

WOMEN'S RIGHTS advanced under Communist regime. For first time, women won legal right to divorce and took over some key industrial posts. Below, woman manager of power plant inspects equipment with assistant. Madame Sun-Yat-sen was given high political post as vice-chairman of People's Republic.

SOVIET EXPERTS helped Chinese map first five-year plan in 1953 *(above)*. Plan, which Peking described as a great success, put emphasis on birth of industrial base for backward nation. At expense of agriculture and consumer production, Reds forged ahead quickly in production of capital goods, with the USSR supplying technical help.

MAJOR QUESTION in 1960 was whether Chinese leader Mao Tse-tung and Soviet Union's Krushchev *(l.)* were engaged in battle for ideological leadership of Communist world. Both leaders took indirect slaps at the other's policies — Moscow criticizing China's commune system and Peking, the Soviet Union's policy of "peaceful" coexistence.

AMBITIOUS PLANS to harness China's rampant rivers got under way in earnest in late 1950s with huge Sanmen Gorge project on Yellow River *(right)*. By 1960, an estimated 40 million Chinese were working to tame and distribute the rivers that caused centuries of sorrow to China's farmers. Aim of Yellow River project was to dot waterway with flood control and power stations and make it navigable for 2000-mile trip by ship from mouth in Shantung Province to industrial complex of Lanchow in far northwestern China.

HAPPIER DAYS in Indian-Chinese relations were represented in visit of Chinese Premier Chou En-lai to New Delhi in 1954 *(below)*. Relations took sharp turn for worse in 1959 when Chinese brutally wiped out Tibetan revolt and encroached on Indian territory. Chinese seized 10 Indian soldiers and killed nine others in an attack in eastern Ladakh (October 1959), making relations even worse. Chou returned to Delhi in 1960 to seek solution of border difficulties, but talks deadlocked over what constituted border in area.

VISITORS FROM U.S. were rare in Communist China during decade, but group of young American students defied State Department warning in 1957 and went to China after visit to Moscow. Premier Chou En-lai himself greeted group, *(above)* and led singing of "*Ain't Gonna Study War No More.*" Reds later tightened issuance of visas, refused to allow U.S. newsmen on mainland unless Washington reciprocated. State Department refused. "Hate America" campaign resulted in arrest of U.S. Catholic Bishop James Walsh in '60.

FREEDOM CAME in 1955 to four U.S. pilots shot down during Korean War. Communists maintained they fell in Manchuria and held them as spies, but released four without explanation at Lowu Bridge into Hong Kong *(l.)*. By end of decade, Peking still held at least four Americans on spying charges. Washington kept alive talks at Warsaw with Chinese envoy to Poland, but meetings had no apparent success in winning freedom for imprisoned Americans. It was lone diplomatic link Washington had with outlaw Red regime.

FORMOSAN EXILE

Pushed off China mainland, aging Chiang Kai-shek devoted decade to strengthening army in hope of striking back at Reds

DISORGANIZED and defeated in 1950, Chiang Kai-shek's Nationalist regime achieved remarkable economic success in its decade of exile on the island of Formosa.

A sweeping land reform program underwritten by the U.S. turned over most of Formosa's farmland to peasants. Crop production increased, and the island's 10 million residents enjoyed one of the highest standards of living in poverty-stricken Asia.

The key to the success was heavy U.S. aid that totaled 3.1 billion dollars. Although there was no official breakdown, perhaps half went to bolster Chiang's 600,000-member military force.

The generalissimo, meanwhile, observed his 73rd birthday in 1960 and still kept alive his dreams of retaking the China mainland. But the dream was as out of reach at decade's end as it was when the demoralized Nationalists were swept from the mainland in 1950.

In 1954, the U.S. and Nationalist China signed a treaty that limited the use of Chiang's military establishment to the defense of Formosa alone, thereby tying the old warrior's hands. Only total war, it appeared, would induce the government in Washington to unleash Chiang again.

INEXORABLY LINKED with the destiny of Nationalist China was Generalissimo Chiang Kai-shek (top *l.*), shown strolling with youngest son, Gen. Chiang Wei-kuo. Aide is in background. Chiang bitterly opposed evacuation of Nationalist-held Tachen Islands *(center)* in 1955 to Communists, but U.S. pressed him to withdraw in fear that friction over tiny isles might lead to war. U.S. Navy guarded evacuation from possible Red attack. Chiang's air army *(right)* was turned by heavy U.S. aid into one of best in Asia, repeatedly whipped Red Chinese jets in dogfights over Formosa Strait. U.S. stationed Matador guided missiles on Formosa in 1957 for defense.

NIPPON RISES FROM WAR RUIN

Enemy transformed into U.S. ally; prosperity reaches all-time peak

JAPAN entered the decade under strict U.S. military occupation, but 10 years later was again claiming its pre-war position as the leading Far Eastern power.

It was a success story that rivaled that of West Germany's post-war boom. But there was one major difference—politics.

Japan's U.S.-imposed democratic procedures led the heavily-populated island nation into bitter ideological splits that erupted in 1960 into violent rioting.

The outbreaks, sparked by the ratification of a U.S.-Japanese defense treaty, forced the cancellation of a goodwill visit by President Eisenhower and the resignation of the pro-Western government of able Premier Nobusuke Kishi.

But the riots, led primarily by Red-tinged labor unions and a radical student organization known as Zengakuren, were only a minor punctuation of Japan's recapture of its pre-war eminence as a major industrial nation.

Its success story started in 1950 with the Korean War. Japan supplied the United Nations forces with the materials of war. Industry thrived, and from the ashes of World War II grew a powerful industrial complex that far outstripped Japan's pre-World War II production.

The Gross National Product rocketed from $11.3 billion in 1950 to an estimated $30 billion in 1960. Wages likewise more than doubled during the period. Japan, by 1960, boasted the highest standard of living in Asia.

Yet the road was paved with obstacles. Because of its close ties with the U.S., Japan was barred from trading with Communist China until 1957. The Chinese mainland, before the war, had been Japan's best customer.

Japan turned instead toward the U.S. and exported heavily—textiles, machinery, electronic equipment, even automobiles. Howls of protest rose from U.S. producers, and Japanese industrialists imposed voluntary quotas on exports that competed with American-made products.

There was bitterness in Japan over the restrictions, but it was only one of a number of friction points that scarred the alliance between Tokyo and Washington during the decade.

In 1957, the case of a U.S. soldier charged with killing a woman scrap-metal scavenger made black headlines in Japan. His name was William Girard. The Japanese insisted he be tried by a Japanese court: the U.S. wanted him before an Army court -martial.

Finally, the U.S. gave way. Girard was convicted by a

RIOTING STUDENTS, protesting scheduled visit of President Eisenhower in June, 1960, surround car of White House Secretary James C. Hagerty. Mob kept him "imprisoned" for 80 minutes before helicopter rescued him. Visit was cancelled later when safety of the President seemed doubtful.

BITTER PILL for Japanese leftists was signing of mutual defense treaty of Premier Kishi during '60 visit to Washington. Treaty was victory for Japan in that it obligated U.S. to consult one-time enemy on deployment and use of troops and weapons in Japan. Ratification touched off month-long riots.

Japanese court and sentenced to a three-year suspended prison term. He returned to his home in Ottawa, Ill. But it was not so much the shooting of an obscure scavenger that inflamed Japanese opinion as the possibility of being caught in the middle of the Cold War. Remembering the atom bombing of Hiroshima and Nagasaki, many Japanese felt neutrality was the only course.

But Japan's premiers, with a majority of the voters supporting them, kept the nation on a firm pro-Western course. Premiers were, successively, Shigeru Yoshida, Ichiro Hatoyama and Nobusuke Kishi, all members of the conservative Liberal-Democratic Party.

The Socialist Party—aided by a clamor for trade with Red China—kept the nation in political turmoil. Fights often flared in the Diet as Japan tasted democratic procedures instituted under U.S. occupation.

The first official step toward Japan's post-war freedom came on September 8, 1951, at San Francisco, where the U.S. and 48 other nations officially made peace with Japan by treaty. The occupation was over, but U.S. troops remained in Japan under a security treaty.

Japan was fully accepted back into the community of nations on December 18, 1956, when the U.N. unanimously voted to grant it membership.

By then, Japan was well on its way to economic success. A sustained foreign trade offensive was carrying Japanese goods to every corner of the earth. It became the world's largest shipbuilder and largest exporter of cotton textiles, and was pushing hard, as the decade ended, for a leading position in designing and producing electronics equipment.

By 1959, Japan was drilling for oil in the Middle East in competition with entrenched U.S. and British cartels. The one-time Axis partner likewise was giving aid to underdeveloped Southeast Asian neighbors.

Much of the credit for the success went to Premier Kishi, who was stabbed by a rightist fanatic in an unsuccessful assassination attempt on July 14, 1960. His government resigned the following day after pushing through the controversial mutual security pact with the U.S., giving Washington the right to continue to station troops in Japan.

Kishi was replaced by Hayato Ikeda, former international trade minister and avowed supporter of the West.

OUTBREAK OF Korean conflict prompted Supreme Allied Commander Douglas MacArthur to allow Japan to establish "police" reserve of 75,000. Reserve, actually military arm, was increased to 164,000 in later years. Fears by civilian populace of return to militarism kept defense force small.

STATE OF WAR between Soviet Union and Japan came to end Oct. 19, 1955, with Japanese Premier Hatoyama *(above)* signing for Japan. Agreement provided that USSR renounce all reparation claims and return Japanese prisoners. Two countries later signed trade agreement *(below)* that allowed each to establish trade mission in the other's country. Japanese booted out some Red delegates on charges of espionage.

Crown Prince's marriage to "commoner" symbolizes new democracy

Women, under the new constitution, voted for the first time. Strong pressure from women's organizations spelled the end of legalized prostitution. In April, 1958, a law banning brothels went into effect, and an estimated 200,000 prostitutes were thrown out of "work." They returned in thousands to their rural homes—most were country girls "leased out" by their parents.

Disaster, common in earthquake and typhoon-prone Japan, struck fiercely in September, 1959, when the worst storm in 25 years killed more than 2000. One million Japanese lost their homes.

Earlier in that year—in February—all Japan celebrated the birth of a 5-pound, 9-ounce boy. The father was Crown Prince Akihito, who shattered centuries-old tradition by taking as his bride in April, 1958, a nominal "commoner," Michiko Shoda, daughter of a prosperous grain merchant.

The wedding delighted the nation and proved another step toward the emergence of a "New Japan" that had abandoned its traditional militaristic concepts during a dazzling decade that left its imprint on almost every aspect of Japanese life.

YOUNG GI William Girard, (*l*), was discharged and sent back to the U.S. after trial in which he was convicted of shooting a Japanase scrap picker on an Army firing range. Shooting aroused anti-U.S. feeling.

STRONG ECONOMIC advance was pushed by heavy output of electronics equipment and shipbuilding industry. Japan ousted Britain in 1956 as world's number one shipbuilder (*above, right*). Tonnage amounted to 1,746,429 tons, 26% of world's total that year, and helped carry the nation's mushrooming electronics output to buyers around world. Among many exports were TV sets (*above, left*), shown being tested by technicians.

DEMONSTRATIONS greeted the ouster of Red-lining mayor of Naha, Okinawa, by U. S. military occupation in 1957. U. S. first stopped aid funds in an unsuccessful attempt to freeze out Kamajiro Senaga, then finally fired him in quick move that sparked wild, swinging demonstration (*above*) in front of Tokyo embassy.

STRICT SHINTO ritual guided royal ceremony that saw Prince Akihito marry commoner Michiko Shoda in 1959. Akihito is first in line to throne held by his father, Emperor Hirohito. Once worshipped as descendant of sun goddess Amaterasu, Hirohito repudiated divinity after World War II, retains little power.

LOST LEADER

Magsaysay death stuns Philippines; U.S. bases irk some nationalists

HANDS CLASPED in victory, Ramon Magsaysay acknowledges cheers after he swept to Presidency by landslide in 1953. Magsaysay won reputation as Huk-busting defense minister under President Quirino. He bolted Liberal Party, however, because of corruption and joined opposition Nationalists.

THE NAME RAMON MAGSAYSAY was magic in the Philippines. The peppery son of a blacksmith was a shining beacon in an island-nation where corruption and fraud had sapped the economic strength and left the people politically disillusioned.

Magsaysay rose to the presidency in November, 1953, by an astounding 2-1 victory over incumbent Elpidio Quirino. He promptly put into effect numerous reforms that startled the slow-moving nation. He endeared himself to the public by throwing open the presidential palace to the poor bringing him their complaints.

But on March 17, 1957, a plane carrying the 49-year-old president crashed at Cebu City; Magsaysay was dead. With him went the dreams of millions.

Vice-President Carlos Garcia, a long-time Nationalist Party politician, assumed the presidency and almost immediately cries of fraud were heard again. Corruption so sapped the national economy that in 1959 Garcia acknowledged publicly that "not much is left in the Government till to pay bills."

Aware of rising discontent, Garcia put into effect a "Filipino First" policy that had a tinge of anti-Americanism. He likewise called for a graft-busting commission, but few Filipinos took the proposal seriously.

The new policy, although satisfying the nationalistic desires of Filipinos, failed to exploit the mineral and agricultural wealth of the islands. Much of the land lay untilled and the mines untapped.

By decade's end, rank-and-file Filipinos were casting about for a new Magsaysay but none was in sight.

DIFFICULT negotiations over use of U.S. bases in Philippines were handled by Ambassador Charles Bohlen, shown lighting cigarette for President Garcia. U.S. agreed to give Filipinos more voice in the operation of the installations.

DESPITE CLAIMS HUKBALAHAP revolt was virtually at end, reports kept coming to Manila as decade ended of further devastation of rural villages by Communist insurgents. Rebellion began in 1948, spread stubbornly until Magsaysay, as defense minister and then president, took personal charge of anti-Huk drive. He backed army action with land reforms to eliminate rural grievances. Huk chief Luis Taruc gave up in 1954, but revolt flared again when Magsaysay was killed.

VANGUARD OF RED forces marched into Hanoi on October 9, 1954, to occupy big northern city under terms of Geneva agreement. By 1960, Hanoi had turned into a ghost of once prosperous, gay city.

NERVOUS PEACE ruled war-torn Indochina in 1960 after a decade of turbulence that rewrote the map of this Southeast Asian land.

At Geneva, on July 12, 1954, the French signed away more than 60 years of control over the Associated States of Indochina. For almost five months 14,000 crack French troops had withstood a seige by overwhelming numbers of Communist-led Vietminh forces at the fortress of Dien Bien Phu in Laos.

U.S. planes airlifted French paratroopers into the battle, but the aid was too little and too late.

By June, 1954, Dien Bien Phu had fallen, and French power with it. After the Geneva capitulation Red troops poured into North Vietnam.

STRIFE IN INDOCHINA

Battle of Dien Bien Phu brings end of French rule

The Geneva agreement split Indochina into four nations. Laos and Cambodia emerged as independent kingdoms, while Vietnam was divided into Korea-like halves—the Communists in the north and a Western-supported regime in the south.

Yet peace did not come after eight years of war. South Vietnamese strongman Ngo Dinh Diem was threatened by Red guerrillas, bandits, and power-hungry religious sects. In Laos, Communist-supported rebels fought Royal Laotian troops in the mountainous northern provinces. Cambodia, its wary eye on Red China, wavered toward "neutralism."

By late 1960, trying to stand on its own feet, Indochina was at a truce, but a truce which was at best uneasy.

SOME 60,000 FRENCH soldiers were killed during Indochina War. Many, such as these infantrymen, met death in defending villages against Communist rebels using hit-and-run jungle tactics.

WITH MOST of major nations attending, Geneva participants partitioned Vietnam at 17th parallel, gave Reds fertile plains and 60 percent of land in N. Vietnam.

GUIDING LIGHT OF Communist victory in Indochina was wily Ho Chi-minh, who spent three decades in exile plotting rebel cause. His Red government became riddled with food shortages, small-scale uprisings after assuming power.

HEROINE OF Dien Bien Phu was French nurse Genevieve de Gallard-Terraube, who refused to evacuate and remained until wounded were airlifted from fort.

CAMBODIA'S NEUTRALIST Prince Norodom Sihanouk got royal treatment in 1957 visit to Moscow. Sihanouk favored India-like foreign policy since assuming power, but struck out late in decade against aggressive policies of Red China.

NAMED AS FIRST Paramount Ruler of Malayan Federation was Tuanku Abdul Rahman, ruler of Negri Sembilan State. Under Constitution, each of Federation's nine states would take turns as titular head of state. The Tuanku died on April 1, 1960, and Sultan of Selangor became new ruler.

SELF RULE FOR ASIANS

Independence comes to Malaya and Singapore; Burma and Thailand accept U.S. aid

SOUTHEAST ASIA, the rice bowl of the Orient, underwent sweeping political transformations during the decade and emerged in 1960 with relative stability.

Malaya, which had fought a 12-year battle with Communist guerrillas in the jungles, announced in July, 1960, that the emergency was over. British and native troops had virtually eliminated the insurgents. The death toll: some 12,000 rebels and 5000 government troops.

On August 31, 1957, amid pomp and ceremony, Great Britain formally turned over to Malaya the reins of government. Under the able leadership of Tuanku Abdul Rahman, the first prime minister, Malaya moved ahead both economically and politically.

His anti-Communist Alliance Party won endorsement at the polls in 1959.

Malaya's neighbor to the south—the island of Singapore — likewise achieved self government from Great Britain. On June 3, 1959, the onetime key British bastion in Asia was cut loose under Prime Minister Lee Kuan Yew, leader of the People's Action Party.

But independence came hard. Negotiations twice broke down over the knotty problem of Singapore's internal security. With the bulk of Singapore's population Chinese, Great Britain feared the island might turn toward Peking.

The fears appeared unfounded. Lee guided Singapore along a non-Communist course. But his chief goal, that of uniting with Malaya, remained unaccomplished. The Malays feared that Singapore's large Chinese population would affect Malaya's delicate political balance.

North of the Malay peninsula, pro-Western Thailand underwent a swift, bloodless coup in September, 1957, that deposed strongman Pibul Songgram and sent him into exile. His successor was Field Marshal Thanarat.

It was only one in a long history of bloodless coups which the peace-loving Thais accepted without dissent.

In 1958, Thanarat, dissolved an elected parliament and replaced it with a handpicked assembly of which 181 of the 240 members were military figures.

FIERY SINGAPORE attorney Lee Kuan Yew led battle for self-government, was named first Prime Minister in 1956. At first thought pro-Communist, Lee led his party along non-Red path, insisted, in broad five-year plan, that his aim was to industrialize island and encourage free trade unions.

Thailand's neighbor, Burma, played a neutral role through most of the decade, but in 1959 broke this policy to accept U.S. aid. Although it amounted only to $30 million, it gratified U.S. officials who hoped it would portend a swing toward the West.

The reason for Burma's acceptance, probably, was strong resentment against Communist China for (1) incursions into Burmese territory in 1956 and (2) brutal smothering of the Tibetan revolt.

Burma, like Malaya, had its internal problems with insurgents. Karen tribesmen in Northern Burma killed thousands and cost the government millions in futile attempts to wipe out the rebels. Communist dissidents likewise remained a problem.

Within the political realm, Prime Minister U Nu faced opposition within his faction-riddled Anti-Fascist Peoples Freedom League. He stepped down for one year in an attempt to end dissent. Army Gen. Ne Win took over.

In February, 1960, U Nu regained a majority in Parliament and returned again as prime minister of Burma.

WAVE OF INDIGNATION swept Burma when Communist Chinese troops entered Burmese territory and occupied some 1000 square miles of territory in Shan states. Premier U Nu, shown *(above)* talking with Red Chinese Foreign Minister Chou En-lai, journeyed to Peking to settle border dispute. U Nu won agreement by Reds to withdraw troops, but later violations occurred. Burmese newspapermen *(r.)* indignantly picketed Soviet Embassy after being manhandled by guards when attempting to interview a Red diplomat being flown to Peking. He had tried to flee hospital following suicide try.

VIOLENT RIOTING swept Singapore in 1955 and 1956 and the government blamed it on Communist-led students. Disorders also flared in wake of series of strikes. With some 1.5 million residents of various groups (majority Chinese) crowded onto 224-square mile island, it took little to touch off rioting. One of major problems facing the government was rocketing birth rate. In 1959 births totaled 70,000, highest per capita rate in world. Scene above, showing police carting off water-soaked rioter, was repeated often during mid-decade. One United States correspondent, Gene Symonds of United Press, was killed in strike rioting by mob in May, 1955.

BUDDHISM PLAYED an important role *(above)* in the lives of Burmese, but friction broke out inside Premier U Nu's political party when he decided in 1959 to become priest. Opponents feared he would guide country into theocracy.

REVOLT RIPS INDONESIA

Sukarno's "Guided Democracy" battles rebels and inflation

BANDUNG CONFERENCE brought together at Indonesian resort in April, 1955, leaders of 29 Asian and African nations, with Sukarno *(above)* as host. His guests included (seated, second *l.* to *r.)* Egypt's Nasser, India's Nehru, Burma's U Nu. Conference was intended to be historic milestone, but bogged down into separate Neutralist, pro-Communist and pro-West blocs, accomplished little. Comment of a diplomatic observer was: "Bandung showed there is no Afro-Asian unity."

IT WAS A difficult decade for the Republic of Indonesia, but the government of President Sukarno managed to survive bloody revolution, mounting economic problems, inflation and a dozen political crises.

By mid-1960, Sukarno had emerged as a powerful political tightrope walker. He was undisputed head of Indonesian nation of 80 million, despite bitter opposition to his self-proclaimed policies of "guided democracy."

Sukarno, chosen Indonesia's first president on December 16, 1949, faced a serious threat to unity in 1955 when the South Moluccas declared their independence from the central government.

But the major revolt erupted December, 1956, on mineral-rich Sumatra when Army Col. Ahmad Hussein proclaimed autonomy for the island. Loyal troops contained the revolt, but four years later it still flickered on.

Politically, Sukarno faced growing dissatisfaction. Popular anti-Communist, Mohammed Hatta, co-founder of the republic, resigned the vice-presidency in 1955 in protest against Sukarno's dictatorial policies. But Sukarno pressed ahead.

In 1959, he dissolved the Constituent Assembly and established a 45-member advisory council to help him run the government. He likewise assumed the premiership.

Then, on Jan. 12, 1960, he gave himself the power to dissolve political parties opposed to the "aims of the State." Three months later, he suspended Parliament and appointed a new 261-member group, among them some 55 Communists or sympathizers.

Although Sukarno fought a verbal battle with Red China over his decree barring non-naturalized Chinese from engaging in business in rural areas, he maintained good relations with the Communist orbit. In 1960 he accepted a $250 million grant from the USSR. The price: Keep the Republic of Indonesia on a neutralist course.

FIRST FREE ELECTIONS in 1955 saw some 6 million Indonesians voting Communist ticket, presaged fears that island nation would go Red. Although Communists later picked up little strength, President Sukarno needed Red support for his coalition and named Communists to cabinet positions.

REBEL TROOPS, equipped with guns and planes, fought Army on many fronts on Sumatra, in Celebes and Moluccas in last half of decade. One of dissident leaders was former Army colonel Hasanuddin, shown addressing troops on Sumatra in 1959. Most Army troops remained loyal to central government.

ANZUS PACT in 1952 bound Australia, New Zealand and the U.S. to provide for joint military security in the event of Communist attack in the Pacific. Secretary of State Dean Acheson is shown addressing delegation at first conference.

SIDNEY SKYLINE reflects U.S. brand names, many now made in Australia, and highlights the post WW II commercial revolution which turned the eyes of Australian industrialists toward the United States for necessary investment capital.

NEW LOOK "DOWN UNDER"

Australia, New Zealand industrialize as wealth mounts

AUSTRALIA and New Zealand, with the beginning of the '50s, entered a dynamic period of growth.

Sharing a common background, the two southernmost members of the British Commonwealth "Club" also shared important strides in industrialization, education and social welfare.

Anzac political activity mainly centered upon a labor-conservative struggle. During the decade a double switch occured in the two nations. Ousting the Labor Party in 1951, Australian Prime Minister Robert Menzies' Liberal-Country Party coalition increased its plurality in 1955, again in 1958. In the 1957 New Zealand elections, however, control shifted from the National Party to Labor.

R. G. MENZIES Australian PM during the past decade of change and growth.

Aided by accelerating U.S. and British investment, Australia and New Zealand arrived at full partnership among Free World nations. Australia, for example, had the largest steel mill in the British Commonwealth and produced 29% of the world's wool.

Australia and her neighbor New Zealand were visited by most of the Royal Family, including Queen Elizabeth II and her husband Prince Philip; also, a host of movie stars.

In 1956 Australia was site of the Olympic Games, won by the USSR in a surprising upset of the U.S.

Prospering economically and socially under stable governments, Australians and New Zealanders looked ahead to increased growth in the '60s.

Both countries widely expanded their international operations. In 1951, Australia signed a Mutual Defense Assistance Agreement with the U.S., signed the Pacific Security Treaty and announced full support of the Columbo Plan, designed to raise Southeast Asia's living standard. Although already joined in defense by the ANZUS pact, Australia and New Zealand decided against parochialism by joining the Southeast Asia Treaty Organization in 1954.

Australia's abundant natural resources, skilled labor force and attractive tax structure were primarily responsible for the 1959 $14 billion Gross National Product, unmatched in its history. British immigrants had always been preponderant, but an easing of restrictions drew pilgrims from other parts of Europe, strengthening the labor force and the economy. New Zealand, also on a swift road to industrialization, was blessed in 1959 with a record $3.2 billion Gross National Product and seized the world lead position in the mechanization of the dairy industry.

NEW ZEALAND CATTLE on the way to market. Dairy products and livestock continued to account for nearly 80% of New Zealand's export trade. However, recent rich uranium ore discoveries promised to open new vistas for introduction of capital from outside the country and added exports.

INDIA QUESTIONS "COEXISTENCE"

Red Chinese aggression shatters neutralist dream; Communists ousted in Kerala after winning election plurality; Congress Party hold weakens

MID-1960 SAW India's policy of "peaceful coexistence" with Communist China almost shattered, even though its first and only Prime Minister, Jawaharlal Nehru, still stubbornly advocated United Nations membership for Peking.

When the decade ended, the Chinese juggernaut not only had crushed the autonomy of Tibet, which the Mao Tse-tung government had solemnly promised Nehru to respect, but had rolled across the frontiers in 1959 to occupy 51,000 square miles of territory recognized for more than a century as Indian.

Meanwhile, near India's southern tip, native Communists had won power in a free election (so far, the only instance on record) in the unemployment-blighted state of Kerala. But they were ousted July 30, 1959, by India's President, Rajendra Prasad, in a welter of administrative collapse and massive popular resistance, and were soundly beaten in the subsequent election.

China's drive to assimilate and Communize doggedly Buddhist Tibet—despite repeated pledges to India that it would respect the state's autonomy and religion—led to a 1959 rebellion in which at least 65,000 Tibetans were killed, 1000 monasteries destroyed and thousands of refugees, including Tibet's sacrosanct ruler, the Dalai Lama, fled across the Himalayas to India. (Late in 1960 the outbreaks—and slaughter—were still continuing.)

In April, 1960, talks between Nehru and Chinese Red Foreign Minister Chou En-lai failed to bring a settlement, and Indian troops massed in the border areas.

Although Nehru's Congress Party, in two elections, retained three-fourths of the seats in the Union Parliament, it lost ground in the states. Continuous power since independence had made it complacent, flabby and, some charged, corrupt. India's big political puzzle was: after Nehru, 71 in 1960, who—and what?

Economically, the First Five Year Plan, ended in 1956, raised national income 15% and brought self-sufficiency in foodstuffs. The second, ending in 1961, called for total investment of $14.6 billion.

Huge grants of aid, mostly from the U.S., played a vital role in the plans. U.S. assistance since 1950 totaled $2 billion, including $927 million in surplus agricultural commodities. A $1.3 billion wheat loan (17 million tons) concluded in May, 1960 reflected the importance the U.S. attaches to India. Soviet aid, mainly a million-ton-per-year steel mill, totaled $678 million.

However, India's 400 million, growing at the rate of 7 million per year, threatened to outrun existing food supplies. Average per capita income was $62 yearly.

India's 13 year dispute with Pakistan over their common claims to Kashmir continued to smolder, despite efforts for a plebiscite. Nehru feared that in a free vote he might lose this 80% Muslim territory. However, there were hints that India and Pakistan might resolve their differences to face Red China.

SEEKING REFUGE, Tibet's Dalai Lama arrived in India in April, 1959. Red China took complete control, installed his chief native rival, the Panchen Lama, as figurehead leader.

ILL-DEFINED BORDER along the snowy crest of the Himalayas, formerly a dispute only among map-makers, became a hot issue when Chinese troops occupied 51,000 sq. miles in 1959.

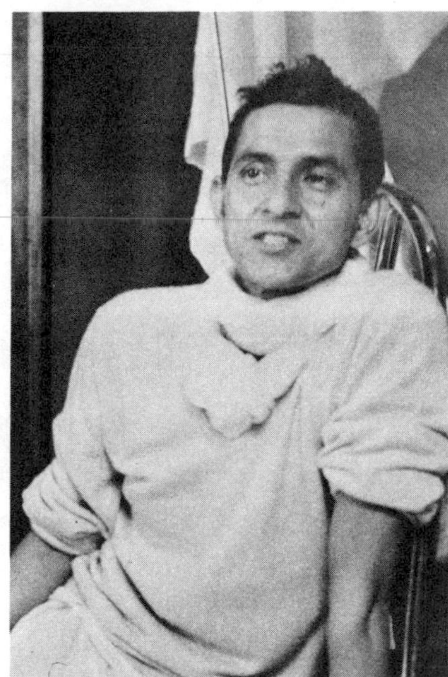

FACING Chinese border claims and feudal politicians at home, B. P. Koirala won Nepal's first elections in 1959.

PRESIDENT EISENHOWER looks on as Nehru speaks at opening of U.S. exhibit at 1959 World Agricultural Fair in New Delhi. Thousands of Indians lined the streets to greet the U.S. President during his December visit.

BROODING PREMIER Nehru, already 71, wrestled with complacent party, divisive nation, growing Chinese threat.

TRAGIC STAMPEDE at Allahabad's Hindu festival in 1954 trampled 500 to death, injured thousands, scattered belongings.

COMMUNIST RULE ends in tragedy. Here, an Indian mourns his wife shot by Communist police as they demonstrated against state control of Kerala's 4000 private schools. Elected in 1957, Red government alienated majority of populace by 1959.

STUDENTS PROTEST outside Chinese embassy on Nov. 4, 1959. Angrily shouting "Death to Chou En-lai," 3000 condemned border encroachment on India.

BEFORE THE SPARRING, India's Prime Minister Nehru and China's Premier Chou En-lai greet each other with smiles upon the latter's arrival in New Delhi April 19, 1960. Six days of talks failed to solve their border dispute. Nehru firmly refused to barter away territory occupied by Chinese troops.

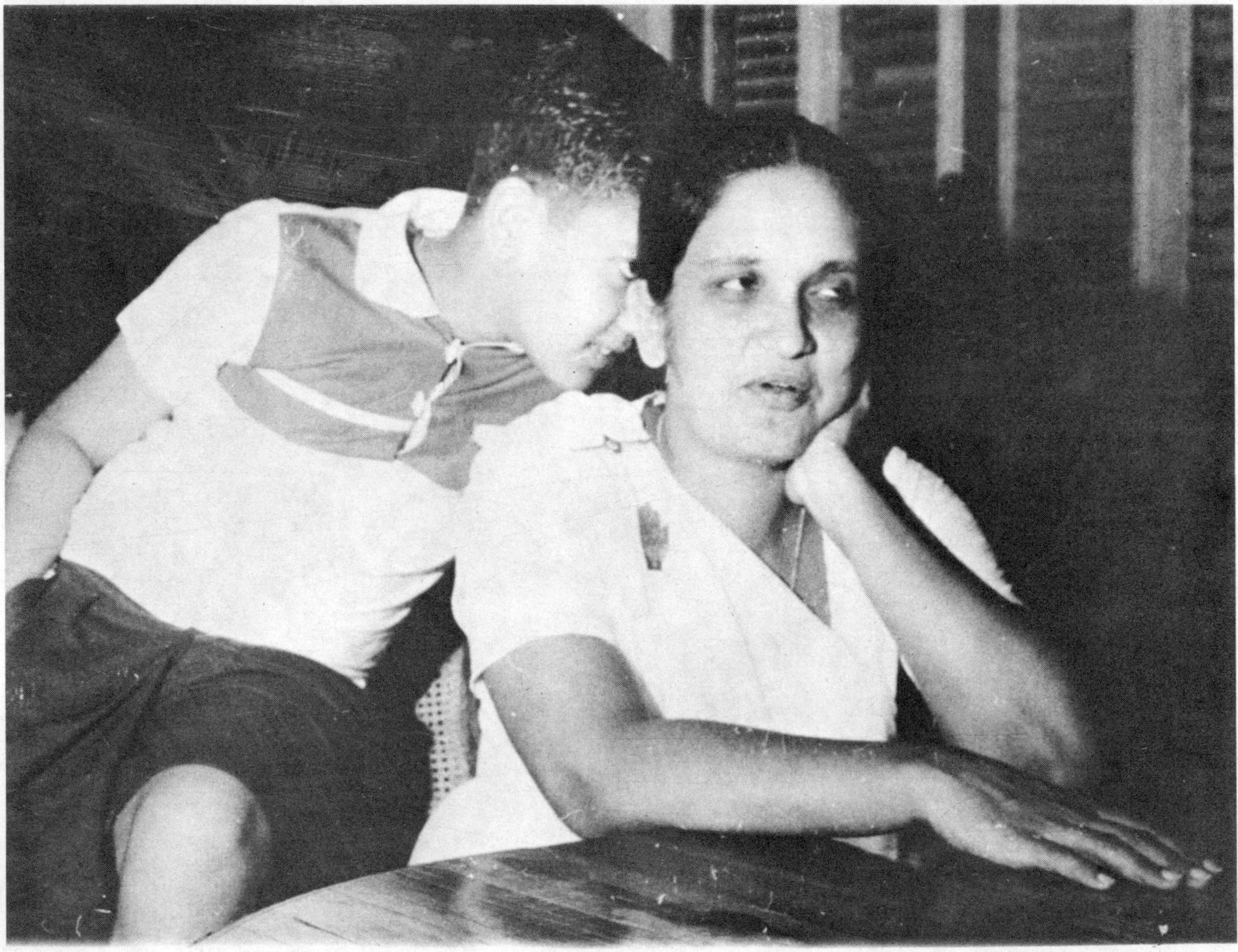

WORLD'S FIRST WOMAN prime minister was Ceylon's Mrs. Sirimavo Bandaranaike, widow of Prime Minister Solomon W.R.D. Bandaranaike, assassinated by fanatic Buddhist monk in 1959. She vowed to replace him, swept Freedom Party to upset victory after highly emotional campaign. Shown with son, Anura, she listens to July 20, 1960, election returns.

PAKISTAN SEEKS STABILITY

Ayub Khan ousts Mirza; Army regime tightens reins, begins new five year plan, strengthens ties with West

PAKISTAN'S new Constitution, adopted February 29, 1956, set up a republican form of government within the British Commonwealth.

Faced with perennial political instability, Iskander Mirza, its first president, was forced, Oct. 7, 1958, to suspend the Constitution, dismiss the legislatures and declare martial law. This centralization of control was tightened by Gen. Ayub Khan who ousted him three weeks later.

In spite of political turmoil, Pakistan boosted its national income 20% between 1949 and 1957. A 10 million expansion in population, however, cut the per capita gain to 7%. A $2.5 billion second Five Year Plan, started in 1960, hoped to add another 20% to national income and create two million new jobs.

U.S. aid by the end of 1957 reached $693 million. Of this, $94 million was defense and $163 million agricultural commodities. Two loans in 1959 provided $31 million for railway improvement. In September 1959 Pakistan announced that a consortium of four British and American companies would build a $31 million oil refinery in Karachi.

Political changes at no time altered Pakistan's firm pro-West orientation.

By the end of 1959 Pakistan and India were able to resolve minor border issues. However, Kashmir and the Indus River issues remained unsolved: Pakistan needed the waters of the Indus, which rise in India, to water its own arid plains.

OLD ASIAN VIRTUES, simplicity and austerity *(above)*, reflect the determination of the Ayub government to tighten the national belt in order to build a 20th Century economy. The results are shown *(below)* in the construction boom in Karachi. With generous foreign aid, largely from the U.S., Pakistan had modernized its railways, expanded port facilities, launched new industries, raised food output.

RULING BY DECREE since 1958, Gen. Ayub Khan closed black markets, pushed land reform, promised elections "soon."

SECRETARY DULLES confers with Governor-General Ghulam Mohammed *(l.)* and Prime Minister Mohammed Ali *(r.)* on his May 1953 visit. A staunch American ally, Pakistan was a member of both the Baghdad Pact and the SEATO alliance.

FIDEL CASTRO'S triumphant entry into Havana in January, 1959, may well have been high point of his career. A year later, many of the men who had fought beside him had lost hope for future of revolution, were fleeing to U.S. In mid-1960, reports from Cuba were that Castro was seriously ill, might give government to his radical younger brother, Raul.

LATIN AMERICA TURNS TOWARD DEMOCRACY

Old line dictatorships fade out; but Reds gain Cuban foothold

At the end of a turbulent decade, most of the nations of Latin America were, on balance, better off—politically, economically and socially—than they had been at its beginning.

In the early '50s, democracy had collapsed in Argentina and Venezuela and was collapsing in Colombia; the small nations of Central America were on a merry-go-round of revolution and counter-revolution; the political tide seemed to be running toward totalitarianism, instead of away from it, and hardly a nation had a government so stable that it could say "it can't happen here."

By 1960, there was reason to hope that the tide had turned.

Three small nations (the Dominican Republic, Nicaragua, Paraguay) were still ruled by dictators, and Cuba was in revolutionary upheaval; but everywhere else, democratic regimes were in office, and had at least a fighting chance to survive.

In most countries, the military still held the balance of power, as it had done down through the generations. It would continue to do so until politicians—and the electorate—had time to learn the habit of solving their difference at the polls, not on the barricades.

But, in the democratic revolutions of Argentina, Venezuela and Colombia, and in lesser political upheavals elsewhere, the leaders of the armed forces had behaved with a new sense of political responsibility.

It could only be hoped that the military men of the '60s would, if they had to intervene in politics, follow the example of officers like Aramburu of Argentina, Larrazabal of Venezuela, Texeira Lott of Brazil.

While Latin America's political upheavals were making headlines, its economic and social revolution was moving quietly forward. The progress of the '50s was often painful and erratic, but it was a real progress.

JUAN PERON, in exile in Panama, had more reason to grin than most ousted dictators; he still had some 2 million loyal supporters in Argentina. However, chance of his comeback was slim.

The basic problem confronting the Latin American states was the vast gulf between a small, wealthy, highly educated upper class, of predominantly European stock, and the hungry, semi-literate masses.

This problem was least acute in Argentina, Chile and Uruguay, whose social patterns had been changed by substantial European immigration in the 19th and 20th centuries, and in relatively wealthy Venezuela and Brazil; Latin America badly needed a middle class.

Everybody knew how to close the gap—industrialization, diversification of agriculture, heavy government spending on public works, health, education, etc.

But all of this cost money—more than most of the Latin American states had, even more than they could hope to raise in the near future by wooing foreign investors (often a politically dangerous course, since ultranationalist sentiment was strong), or receive in grants and aid from the U.S. and the United Nations.

All of it required honest, efficient, imaginative administrators—hard to find when governmental corruption and bureaucratic mediocrity were hallowed by tradition.

And, above all, the process of economic expansion, where it was underway, caused such severe growing pains—in inflation, trade deficits and unbalanced budgets—that the cure seemed almost worse than the disease.

MARCOS PEREZ JIMENEZ was among dictators whose regimes were overthrown in '50s. The mild-looking, bespectacled Venezuelan ran one of hemisphere's harshest police states from 1952 to 1958.

ORGANIZATION OF AMERICAN STATES *(above)*, first meeting of heads of state, Panama, 1956, was kept busy during '50s with problems ranging from economic woes of member states to charges of "aggression" against U.S. by Cuba's Castro.

The evidence of the '50s showed, however, that there could be a middle course between economic stagnation—which would perpetuate social inequality—and economic chaos, and that the nations of Latin America were learning to steer it.

Foreign capital, public and private, poured into the continent, although there was need for still more. New mines and oil fields were opening up vast stores of underground wealth; factories were going up; highways, railroads and power plants, schools, hospitals and homes were being built faster than ever before—though still not fast enough to meet all the needs of countries with soaring birth rates.

And by the end of the decade, although economic instability was still a very serious problem, it was less rampant than it had been in the earlier years.

Men like President Frondizi and Finance Minister Alsogaray of Argentina, President Prado and Finance Minister Beltran of Peru, President Allessandri of Chile, were instituting programs that worked.

Budgets were being balanced, and inflation—though still bad enough to rob urban workers of most of the fruits of progress—was being brought slowly under control.

Of course, Latin America's political problem and its social-economic one were chicken and egg.

Without reasonable political stability, hopes for real economic progress would be dim; governments had to be able to launch long-range programs, get in four or six years of work on them, and turn them over to competent successors; foreign investors had to be given confidence that their investments would be safe. And, without economic progress, and the resultant growth of a responsible electorate with a real stake in its country's welfare, the danger of revolution could not be expected to vanish.

Latin America needed money, time and peace—a big order for the 1960s, but not an entirely impossible one.

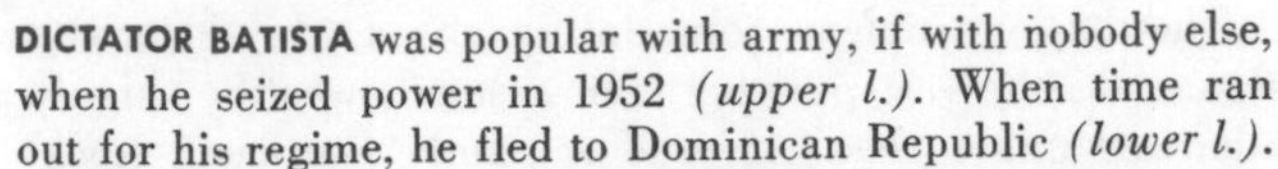

DICTATOR BATISTA was popular with army, if with nobody else, when he seized power in 1952 *(upper l.)*. When time ran out for his regime, he fled to Dominican Republic *(lower l.)*.

Castro ousts Batista, turns on U.S., moves into Marxist bloc

Of all the revolutions and counter-revolutions that crowded the '50s in Latin America, Fidel Castro's rise to power in Cuba was the most dramatic.

It was also, very possibly, dangerous — not only for Cuba, but for the hemisphere and even the Free World.

The man Castro ousted was Fulgencio Batista, a former army sergeant who had usurped power in 1952 and maintained it with a reign of terror that few other Latin American dictatorships could match.

Castro was one of the students who mounted a tragic and futile attack on a Havana army barracks in 1953; he was seized, released, fled to Mexico, and returned in 1957 with the nucleus of a guerrilla army.

His 26th of July Movement—named for the anniversary of the barracks attack—gained wide popular support, and after two years of bitterly fought civil war, the Batista forces simply collapsed.

On Jan. 1, 1959, Fidel Castro and his bearded revolutionaries came down out of the mountains as heroes.

But in the months after the revolution, the unshaven, ebullient Castro took charge in a way that disturbed most outside observers — and many Cubans.

STUDENT RIOTS *(r.)* were frequent during years of Batista rule. Not only the liberal intellectuals of Cuba, but the vast majority of the middle class, were strongly anti-Batista; Fidel Castro's revolutionaries had almost universal support.

CASTRO fought guerrilla war against Batista from hideaway in Sierra Maestra mountains of eastern Cuba *(l.)*. One of history's most public relations-conscious revolutionaries, he let a number of sympathetic U.S. journalists into his camp for long visits. His men's skilled now-you-see-them-now-you-don't guerrilla tactics and fine relations with farmers frustrated regular army attacks.

His "utopian radical" program called for such measures as distribution to the peasants of more arable land than there actually is in all of Cuba.

Before his first year in office was over, he had launched a series of vitriolic attacks against U.S. "imperialism"—although Washington had given his regime friendly recognition and taken no reprisals against the expropriation (with compensation only vaguely promised) of large U.S.-owned sugar plantations and ranches.

And, as his second year began, he appeared to be moving closer and closer to Soviet communism. When the USSR's star salesman, Anastas Mikoyan, visited Cuba early in '60 *(above)*, he was showered with official honors.

Tension reached its height when, on June 29, Castro expropriated (without even an offer of compensation) U.S.-owned oil refineries *(below)* which had refused to process Soviet oil. Washington retaliated by slashing U.S. imports of Cuban sugar—and Soviet Premier Khrushchev immediately offered to buy all the sugar Cuba could sell, and to defend the country, militarily if necessary.

Most cool-headed observers seriously doubted that Khrushchev would make good on either his promises or his threats. But even the remote possibility that Cuba, just a few miles from U.S. territory, might fall into the Soviet orbit was seriously disquieting. And so was the much greater chance that the Castro regime would do much to encourage Communism elsewhere in the hemisphere.

ARGENTINE LABOR idolized Peron *(r.,* a Peronista union rally), and he returned their affection. Nothing was too good—or too expensive—for the *descamisados,* or "shirtless ones," as he called his supporters. His regime encouraged wage increases, spent billions on social services, while ignoring agriculture, traditional mainstay of nation's economy.

Argentine Army overthrows Peron; Frondizi wins in free ballot

ARGENTINA'S JUAN PERON, one of the most spectacularly successful demagogues of the 20th Century, was at the height of his power and popularity as the decade began.

The fact that he was fast driving the nation into bankruptcy (at the end of World War II, when Peron rose to power, Argentina was one of the world's wealthiest countries and a major exporter of beef and wheat; by 1953, beef was rationed and wheat was on the import list) did not bother his fanatically loyal working class supporters

His downfall may have begun when his wife and shrewd political partner, Eva, died in 1952; however, he successfully crushed all opposition for another two years.

Then, in October, 1954, he launched a cold war against the Catholic Church. This tipped the scales against him; revolts began in June, 1955, and continued through the summer until the army decided that enough was enough.

JUAN AND EVA PERON made an unbeatable political team *(above),* on which blonde Evita may well have supplied more than half the brains. She took charge of social services for women and children, spent as freely—and was as popular—as her husband. She almost ran for vice president with him in 1951, but opposition from conservative members of government was too great. Shortly thereafter, she fell ill; ravaged by cancer *(r.),* she cast her last vote from a hospital bed.

CATHOLIC LAYMEN *(l.)* paraded in Buenos Aires on Holy Thursday, 1955, to protest Peron's anti-clerical drive. Fearing growing influence of church, possible formation of Catholic party, he banished religious leaders, legalized divorce, fired priests from teaching jobs, ended government subsidization of religious work. It was his fatal mistake.

Peron was ousted by the military in September, 1955, and a military junta, headed first by Gen. Eduardo Lonardi and then by Gen. Pedro Aramburu, took over.

The nation's first post-Peron election was held in 1957, to choose delegates for a constitutional convention. Peron, from his exile in Venezuela, urged his supporters to cast blank ballots (voting is compulsory in Argentina), and 2 million of them did. Delegates favoring the government's reform constitution won by narrowest of margins.

In the presidential election of 1958, the 2 million Peronista voters swung the balance to Arturo Frondizi, and the world watched him take office with extreme apprehension.

However, Frondizi soon proved that he had no intention of paying his political debt to the former dictator. In two stormy years, he rammed through an austerity program that, by decade's end, was beginning to repair the greater part of the damage of Peron's economic orgies.

ARTURO FRONDIZI *(above)*, Argentina's first post-revolutionary president, turned out to be a shrewd and courageous politician and a grave disappointment to his Peronista supporters, who expected him to reinstitute national giveaway program. His stiff austerity measures led to a wave of strikes in 1959; the army, which could have deposed him as easily as it had Peron, forced him to appoint a new cabinet, but let him stay in power. A year later, he was still hanging on, even slightly stronger.

"PERON OR DEATH" smeared on Buenos Aires wall *(r.)* symbolizes continuing influence of absent dictator in Argentine politics. Two million voters, or approximately one-fourth of the electorate, were still loyal to him in the 1960 parliamentary elections, showed their dissatisfaction with Frondizi regime by casting blank ballots. In Argentina's multi-party system, they held the balance of power, and could almost certainly elect any candidate unscrupulous enough to solicit their voting support

ROJAS PINILLA tried to win support of Colombian workers in his bid for permanent power, but failed. Organized labor joined all other groups, including the powerful Catholic church, to bring about his downfall. At decade's end, two years after revolution, Colombian democracy was again running smoothly.

Colombia, Venezuela expel dictators, restore democratic rule

VENEZUELAN revolution began on New Year's Day, 1958; rioting in the streets of Caracas was followed by a general strike on January 21. Then, after two bloody days in which government forces fought civilian rebels *(above)* and hundreds died, top military brass told Perez Jimenez to get out.

VENEZUELA entered the '50s under the rule of a military junta which had ousted a weak democratic regime in 1948. In 1952, a presidential election was held; but the junta stopped counting ballots when the vote was running two to one against it, and announced the "victory" of its candidate, Marcos Perez Jimenez. For the next six years, Perez Jimenez ran an increasingly oppressive dictatorship. Popular resentment was lulled by the oil rich nation's spectacular prosperity, but it finally flared in 1957, when the dictator returned himself to power for another six years on the basis of a "yes or no" plebiscite. In January, 1958, the dictator was ousted by a popular uprising and another military junta took over. But this one was headed by honest. conscientious Adm. Wolfgang Larrazabal, who called for free elections within months, accepted his own defeat, and did all he could to help the new president, Romulo Betancourt, get on with the assignment of restoring democracy to Venezuela.

TRADITIONALLY democratic Colombia began the decade in a state of political chaos. The inability of either of the major parties — Liberals and Conservatives — to maintain control led to an army coup in 1953, and the rise to power of Gen. Gustavo Rojas Pinilla. Four years later, he had still not gotten around to calling elections; late in 1957, his puppet National Assembly endorsed him for a second term. The nation then staged an almost bloodless revolution; students rioted, workers struck, businessmen closed stores and plants, and the Army simply advised the dictator to leave quietly. Liberals and Conservatives appeared to have learned their lesson; they stopped squabbling, agreed to a 12-year plan for bipartisan government drawn up by provisional regime, and in 1958 elected Liberal Alberto Lleras Camargo president.

ROMULO BETANCOURT, Venezuela's post-revolutionary president, had kept his Democratic Action Party alive underground during 11 years of military rule and dictatorship; it swamped opponents at the polls in '58. Revolutionary leader Larrazabal's presidential bid was hurt by Communist ties.

EVEN in the countries where major political upheaval was avoided, the forces of growth and change were at work and tension was high.

Chile, politically one of the most stable and economically one of the most advanced of the Latin American states, battled inflation and labor troubles throughout the decade, and made some strides toward diversification of its copper-and-nitrate-based economy with oil, steel production.

Peru, also relatively stable and prosperous, nevertheless also suffered acute economic growing pains throughout most of the '50s. In 1959, however, it launched a well-planned austerity program; a year later, currency was stable, the budget balanced and the outlook bright.

Landlocked, leftist Bolivia was plagued by the worst inflation of all, and heavily dependent upon U.S. aid. But there, too, government efforts for stabilization were bearing some fruit by decade's end.

A boom in bananas helped another nearby country, Ecuador, along the uphill road to prosperity.

Backward Paraguay, under the little-publicized but firmly established dictatorship of Alfred Stroessner, enjoyed remarkable stability at the price of extremely slow economic development.

Neighboring Uruguay, which, with its political and cultural sophistication and high living standard, provided a striking contrast, was the scene of an interesting governmental experiment. In 1952, it abolished the presidency and established a Swiss-style nine-man executive council.

PERENNIAL MAVERICK of Peruvian politics, Victor Raul Haya de la Torre *(l.)* left Lima for Mexico City in 1954, after five years in the Colombian embassy, which he was not allowed to leave after seeking political asylum there in 1949.

NATIONALIZATION of tin mines was one of first official acts of Bolivia's 1952-1956 president, Victor Paz Estenssoro *(r.)*. His Nationalist Revolutionary party stayed in power with Hernan Siles Zuazo (1956-60), was expected to win handily in 1960 campaign. Bolivians *(lower r.*, a typical group at polls) were vehemently nationalistic, anti-U.S., in spite of—or because of—their economic dependence on Northern neighbor. Anti-Yankee sentiment flared most dramatically in 1959, when *Time* Magazine quoted U.S. embassy official in La Paz, saying nation should be 'abolished.'

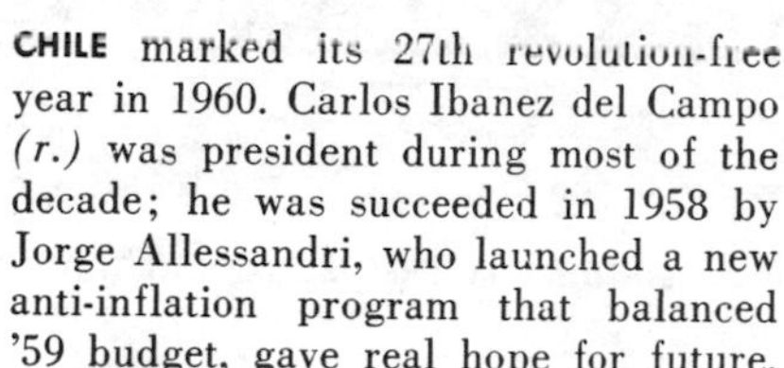

CHILE marked its 27th revolution-free year in 1960. Carlos Ibanez del Campo *(r.)* was president during most of the decade; he was succeeded in 1958 by Jorge Allessandri, who launched a new anti-inflation program that balanced '59 budget, gave real hope for future.

OIL loomed large in Peruvian plans for economic expansion. All over the continent, vast stores of underground wealth—petroleum, metals and minerals — promised a future prosperity.

GETULIO VARGAS *(l.)* ruled Brazil as dictator from 1930 to 1945, performed astonishing feat of making comeback as freely elected president in 1951. Threat of coup by army officers who feared that he planned to re-usurp dictatorial powers drove him to suicide in 1954. His economic policies were more conservative than those of next elected President, Juscelino Kubitschek *(r.)*. Under both regimes, U.S.-Brazilian relations were excellent, private foreign investment encouraged, although Kubitschek flirted briefly with extremists.

Brazil builds new capital; inflation hampers industrialization

EVERYTHING went up in Brazil during the '50s—including, unfortunately, the cost of living.

The giant nation's population soared to 66 million. Its cities mushroomed; a new capital, Brasilia, rose out of the wilderness of its central plateau; it boosted industrial and agricultural output to new highs, attracted millions of dollars in private foreign investment and spent millions more in loans from the World Bank, Export-Import Bank and International Monetary Fund on development of its vast potential in steel, oil, mining and other industries. And, from 1950 on, it battled runaway inflation that grew worse year by year.

BUILDING TYPIFIES MODERN ARCHITECTURE OF NEW BRAZILIAN CAPITAL

Economic expansion and its accompanying growing pains were the major preoccupation of Brazil's political leaders, Getulio Vargas, who committed suicide during his presidential term in 1954, Joao Cafe Filho, his successor, and Juscelino Kubitschek, chief executive from 1956 to 1960.

Kubitschek, a likeable leader whose ambition and optimism for his country seemed to know no bounds (Brasilia, a multi-million dollar monument to faith in the nation's future, was his pet project), tried to fight inflation by riding it out—legislating frequent wage increases, spending huge sums on public works, and keeping more money rolling off the government printing presses.

When cost of living rose 50% in 1959 over 1958 and hard-pressed workers began rioting in Brazil's major cities, it appeared that the inflation issue might play a key role in the defeat of the government party's 1960 presidential candidate, Marshal Texeira Lott, 65-year-old soldier.

Julio Quadros, the opposition candidate, was a former school teacher whose meteoric rise in politics had begun only in 1953, when he ran for, and was elected mayor of Sao Paulo.

One of the most popular and deserving men in Brazilian public life, Quadros, in mid-1960, was fighting for the chance to lead Brazil into the new decade — his chance was good.

COFFEE was one of mainstays of Brazilian economy *(l.,* shipment ready to load at Santos). 1959 was a bumper year with record 17.7 million bags sold.

British Caribbean colonies form new Commonwealth

A NEW NATION was born in the Caribbean in April, 1958, when the West Indies Federation—made up of 10 small islands and island groups—became a member of the British Commonwealth.

In its first parliamentary elections, the leftist Federal Labor Party won a slim majority, and Sir Grantley H. Adams, former Prime Minister of Barbados, became the first Prime Minister of the new state.

The members of the Federation are Jamaica, Trinidad-Tobago, Barbados, St. Lucia, St. Vincent, Grenada, Monserrat, St. Kitts-Nevis-Anguilla, Dominica and Antigua.

They arch over 7700 miles of the Caribbean *(see map, r.)*, with Trinidad and Jamaica 1000 miles apart. Their total population is about 3 million, and their total land area no bigger than that of Massachusetts. Sun, sea, calypso songs and rum make the West Indies one of the world's pleasantest playgrounds.

Among their other commodities are sugar, bananas, bauxite (on Jamaica), asphalt (on Trinidad) and spices. However, most of the islands' people are poor, and the new government planned an ambitious program of industrial development and agricultural diversification.

It was hoped that union would in itself bolster the West Indian economy by eliminating the problem of complex customs and immigration laws for each tiny island, thus permitting a free flow of goods and people throughout the Federation.

However, after the Federation's first two years of statehood, it was clear that union was easier to achieve on paper than in reality.

The islands were plagued by parochialism, squabbling and inept leadership; it was feared that Jamaica, the largest and most prosperous, might be leaning toward secession.

CHIEF MINISTERS of Jamaica and Trinidad, Norman Manley *(l.)* and Eric Williams *(r.)*, refused to run for Federal parliament in '58, preferring to stay home, keep their parties under control.

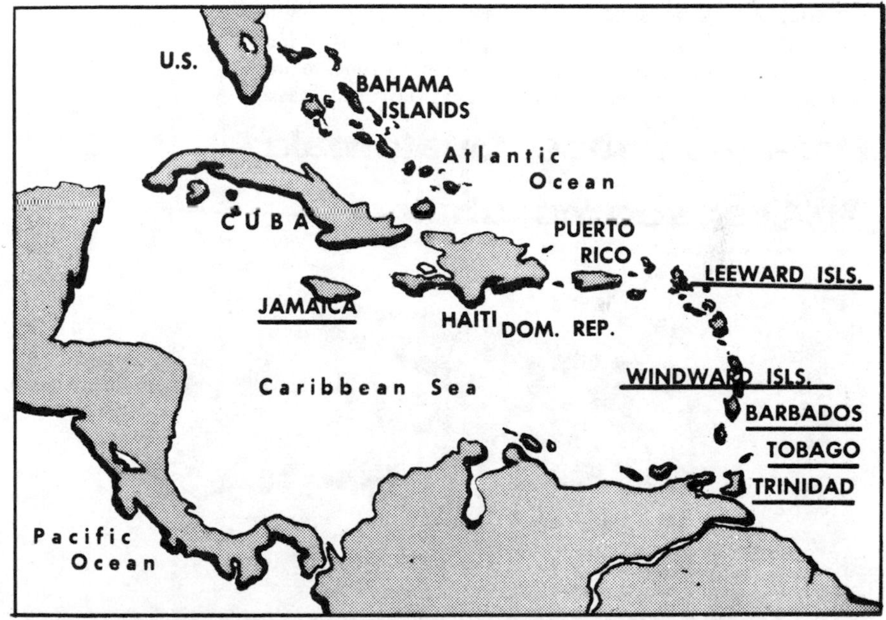

HINDU PRIEST FROM TRINIDAD, BARBADOS REGIMENTAL BUGLER, BRITISH-BORN SUGAR PLANTER ARE TYPICAL CITIZENS OF FEDERATION

VIOLENCE AND BLOODSHED marked the years of Communist domination in Guatemala. *(Above)*, a 1951 riot in Guatemala City. Supporters and foes of the Arbenz regime, equally fanatic, rioted whenever a controversial law was passed.

Pro-Reds lose Guatemala; Trujillo seems shaky

CENTRAL AMERICA's most critical political crisis of the decade was the rise to power, in the early '50s, of a strongly Communist-oriented regime in Guatemala. In March, 1951, popular young Jacobo Arbenz Guzman *(lower r.)* won the presidency in free elections. Within months, his government was veering sharply to the left. Many of the reforms it instituted, such as land distribution, were badly needed and long overdue; but what soon began to alarm U.S. observers—and many Guatemalans—were its obviously pro-Soviet sympathies. By 1953, when Arbenz expropriated 240,000 acres of United Fruit Co. land, pro-Communist and anti-Communist demonstrations were rocking the country. A year later, a successful revolt, which almost certainly had U.S. backing, was mounted by Col. Carlos Castillo Armas *(above)*, and Communism had lost its first foothold in the Western Hemisphere. As President, Castillo Armas struggled to steer a middle course between reaction and radicalism and return the nation to stability; he had achieved some measure of success before his tragic assassination in '57.

THE SIX tiny nations of Central America (Guatemala, Panama, Costa Rica, El Salvador, Nicaragua, Honduras) and their Caribbean neighbors (the Dominican Republic, Haiti) spent the '50s inching painfully toward a place in the sun.

Poverty and political unrest were endemic throughout the area. The violent rise and fall of governments was so much a matter of routine that a president who served out his term and turned his office over to a successor chosen in reasonably free elections was a rare phenomenon.

(Exceptions to the rule of political chaos were reliably democratic Costa Rica on the one hand, totally totalitarian Nicaragua and the Dominican Republic on the other.)

An agricultural economy based on a few all-important export crops (coffee, cotton, bananas), an unfavorable export-import balance and governmental extravagance and corruption were the chief causes of economic ills.

At decade's end, however, the outlook seemed to be brightening.

Political tensions were down from a boil to a simmer. Governmental austerity programs and drives for diversification were in full swing.

Most of the little nations received a valuable economic shot in the arm when the U.S. agreed to split United Fruit Co.'s taxes on Central American operations 60%-40% with producing countries instead of 50-50.

And, most importantly, Central America — like Latin America as a whole — appeared to have realized that its hopes for economic strength lay in union. Plans for a common market and a cooperative drive to stimulate manufacturing were taking a definite shape throughout 1960.

At the end of the decade, by far the most powerful of Latin America's few surviving dictators was Trujillo of the Dominican Republic.

Trujillo had held the island nation in an iron grip since 1930, and he showed no intention of loosening it.

He had instituted a "cult of personality" that dictators of bigger countries might well have envied. The capital city was named for him; so were roads, bridges, dams, schools, factories. His portrait hung in virtually every Dominican home. Newspapers published fulsome articles about him, and their letters columns were crowded with messages from citizens who found it advisable to praise "El Benefactor."

There was no doubt that the Trujillo years had been one long reign of terror for those who opposed him, or that much of the wealth that 30 years of stability had brought to the country had gone straight into the pockets of the large Trujillo family. (His brother was nominal president.)

However, he still had the support of the masses, whose standard of living he had undeniably raised.

The growing opposition to his regime came from the business and professional classes, and was winning the support of the Catholic hierarchy.

The giant question mark was the military, loyal for how long?

A pattern very similar to the one that had led to Juan Peron's downfall in Argentina may be forming.

A revolt in January, 1960, was put down, but many observers believed that Trujillo's days were numbered.

GENERALISSIMO Rafael Leonidas Trujillo Molina was 68 in 1960. He had nominally relinquished presidency to brother Hector, but was still "Supreme Chief."

MEXICO was the exception that proved the rule on the Latin American political scene; orderly democracy prevailed, as it had since the early 1930s. *(Above)*, retiring president Miguel Aleman *(r.)*, rides in parade with incoming chief executive Adolfe Ruiz Cortines on inauguration day in 1952.

Perennial Panamanian resentment over U.S. occupation of the Panama Canal Zone exploded briefly into violence in late 1959, when young nationalist agitators *(above)* tangled with U.S. troops.

Panama's president, Ernesto de la Guardia, had won substantial concessions from the U.S. on jobs and pay for Panamanian workers in the Canal Zone, but had failed to win the right to fly the Panamanian flag beside the U.S. flag in the Zone, which was what the nationalists wanted most. His successor, Roberto Chiari, who took office in June, 1960, was expected to press the flag demand harder; the possibility that he might go so far as to attempt nationalization of the Canal was remote but disquieting.

Chiari had taken office in orderly fashion, but earlier in the decade, Panama had its share of political turbulence. Arnulfo Arias was deposed when he tried to establish a dictatorship in 1951; his successor, Jose Antonio Remon, was assassinated in 1953.

PUBLIC PROJECTS like waterworks, beautified by Diego Rivera mosaics, in Mexico City suburb of Lerma *(r.)* helped boost Mexico's expanding economy. Although the rural masses were still poor, Mexico had progressed much farther along the road to stable prosperity than had most of its neighbors.

CANADA COMES OF AGE

Unprecedented prosperity, major world role reinforce nationalism of U.S. northern neighbor. But economic and defense ties grow stronger despite Conservative victory over Liberals on "Canada First" platform.

IN THE 1950s, Canada, while retaining membership in the British Commonwealth, came to full maturity as an independent nation, adding a new, fresh voice to the councils of the Free World.

Its economic advance was equally rapid. Its population rose from 14 million to 18 million; its Gross National Product doubled ($35 billion from $18 billion); industrial production increased two-thirds, making it the sixth largest nation in industrial output; and immense new mineral wealth was opened up, oil and natural gas in the West, iron and copper in the bleak Northeast.

Canada's coming of age was symbolized when Queen Elizabeth, in late 1952, appointed as Governor General the first native-born Canadian, Vincent Massey (instead of a connection of Royalty or a British peer.)

It received further recognition when Massey was succeeded, in 1959, by Maj. Gen. Georges P. Vanier, the first French Canadian and Roman Catholic to hold the office, and when, in 1957, the Queen herself opened Parliament in Ottawa as "Queen of Canada." (Elizabeth also visited Canada in 1952, while still princess, and in 1959, to open the St. Lawrence Seaway.)

Internationally, Canadian troops played an important role in Korea, and in the UN force sent to Suez following the 1956 cease-fire. This was largely arranged by Nobel Prize Winner Lester Pearson, External Affairs Secretary during the long years of Liberal power.

Politically, the major event was the overthrow of the Liberals, after 22 years of continuous power, by the Progressive Conservatives headed by Saskatchewan lawyer John Diefenbaker. The Liberals lost their majority in June, 1957, and were overwhelmed 222 to 65 in a second election in March, 1958.

An equally stunning upset followed the death, late in 1959, of Maurice Duplessis, for 15 years "strong man" premier of Quebec as head of the French Canadian nationalist *Union National*. After two stop-gap Nationalists, a Liberal, Jean Lesage, became premier in June, 1960, following an election which Liberals hoped pointed to a national comeback.

Diefenbaker, in his two victorious campaigns, spoke out against U.S. dominance. (U.S. industry, by 1960, had at least $14 billion invested in Canada, owned stock majorities in many leading corporations.) In office, however, he continued virtually complete defense cooperation, and the economic links grew ever stronger. (The U.S. took 55% of all Canada's exports, supplied 65% of all imports; Canada accounted for more than a fifth of all U.S. foreign trade.)

But the decade had transformed these ties, like those with Great Britain, into full, equal partnership—during it, Canada fully came of age.

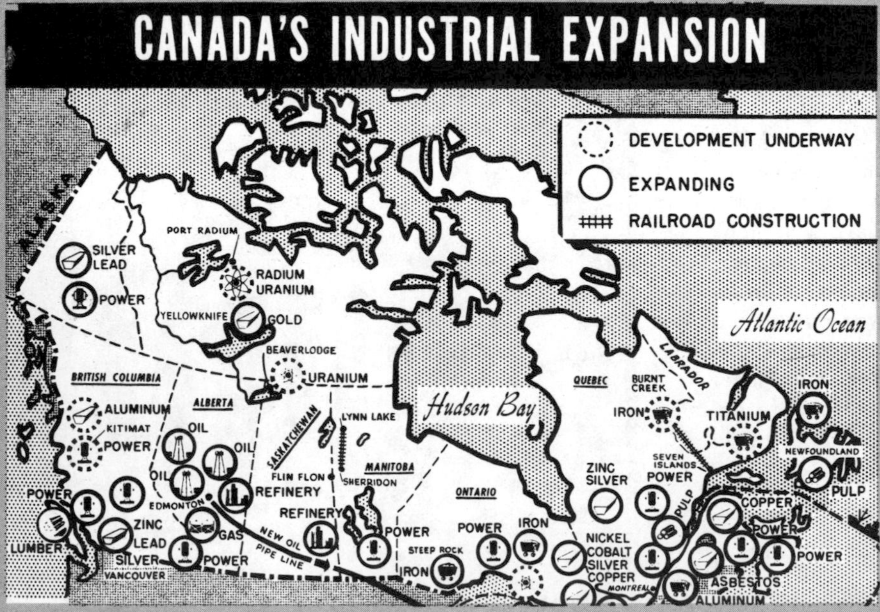

CANADA'S ECONOMIC PROFILE

	1950	1959
Population (millions)	13.7	17.8
Gross National Product ($ billion)	18.1	34.6
Employment (% of Labor Force)	87	95
Average Hourly Earnings ($)		
(Manufacturing)	1.04	1.72
Total Industrial Production		
(1949=100)	106.0	166
Mining	116.0	244
Manufacturing	107.0	153
Electrical Power (billions KWH)	54.4	103.8
Foreign Trade ($ billion)		
Exports	3.2	5.6
Imports	3.2	5.7
Balance	....	—.1
National Budget ($ billion)		
Revenue	2.6	4.7
Expenditures	2.4	5.3
Balance	—.2	—.6
U.S. Direct Investments ($ billion)	6.7	14.6

NATIONAL UNITY was strengthened by completion, in 1960, of 5000-mile Trans Canada Highway, modern motor link between East, prairies, Pacific Coast. New road will open up large additional areas to vacationing Canadians and tourists, whose annual expenditures jumped during decade from $220 million to $400 million. About two-thirds came from the U.S.

DIEFENBAKER's rise to Prime Ministership was not only Conservative triumph, but first time post went to leader who came from outside big eastern provinces.

DEATH of Maurice Duplessis, for 15 years "dictator" of Quebec, signalized weakening of French particularism, increased sense of Canadian nationhood.

DEFEAT of liberals in 1957, ended 22 years in power. Lester B. Pearson, former External Affairs Secretary, then became the leader of the opposition.

CANADIAN-U.S. cooperation continued despite political changes. Important 1953 talks were held between President Eisenhower, Prime Minister St. Laurent, assisted by Pearson, *(c.)* Secretary of State John Foster Dulles, Hume Wrong, Ambassador to U.S. Topics included wheat surpluses, seaway plan.

CANADIAN ICEBREAKER Earnest Lapointe, in April, 1959, was first ship to enter St. Lawrence Seaway, which brought ocean into vast interiors of Canada, U.S. After June dedication, Queen, with Eisenhowers and Diefenbakers as guests, led nautical parade through jointly-built Seaway aboard yacht.

NATIONHOOD did not weaken strong ties with Commonwealth, great affection for Elizabeth, Queen of Canada as well as Great Britain. High point of first of her three visits during '50 s, on all of which her husband, Prince Philip, accompanied her, was first square dance. The Duke wore plaid shirt.

CANADA'S FIRST native born Governors General were Vincent Massey *(l.)* and Maj. Gen. Georges Vanier. Their 20th Century predecessors in Vice Regal post included Queen Victoria's son, Duke of Connaught, British novelist Lord Tweedsmuir (John Buchan) and World War II hero, Lord Alexander of Tunis. But Canada came to prefer native sons.

CANADA FORGED AHEAD in manufacture of automobiles (Ford assembly plant, *above)*, aircraft, farm machinery, rubber and electrical goods, as well as the processing industries, led by paper and pulp, petroleum products, nonferrous smelting and refining, iron and steel, sawmill products, meat packing. Eighty per cent of manufacturing was in Ontario and Quebec provinces. Agriculture depended on mechanization of larger farms (550 acres average grain farm) to hold its own in world trade. Cash income of Canadian farmers for 1959 was $2.8 billion—$423 million from wheat. (A typical Alberta wheat field with an oil rig pumping is shown at right.) Canada abandoned all agricultural price supports.

AMERICAN SCENE

U. S. conquers economic Everests; mood turns serious as the decade draws to end

EARLY in the decade, in 1954, Edmund P. Hillary of New Zealand and his Sherpa guide, Tenzing Norkay, scaled the world's highest mountain, Himalaya's Everest.

Throughout the decade the U.S. people were triumphantly scaling other equally awesome (if less tangible) unconquered peaks, peaks of production, of output, of unprecedented prosperity.

Gross National Product (total of all goods and services) rose from $329 billion in 1951 to well over $500 billion in 1960; disposable personal income, the amount after taxes and similar deductions Americans could actually spend, jumped from $226.1 billion in 1951 to 1960's estimated $350 billion. This meant an average, in 1960, of just under $2000 in the pockets or purses of every man, woman and child in the U.S.—and they were spending it!

They were riding, for example, in some 58 million automobiles (approximately one to every three persons and more than in all the rest of the world), taking to coastal and inland waters on 7.8 million pleasure craft and talking over 72 million telephones (again, more than half the world's total).

They were listening on 156 million radio sets (three to a home and almost one to a person) and viewing on well over 50 million television sets.

Bolstering their urge to buy, advertisers during the decade spent $98 billion, $12 billion in 1960 alone. (TV's share of the total rose from 3% in 1950 to 13.7% in 1959, while radio's dropped from 10.6% to only 5.8%; newspapers remained far in the lead, averaging one-third.)

TELEVISION CAST SPELL OVER GROWNUPS, TOO

Individuals' total assets, as the decade ended, were approaching $1000 billion, a fact which made their instalment debt, well over $35 billion, a matter which did not unduly worry economists.

TV not only showed its muscle in advertising but, in entertainment, had the once omnipotent movies staggering on the ropes.

Attendance at motion picture theaters kept on plunging downward despite desperate efforts to lure back patrons by everything from wide screens to free baby-sitting and simultaneous scents as well as sounds. As the '50s ended, Hollywood was drawing a growing portion of its total revenues from the hated upstart, both by making new films for it (not all were Westerns) and by selling or leasing its precious libraries of old pictures.

Prosperity, with its inevitably attendant high prices and costs, produced an actual shrinkage in the number of Broadway offerings. Initial production expenses rose so high "angels" were reluctant to underwrite them unless virtually assured of a hit. But this trend was more than compensated for by, in New York City itself, the mushrooming of the "Off-Broadway" stage and, in the country at large, by the rebirth of repertory.

Music was a beneficiary of accelerating prosperity, and of a deepening cultural awareness. Concert seats, for the first time in U.S. history, outsold baseball tickets. (Baseball, like the movies, was in a state of flux; attendance fell off, and teams moved skittishly around the country, with such apparent fixtures as the New York Giants and the Brooklyn Dodgers traipsing to, respectively, San Francisco and Los Angeles. And, as with the movies, TV was blamed; it was agreed that by bringing big league games to every whistle stop, it had "murdered the minors.")

Books, too, boomed, with the inexpensive paperbacks, the decade's publishing phenomenon, on sale on every newstand and in every drugstore. If, in too many cases, they were lurid sensationalism or downright pornography, they also were making the greatest literature, the whole record of human achievement, available to every American.

Evidence of growing seriousness, at least of growing awareness of the rest of the world, was foreign travel, on which during the decade 90 million Americans spent $17 billion, and increasing concern with the potential enemy, the Soviet Union. This manifested itself in exchanges of official visitors ranging from ballet dancers to atomic scientists, and included, in 1959, a momentarily mellow Khrushchev.

Serious, too, and stimulated by Soviet scientific accomplishments, was the renewed emphasis on education fundamentals, too long neglected for dubiously useful "social training" which often failed to teach children even how to read. (Most important single educational development was the Supreme Court's desegregation of public schools.)

The U.S. ended the old decade, and entered the new, unimaginably rich, but no longer complacent—aware it must earn and hold, under challenge, its place in history.

SHIFT TO SUBURBS CHANGED FACE OF U.S. LANDSCAPE, GAVE NEW SPACIOUSNESS TO LIVES OF MILLIONS OF PROSPERING AMERICANS

THE BURGEONING CLOUD of radioactive dust blasted into the atmosphere by a force hundreds of times greater than that of the Hiroshima bomb overhung the scientific and political life of the '50s. Twenty-three men on a simple Japanese trawler, the *Lucky Dragon,* inadvertently spent two weeks at sea while highly contaminated debris rained down on them from the skies. On March 1, 1954 at 4 a.m. the U.S. had detonated its "super-bomb" at Bikini, 85 miles away.

SCIENCE TRANSFORMS LIFE

Research makes man healthier, adds years to life expectation, but it also opens up dread possibility of destruction of all human accomplishments, all life on planet

SCIENCE, once considered worthy of only back-page news space, leapt on to the front page in the "historic decade" and stayed there.

There were good reasons for the average man's increased interest in scientific developments. Science in the '50s made man healthier, giving him longer life to enjoy the "good life" brought by a higher standard of living. Drugs dispelled aches, real or imaginary, and tranquilized the troubled mind of modern man. His diet was enriched with tastier, better meats, fruits and vegetables, all made possible by hormones and genetics.

Technology moved man further and faster. Record after record was broken as the highest mountains and lowest depths of the sea were explored. Research and investigation ranged from the minute core of the atom to the wilderness of outer space. The universe was no longer spoken of as the "great unknown." Science did not yet have all the answers, but now time and money seemed the only deterrents.

But while science had immeasurably helped man, it also put into his hands the weapons of ultimate destruction. It seemed to many that science had created a "Frankenstein," a terrible monster it could not control.

In 1952, as if the atom bomb were not deadly enough, the U.S. exploded a weapon with even more dire potential, the hydrogen bomb. Soviet scientists soon followed suit. Before the three nation (U.S., USSR, Great Britain) moratorium on nuclear testing began on November 1, 1958, the earth had been shaken with the blast and debris of over 300 explosions — explosions varying in power from the "small" Hiroshima-size (20,000 tons of TNT) to 20 or 30 megatons (30 million tons of TNT) at Eniwetok. The atmosphere was tainted with the resulting radiation. France attained the questionable prestige of membership in the "atomic club" with the 1960 Sahara blasts.

Progress was made, however, toward peaceful uses of atomic power. Chinks in the Iron Curtain were large enough by 1959 to allow small groups of scientists from both the U.S. and USSR to tour their opposites' laboratories. The year before, beginning July, 1958, 64 nations took part in the International Geophysical Year, supplying equipment and scientists for an 18-month study of the earth, its oceans, atmosphere, sun, and outer space. The data collected promised to keep scientists busy for the next five or six years.

The past decade also produced numerous scientific advances that probably went unnoticed by most of the general public but were nonetheless important.

The basic "parity law" of nuclear physics was shattered by experiments showing seemingly identical sub-atomic particles to possess unexpected right and left hand properties.

Earth's "electric blanket," the ionosphere, was found to extend 1000 times further out than previously thought.

Coordinating the newer science of radio-astronomy with older optical astronomy, an international team of scientists found a new galaxy—5 billion light years distant (1 LY=7 trillion miles). Its "age-old snapshot" was compared with galaxies nearer earth in an attempt to solve one of science's most crucial problems, one that philosophers have been debating for almost 2500 years: did the universe expand from one beginning, or is it in a "steady state" with matter continually being created?

The world's most powerful cyclotron (at the AEC's Brookhaven National Laboratory) pulled protons around a circular, half-mile long magnet, accelerating them up to 30 BEV (billion electron volts). The machine will serve as an atomic microscope for 30 BEV bullets, making it possible to explore the minute, fifty quadrillionths cms., radius of a proton.

During the '50s man used the sun to heat his homes, made diamonds in high-pressure laboratories, studied the language of ducks, bees and porpoises, bred fatherless chickens and rabbits, and subjected his own body to extremes of heat, cold and pressure.

Science, in many ways, made the world a better place. People lived longer and more abundantly. But a double-edged sword dangled over mankind, one side ready to annihilate it in a nuclear blast, the other to stifle man with a world population that might reach 13 billion by the year 2050, as compared to the present 2.9 billion.

At decade's end the question was—even if man escaped the nuclear threat, would there be enough room for him?

PRESIDENT EISENHOWER'S 1953 U. N. speech led eventually to two major atomic energy conferences in Geneva, '55 and '58. The atom's role in medicine, biology, agriculture, basic research and as power source was explored. Upshot was much declassification by Atomic Energy Commission when it found many 'secrets' widespread.

ALBERT EINSTEIN, via TV, warned the U.S. people: "The hydrogen bomb has appeared on the public horizon as an attainable goal. It hints that the annihilation of any life on earth has been brought within the range of technical possibilities." His famous 1939 letter to Roosevelt urged a go-ahead on the atomic bomb. Einstein died in 1955.

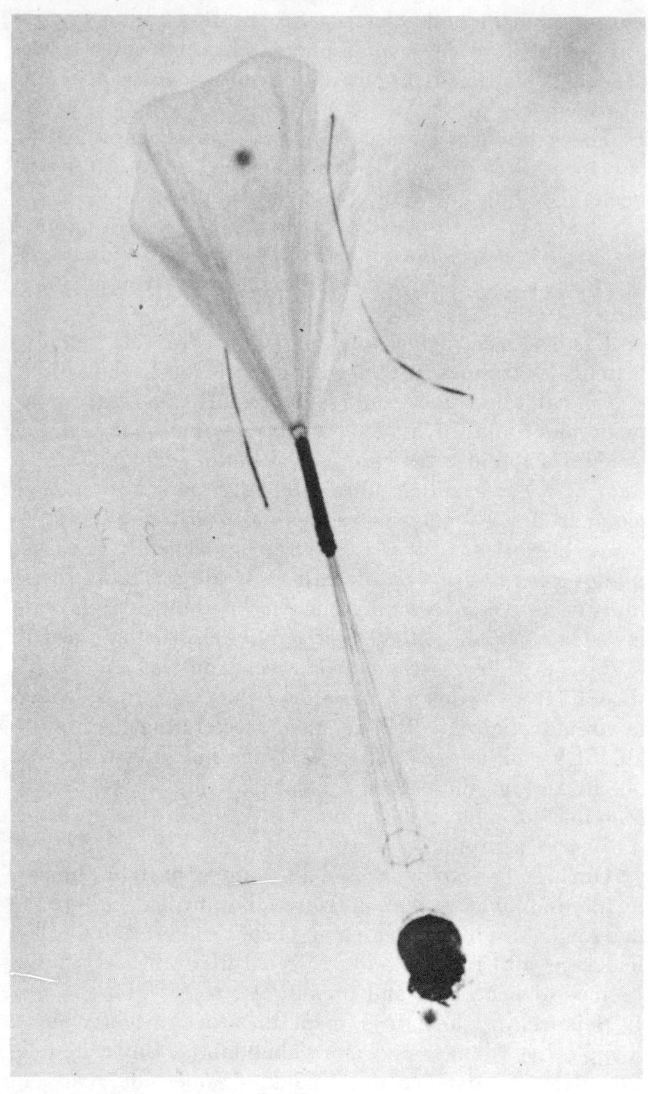

"STRATOSCOPE" BALLOON carried two men up to 80,000 ft. in a sealed gondola in the fall of 1959. Navy Cmdr. Malcolm Ross and Charles Moore of John Hopkins went aloft to make telescopic studies of Venus without interference from 90% of earth's atmosphere. Finding: Water vapor near Venus.

VIVIAN FUCHS, later knighted, was met at the South Pole by Everest's Edmund Hillary *(r.)*. Fuchs completed first overland Antarctic crossing in 2100-mile, 98-day icy race.

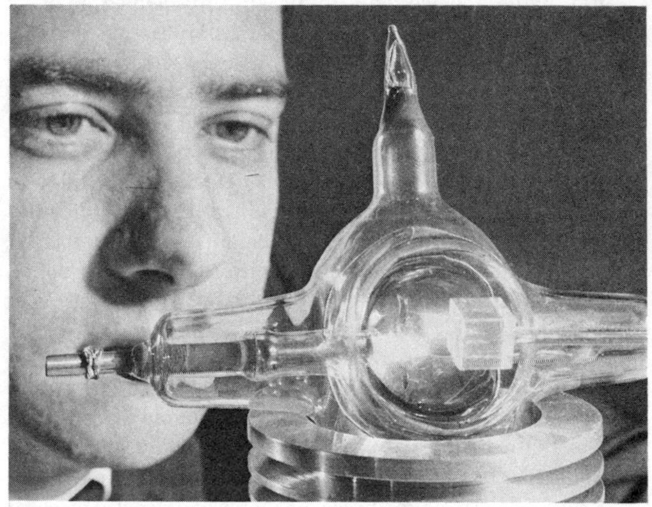

A "COHERENT" LIGHT source—one which no longer is random waves vibrating at different frequencies—was a scientific "first" by Dr. Theodore Maiman. The cube-shaped ruby (called Laser) absorbs random light, later emits it as a parallel beam of great intensity and precise color purity.

CHOPPY JANUARY DAWN off Guam tosses the U.S. Navy's bathyscaph *Trieste* before it dives beneath the surface of the Pacific. Inside the cramped sphere attached beneath a larger float of gasoline (lighter-than-water to enable them to rise), Lt. Don Walsh and Jacques Piccard, of famous scientific family, sank into total darkness of the virgin sea. After five hours they were resting at the bottom of the Mariana Trench, 36,000 feet down—man's deepest dive yet.

"LIVING FOSSIL" dating back to the Devonian period 300 million years ago, a Coelacanth was found alive off the Comoro Islands near Madagascar in 1952. Thought extinct for 70 million years, the features of this anachronistic creature (paired leg-like fins, rudimentary lung) hint a relationship to land vertebrates.

LISTENING POST for messages sent by intelligent life on planets of nearby stars is this 140-ft. radiotelescope stationed in the remote hills of West Virginia

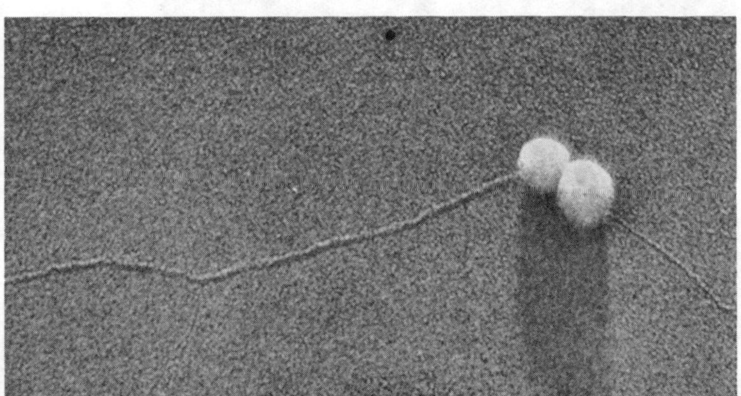

ELECTRON MICROGRAPHS show thread-like DNA (deoxyribonucleic acid protons, magnified 112,000 times. Sequence of just four chemicals within DNA may determine genetic differences between individuals in animals, plants and bacteria. Scientists seek to break code, see how the genes work.

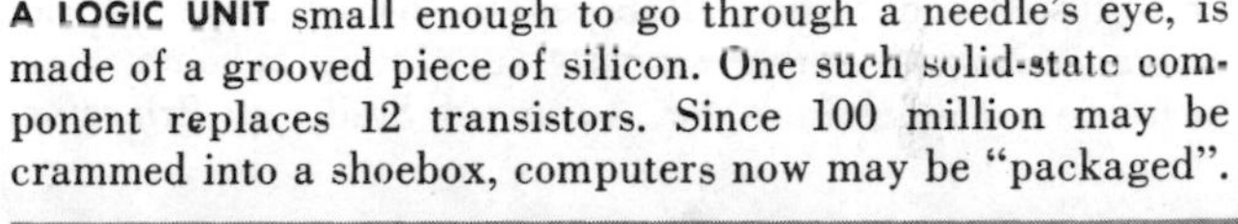

A LOGIC UNIT small enough to go through a needle's eye, is made of a grooved piece of silicon. One such solid-state component replaces 12 transistors. Since 100 million may be crammed into a shoebox, computers now may be "packaged".

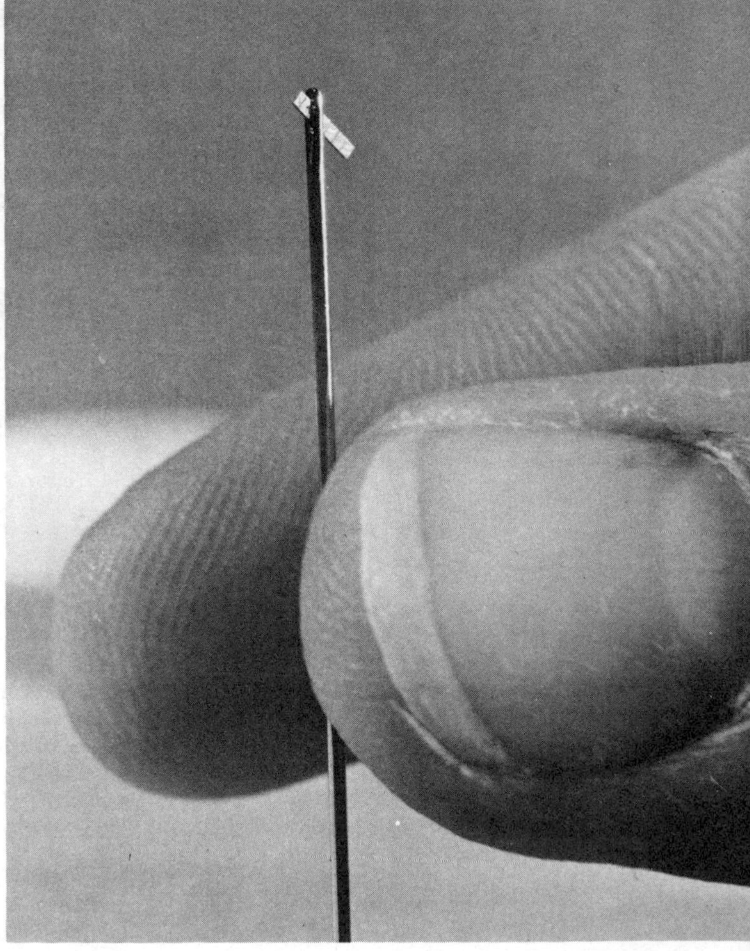

ELECTRONIC COMPUTERS came into their own in the '50s. They were used to sift out radar signals bounced off the sun and for projecting outcomes of national elections. The first air defense computer *(above)* at Lincoln Lab near Boston culls over information in the event of a raid, solves the problems and gives answers for immediate defense procedures.

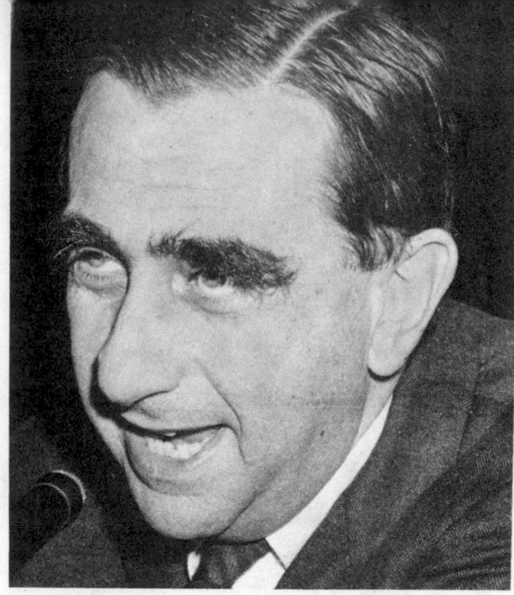

DR. EDWARD TELLER, father of the H-bomb, adamantly advocated continued nuclear tests: his goal was first, a "clean" bomb, then small, tactical weapons, then peaceful A-bomb explosions for blasting out harbors or releasing oil. Dr. Robert Oppenheimer *(r.)*, prime mover in the Los Alamos A-bomb development, warned in 1953 that U.S. and USSR "are like two scorpions in a bottle, each capable of killing the other but only at the risk of his own life . . . The atomic clock ticks faster and faster." Relieved in '54 of AEC security clearance for not enthusiastically supporting H-bomb work, he headed in'60 Institute for Advanced Study at Princeton.

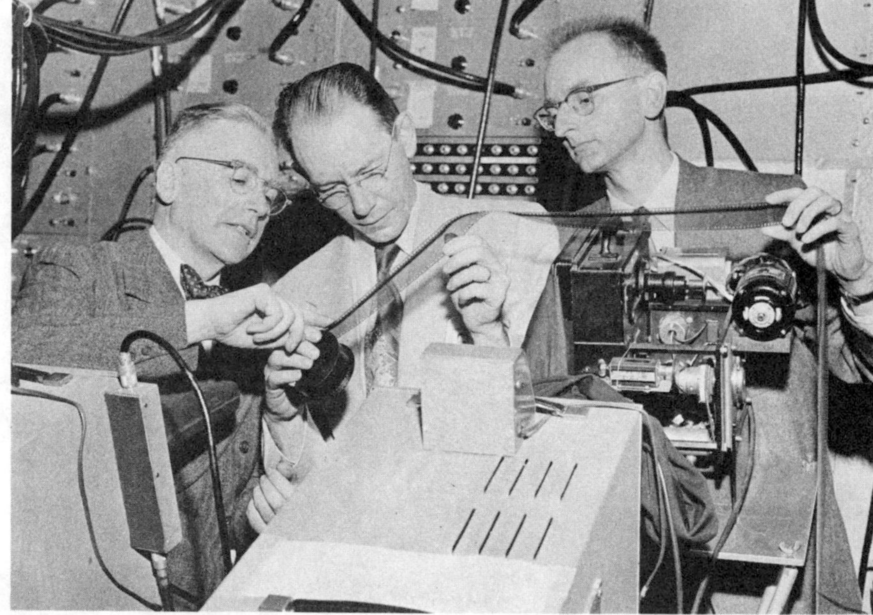

"THE ITALIAN NAVIGATOR has landed and the natives are friendly" let Washington know, Dec. 2, 1940, that Enrico Fermi's work under the west stands of Chicago's Stagg Field had paid off, and a controlled atomic chain reaction had been sustained for first time. In 1954, "world's outstanding nuclear physicist" (who at 37 won the Nobel Prize for discovery of atomic transmutation by the addition of neutrons to the atomic nucleus) died of cancer at his home at the age of fifty-three.

A NUCLEAR GHOST which had haunted world's physicists for a generation was finally snared in the giant Bevatron in 1955 at the University of California. Discoverers of the tiny antiproton (Emilio Segre, Clyde Wiegand and Owen Chamberlain) examine oscilliscope photographs which show subatomic particle's rate of travel. Pinpointing first anti-matter particle brought to public mind the question whether whole anti-matter universes represent annihilation threat to our positive world.

RADIOACTIVE CARBON-14 is taken up by all living matter. Once there, it begins to decay and its radioactivity is halved every 50,000 years. This knowledge, elaborated by Willard Libby, has become archeologists' most cherished tool. By calculating present C14 levels, they can extrapolate the time at which the prehistoric or archeological plant or animal was living. Six-ton apparatus *(right)* keeps out contamination by air during the precise extraction of the C14.

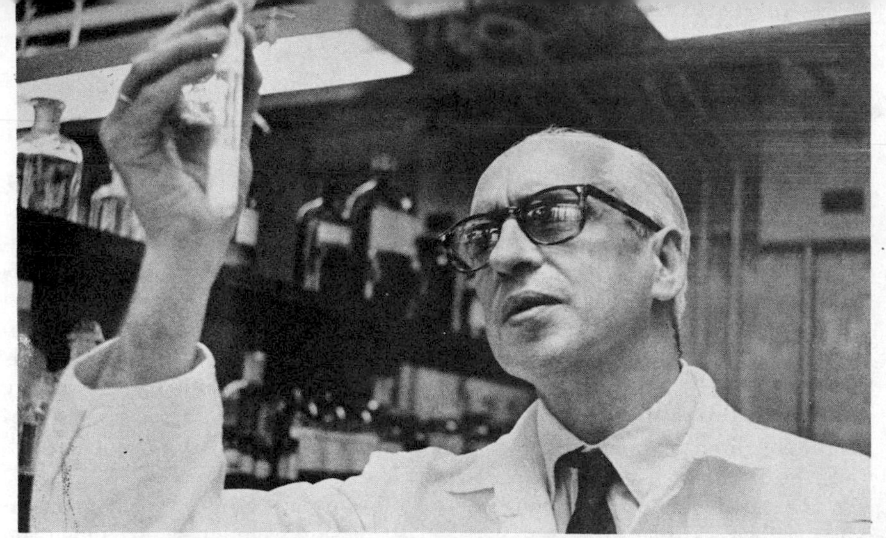

MAN-MADE GIANT molecules of RNA (ribonucleic acid), the complex cell chemical which controls the growth of proteins necessary to life, brought fame to laboratory of modest New York University biochemist. In 1959, Dr. Severo Ochoa was awarded Nobel for medicine. One of his most promising students, Arthur Kornberg of Stanford U., shared the prize for synthesizing a molecule like natural DNA (see p. 165).

CALDER HALL, clean, quiet array amongst sheep of the Northern English countryside, was the world's first commercial nuclear power plant. Queen Elizabeth in Oct., 1956, pulled the switch which sent 70,000 nuclear-made kilowatts of electricity to the grid. By 1975 "atomic" electricity should be economically competitive there. The largest U.S. power installation is at Shipingport, Pa. (60-000 kw.). USSR claims a 600,000-kw power station but has neglected to tell where huge A-powered city is located.

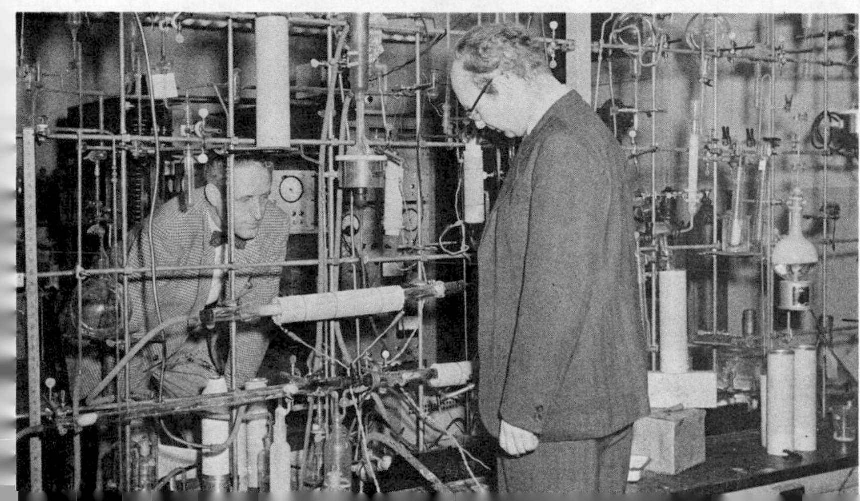

MEDICINE TAKES OFFENSIVE

Anti-polio vaccines found, progress made in circulatory and cancer research

DR. JONAS SALK, following on the heels of such virus-probers as Goodpasture, Huang, Weller, Robbins and Enders, produced the dramatic break-through of the decade—an effective polio-vaccine.

By 1960, over 91 million Americans had received Salk vaccinations. However, almost 87 million had none.

A surge of optimism swept the U.S. when the incidence of paralytic polio hit a record low of 2499 in 1957, compared to 13,580 in 1955.

Disappointment and controversy followed as the "crippler" rallied in 1958, reached epidemic proportions in 1959. Immunologists split into two camps, backers of the Salk killed-virus vaccine and proponents of the oral, live-virus vaccine.

As the 1960 polio season approached, two facts emerged: (1) polio had not been eradicated, (2) the Iron Curtain countries had adopted the live-virus vaccine while the U.S. continued to evaluate the massive 1958-1960 trials.

Revolutionary progress in mental health during the 1950s had resulted from the widespread use of such tranquilizing drugs as the mephenesins, meprobamates, chlorpromazines and rauwolfia. These had enabled therapists to "reach" and help many thousands of the mentally disturbed who before had been utterly withdrawn from reality.

The growing trend towards "open door" and out-patient therapy expedited the adjustment of patients from institutionalized to home life.

In heart disease, leading killer in the U.S., artificial heart and lung devices enabled cardiac surgery to save lives by operations never before considered possible.

Drugs also made their vital contribution. The rauwolfia group effectively lowered blood-pressure in hypertensive patients. The diuretic action of the chlorthiazide family was a boon to cardiac patients suffering from excessive tissue fluid retention.

Other developments were the replacement of faulty blood-vessels with man-made substitutes and the successful scraping, or reaming, of clogged coronary arteries of the heart.

Research on the relationship of cholesterol to circulatory disease (especially atherosclerosis) did not produce common agreement as to the basic causative factor. The public, however, moved toward revamping its diet and a rash of low, and anti-cholesterol products invaded markets and homes.

The U.S. Government, drug companies, hospitals and medical schools spent increasing millions, in money and man hours, in research on cancer, the nation's hydra-headed No. 2 killer.

The decade also saw refinements in diagnostic techniques, expanded facilities for radiation treatment and improved radical surgery methods.

A striking trend was the rise in the virological approach to cancer and mounting evidence that some types, including leukemia, may be caused by — among other factors — viruses.

An exciting highlight was the development of chemical agents which destroy specific cancer cells, delaying, at least for a time, malignant growth. Greatest need remaining, however, was for an agent that would be non-toxic to the surrounding healthy cell-tissue.

An interesting fact, perhaps symbolic, was that Dr. Albert Sabin, a leading developer of oral-type, live-virus polio-vaccine, planned at the end of 1960 to change his focus of research from polio to cancer.

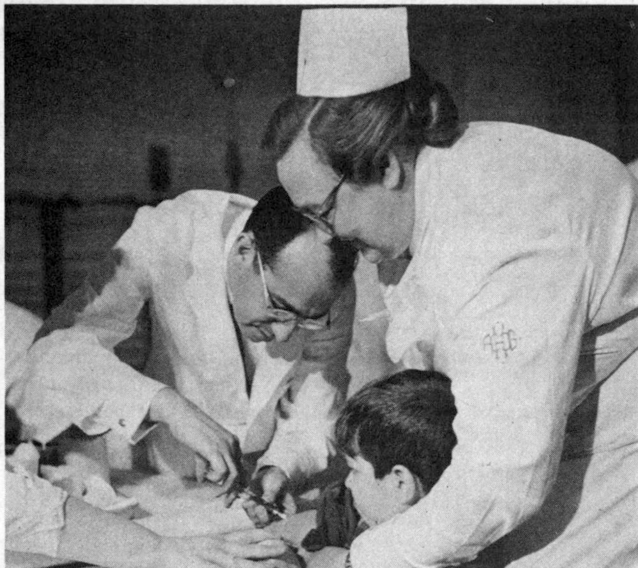

DR. JONAS SALK injected 320,000 Americans with his killed-virus polio vaccine in 1954 field trials. Results led to U.S. Public Health Service acceptance, Salk immunization cam paign, popular belief after 1957 that polio was conquered.

ORAL, LIVE VIRUS vaccine research was conducted independently by Drs. Sabin *(above)*, Harold R. Cox. Hilary Koprowski. While 60 million Russians had received innoculations by 1960, the U.S. authorities were still evaluating method.

SMOKING-MACHINE (above), used in lung cancer research, also symbolizes prevailing medical opinion on smoking and health: "Too many cigarettes won't hurt the machine." Statistical evidence, however, still links lung cancer with excessive cigarette-smoking. Tobacco companies reply: "No direct evidence of causation," yet continue trend to filters.

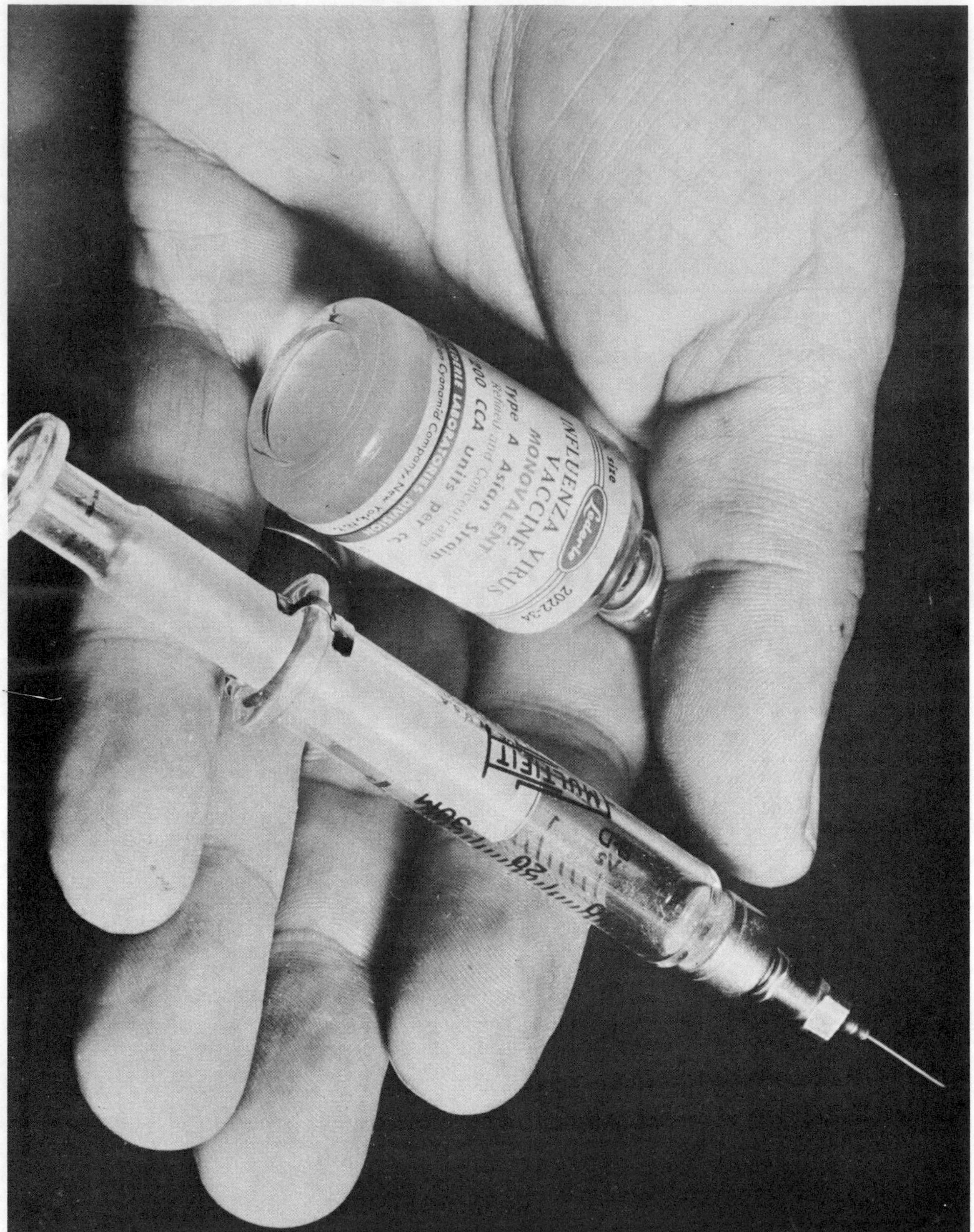

PANDEMIC OF ASIAN FLU in 1957-58 left a worldwide memory of aches, sneezes, absenteeism. Health Service estimated incidence in U.S., for peak year (1957), at 20 million—deaths due to the virus, complicated by pneumonia and other factors, at over 10,000. Vaccine *(above)* was immunologists' attempt to stem the tide. This was first pandemic in which a relatively new type of virus was identified early enough to predict its spread and enable timely preparation of a vaccine.

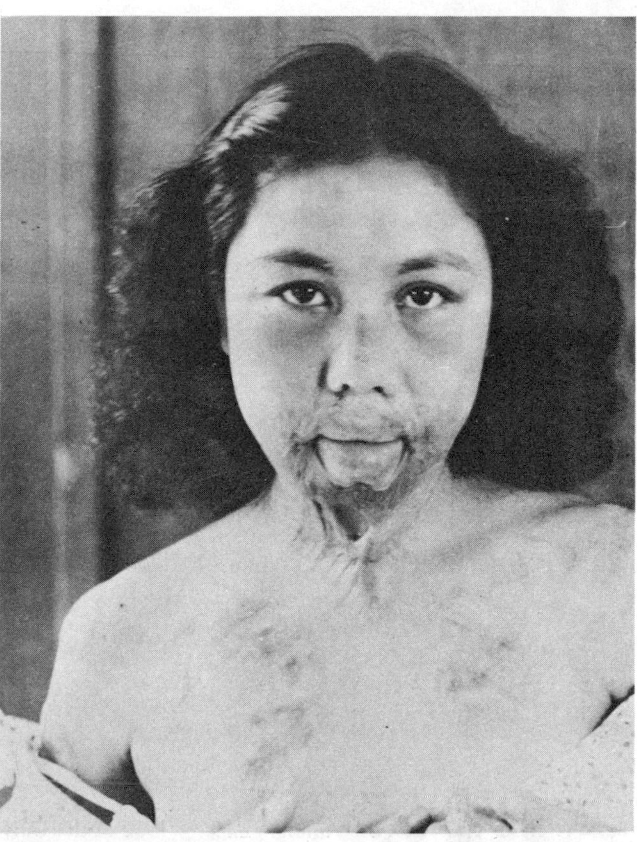

HIDEOUS RAVAGES of nuclear warfare yielded externally to science of plastic surgery in 1956-7. U.S. doctors at Mt. Sinai Hospital, N.Y., transformed 25 Japanese "Hiroshima Maidens" from bomb-casualty gargoyles into reborn human beings. Before *(r.)* and after *(l.)* pictures of Shigeko Niimoto give proof of man's skill at destruction and salvation.

DRUGS A BARGAIN OR FRAUD? Dr. Austin Smith *(above)*, president of Pharmaceutical Manufacturers Assn., defended drug companies in 1960 Senate hearings against charges of profiteering, monopolistic practices. He hailed drugs and medicines as "real bargain" for the American public, which spends annually five times more on alcohol than medications.

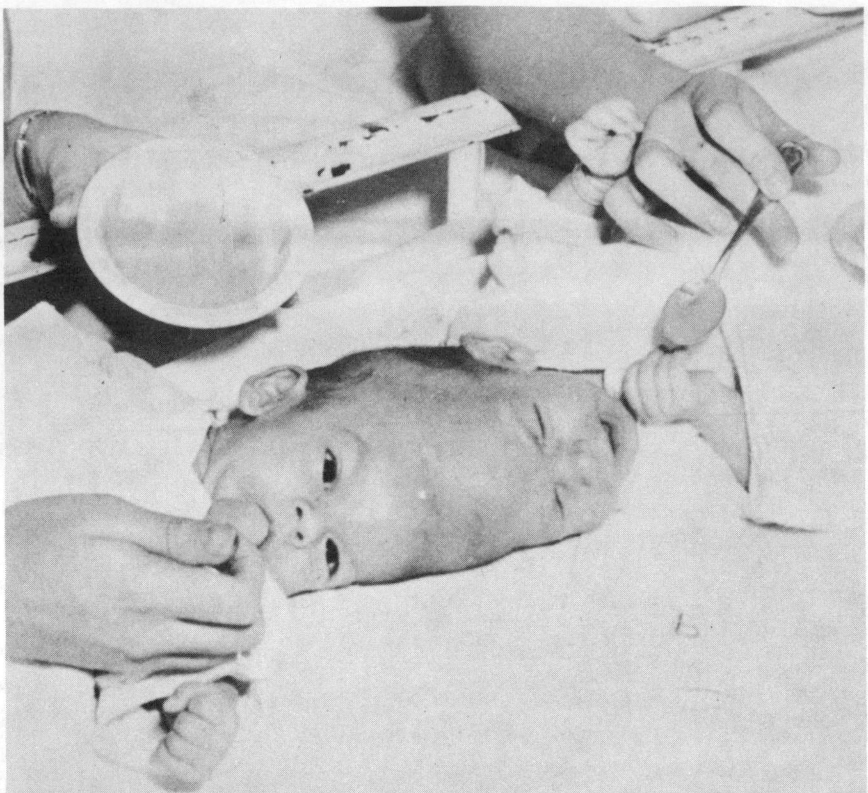

HEAD-TO-HEAD SIAMESE TWINS underwent the first successful separation surgery of its kind in medical history. The unprecedented operation, performed in 1952 at the Univ. of Illinois Educational and Research Hospital, took 12 hours, 40 minutes. Picture *(above)* shows twins being fed months before the operation.

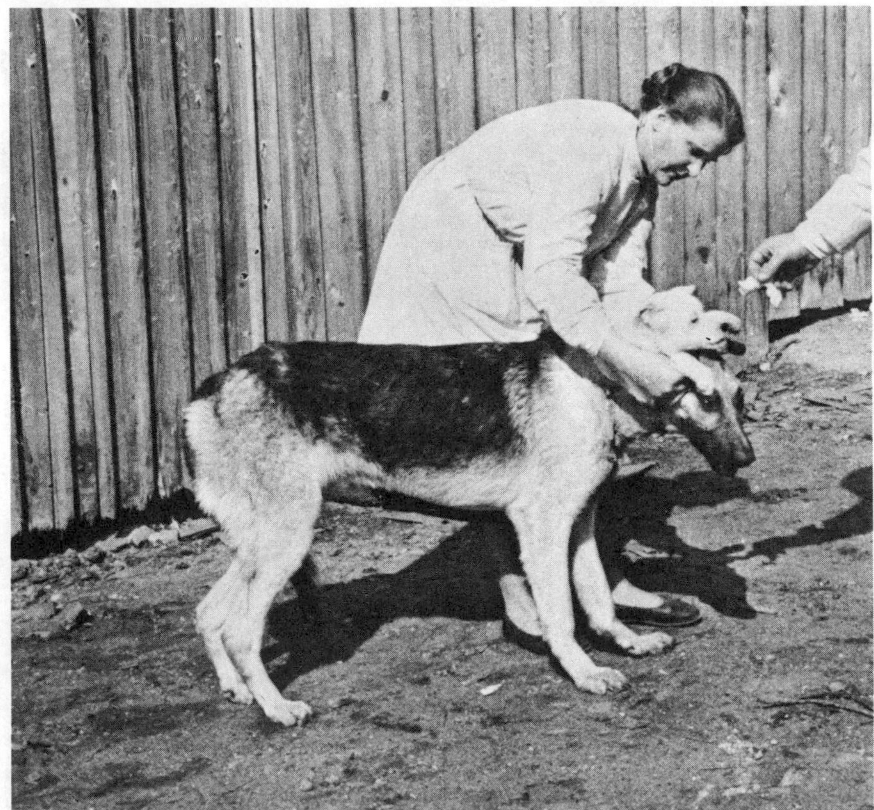

RUSSIAN DOUBLE-HEADER coexisted 30 days. Head, forepaws of puppy, grafted by Dr. Vladimir Demikhov onto full-grown Shepherd, received ample nourishment from larger dog's system, but puppy liked to lick candy on the side.

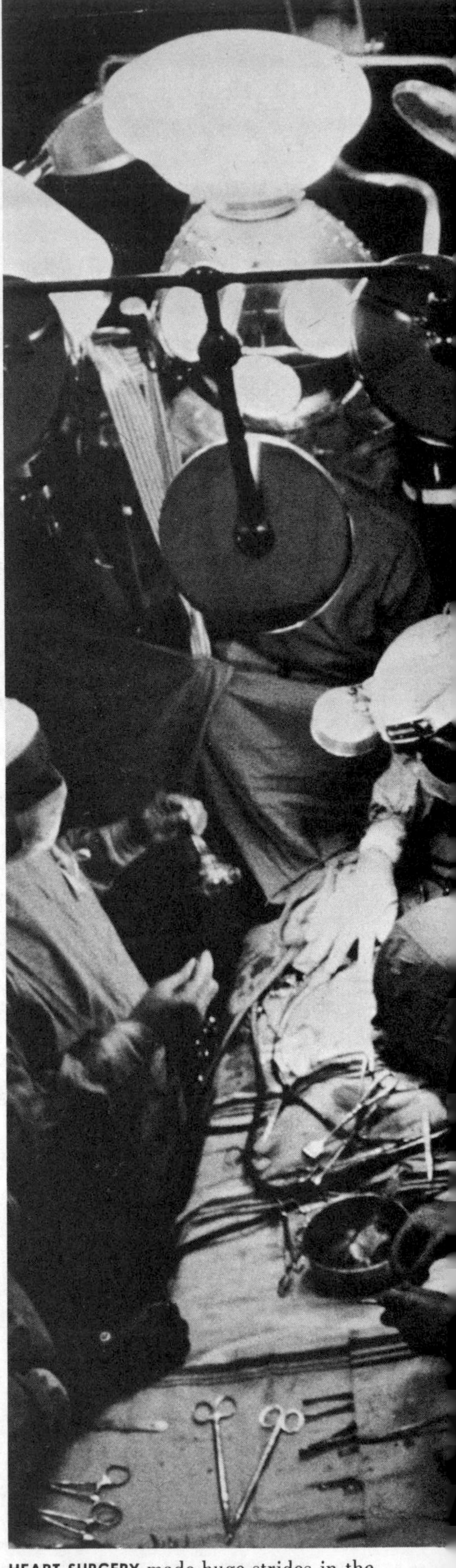

HEART SURGERY made huge strides in the last decade. Operations, formerly impossible, succeeded as scientists de-

veloped artificial hearts, lungs and other devices to maintain circulation of blood while a defective heart received surgery. Surgeons *(above)* join the bloodstream of a mother *(r.)* to that of her 5-month baby *(l.)* to sustain life while they mend a hole impairing child's circulation. This dramatic scene took place in 1955 at the Univ. of Minnesota Hospital.

SOVIET SATELLITE streaking over Tokyo symbolized lead in race for space. The space voyager served as reminder of Soviet's expert technology, prompted U.S. spacemen to work around the clock, but, month after Sputnik I in '57, Sputnik II with dog was launched.

AMERICANS once thought of "space" as a mysterious realm that belonged between the covers of lurid science-fiction magazines. As recently as 1957, an Air Force directive went out to all personnel; "refrain from speaking in a way which makes valid Air Force projects sound like space flight or trips to the moon, lest the public lose confidence in us."

All too soon afterwards, the U.S. public learned just how much confidence they should have had in the "crazy" space-minded people. When the USSR launched the world into the space age, Oct. 4, 1957, the U.S. looked at itself and wondered.

The U.S. had money, brains, big universities, competent engineers, yet it had already been out-paced in a contest where to be second best was, at the beginning at least, to be the loser. Like it or not, the U.S. was being dragged by its heels into the race, not only in space, but to recoup its lost international prestige.

A principle Soviet asset had been a careful, long-term program leading to the conquest of space. Since 1934

RACE FOR SPACE BEGINS

USSR takes initial lead over U.S. with "Sputniks" satellites

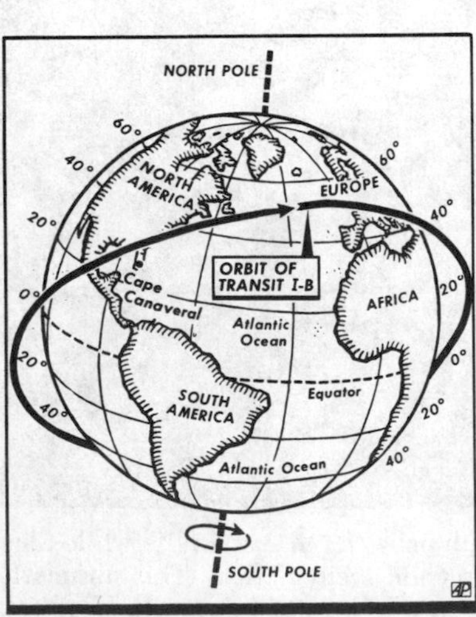

U.S. SATELLITE launched from Cape Canaveral April 13, 1960, circled the globe every 94 minutes—an average speed of approximately 17,000 miles per hour. Orbit passed over world's great oceans.

A. A. BLAGONRAVOV, chief Soviet satellite scientist, was in Washington for space "cooperation" conference when he electrified world with news that USSR had successfully launched a satellite.

they had had a full-scale rocket program. Top level space planners were a feature of centralized government planning. Stalin, himself, took a personal interest in missiles —one possible reason for emphasis on that branch of military research. Their scientists enjoyed the highest esteem, high pay, access to rationed luxuries and a preferred status that made them a "new elite."

In contrast, U.S. science professors often earned little more than university maintenance men. And, despite the enormous complexity of American technological life, they were still considered a group of oddities.

It was not that the U.S. had no rocket program. Since the middle of World War II, when the devastating power of the V-2 rockets was launched against England from Peenemunde on the north coast of Germany, the military services had been all too conscious of the incredible power behind the "rockets' red glare." A rocket research

AFTER VICTORY in orbiting 30.8 lb. Explorer I, anxious press gets questions answered by Dr. William Pickering (propulsion), Dr. James Van Allen (designer of scientific experiment), and Dr. Wernher von Braun, chief of Jupiter team.

program was initiated, but for more than 10 years it lacked most of the elements vital to success. It was a program without high priority, without assurance of continuing and generous financial support, and without a group of dedicated men in positions of authority.

In July, 1950, when the Atlantic Missile Test Center was inaugurated, the supporting equipment for the first "shoot" was not too much more elaborate than that used in the mid '20s on a Massachusetts field, when Robert Hutchins Goddard shot off the world's first liquid rocket. The 1950 missile-men crouched in a tarpaper bath-house fortified with sandbags and watched their 56 foot Bumper 8 rocket (made from the quick amalgam of an old V-2 and a WAC Corporal), surge off the pad, rise to a height of 50,000 ft. and plop safely into the Atlantic 200 miles away.

Since then, the Cape Canaveral site had become the Free World's greatest missile test center. Some 23,000 people worked on the 1500 acre launch area and the 12

AMERICAN EXPLORER I put the U.S. into the space game on January 31, 1958. The Army's Jupiter IRBM rocket performed perfectly in its first satellite-boosting task.

VISIT TO IOWA LAB by top Russian space scientists came in fall of 1959 after American Rocket Society meeting, when Academicians Sedov, Krassovsky and Blagonravov were invited by Dr. James Van Allen *(l.)* whose Explorer experiments discovered two giant bands of radiation around earth.

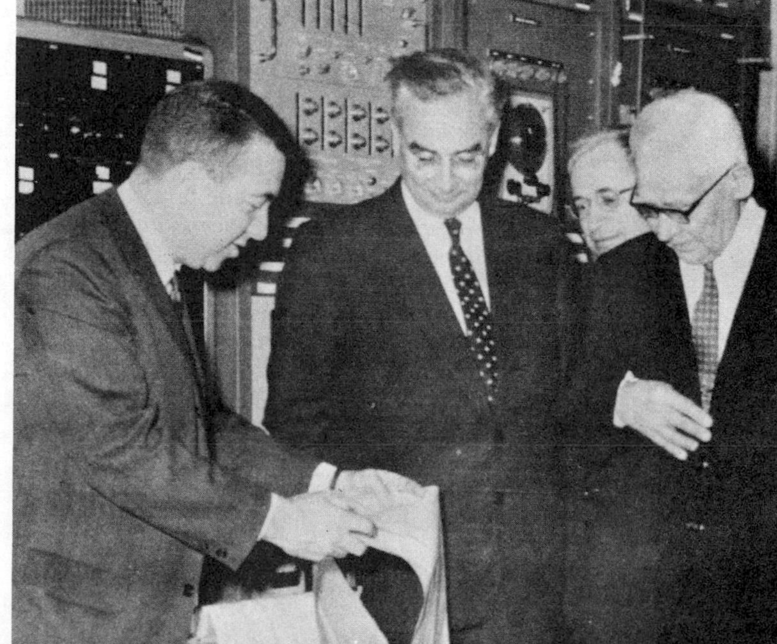

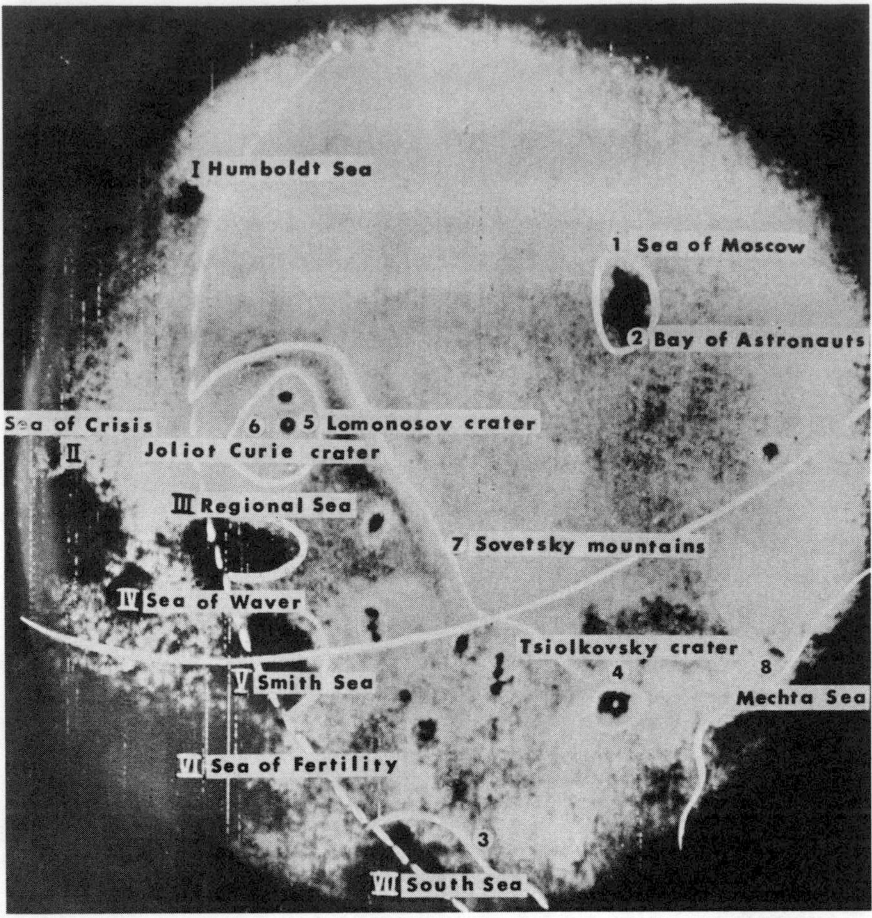

HIDDEN FACE OF MOON is shown for the first time after Soviet's second moon rocket (first hit on near side) relayed back 40 minutes of pictures shot when the satellite swung near dark side.

Dog, monkeys first voyagers

isolated sites on the 6000 mile flight range.

In 10 years over 800 missiles had been fired, mostly after 1954 (until then the experimental rocket program was, at best, rudimentary), when component flight testing began on Thor and Jupiter intermediate range ballistic missiles and the Atlas Intercontinental missile. All three of these military missiles, which in 1960 were "operational," had been used to boost scientific payloads in ballistic curves down the Atlantic range and into orbit. But in both the USSR and the U.S. military missile programs came first, scientific rocket research programs second.

At the time the Russians launched their Sputnik I into orbit they claimed that the Red Army had "at its disposal" an ICBM. Any doubts that the Reds did, in fact, have a giant rocket capable of long range target accuracy were dispelled when a 1200-lb. dog-carrying satellite hurtled into orbit early in November, 1957, boosted by 500,000 lbs. of thrust. The Atlas could only generate 360,000 lbs. but had successfully sent a nose cone into the Atlantic after traveling 1200 miles.

Early in December, 1957, the first U.S. satellite attempt failed. The slim 72-foot Vanguard rocket that was to have orbited a four-pound, six-inch satellite lifted four feet off the pad, settled back awkwardly on the beach, and exploded. In 1958 Werhner von Braun's Army Jupiter team successfully put the U.S. back into the race. A 31-lb. Explorer satellite, carrying cosmic ray counters, was looping around the earth once every 118 minutes. Six weeks later the Navy's Vanguard was successfully launched, equipped with batteries charged with energy from the sun. Its signals were still heard in 1960.

Studies of its orbit "drag" revealed that the earth, once thought to be a slightly oblate sphere, was actually shaped a little like a flat-bottomed pear. Space radiation was discovered to be a thousand times more intense than was expected.

In May, 1958, Moscow crowed about its Sputnik III, weighing one-and-one-half tons, and sneered at U.S. "grapefruit." To coordinate U.S. space efforts the National Aeronautics and Space Administration was created by Congress that summer.

Air Force Pioneer moon shots in the fall continued to fail, but reached a record 71,300 miles. An Atlas ICBM was orbited at Christmas, how-

ORBITING AT 450 MILES Tiros I, America's superb weather satellite, takes picture of the Red Sea and Mediterranean.

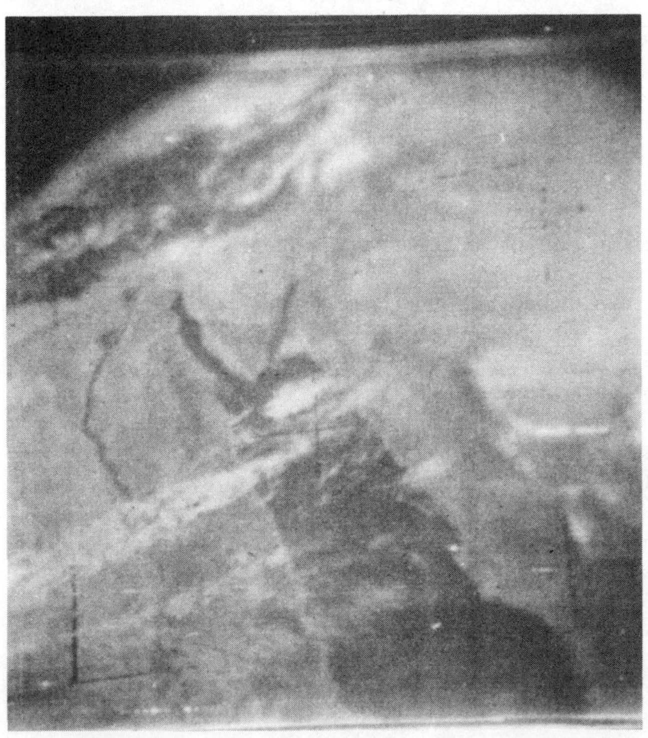

ever, and broadcast a human voice, "this is the President of the U.S. . . . Peace on Earth."

In 1959 man-made planets joined the galaxy. Bearing a plaque with the legend "USSR January, 1959," a 796-lb. cosmic rocket blasted free of the restraining forces of the earth's gravity field and circled in orbit around the sun. It was joined three months later by a Pioneer IV.

NASA announced in April, 1959, that seven experimental test pilots representing all the military services, would begin training as spacemen, one of whom would someday be thrust into space atop an Atlas in a two-ton Mercury capsule which would orbit earth four times at 18,000 mph, following which he would eject himself out of orbit and parachute back to the Atlantic Ocean. The expected date was "sometime in 1961."

In the late summer of 1959, Explorer VI was orbited carrying a TV scanner to take relay pictures of the earth's cloud cover.

Almost perversely, by mid-September, the Russians proudly announced that a vehicle with 860 pounds of equipment was "flying to the moon" at 37,500 mph. Fifty-nine hours after take-off, it hit, spreading pennants marked "USSR-September-1959-September" near the once inviolate "Sea of Serenity."

By November the world's newspapers and scientific journals carried on their lead pages a view of the "dark side" of the moon that no human eyes had ever seen before. Looping behind the moon, Lunik II's camera eye focused on the sunlit other side of the moon. A photocell scanner "broke up" the picture and transmitted it bit by bit over 300,000 miles to Moscow, where it was reassembled.

In January, and again in July, 1960, the Russians caused an international stir by sending "super rockets" 8000 miles into the Central Pacific. U.S. scientists specu-

"PRE-HUMAN" TEST was "boiler plate" Mercury capsule shown hoisted from Atlantic after a fifty mile trip through sky with Rhesus monkey Sam inside.

PRECEDING HUMAN ASTRONAUTS, trained animals were rocketed into space by both U.S., USSR, to determine what future hazards hostile space environment might present to man. "Space-monkey" Sam, *(l.)* pulled lever all during the capsule ride. Laika, the Soviet's "space-dog" *(c.)* became history's first space traveller aboard Sputnik II. She died seven days after blastoff from "oxygen starvation." "Able" monkey *(r.)* holds 'conference' after ride in Jupiter nose cone.

SWIMMING IN AIR, three pressure-suited Astronauts experience short period of weightlessness, or zero G, while plane executes parabolic curve. In orbit, first spaceman will spend four hours free of gravity's pull without harm, it is hoped. But possible situation cannot be tested on earth, where gravity prevails.

lated whether this was a prelude to recovery of a human space-traveler.

U.S. technology began to pay off in 1960. A Thor Able Air Force combination sent nearly a hundred pounds of cosmic ray counters, magnetometers, solar paddles into orbit around the sun. Before its second radio voice faded away, scientific data had been transmitted a staggering 27.5 million miles.

The Tiros weather satellite was then launched, and in its first three months had transmitted 25,000 "bird's eye" pictures of the weather from over 400 miles up.

This was followed by the successful launching of Transit navigational satellites. Looking like gaudy Christmas ornaments, the satellites, and later a full system, announced their position every minute in code.

Ships on the high seas, properly equipped, would be able to use the "man-made star" to chart their course with greater accuracy than in the past.

This would be a boon to missile-launching subs, which, to hit a target precisely, must be able to program their own position into the missile's computer guidance systems.

The near goal in the space struggle for both the U.S. and USSR was conquest of the moon. Although the Soviet Union held a definite lead at the decade's close, an awakened U.S. was striving to close the gap.

FIRST STAGE of the mighty Saturn rocket engine (von Braun with model) was tested in '60. Full rocket will be four times heftier than Soviet's had.

JET TRANSPORT ERA began January 1959 when Pan American World Airways inaugurated commercial service with the Boeing 707. Cruising at 600 mph, the giant jetliner could carry 175 tourist passengers NYC to Paris—3680 miles—in 7 hours.

JETS SHRINK WORLD

Atlantic crossing cut to seven hours, trans-U.S. to under five; traffic control problem grows; military planes increase range

PROGRESS in the field of aviation during the 50s changed the entire course of human development.

Jets screamed overhead with a familiar roar, scarcely attracting any attention. But that roar had made possible an overwhelming alteration in travel-time. In ten years the world had shrunk by one-half in terms of time.

The 1953 promise of 7-hour Atlantic flights and four and a half hour transcontinental dashes was a reality by the end of the decade. Pure jet airliners were carrying passengers between key cities in the U.S. and throughout the world. Advances in aviation had, in fact, made it often necessary for the traveler to spend as much time going to and from airports as flying halfway across the country—and the absurd situation was getting worse.

The same jets which devoured inter-city distances required larger and larger airports, land which no longer could be found within reasonable distances of cities.

Helicopters could take care of some of the problem by ferrying passengers downtown. After the first heliport was opened in New York City in 1956, the low rumble of the "whirlybirds" became an everyday part of the metropolitan zone.

Other VTOL (vertical takeoff and landing) techniques aimed at attaining speeds sufficiently high to cover short inter-urban hops efficiently. Tilting wings and tilting ducted propellers kept the cabin horizontal. The Ryan X-13 turbojet was one of the "tailsitters." In takeoff it zoomed directly upward; landing, it eased itself down, hooking its nose on a guide wire.

The Armed Services, eager to protect retaliatory power in the event of runway or flight-deck destruction, successfully used the brute force of rocket power to blast fighters 400 feet high at 300 mph, in three seconds.

Military fighters increased their range (and therefore

DISPUTED PILOT'S seat *(l.)* in cockpit of DC-8 jetliner (chief 707 competitor) led to pilots' strike protesting ruling of Federal Aviation Agency that FAA inspectors should ride behind pilot. E. R. "Mike" Quesada *(r.)*, first administrator of the new regulatory agency, charged that a "small hard core" of airline pilots was fighting his efforts to make aviation safer. Other FAA moves balked by pilots: compulsory retirement at 65; revision of seniority system to prevent older pilots from first flying (for higher salaries and better hours), the faster, newer models.

SLEEK SWEPT-BACK airframe marked the appearance of the Russian-built MIG-15 *(l.)*, capable of supersonic speed in level flight and of pulling away from the early versions of the F-86 Sabrejet fighter in Korean skies, but range and pilot safety were often sacrificed. Korea's final tally: 208 MIGs confirmed downed, 58 U.S. F-86s lost. Not until 1953 did the first U.S. supersonic combat F-100 Supersabre *(below)* with 50,000-foot ceiling and a combat range of more than 600 miles, give the USAF air superiority. This plane was followed by others in the F-100 series, the F-104, F-106.

their elusiveness) by re-fueling in mid-air. A "flying boom" from air tanker to fighter piped in jet fuel at 15,000 foot altitudes.

Even the infantryman, it seemed, would soon be taking to the air. Individual helicopter blades attached to the soldier's back and rocket-powered "jump belts," were offering more mobility than the traditional weary-soled "dog soldiers."

Military spending for aircraft, which accounted for 80% to 90% of the aircraft industry's sales in 1955, was going to the missile-makers. Fiscal 1960 aircraft expenditures were over half a billion down from the $7.1 billion of 1959, which in turn was a considerable drop from the '58 figure of $7.5. billion. Aircraft industry employment dropped 125,000 between 1957 and 1960.

The private plane industry boomed throughout the last half of the decade, as fast executive travel was made possible by 8,000 company aircraft. This swelled the sub-industry to $100 million proportions.

The need for traffic control became evident when two aircraft, mere specks when 10 miles apart, would meet in 36 seconds if flying at common speed of 500 mph. A 1957 survey of air traffic in New York City showed 123 planes in the air simultaneously. It was expected that this number would be quadrupled by 1975, a major problem for traffic specialists.

Commercial jet travel and utility flying were here to stay and, it was estimated, military flying would continue for at least another 15 years.

But space was the new realm. Man would be led there by the pioneering work of Scott Crossfield, test pilot of North American's X-15, which would take man to the borders of space at 4500 mph, and by the 7 Mercury Astronauts who would be rocketed into the black reaches of space by an Atlas ICBM.

Indicative of the changing spirit of the aircraft industry was the revision of the Institute of the Aeronautical Sciences' title — to Institute of the Aerospace Sciences.

HIGHEST JUMP in history was made in November, 1959, by AF Capt. Joe Kittinger from balloon 76,400 feet (15 miles) above New Mexico. His small drag chute failed to steady, slow his descent, so he fell for 13 miles at 423 mph through − 40° cold. At 10,000 feet his chute opened, his safe landing proving pilots could safely bail out above 55,000 feet altitude.

VERTICAL TAKEOFF and landing was close to a commercial reality with the British Fairey Rotodyne. The dual-prop aircraft has a rotor above fusilage for takeoff and landing and conventional propellers for horizontal flight. When put into operation, carrying 50 people, it will halve the present 4-hour plane-bus trip from London to Paris, France.

JET ACE Ivan C. Kincheloe, flew the fantastic, pint-size Bell X-2 rocket-plane to 126,200 feet (23.86 miles) for world altitude record. Later he said that the plane plummeted 86,000 feet in 62 seconds while the stick was completely ineffective. Slated to fly X-15, Kincheloe (with 10 MIG kills, 101 combat missions, 5 years testpiloting) died at 29 years of age on routine F-104 mission.

UNDER THE WING of its mother ship, a B-52 bomber, the X-15 rocket ship is carried safely to the necessary altitude for detachment and flight. On a given signal from monitoring system on the ground, the X-15 falls away rapidly to 4000 feet. After the initial loss of speed, the X-15 turns on the force that makes it the world's fastest manned plane.

DECADE ACCEPTS ABSTRACT ART

New forms, old classics, dominate '50s

"CHRISTOPHER COLUMBUS DISCOVERS AMERICA" was another forceful painting by cane-carrying mystic Spaniard Salvador Dali. Once a surrealist, he now insisted that he intended to concern himself more in the future with religious thought and art.

THE WORLD'S artistic eye was sharpened and shocked during the 1950s.

The decade began with frauds, fads and fancies. Patrons became artists by paying firms of "ghosts" to create works in their names. In the wake of increasing abstractionism, standards became so confused that monkeys and small children caused widespread interest by aimless spatterings of paint on cardboard.

In the U.S. a nation-wide clamor for western art began when the famous art collection of cowboy painter Charles M. Russell was bought by a Texas oilman. The stampede for range art was on.

Diego Rivera, famed Mexican left-winger, continued to produce red-tinged frescos until his death in 1958. Among them was "Nightmare of War and the Dream of Peace," which portrayed U.S. soldiers crucifying Korean workers.

Across the Pacific, moderns under the guidance of Hasui Kawase and Shinsui Ito, in complete contrast to such early Japanese classicists as Hiroshige who painted landscapes in the traditional manner, developed a new national school called Nippon-Ga (Japanese Style). Other Japanese like Kiyoshi Saito followed European styles, much to the distaste of some Japanese critics.

The slight political thaw behind the "Iron Curtain" permitted Polish artists to turn from "Socialist Realism" to Impressionism and Abstractionism.

By mid-decade amateur art had gained new and unprecedented popularity. The most noted exhibitors were Pres. Dwight D. Eisenhower and Sir Winston Churchill.

Art interest had reached a new peak by 1956. Over one million people flocked to Rotterdam in the Netherlands to see a $50 million collection of paintings by the famous Dutch artist, Rembrandt, shown to celebrate his 350th anniversary.

Jacques Villon, 80-year-old French cubist, captured the painting prize at the 1956 Venice Biennale, the largest international art show. The award for sculpture went to Great Britain's Lynn Chadwick; for engraving to Japan's Shiko Munakata and for drawing to Brazil's Aldemir Martins.

French archaeologists discovered 6000-year-old ivory sculptures and the sculptor's studio in Israel's Negev desert. Other Gallic "diggers" uncovered at Tassilli, in the African Sahara, skilled rock paintings which were executed between 8000 and 3000 B.C.

In Munich the famed Alte Pinakothek museum was opened to the public. Closed since 1939, it had been completely destroyed in a 1944 bombing. The rebuilt structure displayed its 900 original masterpieces, which had been preserved for the duration of the war in a salt-mine.

By 1960, welded, twisted or hammered steel, bronze and chrome emerged into elegant patterns and often intricate, confused forms of sculpture. The 10 years ended as they had begun, with art that claimed to reflect the confusion and chaos of the atomic age in which it was born.

"CHRISTINA'S WORLD" was painted by Andrew Wyeth. His masterful use of egg temper and "magic realism" made the Pennsylvanian the highest paid living artist.

"JUNGLE" by Irish-born New Yorker Colleen Browning captures slum's spirit and exemplifies new tradition in modern realism. Swiss cubist Paul Klee's "Departure of Ships" *(r.)* was one of his paintings which gained him popularity.

"OCEAN GREYNESS" typifies the work of the late leader of the "drip" school, Jackson Pollock. Although his canvases were often under heavy criticism, his new style brought him fame and widespread influence. He died in an auto crash in 1956.

Wide promotion by U.S. museums and the leadership of such artists as American abstractionist Jackson Pollack gave to modern and abstract works increased popular acceptance in the art world. Around the globe millions gathered in bewildered interest to view "nouveau art."

Such abstract ceramic murals, as "The Wall of the Moon" by Joan Miro and Josep Llorens Artigas decorated the UNESCO Palace in Paris, supplanted traditional wall decorations depicting man and beast.

Artist Frenchman Bernard Buffet created a sensation by personifying post-war man and life with modern interpretations.

Moderns and impressionists of the 19th Century like Claude Monet, father of impressionism, and Georges Seurat, founder of pointillism, continued to grow in importance. "Portrait of a Young Woman," by Frenchman Amedeo Modigliani, was sold at Sotheby's Galleries, London, in 1960 for $67,000. Paul Cezanne's "Peasant in a Blue Blouse," was bought at the same gallery in 1959 for $406,000. Paul Gauguin's "I Await the Letter," at the same sale brought $364,000, the highest ever paid for a French post-impressionist at a public auction. A portrait of "Mr. and Mrs. Robert Andrews" by Englishman Thomas Gainsborough was sold at Sotheby's in 1960 for the same amount.

After criticism and disrepute. modern artists and their work were finally endorsed universally. The acceptance carried so much impetus that traditional and classical works were often slighted or overlooked completely.

"COMPOSITION #3" by Russian pioneer abstractionist Wassily Kandinsky was painted in 1914. It was finally shown in 1956 and re-evaluated along with three other works at tens of thousands.

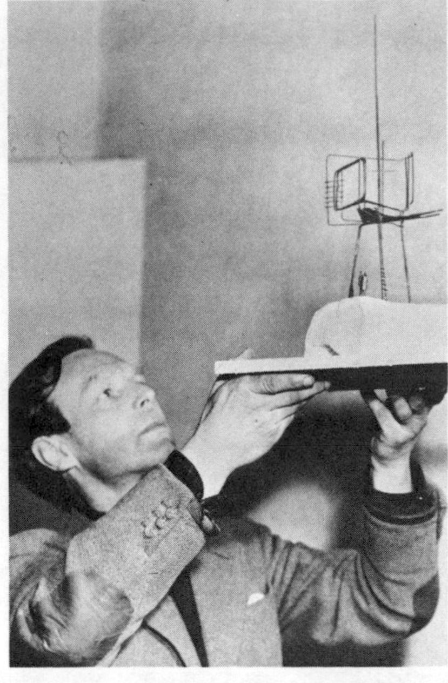

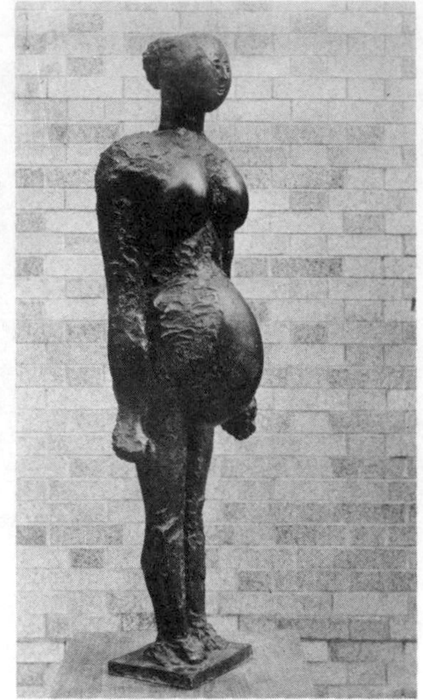

"CLASS CONSCIOUSNESS" typifies work of controversial Sir Jacob Epstein, who died in 1959. Admirers considered him greatest modern sculptor. Object of Epstein's scorn was Reg Butler, whose "Political Prisoner" *(above)* won $32,000 prize.

"PREGNANT WOMEN," by world famous Spaniard Pablo Picasso, represents his shift to sculpture from abstract work.

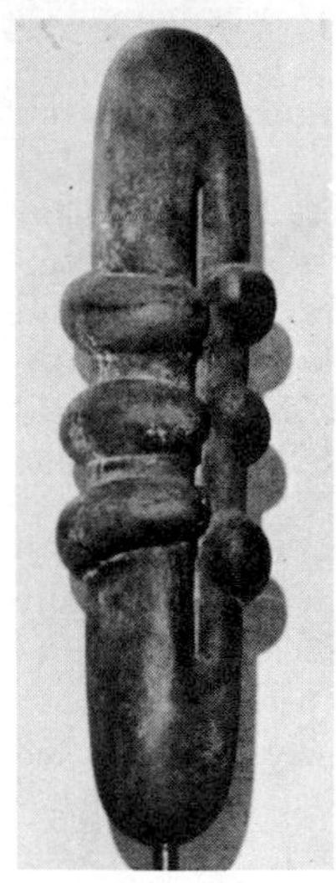

"THE SELF," a rust-brown iron sculpture by Japanese Isama Noguchi, won the 1959 Logan Award at the Chicago Art Institute. Italian Marino Marini's bronze "Curt Valentin" *(below)* represented trend toward detailless figures.

Sculpture Regains World Popularity

One focus of interest during the decade was sculpture.

Such smooth, detail-lacking stone representations as the West German sculptress Katherine Singer's "Rubble Women," which typified the thousands of German women who cleared tons of debris from war-torn Berlin, have become common in public parks and galleries.

Great Britain's Henry Moore, at first considered a "revolutionary," became the leader of the "smooth school" and achieved recognition when he was commissioned to carve a symbol of family life which he entitled "Family Group." Completed in 1956, it was placed in Harlow in Hertfordshire, Great Britain.

The popularity of such welded metal sculpture as "The Devil With Claws," a rough bronze statue by Germaine Richier, also increased during the past ten year period.

"STEEL WELDED KING," by Barbara Lekberg, won recognition at a showing in Sculpture Center, New York. "Family Group" *(below)* was carved by Moore.

BERNARD BERENSON, U.S.-educated Lithuanian-born art critic, authority on Italian Renaissance paintings, died in Italy at 94 in 1959. Great collections were built on famed savant's advice.

"WATER LILIES," valued at $1 million was totally destroyed in a fire that caused $320,000 worth of damage at New York City's Museum of Modern Art in 1959. It was painted by one of the world-renowned French Impressionists, Claude Monet. Other Monet paintings were exhibited at the Museum of Modern Art in 1960.

Both deaths of famous artists and the discovery of lost and hidden masterpieces were seen in the decade.

Notable among those who died, was one of the foremost U.S. painters, John Marin, a water colorist. He influenced his field with unique, chart-like linear effect paintings.

On the West Coast the finding of "Leda and the Swan," a painting believed to be by 16th Century Italian, Paolo Cagliar Veronese, caused universal interest. But some experts, both in the U.S. and England, held that the reported $1 million find was merely a copy.

A dozen Rembrandt etchings, valued at $4000-$5000 for the group, were found in two books purchased for $10 by a San Francisco commercial artist. The volumes were part of a 1200-book shipment from England to the United States.

In 1959 a bust of Cosimo dé Medici, Renaissance ruler of Florence, was found after a two-year search by Dr. Walter Heil, director of the M. H. Young Memorial Museum. The $500,000 portrait sculpture was the work of 16th century Italian sculptor Benvenuto Cellini.

An original "Madonna and Child," work by Leonardo da Vinci, was found in 1956 in a New York antique shop. It was valued at $1 million.

The period of artistic discovery was brought to a close in 1960 with the announcement of the finding, in Mexico, of the oldest American art. Impressions of animals were found by Dr. Jaun Armenta on a 30,000-year-old mastodon pelvic bone fossil.

"CHRIST MOCKED BY SOLDIERS," was painted by French religious-expressionist Georges Roualt. He died at 87 in 1958. Henri Matisse *(below)*, modern French painter, died Nov. 4, 1954. During his life he had survived criticism to become France's most respected master.

"RAPE OF DIJANIRO" by Italian Luca Giordano, was one of ten Renaissance paintings found in a Pasadena, Calif. home, claimed to be worth $10 million.

A SENSATIONAL FIND, of original and forceful painting by Spanish artist Francisco Goya, was valued at $6000. It turned up in a Bilboa, Spain art shop.

PAPERBACKS, BESTSELLERS, DOMINATE '50s

Themes range from learned to lurid

CARL SANDBURG, still active in his early eighties, published his early autobiography *Always the Young Strangers* at 75. Later he received awards from the Poetry Society of America and recognition for his 1953 publication *Abraham Lincoln.*

NOBEL PRIZE for literature went to Sir Winston Churchill for his six-volume "personal narrative" of World War II. *Triumph and Tragedy* told of the final conferences with Truman and Stalin and the breakup of the powerful wartime alliance.

By the end of the 1950s, book publishing, after seven years of steady improvement, for the first time topped the $1 billion mark. First-class reading was available in a profusion notable for its variety and vitality. Although the U.S. reading public decreased from 21% of the total population to 17%, as a result of the advent of television, publishing houses declared that at the close of the decade sales had increased by 60% over '52 figures. The volume of books sold annually rose well past 550 million. Many of the books sold were condensed (the Reader's Digest Condensed Book Club alone distributed 16.5 million books in one quarter) or book-club editions (64 million copies in 1958). Neither of these put dollars into the tills of bookstores.

All that was published was not good. Many lurid, badly written and often dull works were found in the bookstalls. *From Here to Eternity*, a top seller by James Jones, and Herman Wouk's Pulitzer Prize winner *The Caine Mutiny*, along with *The Cruel Sea* by Nicholas Monsarrat, were among the better books. *The Cardinal,* by Henry Morton Robinson, out-sold all other fiction in the early '50s. J. D. Salinger's first novel, *The Catcher in the Rye*, made a smashing hit. Giuseppe di Lampedusa's *The Leopard*, published posthumously in 1960, was enthusiastically received and scored a sweeping success. Small town America appeared in James Gould Cozzens' *By Love Possessed*, and big-town Washington was dissected in Allen Drurys' *Advise and Consent.*

One of the most important literary pieces to steal past the Iron Curtain was the late Russian Boris Pasternak's novel *Doctor Zhivago*, which was first printed in Italy in 1954. The Nobel Prize was offered to Pasternak for the novel but Party pressure forced him to refuse the honor.

John O'Hara's *From the Terrace*, a long chronicle of the status and sex of 20th Century man, sold briskly. But despite public approval, some of his critics believed that this was his poorest work.

Interest in authenticated and colorful historical works continued through the 1950s. Garrett Mattingly's *The Armada* jumped to prominence on the best seller lists. *Exodus,* Leon Uris' glowing saga of the birth of Israel provoked Prime Minister David Ben Gurion to comment, "As a literary work it isn't much, but as a piece of propaganda, it's the greatest thing ever written about Israel." It was scooped up by millions and increased Israel's tourist rate by 11%.

Diaries, memoirs and biographies poured from the printing presses. *The Diary of Anne Frank* (written by a Jewish teenager while she and her family hid from the Nazis in occupied Amsterdam) recaptured for the '50s the horrors of World War II. Anne died in a death camp.

Old military and political campaigners, with the advantage of hindsight, returned to re-fight World War II controversies in a flood of memoirs. Great Britain's Field Marshal Lord Montgomery fired a volley at General Eisenhower for what he claimed was mis-management of the European campaign. Sir Winston Churchill in 1953 completed his six-volume personal history of World War II with *Triumph and Tragedy*. His latest monumental work was the third volume of *The History of the English Speaking People*, published in 1958.

Another book of lasting importance and enduring beauty was Anne Morrow Lindbergh's collection of reminiscences, *Gift from the Sea*.

Adventure-seeking readers scaled the heights of Everest with Sir Edmund Hillary in *The Conquest of Everest. The Spirit of Saint Louis*, a gripping narrative by Charles A. Lindbergh, vicariously carried thousands across the Atlantic.

A new trend in cold realism emerged during the decade. Such vivid, vibrant works as Ernest Hemingway's Pultizer Prize winner *The Old Man and The Sea* and Lawrence Durrell's latest Alexandrian novel, *Clea*, led the market.

The first book ever printed, *The Holy Bible*, remained the world's best seller. Early in the '50s the *Revised Standard Version* brought denunciations from fundamentalist Protestant sects. They complained that this new edition of *The King James Version* altered traditional interpretations.

Inspirational books of both religious and philosophical intent were very much in demand. The most successful was Norman Vincent Peale's all-time best seller *The Power of Positive Thinking.*

The musty campaigns of the Civil War were given fresh reinforcement by such Pulitzer prize winners as MacKinlay Kantor's novel *Andersonville* and Bruce Catton's *A Stillness at Appomattox*. The endless flow of works on Lincoln was highlighted by Benjamin P. Thomas' *Abraham Lincoln*. Carl Sandburg, in 1953, published his prize-winning *Abraham Lincoln.*

The decade, gaining a multitude of books, also lost great men. The great playwright George Bernard Shaw died in 1950. Eugene O'Neill, who died in 1953, was awarded his fourth Pulitzer Prize for *Long Day's Journey Into Night*. This was the first time the prize was ever given posthumously. Frenchman André Gide died in 1951 and H. L. Mencken, quackery lambaster, died in 1956.

FRENCH EXISTENTIALIST Albert Camus gained wide U.S. audience with *The Fall*, symbolic masterpiece relating man's (i.e., Lucifer's) heritage of guilt.

BORIS PASTERNAK "refused" a Nobel prize for *Doctor Zhivago*, story of individual's reactions to Soviet Revolution. He died of cancer in Russia in 1960.

SUPERMARKET-STYLE BOOKSTORES began to crop up all over the country—places where, for 25¢ to $1.95 people could buy quality paperback reprints or originals. Perhaps the outstanding facet of the book publishing business was the mushrooming of paperback books into a $60 million business—300 million copies under 1912 titles.

ERNEST HEMINGWAY *(shown above with his wife)* received first Pulitzer Prize of his long career for his short, vivid saga of a fisherman and a fish: *The Old Man and the Sea.* In 1955 the same book won him the Nobel Prize for literature.

NORMAN VINCENT PEALE'S book, *The Power of Positive Thinking*, set an all-time record of 186 weeks on the best-seller list. He suggested everyday problems of living can be successfully overcome with faith, prayer and positive thoughts.

A "PERMANENT FIXTURE" in Western intellectual life disappeared in 1952. George Santayana died in Rome at 88. A brilliant outpouring of poems, letters and philosophy showed his search for a civilized, permissive attitude toward life.

AN EIGHTY-FIFTH BIRTHDAY cake feted the strong, witty, wise, four-time Pulitzer Prize winner, Robert Frost. Since 1915 he had earned his living (a million volumes sold) as a poet. "I write for two reasons: to be quoted and talked about."

HAROLD ROSS, editor of *New Yorker,* died in '51, was affectionately portrayed in *The Years With Ross* by James Thurber, who also wrote *Wonderful O.*

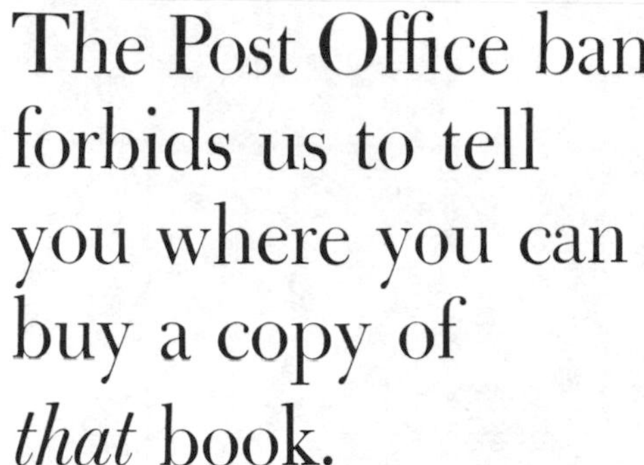

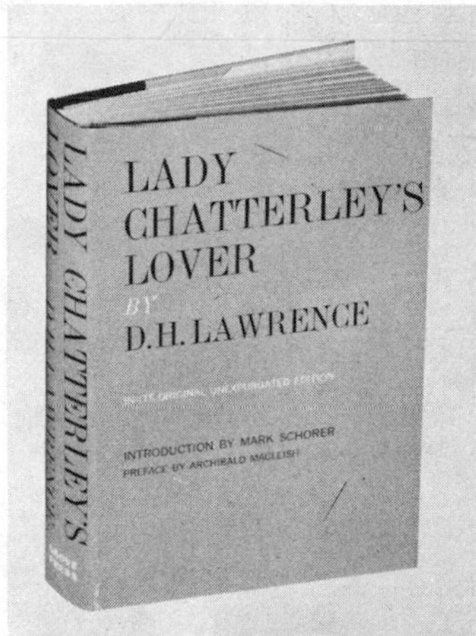

"THAT BOOK" was the unexpurgated edition of D. H. Lawrence's *Lady Chatterley's Lover*—a book which, for 31 years, had been banned in the U.S. When the Grove Press published it in the spring of 1959 the Post Office banned it from the mails due to explicit sexual language. A federal court upset ban—"that" book was legal.

RELEASE FROM TREASON indictment, 13 years in mental hospital came at 72 to Poet Ezra Pound. Accused of WW II treason, he later went to Italy.

VLADIMIR NABOKOV'S witty, well-written tale of a middle-aged man's affair with *Lolita,* his 12-year-old "nymphet," shocked its way to best-seller success.

ENFANT TERRIBLE Françoise Sagan, who published *Bonjour Tristesse* at 18, finished off three more novels, a ballet, a play and her marriage in five years.

29-YEAR-OLD EX-BOXER James Jones' *From Here to Eternity,* written in a house trailer, sold four million copies in seven years. Robert E. Lee Prewitt's life in Hawaii's Schofield Barracks reflected the seaminess and the heroic, the comradeship and the brutality, of life in Uncle Sam's peacetime army before the Pearl Harbor attack.

NEW ERA began for the N.Y. Philharmonic with the appointment of Leonard Bernstein as music director. The still-young maestro also won acclaim as *West Side Story* composer, TV performer.

SOUND OF SUCCESS

A changing musical scene arouses increasing interest, large audience

DEFENDERS of the cultural level of the U.S. eagerly seized on a statistic announced early in the '50s; Americans were spending more money for concert-hall admissions than for baseball tickets.

There were other signs, too, of the increasing interest in music. The number of orchestras in the U.S. rose to over 700 during the decade. The publishers of the *Schwann Long Playing Record Catalog* reported in 1958 that the booming record industry was releasing some 400 new LP records a month. The terms "hi-fi" and "stereo" became a part of everyday language. Summer music festivals, long a special European attraction, began to spring up from Vancouver, B. C., to Newport, R. I. and offered vacationers their choice of opera, symphonies, folk music, jazz or chamber music.

In the orchestral world, three famous ensembles made news. The Chicago Symphony Orchestra found a new lease on life under the baton of Fritz Reiner, who became its conductor in 1954. In similar fashion, the New York Philharmonic was rejuvenated by its new director, Leonard Bernstein, who also brought new life to the Carnegie Hall box office. Composing, conducting, playing the piano and harpsichord, writing *(The Joy of Music)*, lecturing (in the concert hall and on television), the inexhaustible Bernstein was probably the most talked-about musician of the decade.

The NBC Symphony suffered an irreparable loss when Arturo Toscanini, saying, "The sad time has come. . . ." laid down his baton in 1954. The orchestra reorganized itself as the Symphony of the Air and performed without any conductor until after the Maestro's death in 1957.

Ending his tenure as music critic of the *New York Times* with the end of the decade, Howard Taubman became the paper's drama critic. He was succeeded as music critic by Harold C. Schonberg.

Opera lovers generally agreed with

END OF AN ERA came when Arturo Toscanini retired in 1954 after 68 years on the podium. Final years were spent as conductor of the NBC Symphony, an orchestra created especially for him.

UNEXPECTED TREAT for opera lovers waiting to buy standing-room tickets for the Met's 1955 season opening was free coffee dispensed by Met general manager Rudolph Bing. Sale of subscriptions reached a new high during the first decade (1950-60) of Bing's tenure as manager, and the majority of revivals, new productions and new singers he introduced met with favorable reaction from both critics and public.

SOPRANO MARIA CALLAS AS NORMA

SOPRANO RENATA TEBALDI AS TOSCA

Lively Decade at the Metropolitan

critic Howard Taubman, who summed up the first 10 years of Rudolph Bing's career as general manager of the Metropolitan Opera as a "provocative and often exciting decade."

Although the repertoire of the Bing decade was not particularly adventurous, several important contemporary works received Met premieres, notably Alban Berg's *Wozzeck*, Igor Stravinsky's *The Rake's Progress,* and Samuel Barber's *Vanessa.*

TRAGIC FINALE to the career of great baritone Leonard Warren came on Mar. 3, 1960. Appearing as Don Carlo *(below)* in *La Forza del Destino,* he collapsed on stage, died minutes later.

Perhaps the greatest excitement, however, was aroused by four headline-making debuts.

With the 1955 debut of Marian Anderson as Ulrica in *Un Ballo in Maschera,* the Met's color line was broken. Dispelling any suspicion that this was only a sentimental gesture in tribute to the contralto's international reputation, Bing proceeded to engage three other Negro singers (Mattiwilda Dobbs, Gloria Davy, Leontyne Price) in the following years.

The Met's Italian wing was brightened by the debuts of Renata Tebaldi (1955) and Maria Callas (1957), although the latter parted company with the Met in 1959 following a row with manager Bing, and won as many headlines for her temperamental outbursts as for her singing. Newest debut sensation was Birgit Nilsson, whose Isolde was greeted with an avalanche of critical superlatives and gave new hope to Wagnerians.

The impressive list of outstanding newcomers during the decade also included Victoria de los Angeles, Roberta Peters, Leonie Rysanek, Giulietta Simionato, Mario del Monaco, Cesare Siepi and George London.

NEWEST MET STAR BIRGIT NILSSON

PRECEDENT-SETTER MARIAN ANDERSON

PERSONAL TRIUMPHS in the U.S.-USSR cultural exchange program were won by Soviet ballerina Galina Ulanova *(l.)* and U.S. pianist Van Cliburn *(above)*. Ulanova was hailed a "true wonder of her time" by U.S. critics. Cliburn's Moscow triumph brought him a New York ticker-tape welcome, the first time that honor had ever been extended to a musician.

Musical Thaw in Cold War

The U.S. and the USSR found at least one topic on which they could agree during the decade: both nations produce first-rate musical talents.

The USSR led off in the cultural exchange program instituted in the '50s by sending three of its finest instrumentalists to the U.S. in 1956—pianist Emil Gilels, violinist David Oistrakh and cellist Mstislav Rostropovich. They were received with cheers from packed houses and delighted critics, while in Moscow Soviet music lovers were giving an equally warm reception to U.S. tenor Jan Peerce and violinist Isaac Stern.

Eugene Ormandy (in 1958) and Leonard Bernstein (in 1959) led the Philadelphia and New York Philharmonic orchestras, respectively, through successful engagements in the Soviet Union. The first Soviet orchestra to be heard in the U.S., the Moscow State Symphony, arrived during the 1959-60 season.

Moscow cheered U.S. singers in *Porgy and Bess*, and New York applauded Soviet baritone Pavel Lisitsian (singing in Russian) in a Metropolitan Opera performance of *Aida* (sung in Italian).

Enthusiastic U.S. audiences competed in one of the fiercest ticket races on record to see Moscow's famed Bolshoi Ballet and its almost legendary prima ballerina, Galina Ulanova, in 1959. Enthusiastic Soviet audiences catapulted a little-known U.S. pianist, Van Cliburn, into international fame in 1958, when he won first place in the International Tchaikovsky Piano Competition. Neither a dancer's grace nor a pianist's virtuosity seemed affected by political theories of the day in any country.

NEW HOME *(l.)* for N.Y. Philharmonic was under construction in 1960, will be the first structure in new Lincoln Center for the Performing Arts. Orchestra's planned departure from Carnegie Hall threatened destruction of the historic building, but a "Save Carnegie Hall" drive succeeded in winning city and state help needed to save the landmark.

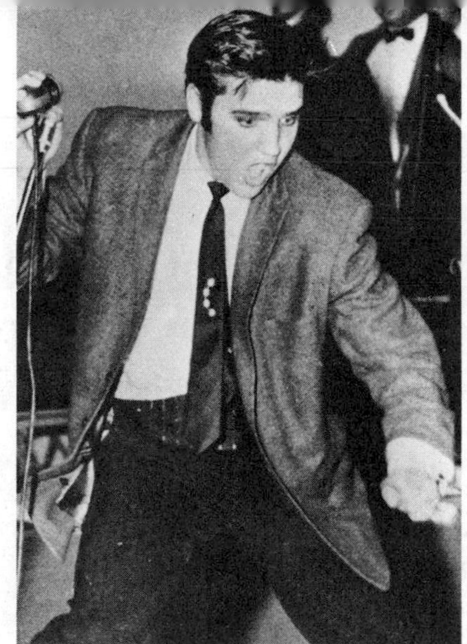

POPULAR MUSIC field was overwhelmed by the rock 'n' roll craze. First and biggest rock 'n' roll success was Elvis Presley *(r.)* whose hip-swinging gyrations shocked parents, delighted teens.

The music scene in the '50s contained something to suit almost any taste. Furthermore, it contained something to offend almost any taste.

In the field of popular music, the great success was rock 'n' roll. A mixture of unvarying rhythm and often suggestive lyrics, rock 'n' roll developed an enormous and frenzied following, chiefly among teen-agers. The antics of rock 'n' roll performers, and the wild enthusiasm of their audiences, produced cries of alarm and condemnation from some adults, with no discernible effect on rock 'n' roll's popularity.

Jazz, which had shocked an earlier generation in much the same way as rock 'n' roll, continued to become more and more respectable. Jazz combos turned up with increasing frequency in staid concert and recital halls, and a church in Connecticut made news by serving communion to the accompaniment of a "Jazz Mass." Some of the ground gained toward respectability was lost in the summer of 1960 when youths unable to crash Newport's Jazz Festival broke into a riot. Marines from the Newport Naval Base had to be called in, and the remainder of the festival was cancelled.

Folk music, previously given little attention in the U.S., began to attract a devoted and increasingly large following. Folk song artists began filling recital halls—and making money. Biggest success of the group was ex-pop singer Harry Belafonte, whose arrangements outraged purists.

Devotees of "longhair" music continued their age-old controversy over the quality of contemporary composers. Some admirers of the early music of veteran composer Igor Stravinsky were disappointed in the increasing tendency toward atonality displayed in the composer's newest works; others were encouraged by the same tendency. Much further "out" than Stravinsky, however, was the music of John Cage and others of his school. A Cage concert featured such musical instruments as a bathtub full of water, a group of radios (turned off and on at random), tape recorders and "prepared" pianos. Opinions varied as to whether the result was the latest thing in music, or just shouldn't be considered music at all.

NEW MUSIC continued to flow from the pen of composer Igor Stravinsky *(l.)*. The output of the 78-year-old composer in the '50s included a cantata (in 1952), *Threni*, based on the Lamentations of Jeremiah (1957-8), a septet (1953) and opera *The Rake's Progress*.

FOLK MUSIC field was entered by singer Harry Belafonte (r.) with tremendous success. His performances featured carefully planned costumes, lighting and staging combined with effective arrangements of folk song material. Purists were outraged; audiences loved it.

HIGH COST OF HITS

Expensive productions, established stars dominate decade as ticket prices soar to Broadway sky; foreign troupes add variety; off-Broadway wins new audiences

The critics, amateur and professional, spent most of the '50s bewailing the decline of the U.S. theater.

Nevertheless, there was hardly a season in which a reasonably discriminating playgoer did not have a choice among at least two or three really good plays (often, admittedly, of foreign origin), half a dozen solidly entertaining ones and several colorful and tuneful musical shows.

Broadway's biggest problem was, undeniably, the old one of money.

Sky-high production costs made "angels" extremely wary about backing any play, however artistically sound, not promising sure success.

And tickets were so expensive ($8.60 for an orchestra seat at an evening performance was not exceptional, and it was hard to find any seat at any time for under $2.50) that theater-going became a luxury for many who would have liked to make it a habit.

However, Broadway ticket prices and the built-in conservatism of the hit system were partially responsible for the exciting revival of "off-Broadway" theater.

In converted movie houses, basements and lofts all over Manhattan, small companies on shoestring budgets offered revivals of the classics, *avant garde* works by established contemporary playwrights and new plays by new writers.

Theater-goers of the '50s had another new development to applaud in the increasing frequency of visits by such outstanding foreign companies as the Comedie Francaise and the Jean-Louis Barault-Madeleine Renaut repertory company from France, the Old Vic from England, the Moiseyev dancers and Bolshoi Ballet from the Soviet Union and the Grand Kabuki from Japan.

Established stars like Helen Hayes, Katherine Cornell, Shirley Booth, the Lunts, the Oliviers and, on the musical stage, Mary Martin, Ethel Merman and Gertrude Lawrence (until her death in 1953) still made news.

So did new plays by established playwrights like Tennessee Williams, Arthur Miller and Lillian Helman, and new musicals by Cole Porter and Rogers and Hammerstein.

But the decade had its share of new talent, too. Yul Brynner rose to stardom in *The King and I*, Audrey Hepburn in *Gigi*, Julie Harris in *I Am A Camera*, Geraldine Page in *Summer and Smoke*, Julie Andrews in *The Boy Friend*, Gwen Verdon in *Damn Yankee*, Susan Strasberg in *The Diary of Anne Frank*, Anne Bancroft in *Two for the Seesaw.*

Among the promising new playwrights of the '50s were William Inge *(Picnic, Bus Stop, The Dark at the Top of The Stairs)*; Englishmen John Osborne *(Look Back in Anger)*, Peter Shaffer *(Five Finger Exercise)*; and Lorraine Hansbury *(Raisin in the Sun)*, first Negro Broadway author.

THEATRICAL WORLD threw a party at one of its favorite hangouts, Sardi's, for *N.Y. Times* drama critic Brooks Atkinson in 1958. *(Above,* guest of honor watches as Helen Hayes embraces Mrs. Atkinson.) The party marked Atkinson's 33rd year as an aisle-sitter; he went into retirement two years later.

BEST MUSICAL of the decade—and, many of its admirers insisted, of any decade—was *My Fair Lady*, the Alan Jay Lerner-Frederick Loewe adaptation of Shaw's *Pygmalion*. For many months after its 1956 opening, practically the only way to get a ticket was to join box office queue *(below)* at four in the morning. Rex Harrison and Julie Andrews (who had skyrocketed to stardom a year before in *The Boy Friend)* were the original characters of Henry Higgins, Liza Doolittle.

THREE PENNY OPERA proved that an off-beat, off-Broadway show could be a Broadway-style box office hit. A revival of a bitter, touching, iconoclastic and irresistibly funny German musical play of the '20s (music by Kurt Weill, book by Bertholdt Brecht) it was translated and adapted by Marc Blitzstein. After a brief first run at Greenwich Village's Theatre de Lys, it reopened there in 1956, was still running in 1960. For a time, it starred Weill's widow, Lotte Lenya.

DIARY OF ANNE FRANK starred 17-year-old Susan Strasberg as the teen-age Jewish victim of Nazi persecution whose real diary was basis of play, Joseph Schildkraut as her father. It was most successful serious offering of the 1955-56 season.

TENNESSEE WILLIAMS was in top form as he returned to his favorite theme, the seamy side of Southern life, in Pulitzer-Prize winning *Cat on a Hot Tin Roof.* It starred Barbara Bel Geddes, Ben Gazzara, Burl Ives, was directed by Elia Kazan.

No two theater-goers would agree on any list of the best plays of the decade; but among those that won popular and critical acclaim were:

1950-1951: *The Rose Tattoo; The Moon Is Blue; Guys and Dolls; Call Me Madam; The King and I.*

1951-52: brightening an exceptionally poor year, Shaw's *Caesar and Cleopatra* and Shakespeare's *Antony and Cleopatra*, presented on alternate nights by Sir Laurence Olivier and Vivian Leigh; another Shaw revival, *Saint Joan; Mrs. McThing*, a fine vehicle for Helen Hayes.

1952-53: *Time of the Cuckoo; Picnic; The Crucible; The Children's Hour* (revival); *Wonderful Town.*

1953-54: *Tea and Sympathy; Teahouse of the August Moon; Ondine; Pajama Game; Solid Gold Cadillac.*

1954-55: *Cat On a Hot Tin Roof; Bus Stop; The Rainmaker; The Desperate Hours; Witness for the Prosecution; The Boy Friend; Damn Yankees.*

1955-56: *Diary of Anne Frank; Waiting for Godot; Tiger at the Gates; The Lark; My Fair Lady.*

1956-57: *Visit to a Small Planet; Waltz of the Toreadors; Long Day's Journey Into Night; Bells Are Ringing.*

1957-58: *The Visit; Time Remembered; The Dark at the Top of the Stairs; Look Homeward, Angel; Look Back in Anger; Two for the Seesaw; West Side Story; Music Man.*

1958-59: *Raisin in the Sun; Sweet Bird of Youth; J.B.; A Touch of the Poet; Take Me Along; La Plume de Ma Tante.*

1959-60: *Five Finger Exercise; Toys in the Attic; The Miracle Worker; Fiorello; Bye Bye Birdie; Sound of Music.*

OUTSTANDING EVENT of the 1958-59 season was *J.B.*, a modern retelling of the story of Job by poet Archibald MacLeish. Pat Hingle gave a brilliant performance in the title role.

DAMON RUNYAN'S Broadway characters of the '30s delighted theater-goers of the '50s in *Guys and Dolls*, one of the decade's best musicals. Its stars were Vivian Blaine, Robert Alda *(center*, white tie), Sam Levene (in pin stripe suit). Frank Loesser wrote the score; choreography was by Michael Kidd; George Kaufmann was the director. Producers Cy Feuer and Ernest H. Martin raked in close to $700,000 on advance sales, settled back to enjoy long, prosperous run.

FILMS REEL IN TV GALE

Stress shifts to fewer, better pictures as costs mushroom, theater attendance drops

As the curtain rose on the '50s, the movies were down for the count of nine. Strong left hook of the brash new challenger, TV, had made itself felt.

1951 rang with the hollow echo of empty movie houses—55 closed down in Manhattan alone that year, 64 in Chicago and 134 in the Southern California area.

Jittery movie moguls were reluctantly weighing the possibilities of some sort of alliance with TV and, at the same time, experimenting with wide screen and three-dimensional techniques which promised to provide the much needed shot-in-the-arm. By 1954 the success of 20th Century's Cinemascope, with its wide angle curving screen, was firmly established; Paramount's Vista Vision and Todd-AO processes were runners-up.

Having decided, "if you can't lick 'em, join 'em," most of the major studios had made their peace with TV by 1955. Warner Bros. and Metro-Goldwyn-Mayer signed to make films for the American Broadcasting Co., 20th Century signed with the Columbia Broadcasting System, Columbia and Paramount formed their own TV subsidiaries.

Drastic economy measures brought an end to the stable system, under which studios kept a large number of stars under contract. Out on their own, many of the stars, attracted by the tax benefits of switching from salaried to investment status, went about happily forming their own production companies.

With nothing left but empty movie lots, the studios' modus operandi changed from that of movie production, with all its attendant glamour, to the business of financing and distributing films made by independent production units. More than half of the 1960 releases were independents.

The change manifested itself in many ways—reduction in the number of releases (approximately 250 in 1960, 429 in 1950), rise in average production costs ($1.4 million in 1960, $600,000 in 1950) and the consequent emphasis on "blockbusters," big pictures planned to gross over $4 million in rentals. The pace was set in 1957 by Paramount's $13 million *Ten Commandments*.

The trend to shoot films abroad snowballed during the decade—35% of all 1960 releases were shot on location overseas. Many stars and producers preferred the arrangement for reasons of tax or pleasure, and there was the artistic asset of greater background authenticity.

Foreign films gained wide audiences in the '50s—500 "art" theaters, devoted exclusively to showing imports with subtitles, sprang up. International stars gained as many U.S. fans as did Hollywood luminaries.

Union difficulties provided a blood and thunder climax to the decade. In January, 1960, the Screen Writers' Guild went on strike and was joined in March by the Screen Actors' Guild. Both actors and writers wanted to share studio profits from sale of post-1948 movies to TV. By June, both walkouts had been settled, closing the script for the '50s with a conventionally happy ending.

MOST EXPENSIVE FILM ever made was *Ben-Hur.* Produced in Rome, it cost $15 million (1927 *Ben-Hur* cost $4 million), had cast of 25,000, was five years in the making and had an arena that took a year to build. It won nine of the 1959 "Oscars," including Best Film, Best Actor (Charlton Heston), Best Director (William Wyler).

SECOND "TEN COMMANDMENTS," produced by late Cecil B. De Mille in 1957, was first of new "blockbusters"—cost $13 million (first version cost $1 million), by 1960 had already grossed $32 million, nosing up on all-time winner, *Gone With the Wind* ($33.5 million). It starred Charlton Heston *(c.)* as Moses; filmed in Vista Vision.

STAR OF "ROOM AT THE TOP," Simone Signoret *(below)* had distinction of receiving first Academy Award for Best Actress ever given to player in British film. Movie, which also won British Film Academy award, was sensitive story of an ambitious young man, his swift rise to power and his love affair with unhappy, older woman.

Major studios finance, distribute "blockbusters" independents produce

HAIR RAISING ROLLER coaster ride left viewers gasping in *This Is Cinerama*, produced by Lowell Thomas in 1953. Though highly effective, Cinerama's defects included high installation costs, imperfect blending of three images

"AROUND THE WORLD IN 80 DAYS," produced by the late Mike Todd, had 50 stars in brief appearances. It won five "Oscars" in 1957, including Best Film award. David Niven and Cantiflas are shown above as they are taking off on their world tour. The movie holds the third highest box office record.

FIRST TV PLAY ever made into a movie and first U.S. film to win the Cannes Festival, *Marty* won four '55 Academy awards. Story of a shy, lonely young man was typical of author Paddy Chayefsky. Originally a TV writer, Chayefsky emerged as an important dramatist, set a trend for dealing with ordinary people in everyday situations. Ernest Borgnine, formerly featured in rough-tough heavy roles, played the part of Marty, a bashful butcher who fell in love with a plain school teacher (Betsy Blair). Other award winners in '50s included *From Here To Eternity*, *On the Waterfront*, *Room at the Top*.

thrown on one screen. Some of the three-dimensional techniques first tried in '52 required use of polarized glasses.

DECAY AND DEGENERACY in the South was the theme of *Streetcar Named Desire*, with *(l. to r.)* Kim Hunter, Marlon Brando, Vivian Leigh. Author Tennessee Williams carried same morbidity through later years with *Cat On A Hot Tin Roof*, etc.

BREEZE FROM SUBWAY grating temporarily cooled Marilyn Monroe, co-starred in *Seven Year Itch* with Tom Ewell. Her come-on look established her as sex symbol of the '50s. After marrying dramatist Arthur Miller, she shocked her many fans by turning intellectual.

FRANCE'S MOST DESIRABLE export was Brigitte Bardot shown *(r.)* in *And God Created Woman*. Combining basic sex with piquancy, BB threatened U.S.' MM, eclipsed such other international beauties as Italy's Sophia Loren, Gina Lollabrigida and Sweden's A. Eckberg.

INFLUX OF FRENCH COMEDIES was best represented by *Mr. Hulot's Holiday*, 1954 Cannes winner, produced and directed by Jacques Tati, who was also the star. Quality of such Japanese films as *Roshomon* and *Hiroshima* earned four festival prizes for Japanese producers in 1954. Great Britain's *Lavendar Hill Mob*, Italy's *La Strada* were among the many notable imports. On the other side of the ledger, more than 50% of U.S. movie revenue was derived from foreign markets.

SEVEN ACADEMY AWARDS went to *Bridge on the River Kwai* in 1958, including ones for Best Film and Best Actor (Britain's Alex Guiness, *above).* It was one of Columbia's first big films—cost $3 million and grossed $30 million—helped bridge crucial period during which studio switched to releasing independent productions.

PEACE IN HOLLYWOOD was restored with end of Screen Actors' Guild strike in April, 1960. Studio executives shook hands with guild negotiators *(r.)* Ron-

SWEDISH FILM DIRECTOR Ingmar Bergman made a name in U.S. with sensitive films like *The Magician* and *Wild Strawberries,* a winner at Int'l Festival.

FUN FOR THE WHOLE FAMILY was offered by drive-ins, which grew to comprise 25% of all theaters. Car hop *(above)* serves refreshments from "Foodmobile." Other services included baby sitters, portable bottle warmers. To lure TV viewers back to movies all theater owners offered extra services, many spent millions redecorating.

ald Reagan and Charlton Heston. The month-long strike interrupted production on eight pictures. Actors gained percentage of new films used on TV.

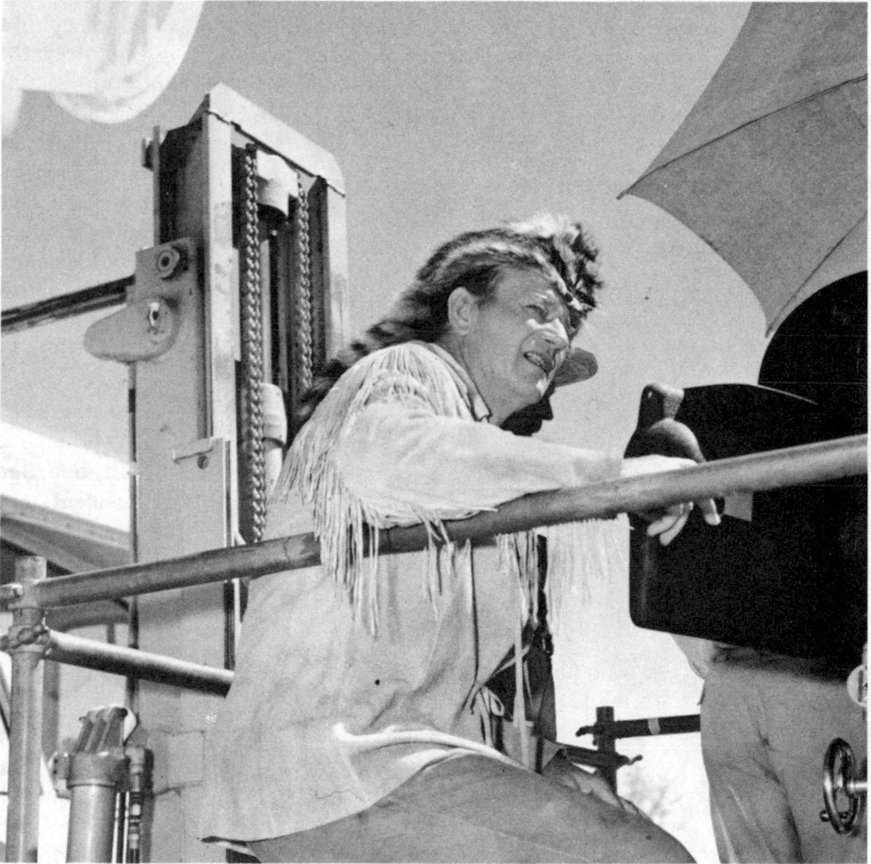

TRIPLE THREAT MAN John Wayne produced, directed and played lead as Davy Crockett in *The Alamo.* Film, released by United Artists, typified trend to independent productions headed by stars, was also classic example of a "blockbuster"—cost $12 million. Others stars turned producers included Burt Lancaster, Kirk Douglas.

TV SPURTS TO ENTERTAINMENT TOP

Westerns thrust aside personality shows; film, tape replace "live" broadcasts. Radio shifts emphasis to music, news as lavish network "hours" disappear

1960 BROUGHT the electronic communication industry to the end of the most significant decade of its development. TV became the dominant medium—but did not drive radio out of business. But radio did change its character completely, dropping its all-around entertainment format to predominantly music and news.

TV broadcasting burgeoned from an embryo industry of 102 stations in 1951 into a business billing $1.5 billion in advertising revenue through a complex of nearly 600 stations and three major networks. Nearly 90% of U.S. homes now have TV sets (an estimated 50 million) and there are a substantial number of "two set homes." TV programs have reached a single audience of 65 million.

Radio's growth has been even more phenomenal. There are now 3491 AM stations and 744 FM stations on the air. Americans own some 156,394,550 radio sets, an average of three per home. Car radios are estimated at 40 million. During 1959, sales of over 18 million sets of all types were reported by manufacturers.

There were several questions about the future of broadcasting still unresolved at the end of the decade. Some phases of the industry were still in the developmental stage—color TV, subscription TV, FM broadcasting and the future of network radio.

EDWARD R. MURROW, CBS commentator, became the prototype of the electronic journalist, giving weighty opinions.

The rise and fall of TV personalities and program formats was rapid during the past 10 years. Names which dominated the medium in the early fifties soon disappeared from starring roles. Milton Berle, the first "Mr. Television," was to start the 1960-61 season as the master of ceremonies on a bowling show. Jackie Gleason, once "Mr. Saturday Night," joined a Broadway musical and returned to TV only in "Specials." Sid Caesar occasionally starred on special shows. Imogene Coca had no regular program, but made some appearances as a guest star. As a team, Caesar and Coca once dominated the important Saturday night prime viewing hours.

Live programming almost completely disappeared from the TV screen. Film and tape shows replaced it. Westerns and "private eye" weekly series formed the bulk of prime time schedules. Re-runs of film shows, sports and quiz game programs and audience participation formats took the major portion of daytime schedules.

Networks devoted much labor, effort and expense to development of the documentary program, but this format did not draw the audience or sponsor interest that straight entertainment fare attracted.

The four major radio networks remained in business though they had been running in the red since TV's impact was felt in the early '50s. At the start of 1960, two networks, Columbia Broadcasting System and National Broadcasting Company, claimed their network radio operations had moved into the black. American Broadcasting Company and Mutual Broadcasting System adopted new radio programming formats in efforts to get on a paying basis: MBS, with 10% of the stations in the country signed as affiliates, became virtually a news service for its members.

TV became a factor in education. Teaching via closed circuit hookups to classrooms proved successful in an experiment in Hagerstown, Md. Networks and stations aired such programming as "Continental Classroom" and "Sunrise Semester" in early morning hours for students and teachers. New York State bought over $300,000 worth of air time on WPIX, New York City, to air educational programs in the day hours of the school year.

At the end of the decade, three of the original four TV networks remained in business. Du Mont Television became defunct in 1955 but the three remaining webs, American, Columbia and National Broadcasting were in healthy condition.

But TV faced the future with many headaches in store for it before its final form would be determined. There would be further investigations, tighter controls, closer scrutiny of programming and more detailed demands that stations and networks fulfill public interest requirements.

"GUNSMOKE" made the transition from radio to TV as the first of a rash of "adult Westerns." This type of programing became the backbone of network evening schedules.

WEEKLY SERIES, "I Love Lucy," started multi-million Desilu Productions, Inc. Lucille Ball *(under table)* and husband Desi Arnaz *(r.)*, built mammoth empire, divorced in 1960.

Payola, Quiz Scandals rock Radio - TV but people continue to look and listen

TV QUIZ scandals reached a climax when Charles Van Doren, of Columbia University, admitted he had been given answers.

PRESIDENTS of the three TV networks testified in quiz hearings. CBS' Stanton conferred with Rep. Oren Harris. *(above)*

PAYOLA scandals hit both radio and TV. Disc Jockeys were accused of violating Sec. 317 of Communications Act. Alan Freed *(r.)*, rock 'n roll pied piper, lost jobs on WABC Radio and WNEW-TV as a result of charges he took payola.

ROBERT E. KINTNER, president of NBC, told Congressional probe laws should make TV quiz cheating a crime.

TV CASTING made strange team mates. Ex-President Truman *(at piano)* appeared on Jack Benny's CBS-TV show.

JACK PAAR succeeded Arthur Godfrey as TV's "enfant terrible," quit NBC-TV program while on camera in protest against "censorship" when a water closet joke was deleted from a tape. After a Far East vacation, he returned to the network.

ARTHUR GODFREY'S stormy career made front page copy across the nation as he fired performer after performer from his various programs. One of CBS's most valuable entertainers, he brought millions of dollars in billings to the web. In 1959, he underwent surgery for lung cancer, came through to resume his career. However, though his tenure of popularity outlasted that of most of his contemporaries, his regularly scheduled programs on CBS Radio and TV were on the wane.

FIRST COAST-TO-COAST telecast (Sept. 4, 1951) brought live coverage of President addressing opening session of the Japanese Peace Treaty Conference in San Francisco. The four major TV networks pooled resources to air the historic event. TV has since become the prime method used by the President for reporting directly to the U.S. public.

IN EARLY days of TV, Sid Caesar and Imogene Coca comedy team dominated the Saturday night ratings with a 90-minute variety show. After team broke up, both performers faded.

MAINSTAYS of NBC Radio Network were its "Monitor" service and its "News-On-The-Hour." Reporting world-wide news, both originated from Radio Central, RCA Bldg., New York.

MUSICAL VERSION of "Peter Pan," not very successful on Broadway, drew record TV audience of 65 million people when televised by NBC-TV in 1955. Program was repeated following year. "Spectacular" starred Mary Martin in title role, Cyril Ritchard as Captain Hook. No single entertainment program has drawn such a TV audience since then.

AD VOLUME DOUBLES IN DECADE

TV adds new dimension, passes $1.5 billion annual volume

ADVERTISERS went on a $98 billion spending spree in the '50s. Their 1960 expenditures, $12 billion, were twice as great as those 10 years earlier.

The staggering increase reflected rising costs, intensified promotion and the coming of age of a new and expensive medium, television.

Competition from the flood of new products during the decade served to make industry more promotion conscious. Advertising was called upon not only to sell but to educate the public on everything from nuclear-generated electricity to chlorophyll toothpaste.

In 1959 an advertiser, to maintain his 1950 advertising schedule, would have had to spend $159 for every $100 spent at the beginning of the decade. Since 1950 magazine costs have increased 74%, newspaper 46%, network TV 212%, outdoor 64%, business papers 59%. Only radio costs decreased—network 50% and spot 2.5%.

A huge chunk of total advertising expenditures was devoured by TV, which seemed to many an electronic money-eating monster. TV costs had tripled since 1950, while those of other major media less than doubled. Advertising history was changed by the Jack-and-the-Bean-Stalk growth of TV during the decade. In 1950 it had only 3.2% of the advertising pie; by 1959 a juicy 13.4%.

"MAN WITH THE EYE PATCH" made a name for Hathaway shirt overnight and fathered many imitators. Agency used eye patch as a memorable device, also associated a personality with the product. Inexpensive campaign proved effective.

ADVERTISING'S DYNAMIC DECADE
(Growth, $ billion)

	1959	%	1958	1957	1955	1950
Newspapers	$3.52	%32	$3.19	$3.28	$3.07	$2.01
Direct Mail	1.57	14	1.59	1.47	1.27	0.76
Television	1.53	14	1.35	1.27	1.01	0.17
Magazines	0.87	8	0.77	0.81	0.72	0.51
Radio	0.64	6	0.62	0.62	0.55	0.61
Miscellaneous	3.00	27	2.78	2.85	2.39	1.65
Total	11.13	100	10.30	10.31	9.01	5.71

All media had to give up some dessert for the new member of the family, but radio gave up the most—its proportionate share of the total fell from 10.6% in 1950 to 5.8% in 1959. The entire structure of radio sales was changed from a single to a multi-sponsor basis, with time divided into small "spot" units. (A one-minute network spot ranged in cost from $725-$1000.)

Newspapers continued to receive the largest portion of all advertising expenditures — $3.5 billion in 1959 — although their share of the total dipped from 36.4 in 1950 to 31.7% in 1959. In dollars, however, newspaper revenue, like that of all other media, increased over the decade.

Magazine revenue rose 13% between 1958 and 1959—the sharpest rise of all media groups last year. Top 1959 ad-getters were Life ($134 million), Saturday Evening Post ($98 million), and Look ($45 million).

Advertising took several well defined creative turns during the '50s. Emphasis of the large majority of ads was on the visual, with dramatic layouts and almost exclusive use of photography for art work.

Ads showed a marked tendency to build an emotional feeling about a product. An image was projected around a shirt, for example, that subtly implied it was worn by the kind of man the reader would like to be. An atmosphere was created around the auto—a fun car, a family car, a prestige car.

Agencies made increased use of research in preparing campaigns—although there was a split vote on its value, genuine or nuisance. Advertisers were even giving campaigns dry runs with newly developed pre-testing techniques. Floods of statistics established such criteria as "most seen," "most remembered," and "most read." (No one had yet devised a way to determine "most sold.")

The two agencies that made the biggest splash during the '50s were Ogilvy, Benson & Mather and Doyle Dane Bernbach. Both started the decade as relatively small newcomers, and both built their reputations by sheer force of creativity, making their mark on the strength of their first campaigns—Hathaway Shirt and Ohrbach's respectively.

Four largest agencies in 1959 were J. Walter Thompson, total billings $328 million; McCann-Erickson, $304 million; Young & Rubicam, $232 million; and Batten, Barton, Durstine & Osborn, $216 million.

Four largest advertisers in '59 were Proctor & Gamble ($54.8 million), General Motors ($53.7 million), Lever Brothers ($37.7 million), General Foods ($37.3 million).

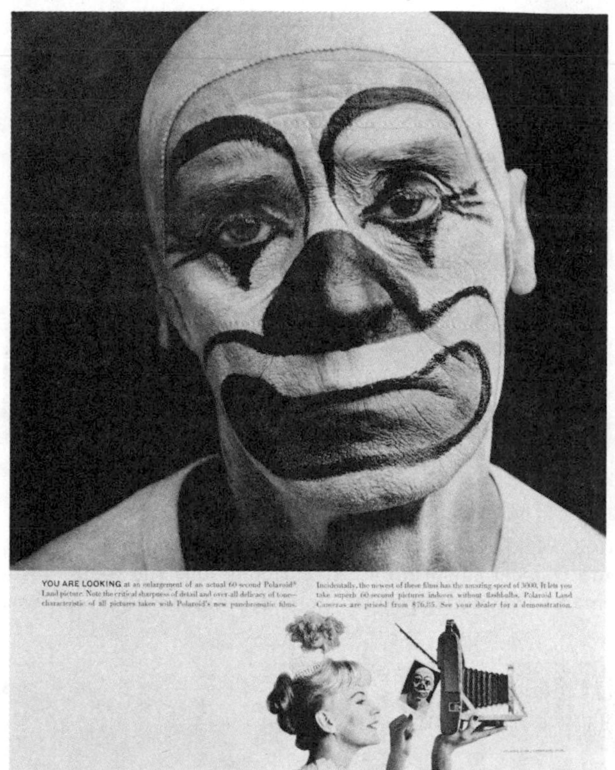

MARVELOUS PHOTOGRAPHY used in Polaroid Camera campaign conveyed better than words fine quality pictures the camera could take, corrected people's conception of it as a gimmicky camera. Sales rose from $23 million to $89 million in 5 years.

EYE CATCHING prestige ads of Ohrbach's department stores aroused not only amusement but highest compliment, widespread imitation. Ads, for first time in retail history, were strictly institutional, never mentioned specific prices or goods.

ARTHUR GODFREY, no. 1 pitchman of the '50s, used a soft, easy sell in his radio and TV commercials, often kidded the sponsor. Although he had built a huge, devoted fan club, he slipped out of favor slightly after firing cast members.

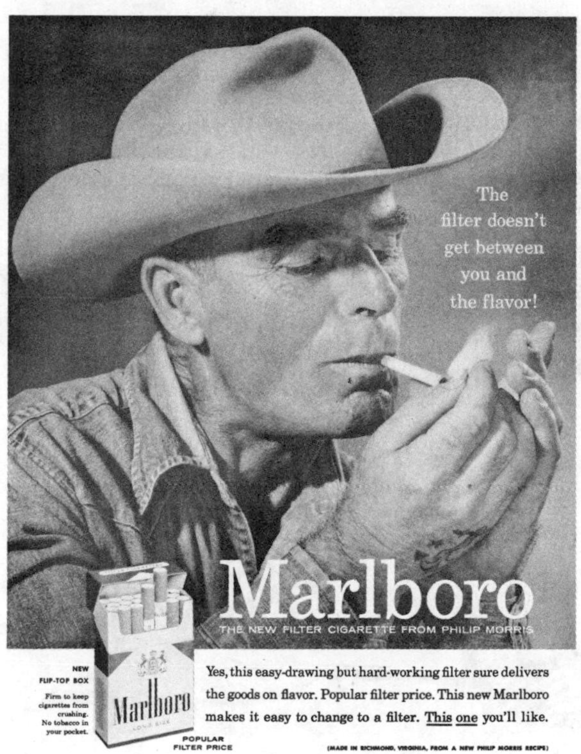

RUGGED COWBOY changed Marlboro's reputation from a smoke for dudes and women to a he-man smoke (women, it was found, prefer a "man's" cigaret). Tattoo by a Bowery artist was added for distinction. Sales rose 120% first year.

A Frank Statement to Cigarette Smokers

RECENT REPORTS on experiments with mice have given wide publicity to a theory that cigarette smoking is in some way linked with lung cancer in human beings.

Although conducted by doctors of professional standing, these experiments are not regarded as conclusive in the field of cancer research. However, we do not believe that any serious medical research, even though its results are inconclusive should be disregarded or lightly dismissed.

At the same time, we feel it is in the public interest to call attention to the fact that eminent doctors and research scientists have publicly questioned the claimed significance of these experiments.

Distinguished authorities point out:

1. That medical research of recent years indicates many possible causes of lung cancer.

2. That there is no agreement among the authorities regarding what the cause is.

3. That there is no proof that cigarette smoking is one of the causes.

4. That statistics purporting to link cigarette smoking with the disease could apply with equal force to any one of many other aspects of modern life. Indeed the validity of the statistics themselves is questioned by numerous scientists.

We accept an interest in people's health as a basic responsibility, paramount to every other consideration in our business.

We believe the products we make are not injurious to health.

We always have and always will cooperate closely with those whose task it is to safeguard the public health.

For more than 300 years tobacco has given solace, relaxation, and enjoyment to mankind. At one time or another during those years critics have held it responsible for practically every disease of the human body. One by one these charges have been abandoned for lack of evidence.

Regardless of the record of the past, the fact that cigarette smoking today should even be suspected as a cause of a serious disease is a matter of deep concern to us.

Many people have asked us what we are doing to meet the public's concern aroused by the recent reports. Here is the answer:

1. **We are pledging aid and assistance to the research effort into all phases of tobacco use and health. This joint financial aid will of course be in addition to what is already being contributed by individual companies.**
2. **For this purpose we are establishing a joint industry group consisting initially of the undersigned. This group will be known as** TOBACCO INDUSTRY RESEARCH COMMITTEE.
3. **In charge of the research activities of the Committee will be a scientist of unimpeachable integrity and national repute. In addition there will be an Advisory Board of scientists disinterested in the cigarette industry. A group of distinguished men from medicine, science, and education will be invited to serve on this Board. These scientists will advise the Committee on its research activities.**

This statement is being issued because we believe the people are entitled to know where we stand on this matter and what we intend to do about it.

TOBACCO INDUSTRY RESEARCH COMMITTEE

5400 EMPIRE STATE BUILDING, NEW YORK 1, N. Y.

SPONSORS:

THE AMERICAN TOBACCO COMPANY, INC. — *Paul M. Hahn, President*

BENSON & HEDGES — *Joseph F. Cullman, Jr., President*

BRIGHT BELT WAREHOUSE ASSOCIATION — *F. S. Royster, President*

BROWN & WILLIAMSON TOBACCO CORPORATION — *Timothy V. Hartnett, President*

BURLEY AUCTION WAREHOUSE ASSOCIATION — *Albert Clay, President*

BURLEY TOBACCO GROWERS COOPERATIVE ASSOCIATION — *John W. Jones, President*

LARUS & BROTHER COMPANY, INC. — *W. T. Reed, Jr., President*

P. LORILLARD COMPANY — *Herbert A. Kent, Chairman*

MARYLAND TOBACCO GROWERS ASSOCIATION — *Samuel C. Linton, General Manager*

PHILIP MORRIS & CO., LTD., INC. — *O. Parker McComas, President*

R. J. REYNOLDS TOBACCO COMPANY — *E. A. Darr, President*

STEPHANO BROTHERS, INC. — *C. S. Stephano, D' Sc., Director of Research*

TOBACCO ASSOCIATES, INC. (An organization of flue-cured tobacco growers) — *J. B. Hutson, President*

UNITED STATES TOBACCO COMPANY — *J. W. Peterson, President*

TOBACCO INDUSTRY placed this ad in 448 newspapers to combat publicity linking cancer with cigarets. It announced establishment of medical committee to investigate charges.

"LOOK SHARP, BE SHARP," Gillette's theme song, *was* sharp, made commercials (animated cartoons and sports-star testimonials) among the most popular on television screens.

SONGSTRESS DINAH SHORE, star of the Chevy TV show, warbled lead-ins for commercials, typified two trends—integrated commercials and association of a personality with a product.

HIGHWAY HUMOUR was provided by Ken-L-Ration billboard. It won a 1956 Chicago Art Director's award. Volume of outdoor advertising increased from $131 million in '49 to $193 million in '59, but share of total revenue decreased 8%.

STAR SALESWOMAN for Westinghouse, Betty Furness, brightened TV commercials for past three elections. Coverage of 1960 conventions, campaigns, election night on CBS radio-TV cost $6 million.

SUCCESS STORY of the decade was that of 33-year-old Hugh H. Hefner *(l.)*, who started *Playboy* magazine in 1953 with a borrowed $11,000. Since then it became a serious competitor to long-established *Esquire* for the leadership of the men's magazine field with a circulation approaching 800,000; moved into its own luxurious building in Chicago. Most popular feature was girl "Playmate of the Month" photograph.

RISING COSTS PLAGUE PRESS

Historic dailies cease publication

COSTLY STRIKES, spiraling costs, and a growing mortality rate did not prevent U.S. newspapers from reaching an all-time high circulation of 58,299,723 copies daily and 47,848,477 Sundays by the beginning of 1960.

This gain of more than 5.5 million daily and 1.5 million Sunday in the decade indicated prosperity—but the evidence was deceptive.

Many of the nation's oldest and biggest papers had gone out of business—18 in 1959 alone—leaving 82% of all towns and cities with one daily. Though there was

TWO OLD-TIMERS, *Collier's Magazine* and *Woman's Home Companion*, went out of business in 1957 despite circulation that was in the millions. Though *Collier's* was one of the Big Four mass magazines, advertising revenue had not kept up with mounting production costs despite readership gains.

CAPITALISTIC TROUBLES caused Red party organ *Daily Worker* to close its doors in January, 1958, when weakened, divided Communist party withdrew its financial aid. Editor John Gates resigned in disillusionment and said that he hoped to be able to "rejoin the American people" in the future.

NEWS HUNGRY New Yorkers crowd in front of a shop window in 1958 where a teleprompter machine displays news during a 19-day Christmas season strike which closed down the city's nine major dailies with combined circulation of 5.7 million. It cost $25 million in advertising revenue, $5 million in wages.

CENSORSHIP BY STEALTH was inaugurated in Georgia in March, 1952, by a three-man board, headed by Baptist minister James Wesberry *(c.)*, which promptly issued secret withdrawal orders to the bookstore and newsstand distributors. Action was challenged by Georgia newspapers as leading to "thought control."

VICTOR RIESEL, blinded by his labor racketeer enemies in acid-throwing attack in April, 1955, continued to write his syndicated column on labor affairs. Indictments were returned against Johnny Dio and others charged with planing crime but presumed acid-thrower Abraham Telvi already had been murdered.

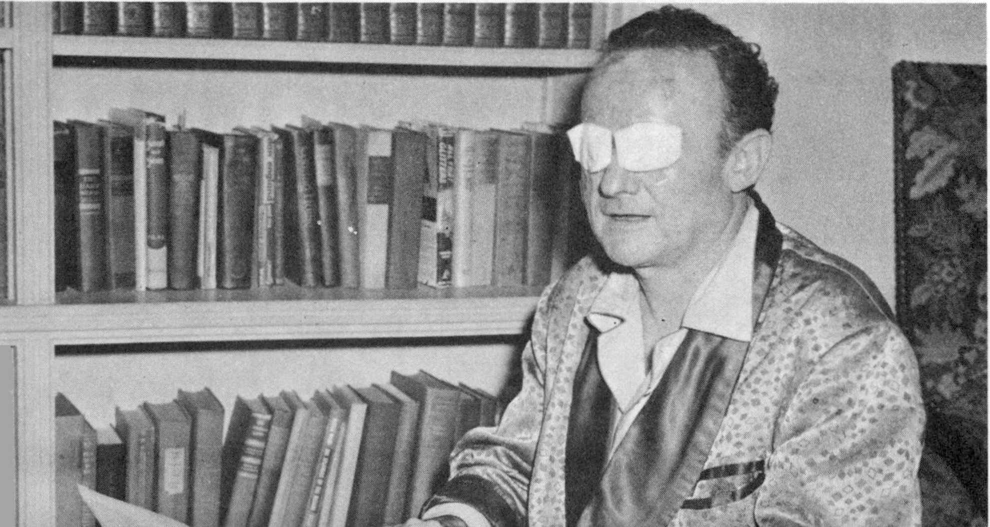

only an over-all decline of 19 daily papers (from 1780 in 1949 to 1761 in 1959), no new major metropolitan paper had been started; the replacements were small suburban papers.

Among the missing were the 114-year-old *Brooklyn Eagle, Boston Post, Los Angeles News,* still others. It was a time of mergers, with the Scripps-Howard chain in particular absorbing its rivals in Columbus, Cleveland and Cincinnati, Ohio, and in San Francisco, where its *News* merged with Hearst's *Call-Bulletin.*

Biggest merger of all was of two of the three giant U.S. news agencies, Scripps-Howard's United Press and Hearst's International News Service in May, 1958.

INS, reputedly losing $1 million every year, was virtually swallowed whole by its more prosperous rival; some 400 INS men lost their jobs.

It gave newly-named United Press International a leg-up in its race with its only remaining competitor, the Associated Press. By the end of 1959 UPI claimed 1656 U.S. newspaper clients against the older agency's reported 1778.

Magazines died, too. *The American Magazine* suspended publication early in 1956 despite circulation of 2 million. And *Collier's Magazine,* born in 1888, died in 1957 (despite its circulation being at an all-time high) due to lack of advertising in its diet, taking with it its sister, *Woman's Home Companion.*

Biggest cloud on the publishers' horizon was increasing number of costly strikes. There were 40 in 1958 and 37 in 1959 alone, ranging from a three-day stoppage on the Washington (D.C.) *Star* to a three-month walkout on the *St. Louis Globe-Democrat.* And, as the decade ended, the *Portland Oregonian* and *Oregon Journal* shut down on Nov. 10, 1959 in a strike that bid to set a duration record. In 1960, it was still unsettled.

War in Korea in 1950 brought 450 U.S. newsmen there; casualties among reporters and photographers were extremely high and several were captured.

As usual, the free world's right to uncensored news was threatened from all sides. In Czechoslovakia in 1951 Associated Press correspondent William Oatis was sentenced to 10 years in prison for "espionage" after a standard Red propaganda trial. Newsmen Russell Jones, UP, and John MacCormac, *New York Times*, were expelled from Hungary in 1957.

Cuba's Fidel Castro, helped to power in 1958 by the U.S. press, took over the papers in Havana. France censored news from revolt-torn Algeria; South Africa expelled newsmen covering its racial riots.

Thorniest problem for newspapers was election coverage after one-party press charges based on elections of 1952 and 1956. In former, some 933 dailies, representing 80% of total circulation, supported President Eisenhower, as against 202 papers and 11% for Stevenson.

(Democrats, however, on this ground alone had no cause for worry, observers said. They pointed out that the vast majority of newspapers had opposed President Truman in his 1948 campaign, and President Roosevelt in three campaigns out of four—and yet they won decisively.)

Prediction for the coming decade was more mergers in face of rising production costs. Sole hope to offset this seemed to be in new typesetting and engraving devices more efficient than antiquated methods and machines now used.

The decade had made it more evident that publishing a big city daily was big business, needing big capital.

PORNOGRAPHY MEANS PROFIT, a special House investigating committee found, after delving into the booming business of publishing magazines and paperback books that titillated and tattled. Unfortunately, the committee was unable to find the cure, fearing restrictive legislation might be a much greater danger.

MARGUERITE HIGGINS *(l.)* chatting with Brig. Gen. John S. Bradley, won the 1950 Pulitzer Prize for her coverage of the Korean War. New York *Times* Washington veteran bureau chief James Reston won his second during 1957.

N.Y. TIMES reporter A. M. Rosenthal was ordered out of Poland in 1959 for the crime of reporting too accurately, displeasing nation's Communist bosses.

COSTLY COLUMN was 1952 one written by Drew Pearson in which he mistook rumor for fact and implied that former U.S. Asst. Attorney Norman M. Littell was acting as propagandist for Netherlands. Court directed Pearson to pay Littell $50,000 damages—the biggest libel verdict in Washington, D.C. history.

THIRD GRADERS, Negro and white, look each other over with wary friendliness on first day of 1954-55 school year at elementary school for service personnel's children at Ft. Myer, Va., Army post. This was first time in modern South children of the two groups sat side by side in same classroom. Defense Department order outlawing segregation in all military installation schools led way toward integration as did firm stand of Roman Catholic bishops on parochial schools.

COURT ORDERS INTEGRATION

South reluctantly accepting ruling; U.S. education, assailed as weak in science, fundamentals, is critically short of teachers, schools, funds

U.S. EDUCATORS, under fire during the '50s as soft, misdirected and inadequate to match the single-minded, no-nonsense Soviet system, nevertheless gave proof that U.S. democracy means what it says.

On May 17, 1954, the U.S. Supreme Court, abandoning its earlier "separate but equal" doctrine, unanimously outlawed racial segregation in the nation's public schools. By decade's end, at least token integration had been accepted everywhere except in the citadels of the deepest South—and even there signs mounted it would come soon rather than late.

Ruling in 1955 that implementation of its decision was task of local authorities, the Court permitted time for adjustment only when communities could give evidence that integration was proceeding with "deliberate speed."

Citizens' Councils and similar diehard segregationist groups sprang up everywhere in the South and, ostensibly restricting themselves to strictly legal measures, encouraged economic pressure and open terror. (Mississippi editor Hodding Carter, a Pulitzer Prize winner, called them a "new incipient Ku Klux Klan.") When the 1956 school year began in Clinton, Tenn., rioters, mostly hoodlum teenagers, filled the streets to protest entry of 12 Negro children into the previously all-white high school. The National Guard was called in; the school was closed and reopened several times; but nine Negroes finished the year, and one, a senior, graduated—and earned a place in history.

Little Rock, Ark., however, was the most publicized focus of resistance. The state's governor, Orval E. Faubus, used the National Guard to prevent the 1957 reopening of Central High School—with Negro attendance—after the local school board had submitted a plan and the court had approved it. President Eisenhower did not

U.S. PARATROOPER, tussling with man who is attempting to wrest his bayoneted rifle from his hand, symbolizes government's determination to protect Negro pupils assigned to Little Rock's Central High School. Army was sent in by President Eisenhower after Arkansas Governor Faubus called out National Guard, closed school, to prevent enforcement of court-ordered plan, drawn by local board. Pro-Faubus group ousted board, later lost to new "moderate" group.

ENRAGED WHITE PUPILS push and heckle two Negro students as latter attempt to enter Central High School. Mob blocked their attempt to attend class that day, but later integrated classes were resumed under the protection of U.S. Army.

take this challenge to Federal authority lying down. He called the Arkansas Guard into Federal service (thus depriving Faubus of authority over it), and sent the Army in. Central remained open under the protection of U.S. troops. Some days only a trickle of white pupils came to school. But the few Negro students assigned came every day. They were spat on, booed, jostled, hated. Their parents were threatened. But they came. By 1960, Little Rock was on the road to full integration (but the events, unleashing popular passions, also had solidified Faubus' hold on state power).

In other areas developments, if less spectacular, were in the same direction. In 1955 the Defense Department integrated all the schools it operated for the children of service personnel. In almost all the border states, integration proceeded with a minimum number of flare-ups and according to schedules adopted by the local boards.

FIXED BAYONETS of Tennessee National Guardsmen clear Main Street in Clinton of mob of teenage hoodlums, many gathered from out of town, who were demonstrating against integration of Clinton's high school. Tennessee authorities handled with firmness all such outbreaks, but situation for a time made town rallying point for racist agitators, similar "crusaders." Isolated bombings of schools took place in South, but, fortunately, there were no casualties, and violence petered out.

GOV. ORVAL E. FAUBUS, champion to the end of segregation, closed down four of Little Rock's high schools for an entire year rather than carry integration into the 1958-59 school year. This came after his plan to transfer the schools to a private corporation was rejected by the courts. (Note sign's misspelling of 'government').

Chief legal hope of the anti-integrationists was Virginia, whose "massive resistance" laws empowered Gov. J. Lindsay Almond to close schools which admitted Negroes in obedience to the U.S. courts. When the 1957-58 school year opened, Negroes were enrolled at Norfolk and other cities. Governor Almond closed the schools. But the courts threw out the Virginia laws, and the schools reopened with Negro pupils attending.

Allied with the school fight was the struggle of Negro college students ("Segregation makes me feel unwanted") to win the same service as whites in stores and lunch counters. The first demonstration was in a Woolworth store in Greenboro, N.C., where four Negro students respectfully but doggedly refused to leave their lunch counter seats.

Such student "sit-downs" mushroomed. By decade's end, Negroes were getting the same service as whites in many Southern cities.

ENCOURAGING SIGN in filling science teaching gap was provided by such teachers as Lon Colburn, retired after 34 years, who returned to teach chemistry in Monroe, La., High School.

MAJOR QUESTION during the decade was — with the harsh nuclear breath of Soviet scientific advances breathing down its neck — what was wrong with U.S. education?

Most criticisms agreed that it was too easy, too diffuse, too concerned with "adjustment to the group" instead of plain, old-fashioned study and learning.

Science—and the basic mathematical disciplines essential to advanced scientific work—were badly neglected.

Even more shocking, it was found that in an enormous number of cases, Johnny, when he reached high school, or even college, literally could not read.

At the root of the crisis were shortages—of building and plant, of skilled teachers and, basic to this last, of adequate teacher pay. (In 1960, despite raises, teachers still were averaging less than production workers.)

The U.S., by 1960, was spending at least $17 billion a year on all education, but many educators were insisting this would have to be doubled. Pupil load of elementary and secondary schools was some 2.5 million above estimated capacity. Many colleges and universities were turning away more applicants than they accepted.

(Meanwhile, the USSR was reported turning out 300,000 scientists, engineers and technicians a year, and the U.S. only 100,000. But the U.S. training level was admittedly higher.)

Higher institutions were being increasingly helped by foundations and the great corporations. (In 1956-57, foundations gave $319 million, corporations some $80 million, and corporate gifts were accelerating.)

But the major financial problem remained. Many felt the only remedy was largely increased Federal aid (which, in the 1960 election year, both parties were promising).

At decade's end, U.S. education was preparing to reeducate itself, and seeking the money to do so.

LOYALTY OATH, vociferously demanded by many organizations, as bitterly opposed by many others, including many of best known private universities, remained both State and Federal problem. In early '50s, California's oath rule (opponents included, second *l.*, then Gov. Earl Warren) was declared unconstitutional. As 1960 ended, oath for all students receiving Federal aid appeared to be on the way out.

"OUR GREAT RACE with the Soviet Union," says Vice Adm. Hyman G. Rickover *(l.)*, "is in education." Incessantly, he sought to awaken the U.S. people to the problem of inferior training for its children. He suggested a "private agency—a Council of Scholars—to set national standards for the high school diploma, and competence of teachers."

EX-HARVARD President James Bryant Conant conducted a $350,000 two-year survey of U.S. high schools. One finding: "Academically talented students ought to be studying five solid subjects in each of 4 years. English, history, mathematics, science and foreign language are solid." He then turned to the junior high schools for similar survey.

"TEMPORARY SCHOOL HOUSE" built more than 25 years ago still serves St. Louis children. In 1959 the nation was 130,000 classrooms short. The education of 8 of 42 million U.S. school children was being affected by obsolete, over-crowded and inadequate classrooms. At a time when 227,000 new teachers were needed annually, only 92,000 were trained. They were being paid as if there were an oversupply: $5025 a year. In 10 years, school expenditures tripled to $14.5 billion a year but shortages remained due to skyrocketing costs and a school population increase of 50% in the past ten years.

NEW YORK CITY teachers picket for more pay for their long hours, often with double sessions and extracurricular duties, in period of rising living costs. Across country some teacher loads were reduced *(below)* by bringing topnotch teachers into many classrooms simultaneously through television.

"THE ROLE OF GOVERNMENT is to help people to help themselves . . . so every child in America has the opportunity to obtain an education so that we can preserve the basic strength of democracy," President Eisenhower told foreign students.

SPUTNIK SHOOK THE ROOTS of the philosophy of American education and led to headline-making re-evaluations of our systems. The USSR was turning out three times as many scientists and engineers. One quarter of U.S. high schools offered no chemistry, physics or geometry. Demand for engineers was so strong, they "could almost write own tickets."

WORLD'S FAITHS DRAW CLOSER

Unity and change mark religious activity in past decade as spiritual heads meet Communist threat

CHILDREN GREET a cheerful Pope Pius XII on his 80th birthday. St. Peter's Square was filled with the faithful from 51 nations, who were also present for the ceremones which marked the 17th anniversary of the Pontiff's coronation.

FIRST ANNIVERSARY celebration of Pope John XXIII as Vicar of 400 million Roman Catholics took place at St. Peter's. Shown here being carried into the Basilica in the gestorial chair, the Pope asked well-wishers to refrain from applause.

A HANDSHAKE between the Rev. Dr. Fred Hoskins *(l.)* of the Congregational Church and the Rev. James E. Wagner of the Evangelical and Reformed Church joined two Protestant sects in '57 to form multi-member "United Church of Christ."

THE YEARS following 1950 found the religions of the world faced with both internal and external dangers.

Communist persecution in Eastern Europe took on a subtle disguise, but was still much in evidence. In China, the parade of foreign missionaries forced across the border to Hong Kong culminated in a complete absence of missionary work. Those who remained behind the "Bamboo Curtain" had their parishes reduced to the four walls of a prison cell.

Although separated by dogma, tradition and centuries of distrust, Catholics, Protestants and Jews were commonly united in their opposition to the Red menace, each coping with it in its own way. The two great Christian bodies concentrated upon a strengthening from within, a reawakening of religious spirit and moral responsibility.

The Roman Catholic Holy Year of 1950 was a move toward this goal. During the year over 3.2 million pilgrims from almost every nation made their way to St. Peter's Basilica. For Roman Catholics it was a year of great changes. Pope Pius XII beatified eight and canonized eight, a record total. The first dogma since 1870, the Assumption of Mary was proclaimed and the Pontiff announced the discovery of the tomb of St. Peter beneath the Basilica.

Of special importance during the Holy Year was the plight of the millions of Catholics suffering behind the

Communist frontier. The world's 400 million Roman Catholics were exhorted to pray and sacrifice for their trapped brethren.

When Pope Pius XII died in 1958 after a long illness the College of Cardinals elected Cardinal Roncalli of Venice as the new Vicar. Taking the name John XXIII, the new Pope soon drew widespread attention because of his liberal and outspoken nature. To meet the needs of the expanding Church he increased the maximum size of the Sacred College from 70 to 85, appointing many new cardinals, among them the first native African. One of his most important steps was to issue a call for an ecumenical council to establish formal unity within Christianity. Aimed chiefly at the Greek Orthodox Church, the council, proposed for 1962, aroused varied reactions among Protestant leaders. Many of them considered the council unnecessary interference, and expressed little enthusiasm for unity on the Pope's terms. But since the doctrinal differences separating the Roman and Eastern churches are minor, hope was held out for a union between the two.

Unity within Protestantism itself was encouraged when a U.S. Episcopalian bishop, the Rt. Rev. Stephen F. Bayne, Jr., became Executive Officer of the world-wide churches in communion with the Church of England. Evangelist Billy Graham also looked for unity, based on increased religious fervor. His plea to his hearers to "declare themselves for God" was a familiar cry in the U.S., Europe, Africa and Asia. His dramatic style of delivery and forceful personality won adherents at every meeting. One of the evangelist's main premises is that Christians cannot win the struggle with Communism by merely opposing it. They must, instead, find courage in a return to God and His truths, an example for all the world.

32 SCHOLARS worked 15 years on the *Revised Standard Version* of the Bible which, when finished in 1953, modernized the King James Version. Dr. Samuel McCrea Cavert *(l.)* and Dr. Roy G. Ross, general secretaries of the National Council of the Churches of Christ, examine the new plates.

LONDON CROWDS fill historic Trafalgar Square to hear American Evangelist Billy Graham preaching his gospel. In Great Britain on an extended preaching marathon, the Southern minister used Europe as a springboard for his world crusade.

CHRISTIAN AND JEWISH heritage was enriched by the discovery of the Dead Sea Scrolls in 1947. Purchased in U.S. in 1955 from a Syrian for return to Israel, the controversial fragments included earliest manuscript of the Book of Isaiah.

NEW AGA KHAN watches 1957 burial rites for grandfather from gilded throne. Chosen spiritual leader of 20 million Ismaili Moslems over father, Ali Khan, who himself died in 1960, young head was 1959 graduate of Harvard University.

SAGHANAYAKA, leader of the sixth great Buddhist Council to be held since the death of Buddha in 483 B.C., presides over the 1954 meeting in Rangoon, Burma. The two-year council attracted 2,500 monks and millions of Buddhist pilgrims.

FORMER DEAN of New York's Cathedral of St. John the Divine, the Very Rev. James A. Pike, Episcopal Bishop of California, posed in 1958 photo with family. Bishop Pike was a strong Protestant voice in U.S. birth-control controversy.

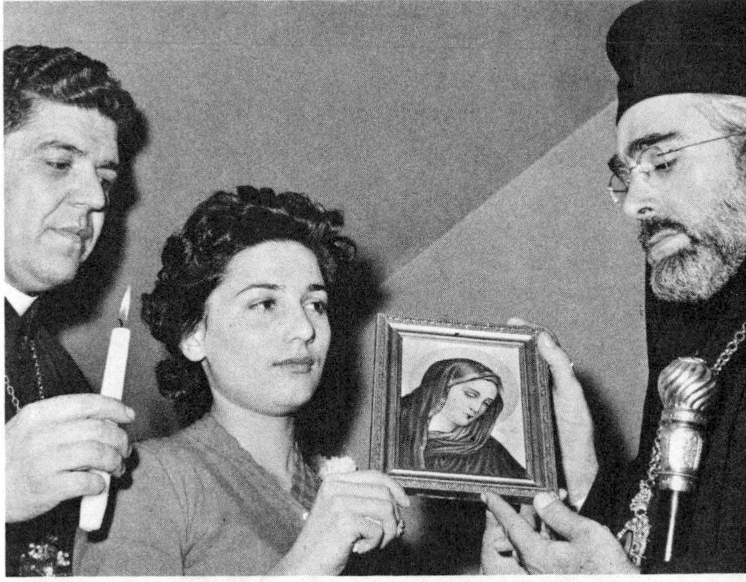

WEEPING MADONNA, claimed to shed tears by its owner, Mrs. Oatsounis of Hempstead, NY, was examined by Archbishop Iakovos *(right)*, Primate of the Greek Orthodox Church of North and South America, and colleague, the Rev. George Papadeas, St. Paul's Greek Orthodox Church, Long Island.

LOURDES CENTENARY was the religious highpoint of 1958 for the world's Roman Catholics. Thousands of physically disabled pilgrims bathed in pool at shrine of St. Bernadette, thought by Catholics to have miraculous powers. Photo shows 50,000 faithful at High Mass in front of Lourdes' Basilica.

FORCED TO FLEE South Africa in 1960 because of his outspoken criticism of police brutality at the Sharpeville "Massacre," the Rev. Ambrose Reeves, *(l.)* Anglican Bishop of Johannesburg, sought refuge from arrest in the British Protectorate of Swaziland, where he awaited further government action.

First native African Cardinal *(r.)* was named by Pope John XXIII in 1960. New church leader, Most Rev. Laurian Rugambwa of Rutabo, Tanganyika, was only 47 at the time of his appointment, making him the second youngest member of the Sacred College. He was born into a pagan Negro tribe.

FOUR AMERICANS were created Cardinals in 1959. Shown above are Richard J. Cushing, Archbishop of Boston *(l.)* and John O'Hara, Archbishop of Philadelphia. Later that year two more Americans received Red Hat, Aloisius J. Muench, Papal Nuncio to Germany, Albert Meyer of Chicago.

THE EARTH SHRANK IN OCT. 1958 WHEN BOTH BRITISH OVERSEAS AIRWAYS AND PAN AMERICAN PUT FIRST JETS IN SERVICE

THE U.S. MOVES ABROAD

During decade 90 million world-traveling Americans spent $17 billion

SOVIET OFFICIAL *(l.)* greets U.S. governors who toured USSR in 1959. Group included *(l. to r.)* LeRoy Collins, Fla.; Cecil Underwood, W. Va.; William Stratton, Ill.; and Luther Hodges, N.C.

A $17 BILLION WANDERLUST drove 90 million Americans to the four corners of the world during the '50s.

The mass exodus, triggered by the economic boom, exploded with the first whoosh of the jet boom. As the earth shrank, the nation's vacation habits expanded — the former two-weeks-in-the-country gave way to a hop to Hawaii or a long weekend in Puerto Rico.

Exotic, out-of-the-way spots suddenly became accessible —the number of U.S. trippers to Hong Kong and East Africa more than doubled.

In 1959, 240,000 Americans spent $100 million in the Pacific, fastest expanding tourist area in the world, and 65,000 spent $35 million just in Japan. The invasion even penetrated the Iron Curtain—20,000 Americans went poking around the USSR in '60.

Western Europe continued in 1960 as the prime overseas magnet — 677,000 tourists spent $625 million in that area. France was still the major attraction—405,000 Americans *parlezvoused* their way about the country. Nearby Canada, however, remained the favorite vacation spot of more Americans—4.8 million—than any other country in the world.

In 1958, for the first time, more tourists went to Europe by air than by sea, largely because of such inducements as economy class fares, fly-now-pay-later plans and credit cards all introduced that year.

During the decade, auto-minded Americans discovered the joys of driving abroad (250,000 honked their way around Europe in 1960 alone), with many purchasing autos at duty-free factory prices abroad and later shipping them home.

Such annual events as the Salzburg Music Festival, Edinburgh Drama Festival and the movie festivals in Venice and Cannes built up a regular U.S. patronage. Special events like Israel's 10th Anniversary in 1957, the Brussels World's Fair in 1958 and the 1960 Rome Olympics attracted additional throngs.

In contrast, the number of foreign visitors to the U.S. was relatively small—5.4 million visitors spent $900 million in 1959 and 4.7 million of them were neighbors from Canada.

To close the $1 billion gap between tourists' expenditures and receipts, the National Assoc. of Travel Organizations sponsored a promotion campaign abroad, "Visit U.S.A. Year —1960." The government obliged by easing visa restrictions.

Americans themselves, however, made up for the lack of foreign tourists—in 1960, 92 million spent $16 billion on vacation and business trips inside the U.S.

Of even wider interest was the sudden mushrooming of motels along the highways, later spreading to resort areas. They grew increasingly luxurious and by decade's end many were offering swimming pools and ultimate luxury of breakfast in bed.

PEACE AND BEAUTY of such Swiss resorts as St. Moritz *(above)* lured 270,000 U.S. tourists to Switzerland in 1959. More than one-third of all passport recipients were over 50 years of age; largest number came from N.Y., Calif., and Illinois.

CARRIBEAN BOOM started in 1954, spurred by faster air service, active promotion and construction of luxury hotels. 581,000 vacationers spent $164 million last year. Nearby Puerto Rico and the Virgin Islands particularly benefited. Tourism was Puerto Rico's third largest industry. In 1956 Laurence Rockefeller gave government 5000 acres on Caneel Bay *(above)*, St. John's Island, one of the three Virgin Islands, for a national park. He later built luxury resort there.

NEON LIGHTS glowed in the middle of the desert on Las Vegas' main street. Hotels began to attract conventions.

CAR-CRAZY AMERICANS hit the open road, filled motels as fast as they were built. New turnpikes and highways cut distances. 75 million people drove through National Forests, 63 million visited National Parks, setting new all-time records.

GLITTERING LINE-UP of such fantastically expensive hotels as the Fountainbleau *(r.)*, Americana and Eden Roc changed Miami Beach shore line in mid '50s. Carribean competition and cool weather chilled hotel owners for awhile, but convention business in the seasonal months and the gradual growth of the off-season summer trade helped fill the hotels.

DECADE SURVIVED THE SACK

Mid '50s made U.S. women shapeless, but return to nature brought back natural look; leisure living brought plethora of pants

FASHIONS in the '50s took on some sensational shapes, set off several minor revolutions, then simmered down and ended the decade in conservative lady-like style.

The early '50s were deceptively quiet. There were no radical edicts from Paris—silhouettes could be slim or full, hemlines stopped at a conservative 15 inches. Clothes had only to be pretty and feminine.

Then in 1955 the late French couturier, Christian Dior, broke things wide open with his introduction of the flat look—a flat denial of feminine curves. The reaction was violent; for once the ladies rebelled. Dior countered with modifications—the "A" look, the "H" look, the "Y" look—all geometrical shapes contrary to nature's plans, with waistlines moved up at the bosom, down at the hips or around the knees.

Although acceptance was only lukewarm and short lived, the groundwork was laid for an even greater revolution—the 1957 Battle of the Sack, which ignored the waistline completely. To compensate for its shapelessness, designers worked out some fit at the hip, concentrated on back interest and moved hemlines way up to the knee. In essence it amounted to a revival of the "razzamataz" of the roaring '20s with a long leg show, ropes of beads, headache bands, pointed shoes and the old Chanel look.

"BUBBLE SILHOUETTE" first appeared in 1958. Variations, most important of which was the harem skirt, all had tight hobble band at knee. Silk model *(r.)* was Tina Leser design.

By the end of 1958 the distorted, displaced and disfigured waistline made a shy reappearance, first in the form of the Trapeze—an elongated lampshade design with narrow shoulders, high waist and short flared skirt—followed by the Empire—a slim, easy line with the waist under the bosom.

The feminine figure was back in good shape by the end of the decade—necklines dipped, waists were nipped and skirts hipped.

Three important new designers appeared on the Paris front—Hubert de Givenchy, Yves St. Laurent and Jules Crahay. Italian couturiers came into their own during the decade and gave French houses a run for their money—Italian knits enjoyed a tremendous vogue.

U.S. designers made increasing use of the miracle fibers. Nylon, orlon and dacron came out of the utility class and showed up in party dresses and town suits. And reflecting the big move to outdoor living, designers emphasized sports collections, offered a plethora of pants—skin tight, short-short and toreador—as well as special outfits for boating, skiing and sports car afficiona das.

PLUNGING NECKLINE of cocktail dress worn at Paris Party by model (l.) was Jules Crahay's most copied number. Designer made headlines after his first show for House of Ricci in '59.

CONTROVERSIAL SACK revived fashion industry, although it was target of much abuse. Even Adlai Stevenson poked fun at Democratic women wearing chemises.

TRAPEZE LINE, successor to the Sack, restored the waist but to an unusually high level. Short, flared skirt as shown on Dior model added to ingenue look.

EMPIRE SILHOUETTE, with its high underbosom waistline, as on this white crepe by Madeleine de Rauch, was last link in change from chemise back to curves.

DEEP POT-LIKE HATS came in with the flapper look, survived the passing of the chemise and, by the end of the '50s, were so deep they almost hid the face.

22-YEAR-OLD DESIGNER Yves St. Laurent *(l.)*, successor to Christian Dior, who died of a heart attack in October 1957, proved himself in his first show. His introduction of the Trapeze was an immediate success and established him as top couturier. The late Dior is shown *(above)* waiting on Britain's Princess Margaret.

WAR ON CURVES was set off by Dior with introduction of the "A" look. The "H" look was narrow with waist at hip, "Y" look was tubular and cocoon-like.

CLAIRE McCARDELL, who died in March, 1958, was one of leading U.S. designers. She specialized in medium to high priced sports clothes, stressed casual look, easy fit. In 1959 she was posthumously named to "Hall of Fame."

ITALIAN FASHIONS made first U.S. appearance after American buyers, fed up with Paris prices, attended Florence fashion show in 1950. Italian designers now rival French, created the popular "Italian Haircut" (a cropped coiffure), specialize in sportswear and sleek evening clothes like two Fontana models above are wearing.

MINIMUM COVERAGE of bikini shocked U.S. women when introduced in 1946. Later, more modest versions won acceptance, dotted beaches by end of '50s.

U.S. SWINGS TO COMPACT CARS

Imports spark Detroit shift

DURING tthe '50s the automobile industry grew to phenomenal proportions and became so vital a part of U.S. economy that, like a barometer, its condition indicated the financial climate of the country. Auto sales, aided by mechanical gadgets and advertising gimicks, reached such heights that talk of the three-car family was no longer absurd.

In its growth the industry followed many unpredictable trends and reversals of trends. Generally the movement was toward bigger, more luxurious and more powerful cars. The race for horsepower between manufacturers was very evident in their advertising pitch, and by mid-decade horsepowe1 had reached 300. Autos had grown in size until fins and trunks kept many garage doors from closing, and parking became a real problem. The standard car colors were replaced by a kaleidoscope assortment. Equally varied was the choice of power operated gadgets which would do everything from raising the radio antenna to adjusting the seat, and the interiors had become almost as plush as the custom cars of royalty.

Before the war, price classes were as varied as body lines, but during the decade this variety diminished and all makes offered more or less the same appearance and performance while the price gap lessened.

The highest advertising budgets in automotive history were allocated in an attempt to spur sales. The heavy post war demand was finally met and then exceeded and it took strong advertising campaigns to move overstocks.

The influx of foreign cars began slowly at the start of the decade and rapidly increased in popularity until in 1959 alone there were 600,000 sold in the U.S. Sport cars appealed to those Americans who enjoyed driving for sheer fun and had not found it in domestic makes. Although limited in size and comfort they found their way into many garages as a "second car."

So many cars were imported from England and the Continent in the early fifties that General Motors in 1953 tested this new market potential, and the following year went into full scale production with the Corvette, with Ford following shortly after with the Thunderbird.

Sport cars gradually influenced a public interest in the possibility of smaller cars being ample for the average family. Low price, mileage economy and ease of parking made an attractive package for buyers of small compact imports Leaders among these cars were Renault, Hillman, Morris, with Volkswagen taking an early lead due to its reliability. By 1958 public acceptance of small economy cars was so firmly established that the little Rambler brought American Motors out of the red. The following year Studebaker-Packard staked its future on the Lark and was also saved. By 1960 the Big Three followed with compacts, Chrysler offering the Valiant, Ford the Falcon and Comet, and GM the Corvair.

REAR ENGINE CORVAIR was Chevrolet's bid for a share of the new compact market. First small car by the Big Three, it had 108 inch wheel base, alloy engine, lowest lines of all.

TYPICAL of the decade's trend to longer, lower, wider shapes was this Ford Starliner *(r.)*. Sales proved a still high demand for the conventional large six passenger family car.

VALIANT boasted liveliest performance with its 100 HP engine. Distinguished as "largest and heaviest of compacts," it was last to join the race but was soon selling as fast as made.

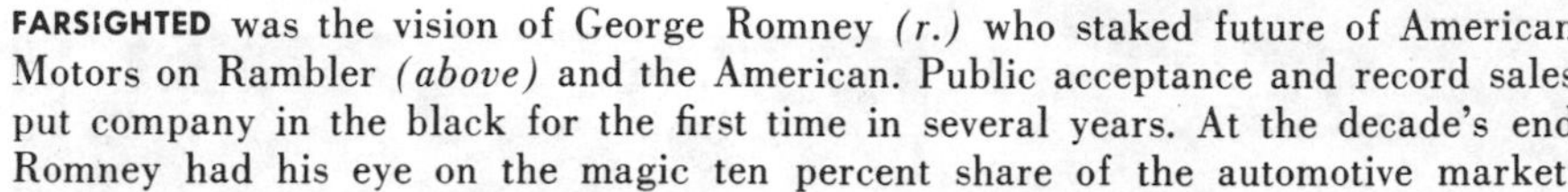

FARSIGHTED was the vision of George Romney *(r.)* who staked future of American Motors on Rambler *(above)* and the American. Public acceptance and record sales put company in the black for the first time in several years. At the decade's end Romney had his eye on the magic ten percent share of the automotive market.

COMPACT market proved the salvation of Studebaker-Packard when they introduced the Lark early *(bottom r.)*. However, its sales slipped when Big Three entered the fray and Ford offered the Falcon *(below)* and Comet *(r.)* which was to be sold by Mercury dealers. Buick, Pontiac and Oldsmobile were planning to come out with larger, more powerful "Luxury Compacts." Detroit also threatened to join the economy small car field, the exclusive domain of imports, if sales continued to rise. Contrary to predictions, import sales had not been affected by the compacts, which were still much larger and more costly.

STILL TOPS in demand despite changing market, Cadillac, symbol of success, sold one for every 40 cars in the U.S. Claims of quality were proven by the fact that one half of their 58 years production was still on the road.

CHEVROLET styling was more opulent than ever as numberless accessories, exteriors, and interiors were offered. The decade's trends found Chevies, Fords looking like Cadillacs.

AMERICAN SPORTCARS, Ford Thunderbird *(above)* and Chevrolet Corvette *(below)* came out in 1954 when market for small high performance cars became evident. Corvette, with its "souped-up" engine, found its way into sports car competition, while the T-Bird evolved as a personal car.

FAMILIAR "beetle" was no longer laughed at as Volkswagen sales were wait-listed up to three months in some locations. Sales of 180,000 during 1960 accounted for 1/3 of import market.

CHIEF CASUALTY in the automotive field was the Edsel. Developed at a cost of $250 million, the line was dropped after 26 months as the sales had not exceeded 110,000 cars.

CONTINENTAL was introduced to the luxury car market in 1956 as a revival of the famed classic. Although sales were poor at first, luxury market has tended to be stable.

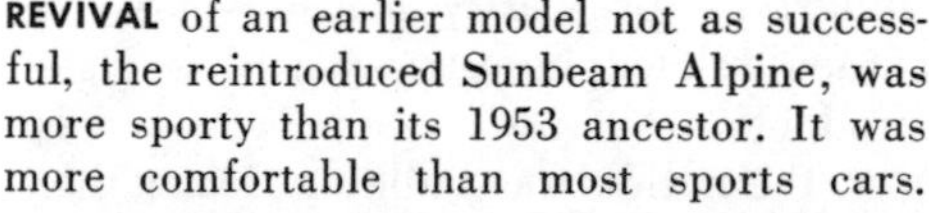

REVIVAL of an earlier model not as successful, the reintroduced Sunbeam Alpine, was more sporty than its 1953 ancestor. It was more comfortable than most sports cars.

SPRITE was introduced in 1959 as one of the lowest priced sports cars from England. Its $1795 price tag made it an immediate success with economy-minded enthusiasts. The 43hp engine gave over 30mpg and 80mph.

POPULAR since 1954 when it first appeared was the high performance Austin-Healey. Other fun cars responsible for the sports car movement were Jaguar, Triumph, and the familiar MG.

NEW YORK'S GUGGENHEIM MUSEUM was the last major work of the colorful, controversial dean of U.S. architects, Frank Lloyd Wright *(insert)*, who died in April, 1959, at age of 89. The cylindrical structure aroused typical Wright furor; his admirers hailed it with delight; his critics compared it to a "washing machine," "marshmallow," or "hot cross bun."

BUILDING SOARS

Construction sets prosperity pace, transforms cities, country areas

BY THE END of the decade, the U.S. building boom appeared to have become chronic.

The construction industry's annual volume soared from just over $30 billion at the beginning of the '50s to a record-breaking $72 billion in 1959.

There seemed to be no end to the demand for skyscrapers and factories, schools and churches, low cost housing projects and luxury apartment houses, and, most significantly, acre upon acre of suburban homes.

In addition, by the late '50s, most cities had embarked upon long-range, multi-million dollar programs to halt creeping obsolescence in their downtown districts—caused, in part, by the flight of business to the suburbs in pursuit of its customers and employes.

The industry suffered only two temporary setbacks—one in 1951, when a rise in prices, down payments and tighter credit slowed new home building, and one in 1957, when the general recession struck.

In 1958, stimulated by a many-sided government program that included increasing funds for mortgages and direct loans, private housing starts and industrial construction began to rise—and by 1959, it could be said that the U.S. had literally built its way out of the slump.

The building industry's prosperity helped spark the comebacks of a dozen related industries such as glass, brick and metal production.

As the '60s began, the nation was building, faster than ever before, on a firm foundation of prosperity.

LEVITTOWN, PA. was among the most spectacularly successful of decade's many mass housing developments. When it opened in 1952, 3000 houses were sold in two months. Contrary to some predictions, the mass developments thrived, did not become "rural slums," even though resale was brisk as original owners were able to afford more expensive homes.

SOUND OF THE '50s for many city dwellers was the clatter of construction as old buildings came down, new ones went up, transforming business and residential districts. Midtown Manhattan's Tishman Building *(above)* was first, in 1954, to be built with prefabricated aluminum walls; the 22-story skyscraper's walls rose at the rate of a floor every 38 minutes.

LUXURY HOMES OF '50s, like California residence *(above)* designed by Richard J. Neutra, were often showpieces of best in modern architecture. U.S. homes in all income brackets were bigger (for larger families), better equipped than ever before. Designed for casual, indoor-outdoor living, they featured patios, "family rooms," and open living-dining areas.

GEODESIC DOMES, easy to erect and offering unobstructed space within, began sprouting like mushrooms during the late '50s. They made ideal auditoriums; first of the important industrial domes was Union Tank Car Co.'s, as big as a major league baseball park, built in 1958 at Baton Rouge, La., to house company's regional maintenance and repair facilities.

UNITED NATIONS HEADQUARTERS, designed by international team of architects headed by Wallace K. Harrison of U.S., was perhaps most dramatic architectural achievement of decade. Started in 1946, on land donated by the Rockefeller family, the project was completed in 1953 at a cost of $65 million. Secretariat *(r.)* towers over New York's East River.

A GREAT STRIDE was taken in an ancient sport as the once-awesome four-minute mile was shattered repeatedly. History-maker was Roger Bannister of England, who flung himself into immortality at Oxford on May 6, 1954, in 3:59.4. As Australia's J. Landy (3:58) said, man needed only confidence.

SPORTS STRESS IS ON SIZE, SPECTACLES

U.S., USSR became chief Olympic rivals; four-minute mile fell; big league baseball turned into cross country contest

U.S. SPORTS both grew in size and underwent a series of transformations during the '50s.

Spectator sport audiences (not counting TV) did not keep pace with the growth in population, although they did increase in absolute totals.

Millions more Americans, blessed with both unprecedented prosperity and a doubling of leisure time, turned instead to such participation sports as bowling, boating and fishing.

Meanwhile spectator sports became even more—and more openly—a business, with primary emphasis on gate receipts. In baseball, still sentimentally acclaimed as the "National Game," such historic teams as the Brooklyn Dodgers and the New York Giants, moved to the Pacific Coast, where the profit potential was greater. (Baseball also was hurt by TV which, bringing Big League games everywhere, pulled the economic rug from underneath the minors.)

The result of the baseball shifts was to leave New York, the nation's largest city, without National League representation.

The situation led to plans to set up a third big league, the Continental, which was to be headed by baseball's "Grand Old Man," Branch Rickey, once Dodger owner, and which would of course have a New York team. But the new league was shelved, temporarily at least, when the National and American leagues each agreed to add two teams, raising each league total from eight to 10.

In professional football, the All-American Conference faded from the picture at the beginning of the decade, leaving the National Football League without a rival. But, as the '50s ended, a new and vigorous contender, the American Football League, came on the scene, backed by potentially lucrative TV contracts.

Meanwhile college football was being rocked by repeated revelations that star players on many teams, in open violation of eligibility rules, were being subsidized.

In tennis, the stars, and hence the interest, shifted from a technically amateur to an openly professional status. Those making the change included Jack Kramer and Pancho Gonzales of the U.S. and Lew Hoad and Ken Rosewall of Australia.

Boxing found itself in much the same position as baseball. The big championship bouts were well attended, but the little "clubhouse fights" which gave novices their chances were, like baseball's minor league, losing out to TV. (Boxing also ended the decade under the usual cloud of alleged underworld links; after the first Patterson-Johansson fight, the courts were called in to find out who really owned what contract and who was to get what money.)

But the purest amateurism, in keeping with the original Olympic spirit, characterized the U.S. Olympic Games entries, while Soviet and satellite athletes were acknowledged professionals in fact if not name.

The USSR, determined to "win" in total points (no official scores by nation are kept), had subsidized them while they devoted all their time and energy to years of intensive training. As the Rome games opened, the U.S. was expected to sweep the traditional male field sports, but the USSR to amass more points by triumphs in other phases, especially the women's events.

RUSSIAN GIRLS took first, second and third places in the 1952 Olympic women's discus event. The winner was blonde Nina Romaschkova *(above)*, who heaved 4 lb. 6.4 oz. discus 168 feet 8½ inches, to set a new women's world record.

AMERICA'S ANSWER to Russia's state-supported athletes were Parry O'Brien *(above)*, Bill Nieder, Dallas Long and Dave Davis, all of whom put the shot over 62 feet. The American men also dominated the other field events.

TO LEAP SEVEN FEET, straight up, is fantastic, but John Thomas of Boston University did it many times. He broke the record held by Soviet pride Yuri Stepanov, who was equipped by his propaganda-seeking sponsors with built-up shoes. John's record by mid 1960: 7 ft. 3¾ in. Going up!

EMIL (THE CHARGING CZECH) Zatopek, whose form was questionable, but who always seemed to get there first, was the decade's greatest distance runner. He won the 1952 Olympic 5000 and 10,000 meters, plus the grueling marathon, all in record time. Footnote: His wife also won the javelin.

A RUSSIAN CHAMPION who earned it the hard way, without the help of the Ministry of Propaganda or the Ministry of Adding Up Scores was Arkadi Vorobiev, Olympic middle-heavyweight champ lifter in 1956. His 3-lift total: 1019¼ pounds.

ONE OF ELEVEN world records established at '56 Olympics was this 287 ft. 2¼ in. javelin throw by Norway's Egil Danielsen.

LATEST AUSSIE WONDER, in the continuing parade of outstanding athletes from "Down Under" in tennis, swimming and track and field, was Herb Elliott, who dieted on nuts and juices and ran a mile in unprecedented time of 3:54.5.

FIRST AMERICAN to break the four-minute mile was Don Bowden of the Univ. of California when he ran it in 3:58.7 at Stockton, Calif., on June 1, 1957. By mid-1959 twenty-two athletes had broken the 4-minute mile 51 times.

WORLD RECORD in the shot put was set by Bill Nieder of Lawrence, Kansas, who flipped those 16 pounds a huge 65 feet, 7 inches at the Texas Relays April 2, 1960. His rivalry with Parry O'Brien glamorized shot-putting.

ALL-OUT effort by U.S. broad jumper Greg Bell, for a 25 ft. 8¼ in. leap, won gold medal in '56 Melbourne Olympic Games.

NO "SOONER" in land-rush days ran faster than Tommy McDonald *(above)* as Oklahoma won 47 straight. Fullback Jimmy Brown *(below)*, great at Syracuse, set rushing records for Browns.

SCORING ON SNEAK plays and passing to spectacular Cleveland Brown receivers (including a racehorse with Li'l Abner name of Mac Speedie), was Otto Graham *(above)*, named Mr. Pro Quarterback of early '50s. Tough Big Ten teams *(below)*, dominated the Rose Bowl. Iowa's Kenny Ploen sparks a 35-19 win over Oregon St.

NEW KINGS of pro football as the '50s ended were the huge, hustling Colts. Adoring Baltimore fans sang fight songs to heroes like the aptly named Alan (The Horse) Ameche, shown here as he gallops over two Green Bay Packers for a touchdown.

THIS MAN started out as a left-handed pitcher. Then his arm went dead. So he taught himself to throw right-handed and play the outfield. In 1960, at 39, he played on his 16th NL All-Star team—and hit a home run. So you see why they call Stan Musial (7 batting championship, 3 MVPs) THE MAN.

BIG HIT of '51 was this homer by Bobby Thomson (*below*) of the NY Giants. The Giants trailed Brooklyn by 13½ games in August, but won pennant on this last-gasp playoff clout. Controversial hero Ted Williams *(r.)* never tips his hat, but there's nothing controversial about two combat hitches as Marine pilot, over 500 homers, 16 all-star selections.

IKE WATCHES (*arrow*) American League's most valuable '56 player, New York Yanks' Mickey Mantle, tee off on 47th homer at Washington. Mantle led in HRs (52), RBIs (130); batting (.353).

GREATEST BASEBALL SHOWMAN of all time was Bill Veeck, who (1) sent a midget up to bat, (2) staged a "night" for a fan, (3) installed an exploding scoreboard in Chicago that acts like Cape Canaveral every time the White Sox hit homers.

PARTICIPATION sports swept the nation during the decade. By 1960, more than 12 million pleasure craft were afloat, and total annual expenditures on boating had reached a record $2 billion.

TRAILBLAZER for Negroes in tennis was Althea Gibson, here congratulated on winning at Wimbledon. Negroes are active in baseball, basketball, boxing, football and track.

LEADING LADY of 1952 Olympics was 19-year-old Andrea Mead Lawrence *(above)*, first U.S. skier to win two Olympic gold medals. Colorful Pancho Gonzales *(below,* far court) was decade's top tennist; toughest challenger, Lew Hoad.

HEARTTHROB of 1956 Winter Olympics was Toni Sailer, handsome mountain villager from Austria. Toni won the downhill slalom and giant slalom, and many feminine hearts. Russia dominated the games, however, winning seven gold medals.

RACE DRIVER'S STORY: *(l.)*, Bill Vukovich, winner, 1954; *(r.)*, Bill Vukovich, loser, 1955. Trying for third straight Indianapolis 500 victory, the little man with the lead foot and iron nerve died in a flaming crash. Some other great drivers killed during the decade were: Jack McGrath, Pat O'Connor, Mike Nazaruk and Bob Sweikert.

MOST SPECTACULAR Kentucky Derby finish of the decade came in 1957. Jockey Willie Shoemaker *(above)* mistook 16th pole for finish, stood up in Gallant Man's Stirrups, blowing the race to Iron Liege. Top Winner among jockeys was veteran Johnny Longden. Racing strictly on West Coast, he rolled up 5000th victory *(below)* at age 47, aboard Bente.

DESPITE DEATHS in sports cars of prominent personalities James Dean, Ali Khan and Marquis de Portago, boom continued. America's Carroll Shelby *(below)* wins at Le Mans.

CLASSIC FIXTURE of trotting, the Hambletonian, was moved from Goshen, N.Y. to DuQuoin, Ill. *(below.)* Change was dominant aspect of harness racing; air-conditioned, escalatored "dream tracks" soon at Yonkers and Roosevelt, N.Y.

THE BIG FIST in boxing during the early '50s was heavyweight champ Rocky Marciano's. Ex-champ Charles *(left)* and others tried gallantly to topple him, but the durable Rock out-bombed them all, retired unbeaten. Last Great Fight by Sugar Ray Robinson, 20 years a superb boxer, was this victory *(above)* over courageous Carmen Basilio. Ray then faded, lost to such boxers as plodder Paul Pender.

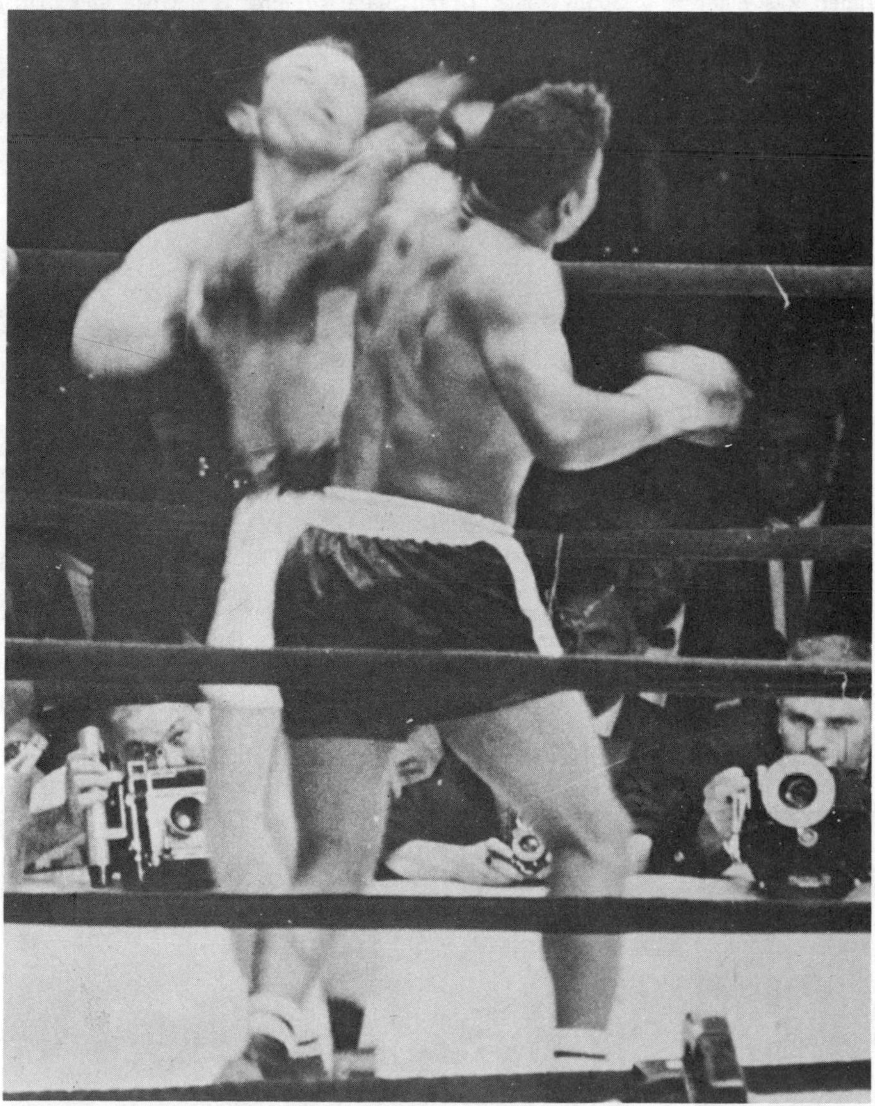

BLURRY WAS THE WAY the whole world looked for Ingemar Johansson when aroused Floyd Patterson caught him with this head-tearing left hook in 1960 return bout. Ingo was out for 10 minutes. This picture was taken from official fight films.

TREMENDOUS BOUNCE was shown by Floyd Patterson, who lost world's heavyweight title by 1959 kayo to Sweden's Ingo Johansson *(above)*, but bounced back to knockout Ingemar, June '60 *(below)*.

GREAT SHOT by both golfer and photographer was made during first round of 1953 Masters Tournament in Augusta, Ga. Ben Hogan *(above)* was having the greatest year since Bobby Jones' Grand Slam, copping U.S. Open and British Open as well as the Masters. He belted this guided missile from trap to green on his way to Masters' record of 274.

NEW SENSATION of golf as the decade closed was husky 30-year old Arnold Palmer of Latrobe, Pa. Taking over from aging Sam Snead and Hogan, he won the 1960 Masters and U.S. Open. He looked like solid bet to be top golfer of '60s.

TRAGIC QUEEN of sport world, Babe Didrikson Zaharias, shown here in 1954 Women's National Open Golf Championship, died in her early 40s. When told she had cancer, the great woman athlete philosophized, "It's the rub o' the green."

THE ROCKET BLASTS OFF as Maurice (The Rocket) Richard soars through the air *(left)* in pursuit of puck during the Stanley Cup playoff against Detroit. His Montreal Canadiens were decade's top team in National Hockey League.

SMASHING UPSET was turned in by U.S. hockey team at 1960 Winter Olympics at Squaw Valley, Calif. Given little chance against crack Canadian, Russian and Czech teams, they took the gold medal. Goalie Jack McCartan *(below)* starred.

WILT "THE STILT" Chamberlain, basketball's "Man Who Has Everything," took the game by storm. Seen here as a Kansas All-American, the 7′2″ wizard broke all scoring records as a 1959-60 rookie with the professional Philadelphia Warriors.

"LITTLE" MAN at 6′1″ in a league of giants, Bob Cousy's fantastic ball-handling and shooting made him player of the decade. Here, he leads Boston Celtics to 1960 NBA championship in playoff victory over St. Louis Hawks.

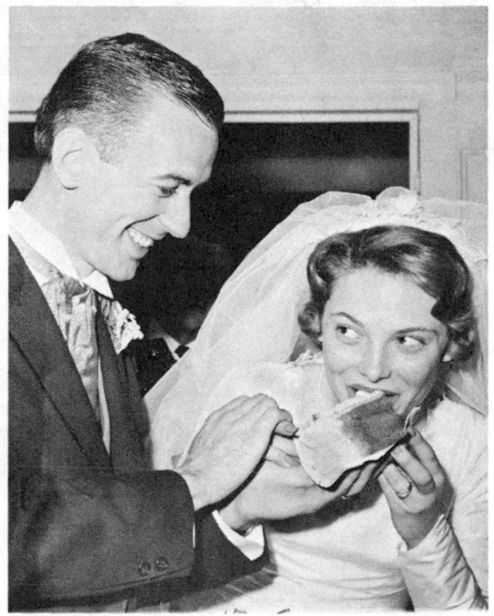

SWEETHEART of U.S.A. after winning 1960 World and Olympic figure skating championships, Carol Heiss was special darling of Hayes Jenkins, a former World and Olympic champion himself. Soon after Olympics they were married.

GALLANT GIRL swimmer was Shelly Mann, record-smashing 1956 Olympic butterfly-stroke champion. Shelly's was classic story of athlete's triumph over illness. As a child she was told that polio had doomed her to an invalid's life.

BOWLING BOOMED. Don Carter, here with 1957 ladies' match game champ Merle Matthews, was No. 1 player, despite unorthodox form. Sport zoomed to No. 2 spot in popular participation. No. 1 was hunting, fishing. No. 3, golf.

THE GAME IS A RUMOR if you are sitting in the far end zone, but Los Angelenos do not care. A record 93,000 fans are watching Walter O'Malley's Dodgers win the 1959 World Series with Chicago in the mammoth Coliseum, a football stadium.

TWO HAPPY BUSINESSMEN, Walter "Cigar" O'Malley, Horace Stoneham, flank one unhappy mayor, New York's Wagner, in 1957. Unsmiling reporters ask classic question "Is Brooklyn still in League?" It was not; the California gold rush was on.

KING QUARTERBACK as '60s began was the nervy Johnny Unitas (*above*). He played on sandlots for ten bucks while waiting chance, got it, drove Baltimore Colts to two straight championships. Star attraction of new American Football League was LSU's Billy Cannon (*below*), a Heisman Trophy winner. League won court fights with NFL over him, also fullback Charley Flowers.

BASEBALL IS A BUSINESS, he learned. A nation was touched, owners embarrassed by photo of tough veteran Enos Slaughter in tears when told he had been sold to Yanks by his beloved Cardinals. Eddie Stanky, St. Louis manager, comforts disillusioned old-timer.

PULITZER PRIZE winning photo shows John Bright of Drake (43), the nation's record- breaking yardage gainer, being deliberately injured in a 1951 game with Oklahoma A&M when he did not even have the ball. Bright's jaw was broken. In 1959 a similar foul, also caught by the camera, cost a Pacific Coast football star an All-American nomination.

NEMESIS of monopolistic boxing empire set up by Jim Norris *(above)* was N.Y. Boxing Commissioner Julius Helfand, wearing victory smile *(below)*. Norris' International Boxing Club was dissolved by Fed. Judge Sylvester Ryan's order.

GRIM SCENE. Detectives question former Kentucky basketball greats. Alex Groza looks glumly at fix evidence, Ralph Beard stares into space, contemplating career smashed by "dumping" practiced in collusion with crooked gamblers.

HE'S SURPRISED, world is delighted. Ed Furgol, born with withered left arm, was given no chance in 1954 U.S. Open. Here, he takes daring shot onto unused fairway. He made it, winning an immensely popular victory by a single stroke.

ROMANCE of the decade occurred when Olga Fikotova *(above)*, Czech discus thrower, and American hammer throw champ Harold Connolly *(r.)*, fell in love during 1956 Olympics in Melbourne. Despite language difference, they started with one thing in common;

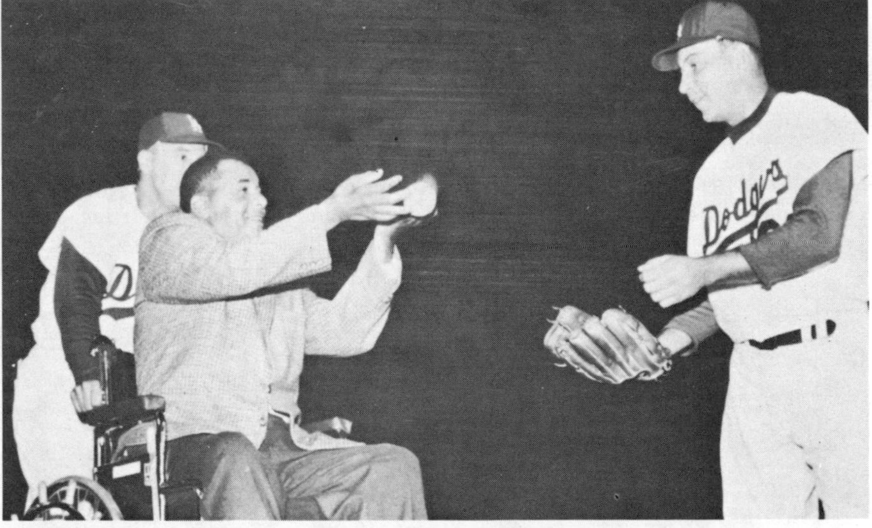

TRAGEDY AND TRIUMPH. Roy Campanella, 3-time MVP Brooklyn catcher, was paralyzed in auto accident, fought way back to regain most of faculties, became radio commentator. Here Johnny Podres, battery mate in historic victory over Yankees in 1955 Series, catches one from Campy. Occasion was 1959 Campanella Night at Los Angeles Coliseum, attended by crowd of 93,103.

BROTHERHOOD OF MAN. Giant Maurice Stokes was outstanding rookie in pro basketball, then suffered rare brain disease, was totally paralyzed. Jack Twyman, Cincinnati Royals star, worked with teammate night and day, raised needed funds. After two years Stokes could sit up, attended game, posed with pal and Wilt Chamberlain.

both broke Olympic records. The Iron Curtain regime in Czechoslovakia said "No wedding," but big Hal went to Prague and won fight for his bride. Other sports world sweethearts were world, Olympic figure-skating champs, Hayes Jenkins, Carol Heiss (p. 247).

FOOTBALL ODDITY of decade came when a substitute, Tommy Lewis, of Alabama, lost his head at the sight of Rice's Dickie Moegle dashing goalward. Lewis (42) rushed onto field, tackled amazed Moegle. Referee awarded touchdown. Rice won 1954 Cotton Bowl, 28-6. "12th Man" incident got bigger headlines than result.

HIGHEST HONOR an athlete can win in Great Britain was conferred upon Gordon Richards, who became Sir Gordon when knighted by Queen in 1952. Sir Gordon, seen sharing a quip with the Queen, Prince Philip, at storied Epsom Downs, is top race winner.

SPORTS OF FUTURE will be played in settings to match this luxury plant at Aqueduct, New York. N.Y. Racing Assn. spent $33 million, completely remodeled old track. Note saddling sheds in front of grandstand. New dream track opened Sept. 14, 1959, set all-time record when 70,000 attended, bet $5 million on Memorial Day, 1959. Meanwhile, football promoters planned all-weather stadia with retractable roofs, rotating grandstands adaptable to many different sports.

CRIME RATE CONTINUED HIGH DESPITE U.S. PROSPERITY

Murders, kidnappings, underworld revenge kept headlines of '50s filled; juvenile delinquency became ever graver problem; Chessman fight against execution drew world attention; spy cases highlighted Communist threat

PROTAGONISTS in life-and-death drama that created international storm were convicted rape-kidnapper Caryl Chessman *(r.)*, California Governor Edmund G. "Pat" Brown *(l.)*. Chessman, sentenced to die in San Quentin's gas chamber in 1948, fought 12-year legal battle for his life, won eight reprieves, but was finally executed in April, 1960, after Gov. Brown could not grant plea for one more stay. Chessman, who wrote three books while on Death Row, won wide sympathy both in U.S. and abroad; many believed his protestations of innocence, others felt that 12 years in shadow of gas chamber were punishment enough in themselves. His death gave fresh ammunition to foes of capital punishment.

DARK WORLD of a troubled child's mind was revealed when the parents of eight-year-old Melvin Dean Nimer *(above)* were stabbed in their Staten Island, N. Y., home in 1959. Melvin's conflicting stories raised suspicion that he was the murderer, but police and psychiatrists were never quite sure.

MYSTERY SLAYING of millionaire playboy Serge Rubenstein *(above)* in January, 1955, was as sensational as his exploits in the world of finance. The 46-year-old, Russian-born banker was bound and strangled in his Fifth Avenue town house; the New York police were unsuccessful in finding the killer.

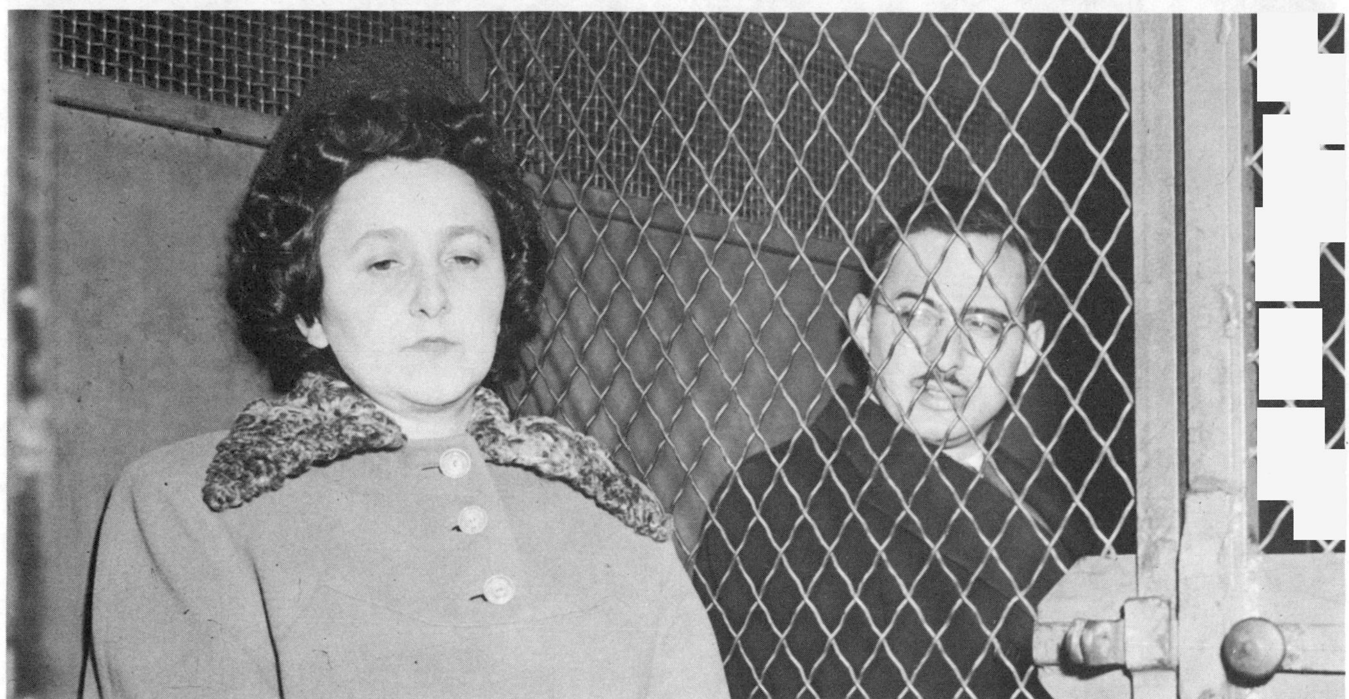

ATOM SPIES Julius and Ethel Rosenberg were first U.S. civilians ever to receive peacetime death sentence for espionage. They were arrested in June, 1950, after arrest in Great Britain of atom scientist Dr. Klaus Fuchs uncovered a trail of conspiracy that led back to Los Alamos, N. M., where, during World War II, Ethel Rosenberg's army sergeant brother had stolen vital atomic data for Soviet Union at his sister's bidding. In the words of Federal Judge Irving Kaufman, who sentenced them to electric chair in April, 1951, they had "altered the course of history" by speeding Soviet development of atom bomb. In spite of appeals for clemency from all over the world, they died at Sing Sing on June 19, 1955.

HOLLYWOOD TRAGEDY of decade was 1958 stabbing of shady Johnny Stompanato *(above, c.)*, boyfriend of Lana Turner *(l.)* by actress' 14-year-old daughter, Cheryl Crane *(r.)*, in her Beverly Hills home. Cheryl told police she had killed him to "protect" her mother; famous Hollywood defense attorney Jerry Geisler won verdict of justifiable homicide.

RACE HATRED in the South exploded into violence many times in the '50s. Most southern courts came far closer than ever before to granting equal justice to whites and Negroes; but 22-year-old Negro truck driver Mack Parker, accused of raping a pregnant white woman, never reached the courtroom. His bullet riddled body was pulled from Pearl River on Mississippi-Louisiana border on May 5, 1959 *(above)*; a lynch mob had dragged him from jail in Poplarville, Miss.

BOBBY GREENLEASE, son of wealthy Kansas City, Mo., automobile dealer *(above)*, was kidnap victim in 1953. The six-year-old was killed after $600,000 ransom had been paid. His abductors, Bonnie Healy, Carl Hall, died in the gas chamber.

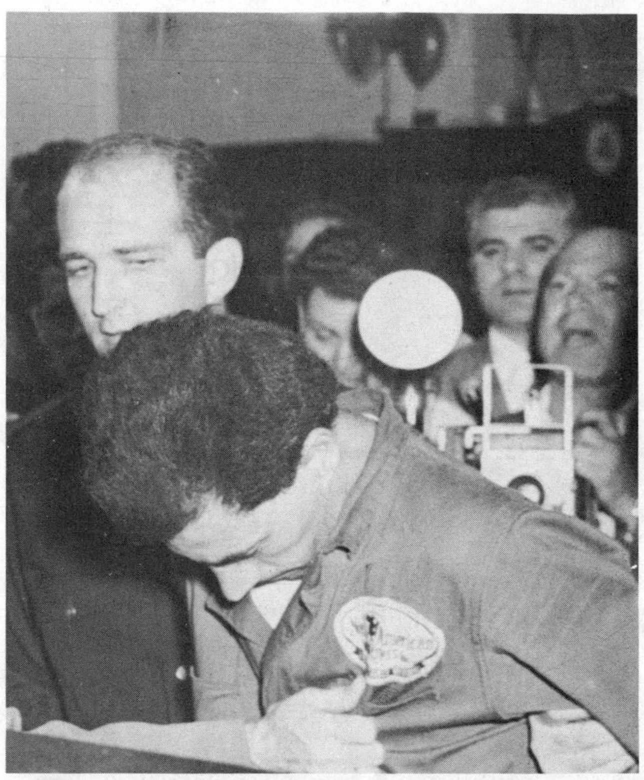

CONFESSION of Angelo John LaMarca *(above)* closed one of decade's most pathetic kidnapping cases. He had stolen 32-day-old son of Mr. and Mrs. Morris Weinberger from their Westbury, N. Y., home, July 4, 1956; abandoned baby to die.

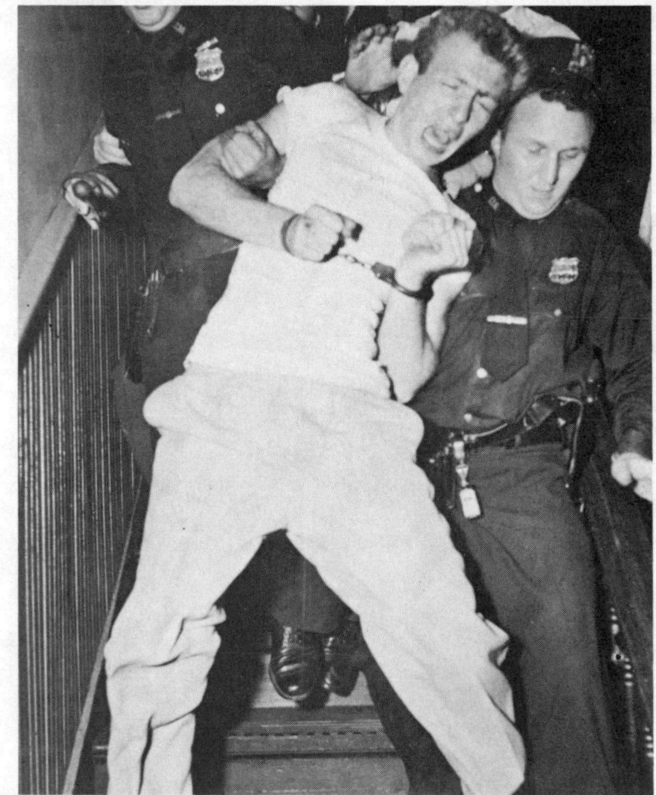

JUVENILE CRIME RATE rose steadily throughout decade to become one of nation's most painful problems. Face of 17-year-old New Yorker charged with assault *(above)* reflects the tormented violence of thousands of teen-age lawbreakers.

YOUNG MAN ABOUT TOWN Mickey Jelke was convicted of procuring in sensational 1953 trial, sentenced to three to six years in Sing Sing. The 23-year-old oleomargarine heir's father claimed after arrest, "he just likes good looking girls."

AIR AGE GET-RICH-QUICK SCHEME for insurance beneficiaries: blow up plane on which policy holder is traveling. Robert Spears *(above, l.)* in 1960 was suspected of neat variation—planting bomb in plane he was scheduled to take, leaving before takeoff, disappearing to let wife collect insurance after crash. (In other cases, saboteurs actually did commit

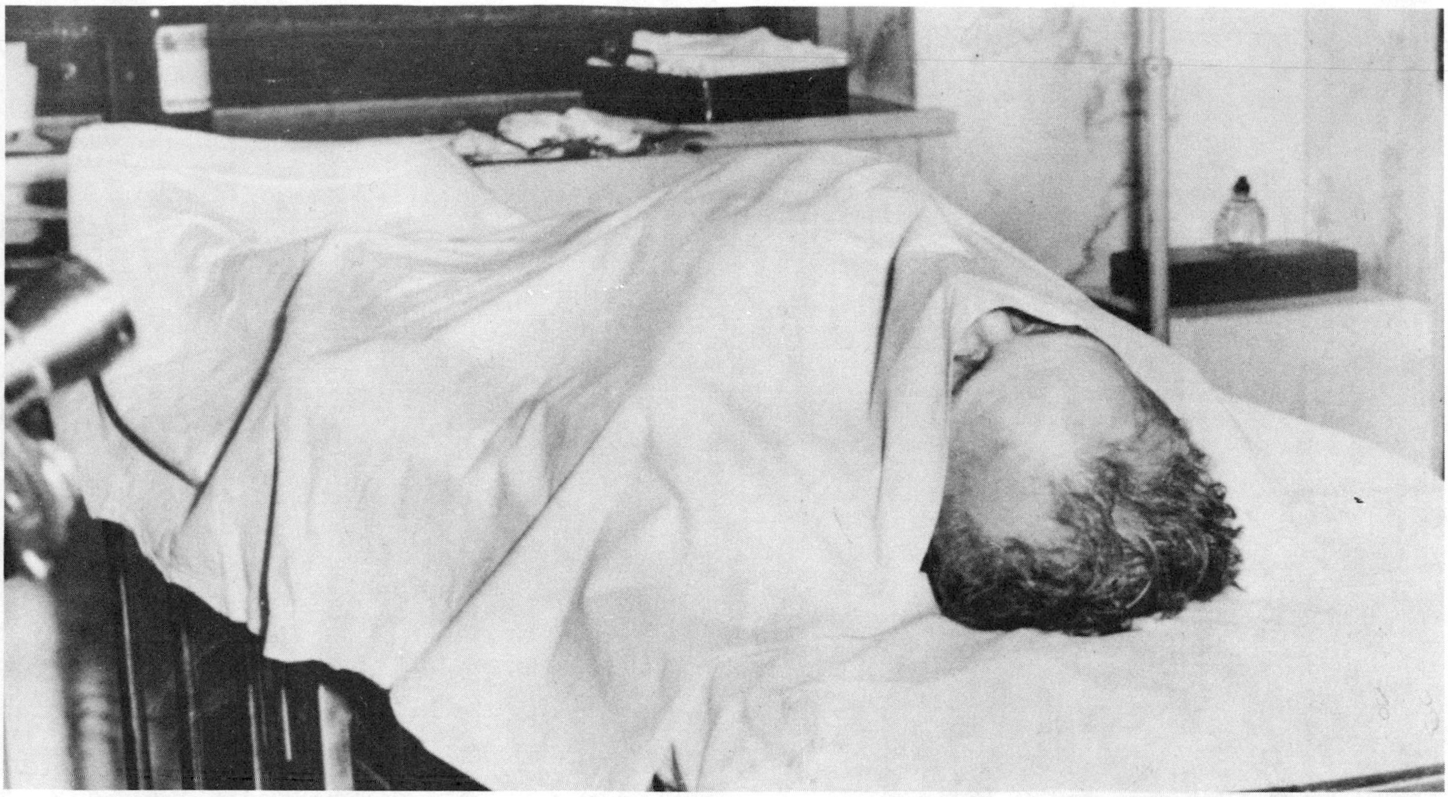

UNDERWORLD REVENGE caught up with prohibition-era gangster Roger Touhy *(above)* when he was paroled in December, 1959, after serving 25 years in prison. He was shot and killed on a Chicago street in traditional gangland fashion. Motive was unknown, but police suspected link with fact that Touhy had been working on a perhaps-too-outspoken autobiography.

suicide.) In 1955, an airliner crashed in Colorado, killing 44 *(above, c.)*, because 23-year-old John Gilbert Graham had planted a bomb in his mother's luggage for insurance money.

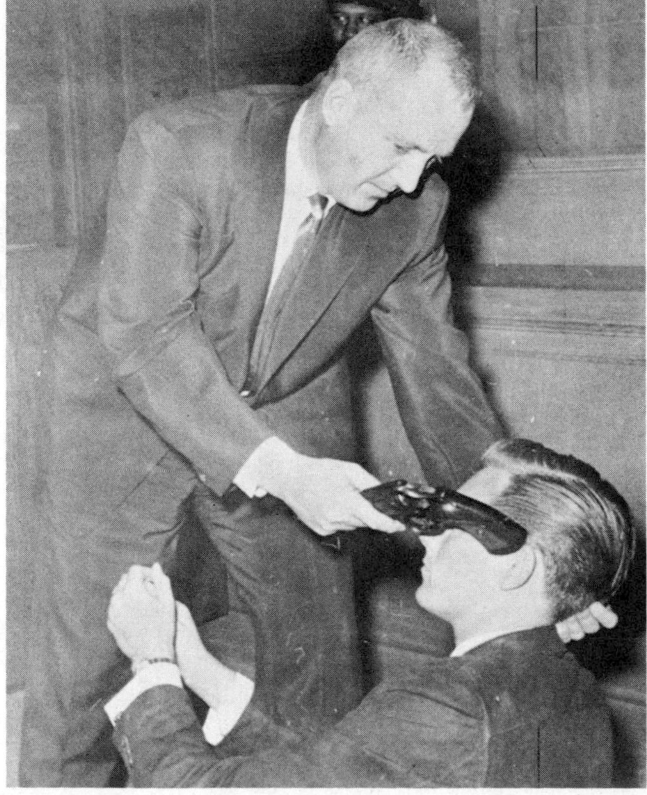

COURTROOM DRAMA of 1960 was trial of Dr. Bernard Finch *(above, l.)* and his girl friend, Carole Tregoff, for murder of his wife. Jury was "hung," second trial was scheduled.

THE FACE OF TRAGEDY stares over the ruins of 2 million homes and the rubble under which nearly 20,000 were buried in South-Central Chile. The worst earthquakes of the decade devastated the country in the spring of 1960, and tremors continued to be felt as a herculean rescue and relief program was carried out. So violent were the quakes that enormous waves not only wiped out villages in Chile, but swamped the coasts of Japan and the Hawaiian Islands across the Pacific.

ANGRY NATURE SHOWS ITS POWER

DISASTERS caused by nature took the highest toll of life and property during the decade, but air, sea and highway crashes ran a devastating second-best.

Typhoon Vera washed away the homes of 1 million Japanese in 1959, left 5000 dead in its rampaging floods and landslides. Violent earthquakes rocked Asia and South America, burying thousands in India, Afghanistan, Iran, Chile and Morocco.

In 1951 an avalanche swallowed whole Swiss towns, and high tides in the North Sea washed over the vulnerable Lowland countries in 1953, smashing Netherlands dikes which had stood for 500 years. In the U.S., tornadoes in the Southwest in 1952-53, hurricanes in the Northeast in 1954-55 and river floods in the West in 1951-52 became rivals of each other in their destructive intensity.

The typhoon sinking of the Japanese ship *Toya Maru* in 1954, drowning 1218, was worst of many ferry disasters which plunged thousands to death in the British Isles, Korea, India, Yugoslavia, Burma, Turkey, Egypt.

Human and mechanical failures continued to wreak havoc throughout the world. Military and civilian planes crashed with tragic frequency, and rail collisions mangled scores of commuters. A dynamited military truck blew up eight city blocks in Bogota, Colombia, killing 1100 in 1956, and mine explosions buried over 700 Belgians, Indians and Africans.

But carelessness on U.S. highways continued to take the highest accident toll, claiming its 1 millionth victim near Cleveland in 1951, and slaughtering 37,800 in 1959 alone. The 1960 death toll has been estimated at 40,000.

TWO RENDING EARTHQUAKES destroyed the Moroccan port and resort city of Agadir in early 1960, leaving 12,000 dead in their wake. In the aftermath—a tidal wave, fires and 45,000 homeless. U.S. and French rescue planes air-lifted victims to hospitals and the wrecked city was evacuated, leaving only a military contingent to guard against looting. King Mohammed V pledged his personal fortune for collateral on a loan to begin the $100 million rebuilding program.

HURRICANE DIANE deluged the Northeastern U.S. in 1954, causing flood emergencies in Pennsylvania, Massachusetts, Rhode Island and Connecticut. Driving rains and swollen rivers took 200 lives, broke all previous flood records.

COFFINS piled upon coffins await burial at funeral services in Frejus, France, after the Malpasset Dam burst its walls and drowned 274 in December, 1959. A Spanish dam broke earlier in the year after month-long rains, took 132 lives.

DEATH IN THE NIGHT came to 176 sleeping crew members of the minesweeping destroyer *Hobson* when it was suddenly rammed and cut in half by the aircraft carrier *Wasp* during peacetime maneuvers in mid-Atlantic in 1952. The *Hobson* sank in a record four minutes. Only 61 men were able to get free, were pulled from the oily water by *Wasp's* crew.

GRAND CANYON, Ariz., was the site of the worst crash in commercial aviation history when a United Airlines DC-7 smashed into a Trans World Airlines Super Constellation in mid-air after leaving Los Angeles only 3 minutes apart. The 128-death toll was equalled only when a U.S. Air Force C-119 crashed, burned 129 to death in Tokyo in '53.

LISTING HEAVILY is the Italian luxury liner *Andrea Doria* just before it went to a watery grave after colliding with the Swedish ship *Stockholm* in a thick night fog 45 miles south of Nantucket in 1956. The *Stockholm*, suffering only a crushed bow, took 533 survivors aboard, was assisted by 12 other ships. The death toll in this disaster was 50.

THREE-WAY COLLISION crushed and scalded 111 to death in a 55-foot-high mound of twisted steel when two express trains, running in opposite directions, plowed into a packed commuter train at a railway station 10 miles north of London Oct. 8, 1952. Passengers on the crowded platform also were injured as two locomotives were hurled at them.

SCHOOL BUS bearing the bodies of 26 children is inspected grimly as it is dredged up from the rain-swollen Big Sandy River in Kentucky after it crashed into a wrecking car and a truck. Only 20 children could make their way to safety after the bus careened into the raging torrents which carried it 200 ft. downstream, defying searchers for days.

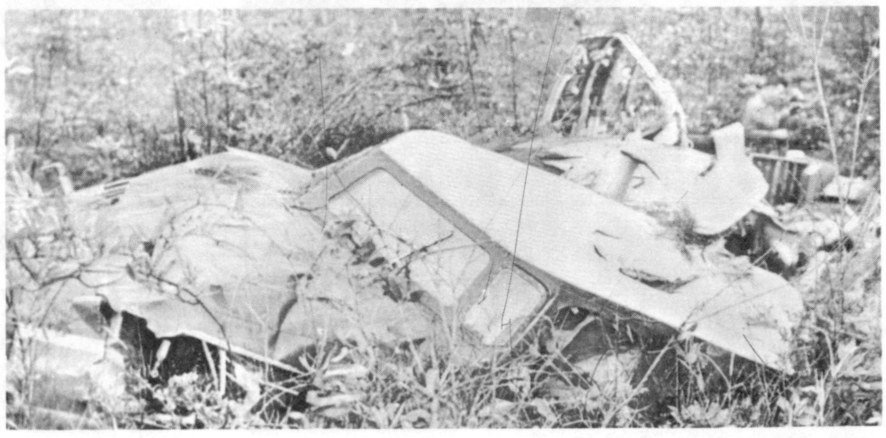

SUICIDE BOMB was suspected cause of 1960's first major air crash, killing 34 over Bolivia, N. C. Evidence of dynamite was found near seat of lawyer Julian Frank, who held insurance worth $1 million. This was the second National Airlines crash in two months, a DC-7 having plunged 42 to their death over Gulf of Mexico in November, '59.

NEW YORK CITY CRASH during blinding snow storm Feb. 1, 1957, which killed 20 aboard Northeast Airlines DC-6 one minute after taking off from LaGuardia Airport, was only one of series of crashes in populated areas. Elizabeth, N. J. was three-time victim in eight weeks (1951-52). Reaction was temporary closing of Newark Airport, though pilots called it safest field in U.S. An emergency landing failure in 1959 left ruins of houses near Midway Airport, Chicago.

DEATH ON THE RAILS crushed 78 commuters on Thanksgiving Eve, 1950, when one Long Island train rushed headlong into another which had halted for caution signal. Reacting heroically, many survivors returned to wreckage to help. Unidentified doctor *(below)* gives plasma to one of the victims.

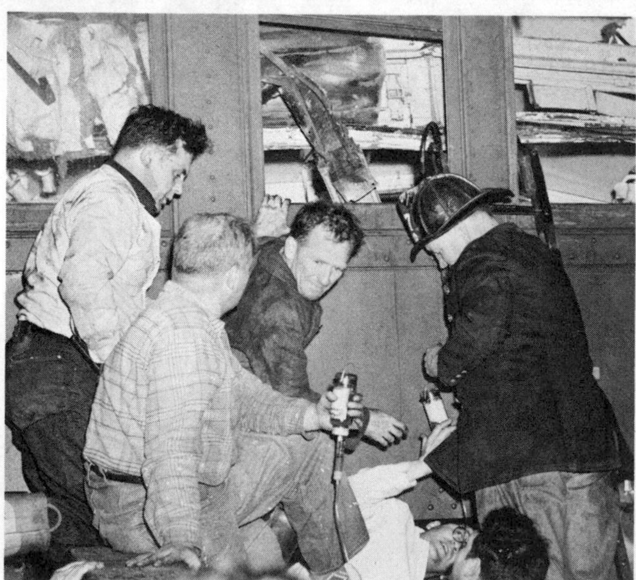

MORNING AFTER view shows where 84 were killed and 500 injured when Pennsylvania Railroad commuter train plunged from the tracks of temporary wooden overpass at Woodbridge, N. J., Feb. 6, 1951. The engineer admitted speeding beyond regulation; no warning signal marked detour area.

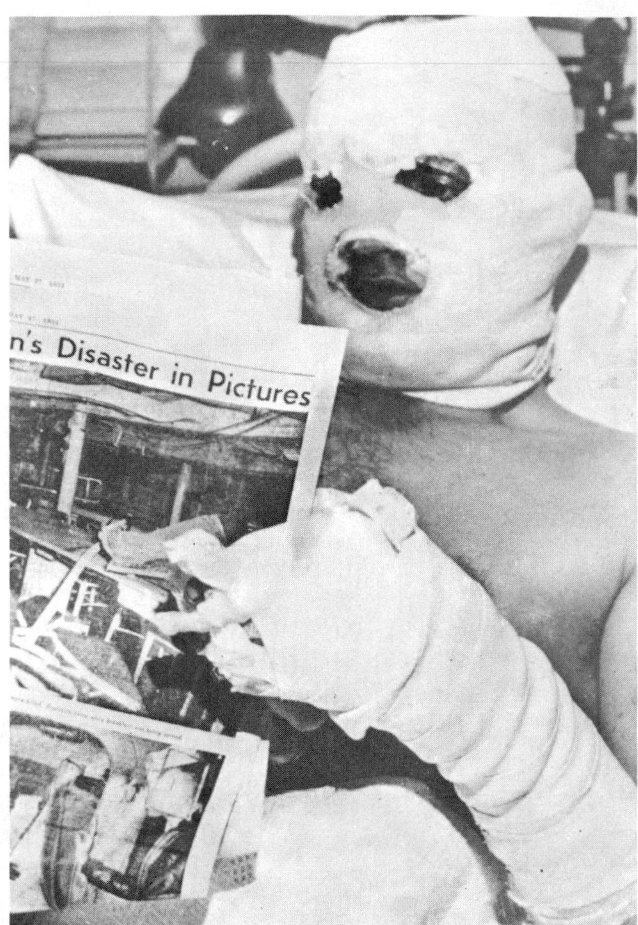

READING ABOUT the explosion and fire which ripped open his ship, the *USS Bennington,* is Cecil Carrier, one of the 201 wounded in the May, 1954, blast. It was so powerful that dental charts had to be used to identify some of the 93 victims, many of whom died when escape hatches became sealed.

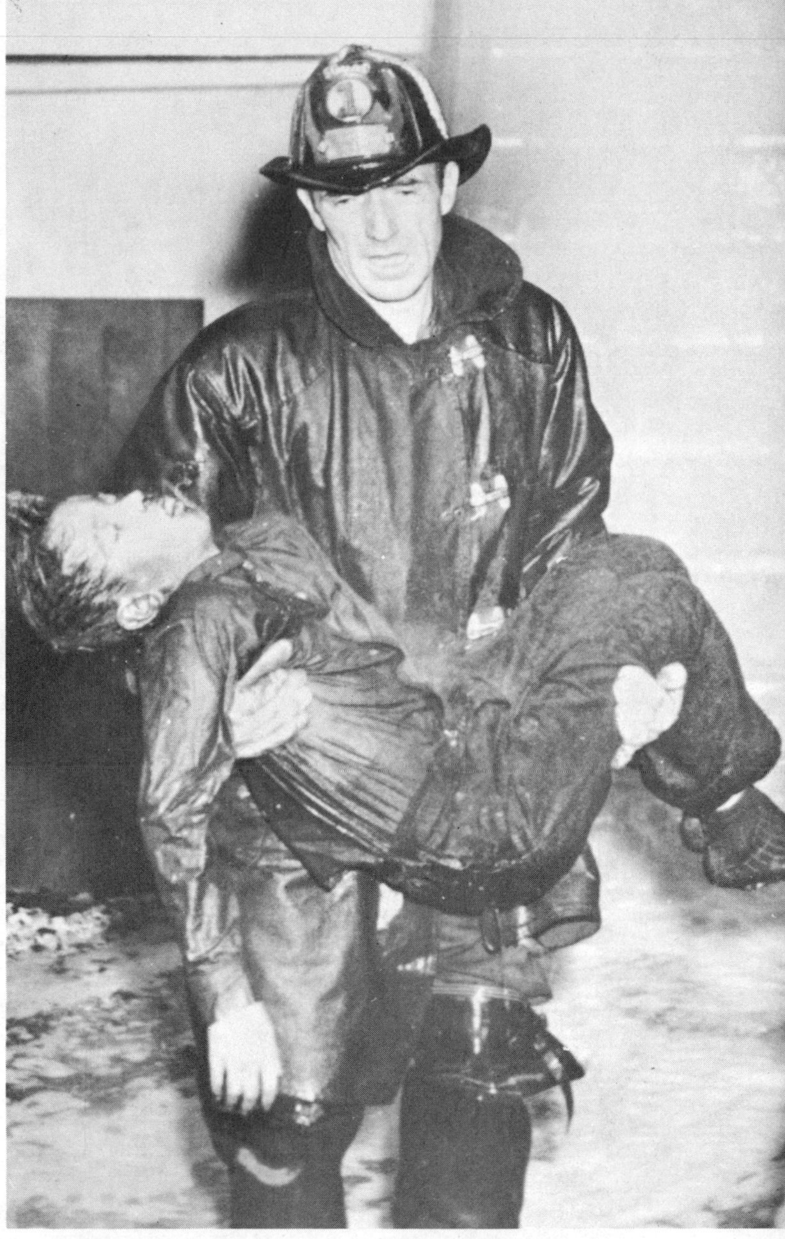

FIREMEN SEARCH CHARRED RUINS of Our Lady of the Angels Parochial School in Chicago for the bodies of children after a furious blaze Dec. 2, 1958, which claimed the lives of 89 school children and three nuns. Scores of pupils leaped frantically from the burning building and were hospitalized with injuries. The worst school fire in the city's history, the tragedy was heightened by a 20-minute delay in sounding the alarm, prompted many other U.S. cities to begin investigation of their own fire hazards to avoid like tragedies.

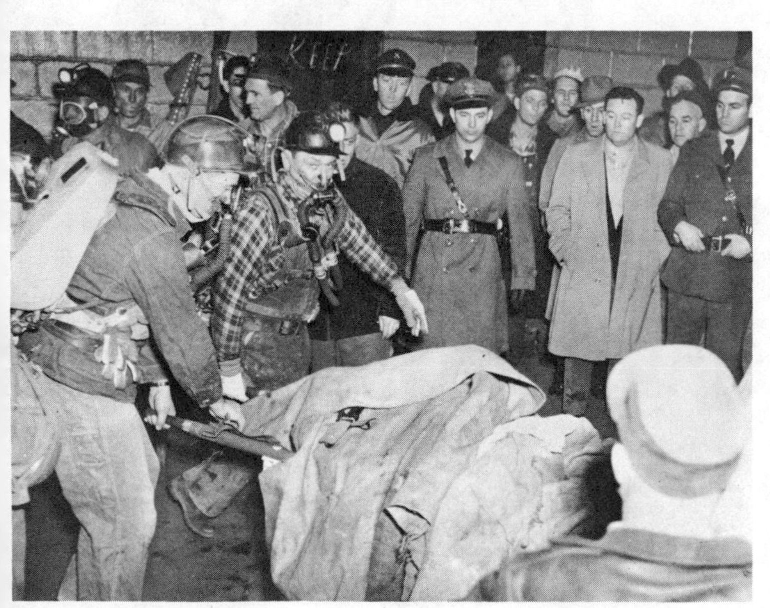

GAS MASKED rescue workers still carrying out victims 58 hours after a 1951 mine blast in West Frankfort, Ill., are watched by grim observers who remember the three other explosions in the same New Orient mine during the last 30 years. The death toll—119. In the South, two explosions rocked the Pocahontas Fuel Co. mine in Virginia, fatally trapping 37 in 1957 and 22 in 1958. In 1960, 18 died in a coal mine fire in Logan, W. Va. Coalbrook, South Africa, mines were decade's hardest hit, losing 417 in 1960 slides.

Passing

SECOND "MAYFLOWER" sails into New York Harbor to spend the summer months of 1957 on display. The 190-ton replica of the pilgrim ship set sail from Plymouth, England on April 22, reached Provincetown, Mass., 53 days later, 14 days less than its predecessor.

REFUGEES STILL SWARMED across borders fifteen years after WW II ended. Some 15 million were still unsettled in 1960. Oldest refugee on record *(l.)*, 105, smokes while waiting for next plane.

ROCK 'N' ROLL RIOT in NYC demanded all the efforts which over a dozen policemen could muster when Alan Freed fans tried to crash the already lengthy lines outside the theatre in 1958.

ONE OF RICHEST MEN in world, John D. Rockefeller, Jr., died May 11, 1960, was buried in quiet ceremony, left $150 million estate. Half went to widow Martha *(below)*, whom he wed in 1951.

Scene PEOPLE AND EVENTS THAT MADE BIG OR SMALL HEADLINES DURING THE DECADE

JIMMY BOYD SANG AND STRUMMED "I Saw Mommy Kissing Santa Claus" to tune of $100,000 in 1953, when over 1 million copies of the Christmas record were sold the first year.

READY TO SURRENDER in 1953 after nine years of jungle hiding, Japanese Pfc. Eguchi, still carrying rifle, found war ended in the Philippine Islands, decided to settle down there.

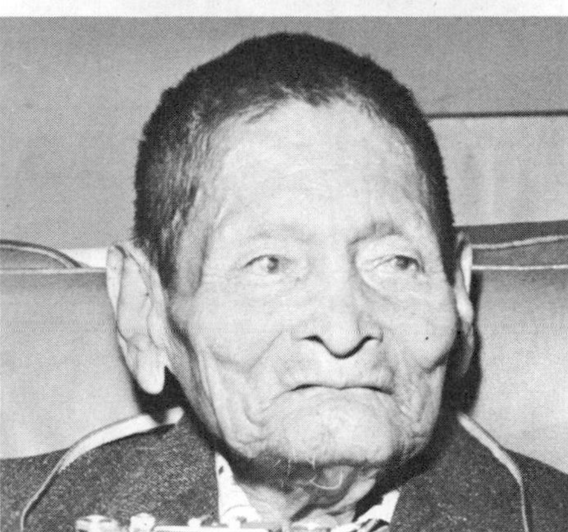

OLDEST MAN IN WORLD was Javier Pereira, or so it was claimed by those who believed him to be 168 when he died Mar. 30, 1956, at Monteria, Colombia. Experts stated there was no way to fix the exact age of the 4-foot-4 Indian.

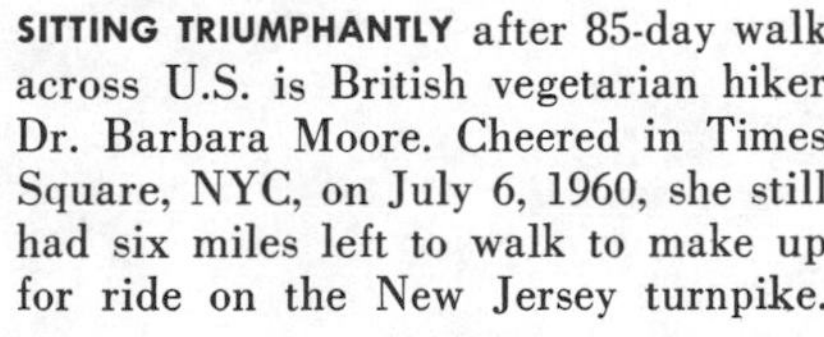

SITTING TRIUMPHANTLY after 85-day walk across U.S. is British vegetarian hiker Dr. Barbara Moore. Cheered in Times Square, NYC, on July 6, 1960, she still had six miles left to walk to make up for ride on the New Jersey turnpike.

LAST UNION ARMY VETERAN, Albert Woolson, former drummer boy, smokes cigar shortly before death in 1956 at age of 109. He was outlived by last Confederate soldier Walter Williams, who succumbed in 1959 in Texas at age 117.

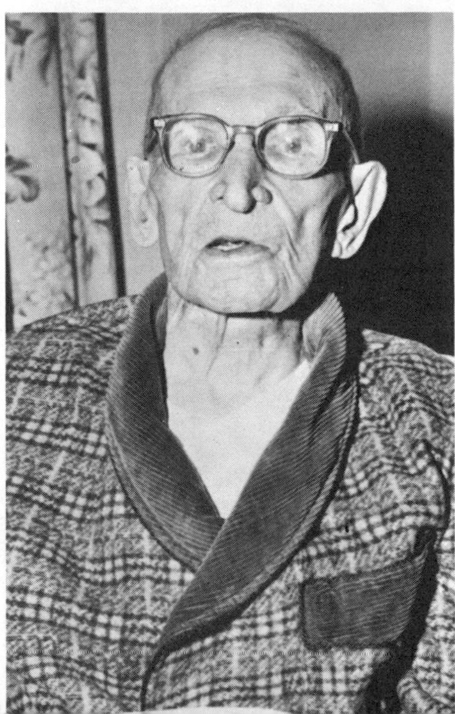

A LESS FORMIDABLE Mt. Everest looms in the distance, made so through bravery of Sir Edmund Hillary *(l.)* and Sherpa guide Tensing Norkey. They reached summit in 1953, climaxing assaults on 29,000 foot peak which had taken many lives.

STILL FIRST LADY for many, Mrs. Eleanor Roosevelt, looking forward to 75th birthday, cheerfully posed in New York hotel in this 1959 pre-birthday picture.

MAKING THE SCENE in Capri is "world citizen" Garry Davis, who "digs" internationalism, was given shelter by sympathetic widow for his "world republic."

MORNING CONSTITUTIONAL of Pres. Truman became part of the American scene. Early Missouri morning in 1953 shows ex-President strolling without usual crowd.

CRUEL SEA lashes doomed Flying Enterprise. Trying to save his ship from salvagers, Capt. Kurt Carlsen *(r.)* refused to abandon his ship, stayed with it till final moments came.

GRAND OLD MAN of the "Grand Old Party," oldest living ex-president, Herbert Hoover, celebrates 86th birthday in Waldorf Astoria, surrounded by cards, but still hard at work.

CLIPPED HOUND DOG, Pvt. Elvis Presley in '58 wryly contemplates next two years of Army life, in which most of "swinging" will be done with a rifle.

THE LATE AGA KHAN III, spiritual head of 20 million Ismaili Moslems, arrives at Excelsior Hotel in Rome with his wife, the Begum. The ebullient Khan died in France in 1957.

MILLIONTH REFUGEE, Andres Suritis, 10, was brought to the U.S. via Latvia and German refugee camp with the aid of the International Committee for European Migration.

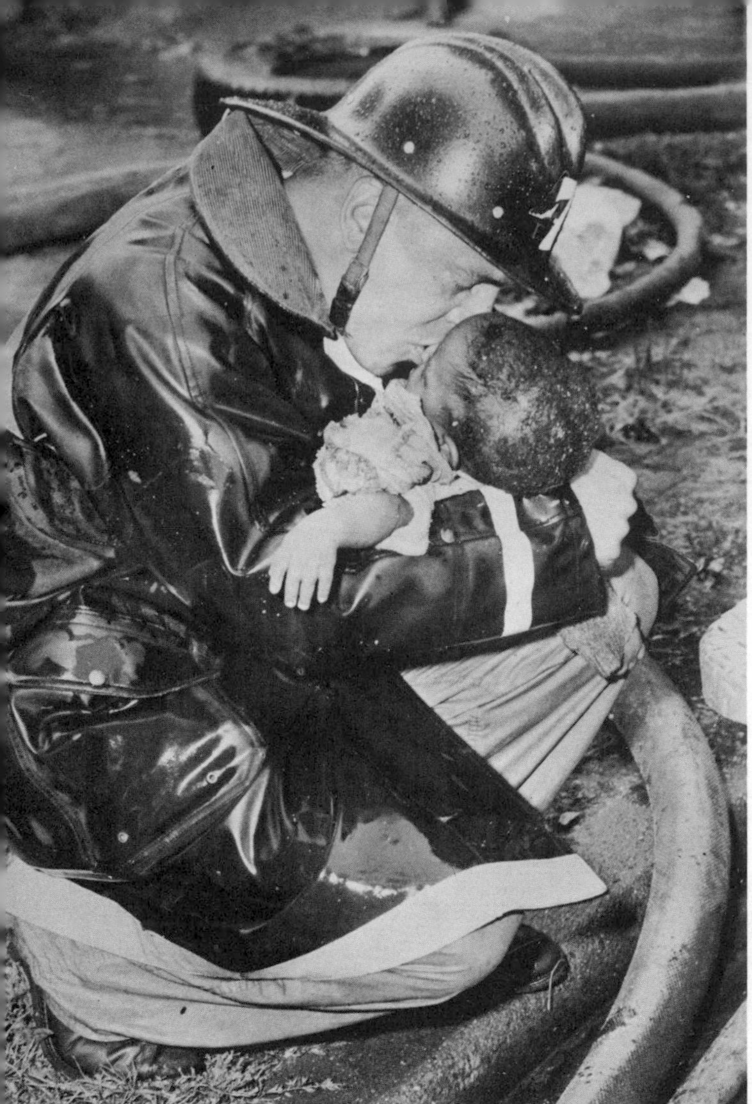

KISS OF LIFE was fruitless, despite valiant attempt by Erie, Pa. fireman, Albert Anderson. The nine-month-old baby suffocated in a raging holocaust that enveloped his parents' home. While child died, photo was lesson in brotherhood.

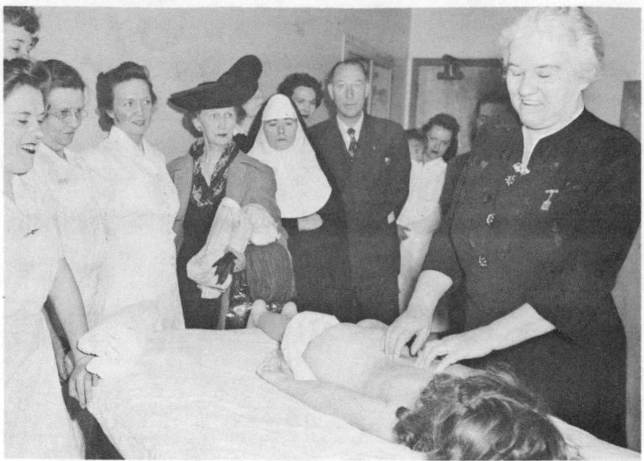

LATE SISTER KENNY, beloved Australian nurse who developed paralysis treatment, shows system of muscle relaxation to nuns and nurses at Chicago's Wesley Memorial Hospital.

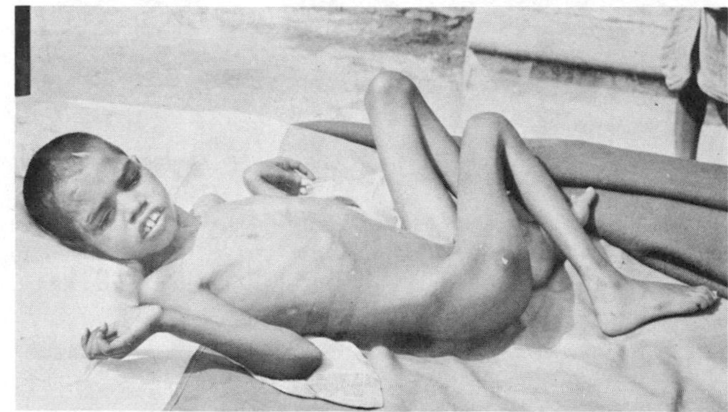

KIPLINGESQUE BUT TRUE was story of "Ramu," Indian "wolf boy," discovered in jungle in 1954 and thought by physicians to have been reared by wild animals, thus explaining boy's savage nature, muteness, deformities, inability to walk.

INVASION FROM SPACE was popular topic during '50s. Many claimed to see "flying saucers" as in above photo. Numerous books, films and articles profited from the hoax, but real proof never given, so most were discounted as odd phenomena.

DIRECT LANDING was made by this auto in 1952; it had "come to the right place." Terrible road death toll in United States continued to mount during the decade, often claiming more than 400 lives on holiday weekends despite police vigilance.

FROM QUEEN TO PRINCESS was no demotion for film actress Grace Kelly, daughter of bricklayer-turned millionaire, John Kelly, when she became bride of Prince Ranier II of Monaco and attained real-life royalty as Princess Grace of Monaco.

PRESIDENT'S DAUGHTER, the former Margaret Truman, emanates bridal joy after her 1956 wedding in Independence, Missouri, to E. Clifton Daniel, Jr., *New York Times* correspondent. Ex-Pres. Truman's comment: "I'm glad he's a Democrat."

THE BEAUTY AND THE BRAIN made a striking couple when they united during the decade. Gracing a N.Y. party, Marilyn Monroe and playwright Arthur Miller show no concern over difference.

NORWEGIAN TRANSLATION OF CINDERELLA was written by Anne Marie Rasmussen, Norwegian bride of Steven Rockefeller, both shown here on motorcycle. Father-in-law was N.Y. Gov. Nelson Rockefeller, in whose home Nordic beauty was once maid.

BRIEF MARRIAGE of Elizabeth Taylor and showman Mike Todd had a tragic final curtain when Todd plunged to death in New Mexico aircrash, 13 months after marriage. Thrice-wed Miss Taylor took a fourth the following year, Eddie Fisher.

PANTIE RAIDS became a craze during the '50s. College students all over the United States (particularly in the spring) scampered into girls' dormitories and absconded with their treasured booty of "unmentionables." Fad soon died out.

QUICK CHANGE has to be made by fortunate fugitive from San Francisco hotel fire in 1953. Alert work by the hotel's personnel, fire department averted a possible tragedy, but caused many unprepared exits in underwear and pajamas.

MAN WITHOUT A JOB suns himself in Capri after the '52 coup in Egypt ended his reign. Ex-king Farouk faces a lifetime of play and relaxation.

QUEENS WERE CROWNED in honor of everything from beer to the universe during the decade. Here Miss World of 1951 justifies the many beauty contests.

IT'S NOT THE HEAT and it may not be the humidity, but nevertheless, "Granny" manages to retain some decorum by keeping her hat on at the beach.

ORIGINAL LADY GODIVA had only one "peeping Tom," while 1951 version attracts hundreds at British pageant in Coventry, England, despite addition of the flesh-colored tights.

IRONIC POSTER affords grim joke to National Guard soldiers patrolling the flooded city of Laredo, Texas, during the 1954 flood in which over 200 lives were reported lost.

BOY MEETS GIRL . . . or does he? Decade produced its share of oddities but none quite so puzzling as status of Christine Jorgenson and her (his) "confreres," who changed sex from male to female and found selves somewhere in between.

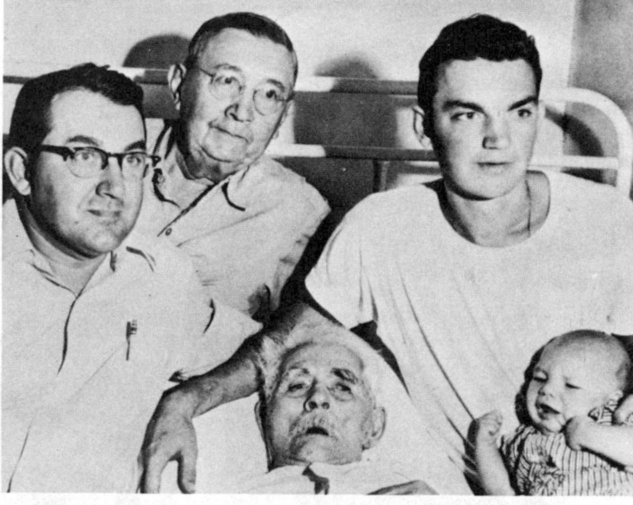

114 YEARS DIFFERENCE in ages is represented by five generations of Kings in California. Joaquin King *(on bed)* was 114 years old and baby 2½ months in '53 at time of photo.

UNSCHEDULED SOLO was made by fledgling pilots Eddie Cates *(seated)*, 13, and "co-pilot" Roy Brosseau, 11, in 1956 when they commandeered a monoplane for hour joyride.

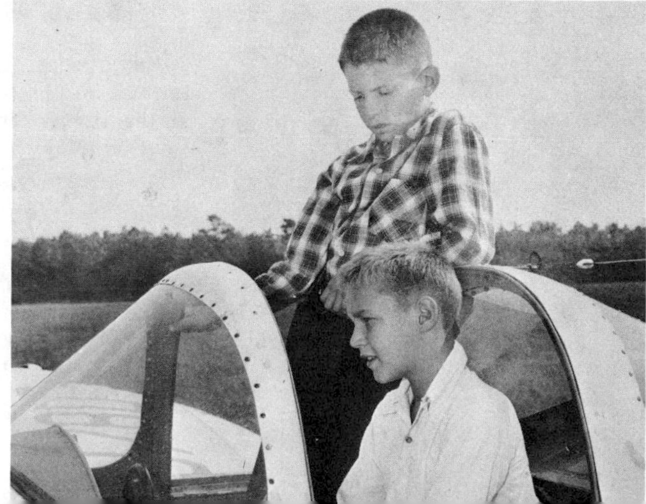

THE EGG AND I. Pensive chick examines machine designed to pick recipes for bigger egg production. Like any worker in 1950s, automation worries chick.

GREATEST ZOO ATTRACTION for many years at Chicago's Lincoln Zoo was "Bushman," massive 22 yr. old gorilla who was found dead in his cage in '51.

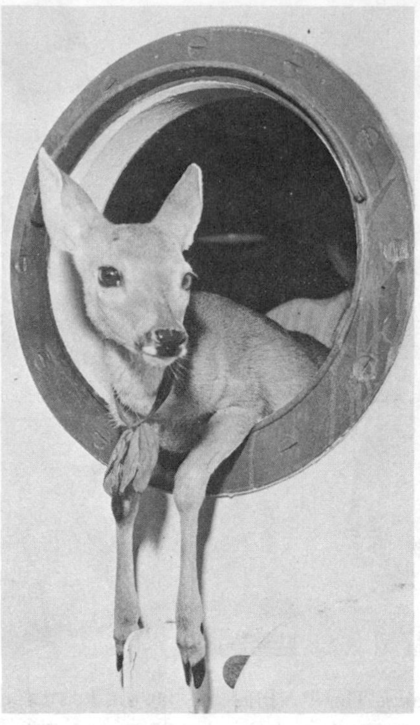

UNDESIRABLE ALIEN, fawn from Ecuador looks balefully at retreating U.S. as it returns home. Deported because of disease, fawn was least sinister deportee.

BLUSHING BRIDE, Sumaili, a lady gorilla, retreats into protecting arms of keeper at the Bronx Zoo after first catching sight of Mambo, her intended mate.

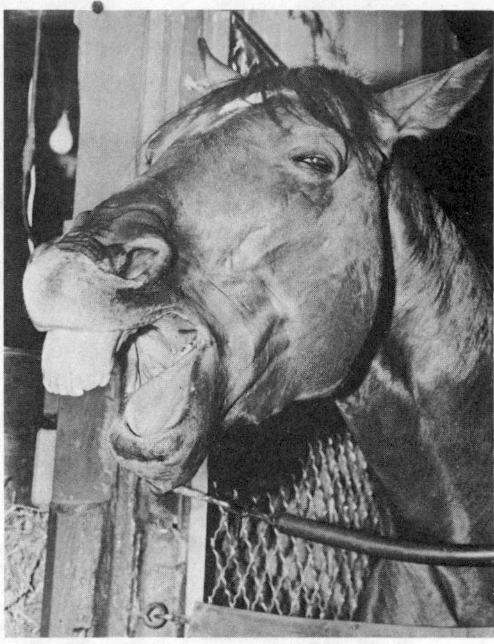

HORSE LAUGH is given by Silky Sullivan, West Coast race-horse who, in 1958, repeatedly surprised "smart money" by coming from behind in important races.

LACK OF PRIVACY disturbs orangutang "Andy" at Bronx Zoo more than heat. It's bad enough that a fellow must dress scantily without being stared at.

THE DECADE'S TOP AWARDS

1951 *NOBEL PRIZE:* Edwin M. McMillan, Glenn T. Seaborg (U.S.), Chemistry; Par Lagerkvist (Swe.), Literature; Leon Jouhaux (Fr.), Peace.

PULITZER PRIZE: Conrad Richter, Fiction *(The Town)*; William H. Fitzpatrick *(New Orleans States)*, Editorial Writing; Carl Sandburg, Poetry.

ACADEMY AWARD: Humphrey Bogart, Best Actor *(The African Queen)*; Vivien Leigh, Best Actress *(A Streetcar Named Desire)*; *An American in Paris*, Best Film.

1952 *NOBEL PRIZE:* Selman A. Waksman (U.S., Medicine; Francois Mauriac (Fr.), Literature; Albert Schweitzer (Fr.), Peace.

PULITZER PRIZE: St. Louis Post-Dispatch, Meritorious Public Service; John M. Hightower *(Associated Press)*, International Reporting; Herman Wouk, Fiction *(The Caine Mutiny)*; Marianne Moore, Poetry.

ACADEMY AWARD: Gary Cooper, Best Actor *(High Noon)*; Shirley Booth, Best Actress *(Come Back Little Sheba)*; *The Greatest Show on Earth*. Best Film.

1953 *NOBEL PRIZE:* Fritz Zernike (Den.), Physics; Herman Staudinger (W. Ger.), Chemistry; Winston Churchill, Literature; Gen. George C. Marshall (U.S.), Peace.

PULITZER PRIZE: Don Whitehead *(Associated Press)*, National Reporting; Vermont C. Royster *(Wall St. Journal)*, Editorial Writing; William Inge, Drama, *(Picnic)*; Archibald MacLeish, Poetry.

ACADEMY AWARD: William Holden, Best Actor *(Stalag 17)*; Audrey Hepburn, Best Actress *(Roman Holiday)*; *From Here To Eternity*, Best Film.

1954 *NOBEL PRIZE:* Linus Pauling (U.S.), Chemistry; Thomas H. Weller, Frederick C. Robbins and John F. Enders (U.S.), Medicine; Ernest Hemingway, Fiction.

PULITZER PRIZE: Newsday (Garden City, N. Y.), Meritorious Service; Richard Wilson *(Cowles Newspapers)*, National Reporting; Bruce Catton, History *(A Stillness At Appomatox)*; Charles A. Lindbergh, Autobiography *(The Spirit of St. Louis)*.

ACADEMY AWARD: Marlon Brando, Best Actor *(On the Waterfront)*; Grace Kelly, Best Actress *(The Country Girl)*; *On the Waterfront*, Best Film.

1955 *NOBEL PRIZE:* Polykarp Kusch, Willis E. Lamb (U.S.), Physics; Hugo Thorell (Swe.), Medicine; Halldor Kiljan Laxness (Ice.), Literature. No Peace award.

PULITZER PRIZE: Harrison Salisbury *(New York Times)*, International Reporting; William Faulkner, Fiction *(A Fable)*; Tennessee Williams, Drama *(Cat on a Hot Tin Roof)*; Gian-Carlo Menotti, Music *(Saint of Bleecker St.)*.

ACADEMY AWARD: Ernest Borgnine, Best Actor *(Marty)*; Anna Magnani, Best Actress *(Rose Tattoo)*; *Marty*, Best Film.

1956 *NOBEL PRIZE:* William Shockley, Walter H. Bratain, John Bardeen (U.S.), Physics; Cyril N. Hinshelwood (G.B.), Nikolai N. Semenov (USSR), Chemistry. No Peace award.

PULITZER PRIZE: William Randolph Hearst, Jr., J. Kingsbury Smith, Frank Coniff *(Hearst Newspapers)*, International Reporting; MacKinlay Kantor, Fiction. *(Andersonville)*; Richard Hofstadter, History *(Age of Reform)*.

ACADEMY AWARD: Yul Brynner, Best Actor *(The King and I)*; Ingrid Bergman, Best Actress *(Anastasia)*; *Around the World in 80 Days*, Best Film.

1957 *NOBEL PRIZE:* Sir Alexander Todd (G.B.), Chemistry; Albert Camus (Fr.), Literature; Lester B. Pearson (Can.), Peace.

PULITZER PRIZE: Russell Jones *(United Press)*, International Reporting; Kenneth Roberts, Special Citation for historical novels. Eugene O'Neill, Drama *(Long Day's Journey into Night)*; Sen. John F. Kennedy, History *(Profiles in Courage)*.

ACADEMY AWARD: Alec Guinness, Best Actor *(The Bridge on the River Kwai)*; Joanne Woodward, Best Actress *(The Three Faces of Eve)*; *The Bridge on the River Kwai*, Best Film.

1958 *NOBEL PRIZE;* Pavel A. Cherenkov, Igor E. Tamm, Ilya M. Frank (USSR), Physics; Frederick Sanger (G.B.), Chemistry; Boris Pasternak (USSR), Literature.

PULITZER PRIZE: The New York Times, International Reporting; Harry S. Ashmore *(Arkansas Gazette*, Little Rock), Editorial Writing; Samuel Barber, Music *(Vanessa)*.

ACADEMY AWARD: David Niven, Best Actor *(Separate Tables)*; Susan Hayward, Best Actress *(I Want to Live)*; *Gigi*, Best Film.

1959 *NOBEL PRIZE:* Emilio Segre, Owen Chamberlain (U.S.), Physics; Jaroslav Heyrovsky, Chemistry; Salvatore Quasimodo, Literature; Philip John Noel-Baker (G.B.), Peace.

PULITZER PRIZE: Joseph Martin, Philip Santora *(New York Daily News)* International Reporting; Bill Mauldin *(St. Louis Post-Dispatch)*, Cartoon; Archibald MacLeish, Drama *(J.B.)*; Stanley Kunitz, Poetry.

ACADEMY AWARD: Charlton Heston, Best Actor *(Ben Hur)*; Simone Signoret, Best Actress *(Room at the Top)*; *Ben Hur*, Best Film.

1960 *PULITZER PRIZE:* George Abbott, Jerome Weidman, Sheldon Harnick, Jerry Bock, Drama *(Fiorello)*; Allen Drury, Fiction *(Advise and Consent)*; Samuel Eliot Morrison, Biography *(John Paul Jones)*; Abraham Rosenthal *(New York Times)*, International Reporting; Vance Trimble *(Scripps-Howard)*, National Reporting.

In Memoriam

ARTS AND LETTERS

MAXWELL ANDERSON, 70, U.S. Playwright, *(Winterset)*, Feb. 28, 1959.

SHOLEM ASCH, 76, author, July 10, 1957.

ALBERT CAMUS, 46, Nobel Prize winner, French author, Jan. 4, 1960.

PAUL CLAUDEL, 88, French diplomat, author, Nov. 23, 1955.

SIDONIE GABRIELLE COLETTE, 81, French authoress, Aug. 3, 1954.

JOHN DEWEY, 92, U.S. philosopher, educator, June 1, 1952.

CHRISTIAN DIOR, 52, French fashion designer, Oct. 24, 1957.

SIR JACOB EPSTEIN, 78, controversial sculptor, Aug. 19, 1959.

JOSE ORTEGA Y GASSET, 72, Spanish writer, philosopher, Oct. 13, 1955.

WANDA LANDOWSKA, 80, world famous harpsichordist, Aug. 16, 1959.

THOMAS MANN, 80, author, Aug. 12, 1955.

JOHN PHILLIPS MARQUAND, 66, U.S. novelist, July 16, 1960.

HENRI MATISSE, 84, French painter, Mar. 3, 1954.

EUGENE O'NEILL, 65, U.S. playwright, Nobel Prize winner, July 27, 1953.

ROBERT E. SHERWOOD, 59, U.S. playwright, *(Petrified Forest)*, Oct. 13, 1955.

NEVIL SHUTE, 60, Australian novelist, Jan. 12, 1960.

JOHN SLOAN, 66, U.S. painter, *(Haymarket)*, June 24, 1954.

MAURICE UTRILLO (VALADON), 71, French painter, Nov. 5, 1956.

FRANK LLOYD WRIGHT, 89, architect, April 9, 1959.

BUSINESS AND INDUSTRY

PHILLIP DANFORTH ARMOUR, 64, ex-Vice Pres. of Armour Meat Co.; Jan. 18, 1959.

VINCENT ASTOR, 67, millionaire philanthropist, board chairman of *Newsweek;* Feb. 3, 1959.

CLARENCE BIRDSEYE, frozen food king, founder of Birdseye General Food Co.; Oct. 7, 1956.
MARSHALL FIELD III, 63, heir to Chicago store millions and one-time publisher; Nov. 8, 1956.
GLENN S. MARTIN, 69, aviation pioneer and manufacturer; Dec. 4, 1955.
JOHN D. ROCKEFELLER, Jr., 86, millionaire philanthropist; May 11. 1960.
HARRY F. SINCLAIR, 80, founder of Sinclair Oil Co.; Nov. 10, 1956.
GEORGE ARTHUR SLOAN, 61, industrialist; May 20, 1955.
ROBERT R. YOUNG, 60, New York Central board chairman, financier; Jan. 25, 1958.

ENTERTAINMENT

ETHEL BARRYMORE, 79, famed actress sister of Lionel and John Barrymore; June 18, 1959.
LIONEL BARRYMORE, 76, stage, screen and radio actor; Nov. 15, 1954.
LOU COSTELLO, 53, film comedian; Mar. 3, 1959.
CECIL B. deMILLE, 77, pioneer movie producer; Jan. 21, 1959.
ROBERT DONAT, 53, British actor *(39 Steps)*; June 9, 1959.
ERROL FLYNN, 50, film star, noted for swashbuckling roles; Oct. 14, 1959.
OLIVER HARDY, 65, portly half of Laurel and Hardy comedy team; Aug. 7, 1957.
LOUIS B. MAYER, 72, film mogul; Oct. 29, 1957.
TYRONE POWER, 44, film actor; Nov. 15, 1959.
LAWRENCE TIBBET, 63, opera star; July 21, 1960.

POLITICS AND GOVERNMENT

MARSHALL PIETRO BADOGLIO, 85, Italian conqueror of Ethiopia, 1st premier after *Il Duce's* assassination; Oct. 30, 1956.
ALBEN W. BARKLEY, 78, U.S. Vice Pres. under Truman; April 30, 1956.
ANEURIN BEVAN, 63, stormy leader of British Labor Party; July 6, 1960.
CAROL II, 59, ex-King of Rumania; April 4, 1953.
LT. GEN. CLAIRE CHENNAULT, 67, WW II leader of Flying Tigers; July 27, 1958.
JOHN FOSTER DULLES, 71, U.S. Secy of State under Eisenhower; May 25, 1959.
WILLIAM "BULL" HALSEY, 76, U.S. Fleet Admiral in Pacific during WW II; Aug. 16, 1959.
CORDELL HULL, 83, Secy of State under FDR; July 23, 1955.
ABDULLAH IBN UL-HUSSEIN, King of Jordan, assassinated July 31, 1951.
FIELD MARSHALL ALBERT KESSELRING, 79, top Nazi strategist during WW II; July 22, 1960.
PRINCE ALY KHAN, 48, Pakistan ambassador to UN; May 11, 1960.
MARY OF TECK, 85, Dowager Queen of Great Britain; March 24, 1953.
JOSEPH R. McCARTHY, 49, controversial U.S. Senator, (R.-Wis.); May 2, 1957.
VITTORIO EMMANUELE ORLANDO, 92, ex-Italian premier, drafter of Versailles Treaty; Dec. 1, 1952.
DR. ERNST REUTER, 64, anti-Communist mayor of Berlin; Sept. 29, 1953.
MAMORU SHIGEMITSU, 63, Japanese Foreign Minister who surrendered Japan to Allies; Jan. 25, 1958.
JOSEPH V. STALIN, 73, Soviet Premier; March 5, 1953.
ROBERT A. TAFT, 63, U.S. Senator (R.-Ohio); Aug. 4, 1953.
FREDERICK M. VINSON, 63, Chief Justice of the Supreme Court; Sept. 8, 1953.
ANDREI VISHINSKY, 70, Soviet diplomat; Nov. 22, 1954.
GEN. JONATHAN M. WAINWRIGHT, 70, defender of Corregidor; Sept. 2, 1953.

RELIGION

GEORGE, PATRIARCH OF THE ARMENIAN CHURCH, 86, May 10, 1954.
AGA KHAN III, 79, spiritual leader of 20 million Ismaili Moslems, July 11, 1957.
KENNETH E. KIRK, 68, Anglican Bishop of Oxford, June 8, 1954.
POPE PIUS XII, 88, Vicar of the Roman Catholic Church, Oct. 9, 1958.
ALOJZIJE CARDINAL STEPINAC, 61, Roman Catholic Primate of Yugoslavia, long-time prisoner of Communists, Feb. 10, 1960.

SCIENCE

DR. ROY CHAPMAN ANDREWS, 76, U.S. naturalist, explorer, Mar. 11, 1960.
DR. WALTER BAADE, 67, German-born astronomer, June 25, 1960.
KARL F. BONHOEFFER, 58, professor, discoverer of two forms of hydrogen, May 20, 1957.
ALBERT EINSTEIN, 76, famed physicist and mathematician, Mar. 14, 1955.
ENRICO FERMI, 53, Italian-born physicist, Nov. 28, 1954.
SIR ALEXANDER FLEMING, 73, British discoverer of penicillin, Mar. 11, 1955.
MME IRENE JOLIOT-CURIE, 58, French physicist, daughter of Pierre and Marie Curie, May 17, 1956.
DONALD J. HUGHES, 45, nuclear physicist, April 23, 1960.
DR. ERNEST O. LAWRENCE, 57, inventor of the cyclotron, Aug. 27, 1958.

SPORTS

LUIS ANGEL FIRPO, "The Wild Bull of the Pampas," 65, ex-Argentine Heavyweight, Aug. 3, 1960.
HERMAN HICKMAN, 46, football star, coach, sports commentator; April 25, 1958.
WILLIE HOPPE, 71, winner of 51 world billiard championships, April 1, 1959.
MEL OTT, 49, baseball star, Nov. 21, 1958.
TRIS SPEAKER, 70, baseball "immortal," Dec. 8, 1958.
JIM THORPE, 71, world famous U.S. athlete and Olympic champion, Mar. 28, 1953.
BABE DIDRICKSON ZAHARIAS, 42, U.S.'s greatest woman athlete, Sept. 27, 1956.

CRISIS OF CHANGE

THE INCREDIBLE DECADE 1960-1970

Change is nothing new. We all accept it; we even claim to welcome it. But change in the Sixties *was* something different, something truly incredible. Not only did it hit us over the head and knock us down — once down, it proceeded to knead us into the ground.

Reflect a moment. Recall the Eisenhower years. Student riots hadn't happened. Vietnam was as relevant to our daily lives as Afghanistan. "Black Power" not only wasn't a cliche — it was a fantasy. And if we heard the term "political assassination," our first thoughts would have been of Abe Lincoln and John Wilkes Booth.

All that has changed. We've experienced the Sixties, and our frames of reference have shifted as they never have before. Now we anticipate the Seventies with mixed feelings of excitement, awe and trepidation. There will be no respite from further change; History has taught us that change feeds upon itself and accelerates until the forces behind it find a new state of equilibrium.

With technology advancing in giant steps each day, with student and black unrest, with urban frustration and rural backlash, with nationalism struggling against the Utopian concept of a world community, that equilibrium is not likely to be reached in the near future.

"That's one small step for a man, one giant leap for mankind."

HISTORIC HIGHLIGHTS 1960-1970

It was a decade of paradoxes. The Incredible Sixties saw both the fulfillment of mankind's greatest dream and the violent deaths of humanity's greatest dreamers. American astronauts landed on the moon and the entire world basked in the resurrection of a world communal spirit which for too long had been absent from the human heart. But even the accomplishment of that centuries-old dream did little to ease the troubles of a schizophrenic planet. Divisions ruled everywhere — between nations, within nations, and within men. Czechoslovakia, Vietnam, the Middle East, assassinations, crime — wherever one looked, the greatest paradox still remained man's inhumanity to man.

Astronaut Edwin Aldrin stands beside an American flag at Tranquility Base, the Moon. The lunar landing represented the decade's greatest scientific feat.

Shown here joking with the quarantined Apollo 11 astronauts, President Nixon was the first President to greet returning spacemen aboard a recovery ship.

New York City treated the three moonmen to a hero's ticker tape parade.

Paratrooper rests atop battle-scarred Hamburger Hill, which U.S. forces captured after a ten-day long assault.

U.S. armored personnel carriers in Vietnam not only carried troops into battle, but brought them back as well.

Barefooted Vietnamese mother and her children flee from their burning home. Their village, a suspected NLF supply depot, was set afire by ARVN rangers.

As U.S., Saigon, Hanoi and NLF negotiators talked in Paris, the war dragged on unabated. On the left, representing the U.S., are A. Harriman and C. Vance.

North Vietnamese negotiators came to Paris to participate in peace talks.

John Kennedy fell victim to an assassin's bullet in Dallas, Texas, on November 22, 1963. The white arrow points to the dying President's foot; the black arrow points to Mrs. John Connally, wife of the Texas governor.

A grim and stunned inaugural party watched as Lyndon B. Johnson was sworn in aboard Air Force One.

Smoke billowed skyward from burning vehicles in the center of Prague on August 21, 1968, as Soviet and Warsaw Pact armies captured the Czech capital.

Shortly after winning his party's California primary, Robert Kennedy was assassinated by a young Jordanian.

An assassin's bullet also ended the career of Dr. Martin Luther King.

His hopes buoyed by LBJ's sagging popularity, Robert Kennedy announced his candidacy for the Dem. Presidential nomination on March 16, 1968.

Campaigner Richard Nixon claimed that he was becoming a favorite with American youth — not with the revolutionary few, but the forgotten many.

Senator Eugene McCarthy led a "children's crusade" as a peace candidate in 1968. He helped to unseat LBJ but VP Humphrey won the Dem. nomination.

Democratic nominees Hubert Humphrey and Edmund Muskie could not recover from the Chicago convention debacle in time to catch Nixon's lead.

Richard Milhous Nixon was sworn in as 37th President of the U.S. by Supreme Court Chief Justice Earl Warren on January 20, 1969. Nixon received 302 electoral votes in the November, 1968, election as opposed to runner-up Humphrey's total of 191, and third party candidate George Wallace's total of 45.

The Battle of Chicago, August, 1968, took place outside the Democratic National Convention site. Antagonists were Mayor Daley's armed police units and anti-war, pro-McCarthy demonstrators. Many political observers felt that this battle sorely intensified the Democratic Party's internal split and ultimately cost nominee Humphrey the election.

The first major civil rights march on Washington occurred in 1963. Demonstrators were well-treated by the Federal government, and the march served to unify the various civil rights factions. It was there that Dr. Martin Luther King Jr. presented his famous "I Have A Dream" speech.

Martin Luther King, a man with unshakeable faith in the power of love, delivered this speech during a voter registration rally in Mississippi in 1966.

Black Panther leaders Bobby Seale and Huey Newton both ran afoul of the law. Newton was convicted of manslaughter, while Seale faced charges of murder and inciting to riot.

Reverend Ralph Abernathy, Martin Luther King's top aide became President of the Southern Christian Leadership Conference after Dr. King's assassination. Here he drives a mule-drawn wagon in Poor People's march in 1968.

Looters, guarded by Military Police share the attention of curious onlookers and children who walk amidst battered stores and debris in Newark. National Guardsmen and local police joined in efforts to quell the July 1967 race riots.

New York City's Tactical Patrol Force ended a sit-in at Columbia University in April, 1968, one of many disturbances which rocked American campuses as radical youth protested Establishment policy.

Soldiers engaged in a sit-in at the Presidio stockade are being read the Army's Mutiny Act. The Army faced unprecedented dissent from soldiers opposed to the Vietnam War and the inhumane treatment of military prisoners.

Rough police treatment of anti-war demonstrators became a familiar sight in the news media in the late Sixties. Above, draft card-burners and sympathizers are being rounded up outside the Supreme Court in 1968.

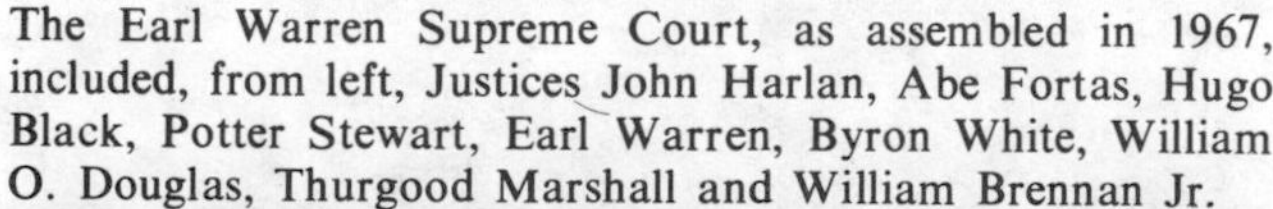

The Earl Warren Supreme Court, as assembled in 1967, included, from left, Justices John Harlan, Abe Fortas, Hugo Black, Potter Stewart, Earl Warren, Byron White, William O. Douglas, Thurgood Marshall and William Brennan Jr.

Reign of Pope Paul VI marked a return to conservatism, largely reversing the liberalizing trends of his predecessor, Pope John XXIII. Lay opposition to his rigid birth control stand caused a serious split in the Church.

RECORDS

National Affairs

Deep divisions, largely about an unpopular foreign war, rock the stability of the nation

Vietnam, political assassinations, the New Left, the Far Right, high crime rates, violence, student demonstrations, anti-war offensives, racial riots, alienated youth — such was the picture of the United States at the end of the 1960's.

The Sixties began peacefully enough. In his inaugural address of January 20, 1961, the nation's youngest President implored Americans to look into their hearts and, "Ask not what your country can do for you. Ask what you can do for your country." John Fitzgerald Kennedy, symbol of the New Politics led by America's articulate intelligentsia, was assassinated in Dallas, Texas, on November 22, 1963.

Lyndon Baines Johnson, Vice President, was sworn in as 36th President of the U.S. aboard the Presidential plane on the same day, and retained that office for the next five years. Johnson won a landslide victory in the 1964 elections, defeating his Republican Conservative opponent Barry Goldwater by one of the largest pluralities ever recorded in a Presidential election.

This same President's popularity fell so low during the ensuing five years that he declined to seek re-election in 1968. The reason, for this and for so much of the change in the American psyche during the Sixties, was Vietnam.

Several potential leaders emerged during the 1968 Presidential campaign: Democratic Senators Kennedy, McCarthy, and McGovern were the peace candidates, while Vice President Hubert Humphrey and Republican Richard Nixon offered continuity with past policies. In the end, almost anti-climatically (after the assassination of Robert Kennedy, and after the Chicago Democratic convention debacle which saw Mayor Daley's police force riot and brutally attack pro-McCarthy demonstrators, convention delegates, reporters and innocent bystanders), Republican nominee Nixon emerged victorious, riding high on his promises to "re-enfranchise" the common man, the "Forgotten American." But at the decade's end, it was apparent that President Nixon would continue to face the nationwide unrest that, if anything, had increased since President Johnson left office.

At the same time, Mr. Nixon had to deal with a revitalized Congress which had unshackled its traditional Conservative chains and finally become a viable legislative body for contemporary America. Not only was a staggering volume of important legislation passed in the Sixties (Medicare, Civil Rights Bill of 1964, aid to education, immigration revision, anti-poverty program, etc.), but Congress began to assert its prerogatives in such formerly "rubber stamp" areas as military appropriations and judicial selection.

As public opinion soured on the concept of an all-powerful "military-industrial complex," Defense Department planners could no longer expect unlimited funds for sometimes overpriced, unnecessary, weapons systems from a publicly-responsive legislature.

The end of the 1960's also marked the end of the Earl Warren Supreme Court which played a major role in the dynamic social changes of the decade with landmark decisions in such fields as civil rights, criminal law and legislative apportionment.

The national economy almost doubled in 10 short years — $503 to $920 billion GNP. Gradually, U.S. business and the public came to accept the "new economics," in which the government managed the economic structure to insure steady growth, hopefully, with minimum inflation.

The Civil Rights movement began quietly in the early Sixties. But after Watts, Detroit and Newark, it became clear that things had drastically changed.

Three Presidents, and Three Styles

White House leadership in the '60s is symbolized by JFK's New Frontier, LBJ's Great Society, and Nixon's Forward Together

President John F. Kennedy, displaying his characteristic charismata, boards a plane at Washington's National Airport in June 1963 for a flight to Charleston, West Va., where he was to join in state centennial festivities.

Americans met the changes and challenges of the decade under three Administrations of markedly different style.

In his 1961 Inaugural Address, President John F. Kennedy set a tone of bold commitment with the words, "Ask not what your country can do for you, but what you can do for your country."

Beginning his first full term as President in 1965 after his smashing defeat of Republican Barry Goldwater, Lyndon Baines Johnson declared that his hoped-for Great Society was "the excitement of becoming — always becoming, trying, probing, falling, resting and trying again — but always trying and always gaining."

In his 1969 Inaugural, Richard Milhous Nixon told the war-weary country: "The greatest honor history can bestow is the title of peacemaker." And to a country wracked with dissension, he urged delivery "from inflated rhetoric that promises more than it can deliver; from angry rhetoric that fans discontents into hatreds; from bombastic rhetoric that postures instead of persuading."

The changing styles reflected the developing mood of the country

The late poet Robert Frost exchanges confidences with the First Lady while Pearl Buck talks with the President after a 1962 White House dinner honoring Nobel Prize winners.

Kennedy liked to transact official business from his rocking chair in the White House. This typical picture of the President with "a special grace" was taken in 1962.

from one of high adventure, to mighty effort and disillusionment, to reappraisal and retrenchment.

In 1961, his first year as President, the 43-year-old Kennedy faced the Bay of Pigs disaster when an encouraged invasion of Castro's Cuba by Cuban exiles was smashed. Then in October, 1962, came the sharp confrontation with Russia over the Soviet missile bases in Cuba — when the Kremlin backed down and removed the missiles.

The New Frontier finally got going in November, 1962, when Kennedy signed the executive order ending racial discrimination in Federally subsidized housing. In October, 1963, he signed a limited nuclear test ban treaty with Russia and Britain.

Kennedy was just getting into his stride when, as his triumphant motorcade passed through Dallas streets on Nov. 22, 1963, three shots rang out, and the 35th President was dead. For four days stunned citizens watched television and mourned.

Taking over the Presidency, Lyndon Johnson retained most of the Kennedy Administration members, although some advisers, including Theodore C. Sorenson and Arthur M. Schlesinger Jr., shortly departed. Among the Cabinet stalwarts who continued were Secretary of State Dean Rusk and Defense Secretary Robert McNamara, former Ford executive.

It was Johnson's aim to carry forward, and expand on, all the Kennedy commitments — including one to put a man on the moon within the decade. As a distinguished Congressional alumnus, LBJ used his skill and contacts to push through Congress in 1965 more major liberal legislation than at any time since the early 1930s.

But he began to run into dissatisfaction over the increasingly costly war in Vietnam. Calling for guns and butter in a fiscal 1967 budget that crossed the $100 billion line for the first time, LBJ held fast to all his commitments. But the country was tired of the bloody, hopeless Vietnam conflict, worried about proliferating race riots, sick of high taxes and inflation. In August, 1967, polls showed that he had only 39% approval of the American voters.

As the 1968 Presidential campaign began to warm up, Johnson surprised the nation, and the world, by announcing on March 31 that he was ending most of the bombing in North Vietnam as a peace gesture and that "I shall not seek, and I will not accept, the nomination of my party for another term as your President."

The shocking assassination of Sen. Robert F. Kennedy on June 5 then made the nomination of Vice President Hubert Humphrey as the Democratic candidate inevitable. But the weight of the unpopular Johnson Administration was too much for Humphrey to overcome in his close race with GOP's Nixon.

The new President promptly staffed his Administration with cool, competent men much like himself. Replacing the durable Rusk as Secretary of State was Eisenhower's onetime Attorney General William Rogers.

Another important era ended in Nixon's first year with the retirement of Chief Justice Earl Warren whose court had made landmark liberal decisions in race relations, criminal justice, and reapportionment. To replace him Nixon chose D.C. Court of Appeals Judge Warren Earl Burger, believed to hold more conservative views on constitutional interpretations.

1. Adieu to an administration . . .

2. Efficiency expert exits . . .

3. Happy homecoming . . .

1. Secretary of State since 1961, imperturbable Dean Rusk comforts his wife, Virginia, as Department employees sing "Auld Lang Syne" at a farewell reception in January 1969.

2. The man who brought industrial efficiency to the Pentagon, Defense Secretary McNamara, former Ford whiz kid, winds up his stint. Left, Joint Chiefs Chairman, Gen. Earle Wheeler; right, Deputy Sec. Paul Nitze.

3. After being confirmed 69-11 by the Senate as a member of the U.S. Supreme Court, Justice's Solicitor General Thurgood Marshall greets his chauffeur for a happy ride home.

4. At long last Secretary of State Dean Rusk appears before the Senate Foreign Relations Committee in March 1968 to be quizzed on Vietnam War policy. Chairman J. W. Fulbright is recognizable, center Senatorial row.

5. As Johnson's adviser on consumer affairs, former TV star Betty Furness, here testifying before a Senate subcommittee, startled industry with her aggressive approach to protecting the public from exploitation.

6. The top ranking Negro in the LBJ Administration, Robert C. Weaver, Secretary of the new Housing and Urban Development Department, appears before a Senate Banking subcommittee in a 1966 hearing on housing.

7. In front of Hollybush, home of Glassboro State College's President Thomas E. Robinson, where Johnson and Kosygin first met, the leaders hold a press conference on June 23. At Kosygin's left, Ambassador to Washington Anatoly Dobrynin; next to trooper, Gov. and Mrs. Hughes of New Jersey.

8. The first outgoing President in 169 years to deliver a State of the Union message personally, Johnson called on Congress for a continued commitment to the policies of his five-year term. Left, Vice President Humphrey; right, Speaker of the House John McCormack of Massachusetts.

4. Rusk replies . . .

5. Let the buyer beware . . .

6. Weaver on housing . . .

7. 'Til we meet again . . .

8. A personal president . . .

1. The Nixons have it made ...

2. Not yet a household word ...

3. Now it's the Burger court ...

4. A new hand at State ...

1. Greeting guests at the first of six Inaugural Balls on Jan. 20, 1969, here at the Smithsonian Institute, President and Mrs. Nixon enjoy the fruits of a long, hard battle to win the nation's top political post.

2. In his earnest campaign to fix his identity, the little-known Vice President Spiro Agnew, Maryland's former governor, appears here before an increasingly friendly press in July 1969 for give-and-take with Treasury Secretary David Kennedy.

3. Changing of the legal guard is symbolized here as Warren Earl Burger, right, poses with friends after being sworn in as Chief Justice of the U.S. Waving farewell after sixteen years in the post is retiring Earl Warren.

4. Assuming the heavy load of U.S. foreign policy management, attorney William P. Rogers is sworn into office by Chief Justice Warren in January '69 as his longtime friend, the President, and his wife, Adele, look on.

Warren Leads Court's Liberal Decade

High tribunal forges impressive advances in civil rights, criminal law, legislative apportionment; Fortas is resignee

Responding to the liberal leadership of Chief Justice Earl Warren, the Supreme Court of the United States played a major role in the dynamic social change that swept the nation during 1960-70.

Landmark decisions were handed down in such fields as civil rights, criminal law, and legislative apportionment. Overall, the decade was marked by the court's vigor, its liberalism, and its willingness to enter controversies previously reserved to Congress and the Executive Branch.

One storm swirled around Justice Abe Fortas, who became the first member in history to resign under fire. More generally, critics lashed the court for its "legislative" approach to the law and its "activist" philosophy.

But as the decade neared its close, most Americans seemed agreed that the Warren court had been a constructive factor in the extension of full constitutional rights to all Americans.

In the early 1960s, the court made clear its pioneering intent by ruling it held jurisdiction over the apportionment of State legislatures. The "one-man, one vote" principle was applied to both houses of a legislature in the 1964 case of Reynold v. Sims — an opinion which the Chief Justice reportedly felt was the most significant one of his career in the Supreme Court.

The rule was extended by 1967 to Congressional and local districts as well, and in 1969 the court ruled that districts must be mathematically equal in population — unless variations are unavoidable despite a "good faith" effort.

A noisier upheaval was caused in 1962 with the decree that a 22-word non-sectarian prayer prescribed by a State board for New York schools was a "restricted activity" and therefore unconstitutional. Decisions in 1962 and 1965 also struck at required exercises in public schools.

Protestors said the court had "banned God from the schools," but such was not the case. Each pupil still had the right to pray or read the Bible in school as he wished, but authorities could not compel this for all students.

The court wrestled with cases involving the rights of accused criminals, and was criticized by many police and some prosecutors for decisions favoring the suspect or criminal.

The most controversial ruling was in *Miranda v. Arizona* (1966) that police had to advise suspects of their right to remain silent and to have counsel before proceeding with interrogation.

Federal Bill of Rights protections were applied to State criminal proceedings: the right against self-incrimination (1964); the right of the accused to be confronted by the witness against him (1965); and the right to a jury trial for serious crimes (1968).

A significant 1965 decree upheld the public accomodations section of the 1964 Civil Rights Act. In 1968 the court went further by ruling that an 1866 law forbids all discrimination in the sale and rental of real estate.

The Federal voting rights act of 1965 was upheld in 1966, and a 1969 voting rights decision struck down new State voting procedures designed to evade the act.

A dubious 1968 decision upheld State aid for parochial school textbooks, but the court also removed legal barriers to taxpayer suits against tax aid for religion.

After drawing fire for its "contemporary community standards" test of obscenity, the court upheld the obscenity conviction of Ralph Ginzburg and another New York publisher.

After taking such a large part in bringing about progress of the 1960-70 decade, Chief Justice Warren in 1967 announced his intention to retire. He stayed on, however, when the Senate in 1968 refused President Johnson's request to promote Justice Fortas to Chief Justice.

Fortas was subsequently involved in a controversy over a $20,000 payment for outside services which he accepted from, and later returned to, a foundation linked to embattled financier Louis Wolfson. His resignation gave President Nixon the chance to name two conservative members to the court.

In 1967 Justice Thurgood Marshall became the first Negro member of the court. It seemed a fitting step for a decade which saw the court further emerge as an effective champion of the rights of minority groups and all Americans in the pursuit of their constitutional freedoms and liberties.

Congress Compiles an Impressive Record

Under LBJ, JFK proddings, lawmakers finally burst through old conservative barriers; Powell, Dodd, Bobby Baker cause ethics snarls

John Kennedy, Robert Kennedy and Ted Kennedy: these three men, brothers, sons of tycoon Joseph P. Kennedy, personified the new American politics of the Sixties. Whether because of the Kennedy wit, the Kennedy good looks or the Kennedy initiative, they captured the imagination and loyalty of the American public as no others could, and there was much speculation, in happier days when all three were alive, of a Kennedy dynasty in the American Presidency. In those days, people looked forward to many years of touch football on the White House lawn. Now, John is dead, Robert is dead, and Ted's political future is doubtful in the aftermath of a tragic 1969 automobile accident in Mass.

Congress tried valiantly to break into the 20th Century during the 1960-70 decade, and succeeded to a large degree.

The modernization struggle began with House of Representatives Speaker Sam Rayburn's epochal 1960 effort to expand the House Rules Committee, which had long stood as a key conservative bastion against progressive bills. The veteran Texan's last great battle was fought to help the nation's young new President, John F. Kennedy, who was elected on a promise to bring in a "New Frontier" of Progress.

"Mr. Sam" correctly judged that the Rules group, under testy Chairman Howard W. Smith, of Virgina, would block most liberal proposals unless enough Administration supporters were added to tip the balance of power. Rayburn finally defeated "Judge" Smith, by 217 to 212 votes, after three weeks of heated backstage maneuvering.

While the Rules "packing" gave the White House dominant power on Capitol Hill, Kennedy still had to combat a House floor coalition of Smith's conservative Democrats and the Republicans, led by Indiana's hardy perennial, tough-talk-

The late Senate Minority Leader Everett Dirksen tells reporters the "Ev & Gerry Show" has folded. He and his House counterpart, Congressman Gerald Ford, quit their weekly confabs with press when Nixon was elected President.

Just plain 'bobby'. At Senate probe, ex-Senate aide Bobby Baker tries to explain how he acquired his wealth.

ing Representative Charles Halleck.

The Senate leadership also changed when Majority Leader Lyndon B. Johnson was elected Vice President. Cloakroom cajoler LBJ's place was taken by Montana's Mike Mansfield, a pipe-puffing former professor. Minnesota's Hubert H. Humphrey, a dynamic liberal who had penetrated the crusty Senate "Establishment" under LBJ's tutelage, moved up to Democratic Senate Whip.

After Johnson became President, Arizona's conservative Senator Barry Goldwater challenged him in the 1964 Presidential election but lost heavily. (Goldwater returned to the Senate in 1968.) Minnesota's Senator Eugene McCarthy, running as a "Peace" candiate, won a striking victory in the 1968 New Hampshire Presidential primary. Senator Robert F. Kennedy entered the Presidential race, and as Johnson withdrew, Humphrey won his party's nod.

During President Kennedy's first two years in office, Democrats had margins of 263-174 over the GOP in the House and 64-36 in the Senate — not enough to surmount conservatives on every vote. The party ratio shifted little in the next Congress, but with adoption of the momentous Civil Rights Act of 1964, the logjam of pent-up bills began to break.

JFK's other accomplishments included anti-poverty programs, a strong foreign aid bill, Federal pay hikes, and tax improvements.

Congress really got cranked up after the 1964 elections, when the LBJ sweep brought in Democratic margins of 295-140 in the House and 68-32 in the Senate.

The "Johnson Congress" produced an amazing volume of legislation, including: Medicare, major federal aid to education, excise tax cuts, minority voting rights, the anti-poverty program, immigration revision, college scholarships, a new farm program, a Department of Urban Affairs, highway beautification, and a constitutional amendment on Presidential succession and illness.

Republicans picked up 47 House seats in 1966, and elected such Senate "stars" as Massachusetts' Edward Brooke, Oregon's Mark Hatfield, Illinois' Charles Percy, and Tennessee's Howard Baker.

Led in the Senate by majestic orator Everett McKinley Dirksen, and in the House by Michigan's Gerald Ford, who had deposed Halleck, the GOP slowed down the pace considerably. It took Congress a year and a half to pass LBJ's tax surcharge, and it cut spending by $6 billion before doing so. Former lawmaker Richard Nixon, elected President in 1968, did not speed things up.

Much of Congress' record was marred by the ethics cases, and a bill to modernize procedures foundered as Capitol Hill seemed undecided about entering the 20th Century.

There was frustration, too, over the Vietnam war and the toll it was taking on domestic priorities. "Doves" led by Senate Foreign Relations Committee Chairman William Fulbright kept up constant criticism. In 1969, solons approved a treaty against proliferation of nuclear weapons and pressured the President for disarmament talks with Russia.

For all its troubles, Congress did burst through the ties which had held back most progressive legislation since New Deal days. It proved that the Legislative Branch of government could respond to modern needs if the voters are concerned enough to demand action.

1. Joe and John . . .

2. Hoosier battler . . .

3. Any arguments? . . .

4. Mr. Sam's last gavel . . .

1. Former House Speaker Joe Martin is congratulated by Speaker John McCormack at unveiling of Capitol bust of longtime GOP leader Martin.

2. Indiana Congressman Charles Halleck, House GOP leader, assumes rostrum at party convention.

3. New House GOP chief Gerry Ford wields own gavel after ousting Halleck from his party position.

4. Attending Bonham, Tex., funeral services for House Speaker Rayburn are JFK, Lyndon Johnson, former Presidents Ike and Truman.

5. New Rayburn House Office Building towers over Capitol Hill landscape amid criticism of its cost.

6. John McCormack of Massachusetts takes over gavel of House after death of Sam Rayburn of cancer.

7. Democratic Senator Thomas J. Dodd of Connecticut talks to reporters during a recess in the Senate Ethics Committee Hearing in 1966. His extra–curricular junketing at the taxpayer's expense led to a formal censure of his activities by Senate colleagues.

8. Democratic Representative Howard W. Smith of Virginia, Chairman of the powerful House Rules Committee, was perhaps the single most influential Congressman during the 60's. All legislation first had to pass his committee before it could reach the House floor.

9. Senator William Fulbright reads mail from 12,000 supporting his stand against Vietnam War.

10. Arizona's Senator Carl Hayden waits as aide slices cake at party marking his 91st birthday.

11. Banker foe Rep. Wright Patman confers with tax chief Mills.

12. Senator Russell tells press treatment removed lung tumor.

13. Harlem's embattled Adam Powell discusses court victory.

5. The big one . . .

6. The new Speaker . . .

7. Sen. Dodd fights censure . . .

8. Rep. Smith is defeated . . .

9. Pleas for peace . . .

10. Senator at 91 . . .

11. Tax reform . . .

12. Cancer cured . . .

13. Powell reprieve . . .

A Decade of Political Chaos

Multiple assassinations and increasing discontent on campuses and in ghetto streets generate a bewildering mixture of liberalism and conservatism

Chicago's Mayor Richard Daley played host to the Democratic Convention — and, unwillingly, to hordes of discontented youngsters. Riot was inevitable.

The old definition of politics — that it is the art of the possible — was still valid. But the word "possible" needed redefining.

John F. Kennedy's "new frontier" concept certainly seemed practicable. Yet President Kennedy's thousand days in office produced few significant new programs.

And Lyndon Johnson was certainly no visionary dreamer: Johnson's pre-presidential career indicated that he would attempt little outside the realm of immediate possibility. Yet his excellent domestic plans were lost in a labyrinth of foreign commitments.

The 1960's were the years when the rules were changed, the shape of political reality altered.

At the beginning of the 70's, both major parties were in the midst of factional quarrels — disagreements which had been developing for the past 10 years.

Since the end of the Second World War, accepted lines between party ideologies had been blurring. Several young liberals became prominent in the Republican Party, and a number of Conservatives marched under the Democratic standard. These schisms were, at

In an age of Electronics, Nixon found that some old-fashioned whistle stopping could be an effective tactic.

Many dissidents saw the assassination of President John F. Kennedy as proof that the old political systems had degenerated into destructive parodies of democracy, and sought alternatives in non-Establishment leaders.

first, slight but later threatened to make party conventions verbal exercises in character assassination.

Seasoned political professionals were beginning to realize that they must reckon with third parties. While it appeared doubtful that any third party candidate could win a major national election, their influence was steadily growing. Candidates from the various "New Left" coalitions and rightist groups demonstrably influenced elections by siphoning off votes from more prominent candidates, and by forcing Democratic and Republican champions to respond to challenges and criticism.

More than the categories and issues of politics changed in the 60's: the very style of the art was altered. Show-biz became a paramount — perhaps *the* paramount — political craft.

Crude showmanship had, of course, always been part of the American political experience, and few men were ever elected without a platform manner and/or theatrical charisma at least the equal of their potential statesmanship. But in 1952, campaign managers fully realized the potency of Madison Avenue imagebuilding techniques, and initiated a policy of handling office seekers as products. In the 60's, that policy became standard practice. Advertising agencies were routinely consulted before a candidate made even initial campaign statements. A candidacy was *merchandised* like a new brand of soap, and some observers feared that if this trend continued, Americans would no longer elect *Presidents* but cast their ballots for leading men.

More than kaleidoscopic ideologies, more than the infusion of manufactured glamor, the central fact of American politics was that it no longer worked. This jerry-built system of choosing leaders, cobbled together from reassuring national myths and shrewd practical maneuvering, did not perform its function: in the 60's, leaders discovered that people had stopped accepting their rhetoric.

Scandals disgraced all levels of government — outrages possibly no worse, but certainly far better publicized, than historical counterparts. And the population expressed disillusionment and contempt.

At the Republican convention in 1968, there were rumblings of violence; at the Democratic meeting, there was terror in the streets. Candidates appearing at campaign rallies withered under a barrage of insult. It was obvious that general respect for political institutions was dying a sordid death.

Three good men fell to assassins' bullets.

Pundits agreed that the election of Richard M. Nixon in 1968 symbolized the willingness of a substantial portion of the country to give traditional methods a final chance. Mr. Nixon represented conventional intelligence and proven methods.

Disaffected intellectuals, angry students, middle-class individuals whose life styles had been swept away by a relentlessly advancing technology and mutated social systems — these held no hope for the new President. But the bulk of the voting population, those still stable, still prosperous, could see in Nixon's common-sense Republicanism a possible path back to a world where beloved Presidents did not die on television, where their children did not express hostilities in open revolt.

1. Before the killing ...

2. The second man ...

3. Man from Maine ..

1. Flushed and happy, Senator Robert Kennedy flashed a victory sign to his supporters after winning the California Democratic primary. Minutes later he was assassinated.

2. Although former Vice President Hubert Humphrey campaigned long and valiantly, he could not obliterate his image of the then unpopular Lyndon B. Johnson's echo and all-purpose yea-sayer.

3. Senator Edmund Muskie of Maine, unsuccessful running mate of Presidential nominee Hubert Humphrey, emerged from the 1968 campaign as one of his party's leading figures.

4. In Senator Eugene McCarthy, disaffected youth and peace-people found an almost perfect champion — a quietly charismatic poet-politician. But McCarthy's charm did not touch the Democratic regulars.

5. Ex-Governor George Wallace of Alabama projected countrified wholesomeness and folksiness to his supporters — and reactionary bigotry to his critics. Folksiness did not carry the election.

6. Among the reasons liberals deserted Lyndon B. Johnson were his outspoken determination to prosecute the war in Vietnam and his tacit support of the unpopular House Unamerican Activities Committee.

7. After the disturbances at Chicago, feelings were mutual — Yippee leader Abbie Hoffman called Mayor Daley's police "pigs" and the officers called Abbie and his followers dirty, disrespectful rioters.

4. Peace candidate . . .

5. Just plain George . . .

6. Liberals vs. Lyndon . . .

7. The last yippee . . .

1. Barry balks . . .

2. Reagan — a future role?

1. Although many Republicans urged Barry Goldwater to seek the 1968 GOP nomination, the champion of moderate conservatism declined.

2. California Governor Ronald Reagan was mentioned as a possible candidate for the role of President, or as a Vice Presidential running mate.

3. Cleveland Democrat Carl Stokes was the first black man in history to campaign for — and win — the mayoralty of a major city.

4. Mayor John V. Lindsay of New York — the most Kennedy-esque of the young Republicans — lost the GOP primary, ran as a Liberal and won.

5. Awesome problems of urban blight as well as rivalry for political power and prestige were temporarily shelved at the Governors' Conference in Colorado Springs as they posed for a formal portrait.

3. Success for Stokes . . .

4. "If at first you don't succeed" . . .

5. Forty-two heads are better . . .

"Two Nations, One Black, One White"

Racial tensions mount during the 60's as Negro Americans battle for equal rights and equal opportunities

A San Francisco policeman, with shotgun at the ready, stops a passing Negro following day-long rioting in front of Bayview Community Center in 1966.

Of all the crises of change that confronted the nation in the '60s, none was more agonizing than the crisis in race relations.

For almost 100 years after the abolition of slavery, the second-class citizenship of Negro Americans had been accepted as a fact of life by black and white alike. Segregation and discrimination had effectively cut the vast majority of Negroes off from the social and economic mainstream of American life. And honest dialogue between blacks and whites had been so rare as to be almost non-existent.

The Negro protest movement of the '60s was simply a rebellion against an intolerable status quo.

Some seeds of change had been planted in the '50s: most notably, by the 1954 Supreme Court decision outlawing deliberate racial segregation in public schools, and by the 1956 bus boycott in which the Negroes of Montgomery, Ala., led by a young minister named Martin Luther King, Jr., won the integration of their city's public transportation facilities.

But most Americans were taken by surprise when, on February 1, 1960, four black college students sat down at a lunch counter in

Rap Brown, Stokely Carmichael's successor as leader of SNCC, became a symbol of black power in late '60's.

The assassination of Dr. Martin Luther King in Memphis, Tennessee, on April 10, 1968, precipitated widescale Negro rioting throughout the entire nation and swayed many blacks away from Dr. King's own policy of non-violence.

Greensboro, N.C., and refused to leave until they had been served.

Within a matter of weeks, "sit-ins" were sweeping the South, and the sit-in kids proved to be the vanguard of an army. In the months and years that followed, thousands upon thousands of Negroes demonstrated in southern towns and cities. Their immediate objective was generally the integration of places of public accommodation, but the cup of lunch counter coffee became the symbol of a far greater goal — full equality before the law and in all areas of daily life.

The demonstrators were abused and set upon by mobs, beaten and jailed by the hundreds. But, following the doctrine of non-violence preached by Martin Luther King, they almost never struck back. They won the sympathy and admiration of millions of white Americans. So did the voter registration workers who risked their lives in rural areas where no black man had ever cast a ballot, and the black students fighting for acceptance in white schools and colleges.

By 1963, civil rights had become a major national issue.

In June of that year, President John F. Kennedy sent Congress a legislative package designed to guarantee Negro voting rights, end discrimination in hiring and in most places of public accommodation, and hasten school integration.

And in August, when the March on Washington drew a quarter of a million peaceful demonstrators to the nation's capital, it was possible to believe that the goal of racial justice was within reach.

A year later, under President Lyndon B. Johnson, most of the Kennedy civil rights legislation was passed. With the Civil Rights Act of 1964 and others that came after it, black Americans had finally won equality before the law.

But true equality in everyday life and the elimination of prejudice in everyday relationships between blacks and whites were more elusive. The nation's time of racial troubles was just beginning.

Militant protest spread throughout the north, directed against discrimination in jobs and housing and inferior education in ghetto schools.

The "white backlash" that was to play a major political role during the last years of the decade began to develop. And an increasing number of Negro leaders called for "black power" as the only defense against white hostility. There was some racial progress in the late '60s, political, social and economic, but it was overshadowed by mounting tension.

In the summer of 1964, the Northeast was struck by the worst racial rioting since World War II, and every succeeding year brought a new wave of ghetto uprisings.

The riots made it painfully clear that the problem of race was inextricably linked with the problem of poverty. Millions of black Americans were trapped in the ghettos, the TV set, bought on time payments, their only link with the affluent and complex society outside. To end their imprisonment would require a major national commitment of funds, energy and creativity.

This was the message of the Report of the National Advisory Commission on Civil Disorders, which warned in 1968 that "Our nation is moving toward two societies, one black, one white — separate and unequal."

To many concerned Americans, it seemed that the task of making those two societies one would be the greatest challenge of the '70s.

1. Woolworth sit-in . . .

2. Freedom Rider bus in Alabama . . .

3. Medgar Evers burial . . .

1. The sit-in movement at Southern lunch counters marked the beginning of the decade's civil rights actions.

2. White crowds fire-bombed this "Freedom Riders" bus in Alabama in 1961.

3 Assassinated Civil Rights leader Medgar Evers, a World War II veteran, was buried in Arlington National Cemetery on June 19, 1963.

4. Police officials with grappling hooks search for the missing bodies of three civil rights workers near Philadelphia, Mississippi.

5. Bull Connor, Sheriff of Birmingham, Alabama, won international notoriety in 1963 for his violent handling of civil rights demonstrators.

6. Montgomery, Alabama, residents lined the streets as civil rights marchers passed by on their way to the state capitol.

7. Elderly Negroes who had never dared approach a voter registration office were led to county court houses all over Mississippi by CORE volunteers.

8. Clergymen and laymen of all faiths marched past Capitol Building on May 18, 1964, to urge passage of a new Civil Rights Bill.

9. Mrs. Malcolm Peabody, mother of the governor of Massachusetts, was arrested in 1964 while participating in a motel dining room sit-in.

10. Young Negro in Kansas City gets a haircut in a newly integrated barber shop on the day after passage of the Civil Rights Bill of 1964.

11. The first two Negroes ever to attend the University of Georgia received their diplomas in 1963.

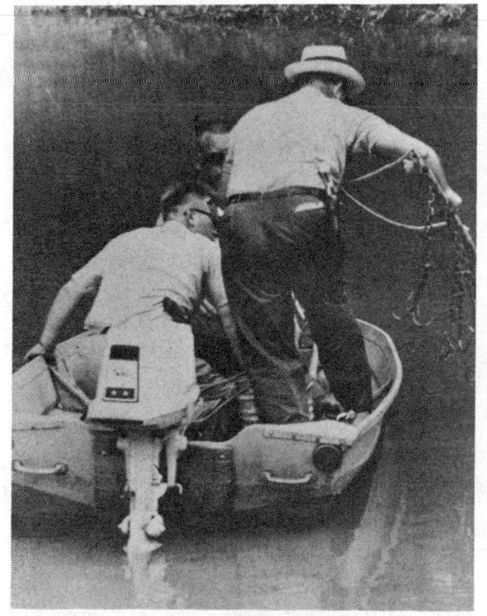

4. Missing civil rights workers . . .

5. Birmingham hosing . . .

6. White sentiments . . .

7. Voter registration . . .

8. Civil rights march . . .

9. Governor's mother arrested . . .

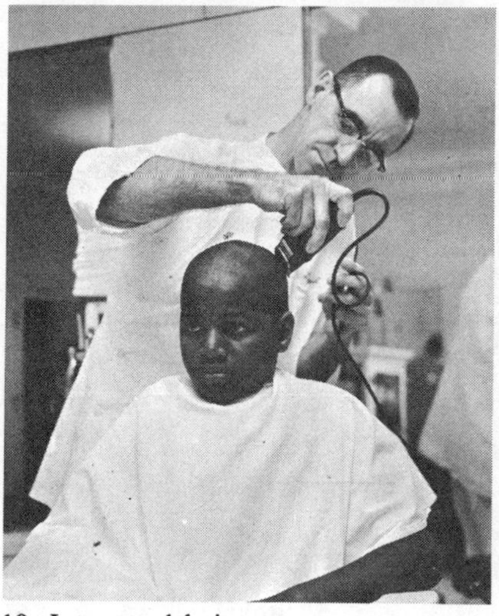

10. Integrated haircut . . .

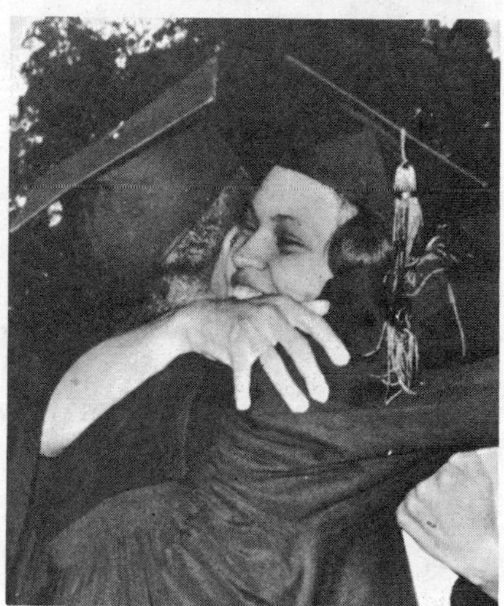

11. First Negro graduates . . .

1. March on Montgomery...

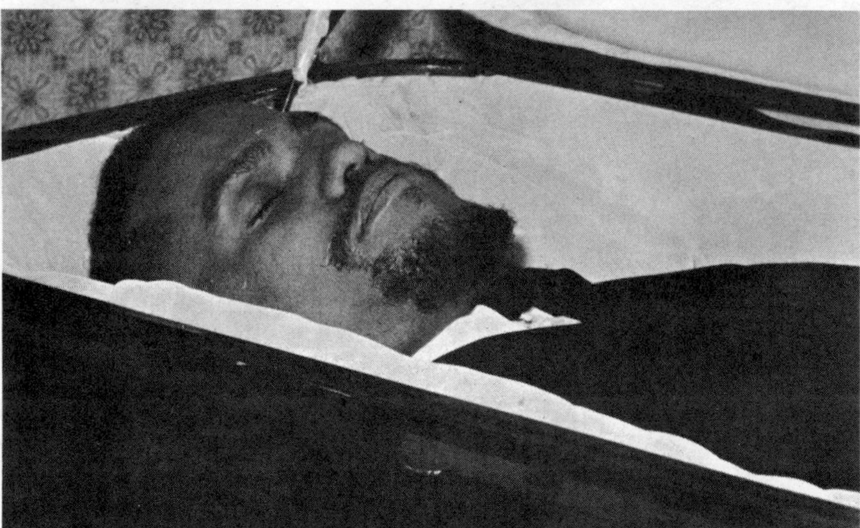

2. The body of Malcolm X..

3. Panther leader...

4. Militant blacks...

5. Stokely at war...

1. Arms locked and singing in the rain, Civil Rights leaders from different groups led a march on the Montgomery, Alabama, courthouse in 1965.

2. The body of Malcolm X, Negro nationalist leader who was assassinated Feb. 21, 1965, was displayed for public viewing in New York City.

3. Black Panther leader Huey Newton, alleged killer of an Oakland policeman, became a rallying point for black power advocates in the late 60's.

4. Black Americans displayed a new mood of angry militancy as racial tensions mounted during the last half of the decade.

5. Black power militant Stokely Carmichael urged Negroes to get guns and take to the streets in retaliation for the assassination of Dr. King.

6. Roving bands of Negroes looted and set fire to buildings in many cities following Dr. King's assassination.

7. 50,000 people came to Washington in 1968 to join the Solidarity Day program in support of the Poor People's March on Washington.

8. With their fallen leader at their feet on a Memphis balcony, Dr. King's aides point to the source of the shot that felled him.

9. Black Panther groups set up tables at universities across the country to gain support for the black power movement.

6. Looting and burning in the aftermath...

7. Poor people solidarity...

8. Death of a great man...

9. Panthers seek grass roots...

A Decade of War in Vietnam

U.S. forces move into the tiny Southeast Asian nation as advisers to the pro-western government; stay to fight one of the most unpopular wars in American history

Ho Chi Minh, wily, tough leader of North Vietnam, died late in 1969, leaving no clear heir to his position.

According to a bit of popular political folk-wisdom, Republicans create the conditions for war, Democrats then prosecute them, and, finally, Republicans end them.

In the last months of 1969, the conflict in Vietnam seemed to be following that scenario exactly.

U.S. involvement in the long, unpopular struggle began during the Eisenhower administration, when a handful of experienced American combat specialists were sent to the tiny Southeast Asia nation to help pro-Western forces in its southern half erect bulwarks against northern Communists.

Gradually, U.S. participation increased, possibly because the chief of the Saigon government Ngo Dinh Diem, had powerful friends in this country.

The Diem years were marked by conflicts within Saigon itself. Buddhist leaders, representing about 90 percent of South Vietnam's population, accused the Catholic Diem of injustice and religious repression. To demonstrate their grievances, several Buddhist monks publicly immolated themselves.

Early in 1964, Diem was assas-

U.S. diplomats Averell Harriman and Cyrus Vance led the Paris peace mission. After comic-opera beginning, negotiators settled down to serious discussion.

President Van Thieu and chief Xuan Thuy represented Hanoi.

sinated and a military junta led by Gen. Duong Van Minh seized the government. A few months later, Minh was toppled by another leader, Gen. Nguyen Khanh.

The chaos in Saigon worked to the advantage of the Communists and their leader, Ho Chi Minh. North Vietnam guerillas — the Viet Cong — carried the war to the capital city itself.

President Kennedy's military advisers responded with thousands more U.S. troops and hundreds of tons of equipment. It was becoming clear that the war was, in every aspect save the rhetorical, a U.S. affair.

Then, on August 4, 1964, Navy officials announced that U.S. destroyers had been attacked in the Gulf of Tonkin by Viet Cong torpedo boats. Congress speedily endorsed the "Tonkin Bay Resolution" which enabled President Johnson to act on his own discretion in furthering the action in Vietnam.

Meanwhile, Saigon leadership had changed several more times. The winner of what must have been a fierce power struggle was peppery, dapper little Nguyen Cao Ky, former Air Force Vice Marshall. Ky swiftly repressed dissident elements within his regime.

President Johnson was far less successful in calming *his* critics. Huge anti-war rallies were held in every U.S. city. A small, but very articulate, body of Congressmen demanded that Johnson initiate peace conferences and an equally vociferous group demanded that the U.S. declare full-scale war on the Vietnamese rebels. This Johnson refused to do, but he *did* sanction mass bombings of suspected Viet Cong supply depots, usually small villages.

On March 31, 1968, Johnson stunned the nation with a double announcement: he would not seek reelection — and he had ordered the bombings halted. Two months later, representatives of Ho Chi Minh said the Viet Cong were willing to negotiate peace terms.

After some comic-opera haggling over the site of the talks, both sides agreed to meet in Paris. Once there, the diplomats treated the world to more unintentional black humor as they argued over the type of table they would sit at. Finally, the U.S. delegation chief, W. Averell Harriman, and his opposite number from Hanoi, Xuan Thuy, shook hands and began the negotiations.

The diplomacy in France, however, was not affecting combat in Vietnam. War continued to rage. Closed coffins continued to return to the U.S.

Democrats and Republicans both said little about the war during the 1968 presidential campaigns. Richard Nixon claimed he had a plan for ending the conflict, but would not divulge it because, he said, it might interfere with the Paris talks.

During the first six months of his administration, President Nixon furthered the policies of his predecessor with regard to the war. Then, in June, 1969, he suddenly ordered the withdrawal of 25,000 U.S. soldiers from Southeast Asia. He promised that before the end of the year, 100,000 Americans would be ordered off the battlefields.

Reaction to the announcements was mixed. Senate Hawks decried what they claimed was capitulation to Communism. Doves remarked that Nixon's peace plan was simply the action they had been asking for since the beginning of hostilities — sending U.S. military forces home.

1. The battle's end ...

2. Death on a hill ...

3. The defeated ...

1. After a long, bloody battle between North and South forces, soldiers mingled with civilians in the ruined streets of Hue.

2. Devastation came also to rural areas of Vietnam: some of the most prolonged action occurred at "Hamburger Hill."

3. South Vietnamese rangers took dozens of prisoners following an intense fire-fight at Ben Hoa, a southern town.

4. U.S. Navy destroyers and aircraft carriers cruised in coastal waters, lending artillery support to land forces.

5. Paratroopers sustained heavy casualties after a spate of especially bitter combat in spring and early summer.

6. Marine helicopters were extensively used in "touch and go" operations, spotting and picking up troops, and pouring down low-level machine gun fire.

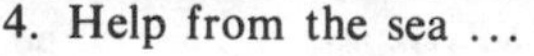

4. Help from the sea ...

5. Spring casualties ...

6. "Touch and go" ...

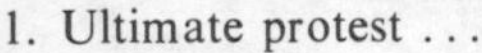

1. Ultimate protest ...

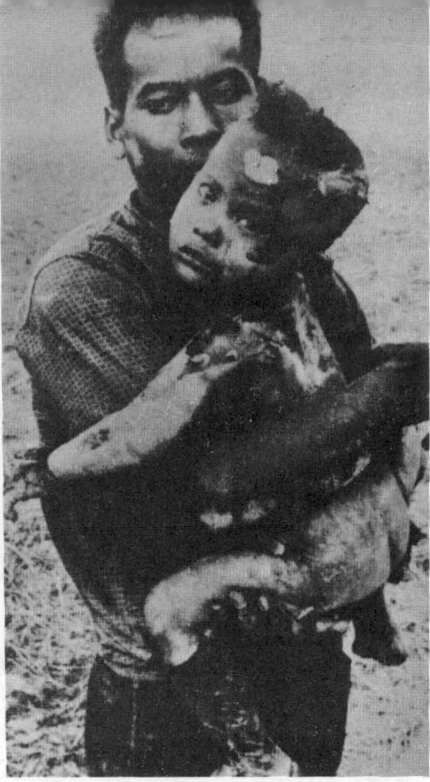

2. Napalm and children ...

1. To demonstrate their grievances with the U.S. supported Diem government, several Buddhist monks publicly immolated themselves on Saigon streets.

2. U.S. bombers dropped hundreds of tons of napalm, a mixture of jellied gasoline and explosives, on suspected Cong areas. Bombs were not selective.

3. Niceties of war were not always observed by the South Vietnamese: a police chief executed a Viet Cong officer without benefit of trial.

4. Quakers were among the groups protesting the Asian action, holding weekly vigils at Federal installations in major U.S. cities, including Washington.

5. Vietnamese peasants, caught between opposing, hostile armies, often watched terrified as Marine helicopters descended on fields and rice paddies.

6. General William C. Westmoreland, then commander of U.S. forces in Vietnam, pled the hawk's case to a joint session of Congress in April, 1967.

7. Perhaps the only happy moments the war generated occurred when servicemen returned to home and family with mind and body both intact.

3. Saigon "justice" ...

4. Unhappy Quakers ...

5. Waiting for the choppers ...

6. The General speaks ...

7. Johnny comes marching home ...

Vietnam Dominates Defense Picture

Military spending skyrockets to $80 billion annual level, but public scrutiny may slow Safeguard anti-ballistic missile

B-70, conceived as the ultimate manned bomber of the 1970s, turned out to be a $1.3 billion fiasco. One crashed; the other is in a museum.

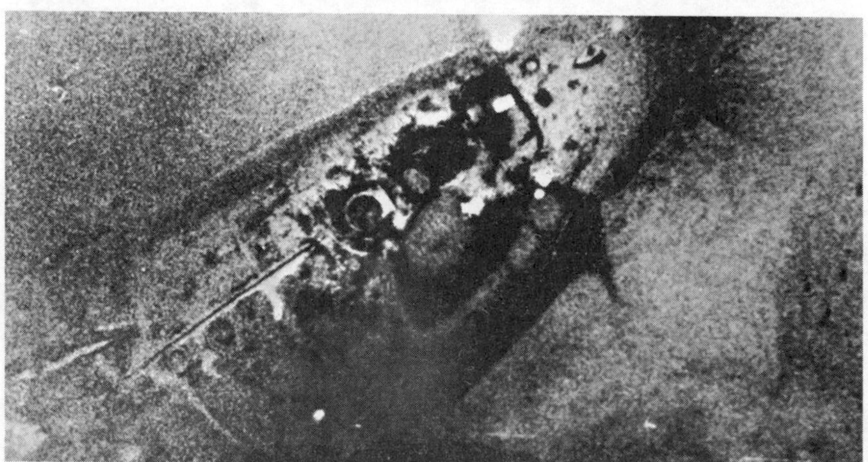

Fragments of nuclear sub *Scorpion*, lost near Azores in mysterious accident spurred efforts for improved deep sea search and rescue system.

One factor completely dominated the U.S. defense picture in the late 1960s: Vietnam. In cascading fashion it threatened the stability of American society:

- American troop commitments topped 500,000 and casualties, 30,000 (surpassing even the Korean war by early 1969).
- Annual expenditures in Southeast Asia ran around $30 billion and forced defense spending up to what many feared would become a permanent level of $80 billion.
- The war toppled one administration and was the No. 1 challenge to its successor.
- The increasingly divisive trends at home were linked to public disenchantment with Vietnam.
- And the "military-industrial complex" that President Eisenhower warned about in his farewell speech had become the target of greater public and congressional scrutiny, a scrutiny that could lead to a major overhaul of U.S. strategic military policies.

As the decade began President Kennedy took office on the promise to erase the "missile gap" supposedly being widened by the Soviets. The existence of that gap was never

Safeguard anti-ballistic missile became focal point of hawk-dove confrontation as Vietnam fighting cooled.

Top Pentagon brass Laird (seated) and Packard bombarded Congress with statistics to keep ABM alive.

Adm. Rickover's secrecy-shrouded NR-1 research sub was launched publicly after mounting costs were uncovered.

really proven, but his stress on a wide range of military responses to enemy threats reduced the chances of a direct nuclear confrontation between the two superpowers.

Part of that policy of flexible response called for what became known as counter-insurgency forces (nicknamed COIN by the Pentagon) to deal with local hot spots such as Vietnam.

Thus, out of this search for flexibility, the U.S. found itself rigidly involved in a guerilla war half way around the globe — and with no apparent way to get out gracefully.

Eight years later the man Kennedy defeated took office on the promise that he could get the country out of Vietnam. The stalemated peace talks in Paris began to move almost imperceptibly toward a solution after Nixon held out the possibility of Communist participation in a South Vietnamese government.

But as the pendulum began swinging back from the stress on tactical warfare such as Vietnam to improved strategic capability, new controversies arose. They centered on the kinds of weapons needed for defense in the '70s — and their cost and effectiveness.

At the heart of this debate was the Safeguard anti-ballistic missile. It had become almost the symbol of the division between the "hawks" and "doves" who earlier focused their quarrels on Vietnam.

Safeguard had a long and unhappy history. It began as Nike-Zeus in the late 1950s in an attempt to extend the technology of anti-aircraft missiles to missile defense. It was renamed Nike-X by the Kennedy Administration to emphasize its experimental nature and under that name remained on the shelf until 1967.

Then Defense Secretary Robert McNamara announced his half-hearted approval of a limited ABM system, renamed again to Sentinel. The argument for the system was that it would defend U.S. cities against a potential Communist Chinese nuclear missile threat.

The Nixon administration inherited the controversial project and sought to placate all sides by renaming it Safeguard, cutting back initial expenditures to only a billion dollars for research (out of a total estimated at more than $7 billion) and reorienting it to defense of strategic missiles.

This approach seemed to satisfy nobody. Opponents said it would never work and therefore was both a waste of money and a new step in the arms race. Defenders said it wasn't enough if the Soviets were really beefing up their offensive weapons, as intelligence reports indicated.

But in the new climate of public questioning of defense expenditures, Safeguard appeared to be in for a hard time. The decade of the '60s was strewn with the corpses of other glittering weapons systems. The B-70 bomber, Skybolt missile, mobile medium-range ballistic missile and the TFX aircraft (later renamed the F-111), are examples.

In addition, recent revelations that the Air Force C-5A military cargo jet may have cost as much as $5 billion more than originally planned further alienated the public.

Defense planners already were talking about the nation's defense posture after the Vietnam war, and the outlook appeared that this posture in the '70s would concentrate on improved offensive weapons to deter aggression rather than more limited warfare capability or an ABM system.

U.S. Apollo 11 Lands Men on Moon

The U.S. surpassed the early Russian space lead with a manned lunar landing on July 20, 1969

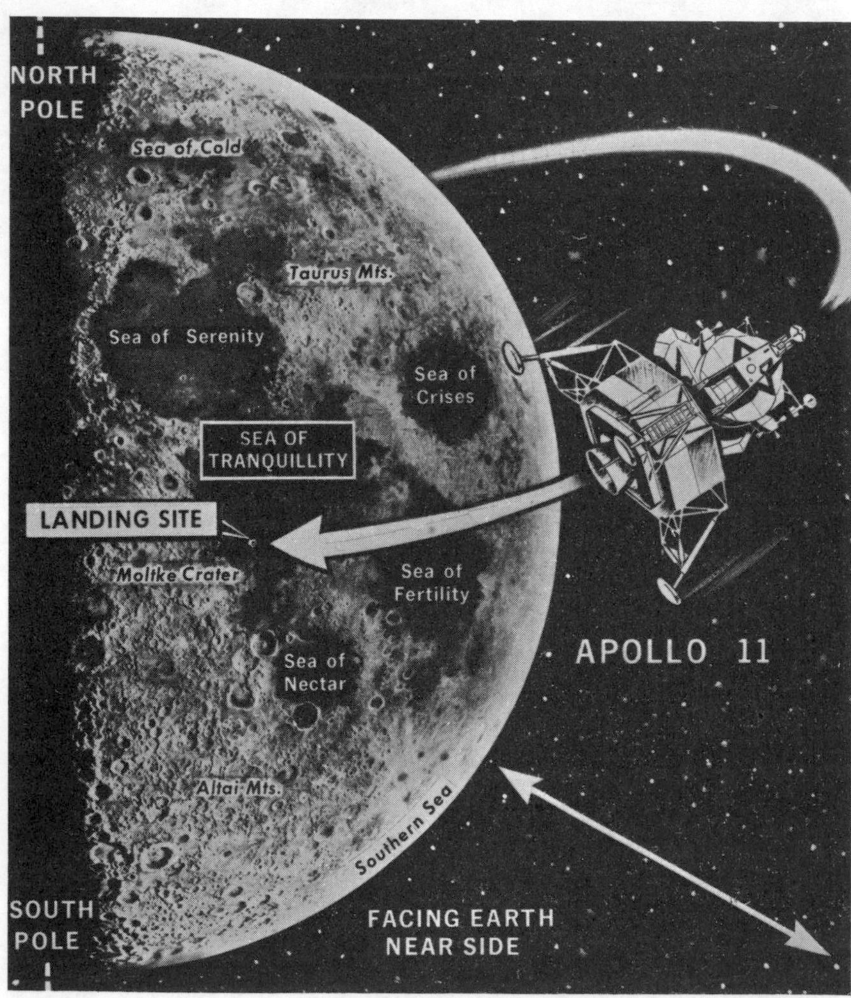

This artist's conception shows the trajectory of the manned Apollo II lunar module as it approached its moon landing site in the Sea of Tranquility.

The decade of the 1960s in space exploration was conveniently bracketed between Russian Cosmonaut Yuri Gagarin's pioneering, 1.8-hour orbital flight April 12, 1961, and the U.S. Apollo moon landing on July 20, 1969.

With the completion of the letter perfect Apollo 10 "dress rehearsal" on May 26, American astronauts had accumulated more than 4,000 man-hours in space — some five times as many as their Soviet counterparts. Leadership in space had clearly gone to the Americans.

The U.S. had started the decade behind in the size of its space boosters and, more important, appeared to be behind in its will to make bold ventures into space. All that changed when President Kennedy on May 25, 1961, committed the nation to landing a man on the moon within the decade.

The challenge was the spur the lagging U.S. space program needed. So was the orbiting of the first American, John Glenn, on Feb. 20, 1962.

Although the Russians scored another coup with the first "space walk" by Cosmonaut Aleksei Leonov during the Voskhod 2 mission on March 18, 1965, the U.S. forged ahead with five major triumphs:

• Longest space flight to date —

Astronaut Edwin Aldrin prepares to deploy the Early Apollo Scientific Experiments Package on lunar surface.

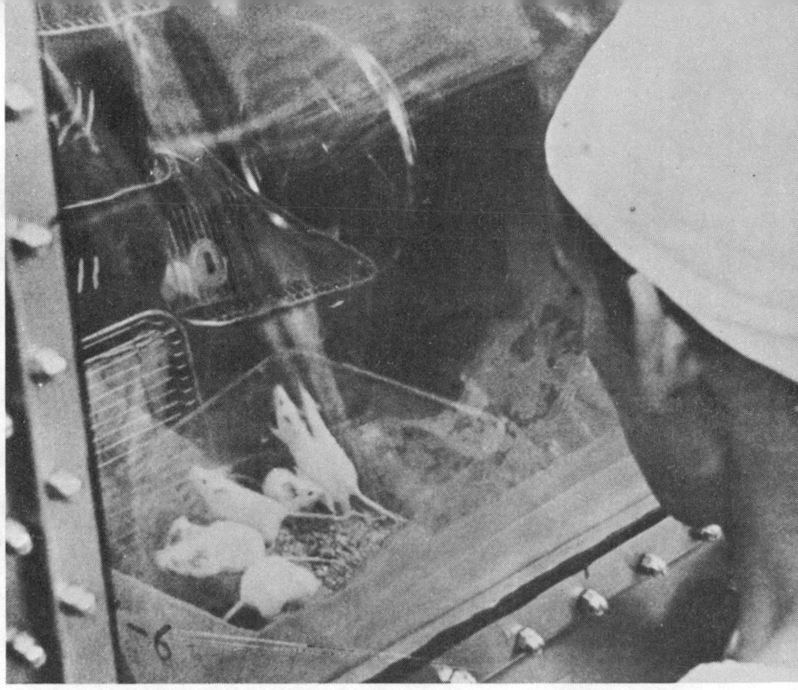

NASA injected 264 white mice with specks of moon dust to determine whether toxic organisms existed on the moon.

the two-week mission of Gemini 7 on Dec. 14-28, 1965.

• First rendezvous mission — Gemini 6, which approached to within a foot of Gemini 7.

• First docking in space — Gemini 8, which linked up with its Agena target vehicle on March 17, 1966.

• First manned flight around the moon — Apollo 8, which sent back TV pictures of the moon on Christmas Eve, 1968.

• And, finally, the electrifying moon walks of astronauts Neil Armstrong and "Buzz" Aldrin in Apollo 11.

In the process, the U.S. leap-frogged over the Soviets in the critical area of "weightlifting" capability. Early manned flights — both U.S. and Russian — relied on missiles originally developed for military purposes. But once the Apollo goal was announced, the U.S. launched a multi-billion dollar program to develop a rocket specifically for space flight.

The result was the 36-story-high Saturn 5 rocket/Apollo spacecraft combination. With 7.5 million pounds of thrust in its booster stage, the Saturn 5 was more than twice as powerful as the largest known Soviet vehicle although the existence of a yet unflown 10 million-pound-thrust Soviet rocket was long rumored.

The one catastrophic setback, the deaths of Astronauts Virgil Grissom, Edward White and Roger Chaffee in their Apollo spacecraft on the pad Jan. 27, 1967, was overcome in record time.

Ironically for the U.S. space program, however, success was steadily putting that program out of business. Debates in Congress and in the executive branch on what the country should do after the moon landing began in earnest in 1966 and at the start of the 70's had never really been resolved.

In that year, spending by the National Aeronautics and Space Administration (NASA) reached a peak of $6 billion and then steadily declined to the 1969 level of slightly less than $4 billion. Numerous proposals to establish camps on the moon (patterned after those of the Antarctic explorers) or mount a manned expedition to Mars were rejected by Congress.

Overlooked in the glamour that surrounded the manned flights was more than 900 unmanned spacecraft launched since Sputnik 1 on Oct. 4, 1957. Nearly two-thirds of these were American, but the "space club" was no longer the exclusive province of the two super powers.

In addition to more than 300 Soviet satellites, Australia had launched one; Canada, two; France, five; Italy, two; and the United Kingdom, three. Three others were launched by the U.S. for the European Space Research Organization, and Japan and West Germany were due for satellites in orbit soon.

These unmanned spacecraft could be placed into three major categories: *reconnaissance,* or "spy," *satellites* employed by the U.S. and USSR to keep tabs on each other's military activities; a wide variety of *scientific spacecraft* to study the earth, moon, planets and phenomena of outer space; and the so-called *applications satellites* for weather forecasting, communications, navigation, geodesey and natural resources observations.

The real future of the space program may lie in this third category — applying space technology to earth-bound problems. In this area the U.S. has been the leader from the beginning and completely dominates the international satellite communications consortium through its quasigovernmental Communications Satellite Corp. This aspect of space flight has already evolved from a research program to operational status, and weather satellites may soon follow.

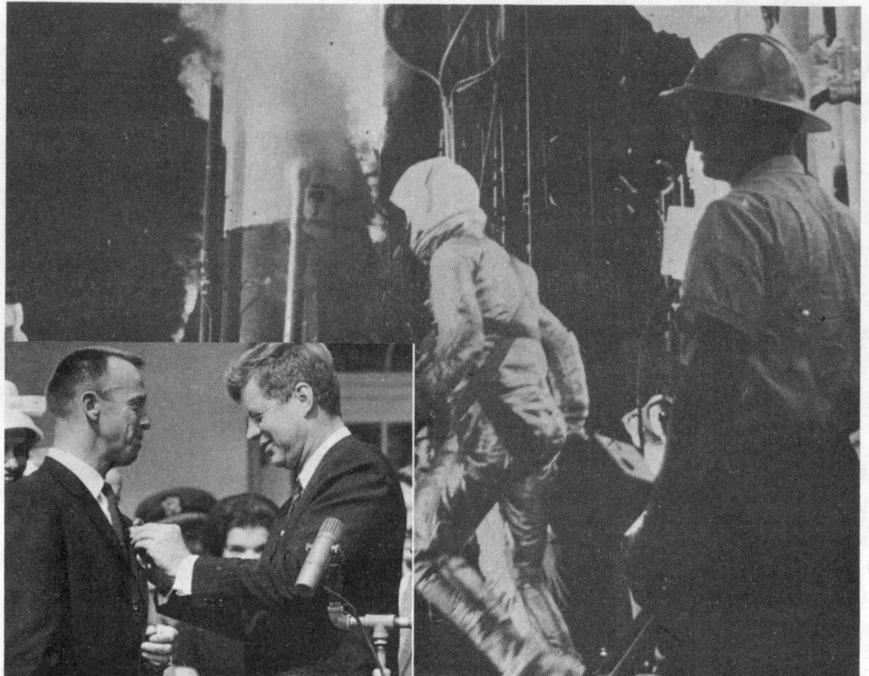

1. Hero's reward for Shepard . . .

2. And more of the same for Glenn . . .

4. TV from space, courtesy of Apollo 8

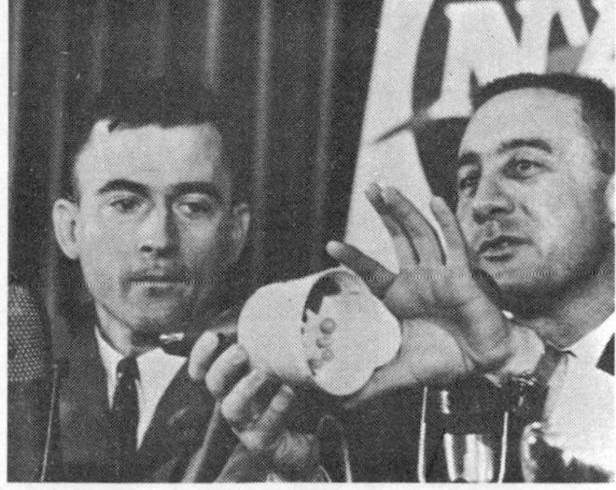

3. Gemini veterans explain maneuvers . .

5. Apollo 9 team reports . . .

6. Frogmen greet Apollo 10 crew . . .

1. Alan B. Shepard Jr., America's first man in space receives the thanks of President Kennedy after his suborbital Mercury flight in May, 1961.

2. The traditional tickertape parade up Fifth Avenue in New York obviously delights John Glenn after his first orbital Mercury flight.

3. Virgil (Gus) Grissom, who later died in the Apollo fire, describes workings of Gemini craft after he commanded its first flight in March, 1965. John Young looks on.

4. Apollo 8 astronaut Bill Anders is seen in this live TV transmission from space during the 1968 mission.

5. Apollo 9 crew of David Scott, Russell Schweickart and James McDivitt describe their 10-day mission during post-flight conference.

6. Apollo 10 crewmen await recovery helicopter that will take them to the carrier *Princeton* after Navy frogmen attach flotation collar to spacecraft.

7. Apollo 10 crew of Eugene A. Cernan, Thomas P. Stafford and John W. Young show varying degrees of apprehension and confidence in the traditional portrait taken on the eve of their May, 1969, flight.

8. Apollo command module, nicknamed "Charlie Brown," orbits moon during Apollo 10 mission.

9. "Snoopy," the Lunar module, meanwhile carries Stafford and Young to within 9 miles of the surface.

10. Stafford poses with the genuine article against a background of a simulated moonscape.

11. Manned Spacecraft Center Director Dr. Robert Gilruth (right) breaks out the traditional flags and cigars to signal another successful mission as premier astronaut Alan Shepard beams. Shepard later was accepted for future flights following a correction of his ear injury sustained in flight.

12. The families of astronauts Cernan (above) and Young (foreground) provide another traditional ceremony at reunion in Houston.

13. Saturn V rocket is wheeled out to the launch pad in preparation for the successful moon-landing mission launched on July 16.

14. A major step on the road to the moon was Ed White's space walk outside Gemini 4 capsule in June, 1965.

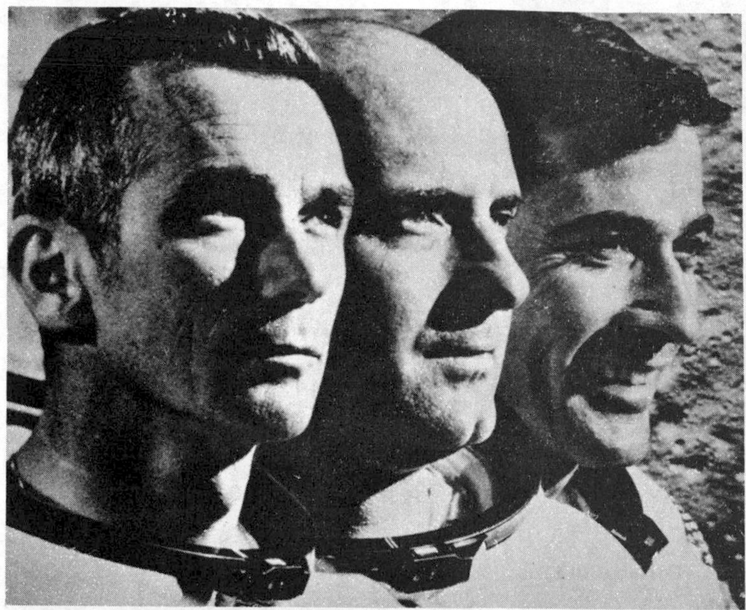

7. Cernan, Stafford and Young manned Apollo 10 ...

8. Command module

9. Lunar Module

10. "You're a good man, Tom Stafford" ...

11. Cigars and flags for another mission ...

12. .. Welcome home from the families.

13. First step to the moon ...

14. Take a walk ...

Cities: Struggle for Survival

Explosion of "inner city slums" forces recognition of needs of the poor; Congress gives pittance to urban aid programs.

"Help"

— © 1966 *Herblock in the Washington Post.*

In the 1960s, the country discovered "urban problems," catch-phrase for the gravest combination of malignant ills to confront the nation since the Civil War.

Chief among them was the ghetto, pitting the body politic, and spreading. It was also — for 70% of the population living in cities — inadequate housing and street crime, traffic snarls and the mess in mass transit; it was air, noise, and water pollution, and a decline in services.

The government's approach to these ills, early in the decade, was consistently piecemeal as it had been for years. Crime was left to the states; housing help (rooted in the '37 Housing Act) trickled dollars down through a hodgepodge of authorities; welfare problems were treated with outdated welfare concepts; and poverty, isolated in ghettoes, or in Appalachia — was swept under the carpet.

A typical early '60s cry of liberal politicians was for "public housing," as if it might cure all urban ills. It didn't begin to cure the housing problem.

As a '62 survey showed, 148,000 families had been uprooted as of then but only a fraction of the poor and ill-housed had been helped.

A stagnant air mass blanketing Manhattan in smog is seen in this 1966 view from Empire State Building. Slight relief was afforded when utilities began burning low sulphur-content fuel. However, autos, as in typical scene of congestion, spew out 85% of air pollutants, pointing up the need for a radically altered mass-transit system.

In August, 1969, HUD head George Romney, while pledging implementation of the '68 Housing Act and pressing for full funding of $3 billion, candidly admitted that Federal Housing had been a failure: "it's been trying to build while Urban Renewal reduced the number of units available."

What had happened was that, almost mid-way between those two dates, the ghettoes had exploded.

City slums everywhere, Watts in Los Angeles, in Detroit, in Newark, were left smoking ruins.

The Center for the Study of Urban Violence at Brandeis University reported that in 1967, "riot type ghetto disorders" had occurred in 168 cities; about 18,800 persons were arrested, 3,400 injured and 82 killed.

In the April '68 riots in 172 cities following the assassination of Martin Luther King, Jr., 27,000 were arrested, 3,500 injured and 43 killed.

Across the country, urbanologists like Daniel (Pat) Moynihan, chief cities man for LBJ and in President Nixon's Urban Affairs Council, and Professor Edward Banfield of Harvard, saw it as coming from an amalgam of all city ills, fueled by racial intolerance. It was also characterized as the breakdown of the cities' 18th and 19th century physical plants, and due, in large measure, to the carryover of 19th century attitudes and government instrumentalities.

Integrated programs were first offered in 1967-'68 by President Johnson, and in 1969 by President Nixon, that were attempts to treat urban problems as a whole.

There were private groups formed, such as John Gardner's Urban Coalition in which private industry took part in the rehabilitative process. By late '69 however, the interest of private industry seemed a lagging expedient, as funds for promised projects were raised only in small part. In legislation, the '68 Housing Bill was a distinct improvement over the past; though funded in a bare bones manner, it asked for construction of 6 million new housing units over a 10 year period. Most imaginative was LBJ's Model Cities program, later continued in an expanded version by President Nixon.

But treatment of the vast tangle of slum employment, housing, crime, and other city woes depended on how much of the national budget went for defense and Viet Nam.

LBJ's programs were drastically cut. Head Start and Job Corps which spent $271.2 million in 1967 were forced to share a mini-grant of $5 million appropriated in 1968 for the entire Office of Economic Opportunity. And radical community experiments in some O.E.O. units soon had a fire-breathing conservative Congress attempting to dismember a number of its limbs. By mid-July 1968, Head Start was severed from the body and given to a less-than-sympathetic Department of H.E.W.

President Nixon, to the surprise of many, offered a fair packet of nostrums to the cities in August 1969. Proposals for revamping the country's Welfare system were forward-looking. One major change suggested was to allow families to keep a $720 annual portion of outside income against a pro-rated drop of one-half dollar benefit for each dollar earned above that amount. President Nixon's mass-transit plan, and his scheme to have tax dollars returned to the states with a tidy amount earmarked for cities, was indication that at least the executive branch took the cities' troubles seriously. Enough so to put liberal principles into an old Tory. The rest remained up to Congress.

1. Riots, riots, riots . . .

2. Fire sale . . . ?

1. The face of the riots that spread through American cities could be seen in microcosm during the arrest of a beaten and bloodied Newark Negro in July, 1968.

2. An open door policy prevailed during the '66 riot in Cleveland, Ohio, as officers, to prevent inflamatory moves, stood by while looters carried off booty.

3. Mothers in Ann Arbor, Michigan, link arms to prevent arrest by Sheriff's deputies during a 1968 protest over welfare cuts.

4. Harlem parents picket a local school demanding a voice in its administration during the 1968 fight for school decentralization.

5. The problem of garbage disposal, complicated by strikes of sanitation workers, reached crisis proportions in the 60's as more consumer goods than ever came packaged in disposable containers.

6. A slum backyard in Washington D.C. is a classic example of what housing evangelist George Romney called the failure of urban renewal under the Federal Housing program.

7. Former Welfare Secretary John Gardner met the country's mayors in 1968 at a major conference devoted to the topic: Is the Big City Dying? From left to right: Stokes of Cleveland, Gardner, Alioto of San Francisco, and White of Boston.

8. Here would-be plasterers are shown how by their instructor in one of the programs under Office of Economic Opportunity control. These much-heralded programs were crippled by Congressional paring of funds.

3. Let my people go ...

4. Demand a say in schooling ...

5. What a waste ...

6. Slumming it ...

7. Mayors talk over mess ...

8. Keeping cities plastered ...

Economy's Big Change Is Psychological

Acceptance of government management overshadows dazzling growth record but decade begins and ends with uncertainty

Waves of speculative gold buying reached a crest in March, 1968, raising a threat of an international monetary collapse. U.S. reserves were severely depleted Seven nations met in Washington, agreed on two-tier gold price.

The decade began with uncertainty as to how business would be affected by the policies of a new Administration — and ended the same way.

During the years between, there were profound quantitative changes in the economy. Gross National Product leaped from a mere $503 billion in 1960 to an expected $920 billion in 1969.

But perhaps an even greater change was psychological. The decade saw the gradual acceptance of the "new economics," in which the government is expected to manage the entire economic structure so as to insure steady growth without serious disruption.

"Recessions are not inevitable," declared the President's Council of Economic Advisers in 1965. Events appeared to bear them out in the latter part of the decade, but not without considerable strain.

It turned out to be much easier to "manage" the economy when the situation called for deficit spending and tax cuts than when it called for tight budgets, tight money and an increase in taxes.

In 1962, President Kennedy stimulated the lagging economy by putting over a 7 percent investment tax

Embattled Treasury Sec. David Kennedy saw the first dollars with his signature in June, 1969.

May 29, 1962, was the day when N.Y. Stock Exchange reversed panic selling; clock showed ticker 2½ hours late.

Office construction boomed, but in 1969 residential construction still waited fruition of rosy predictions.

credit for business. In 1964, President Johnson had little difficulty putting through an $11 billion tax cut, and thus guaranteed effective demand, as it turned out, for years to come. The budget deficit that year was only $5 billion.

There were those who said that this kind of manipulation would work only if the President were given the power to raise or lower taxes and make other adjustments without having to deal with Congress. And in 1967 and early 1968, Congress bore them out by balking at passage of a tax rise despite dangers of an overheated economy and pressure on the dollar.

The 10 percent tax surcharge was finally agreed to by reluctant legislators in mid-1968. Did it come too late? Inflation, held in check in the early part of the decade, re-appeared in ugly strength. The cost of living rose 4.6 percent in 1968, the largest yearly rise since the Korean War year of 1951. The nation's balance of payments situation worsened.

In 1969, President Nixon attempted to bring the Federal budget into near balance, and proposed retaining the 10 percent surcharge. The Federal Reserve Board, on April 3, raised the discount rate to 6 percent, a 40-year high, and also raised the level of required reserves of banks, further reducing their lending abilities.

A debate raged as to whether such measures were too mild to control inflation or were, in fact, too strong — an "economic overkill."

The stock market did its usual spotty job of anticipating business trends. Its three bad years of the decade were 1962, 1966 and 1969.

On May 29, 1962, when the market began to recover from the JFK-steel industry confrontation, volume reached 14.8 million shares on the Big Board, and the figure was regarded as astounding. By 1968 that volume was merely "active" and brokerage houses were swamped by paperwork, necessitating shorter market hours.

Most key industries benefitted from the prolonged boom. Housing, however, remained in a slump until late in 1968. Housing starts were expected to reach 1,650,000 in 1969 — the first good year since the 1,610,000 of 1963. The crucial problem remained, however, of finding a way to decrease construction costs to offset both the credit crunch and the spiraling costs of land, construction materials and wage increases.

The Nixon Administration at first attempted to keep its options open on the gold question. But by February, 1969, Treasury Secretary David Kennedy had assured the world that the U.S. would not raise the price of gold — consequently, in Europe, gold speculators suffered.

By April 4, President Nixon was ready to slightly relax the controls on overseas investment, stating that the balance of payment problem would be solved by attacking "fundamentals," not by maintaining a "patchwork quilt of controls." He advocated a strong budget surplus and monetary restraint as the cures both for payments problems and inflation.

As the new decade approached, the outcome of these efforts remained in doubt, and few observers were in a position to challenge one of President Johnson's last official statements on economic matters: "We cannot hope to reach in a single year the goal that has eluded every industrial country for generations — that of combining high employment with stable prices."

Affluence and Status Change The Face of Labor

Unions abandon confrontation tactics as business-like bargaining brings job security and big pay checks for skilled; Strikes hit public as service workers organize.

Convicted of jury tampering, Teamsters Union president James R. Hoffa enters the Federal Penitentiary at Lewisburg, Pa., to begin jail term.

It was the decade in which organized labor merged into the great American middle class.

An increasingly conservative rank-and-file abandoned the violent tactics of yesteryear, and a new breed of corporate-type union leader emerged to pursue in hard but business-like bargaining sessions the solid goals of job security, higher pay and a shorter work week.

In a climate of rising prices, higher taxes, and prosperity fueled by military-industrial spending, big wage settlements became common. When, in September, 1967, the United Automobile Workers struck Ford Motor Company and won an increase of 7% — the biggest ever negotiated by the union — it was scarcely headline news. By 1968, some 46% of union families were earning between $7,500 and $15,000 annually.

With its collective eye on a home in the suburbs, education and upward social mobility, labor understandably put major stress on job security.

One pattern for dealing with technological unemployment was set by a 1963 steel industry contract which kept more workers on the job by giving senior union men a 13-week vacation every five years.

New York City's Welfare workers went on strike for higher pay and reduced case loads.

A strike by 5600 members of the Transport Workers Union sends Philadelphia commuters scurrying for space on the Pennsylvania railroad.

Jailed during paralyzing N.Y. transit strike, TWO Pres. Michael Quill told judge to drop dead, then died himself.

John DeLury led N.Y.C. sanitation strike that led to health emergency.

AFL-CIO Pres. George Meany (l) condemns state laws outlawing union shops.

Less pleasing to labor was the April 1964 arbitration panel ruling on railroad featherbedding which eliminated 90% of all firemen's jobs through attrition.

In 1964 the Labor Department took a dim view of long-term job security, reporting automation was eliminating 200,000 jobs a year. By 1968, however, a galloping economy had brought unemployment down below the 2.5 million mark for the first time since 1953.

But if the automation bogey ceased to haunt the trade union halls, it virtually made its home in the ghettos. At a time when only 3.1% of all white workers were out of jobs, the unemployment rate for Negroes, with fewer of the technical skills now required by industry, remained at 6.7%.

Automation became a factor in increasing government intervention in labor-management disputes, job training and anti-poverty measures.

The Kennedy Administration got involved in working for settlements almost immediately and sought to combat technological unemployment by forming a job training program under the 1961 Area Development Act. But the big admission that a high-riding economy alone couldn't solve the jobs and income problem came with the passage of President Johnson's massive anti-poverty bill in 1964.

Strikes did more to inconvenience the public than roil labor-management relations. In 1966, a 43-day walkout of machinists at 5 airlines caused some 150,000 persons a day to find alternate means of transportation. New York City experienced a 13-day strike against the city's combined subway and bus system. And hospitals were hit by mass resignations in New York and San Francisco.

In 1967, the time lost to work stoppage was 50% over the previous year and the highest since 1959. Significantly, militancy increased among the nations 10.5 million government employees and teachers and was brought into tragic focus in 1968 when Dr. Martin Luther King was murdered while leading a demonstration in support of striking garbage workers in Memphis.

Despite big wage hikes and an all-time high for union membership (17.9 million in 1967), neither chiefs nor rank-and-file were satisfied with the state of the union. One reason was that total growth of the movement since 1956 was only 400,000, while in the same period the non-farm work force grew by 11.5 million. Another was impatience with old-time leaders and philosophy.

In 1965, rank-and-file discontent swept from power Steel Workers' President David McDonald and Electrical Workers' President James B. Carey.

The United Automobile Workers, in May 1968, was suspended from the AFL-CIO, bringing to a head the long-smoldering feud between its president, Walter Reuther, and Federation president George Meany, over Reuther's demand for a more progressive social policy and internal reforms.

Scandals rocked the unions during the decade. In 1964, labor's greatest maverick, Jimmy Hoffa, was convicted of jury tampering, mail and wire fraud, and conspiracy to appropriate $25 million in union funds for private use. And in 1967 it was revealed that the CIA had been secretly channeling funds to unions through foundations.

At the close of the 60's, labor took for granted many of the benefits which had led to violent confrontation a decade earlier. With a big stake in the economy, it turned its attention to protecting its newfound status against the encroachments of the less privileged and less skilled.

World Affairs

Conventional wars, and the threat of nuclear war, ruled the Sixties

While the planet Earth did manage to avoid world war and nuclear confrontation, wars of a smaller scale pervaded the decade of the Sixties. Uppermost in most American minds, of course, was the war in Viet Nam which, by the end of the decade, was draining approximately $20 billion annually from the U.S. economy, and cost the U.S. over 40,000 young casualties since the American military buildup began there in 1965.

Throughout the rest of the world, virtually every major power was involved either in war, invasion, or violence which attracted international attention during the Sixties. India invaded the Portugese colony of Goa in 1961; China fought a border war with India in 1962; the USSR-Chinese ideological split grew to such mammoth proportions that by the end of the decade the two countries were embroiled in an on-going border confrontation in Asia; the USSR and five Eastern European satellite nations invaded Czechoslovakia in 1968; France was embroiled in an Algerian colonial war until 1962 when DeGaulle managed to extricate his country. Other major limited wars included the Mid-East war of 1967, the famed Six-Day war which saw tiny Israel defeat her larger Arab neighbors and establish her military superiority in the area; the Nigerian civil war; the Greek-Turkish conflict over the fate of the island nation of Cyprus; numerous coups and countercoups on almost every continent; and assorted border conflicts.

Major confrontations also played their role in establishing the Sixties as a decade of military might. The U.S.-USSR confrontations included the Cuban Missile Crisis of 1962, the building of the Berlin Wall (with President Kennedy's subsequent callup of reservists to bolster U.S. German-based forces) in 1961, and numerous diplomatic confrontations.

Diplomatic confrontations have been easy enough for any nation to participate in, since any nation can command the attention of the technologically advanced international news media. Witness little Albania's rise to the forefront of "diplomacy" as a staunch ally of, and rather loud mouthpiece for, the People's Republic of China.

All in all, it was a good decade for war, but a bad one for humanity and peace. It seemed that humanity and peace too often interfered with other, more expedient goals. There was always the promise of peace in the future, but history spoke too often, and too tragically for our best hopes to lie in building upon the peace prospects of the Sixties.

Many national and world leaders called upon men to rededicate themselves during the Sixties. And, in fact, there was some rededication to the overwhelming problems faced by all of mankind — the problems of overpopulation, hunger, disease, a dangerously misshapen ecological balance. But the still overwhelming massiveness of these problems point out all too clearly that there has not been nearly enough of this kind of activity — too much potentially constructive human energy was still expended in war, too many scientific minds were still engaged in developing weapons of destruction instead of instruments of life.

Undoubtedly, a rededication, a change of priorities, is necessary — not only to peace but to basic survival. As long as nationalistic goals take precedence over human goals, as long as the golden rule is not uppermost in the men's minds, a golden world is still far in the future.

Plausible reasons are usually given for wars. Leaders in all camps stated that war meant ultimate peace. Whatever else war meant, it also meant death.

U.N. Survival a Cause for Hope

Amid international crises and internal dissension it remains the world center for negotiation and useful cooperation

Relaxed and youthful appearing, the former Burmese school teacher, U Thant, is sworn in as U.N. Secretary General in 1961 ...

... following the death of Dag Hammerskjold, here (l) with Ireland's Fred Boland.

In his native Sweden crowds thronged the funeral of the peace-loving U. N. leader.

Departed Greats: In 1961, at the peak of their influence, Chief U. S. Delegate Adlai Stevenson visits delegate Eleanor Roosevelt.

More than 400 dignitaries in the diplomatic world were invited to ceremonies on July 5, 1969, to celebrate the 50th anniversary of the creation of the League of Nations. They were to be held at the former home of Woodrow Wilson, now a museum filled with exhibits relating to the League and memorabilia of the President, its main architect. But the event was called off because only 35 persons accepted the invitation. U.N. Secretary General U Thant declined, as did Hubert Humphrey, board chairman of the Woodrow Wilson Center for scholars at the Smithsonian Institution; no acceptances came from top officials of the U.S. State Department, nor from members of the Senate Foreign Relations Committee, nor from more than 10 ambassadors of the 50 envoys of former League member states.

Although the memory of the first world organization had all but died, the new one, the United Nations, was alive and fairly well as it approached the 35th anniversary of the 26th day of June, 1945, when 46 nations signed its charter in San Francisco. The U.N. now had 126 members and had miraculously, even with some effectiveness, survived a decade of war, crisis, and

Arthur J. Goldberg, former Supreme Court Justice, becomes chief delegate after Stevenson's death.

James Russell Wiggins (c), a former Washington Post editor, became chief delegate as the Johnson era ended.

Goldberg resigned in 1968 to be followed briefly by George W. Ball, former Under Secretary of State.

Nixon's appointee as chief delegate was a career diplomat, Charles W. Yost, seen here (1) during a Middle East debate.

Since 1964 U. N. forces like these have been trying to keep peace between Greeks and Turks on Cyprus.

near fatal internal squabbling.

In 1960 there were but 82 members; the world was beset with troubles in the Congo, Algeria, Tunisia, Angola, and South Africa, and Russia's Premier Khruschev was demanding that the even-handed Secretary General Dag Hammarskjold resign to make way for a three-man secretariat composed of a Westerner, a Red bloc delegate, and a representative of the uncommitted or neutralist nations.

On Sept. 18, 1961, Hammerskjold was killed in a plane crash in Northern Rhodesia while on a mission to try to stop the fighting between U.N. Peace Forces and troops from the rebellious Katanga province in the Congo. Russia's potentially enfeebling troika plan of secretaryship was thwarted by the election of former school teacher U Thant of Burma as Secretary General.

In 1963 the U.N. received two blows to its prestige: the crisis over Russian bases in Cuba was settled between the Soviet Union and the U.S. beyond the jurisdiction of the U.N. And the big powers concluded a nuclear test ban treaty outside its councils. But finally a precarious peace was established in the Congo, and in 1964 the U.N. forces withdrew. That same year, 7,000 U.N. troops went to Cyprus to keep the peace between the Greek majority and the Turkish minority, some of them remaining through 1969, although the situation finally cooled.

Another crisis year was 1965 when the Soviet Union, six other communist bloc nations and France refused to pay their share of the peace-keeping operations voted by the General Assembly. Since their charter clearly specified that nonpayers could not vote, the Assembly was bogged down in futile debate.

On July 14, 1965, the well-liked chief U.S. delegate Adlai Stevenson died in London at 65. He was succeeded by former U.S. Supreme Court Justice Arthur Goldberg, who worked out a compromise whereby the U.N. deficit could be met by voluntary contribution, avoiding the no-pay, no-vote issue.

Also in that year, a member nation for the first time resigned — Indonesia. But there were no other departures and Indonesia soon returned.

Increasingly, the attention of the U.N. turned to the Vietnam war, but efforts to mediate it came to no avail. Frustration over this situation was a major factor in U Thant's declaration that hc would not seek another five-year term when his first one expired in November 1966. However, he was prevailed upon to accept re-election.

In the closing days of 1966, the U.N. Security Council on Dec. 16, in a historic first, imposed mandatory economic sanctions against Ian Smith's rebel regime in Rhodesia, and the Assembly passed significant covenants on human rights — economic, social, civil, and political — and unanimously approved a treaty barring nuclear weapons from outer space. Then, after ten years of effort, the Assembly on June 12, 1968, passed a treaty limiting the spread of nuclear weapons to the present "nuclear club:" the U.S., Russia, Great Britain, Red China, and France (the latter two not signing).

In 1969, with President Nixon's selection of career diplomat Charles W. Yost as chief U.S. delegate, the U.N. was working quietly behind scenes mainly on how to preserve peace in the Middle East crisis. As a sponsor and headquarters for private four-power talks between the U.S., Russia, Great Britain, and France on this sticky issue, the U.N. seemed to be cast in what might be its most effective role.

China: Enigma With the Bomb

Internal power struggle brings economic chaos, but nuclear capacity gives new thrust to anti-U.S. and anti-USSR foreign policy.

Recurrent clashes along the 7,000-mile Sino-Soviet border raised prospects of all-out war between the two Communist giants. This sign on Chen Pao island warns "never to violate Chinese territory."

Red China remained a disturbed and disturbing giant throughout the 60's. Plagued by food shortages, lagging industry, and internal dissension, the Communist regime of Chairman Mao Tse-tung nevertheless continued to call for world revolution against the policies of both the U.S. and the USSR.

By 1961, the nation was in deep trouble from successive crop failures and was forced to buy 5 million tons of wheat from the West. It was to be the first of many such purchases.

With factory workers near starvation, industrial production dropped to 30 percent of capacity. In 1962, Peking responded to the crisis by ordering 30 percent of China's urban population back to the farms. The edict was widely opposed and the tiny British Colony of Hong Kong was deluged with 70,000 refugees.

The army cut off the exodus but the rumblings of discontent among peasants and transplanted factory workers grew.

Internal crises did nothing to abate Mao's tough foreign policy, which brought about the attack on India on Oct 22, 1962, and the break with the USSR the same year. Mao also managed to woo away from Moscow all Communist parties in Asia except Outer Mon-

In 1969, Chairman Mao named Defense Minister Lin Piao his heir apparent. China-watchers predicted little change in policy with the new appointment.

Cultural Revolution's rampaging Red Guards brought the economy to a halt.

golia and India.

Despite its extreme poverty, Red China indulged its own form of "dollar diplomacy" with loans and aid to Laos, Syria, Cambodia, Algeria and Albania.

Following the break with Russia, tension mounted along the 6000-mile Sino-Soviet border, and in 1963 Peking hinted it might take back the 1.5 million square miles wrested from it by Russia in the 19th Century.

In response, the USSR began shifting troops from East Europe to the troubled area. By the close of the decade, border incidents between the one-time comrades had become frequent.

China moved further still from the USSR in 1964 by seeking new trading partners around the globe, particularly in Japan and Western Europe.

Peking also sought to undermine Soviet influence by posing as the champion of the non-white underdeveloped world, with Chinese Premier Chou En- lai personally carrying the message of pure revolution to the nations of Asia and Africa.

Then on Oct. 16, 1964, Red China exploded its first atom bomb. By existing standards of nuclear technology, the bomb was primitive, but the fact that it had been developed at all within China's backward economy was impressive evidence of China's determination to achieve world power status.

The bomb helped China persuade neutralist regimes in Burma and Cambodia that China, rather than the USSR, would be the dominant force in Asia during the years ahead.

Simultaneously, China expanded its trade with the non-Communist world by 25 percent, while at home it gave new impetus to the drive against "revisionists" and those trying to undermine the teachings of Chairman Mao.

At first the anti-opposition drive seemed no more than the usual moves to curb dissent. Then in July, 1966, Mao announced that the Great Proletarian Cultural Revolution was in full swing and would purge all those "taking the capitalist road."

The Red Guard, an organization of teenagers, served as Mao's political weapon as they rampaged through the cities denouncing the bourgeoisie, the intellectuals and the bureaucracy.

But by unleashing the Red Guards, Mao had also opened the door to the voice of disaffection everywhere. Respect for authority was eroded, production schedules were ignored, and roving bands of youths attacked local administrations. With economic and political chaos threatening, Mao called in the army to stem the tide of revolt.

By 1968, the Cultural Revolution had receded but a considerably weakened China faced the world. Continued sword-rattling speeches were made about the U.S. in Vietnam and "revisionist" Russia with whom war was said to be "inevitable," but Mao shied away from battlefield commitments.

As the decade closed, the chance of an accommodation with the U.S. seemed a possibility — but a remote one. Mao had finally appointed a successor, Defense Minister Lin Paio, and the new Nixon Administration in Washington lowered trade and visiting barriers to Red China.

On Formosa, the Nationalist regime of Generalisssimo Chiang Kai-shek virtually abandoned all hope of a return to the mainland. But the ageing Chiang still gave 80 percent of his budget to the military and maintained a 600,000-man army.

And despite a fast-growing economy and seeming prosperity, Chiang maintained an iron hand over the island. Opposition and free expression were as remote in 1969 as in 1960.

1. To the Indian frontier ...

2. Soviets walk out ...

3. China gets The Bomb ...

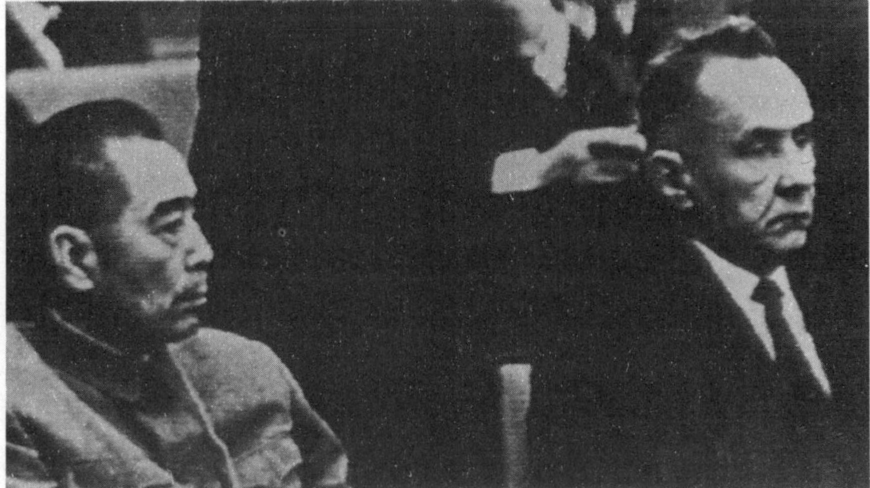
4. Friends no more ...

1. Chinese Communist medium tanks played important role in frontier battle with India over disputed territory.

2. When Soviet Representative Valerian Zorin walked out of United Nations General Assembly during speech by Nationalist China delegate, relations between Russia and Red China were still cordial, but by the decade's end the Russians had lost all enthusiam for the seating of Mao's China in the international body.

3. China made a determined bid for world power status in October, 1964, when she exploded her first crude atomic device.

4. The growing chill in Sino-Soviet relations is evident from the grim expressions worn by Red Chinese Premier Chou En- lai and Soviet Premier Alexei Kosygin during 1964 Moscow meeting of world Communists.

5. During Red China's agricultural crisis, 70,000 refugees deluged Hong Kong, but the Crown Colony, which had absorbed a million refugees previously, was forced to turn back 60,000.

6. The cult of Chairman Mao and his Thoughts was propagated everywhere. Here the sign above a Shanghai theatre reads "Bravo Mao!" but others exhorted the populace to attack Mao's enemies, the "bourgeoisie" and the "revisionists."

7. Red Guards hold leaders of "Anti-Revolutionary" groups to public shame during Cultural Revolution which toppled many old-line Communists from power.

8. To achieve rapid industrialization, China converted illiterate peasants into partially skilled factory workers, recruited men and women to work together in peoples' communes.

9. Chinese students in Moscow clashed with Soviet police in Red Square, claimed they were attacked without provocation.

10. On Matsu, 33 miles from the Communist mainland, Nationalist Chinese troops kept in shape but their maneuvers were mostly defensive.

11. His hopes of regaining the mainland vanishing, President Chiang Kai-Shek ruled Nationalist China with almost dictatorial powers. The economy rode high but political opposition invited censorship or prison.

5. Fleeing starvation ...

6. The Chairman was everywhere ...

7. The price of opposition ...

8. No sex discrimination ...

9. "Chinese go home" ...

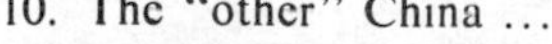

10. The "other" China ...

11. Aging Generalissimo ...

Sino-Soviet Dispute Heats Up

Khrushchev's deStalinization campaign stirs illusion of freedom; Brezhnev-Kosygin oust "K", clamp down on liberties

China-Russia enmity over control of the Red world drew harsh words at meetings of the two early in the decade. But by March 1969, anger had flared into open clashes between their armed forces along the Sino-Soviet border.

There's a liberal saying that U.S. "hard-liners" are like Bible-belt fundamentalists — they see Russian "commies" as demons in a sort of medieval morality play.

But when, in June '69, Ambassador Dobrynin complained to Secretary of State Rogers that he wasn't taking the "Chinese threat" seriously enough, it grew clear that a whole new stage set of devils had cropped up.

Not that the scenario featuring "yellow peril" protagonists was new to Americans, but it was certainly new for the Russians. In late '69, the often-mentioned possibilities of new alignments in the following decade — particularly of the U.S. and the USSR — against Red China were mind boggling.

The latent Sino-Soviet dispute, running through the 60s like a nervous tic, got its first big shove toward confrontation from Khrushchev's policy of de-Stalinization.

As early as 1956, the burly, charismatic Premier had assailed Stalin's "cult of personality." And, as Stalinist members of the Presidium — Kaganovich, Molotov, Malenkov — dropped out of sight, it became evident that Khrushchev was con-

Two-stage intermediate missiles, as well as giant ICBMs, were paraded around Moscow's Red Square in the usual display of military might on Russia's 50th anniversary of the revolution.

USSR's ruling duo, Leonid Brezhnev, party chief (2nd left) and Premier Alexei Kosygin (r.) welcome Hungary's head, Janos Kadar, to Moscow in 1969.

solidating his position.

Meanwhile, from Port Arthur to Prague, Stalin statues were toppling and Stalin Allées everywhere were renamed. But it wasn't until 1961 that the anti-Stalin policy was formally consecrated — one blustery November day the late Dictator's remains were removed from the Kremlin's Walls.

At the same time that this political in-fighting went on, Khrushchev was preaching "peaceful coexistence" with the West. In order to appease party hawks, however, he maintained an aggressive posture vis-a-vis the U.S.

In '61 he broke the three year moratorium on nuclear tests. Then, in the fall of '62, misjudging U.S. temper, he tried to set up Cuba as a giant launching pad for missiles aimed at the U.S. The world teetered on the brink during the Cuban crisis until Khrushchev was faced down by President Kennedy.

This lost gamble, plus a series of domestic crises — wheat crop failures and lagging industrial growth over the next two years — were all his enemies needed. He was ousted in 1964.

The period before his fall, however, saw an unprecedented thaw in Russian-American cultural relations. Poets, for example, like Yevtushenko, who visited the U.S. often in the first half of the decade became near heroes to academic America via educational TV.

Unhappily this climate changed quickly under the new First Secretary, Leonid Brezhnev, and the incoming Premier, Alexei Kosygin.

The first signs of their repressive temper were seen in attempts to stifle what little intellectual freedom there was. It began innocently enough. There were debates and polemical arguments in the party sanctioned press.

Yuli Daniel's and Andrei Sinyavsky's trials, for example, drew impassioned protests from the West's intellectual community and from some brave Russians. Their imprisonment however, was only the start. And though it became obvious to outsiders that Soviet intellectuals were clamoring for more freedom, continued arrests and trials in '68 and '69, drove home the fact that neo-Stalinism was in the saddle.

On the foreign front, unavailing attempts were made for a rapprochement with China. At the same time pressure was put on Red bloc countries to heed the Soviet diktat.

As the world soon saw, tyranny, through the use of armed might, was the answer to dissidents. On August 21, 1968, following Czechoslovakia's failure to curtail political liberties of the Dubcek regime, Soviet tanks overran the country.

In an attempt to shore up the fragmenting Soviet bloc, a World Congress of Communist Parties was convened in Moscow in mid-June '69. One purpose — a show of solidarity to cauterize wounds opened by the invasion of Czechoslovakia. Another, perhaps overriding, reason: to read Red China out of the Communist movement. Neither met with much success. Clashes continued along the Sino-Soviet border. Troop build-ups on both sides of the border were seen.

The 60s ended like a cliff-hanger for the USSR. What will Red China do? Will the Czechs lie doggo or explode to become another bloody Hungary? And at home, how to keep moving toward that bourgeois goal of more consumer goods? The 70s will tell.

1. Tovarich, ban that bomb! ...

2. Dictator's bones downgraded ...

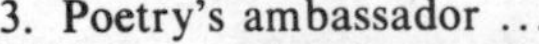

3. Poetry's ambassador ...

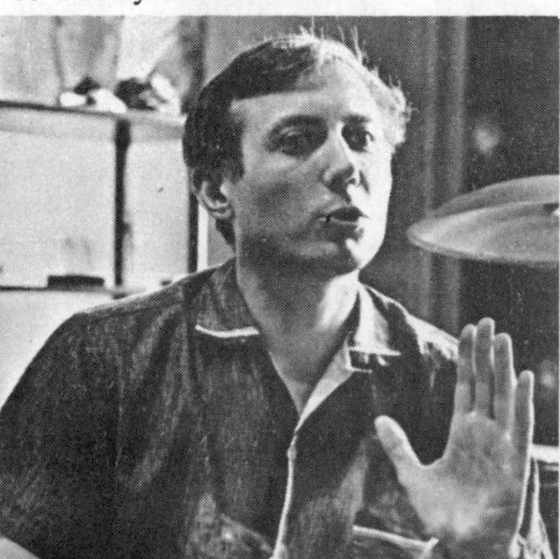

4. Defector declares: dad was dreadful ...

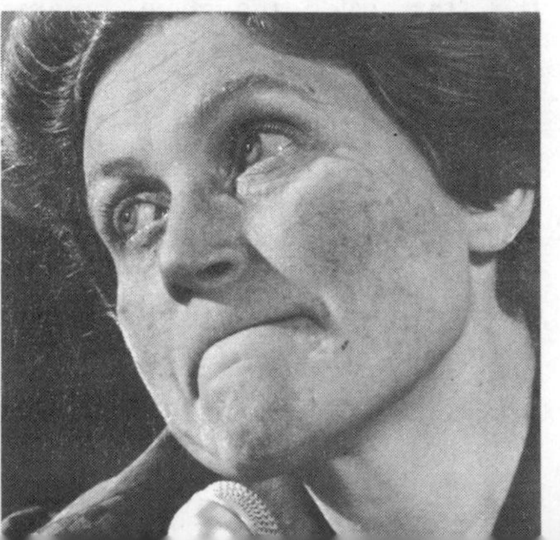

1. American and Russian "peace-niks" march through Red Square in a rare instance of an officially sanctioned parade in 1962. The signs read "Ban the bomb."

2. Stalin's bones lie under the stone slab (foreground) to which he was removed — at the height of Khrushchev's de-Stalinization campaign in 1961 — from the tomb he shared with Lenin in Moscow's Red Square.

3. Poet Yevgeny Yevtushenko was the darling of American intellectuals and one of the more charismatic Soviet culture figures to appear in the U.S. during the years of greatest inter-cultural exchanges.

4. Stalin's daughter. Svetlana Alliluyeva was the U.S.S.R.'s most notorious defector of the decade. Here she is seen at her first press conference in New York City, April 25, 1967.

5. Soviet Premier Nikita Khrushchev before he became a "non-person" is shown welcoming space heroes Valentina Tereshkova, first female astronaut, and Lt. Col. Valery Bykovsky, June 22, 1963, at a Moscow celebration.

6. Colonel Yuri Gagarin, the world's first "cosmonaut" died in a plane crash on March 27, 1961.

7. In solemn ceremony, Gagarin's remains are carried by Russia's top leaders during the State funeral to which all the world sent expressions of condolence. Pallbearers include Kosygin (L.) and Brezhnev (center, front).

8. The U.S.S.R.s mach 2 supersonic jetliner, the TU-144, is shown to foreign newsmen and dignitaries at Sheremyetevo Airport, Moscow, just before its successful demonstration flight on May 21, 1969.

9. The trial of Yuli Daniel (L.) and Andrei Sinyavsky was an earnest of repressive measures to follow. Although the world's intellectual community denounced the 1966 imprisonment of the two writers, dissidents continued to be harshly suppressed. Their defense attorney, Mark Kogan, is at the right.

5. K and the high flyers ...

6. First human in space ...

7. ... is mourned by all!

8. Twice faster than sound ...

9. The brave and the jailed ...

East European Nations Sound Independent Note

Communist "commonwealth" crumbles; Russia seeks to maintain power by arresting liberalization trend with Czech invasion

Prague student waves Czech flag atop one of Soviet tanks which invaded the city in Aug. 1969.

The myth that the nations of East Europe formed a monolithic "Red bloc" subservient to the dictates of Moscow suffered an uneasy death during the '60's.

Except for Albania and East Germany, a fresh liberal wind swept through the Communist-orbit lands, and Poland, Hungary, Czechoslovakia, Rumania and Yugoslavia all escaped, to a greater or lesser extent, from total economic dependence on the USSR.

But the limits to which the satellites could strike out on their own were clearly defined in 1968 when Soviet troops marched into Czechoslovakia to terminate a liberalization program that went "too far."

Impetus for the independent line in the Balkans derived from Soviet Premier Nikita Khruschev's de-Stalinization program and the dispute with Red China, formalized at the Communist Party Congress of 1961 when Red China Premier Chou En-lai walked out.

In Poland and Hungary, the downgrading of Stalin only sanctioned trends in progress since 1956. But in East Germany, Bulgaria, Rumania and Czechoslovakia, it aggravated ideological splits and produced a frantic search for scape-

Alexander Dubcek led Socialist Republic of Czechoslovakia to period of liberal reforms, which provoked Soviet repression restoring hard-line Communists to power.

Policeman inspects wreckage of Yugoslav Consulate in Bad Godesberg, Germany, bombed by refugees from Croatia.

goats.

Tiny Albania broke completely with the USSR, becoming an increasingly bellicose satellite of the Chinese.

Economic difficulties also played a role in the breakup of the satellite empire. Industrial and agricultural production lagged. To combat the decline, the Czechs, Bulgarians and even the East Germans began to rely on market mechanisms.

The Yugoslavs decollectivized their farms and the Poles followed, putting 85 percent of their agriculture on state-managed private farms, while the Hungarians resorted to incentive systems.

Khruschev attempted to halt the break-up as early as 1961 when he called to Moscow the leaders of Comecon, the East Europe counterpart of the Common Market, in an effort to weld the loosely organized group into one central agency.

But resistance to this economic colonialism was sharp, particularly from Poland and Czechoslovakia, who preferred an arrangement that would enable them to profit from trade with the West. Subsequently, the U.S. signed trade agreements with Yugoslavia, Poland and Rumania.

The satellite nations took different ways of manifesting their growing independence. Rumania, the only East European nation to congratulate China on its first atom bomb in 1964, called in 1966 for the abolition of both NATO and the Warsaw Pact.

Rumania again broke ground in 1967 when she became the first Balkan nation to recognize West Germany. She then refused to join the Communist bloc in condemning Israel in the Middle East. She antagonized Moscow again in Aug. 1969 when she played host to President Nixon during his historic "bridge-building" visit, the first to a Communist nation since the close of World War II.

Yet for all his independence in international and economic affairs, Rumania's party chief Nicolae Ceausescu maintained a policy of domestic repression matched in severity only by that of East Germany.

Under Walter Ulbricht, the latter remained throughout the decade a closed society dependent upon the USSR for military and economic support.

Part of the change in East Europe was evident by the shift in relations with the Roman Catholic Church. In 1964, Hungary restored the Church's right to form a hierarchy and communicate with it and in 1966 Yugoslavia became the first Communist nation to open full diplomatic relations with the Vatican.

In 1966, however, a struggle between the Polish government and the Church over the latter's right to free expression threatened to divide the nation's 31 million citizens.

East Europe experienced its biggest crisis in 1968. On Jan. 5, insurgents ousted Czech President Antonin Novotny as head of the Communist Party and replaced him with Alexander Dubcek.

Dubcek began putting through a series of reforms that included greater press freedom, curtailed military power, and changes in the rigid Marxist economy.

On Aug. 21, nearly half a million Soviet troops invaded Czechoslovakia. Under urging from their leaders, the Czechs put up no significant resistance. When the latter promised to end their reforms, the Russian troops slowly withdrew.

Yugoslavia and Rumania had voiced their support for the Czechs, but the message to the satellites was clear: the Brezhnev Doctrine under which Moscow asserted the right to intervene in the affairs of members of the socialist "commonwealth" would be implemented by force.

1. "Russians go home" ...

2. Defeated Czech leaders return from Moscow ...

3. Tito turns East ...

1. Road signs pointing to Moscow are accurate. Others were deliberately misleading as Czech youths sought to confuse Soviet occupation troops.

2. Alexander Dubcek and Ludvik Svoboda confer at Prague Castle after return from enforced visit to Moscow where they learned of harsh Soviet terms.

3. Thaw in Soviet-Yugoslav relations was signalled by 1962 visit of President Tito (right) to Moscow. But Tito also kept lines open to West.

4. Resurgent Czech nationalism followed on Soviet invasion and government leaders like Smirkovsky got rousing welcome from factory and farm workers for their stand.

5. Stefan Cardinal Wyszynski led Polish bishops in continuing counter-attack on government efforts to silence Catholic Church in predominantly Catholic Poland. At 1966 Krakow celebration of Polish Christian Millenium, he reaffirmed right to free expression.

6. Polish state-run supermarket in Warsaw is biggest in Eastern Europe, including Soviet Union. Limited selections and some high prices made it more of a showcase than a mass consumer phenomenon.

7. Unpopular throughout Eastern Europe for his hard-line Marxist policy, East German Communist Party Chief Walter Ulbricht (left) got a rousing welcome from Egyptian President Nasser during 1965 Cairo visit.

8. Mini skirts invaded Eastern Europe and brightened Belgrade streets but drew disapproving stares from older generation. Balkan youth generally combined strong anti-Vietnam sentiments with enthusiasm for U.S. music, fashions, life-styles.

4. Workers acclaim stand of Czech leaders . . .

5. Poland's defiant cardinal . . .

6. Shopping at "Super Sam" . . .

7. A rare welcome for Ulbricht . . .

8. The generation gap in Yugoslavia . . .

Great Britain's Eight-Year Ordeal

Hopes for European economic and political unity soar as de Gaulle government is replaced by more amenable regime

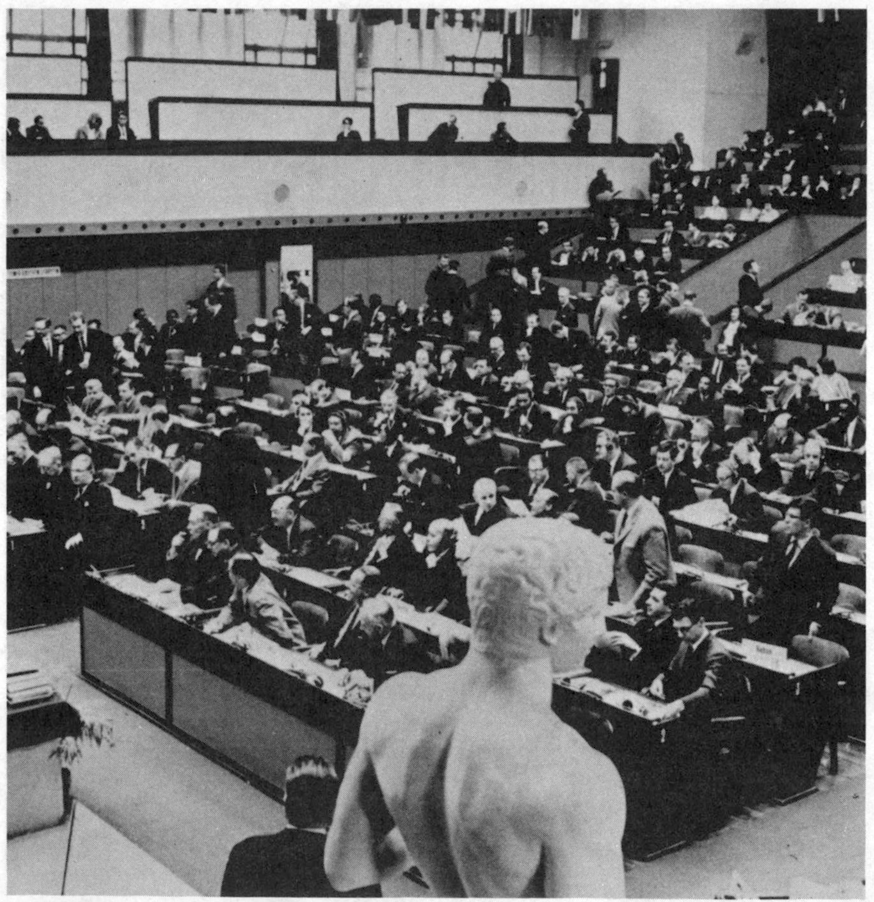

Transatlantic trade talks were a major concern of the Common Market during entire decade. First session of the "Kennedy Round" convened May 4, 1964. In 1966, Market nations finally agreed on a common bargaining position.

It was in July, 1961, that an economically hard-pressed Great Britain rather reluctantly opened negotiations to join the new European Economic Community (Common Market). Eight years later the British were still trying.

This time, of course, their hopes were high. So were those of the "Friendly Five" nations of the Common Market that had always favored British membership. In fact, hopes and even dreams of a rebirth of European unity were rushing to fill the vacuum caused by the ultimately burst bubble of Charles de Gaulle.

The new French government of President Georges Pompidou was widely believed to be willing to drop the opposition that had kept Britain out of the Market all those years, and the English were pressing for talks "at the earliest possible moment."

Nevertheless, hard bargaining still lay ahead. The recalcitrance of de Gaulle was partly based on substantive issues such as Britain's relationship to its Commonwealth, its "special relationship" with the U.S., and with Britain's own economic problems.

Ironically, most observers had

Until retirement of De Gaulle in 1969, this study of Prime Minister Harold Wilson said all there was to say about British efforts to gain entry to the Common Market.

Britain had many supporters on the continent. Here West Berlin students carry anti-De Gaulle slogans: "We want unity, not grandeur"; "Europe doesn't want a Fuehrer."

expected back in 1961 that the British would have relatively little difficulty in gaining admission. The first de Gaulle veto, in 1963, after difficult and prolonged negotiations, was received with astonishment. As the French president exercised his veto repeatedly over the years, the other five (West Germany, Italy, Belgium, the Netherlands and Luxembourg) were in a dilemma. They knew the Common Market could not succeed without France but were afraid that it also could not succeed without England.

Just before Christmas, 1963, there was a real possibility that the Market would break up. One divisive issue was farm policy, which also had been a key problem in the early negotiations with Britain. By mid-1965, de Gaulle was so angered at the failure to achieve agricultural agreement that he boycotted EEC meetings. At the time he was also believed to be concerned that the Market's movement toward simple majority rule would offset individual veto powers. The others agreed to retain the veto, however, and in 1966 progress toward economic unity picked up considerably. In July, the Market agreed on uniform farm price levels and on forming an EEC agricultural fund to handle support buying and subsidies on an international basis.

This achievement came along with another far-reaching decision to unify tariffs. Beginning on July 1, 1968, the six nations declared they would stop charging customs on each other's industrial exports and would surround themselves with a single tariff wall.

Europeans were buoyed in the mid-60s by predictions that their standard of living was rising so fast that it would all but catch up with that of the U.S. by 1975. Experts congratulated the various countries for their adroit use of monetary and taxation devices to stimulate their economies. Less welcome were observations about the growing economic power of U.S. interests in Europe.

The Common Market began 1969 with an important agreement on transportation policy. By March, the French dropped opposition to a common patent system.

The problem of British admission, however, grew acute. Chancellor Kurt Kiesinger of West Germany met with Prime Minister Harold Wilson and declared: "For both our countries, a united Europe is inconceivable without Britain."

Then came the downfall of the de Gaulle government and the final election, in late June, of Georges Pompidou. Though Gaullist, the new government issued on June 26 an initial policy statement that appeared to contradict de Gaulle's assertion that British membership would change the nature of the Market and weaken it. Pompidou repeated his campaign offer to meet with other Market members on the British question and said France would go "as fast and as far as our partners" in building a united Europe.

Still to come were the hard negotiations with Britain, and also with the U.S. over tariff reductions. Still to come were solutions to European money crises. But economic unity and progress seemed possible once more.

The Common Market was originally formed not only for economic cooperation but for eventual political unity. Hopes for this had disappeared during the long years of Gallic contentiousness, but in the latter part of 1969 even this forgotten dream was brought out and dusted off.

End of an Era: de Gaulle Bows Out

An incarnation of French power, the 78-year-old general leaves the field to younger, hopefully more flexible, men

General Charles Andre Joseph Marie de Gaulle, leader of the Free French in World War II and president of the Fifth Republic, his own creation, from Jan. 1959 to April 1969, when at 78 he resigned after a referendum defeat.

The '60s were for France, and to some degree for the world, the decade of de Gaulle. After a series of weak governments, the French elected Charles de Gaulle Prime Minister on June 1, 1958. Three months later they adopted his proposed constitution for the Fifth Republic, and on Jan. 1959 elected him president, endowed with constitutional powers unusual for an elected Chief of Staff. He had served in that role as an absolute monarch for ten years, ten months and 28 days when he resigned on April 28 following a defeat on a relatively unimportant referendum.

He had survived a series of crises and conspiracies — including a half dozen attempts on his life — and had made France's influence count in world affairs far more than its resources and 50 million population perhaps warranted. By courting the Communist bloc and trying to reduce U.S. influence in Europe, he tried to make France the leader of a Third Force between the West and the East, and he developed his own nuclear *force de frappe* to emphasize this leadership. Bringing France into the Common Market

Georges Pompidou, de Gaulle's premier (1962 to 1968) succeeds him as president on June 15, 1969, at 57.

Waving the tricolor, youthful supporters of de Gaulle organized as "L'Union des Jeunes pour le Progres" move into the streets of Paris during the 1968 Revolution to show their allegiance.

— from which he barred U.S.-oriented Britain — he presided over a wave of prosperity that was only lately beginning to come unstuck because of inflation, wage inequalities, and farmer unrest — plus a neglect of education, housing, and other domestic needs.

President de Gaulle's first major service to France had been to grant independence to Algeria on July 3, 1962, ending eight years of brutal civil war that took some 350,000 French and Moslem lives and cost the nation $20 billion.

Western diplomats were startled when on Jan. 27, 1964, de Gaulle recognized Red China, breaking ties with Nationalist China. Later that year he made triumphal tours of Mexico and South America as part of his strategy to encourage smaller nations to turn to France rather than the U.S. or the Soviet Union. In a February, 1965, broadcast he startled the world by proposing a five-power conference to revise the U.N. charter, with non-member Red China participating, and called for a return to the gold standard, which clearly would reduce dependence on the dollar and the pound sterling by all countries.

Withdrawing from the NATO command structure, he ordered all U.S. forces out of France by April 1, 1967. But signs of disaffection began to be felt at home. In the December, 1966 Presidential elections he was forced into a humiliating run-off before finally defeating the Socialist-Communist candidate Francois Mitterand to gain a new seven-year mandate. Then in the March 12, 1967, Parliamentary elections, the Gaullists and their allies emerged with only a shaky one-vote margin.

Then came the French Revolution of 1968, starting out in mid-May as a student protest against educational inadequacies and escalating into violent rioting and a massive general strike. Dissolving the Assembly to force new elections, de Gaulle called on the people to support his party to avert a Communist takeover in France. It was the last hurrah, but the old magic worked and the Gaullists won the heaviest majority ever given to any French party.

But as de Gaulle himself once observed, "There is always an end to everything. Everyone comes to an end." When the French citizens rejected his proposal to provide the provinces with a greater degree of regional autonomy (downgrading the Senate), he promptly fulfilled his promise to quit if defeated.

Elected as his successor on June 15 was Georges Pompidou, 57, de Gaulle's premier from April, 1962, to July, 1968, when despite his brilliant services in the May revolution he was replaced by the more stoutly Gaullist Maurice Couve de Murville — a move that many observers felt contributed to de Gaulle's downfall. As Premier, Pompidou elected Jacques Chaban-Delmas, 54, a tennis player, World War II Resistance veteran, and onetime president of the National Assembly.

Entering a new era, France had leadership that offered less grandeur than Pres. de Gaulle had provided but probably more expertise on the nation's basic requirements. As an editorial in Le Monde commented: "This is the real key to the affair: the French were weary of greatness, weary of challenges and alarums."

1. Violent statement on Vietnam . . .

2. A voice on the left . . .

3. Comeback and putdown . . .

4. An amiable stand-in . . .

5. Rebel with cause . . .

1. Student demonstrators in Paris burn the American flag to dramatize their opposition to U.S. policy.

2. Francois Mitterand, the leader of the French Federation of the Left, forced de Gaulle into a humiliating runoff in the 1965 elections.

3. Onetime (1952) French Premier Edgar Faure as Education Minister in 1968 jammed through a reform bill giving unprecedented freedom to university students, was dropped by Pompidou .

4. Alain Poher, onetime Resistance leader and president of the Senate, became the Interim President briefly after de Gaulle resigned.

5. Leftist rebel Ahmed Ben Bella became Algeria's president in 1963, developed strong ties with Russia, was deposed in a bloodless coup by Col. Houari Boumedienne in 1965.

6. Parisians use the 1967 visit of Vice President Humphrey as an excuse for anti-American demonstrations.

7. Gen. Lyman L. Lemnitzer (right), commander of U.S. forces in Europe, reviews his troops in 1967 as they leave French soil along with NATO.

8. President de Gaulle welcomes West German Chancellor Ludwig Erhard to his country home at Rambouillet in 1965 when the two leaders met for secret talks on European unity.

9. Georges Bidault, head man of the Resistance during World War II and onetime premier (1949-50), returns to France in 1968 after six years of exile in Brazil and Belgium as a strong opponent of the Algerian deal.

10. This scene is in Rue Gay-Lussac after a night of rioting in May 1968.

6. They don't like the U.S. ....

7. Withdrawal to prepared position ...

8. Traditional enemies with common problems ...

9. Back home again ...

10. Desolation and destruction ...

Britain: Lagging Economy, Dwindling Empire

Labor takes power, meets balance of trade crises with austerity and controls

Britain in 1969 enjoyed a brief respite from growing concern with high taxes, frozen wages and wildcat strikes when Queen Elizabeth crowned Prince Charles in age-old ceremony in Wales. The investitute received the full support of the Labor government.

In the '60's, Great Britain's claim to first-rate power status was seriously challenged by economic and political crises at home, diminishing world responsibilities, and repeated failure to gain admission to the European Economic Community or "Common Market."

Conservative Prime Minister Harold Macmillan began the courtship in 1961, and was first rebuffed by France in 1963. The Labor Government was no more successful, and only with the fall from power of General de Gaulle in 1969 did Britain's chance to lose its "splendid isolation" brighten.

Britain had good reasons for wanting to marry into the prosperous EEC. Exports of the group had jumped 30% in 1960. Those of the United Kingdom, which lives on trade, gained only 12%.

Gold reserves hit a 10-year low that same year and unemployment rose steadily, by 1963 reaching 3.9% in England and Scotland and 11.2% in Northern Ireland.

In 1963, the already shaky Tory government was rocked by two scandals. John Profumo, Minister

Prime Minister Wilson's austerity program hit the lower and middle classes, Labor's traditional supporters.

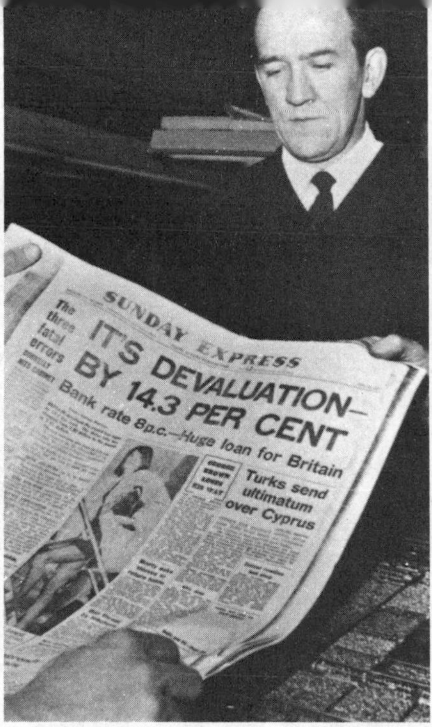

Devaluation of the pound on Nov. 18, 1967, marked a further retreat from world power by Britain.

A coffin was wheeled to Harold Wilson's residence in 1967 to protest his application to the Common Market.

of War, had an affair with "party girl" Christine Keeler (who was also carrying on with Soviet Naval Attache Evgeny Ivanov). And Lord Privy Seal Edward Heath revealed that John Philby, who had resigned from the Foreign Office in 1951, then disappeared, had been a Russian spy.

The major casualty was aging Prime Minister Macmillan, who resigned in 1964 after seven years of power. He was briefly succeeded by his Foreign Minister, the Earl of Home.

But Britain was ready for a change, and in the October 15 elections, Harold Wilson, the 46-year old Labor party leader and ex-Oxford don, captured the post of Prime Minister. His margin of four seats was the smallest of the century.

Wilson had hardly taken office when faced with the now desperate necessity of shoring up an economy on the verge of collapse. The mounting deficit in the balance of payments — a problem which had periodically haunted Britain during the past 50 years — was reaching crisis size.

On November 25, 1964, to avoid devaluing the pound, eleven nations, led by the U. S., put together a record $3 billion rescue fund. At home, the Labor government slapped a 15% surcharge on imports and raised taxes and the bank rate.

The struggle to restore confidence in the pound was continuous. In 1966, Wilson presented the country with a far-reaching austerity program, including defense budget cuts, a 10% hike in excise taxes, and a year-long wage-price freeze.

But by the end of 1967 no significant surplus in the balance of payments had been achieved. Briton's exports totaled $10.77 billion, her imports $12.98 billion.

By the time of the April, 1967, elections, traditional Labor voters were clearly unhappy, boycotting the polls or switching sides. They griped about anti-inflation measures designed to "redeploy" labor from services into manufacturing, which had the effect of raising the number of unemployed to 600,000.

Per capita income was a low $1,500, and taxes on individual and corporate incomes over $2,500 were leveled at 42.5%.

Britain's situation at home was not helped by her dwindling Empire role. In 1961, South Africa quit the British Commonwealth; Cyprus and Sierra Leone became independent members.

On November 11, 1965, Premier Ian Smith of Rhodesia and his white minority government made a unilateral declaration of independence. And on January 16, 1968, Wilson announced that by 1971 all British forces would be withdrawn from Malaysia, Singapore and the Persian Gulf.

Labor had other problems. The party left wing criticized support for the U. S. Vietnam war policy.

But more serious and divisive was the emergence of Enoch Powell, a Tory M. P., in April 1968, as a spokesman for an end to colonial immigration.

In a series of explosive speeches urging that Negro and Indian residents be packed off to their homeland, Powell seemed to portend a serious racial issue for Britain in the '70's.

1. Student rebels take over LSE ...

2. Venerable protester at Ministry of Defense ...

3. Sex at the Ministry of War ...

4. Black Power-London style ...

1. Sacking of two London School of Economics lecturers brought sit-ins-, strikes and police in April 1969.

2. Earl Russell white-haired 88-year old philosopher, joined students and intellectuals in non-violent civil disobedience against weapons of mass destruction.

3. Christine Keeler almost caused downfall of Tory regime when War Minister John Profumo publicly denied having affair with her.

4. Negroes advocated militancy while Conservative Member of Parliament Enoch Powell calls for restrictions on colored immigration.

5. Anti-Vietnam demonstration in London drew 20,000. The 1968 march on U.S. Embassy was one of many protests against government support of U.S. policy.

6. Ill health forced embattled Prime Minister Harold Macmillan (left) to retire. Foreign secretary Lord Home renounced an Earldom, became Sir Douglas-Home to take over House of Commons leadership.

7. Patrick Gordon-Walker the Labor government's highly respected Foreign Secretary, had to resign after racists caused his defeat in two campaigns for seat in Parliament.

8. British troops were called into Northern Ireland in 1969 to quell the violence that broke out between Catholics and Protestants.

5. Protesters marching on American Embassy ...

6. Outgoing conservatives Macmillan and Home ...

7. Ousted by racists ...

8. The Irish revolution continues ...

West Germany, The Modern Phoenix

From the ashes of World War II, West Germany rises to world leadership in finance. industry and politics

The Berlin Wall, constructed in 1961 to separate East and West Berlin, has become the symbol of a Germany divided between the two great world powers.

Throughout the Sixties, Germany remained the focal point of cold war tensions between the U.S. and the Soviet Union. The divided city of Berlin, located 110 miles within the East German border, continued to absorb East German refugees (about 4 million since the establishment of the East German state in 1948) until August 13, 1961, when Russian Premier Nikita Khrushchev inspired the East German puppet government to close the East-West Berlin border with guns and barbed wire and, finally, the concrete Wall.

Octogenarian Konrad Adenauer, West German Chancellor from 1949 to 1963 and leader of the Christian Democratic Party, began to concentrate his diplomatic efforts on strengthening Franco-German friendship as he became increasingly afraid that President Kennedy, in dealing with the USSR on the Berlin issue, would try to "sell Germany down the Rhine."

Meanwhile, post-war West Germany had grown into an industrial giant. The German monetary unit, the Deutsche Mark, was revalued upward 5% in March, 1960, to four marks per dollar, and by the 1969 international monetary crisis had

Adolf von Thadden's neo-Nazi party gained some support in the Sixties, but lost all parliamentary seats in the October, 1969, election.

Leftist West German demonstrators in Frankfurt carry posters of student leader Rudi Dutschke. "Red Rudi" was shot in April, 1968, in Berlin. Student at right carries a placard reading "Vietnam for the Vietnamese."

emerged as one of the world's hardest currencies.

The man largely responsible for the West German post-World War II economic boom was Dr. Ludwig Erhard, Economics Minister during the Adenauer regime and successor to *Der Alte* as Chancellor in 1963. Chancellor Erhard, ruling with a coalition Cabinet and Parliament under the Free Democratic Party, faced the immediate problems of keeping Germany's economic boom going despite fears of inflation, and keeping a viable political balance between two allies, France and the United States.

Erhard won re-election in September, 1965, despite rising sentiment against him over his government's controversial stand on the extension of the statute of limitations for war criminals and his sudden Middle East policy shift. (He established diplomatic relations with Israel in 1965 after Egypt invited East German President Walter Ulbricht to visit Cairo). But Adenauer's Christian Democratic Party and West Berlin Mayor Willy Brandt's Social Democratic Party took their share of parliamentary seats, thus further weakening the Chancellor's coalition.

Erhard's problems mounted as prices rose and consumer demand and jobs dropped. He was also criticized by the growing number of German Gaullists for being a puppet of the U.S.

The end came in November, 1966, as the ruling Erhard coalition finally collapsed. A new coalition between the Christian Democratic Party and the Social Democratic Party formed. Sixty-three-year old Kurt Georg Kiesinger emerged as the compromise CDU Chancellor choice, despite his Nazi past.

At the same time the world viewed with increasing alarm the rise of the neo-Nazi National Democratic Party which won a total of 31 seats in four state elections. Alarmed observers remembered that Hitler's party had even less power 10 years before World War II. Kiesinger said that the election results would hurt Germany's image abroad and called on Germans to "take up the battle" against the National Democrats.

But the Chancellor had other more pressing political problems to handle, among them: the rise of a student leftist movement, headed by Rudi Dutschke; the ever-present threat of an increased Soviet aggressiveness, especially after he had begun trade talks with Communist China; and the danger that it would be necessary for the U.S. to withdraw many of its troops from German soil because of an unfavorable balance of payments. This last dilemma was solved in mid-1967 when Bonn agreed it would not seek gold for the dollars American soldiers spent in West Germany.

By 1968, West Germany had become the world's second biggest money-lender, after the U.S., and the services of German banks were in such great demand that, as one German newspaper editor phrased it, "The foreign borrowers are polishing the brass doorknobs." The country's current wealth stems directly from its huge surplus of exports over imports — a figure running at an annual rate of more than $2.6 billion.

Her place as a world financial and industrial leader established, West Germany stands in marked contrast to her underdeveloped East German neighbor. But without question, the fondest hope for the coming decade of both the people and the government is that the two states can be reunited into one independent German nation.

1. Two Chancellors ...

2. Waiting for East Berlin permits ...

1. Konrad Adenauer and Ludwig Erhard both served as West German Chancellors during the Sixties. Erhard, Economics Minister under Adenauer, succeeded to the Chancellorship in August, 1963.

2. West Berliners waited in line to receive permits to visit East Berlin relatives during the 1963 Christmas holidays.

3. Soviet Premier Nikita Khrushchev, builder of the Berlin Wall, visits his creation in 1963.

4. Above members of the left-wing Extra Parliamentary Opposition give Nazi salute from the balcony of Rhine Hall during demonstrations against West German Chancellor Georg-Kurt Kiesinger. Kiesinger, bottom left, shown with Defense Minister Gerhard Schroeder, called the youths "today's Fascists." Although Kiesinger won a plurality in the 1969 elections, he lost the Chancellorship to a coalition headed by Willy Brandt.

5. The highly successful Volkswagen company, exporting cars all over the world, has become a symbol of West German economic prosperity.

6. West Germany's first submarine since World War II was launched in 1961. During the Sixties, Western Allied nations supervised a cautious buildup of West German Armed Forces.

7. War crimes trials continued throughout the Sixties. A controversial issue in West German politics was the extension of the statute of limitations for these trials until 1970.

8. Willy Brandt, leader of the Social Democratic Party and Foreign Minister under the Kiesinger regime, formed a coalition with Walter Scheel's Free Democratic Party after the October, 1969, elections, thus wresting the Chancellorship away from Kurt Kiesinger and the Christian Democratic Party.

3. Khrushchev at Wall . . .

5. Volkswagen plant on Mittelland Canal . . .

6. West German submarine . . .

8. New Chancellor Brandt . . .

4. Opposition youth protest against Kiesinger . . .

7. War criminals on trial . . .

Northern Europe Meets its Problems

Belgium and Holland reach agreement with former colonies; Denmark refuses Common Market membership; Finland remains friend to East and West

The colors of the participating countries of NATO are hoisted on the masts in front of the new headquarters at Evere in Brussels in 1967, after the move from France.

Swedish citizens, irate over the Vietnam War, demonstrate in Stockholm, the site of the so-called International War Crimes Tribunal held in April and May, 1967.

Belgium was torn by violent Socialist-led riots and strikes in early 1961 protesting the government's austerity program causing the downfall of Premier Eyskens.

Theo Lefevre's new coalition included former NATO Secretary-General Paul-Henri Spaak. Despite the loss of the Congo in 1960, Belgium's GNP and exports were increasing.

Foreign Minister Spaak and Congo Premier Adoula reached an agreement whereby Belgium's former colony would receive a $20 million technical assistance loan in 1964. But by the end of that year, Belgium dispatched a battalion to the Congo to rescue hundreds of whites held captive by rebels.

In what threatened to be a repeat of Belgium's 18-day doctor strike in 1964, King Baudouin reacted swiftly to demands that doctors be permitted to charge 60 cents a visit at seven government clinics.

Shortly after the Netherlands granted independence to Indonesia in 1960, many feared an outbreak of war between the two nations.

By 1964, however, it was clear that war would not come, for Indonesia exported close to $60 mil-

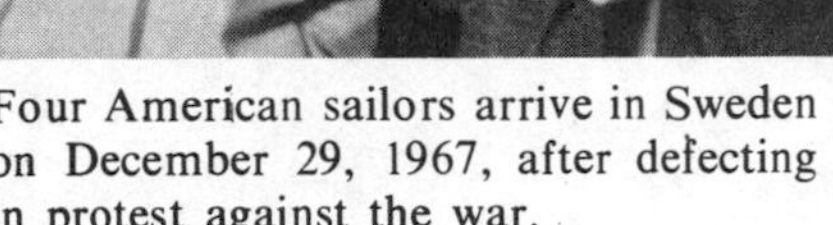

Four American sailors arrive in Sweden on December 29, 1967, after defecting in protest against the war.

Dutch Crown Princess Beatrix and West German diplomat Claus Von-Amsberg are married on Mar. 10, 1966.

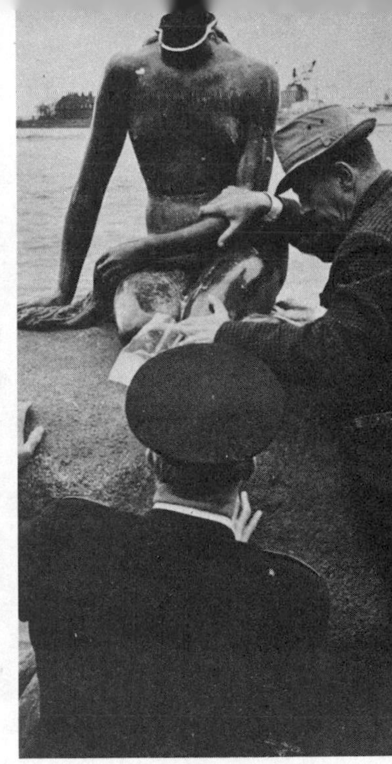

Copenhagen landmark of a mermaid on a rock lost its head in 1964, most probably the work of vandals.

lion worth of tin, oil, rubber and other resources to her former colonial master. The Dutch granted Indonesia $27.4 million in credits for 1965.

On March 10, 1966, Crown Princess Beatrix, heir to the Dutch throne, married 39 year old West German diplomat Claus Von Amsberg. In April, 1967, Beatrix gave birth to a son, the first male heir in four generations. William II had died in 1890.

The rising discontent in Holland was evident by the loss of fourteen seats by the nation's two major parties in the Tweede Kamer, the Dutch equivalent of the U.S. House of Representatives.

Grand Duchess Charlotte of Luxembourg, the longest ruling monarch in Europe (she had ruled since 1919), abdicated in 1965 in favor of her son, Prince Jean.

Grand Duke Jean's promise to strive to "ban all that remains of moral and material misery" in his domain wouldn't be too difficult to fulfill inasmuch as Luxembourg had a booming industry, no unemployment, $70 million in U.S. investments and the highest standard of living in Europe.

Under the NATO alliance, Denmark and Norway approved a joint Baltic command with West Germany in December, 1961.

Denmark applied for Common Market membership in August, 1961, for the bulk of Denmark's trade was with the British and, if excluded from the EEC (European Economic Community), its primary exports would be severely damaged by the protective tariff wall being built around the Common Market if Great Britain gained entry.

After De Gaulle refused to allow British entry, he offered the Danes membership, but Denmark refused.

Inflation in Denmark was so severe that Premier Krag instituted an austerity program. Its apparent success caused Krag to comment in 1964, "Never has Denmark seen her reserves increase so much in such a short time."

Krag was forced to form a minority government after the 1965 elections. The November, 1966, voting gave the Socialists control of Parliament for the first time in Denmark's history. Hilmar Baunsgaard, an opponent of Denmark's NATO membership, became Premier as a result of the December, 1967, election, caused by the rejection of a Social Democratic bill to freeze wages by the Parliament.

Norway's September, 1965, elections brought the nation its first conservative government in 19 years. The unexpected Labor defeat resulted in the removal of Dr. Halvard Lange, key figure in NATO formation, from the Foreign Ministry.

Speaking of Finland's relations with both East and West, Finnish President Urho Kekkonen said, "The better relations with the Soviet Union, the wider our freedom of maneuver in our relations with the West."

Kekkonen, popular with both East and West, was overwhelmingly re-elected in 1962 and 1968 for six-year terms.

Sweden's 1965 elections resulted in the re-election of Premier Tage Erlander who had led his nation since 1946. But the Communists were the only party to increase their overall percentage of the popular vote.

Iceland began to show more pro-Western feeling and heavier support for NATO in the 1960s.

Italy: Economic Boom, Political Bust

As the economy soars, politicians squabble and governments fall; Franco names heir; Salazar stricken

Between demonstrations, Italian workers rest outside Rome's Colosseum. The 1968 wave of strikes and protests exploded with the pent-up frustration of years of government unresponsiveness to social reform.

Italy's history during the last decade was a chronicle of continued prosperity and precarious politics.

The country's industrial growth — motive force for what has been called Italy's economic "miracle" — roared ahead in the 60's at a pace just under that of West Germany, which had the highest rate of growth in Europe. All the while, governments in the "boot" continued to fall at an average rate of one every 10 months (since 1943).

The earliest signs of a booming economy were seen in the sharp drop of unemployment from 1.9 million at the end of the 50's to less than one million in 1961, in the serious shortage of skilled labor, and, more conspicuously, in the highly publicized industrial plants that were built in particular areas of the impoverished South.

By June, 1960, a giant petrochemical plant had begun operating in Gela, Sicily. In July of that year, the Taranto steel mill was launched. By 1964, this $40 million dollar complex — third largest in Europe — was spewing out products for Italy's biggest E.E.C. (Common Market) consumer, West Germany.

Similarly, automobile production — mainly from Fiat — rose from

Italian politics are cynical and operatic. In the '68 election, Rome flaunted banners like an Aida stage setting.

The 29th post-war cabinet in the "boot" was formed December 1968 by Premier Mariano Rumor (l) here being congratulated by President Saragat at swearing-in ceremony.

752,000 units in 1961, to 1,400,000 in '66, and was approaching the 1,800,000 mark in '69.

By late June '69, in fact, the giant Fiat plant had not only outdistanced its nearest competitor in rate of growth, it was extending tentacles into France with a 15% purchase of the Citroen works.

The economy suffered a temporary setback in 1964 due principally to a sharp increase in importing of raw materials (23.4%) compared to the low export rate of 6.6%. At the same time, as gold reserves were depleted by this unfavorable balance of payments, the government clamped down on the price-wage spiral with a credit squeeze. Investors panicked. The value of the *lira* fell. Confidence was restored only by a quick loosening of credit and official bank backing of the lira. With these steps, the inflow of foreign capital, attracted earlier in the decade by tax concessions, was again resumed.

The '65-'69 period confirmed the economy's extraordinary resiliency and basic health. Gross national product rose in the *bad* year ('64) 3%, by '66 it spiked to 5.8%, while industrial growth in '67 shot up 10.2%, the highest rate of growth on the continent.

Unfortunately, social reforms did not keep pace with the economy. A by-product of affluence was increasing student dissent over education's inept bureaucracy, poor physical facilities at the Universities, and professorial "tyranny." Often linked with labor's demands for hastening social reform, a series of student-labor strikes led to a major confrontation in Rome during 1968.

The caretaker government of Giovanni Leone fell at once.

The periodic rise and fall of Italy's cabinet was due mainly to the nature of the coalition between the Christian Democrats (principal, but not a majority party) and the Socialists. Since the 40's and 50's, the Socialists, pushing for social reform, often cooperated with the Communists against the expedient do-nothing interests of conservatives in their own and the C.D. party.

This so enraged the Christian Democrats during the 1950's that they threw out long-time Socialist leader Nenni as Foreign Minister and did not take the Socialists back into the governing councils until 1963. From then on, Communist gains of up to 25% of the Chamber of Deputies in 1969, splits and intra-party feuding among Socialists, and fear of all moderates that a flirtation with the Communists would separate them from the halls of power, caused votes of "no confidence" time after time, and the governments fell.

This, at least, was avoided in Franco's Spain where the Falange ruled with an iron hand. Student mini-riots in '68 resulted in the University of Madrid being temporarily closed. Sporadic labor unrest, from the '62 walkout of the Asturias miners to occasional protests in '67 over devaluation of the peseta, brought no observable change in the Generalissimo's autocratic rule. Biggest news of the decade was Franco's announcement in July '69, that his successor would be Don Juan Carlos, thus returning the monarchy to the land of Cervantes.

Portugal, meanwhile, last of the colonial powers, had its hands full as the 36-year-old despotic regime of Salazar attempted to beat back native uprisings in Angola, Mozambique, and Portuguese Guinea, a struggle continuing through the decade. Salazar's cerebral stroke in '68 brought Marcello Caetano to power, but no change in domestic or foreign policy.

1. Red leader leaves scene . . .

2. Wanting more of the good life . . .

3. Main auto artery . . .

4. Politics makes strange . . .

1. Palmiro Togliatti (in portrait before weeping woman) died on August 21, 1964, while vacationing in the Soviet Union. Millions turned out in Rome for the funeral procession of this long-time leader of Europe's largest Communist Party.

2. The resentment of Rome's workers over low pay in prosperity spilled over in a wave of protests like this one in mid-December, 1968, when they learned that two striking Sicilian compatriots had been slain.

3. Italy's super highway, the Autostrada del Sole, shown here in the breathtaking scenic stretch between Bologna and Florence, opened its last link to the South in 1968, the first *thruway* since Roman times.

4. Premier Fanfani and President Segni embrace in 1962 following Segni's election. Fanfani's attempt to work with the Socialists to broaden the government's base irked fellow Christian Democrats and brought him down in May, 1963.

5. Student protests in December, 1968, over inept University bureaucracy and "tyrannical professors" caught fire from earlier protests in Germany and France, but were less violent.

6. The stern public image of Spain's Generalissimo Franco was mellowed with the release of happy family photos in 1969 as age and ill health brought closer the end of his reign and the need to choose a successor.

7. Franco's heir, Don Juan Carlos, who was named in July, 1969, will restore the Bourbon monarchy to Spain. Here he is seen during his marriage to Princess Sophie of Greece, May 16, 1962.

8. Spain's "red Duchess," 32-year-old protestor for people's rights, resents her nickname. Recently sentenced to one year in jail, the 21st Duchess of Medina Sidonia is properly called Luisa Isabel Alverez De Toledo Maura.

9. Portugal's era under the thumb of dictator Antonio Salazar came to an end with his cerebral hemorrhage in 1968.

10. Premier Marcello Caetano took up the reins of Portugal's tightly controlled dictatorship in early 1969. His first pronouncements offered little hope that democracy might prevail.

5. Demanding to be heard ...

6. The 'Caudillo' and the kids ...

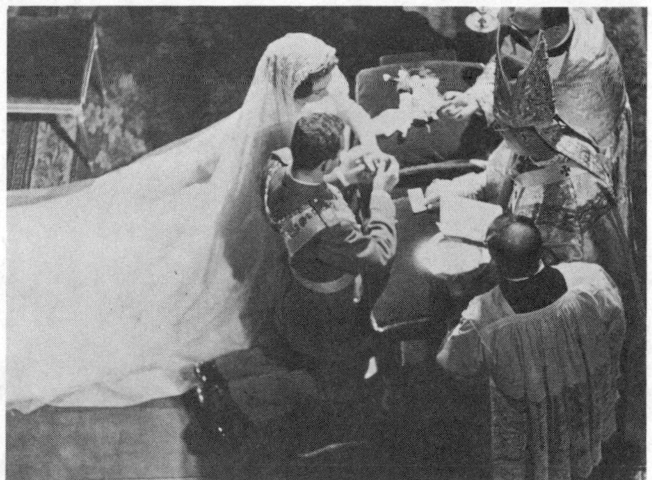

7. La Mancha's future king and queen ...

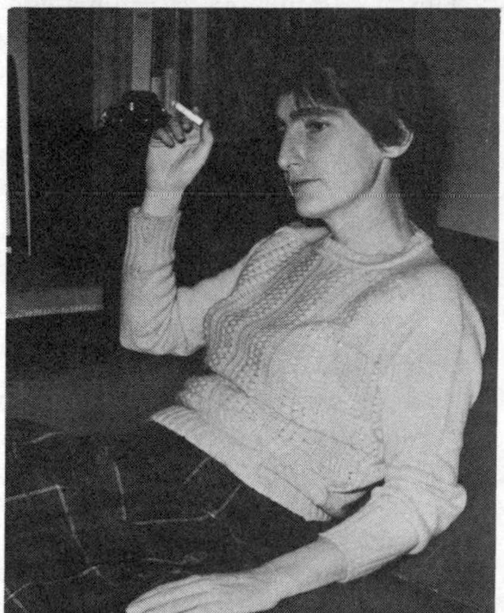

8. A duchess and a dear ...

9. Portugal slips from strong man's grip ...

10. Under the thumb of another ...

Greece, Turkey Clash Over Cyprus

Youthful Greek King and octogenarian Turkish Premier face opposition at home and abroad as Cyprus ends 82 years of British rule

Turkish Cypriots, armed with a variety of weapons, are alert lookouts on the watch for a possible Greek Cypriot attack. Greek Cypriots are also on constant guard in the strife-torn island where friends have become enemies.

On May 27, 1960, General Cemal Gursel led a military junta which, in an almost bloodless *coup*, overthrew the ruling Turkish administration of Prime Minister Adnan Menderes, thus ending 10 years of political continuity in Turkey.

Tension neared the explosion point in the capital city of Ankara on September 17, 1961, as the new government, headed by Gursel, hanged former Prime Minister Menderes and two of his cabinet ministers.

This act fomented a raging controversy throughout the country on the subject of treatment of political prisoners and finally, on May 30, 1962, caused the new Prime Minister, Ismet Inonu, to submit his government's resignation.

Within a month, however, Inonu had formed a new three party coalition government, excluding the late Menderes' Justice Party, and returned to power. In an effort to gain the support of Justice Party members, Inonu agreed to free from prison all but the top leaders of the old regime.

But Inonu could not gain the confidence of his people, and his government's attempts to stabilize

Military junta that took over Greece in 1967 was headed by Premier Col. George Papadopoulos (r), Deputy Premier Brig. Stylianous Patakos.

Greek King Constantine and Queen Anne Marie relax a moment in their Villa Polissena home in Rome with their children, Prince Paul and Princess Alexia, after the failure of his coup against Greek regime.

the currency and cut imports while boosting exports to reduce the $150 million annual trade deficit, were doomed to failure.

Inonu's People's Republican Party was swept out of office in the November, 1963, election, but since the winning Justice Party was unable to muster a majority, Inonu was again recalled to power.

The 80-year old leader was finally succeeded as Prime Minister on February 13, 1965, by Suat Hayri Urguplu, after Inonu's budget was thrown out by the National Assembly.

On October 27 of that year, the Justice Party's Suleyman Demirei won the office of Prime Minister, and Turkey had its first one-party government in four years.

In March, 1966, General Cevdet Sunay succeeded the ailing Cemal Gursel as Turkey's President. Gursel died on September 14, 1966.

Greece, early in the decade, saw Premier Konstantinos Karamanlis returned to power for the third consecutive time in a landslide victory. The opposition parties, however, charging fraud and intimidation, boycotted Parliament. In April, 1962, a brief anti-government riot in Athens signalled the beginning of the end of the eight year rule of Premier Karamanlis.

Demonstrations for the release of political prisoners erupted into rioting. The Premier demanded that King Paul and Queen Frederika cancel their planned state visit to London. They didn't, and Karamanlis resigned on June 11, 1963, his clash with the Greek monarchy proving too severe a blow.

On March 6, 1964, King Paul died and the throne of the Hellenes was inherited by his only son, Constantine. Six months later, the 24-year old monarch married the young Princess Anne-Marie, daughter of Denmark's King Frederik IX.

The still of the Athenian night was suddenly broken on April 20, 1967, by tanks guiding their way through the city. At daybreak, King Constantine was called upon to witness the installation of the new government of Premier Konstantinos Kollias.

The political crisis which had begun with the July 15, 1965, resignation of Premier Papandreou ended with April's military *coup* and the one-day abortive "counter-*coup*" of December 13, 1967, which resulted in the flight of the Royal family to Rome and the reassertion of the absolute power of the ruling military junta.

Cyprus attained full independence from Great Britain on August 16, 1960. Archbishop Makarios III was installed as President, and Fazil Kucuk became Vice President of the newly independent regime.

Fires in Greek schools and the bombings of Turkish mosques typified the overt hostility which existed between the island's Greek and Turkish communities throughout the decade.

By Christmas of 1963, the eruption of four centuries of hatred between the two nationalities had turned the country into a battlefield. United Nations troops arrived to ease tensions, but it was not until August 10, 1964, that a cease-fire agreement was reached.

Finally, after three weeks of U.S. and U.N. mediation in 1967, following years of conflict, Greece capitulated to most Turkish demands for the easing of restrictions on the Turkish-Cypriot minority. The main casualty of the conflict was the Greek dream of *Enosis,* union of Cyprus with Greece.

1. Melina pickets the White House ...

2. Together once again ...

3. "Free Greece" in Holland ...

4. President visits front lines ...

1. Greek actress Melina Mercouri was deprived of her Greek citizenship following her criticism of the military regime in Athens.

2. "Zorba the Greek" composer Mikis Theodorakis visits with his family after having been liberated by the Greek regime he so bitterly opposed. He was freed under the terms of the junta's 1967 Christmas amnesty.

3. Andreas Papandreou, son of the former premier, is flanked by two members of the Dutch committee called "Free Greece" in Amsterdam in 1968.

4. During his inspection tour through the Kyrenia Mountains in 1964, Cyprus President Archbishop Makarios looks towards Turkish lines through binoculars from a Greek Cypriot position.

5. A Swedish United Nations soldier cleans his weapon as a little Greek Cypriot watches. U.N. peace-keeping forces came to Cyprus in 1964.

6. Cyrus R. Vance was sent by Pres. Johnson to meet with Greek, Turkish and Cypriot leaders in an effort to resolve the Cyprus crisis.

7. Turkey's former premier, Adnan Menderes, was hanged on Sept. 17, 1961, after being convicted of a charge of violating his country's constitution and other crimes.

8. "Murders of Turkish Cypriots: America" reads the sign on the gate of the U.S. Embassy in Istanbul, Turkey, following the outbreak of renewed fighting between Greek and Turkish Cypriots on Cyprus in 1967.

9. After resigning his post of Greek Premier on June 11, 1963, Konstantinos Karamanlis chats with reporters upon his arrival in Zurich, Switzerland.

5. Cypriot tension affects both ...

6. In search of peace ...

7. Executed on Imrali island ...

8. The fall guy always to blame ...

9. Result of royal confrontation ...

The Middle East: World's Hotspot Keeps Boiling

During the 1960's, Israel is established as the area's military giant, while Arabs fight among themselves

An Israeli soldier stands guard in eastern Jerusalem on June 5, 1969, a date which marked the second anniversary of the commencement of the Six Day War.

Nationalism was the password in the Middle East during the turbulent decade of the Sixties.

At the close of the decade, the ideological attitudes of the antagonists remained unchanged. The Arab nations, divided on every other point, united behind the position that the Israelis were imperialists who must be driven into the sea, while Israel remained firm in her resolve to maintain her homeland.

The thin shell of Arab unity cracked repeatedly, often even before its myth could be announced to the rest of the world.

Syria broke away from the federation of the United Arab Republic September 28, 1961. Originally, in 1958, it had asked to join Egypt so Nasser could rescue it from the threat of an internal Communist takeover. But by 1961, Syria' bankers, landowners and traders feared that Nasser's reforms and nationalization decrees might end their own careers. A series of coups and counter-coups have ensued, but the trend throughout has been a definite shift away from Egyptian domination of Syria.

The story repeated itself in other Arab countries. While Nasser re-

The Israeli Armed Forces operated with dazzling efficiency on all fronts as its men pushed through and beyond the borders of three neighboring Arab states.

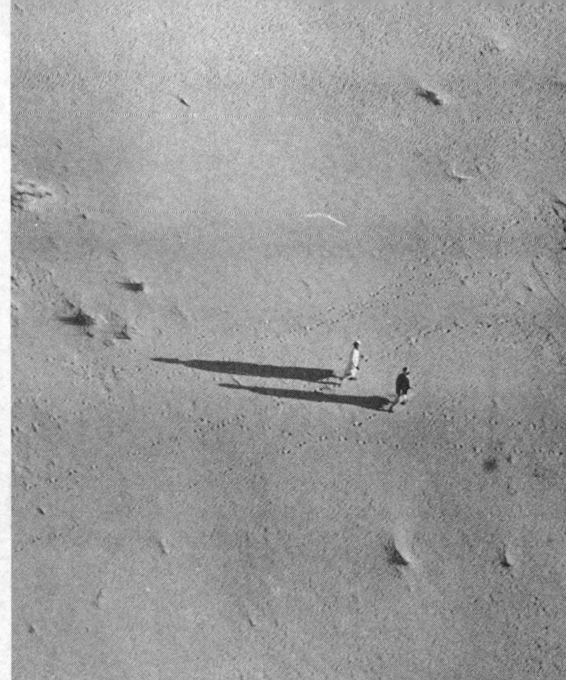

Two men, soldiers of the defeated Egyptian army, cast long shadows as they walk across the Sinai desert trying to reach the Suez Canal and their homes in Egypt.

mained the ideological focal point of the Arab world, he was not able to effectively marshall his followers in any sphere of endeavor , not even in the destruction of Israel.

Other intra-Arabian disputes included:

• An Iraqi attempt to invade the oil-rich sheikdom of Kuwait in July, 1961, just days after the withdrawal of British troops.
• Moroccan-Algerian border war in October, 1964.
• A lingering war which saw Egyptian and Saudi-Arabian troops fighting on opposite sides in Yemen.

While the Arab world polarized and fought, Israel consolidated and advanccd. Premier David Ben-Gurion resigned his office on June 16, 1963, marking the end of an era and thereby underscoring Israel's transition from a basically agrarian state to one relying on trade and specialized industries. Levi Eshkol, former minister of finance, suceeded Ben-Gurion and promised to follow his predecessor's policies.

The Middle East arms race continued in the early Sixties, accelerating sharply on both sides in 1966 and finally exploding on June 5, 1967 into the Six-Day War, the third major Arab-Israeli conflict since the Palestinian partition in 1948.

Within six short days, tiny Israel had established itself as a military giant in the area, capturing substantial portions of Egypt, Jordan and Syria. Israel had demonstrated conclusively that its 2.7 million people were still more than a match for the 55 million neighboring Arabs.

Tension in the area did not abate, however. Israel was enjoying the flush of victory and was making it clear that it had no intention of returning to the status quo. It had reduced the length of its land borders by more than one-half and controlled more than 26,000 square miles of Arab land.

On the other side, the Russians quickly re-armed the Arabs after the war, and Arab guerilla warfare, in the forms of artillery barrages and terrorist raids, began almost immediately. The Israelis in turn adopted the policy of swift, retaliatory raids against the offenders.

One of the most ominous developments in the area has been the increasing Soviet influence, spread largely by military aid programs to the Arabs. The U.S.S.R. now manages the military establishments of Algeria, Syria, the UAR and Yemen. Egypt alone has received well over $1 billion worth of Russian military hardware since the 1967 war, and the equipment is as modern as anything Russian troops are using in central Europe.

Communist military penetration, however, was only part of a many-faceted campaign that also included economic aid (such as Egypt's billion dollar Aswan dam) and swelling trade agreements. Currently, 65 per cent of Egypt's commerce is with the Soviet bloc.

The U. N. has been grossly ineffective at arranging a settlement, while the Big Four summit conferences promise to fare just as badly. The Israelis maintain that, to arrange a lasting peace, they will have to negotiate directly with the Arabs. Arab leaders, however, given the nationalistic mood of their populaces, see any direct negotiation with Israel as the quickest form of political suicide. Resultantly, the determined arms escalation continues, and so does the war of nerves.

1. Armed Al Fatah leader . . .

2. Arab junior commando army . . .

1. Yasar Arafat, head of the Al Fatah guerrilla terrorist movement, wears his commando uniform and carries an automatic weapon as he listens to a speech being delivered at the Palestine Student's union.

2. Two young Jordanians, trained as junior Fatah commandos, guard the entrance to their commando base. Boys between 8 and 15 are given machine guns and live ammunition and are sent on raids into Israeli territory.

3. Israeli troops escort Al Fatah saboteurs to a prison camp. The terrorists were captured during a March, 1968, Israeli armored land attack on Jordanian territory.

4. After the June, 1967, war no place in Israel was immune to terrorist attacks. This Arab saboteur was captured in the Gaza strip.

5. On trial in an Israeli court are seven people accused of plotting to set off a bomb in the Zion Cinema in Jerusalem on October 8, 1967.

6. Children on an Israeli kibbutz survey the damage caused to their kindergarten by Arab shelling.

3. Israel takes prisoners . . .

4. Terrorist caught in Gaza . . .

5. Trial of plotters . . .

6. Kindergarten bombed . . .

1. Bombed supermarket . . .

2. Master strategist Dayan . . .

3. Arab leader Nasser . . .

1. Israeli citizens mill about in front of a supermarket which has just been damaged by a terrorist bomb.

2. Moshe Dayan, mastermind of the Israeli victory during the 1967 Six Day War, is currently one of Israeli's leading political figures.

3. Gamal Abdel Nasser, president of Egypt and the most charismatic figure in the Arab world, peers through binoculars at Egyptian army maneuvers.

4. Members of the Israeli Defense Forces are on maneuvers in preparation for border skirmishes with belligerent Arab states.

5. King Hussein maintained his throne despite widespread unrest and rioting in Jordan during the 60's. Jordan was the heaviest loser of the Six Day War.

6. Iraq conducted public hangings during 1969 of men convicted of spying for Israel and the United States.

7. Jewish demonstrators, protesting the handling in Iraq of alleged Israeli spies, burn an Iraqi flag outside the UN in New York City.

8. Russia increased her military might in the Middle East in the late 60's. Here, framed by big guns, is part of the ever-growing Soviet Mediterranean fleet.

9. Prime Minister Levi Eshkol, Israel's leader during the Six Day War, died in office in 1969.

10. Members of the Knesset and government ministers assembled before Levi Eshkol's coffin on Mount Herzl.

11. This Arab refugee chose to leave his home on Jordan's west bank rather than live under Israeli rule.

12. The Wailing Wall, one of Judaism's holiest places, is located in eastern Jerusalem. The Israelis have declared their intention never to return any part of the Holy City to the Arabs.

13. Golda Meir, Prime Minister of Israel, began her much-heralded state visit to the United States in Washington and continued across the country, wildly acclaimed.

14. The Shah of Iran, already self-crowned, places his Queen's crown on her head. Although Iran is an Arab state, it did not participate in hostilities toward Israel.

4. Battle exercises . . .

5. A young, troubled king . . .

6. Hangings in Iraq . . .

7. Burning of Iraqi flag . . .

8. Russian warships . . .

9. Levi Eshkol . . .

10. Eshkol laid to rest . . .

11. War refugee . . .

12. Wailing wall . . .

13. A very welcome visitor . . .

14. Coronation in Iran . . .

Africa's Racial Border Firms Up

Invisible barrier separates newly independent Black Africa from the continent's white supremacy southern sector

Jogging along a deserted highway in Tanzania, these Freedom Fighters of the Mozambique Liberation Front are on an early morning training run. Mostly refugees, they aim to fight the Portuguese rulers in their native Mozambique.

The change in Southern Africa in the 1960s was mainly strengthening of the status quo. A racial barrier ran from the South Atlantic along the northern border of Angola, Rhodesia, and Mozambique to the Indian Ocean.

Above this barrier lay the restless new nations of Black Africa with some 250,000,000 population. Below, was a white preserve where less than 5 million Europeans kept more than 30 million blacks in serfdom.

South Africa, kingpin of white supremacy, spread across the continent's tip. Curious new exceptions to the region's whiteness were the liberated, black-ruled British territories of Botswana (1966), Lesotho (1966), and Swaziland (1968). They maintained a precariou independence and pragmatic economic relations with their white neighbor states.

As the decade began, South Africa became a Republic, May 31, 1961, and withdrew from the British Commonwealth in the face of other members' objections to the dominant South African Nationalist Party's apartheid (racial segregation) policies. Under Prime Min-

Seeking to modify his image as a hard-faced keeper of apartheid, Prime Minister Vorster shows a sporty side.

Prime Minister Ian Smith and P. Mkudud (left), opposition leader, march to the '67 Rhodesian Parliament.

The fatal stab wounds inflicted on Prime Minister Verwoerd in September 1966 made big news in Johannesburg.

isters Malan, Strijdom, Verwoerd, and (after the latter's 1966 assassination by an insane mulatto) Balthazar Vorster, the nation's 3.5 million whites progressively tightened restrictions on its 12 million blacks, for whom separate residential areas called Bantustans were being set up, and its 1.5 million mixed-blood coloreds. South Africa also in 1969 moved to extend apartheid into South-West Africa, the vast, mineral-rich territory over which it still effectively exercised a mandate legally terminated by the U. N. in 1966.

Despite worldwide disapproval and U. N. condemnation, South Africa continued to prosper. Its \$1.1 billion annual gold production (three-quarters of the free world's supply), and its strong ties with foreign capital (the U. S. alone has \$1 billion invested there) counterbalanced moral pressures.

During 1969 dissension arose in the Nationalist Party over Vorster's commercially-inspired gestures toward nearby black nations and local black workers. Conservative Afrikaners, descendants of the original Dutch settlers, were threatening to start a new party if there was further dilution of apartheid.

To the north, the rebel British colony of Rhodesia in June, 1969, adopted a new constitution. Prime Minister Ian Smith aimed at giving his rebellion legal coloration without breaking his pledge that the black majority would not rule the country "in my lifetime."

Under this constitution the 225,000 whites held 50 seats in the Parliament with the balance of sixteen representing 4 million blacks. The blacks could achieve equal representation by ballot but the income and property restrictions were such that black equality couldn't be achieved until the year 2000 at least.

Following the 1964 breakup of Sir Roy Welensky's Central African Federation — with Northern Rhodesia becoming black Zambia, and Nyasaland, black Malawi — Rhodesia stayed under white rule and unilaterally declared its independence on Nov. 11, 1965. The British refused to accept Rhodesia's independence unless it made provision for majority rule — and the new constitution won't help. Meanwhile, a punitive economic blockade against Rhodesia by Britain and most U. N. members continued in full force.

In the Portuguese territories of Angola and Mozambique, up to 100,000 Lisbon troops continued to be tied down defending the urban centers against black guerillas bent on liberating their homelands. In February, 1969, the Western-oriented guerilla leader Eduardo Mondlane was blown to bits by a bomb (planted by Portuguese secret police or by less moderate associates) in his Dar es Salaam retreat. And the struggle went on unabated, despite Portugual's stubborn efforts, taking 40 percent of its annual budget, to maintain in Africa a viable "multiracial" empire.

As White Africa faced the next decade, the question was largely whether South Africa, the prosperous and powerful leader, by making concessions on trade to its black neighbors and by bringing more blacks and coloreds into the industrial system could provide enough economic benefits to the region to prevent a violent racial explosion. Would the Afrikaners themselves permit it? Would the blacks wait for it or be satisfied with less than freedom?

Independence, Upheaval, Coups, Reform

This was Central Africa in the 1960s as new nations struggled with the perplexing new problems of freedom

Symbolic of the bloody tribal warfare between the Nigerians and the secessionist state of Biafra, this 1968 photo shows a rebel soldier with a Nigerian soldier killed by Biafrans who took his uniform to use.

In 1945 there were four independent nations in Africa: Egypt, Ethiopia, Liberia, Union of South Africa. In 1969 there were 42. Most of them gained independence in the 1960s, most were in Black Africa.

Unfortunately, independence did not necessarily bring the good life. Most of the Black African states had originally been carved out of jungle and wasteland by the 19th century European colonialists without regard for tribal boundaries or economic prospects. Usually there was no common language (except that of the former rulers), no traditions (except conflicting tribal customs), few trained officials or professionals, few local industries or the skills to develop them.

A large nation with heavy copper resources, the Democratic Republic of the Congo was paralyzed by bloody tribal conflict for three years after its Belgian rulers left in 1960, while U. N. forces tried futilely to keep the peace. Under Moise Tshombe, the Katanga province, where Belgian copper-mining operations (later nationalized by the Congolese) were centered, seceded

Among the 180,000 Asians in Kenya where non-citizens are being eliminated from jobs by denial of work permits, these shops close up.

In a scene of typical African political turmoil, Gen. Joseph Ankrah (glasses), who toppled Ghana's Nkrumah in '66, roughly quizzes a man (standing on chair) who claims he masterminded the coup from London.

in 1960; Premier Patrice Lumumba, head of the National Congolese movement, was ousted and in 1961 murdered by Katanga tribesmen, becoming a left-wing martyr. The secession finally ended and the U. N. withdrew, but President Joseph Kasavubu was overthrown by Maj. Gen. Joseph D. Mobutu in 1965 and Tshombe went into exile.

In that same year, army leaders took over the governments of Central African Republics Dahomey, Ghana, Nigeria, and Upper Volta. In 1967 Burundi and Sierra Leone, and in 1968 Mali, fell to military coups. The pattern: Army men took over assertedly to end corruption, waste, and inefficiency and promised elections as soon as conditions stabilized. Some reforms were made, but in 1969 with nine of Black Africa's 36 nations under military rule, no elections were yet in sight.

Rampant tribalism was responsible for the Nigerian civil war, which escalated into Black Africa's first modern war, with far-reaching international implications. Huge Nigeria — with 57 million people, Africa's largest nation — is richly endowed with resources. But its people are split up into 250 tribes, each with its own language. The north is dominated by the Moslem Hausas and Fulani; the west, by the pro-Western Yoruba, and the east, by the gifted and energetic Ibos.

In 1966 Ibo army officers overthrew the corrupt federal government and murdered the Prime Minister, a northerner. His countrymen struck back, killing Ibo coup leaders and installing another northerner, Maj. Gen. Yakubu Gowon, as Prime Minister. Then Hausa tribesmen in the north slaughtered some 20,000 Ibos; a million Ibos fled to the eastern region. On May 30, 1967, this region seceded, setting up the state of Biafra headed by Lt. Col. Odumegwu Ojukwu. In two years of bloody fighting, federal troops had squeezed the Biafrans into a tiny portion of their eastern homeland. But despite widespread starvation they refused to give up.

Federal Nigeria was aided with arms from Britain and the Soviet Union; France had been providing arms to Biafra, as had Communist China, to a small but ominous extent. Biafra was getting food supplies from the Roman Catholic Church and from private groups, notably in the neutralist U. S. Among the African states, few have recognized Biafra. Fearful of further Balkanization of the continent and leery of encouraging tribal revolts, most Black Africa leaders have been striving for a cease-fire and a "united Nigeria."

At mid-1969 no satisfactory end was in sight and the explosive question remained whether the Great Powers would become further involved.

As Black Africa neared the end of its decade of change there were elements of hope. The Ivory Coast, for example, with strong economic ties to France, had an annual economic growth rate of 10 per cent. Kenya, under President Jomo (Burning Spear) Kenyatta, maintained tribal peace. Tanzania was working together with Zambia in the kind of regional economic cooperation that appeared Black Africa's best answer to poverty and political instability.

1. Losers in Nigerian tribal conflict ...

2. Innocent victim of Congo hatreds ...

1. An Ibo mother and her children flee from Lagos during the bloody 1966 riots when some 20,000 Ibos were massacred in the northern region of Nigeria. More than a million of her fellow tribesmen sought sanctuary in the Ibo-homeland Eastern region, which became Biafra.

2. Stopped by trigger-happy Indian U.N. troops advancing along a highway in the Katanga Province of the Congo, a Belgian cement-factory worker, Albert Verbrugghe, wounded by gunfire, pleads for his life. His wife and a woman passenger in his car have been killed already. This was in 1963.

3. Innocent pawn in the savage civil war between Nigeria and Biafra, this baby is one of thousands of children dying of hunger day after day in the beleaguered rebel Ibo homeland. Both sides used starvation as a strategic tool — the Nigerians to weaken their enemy through blockade, the Biafrans to enlist international support.

4. Safe at last from Congo perils, this small child is carried from a plane at the Leopoldville airport by a missionary in 1964 after both had fled Stanleyville, where Belgian paratroopers had rescued them from imprisonment by Congolese rebels.

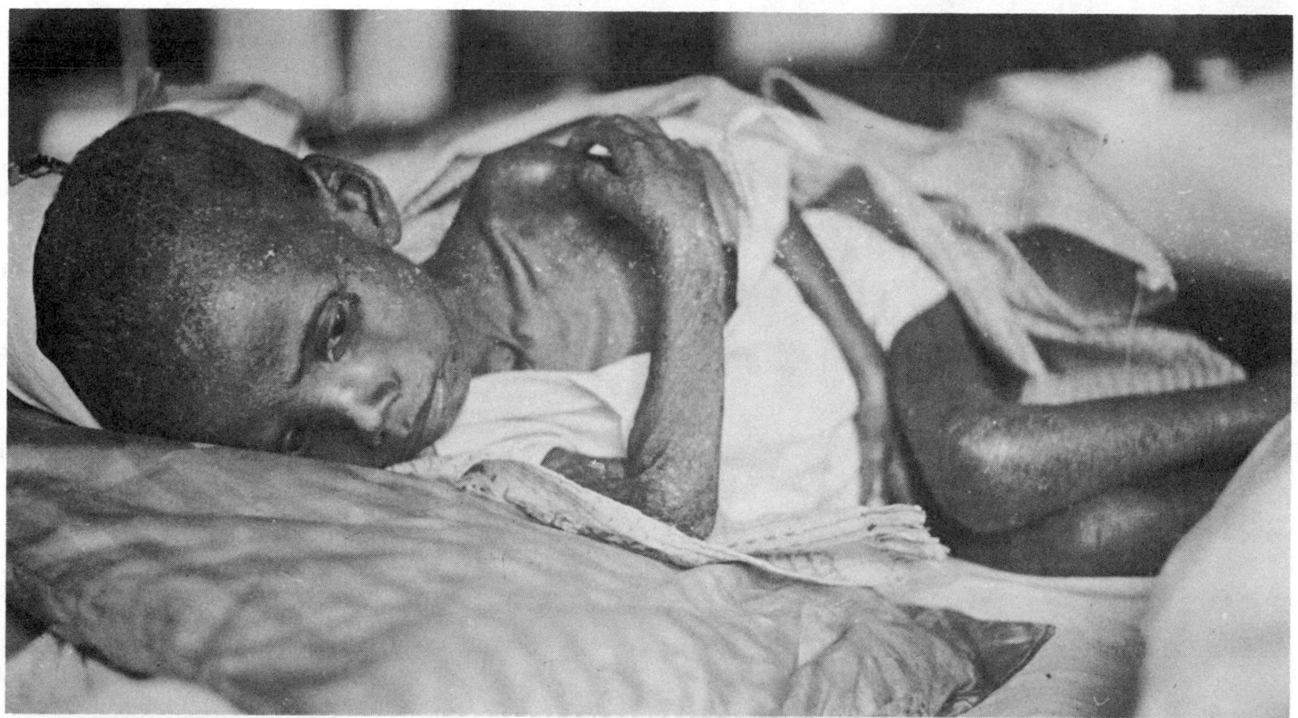

3. Starvation becomes a military weapon ...

4. A tiny war refugee is saved ...

1. Two African strong men ...

2. China's best friend in Africa ...

3. At the Summit, soul brothers ...

1. Taking a salute while on a visit to Kenya is Lt. Gen. Ankrah of Ghana, while his host, President Kenyatta, waves aloft his regal fly whisk.

2. Greeting an admirer, Red China's Chairman Mao Tse-tung welcomes to Peking the president of Tanzania, Julius K. Nyerere, who is gratefully receiving Chinese aid on railroads.

3. A year before his downfall, the anti-British President Nkrumah of Ghana attends the 1965 African Summit Conference in Accra to demand that Great Britain use troops to quell the revolt of the White Government in Rhodesia. Beside him is his leftist friend, President Toure of Guinea, soon to offer him a place of refuge.

4. In the news limelight in 1964 was the former secessionist president of Katanga, Moise Tshombe, here telling of plans to become Congo premier. He did hold the post briefly until he was exiled by General Mobutu. He died mysteriously in 1969 in Algiers where he had been held prisoner for two years after a gunpoint abduction.

5. Smiling warmly, Ethiopia's Emperor Haile Selassie is decorated by an African girl while visiting Kenya, as President Kenyatta applauds the act.

6. Riding to power after a bloody coup in January, 1966, Maj. Gen. J. T. U. Aguiyi-Ironsi was an imposing figure as supreme head of the federal military government of Nigeria. Six months later he was assassinated and succeeded by Lt. Col. Yakabu Gowon.

7. In this typical outdoor market in Lagos, dash — meaning bribe — is the traditional factor making the big difference between getting a favorable location for selling or a so-so one.

8. Each offered leadership of a 1967 revolutionary junta in absentia, these two Sierra Leone army officers took off from London for Freetown on the same plane — Lt. Col. Ambrose Genda (left) and Lt. Col. Andrew Juxon-Smith. Before landing, they learned that the final choice was Juxon-Smith.

4. Upbeat moment for Congolese rebel

5. Greetings to the King of Kings ...

6. Nigerian chief, soon a victim ...

7. Where dash means cash ...

8. Which one will rule Sierra Leone? ...

Divided India Faces Invasion and Hunger

Death of Nehru, clashes with Red China and Pakistan erode unity; soaring population growth remains unchecked

Sikhs demonstrating for a separate state in the Punjab were one of many tribes and religious groups threatening India's unity.

In 1960, Prime Minister Nehru of India prophesied that the 60's would be "the critical phase of our national existence."

After 14 years of independence, India suffered from lagging industrialization, food shortages, disunity and worsening relations with neighboring Pakistan and Red China.

To finance ventures like its $23 billion five-year plan of 1960, India had to turn to Western nations, who promised $2.2 billion in aid, and the Soviet Union, who pledged $500 million.

Plagued by power shortages, transportation difficulties and high taxes, production slowed to a crawl despite massive aid. In 1962, India's foreign trade reserves had dwindled to $212 million.

During the first three years of the decade, India spent some $100 million on birth control, but her population continued to grow at the rate of 10 million per year, leading to predictions of a one billion population by the end of the century.

Agricultural production was not up to the task and in 1966 it was estimated 12 million persons faced starvation and 100 million faced some degree of hunger.

The problem was aggravated by the disunity plaguing India. As the

New Delhi policemen fired tear gas, dodged rocks, during riot over choice of official language for the Punjab.

Prime Minister Indira Gandhi displayed a broken nose after being stoned during an election campaign tour.

decade opened, Sikhs in Punjab clamored for an autonomous state. In the northeast, Naga tribesmen continued a six-year guerilla war against the central government.

In 1965, when Hindi, which is spoken by 40% of the population, was made the official language, riots broke out, instigated by those speaking India's 15 other major tongues and 55 minor languages.

But the sharpest blow of all to India's unity was the death of Nehru on May 27, 1964, after 17 years as Prime Minister.

Although he had been elected to his final term by 114 million votes in the world's largest free election, Nehru's last years were troubled by revolts against his Congress Party. Also, his image as a peace-lover was tarnished when India invaded Goa on Dec. 17, 1961.

Then on Oct. 22, 1962, Chinese troops attacked India, and Nehru had to fire Krishna Menon, his staunch political ally, as foreign minister, for his poor preparation of the Indian army.

A month after its attack, as India braced for retaliation, Peking began a withdrawal and offered to negotiate.

To Nehru's successor, Lal Bahadur Shastri, a former close aide in the Congress Party, was left the task of building the nation's military strength. Military spending was tripled to $1.8 billion, and in a land where income averaged $65 yearly, citizens were called to contribute an additional $500 million.

When in 1965 Pakastani troops crashed into disputed Kashmir, India was ready and responded with a thrust toward Lahore and the two countries were at war. At issue was a barren 8,000 square mile area known as the Great Rann of Cutch beneath which, it was suspected, lay great reserves of oil.

In 1966, the Soviet Union got Shastri and Premier Ayub Khan of Pakistan to meet in Tashkent and both sides agreed to withdraw. But on Jan. 11, just a few hours after peace had been restored, Shastri succumbed to a heart attack.

Mrs. Indira Gandhi, Nehru's daughter, was named Prime Minister and was immediately faced with revolt against her Congress Party, which had ruled India since independence. Protesting food shortages, high prices, poor government services and the Party's complacency in initiating reforms, insurgents reduced its 221-seat majority in the lower house of Parliament to 35 in the Feb. 1967 elections.

By 1968, strikes and riots plagued India and six of the country's 16 states were unable to create stable governments.

During the decade, India's neighbor, Pakistan, sought continued economic aid from the West, better relations with Red China, and a measure of independence which would enable it to balance the two forces on which its fate depended.

In Dec. 1962, Pakistan settled its border dispute with China, and pursued its continuing dispute with India over Kashmir.

Internally, the nation transferred power from a military dictatorship to civilian rule in a new constitution adopted on June 8, 1962. In 1965, Ayub Khan won the country's first presidential election against opposition since he seized power in 1958. In 1969, however, Ayub Khan stepped down under pressure of rioting mobs and a military man was once more in power.

Industrial growth during the decade surpassed expectations at 17% per year, as did private investment.

In April 1968, Soviet Premier Kosygin visited Pakistan and pledged more economic aid but gave no indication of slowing down military assistance to India, the promise most sought by Pakistan.

1. Improving Chinese relations . . .

2. Hours before death . . .

3. Peace for Kashmir . . .

4. Portuguese prisoners of war . . .

1. Pakistan President Ayub Khan saluting at Cairo Airport while on way to Afro-Asian Conference in Algiers, was greeted by Red Chinese Premier Chou En-lai, United Arab Republic President Gamel Abdel Nasser and Indonesian President Sukarno.

2. At Tashkent, Indian Prime Minister Shastri signed agreement with Pakistan for both sides to withdraw troops from disputed Kashmir. Hours later, Shastri succumbed to heart attack.

3. For Pakistan's Ayub Khan peace meant greater freedom to balance East against West and maintain independence.

4. India shocked the world by invading Portuguese Goa. During the 48-hour conflict, 67 lives were lost, 45 of them Portuguese.

5. To curb its soaring birth rate by voluntary sterlization, India turned to billboard campaigns proclaiming four as the ideal family.

6. Prime Minister of India since it became independent in 1947 until his death in 1964, Nehru saw himself as "a queer mixture of East and West, out of place everywhere, at home nowhere."

7. Communist-led students demonstrate against Nixon's visit to India by burning him in effigy in Calcutta.

5. Four is enough . . .

6. Dead at 74 . . .

7. The heat's on . . .

1. Poverty and affluence ...

2. Fired for unpreparedness ...

1. A sleeping girl with no home of her own passes unnoticed on busy Calcutta street.

2. Defense Minister V. K. Krishna Menon (left), frequent champion of Red China, was ousted by Nehru when Indian army was found unprepared for Chinese attack.

U.S.-China Power Struggle Dominates Southeast Asia

Indonesia's Sukarno loses power; U.S. decision to negotiate Pueblo crisis disappoints South Korea; Pro-West Malaysia Federation emerges

Recurrent crises became a way of life throughout Southeast Asia during the decade. Small nations rocked under the impact of internal power struggles and growth problems while the larger were caught up in the Cold War between the U.S. and China for political and diplomatic supremacy in the area.

Typical was the plight of South Korea, which entered the 60's as a divided country with few resources, an exploding population and a long heritage of administrative corruption.

Here democracy was sacrificed to efficiency in May, 1961, when a military junta ousted the elected regime of John M. Chang.

He was replaced by army strongman Gen. Chung Hee Park who launched a five year plan in 1963 to increase electric power, farm output and employment. Although the plan made little inroads on South Korea's major economic problems Park was confirmed in power in open elections in 1963 and again in 1967.

Seeking to improve South Korea's relations abroad, Park accepted Japan's offer to pay $500 million as compensation for its 35-year occupation of Korea.

This move also misfired, triggering nationwide riots protesting the "humiliating settlement" as well as corruption within Park's regime. Faced with demands for his resignation, Park declared martial law and dismissed 576 government officials for misconduct.

Sustaining Park's regime was South Korea's strategic role in the cold war between the U.S. and China. In 1966, President Johnson visited Korea and each year the U.S. provided $200 million in military aid to help pay for the fourth largest standing army in the world.

In addition to supplying 45,000 troops to the U.S. cause in Vietnam, South Korea also stood ready to respond to increasing hostilities from the North with force. It was also disappointed over the U.S. decision to negotiate the Pueblo incident when the Communists seized the U.S. spy ship on Jan 23, 1968.

The North Koreans claimed the electronically-equipped surveillance craft had been captured while violating their 12-mile territorial limit, but Washington completely denied the charges and called the Pueblo's seizure an act of piracy.

Private negotiations with the North Koreans took place at Panmunjon, the village in Korea's demilitarized zone that had been used for armistice talks since the Korean conflict 15 years earlier.

Plagued by Communist pressure and internal conflicts between its Chinese and Malayan citizens, Malaya sought a solution to its problems by merging with Singapore in 1963 to form the democratic Federation of Malaysia. Singapore, however, seceded from the Federation in 1965, and the May, 1969, ethnic riots caused the government to dissolve in favor of a National Operations Council which now runs the Federation as an emergency state.

In spite of this, Malaysia continues as one of the most economically robust areas in Southeast Asia, producing one third of the world's raw rubber, 40 percent of its tin, and having a per capita income of $200 annually.

This was not the case with neighboring Indonesia, where President Sukarno, seeking to divert attention from a faltering economy, and experiencing strong pressure from the Indonesian Communist Party (the world's third largest), mounted a campaign to "crush Malaysia."

Sukarno further signalled his hostility to the West by making Indonesia the first nation to withdraw from the United Nations on Jan 7, 1965.

Sukarno's policies backfired, however, and in a months-long bloodbath in 1965-66, during which up to half a million persons, most of them Communists, were slaughtered, he was replaced by army-supported General Suharto.

Suharto broke with Peking, returned Indonesia to the U.N. and announced a policy of peaceful cooperation with Southeast Asia, including Malaysia.

During the 60's, Laos retained an uneasy neutrality which was frequently threatened by war between government troops and the pro-Communist Pathet Lao. With the latter controlling some 35 percent of the country, the Laotians were unable to control the flow of Viet Cong men and materials on the Laos section of the Ho Chi Minh trail and U.S. planes took over the job.

Burma continued to be neutral, although critical of U.S. involvement in Vietnam.

Thailand stayed a staunch ally of the U.S. and served as a major base for operations in Vietnam. But U.S.-Cambodia relations deteriorated as Washington charged the Viet Cong were being allowed to use that nation as a staging area in the Vietnam war.

1. Blood bath for Communists ...

2. Dark glasses wont help ...

1. Anti-Communist Moslems in Jakarta burn Communist Youth Headquarters in drive against Indonesian Reds. Close to half a million Communists died in the blood bath.

2. Indonesia's President Sukarno (left) tried to divert attention from a failing economy with an anti-Western foreign policy. Here he attends an Indochinese people's conference with Cambodia's chief of state Norodom Sihanouk.

3. To bolster his "crush Malaysia" campaign, Sukarno recruited pre-teen girls and matrons into his army.

4. Caught between government troops and the pro-Communist Pathet Lao, Buddhist monks join the stream of refugees crossing the Mekong River border into Thailand.

5. Russian plane drops supplies to rebel Pathet Lao forces as they drive against the neutralist Laotian government.

6. U.S. and North Korean officials silently confront each other at Panmunjon during the longest Korean truce meeting on record — 11 hours and 35 minutes.

7. When the USS Pueblo, an electronic spy ship, was captured by the North Koreans, it became the Navy's first ship surrendered in peacetime without a fight in 161 years.

8. With military backing, Gen. Chung Hee Park turned out Korea's elected government and took control, but the strongman's pro-U.S. stance still won him a warm welcome in Washington.

9. Although not formally charged, Pueblo skipper Comdr. Lloyd Bucher (center) still faced a Naval Court of Inquiry for "giving up the ship."

10. Meeting in London to announce the creation of a new nation, the Federation of Malaysia, were (left to right) British Prime Minister Harold Macmillan, British Commonwealth Relations Minister Duncan Sandys and Malaya Prime Minister Tunku (Prince) Abdul Rahman.

3. Distaff brigade ...

4. Fleeing Buddhists ...

5. Reds over Laos ...

6. Silent hostility ...

7. Pueblo: the ship that was given up ...

8. Army strongman welcomed ...

9. "Suspect of a violation of Navy regulations" ...

10. Birth of a Nation ...

Japan Becomes a Consumer Society

Prosperity changes face of nation, gives independent thrust to foreign policy, maintains conservative leaders in power

Students of Zengakuren Federation which toppled Kishi Government in 1960 burn Japanese and U.S. flags to protest 1968 U.S. nuclear submarine visit.

During the 60's, Japan enjoyed the world's fastest growing economy and became the first Asian nation to achieve status as a consumer society with wage levels and living standards approaching those of Europe.

The rising sun of prosperity transformed almost all aspects of society, including the physical stature of the Japanese. Thanks to richer diets, 15-year old boys entered the decade 3.15 inches taller than their counterparts of 1947.

In politics, cries for revolutionary change were drowned out by the rising jingle of cash registers; and in gratitude, voters in 1960 gave to Premier Hayato Ikeda's business-oriented Liberal-Democrats the largest majority won by any Japanese party since the war.

In 1962, even dissident youth found itself too busy choosing among 1.2 million job vacancies to continue the pattern of street riots which plagued the late 50's.

Prices rose, and in 1964 were 23% over 1960, but per capita income was up $520 from $417 in 1961, and people spent lavishly. By the mid 60's, over 90% of city families had television sets.

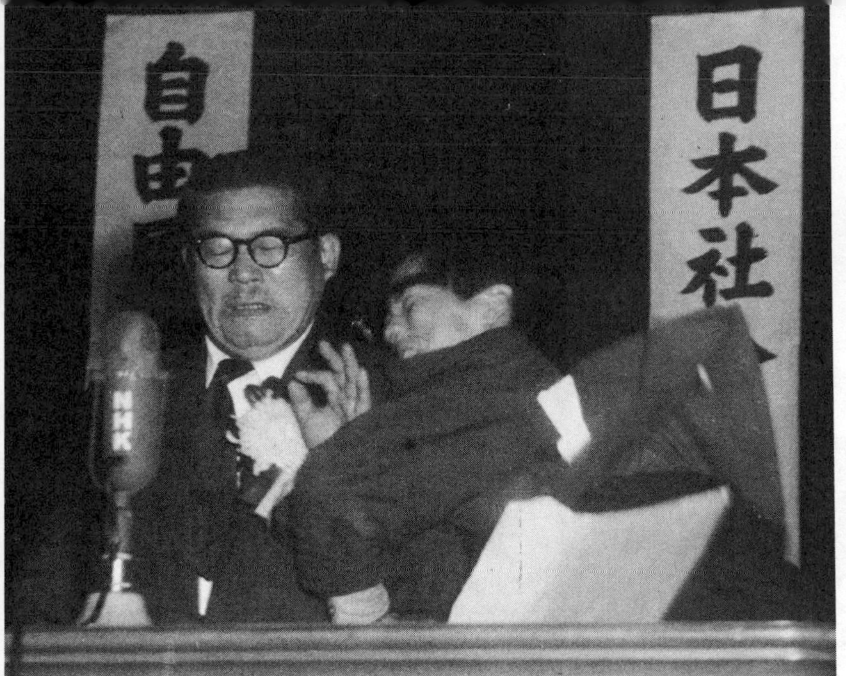

Inejiro Asanuma, chairman of the Japan Socialist Party, is assassinated during his October, 1960, election speech.

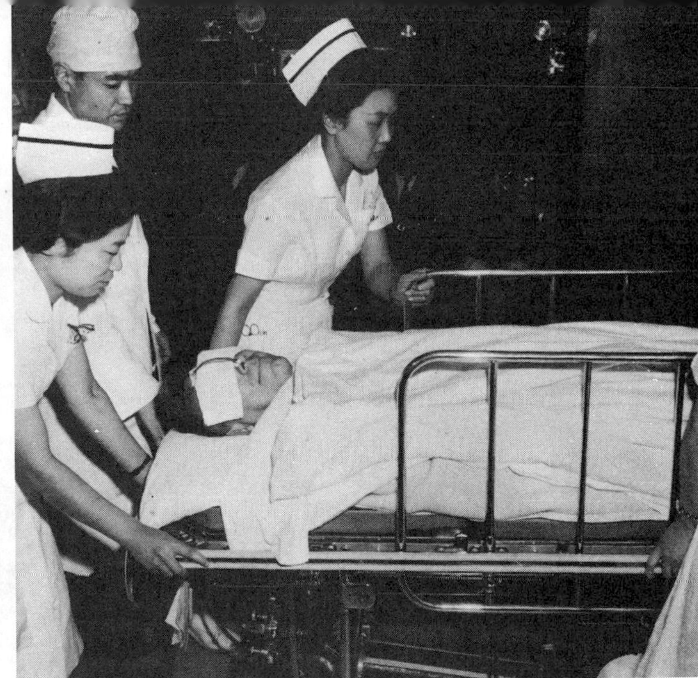

U.S. Ambassador, Dr. Edwin O. Reischauer was operated on for stab wounds received from Japanese youth in 1964.

But while higher wages and better jobs brought record marriages, they had the opposite effect on birth rates, which by 1962 had declined 50% since the war.

From the first year of the decade, expansive exuberance characterized the business-financial community. By 1961, industry was expanding so fast it created a $1.6 billion trade deficit, the biggest in Japan's history. In that same year, Japanese firms splurged some $540 million on expense account entertainment.

With a gross national product growing 9% annually, Japan had a record to boast of, and found plenty of ways of doing so.

In 1963, it built an atomic reactor to supply cheap electricity, and in 1965, when it hosted the Olympic games, Japan showed visitors a new 54,000 seat stadium in Tokyo, a super-highway from the airport to the city, the world's first commercial monorail, and a complete face lifting for Tokyo.

The power of prosperity was manifested in more significant ways also. In 1965 Japan was elected to the United Nation's Security Council and affirmed its new role as a "have" nation with a pledge of $200 million to the Asian Development Bank, a contribution matched only by the U. S.

Japan's leaders during the decade reflected the generally conservative mentality of the country. In November 1964, Eisaku Sato, a career bureaucrat who had the backing of the business community for his hard line on radicals, succeeded Ikeda as Premier.

Sato pursued a vigorous foreign policy on all fronts. Wary of Communist China's nuclear testing, he increased Japan's defense spending by some 12% and instituted a major modernization of defense plans.

Sato also managed to increase Japan's trade with the Reds to $400 million. Although a small amount when compared to the $5 billion annual trade with the U. S., it was a significant step on the road to Japan's increasingly independent international stance.

In 1968, Sato affirmed Japan's responsibility for its own self-defense, including the use of nuclear weapons, and began a drive for the return of Okinawa, the most complex U. S. military base in the western Pacific.

Power and prosperity did not eliminate all of Japan's problems. Rumblings of discontent could occasionally be heard and violence erupted. The Socialist party was relatively powerless but a new militant group called the Soka Gakkai, claiming over 12 million members, threatened to become a disturbing force.

In 1964, the popular American Ambassador, Erwin O. Reischauer, was stabbed in the thigh by a youth, and whenever U. S. nuclear submarines visited Japan, riot police battled anti-American demonstrators in the streets.

Tokyo suffered from transportation overloads and housing shortages, and in his first budget Premier Sato allocated $727 million for new construction. But much more would be needed to produce a significant improvement.

More ominous to observers were what they saw as the shaky underpinnings of the upward-thrusting economy. There was a serious shortage of capital and borrowing had become part of the Japanese way of life. There was an ample supply of confidence, however, and the nation looked forward to the 70's for more of the same.

1. Japan builds Orient's highest bridge over River Sako on Tokyo-Nagoya Super Highway.

2. New Super Express, left, of Japanese National Railways glides into Tokyo at end of high-speed run from Osaka.

3. Japanese Prime Minister Eisaku Sato, right, celebrates victory of his Liberal Democratic Party in Parliamentary election.

4. Anti-U.S. demonstrations at Sasebo bring swift police crackdowns.

5. Illustrating Japan's prosperity is this new oil tanker, the Idemitsu Matsu, the world's largest tanker and the first ship to exceed 200,000 tons.

1. Highest bridge in the East ...

2. Super Train ...

3. Victory in Parliament ...

4. Demonstrators clash with police ...

5. The biggest yet ...

An Upbeat Economic Decade For "Down Under"

Australia, New Zealand build expansion in industry, exports, while ending isolation in face of Southeast Asia turmoil. Philippine problems mount.

It was a decade of profound economic, political and social change "down under."

Traditional patterns of Australian and New Zealand national life — a rural-farm economy, rigid racial structures, isolationism — crumbled beneath the impact of booming industrialization, the combination of widespread affluence and drastic labor shortages, and wars and revolutions in nearby Southeast Asia.

The changes occurred against a background of booming expansion. Both nations extended their markets throughout Southeast Asia.

The two countries got a significant economic boost in 1962 when each discovered mineral deposits, the major one being a huge iron ore deposit in Western Australia estimated at 1.8 billion tons and called "a major turning point for Australian industry."

The discovery only added impetus to an accelerating farm-to-factory shift. By 1963, some 30% of Australian workers were in industry.

By the end of the 1962-63 fiscal year, Australia had record overseas reserves of $1.4 billion and a cash surplus of $35 million. Exports of wool, beef and sugar set new records as Japan displaced Britain as the number one customer.

For the same year, New Zealand's overseas reserves stood at $258 million as compared to $132.3 million for the previous year. Factories produced goods valued at more than $2.25 billion, up 6.6% over the previous year.

One problem was a growing balance of payments deficit. In 1965, to remedy the situation, the New Zealand government approved creation of a national steel industry designed to save $56 million a year in imported steel costs. It became the biggest industrial project in the nation's 125-year history.

The booming economy in both countries created drastic labor shortages, and when New Zealand's Tories defeated Laborites at the polls in 1961, the new Prime Minister, Keith J. Holyoake, strove to abolish compulsory unionism and step up immigration.

Full employment and the move from farm to city also had their effect on Australia's restrictive racial laws. In 1962 the country's 40,000 Aborigines won the right to vote but were still forbidden to drink alcohol, own land or intermarry with whites. Then in June, 1964, state legislatures began abolishing all discriminatory laws.

Another step toward modernization was taken in February, 1966, when Australia shifted to the decimal system of currency from the British pound-shilling-pence method.

Some of the fuel powering the "down under" boom came from Southeast Asia's turmoil. Uncomfortably aware that in 1964 Indonesia's President Sukarno possessed a fleet of Soviet-made jet bombers within two hours striking distance of its cities, and of the growing conflagration in Vietnam, Australia embarked on a major program to beef up its arsenal of military hardware.

The renewal of guerilla warfare in the Philippines was another factor in Australia's record 1965 defense budget of $2.7 billion. But the nation's most controversial defense measure was the draft it instituted in 1965, the first peace-time conscription in its history.

Throughout the last half of the 60's, both Australia and New Zealand supplied India and South Vietnam with arms, supplies and personnel, thus ending their traditional isolationism with a major commitment to support the independence of non-Communist neighbors.

Changes of leaders brought little change in major policies. In 1966, Sir Robert Menzies, Australia's oldest Prime Minister in point of service, stepped down after 16 years in office and was succeeded by Harold Holt, deputy Liberal Party leader.

When Holt drowned while swimming on December 17, 1967, he was succeeded by John Gorton, a veteran politician who reaffirmed the policy of strong ties with the United States. Reiteration of U.S. ties had also insured the reelection of Holyoake as New Zealand Premier in 1966.

The Philippines could produce no comparable record of stability and growth. The failure of President Diosado Macapagal in the first half of the '60's to make headway in improving the poverty-striken condition of the masses had gained wide popular support for left-wing groups like the People's Liberation Army (Huks).

In an atmosphere of bitterness, election campaigns turned violent, and when Ferdinand Marcos defeated Macapagal in 1965, 48 killings were recorded. Marcos' National Party scored an impressive victory in April, 1968, and used its power to institute a moderate land reform program.

The 60's also saw the rise of an intense nationalism among Filipinos who sought to break away from U.S. domination.

1. Guests in London ...

1. Attending British Prime Ministers' conference in London, Premier Keith Holyoake, left, of New Zealand and Robert Menzies of Australia visit with former British Prime Minister Anthony Eden (Lord Avon).

2. Harold Holt, Australian Prime Minister, was to drown during vacation swim.

3. Australian anti-war demonstrators protest support of U.S. Vietnam policy during Canberra visit of Vice President Humphrey.

4. Australia's big defense budget, new additions to Royal Navy like anti-submarine frigate H. M. A. S. Yarra, reflect concern with conflicts in Vietnam and Malaysia.

5. New Philippine President Ferdinand Marcos during election campaign in which he defeated Diosdado Macapagal.

2. Drowned Prime Minister ...

3. Vietnam Yankee, Go Home ...

4. New addition to Royal Australian Navy . . .

5. Marcos appeals for support . . .

Latins on Treadmill to Revolution?

Economic and social progress continue at slow pace, as U.S. fear of Communism obscures the need for basic reforms

Attempts of Fidel Castro to spread communism through the Hemisphere set the tone for relations between the U.S. and the Latin republics for the entire decade.

It has often been said that "when Uncle Sam sneezes, Latin America catches cold."

This historical truth was particularly relevant in the 1960's — and the germ was the U.S. preoccupation with Communism in the Caribbean and Southern Hemisphere.

Hoping to overthrow the regime in Cuba, the C.I.A. convinced the new Kennedy administration to support an invasion in April 1961. The resulting fiasco at the Bay of Pigs was a tremendous blow to American prestige, and led to Fidel Castro's declaration on December 2, 1961, "I am a Marxist-Leninist."

In response, the OAS Foreign Ministers, meeting at Punta del Este in January 1962, voted to exclude the government of Cuba from participation in the Inter-American system.

The establishment of a Communist regime only 90 miles from Florida had a more important effect: it made the U.S. treat Latin America more seriously.

Given this new perspective, President Kennedy launched the Alliance for Progress in 1961, "to assist free men and free governments in cast-

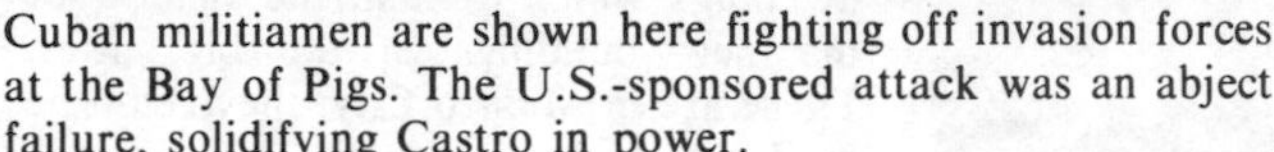

Cuban militiamen are shown here fighting off invasion forces at the Bay of Pigs. The U.S.-sponsored attack was an abject failure, solidifying Castro in power.

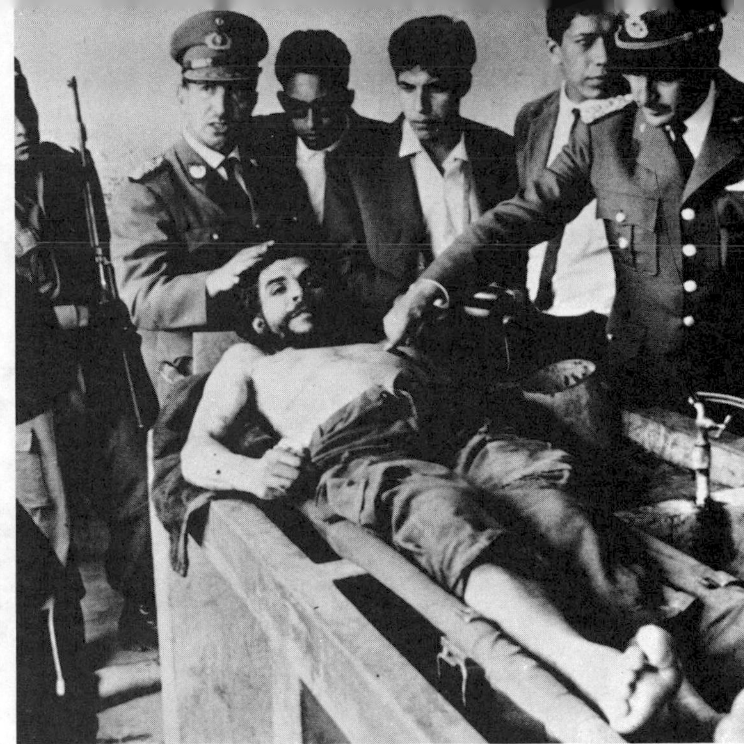

Castro's efforts to mount a guerrilla-led peasant revolution in Bolivia failed with the capture of Che Guevara. A Bolivian official shows the mark of the fatal bullet.

ing off the chains of poverty."

Although the fear of communist infiltration was exaggerated by many, it was not entirely unfounded. Castro did encourage guerrilla movements in other Latin countries, and the shipment of Soviet troops and missiles to Cuba in 1962 was a genuine threat to the peace and security of the entire world (see *Defense* section).

The problem was that a U.S. policy based on anti-communism was not very appropriate to the urgent problems of Latin American development, did not usually coincide with Latin needs, and was often overstated.

In April of 1965, for example, the U.S. sent troops to the Dominican Republic because it feared a Communist takeover, but most every on-the-scene observer disputed the State Department's list of "communists" supposedly in charge.

The Dominican intervention had grave consequences for U.S.-Latin American relations. It antagonized many Latin liberal leaders who believed that the U.S. would now unilaterally intervene anywhere, even if it had only a suspicion of communist influence. Since the Latin American countries had fought for years to uphold the principle of nonintervention — and for just this reason, to keep a check on the power of the "Colossus of the North" — the military action was especially distasteful.

Equally critical were progressive forces in Latin America who saw that the U.S. was so obsessed with fighting communism that it would even support reactionary interests to do so, rather than put its weight behind political and social change.

By the mid-'60 s, then, the initial enthusiasm sparked by the idea of the Alliance had disappeared. There had been some advances — in literacy, in health services, in working out economic plans — but the original hopes were not realized.

The plan stagnated because basic reforms were prerequisites of growth and were not accomplished. The U.S. contributed over $1 billion a year to Latin American development programs during the 60's, but could have done much more to support the forces of change.

The rapid migration of rural masses to the big cities mushroomed the number of urban slums, and caused many to starve due to the lack of jobs and decrease in agricultural productivity. The exploding population dimmed the hope for increasing standards of living: Latin America with less than 200 million people in 1960 would be more than 360 million by 1980.

Dissatisfaction with the rate of economic and social progress was expressed in many Latin American states in the '60 s by a rise in militarism. There were actually fewer democratically elected governments in power in 1969 than 1961.

Some form of dictatorship — either military or civilian — existed at the turn of the 70's in Argentina, Bolivia, Brazil, Cuba, Haiti, Nicaragua, Panama, Paraguay, and Peru — in other words, over most of the area and population of South America.

Yet even the democratic governments did not seem to have the enthusiastic support of the masses; in only a few countries did they make significant progress on the major social and economic problems. The decade of the '70 s could well be the turning point: either evolution or explosion in Latin America by 1980.

1. A familiar sight in the Caribbean ...

2. The all-purpose Secret Weapon ...

3. Vacuum filled by the Military ...

1. Scenes such as these were common in Santo Domingo in 1965, when President Johnson sent American Marines to the Dominican Republic. Here, they are attempting to flush out rebel snipers.

2. A bulldozer masquerading as a tank is used by Honduran troops preparing to move against Salvadoran positions near Nueva Ocotopeque. O.A.S. mediators attempted to settle the recurring border dispute.

3. Brazilian President Arthur Costa e Silva (center) suffered a stroke on August 30, 1969. A military triumvirate immediately announced that it would run the country until the ailing President recuperated.

4. The economic problems of Latin America are symbolized by the slum dwellings which exist in the shadow of the new buildings in the big cities. These are in Mexico City; they could be in Rio or Caracas as well.

5. The hated dictator of the Dominican Republic, Rafael Trujillo, was ambushed in 1961 by officers of his own army. The car in which he was riding was shot through with over 60 bullet holes.

6. Pro-American Chilean President Eduardo Frei, head of the Christian Democrat Party, will face a hard reelection battle in 1970. Because of inflationary trends and high taxes, his middle class support has been steadily eroding away.

7. An embarrassing deadlock was broken by the election in May 1968 of Galo Plaza Lasso of Ecuador (right) as Secretary-General of the OAS. His predecessor, Dr. José Mora (center) embraces him on his inauguration.

8. An example of the brutal rule of President Duvalier is the "trial" of David Knox, shown here in a Haitian courtroom. Knox, a Britisher from the Bahamas, is accused of being "a second-rate James Bond."

9. Rafael Caldera succeeded the rival Democratic Action Party's Raul Leoni (bkgrd) as president of Venezuela in one of the rare peaceful changes of power ever in Latin America.

4. The rich and the poor . . .

5. Death to the Generalissimo . . .

6. Girding for the fray . . .

7. The new head of OAS . . .

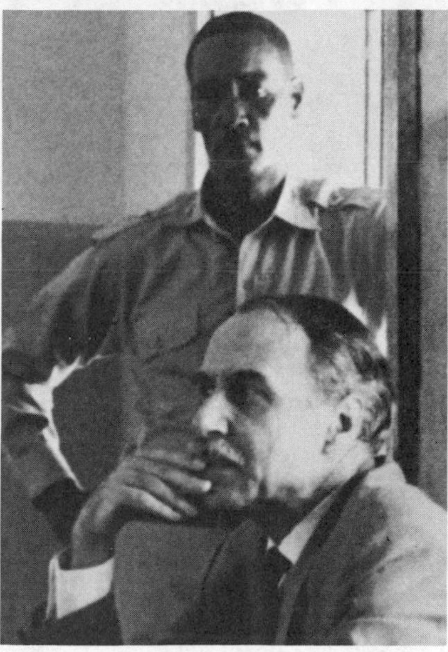

8. Dictatorship over Haiti continues . . .

9. Democratic rule in Venezuela . . .

Canada Moves Into Her Second Century

Centennial Celebration strengthens national ties; world role reassessed; separatism spurs need for official language act

Man with the mandate, Canada's youthful Prime Minister Pierre Elliott Trudeau sniffs his carnation and the sweet smell of success at Liberal party convention in Ottawa at which he was chosen party leader in June, 1968.

During the sixties this nation of nearly 22 million people living between the Atlantic and the Pacific, the United States border and the far reaches of the Arctic experienced a decade of unprecedented changes in political, economic and cultural life.

However, the years 1960 and 1961 gave little promise of better things to come. The nation was caught in a recession. The Federal deficit budget continued to escalate. Popular disenchantment with Prime Minister John Diefenbaker and his Conservative government was widespread. Despite awareness of many benefits of large United States capital investments in the nation's manufacturing and mineral industries, Canada was eager for more economic independence. In June, 1962, Diefenbaker announced an austerity program and loans totaling over $1 billion, and a cut of $250 million in spending for the current fiscal year.

In January, 1963, the United States publicly urged Canada to accept nuclear warheads under U.S. custody. Washington criticized Diefenbaker for failing his allies and endangering North American air defense. In February, under

With the provocative shout "Long live Free Quebec," French President Charles de Gaulle delighted Separatists and angered official Ottawa. He cut short his official visit to Canada in 1967.

Montreal University students hoist the banner of Separatism during President de Gaulle's historically embarrassing Canadian visit.

pressure from the Liberal party, Commons passed a "no confidence" vote. Parliament was dissolved and elections were called for April 8, 1963. Liberal Leader Lester B. Pearson was elected Prime Minister.

The early 60's found a rapidly escalating demand for "separatism" by many of Quebec's 6 million French who claimed they were being treated like "second class citizens." Prime Minister Pearson first worked with the Royal Commission on Bilingualism and Biculturalism to meet the crisis. During his second year in office, he substantially increased the number of French Canadians in his Cabinet. In 1964, as a further move to national unity, Pearson went before Parliament to propose the adoption of a distinctly Canadian flag, with maple leaf design. After lengthy debate, and approval by Queen Elizabeth II, the flag was adopted, with the provision that the British flag could also be flown with it, if desired.

In January, 1964, Pearson visited President de Gaulle in France. The two leaders agreed to closer cultural and trade ties. Pearson then went to Washington where he and President Johnson signed agreements for a multi-million dollar power and flood control project for the Columbia river basin.

The decade of the sixties also stressed Canada's cultural concerns. In May, 1960, Toronto opened its new $12 million O'Keefe Center for the Performing Arts. In 1963, Montreal's beautiful new Place des Arts was dedicated. The Centennial year of 1967, with its theme, "Man and His World" showcased Canada's cultural place in the international scene. Crowning cultural event of the decade was the dedication and premiere performance in Ottawa on May 31; 1969, of the new $46.5 million National Arts Center.

At midnight on December 31, 1966, Canada's Centennial Celebration of Confederation was ushered in on Parliament Hill, Ottawa, as Prime Minister Pearson lighted a symbolic torch. He repeated the ceremony before a distinguished audience at Place des Nations, on April 28, 1967, to officially open Expo '67. The preparation of the 1,000 acre site in the St. Lawrence River near Montreal had been an engineering feat. Seventy nations participated in Expo '67. Its success was tremendous — total visitors clocked admissions of 50,306,648.

On April 4, 1968, shortly before his 71st birthday, Prime Minister Pearson retired, naming as his choice as successor 48-year old Minister of Justice Pierre Elliott Trudeau. Soon after being sworn in as Canada's 15th Prime Minister he chose to dissolve Parliament and call for an election on June 24, 1968, hoping for a mandate. His whirlwind campaign against Nova Scotia's Conservative leader Robert Stanfield ended in a decisive victory with a majority government for the first time in six years. The Liberals won 154 of the 264 seats in the House of Commons.

Both in February 1968 and 1969 provincial Prime Ministers met in Ottawa with Prime Minister Trudeau for a Constitutional Conference to update the constitution, with particular concern for a charter of human rights and for establishing rules for closer federal-provincial cooperation.

As the '70s neared and politicians clamored for new national programs, Trudeau announced a new round of austerity to combat the dangers of inflation.

1. The Queen feted . . .

2. Separatists demonstrate . . .

1. Queen Elizabeth and Prince Philip were honored at a State dinner during their visit to Canada in 1964. The most notable aspect of the royal visit was the demonstrations it provoked in Quebec.

2. Extraordinary security precautions were required all during the Queen's visit as sign-carrying Separatists demonstrated in Montreal.

3. The United States pavilion designed by Buckminster Fuller was one of the most spectacular of the buildings of 70 nations at Expo '67, especially since it was the only one through which the mini-rail ran.

4. Spring 1966 marked the strike of members of railroad unions shown picketing Toronto's Union Station. Crippling Canada's major railroads, 120,000 striking employees were only persuaded to go back to work because of the passage of an emergency bill.

5. Moment of warm rapport as Prime Minister Lester B. Pearson emerges from a diplomatic reception. Following his retirement as Prime Minister in April 1968, Pearson has been Chairman, Commission on International Development, The World Bank; and since Spring 1969, Chancellor of Canada's Carleton University.

6. As the Beatles dramatically emerged from their plane at Montreal's Dorval airport, September 9, 1964, rock history was about to begin for thousands of Canadian fans.

7. No mistaking the frenzied welcome of distaff fans of the Beatles, though one or two appeared puzzled, even stunned.

8. Montreal's dynamic Mayor Drapeau, strong motivating force behind the plans and completion of the city's sleek, smooth-riding new subway, the Metro, must have been happy on October 16, 1966 at the opening day crowds at Henri Bourassa Station.

3. Fuller's soaring sphere . . .

4. Canada's rail crisis . . .

5. Pearson's own aura . . .

6. The Beatles arrive . . .

7. Frenzied female reaction . . .

8. Drapeau's dream-come-true . . .

American Scene

Youth spearheads change in American life; the Puritan ethic is dropped in favor of self-fulfillment

In a decade pervaded with change, perhaps the biggest change, the causal factor of all others, was the direct involvement of American youth, the "Now" generation, in all levels of American life. Unlike their predecessors of the Silent Fifties, they were far from reticent about expressing their opinions on everything: civil rights, the role of the University, the technocratic society, the war in Vietnam, and the behavior of Presidents.

The war babies finally came of political and oratorial age. They were a new generation who had grown up under the influence of the atom bomb, the cold war, television and, most importantly, middle class values. More than anything else, their parents' middle class values caused them to re-examine their own personal priorities in terms of who they were, what they wanted and where they were going. Materialism ceased to be the end-goal of living; the Now generation sought nothing less than complete self-fulfillment.

All this led, among other things, to confrontations, beginning with the Free Speech movement at the University of California's Berkeley campus in 1964, though the embryonic germs for this could be traced back to the Freedom Riders and the non-violent civil rights protests of the early Sixties.

Youth's most popular medium for expression was music — hard rock, acid rock, protest songs, protest chants and protest ballads. Among the most eloquent spokesmen of this modern counterpart to poetry were the Beatles, The Rolling Stones, Bob Dylan, Joan Baez and Judy Collins.

Another major development was the adoption by the young of movies as their own contemporary art form. During the Fifties, Hollywood studios fairly monopolized the medium, largely with mediocre productions, but by the end of the Sixties directing or producing the Great American Film became tantamount to writing the Great American Novel. Movies, undisputedly, was the art form for the Now generation, and underground and overground endeavours alike reflected their tastes.

One of their tastes was nudity in the arts — but not for pornography's sake. The popular Broadway musical "Hair" best explained the new attitudes toward nudity; performers removed their clothes after most performances in an effort to "re-humanize" the theatre experience.

Television, as always, lagged behind the other media and, for the most part, remained a "vast wasteland" during the Sixties. Notable exceptions were the network news departments and the birth of the National Educational Television (NET) network.

Television commercials came into their own as an art form, employing all the latest cinematic techniques, and earned a berth in New York City's Museum of Modern Art.

In sports, the Cinderella New York Mets won the 1969 World Series, but baseball nonetheless waned as a national pastime to be supplanted by professional football.

Crime grew to mammoth proportions in the Sixties. Law and order became a popular election banner for conservative politicians, and harried urban residents learned the meaning of fear as they walked from their bus stops at night.

Heart transplants became the new medical wonder, skirts rose to mini and micro-mini length; Americans travelled abroad more than ever before, used drugs in "epidemic proportions," and began to experiment more openly with sex. The American puritan ethic was clearly on the wane.

America in the Sixties was a nation psychologically divided against itself. Values polarized, and confrontations became regular occurrencies.

"Big Science" Emerges in Decade

Man on the moon, heart transplants headline period of burgeoning federal support, but slowdown looms in '70s

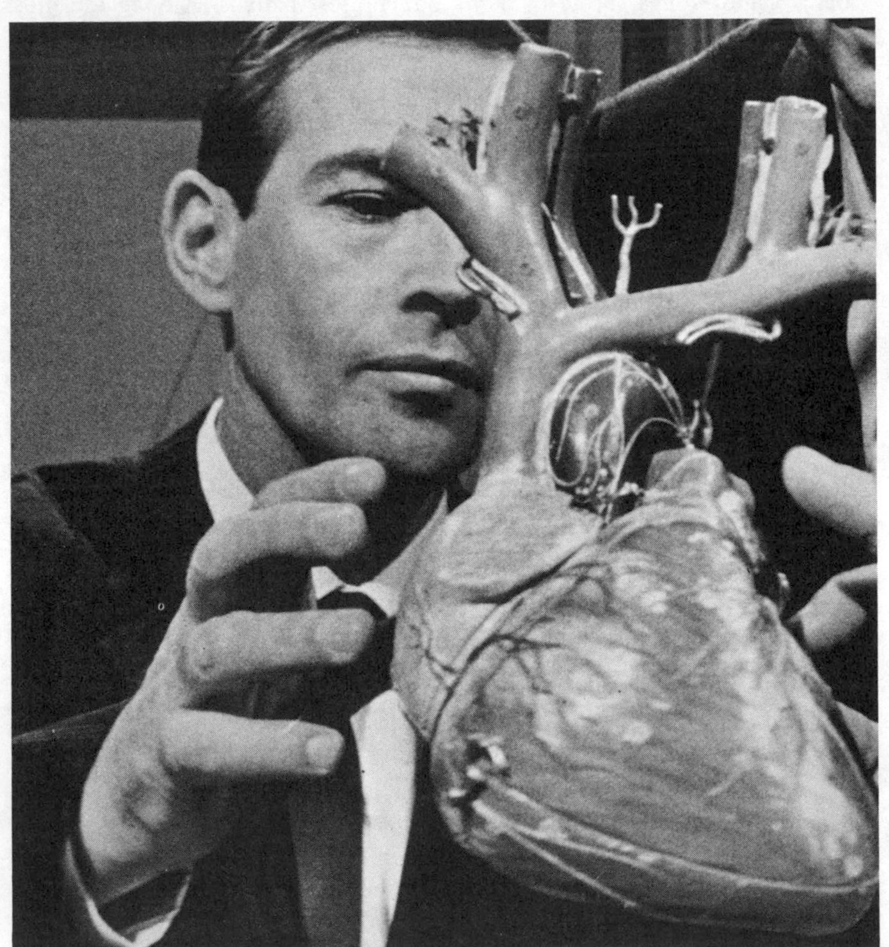

Heart expert Dr. Christiaan Barnard, South African surgeon who performed history's first heart transplant, describes process to American TV viewers.

The period following World War II in general — and the decade of the 1960s in particular — has been called a renaissance of American science. By almost any criterion, this period measures up as the one that marked the emergence of "big science."

One good indicator is the increased federal funds poured into research and development. These funds more than doubled from $7.7 billion in Fiscal Year 1960 to $16.4 billion in Fiscal Year 1969 for a total of $135 billion over the decade. Private industry spent about another $50 billion on R&D.

But as the decade came to a close thoughtful scientists began to wonder if the renaissance wasn't playing itself out. Federal support had hovered around the $16 billion annual plateau since 1966 and Congress grew increasingly restive about expensive new projects. The Vietnam war took much of the blame for this disenchantment, but the real reason could be a growing public dissatisfaction with the results of these billions.

Probably the most dramatic example of big science was the successful Apollo project to land a man on the moon. Despite the sev-

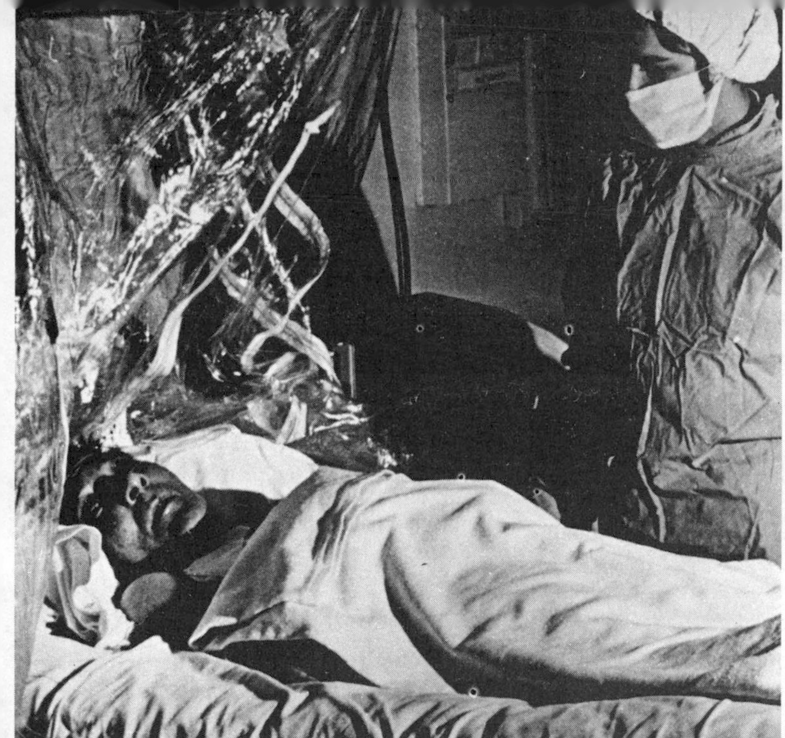

Historical moment — Nurse watches over transplant patient Louis Washkansky at Groote Schuur hospital in Capetown.

Philip Blaiberg enjoyed life for over 18 months before succumbing from organ rejection in August 1969.

ere setback caused by the deaths of three astronauts in January 1967, the project neared completion on schedule in the summer of 1969, and the $23 billion price tag was at the low end of the estimates at the time President Kennedy announced the project in May 1961.

But other criteria of scientific progress were just as dramatic. The invention of the integrated circuit by Jack Kilby of Texas Instruments in 1961 signaled a revolution in ultra-miniature electronics. The late 60's phase of that revolution was known as large-scale integration (LSI) in which hundreds — and some day perhaps thousands — of electronic components are built into a finger nail-sized chip.

The vacuum tube, which launched electronics at the turn of the century, became a museum piece except for the television picture tube — and the industry was even working on that.

The decade also saw the emergence of the laser (light amplification through stimulated emission or radiation), a device that directs an extremely precise beam of light and may have vast implications in communications, medicine and data processing. For the present, however, it has yet to live up to its bright promise.

Peaceful uses of the atom also had to be classed as only qualified successes. A limited amount of electric power generation was achieved (though not as cheaply as with hydrocarbons) and the use of underground nuclear explosions to retrieve petroleum passed a feasibility test in December, 1967 with the Project Gasbuggy detonation at Farmington, N.M.

Computers, the bulky and unreliable giants of the late 1950s, capitalized on the new electronics technology to pervade every segment of society. Their most challenging job in the 1970s will be in the controversial anti-ballistic missile system to pick out incoming enemy warheads from among hundreds of thousands of decoys.

Conversion of the nation's commercial airline fleet to jets had just started in 1960 and by 1970 was nearly complete as the aircraft industry began to wrestle with the financial problems — not the technology — of introducing a supersonic transport flying nearly three times the speed of sound. The U.S. SST is due to go into service around 1977, but by that time Anglo-French and Russian versions already would be flying.

Aerospace technology also filtered down to the dying passenger railroad business as high-speed trains began demonstration service during 1968 along the congested Washington-Boston corridor.

Despite this emphasis on big science, the advance that probably captured the most public interest came from an individual researcher, South African heart surgeon Christiaan Barnard, who made the first successful heart transplant in November, 1967.

The real sleeper of the decade in science may be the discovery of element 104 by Albert Ghiorso and his associates at Lawrence Radiation Laboratory in 1969. Fittingly discovered on the 100th anniversary of Dmitri Mendeleyev's periodic table of elements, it opened vistas of an expanded list containing up to 168 elements.

But the real challenge to science as the decade drew to a close was how man could live in his new environment. The science that put man on the moon in the '60s will be turned to the No. 1 problem of the '70's, the increasing pollution of the earth.

1. Tektite I . . .

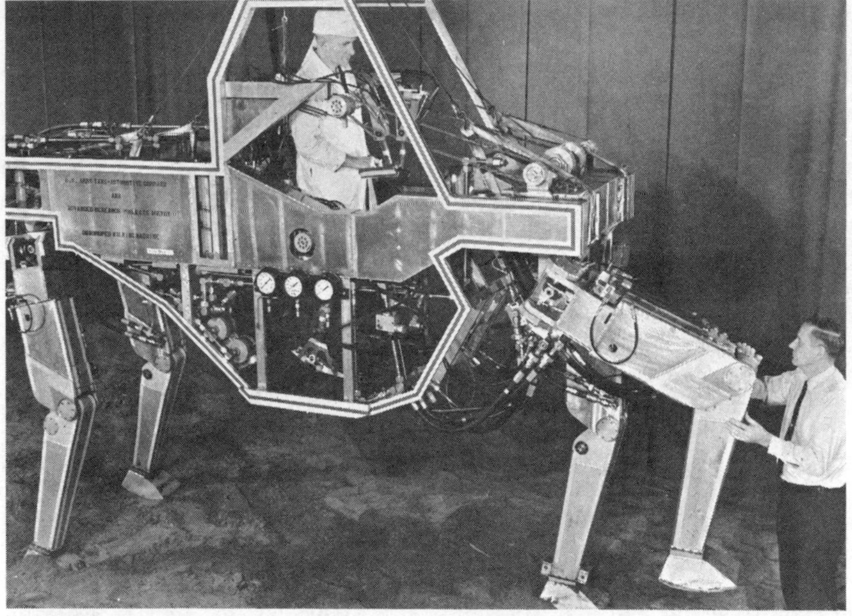

2. Walking machine . . .

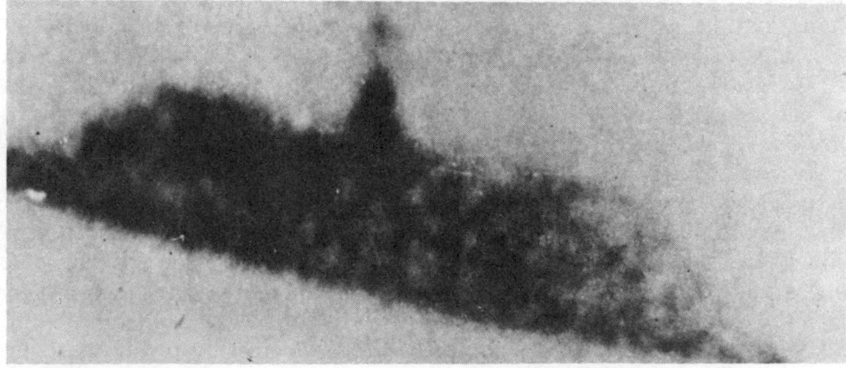

3. Flying saucer (?) . . .

1. Undersea habitat developed by General Electric for civilian agencies was a whopping success during a two-month test in the Virgin Islands, while a similar Navy project, Sealab 3, flopped.

2. Another GE project, a four-legged quadruped machine, underwent initial tests under an Army research contract.

3. Flying saucer buffs list this photo taken at McMinnville, Ore., on May 11, 1950, as "authenticity: probable." They took their case to Congress, which gave them a sympathetic hearing but nothing more.

4. Cameraman prepares for underwater filming outside Moray research vessel.

5. Dr. Lee A. DuBridge, nonpolitical president of California Institute of Technology, takes the reins as President Nixon's science advisor. He immediately marched up Capitol Hill to do battle for bigger science budgets.

6. House Science and Astronautics Committee's Emilio Q. Daddario, Rep. from Conn., is warmly greeted by Brig. Gen. Leo A. Kiley, Commander of Holloman AFB Missile Development Center, on his visit to the Aeromedical Research Laboratory near Alamogordo, N.M. in January 1966. The trip evinced legislative concern with new scientific developments.

7. Hippies seemed to think that Icarus would hit the Earth on June 15, 1968, so many of them came to Boulder, Colorado, to prepare for the end. They felt that the Boulder area might be saved from destruction.

8. New electronics technology known as LSI (large-scale integration) swept the industry with ultra-miniature devices. The 80-gate LSI circuit on the left, from Fairchild Semiconductor, does the same job as the integrated circuit version on the right.

9. Pigtail monkey prepares for flight in the space agency's Biosatellite series to study physical stresses of long-duration missions before man takes the next major steps to Mars and beyond.

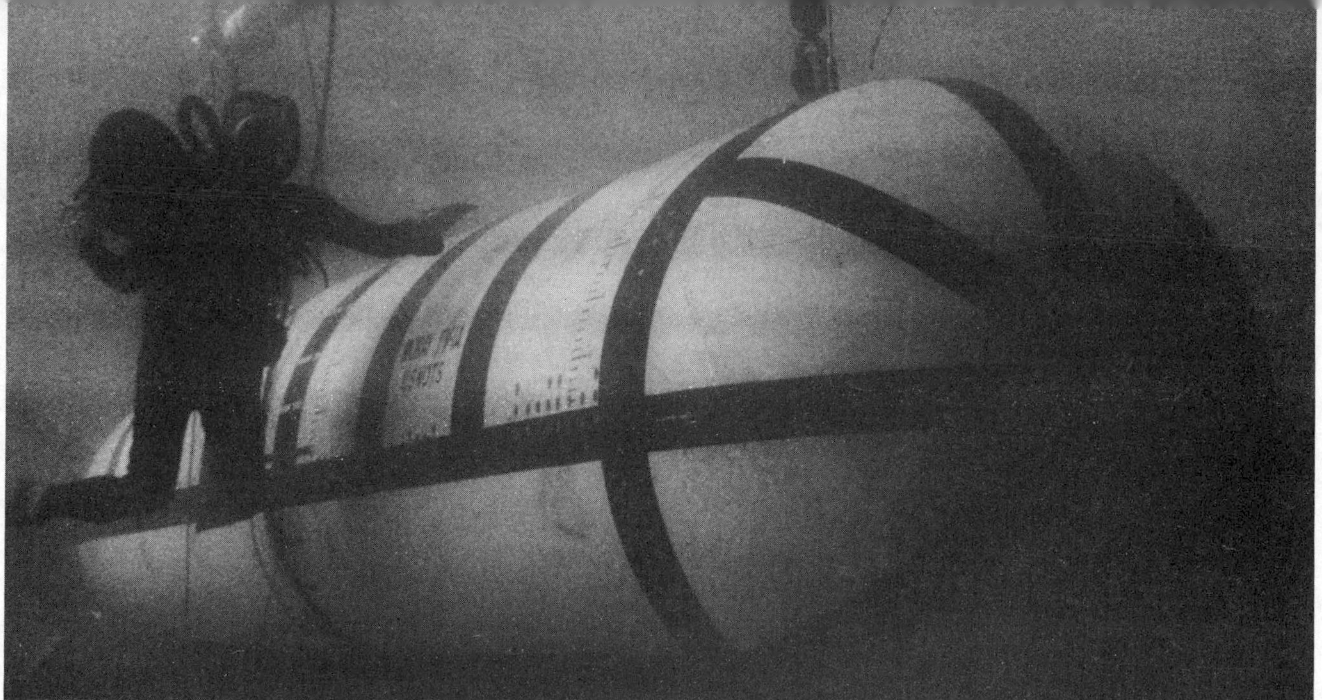

4. Underwater research ...

5. New science chief ...

6. An exchange of information ...

7. They thought it would crash ...

8. Shrinking electronics ...

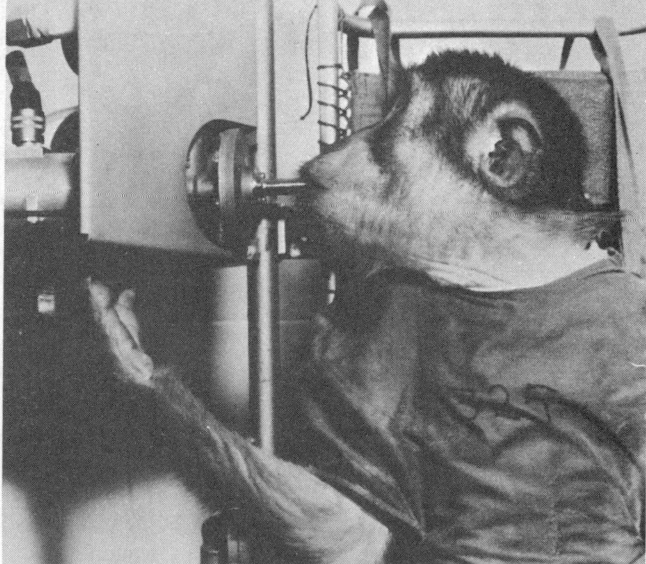

9. Space pioneer ...

Confrontation Politics On the Campus

Students challenge the affluent society; teachers take to the streets; massive Federal aid makes little dent in ghetto educational needs

Symbolic of widespread student protest over "dehumanizing" university regulations was this attention-getting rallying point at the Berkeley campus.

A succession of sharp crises ripped through the expensive fabric of American education during the '60's as schools and universities became microcosmic battlegrounds for the big issues dividing society.

While arson and violence by small groups of militants grabbed the headlines and brought club-swinging police onto the campus, the significant news was the widespread and smoldering student impatience with the continuing war in Vietnam, the slow pace of racial progress, and what many felt were the dehumanizing trends in education.

Student activism opened the decade with the first student lunch-counter sit-in at Greensboro, N.C., on Feb. 1, 1960, slowly gathered momentum and then exploded in December of 1964 at the University of California's Berkeley campus, when the Free Speech Movement, led by Mario Savio and overwhelmingly supported by students and faculty, managed to paralyze the University in a series of demonstrations.

In 1965, the radical Students for a Democratic Society and a number of professors began organizing op-

Protesting restrictions on political activity, Free Speech demonstrators led by Mario Savio paralyzed UC.

Black Power leaders Stokely Carmichael (l) and H. Rap Brown denounced "racist policies" at Columbia.

Ideology for young radicals was provided by Prof. Herbert Marcuse, whose books became campus guides to revolt.

position to the Vietnam War. By 1967, the anti-war movement had replaced civil rights as the major focus of protest, with much of it centered on university participation in chemical, biological and germ warfare research. Their argument: the university will be a military-industrial captive as long as two-thirds of its research funds come from the Defense Department, the Atomic Energy Commission and NASA.

Students from coast to coast in 1968 played confrontation politics. New York's Columbia, San Francisco State (where acting president S. I. Hayakawa called in 600 police to keep the campus open), and the University of California at Berkeley were just three of many institutions rocked by the revolt of a generation called by the Cox Commission Report on Columbia "the best informed, the most intelligent and the most idealistic this country has ever known."

One revolt at Berkeley centered on the regents' refusal to permit credit for an experimental course that included lectures by Black Panther leader Eldridge Cleaver. Increasingly during the decade, the street cry of "black power" was heard on campus in support of black studies, preferential treatment and waiving of entrance exams.

In 1962, for the first school year since the Supreme Court desegregation decision in 1954, integrated schools made it through without violence. But by 1967, urban schools were under harsh attack by educational critics for their failure to meet the needs of the ghetto child.

New York City, the country's biggest school system, sought a remedy in radical reorganization. In December 1967, Mayor Lindsay proposed to decentralize education by grouping the city's 900 schools under 30 to 60 autonomous community school boards with power to hire administrators and teachers, plan curriculum and allocate funds.

The plan touched off one of the bitterest teacher strikes during a decade plagued by labor unrest in the schools. In September 1968, 53,000 of New York City's 57,000 teachers walked out over decentralization.

Ostensibly, the dispute centered on the right of Negro parents in Brooklyn's Ocean Hill-Brownsville section to remove ten "unsatisfactory" teachers, but from the parents' point of view, the major issue was whether black parents could have a voice in neighborhood schools.

Work stoppages by teachers seeking higher pay also hit New York in 1962 and 1968, when Florida was also struck. Strikers claimed that while average salary for full professors had climbed to $19,700, that for teachers stayed at a low $6,500.

Both teachers and space were in short supply throughout the decade. In 1960, the U.S. Office of Education reported 1.87 more pupils per class than could be accommodated, and a need for 135,000 more teachers and 127,000 classrooms.

Although over 200,000 new teachers took jobs in 1966-67, at term's end half were gone. Elementary schools were hardest hit of all, with 66,000 unfilled posts.

With little fanfare, technology invaded the classroom when computer teaching went into effect for the first time in 1966 at a Brentwood, Calif. school. 100 first-grade pupils began learning math and reading from an IBM machine in what might be the most significant educational event of the decade.

1. Teachers walked out ...

2. Students sat in ...

3. New York's first of many strikes ...

4. Shanker: Job security for teachers

5. McCoy: Neighborhood control ...

1. Chicago's first teachers' strike in May, 1969, brought demands for a $150 monthly increase, improved classrooms and guarantees against layoffs.

2. At a 1965 "Teach-In" at the University of Wisconsin, students and faculty discussed Vietnam — and agreed U.S. should get out.

3. A decade of turbulence in New York's schools opened with the first teachers' strike in the city's history in 1961.

4. United Federation of Teachers' President Albert Shanker drew jail sentence in 1969 for disobeying injunction during strike for teacher job security.

5. Rhody McCoy led Brooklyn's Ocean Hill-Brownsville black parents in drive for greater local control of schools, precipitating clash with mostly white teachers' union.

6. When "confrontation politics" hit San Francisco State College in December, 1968, acting president Dr. S. I. Hayakawa promised to keep campus open and maintain order.

7. Hayakawa's warning went unheeded. With 600 police on campus, 150 arrests, 25 arson reports, three small bomb explosions and hundreds of injuries, San Francisco State resembled a battlefield.

8. Student integration by bussing drew irate white parents to Brooklyn Board of Education for mass protest.

9. While social activists sought to radicalize the campus, former Harvard professor Timothy Leary invited thousands of San Francisco "Hippies" to "turn on, tune in and drop out."

10. Columbia University strike leader Mark Rudd at 1968 rally promised continued militant action. Of middle-class background, Rudd was typical of the campus radicals who sought to impose a more responsible community role on the universities.

11. In 1965, a new physical science lecture hall with pioneering features for economy and teaching effectiveness went into full operation on the Berkeley campus of the University of California.

6. Hayakawa delivers the message ...

7. San Francisco State students respond ...

8. White backlash? ...

9. Leary: Get out of "the system" ...

10. Big man on campus ...

11. Electronic classrooms ...

Christendom Bows To Dramatic Changes

Traditions shattered; Communions separated for centuries seek understanding, take joint action in areas of crisis

In a procession of pomp and pageantry on October 11, 1962, Pope John XXIII is borne aloft as some 2500 prelates, bishops and world religious leaders cross St. Peter's Square to the Bascilica for opening session of Vatican II.

The decade saw an exodus from cloister, cathedral, church and synagogue for direct involvement in the secular side of life. New unity was stimulated before problems of mutual concern.

Winter of 1961 in New Delhi, India, found Roman Catholics attending the assembly of the World Council of Churches for the first time as observers. A phenomenon of the decade was the "kiss of peace" exchanged by Pope Paul VI and Patriarch Athenagoras in 1964 in Jerusalem when they prayed together at the Mount of Olives for the reconciliation of Christians.

Ecumenism in 1969 in New York City reached new hospitable heights when the Broadway Church (Protestant) deserted its worn out building to hold Sunday services in the Roman Catholic Church of St. Paul the Apostle.

Beginning in the fall of 1962 many changes emanated from Rome. Pope John XXIII's inspired call for Vatican II, first ecumenical council in nearly a century, brought 2400 Roman Catholics, the Curia, bishops and prelates, as well as Orthodox and Protestant observers to the colorful opening ceremonies of the first session of the Council at

In the first such visit since the Reformation, former Archbishop of Canterbury Geoffrey Francis Fisher meets privately with Pope John at the Vatican, December 3, 1960.

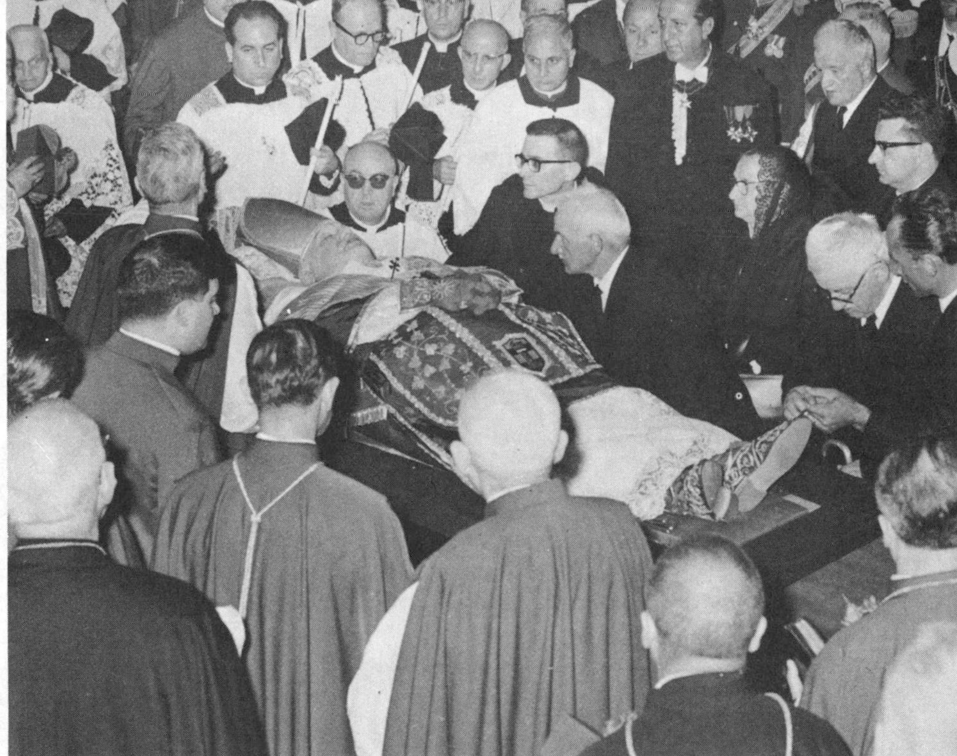

Beloved in life, revered in death, Pope John XXIII's Vatican II encyclical, *Pacem in Terris,* was addressed "to all men of good will" rather than to Roman Catholics alone.

St. Peter's Basilica on October 11, 1962. Pope Paul VI called three more sessions as successor to Pope John XXIII who died on June 3, 1963.

Self imposed task of the Council was "aggiornamento," to bring the church in tune with the 20th century. Guiding light for Vatican II was Pope John's encyclical, *Pacem In Terris,* peace on earth. Opening the third session in September 1964, Pope Paul broke with tradition by con-celebrating mass with 24 bishops as a symbol of their new council – approved role of sharing with him in the government of the church.

On Advent Sunday, November 29, 1964, by council-rule, Catholic churches all over the world replaced time-honored Latin with English or local vernacular in the mass.

By the late 60's celibacy became an increasingly debatable issue. Priests were leaving the church at the rate of fifty a month to marry. Although defrocked, some priests held underground masses in the homes of Catholic friends. Even among the faithful, civilian "mufti" often replaced religious garb of both nuns and priests as they grappled with the problems of the day on urban levels.

In 1964, the National Council of Churches had given approval to birth control as a curb against world population explosion. The decade's end, however, found the traditional Roman Catholic stand on contraception a highly controversial one. In 1968 in Washington, D.C. Patrick Cardinal O'Boyle disciplined dissenting priests by demanding they repudiate their public defense of the Catholic right to regulate birth according to conscience. At St. Mathews' Cathedral, attended by 1200, as O'Boyle read his statement on birth control during mass, 150 parishioners staged a walk-out.

Evangelism continued to flourish in the sixties. The Reverend Billy Graham crusaded from Africa to New Zealand. In West Berlin, East Berliners defied border guards to hear him.

Youth's revolt against "packaged religion and church members' hypocrisy" took many forms. In 1966 ex-Harvard professor Timothy Leary, reporting on profound religious experience induced by LSD and other drugs, gathered followers for his League of Spiritual Discovery. Jazz masses were heard in such sacrosanct places as Boston's Old South Church.

The explosive issues of race and the Vietnam war concerned religion. On May 4, 1969, black militant leader James Forman invaded New York's Protestant Riverside Church during a Sunday communion service to demand that the church turn over 60 percent of its investment income as its share of the $500 million demanded by the National Black Economic Development Conference as "reparation to U.S. Negroes from white Christians and Jewish synagogues." Forman next posted a copy of the NBEDC "manifesto" on the door of the Lutheran Church in America headquarters; then appeared at the New York Archdiocesan chancery to demand $200 million from United States Roman Catholics.

The decade was ruled by two dominating trends: the challenge to religion to be relevant, and the continuing growth of ecumenism. The Roman Catholic Church was suffering its greatest crisis as parishioners and the hierarchy alike, in voices of unfettered persistence, demanded tradition-shattering changes.

1. Pope Paul's first appearance . . .

2. Historic embrace . . .

1. Cardinal Giovanni Montini, Archbishop of Milan, elected to succeed Pope John XXIII, makes his first public appearance as Pope Paul VI on June 21, 1963.

2. During his first visit to Jerusalem in 1964, Pope Paul VI exchanges an embrace with Patriarch of Constantinople (Istanbul) Athenagoras before the altar.

3. Shown at the press conference that followed the Grace Cathedral service on December, 1960, at which Presbyterian Dr. Eugene Carson Blake (r) launched his proposal for Protestant Church union is the then Bishop of the Cathedral, James Pike, during the 10th General Assembly of the National Council of Churches, San Francisco.

4. Five World Council of Churches leaders at fourth Assembly in Uppsala, Sweden, July 4-19, 1968: Dr. Martin Niemoeller, Germany, a WCC president; Dr. Ernest Payne, retired general secretary, Baptist Union of Great Britian and Ireland; Dr. Eugene Carson Blake, an American, and WCC general secretary; Metropolitan Nicodim, chairman, foreign affairs department, the Russian Orthodox Church; and Bishop Hanns Lilje, Evangelical Lutheran Church of Hannover, Germany.

5. In a rare moment of personal exchange during the visit of the Archbishop of Canterbury to Rome in March, 1966, he is shown in warm conversation with Pope Paul.

6. Protesting the participation of Roman Catholic Archbishop of Westminister, Cardinal John Heenan, in a church unity service at St. Paul's Cathedral, London, on January 22, 1969, sign carrying demonstraters register disapproval in no uncertain terms.

7. America's first Negro bishop, appointed auxiliary bishop of New Orleans by Pope Paul in October, 1964, the Rev. Harold R. Perry emerges from the historic St. Louis Basilica following his consecration in January, 1965.

8. Surrounded by a startled congregation at Old South Church, Boston, during a contemporary worship service in this sacrosanct sanctuary, fall 1966, rock enthusiasts spill over into the aisles.

9. Losing his standing as 11th ranking cleric in the papal household by forsaking celibacy for marriage to Giovanna Carlevaro at the Church of the Santa Maria della Pace on March 29, 1969, Mnsgr. Giovanni Musato relinquishes chaplaincy to Pope Paul VI.

3. Sunday Service makes headlines ...

4. Ecumenism at Uppsala ...

5. Two religious leaders relax ...

6. Unecumenical protest ...

7. First Negro Bishop ...

8. Explosion in the aisles ...

9. Roman Holiday for Roman cleric ...

Ten Years of Aesthetic and Social Change

Designers reject International Style; social change affects building and architecture, but progress is slow.

During the past decade, cartoons like this appeared to point up increasing public interest in the preservation of the architectural heritage of cities.

During the decade of the 1960's, the greatest change in architectural design was a movement away from the steel-framed, glass box of the International Style, considered a crowning achievement of the Industrial Age ever since the 30's, when architects like Walter Gropius and Mies van der Rohe introduced it to the U.S.

Stressing simplicity of space and structure, the International Style depended for aesthetic value chiefly on proportion and careful detailing. But by the 60's, in the hands of speculative builders and architects less conscientious than a Mies, the glass box had become a structure more simplistic than simple. It epitomized the cold, clean, and deadly dull atmosphere of the big business environment.

As the decade opened, Minoru Yamasaki was already popularizing a more romantic style, one of arches, curves, and spires. Then came Eero Saarinen's TWA Terminal at New York's JFK Airport and his Dulles Airport in Washington, D.C.

1968 saw the opening of a huge sports-recreation-office complex over former site of New York's Penn Station.

Eero Saarinen's TWA Terminal at Kennedy International Airport, New York City, heralded a new romanticism in architectural design, and lent new meaning to the aphorism, that "form follows function."

(completed in 1962 and 1963, respectively.) These designs departed radically from the angularity of glass and steel, and their curved roof lines represented visually the function of the facilities they housed.

The trend away from the rectangle was carried on by Bertrand Goldberg in his Marina City Apartments (Chicago, 1965), by the designers of New York's Lincoln Center (1965-66), who put together a modified mixture of modern and classical styles in massive marble, and by architects who leaned on the Brutalist tradition (see R. Banham, *The New Brutalism,* 1966) and the work of Louis I. Kahn.

Buildings like Paul Rudolph's Arts and Architecture Building at Yale (1964), Kallman & McKinnell's Boston City Hall (1968), and I.M. Pei's Center for Environmental Research (Denver, 1967), were, like buildings of the new romantic style, sculptural in effect, but instead of delicate curves, they offered the juxtaposition of voluminous masses and columns that created surprising combinations of line, texture, and angle. Both styles were made possible by tremendous improvements in concrete technology.

Subordinately, the new emphasis on freedom in design extended to a phenomenon known, in the second part of the decade, as Pop Architecture, and expounded by architect Robert Venturi *(Complexity and Contradiction in Architecture,* 1967.) This development placed a new value on the happenstance, the environment that occurred without planning. Its derivation may have been, in part, a reaction to the heavy emphasis on planning urban environments and the increasing complexity of such planning, as the decade wore on.

During the 60's, architects and planners were called on to cope with ever larger problems, and to find solutions on an increasingly large scale. As urban problems worsened, with the summer riots of 1967 providing the best evidence, the Federal Government initiated two additional Cabinet Departments: the Department of Housing and Urban Development and the Department of Transportation. Designers and builders were asked to think of planning in terms of interacting systems of a total environment. Illustrations of the trend toward large-scale planning were the experimental new towns, such as Reston, Va. (1965) and Columbia, Md.(1966-67), or the fad for cultural and civic centers.

To cope with the vast and growing need for middle and low-cost housing (Presidents Johnson and Nixon set the goal of creating 26 million new homes within the next decade), large industrial corporations as well as architects and builders began adapting computer techniques and the methods of mass production to the housing field. Pre-fabrication of dwelling units became the watchword, although potential success was hampered by out-moded building codes, labor union demands, and inexperience.

1. New York's Lincoln Center, night view . . .

2. Interior, Metropolitan Opera House, Lincoln Center . . .

3. Migrant workers' housing, made of plastic . . .

1. The trend toward large-scale, multi-purpose building projects is illustrated by New York's Lincoln Center for the Performing Arts, designed by several teams of architects.

2. Classical marble, Viennese chandeliers, and distinctively modern curves are thrown together inside Metropolitan Opera, a part of Lincoln Center designed by Wallace K. Harrison.

3. Example of the attempt to cope with increasing social problems is this design by a group of California architects for migrant workers' camp, which experiments with the use of a new building material — plastic.

4. Design for this seaside resort was based on thorough ecological studies of the land. Buildings illustrate shed roofs, which enjoyed great popularity during the 60's.

5. Interior at Sea Ranch shows strong, form-giving structural elements left exposed, and bold graphics used both as decoration and as expanders of apparent space.

6. Overwhelming masses, juxtaposed to create surprising textures, forms, and spaces form a "sculpture in concrete," designed by Paul Rudolph.

7. Architects Kallman & McKinnell won a national competition with their complex, concrete contribution to Boston's new Government Center.

8. The glass box did not totally disappear, but took on new variations as designed by Skidmore, Owings & Merrill. Cross-diagonal wind bracing is structural element exposed to view and left to rust and take on a reddish patina.

9. Not all architectural landmarks succumbed totally to the wrecker's ball; New York's Grand Central Terminal merely allowed itself to be subdued by the monstrous office building on its roof.

4. Sea Ranch resort, by MLTW Moore/Turnbull ...

5. Interior, Sea Ranch ...

6. Art and Architecture Bldg. at Yale ...

7. Boston's new City Hall ...

8. Alcoa Building, San Francisco ...

9. Pan Am atop Grand Central Terminal ...

Familiar Names Go in Stormy Era

Herald Tribune and Saturday Evening Post among the casualties; more growth than profits for busy, beleaguered press

Broadway columnist, Dorothy Kilgallen, here with convicted wife-murderer, Finch, died of a pill overdose in 1965.

Hollywood columnist Hedda Hopper, former actress known for her hats and refreshing candor, died at 75 in 1966.

Sentiment and tradition went by the boards in the 1960s as the press faced up to harsh economic realities — all this in a period of shattering, exacting news events including the assassinations of President John F. Kennedy, the Rev. Martin Luther King, and Sen. Robert F. Kennedy along with the running stories of the Vietnam war, ghetto riots, crisis and pollution in the urban areas, and a Presidential campaign and election.

The industry was expanding, but costs were mounting faster, and publications had to be sure of their readership and their appeal, or their mission, to stand the pace. The weaker ones were dropping out.

Newspaper circulation continued to hit new highs — 62,535,394 at the end of 1968 compared with 58,881,746 in 1960. But while there was a net gain of three dailies during 1968 for a total of 1752, that was 11 less than there were at the beginning of the decade, and some big names had disappeared. What happened in New York City was most dramatic, and symptomatic.

At the turn of the century New York had 15 major dailies; by 1930 there were 12; as the 1960s began there were seven. As the printing unions got increasingly tough about wages and distribution of profits from automation, the city's papers were hit by a 114 day strike ending on March 31, 1963. Cleveland, meanwhile, had a 129-day strike and Minneapolis a 116-day shutdown, but New York's was the costliest, destroying an estimated $190 million in newspaper revenue plus millions more in business and government income.

This was a final death blow to Hearst's New York *Mirror,* with its 850,000 circulation the nation's second largest newspaper. The *Mirror* sold its goodwill to No. 1, the competing *Daily News.*

By 1965 more than 60 newspapers across the country were successfully using computerized typesetting equipment. But in New York the printing unions had a costly deal on automation with a virtual veto on the installation of new equipment. In the fall of 1965, the Newspaper Guild, concerned about the effects of automation on its commercial members tried to get the same powers in a 24-day strike against the N.Y. *Times.* All of the

World Journal Tribune

SPORTS FINAL

World Journal Tribune Ends Publication Today

Marines Mop Up on Hill 881

Act to Bar Apartment Walkouts

Kidnaper's Beating Of Boy Revealed

Decoys Kill Cab Bandit

Statement Issued By Matt Meyer

Wall Collapses, 20 Buried

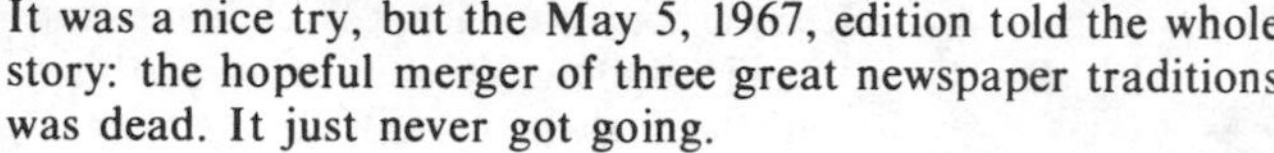

It was a nice try, but the May 5, 1967, edition told the whole story: the hopeful merger of three great newspaper traditions was dead. It just never got going.

At Time's 40th anniversary party in 1963, founder Henry R. Luce chats with, from the left, Sen. Humphrey, French ex-Premier Mendes-France, Jean Monnet, Sen. Dirksen.

other papers except the N.Y. *Post* shut down in sympathy, and the Guild won major concessions. This was a last straw for the ailing *Herald Tribune,* which in March, 1966, merged with two other weak oldsters, Hearst's *Journal-American* and Scripps-Howard's *World Telegram & Sun.* Plans to put out a joint newspaper were delayed by a Newspaper Guild strike to force all rehiring on a seniority basis.

Publication of the *World Journal Tribune,* descendant of a dozen great papers and journalistic powers such as Joseph Pulitzer, William Randolph Hearst, and Horace Greeley, began on Sept. 13, 1966 — and after a futile struggle ended on May 5, 1967. The city now had three general dailies: the morning *Times,* the tabloid *News,* and the evening tabloid *Post.*

It was the survival of the fittest, and a symbol of the trend was the chain of Samuel I. Newhouse, who consistently put operations ahead of editorial policy. With the 1962 purchase of both of New Orleans' papers, the *Times-Picayune* and the *Statesman-Item,* the Newhouse chain became the nation's largest with 19 papers; purchase of the prestigious Cleveland *Plain Dealer* in 1968 made the total 20.

Magazines in 1968 continued to fight back against television with increased success, topping $1 billion in advertising revenue for the fourth consecutive year. But the competitive struggle between individual magazines increased sharply with the race going largely to those with basic specialties and wide current appeal — those devoted to women's interests, shelter, news, hobbies, young people.

The end came for one of the oldest, biggest, best known general magazines, the *Saturday Evening Post.* Starting in 1961 the venerable parent company, Curtis Publishing, began to show a loss; by 1968 losses had totaled $55 million.

Along the line Curtis was shaken with internal executive and editorial upheavals. Efforts to recapture the *Post's* oldtime appeal as a mirror of heartland America, largely with new muckraking and exposé stunts, did not impress readers, and particularly the buyers of advertising. In 1965 the Post became a biweekly; in 1968 merchandiser Martin S. Ackerman came in as Curtis president with new money. He sold the 85-year-old *Ladies Home Journal* and the *American Home,* turned the Post from a "mass" to a "class" magazine by lopping off 3 million of its 6.4 million subscribers. But it was too late. The Feb. 8, 1969, issue became the last for a magazine bought for $1,000 in 1897 by the great Cyrus H. K. Curtis and turned into one of the most successful ever published.

Death also came during the decade to a notable publisher, Henry R. Luce, on Feb. 28, 1967. Cofounder, with the late Briton Hadden of *Time* (1923) and of a new journalistic format, he started *Fortune* (1930), *Life* (1936), and *Sports Illustrated* (1954). As the 1960s ended, under his handpicked successor, Hedley Donovan, the vast and until recently highly profitable Time Inc. empire was undergoing soulsearching reappraisals. *Life's* revenue was slipping; *Time's* rival, the smaller circulation but fast-moving *Newsweek* (bought by the affluent Washington Post Company in 1961) was ahead in advertising.

As always, nothing was certain in the world of newspapers and magazines except the certainty of change.

1. In a party mood ...

1. For reasons known only to his own whimsically complex mind, best-selling author Truman Capote ("In Cold Blood") gave a big masked ball at New York's Hotel Plaza in November 1966 in honor of Katharine Graham, president of the Washington Post Co. (also owners of Newsweek), to which everyone who is in the swim was invited. Here host and honored guest enter the scene.

2. When the N.Y. Times home office tried to change the Washington setup in '68, editor-columnist James Reston protested with vigor, moved up to Manhattan as executive editor with clear control of news operations, in '69 moved back to Washington as vice president in charge of news coverage and in a better spot to continue his column.

3. Protected in his hegemony by the Reston coup was Tom Wicker, veteran Washington bureau chief, who was thus confirmed as the man in charge when it came to covering the Capitol.

4. 148-year publishing history ended with the demise of the Saturday Evening Post on Jan. 10, 1969. It had known impulsive youth, the vigors of middle-age, the agonies of slow decline and would now be buried in the subscription lists of Life and other magazines.

2. Winner of a palace revolution ...

3. Survivor in a tough spot ...

Magazine Company to Merge With Lin Broadcasting

By ROBERT E. BEDINGFIELD

The end will come today for The Saturday Evening Post.

Directors of the once-dominant publication—it still has about 3.5 million subscribers—will declare it officially dead this morning and arrange for its burial in the subscription lists of Life and other magazines.

Thus will end the 148-year publishing history of a magazine that has outlived the more rural, more insular America it once served.

Martin S. Ackerman, president of the Saturday Evening Post Company and of its parent, the Curtis Publishing Corporation, has called a news conference for this afternoon at which, he said, he may have "something to announce" about merging the Post company with the Lin Broadcasting Corporation of Nashville.

Mr. Ackerman yesterday rejected an offer he had received

Mirrored U.S. Idea and Changes Sinc Its Birth in 1821

By ISRAEL SHENKER

The Saturday Evening P has known impulsive youth, vigor of middle-age and agonies of slow decline.

In the beginning it made mark with fiction that sometimes compelling sometimes uncomplicated, in middle age it was high conservative values.

But the new readership tried desperately to attract through a brighter format articles designed to make he lines ,or a least to make continue reading—was neit big enough nor faithful enou

The Saturday Evening P memorialized a country dou ful about world destiny confident of its own virtu The magazine's fiction, artic and advertising, even its cov of sweetly imaginative realis consecrated the simple deligh

Its presence in dentis waiting rooms testified to

4. Never on Saturday ...

Mergers Highlight The Decade

Book houses are taken over by industrial giants; rise of the Jewish hero, black literature, and the non-fiction novel are trends

It was the decade when McLuhan announced that print was no longer the medium for the message, when novelists proclaimed the death of the novel, and when book publishers made more money than ever — as publishing highballed into the corporate world of mergers, takeovers, and consolidations.

At the outset, the signs of bigness were limited to mergers among book houses: Harcourt, Brace & Co. with World Books, Random House and Alfred A. Knopf early in '61.

But as sales went from $1.3 billion in '61 to almost $2 billion in '69, book firms caught the eye of the electronic giants. Between 1967 and 1968, CBS snared Holt, Rinehart and Winston, RCA snapped up Random House, and Xerox, Raytheon, and others entered the field.

In the late 60s there was an unprecedented shifting of top editing personnel as the inevitable corporate shake-ups took place. Many editors sought refuge in the few remaining *quality* houses, but they feared that the days of the small quality publisher were numbered.

The decade witnessed the end of quality also in the deaths of the last literary giants: Hemingway in '60, Faulkner in '62, John Steinbeck in '68; and the poets Robert Frost, Wallace Stevens, Ted Roethke, and William Carlos Williams.

Eminent younger poets continued to produce major works, most notably Robert Lowell and John Berryman. But there were no instant successors to the late greats among younger prose writers, although press-agentry demanded names. John Updike, whose *Centaur* won the '64 National Book Award, was most often mentioned. John Cheever entered the lists in '69 with his highly acclaimed *Bullet Park.*

Other writers of distinction during these years included: Joseph Heller *(Catch 22),* Saul Bellow *(Herzog),* Bernard Malamud *(The Fixer),* and Philip Roth *(Portnoy's Complaint).*

In retrospect, critics saw in these books "the rise of the Jewish literary hero." More accurately, what was chronicled was the vogue of the anti-hero, or the hero as *schlemiel.*

Another trend was begun in the mid 60s as the civil rights struggle waxed: publishers began scrambling to add black writers to their lists. Although excellent little-known authors like James McPherson *(Hue and Cry)* and Ishmael Reed *(The Free-Lance Pallbearers)* considered themselves artists striving for self-expression, most young black writers felt that it was their responsibility, as one put it, "to deniggerize the world" by helping the black revolution.

Most popular were books affording whites a look into the black experience: Cleaver's *Soul on Ice,* Baldwin's *The Fire Next Time,* Malcolm X's *Autobiography.*

A belief that the novel's form had outlived its usefulness, however, inspired new modes — most notably the "non-fiction" novel. The genre got a major kick-off in '66 with Truman Capote's *In Cold Blood.* But his cool, journalistic technique seemed curiously bloodless in comparison to the baroque splendors — in the same genre — of Norman Mailer's *Armies of the Night,* 1968 winner of both the Pulitzer Prize and the National Book Award.

A better index of the average reader's taste was seen in the long-run best sellers. Jacqueline Susann's *Valley of the Dolls,* reportedly a roman à clef based on freaked-out Hollywood types, made the N.Y. Times best seller list for 65 weeks. Her '69 best seller *The Love Machine* promised to run it a close second. And following the '63 vindication of *Fanny Hill* as non-pornographic by the N.Y. State Court of Appeals, a spate of titillating would-be 'sexational' books appeared — *Candy, The Exhibitionist, The Voyeur* — all promptly aimed at best-sellerdom.

The deaths of great Americans — John F. and Robert Kennedy and Martin Luther King — brought their life stories, like instant replay, to the book stalls.

But an affirmation of the novel's vitality, and the pleasure of the written word, came despite TV and the critics' gloom, toward the decade's end. Vladimir Nabokov's *Ada* proved that only genius is needed to keep life in the old form.

1. A poet is honored . . .

2. Intimate look at J.F.K.'s death . . .

3. Claimed invasion of privacy . . .

4. " . . . is dandy but liquor is quicker."

5. An early word for militant brothers

1. One of the few presidents to honor poets, J.F.K. acclaimed Robert Frost on his 88th birthday. Rear, left, is Senator Saltonstall; right, Interior Secretary Udall.

2. William Manchester's book about J.F.K. became an inflated press sensation when the President's widow withdrew her initial support of the author and tried to stop publication of the book.

3. In December, 1966, Jacqueline Kennedy, shown here with legal advisers, failed in her attempt to stop serial publication of *The Death of a President,* in *Look* magazine. She claimed it was an invasion of her "emotional privacy."

4. With the tandem authorship of *Candy,* a trend was begun in writing a "put down" of the popular sexational books of the decade. A similar late 60s spoof of the genre is group authored *Naked Came a Stranger.*

5. James Baldwin, one of the decade's noted black writers, was an early proponent of black militancy among Negro authors.

6. The "march on Washington" was the source of Norman Mailer's *Armies of the Night,* one of the finest examples of reportage-novels of the decade. Here author Mailer, center, clasps the arm of noted poet Robert Lowell, to his left.

7. Saul Bellow was one of the best of the decade's novelists and representative of a group of writers who created a major fictional trend in the 60s the Jewish anti-hero.

8. Herzog, by Saul Bellow, is a watershed work in the creation of its central character, an academic who writes interminable letters to figures in history, the prototypical hero-'schlemiel'.

9. In 1968 the first computer-controlled book, from manuscript to printed page, was produced. Here is one machine of the production complex.

10. "Papa" Hemingway's suicide in 1960 brought an end to a world literary figure whose life often seemed like his fiction. Here, a few months before dying, he watches his matador friend Antonio Ordonez perform in a small town in Spain.

11. Truman Capote was first on the scene with *In Cold Blood* in the area of the journalistic novel.

12. Notable publishing figure Bennett Cerf heralded the take-over of book houses by the electronic giants. His claim that books would gain in quality was widely disputed by most editors.

6. To arouse the nation's conscience . . .

7. A Bellow easy on the ear . . .

8. Hallmark of the genre . . .

9. Computers click in book whirr-ld . . .

10. Last of a giant . . .

11. Probed murderers' minds . . .

12. Claims bigger is better . . .

Art: Something for Everyone

Cultural explosion hits art market; prices of Old Masters and 19th century Americans soar; contemporaries strive for new styles and new media

Crowds, pickets and politicians hit the Metropolitan Museum's controversial multi-media Harlem "history".

Masses, money and movement shaped the art world of the '60s as the affluent society launched the nation's biggest cultural binge ever.

Art was everywhere: in big-city museums, in ghetto stores, in supermarkets and banks, in homes, offices and schools; and wherever it was, people flocked by the millions to view, to touch, to buy.

At the start of the decade, some two million annually visited the Metropolitan Museum of Art. By 1968, annual visitors topped 6 million and the figure was rising.

That same year, 20 new museums sprang up nationwide, while 49 more were under construction at a cost of $230 million.

The crowds that came to look stayed to buy. Museum Craft Shops featuring $.05 postcards and $1,000 pottery thrived. At the Cleveland Museum, gift sales jumped from $95,000 in 1960 to $194,000 in 1966; Washington's Smithsonian got $500,000 in one year from the sale of reproductions and publications; and the Metropolitan took in $1.6 million the same year.

Attracted by the "hot" art market, mass merchandisers stepped boldly into the field of original paintings. Woolworth's offered a Dali at $74,000 and a Gains-

In his life-size sculpture-environment, Edward Kienholz froze a moment of contemporary America.

Scale became content in Ronald Bladen's huge "X" at the Corcoran Gallery in the nation's capital.

borough at $24,000, while Korvette's set up suburban art galleries.

Spectacular prices breathed a feverish current through the markets. Art buyers paid $3,044,500 at a single New York sale in April, 1968, and $2,500,000 at another in London in June. In 1966, the world's leading auction houses had a record turnover of $80 million.

Individual items set new highs. In Nov. 1961, the Metropolitan paid $2.3 million (the highest ever paid for a painting) for Rembrandt's "Aristotle Contemplating the Bust of Homer." A post-card size Flemish painting by Roger Van der Weyden went at $26,552 per square inch. And $532,000 was paid for Picasso's "Mother and Child," the highest ever paid for a work by a living artist.

With much European art priced outside the range of even wealthy collectors, the market turned with renewed interest to American artists of the 19th and early 20th Century. The museums discovered the American heritage, as did Madison Avenue galleries. The result was predictable: a boom in American art that raised the price of a Thomas Cole from $2,500 in 1950 to $100,000 in 1968, to take just one example.

Also attracted by the big money in art was the Internal Revenue Service, which started a crackdown on inflated income tax deductions on donated works of art, and the forgers.

Biggest art scandal was the Metropolitan's discovery that its world famous fifth-century B.C. bronze horse was a fake less than 50 years old. But more harmful in the long run was the proliferation of fakes flooding the market.

Beneath the glitter of dollars and markets lay a more abiding interest in art, producing fine work and scholarly exhibitions. In 1963, for example, half a century after the exhibition which launched U.S. art into the 20th century, thousands flocked to a restaging of the event at the original site, Manhattan's 69th Regiment Armory. Here in 1913 Arthur B. Davies, Walt Kuhn and others had organized the "Armory Show" which opened America's doors to the European Avant Garde.

No event of similar importance took place in the '60s, although Pop Art did provide a modicum of amusement and controversy. Mildly satirizing the American scene, it yet displayed a kind of establishment affection for the American scene, celebrating in outsize form the ikonography of the movies, TV and advertising.

James Rosenquist (giant billboards with social comment), Claes Oldenburg (soft sculptures of mammoth hamburgers and plastic environments), Roy Lichtenstein (huge facsimilies of comic strips) were its star performers, with Andy Warhol (Brillo boxes and Campbell Soup cans) serving as the sad-eyed court jester to the whole Pop "scene."

Contemporary with the "new vulgarity" of Pop arose a new classicism, wherein precisionists like Briget Riley, Josef Albers and Ellsworth Kelly explored the world of optical response and "after image." Somewhat akin were the "minimal" artists, craftsmen-technicians who concentrated on developing simple geometric forms to sometimes gigantic scale.

Artists also invaded the world of technology in search of new materials and styles, and Tech/Art emerged towards the decade's end, where laser beams, programmed TV sets, and kinetic light displays promised a new kind of art.

The giants of the '60's remained those of previous decades: Marcel Duchamp, who died, and Pablo Picasso, who continued to paint.

1. The social responsibility of a museum . . .

2. Searching for roots . . .

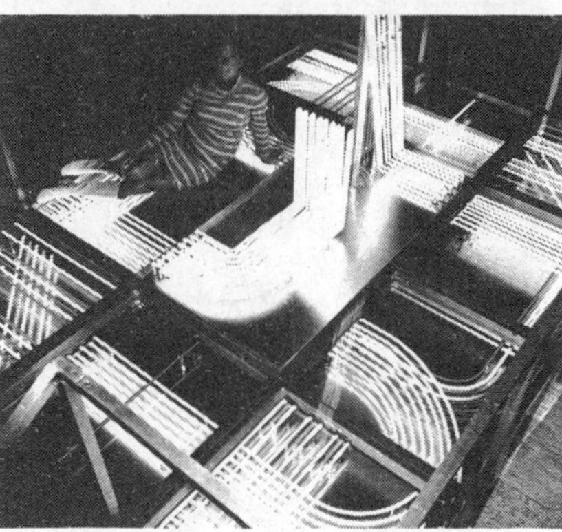

3. "The most spectacular . . .

4. Price: $5 million . . .

1. Stark photographs and recorded Negro jazz lent documentary realism to the Metropolitan Museum's "Harlem on My Mind" exhibition but purists questioned what it had to do with art.

2. While Director Thomas Hoving fought off critics, blacks and whites swarmed through the Met to make the "Harlem" show one of the best attended in the museum's history.

3. Antonakos's glass-decked platform with giant candy-colored neon tubes flashed on and off in programmed patterns at the Nelson-Atkins Gallery's $400,000 spectacular.

4. The only authenticated painting by Leonardo da Vinci, "Beauty Enhances Virtue," was exhibited at the National Gallery in Washington. It was purchased from the private collection of Prince Franz Josef 11 of Lichtenstein.

5. Remaining aloof from trends and fashions were a few artists like Frank Gallo whose individual probings of the human form gave a particular vitality to American sculpture.

6. Pop Art's comic-strip parodies acquired an authenticity of their own with Roy Lichtenstein's skillful and exaggerated simplifications.

7. Pop Art also rated serious attention from critics and top prices from buyers. Andy Warhol's reproductions of Brillo and Mott's boxes brought over $300 each.

8. Bridget Riley's "Current" at the Museum of Modern Art's Responsive Eye exhibit was one of the more successful efforts to use optical science to create illusion.

9. George Segal's alienated figures haunted the '60's. Amidst the glare and color of op, pop and psychedelic art, their sculptured whiteness stood out in eerie contrast.

5. An individual voice . . .

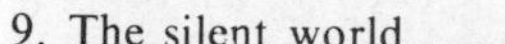

6. "Art is what happens . . .

7. Sad court jester to the '60's . . .

8. Visual dynamics . . .

9. The silent world . . .

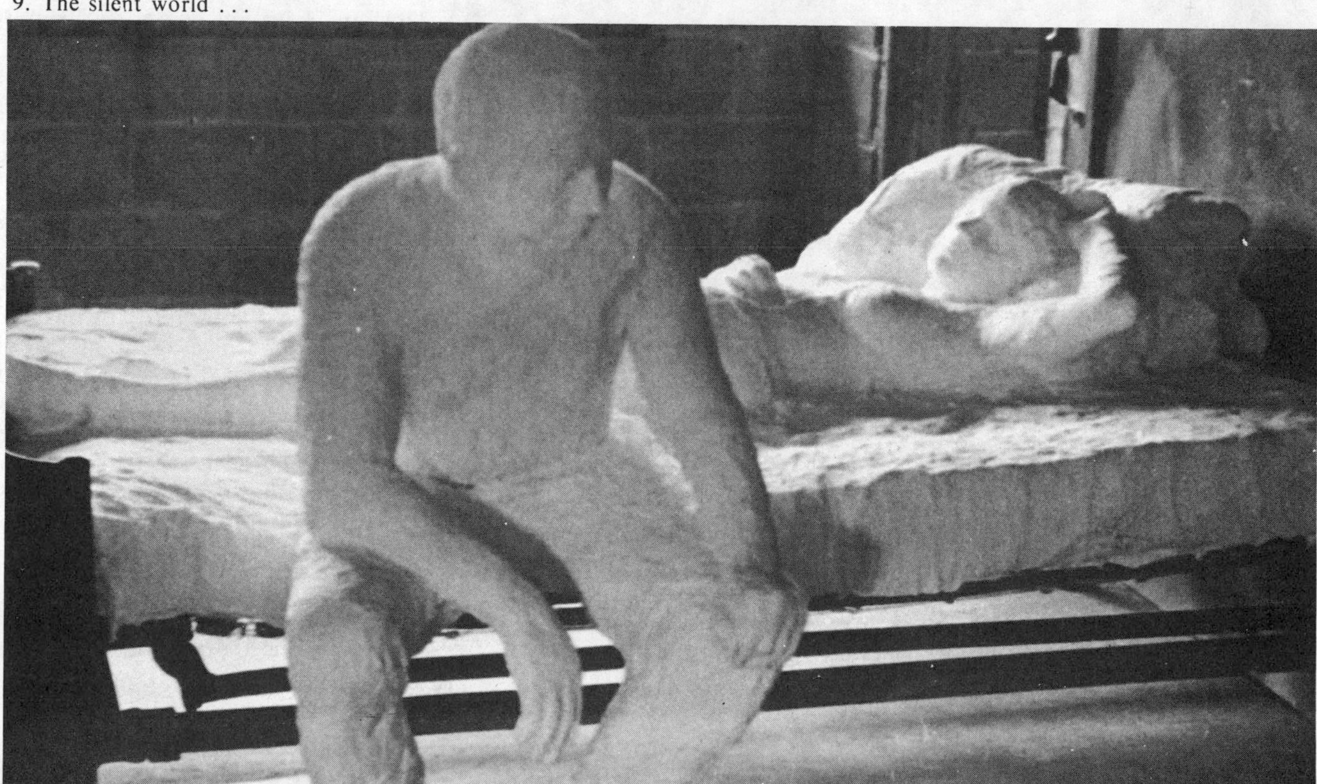

Theater: Barometer of Change

Broadway staggers along; but Off-Broadway's nudity, coarseness, and vigor reflect youth's profound discontent with the establishment

Oh! Calcutta! was first show performed by all nude actors. While winning plaudits for forms like this, it took critical buffeting for showing little else. Title is from old French saying that begins: Oh quelle. . . .

The theater refused to attend its own funeral in the last decade despite all the critics who volunteered to act as pallbearers.

Those who announced *doom* under the flies, each season of the commercial theater, had cause for alarm, however. The economics of Broadway made it increasingly tough to mount a show that might attract its own audience, and might enjoy a modest run, without entertaining instant death. But it must either be a hit — or curtains.

As usual, musicals and comedies were the great medicine for the ills of the tired business man. Financial returns from these shows, if they became hits, were enormous. But the hazards were equally sizeable and grim, as statistics showed.

The number of straight plays declined from 36 in 1961 to only 28 in 1969. The average number of musicals remained fairly constant at about 15 per season. But the flops remained fairly constant as well. In 1964-65, one half of all the entries failed. In the '65-'66 season, only one show out of three was profitable. In '66-'67, there were 12 successes, 25 flops.

Why Broadway is considered so

Hair, a "tribal folk-rock musical," bruised some audience ears with its easy flow of four-letter words while warming others with its driving rhythms and lyrical miming of the hippie life-style.

Ellen Stewart in front of the new home for the La Mama troupe was the 'mother of 'em all' in her original cafe-theatre, spawning ground for a new generation of playwrights.

risky a gamble for investors can be seen in dollars and cents terms in the failure of some typical musicals. *Kelly* in 1964 closed after one performance with a loss of $650,000. In the '66-'67 season, *A Joyful Noise* went dark after 12 performances, losing $500,000; and *Breakfast At Tiffany's* never outlasted its previews, and lost David Merrick $425,000.

The decade brought a number of first-class playwrights, notably Harold Pinter, an English import, first seen here in '61-'62 in *The Caretaker,* the native Neil Simon, master comedy craftsman of *Come Blow Your Horn, The Odd Couple, Plaza Suite,* and the inestimable Edward Albee, whose comedy-drama *Who's Afraid of Virginia Woolf* was the only hit of the '61-'62 season — probably the blackest season of the century with a total loss of $6 million dollars.

Albee's career was an example of the circuitous route sometimes taken by young playwrights before recognition and the large returns of Broadway. His one-act first plays, *The Death of Bessie Smith,* and *The Zoo Story* — turned down for U.S. production — were first seen in Berlin in 1959 before they hit the boards Off-Broadway in 1960.

As in the theater's best years — the time of the Provincetown Playhouse and Eugene O'Neill in the 20s, and the Group Theater and Federal Theater days in the 30s — so that ferment that kept the fabulous invalid more than alive was found not in the commercial theater but in the Off and Off-Off Broadway scene.

Sparks were first emitted in the 60s by Albee's *The Zoo Story* produced in tandem with Beckett's *Krapp's Last Tape.* Then in 1961, The Living Theater titillated the bourgeoisie with *The Connection,* a play about drug users. Shortly afterward, an enterprising young producer began to show the works of fledging dramatists at a Greenwich Village bistro, Cafe La Mama. It was from these environs that the new theater took wing.

Based sometimes on esoteric ideas — like Artaud's Theater of Cruelty, which underlay the sensational Peter Brook production of *Marat-Sade* (brought over from England in '66), or on ideas of audience involvement as in *Dionysus* '69 — the era of the love-in and freak-out was at hand.

Hippie musicals *Hair* and *Your Own Thing* in 1968-69 had Gothamites rocking; *Boys in the Band, Tom Paine, The Indian Wants the Bronx,* brought audiences Off-Broadway as never before.

Finally, 1969 seemed destined to *blow the mind* of conservative theater-goers as nudity hit the boards. *Sweet Eros* had a sweet young thing in the buff all evening as her psycho-swain tried to turn her on; *Che* was labeled pornographic and shut down (it returned fully clothed) because of its simulated fornication and the scrutiny, by the actors, of one another's genitals. But Kenneth Tynan's *Oh Calcutta!* proved to be the apotheosis of nudity on stage as all the performers did their thing in the highly visible altogether.

From the sweet simplicity of the decade's outstanding musicals, *Hello Dolly!* and *Fiddler on the Roof,* to the talent and hatred of Leroi Jones's *Dutchman,* as the civil rights movement gave the negro theater wings, to the ultimate confrontation of the establishment in the nose-thumbing, enlivening, nude plays, the theater entered a period of profound change.

1. Theater of cruelty . . .

2. Hello, Carol!

3. Zero makes thousands happy . . .

1. Peter Brook's production of *Marat/Sade* in 1966 was the touchstone for a decade of theatrical daring. Though rebuffed as "sensational" by some critics, it had at least the virtue of stirring up debate, and at best of the greatest display of ensemble acting in many a season.

2. Carol Channing and David Burns created the lead roles in *Hello, Dolly!,* biggest musical money-maker of the decade. In 1968, Dolly underwent a color change with PearlBailey and Cab Calloway taking over the principal parts.

3. Zero Mostel garnered kudos when he opened as Tevye in *Fiddler on the Roof* six seasons ago. The second biggest musical winner of the decade, *Fiddler* had earned almost $6,000,000 by 1970.

4. The Great White Hope, Howard Sackler's poetic drama about the rise and fall of Jack Johnson, first black heavyweight boxing champ, catapulted James Earl Jones to stardom.

5. A literate "Man For All Seasons," Robert Bolt's drama about Thomas More was raised to particular eminence by the performance of Paul Scofield.

6. Uta Hagen and Arthur Hill raised Edward Albee's *Who's Afraid of Virginia Woolf* to its proper prize-winning height. The Pulitzer Committee, however, backed away from this brilliant, though brutal, dissection of a marriage, causing a great outcry.

7.Donald Pleasance as the crotchety old vagrant, shone in Harold Pinter's brilliantly mordant drama *The Caretaker* in 1962.

8. The Boys in the Band by Mart Crowley was the first play to present the self-wounding world of homosexuals in a sympathetic light. Frederick Combs (1.) and Kenneth Nelson are seen at a moment of crisis and comfort.

4. The winnah ...

5. Here heedless; soon headless ...

6. Marriage Albee style ...

7. Pleasance pleasures as cadging codger ...

8. Inverts invoke pity ...

Financial Ills Plague Music Centers

Programming cut despite audience boom; The Beatles arrive; intellectuals ponder "Pop" as middle class finds it fashionable

Opening of a "stately pleasure-dome" on September 16, 1966, had crowd and TV cameras awaiting celebrities coming to the gala premiere of the Metropolitan Opera Company in its new Lincoln Center home.

The great culture craze that swept the country in the 60s left one obvious sign of its passing: an urban landscape dotted with dazzling glass-and-marble music palaces.

New York's Lincoln Center marked its debut with the opening of Philharmonic Hall in '62, and the Metropolitan Opera's new home bowed there in '66; Houston's Jesse Jones Hall won first plaudits in '67; Atlanta's Arts Center in '68. At the decade's close, Washington was touting its JFK Center, scheduled for a '70 opening, as a culture package guaranteed to outshine Lincoln Center in importance.

And yet, despite all the hoopla and the boom in concert going, the 60s ended on a sour note:

Early in '69, Atlanta's Memorial Arts Center shut down; Lincoln Center teetered on the verge of bankruptcy — despite record attendance, the Met's Mr. Bing was forced to cancel visits of the Stockholm and Vienna Opera Companies; and the Los Angeles Musical Center, known for being economy-minded, complained of hardening of the financial arteries.

Traditionally, such centers have relied on private philanthropies, but by '69 they found themselves getting short shrift from their usual

Visiting ballet stars Margot Fonteyn and Rudolph Nureyev, after 33 curtain calls, sit out a 35 minute ovation after their 1965 N.Y. debut in *Romeo and Juliet*.

Leonard Bernstein (1) greets Lauritz Melchior at the reception following 125th N.Y. Philharmonic anniversary concert Dec. 7, 1967. Pianist Loren Hollander looks on.

benefactors as urban problems siphoned off much of the money earmarked for them.

These problems renewed the age-old debate over government subsidy of the arts: is it a good thing or bad?

The mainstay of any center is its orchestra, and this country's symphony orchestras, despite their financial woes, won more praise in the 60s than ever before. In fact, a '63 survey found that many critics regarded only the London and the Berlin as "occasional equals" to the top five US ensembles: New York, Philadelphia, Cleveland, Boston and Chicago.

By '69 though, some listeners feared a decline as conductors began to move about in what one critic called a "game of musical chairs": Bernstein announced he'd leave New York's Philharmonic; Mehta, L.A.'s leader, tried out for Bernstein's post but flunked; Szell curtailed work at Cleveland to take a guest spot with New York; Martinon quit the Chicago; and Leinsdorf planned to leave Boston.

In the world of opera, The New York City Opera Company came into its own as choristers of the first rank, paced by the growing acclaim for Beverly Sills. Called the "greatest singing actress in the world," her '66 performance as Cleopatra, in Handel's *Julius Caesar,* followed by an incomparable *Manon* in '67 brought Sills to the summit.

The Met, on the other hand, even in its sumptuous new setting at Lincoln Center, sang along in its usual stodgy way. Occasional production highlights — Joan Sutherland's '62 debut in *Lucia di Lammermoor, Falstaff* in '64, *Luisa Miller* in '68 were marked by that grand manner in which the Met, at its best, excels. Often, however, the management was faulted for its dull repertory, poor staging and for putting third rate singers into first rate parts.

As for the dance, 1965 was the year when "balletomaniacs" nearly "blew their minds"...The cause: arrival of Rudolph Nureyev and Margot Fonteyn with Britain's Royal Ballet. End result: 33 curtain calls after *Romeo and Juliet* for this matchless duo. For consistent excellence, however, kudos went to George Balanchine whose impeccable art was embodied in the speed, grace, and sensuality of his New York City Ballet Company.

Debuts of note included that of outstanding cellist Jacqueline Du Pre. The blonde, British born performer delighted music (and other) lovers when she married the gifted young pianist Daniel Barenboim (debut in '57).

Lovers of keyboard fireworks delighted in the return — after a 12 year silence — of Vladimir Horowitz ('65), considered by many the greatest virtuoso of his time.

In "pop" music, the signal event of the decade was the arrival in '64 of the Beatles. Their music's seminal effect on "rock" and its derivatives was incalculable. By the late 60s, they had become darlings of the middle class as well as the anti-establishment young. Turning toward serious music then, their "tape collage" (using "found music," i.e. snatches of street sounds) paralleled the work of such satirists as John Cage and Stockhausen.

In the area of folk music, a wave of youthful enthusiasm early in the decade made a Mecca of the Newport Folk Festival. It also made millionaires of the more adept folk singers: Bob Dylan and Joan Baez, for example, and of such practitioners of black "soul" music as Aretha Franklin. Nonetheless, much chaff was palmed off as gold by disc jockeys and other promoters of the musical young.

1. Cellist at the capitol ...

2. Sexational song-spectacular ...

3. The boss gives pointers ...

4. Charisma on the keys ...

5. Symphony's baton goes to Boulez ...

1. Government interest in the arts was at its highest during JFK's administration. Here the President and first lady honor Pablo Casals at a White House musicale.

2. One operatic high-light of the 60s was Albert Ginastera's sexational *Bomarzo* presented by the N.Y. City Opera Co. in 1968. Salvador Novoa and Joanna Simon are the lustful Duke and lush Pentaselia.

3. Master of the dance, George Balanchine built the N.Y. City Ballet Co., over the decade, into the country's foremost dance ensemble. Here (foreground) he directs members of the company at a rehearsal.

4. Vladimir Horowitz, who is considered by many the world's top-flight keyboard virtuoso, returned to the concert stage May 9, 1965, to display his extraordinary technique after a 12 year absence.

5. Until Pierre Boulez was appointed Musical Director of the N.Y. Philharmonic in 1969, to fill the vacancy left by the resignation of Leonard Bernstein, there had been much 'catty' comment by the cognoscenti and infighting among conductors for the illustrious post.

6. Beverly Sills, here seen as Manon in the N.Y. City Opera's 1968 presentation, was acclaimed the greatest singing actress of the decade, perhaps of the last half-century.

7. An avant-garde musical happening is effected by showing Electric Circus dancer Ray Taylor in strobe lights as he hoofs to the music of the Beatles, a 1968 mind-blowing affair.

8. Folk-singer and youth idol Bob Dylan returned to the stage in 1969, mellower and with shorter hair, after a long absence due to a near-fatal motorcycle accident.

9. The Beatles, pop-music prodigies and symbols, for a whole generation of young people, of an anti-establishment life style.

6. Sills at the summit ...

7. A psychedelic wha ...?

8. Folk singer strums again ...

9. Beatlemaniacs' delight ...

Movies Remain A Major Medium

Responding to the challenge of television and foreign competition, American film-makers widen screens and broaden subject matter.

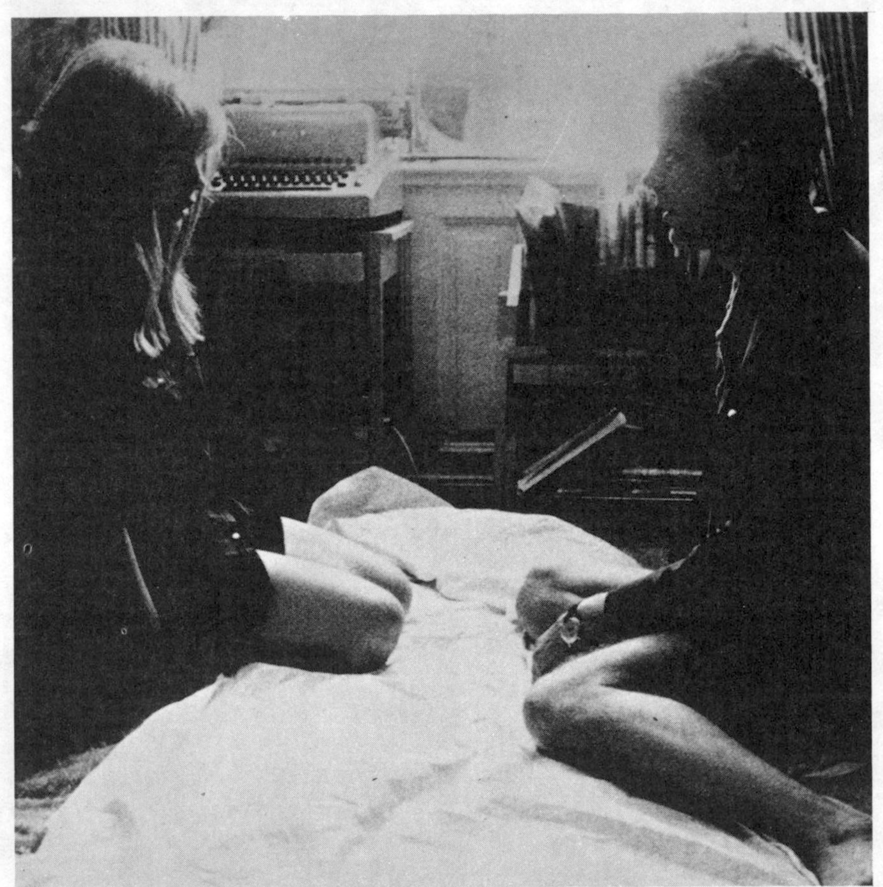

In matters erotic, the Swedish import, *"I Am Curious (Yellow)"* left nothing to the imagination. Director Vilgot Sjoman's far-left political proselytizing was virtually ignored.

Moviegoing lost its informality during the 60's. Most of the nation's neighborhood theaters became pizza parlors and dad no longer took the family to the flicks to pleasantly kill a few Friday night hours, unless dad owned an oil well, because admission prices rose to match the gaudy, big-screen kind of entertainment movies became.

The film industry first reacted to the threat of universal television with size. Theater screens elongated and grew taller, and advertising seemed designed to convince audiences that *big* equalled *good.*

All that space couldn't be filled with two people talking to each other, or even a bevy of gangsters gunning each other, so Hollywood began concentrating on spectacle, and often old-fashioned film virtues like plot and performance got lost in the familiar "cast of thousands."

"Hollywood," incidentally, became more a state of mind than a geographical location. Picture companies trekked to every corner of the globe searching for authentic backgrounds and a supply of people willing to impersonate crowds for nominal payment. Very few films were shot entirely in California

"Guess Who's Coming To Dinner?" Sidney Poitier, that's who. Hailed by liberals, some black groups found the "super Negro" doctor Poitier portrayed condescending.

Dustin Hoffman, *"The Graduate,"* is verging on rebellion while rejecting his parents' life style.

because sophisticated audiences sneered at phony stage sets, and because extras there demanded a full U.S. wage.

Ironically, the facilities of the giant film companies were usurped by television: small-screen shows were manufactured where once theater features were made. More than one film corporation survived because it was able to rent equipment to TV producers.

The modest, small-budget movies designed to occupy the bottom half of double bills were no longer shot, but their equivilant began to fill prime television time — crime melodramas, situation comedies. Like the earlier movies, TV shows served as on-the-job training for writers, actors, directors, cameramen. Thus, the film and television industries, once arch-enemies, gradually became mutual parasites to the profit of both.

Indeed, they were no longer rivals: they weren't selling the same product. Television offered "family entertainment" — froth — and the movies provided lavishness and "adult" stories.

The maturity of theme that characterized many Hollywood products — both good and bad — in the late 60's, was partially a result of the influence of foreign films. During the earlier years of the decade, educated moviegoers wearied of the perpetual diet of sentiment and mock heroics served by their local theaters, and began patronizing "art houses" — tiny theaters often located close to college campuses that screened French, Italian and Scandanavian imports.

Though the prints were frequently murky and anyone without a working knowledge of the movie's native language missed the dialogue (superimposed translations confused more than enlightened), Americans responded to the films' unconventional subject matter and technical innovations.

American directors quickly appropriated such techniques as they could use and, as censorship loosened in the mid 60s, also began dealing with topics treated by their foreign counterparts.

Eventually, foreign and domestic patrons mingled as movies became international endeavors. It became common for U.S. and foreign companies to cooperate on film projects. Actors would speak their lines in their native tongue and later, in the cutting room, their words would be transformed into the language of whichever nation would release the picture. More and more foreign works were being shown in mainstem first-run theaters.

But the intellectual community emerged hugely influential in movie-appreciation circles. Within the decade, movies became respectable, recognized as an important art form. Most colleges were sponsoring showings of "classic" films, and many were providing classes where frames of celluloid were being scrutinized as closely as Shakespearean sonnets. A few large institutions — notably UCLA and NYU — had courses in the making of movies.

During the 60's, the movies grew up. Few considered them proletariat pap, and nearly everyone in civilized countries was affected by them. At their best, they were the most powerful art ever devised. And at their worst they were exactly what turn-of-the-century critics predicted they would become — the biggest portion of sheer vulgarity ever shoved onto an unresisting citizenry.

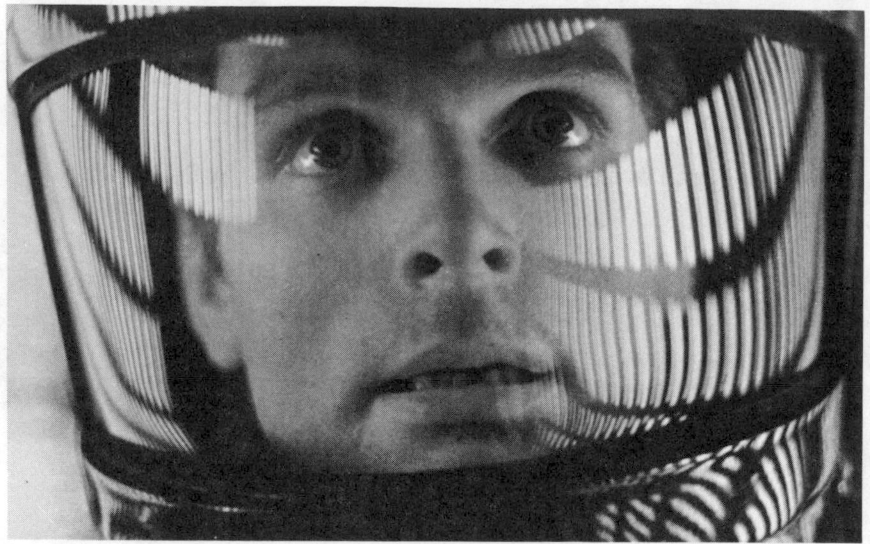

1. Far away places . . .

2. Before the flood — and cameras . . .

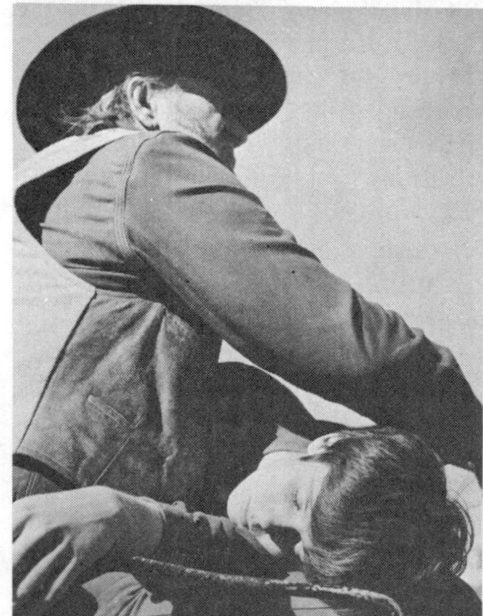

3. The Duke and friend . . .

4. Bad guys on bikes . . .

1. Stanly Kubrick's "2001 : A Space Odyssey" was visually stunning and philosophically exciting — the best cinematic monument to the dawning space age.

2. "The Bible . . . In The Beginning" retold the story of Genesis. Despite an enormous budget, director John Huston's film was another ho-hum Hollywoodization.

3. After a career of more than 30 years, John Wayne was finally hailed as an actor for his work in "True Grit."

4. A series of low-budget films portraying the doings of motorcycle gangs mythologized hoods and garnered box-office cash.

5. Paul Newman emerged as a star who could also act. One of his finest roles was "Cool Hand Luke," an uncompromising movie about a southern prison.

6. Clint Eastwood found super-star-status in Italian-made, very bloody, westerns.

7. Clark Gable's last film was "The Misfits," opposite the doomed Marilyn Monroe.

8. "Dr. Strangelove," the blackest of black comedies, satirized the cold war and made the prospect of world-wide atomic annihilation gruesomely funny.

9. "I, A Woman" was the harbinger of a series of sexy — and successful — foreign films.

10. "Help" helped millions of non-rock fans understand the appeal of Britain's Beatles.

11. Dust-bowl derring-do, fine acting and sharp direction characterized "Bonnie and Clyde."

5. An egg-straordinary performance ...

6. Mediterranean gun-slinging ...

7. Gable's valedictory ...

8. Humorous H-bombs ...

9. A Swedish pout ...

10. The lads from Liverpool ...

11. Beautiful gangsters ...

Few Oases in TV Wasteland

Video wins high marks for on-the-spot news and educational programs; irreverent humor makes Laugh-In the "in" show, knocks Smothers Brothers out

Rowan and Martin, *Laugh-In's* stars, found a format that especially suited the medium. Filmed bits of comic business were cut up and inserted throughout the show to lend it a freshness, rare in a decade of stale comedies.

Chroniclers of TV history will remember the 60's as the decade when former F.C.C. Chairman Newton Minow blasted the TV scene in '61 as a "vast wasteland."

By mid '69 even friendly critics admitted that real nuggets were hard to find in all the fool's gold of video-land.

The few developments, they noted at a Public Broadcasting symposium, were mainly in educational TV — which staggered along each year on a cruelly inadequate budget — and in the medium's capacity for on-the-spot news.

Video's unique ability — to show an event happening *now* was early seen at its best during the '63 coverage of John F. Kennedy's funeral.

Subsequently, the Martin Luther King and Robert Kennedy rites, and the Apollo moon shots — confirmed the medium's power.

Commentators in print noted with approval the "shared experience" provided by the camera, and the "national catharsis." The praise was not wholly without blemish, however, as some spied a "serious danger in selective camera viewing" and opined that the "camera might mold public opinion."

1962 Nixon-Kennedy TV debates, say many news analysts, were instrumental in bringing JFK to the White House.

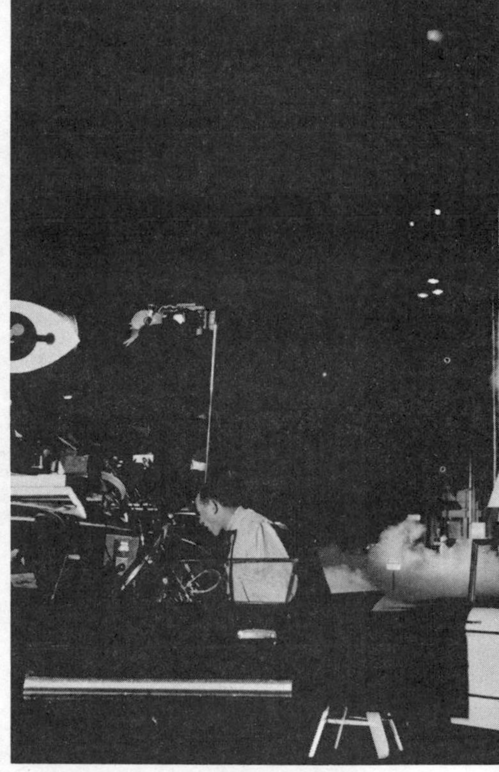

TV's talents showed during coverage of such dramatic news events as this early orbital space shot in 1962.

For example, during the 1968 Democratic Party Convention in Chicago, Mayor Daley's partisans denounced the scenes of police brutality as distortions of the news. They claimed that if, as cameramen admitted, the TV cameras go "where the action is," the news is being manipulated.

More serious complaints were to follow.

In early 1969, a documentary purporting to show *pot*-smoking delinquents was, in fact, staged by a major network. And later that year the license renewal of WPIX was held up when it was alleged that '69 Czechoslovakian riot scenes were actually stock film footage of the Hungarian uprising years earlier.

These charges gave leverage to TV's gadflies in their perennial tilt with the networks over the insipid quality of overall programming.

In the 61-62 season, out of 73½ hours of weekly prime time, 30½ were filled with westerns, private-eye and action-adventure series.

Through most of the decade, the percentages remained much the same; only the types of shows changed to suit changing popular tastes.

Two *shamus* shows, for instance, 77 *Sunset Strip* and *Hawaiian Eye* (62), gave way to James Bond mimicry with the *Man From UNCLE* (65) and *Mission Impossible* (67). Then as the hippy scene grooved into view, up popped those coppers' little helpers, *Mod Squad* (69).

Proving that imitation is the sincerest form of flattery, the top rated *Beverly Hillbillies* (62), king of the jes folks shows, spawned *Petticoat Junction* (63), and of the dumb-family-head-but-what-a-smart- man shows, *Hazel* (62), a winner with Shirley Booth, bred simpering *Grindl* (63), a loser with Imogene Coca.

Taste to the contrary notwithstanding, the ratings told it like it was, as did the TV moguls: "this is what the people want."

For a while it seemed that reliance on ratings would be discredited as Congress took a hard look at the rating system in 1963. But by 1969, Congress had long succumbed to lobbying pressure from broadcasters, and Newton Minow was six years gone from the video scene. Ratings stood as tall in the saddle as ever.

The first adult entertainment series to break through the encrusted formulas of the 60's was *That Was The Week That Was* (64). Though it lasted only two seasons as censors blue-penciled it out of existence, TW3 trailblazed the way for *The Smothers Brothers* (67) and for *Rowan and Martin's Laugh-In* (68), the brightest spot on the video horizon in many years.

But by '69, TV proved to be as timid as ever. Controversy was still verboten. And since politics is, if anything, controversial, when the Smothers Brothers liberal sting goaded the CBS ox once too often, the show was dropped in early '69.

Radio throughout the decade was not any better in the area of public service. Except for increased revenue from advertisers — which thwarted the forecast of a lingering death by television — it remained largely what Minow had called it in '61, "a bazaar of pitchmen and commercials which plead, bleat, pressure and shout."

Goaded beyond patience, vocal opponents of commercial TV's inadequate programming took a radical step in June '69.

The National Citizens Committee for Public Broadcasting planned to picket the major networks when the September season began. Crisis may be coming to video-land.

1. Camera eye on rights marchers . . .

2. Modern day musketeers . . .

3. Cute 'n' rich, but jes' folks . . .

4. Naow I'd like tew bring yew . . .

1. Coverage of the 1964 march on Washington proved that television had no peer in bringing the immediacy and excitement of events to the viewing public.

2. The popular "Man From UNCLE" was inspired by the James Bond craze and its use of way-out hardware. Here, actors Robert Vaughn (L) and David McCallum (R) prepare to zap their enemies.

3. America's dream of "shucks, us folks can be millionaires too" took on aspects of a self-parody in the *Beverly Hillbillies.* It zinged its way to the hearts of millions as the number one show for several seasons.

4. Ed Sullivan spotted the trend before Beatle-mania swept the country. He brought the mop-haired Liverpudlians to the U.S. for their first guest appearance on his show in 1964.

5. TV coverage of the Vietnam war, though superficial at best, caught the bewilderment of many young G.I.s about the home front conflict over an unpopular war.

6. Talent and experimentation on Channel 13 enlivened many a dull season. Here, James Coco, in Terrence McNally's play *Next,* suffers indignity after indignity — an Everyman trapped in an army induction nightmare.

7. The famous first emblem of National Education Television, whose hoot delighted many as it went from "who-o-o" to "he-e-elp" in its cry for funds from viewers.

8. The most outspoken FCC chairman of the decade, Newton Minow, will be remembered for coining the phrase that described TV programming as a "vast wasteland."

9. Running afoul of network censors for their controversial, and liberal opinions, the Smothers Brothers' show was cancelled for 1969 after two seasons of popular success.

10. TV's gingerly approach to integration is exemplified by Julia, starring Diahann Carroll, shown here with Lloyd Nolan. Its distance from life is revealed in a soap opera plot and the choice of star, one of the best-looking women around, black or white.

5. Eye on Vietnam . . .

6. . . . take off everything?

7. Whooo? Check channel 13 and see

8. Overseer of the boob tube . . .

9. Tom, Dick, and Inger . . .

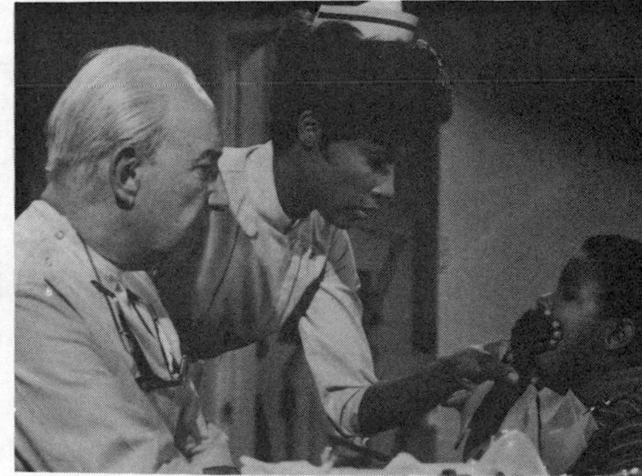

10. No 'soul food' served here . . .

Social Issues Hit Madison Avenue

Cigarette ads under attack but industry volume soars as agencies go public and new talent reshapes image

Dubbed Yellow Submarine Art, a new visual style hit the ad world. Flat, two-dimensional, with swirling lines and hot colors, it aimed right at the youth market.

Madison Avenue experienced both profits and problems on a big scale during the past decade.

Budgets soared, but so did criticism of the advertising industry's lagging acceptance of social responsibilities. In the background, the threat of government controls loomed large.

Precipitating the hottest controversy was the January, 1964, report by the U.S. Surgeon-General Luther Terry, linking cigarettes and illness. The health issue was not new, but the report raised the possibility of government regulation of all cigarette promotion, which at the time amounted to some $250 million annually.

Response within the industry was mixed. In 1965, Doyle Dane Bernbach and Ogilvy Benson and Mather announced they would no longer handle cigarette advertising and Emerson Foote resigned as Chairman of McCann-Erickson rather than have anything to do with the sale of cigarettes.

Other agencies went after the business, however, and by 1969 cigarette advertising had risen to $300 million. That same year efforts by the FTC to enforce drastic health warnings on cigarette packages were vetoed by the U.S. House of Representatives.

Lyndon Johnson said this Doyle Dane Bernbach ad gave important support to his Rat Extermination Bill.

He might as well. Because the polluted air in Philadelphia has about the same effect on him as smoking 8 cigarettes a day.

What causes the high pollution? Much of it is due to industries and large apartments. All burning high-sulfur fuel. This creates tiny drops of sulfuric acid that enter the air. They're highly corrosive—irritating to eyes, throat and lungs.

That's why government officials urge a ban on high-sulfur fuels. And recommend Natural Gas. It contains no sulfur and is a non-pollutant.

PGW is doing its share to help. We've encouraged the use of gas by cutting rates for heavy users.

What can you do? Support proposals and legislation to restrict any activities that pollute our air.

Our babies need clean air to breathe. So do we.

PHILADELPHIA GAS WORKS

DOES YOUR BABY SMOKE?

The twin villains smoking and pollution were hit in Philadelphia Gas Works ad, one of many on social issues.

To keep the ghetto cool, the American Association of Ad Agencies created a campaign aimed at affluent America.

Most likely action for the early 70's appeared to be an FCC ban on TV cigarette commercials.

Other problems plagued the industry and tarnished its image.

In 1962, the FTC held Colgate-Palmolive Co. and its agency, Ted Bates, guilty of deceptive advertising when they substituted materials in a TV commercial. The Supreme Court agreed and in 1965 ruled that advertisers may not willfully deceive the public when presenting an ad.

More regulations were imposed in May, 1967, when the Food and Drug Administration prohibited any claim for prescription drugs that could not be substantiated by evidence. And in July, 1968, New York became the first city in the U.S. with a "truth in advertising" law.

Censorship became an issue when TV commentator Howard K. Smith interviewed convicted perjurer Alger Hiss in 1963. Eversharp and Kemper Insurance — neither connected with the show — asked ABC to cancel their sponsorship of several other of the network's programs. In the wake of the assassination of Senator Robert Kennedy, renewed impetus was given to the cry against violence on TV.

Perhaps even more troubling to the ad agencies was the evidence produced by a House Commerce Committee Investigation in 1963 that the TV and radio audience reports, on which advertisers based their decision to pay up to $40,000 for a minute of prime TV network time, were warped, with dogs and babies included as "viewers" in some of the counts.

Racial tension also threatened the agencies, several of which admitted in May, 1968, that they had been using far too few Negroes on TV spots. Of the 7,432 commercials produced in the year ending August 31, 1967, only 314 used Negroes and Puerto Ricans.

Continuing criticism and controversy did little to alienate the advertisers, who upped their spending from $11 billion annually in 1960 to $17 billion in 1967. Network TV accounted for $1.26 billion of that figure and spot TV for $820 million.

The lion's share went to the giants of the industry. The 102-year old J. Walter Thompson Company and Interpublic, Inc. both billed close to $380 million in 1962. By 1967, JWT had raised its volume to $580 million, but Interpublic, with billings of $711 million, ended the year $9 million in debt and with a $3 million deficit.

Despite the prominence accorded TV and the demise of the *Saturday Evening Post* in 1969, a surprising amount of the big spending went to magazines. The *Ladies Home Journal* had 1967 ad revenues of $35 million, *Good Housekeeping*, $36.5 million, and *McCalls*, with a top circulation of 8.5 million, had ad revenues of $43.5 million. On the male side, *Playboy* closed 1967 with an ad revenue of $20.4 million.

The biggest operational change along Madison Avenue was heralded in 1962 when a small new agency, Papert Koenig Lois, Inc., took the revolutionary step of making a public offering of its stock.

Major agencies Foote Cone & Belding and Doyle Dane Bernbach followed in 1963 and 1964.

Account switching continued unabated (as many as 247 in a year). Benefitting were aggressive new agencies like Wells Rich Greene whose billings in 1967 totaled $70 million.

The newcomers and mavericks turned to humor, mixed media, and the psychedelic underground for ideas and new ways to get and hold the consumers' attention in the affluent, permissive society. Whether or not their off-beat approach would succeed in building sales remains for the 70's to decide.

1. Two in one . . .

2. It could happen to you . . .

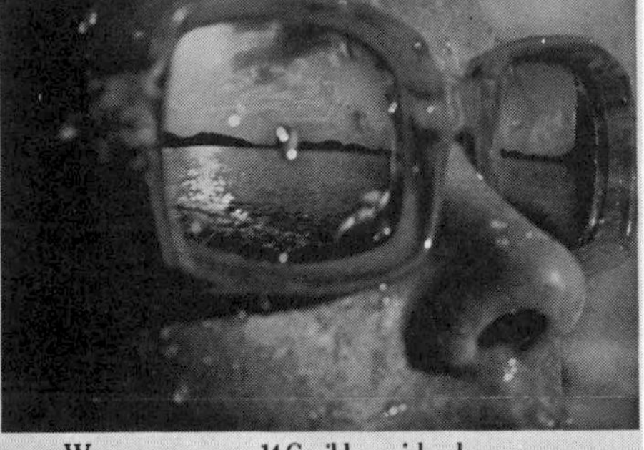

3. Reflections in a consumer's eye . . .

If you get a bad meal on a plane you can't walk out.

Northeast Yellowbirds to Florida. You'll wish we flew everywhere

4. Bucking the trend . . .

5. Making the best of it . . .

1. Jack Tinker and Partners dovetailed tourism and tummy-ache in this double-play ANDY-winning poster.

2. On this subway poster, minimal copy and strong visual identification delivered a subtly effective sales pitch for School of Visual Arts.

3. Through glasses colored by J. Walter Thompson, viewers got a personalized but glamorous view of what Pan Am had to offer.

4. Carl Ally's award-winning newspaper ad for Northeast Airlines ran counter to the trend of striking visuals and tight copy, instead gambled on reader's interest in the basic message.

5. Poster series by Batten, Barton, Durstine and Osborn made light of the unwieldly weight of *The New York Times* and stressed something-for-everyone theme.

6. Political ad campaigns showed few innovations. One of the better newspaper ads was Doyle Dane Bernbach's series which won an ANDY award — but not the election for Senator Eugene McCarthy.

7. In Volkswagen ads Doyle Dane Bernbach combined whimsy with fact. Its kidding approach won high readership for a hard-hitting message.

8. Edward H. Weiss & Co. used "vanishing American" on dollar bill segment as sure-fire attention getter for GATX.

9. The Economic Development Council of New York didn't mean it when they suggested Central Park be turned into a parking lot . . . but the scary visual of what might happen served to dramatize the Council's theme of involvement in the city and its problems.

10. In 1967 Wells, Rich, Greene's TV commercial for Benson & Hedges won kudos along Madison Avenue but two years later practically all cigarette advertising was vanishing from the air.

11. Young & Rubicam, capitalizing on the publicized benefit of a switch away from cigarettes, indulged in hyperbole in suggesting that ladies would have to wait in line to smoke cigars.

12. Jamaica: more than a fun stopover, was visual theme of consumer magazine ads by Doyle Dane Bernbach for Jamaica Tourist Board.

13. Campbell-Ewald/New York won attention for *Forbes,* the financial magazine, by portraying today's youthful rebel as tomorrow's establishment leader.

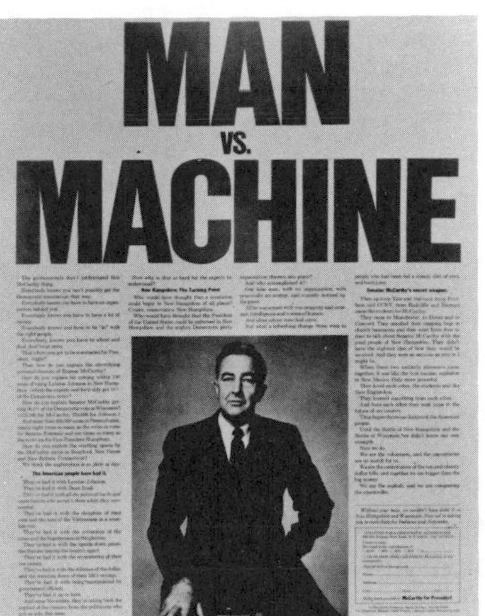

6. The format was familiar . . .

7. Big campaign for small car . . .

8. Visual message . . .

9. Funny — and frightening . . .

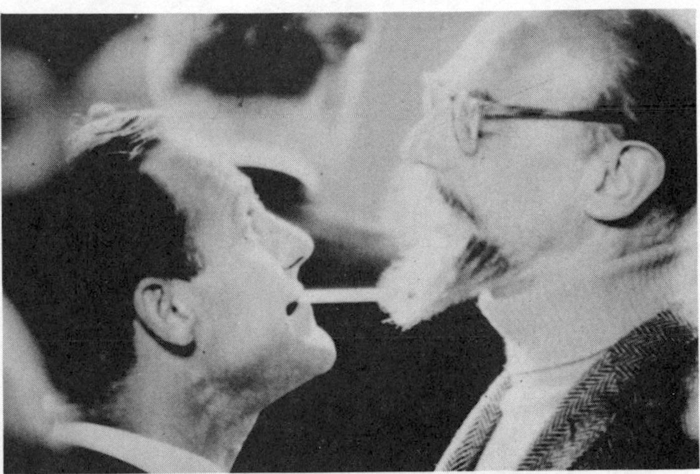

10. Vanishing smoke . . .

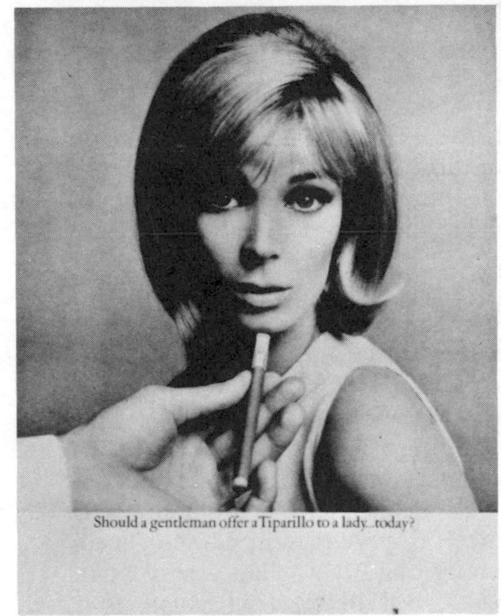

11. Equal rights for women . . .

JAMAICA

12. Focus on a culture . . .

13. Chairman of the Board . . .

From Up Tight To Do Your Own Thing

Fashion is democratized, the young take over and anything goes — from micro-minis to maxi skirts, with plenty of pants

For the first time in history, hemlines rose a handspan above the knees in the mid-1960's — and stayed there. Young people started it, mothers followed.

A decade ago, Paris was securely ensconced at the head of the world of fashion as it had been for centuries. Balenciaga, Givenchy, Dior, Chanel and a few lesser lights called the shots, set the shapes and established the hemlines worn round the world.

Jacqueline Kennedy was the first lady of fashion and despite her appointment of Oleg Cassini as official dressmaker she followed the Paris mode — and everybody else followed her.

By the end of the decade, the Paris couture was gasping for breath. Ready-to-wear clothes had taken over. Fashion was being set in London, Scandinavia and the streets of New York. Custom-made couture clothes had become too staid, too safe. Even the woman who could afford them did not care to wait around for fittings.

Balenciaga had gone out of business, the Chanel suit was as passé as the bustle and Oleg Cassini was better known for his men's clothes than his women's designs.

So were a lot of other women's designers who had moved into the men's field. Pierre Cardin in Paris and Hardy Amies in London were among the first. Then came John Weitz, Bill Blass, Jean Louis, Luis Estevez and Geoffrey Beene in the

Margie Lindsay, daughter of N.Y. City's mayor, modelled a fur coat and boots at fashion show, left in uniform of the young: pants, military shirt.

Paris tried to keep its place in the sun with fashions like St. Laurent's see-through gown.

Men edged into the fashion game with way-out outfits like chain vest, sheer shirt.

United States.

They were replacing the dull, drab sack suit that men had worn for years with bright colors, more shapelines, more daring accessories. Men's wear had become the new frontier in fashion. Even conservative men were daring to be noticed.

Meanwhile, a kind of joyous anarchy was taking place in the women's arena. The rule-book was being thrown away, along with bras, girdles, garters, white gloves and any kind of restrictive dressing.

Hemlines varied from microminis to ankle lengths. Slithery, clinging fabrics were the rule and nobody worried about her slip showing. Hardly anyone was wearing one.

After all, a slip wasn't necessary with pants — and everybody was wearing those. Towards the end of the decade, even the better restaurants weren't insisting their customers wear a skirt and it was possible to go to a formal party and find almost as many women wearing pants as men were.

It all started around 1963 when André Courrèges, a former Balenciaga disciple, opened his own salon in Paris with a space age look. His white shift stopped a few inches above the knees, was worn with calf-high white boots and a motorcycle type helmet. It set off an explosion that was felt around the world.

Influential designers here like Jacques Tiffeau and Rudi Gernreich were quick to follow the upward march of hemlines. By the mid-1960's, skirts were shorter than they ever were in the 1920's, the previous high point in recorded fashion.

The most influential designers were not those making expensive made to order clothes or even expensive ready to wear. The fulcrum had shifted to Seventh Avenue where Stanley Herman of Mr. Mort, Anne Klein and Victor Joris of Cuddlecoat, the Coty Award winners for 1969, were letting their hemlines fall where they may, and making clothes priced within the reach of the masses.

Sign of the times were the names inscribed on the scarves that women draped around their heads in place of hats or tied around their necks. The names were no longer those of the Paris couturiers. Seventh Avenue mass-produced designers were well represented.

The young were setting the pace, and nobody was dictating to them. They wore their hair long and straight and their elders followed as best they could. The status hairdo at the end of the 1960's was a kind of pony tail or George Washington, tied with a bit of wool or a status scarf.

Make-up was natural, except for the eyes, which were fringed in false lashes day or night. Rings on all the fingers, doubling up sometimes, and clock-size wrist watches were the prominent jewels, along with love-beads or early-Greenwich Village medallions slung on thongs or chains.

Dressing tended to be in layers, involving such parts as shirts, T-shirts, vests, tunics, skirts and pants. Cable knit sweaters could go down to the floor and glittery fabrics worn during the day. Jumpsuits were turning up for both men and women and boys and girls had a tendency to dress alike. They went shopping together in the same place and often bought the same things.

By the end of the decade nobody was shocked by the see-through dresses and blouses some designers were showing. In 1964, Rudi Gernreich had startled the world with his topless bathing suit. But nudity no longer had the capacity to startle. It was prevalent in the theater. How far it would go off-stage was anybody's guess. The old guidelines had disappeared.

1. When the wind blows . . .

2. For country living . . .

3. Chanel, anyone?

1. By the end of the decade, designers had grown restless with short hems and began producing floor-sweeping coats, this one by Valentino.

2. Pants turned up everywhere. Pierre Cardin gave his pizazz with the addition of a fringed tunic.

3. Baby Jane Holzer wore Chanel coat, a fashionable uniform of the mid-60's.

4. Asymmetric line of Vidal Sassoon haircut decorated sleek young heads in the 60's. A $60,000 diamond rises out of Cardin's sculpted silver necklace designed as a built-in halter for long crepe evening gown.

5. Courrèges's cool, spare, knee-baring shifts were startling when they first appeared in the early 1960's. A few years later, they had become classics.

6. Eyeglass frames — sunglasses too — became part of the craze for accessories.

7. Pierre Cardin buttons actor Laurence Harvey into a long-haired fur jacket designed for film "A Dandy in Aspic."

8. Yves St. Laurent, Paris couturier, chats with his fan, Lauren Bacall and her daughter, Leslie Bogart.

9. André Courrèges, innovator of the mini-skirt, jokes with his Paris associate, Coquelin.

10. Giant necklaces, bold earrings and bracelets decorated simple clothes.

11. Jewelry wasn't limited to necks or wrists — it sprawled all over body.

12. Discs and circles were strung along waistlines or as shown here as a necklace.

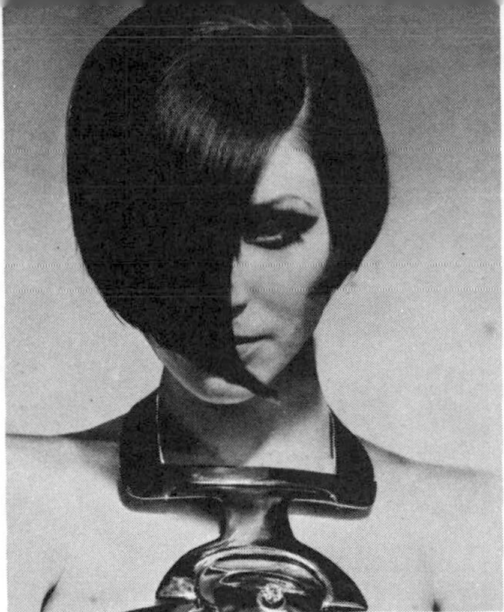

4. Now you see me . . .

6. Eyeglasses for beauty . . .

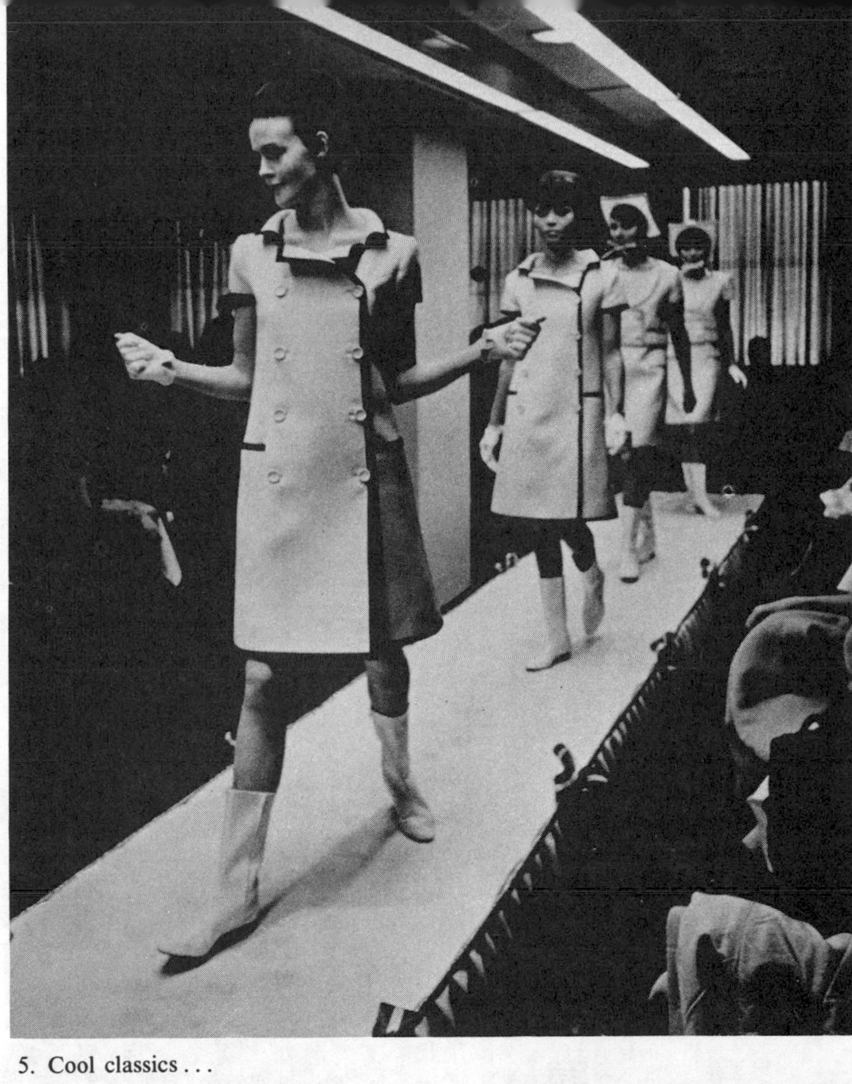

5. Cool classics . . .

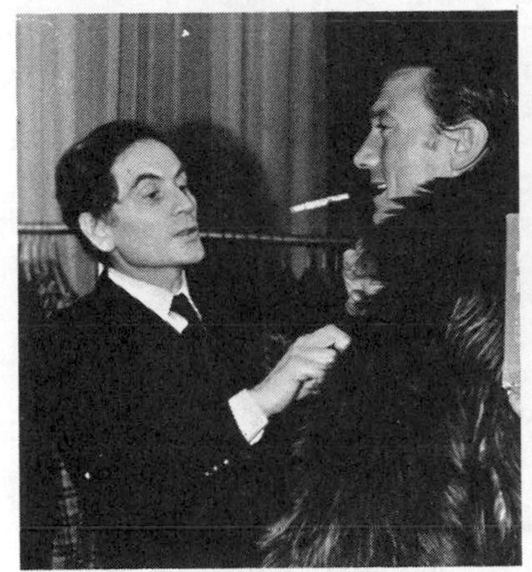

7. Man or beast?

8. Laurels to St. Laurent . . .

9. The "mini" king . . .

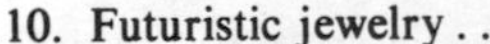

10. Futuristic jewelry . . .

11. Glittery vest . . .

12. Switchabout . . .

Jets and Affluence Spur 60's Travel

The world shrinks as jets bring personal meccas closer; London-Paris-Rome circuit favored; Europe's '67 troubles halt boom

Travel was largely a pastime for the rich until the 1960's when the jet air age and low group fares brought mass travel to the multitude.

White collar affluence was one contributor to the travel upsurge. Another, and more immediate, cause was the advent of the jet air liner. Suddenly it was easier to get there, *there:* the mecca hitherto only dreamed of by American stay-at-homes.

The sight-seeing boom of the 60's actually began in January, 1959, when Pan American inaugurated commercial all-jet passenger service with the first Boeing 707s. Suddenly two week vacationers found that Europe was within reach, that they could reach London in 6 hours, Paris in 7, Istanbul in 12. Travel clubs sprang up across the country, group tours at reduced rates multiplied, and charter flights abounded.

The profound change in America's vacation habits was reflected in the sharp annual rise in the number of U.S. travellers abroad.

In 1960, when jet travel was in its infancy, only 861,000 U.S. birds of passage visited Europe; by 1966, when jets were almost commonplace, the travel wave crested and the number of travelers soared above the 3 million mark.

By then Washington had begun

Visitors to Stratford-on-Avon soared to 2 million mark in '64 on the bard's 400th birthday. Classroom (c) is where Shakespeare learned his "small Latin."

Corsica, little known until 1966, then became one of Europe's "in" spots. This French island province has 600 miles of coastline, and mountains rising to 8,500 feet.

to seriously worry about the effect dollars spent abroad by American tourists would have on the U.S. balance of payments. Although a "See America" campaign had been launched in '62 in a double-pronged attempt to cut spending abroad and to promote home country touring, it wasn't until the peak travel year of '65-'66, when American travellers spent $3.8 billion overseas compared to the $1.2 billion dropped here by foreign visitors, that the first really tough Presidential program to clamp down on tourist spending abroad was sent to Capitol Hill.

Congress wouldn't act upon the program, though, since the chief restraint suggested by LBJ — limiting the amount of duty free goods brought home from $100 to $10 — would not have affected the really big spenders, anyway.

It took European political unrest, student riots, and a Mid-East war to keep Americans down on the farm in '67.

Until that year of troubles, the London-Paris-Rome circuit was the odds-on favorite of travellers.

The spill-over of tourists who were frightened away from Europe and the Mid-East benefitted the North, Central and South American archipelagos. Never had so many Americans gone on forest rambles, or gone geyser and grizzly watching before.

The U.S. National Park Service counted 150 million visitors to their preserves by late summer of 1968 — an increase of 10 million over 1967.

Caribbean cruise ships found favor and new ports of call opened, adding to Puerto Rico, the Virgin and West Indian Islands, such exotic new names as Aruba, Guadeloupe, Surinam, and Grenada, all competing for the Yankee dollar.

During the decade, jet-setters and jaded others in search of new lands were the fashion trend-setters of "in" spots each year.

Thus in 1960, the Greek Isles — long a favorite of avant-garde travellers — were spot-lighted as jets brought them closer; in '62, the Spanish and Portuguese beaches (and the countries' low cost of living) were popular; Africa was stage front in '63; the Japan-held Olympics of '64 attracted visitors to the Far East — with Hong Kong an ever-growing crowd pleaser. These vacationlands were followed in popularity during '65 and '66 by scenic (and bandit-ridden) areas of Corsica and Sardinia, while Tunis and other parts of North Africa saw a mini-boom of tourism by the decade's end.

Although the tourist upsurge had slowed in '67, its economic and inter-cultural values were recognized by the U.N. which declared 1967 the first "International Tourist Year."

By the end of the 60's, one trend had emerged as an institution: jet air travel. It had knocked the bottom out of luxury ships as vehicles for mass transportation. The Queen Mary was sold to Long Beach, California, for $3,450,000; the Queen Elizabeth went to Florida. Though replacements were built, such as the Queen Elizabeth II, launched in '69, the spare look about them when contrasted to the late grand dames of the sea revealed a ship clearly aimed at the new mass tourist market. With the 747 jumbo jets poised for the 70's, and the supersonics in the wings, it was obvious that the last gracious and easy means of travel would soon be as extinct as other amenities of the onrushing space age.

When the great tunnel-cut Wawona Redwood tree in Yosemite was found to have been downed by spring rains in '69, it marked the end of an era. Unless you count a wag in a tourist office, selling a return trip to Italy: "See Venice," he said, "it's sinking."

1. Colorado River canyon...

2. Mexican fauna...

1. Glen Canyon, part of man-made Lake Powell, is only one of the awesome cliff-sided waterways of the giant water-storage site between Utah and Arizona. "See America" tourists and boaters found much to beguile them here in the late 60's.

2. Mexican nightlife performers took the American tourists to their bosoms during the '68 influx of visitors to the site of the Olympics. Here is a favorite view of fauna in an Acapulco hotel.

3. This Indian girl is framed within the colossal wall of Peru's fabled lost city of Machu Picchu. Double the number of tourists sought this and other sights south of the border due to Europe's troubles in '68.

4. The 2000 year-old Wawona tree, a giant Sequoia, was a major attraction in Yosemite National Park during the great westward trek of tourists in '68. Spring rains and disease felled the giant in 1969.

5. New York's World's Fair recorded a half million visitors for its two-season run. Here is an aerial view of the Unisphere and fountains on the Fair's last day, October 17, 1965.

6. Bulgaria's miles of unparalleled beaches at its Black Sea "Golden Sands" resort became better known to the West in 1965 as iron curtain countries began plumping for the tourist dollar.

7. Stopping of the American side of Niagara Falls brought gasps to tourists with honeymoon memories in 1969 as engineers diverted the flow to the Canadian Falls. Their plan is to reinforce the underlying escarpment.

3. Peru's fabled lost city...

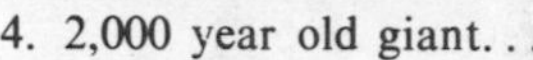

4. 2,000 year old giant...

5. New York World's Fair...

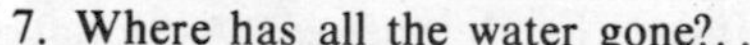

7. Where has all the water gone?...

6. Iron Curtain resort...

Transportation: Decade of Crisis

Overcrowded skies, roads, faltering commuter railroads reach crisis stage; pollution, safety problems hit Detroit

Ralph Nader won fame in 1966 as a critic of the auto industry's unconcern with safety. His testimony before Senate subcommittee that General Motors was having him "investigated" caused a furore, elicited an apology from GM.

First Secretary of Transportation, Alan S. Boyd, warned the U.S. Chamber of Commerce against expecting immediate changes. His prophecy held true except for a slight upgrading, via the "Metroliner," of Eastern rail transit.

"From mass transportation to a transportation mess," might read the short and woeful chronicle of an average commuter in the 1960s.

As aircraft grew in sophistication, number, and size through the 60's, there were increasing bottlenecks and breakdowns on the ground. Airports had become too small, they had inadequate radar systems for instrument landings, there were personnel problems as air traffic controllers were overworked and underpaid.

Similarly, anomalies and contrasts developed in ground travel. Take railroads.

After years of neglect, public outcry forced lines serving the Eastern seaboard to better their passenger service by installing high-speed trains. What happened? Antiquated road beds forced these trains to travel at considerably less than their optimum speed.

It was a time, too, of a sea change: a decade that marked the death of luxury tripping by water (Cunard, for example, sold its two *Queens, Elizabeth* and *Mary*, replacing only one; American Export retired the *Constitution* and the *Independence*, replacing neither) while it witnessed the birth of a new over-water vehicle, the Hovercraft.

And, of course, man did travel to

Chevrolet's Corvair, earlier winner, was dropped in '69.

Ford's Mustang copped sportster market, caused Corvair's demise.

Volkswagen enjoyed lion's share of import sales.

Ford's 1969 Maverick vied for "sub-compact" market.

Chevrolet's Nova sales showed smaller car trend.

Studebaker's Avanti failed to attract buyers despite racy lines.

Pontiac's Grand Prix was good '69 sample of racy, conservative blend that proved a style favorite.

the moon and back, bringing hundreds of requests to airlines for passage on the first commercial moon flight.

The 60's revolution in air transport began actually in January, 1959, when Pan Am inaugurated all-jet passenger service with the first Boeing 707s.

Other major carriers quickly followed suit. However, the enormous cash outlay needed to build up a jet fleet brought a typical cash-profit squeeze.

In 1960, Capital was taken over by United; in '62, a merger between Continental and United fell through at the last minute due to an executive squabble; American and Eastern wooed each other but the C.A.B. refused to sanction the match. By '66, however, the peak travel year of the decade, the jets had paid for themselves.

Now interest centered on air traffic problems as stacked aircraft created a skyful of hazard. By 1968, a 2-1/2 hour wait in a holding pattern was not uncommon.

Since most metropolitan areas resisted putting jetports anywhere near their populous centers, the development of a new kind of aircraft shot ahead. The V/STOL (vertical, or short take off and landing craft) came into being as one answer to the problem. At the same time that noisier jets and jetports were decried and noise abatement was spurred, the SST (supersonic transport) race went on — with, of course, promise of a shock wave (sonic boom) of devastating consequences. Here both the Russian, and the British-French joint venture stole a march on the U.S. with mach 2 SSTs up and flying by '69. Boeing's mach 3 variable-wing plan had to be redesigned because of weight-cost problems.

Meanwhile, by mid-decade, a revolution afloat was taking place. Merchant shipping via containerized transports promised to change the nature of sea freighting despite strong union protest. And ocean-going tankers hit the 300,000 ton deadweight class with the *Universe Ireland* in '68.

The automobile industry weathered several slumps during the decade, the '60-'61 low and the '66 recession, with one fatality, the death of Studebaker-Packard as a U.S. producer (moving to Canada), and one chronic invalid, American Motors.

Although Detroit consistently pushed its large, splashy moneymakers, the incursion into the U.S. market of small foreign cars, especially the Volkswagen, did not go unnoticed. To satisfy native tastes, however, small was wed to sporty. The result, early in the decade, was the Corvair, out of Chevrolet, and thereby hangs a tale. Although G.M. dropped the model in 1969 because sales went from a peak 304,000 in '62 to 15,000 in '68, as it was outsold by Ford's classier-looking Mustang, it succumbed as much to Ralph Nader's onslaught.

In 1965, using the Corvair as the focal point of his book "Unsafe at Any Speed," and as focus of his testimony before a Senate subcommittee, Ralph Nader made automobile safety a matter of public and industry concern. From then on, seat belts, head supports, collapsable steering columns, and padded dash boards grew common, some mandated by law, others developed optionally by an industry wary of its tarnished image.

Washington's awareness of the magnitude of the problem was expressed in 1967 with the creation of a cabinet-rank Department of Transportation.

But as 1970 rolled around with most of the national budget still aimed at defense and Vietnam, the moveable sidewalks and battery-operated automated computer-run cars of the future still seemed a long way off.

1. Twice faster than sound ...

2. The Flying whale ...

3. It rests on air ...

4. Could set track record but ...

1. The British-French SST (supersonic transport) Concorde is shown here lifting off from an airport in Toulouse, France, on its maiden flight, March 2, 1969.

2. Boeing's 747, Jumbo-jet, undergoing taxi tests on February 6, 1969, is the world's biggest commercial jetliner. Carrying up to 490 passengers, the giant double-decker jet dwarfs the "chase car" that tags along on these tests.

3. This largest model Hovercraft plies between Dover and Boulogne, serving the British railway system. At 70 knots top, carrying 255 passengers and 30 cars, the *Seaspeed* makes the channel crossing in 35 minutes. The conventional ferry takes two hours.

4. Penn-Central's high speed Metroliner runs the 226 miles between Washington D.C. and New York in less than three hours. Although it has a top speed of 165 m.p.h., it is forced to run at 75 m.p.h. because of an inadequate road-bed.

Sports World's Sprouting Sixties

In sports, quantitative changes were the most significant, as expansion became the password of the decade

Most of the decades in this century have had their own sports labels. There were the Golden Twenties with Bill Tilden, Jack Dempsey, Babe Ruth and Bob Jones. Then came the Terrific Thirties with Notre Dame in football and the St. Louis Cardinals in baseball. In turn, they were followed by the Furious Forties of war and recovery. The 1960s may well be cataloged as the Sprouting Sixties.

Never, previously, had there been the growth and expansion shown by the sports world as during the 1960s. Major league baseball greeted the start of the decade with 16 teams. It closed it with 24. Professional basketball had 11 clubs in a single league at the start but grew to 25 in two rival leagues during the ten years. Hockey had hung stubbornly to six teams in its National League for years as the ice sport entered the decade but had swollen to twice that number before 1970. Professional football closed out its 1959 schedule with 12 teams but took over the autumnal sports stage of 1969 with 26. Open tennis, in which amateurs and professionals play in the same tournament, became a reality and revived the sport. Professional golf multiplied its prize list six-fold and spawned such household favorites as Gary Player, Arnold Palmer, Jack Nicklaus and Bill Casper, all of whom became virtual millionaires and internationally famous.

Among the amateurs, primarily on the college level, things grew at the same rate. Each year during the decade the National Collegiate Athletic Association (NCAA) reported an attendance increase at the football games under its jurisdiction.

Television, with its mountains of dollars provided by sponsors, aided the expansion by bringing programs into virtually every home.

To combat the possible loss of fans to the ease of fireside viewing, the sports world countered with new arenas that surpassed the billion dollar mark in costs for those who watched the contests in the flesh. New stadiums that could be used for various sports were built in Minneapolis-St. Paul, Atlanta, Los Angeles, San Francisco, New York, Washington, St. Louis, Anaheim, San Diego and Oakland. The building frenzy was climaxed by the Astrodome at Houston where 60,000 fans can watch a major league baseball game in air-conditioned luxury in a roofed building that covers 9 1/2 acres.

New indoor arenas also dotted the landscape with New York City dedicating a new $26,000,000 Madison Square Garden late in the decade. Similar structures also were built in Philadelphia, Oakland and Los Angeles. Racing, in the New York City area alone, contributed four plants, either entirely new or greatly refurbished, that rivaled the palatial homes of the ancient kings .

On the field of play, the athletes also did well.

In 1961, Roger Maris, an outfielder for the New York Yankees, eclipsed the home run record of the immortal Babe Ruth by striking 61 in a single season. Ruth's total of 60 was set in 1927 and had been expected to stand for all time.

Bob Beamon, a lanky athlete from the University of Texas at El Paso, went into orbit during the 1968 Olympic games in Mexico City and added almost 14 inches to the world long jump record in a single effort, moving the standard from 27 feet, 4 3/4 inches to 29 feet, 2 1/2 inches. Joe Namath, a confident quarterback at the University of Alabama in his undergraduate days, was paid $400,000 to sign a contract by the New York Jets of the American League at the start of the 1965 season and in January of 1969 guided the club to a 16-7 victory over the Baltimore Colts of the National Football League in the third annual Super Bowl game.

Lew Alcindor, a 7-foot, 1 1/2-inch product of the Sidewalks of New York, starred as the University of California at Los Angeles won two national titles and 88 of 90 games in basketball during a three-year span; then became an instant millionaire by agreeing to play professionally for the Milwaukee team for five years at a total salary of $1,400,000.

1. Nicklaus power at play . . .

2. Pain in back, money in bank . . .

1. A collegiate amateur at the start of the decade, Jack Nicklaus' powerful golf game brought him U.S. Open titles in 1962 and 1967, the British Open crown in 1966 and three Masters triumphs before the period ended.

2. Arnold Palmer combined a natural golfing ability with a theatrical flair that endeared him to his Army and pyramided his successes into a multi-million dollar business.

3. Houston's Astrodome has foul lines 340 feet long for baseball and also has been the scene for college and pro basketball, football games and rodeos plus many less athletic events.

4. Texans, as well as visitors from afar, leave their ponies at the ranch as they flock in cars to Houston's domed stadium by the millions. The Astrodome may be the most significant gift of the '60s to athletics.

3. Man-made sky, man-made grass . . .

4. Ride'em in comfort, cowboy . . .

1. With tears in his eyes ...

2. A little present for you ...

3. The smile of victory ...

1. Joe Namath, flamboyant quarterback of the Superbowl champion New York Jets, tells with tear filled eyes why he would quit football rather than sell his bistro as ordered by Commissioner Pete Rozelle. He later relented.

2. Here Namath deftly hands off ball to Matt Snell as New Yorkers scuttle Baltimore, 16-7, in Superbowl, Jan. 12, 1969. He had brazenly predicted his underdog mates would win.

3. Vince Lombardi, former high school teacher of Latin and Greek, created a Pro football dynasty as boss of Green Bay Packers.

4. Roger Maris of the New York Yankees exceeds Babe Ruth's record of 60 by smashing 61 on Oct. 1, 1961. Homer came off pitch by Tracy Stallard of Boston Red Sox.

5. Sandy Koufax, lefthanded pitching ace of the Los Angeles Dodgers, virtually was unbeatable until stopped by an arthritic elbow.

6. Whitey Ford, greatest of all New York Yankee lefthanded pitchers, stands near mound again after his retirement, May 30, 1967, following 15 glittering seasons.

7. Wilt Chamberlain, 7 foot star of the Philadelphia team, scans floor for receiver while crowded by Bill Russell (6-10) of Boston in 1966 National Basketball Association game.

8. Lew Alcindor, 7 foot 1⅜ inches of basketball ability, helped bring UCLA three straight national collegiate basketball titles and earned himself three consecutive All-America designations. He now is a pro with Milwaukee of the NBA.

4. No. 61 in 1961 ...

5. Enemy of the batters ...

6. Saying goodbye ...

7. Down and under ...

8. Higher and higher and higher ...

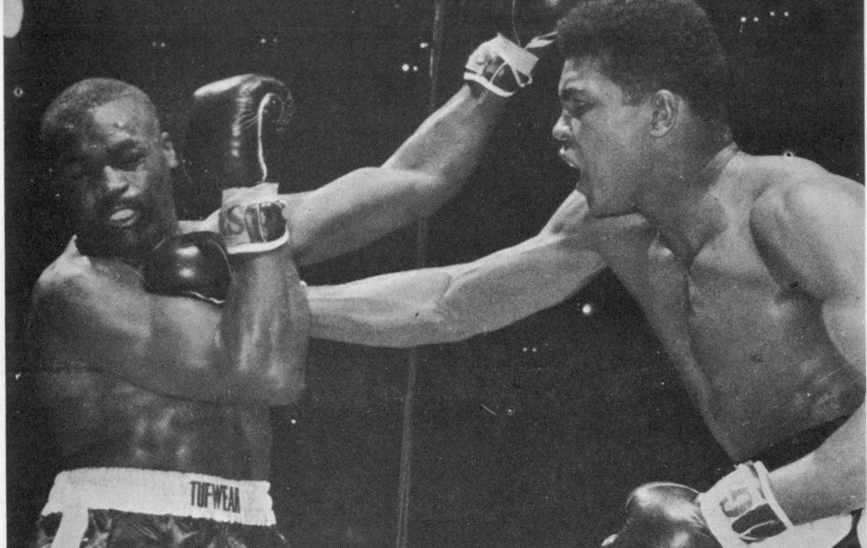

1. The word more powerful than the fist ...

2. The king is dead, long live the king ...

3. Death is the victor ...

4. Something new in racing ...

5. With cool poise ...

1. Cassius Clay battered his way to the heavyweight boxing title but by decade's end he was a convicted draft dodger, shorn of his ring honors and living as an Islam minister with the name of Muhammad Ali.

2. With Cassius Clay dethroned by edict of various athletic commissions because of his hassle with U.S. draft boards, Joe Frazier (left) inherited a part of the title and defended it successfully against Mexico's Manuel Ramos.

3. Davey Moore lost his world featherweight title to Sugar Ramos of Mexico in tenth round of their 1963 bout. Moore died of severe beating a few days later.

4. Adapting aerial thinking to the racing car produced the turbine engine which was introduced to Indianapolis Speedway with considerable success and controversy.

5. Peggy Fleming of Colorado Springs, Colo., poised and graceful, glides to gold medal in women's figure skating at 1968 Winter Olympics at Grenoble, France.

6. George Foreman waves small United States flag as he marches around the ring after winning heavyweight boxing title at 1968's Olympic Games in Mexico.

7. Negroes Tommie Smith (center) and John Carlos show their disdain of United States racial policies by saluting with black gloved fists and averted glances at ceremonies honoring their first-third finish in the 200-meter dash at Mexico City. They were suspended.

8. Tom Okker of Holland, lithe and agile, gives his all in tennis defeat at London Grass Court championships during 1967 tournament.

9. Northern Dancer (right) wins 1964 Kentucky Derby with Bill Hartack in saddle. Hill Rise, with both front feet off ground, is second.

10. Arts and Letters was second to Majestic Prince in both the 1969 Kentucky Derby and Preakness but shown here winning Belmont Stakes over arch rival.

11. Arthur Ashe, first male Negro to gain international tennis ranking, was the surprise winner of the first U.S. Open in 1968 at Forest Hills, N.Y.

12. Racing's biggest innovation of the decade was the appearance of girl jockeys in 1969. Here Bobby Ussery shows how he feels about it.

6. A tiny flag, a giant man ...

7. A salute of derision ...

8. No wooden shoes for nim ...

9. Which is the dancer? ...

10. Turn about is fair play ...

11. First of his kind ...

12. Another bastion falls ...

1. It was nice being here . . .

2. An entirely new kind of bait . . .

1. Thousands of fans attend 1969 ceremonies in Yankee Stadium as Mickey Mantle's uniform number is retired after having been worn for 18 years by the slugging outfielder.

2. Ted Williams, famed Boston Red Sox outfielder, spent eight years fishing after retiring as a player but returned to baseball in 1969 as manager of Washington Senators under a deal that could make him a millionaire.

3. Jean Claude Killy of France dominated men's Olympic skiing in 1968 games at Grenoble and became an international hero. He turned professional shortly afterwards.

4. Billie Jean King, California housewife, was named the world's outstanding woman athlete after winning U.S., Wimbledon and Australia singles tennis championships in 1967.

5. Soccer is played in more countries than any other sport and Pele (in white uniform) is regarded as the best player of them all. His team is Santos of Brazil.

3. Superman on skis . . .

4. Now she knows she is good . . .

5. World's most widely known athlete . . .

The Nation and the World Honor their Best

Rev. Dr. Martin Luther King, Jr., Mikhail A. Sholokhov, Pablo Casals and J. Robert Oppenheimer are among decade's winners

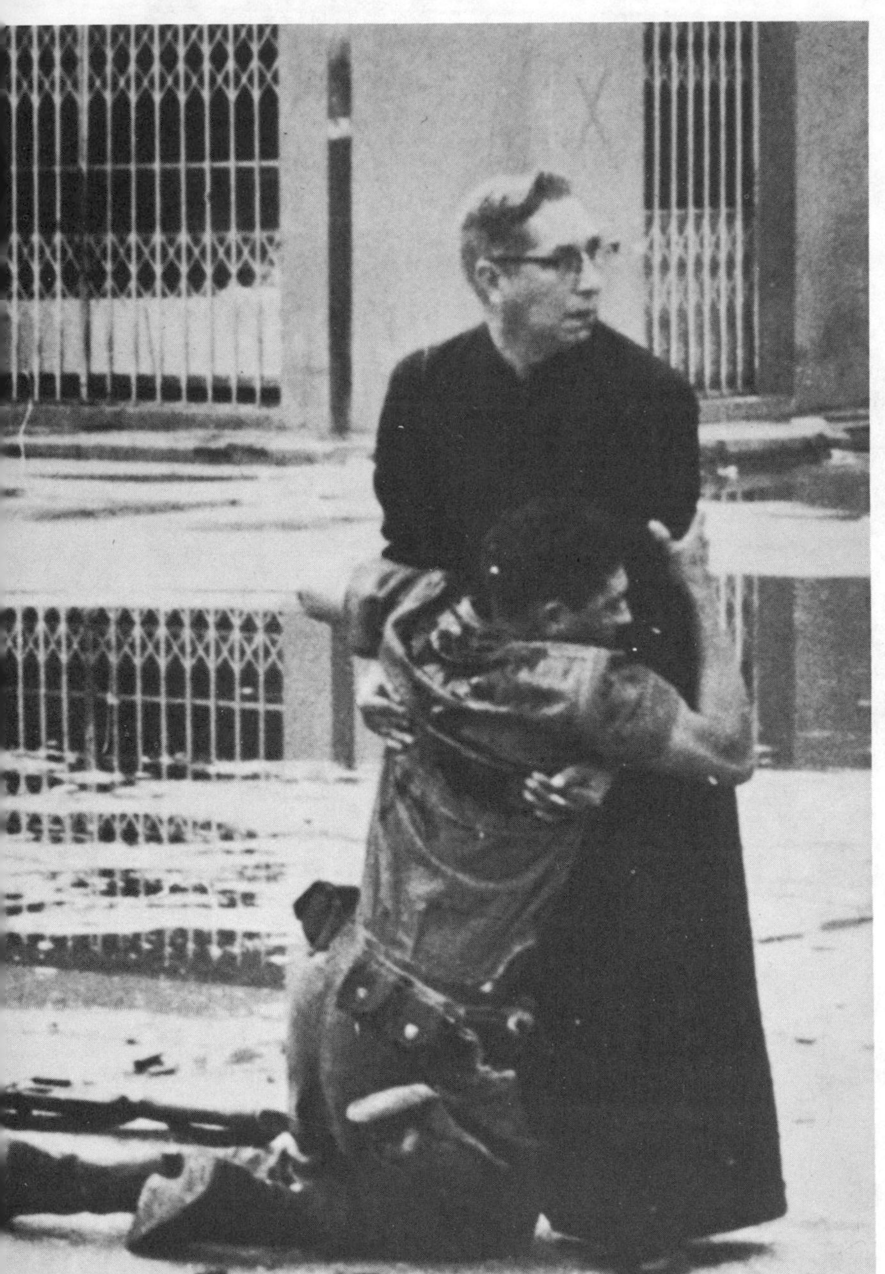

Hector Rondon was awarded the 1962 Pulitzer Prize for News Photography for his photo showing a priest aiding a wounded soldier during a two-day revolt in Venezuela.

Dr. Maria Goeppert-Mayer, first American woman awarded a Nobel Prize in Physics, chats with Sweden's King Gustav Adolf VI in 1963.

The Rev. Dr. Martin Luther King, Jr. received the Nobel Peace Prize in Oslo, Norway, on December 10, 1964.

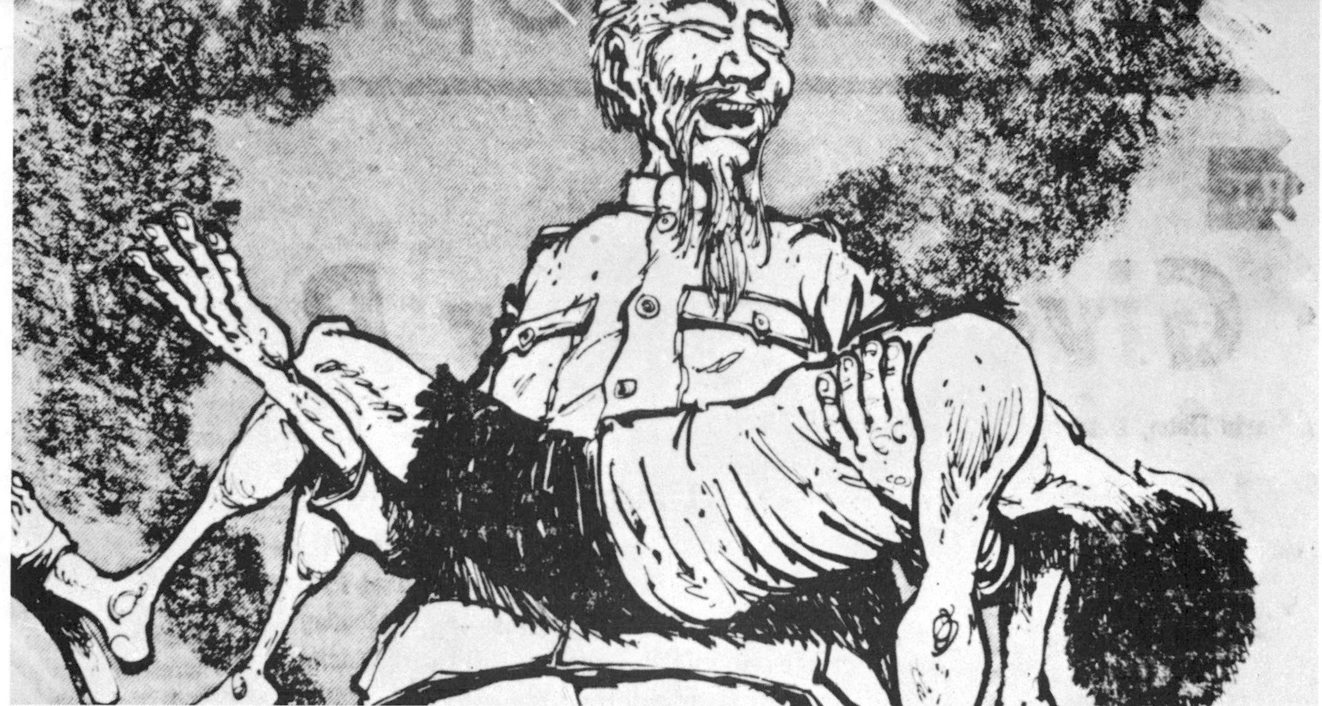

1967's Pulitzer Prize for Editorial Cartooning went to the Denver *Post's* Patrick Oliphant for this cartoon picturing Ho Chi Minh saying, "They won't get *us* to the conference table ... will they?"

Pablo Casals, 93-year-old Spanish-born cellist residing in Puerto Rico, was awarded the 1968 Freedom House award.

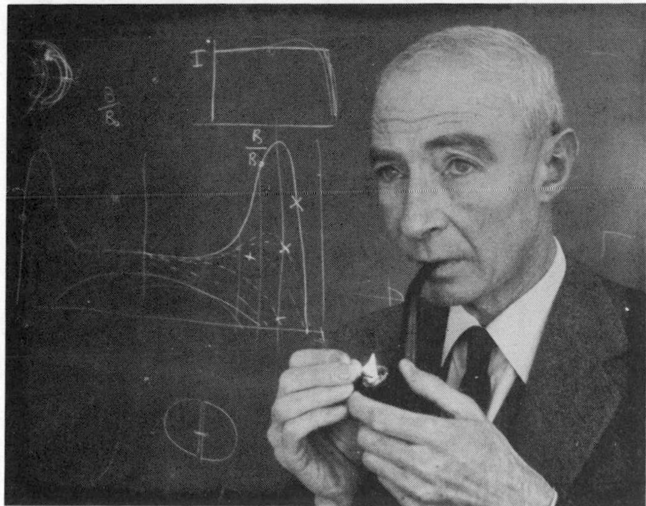

Atomic physicist J. Robert Oppenheimer won the Atomic Energy Commission's $50,000 Enrico Fermi award in 1963.

Russian author Mikhail A. Sholokhov smiles after learning he had been honored with 1965's Nobel Prize in Literature.

Crime Rise Reflects Social Ills

Political assassinations, race riots, street crimes plague the nation; militants' tactics bring demands for law and order

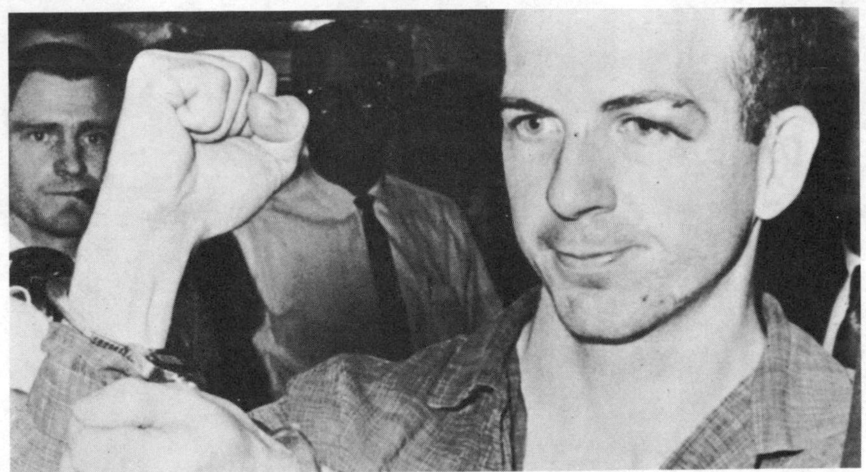

Manacled Lee Harvey Oswald gestures triumphantly as he is led to a cell in Dallas, Texas. His motives unexplained, Pres. Kennedy's defiant assassin took his reasons to the grave when he was shot to death by Jack Ruby.

Dallas night club operator Jack Ruby is surrounded by newsmen and his seated attorneys, Joe Tonahill (l), and Melvin Belli (r). Acting out of hysteria and grief, Oswald's killer spotlighted slipshod police security.

As war is said to be too important to be left to the generals, crime is too important to be left to the police.

What events in the 1960's underscored was the need for more than conventional wisdom: better crime detection methods, or more police.

In the first major presidential address on crime ever presented to the Congress, Lyndon Johnson in 1967 stressed the need for a double-pronged attack on criminal activity. As outlined in his Crime Commission's exhaustive study, one essential was the development of more sophisticated police techniques; but the second — and perhaps paramount need — was prevention of crime by attacking the underlying social roots.

In a '69 interview, New York's Police Commissioner Leary said: "When people are upset about crime, they very seldom go to the judges, or to the prisons." Nor, he might have added, do they take a long, hard look at the society in which crime flourishes on such a large scale.

It took a handful of deaths, and the specter of violence as an American way of life, to highlight the underlying social malaise.

On June 6, 1968, in Los Angeles,

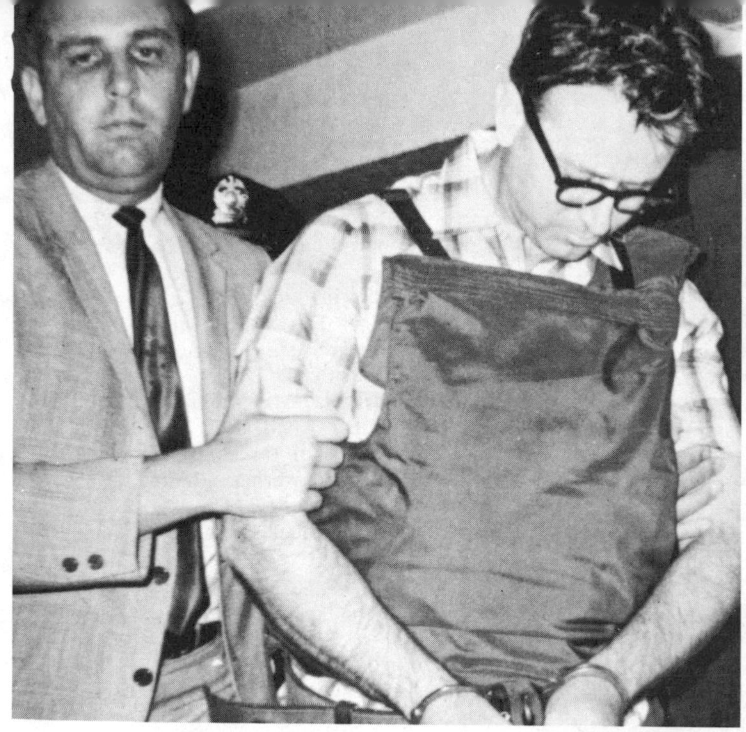

James Earl Ray, drifter, small-change stick-up artist and four time loser, achieved his dream with the murder of Martin Luther King, Jr.: no one would ever forget him.

Squirming Sirhan Sirhan, assassin of Sen. Robert Kennedy, adds another portrait to "murderer's row," a paranoid who acted out his fantasy with real bullets.

Robert Kennedy was cut down by an assassin's bullet, the third great U.S. leader to be killed in less than five years.

Earlier that year, Martin Luther King was shot to death; in 1963, President John F. Kennedy was struck down by Lee Harvey Oswald.

"My God," said one horrified witness after the shooting of Robert Kennedy, "what's America coming to?"

An attempt to answer that question was made by LBJ in his TV address to the American people that evening.

A Commission on Violence was being set up, he said, and was asked to determine "what in the nature of our people and the environment of our society makes possible such murder and such violence?"

The report, released in June '69, called the nation "bloody-minded" and documented a violent tradition, obscured by a "kind of hysterical amnesia." It did not point the finger at the underlying social ills, however, as had the Kerner Commission's study of civil disorders, for fear, as a Commission member put it, of "increasing dissension."

But if no answers were given, at least the necessary question had been definitively proposed.

Meanwhile, the fight against organized crime continued as it had for years, with the knowledge, stated candidly in the Crime Commission's report, that it flourished only with the connivance of local officials.

The size of the boodle taken by syndicated crime was long known to be enormous. Light was thrown on the mechanics of its operation for the first time, however, when in '63 Joseph Valachi blew the whistle on crime kings of America's own Mafia, known as the Cosa Nostra (our thing). Doing their thing meant collecting illicit gains of $7 billion a year ('69 estimates) from illegal gambling, $350 million from narcotics, and lesser amounts from vice and loan sharking.

Killings set off in the struggle for mob control were fairly common during the 60's as boss elders died off, (some like Vito Genovese of natural causes) and their heirs vied for top job.

Other less tangible motives than mob rule were sought in killers like Richard Speck — murderer of eight Chicago nurses in 1966. One theory, advanced by French geneticists, held that such men shared a chromosome imbalance. When this genetic anomaly was found among other killers, the theory gained ground.

By the end of the decade, however, a mood swing, away from understanding, had set in. "Law and order" became the rallying cry of the man in the street who cared less for motives than for catching criminals.

Some blamed the crime rise on the permissiveness of the courts.

While the Supreme Court's liberal trend had curtailed some free-swinging police methods, it had not — as reflective police officials admitted — "handcuffed the police."

Nonetheless, with the swing toward a conservative temper, it was expected that strict observance of a defendant's rights during interrogation would be more honored in the breach in the 70's.

The saddest note of the decade was the failure of Congress to push through a meaningful gun control law despite the intensity of feeling after Robert Kennedy's death. In early '69 it was estimated that there were 50 million private small arms in the country — two million of them purchased in 1968.

Plautus, in the 2nd century B.C. said: Man is a wolf to man — a fitting epitaph for the violent 60's.

1. Slain NAACP leader . . .

2. Evers' accused killer . . .

3. Three bodies sought . . .

4. Militant black foresaw his death . . .

1. Casket of slain NAACP integrationist leader, Medgar Evers, arrives in Washington D.C., June 17, 1963, for burial in Arlington National Cemetery.

2. F.B.I. man in Jackson, Mississippi, brings in Byron De La Beckwith, Medgar Evers' accused slayer, later set free by all-white jury.

3. In Philadelphia, Mississippi, on June 27, 1964, F.B.I. men drag the Pearl River for bodies of three missing civil rights workers: Schwerner, Chaney, and Goodman.

4. Malcolm X, Black Muslim leader, was murdered by rival blacks on February 21, 1965.

5. Joseph Valachi, former syndicate underling, enjoys the spotlight before testifying to workings of the "Cosa Nostra" before the Senate Investigations Subcommittee in 1963.

6. Last of the "Cosa Nostra" kings, Vito Genovese ran the shop, even ordered murders from behind bars until he died of natural causes.

7. Charles Lucania, alias Lucky Luciano, vice czar of the 30's, dead at 65 in a Naples airport. Deported in 1946, he pulled "mafia" strings until boss power passed to Genovese.

8. Flamboyant trial lawyer, F. Lee Bailey rocketed to fame with his defense of Carl Coppolino and Dr. Sam Sheppard.

9. Room where 8 of 9 student nurses lived as it looked after their brutal deaths at the hands of Chicago murderer Richard Speck.

10. Acne-scarred killer Richard Speck is returned to prison after his arraignment for the killing of eight student nurses.

11. N.Y. City residents were shocked to learn that no one had answered Catherine Genovese's cries for help — heard by many — as she staggered, bleeding from stab wounds, into a doorway a few steps from home.

12. Mace fell into disrepute as a humane police weapon when physicians testified that it left permanent eye injuries.

13. Boston Strangler, Albert De Salvo, moments after he was recaptured in a Lynn, Mass. clothing store on February 26, 1967. He had fled from Bridgewater State Hospital.

5. Mafioso tells all . . .

6. Ran mobsters from jail . . .

7. His luck ran out . . .

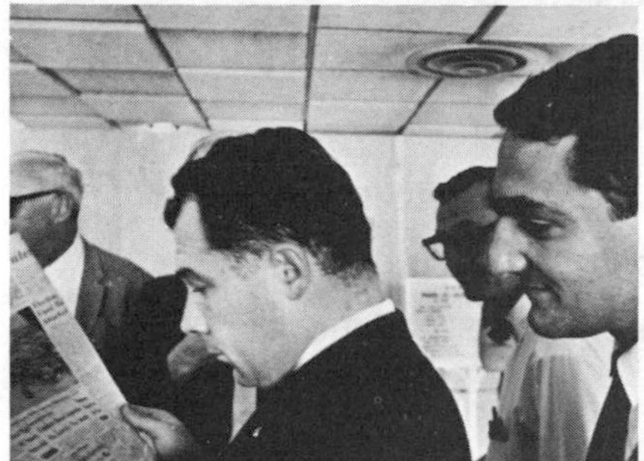

8. Bar's star performer . . .

9. Scene of carnage where . . .

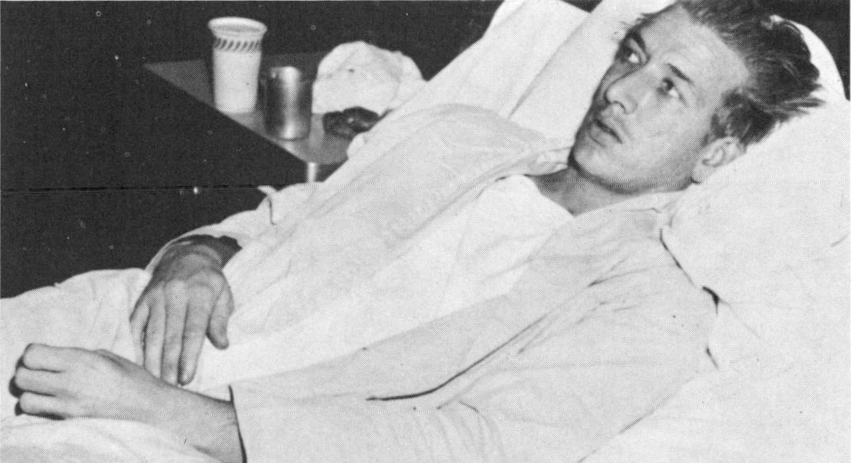

10. . . . killer slew eight

11. So near and so far . . .

12. The anti-Mace case . . .

13. Nemesis of Boston . . .

Decade's Diary of Death and Destruction

New York City has its worst plane crash; scores of children die in Welsh avalanche; hundreds burn to death in Belgian department store blaze

A mid-air collision over New York City brought death to 133 persons, as a United Airlines DC-8 collided with a TWA Super Constellation on Dec. 16, 1960. The United jet fell in Brooklyn, the TWA in Staten Island.

Death came to many in cars as a bridge over the Ohio River collapsed on the afternoon of Dec. 15, 1967.

A grief-stricken mother carries the body of her twelve-year-old child from the ruins of her Varto, Turkey, home after Aug. 22, 1966, earthquake destroyed the town.

Crude oil from the tanker *Torrey Canyon,* aground Mar. 18, 1967, flowed to England and Brittany, France, where birds were caught helplessly in the oil.

Rain-soaked slag heap avalanched down upon Aberfan, Wales, Oct. 21, 1966, burying a school and many homes. Mourners file past coffins of 81 children who perished.

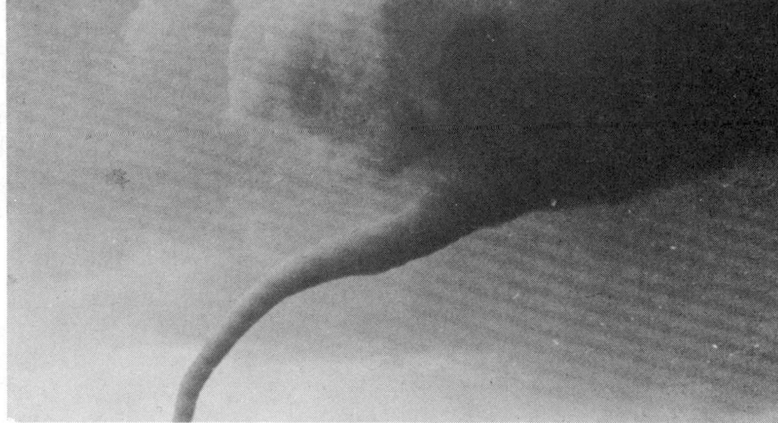

A tornado funnel churns over the countryside of Tracy, Minnesota, in mid-June, 1968, leaving nine persons dead, one hundred injured and extensive property damage.

An estimated 300 people burned to death and scores were injured in a spectacular fire that swept Brussels' chic "A L'Innovation" department store on May 22, 1967.

Torrential rains flooded northern Italy from November 4th through November 6th, 1966. Thousands of art treasures were ruined as the hardest hit city was Florence.

More than 500,000 tons of mud seeped into the many museums and churches of Florence, Italy, damaging valuable books and paintings, some beyond repair.

An outdoor mass is held outside the ruins of St. Thomas Catholic Church, Long Beach, Mississippi, after Hurricane Camille hit the Gulf Coast on August 17, 1969.

An estimated 1,800 persons were killed when an avalanche of earth and rock caused the Vaiont dam to burst, destroying Longarone, Italy and nearby hamlets on October 8, 1963. A priest stands by two of the bodies.

A tremendous earthquake hit western Sicily on January 15, 1969, leaving an estimated two hundred dead and 80,000 homeless. Villages such as Gibellina (above) were almost totally destroyed and most inhabitants killed.

On the day after the Aberfan, Wales, slag heap avalanche, rescue workers search wet coal waste at Pantglas Junior School for bodies. Of the 144 persons who perished here on October 21 1966, 116 were children.

The Passing Scene

People and events that made big and small headlines during the decade.

Dr. Timothy Leary, exponent of hallucinatory drugs, announces at a May, 1969, press conference the formation of a new political party called *Fervor*. His wife is at right.

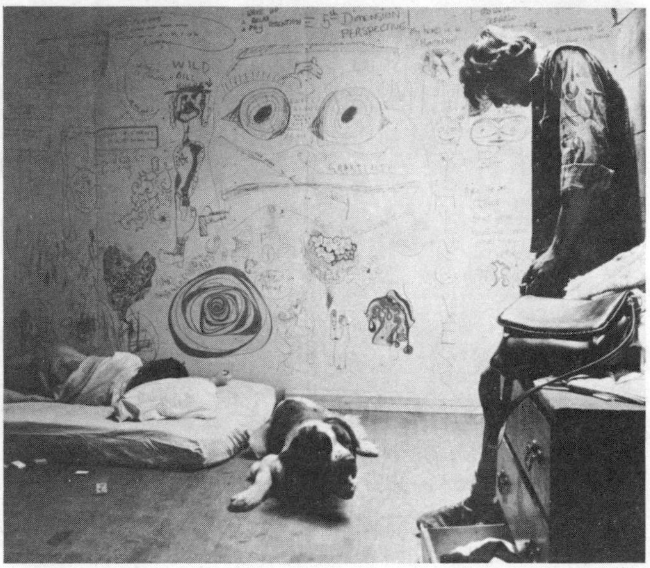

Psychedelic art work is scrawled on the wall and a runaway girl sleeps on a mattress at a communal-living hippie group haven in New York as a hippie and a large dog stand vigil.

Maharishi Mahesh Yogi is flanked by Beatles George Harrison, left, and John Lennon at a UNICEF gala in Paris, Dec. 16, 1967. The Maharishi was considered to be the Beatles' "spiritual father."

Yippie leader arrives at 1968 House Un-American Activities Subcommittee hearing investigating the Democratic National Convention disturbances.

An estimated 400,000 youngsters turned out to listen to the Woodstock Music and Art Fair, White Lake, New York, Aug. 22-24, 1969. The long-haired and wildly dressed kids lived in love, trust and tranquility for three days.

Richard Burton and Elizabeth Taylor, the sixties' most celebrated lovers were peeped at, spied on, and otherwise followed by a horde of photographers and press-men, from Roman night clubs to Spanish bull fights.

Mrs. Aristotle Onassis, former Jacqueline Bouvier Kennedy, and her husband walk with her son, John F. Kennedy, Jr., on New York's 5th Avenue.

Italian actress Sophia Loren, home after birth of a son in Switzerland.

Crown Prince Harald, 31, of Norway wed Sonja Haraldsen, 30, in Oslo on August 29, 1968.

The Duke and Duchess of Windsor stroll in New York City where they have a home. "The King's Story" movie about them has been made

King Constantine of Greece weds Princess Anne-Marie of Denmark on September 18, 1964, in Athens.

New York's Mayor John Lindsay often enjoyed his job, but also found it laden with such horrors as teacher strikes, sanitation strikes and unruly snowstorms. In 1969, the Mayor was denied his party's nomination for re-election.

Senator Edward Kennedy, youngest and last of the Kennedy brothers, seemed the perfect choice for the Democratic Presidential nomination in 1972 until July 20, 1969, when he was involved in an automobile accident which killed his female passenger, Mary Jo Kopechne. The senator escaped physical injury.

In 1964, Pres. Johnson caused considerable furor over the proper treatment of beagles when he lifted one of the White House pets by its ears.

The generation gap stretched wider than ever in the Sixties as both the young and the old found it increasingly hard to understand each other.

Following the trend for show business stars to enter politics, Shirley Temple Black became a member of the U.S. delegation to the U.N. in 1969.

Fashions exposed more and more of the human body in the Sixties. In 1964, Carroll Baker wore this Oleg Cassini transparent gown to a film premier.

Dressed in African garb and wearing her hair Afro-style is Miss Black America of 1969 — alias Gloria Smith, a 24-year-old New York City model.

"Traditional" 1969 Miss America was Pamela Anne Eldred of Michigan. Note of changing times: event was picketed by Women's Liberation Front.

Designer Yves Saint Laurent was Fashion's success story of the decade. He began by working for Dior, and was soon manager of the Dior business.

Students occupied the Sorbonne in May, 1968, as part of France's massive uprisings. Above, students perch upon a statue of Victor Hugo.

Sen. Strom Thurmond of S. Carolina addressed 2,000 students at the Univ. of Mass. while black students and whites dressed in sheets heckled him.

Amazin' — purely amazin'. The New York Mets, clown princes of the National League, lovers of lost causes idols, went all the way to the championship, taking the World Series from the Baltimore Orioles.

Actress Sharon Tate was found shot to death in Beverly Hills. Police hinted at drug-ridden bizarre rituals. Ironically, Miss Tate's husband, Roman Polanski (r), made a specialty of popularizing such Gothic horror stories.

Senator Everett Dirksen, perhaps the last of the old-time politicians of grand manner and flowing rhetoric, died in early September, 1969. The body of the Republican Senate minority leader was returned to his home town, Peoria, Ill.

Millions of Americans paused to express dissatisfaction with the U.S. action in Vietnam during Moratorium Day, October 15, 1969. Observances were held in virtually every town and city across the country.

In Memoriam

ARTS & LETTERS

Jean Cocteau, 74, French poet, playwright, critic, artist and film director; Oct. 11, 1963.

T. S. Eliot, 76, American-born poet ("The Waste Land") who became a naturalized British citizen; Jan. 4, 1965.

Edna Ferber, 82, portrayer of American life in novels, short stories and plays; April 16, 1968.

Ian Fleming, 56, best-selling British writer of spy stories and creator of James Bond; Aug. 12, 1964.

Robert Frost, 88, considered unofficial poet laureate of the U.S., winner of more Pulitzer Prizes than any other American poet (1924, '31, '37, '43); Jan. 29, 1963.

Alberto Giacometti, 64, internationally acclaimed sculptor; Jan. 11, 1966.

Moss Hart, 57, playwright, co-author of Pulitzer Prize winning "You Can't Take It With You;" Dec. 20, 1961.

Ernest Hemingway, 61, Nobel Prize winning novelist for literature (1954); July 2, 1960.

James Langston Hughes, 65, one of the first Negro writers to "tell it like it is;" May 22, 1967.

Helen Keller, 87, born blind and deaf, became a lecturer and writer; June 1, 1968.

Somerset Maugham, 91, best-selling novelist whose books included "Of Human Bondage;" Dec. 16, 1965

Anna Mary Robertson (Grandma) Moses, 101, beloved American "primitive" painter who began painting at age of 76; Dec. 13, 1961.

Carl Sandburg, 89, biographer of Lincoln and poet of the American way of life; July 22, 1967.

Upton Sinclâir, 90, American social and economic reformer and author ("The Jungle"); Nov. 25, 1968.

John Steinbeck, 66, Nobel Prize winning novelist ("Of Mice and Men," "Grapes of Wrath"); Dec. 20, 1968.

ENTERTAINMENT AND SPORTS

Eddie Cantor, 72, comedian whose career spanned vaudeville, Broadway films, radio and TV; Oct. 10, 1964.

Ty (Tyrus Raymond) Cobb, 74, considered baseball's greatest player; July 17, 1960.

Nat King Cole, 45, velvet-voiced popular singer; Feb. 15, 1965.

Ernie Davis, 23, all-American halfback at Syracuse Univ., only Negro ever to win Heisman Trophy, college football's highest award; May 18, 1963.

Walt Disney, 65, creator of Mickey Mouse and a whole wonderful world of fantasy; Dec. 15, 1966.

Jimmy "Double X" Foxx, 59, Baseball's Hall of Fame infielder, powerhouse home run hitter; July 21, 1967.

Oscar Hammerstein, 2nd, 65, Broadway librettist, lyricist and producer ("Showboat", "Oklahoma"); Aug. 23, 1960.

Bert Lahr, 72, brilliant comic actor of stage and screen; Dec. 4, 1967.

"Big Daddy" Lipscomb, 31, National Football League star; May 10, 1963.

Cole Porter, 71, one of America's most beloved songwriters ("Night and Day"); Oct. 15, 1964.

Otis Redding, 26, gifted Negro "soul" singer; Dec. 10, 1967.

Billy Rose, 66, flamboyant Broadway and Wall Street entrepreneur; Feb. 10, 1966.

Spencer Tracy, 67, sensitive and wise actor known for his portrayals of lawyers and priests; June 10, 1967.

Albert Warner, 84, movie tycoon and a founder of Warner Bros. Pictures; Nov. 26, 1967.

BUSINESS, INDUSTRY AND LABOR

Anthony Anastasio, 57, Italian-born vice president of the International Longshoremen's Assn., known as "Tough Tony," Mar. 1, 1963.

Elizabeth Arden, 81, turned the business of looking beautiful into a big business; Oct. 18, 1966.

Bernard Baruch, 94, financier, philanthropist, and advisor to Presidents; June 20, 1965.

James Ford Bell, 81, founder and former Chairman of Board of General Mills; May 7, 1960.

Sir Winston Churchill, 90, former British Prime Minister, author, prominent Parliamentary speaker; Jan. 24, 1965.

Dwight D. Eisenhower, 79, Army General and 34th President of the United States; March 28, 1969.

King Farouk, 45, former monarch of Egypt who was forced to abdicate in 1952; Mar. 18, 1965.

Walter Gifford, 81, president and later chairman of A.T.&T. from 1925 to 1950; May 7, 1966.

Bernard Gimbel, 81, head of Gimbel's and Saks, leader and innovator in retail chain marketing; Sept. 29, 1966.

Clinton Strong Golden, 72, co-founder of United Steel Workers of America; June 12, 1960.

Dag Hammarskjold, Swedish statesman and United Nations secretary-general until death; Sept. 18, 1961.

Judge Learned Hand, 89, Judge of the United States Court of Appeals, Second Circuit, most famous jurist of his time who wrote more than 2,000 opinions; Aug. 18, 1960.

John Fitzgerald Kennedy, 46, 35th President of the United States; Nov. 22, 1963.

Continued on page 826

John F. Kennedy, served from 1961 as youngest U.S. President until his assassination on Nov 22, 1963, in Dallas, Texas.

Robert F. Kennedy, ex-Attorney General and N.Y. Senator; slain by an assassin's bullet on June 6, 1968, after winning Cal. primary.

Dr. Martin Luther King Jr., non-violent civil rights leader; shot to death in Memphis at 39, April 4, 1968, while supporting strike.

Sir Winston Churchill, 90, Prime Minister, British statesman and author, also prominent Parliamentary speaker; Jan. 24, 1965.

Paul Tillich, eminent German Protestant teacher and world-renowned theologian, died October 22, 1965 at the age of 79.

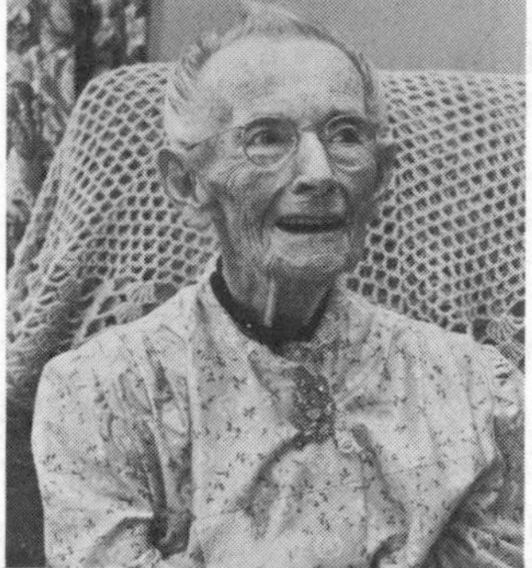
"Grandma Moses," 101, naively simplistic American artist who began career while in her seventies, died Dec. 13, 1961.

Albert Schweitzer, famed humanitarian Dr. in Africa; renowned musician, French Protestant theologian Sept. 4, 1965.

J. Robert Oppenheimer, American physicist noted for the atom bomb and contributions to relativity; Feb. 18, 1967.

Yuri A. Gagarin, Russian, the world's first visitor to outer space; killed March 27, 1968, in an air accident at the age of 34.

John Steinbeck, American novelist, recipient of 1962 Nobel Prize for Literature and the 1940 Pulitzer Prize; died Dec. 20, 1968.

Walt Disney, versatile and successful salesman of fantasy, creator of Mickey Mouse, and Donald Duck; died Dec. 15, 1966.

Norman Thomas, 84, American socialist leader who repeatedly ran unsuccessfully for President, Socialist ticket; Dec. 19, 1968.

Pope John XXIII, 261st Pope of the Roman Catholic Church; organized Catholic Action groups; died June 3, 1963, at age 81.

Robert Frost, major 20th century American poet, master of the New England voice, multiple Pulitzer winner; died Jan. 29, 1963.

Auguste Piccard, made first balloon ascension into stratosphere; developed ocean vessel bathyscaphe; Mar. 24, 1962.

Spencer Tracy, actor famous for his character portrayals of "down-to-earth" American men; died June 10, 1967 at 67.

Dwight D. Eisenhower, Allied Forces Commander-in-Chief in European theatre; former U.S. President; March 28, 1969.

Konrad Adenauer, *der Alte,* 91, West Germany Chancellor for four successive terms; revived post-war economy; April 19, 1967.

Dag Hammarskjold, U.N. Secretary General, posthumously awarded Nobel Peace Prize in 1961 died Sept. 18, 1961.

Adlai Stevenson, 65, American statesman and two-time Democratic Presidential nominee; died in London July 14, 1965.

Ernest Hemingway, 61, American award-winning novelist; big-game hunter; bull fight expert; committed suicide July 2, 1960.

Margaret Sanger, single-handed crusader for the birth control movement in 1912; died on Sept. 6, 1966, at the age of 83.

Douglas MacArthur, U.S. Army General; commanded the United Nations forces in Korean War; died April 5, 1964.

Eleanor Roosevelt, 78, American writer and humanitarian; wife of Franklin Roosevelt, 31st President of U.S.; died Nov. 8, 1962.

T.S. Eliot, one of the greatest English-language poets, recipient of 1948 Nobel Prize; died January 4, 1965.

Helen Keller, blind and deaf from the age of two, became author, lecturer, and symbol of courage to all; June 1, 1968.

Carl Sandburg, 89, Pulitzer Prize-winning author, poet and well-known biographer of Abraham Lincoln; July 22, 1967.

William Faulkner, contemporary Mississippi writer who wrote mainly about the South and its decadence; died July 6, 1962.

Vivien Leigh, 53, English actress; former wife of Sir Lawrence Olivier; star of "Gone With the Wind;" died July 8, 1967.

Nat "King" Cole, well-loved American Negro singer and album favorite; died of cancer at 45 on February 15, 1965.

Judy Garland, famed singing actress; childhood star of movie classic "The Wizard of Oz;" died on June 22 1969, at age 45.

Marilyn Monroe (Norma Jean Baker), much publicized Hollywood actress and sex symbol; died August 4, 1962.

Adlai E. Stevenson, 65, U.S. Ambassador to the United Nations and twice-defeated candidate for presidency; July 14, 1965.

Robert Francis Kennedy, 42, Democratic Senator of New York, sought Presidential nomination for 1968 election when assassinated; June 6, 1968.

Henry Morgenthau, 75, Sec. of Treasury, 1934-45 and friend of FDR; Feb. 6, 1967.

Malcolm X, 39, leader of black militant Nationalist movement; Feb. 22, 1965.

William O'Dwyer, 74, controversial mayor of New York City from 1946-50 and later Ambassador to Mexico; Nov. 24, 1964.

George Papandreou, 80, the "Old Fox" of Greek politics; former Premier who opposed military junta in Greece in 1967; Nov. 1, 1968.

Sam Rayburn, 79, House Speaker; served longer as Representative and Speaker in U.S. Congress than any other man; Nov. 16, 1961.

Mrs. Eleanor Roosevelt, 78, famous wife and widow of Franklin D. Roosevelt, 32nd President of U.S.; Nov. 8, 1962.

Lal Bahadur Shastri, 61, Prime Minister of India who engineered peace treaty with Pakistan; Jan. 11, 1966.

Alfred Sloan Jr., 90, builder of General Motors and great philanthropist; Feb. 17, 1966.

William Richard Steinway, 78, piano manufacturer; Sept. 22, 1960.

MILITARY & SPACE

Lieut. Commander Roger Chaffee, 31, rookie astronaut testing the Apollo space craft; Jan. 27, 1967.

Gen. Dietrich von Choltitz, 71, Nazi commander who defied Hitler's command to burn Paris; Nov. 5, 1966.

Lieut. Col. Virgil I. Grissom 40, veteran of two missions in space and one of the original seven; Jan. 27, 1967.

Adm. Husband E. Kimmel, 86, Pearl Harbor Commander of the Pacific Fleet; May 14, 1968.

General Douglas MacArthur, 84, five-star General of U.S. Army who led the Allied victory over Japan in WWII; April 15, 1964.

Gen. Walter Bedell Smith, 65, Chief of Staff, ETO, World War II, former Ambassador to USSR, Under Secretary of State, head of Central Intelligence Agency; Aug. 9, 1960.

Lieut. Col. Edward H. White, 36, first American Astronaut to walk in space; Jan. 27, 1967.

RELIGION AND EDUCATION

Martin Buber, 87, Jewish philosopher and educator; June 13, 1965.

Dr. A. Whitney Griswold, 56, president of Yale University; April 19, 1963.

Dr. Martin Luther King Jr., 39, great American civil rights leader; April 4, 1968.

Pope John XXIII, 81, 261st Pope of the Roman Catholic Church; June 3, 1963.

Rabbi Abba Hillel Silver, 70, leader in U.S. Jewish affairs and in the world Zionist movement; Nov. 28, 1963.

Francis Joseph Cardinal Spellman, 73, of New York; Dec. 2, 1967.

Theoclitos, 71, Archbishop of Athens and head of Greek Orthodox Church; Jan. 8, 1962.

SCIENCE & MEDICINE

Peter Joseph Debye, 82, Dutch physicist, chemist and Nobel Prize winner for molecular structure; Nov. 2, 1966.

Otto Hahn, 89, discovered that an atom could be split, won Nobel Prize for chemistry in 1944; July 23, 1968.

Dr. Carl Gustav Jung, 85, co-father of psychoanalysis, coined terms "introvert and extrovert"; June 6, 1960.

Hermann Joseph Muller, 76, U.S. geneticist and Nobel Prize winner for effect of radiation on genes; April 5, 1967.

J. Robert Oppenheimer, 63, controversial head of the Manhattan project. Responsible for the atomic bomb; Feb. 18, 1967.

Dr. Theodore Von Karman, 81, Hungarian-born aviation expert, developed the jet plane; May 7, 1963.

Prof. Auguste Piccard, 78, pioneer Swiss explorer of the stratosphere and ocean depths; March 24, 1962.

Dr. Jean Felix Piccard, 79, famed stratosphere balloonist and cosmic ray researcher; Jan. 28, 1963.

Dr. Bela Schick, 90, devised the Schick test for diptheria; Dec. 6, 1967.

Dr. Norbert Weiner, 69, mathematician called the "father of automation"; March 18, 1964.

PRESS & PUBLISHING

Lord Beaverbrook, 85, founder of a British newspaper empire ("The Daily Express" and others); June 9, 1964.

Whittaker Jay David Chambers, 60, former Communist who testified against Alger Hiss; July 19, 1960.

Sir William Neil Conner, 57, Britain's favorite acid-tongued columnist; April 6, 1967.

Jay Norwood ("Ding") Darling, 85, cartoonist, winner of two Pulitzer Prizes; Feb. 12, 1962.

Stanley Hoflund High, 65, "Reader's Digest" editor; Feb. 3, 1961.

Henry R. Luce, 68, founder of "Time-Life-Fortune" empire; Feb. 28, 1968

Dorothy Parker, 73, columnist, critic and leading wit at the Algonquin Round Table; June 7, 1967.

Emily Post, 86, leading authority on etiquette, Sept. 25, 1960.

INDEX

C

I

J

K

L

N

O

P

Q

R

S

T

U

V

W

X

Y

Z

PICTURE CREDITS

The following list credits the source of each picture used. Credits are listed picture by picture for each page—left to right, top to bottom. Each picture starting a new line across each page is preceded by a dash (—); each picture on that same line is preceded by a comma (,).

Abbreviations used are:

Acad MP A and S, Academy of Motion Picture Arts and Sciences; **Bet.**, Bettmann Archive; **BB**, Brown Brothers; **BS**, Black Star; **Cul.**, Culver; **DD**, Defense Dept.; **Eur.**, European; **INP**, Internat'l News Photos; **Key**, Keystone; **MGM**, Metro-Goldwyn-Mayer; **NA**, National Archives (Wash., D.C.); **PP**, Picture Post Library (London); **PPS**, Professional Picture Service; **Sov.**, Sovfoto; **Ullstein**, Ullstein, Bilderdienst (Berlin); **UN**, United Nations; **UP**, United Press; **UPI**, United Press International; **UU**, Underwood and Underwood; **WW**, Wide World.

102—BB. 103—"Los Angeles Times". 104—Sov., BB—Pix Inc., UP—Key., ©Karsh Ottawa, Beacon Press. 105—Pix Inc., INP—BS, Pix Inc.—Graphic House, BB, ©Karsh Ottawa. 106—UU. 107—UU. 108—BB. 109—BB, BB—INP, Library of Congress—BB, UU. 110—WW—BB—INP, BB, BB. 111—BB—BB, BB, BB. 112—BB, INP—BB. 113—Ford Motor Co. Archives, WW—BB, BB—BB, BB. 114—"St. Louis Post Dispatch," WW—BB—BB—UP, BB, BB. 115—BB—BB, Bet., INP—BB, BB. 116—BB—UU—BB. 117—Library of Congress, BB—BB, BB, BB. 118—BS, INP, BB—BB—Eur., BB. 119—BS, INP—UU—N.Y. Public Library. 120—BB, WW, Key.—BB—Bagby Photo. 121—UP, Key., INP—INP, BB, Springfield College—BB, BB, BB. 122—BB, Cul.—INP—UP, Bet. 123—Cul., BB—WW—Eur.—INP, WW, BB.

124—Curtis Pub. Co., same—Bet., Sears Roebuck and Co., same. 125—BB, BB, BB—Alinari (Florence), Christian Science Pub. Co., INP. 126—BB—WW, BB—Key.—WW—WW, BS, BB. 127—UU—BB—WW, BB—BB, BB, Historisches Bildarchiv (Bad Berneck, Germany) 128—BB, UP, BB—Cul.—BB, BB, BB. 129—BB, INP, BB—Cul., PP—Cul. 130—WW, Mus. of Modern Art—INP—BB—BB. 131—BB—Cul., INP, BB—Cul., UP. 132—Mus. of Modern Art—BS—Met. Museum of Art, same. 133—BB, BB, UP—BB—BB, WW, INP. 134—Ewing Galloway—same, INP, BB. 135—UP—Cul.—UP—UP, UP, BB—INP, BB, BB. 136—WW, BB, Cul.—BB, WW—"Collier's"—BB, BB—BB. 137—BB, BB, Cul.—BB—BB, BB—BB, BB—Eur. 138—WW. 139—BS 140—Harris and Ewing—WW, BB. 141—WW, BB—PP, BB, NA—BB, WW. 142—Ewing Galloway—BB, NA—INP—BB, BB, Photo Viollet (Paris). 143—WW—BB—BB, BS—Imperial War Museum (London), BB. 144—Ullstein, BB—BB, Historisches Bildarchiv (Bad Berneck, Germany)—BS—BB. 145—BB, WW—BS—Eur.—WW. 146—INP, BB—Eur., BB. 147—WW, WW—BB, UP—UP, BB. 148—BB—BB, WW. 149—BB., Cul.—INP, INP—BB, UP. 150—INP, NA—INP, Imperial War Museum (London), PP—INP, BB, WW. 151—BB, UP—BB, WW, INP, WW—BS—Ullstein—USAF, NA—USN—DeMarcy, USAF. 152—BB, BB—NA, BB—Ewing Galloway. 153—Key.—BB. 154—Ewing Galloway, BB—WW, BB—BS, WW—NA, Sov. 155—WW—Library of Congress, BS. 156—NA—League of Nations. 157—USN, INP—BS—Key., WW. 158—WW—BB—WW, BB. 159—BB, INP, BB—UP—BB. 160—Acad. MP A and S, Cul., Cul.—BB, BB—UP, Cul.—Mus. of Modern Art, Cul. 161—Cul., Cul.—Cul., WW, INP—"N. Y. Times," BB—Cul. 162—Cul., Cul.—BB—UP, BB—USN. 163—UU, BB, BB—Univ. of Minn., BB—WW, BB. 164—WW, INP, UP—Eur., "N. Y. News," Eur.—INP, WW, INP. 165—BB, Irene Castle Enzinger—WW—BB, ©Martin Ves, Key., INP. 166—Ford Motor Co. 167—BB. 168—Ford Motor Co., Gen. Motors—INP. 169—INP—BB, INP—WW, WW—Ewing Galloway. 170—BB—INP, INP—INP, BB, INP. 171—WW—WW, INP—INP, WW. 172—UP, UP—Ullstein, BS—UP 173—Sov., INP, Eur.—INP, UP, INP. 174—WW, WW—WW, PP, WW—NA, INP. 175—INP, Cul., Cul.—INP, WW, INP—INP, Key. 176—Cul., BB, INP—Cul., ©"Life"—BB, UP, BB. 177—WW, WW—BB, BB—Cul., INP. 178—Mus. of Modern Art, WW—BB, INP, WW—Mus. of Modern Art, same, WW. 179—BB, WW—WW, UP—INP, WW. 180—Inst. of Aeronatucal Sciences, WW—BB, WW—BB, BB. 181—UP, WW—WW—INP. WW. WW. 182—INP, Eur., BB—UP, WW—INP, INP—INP, WW. 183—WW, WW—BB, WW—WW, INP, WW, WW—INP, INP.. 184—UP. WW—WW, INP—UP, Cul., INP. 185—BB, BB—UP—UP—Cul., UP, WW. 186—WW, Freer Gallery of Art—INP. 187—BS—Whitney Museum of American Art, Met. Museum of Art—WW. 188—BB—WW, 20th Cent.—Acad. MP A and S, Cul. 189—Acad. MP A and S—WW, Acad. MP A and S—WW, Acad. MP A and S, same. 190—BB, Cul.—Key., Acad. MP A and S, same—same, Mus. of Modern Art, MGM. 191—WW, Cul.—Cul., BB—Cul., WW, Cul. 192—WW, UU, WW—WW, WW, WW—Ullstein, WW, BB. 193—INP, WW—©"Time" Inc., INP—INP, "New York Times". 194—WW, INP—WW, UP. 195—WW, INP—INP, WW, WW—WW, WW. 196—BB, UP—WW, WW—US Army, WW, UP. 197—Liggett and Meyers Tobacco Co.—R. J. Reynolds, Jordan Car Co. 198—Chrysler Corp., Ford Motor Co.—BB, INP—BB, INP—WW, INP. 199—BB, Westinghouse—UU, Key., WW, BB, Cul. 200—Eur.—INP, UP—WW, WW, UP. 201—WW, Key.—WW, INP, UP. 202—WW. 203—BS 204—INP—WW. 205—UP, WW, UP—WW, WW—WW, WW. 206—INP, WW—Key., UP—UP. 207—WW, UP—Harris and Ewing, same—Key., Ewing Galloway. 208—UP, BS—INP, UP—Cul.' Cul. 209—TVA—Triangle Photo, Harris and Ewing—INP, WW. 210—Triangle Photo, WW, UP—WW, UP. 211—BB, INP—Triangle Photo—Earl Leaf. 212—WW, Harris and Ewing—BB, Key. 213—213—UU, UU—Canadian Nat'l Railways—Canadian Nat'l Film Board—same, same, same. 214—Library of Congress. 215—UP, BB, WW—BB, BS—UP, Pix Inc.—Eur. 216—Sov., Sov.—Sov.—INP, Sov.—Anderson (Florence), WW. 217—UU, INP—Key.—WW—INP. 218—UP—UP WW. 219—INP, INP—WW, BB—WW, Pan American Airways. 220—UP, WW—WW, BS, WW—WW. 221—WW, UP, Key.—N. Y. Yankees, UP, WW—UP, WW. 222—UP, WW, WW—WW, WW, UP—BB, UP, WW. 223—Triangle Photo, UP—INP, INP—UP, WW—INP, Dept. of Comm., same. 224—WW, WW, INP—WW, Ewing Galloway—WW, WW, WW. 225—WW, UP—WW, WW—WW, WW. 226—20th Cent., Universal Int'l.—MGM, Cul., Warner Bros.—WW—Warner Bros., Universal Pictures. 227—Cul., MGM—MGM—MGM, Acad. MP A and S—same, same, Cul. 228—Acad. MP A and S, same—Cul.—Cul., Cul., Acad. MP A and S—same, same, same. 229—Acad. MP A and S, same, Cul.—Cul.—20th Cent., Cul.—BB, Acad. MP A and S. 230—WW, UP, Cul.—Cul., Key.—Cul. NBC, WW. 231—UP, UP, Cul.—UP—WW, WW, UP—BB, WW, Harris and Ewing. 232—INP, Key., WW—WW—WW, WW, INP—Key., UP, WW. 233—Key., Key.—WW, Ewing Galloway—BS, UP, WW. 234—Cul., Cul., Vandamm—Key.—BB, Cul.—Cul., Cul., BB. 235—Cul., BB—Vandamm—same, WW, Cul.—Cul., Cul., Vandamm. 236—WW, Met. Museum of Art—YEAR, WW—BB, WW. 237—Cul., WW—UP—WW, CBS, WW—WW, RCA. 238—WW, Key.—WW, WW—BB, WW. 239—INP, INP—WW, WW—INP, BS, INP—Ewing Galloway. 240—UP, UP—WW, INP, Harris and Ewing—Carl Byoir and Assoc., Acad. MP A and S. 241—WW, INP—UP, INP, UP—Radio City Music Hall, Key. 242—©Karsh Ottawa. 243—BB. 244—WW, UP—YEAR, WW.

245—WW—UP, WW—Eur. 246—WW—INP—Ullstein, Pix Inc., BS—USAF, USAF. 247—WW, Brit. Info. Serv.—UP—INP, WW. 248—Brit. Info. Serv., same—WW, WW—WW, WW. 249—Key., WW—Ewing Galloway—Sov., WW. 250—UP—BS, INP, WW. 251—INP, WW—WW, UP—Pix Inc. 252—WW, Eur.—US Army. 253—WW—BB, INP. 254—USN. 255—USN—Pix Inc., INP—WW, USN. 256—USN—US Army, Imperial War Museum (London)—WW, US Army. 257—US Army, same—same—WW, UP. 258—WW, Australian News and Info. Bureau—INP, USAF—INP, INP, WW. 259—WW, WW—UP, US Army—WW, UP, WW. 260—N.Y. Central, WW, WW—UP, WW. 261—Ewing Galloway, same, WW. Ewing Galloway—USO, WW—US Army, Library of Congress—UP. 262—UP, INP—INP—WW, UP, BS—Eur., UP. 263—UP, WW, WW—Ewing Galloway, WW—Lockheed, UP. 264—UP, UP—UP—WW—UP, UP 265—DD—US Army, BS. 266—US Army, WW—US Army—INP, WW. 267—Ullstein, WW—BS, US Army—UP, US Army. 268—UP, WW—Sov., Boeing Aircraft, North American Aviation—INP, North American Aviation, YEAR—Republic Aviation, Glenn Martin Co. 269—WW, INP—US Army, UP, WW—INP, WW, UP. 270—WW, WW—USMC, Ward—WW, Pix Inc. 271—WW, INP—WW—WW, UP. 272—WW, US Army—WW, US Army, Sov. 273—INP, Pix Inc.—INP, US Army—INP, INP, INP. 274—INP, UP, WW—Key., Eur.—WW. 275—UN—Post Office Dept., USN. 276—MGM—20th Cent., Los Angeles "Evening Herald"—MGM. 277—Cul., S. Goldwyn, Los Angeles "Evening Herald"—Cul., Paramount—Acad. MP A and S, Paramount, Warner Bros. 278—WW, WW, USMC—BB, WW—WW, INP, BS. 279—WW, BB—WW, WW—UP, UP, UP. 280—UP, UP—WW, UP, WW—UP, WW, WW. 281—WW, WW, USN—WW, Pix Inc., INP—WW, BB, Key. 282—WW, WW—INP, INP. 283—Ice Follies, ©"Life"—UP—INP, Acad. MPW A and S, National Gallery of Aft (Wash., D.C.) 284—UP—Key.—WW. 285—INP, UP, WW—INP, WW—WW, WW. 286—INP. 287—UN. 288—WW, INP—INP. 289—US Army—WW, Army Sig. Corp.—UP, INP. 290—INP, INP—WW, UP—UP. 291—WW. 292—INP, WW—INP, WW—INP. 293—UP, WW—INP, WW. 294—INP, WW—INP—INP, ©Karsh Ottawa. 295—WW—Sov., WW. 296—Alexanderson—Leonard Lefkow. 297—WW, UPI—©"Life" INP—Eastfoto. 298—INP—UP, INP. 299—James Hornick, INP—UN, same, same. 300—WW, WW—UN, UNICEF—WW. 301—News Front—INP, WW. 302—UP—WW, WW. 303—UP, WW—WW, WW—INP, WW. 304—WW, WW. 305—INP, UN—Ewing Galloway. 306—WW, INP—WW, DD—WW, WW. 307—WW, DD—DD, WW—UP, DD. 308—INP, DD—UN, INP—UN, DD. 309—INP, WW—U.S. Army, WW—WW. 310—INP. 311—WW, INP—WW, WW, INP—UP, WW. 312—WW, WW. 313—UP, WW—UPI, UPI—WW, UPI. 314—INP, UP—INP, UP. 315—WW, WW, INP—WW. 316—SOV.—UPI, UPI, WW. 317—WW—Conrad courtesy of Denver "Post," WW—UP. 318—UP—UP. 319—Eastfoto—WW, INP—UPI. 320—WW, Israel Office of Information—UP, UN. 321—INP—UPI, WW—WW. 322—WW, WW—WW, Frank Novotny—UP, WW.

323—BS, WW—Consulate General Japan (N.Y.), UP—WW, WW. 324—INP, WW—WW, WW, INP—UPI, WW, INP. 325—WW, INP INP, Eur., WW—WW, WW. 326—Canadian Consulate General (N.Y.) WW, UN—Canadian Consulate General—WW, Keystone. 327—INP, WW—WW—INP, Brazilian Gov. 328—INP—Paul Hess—WW—INP, WW. 329—INP, Year, INP—INP, WW, BB. 330—INP, WW—Andre Ostier—UP, Key. 331—BS, Cul., NBC—UP, UP—Black Star, New York Philharmonic. 332—Acad. MP A and S, same—20th Cent.—Columbia Pictures, Los Angeles "Evening Herald," Paramount. 333—United Artists, same, Year—Year, same—INP, Paramount—WW. 334—John Swope, Levin and Smith, John L. Toohey—Fred Fehl, Jacobson and Harmon—WW, Roderick MacArthur from Bill Doll and Co. 335—CBS, CBS, CBS—WW, CBS—WW, WW. 336—WW, Year—WW, WW, INP—INP, R. Clarkson. 337—WW, WW—WW—UP, WW. 338—"New Yorker," Carven, Bill Mauldin—Craven, same—"New Yorker," Cul. 339—WW, WW—UPI, The Weekly News (NZ), WW, Roy Bernard Co.—INP, UPI, INP. 340—WW—WW, USN—WW, Convair 341—USAF—WW—WW, WW, INP. 342—Associated Press Asian Photos, UP—courtesy "Life," Nat'l Found. Infantile Paralysis. 343—UPI, WW—E. W. Bliss Co., AP—American Museum of Natural History, WW. 346—WW. 347—Columbia Univ. 348—WW. 349—UPI, WW. 350—WW—UPI, WW—WW. 351—WW, UPI—UPI, WW, UPI. 352—WW, WW—WW—UPI, WW. 353—WW—UPI—UPI. 354—WW, PUI. 355—Harris Ewing, UPI—WW. 356—All WW.

357—UPI—WW, WW—UPI. 358—UPI—UPI, WW. 359—WW, WW—WW—WW, Black Star. 360—All WW. 361—WW—UPI, WW—WW, WW. 362—WW—UPI—UPI—UPI. 363—WW—UPI—WW. 364—WW, WW—WW—WW, UPI. 365—All WW. 366—WW. 367—UPI, UPI—WW—WW. 368—Convair—WW. 369—All WW. 370—WW—UPI—U.S. Dept. of Defense. 371—U.S. Dept. of Army, Same—U.S. Dept. of Navy, U.S. Dept. of Defense.

372—U.S. Dept. of Army—UPI—UPI. 373—UPI—WW—WW, WW. 374—American Telephone & Telegraph—UPI—UPI. 376 UPI, UPI—Bethlehem Pacific Coast Steel Corp, WW. 377—Carl Byoir & Assoc. (Los Angeles). 378—Drake Museum—Standard Oil Co. (N.J.). 379—Karsh (Ottawa), WW. 380—UPI—WW, UPI. 381—Gib Brush (L.A. Daily News)—UPI, UPI—UPI. 382—All WW. 383—UPI,

WW—Birdseye Frozen Food Corp. 384—James Hornick (Toronto). 385—UPI. 386—All WW. 387—Same. 388—WW, UPI—WW. 389—WW, UPI—WW, WW. 390—All United Nations. 391—UPI—United Nations—Charles Hewitt (Picture Post). 392—WW. 393—NEWS FRONT—WW, Keystone—UPI. 394—WW. 395—UPI. 396—Sovfoto—Same—UPI, UPI. 397—Sovfoto—UPI, UPI. 398—

Sovfoto—WW, WW. 399—UPI. 400—UPI, WW, WW—UPI. 401—UPI—WW—WW, UPI. 402—Eastfoto, WW—WW, UPI—WW. 403—WW—WW, UPI. 404—Katherine Young. 405—UPI, WW—WW, The Associated Press (Bilderdienst). 406—WW, WW—UPI. 407—WW, Roy Bernard Co. —Frank Novotny, WW. 408—British Information Services. 409—WW, UPI—Keystone, Black Star—

UPI, UPI. 410—UPI, WW—WW. 411—British Information Services—WW—WW, UPI. 412—UPI. 413—All UPI. 414—All WW. 415—UPI—UPI—WW, WW. 416—WW—UPI. 417—WW, Jean Manzon for European Photo—WW, Black Star. 418—WW, WW—Gillon Agency, WW. 419—UPI, WW—WW—WW. 420—UPI—ANP Foto (Amsterdam). 421—All WW. 422—UPI, UPI—WW—WW. 423—

WW, UPI, European Photo—Black Star. 424—UPI—WW. 425—All WW. 426—WW, Acme Photo—WW. 427—Acme Photo, Same, WW—UPI. 428—Israel Office of Information. 429—WW, WW—Israel Office of Info. (N.Y.), UPI—WW, WW. 430—WW—Israel Office of Info. (N.Y.), WW—WW, WW. 431—UPI—Acme Photo, Paris-Match (Gamma). 432—WW—UPI. 433—WW, WW—United Nations—UPI. 434—UPI, WW—UPI. 435—

UPI, WW—UPI. 436—All UPI. 437—All WW. 438—Acme Photo, UPI—WW. 439—UPI—WW. 440—UPI—UPI—WW. 441—Acme Photo—WW, Robert Y. Richie for California Texas Oil Co. 442—Paris-Match (Gamma). 443—UPI—WW—UPI. 444—UPI—WW—UPI, WW. 445—WW, WW—WW—UPI. 446—Keystone—WW. 447—WW, UPI—UPI. 448—UPI. 449—WW—UPI, WW—UPI, WW, WW. 450—WW, Information Services—

Govt. of Ghana—WW, UPI—British Information Service, WW. 451—Federal Information Dept. of Southern Rhodesia, European Photo—Associated Press—WW—WW, WW—WW, WW, WW. 452—WW—WW, WW—WW—WW, Ewing Galloway. 453—WW—WW—Alastair Matheson (Nairobi). 454—U.S. Dept. of Army. 455—WW. 456—WW, UPI—UPI. 457—WW, WW—UPI, WW. 458—All WW. 459—Leonard Lefkow—WW

—Life. 460—Eastfoto, WW. 461—UPI—Eastfoto, Same—Same. 462—Eastfoto—UPI, UPI—WW. 463—All WW. 464—WW—WW. 465—UPI, WW—UPI. 466—WW—Tokyo Shibaura Electric Co. 467—Rep. of the Philippines (Office of the President)—UPI, WW. 468—WW—UPI. 469—WW, UPI—UPI, Sovfoto. 470—WW—UPI. 471—Eastfoto—WW—Black Star, Same. 472—WW, UPI—WW—UPI. 473—WW, Albert E. Norman (Australia)

—WW—J. Erne Adams, courtesy New Zealand Herald. 474—Information Service of India. 475—WW, UPI—WW—UPI—J. M. D'Souza, The Times of India. 476—WW. 477—WW—Black Star—WW, Black Star. 478—UPI—WW. 479—Hamilton Wright—UPI. 480—WW—UPI—WW—UPI. 481—WW, UPI, WW—UPI—WW—WW, WW. 482—Black Star—WW—UPI. 483—WW—UPI—WW. 484—UPI

—WW—UPI. 485—UPI, UPI—UPI—Torente "Ercilla" (Santiago. Chile)—Black Star. 486—UPI, WW—WW—Brinton for Pix Inc. 487—WW, British Information Services—Pan American World Airways, Barbados Publicity Committee, Frederick Lewis (N.Y.). 488—WW—WW—UPI. 489—WW—UPI, UPI—Graphic House. 490—Ron Laidlam. 491—Canadian Govt. Travel Bureau—Canadian Consulate

General (N.Y.), WW, United Nations. 492—WW, WW—Keystone. 493—Canadian Consulate General (N.Y.), Same—Ford Motor Co. of Canada, National Film Board (Canada). 494—WW. 495—WW. 496—U.S. Air Force—WW. 497—WW. 498—UPI, WW—Henry W. McAllister for Carl Byoir & Assoc.—WW. 499—WW. E. W. Bliss Co.—Dr. C. E. Hall (M.I.T.)—WW, Martin Co. 500—WW, UPI

—WW, UPI. 501—UPI—Henry Maule (London)—U.S. Geological Survey. 502—National Found. for Infantile Paralysis, WW. 503—Life Photo by Fritz Goro. 504—UPI. 505—Courtesy Mrs. E. H. Benenson, Same—WW. 506—All UPI. 507—Life Photo by Albert Fenn. 508—Associated Press Asian Photo—WW, UPI. 509—UPI, WW—UPI. 510—UPI—National Aeronautics and Space

Administration. 511—WW—UPI, UPI, WW. 512—All WW. 513—Boeing—WW, WW. 514—WW—WW—UPI. 515—Kaman Aircraft Corp.—UPI—UPI. 516—WW. 517—Museum of Modern Art—Edwin Hewitt Gallery, Museum of Art—WW, Museum of Modern Art. 518—Life, WW, Museum of Modern Art—UPI—Museum of Modern Art, Same, Sculpture Center. 519—Museum of Modern Art—Associated Press—Museum of

Modern Art—WW, UPI, WW. 520—Post-Dispatch—British Information Services. 521—Knopf Publishing Co., Paragon Art Studio Inc.—WW. 522—Pix Inc. (N.Y.), WW—WW, UPI. 523—Fabian Bachrach, Criterion Photocraft, Scribner's—Simon & Schuster, UPI, Clayton—Smith—Gamma Picture Agency, Look. 524—New York Philharmonic—National Broadcasting Co. 525—WW, Metropolitan Opera Co.—

Same, WW—WW, Metropolitan Opera Co. 526—S. Hurok, UPI—Lincoln Center. 527—UPI—Joe Covello for Black Star, Archie Lieberman for Black Star. 528—New York Times. 529—Friedman-Abeles—WW. 530—Roderick MacArthur for Bill Doll & Co.—Fred Fehl courtesy James Proctor, Zinn Arthur for The Playwright's Co. 531—WW, Graphic House. 532—Paramount. 533—Metro Goldwyn Mayer—Continental

Distributing Co. 534—Lynn Farnol—Michael Todd Prod., United Artists. 535—Warner Bros.—20th Century-Fox, French Embassy Info. Service. 536—GBD International Films—WW, WW. 537—WW, Loew's Theaters—United Artists. 538—Columbia Broadcasting System. 539—Same—WW. 540—All WW. 541—WW, UPI—WW. 542—WW—WW, National Broadcasting Co. 543—George Cord. 544—Ogilvy, Benson & Mather. 545—

Doyle Dane Bernbach, Benjamin Sonnenberg & Co.—Doyle Dane Bernbach, Leo Burnett Co. 546—Tobacco Industry Research Committee, Gillette Safety Razor Co.—Maurey Garber—Needham Louis & Brorby (Chicago), Ketchum MacLeod & Grove. 547—Playboy, Colliers, Playboy—YEAR. 548—UPI—Atlanta Constitution—WW. 549—Budd Mourer—UPI, WW—WW, Black

Star. 550—UPI. 551—All WW. 552—UPI—WW. 553—WW—UPI. 554—WW, Conant—Post Dispatch photo by Black Star. 555—UPI, UPI—Met. Pittsburgh Educational Television—YEAR. 556—UPI, UPI—WW. 557—WW, UPI. 558—Consulate General of Israel (Calif.), UPI—WW, WW. 559—UPI, WW—WW, WW, WW. 560—All WW. 561—Swiss National Tourist Office—Jackson Hole

Preserve Inc. 562—WW, Keystone—WW. 563—Couture Group of N.Y. Dress Institute—UPI. 564—WW, WW, UPI—WW, UPI. 565—UPI, WW—WW, Lyn Armstrong. 566—General Motors—Chrysler Corp. 567—American Motors Corp, Same—Ford Motor Co.—Same—Same, Studebaker Packard Co. 568—General Motors—Ford Motor Co., General Motors—Same, Charles F. Campbell for

Roy Bernard Co. (N.Y.). 569—Ford Motor Co., Same—Austin Healy—Sunbeam Alpine, Austin Healey. 570—WW, WW—WW, YEAR. 571—Richard J. Neutra, Ewing Galloway—UPI. 572—WW. 573—UPI—WW—WW, WW. 574—Sovfoto—WW, WW, WW. 575—WW—UPI—WW, UPI, WW. 576—UPI—WW, WW—UPI. 577—WW—WW, UPI—UPI. 578—UPI, WW—WW, WW—UPI, UPI. 579—

WW, UPI—UPI, WW—WW. 580—WW—WW, WW—UPI, WW. 581—R. Clarkson, WW—WW—UPI. 582—WW, WW—WW, UPI—UPI. 583—WW—WW—UPI, WW. 584—UPI, UPI—UPI, WW. 585—UPI, UPI—European Photo, WW. 586—WW, UPI. 587—WW, WW—UPI. 588—All UPI. 589—All UPI. 590—WW, WW—UPI. 591—UPI—WW. 592—WW. 593—WW—WW, UPI. 594—Keystone—UPI—UPI. 595—Keystone, UPI—WW.

596—UPI—WW, WW. 597—WW, UPI—WW. 598—UPI—WW, WW—WW, WW. 599—All WW. 600—Life (c) Time Inc., The Weekly News (N.Z.), WW—UPI, WW—UPI. 601—WW, UPI, UPI—WW—WW—WW. 602—UPI, UPI—UPI—WW, WW. 603—UPI, WW—UPI, UPI—UPI. 604—UPI, UPI—WW, YEAR, Ruth Marion Baruch (San Francisco). 605—European Photo, UPI—WW, WW, UPI. 606—UPI, WW, UPI—Chicago

Park District, WW, UPI. 607—UPI. 612—NASA, WW—NASA. 613—UPI, WW—UPI—PPS, PP. 614—WW, UPI—WW, UPI—WW. 615—WW, UPI, WW—WW, UPI—UPI. 616—AFP-DPA Photos, WW—WW—UPI, UPI. 617—Daily News—UPI, WW—WW. 618—UPI. 620—UPI. 621—UPI, WW. 622—UPI—WW, WW. 623—UPI—UPI, WW—YEAR, Inc., UPI. 624—UPI. 626—WW. 627—WW, PP. 628-29—

WW. 630—WW. 631—UPI, WW. 632—UPI—UPI, WW. 633—WW, UPI—WW, UPI. 634—WW. 635—YEAR, Inc.—WW—UPI. 636—WW. 637—UPI, YEAR, Inc. 638-39—WW. 640—WW—WW—UPI. 641—UPI—PP, WW—UPI. 642—WW. 643—PPS. 644—WW—Defense Dept.—UPI. 645—UPI, UPI—Defense Dept. 646—WW, WW—WW—UPI. 647—WW. 648—NASA—UPI. 649—UPI, WW, General Dynamic Corp. 650-51—

NASA. 652-53—NASA. 654—Herblock, The Washington Post. 655—WW. 656-57 WW. 658—New York Times. 659—UPI, WW. 660-61—WW. 662—PPS. 664-65—WW. 666—PPS. 667—PPS, WW. 668—WW—WW, PPS—PPS. 669—WW. 670—UPI. 671—WW, UPI. 672—WW. 673—WW—YEAR, Inc., Sovfoto—UPI, WW. 674—WW. 675—PPS, WW. 676—WW—PPS—PPS. 677—PPS—WW,

WW, WW, Yugoslavia Information. 678—WW. 679—PP, WW. 680-683—PPS. 684—PPS. 686—WW, WW, PP. 686—PPS—PPS—PPS, UPI. 687—PPS—WW, PPS—UPI. 688—German Information Center. 689—UPI, WW. 690—WW. 691—WW, UPI—WW—German Information Center, WW. 692—Belgian Consulate General—PPS. 693—PPS, WW, PPS. 694—PPS. 695—PPS. 696-97—PPS. 698—WW.

699—WW, WW. 700—WW—WW, PPS—WW. 701—UPI, UPI—WW, UPI—PPS. 702—PPS. 703—PPS, WW. 704—PPS—UPI. 705—PPS. 706—PPS—PPS—WW. 707—PPS, PPS—UPI, WW, PPS, UPI, PPS-PPS, WW, PP. 708-709—WW. 710—PPS. 711—PPS, PP. 712—UPI—WW. 713—PPS—WW. 714—PPS—PPS—WW. 715—WW, PPS—PP, WW—PP. 716-717—WW. 722-723—WW. 724-725—PPS.

726—PPS, Japan National Tourist Organization—WW, PPS—Japan Consulate General of Japan, N.Y. 728—WW—WW, UPI. 729—Australian News & Information Bureau—WW. 730—UPI. 731—WW, UPI. 732—WW—UPI—WW. 733—WW. 734—PPS. 735—PP, WW. 736—PPS. 737—Fuller & Sadao—WW, PPS—PPS, PPS, PPS. 738—WW. 740—WW. 741—UPI, PP. 742—General Electric—General

Electric—NICAP. 743—US Navy—UPI, UPI, UPI—Fairchild Development Laboratories, NASA. 744—UPI. 745—WW, UPI, WW. 746—UPI, WW—WW—WW, WW. 747—WW,WW—WW, WW—UPI, WW. 748-749—PPS. 750—PPS. 751—National Council of Churches, Religous News Service—PPS, UPI—WW, WW, PPS. 752—Alan Dunn-The New Yorker Magazine, Inc. 753—Alexandre Georges, TWA by Ezra Stoller Assoc's. 754—

Lincoln Center for the Performing Arts, Inc. Photo by Morris Warman—Harrison & Abramovitz—Joshua Freiwald. 755—Morley Baer, Morley Baer—Paul Rudolph, Cervin Robinson—Morley Baer, Pan American. 756—WW. 757—WW, Time, Inc. 758—WW—New York Times, same—Same. 760—WW—WW, WW—YEAR, Inc, Dial Press 761—Jill Krementz—Jeff Lowenthal, YEAR, Inc., Don Soucy—WW, WW, Random House.

762—Murray Radin. 763—Los Angeles County Museum of Art, Corcoran Gallery of Art. 764—UPI—John Launois Performing Arts Foundation of Kansas City—National Gallery of Art, Washington, D.C. 765—Graham Gallery—Leo Castelli Art Gallery, Life Magazine, Museum of Modern Art, N.Y.—Collection: Art Institute of Chicago, Photo courtesy of the Sidney Janis Gallery, N.Y. 766—Friedman-Abeles. 767—

Ganshaw & Prescott, Morris Warman. 768—Nancy Palmer Photos—PPS, YEAR, Inc. 769—Friedman-Abeles, PPS. Alix Jeffry—PPS, Friedman-Abeles. 770—UPI. 771—WW, N.Y. Philharmonic. 772—WW—Beth Bergman, New York State Theater—WW, WW. 773—New York City Opera Co.—Tom Monaster, CBC, WW. 774—Grove Press, Inc. 775—Columbia Pictures Corp., Embassy Pictures Corp.

776—New York Public Library—20th Century-Fox—Paramount Pictures Corp., American International Pictures Export Corp. 777—New York Public Library, United Artists Corp.—New York Public Library, Columbia Pictures Corp.—Audubon Films, United Artists Corp., Warner Bros.—Seven Arts. 778—NBC. 779—WW, CBS. 780—NBC, CBS—WW. 781—NBC—WNET, WNET, CBS—UPI, NBC. 782—AMR International, Inc. 783—Doyle, Dane & Bernbach, Lewis & Gilman, Young & Rubicam. 784—Advertising Club of New York, Same—Pan Am, Carl Ally, Inc.—Batten, Barton, Durstine & Osborn. 785—Advertising Club of N.Y., Doyle, Dane, Bernbach, Edward H. Weiss & Co.—Young & Rubicam, Wells, Rich Greene—Young & Rubicam, Doyle, Dane, Bernbach, Campbell-Ewald. 786—YEAR, Inc. 787—WW. 788—Lord & Taylor—WW, New York Times. 789—WW, New York Times—Vision Unlimited—UPI, WW, PP—UPI, UPI, UPI. 790—Shoe-Maker, Chicago's American. 791—British Travel Association, French Government Tourist Office. 792—U.S. Department of the Interior—Braniff International. 793—Grace Line, U.S. Department of the Interior—WW, Bulgarian Mission to the UN—PPS. 794—WW—WW. 795—General Motors, Ford Motor Co., Volkswagen, Ford Motor Co.—General Motors, Studebaker, General Motors. 796—British Government Tourist Office—WW—PP—Penn-Central. 798—WW—UPI. 799—Astrodome—Same. 800—UPI—UPI—WW. 801—UPI, WW—WW, WW—WW. 802—WW. 803—WW, WW—WW, UPI, UPI—UPI, UPI. 804—UPI—WW. 805—WW, WW—UPI. 806-807—WW. 808—UPI, UPI. 809—WW, WW—UPI—WW. 810—WW, UPI, UPI—WW, WW, WW—WW, Pittsburgh Chemical Co., WW. 811—WW, WW. 813—WW, PP—WW—WW. 814—Paris Match, PPS—PPS, WW—PPS. 815—PPS—WW. 816—UPI, WW—WW, UPI. 817—WW. 818—PPS—WW, PPS. 819—WW, World Journal Tribune—PPS. 820—WW, WW—UPI—UPI, UPI. 821—UPI, UPI, WW—WW, PPS, WW. 822—UPI. 824-825—WW.

Illustrated Daily News
GERMANS BLOCK SIGNING OF TREATY
Newport to Entertain Prince of Wales in August
KABO CORSETS
NO BRASS EYELETS
Ladies Sin
against themselves in failing to note the Fall Line of
KABO
Bias-Gored Straight Front and Modified CORSETS
Scores of Gracious Models, with
LONG SKIRT
LOW BUST
DEEP HIP
PARIS CLASP
All Hand Finished, at
$1.00 to $5.00
Write for Catalog
Very Little
argument is needed to convince those of too ample form that
The Form-Reducing
KABO
in moulding such figures to lines of Happy Symmetry, and reducing too high and too full abdomen to Absolute Flatness, accomplishes that which no other corset made does accomplish.
Price, $2.50
CHICAGO CORSET CO.
215 Monroe Street, Chicago
388 Broadway, New York
Our Handsome $3.10 Dress
$3.10
This Becoming and Latest Dress Turban, $2.88.
These IMMORTAL CHAPLAINS ...
INTERFAITH IN ACTION
S.S. DORCHESTER
3¢ UNITED STATES POSTAGE 3¢
AMERICA THE LAND OF THE WOMAN - THE HOME OF THE GIRL!
OUR SLAVES!
It is goot to hear Americans are now pudding 10% of der pay into Bunds!
Herman, you tell him it iss BONDS- not BUNDS!
For VICTORY... put at least 10%
The Whole Range of Music
"VICTOR"
TALKING MACHINE
CHOPIN
SOUSA
"HIS MASTER'S VOICE"
Awarded Gold Medal
Pan-American Exposition
ELDRIDGE R. JOHNSON, Maker
U.S.
SANTO DOMINGO